Mergers and Acquisitions

Understanding the Antitrust Issues

Second Edition

Robert S. Schlossberg, Editor

Section of Antitrust Law

This volume should be officially cited as:

ABA SECTION OF ANTITRUST LAW,
MERGERS AND ACQUISITIONS: UNDERSTANDING THE ANTITRUST ISSUES, 2D EDITION (2004)

Cover design by ABA Publishing.

Printed in the United States of America.

Library of Congress Control Number: 2004101834
ISBN: 1-59031-373-9

Discounts are available for books ordered in bulk. Special consideration is given to state bars, CLE programs, and other bar-related organizations. Inquire at ABA Book Publishing, American Bar Association, 750 North Lake Shore Drive, Chicago, Illinois 60611.

06 05 04 03 02 5 4 3 2 1

ababooks.com

CONTENTS

FOREWORD

The Section of Antitrust Law is pleased to publish the second edition of *Mergers and Acquisitions: Understanding the Antitrust Issues*, a comprehensive review of United States substantive merger law. Since the publication of the first edition, the federal agencies and state attorneys general have continued an active agenda and have refined merger analysis through settlements, litigated cases and speeches.

Like the first edition, this second edition serves as a fundamental reference to all sources relevant to merger analysis. It has been completely updated to capture the most important developments in this area. No other book or treatise provides the comprehensive and up-to-date analysis available in *Mergers and Acquisitions: Understanding the Antitrust Issues*.

The Section is indebted to the many attorneys who contributed to a work of this scale and scope. The Section's Mergers and Acquisitions Committee, and particularly its current Chair, Joe Krauss, devoted time and attention to this project. In addition, I want to thank Council members Ilene Gotts and Debbie Pearlstein, who reviewed this book before publication and provided valuable insights.

I want to extend special thanks to editor Bob Schlossberg, who was co-editor of the first edition and who coordinated the work of all contributors in preparing this second edition.

Kevin E. Grady
Chair, Section of Antitrust Law
American Bar Association
March 2004

PREFACE

The first edition of *Mergers and Acquisitions: Understanding the Antitrust Issues* published in 2000, replaced the Section's Monograph #12 on horizontal mergers that was issued in 1986. Like its predecessor, the current edition is designed to be a comprehensive review of United States substantive merger law for use by counsel evaluating or advocating a transaction. The book guides the reader through the substantive analysis applied to transactions, commencing with market definition and measurement (Chapter 3), transitioning to a discussion of possible coordinated and unilateral effects arising from a transaction (Chapter 4), and then focusing on the various mitigating factors potentially available to the parties (Chapter 5), as well as efficiencies (Chapter 6) and potential defenses (Chapter 7). Separate chapters are devoted to the issues arising in the joint venture context (Chapter 8) and in vertical (Chapter 10) and conglomerate mergers (Chapters 10 and 11, respectively). The book also addresses theories of potential competition (Chapter 9) and issues particular to international transactions (Chapter 12). Judicial relief and remedies are discussed in Chapter 13.

The book does not seek to detail the process and procedures of merger review at the federal agencies, although Chapter 2 touches upon the topic; for that, the ABA Section of Antitrust Law issued the second edition of its practice guide entitled, *The Merger Review Process: A Step-by-Step Guide to Federal Merger Review* in 2001. In addition, while it briefly discusses state merger enforcement, a more in-depth discussion of that topic is available in the Section's *State Antitrust Practice and Statutes* (3d ed. 2003); it also does not address foreign review of mergers, for which the reader is directed to the Section's treatise, *Competition Laws Outside the United States*.

This book is the product of numerous individuals. We owe a special thanks to Bob Schlossberg, who was responsible for editing the entire second edition. Bob was assisted by a number of individuals at his firm and, in particular, Christopher Tierney, who spent long hours seeing the book through to publication. In addition, the following individuals contributed to the drafting of this second edition:

Daniel M. Abuhoff	Elizabeth Averill	David T. Beddow
David A. Applebaum	Nicholas W. Bath	Linda Blumkin

Logan M. Breed
Stacey C. Burton
Ana Maria Cabassa-Torres
Jay Campbell
Dando B. Cellini
Robert N. Cook
Tom Fina
Kerrie Freeborn
Ilene K. Gotts
Peter Guryan
Burney P.C. Huber
Ray Jacobson
Robin Lin
Marni B. Karlin
J. Robert Kramer II
Tad Lipsky
Joseph Miller
Danielle Monnig
Suzanne Morris
Ora Nwabueze
Nana Osafo
Frederick H. Parmenter
Leslie D. Peritz
Tom Smith
Stephen Spiegelhalter

Finally, the book could not have been published without the hard work of the secretarial staff at Morgan Lewis & Bockius LLP, especially Linda Hamilton, Debbie Smith and Sheila Wood.

Joseph G. Krauss
Chair,
Mergers and Acquisitions Committee
Section of Antitrust Law
American Bar Association
March 2004

CHAPTER 1

OVERVIEW OF THE APPLICABLE U.S. ANTITRUST LAWS

The U.S. antitrust laws seek to preserve competition in the U.S. economy and to ensure that U.S. consumers continue to enjoy the benefits of that competition. The antitrust laws are not, however, designed to protect individual competitors from the "rough and tumble" of vigorous competition or to thwart business efficiencies that may be achieved through the combination of two firms' resources.[1] As applied to mergers and acquisitions, the antitrust laws seek to ensure such transactions do not create, enhance, or facilitate the exercise of market power, thereby giving one or more firms the ability "to raise prices above competitive levels for a significant period of time."[2]

A number of federal and state statutes regulate the competitive effects of mergers and acquisitions.[3] The principal federal statute is

---

1. *See* Brunswick Corp. v. Pueblo Bowl-O-Mat, Inc., 429 U.S. 477, 488 (1977) ("the antitrust laws . . . were enacted for 'the protection of competition, not competitors'") (quoting Brown Shoe Co. v. United States, 370 U.S. 294, 320 (1962)); Northeastern Tel. Co. v. AT&T, 651 F.2d 76, 79 (2d Cir. 1981) ("dominant firms, having lawfully acquired monopoly power, must be allowed to engage in the rough and tumble of competition") (citing Berkey Photo, Inc. v. Eastman Kodak Co., 603 F.2d 263 (2d Cir. 1979)).
2. United States v. Long Island Jewish Med. Ctr., 983 F. Supp. 121, 136 (E.D.N.Y. 1997) (quoting United States v. Archer-Daniels-Midland Co., 866 F.2d 242, 246 (8th Cir. 1988)).
3. The Hart-Scott-Rodino Antitrust Improvements Act of 1976 (HSR Act), 15 U.S.C. § 18a, requires the parties to reportable transactions to notify the Antitrust Division of the U.S. Department of Justice (DOJ or the Division) and the Federal Trade Commission (FTC or the Commission) prior to consummating the proposed transaction and to observe the applicable waiting period. See part C of Chapter 2 for a discussion of the HSR Act and its administration. Furthermore, various federal statutes are applicable to mergers and acquisitions involving specific industries. See part C of Chapter 7 for a discussion of the federal statutes applicable to the banking, energy, transportation, communications, and newspaper industries. In addition, the National Cooperative Research and Production Act of 1993, 15 U.S.C. §§ 4301-06, applies to research and

Section 7 of the Clayton Act (Section 7),[4] which prohibits the acquisition of voting securities or assets when "in any line of commerce or in any activity affecting commerce in any section of the country, the effect of such acquisition may be substantially to lessen competition, or to tend to create a monopoly."[5] In addition, the competitive consequences of a merger or an acquisition may be challenged under Section 1 of the Sherman Act,[6] which prohibit contracts, combinations, or conspiracies in restraint of trade, or under Section 2 of the Sherman Act,[7] which prohibits monopolization, attempts to monopolize, and conspiracies to monopolize. Furthermore, Section 5 of the Federal Trade Commission Act,[8] which empowers the Federal Trade Commission (FTC or Commission) to challenge "any unfair method of competition or unfair and deceptive act or practice," is used by the FTC, accompanied by a Section 7 claim, to challenge mergers and acquisitions on competition grounds. Finally, numerous state statutes regulate the competitive effects of mergers and acquisitions in the enacting states.

A. Section 7 of the Clayton Act

1. Section 7 Applies to Acquisitions of Stock or Assets and to Mergers

As enacted in 1914, Section 7 of the Clayton Act originally prohibited only the acquisition by one corporation of the stock of another corporation when such an acquisition would likely result in a substantial lessening of competition between the acquiring and the acquired firms.[9]

---

development and production joint ventures and is discussed in part D.2 of Chapter 8.

4. 15 U.S.C. § 18.
5. *Id.*
6. *Id.* § 1.
7. *Id.* § 2.
8. *Id.* § 45.
9. In pertinent part, the original Section 7 provided: "No corporation engaged in commerce shall acquire, directly or indirectly, the whole or any part of the stock or other share capital of another corporation engaged also in commerce, where the effect of such acquisition may be to substantially lessen competition between the corporation whose stock is so acquired and the corporation making the acquisition, or to restrain such commerce in any section or community, or tend to create a monopoly in any line of commerce." *See* United States v. Philadelphia Nat'l Bank, 374 U.S. 321, 340 n.18 (1963). In addition, Section 7 applies to acquisitions in which the stock of the acquired firm is turned in and extinguished. *See* Midwestern Machinery, Inc. v. Northwest Airlines,

By its explicit terms, the original Section 7 did not apply to asset acquisitions.[10]

In *United States v. Celanese Corp. of America,*[11] the court described the rationale behind applying Section 7 only to stock acquisitions. The principal concern of the drafters of Section 7 was the amalgamation of power in the hands of holding companies.[12] These powerful firms voted the stock of the various companies they controlled, often allowing them to align the interests of direct competitors, thereby stifling competition. Section 7 was designed to thwart clandestine acquisition of voting power via stock purchases, thereby preventing the holding companies from gaining control of firms that were in competition with one another.

Moreover, as interpreted by the U.S. Supreme Court, the original Section 7 did not apply to mergers, even when mergers supplanted stock acquisitions as the prevalent means of corporate amalgamation.[13] Before long, Section 7 as it was originally enacted became a "dead letter."[14]

Recognizing the deficiencies in the original Section 7, the FTC as early as 1928, began suggesting amendments to the act to draw asset acquisitions within its scope and to require companies proposing a merger to give the Commission prior notification of their plans.[15] Sixteen bills to amend Section 7 were introduced during the period from 1943 to 1949, revealing the growing legislative interest in this area of antitrust law.[16] This interest was fueled by concerns over increasing concentration in U.S. industries, exemplified by a merger wave following

---

167 F.3d 439 (8th Cir. 1999).

10. *See* United States v. Columbia Steel Co., 334 U.S. 495, 507 n. 7 (1948) (citations omitted); *Philadelphia Nat'l Bank*, 374 U.S. at 337-38.
11. 91 F. Supp. 14 (S.D.N.Y. 1950).
12. *See id.* at 16. *See generally* A.D. NEALE, THE ANTITRUST LAWS OF THE UNITED STATES OF AMERICA 180-82 (1970).
13. *See Philadelphia Nat'l Bank*, 374 U.S. at 337-39; Arrow-Hart & Hegeman Elec. Co. v. FTC, 291 U.S. 587, 595 (1934); FTC v. Western Meat Co., 272 U.S. 554, 561 (1926); *Celanese Corp.*, 91 F. Supp. at 15-17.
14. *See Philadelphia Nat'l Bank*, 374 U.S. at 339-40.
15. *See* Brown Shoe Co. v. United States, 370 U.S. 294, 314 & n.25 (1962). By the time of the *Brown Shoe* decision in 1962, the FTC had "continued unsuccessfully to urge adoption of the prior notification provision." *Id.* at 314 n.25. Persistence ultimately paid off, however, in the 1976 enactment of the Hart-Scott-Rodino Antitrust Improvements Act of 1976, 15 U.S.C. § 18a, which provides for prior notification of certain mergers and acquisitions.
16. *See Brown Shoe Co.*, 370 U.S. at 311-12.

the Second World War. Additionally, two influential reports, one by the FTC and the other by the Temporary National Economic Committee, offered statistical evidence of the mergers' concentrative impact on American business and recommended government intervention.[17]

Acting against this backdrop, Congress amended Section 7 by passing the Celler-Kefauver Antimerger Act of 1950.[18] In *Brown Shoe Co. v. United States,*[19] the U.S. Supreme Court reviewed the legislative history and the purposes of the amendments.[20] The Court noted that Congress intended the amendments to "plug the loophole" exempting asset acquisitions from coverage of the Clayton Act, and to expand the scope of Section 7 to cover vertical and conglomerate mergers. The removal of the "acquiring-acquired" language of the original Section 7 accomplished this goal.[21] Further, the Court concluded that the amendments distinguished Section 7 analysis from Sherman Act analysis in the merger context. First, Section 7 was to be applied to mergers[22]

---

17. *See* FTC, REPORT ON THE MERGER MOVEMENT: A SUMMARY REPORT v (1948) (chronicling the impact of merger activity on concentration in American business and warning against the potential power of the remaining firms); Temporary Nat'l Economic Comm., *Final Report and Recommendations,* S. Doc. No. 35, 77th Cong., 1st Sess. (1941) (statistical studies of the merger trend). *But see* John Lintner & J. Keith Butters, *Effect of Mergers on Industrial Concentration, 1940-47*, 32 REV. ECON. & STATISTICS 30 (1950) (arguing that the postwar merger movement, while involving numerous transactions, had little concentrative effect). *See generally* Derek C. Bok, *Section 7 of the Clayton Act and the Merging of Law and Economics*, 74 HARV. L. REV. 226, 228-38 (1960) (discussing these reports in the context of an overview of the merger trend and the legislative history of the 1950 amendments to Section 7); THE LEGISLATIVE HISTORY OF THE FEDERAL ANTITRUST LAWS AND RELATED STATUTES 3387-89 (Earl W. Kintner ed. 1980) (discussing the FTC report and the legislative history of the 1950 amendments).
18. *See* Celler-Kefauver Antimerger Act of 1950, 15 U.S.C. § 18.
19. 370 U.S. 294 (1962).
20. *See id.* at 315-23.
21. *See id.* at 316-17. (By the deletion of the "aquiring-acquired" language, the amendment hoped to make clear "that § 7 applied not only to mergers between actual competitors, but also to vertical and conglomerate mergers whose effect may tend to lessen competition in any line of commerce").
22. Though the language of the amendments did not make specific reference to mergers, the U.S. Supreme Court inferred, from the legislative history of the amendments, the intent of Congress to expand Section 7 to cover

where the "trend to a lessening of competition in a line of commerce was still in its incipiency," whereas the Sherman Act required proof of extant harm to competition.[23] Second, Sherman Act precedent was not to be determinative in merger cases under Section 7.[24] Finally, Congress used the language "*may be* substantially to lessen competition," indicating that Section 7 illegality was based on a probable, rather than a definite, lessening of competition.[25] In addition, the amendments clarified some of the limits of Section 7's application to mergers. Congress intended that Section 7 not be used to hinder two small firms merging in order to compete with a larger, dominant competitor, or to hinder a merger in which one of the parties was a failing firm.[26]

In 1980, Congress further amended Section 7 to expand the scope of its coverage. First, the act's prohibitions were extended to acquisitions among "persons" rather than "corporations."[27] This change allowed the act to capture acquisitions by natural persons, partnerships, and other unincorporated associations and business entities rather than just corporations. Second, the act's coverage was broadened to include those transactions that "affected" interstate commerce.[28] Previously, the act only covered those transactions that were "in" interstate commerce.[29]

---

mergers. *See Philadelphia Nat'l Bank*, 374 U.S. at 341.

23. *See Brown Shoe Co.*, 370 U.S. at 317-18; *see also Philadelphia Nat'l Bank*, 374 U.S. at 362; United States v. E.I. du Pont de Nemours & Co., 353 U.S. 586, 589 (1957).

24. *See Brown Shoe Co.*, 370 U.S. at 318.

25. *See id.* at 323; *see also E.I. du Pont de Nemours & Co.*, 353 U.S. at 589 ("Section 7 is designed to arrest in its incipiency not only the substantial lessening of competition from the acquisition by one corporation of the whole or any part of the stock of a competing corporation, but also to arrest in their incipiency restraints or monopolies in a relevant market which, as a *reasonable probability*, *appear at the time of suit likely to result* from the acquisition by one corporation of all or any part of the stock of any other corporation") (emphasis added).

26. *See Brown Shoe Co.*, 370 U.S. at 319.

27. *See* Act of Sept. 12, 1980, Pub. L. No. 96-349, § 6(a), 94 Stat. 1157 (codified as amended at 15 U.S.C. § 18); H.R. REP. NO. 871, 96th Cong., 2d Sess. 1980, 1980 U.S.C.C.A.N. 2732, Apr. 11, 1980.

28. *See* Act of Sept. 12, 1980, Pub. L. No. 96-349, § 6(a), 94 Stat. 1157 (codified as amended at 15 U.S.C. § 18); H.R. REP. NO. 871, 96th Cong., 2d Sess. 1980, 1980 U.S.C.C.A.N. 2732, Apr. 11, 1980.

29. *See* United States v. American Bldg. Maintenance Indus., 422 U.S. 271 (1975). The 1980 amendment explicitly overruled the holding in *American Building Maintenance*.

2. *Section 7 Applies to Acquisitions of Less Than 100 Percent of Voting Securities*

Consistent with the Clayton Act amendments' aim of capturing all anticompetitive mergers and acquisitions, the courts have interpreted Section 7's prohibitions to cover partial acquisitions that may produce anticompetitive effects. The acquisition of "any part" of another company's stock is subject to Section 7.[30]

The Clayton Act's coverage of partial acquisitions is limited, however, by the act's exemption for acquisitions made "solely for investment." An acquirer of stock may avoid the substantive prohibitions of the Clayton Act, by demonstrating that the acquisition was made without any intent to exercise control over or influence the corporation whose stock is being acquired.

Acquisitions may be exempt from the Hart-Scott-Rodino Antitrust Improvements Act of 1976 (HSR Act)[31] reporting requirements if the acquirer can show that (1) the acquisition was made solely for the purpose of investment and (2) the acquisition will result in ownership of 10 percent or less of the voting securities of the issuer.[32]

The Section 7 solely-for-investment exemption is not limited by the HSR Act 10 percent ownership cap.[33] The defendant must, however, show that the purchase is being made solely for investment purposes. For example, in *United States v. Tracinda Investment Corp.*,[34] the parties' contract specifically stated that the defendant's acquisition of stock was being made solely for investment purposes and not with the

---

30. *See* United States v. E.I. du Pont de Nemours & Co., 353 U.S. 586, 589 (1957). *See generally* 5 PHILLIP AREEDA & DONALD F. TURNER, ANTITRUST LAW ¶¶ 1203-04 (1980).
31. 15 U.S.C. § 18a.
32. *See* 15 U.S.C. § 18a(c)(9). For institutional investors, the solely-for-investment threshold is 15% or less of the outstanding voting securities of the issuer *or* voting securities of the issuer valued at $25 million or less. *See* 16 C.F.R. § 802.64(b); *see also* Ilene K. Gotts & Robert C. Weinbaum, *Partial Ownership Interests: The Antitrust Concerns and Structural Techniques for Minimizing Them*, ANTITRUST REPORT, Oct. 2000 at 18.
33. *See* United States v. Tracinda Inv. Corp., 477 F. Supp. 1093 (C.D. Cal. 1979) (acquisition allowed under investment exemption where acquiring party acquired 25.5% of issuer); Anaconda Co. v. Crane Co., 411 F. Supp. 1210, 1217 (S.D.N.Y. 1975) (acquisition allowed where 22.6% of issuer's stock acquired).
34. 477 F. Supp. 1093 (C.D. Cal. 1979).

intent to exercise control over the target company.[35] In addition, the defendant in that case was contractually limited regarding the voting of the acquired stock and the percentage of that stock that he could purchase.[36] Once the acquirer makes such a showing, the burden is shifted to the plaintiff, who must then show that the defendant does not fall within the exemption.[37]

3. Section 7 Applies to Not-for-Profit Corporations

Courts have applied Section 7 to acquisitions by nonprofit corporations[38] with recent decisions pausing only to consider what impact the acquiring firm's nonprofit status will have on the Section 7 competitive effects analysis.[39] One court has held that nonprofit status

---

35. *Id.* at 1098.
36. *Id.* at 1098-99.
37. *Id.* at 1098.
38. Section 44 of the FTC Act defines a "corporation" for purposes of the act's coverage. *See* 15 U.S.C. § 44. Although the U.S. Supreme Court has distinguished nonprofit entities for purposes of the FTC's jurisdiction under Section 44, *see* California Dental Ass'n v. FTC, 526 U.S. 756, 766-69 (1999) (nonprofit association falls within Section 44 when it confers economic benefit on its members, but "proximate relation to lucre must appear" before the Commission will have jurisdiction), the FTC may proceed against mergers involving not-for-profit entities under Section 7 of the Clayton Act, using the jurisdiction conferred by Section 11 of the Clayton Act. *See* FTC v. University Health, Inc., 938 F.2d 1206, 1214-17 (11th Cir. 1991); United States v. Rockford Mem'l Corp., 898 F.2d 1278, 1280-81 (7th Cir. 1990).
39. *See* United States v. Long Island Jewish Med. Ctr., 983 F. Supp. 121, 145-46 (E.D.N.Y. 1997); FTC v. Butterworth Health Corp., 946 F. Supp. 1285, 1296 (W.D. Mich. 1996), *aff'd*, 121 F.3d 708 (6th Cir. 1997); FTC v. Freeman Hosp., 911 F. Supp. 1213, 1227 (W.D. Mo.), *aff'd*, 69 F.3d 260 (8th Cir. 1995). *But cf.* United States v. Carilion Health Sys., 707 F. Supp. 840 (W.D. Va.), *aff'd without opinion*, 892 F.2d 1042 (4th Cir. 1989). In *Carilion*, the court dismissed the Section 7 claim because the acquisition involved no stock, and therefore was not captured by the stock clause of Section 7, and because the assets clause of Section 7 did not apply to nonprofit companies. *Id.* at 841 n.1. The court proceeded to analyze the merger under Section 1 of the Sherman Act. The court held that the merger did not constitute an unreasonable restraint of trade and found it unnecessary to rule on whether nonprofit status exempts a merger from Section 1 analysis. *Id.* at 849. The Seventh Circuit, in *Rockford Memorial*, expressly rejected the district court's analysis in *Carilion* and declined to follow the Fourth Circuit's unpublished opinion

will have "limited and non-determinative effect,"[40] another held that nonprofit status is material but not dispositive,[41] and a third court held that nonprofit status must be considered.[42]

B. Sections 1 and 2 of the Sherman Act

For practical purposes, the 1950 and 1980 amendments to Section 7 all but eliminated the Sherman Act as a necessary tool for antitrust merger enforcement. Prior to 1950, the Sherman Act could be used to capture asset acquisitions, as the Clayton Act did not reach such transactions. Before 1980, the Sherman Act could be used to capture acquisitions involving entities other than corporations or entities that were not "in" interstate commerce. With the passage of these amendments, however, the role of the Sherman Act in merger enforcement largely has been supplanted by the Clayton Act.

Section 1 of the Sherman Act proscribes "every contract, combination . . . or conspiracy . . . in restraint of trade or commerce,"[43] and courts have interpreted this language to bar only unreasonable restraints.[44] The Clayton Act's effects test obviates the need to show an unreasonable restraint to prove a Clayton Act violation.[45]

The U.S. Supreme Court has alluded to the differing standards under Section 1 and Section 7,[46] but the Seventh Circuit has more recently

---

affirming the district court. *See Rockford Memorial*, 898 F.2d at 1286.

40. *See Long Island Jewish Med. Ctr.*, 983 F. Supp. at 146.
41. *See Butterworth Health Corp.*, 946 F. Supp. at 1296.
42. *See Freeman Hosp.*, 911 F. Supp. at 1227.
43. 15 U.S.C. § 1.
44. *See* Standard Oil Co. v. United States, 221 U.S. 1, 60-70 (1911).
45. Section 7 provides, in pertinent part, that "no person engaged in commerce . . . shall acquire the whole or any part of the assets of another person . . . where . . . *the effect of such acquisition may be substantially to lessen competition, or to tend to create a monopoly*." 15 U.S.C. §18 (emphasis added).
46. *See* Minnesota Mining & Mfg. Co. v. New Jersey Wood Finishing Co., 381 U.S. 311, 323 (1965) ("the Commission's Clayton Act proceeding required proof only of a potential anticompetitive effect while the Sherman Act carries the more onerous burden of proof of an actual restraint"); United States v. Penn-Olin Chem. Co., 378 U.S. 158, 170-71 (1964) ("The grand design of the original § 7, as to stock acquisitions, as well as the Celler-Kefauver Amendment, as to the acquisition of assets, was to arrest incipient threats to competition which the Sherman Act did not ordinarily reach. It follows that actual restraints need not be proved"); *see also* United States v. Columbia Steel Co., 334 U.S. 495

held,[47] and scholars have argued,[48] that the standards for Section 1 and Section 7 have coalesced into the Section 7 standard. This conclusion has not been adopted by all courts.[49]

Section 2 of the Sherman Act[50] prohibits monopolization, attempts to monopolize, or conspiracies to monopolize, and a merger may be challenged under Section 2 where the transaction is a vehicle for monopolization, attempted monopolization, or a conspiracy to monopolize.[51] Section 2, however, unlike Section 7, requires a showing of intent to monopolize (monopolization and attempted monopolization), the possession of monopoly power in the relevant market (monopolization), predatory or anticompetitive conduct designed to monopolize (monopolization and attempted monopolization), or a dangerous probability of success in monopolizing (attempted monopolization).[52] These requirements, as compared to the breadth of the Clayton Act, render Section 2 a more unwieldy and far less frequently used tool in merger enforcement.

C. Section 5 of the Federal Trade Commission Act

Section 5 of the FTC Act authorizes the FTC to challenge "any unfair method of competition or deceptive act or practice."[53] The U.S. Supreme Court has interpreted this grant of authority to allow the FTC to

---

(1948) (a showing of an unreasonable restraint of trade is required for a merger to be found illegal under Section 1 of the Sherman Act).

47. *See* United States v. Rockford Mem'l Corp., 898 F.2d 1278 (7th Cir. 1990).

48. *See* 4 PHILLIP AREEDA, HERBERT HOVENKAMP & JOHN L. SOLOW, ANTITRUST LAW ¶ 906 (rev. ed. 1998).

49. For example, some district courts have followed *Penn-Olin* and noted a distinction. *See* Bon-Ton Stores v. May Dep't Stores, 881 F. Supp. 860, 867 (W.D.N.Y. 1994); SCFC ILC, Inc. v. Visa USA, Inc., 819 F. Supp. 956, 991 (D. Utah 1993), *aff'd in part, rev'd in part*, 36 F.3d 958 (10th Cir. 1994).

50. 15 U.S.C. § 2.

51. *See, e.g.*, Nelson v. Monroe Regional Med. Ctr., 925 F.2d 1555, 1563 (7th Cir. 1991); Volvo N. Am. Corp. v. Men's Int'l Prof'l Tennis Council, 857 F.2d 55 (2d Cir. 1988); Santa Cruz Med. Clinic v. Dominican Santa Cruz Hosp., 1995-2 Trade Cas. (CCH) ¶ 71,254 (N.D. Cal. 1995).

52. *See* Spectrum Sports, Inc. v. McQuillan, 506 U.S. 447, 456-59 (1993) (elements of attempted monopolization claim); United States v. Grinnell Corp., 384 U.S. 563, 570-71 (1966) (elements of monopolization claim).

53. 15 U.S.C. § 45.

challenge under Section 5 any conduct that would constitute a violation of the Sherman Act or the Clayton Act.[54]

The vast majority of the mergers challenged by the FTC proceed in this fashion, with the alleged Section 7 violation forming the basis of the FTC's Section 5 claim. Judicial decisions that have reviewed the FTC's merger cases with Section 5 and Section 7 claims have focused on the Section 7 claim, using that claim as the basis of the substantive analysis.[55]

Although no court has determined whether a merger could be halted under Section 5 alone,[56] Section 5 has been found to be a possible supplement to Section 7 of the Clayton Act where the FTC has not been able to establish jurisdiction, e.g., prior to the 1950 and 1980 amendments to the Clayton Act.[57] Passage of the 1950 and 1980 amendments, however, has diminished the importance of this supplementary role.

D. State Antitrust Laws[58]

Every state, as well as the District of Columbia, Puerto Rico, and the Virgin Islands, has some form of antitrust statute.[59] Among these

---

54. *See* FTC v. Motion Picture Adver. Co., 344 U.S. 392, 394-95 (1952); FTC v. Cement Inst., 333 U.S. 683, 691 (1947).
55. *See, e.g.*, FTC v. Cardinal Health, Inc., 12 F. Supp. 2d 34 (D.D.C. 1998); FTC v. Tenet Health Care Corp., 17 F. Supp. 2d 937 (E.D. Mo. 1998), *rev'd on other grounds,* 186 F.3d 1045 (8th Cir. 1999); FTC v. Staples, Inc., 970 F. Supp. 1066 (D.D.C. 1997).
56. *See* FTC v. Atlantic Richfield Co., 549 F.2d 289, 291-92 n.1 (4th Cir. 1977) ("Certainly there is no case holding that a merger may be enjoined solely on the basis of a violation of § 5").
57. *See* Dean Foods, 70 F.T.C. 1146, 1291 (1966) (Section 5 claim may allow the FTC to capture mergers where the conduct falls outside the jurisdictional reach of Section 7), *modified by consent and enforced*, 1967 Trade Cas. (CCH) ¶ 72,086 (7th Cir. 1967); Beatrice Foods Co., 67 F.T.C. 473, 726 (1965) (Section 5 may be used to capture noncorporate acquisitions where pre-1980 Section 7 was powerless), *modified*, 1967 Trade Cas. (CCH) ¶ 72,124 (9th Cir. 1967).
58. A thorough examination of state merger enforcement can be found in the ABA's monograph on the subject. *See* ABA SECTION OF ANTITRUST LAW, MONOGRAPH NO. 21, STATE MERGER ENFORCEMENT (1995); *see also* ABA SECTION OF ANTITRUST LAW, STATE ANTITRUST ENFORCEMENT HANDBOOK (2003); ABA SECTION OF ANTITRUST LAW, STATE ANTITRUST PRACTICE AND STATUTES (3d ed. 2003).
59. *See* 6 Trade Reg. Rep. (CCH) ¶ 30,000 (reprinting the statutes); *see also*

antitrust statutes, there are fourteen that deal directly with mergers and acquisitions. Of those fourteen, eight have provisions comparable to Section 7,[60] while the remainder are more targeted in their coverage, applying only to merged monopolies, mergers in particular industries, stock (but not asset) acquisitions, or horizontal mergers.[61] State attorneys general have brought cases under their respective state laws,[62] under Section 7,[63] or under a combination of both state and federal statutes.[64]

In recent years, there have been numerous cases jointly brought by one of the federal agencies and one or more of the state attorneys general, and such cases have been brought under both the state law and Section 7,[65] or under Section 7 alone.[66] When such a claim is brought by

---

ABA SECTION OF ANTITRUST LAW, STATE ANTITRUST PRACTICE AND STATUTES (3d ed. 2003).

60. *See* ALASKA STAT. § 45.50.568 (Michie 1998); COLO. REV. STAT. § 6-4-107 (1997); HAW. REV. STAT. § 480-1 (1997); ME. REV. STAT. ANN. tit. 10, § 1102-A (West Supp. 1997); NEB. REV. STAT. § 59-1606 (1995); TEX. BUS. & COM. CODE ANN. § 15.05(d) (West 1998); WASH. REV. CODE ANN. § 19.86.060 (West 1989); P.R. LAWS ANN. tit. 10, §261 (1997).

61. *See* ARK. CODE ANN. § 4-75-301 (Michie 1996); LA. REV. STAT. ANN. § 51:125 (West 1987); MISS. CODE ANN. § 75-21-13 (1997); N.J. STAT. ANN. § 56:9-4 (West 1989); OHIO REV. CODE ANN. § 1331.02.1 (Page 1993 & Supp. 1997); S.C. CODE ANN. § 39-3-110 (Law Co-op. 1985 & Supp. 1997).

62. *See, e.g.*, Maine v. American Skiing Co., 1996-2 Trade Cas. (CCH) ¶ 71,478 (Me. Super. Ct. 1996); Maine v. Connors Bros., Ltd., 1988-2 Trade Cas. (CCH) ¶ 68,237 (Me. Super. Ct. 1988).

63. *See, e.g.*, California v. Sutter Health Sys., No. C99-03803 MMC (N.D. Cal. Jan. 5, 2000)); Wisconsin v. Kenosha Hosp. & Med. Ctr., 1997-1 Trade Cas. (CCH) ¶ 71,669 (E.D. Wis. 1996); Pennsylvania v. Providence Health Sys., 1994-1 Trade Cas. (CCH) ¶ 70,603 (M.D. Pa. 1994); Pennsylvania v. Russell Stover Candies, Inc., 1993-1 Trade Cas. (CCH) ¶ 70,224 (E.D. Pa. 1993). The states may seek divestiture under Section 16 of the Clayton Act, *see California v. American Stores Co.*, 495 U.S. 271 (1990), or treble damages, under Section 4, for injury suffered to their proprietary interest, *see Hawaii v. Standard Oil Co.*, 405 U.S. 251, 262 (1972).

64. *See, e.g.*, Massachusetts v. Doane Beal & Ames, Inc., 1994-1 Trade Cas. (CCH) ¶ 70,516 (D. Mass. 1994); Stanley Works v. Newell Co., 1992-2 Trade Cas. (CCH) ¶ 70,008 (D. Conn. 1992).

65. *See, e.g.*, FTC v. Tenet Health Care Corp., 17 F. Supp. 2d 937, 939 (E.D. Mo. 1998), *rev'd on other grounds,* No. 98-3123, 1999 WL 512108 (8th Cir. July 21, 1999).

a federal agency and one or more of the states, the analysis under the state statute is likely to parallel Section 7 analysis.[67]

66. United States v. First Data Corp., No. 1:03CV02169 (D.D.C. filed Oct. 23, 2003); United States v. Echostar Communications Corp., No. 1:02CV02138 (D.D.C. filed Oct. 31, 2002) (complaint); United States v. Waste Mgmt., Inc., No. 98 CV 1768 (FB) (MDG) (E.D.N.Y. filed June 25, 2002) (modified final judgment); United States v. Vail Resorts, Inc., 1997-2 Trade Cas. (CCH) ¶ 72,030 (D. Colo. 1997); United States v. Thomson Corp., 1997-1 Trade Cas. (CCH) ¶ 71,754 (D.D.C. 1997); United States v. USA Waste Serv., 1997-1 Trade Cas. (CCH) ¶ 71,692 (D.D.C. 1996).

67. *See Tenet Health Care Corp.*, 17 F. Supp. 2d at 941 ("The parties have assumed that the state-law claim should be analyzed by the same standards governing the Clayton Act claim, and the Court agrees with that assumption and discusses the case accordingly").

CHAPTER 2

U.S. ENFORCEMENT POLICY AND PROCEDURE

A. The Concurrent Enforcement Authority of the U.S. Department of Justice and the Federal Trade Commission

The Antitrust Division of the U.S. Department of Justice (DOJ or the Division) and the Federal Trade Commission (FTC or the Commission) share jurisdiction for challenging mergers, acquisitions, and joint ventures under Section 7 of the Clayton Act.[1] The agencies' concurrent enforcement authority has evolved since the passage of the Federal Trade Commission Act in 1914.

Between the enactment of the Sherman Act in 1890 and the enactment of the Clayton and Federal Trade Commission Acts twenty-four years later, the DOJ was the sole federal government agency charged with antitrust enforcement responsibility. During that time, the Sherman Act was the only statutory weapon the Division had for challenging mergers on the basis of their effect on competition.

In 1914, Congress passed the Clayton Act to deal more directly and effectively with mergers and the Federal Trade Commission Act to establish the FTC as a separate agency to enforce certain of the nation's competition laws, including the merger laws. The FTC did not supplant the DOJ as the federal government's antitrust enforcer, but became an additional source of antitrust enforcement authority and expertise. As the U.S. Supreme Court later explained, it was "the congressional intent to create a body of experts who shall gain experience by length of service; a body which shall be independent of executive authority, except in its selection, and free to exercise its judgment without the leave or hindrance of any other official or any department of the government."[2]

In 1948, the DOJ and the FTC signed a formal liaison agreement creating a mechanism for resolving conflicts that arise from the agencies'

1. 15 U.S.C. § 18. For a discussion of the strengths and weaknesses of the current dual system, see Report of the American Bar Association Section of Antitrust Law, Special Committee to Study the Role of the Federal Trade Commission (1989).
2. Humphrey's Ex'r v. United States, 295 U.S. 602, 625-26 (1935).

concurrent jurisdiction over Section 7 enforcement.[3] Though the 1948 liaison agreement does not "in any way limit either agency in making an independent decision as to what investigation it will undertake,"[4] it nonetheless seeks to avoid duplicative investigations. The process established by the 1948 agreement has been revised and refined over the years, but the basic framework remains.

The determination of which agency will handle a particular prospective investigation is known as "clearance." Before initiating a new investigation, each agency briefly describes the scope of the investigation to the other agency and provides the other agency with the names of the potential targets of the investigation and the relevant product and geographic markets involved.[5] Generally, the prospective investigation will be "cleared" to the agency with the greater expertise in the relevant product.[6]

In this regard, the DOJ has historically taken the lead in investigating mergers and acquisitions involving telecommunications, banking and finance, steel, electric power, air transport services, beer, and newspapers. The FTC has historically taken the lead in investigating mergers and acquisitions involving chemicals, oil and gas pipelines, food and food distribution, cable television, pharmaceuticals, retailing, and textiles. The agencies have shared jurisdiction in computer software and

---

3. *See Liaison Agreement of the FTC and the Antitrust Division, reprinted in* 4 Trade Reg. Rep. (CCH) ¶ 9,565.05 *and* www.usdoj.gov/atr/foia/divisionmanual/ch7.pdf (collectively discussing concurrent jurisdiction).
4. *Id.*
5. Under the 1948 liaison agreement, the agencies exchanged index cards with information regarding any new proposed investigations. If the other agency did not have an investigation of the matter pending, the agency sending the notification could proceed without further liaison. This exchange of information is now computerized.
6. FEDERAL TRADE COMM'N & U.S. DEP'T OF JUSTICE, FTC/DOJ CLEARANCE PROCEDURES FOR INVESTIGATIONS (1993), *reprinted in* 65 Antitrust & Trade Reg. Rep. (BNA) 746 (1993). The 1993 memorandum elaborates that "product" means, in order of significance, the same product, a substitute, an input or output, and a product used in the subject product in a single manufacturing process. The agency's expertise is evaluated in terms of its having engaged in a "substantial antitrust investigation" in the relevant industry within the preceding five years. A "substantial antitrust investigation," in turn, means one in which requests for additional information under the Hart-Scott-Rodino Antitrust Improvements Act of 1976, 15 U.S.C. § 18a, civil investigative demands, or subpoenas were issued and documents submitted and reviewed.

health care (including hospital) cases. While these areas of expertise serve as a general guide to the expertise of the respective agencies, the agencies on occasion agree, for reasons that may have nothing to do with their respective expertise, that one of them should pursue an investigation in an industry where the other has traditionally had expertise.[7]

In 1993, the liaison agreement was updated and clarified to establish interagency procedures for determining which agency would investigate a matter in which both have expressed an interest.[8] Under these 1993 procedures, the agencies undertook to try to resolve clearance issues within ten calendar days after receipt of notification of a transaction under the Hart-Scott-Rodino Antitrust Improvements Act of 1976 (HSR Act) or within ten days of a request by one of the agencies relating to a transaction that was not reportable under the HSR Act.[9]

In March 1995, the antitrust agencies jointly announced the implementation of additional procedures to improve the clearance process in HSR Act matters, including the increased use of e-mail communications between the agencies.[10] Under these new procedures, clearance decisions must be resolved within nine business days after receipt of notification under the HSR Act.[11]

On March 5, 2002, the agencies announced they had entered into a Memorandum of Agreement establishing revised clearance procedures for merger reviews.[12] The agreement attempted to reduce greatly the number of clearance disputes between the agencies by allocating all mergers in certain industries to each agency based on their historical

---

7. Clearance disputes between the agencies sometimes arise because one agency is concerned that granting clearance to the other "would permit the other agency to gain experience, and, perhaps, 'capture' that industry." Deborah Majoras, Remarks Before the Houston Bar Association Antitrust and Trade Regulation Section, Houston, We Have a Competitive Problem: How Can We Remedy It? (Apr. 17, 2002), *at* www.usdoj.gov/atr/public/speeches/11112.htm.
8. *See* FTC/DOJ CLEARANCE PROCEDURES, *supra* note 6.
9. *Id.*
10. U.S. DEP'T OF JUSTICE & FEDERAL TRADE COMM'N, HART-SCOTT-RODINO PREMERGER PROGRAM IMPROVEMENTS (1995), *reprinted in* 6 Trade Reg. Rep. (CCH) ¶ 42,522.
11. *Id.*
12. Memorandum of Agreement Between the Federal Trade Commission and the Antitrust Division of the United States Department of Justice Concerning Clearance Procedures for Investigations (2002), *at* www.ftc.gov/opa/2002/02/clearance/ftcdojagree.pdf.

expertise. The revised clearance procedure seemed largely successful at first: investigations commenced within a matter of days and there were no clearance disputes between the agencies.[13] However, the Agreement met intense political opposition on Capitol Hill, and DOJ therefore announced on May 20, 2002 that it would no longer follow the Agreement.[14]

Generally, the clearance process enables the agencies to avoid duplicative investigations.[15] Disputes may arise, however, over which of the two agencies has expertise that is more directly applicable to a particular matter. These disputes are typically resolved by agency staff assigned to liaise with each other, but may require review at higher levels of authority—ultimately to the level of the Chairman of the FTC and the Assistant Attorney General of the Antitrust Division, if necessary.[16]

B. The History and Use of the Federal *Merger Guidelines*

The *Merger Guidelines* are the enforcement agencies' public explanation of how and why the agencies make the decisions they do regarding merger enforcement. The *Merger Guidelines* are both an outline for the agency staffs conducting investigations and a series of guideposts for companies and lawyers involved in planning and overseeing mergers and acquisitions. The *Merger Guidelines* set forth the specific factors that the agencies will examine in seeking to determine the likely effects on competition of a merger or acquisition. Although the *Merger Guidelines* do not have the force of law, courts have found them to be useful tools for their own merger analyses.

1. The Purpose of the **Merger Guidelines**

The DOJ first published *Merger Guidelines* in 1968.[17] The purpose of those *Merger Guidelines* was to "acquaint the business community,

---

13. *See* Enforcement: DOJ/FTC Clearance Agreement Succumbs to Political Inflammation, 82 Antitrust & Trade Reg. Rep. (BNA) 467 (May 24, 2002).

14. Press Release, U.S. Dep't of Justice, Statement by Charles A. James Regarding DOJ/FTC Clearance Agreement (May 20, 2002), *at* www.usdoj.gov/atr/public/press_releases/2002/11178.htm.

15. Majoras, *supra* note 7.

16. *See* HART-SCOTT-RODINO PREMERGER PROGRAM IMPROVEMENTS, *supra* note 10.

17. U.S. DEP'T OF JUSTICE, MERGER GUIDELINES (1968) [hereinafter 1968 MERGER GUIDELINES], *reprinted in* 4 Trade Reg. Rep. (CCH) ¶ 13,101.

the legal profession, and other interested groups and individuals with the standards currently being applied by the U.S. Department of Justice in determining whether to challenge corporate acquisitions and mergers under Section 7 of the Clayton Act."[18]

The 1968 *Merger Guidelines* were superseded by the 1982 *Merger Guidelines*,[19] which, while differing greatly in substance from the 1968 *Merger Guidelines*, had very much the same purpose: to provide guidance to the business community on the Division's enforcement intentions and mode of analysis.[20] The 1982 *Merger Guidelines* also expanded discussion of the definition of relevant markets.[21]

The current *Merger Guidelines*? in effect, with one limited amendment, since 1992[22]? were intended to help "prevent anticompetitive mergers yet avoid deterring the larger universe of procompetitive or competitively neutral mergers . . . by providing guidance enabling the business community to avoid antitrust problems when planning mergers."[23] Although the agencies anticipated that the *Merger Guidelines* would cause the legal and business communities to be somewhat more selective in their choices of possible mergers or merger partners, the agencies also expected that the *Merger Guidelines* would reduce the "deterrents to efficiency-enhancing business conduct that will promote U.S. competitiveness."[24]

---

18. *Id*. at 1.
19. U.S. DEP'T OF JUSTICE, MERGER GUIDELINES (1982) [hereinafter 1982 MERGER GUIDELINES], *reprinted in* 4 Trade Reg. Rep. (CCH) ¶ 13,102.
20. *See id*. at 20,528.
21. *See id*. at 20,529.
22. *See* U.S. DEP'T OF JUSTICE & FEDERAL TRADE COMM'N, HORIZONTAL MERGER GUIDELINES (1992) [hereinafter 1992 MERGER GUIDELINES], *reprinted in* 4 Trade Reg. Rep. (CCH) ¶ 13,104 and in Appendix I; U.S. DEP'T OF JUSTICE & FEDERAL TRADE COMM'N, REVISION TO SECTION 4 OF HORIZONTAL MERGER GUIDELINES (1997) [hereinafter REVISED MERGER GUIDELINES], *reprinted in* 4 Trade Reg. Rep. (CCH) ¶ 13,104, at 20,573-11.
23. U.S. DEP'T OF JUSTICE & FEDERAL TRADE COMM'N, STATEMENT ACCOMPANYING RELEASE OF REVISED MERGER GUIDELINES (1992), *reprinted in* 4 Trade Reg. Rep. (CCH) ¶ 13,104, at 20,569.
24. *Justice Department and FTC Issue Horizontal Merger Guidelines,* U.S. Newswire, at 2 (Apr. 2, 1992).

2. *The Evolution of the* Merger Guidelines

a. The 1968 *Merger Guidelines*

The 1968 *Merger Guidelines* attempted to define a limited focus to the government's enforcement policy, informing the legal and business communities that "[m]arket structure is the focus of the Department's merger policy chiefly because the conduct of the individual firms in a market tends to be controlled by the structure of that market."[25]

The 1968 *Merger Guidelines* employed the "reasonable interchangeability" test for defining the relevant product market, but did not provide much guidance as to how the test was to be applied.[26] Similarly, the 1968 *Merger Guidelines* explained that "[t]he total sales of a product or service in any commercially significant section of the country (even as small as a single community), or aggregate of such sections, will ordinarily constitute a geographic market if firms engaged in selling the product make significant sales of the product to purchasers in the section or sections."[27]

In addition to horizontal mergers and acquisitions, the 1968 *Merger Guidelines* also addressed vertical relationships, conglomerate mergers, and potential competition analysis.[28]

b. The 1982 *Merger Guidelines* and FTC *Statement*

The 1968 *Merger Guidelines* remained in place until June 14, 1982, when the Division announced new merger guidelines to outline the standards in use at the Division to determine what mergers to challenge.[29] At the time of the announcement, the Division stated that the 1982 *Merger Guidelines* did not mark a revolutionary change from the earlier analysis, but simply codified the evolutionary changes that had already been adopted in practice during the fourteen years since 1968.[30] The 1982 *Merger Guidelines* provided a more detailed

---

25. 1968 MERGER GUIDELINES, *supra* note 17, § 2.
26. *See id.* § 3(i).
27. *Id.* § 3(ii). The *Merger Guidelines* explained that the geographic market, thus defined, need not be expanded or contracted unless "it clearly appears" that the existence or absence of "economic barriers" necessitates such an adjustment. *Id.*
28. *See id.* §§ 11-20.
29. *See* 4 Trade Reg Rep. (CCH) ¶ 13,102, at 20,528.
30. *See* Statement of Attorney General William French Smith, at 2 (June 14, 1982); 4 Trade Reg. Rep. (CCH) ¶ 13,102, at 20,528.

discussion of the process for defining the relevant market than the 1968 *Merger Guidelines* had provided. This discussion included consideration of the predicted reaction of customers to a small hypothetical price increase to determine whether to include a particular product or firm in the relevant market.[31]

The 1982 *Merger Guidelines* also replaced the 1968 *Merger Guidelines*' use of the four-firm concentration ratio with use of the Herfindahl-Hirschman Index (HHI) as the means of calculating market concentration.[32]

The 1982 *Merger Guidelines* also set forth a number of qualitative factors, including ease of entry, that the Division would examine in addition to the quantitative calculation of market shares and market concentration.[33]

The FTC did not join with the DOJ in issuing the 1982 *Merger Guidelines.* It issued its own *Statement* expressing its collective judgment supporting changes in the 1968 *Merger Guidelines* and highlighting the "principal considerations that [would] guide its horizontal merger enforcement."[34] Although indicating that it would give "considerable weight" to the 1982 *Merger Guidelines*, it refrained from endorsing the *Merger Guidelines*' analytical approach or the specific numerical thresholds for reviewing horizontal mergers. The *Statement* also indicated that the Commission would likely be more receptive than DOJ to arguments related to the efficiencies generated by a particular merger, or to the likelihood that a firm or division would exit the market absent the merger.[35]

---

31. 1982 MERGER GUIDELINES, *supra* note 19, § II(A).
32. *See id.* § III(A). The 1982 MERGER GUIDELINES established three levels of concentration based upon the calculation of the postmerger HHI, defining markets with a postmerger HHI under 1000 points as "unconcentrated," between 1000 and 1800 as "moderately concentrated" and above 1800 as "highly concentrated." The 1982 MERGER GUIDELINES then specified the HHI increase levels resulting from the merger for each classification, the presence of which would render a challenge by the Division as "likely" or "unlikely."
33. *See id.* §§ III(B)-(C).
34. FEDERAL TRADE COMM'N, STATEMENT CONCERNING HORIZONTAL MERGERS (1982) [hereinafter 1982 FTC STATEMENT], *reprinted in* 4 Trade Reg. Rep. (CCH) ¶ 13,200.
35. *See id.* at 8-11.

c. The 1984 Revisions[36]

Two years after it issued the 1982 *Merger Guidelines*, the DOJ announced the refinement of its merger analysis "to incorporate new insights and to ensure the continued relevance of that analysis to a changing economic environment."[37] In general, the 1984 revisions were "intended to correct any misperception that the *Merger Guidelines* are a set of rigid mathematical formulas that ignore market realities and rely solely on a static view of the marketplace."[38]

The 1984 *Merger Guidelines* contained sections on nonhorizontal mergers, including vertical mergers,[39] and mergers raising potential competition issues,[40] which to date have not been superseded. The great majority of prospective mergers that are closely examined by the agencies create concerns about the impact on horizontal competition, but vertical and potential competition issues do nevertheless still arise, and the source for analysis is still the 1984 *Merger Guidelines*.

d. The 1992 *Merger Guidelines*

Following the 1984 revisions, the *Merger Guidelines* were not updated again until April 2, 1992, when the 1992 *Horizontal Merger Guidelines* were jointly issued by the DOJ and the FTC, a development characterized at the time as "a major step forward."[41] "Where, as here, two agencies have concurrent enforcement responsibilities, the standards to be applied should not depend on which agency is analyzing a particular merger."[42]

In their joint statement accompanying the issuance of the 1992 *Merger Guidelines*, the DOJ and the Commission described the joint guidelines as the "next logical step in the development of the agencies' analysis of mergers."[43] The 1992 *Merger Guidelines* reflected the enforcement agencies' experiences in applying the 1982 and 1984 versions and contained "improvements . . . made to reflect advances in

36. U.S. DEP'T OF JUSTICE, MERGER GUIDELINES (1984) [hereinafter 1984 MERGER GUIDELINES], *reprinted in* 4 Trade Reg. Rep. (CCH) ¶ 13,103.
37. *See id.* at 20,551.
38. *Id.*
39. *See id.* § 4.2.
40. *See id.* § 4.1.
41. U.S. Dep't of Justice, Press Release (Apr. 2, 1992).
42. *Id.*
43. STATEMENT ACCOMPANYING RELEASE OF REVISED MERGER GUIDELINES, *supra* note 23, at 20,569.

legal and economic thinking."[44] The 1992 *Merger Guidelines* were also designed to "clarify certain aspects of the *Merger Guidelines* that proved to be ambiguous or were interpreted by observers in ways that were inconsistent with the actual policy of the agencies."[45]

As a practical matter, the 1992 *Merger Guidelines* included a number of revisions that were "largely technical or stylistic."[46] In their "most significant revision," the 1992 *Merger Guidelines* "explain[ed] more clearly how mergers may lead to adverse competitive effects and how particular market factors relate to the analysis of those effects."[47] In addition, the 1992 *Merger Guidelines* sought to "sharpen the distinction between the treatment of various types of supply responses and to articulate the framework for analyzing the timeliness, likelihood and sufficiency of entry."[48]

e. The 1997 Efficiencies Revision of the 1992 *Merger Guidelines*

In 1997, the DOJ and the FTC jointly revised the 1992 *Merger Guidelines*' treatment of efficiencies. The revision reaffirmed the agencies' prior recognition that the potential to generate efficiencies is "the primary benefit of mergers to the economy."[49] Nonetheless, because "[e]fficiencies are difficult to verify and quantify" and because even "efficiencies projected reasonably and in good faith by the merging firms may not be realized," the 1997 revision stated that "the merging firms must substantiate efficiency claims so that the Agency can verify by reasonable means the likelihood and magnitude of each asserted efficiency, how and when each would be achieved (and any costs of doing so), how each would enhance the merged firm's ability and incentive to compete, and why each would be merger-specific."[50] The revision continued: "Efficiency claims will not be considered if they are

---

44. *Id*.
45. *Id*.
46. *Id*.
47. *Id.*; *see* 1992 MERGER GUIDELINES, *supra* note 22, § 2.
48. STATEMENT ACCOMPANYING RELEASE OF REVISED MERGER GUIDELINES, *supra* note 23, at 20,569; 1992 MERGER GUIDELINES, *supra* note 22, §§ 1.3, 3.
49. *Compare* REVISED MERGER GUIDELINES, *supra* note 22, *with* 1992 MERGER GUIDELINES, *supra* note 22, § 4, *reprinted in* 4 Trade Reg. Rep. (CCH) ¶ 13,104, at 20,573-13.
50. REVISED MERGER GUIDELINES, *supra* note 22.

vague or speculative or otherwise cannot be verified by reasonable means."[51]

3. *The Nonbinding Nature of the* Merger Guidelines

Although the *Merger Guidelines* provide the DOJ and the FTC with an analytical tool with which to make civil enforcement decisions in the context of corporate mergers and acquisitions, the *Merger Guidelines* are not binding even with respect to the enforcement agencies themselves.[52] Nonetheless, as a matter of practice, the agencies generally adhere to the principles set forth in the *Merger Guidelines* so that the *Merger Guidelines* retain their usefulness as instructional and planning tools for the business and legal communities.

The enforcement agencies' *Merger Guidelines* are of course not binding on the courts[53] and, in at least one case, the *Merger Guidelines* have been criticized as inconsistent with federal antitrust law. In *Olin*

---

51. *Id.*
52. *See* 1992 MERGER GUIDELINES, *supra* note 22.
53. *See, e.g.*, Prater v. United States Parole Comm'n, 802 F.2d 948, 954 (7th Cir. 1986) ("if the Justice Department issues guidelines for the enforcement of a federal statute that it administers (as it did in the 1984 U.S. Department of Justice Merger Guidelines, for example), this is the performance of an interpretive function that every law enforcement agency has; it is not the enactment of a law"); FTC V. Swedish Match, 131 F. Supp 2d 151 167 n.12 (D.D.C. 2001) ("The Merger Guidelines are not binding on the Court, but as this Circuit has stated, they provide 'a useful illustration of the application of the HHI.'"); Ansell Inc. v. Schmid Labs., Inc., 757 F. Supp. 467, 475 (D.N.J. 1991) ("The Court views the Product Market Definition position of the DOJ in the Merger Guidelines as an advisory aid in determining the relevant product market"), *aff'd*, 941 F.2d 1200 (3d Cir. 1991); Check-Mate Sys., Inc. v. Sensormatic Elecs. Corp., 1986 WL 6207 (E.D. Pa. 1986) ("[T]he merger guidelines, which are not the law, merely indicate when the U.S. Department of Justice is likely to challenge mergers. They are, as the title says, only guidelines, not binding on the Justice Department and surely not binding on the courts"), *aff'd*, 810 F.2d 1162 (3d Cir. 1987); Laidlaw Acquisition Corp. v. Mayflower Group, Inc., 636 F. Supp. 1513, 1521 (S.D. Ind. 1986) ("The agencies' opinion of a merger is not binding on this court, and their enforcement decisions do not necessarily reflect the current state of antitrust law"); Marathon Oil Co. v. Mobil Corp., 530 F. Supp. 315, 325 (N.D. Ohio), ("Obviously, such guidelines are not binding on the courts") *aff'd*, 669 F.2d 378 (6th Cir. 1981).

Corp. v. FTC,[54] the Ninth Circuit rejected the defendant's argument that it was inconsistent to recognize a larger relevant market once a narrower relevant market had been identified, opining that "[w]hile this may be true under the Department of Justice Merger Guidelines, it is not true as a matter of federal antitrust law."[55]

Although not binding, the *Merger Guidelines* have frequently been regarded by district courts[56] and courts of appeal[57] as useful, legitimate

---

54. 986 F.2d 1295 (9th Cir. 1993).

55. *Id*. at 1301.

56. *See, e.g.*, FTC v. Libbey, 211 F. Supp. 2d 34, 52 n.33 (D.D.C. 2002) (citing *Guidelines* on efficiencies); United States v. SunGard Data Systems, Inc., 172 F. Supp. 2d 172 (D.D.C. 2001) (citing *Guidelines* regarding relevant product market definition); FTC v. Swedish Match, 131 F. Supp. 2d 151, 167 n.12 (D.D.C. 2000) ("The Merger Guidelines are not binding on the Court, but . . . they do provide 'a useful illustration of the application of the HHI'"); FTC v. Cardinal Health, Inc., 12 F. Supp. 2d 34 (D.D.C. 1998); FTC v. Staples, Inc., 970 F. Supp. 1066 (D.D.C. 1997); HTI Health Servs. v. Quorum Health Group, 960 F. Supp. 1104 (S.D. Miss. 1997); FTC v. Butterworth Health Corp., 946 F. Supp. 1285, 1293 (W.D. Mich. 1996), *aff'd*, 121 F.3d 708 (6th Cir. 1997); Community Publishers v. Donrey Corp., 892 F. Supp. 1146, 1153 (W.D. Ark. 1995) (while the *Merger Guidelines* "do not have the force of law," they "represent mainstream economic thinking"); New York v. Kraft Gen. Foods, Inc., 926 F. Supp. 321, 358 n.9 (S.D.N.Y. 1995) ("the Merger Guidelines are helpful in providing an analytical framework for evaluating an acquisition, but they are not binding upon the court"); FTC v. Alliant Techsystems Inc., 808 F. Supp. 9, 20 (D.D.C. 1992); United States v. United Tote, Inc., 768 F. Supp. 1064, 1070-71, 1079-84 (D. Del. 1991) (citing *Guidelines* on concentration levels, market power definition, entry, and efficiencies); United States v. Country Lake Foods, Inc., 754 F. Supp. 669 (D. Minn. 1990); United States v. Ivaco, Inc., 704 F. Supp. 1409 (W.D. Mich. 1989); Tasty Baking Co. v. Ralston Purina, Inc., 653 F. Supp. 1250, 1264 (E.D. Pa. 1987) (*Merger Guidelines*, "acknowledged by defendants to be an important tool for assessing acquisitions," supported conclusion that merger would create impermissible increase in concentration); Santa Cruz Med. Clinic v. Dominican Santa Cruz Hosp., 1995-2 Trade Cas. (CCH) ¶ 71,254 (N.D. Cal. 1995); FTC v. R.R. Donnelly & Sons Co., 1990-2 Trade Cas. (CCH) ¶ 69,239 (D.D.C. 1990) ("Well-established precedent and the United States Department of Justice Merger Guidelines recognize that the sophistication and bargaining power of buyers play a significant role in assessing the effects of a proposed transaction"); FTC v. Imo Indus., 1992-2 Trade Cas. (CCH) ¶ 69,943 (D.D.C. 1989); United States v. Central State Bank, 1989-1 Trade Cas. (CCH) ¶ 68,493 (W.D. Mich.

tools for analyzing mergers. In *FTC v. H.J. Heinz Co.*,[58] for example, the D.C. Circuit adopted the *Merger Guidelines*' use of the HHI to calculate market concentration, noting that "[u]nder the Merger Guidelines a market in which the postmerger HHI is above 1800 is considered 'highly concentrated' and mergers that increase the HHI in such a market by over 50 points potentially raise significant competitive concerns."[59] The court noted that the premerger HHI in the relevant product market was 4775 and that the merger in question would raise the HHI by 510 points.[60] The court therefore held that the FTC had "create[d], by a wide margin, a presumption that the merger will lessen competition" in the relevant market.[61]

Occasionally, the courts have criticized the enforcement agencies for not following the precepts of the *Merger Guidelines*. In *United States v. Syufy Enterprises*,[62] for example, the Ninth Circuit upheld the trial court's refusal to enjoin a movie theater merger in Las Vegas on the grounds that entry into the Las Vegas first-run motion picture exhibition market was relatively easy. Noting that, under the *Merger Guidelines*, "if successful entry is likely within two years, there are no significant entry barriers, and the government will not challenge mergers in that market," the Ninth Circuit stated that, "[h]ad the government applied the two-year test here, it surely would not have pursued this suit."[63]

1988); Burlington Indus. v. Edelman, 666 F. Supp. 799, 804 (M.D.N.C. 1987), *aff'd*, [1987 Transfer Binder] Fed. Sec. L. Rep. (CCH) ¶93,339 (4th Cir. 1987); FTC v. Occidental Petroleum Corp., 1986-1 Trade Cas. (CCH) ¶ 67,071 (D.D.C. 1986); United States v. Rice Growers Ass'n, 1986-2 Trade Cas. (CCH) ¶ 67,288 (E.D. Cal. 1986).

57. *See, e.g.*, FTC v. H.J. Heinz Co., 246 F.3d 708, 716-17, 720-22 (D.C. Cir. 2001); Dr. Pepper/Seven-Up Cos. v. FTC, 991 F.2d 859, 865 (D.C. Cir. 1993); United States Healthcare Inc. v. Healthsource, Inc., 986 F.2d 589, 597 (1st Cir. 1993); United States v. Loew's Inc., 882 F.2d 29, 31 (2d Cir. 1989); R.C. Bigelow, Inc. v. Unilever N.V., 867 F.2d 102, 110 (2d Cir. 1989); United States v. Archer-Daniels-Midland Co., 866 F.2d 242, 244, 245 (8th Cir. 1988); FTC v. PPG Indus., 798 F.2d 1500, 1503 (D.C. Cir. 1986); Ball Mem'l Hosp. v. Mutual Hosp. Ins., Inc., 784 F.2d 1325, 1336 (7th Cir. 1986); Deauville Corp. v. Federated Dep't Stores, 756 F.2d 1183, 1190 (5th Cir. 1985).
58. 246 F.3d 708.
59. *Id.* at 716 n.9.
60. *Id.* at 716.
61. *Id.*
62. 903 F.2d 659 (9th Cir. 1990).
63. *Id.* at 666 n.11.

Similarly, in *United States v. Baker Hughes Inc.*,[64] the D.C. Circuit rejected the government's assertion that entry must be "quick and effective," finding "no merit in the legal standard propounded by the government. It is devoid of support in the statute, in the case law, and in the government's own Merger Guidelines."[65] In addition, the court rejected the government's claim that only ease of entry could defeat a prima facie case, reminding the government that its "own Merger Guidelines contain a detailed discussion of non-entry factors that can overcome a presumption of illegality established by market share statistics."[66] Finally, the court noted:

> We refer the government to its own Merger Guidelines, which recognize that "[i]n a variety of situations, market share and market concentration data may either understate or overstate the likely future competitive significance of a firm or firms in the market." . . . Although the Guidelines disclaim "slavish[ ] adhere[nce]" to such data .. . we fear that the Department of Justice has ignored its own admonition.[67]

In sum, the courts have often viewed the enforcement agencies' *Merger Guidelines* as useful tools that, while clearly not binding on the court, provide a helpful analytical model for resolving complex antitrust issues.

---

64. 908 F.2d 981 (D.C. Cir. 1990).
65. *Id.* at 983.
66. *Id.* at 985; *cf.* Jonathan B. Baker, *The Problem with Baker Hughes and Syufy: On the Role of Entry in Merger Analysis*, 65 ANTITRUST L.J. 353 (1997) (arguing that where committed entry is at issue, Section 7 of the Clayton Act requires that the antitrust agencies and the courts evaluate whether entry would be profitable in order to determine whether entry would likely cure the competitive problem).
67. *Baker Hughes Inc.*, 908 F.2d at 992 n.13; *see also* United States v. Waste Mgmt., Inc., 743 F.2d 976, 982-83 (2d Cir. 1984) ("[T]he Merger Guidelines issued by the government itself not only recognize the economic principle that ease of entry is relevant to appraising the impact upon competition of a merger but also state that it may override all other factors. . . . If the U.S. Department of Justice routinely considers ease of entry as relevant to determining the competitive impact of a merger, it may not argue to a court addressing the same issue that ease of entry is irrelevant").

C. Review of Reportable Transactions under the Hart-Scott-Rodino Antitrust Improvements Act of 1976

The HSR Act[68] requires the parties to certain mergers and acquisitions to provide certain information[69] to the FTC and the DOJ and to observe waiting periods prior to consummating the merger or acquisition.[70] For most reportable transactions, the HSR Act requires the parties to wait thirty calendar days after the completion of the HSR filing before closing the transaction.[71] The thirty-day period is subject to

---

68. 15 U.S.C. § 18a.

69. All information submitted in connection with a premerger notification filing, including the fact that a filing has been received, is confidential and exempt from disclosure under the Freedom of Information Act. 15 U.S.C. § 18a(h). The premerger notification and report form allows parties to request early termination of the waiting period. If early termination is requested and granted, a notice is posted on the FTC's website and is published in the *Federal Register*. *See* 15 U.S.C. § 7A(b)(2). This notice makes public the fact that a filing was made and by which parties but not the contents of the filing.

70. *See* 15 U.S.C. § 18a(d); 16 C.F.R. §§ 801-803. Not all transactions are reportable under the HSR Act. The original language of the Act provided that transactions valued $15 million or less were not subject to the reporting requirement. In 2001, the "size of transaction" minimum threshold for reporting purposes was increased to $50 million. 15 U.S.C. § 18a. The HSR Act and its implementing regulations also exempt certain transactions from the reporting obligation. Transactions that are not subject to the HSR Act's notification and waiting requirements are nevertheless subject to the substantive antitrust jurisdiction of the FTC and the DOJ, *see* United States v. United Tote, Inc., 768 F. Supp. 1064 (D. Del. 1991); Mustad Int'l Group NV, 120 F.T.C. 865 (1995); Kiwi Brands Inc., 118 F.T.C. 406 (1994); McCormick & Co., 116 F.T.C. 1230 (1993); Central Soya Co., 113 F.T.C. 786 (1990); Xidex Corp., 102 F.T.C. 1 (1983)), which continue to take action against acquisitions that are not reportable under the HSR Act. *See, e.g.*, United States v. 3D Sys. Corp., No. 1-01-CV01237 2002 U.S. Dist. LEXIS 18377 (D.D.C. Apr. 17, 2002); MSC Software Corp. (FTC Complaint issued Oct. 10, 2001, FTC Docket No. 9299); Monier Lifetile LLC (FTC Complaint Issued Sept. 22, 1998, FTC Docket No. 9290); Shell Oil Co. (FTC Complaint and Consent Order issued Apr. 21, 1998, FTC Docket No. C-3803). Nonreportable transactions typically come to the enforcement agencies' attention through complaints from aggrieved parties or through news reports.

71. *See* 15 U.S.C. § 18a(e). If the thirtieth day falls on a weekend or federal holiday, the waiting period continues throught the next business day.

extension by the issuance of a request for additional information (Second Request) until thirty calendar days after the parties have substantially complied with the Second Request.[72]

The Premerger Office of the FTC's Bureau of Competition advises firms as to their responsibilities under the HSR Act and administers the Act's premerger notification program. If, upon review by the Premerger Office, a filing is found to be deficient in either form (e.g., failure to provide the requisite number of copies to each agency) or substance (e.g., failure to provide all of the required information), the Premerger Office notifies the filing party of the deficiency. The HSR Act waiting period does not start until all required filings are complete and each acquiring person has paid the applicable filing fee.[73]

The Premerger Office prepares a summary of information contained in the HSR Act filings, such as areas of product or geographic overlap between merging companies, to facilitate the determination of the level of scrutiny each transaction should receive. These summaries are circulated to the FTC's Merger Screening Committee (comprised of the management of the Bureau of Competition, the Bureau of Economics and certain regional offices) for a determination of whether the HSR Act's waiting period should be terminated early or whether a preliminary review is warranted to determine the likelihood of anticompetitive effects as a result of the transaction.

At the DOJ, if the staff determines that a transaction does not warrant investigation, the staff member fills out a "No-Interest" form, which is sent to the appropriate Section Chief or Assistant Chief and, if approved, forwarded to the Antitrust Division's Premerger Notification Unit/FTC Liaison Office.[74] The FTC Liaison Office then will notify the FTC of the Division's decision not to investigate further.[75] If both parties have requested early termination and have submitted their notification and report forms, early termination usually will be granted when both agencies do not wish to investigate further.[76]

---

72. *See* 15 U.S.C. § 18a(e)(2); 16 C.F.R. § 803.20. For cash tender offers and acquisitions involving a party in bankruptcy, the initial waiting period is only 15 calendar days, subject to extension until 10 calendar days after substantial compliance with a Second Request, if one is issued. *See* 15 U.S.C. § 18a(e); 16 C.F.R. §§ 801.30, 803.10; 11 U.S.C. § 363(b)(2)(B).
73. The filing fee ranges from $45,000 to $280,000 depending on the size of the transaction. *See* 15 U.S.C. § 18a; 16 C.F.R. § 803.9.
74. *See* Antitrust Division Manual § 3.D.2.d(i), *at* www.usdoj.gov/atr/foia/divisionmanual/ch3.htm.
75. *See id.* § 3.D.1.e(a).
76. *See id.* § 3.D.1.e.

If in either agency the staff determine that a preliminary review is warranted, a staff attorney is assigned to scrutinize the proposed transaction and clearance to investigate the transaction is determined.[77] Once clearance has been received, the staff conducting the preliminary review may seek information, on a voluntary basis, from the filing parties, customers, competitors, potential entrants, and others. Most preliminary reviews do not result in the issuance of a Second Request.

If substantive antitrust concerns remain at the end of the initial waiting period, or if there has been insufficient time to conclude that the transaction does not raise anticompetitive concerns, the investigating agency may issue a Second Request.[78] When the investigating agency has decided to issue a Second Request, the agency typically notifies the parties before the close of business on the last business day of the initial waiting period. (The notification may be made by telephone.)

Prior to the issuance of a Second Request, and prior to the expiration of the initial waiting period, an acquiring party may also withdraw its HSR filing and refile within two business days without paying an additional filing fee.[79] This restarts the initial waiting period from the refiling date, thereby allowing for further discussion with agency staff. The procedure requires that there be no substantive change in the proposed acquisition, and it may only be used once.[80] In addition, the acquiring party must update item 4(c)[81] and recertify the HSR filing.[82]

Contemporaneously with the issuance of a Second Request, the staff normally seeks authority from their respective agency to use compulsory process to obtain documents, testimony, and answers to interrogatories

---

77. *See* part A of this Chapter.
78. For example, out of the 1,187 transactions reported under the HSR Act in fiscal year 2002, only 49 transactions received Second Requests. Early termination was requested in 1,042 of those 1,187 transactions and granted in 793 of them. *See* FEDERAL TRADE COMM'N & DEP'T OF JUSTICE, ANNUAL REPORT TO CONGRESS, FISCAL YEAR 2002; Appendix O.
79. *See* ABA SECTION OF ANTITRUST LAW, PREMERGER NOTIFICATION PRACTICE MANUAL, Interpretation 267 at 327 (3D ED. 2003).
80. *See id.*
81. Item 4(c) of the HSR Notification Report Form requires generally the submission of documents prepared in connection with the transaction and created or reviewed by officers or directors that discuss competition and related issues.
82. The HSR Notification Report Form must be certified by an officer or director of the filing party.

from third parties.[83] The staff may not necessarily use such authority in all cases, but may employ more informal methods, such as in-person and telephone interviews, throughout the investigation to obtain information from third parties.

A Second Request is typically broad in scope. If it appears that the investigating agency is likely to issue a Second Request, or if a Second Request has been issued, the parties can work with the investigating agency to narrow the scope of the request to focus on the areas in which antitrust concerns exist. In fact, the standard language of the Second Request encourages its recipient to propose modifications to expedite the review of the transaction under investigation.[84] In discussing a proposed modification, the agencies typically want to understand what documents or information a proposed modification would exclude and why it is reasonable to exclude such documents or information.[85] Upon receipt of a Second Request, the recipient may also petition for a review of the information sought in the Second Request by a senior agency official to determine whether it is unreasonably cumulative, unduly burdensome or duplicative.[86]

---

83. *See* 15 U.S.C. §§ 49, 50, 57b-1(a)(6); 16 C.F.R. § 2.7-2.8.

84. The FTC generally "encourage[s] the parties to negotiate with the staff in order to obtain modifications to the second request." Statement of the Federal Trade Commission's Bureau of Competition on Guidelines for Merger Investigations, *at* www.ftc.gov/os/2002/12/bcguidelines021211.htm.

85. Other compliance options include "quick look" review or "phased production" of Second Request documents. Quick look review, initiated by the parties or by the agency, allows for the isolation of one or more dispositive issues in an investigation, permitting the parties to produce documents pertaining only to those issues and potentially expediting a resolution of the investigation. *See* U.S. Dep't of Justice, *Merger Review Process Initiative* (Oct. 12, 2001), *at* www.usdoj.gov/atr/public/9300.htm. Phased production, initiated by the parties to the transaction, permits the production of documents thought by the parties to be dispositive of key issues. An investigation may be terminated, therefore, prior to full production, because the documents produced early on satisfy the agency's concerns with the transaction. For a more thorough discussion of quick look and phased production, see ABA SECTION OF ANTITRUST LAW, THE MERGER REVIEW PROCESS 164-68 (2d ed. 2001).

86. 66 Fed. Reg. 8721 (Feb. 1, 2001) (codified at 16 C.F.R. § 2.20). If the FTC is investigating the merger, the parties may seek review by the FTC's General Counsel using an expedited procedure. *See* FTC Statement, *supra* note 84; Federal Trade Comm'n, Requests for Additional Information: Appeal Procedure, *at* www.ftc.gov/bc/hsr/appeal~1.htm.

The required document production and interrogatory responses must be delivered to the agency office specified in the Second Request, along with a notarized certification of compliance from an officer or director of the responding party. In practice, if the agency determines that the response does not substantially comply with the Second Request, it may reject the certification of compliance and refuse to acknowledge the commencement (and subsequent termination) of the second waiting period.[87]

After the parties have substantially complied with the Second Request, the investigating agency has at most thirty days to bring an action to challenge the proposed transaction.[88] The parties to the transaction may agree to delay their closing to conduct further discussions with the agency staff prior to the staff's forwarding of an enforcement recommendation to agency management. Ultimately, if the staff intends to recommend action to block a proposed transaction, the parties to the proposed transaction usually grant sufficient time to present their case to the ultimate decision makers—either the Assistant Attorney General for Antitrust or the individual members of the Commission—before a lawsuit is filed.[89] At the FTC, the complaint must be authorized by a majority of the Commissioners voting. Although not required, the

---

87. *See* FTC v. McCormick & Co., 1988-1 Trade Cas. (CCH) ¶ 67,976, at 57,985 (D.D.C. 1988) (temporary restraining order prohibiting the consummation of the proposed transaction because McCormick had not substantially complied with the Second Request).

88. The investigating agency has 10 days in the case of a cash tender offer and certain bankruptcy transactions. *See supra* note 72.

89. For example, in fiscal year 2001, the agencies challenged 55 of the 70 transactions for which Second Requests were issued. Of those 55 challenged transactions, 23 were investigated by the FTC. The FTC reached 18 consent agreements, and the parties abandoned four transactions. The FTC sought injunctive relief in one of the investigations. The Division challenged 32 transactions, filing complaints in district court for eight of them and threatening to file complaints in the remaining matters. The Division negotiated consent decrees in all eight transactions for which it filed a complaint. In the 24 transactions where the filing of a complaint was only threatened, the parties restructured their deals to the satisfaction of the Division in 20 of the transactions, and the parties abandoned the remaining four transactions after the Division's intent to file a complaint was made clear. *See* Appendix O. For a comprehensive guide to the federal merger review process, see ABA SECTION OF ANTITRUST LAW, THE MERGER REVIEW PROCESS (2d ed. 2001).

agencies increasingly issue statements to explain their decisions not to challenge a transaction.[90]

In cases in which the FTC seeks a temporary restraining order, preliminary injunction, or other relief under Section 13(b) of the Federal Trade Commission Act,[91] the Commission is required to issue an administrative complaint within twenty days after the federal court enters an order granting the relief requested.[92] In some cases, defendants in Section 13(b) actions have agreed not to consummate a challenged acquisition until after the court's ruling on the motion for preliminary injunction, in order to avoid the automatic issuance of an administrative complaint that would follow the granting of a temporary restraining order.

In 1995, the FTC issued a statement announcing that, in cases in which a preliminary injunction is denied after the issuance of an administrative complaint by the Commission, the Commission will reassess whether to pursue administrative litigation, based on a consideration of various factors, including: (1) the factual findings and legal conclusions of the district court or any appellate court; (2) evidence developed during the course of the preliminary injunction; (3) whether the transaction raises important issues of fact, law, or merger policy that need resolution in administrative litigation; (4) an overall assessment of the costs and benefits of further proceedings; and (5) any other matter that bears on whether it would be in the public interest to proceed with the merger challenge.[93]

Unlike the FTC, the DOJ does not conduct administrative proceedings in antitrust matters or issue administrative orders to remedy antitrust violations. When the Division is the party bringing an antitrust enforcement action, the matter is adjudicated to a final disposition in federal court without an administrative proceeding.

---

90. *See, e.g.*, FTC, Press Release, FTC Closes Its Investigation into Caremark Rx's Proposed Acquistion of Advance PCS (Feb. 11, 2004), *at* www.ftc.gov/opa/2004/02/caremarkadvance.htm.
91. 15 U.S.C. § 53(b).
92. *Id.*
93. *See* FEDERAL TRADE COMM'N, STATEMENT OF POLICY REGARDING ADMINISTRATIVE LITIGATION FOLLOWING THE DENIAL OF A PRELIMINARY INJUNCTION (June 21, 1995).

D. Review of Transactions by State Attorneys General

1. *The National Association of Attorneys General* **Merger Guidelines**

In 1993, the National Association of Attorneys General (NAAG) released guidelines "explain[ing] the general enforcement policy of the state and territorial attorneys general . . . concerning horizontal acquisitions and mergers . . . ."[94] The *NAAG Merger Guidelines* are generally consistent with the current federal agency guidelines, but there are some differences. The *NAAG Merger Guidelines*, for example, define the market in a different manner than the federal agencies,[95] although the *NAAG Merger Guidelines* indicate that the federal methodology of defining markets can be used as an alternative method and where the two methods produce different results, the one that appears most accurate or reliable will be used.[96] In addition, the *NAAG Merger Guidelines* indicate that market power is presumed created or enhanced by a merger

---

94. HORIZONTAL MERGER GUIDELINES OF THE NATIONAL ASSOCIATION OF ATTORNEYS GENERAL (1993) § 1 [hereinafter NAAG MERGER GUIDELINES], *reprinted in* 4 Trade Reg. Rep. (CCH) ¶ 13,406 and in Appendix M. A number of commentators have suggested that a division of effort be considered between the federal agencies and the state attorneys general; generally these recommendations suggest that the areas of responsibility be allocated along the lines of probable harm from the merger, with states assuming prime responsibility for investigating mergers whose effects are primarily state specific. *See, e.g.*, Robert H. Lande, *When Should States Challenge Mergers: A Proposed Federal/ State Balance*, 35 N.Y.L. SCH. L. REV. 1047 (1990); Robert Langer, *Should the Antitrust Division, the FTC, and State Attorneys General Formally Allocate the Market for Antitrust Enforcement?* ANTITRUST REPORT, Oct. 1998; Deborah Majoras, Remarks Before the New York State Bar Association Antitrust Law Section, Antitrust and Federalism (Jan. 23, 2003), *at* www.usdoj.gov/atr/public/speeches/200683.htm ("Without question, under the current system, the state attorneys general should enforce the antitrust laws in matters of local reach").

95. *Compare* 1992 MERGER GUIDELINES *supra* note 22, § 1.1 (using the SSNIP test to determine the appropriate product market) *with* NAAG MERGER GUIDELINES, *supra* note 94, § 3.1 (expansion of the product market to include only products that would be considered suitable by 75% of the purchasers of the product(s) produced (in common) by the merging firms). The SSNIP test is discussed in Chapter 3 Section A.1.B. *infra*.

96. *See* NAAG MERGER GUIDELINES, *supra* note 94, § 3.1.

involving at least one firm with a market share of 35 percent, or, between an innovative firm and a firm with a market share of 20 percent.[97] The *NAAG Merger Guidelines* also indicate a more skeptical approach to efficiencies.[98]

2. Premerger Notification

State attorneys general are unable to obtain access to documents and information filed pursuant to the HSR Act from the DOJ or FTC.[99] In addition, no state has passed legislation which requires the filing of premerger notification reports at the state level. In an attempt to coordinate premerger investigations, federal and state antitrust enforcers have entered into agreements to share some information and to collaborate on enforcement efforts.

NAAG has created the *Voluntary Premerger Disclosure Compact*.[100] Under the *Compact*, states agree not to serve the merging parties with any requests for information or make any other compulsory precomplaint

---

97. *See id.* § 4.4.

98. The *NAAG Merger Guidelines* are explicit in rejecting the notion of efficiencies claims as an affirmative defense, but do articulate the circumstances, albeit highly restrictive ones, in which efficiencies will be considered by the state enforcers. *See* NAAG MERGER GUIDELINES, *supra* note 94, § 5.3. To the extent cognizable under the *NAAG Merger Guidelines*, efficiencies must be demonstrated by the merging parties to be "significant," and this demonstration must be made with "clear and convincing evidence." *Id.* The merging parties must also demonstrate "that the efficiencies will ensure that consumer prices will not increase despite any increase in market power due to the merger." *Id.* The *NAAG Merger Guidelines* also note that "the Attorneys General will reject claims of efficiencies unless the merging parties can demonstrate that equivalent or comparable savings cannot be achieved through other means and that such cost savings will persist over the long run." *Id.*

99. *See* Mattox v. FTC, 752 F.2d 116 (5th Cir. 1985) (forbidding disclosure of HSR filings to state attorney general); Lieberman v. FTC, 771 F.2d 32 (2d Cir. 1985) (same).

100. *Reprinted in* 4 Trade Reg. Rep. (CCH) ¶ 13,410 (1987). NAAG has revised the *Compact*. *See NAAG Premerger Compact*, 66 Antitrust & Trade Reg. Rep. (BNA) No. 1647, at 78 (1994). Forty-four states, Guam, the Virgin Islands, Northern Mariana Islands, Puerto Rico, and the District of Columbia have joined the *Compact*. The NAAG has also drafted a model state statute addressing premerger notification. *See* Model State Statute Governing Premerger Notification, 53 Antitrust & Trade Reg. Rep. (BNA) No. 1345, at 944 (1987).

investigatory demands during the HSR waiting periods if the parties agree to provide the designated "liaison state" with a copy of the HSR filings and other materials provided to the federal agencies.

In 1998, the federal enforcement agencies and many state attorneys general agreed to a "protocol" for the conduct of joint federal/state merger investigations.[101] The protocol covers joint treatment of confidential information, strategic planning by the enforcement agencies, document production, interviews with witnesses, settlement discussions, and press statements.

---

101. U.S. DEP'T OF JUSTICE, FEDERAL TRADE COMM'N & NATIONAL ASS'N OF STATE ATT'YS GEN., PROTOCOL FOR COORDINATION IN MERGER INVESTIGATIONS BETWEEN THE FEDERAL ENFORCEMENT AGENCIES AND STATE ATTORNEYS GENERAL, *reprinted in* 4 Trade Reg. Rep. (CCH) ¶ 13,420.

CHAPTER 3

Market Definition and Measurement

A. Defining the Relevant Market

Under Section 7 of the Clayton Act, a plaintiff must show the challenged acquisition will result in a substantial lessening of competition "in any line of commerce or . . . in any section of the country."[1] The statutory phrases "in any line of commerce" and "in any section of the country" require a determination of both the relevant product and geographic markets.[2] Indeed, some courts hold that the

---

1. 15 U.S.C. § 18; *see* United States v. Pabst Brewing Co., 384 U.S. 546, 549 (1966) ("When the government brings an action under Section 7, it must . . . prove no more than that there has been a merger between two competitors engaged in commerce and that the effect of the merger may be substantially to lessen competition or tend to create a monopoly in any line of commerce in any section of the country").
2. *See* Brown Shoe Co. v. United States, 370 U.S. 294, 324 (1962) ("the 'area of effective competition' must be determined by reference to a product market (the 'line of commerce') and a geographic market (the 'section of the country')"); United States v. E.I. du Pont de Nemours & Co., 353 U.S. 586, 593 (1957) (determination of the market is the necessary predicate to a Section 7 case); *accord* United States v. Marine Bancorp., 418 U.S. 602 (1974); United States v. General Dynamics Corp., 415 U.S. 486 (1974); United States v. Continental Can Co., 378 U.S. 441 (1964); Olin Corp. v. FTC, 986 F.2d 1295, 1297 (9th Cir. 1993); Crown Zellerbach Corp. v. FTC, 296 F.2d 800, 804 (9th Cir. 1961); United States v. Atlantic Richfield Co., 297 F. Supp. 1061, 1066 (S.D.N.Y. 1969), *aff'd sub nom.* Bartlett v. United States, 401 U.S. 986 (1971).

   The relevant market as defined in cases under Sections 1 and 2 of the Sherman Act, 15 U.S.C. §§ 1, 2, may have relevance to cases decided under Section 7 of the Clayton Act. *See* United States v. Grinnell Corp., 384 U.S. 563, 573 (1966) ("we see no reason to differentiate between 'line' of commerce in the context of the Clayton Act and 'part' of commerce for purposes of the Sherman Act"); United States v. Syufy Enters., 712 F. Supp. 1386, 1396 (N.D. Cal. 1989) ("The relevant market is generally the same for cases brought under either Section 2 of the Sherman Act or Section 7 of the Clayton Act."), *aff'd*, 903 F.2d 659 (9th Cir. 1990); Kellam Energy, Inc. v. Duncan, 616 F. Supp. 215, 218 n.3 (D. Del. 1985) (geographic market definition standards are the same under

"substantiality" of the effect of the merger on competition can only be gauged in terms of a defined product and geographic market.[3]

Some commentators have suggested that the importance of market definition can be overstated.[4] Central to much of the critical legal and

---

the Sherman and Clayton Acts). *But see* United States v. Bethlehem Steel Corp., 168 F. Supp. 576, 588 (S.D.N.Y. 1958) (suggesting that the purpose of a given antitrust law should guide the market definition process for that law).

3. *See E.I. du Pont de Nemours & Co.*, 353 U.S. at 593 ("[s]ubstantiality can be determined only in terms of the market affected"); *see also* United States v. Marine Bancorp., 418 U.S. 602 (1974); *General Dynamics Corp.*, 415 U.S. at 486; *Continental Can Co.*, 378 U.S. at 441; *Brown Shoe Co.*, 370 U.S. at 324-25; *Atlantic Richfield Co.*, 297 F. Supp. at 1066.

4. *See, e.g.*, Anthony E. DiResta, *Enforcement by the Federal Trade Commission in the Bureau of Competition*, 1117 PLI/Cor. 1085 (May-June 1999) ("When the Commission finds unique relationships among products made by the merging firms, as evidenced by how the firms behave in the marketplace and by quantitative analysis of past pricing behavior, the Commission has a merger that poses problems. And the issue of the precise market definition becomes and should become secondary"); Note, *Analyzing Differentiated-Product Mergers: The Relevance of Structural Analysis*, 111 HARV. L. REV. 2420 (June 1998) ("The traditional structural approach to merger analysis, which begins with market definition, is now well-recognized as better suited for analyzing coordinated interaction than for predicting unilateral effects. Because government enforcement agencies and economists have come to view unilateral effects as the primary danger in differentiated-product mergers, they have increasingly relied on newly developed econometric and empirical techniques that are designed to predict unilateral price effects without the need for defining the market."); James F. Rill, *Practicing What They Preach: One Lawyer's View of Econometric Models in Differentiated Products Mergers*, 5 GEO. MASON L. REV. 393 (1997) ("Some proponents of econometric models suggest that .. . the Guidelines' structural analysis is not required for certain differentiated products mergers. This notion possesses certain theoretical appeal: If harm can be established even absent a formally defined market, why should precise market definition be necessary? However, this reasoning fails to take account of actual marketplace dynamics, which often substantially affect the merged firm's ability and incentive to raise price. Moreover, it places unwarranted (and unnecessary) faith in the ability of the models to accurately predict post-merger behavior."); Jonathan Baker, Director, Bureau of Economics, FTC, Contemporary Empirical Merger Analysis, Remarks Before the George Mason University Law Review

economic commentary has been the view that defining relevant markets has become an end in itself, rather than a tool to use in analyzing competitive impact. Indeed, non-merger cases, the U.S. Supreme Court has shown that proof of actual detrimental effects can obviate the need for an inquiry into market power.[5] Moreover, some courts of appeals have expressed a preference for actual proof of market power over market definition analysis,[6] although the Court of Appeals in *Microsoft* explicitly rejected the argument that actual proof of market power was required for a Section 2 monopolization claim.[7] At the present time, the only method endorsed by the courts to establish that a merger violates antitrust laws is structural analysis, although sometimes a practical alternative in the form of merger simulation may be available.[8]

Symposium, Antitrust in the Information Revolution: New Economic Approaches for Analyzing Antitrust Issues, at 8 (Oct. 11, 1996), *at* www.ftc.gov/speeches/other/gmu5.htm ("if a merger can be shown directly to harm competition, antitrust should not need to spend much effort on market definition").

5. "Since the purpose of the inquiries into market definition and market power is to determine whether an arrangement has the potential for genuine adverse effects on competition, 'proof of actual detrimental effects, such as a reduction of output,' can obviate the need for an inquiry into market power, which is but a 'surrogate for detrimental effects.'" FTC v. Indiana Fed'n of Dentists, 476 U.S. 447, 460-61 (1986) (using direct proof to show market power in a Sherman Act Section 1 unreasonable restraint of trade action) (quoting 7 PHILLIP E. AREEDA, ANTITRUST LAW ¶ 1511, at 429 (1986)).
6. Three courts of appeals have concurred that "market share is just a way of estimating market power, which is the ultimate consideration. When there are better ways to estimate market power, the court should use them." Allen-Myland, Inc. v. IBM Corp., 33 F.3d 194, 209 (3d Cir. 1994); United States v. Baker Hughes, Inc., 908 F.2d 981, 992 (D.C. Cir. 1990) (Thomas, J., joined by Ginsburg, J.); Ball Mem'l Hosp., Inc. v. Mutual Hosp. Ins., 784 F.2d 1325, 1336 (7th Cir. 1986).
7. *See* 253 F.3d 34, 56-57 (D.C. Cir. 2001) (finding that a structural market power analysis was sufficient in the absence of direct proof of monopoly power, even in a changing market).
8. Merger simulation employs standard oligopoly models to predict the effects of mergers quantitatively. For a concise description of the analysis, see Gregory J. Werden, *Simulating Unilateral Competitive Effects from Differentiated Products Mergers*, ANTITRUST, Spring 1997, at 27. For a more thorough explanation of the analysis, see Philip Crooke, Luke M. Froeb, Steven Tschantz & Gregory J. Werden, *The Effects of Assumed Demand Form on Simulated Postmerger Equilibria*, 15 REV. INDUS. ORG. 205 (1999); Jerry A. Hausman & Gregory K.

In most cases presumptions are still made and evidentiary burdens are still established only after the definition of "relevant markets."[9] Under traditional Section 7 analysis, markets and market shares must be defined in order to determine the degree of concentration in an industry and whether, given that concentration, there is a basis for (rebuttable) concerns about collusion or the exercise of unilateral market power.[10] A merger of firms in a defined market that is unconcentrated is unlikely to cause a "substantial" lessening of competition, the theory goes, because collusion will be difficult and the exercise of unilateral market power will be unlikely. In contrast, a merger in a highly concentrated market presents a greater possibility of reducing competition, by facilitating collusion among the remaining firms or allowing one firm to gain pricing power. Given these presumptions, it is not surprising that Section 7 cases are often won or lost on market definition issues.[11]

Leonard, *Economic Analysis of Differentiated Products Using Real World Data*, 5 GEO. MASON L. REV. 321 (1997); Gregory J. Werden, SIMULATING THE EFFECTS OF DIFFERENTIATED PRODUCTS MERGERS; A PRACTITIONERS' GUIDE, IN STRATEGY AND POLICY IN THE FOOD SYSTEM: EMERGING ISSUES 95 (Julie A. Caswell & Ronald W. Cotterill eds., 1997); Gregory J. Werden & Luke M. Froeb, SIMULATION AS AN ALTERNATIVE TO STRUCTURAL MERGER POLICY IN DIFFERENTIATED PRODUCTS INDUSTRIES, IN THE ECONOMICS OF THE ANTITRUST PROCESS 65 (Malcom B. Coate & Andrew N. Kleit eds., 1996). *See also* Gregory J. Werden, *Assigning Market Shares*, 70 ANTITRUST L.J. 67 (2002).

9. *See, e.g.*, FTC v. Staples, Inc., 970 F. Supp. 1066, 1073 (D.D.C. 1997) ("As with many antitrust cases, the definition of the product market in this case is crucial. In fact, to a great extent, this case hinges on the proper definition of the relevant product market."); *see also* United States v. Engelhard Corp., 126 F.3d 1302, 1305 (11th Cir. 1997) ("Establishing the relevant product market is an essential element in the Government's case").

10. FTC v. Proctor & Gamble Co., 386 U.S. 568, 577 (1967).

11. The U.S. Supreme Court decision in United States v. Continental Can Co., 378 U.S. 441 (1964), illustrates this point. Continental Can had a dominant position in the aluminum can market and sought to acquire Hazel-Atlas, the third largest manufacturer of glass containers. The district court considered the glass and metal container industries separate lines of commerce, rejecting the government's argument that they should be considered together based on the end use of the containers. Because the government could not demonstrate a Section 7 violation in the separate markets, the district court dismissed the case. United States v. Continental Can Co., 217 F. Supp. 761, 806 (S.D.N.Y. 1963). The U.S. Supreme Court reversed by finding a combined glass and metal container

Section 7 does not explain how to define relevant markets; that is left to the courts. At its most fundamental level, the relevant market has been defined as the "area of effective competition" within which the merging entities conduct business.[12] Courts usually consider separately the finding of a relevant product (or service[13]) market and a relevant geographic market, but they are in fact closely related concepts. Both involve determining the point at which a seller can no longer coordinate with other sellers, or a monopolist can no longer reap monopoly profits. The determination of both types of markets is a fact issue,[14] on which the plaintiff bears the burden of proof,[15] and typically requires detailed analyses of complex economic and market data.

---

market. *Continental Can Co.*, 378 U.S. at 457. Because Continental Can and Hazel-Atlas ranked among the top six firms in the combined market, the merger was enjoined under Section 7. *See id.* at 461-62; *see also* FTC v. Owens-Illinois, Inc., 681 F. Supp. 27, 34 (D.D.C. 1988) ("Despite their differences on many other issues in this case, the parties agree that [defining the relevant market] ... is the determinative issue in this case."), *vacated as moot,* 850 F.2d 694 (D.C. Cir. 1988).

12. *See* United States v. E.I. du Pont de Nemours & Co., 353 U.S. 586, 592-93 (1957); Standard Oil Co. v. United States, 337 U.S. 293, 299 (1949).

13. *See, e.g.*, United States v. Connecticut Nat'l Bank, 418 U.S. 656 (1974) (commercial banking services); United States v. Grinnell Corp., 384 U.S. 563 (1966) (central station protective services); FTC v. University Health, Inc., 938 F.2d 1206 (11th Cir. 1991) (acute care hospital services); United States v. Household Fin. Corp., 602 F.2d 1255 (7th Cir. 1979) (cash loans); Commander Leasing Co. v. Transamerica Title Ins. Co., 477 F.2d 77 (10th Cir. 1973) (title insurance); Credit Bureau Reports, Inc. v. Retail Credit Co., 476 F.2d 989 (5th Cir. 1973) (insurance credit reporting services); Central Savings & Loan Assoc. v. United Fed. Savings & Loan Assoc., 422 F.2d 504 (8th Cir. 1970) (savings and loan services); Syracuse Broad. Corp. v. Newhouse, 236 F.2d 522 (2d Cir. 1956) (newspaper and radio advertising).

14. *See, e.g.*, *E.I. du Pont de Nemours & Co.*, 353 U.S. 586; *Engelhard Corp.*, 126 F.3d at 1305; Cable Holdings of Ga., Inc. v. Home Video, Inc., 825 F.2d 1559, 1563 (11th Cir. 1987); Monfort of Colo., Inc. v. Cargill, Inc., 761 F.2d 570, 579 (10th Cir. 1985), *rev'd and remanded on other grounds*, 479 U.S. 104 (1986) (definition of relevant market reviewed under clearly erroneous standard); Twin City Sportservice, Inc. v. Charles O. Finley & Co., 676 F.2d 1291,1299 (9th Cir. 1982); Kaiser Aluminum & Chem. Corp. v. FTC, 652 F.2d 1324 (7th Cir. 1981); Jim Walter Corp. v. FTC, 625 F.2d 676 (9th Cir. 1980); Heatransfer Corp. v. Volkswagenwerk, A.G., 553 F.2d 964 (5th Cir. 1977).

15. *See Connecticut Nat'l Bank*, 418 U.S. at 669-70; Avnet, Inc. v. FTC, 511 F.2d 70, 77 n.19 (7th Cir. 1975).

1. The Product Market

In 1962, the U.S. Supreme Court in *Brown Shoe* established an analytical framework that most courts since have used as the starting point in defining the relevant product market. The *Brown Shoe* Court identified two types of product markets: (1) a relevant product market, whose outer boundaries "are determined by the reasonable interchangeability of use or the cross-elasticity of demand between the product itself and substitutes for it";[16] and (2) possibly, one or more "well defined submarkets . . . which, in themselves, constitute product markets for antitrust purposes" within that relevant market.[17] Courts have looked at both types of product markets in analyzing the legality of a merger.

a. Judicial Tests for the Relevant Product Market

The U.S. Supreme Court in *Brown Shoe* articulated two related tests for defining the relevant product market or submarket: "cross-elasticity of demand" and "reasonable interchangeability."[18] The *Brown Shoe* Court also held that cross-elasticity of production facilities was another factor to be considered in determining the product market, though it was not considered relevant in that case.

---

16. Brown Shoe Co. v. United States, 370 U.S. 294, 325 (1962); *see also* FTC v. Swedish Match, 131 F. Supp. 2d 151, 158 (D.D.C. 2000) (finding, in light of *Brown Shoe's* indicia, that loose leaf chewing tobacco constitutes a distinct relevant product market from moist snuff tobacco); United States v. Long Island Jewish Med. Ctr., 983 F. Supp. 121, 139-40 (E.D.N.Y. 1997) (defining relevant product market as "general acute care inpatient hospital services, rather than the provision of these services by anchor hospitals"); United States v. Gillette Co., 828 F. Supp. 78, 83 (D.D.C. 1993) (in proposed acquisition of premium fountain pen company, product market definition included all other premium writing instruments, such as mechanical pencils and refillable pens); R.R. Donnelley & Sons Co., 120 F.T.C. 36, 153-76 (1995) (in proposed acquisition of printing company, product market definition of high-volume printing included both gravure and offset printing).
17. *Brown Shoe Co.*, 370 U.S. at 325.
18. These product market tests were derived from the U.S. Supreme Court's opinion in *United States v. E.I. du Pont de Nemours & Co.,* 351 U.S. 377 (1956) (the *Cellophane* case).

(1) Cross-Elasticity of Demand: Price Movements Between Products

Cross-elasticity of demand focuses on the sensitivity of demand for one product to changes in the price of another product. If a small price increase in one product will induce a substantial number of buyers of that product to switch to another product, there is a high cross-elasticity of demand between the products. Conversely, if the small price increase in the one product induces very few buyers to switch, there is said to be a low cross-elasticity of demand between the products. The same analysis applies to price decreases. There is high cross-elasticity of demand when a small price decrease in one product wins over a high number of buyers of another product.[19] There is low cross-elasticity of demand when a small price decrease has little effect on the amount purchased of other products. The products at issue need not compete at the same price level to exhibit a high cross-elasticity of demand.[20]

As a general rule, where evidence suggests high cross-elasticity, courts have found products to be in the same product market;[21]

---

19. *See E.I. du Pont de Nemours & Co.*, 351 U.S. at 400. The *du Pont* Court explained that if "a slight decrease in the price of cellophane causes a considerable number of customers of other flexible wrappings to switch to cellophane, it would be an indication that a high cross-elasticity of demand exists between them; that the products compete in the same market." *Id.*

20. *See* American Crystal Sugar Co. v. Cuban-Am. Sugar Co., 152 F. Supp. 387 (S.D.N.Y. 1957), *aff'd*, 259 F.2d 524 (2d Cir. 1958). When the ratio of the percentage change in the quantity demanded of one product to the percentage change in the price of another product yields a number less than one, the cross-elasticity between the two products is considered in the inelastic range. When the ratio is one, there is a unitary cross-elasticity. When the ratio is greater than one, the cross-elasticity is in the elastic range. Cross-elasticities, like a product's "own" elasticity (i.e., the ratio of the percentage change in quantity demanded of a given product to the percentage change in that product's own price), are not constants. Instead, elasticities vary as the initial price levels vary. In particular, as one moves from lower to higher prices along a given product demand curve, the elasticity of demand becomes larger. Intuitively, this is because, as a product's price is raised to ever higher levels relative to other products, more alternative products become reasonable economic substitutes.

21. *See, e.g., E.I. du Pont de Nemours & Co.*, 351 U.S. at 400 (preventing du Pont from gaining monopoly control on the basis of customer sensitivity to price or quantity fluctuations); New York v. Kraft Gen. Foods, Inc., 926 F. Supp. 321, 333-35 (S.D.N.Y. 1995) (finding all cereal to be in

conversely, where evidence suggests low cross-elasticity, products are found to be in separate markets.[22] For example, the court in *FTC v. Staples, Inc.* adopted the FTC's approach to market definition, which posited that a small but significant nontransitory price increase by Staples would not cause a considerable number of Staples customers to purchase consumable office products from nonsuperstore alternatives, but instead would cause customers to turn to another office superstore, such as Office Depot, Staples' major rival.[23] As is often the case, there were no direct estimates of cross-elasticities of demand. However, the court relied on the merging parties' own documents and statistical analysis of prices across geographic markets to show Staples' prices were about 13 percent higher in cities where it faced no office superstore

---

relevant market because price increases cause demand-side substitution); FTC v. Owens-Illinois, Inc., 681 F. Supp. 27, 47 (D.D.C. 1988) (finding containers comprised of glass, plastic, metal, and paper are part of relevant market), *vacated as moot,* 850 F.2d 694 (D.C. Cir. 1988); Liggett & Myers, Inc., 87 F.T.C. 1074, 1163 (1976) (finding all dog food to be in the same market in view of interchangeability and cross-elasticity of supply), *aff'd*, 567 F.2d 1273 (4th Cir. 1977).

22. *See, e.g.*, United States v. Archer-Daniels-Midland Co., 866 F.2d 242, 246 (8th Cir. 1988) (low cross-elasticity of demand between sugar and high fructose corn syrup); United States v. Ivaco, Inc., 704 F. Supp. 1409, 1416 (W.D. Mich. 1989) (low cross-elasticity of demand and a low cross-elasticity of supply in tamper market); Grumman Corp. v. LTV Corp., 527 F. Supp. 86, 90 (E.D.N.Y.) (cross-elasticity of demand for two aircraft nonexistent), *aff'd*, 665 F.2d 10 (2d Cir. 1981); United States v. United Techs. Corp., 1977-2 Trade Cas. (CCH) ¶ 61,647, at 72,665 (N.D. Ohio 1977) (gas turbine generating systems and fossil or nuclear steam generating systems not in the same market where econometric model showed "zero cross-elasticity" between them); *see also* United States v. American Technical Indus., Inc. 1974-1 Trade Cas. (CCH) ¶ 74,873, at 95,872-73 (M.D. Pa. 1974) (analyzing factors contributing to a low cross-elasticity of demand between artificial and real Christmas trees); Beatrice Foods Co., 86 F.T.C. 1, 57-59 (1975) (analyzing cross-elasticity of demand between paint rollers and paint brushes), *aff'd*, 540 F.2d 303 (7th Cir. 1976); Brillo Mfg. Co., 64 F.T.C. 245, 253 (1964) (there is little or no cross-elasticity of demand between steel wool and other products, thus the relevant market is steel wool), *modified*, 75 F.T.C. 811 (1969). *But cf.* United States v. Continental Can Co., 378 U.S. 441 at 455-56 (1964) (U.S. Supreme Court found evidence of price differentials and low price sensitivity between glass and metal containers as "relevant" but not "determinative" given other evidence of competition between the products).

23. *See* FTC v. Staples, Inc., 970 F. Supp. 1066 (D.D.C. 1997).

competition than in cities where there were three office superstores.[24] The court further found that Staples' prices were inversely related to the number of superstores in a given geographic area. From these comparisons, the court inferred a high cross-elasticity of demand between disposable office products offered by office superstores and a low cross-elasticity of demand between superstores and other sellers of disposable office supply products, such as mass merchandisers, smaller office supply stores, and mail order houses.[25]

As a practical matter, cross-elasticity can be very difficult to measure and, therefore, difficult to prove. There must be sufficient price and quantity data to construct a statistically significant sample, and the relevant demand elasticity must focus on a time horizon that accurately reflects producer and consumer behavior.

Even when measurement of cross-elasticities is possible, cross-elasticities raise real-world problems for competitive analysis. First, there is no clear line of demarcation indicating when a cross-elasticity is high. Second, the analysis can lead to erroneous results. For example, where the selling price exhibits a high degree of variability and consumers typically maintain an inventory of the product, estimates derived from short-run data may overstate the seller's own elasticity of demand and understate the seller's cross-elasticity of demand.[26] Moreover, where a firm that already has market power raises its prices further above competitive levels, the result may be that consumers respond by switching to less expensive, imperfect substitutes in other markets. Measuring the cross-elasticity of demand between the high-priced product in the monopolized market and the imperfect substitute will suggest a higher cross-elasticity, and greater substitutability, than would exist in a competitive market. At the extreme, it may suggest the two products are in the same relevant market when in fact they are substitutes only because one product's price is already at a monopoly level.[27]

---

24. *See id*. at 1075-76.
25. *See id*. at 1077.
26. Jonathan B. Baker, Director, Bureau of Economics, FTC, Contemporary Empirical Merger Analysis, Remarks Before the George Mason University Law Review Symposium, Antitrust in the Information Revolution: New Economic Approaches for Analyzing Antitrust Issues, at 13 (Oct. 11, 1996), *at* www.ftc.gov/speeches/other/gmu5.htm.
27. For example, over some range of prices above the competitive level, "widgets" could be a relevant market, in the sense that the potential exists to exercise market power in the sale of widgets and profitably elevate prices above the competitive level. Yet, the ability to raise widget prices

This logical error has been referred to as the *Cellophane* trap, for the arguable mistake committed by the U.S. Supreme Court in *United States v. E.I. du Pont de Nemours & Co.*[28] In that case, du Pont's high prices on its superior product caused some consumers to switch to imperfect substitutes. Because of this evidence of switching (and by implication a high cross-elasticity of demand), du Pont was able to convince the Court that the relevant market was broad and that therefore du Pont could not be a monopolist.[29]

A low cross-elasticity also can be misleading, however, if it is not placed in proper context. For example, suppose that the producer of product A is constrained from raising prices above current levels because at higher prices consumers would switch to product B, even though at current prices there is virtually no switching between the two products. Historical price data would likely yield a low measured cross-elasticity of demand, even though product B clearly constrains product A from raising prices further. If two sellers of product A proposed to merge, it would be a mistake to exclude product B from the relevant market if the question is whether the merger will tend to raise prices above current levels, even though the measured cross-elasticity was low.[30]

---

is not without limits. At some point, higher widget prices will be constrained by consumers' willingness to switch to "gadgets," an imperfect substitute. Thus, whether widgets and gadgets are interchangeable in use, and whether the cross-elasticity of demand between them is high, depends on whether the initial price levels are near or far from competitive prices.

28. 351 U.S. 377, 401-03 (1956).

29. The courts, in two non-Clayton Act proceedings, have warned against the *Cellophane* trap. *See* Eastman Kodak Co. v. Image Technical Servs., Inc., 504 U.S. 451, 471 (1992) ("'[T]he existence of significant substitution in the event of further price increases or even at the current price does not tell us whether the defendant already exercises significant market power.'" (quoting PHILLIP AREEDA & LOUIS KAPLOW, ANTITRUST ANALYSIS ¶ 340(b) (4th ed. 1988)); United States v. Eastman Kodak Co., 853 F. Supp. 1454, 1469-70 (W.D.N.Y. 1994) (court described the *Cellophane* trap before finding it inapplicable).

30. As another example, suppose that the cross-elasticities between product A and products B through N were all low, but that the cumulative constraining effect of all these products was sufficient to prevent the price of product A from rising above current levels. It may not be proper to exclude these other products from the relevant market if the question was whether a merger between sellers of product A could result in the power to raise prices above current levels.

Because of these interpretation problems and the problems of proof associated with the measurement of cross-elasticities, both the courts and the 1992 *Merger Guidelines*[31] use cross-elasticity not as the dispositive factor, but only as one important factor to be considered. Beyond cross-elasticity, the courts and agencies have looked at a number of related indicators, including reasonable interchangeability of use, to gain an understanding of the degree of competition between the merging firms' products.[32]

(2) Reasonable Interchangeability

Reasonable interchangeability of use, or demand substitutability, focuses on similarities in uses and characteristics between products—that is, on the buyers' perceptions of whether the products at issue are good substitutes for one another. In a world of imperfect price and quantity data from which to analyze elasticities, qualitative evidence of a buyers' willingness to substitute one good or service for another often provides the principal evidence of the boundaries of a relevant market.

In fact, interchangeability of product use has been called the "fundamental quality of any properly delineated market."[33] If a court

---

31. U.S. DEP'T OF JUSTICE & FEDERAL TRADE COMM'N, HORIZONTAL MERGER GUIDELINES § 1.0 (1992) [hereinafter 1992 MERGER GUIDELINES], *reprinted in* 4 Trade Reg. Rep. (CCH) ¶ 13,104 and in Appendix I.
32. *See* Brown Shoe Co. v. United States, 370 U.S. 294, 325 (1962); FTC v. PPG Indus., Inc., 798 F.2d 1500, 1504-06 (D.C. Cir. 1986) (glass and plastic aircraft transparencies in same market because of sellers' and buyers' perceptions and competition at bidding stage); Hayden Pub. Co. v. Cox Broad. Corp., 730 F.2d 64, 70 n.8 (2d Cir. 1984) (the general question is "whether two products can be used for the same purpose and, if so, whether and to what extent purchasers are willing to substitute one for the other"); Kaiser Aluminum & Chem. Corp. v. FTC, 652 F.2d 1324, 1330 (7th Cir. 1981) ("the clearest indication that products should be included in the same market is if they are actually used by consumers in a readily interchangeable manner"); FTC v. Staples, Inc., 970 F. Supp. 1066, 1074 (D.D.C. 1997) (the general rule when determining a relevant product market is the "reasonable interchangeability of use by customers"); Frank Saltz & Sons, Inc. v. Hart Schaffner & Marx, 1985-2 Trade Cas. (CCH) ¶ 66,768, at 63,719 (S.D.N.Y. 1985) ("The Court must determine 'how far buyers will go to substitute one commodity for another.'" (quoting *du Pont*, 351 U.S. at 393)).
33. United States v. Ford Motor Co., 286 F. Supp. 407, 411 (E.D. Mich. 1968), *aff'd,* 405 U.S. 562 (1972); *see also Kaiser Aluminum & Chem.*

finds that products are reasonably interchangeable, it will likely hold the products are in the same market, even where the products cut across traditional industry lines.[34] Conversely, where there is evidence that products are not deemed by customers to be substantially interchangeable, separate markets are most often found.[35]

In determining the degree of interchangeability, courts (and agencies) look first and foremost at whether the products are actually viewed by participants in the market as substitutes for one another. Thus, courts have found seemingly very different products to be in the same product market based in part on their perceived substitutability.[36]

Corp., 652 F.2d at 1330 ("the clearest indication that products should be included in the same market is if they are actually used by consumers in a readily interchangeable manner").

34. *See, e.g.*, United States v. Continental Can Co., 378 U.S. 441, 453-57 (1964) (glass jars and metal containers sufficiently interchangeable to be in the same market); FTC v. R.R. Donnelly & Sons Co., 1990-2 Trade Cas. (CCH) ¶ 69,239, at 64,854-55 (D.D.C. 1990) (offset and gravure print process interchangeable and in the same product market); FTC v. Owens-Illinois, Inc., 681 F. Supp. 27, 47 (D.D.C. 1988) (glass and plastic containers sufficiently interchangeable for certain applications to be in the same market), *vacated as moot,* 850 F.2d 694 (D.C. Cir. 1988); Robinson v. Intergraph Corp., 1988-2 Trade Cas. (CCH) ¶ 68,138, at 58,942 (E.D. Mich. 1988) (no submarket in a particular line of computer software where other software can be used for the same purpose); Liggett & Myers, Inc., 87 F.T.C. 1074, 1163 (1976) (all dog food found to be in the same market given interchangeability of use), *aff'd,* 567 F.2d 1273 (4th Cir. 1977). *But see* FTC v. Staples, Inc., 970 F. Supp. 1066, 1074 (D.D.C. 1997) (noting, in finding a submarket of consumable office supplies sold through office supply superstores, that "[n]o one disputes the functional interchangeability of consumable office supplies. However, as the government has argued, functional interchangeability should not end the Courts' analysis").

35. *See, e.g.*, FTC v. Warner Communs., 742 F.2d 1156, 1163 (9th Cir. 1984) (per curiam) (prerecorded music and home tapes not sufficiently interchangeable to be in the same market); Beatrice Foods Co. v. FTC, 540 F.2d 303, 308 (7th Cir. 1976) (limited interchangeability in use between paint rollers and brushes on one hand and paint aerosols and sprayers on the other did not prevent the FTC from properly finding that rollers and brushes constituted a separate submarket); Ansell Inc. v. Schmid Labs., Inc., 757 F. Supp. 467, 472-73 (D.N.J.) (limited interchangeability between wholesale and brand name condoms), *aff'd,* 941 F.2d 1200 (3d Cir. 1991).

36. *See, e.g., Continental Can Co.*, 378 U.S. at 456 (glass and metal containers); *Brown Shoe Co.*, 370 U.S. at 326 (men's, women's and

Conversely, courts have placed seemingly related products into different product markets for Section 7 purposes because the products were viewed by consumers as ineffective substitutes.[37] Differentiated consumer products present special problems in terms of placing them in a relevant product market.[38] Following the *Merger Guidelines*, the

---

children's shoes); United States v. E.I. du Pont de Nemours & Co., 351 U.S. 377 (1956) (cellophane and other flexible wrapping materials); Cable Holdings of Ga., Inc. v. Home Video, Inc., 825 F.2d 1559 (11th Cir. 1987) (cable television, satellite television, video cassette recordings, and free television); FTC v. PPG Indus., Inc., 798 F.2d 1500 (D.C. Cir. 1986) (glass and plastic transparencies for aircraft); American Crystal Sugar Co. v. Cuban-Am. Sugar Co., 259 F.2d 524, 530 (2d Cir. 1958) (beet sugar and cane sugar); United States v. Gillette Co., 828 F. Supp. 78, 83 (D.D.C. 1993) (premium fountain pens, mechanical pencils, refillable pens, and other premium writing instruments); United States v. Syufy Enters., 712 F. Supp. 1386 (N.D. Cal. 1989) (various kinds of passive entertainment), *aff'd,* 903 F.2d 659 (9th Cir. 1990); R.R. Donnelly & Sons Co., 120 F.T.C. 36, 153-76 (1995) (gravure and offset printing); *see also Continental Can Co.*, 378 U.S. at 456 ("We would not be true to the purpose of the Clayton Act's line of commerce concept . . . were we to hold that the existence of noncompetitive segments within a proposed market precludes its being treated as a line of commerce").

37. *See, e.g.*, Olin Corp. v. FTC, 986 F.2d 1295, 1303-04 (9th Cir. 1993) (concluding that dry and liquid pool bleaches were in separate markets despite the fact that "both products are used to sanitize swimming pools"); FTC v. Swedish Match, 131 F. Supp. 2d 151, 157 (D.D.C. 2001) (finding a market distinction between loose leaf tobacco and moist snuff); Bon-Ton Stores v. May Dep't Stores Co., 881 F. Supp. 860 (W.D.N.Y. 1994) (finding a "traditional department stores" submarket within the broad general merchandise, apparel and furniture market, in part because of a perception of a traditional department store market); *Ansell Inc.*, 757 F. Supp. at 473-74 (concluding that condoms sold at retail are different from condoms sold wholesale because they have distinct customers); United States v. Rockford Mem'l Corp., 717 F. Supp. 1251, 1259-60 (N.D. Ill. 1981) (concluding that identical inpatient and outpatient health care services could be placed in different markets because third-party insurers limited the cross-elasticity of demand to the least expensive option), *aff'd,* 898 F.2d 1278, 1285 (7th Cir. 1990).

38. For example, does Coca-Cola compete in a branded cola market, in an all cola market, in an all soft drink market, in a cold drink market, or in an all beverage market? *See,* Coca-Cola Co., 117 F.T.C. 795, 931-40 (1994) (rejecting all carbonated soft drink market in favor of branded carbonated soft drink market in part because consumers regarded branded products as being in a separate market from unbranded products).

agencies and the courts look to whether a potential substitute will constrain the price of the relevant product, rather than whether the potential substitute will serve the same function as the relevant product.[39]

A number of factors may bear on product market definition. The *Brown Shoe* Court listed these factors—the "practical indicia"—that could affect product market "boundaries": "industry or public recognition of the submarket as a separate economic entity, the product's peculiar characteristics and uses, unique production facilities, distinct customers, distinct prices, sensitivity to price changes, and specialized vendors."[40] Courts have considered: differences in price or price movements between products,[41] quality differences,[42] existence of

---

39. United States v. UPM-Kymmene Oyj, 2003-2 Trade Cas. (CCH) ¶ 74,101, at *8 (N.D. Ill. July 25, 2003) (memorandum opinion and order), (finding that if, despite functional substitutability, "buyers of one product would not switch to the other product in numbers sufficient to defeat the profitability of a small but significant non-transitory price increase, then those functionally similar products are not in the same market."); United States v. Microsoft Corp., 253 F.3d 34, 347-48 (D.C. Cir. 2001) (citing Rothery Storage and Van Co. v. Atlas Van Lines, Inc., 792 F.2d 210, 218 (D.C. Cir. 1986)).

40. Brown Shoe Co. v. United States, 370 U.S. 294, 325 (1962). See discussion of submarkets *infra* part A1e of this Chapter.

41. *See* United States v. Aluminum Co. of Am., 377 U.S. 271, 275-76 (1964) (finding separate aluminum and copper cable submarkets based on significant price differentials and independence of price movements); United States v. Archer-Daniels-Midland Co., 866 F.2d 242, 246 (8th Cir. 1988) (despite functional interchangeability of sugar and high fructose corn syrup, persistent price difference of 10 to 30% warranted finding of separate markets); *Warner Communs.*, 742 F.2d at 1163 (prerecorded music, excluding home tapes, found to be separate market based on 300% price difference); Kennecott Copper Corp. v. FTC, 467 F.2d 67, 78-79 (10th Cir. 1972) (concluding that price competitiveness between coal and other energy sources alone is insufficient basis for finding product market that includes more than coal); United States v. SunGard Data Sys., Inc., 172 F. Supp. 2d 172, 193 (D.D.C. 2001) (rejecting government's definition of product market "[i]n light of decreasing costs of equipment and telecommunications"); FTC v. Swedish Match, 131 F. Supp. 2d 151, 161 n.8, 165 (D.D.C. 2000) (loose leaf and moist snuff tobacco not in same market because of price differences and independent price movements); FTC v. Staples, Inc., 970 F. Supp. 1066 (D.D.C. 1997) (finding separate market consisting of consumable office supplies sold through office superstores in part due to persistent price differences between office supplies sold by superstores and office supplies sold by other retailers); Bon-Ton Stores v. May Dep't Stores Co., 881 F. Supp. 860, 874 (W.D.N.Y. 1994)

("traditional department stores" are distinct market from other providers of general merchandise, apparel and furniture because "department store prices do tend to be different from other retailers"); Consolidated Gas Co. of Fla., Inc. v. City Gas Co. of Fla., Inc., 665 F. Supp. 1493, 1517 (S.D. Fla. 1987) (natural gas in distinct market from liquid petroleum gas due to significant difference in price), *vacated as moot*, 931 F.2d 710 (7th Cir. 1991); United States v. Black & Decker Mfg. Co., 430 F. Supp. 729, 738-40 (D. Md. 1976) (professional and occasional user chain saws distinguished based on price differential); United States v. Alcan Inc., No. 1:3CV02012 (D.D.C. filed Sept. 29, 2003) (brazing sheet less expensive than "materials it replaced"); United States v. General Elec. Co., No. 1:03CV01923 (D.D.C. filed Sept. 16, 2003) (critical care monitors cost "significantly less" than low-acuity monitors); B.A.T. Indus., 104 F.T.C. 852, 931-32 (1984) ("a substantially and persistently higher price [for one of two products at issue] . . . indicates that a small price change for either product would be unlikely to induce [switching]").

42. *See, e.g.*, RSR Corp. v. FTC, 602 F.2d 1317 (9th Cir. 1979) (secondary lead sold for about 10% less than primary lead); Avnet, Inc. v. FTC, 511 F.2d 70, 77 (7th Cir. 1975) (new automotive electrical units found to be separate market from rebuilt and reconditioned units, where quality differences resulted in price differentials of 25 to 50% and there was an absence of price interaction); A.G. Spalding & Bros., Inc. v. FTC, 301 F.2d 585 (3d Cir. 1962) (high-priced professional grade athletic products); United States v. Gillette Co., 828 F. Supp. 78, 83 (D.D.C. 1993) (defining submarket of writing instruments, based on prestige, image, and quality, as premium writing instruments with retail prices of $40-$400); *Ansell Inc.*, 757 F. Supp. at 473-74 (defining submarket of brand name condoms, based on differences of price and quality compared to wholesale condoms); Monfort of Colo., Inc. v. Cargill, Inc., 591 F. Supp. 683, 698 (D. Colo. 1983) (boxed beef), *aff'd,* 761 F.2d 570 (10th Cir. 1985), *rev'd on other grounds,* 479 U.S. 104 (1986); United States v. Blue Bell, Inc., 395 F. Supp. 538, 542-47 (M.D. Tenn. 1975) (industrial rental garments); United States v. Alcan Inc., No. 1:03CV02012 (D.D.C. filed Sept. 29, 2003) ("In heat exchange applications, no other material matches the combination of strength, light weight, durability, formability, and corrosion resistance of brazing sheet"); Liggett & Myers, Inc., 87 F.T.C. 1074 (1976) (premium dog food), *aff'd,* 567 F.2d 1273 (4th Cir. 1977). *But see* Brown Shoe Co. v. United States, 370 U.S. 294, 326 (1962) (rejecting "price/quality" distinctions in shoe markets because "men's shoes selling below $8.99 are [not] in a different market from those selling above $9.00"); Beatrice Foods Co. v. FTC, 540 F.2d at 309-10 ("professional" and "do it yourself" paint brushes and rollers are in the same market where price and quality differences between them are not sufficient to establish "clearly separate price groupings," but rather show substantial overlap, and where products are distributed by the same retailers); United States v. Long Island Jewish Med. Ctr., 983 F. Supp. 121,

different customer groups,[43] evidence that sellers do not take into substantial account other products in marketing and pricing,[44] specialized

---

138-40 (E.D.N.Y. 1997) (rejecting plaintiff's proposed product market consisting of acute inpatient service provided by "anchor hospitals" – those offering highly sophisticated services and high quality medical staffs – as opposed to general acute care inpatient hospital services); New York v. Kraft Gen. Foods, Inc., 926 F. Supp. 321, 333 (S.D.N.Y. 1995) (all ready-to-eat cereals are in the same market because "there is no clear break in the chain of substitutes" that would permit the definition of a smaller market); United States v. Ivaco, Inc., 704 F. Supp. 1409, 1416-17 (W.D. Mich. 1989) (high technology and conventional automatic tampers in same market despite quality differences resulting in limited substitutability for some customers; price differential offsets quality difference); Pennsylvania v. Russell Stover Candies, Inc., 1993-1 Trade Cas. (CCH) ¶ 70,224, at 70,090-91 (E.D. Pa. 1993) (gift box chocolates and promotional boxed chocolates in same market with other candies such as boxed fudge, peanut brittle, and nut clusters); Frank Saltz & Sons, Inc. v. Hart Schaffner & Marx, 1985-2 Trade Cas. (CCH) ¶ 66,768, at 63,720 (S.D.N.Y. 1985) (declining to find a "better quality suit" market after finding that customers purchase suits in multiple quality markets); R.R. Donnelley & Sons Co., 120 F.T.C. 36, 153-76 (1995) (product market definition of high-volume printing included both gravure and offset printing); Nestlé Holdings, Inc., Dkt. No. C-4082, 68 Fed. Reg. 39564, 39565 (July 2, 2003) (analysis to aid public comment) ("Ice cream also is differentiated on the quality of ingredients, with super premium containing more expensive and higher quality inputs").

43. *See* Lucas Auto. Eng'g, Inc. v. Bridgestone/Firestone, Inc., 275 F.3d 762, 768 (9th Cir. 2001) ("categorical insistence" and "very strong preference" by customers for original equipment major brand tires over private label tires); United States v. Waste Mgmt., Inc., 743 F.2d 976, 980 (2d Cir. 1984) (customer preference for waste removal depended upon quantity of trash produced); United States v. SunGard Data Sys., Inc., 172 F. Supp. 172, 185 (D.D.C. 2001) (rejecting market limited to shared hotsite disaster recovery system because, *inter alia*, "quick ship service is a viable substitute for a shared hotsite for at least some customers with midrange systems"); FTC v. Cardinal Health, Inc., 12 F. Supp. 2d 34, 48 (D.D.C. 1998) (distinct market for the wholesale distribution of prescription drugs because of the existence of a class of customers incapable of distribution internally); United States v. Rockford Mem'l Corp., 717 F. Supp. 1251, 1260 (N.D. Ill. 1989) (distinct markets for inpatient and outpatient care because of the different need for each service among customers), *aff'd*, 898 F.2d 1278 (7th Cir. 1990). *But see* United States Healthcare, Inc. v. Healthsource, Inc., 1992-1 Trade Cas. (CCH) ¶ 69,697, at 67,180 (D.N.H. 1992) ("the distinct preferences of a distinct group of consumers does not suffice for defining a separate product market"), *aff'd*, 986 F.2d 589 (1st Cir. 1993); FTC v. R.R.

vendors,[45] distinct product classes or uses,[46] unique technology or production facilities,[47] industry or public recognition of separate markets,[48] and branded versus private label or generic consumer goods.[49]

Donnelly & Sons Co., 1990-2 Trade Cas. (CCH) ¶ 69,239, at 64,854 (D.D.C. 1990) (same).

44. *See, e.g.*, FTC v. Swedish Match, 131 F. Supp. 2d 151, 162, 164 (D.D.C. 2000) (defendants' documents and other sellers' testimony indicate that loose leaf tobacco sellers do not view moist snuff as being in the same market); FTC v. Staples, Inc., 970 F. Supp. 1066 (D.D.C. 1997) (office supply superstores generally do not consider office supplies sold through other outlets in making marketing and pricing decisions); *Beatrice Foods Co.*, 540 F.2d at 309 (manufacturers of brushes and rollers do not consider aerosols or spray paints when setting price); United States v. Syufy Enters., 712 F. Supp. 1386, 1400 (N.D. Cal. 1989) (distributors of movies consider other channels of distribution when making decisions for release dates), *aff'd,* 903 F.2d 659 (9th Cir. 1990); FTC v. Coca-Cola Co., 641 F. Supp. 1128, 1133 (D.D.C. 1986) (noting that "pricing and marketing decisions [were] based primarily on comparisons with rival carbonated soft drink products, with little if any concern about competition from other beverages"), *vacated mem.,* 829 F.2d 191 (D.C. Cir. 1987); Coca Cola Co., 117 F.T.C. 795, 931-40 (1994) (manufacturers of brand name soft drink concentrate regard branded products as being in separate market from unbranded products); Luria Bros. & Co., 62 F.T.C. 243, 576 (1963), *aff'd,* 389 F.2d 847 (3d Cir. 1968).

45. *See, e.g.*, United States v. Waste Mgmt., Inc., No. 1:03CV01409, 68 Fed. Reg. 47930, 47940 (Aug. 12, 2003) (proposed final judgment and competitive impact statement) (providers of small container commercial waste collection service use specialized equipment and different vehicles from providers of other waste collection services); United States v. Mrs. Smith's Pie Co., 440 F. Supp. 220, 228-29 (E.D. Pa. 1976) (difference in vending between frozen pies and fresh pies).

46. *See, e.g.*, United States v. Aluminum Co. of Am., 377 U.S. 271, 277 (1964) (insulated aluminum conductor products and insulated copper conductors serve "distinctive end uses"); RSR Corp. v. FTC, 602 F.2d 1317 (9th Cir. 1979) (secondary lead sold for about 10% less than primary lead); Reynolds Metals Co. v. FTC, 309 F.2d 223, 229 (D.C. Cir. 1962) (florists' foil and other aluminum foil held to be in separate product markets because of price differences despite the fact the products were virtually identical); *cf.* International Tel. & Tel. Corp. v. General Tel. & Elec. Corp., 518 F.2d 913, 932 (9th Cir. 1975) (no competitive significance for sales to different groups because pricing is the same); Chicago Bridge Iron Co., N.V., No. 9300, 2003 FTC LEXIS 96, at *19 (2003) (LIN/LOX tanks and spheres "serve different functions"); *cf.* United States v. SunGard Data Sys., Inc., 172 F. Supp. 2d 172, 189 (D.D.C. 2001) ("peculiar characteristics and uses of the product . . . support a finding that internal hotsites fall within the

---

same product market as shared hotsite services").

47. *See, e.g.*, Beatrice Foods Co. v. FTC, 540 F.2d 303, 308 (7th Cir. 1976) (paint brushes and rollers found to be manufactured from "raw materials" utilizing a technology vastly different from those employed in the manufacture of aerosols and sprayers); Crown Zellerbach Corp. v. FTC, 296 F.2d 800, 812 & n.8 (9th Cir. 1961) (insufficient production flexibility in paper markets); Gearhart Indus. v. Smith Int'l, Inc., 592 F. Supp. 203, 212 (N.D. Tex.) ("Measurement-While-Drilling" is a distinct technology used in specific oil drilling processes), *aff'd in part, modified in part and vacated in part*, 741 F.2d 707 (5th Cir. 1984); United States v. General Elec. Co., No. 1:03CV01923 (D.D.C. filed Sept. 16, 2003) (critical care monitors distinguished from low-acuity monitors because the former can measure and display more patient parameters and require significant networking capabilities); Chicago Bridge & Iron Co., N.V., No. 9300, 2003 FTC LEXIS 96, at *12-22 (2003) (field-erected tanks distinct from shop-fabricated tanks, and citing testimony that field-erected TVC is "a vastly different technology than what shop-built chamber requires"); *cf. SunGard Data Sys., Inc.*, 172 F. Supp. 2d at 188 ("changing nature of the technology" supported view that internal hotsites should have been included in market with shared hotsites); Weeks Dredging & Contracting, Inc. v. American Dredging Co., 451 F. Supp. 468, 488-89 (E.D. Pa. 1978) (distinct technology relied on in finding separate markets for bucket and hydraulic dredging).

48. *See* Lucas Auto. Eng'g, Inc. v. Bridgestone/Firestone, Inc., 275 F.3d 762, 768 (9th Cir. 2001) (evidence "suggest[s] that manufacturers, retailers and purchasers recognize original equipment major brand vintage tires as a separate economic entity from private label tires"); FTC v. PPG Indus., Inc., 798 F.2d 1500, 1504 (D.C. Cir. 1986) (relevant product market defined based on both buyer's and seller's perceptions); FTC v. Warner Communs., 742 F.2d 1156, 1163 (9th Cir. 1984) (per curium) (record industry recognized prerecorded music as a market separate from recorded music market); A.G. Spalding & Bros., Inc. v. FTC, 301 F.2d 585, 603 (3d Cir. 1962) (sporting good items are recognized by industry as separate products used in a recognized market (e.g., baseball or football)); United States v. UPM-Kymmene Oyj, 2003-2 Trade Cas. (CCH) ¶ 74,101, at *6 (N.D. Ill. July 25, 2003) (memorandum opinion and order) (industry trade association organized paper label stock into two categories); *cf. SunGard Data Sys., Inc.*, 172 F. Supp. 2d at 189 (rejecting product market consisting only of shared hotsite; industry recognition supported view that internal hotsites should be included); *Crown Zellerbach Corp.*, 296 F.2d at 813 (industry recognition of various paper grades); Grumman Corp. v. LTV Corp., 527 F. Supp. 86, 90 (E.D.N.Y.) ("aerospace industry distinguishes between [land-based and carrier-based aircraft] . . . in terms of the product and their producers" (emphasis removed)), *aff'd*, 665 F.2d 10 (2d Cir. 1981).

b. The *Merger Guidelines*' Hypothetical Monopolist Approach

The *Merger Guidelines* do not rely on such indicia to define relevant markets. Instead, the *Merger Guidelines* focus on an analytical framework that makes use of a hypothetical monopolist to try to force evidence of cross-elasticities and interchangeability into a more defined context. Under the *Merger Guidelines*, a "market is defined as the product or group of products and a geographic area in which it is produced or sold such that a hypothetical [monopolist] likely would impose at least a 'small but significant and non-transitory' increase in price, assuming the terms of sale of all other products are held constant."[50] The product market and geographic market should be no bigger than necessary to satisfy this test. In defining the market, the *Merger Guidelines* focus solely on the demand responses of consumers. In defining the market, the *Merger Guidelines* consider supply responses by "uncommitted" entrants in the market participation section,[51] while

---

49. Among the factors considered in determining whether private label goods should be considered as part of the branded good product market are differences in quality or reputation, patents and know-how differences, brand loyalty, frequency of purchase (infrequent purchasers may be less brand loyal), price movements between branded and unbranded goods, and cross-elasticity of demand between branded and unbranded goods. *See* Lucas Auto. Eng'g Inc. v. Bridgestone/Firestone, Inc., 275 F.3d 762, 768 (9th Cir. 2001) (reversing summary judgment for defendant because defendant had offered evidence to raise a genuine issue as to whether there is a separate market for original equipment major brand vintage tires versus private label tires); Coca-Cola Bottling Co. of the Southwest, 118 F.T.C. 452, 534 (1994) (Commission overturned ALJ finding of broad beverage product market including private label and warehouse brands, finding a narrower product market of branded carbonated soft drinks in part due to evidence of high price inelasticity between Coke products and unbranded soft drinks).

50. 1992 MERGER GUIDELINES, *supra* note 31, § 1.0; *cf.* HORIZONTAL MERGER GUIDELINES OF THE NATIONAL ASSOCIATION OF ATTORNEYS GENERAL (1993) § 3.1 [hereinafter NAAG MERGER GUIDELINES], *reprinted in* 4 Trade Reg. Rep. (CCH) ¶ 13,406 and in Appendix M (focusing primarily on evidence of consumer interests and buying patterns instead of the federal guidelines hypothetical price increase; the NAAG MERGER GUIDELINES allows a comparably priced substitute to "expand the product market definition if, and only if, considered suitable by customers accounting for seventy-five percent of the purchases").

51. 1992 MERGER GUIDELINES, *supra* note 31, § 1.0.

"committed" entry is considered separately as to whether it is timely, likely, or sufficient to defeat a price increase.[52]

Although the antitrust enforcement agencies attempt to apply this hypothetical monopolist test, most often, the data simply is not there to do so. Nevertheless, understanding the test is useful in providing common terms and concepts to use in discussing the degree of competition between the parties and others, and how competition will be affected by the transaction.

Under the *Merger Guidelines* test, the agencies begin by identifying each narrowly defined product produced or sold by the merging firms. For each product, the agency will ask what would happen if a hypothetical monopolist in that product imposed a "small but significant and non-transitory" price increase, holding the terms of sale of other products constant. If the price increase would prove unprofitable to the hypothetical monopolist because consumers would switch to the "next best substitute," the agencies will add that substitute product to the original product and begin the analysis again. The agencies will continue to add products until a market is identified in which the hypothetical monopolist could profitably impose a "small but significant and non-transitory" price increase.[53] The price increase postulated in most cases

---

52. *Id.* § 3.0.

53. The small but significant price increase is not a "tolerance level" for price increases. *Inquiry Concerning Commission's Merger Policy Under the Federal Power Act*, 1996 WL 233992 (F.T.C. May 7, 1996) ("The 'small but significant and non-transitory' increase in price is employed solely as a methodological tool for the analysis of mergers: it is not a tolerance level for price increases"). The small price increase (usually 5%) is used to identify the products and areas that a monopolist would have to control to profitably raise price by the postulated amount. Thus, only if there were a merger to monopoly, or a market that would support a perfect cartel, would one expect price to rise by the full postulated amount. Subsequent steps in the analysis identify market participants and consider whether the merger significantly increases the likelihood that some group of firms will exercise market power and raise prices through coordinated interdependence, or whether the merging firm could do so unilaterally. Absent a merger to monopoly, or a market that will support a perfect cartel, any merger-induced price increase will necessarily be less than the small but significant amount used initially to define the relevant market. Therefore, in most instances, when determining whether to challenge any particular transaction, the agencies are concerned with possible price increases much smaller than the small but significant amount used to define relevant markets, unless the product at issue has no close substitutes and demand is relatively inelastic.

will be 5 percent, although the agencies reserve the right to assess a higher or lower price increase depending upon the nature of the product industry.[54]

Thus, the case law's emphasis on both reasonable interchangeability and cross-elasticity of demand is subsumed by the *Merger Guidelines* within this hypothetical monopolist analytical tool. Reasonable interchangeability is factored into the market definition process through consideration of the consumers' likely reaction to the price increase—the agencies will consider evidence of consumer price sensitivity, sellers' estimation of product substitutability, downstream competition faced by buyers in their product market and the timing and cost of switching products.[55] Cross-elasticity of demand is presumed in the selection of the next best substitutes which "would account for the *greatest* value of diversion of demand"[56] in response to the price increase. The agency will select the product with the highest cross-elasticity of demand with the seller's product to include in its market definition.[57]

The postulated small but significant price increase is not necessarily assumed to be uniform. Instead, the hypothetical monopolist is assumed to maximize profits by raising price (by at least the specified threshold amount) of any or all of the products in the postulated market. Thus, there might be a concern that prices of some group of products, but not all products, would be raised. If so, the group for which prices would be raised by the threshold amount would constitute a relevant market. In differentiated product markets, this approach can produce much smaller

---

54. For example, if there is evidence of preexisting collusion or coordinated interdependence among current sellers, indicating that current prices are probably above competitive levels, then a price below current levels may be used as the base price. The government has also run the hypothetical monopolist test based on a 10% price increase. *See* United States v. Country Lake Foods, Inc., 754 F. Supp. 669, 675 (D. Minn. 1990).
55. 1992 MERGER GUIDELINES, *supra* note 31, § 1.11.
56. *Id.* § 1.11 n.9 (emphasis added).
57. A hypothetical monopolist may, however, be more restrained by the existence of many substitute products each with a low cross-elasticity of demand, rather than one or two substitutes with a high cross-elasticity of demand. The hypothetical monopolist's price-setting behavior ultimately rests with its "*own*-elasticity of demand"—what will be the effect on the demand for its own product. Cross-elasticity is only important to the extent that it sheds light on the hypothetical monopolist's own-elasticity of demand. ABA SECTION OF ANTITRUST LAW, MONOGRAPH NO. 12, HORIZONTAL MERGERS, LAW & POLICY 107 (1986).

markets than would emerge if one assumed that the prices of all products must rise uniformly by the given amount.

It is generally assumed in the *Merger Guidelines* that price discrimination is not possible, and markets are defined in terms of products and points of production. Where discrimination is possible, however, the *Merger Guidelines*' market definition focus shifts to groups of consumers against which price discrimination could be directed.[58]

Although courts have noted that they are not bound by the *Merger Guidelines*,[59] many have endorsed or applied its hypothetical monopolist approach,[60] while some have questioned its validity in certain circumstances.[61]

---

58. *See* FTC v. Owens-Illinois, Inc., 681 F. Supp. 27, 48-52 (D.D.C. 1988), *vacated as moot*, 850 F.2d 694 (D.C. Cir. 1988).

59. *See, e.g.,* FTC v. H.J. Heinz Co., 246 F.3d 708, 716 n.9 (D.C. Cir. 2001) ("Although the Merger Guidelines are not binding on the Court, they provide 'a useful illustration of the application of the HHI'"); FTC v. PPG Indus., Inc., 798 F.2d 1500, 1503 n.4 (D.C. Cir. 1986) ("the Department of Justice Guidelines offer a useful illustration of the application of the HHI, but are by no means to be considered binding on the court"); FTC v. Swedish Match, 131 F. Supp. 2d 151, 167 n.12 (D.D.C. 2001) ("The Merger Guidelines are not binding on the Court, but as this Circuit has stated, they do provide 'a useful illustration of the application of the HHI'"); *see also* part B of Chapter 2.

60. *See, e.g.*, California v. Sutter Health Sys., 130 F. Supp. 2d 1109, 1120, 1128-32 (N.D. Cal. 2001) (holding "[a]lthough the Merger Guidelines are not binding, courts have often adopted the [market delineation] standards set forth in the Merger Guidelines in analyzing antitrust issues," and applying the hypothetical monopolist test); FTC v. Owens-Ill., Inc., 681 F. Supp. 27, 34 n.17, 38-46 (D.D.C. 1998), *vacated as moot*, 850 F.2d 694 (D.C. Cir. 1988) (holding that "the Guidelines are not binding on the courts," yet applying the hypothetical monopolist test); New York v. Kraft Gen. Foods, Inc., 926 F. Supp. 321, 359-61 & n.9 (S.D.N.Y. 1995) (holding that the "Merger Guidelines are helpful in providing an analytical framework for evaluating an acquisition, but they are not binding upon the court" and adopting the Guidelines hypothetical monopolist test); Santa Cruz Med. Clinic v. Dominican Santa Cruz Hosp., 1995-2 Trade Cas. (CCH) ¶ 71,254, at 76,091 n.1, 76,094 n.6 (N.D. Cal. 1995) (holding that the "merger guidelines are not binding on the courts" but citing Guidelines treatment of geographic market approvingly).

61. *See* Gregory J. Werden, *The 1982 Merger Guidelines and the Ascent of the Hypothetical Monopolist Paradigm,* 71 ANTITRUST L.J. 253, 264 n. 38 (2003) (discussing cases critical of the Merger Guidelines approach, including FTC v. PPG Indus., Inc., 798 F.2d 1500, 1503 n.4 (D.C. Cir. 1986); United States v. Englehard Corp., 970 F. Supp. 1463 (M.D. Ga.

Courts have often recognized the hypothetical monopolist paradigm by quoting leading treatises. The hypothetical monopolist paradigm set forth in the Areeda treatise has been quoted or paraphrased by circuit or district courts in the First, Second, Third, Fourth, Sixth, Eighth, and Ninth Circuits.[62] The Sullivan treatise[63] has been quoted by the First, Third, Fifth, Eighth, Ninth, Tenth, Eleventh, and D.C. Circuits or courts therein.[64] Courts have also heavily based their reasoning on the hypothetical monopolist paradigm, most notably in *United States v. Archer-Daniels-Midland Co.*,[65] which reversed the district court's grant of summary judgement against the government on the issue of market definition.[66]

c. Competition Between Differentiated Products:
The Continuum Problem

Product market definition can be further complicated by the problem of similar, but not exact, substitutes. "Differentiated products" may exist within the same product market, but offer such distinct advantages or disadvantages to consumers that they cannot be considered perfect substitutes for one another. To include the full range of differentiated products in the relevant market would dilute the effect that merging competitors may have on the market, while omitting substitutes at the margins would understate the potential demand responses.

The *Brown Shoe* Court considered these issues in defining the relevant product markets for shoes of differing prices and quality made for men and women of different ages. While acknowledging that "'price/quality' differences, where they exist, are [not] unimportant in analyzing a merger,"[67] the Court settled on broadly drawn submarkets of men's, women's, and children's shoes regardless of price or quality.[68] The *Brown Shoe* Court sidestepped further subdivisions based on age and

---

1997); Olin Corp. v. FTC, 986 F.2d 1295 (9th Cir. 1993); and Monfort of Colo., Inc. v. Cargill, Inc. 591 F. Supp. 683, 695 (D. Colo. 1983)).

62. *Id*. at 265 n. 41.
63. Lawrence A. Sullivan, HANDBOOK OF THE LAW OF ANTITRUST 41 (1977).
64. Werdon, *supra* note 61, at 264-65.
65. 866 F.2d 242 (8th Cir. 1988).
66. Werden, *supra* note 61, at 265.
67. Brown Shoe Co. v. United States, 370 U.S. 294, 326 (1962).
68. "It would be unrealistic to accept Brown's contention that, for example, men's shoes selling below $8.99 are in a different market from those selling above $9.00." *Id.*

sex by concluding they would not effect the ultimate outcome of the case.[69]

Courts that have considered continuum markets after *Brown Shoe* have split on the issue, with some courts drawing distinctions in markets based on qualitative differences[70] and others rejecting them.[71] Some

---

69. *Id.* at 327.

70. *See* Avnet, Inc. v. FTC, 511 F.2d 70, 78 (7th Cir. 1975) (distinguishing original automotive electrical units from rebuilt units); Reynolds Metals Co. v. FTC, 309 F.2d 223, 229 (D.C. Cir. 1962) (distinguishing markets for florist foil and lower priced decorative foil); A.G. Spalding & Bros., Inc. v. FTC, 301 F.2d 585, 603 (3d Cir. 1962) (distinguishing high-priced professional grade athletic products from low-priced equivalents); United States v. Gillette Co., 828 F. Supp. 78, 81-84 (D.D.C. 1993) (drawing market for "premium" writing instruments priced between $40 and $400 which "afford their users (as well as those who merely put them in their breast pockets) image, prestige and status"); Ansell Inc. v. Schmid Labs., Inc., 757 F. Supp. 467, 472-73 (D.N.J.) (distinguishing condoms sold at retail from condoms sold wholesale based on differences in shape, size, and packaging), *aff'd,* 941 F.2d 1200 (3d Cir. 1991); *see also In the matter of* Nestlé Holdings Inc., 68 Fed. Reg. 39,564 (July 2, 2003) (distinguishing in complaint between super premium ice cream and premium and economy ice cream); Hicks, Muse, Tate & Furst Equity Fund V, L.P., *at* www.ftc.gov/os/2003/06/dreyeranalysis.htm (press release issued by the FTC on October 22, 2003 distinguishing in complaint between refrigerated pickles and all pickles); United States v. Dairy Farmers of Am., 2001-1 Trade Cas. (CCH) ¶73,136 (E.D. Pa. 2001) (distinguishing in complaint between branded butter and private label butter); Pennsylvania v. Russell Stover Candies, Inc., 1993-1 Trade Cas. (CCH) ¶70,224 (E.D. Pa. 1993) (state of Pennsylvania alleged acquisition would substantially lessen competition in "gift boxed chocolates sold nationally through chain drug stores and mass marketers").

71. *See, e.g.*, Liggett & Myers, Inc. v. FTC, 567 F.2d 1273, 1274-75 (4th Cir. 1977) (rejecting distinctions between classes of dog food); Beatrice Foods Co. v. FTC, 540 F.2d 303, 309-10 (7th Cir. 1976) (rejecting significance of price/quality differences between "do-it-yourself" and "professional" paint brushes and rollers); New York v. Kraft Gen. Foods, Inc., 926 F. Supp. 321, 333 (S.D.N.Y. 1995) (ready-to-eat cereals are "so highly differentiated, and compete with one another along so many different dimensions, that there is no clear break in the chain of substitutes that would permit a definition of a market smaller than all RTE cereals"); United States v. Ivaco, Inc., 704 F. Supp. 1409, 1415-17 (W.D. Mich. 1989) (concluding that market includes all automatic tampers, despite differences between conventional automatic tampers and

courts have suggested that the use of price/quality distinctions depends upon the price sensitivity between the products.[72]

Differentiated consumer goods industries exhibit certain characteristics in common which complicate the competitive effects analysis of a merger. First, often products appear over a broad and fairly continuous range of prices and qualities, not clustered around those attributes. Second, competition is localized to some extent because a consumer's second choice product most often is similar to the first choice product in price and product attributes. Third, competition is not entirely localized because some consumers' second choices are not so similar in terms of price and product attributes to their first choices.[73] In such a situation, the indicia listed in *Brown Shoe* may be less meaningful in a heterogeneous market.

The *Merger Guidelines* approach to product market definition may prove helpful in sorting out differentiated product markets.[74] By analyzing demand responses to supracompetitive prices, the agency can sort out those products along the continuum that belong in the product

---

new continuous action tampers); Pennsylvania v. Russell Stover Candies, Inc., 1993-1 Trade Cas. ¶ 70,224, at 70,091 (E.D. Pa. 1993) ("Where the antitrust plaintiff articulates product differences along a spectrum of price and quality, the product market distinctions are economically meaningless and unrealistic." (citations omitted)).

72. *See, e.g.*, Beatrice Foods Co. v. FTC, 540 F.2d 303, 310 (7th Cir. 1976) ("Prior cases indicate that price/quality distinctions in products may play a role in market definitions where articles are sold in clearly separate price groupings that have little or no price sensitivity between them."); *accord Avnet, Inc.*, 511 F.2d at 77 (holding that a 25% to 50% price differential between new and rebuilt automotive electrical units combined with the absence of substantial price interaction between the two lines supported finding of distinct product markets). *But see* United States v. Black & Decker Mfg. Co., 430 F. Supp. 729, 738-40 (D. Md. 1976) (finding separate professional and occasional user chain saws markets on price differential alone absent evidence of low cross-elasticity of demand).

73. Gregory J. Werden & George A. Rozanski, *The Application of Section 7 to Differentiated Products Industries: The Market Delineation Dilemma*, ANTITRUST, Summer 1994, at 40-41.

74. *See id.* at 40; David J. Dadoun & Diana L. Dietrich, Comment, *After Gillette: An Analysis of Premium Product Markets Under the 1992 Merger Guidelines,* 17 HARV. J.L. & PUB. POL'Y 567 (1994). *But see* James A. Keyte, *Premium Fountain Pens and Gift Boxed Chocolates: Market Definition and Differentiated Products*, ANTITRUST, Fall 1993, at 19.

market and those that do not. The *Merger Guidelines*' approach attempts to identify the constraints that influence prices, whether those constraints arise from closely interchangeable products or otherwise. Mergers that remove significant constraints are likely to result in higher prices. A significant constraint might be removed by merging firms selling imperfect substitutes. Conversely, a merger between the only closely interchangeable products might not pose any threat to competition because of the presence of a host of imperfect substitutes.

d. The Cluster Markets Debate

Courts have sometimes defined the relevant product market as a "cluster" of products or services that are not themselves substitutes for one another. This approach departs from the judiciary's traditional reliance on product substitutability to define the relevant product market. It is usually justified by consumer preference for group provision of products or services because of the convenience or savings that accrue to the consumer by dealing with only one supplier.[75]

The cluster market concept was first articulated by the U.S. Supreme Court in its 1963 decision in *United States v. Philadelphia National Bank*.[76] The Court found a product market composed solely of commercial banks, excluding other financial institutions even though they offered some competing products, such as savings accounts. The Court determined that the exclusion was warranted by the distinctness of the services offered by commercial banks, cost advantages, and "settled consumer preferences" which insulated commercial banking products from competition by products of other financial institutions.[77] The Court extended the cluster market concept to services in *United States v.*

---

75. *See* Jonathan B. Baker, *The Antitrust Analysis of Hospital Mergers and the Transformation of the Hospital Industry,* 51 LAW & CONTEMP. PROBS. 93, 123-41 (1988) (discussing the application of cluster markets in hospital merger cases); Ian Ayres, *Rationalizing Antitrust Cluster Markets*, 95 YALE L.J. 109 (1985) (suggesting that court should only define cluster markets when transaction costs are reduced by purchasing them from a single supplier); *see also* Gregory E. Elliehausen & John D. Wolken, *Small Business Clustering Financial Services and the Definition of Banking Markets for Antitrust Analysis*, 32 ANTITRUST BULL. 707 (1992) (positing that empirical data proves small businesses cluster purchases of some financial services due to "settled customer preference").
76. 374 U.S. 321 (1963).
77. *Id.* at 356-57.

Grinnell,[78] where it found that accredited central station security services constituted a cluster market.[79]

The economic principle of complementarity (in demand or supply) underlies the concept of cluster markets. Cluster markets have been most extensively employed in the banking industry, where courts have found the cluster of commercial banking services to constitute the relevant market.[80] Cluster markets analysis also has been used to challenge mergers involving traditional grocery supermarkets[81] and department

---

78. 384 U.S. 563, 572 (1966). The *Grinnell* Court implied that service markets would be treated differently than product markets: "[W]e deal with services, not products." *Id.* However, the distinction was not explained by the Court.
79. Earlier decisions, though not employing cluster market language, had multiproduct markets for much the same reasons. *See, e.g.*, A.G. Spalding & Bros., Inc. v. FTC, 301 F.2d 585, 603 (3d Cir. 1962) (holding that athletic goods industry is the appropriate line of commerce); United States v. United Shoe Mach. Corp., 110 F. Supp. 295, 338-39 (D. Mass. 1953) (aggregating shoe machines which perform 18 different processes into one market); Papercraft Corp., 78 F.T.C. 1352, 1361-64 (1971) (giftwrap, tying materials and tags included in a single market).
80. *See, e.g.*, United States v. Connecticut Nat'l Bank, 418 U.S. 656, 664-66 (1974); United States v. Phillipsburg Nat'l Bank & Trust Co., 399 U.S. 350, 360-61 (1970); United States v. Philadelphia Nat'l Bank, 374 U.S. 321, 356 (1963); *see* United States v. Central State Bank, 621 F. Supp. 1276, 1291-92 (W.D. Mich. 1985) (upholding merger based on effect in commercial banking cluster market, refusing to define markets as transactional accounts and small loans), *aff'd per curiam,* 817 F.2d 22 (6th Cir. 1987); United States v. First Nat'l State Bancorp., 499 F. Supp. 793, 811 (D.N.J. 1980); *see also* Michael A. Greenspan & Jacqueline T. Coldough, *The Relevant Product Market for Bank Acquisitions*, 41 ANTITRUST BULL. 453 (1996) (noting that in their shared responsibility for reviewing bank acquisitions, the DOJ defines product market by disaggregating a cluster into its constituent parts, while the Federal Reserve, Office of the Comptroller of the Currency, and Federal Deposit Insurance Corporation define product market as cluster of services); *cf.* United States v. Household Fin. Corp., 602 F.2d 1255, 1259-60 (7th Cir. 1979) (finance companies offer unique cluster of products and services to a class of high-risk customers that were not financed by other financial institutions).
81. *See* California v. American Stores Co., 697 F. Supp. 1125, 1129 (C.D. Cal. 1988) (enjoining merger of two grocery stores because grocery stores are a market distinct from other providers such as convenience stores and gas stations, who provide similar products), *aff'd in part and rev'd in part*, 872 F.2d 837 (9th Cir. 1989), *rev'd on other grounds*, 495

stores.[82] More recently, cluster markets have been found in the health care field.[83] The range of businesses to which cluster markets can be applied could be quite large.[84] Nevertheless, courts have not always been amenable to cluster market arguments.[85]

U.S. 271 (1990), *reinstated in relevant part*, 930 F.2d 776 (9th Cir. 1991).

82. *See* Bon-Ton Stores v. May Dep't Stores Co., 881 F. Supp. 860, 869-70 (W.D.N.Y. 1994) (enjoining merger of two department stores because relevant market is "traditional department stores" due to the nature of goods and services sold).

83. *See, e.g.*, FTC v. Freeman Hosp., 69 F.3d 260, 268 (8th Cir. 1995) (relevant product market is "acute care inpatient services"); FTC v. University Health, Inc., 938 F.2d 1206, 1210-11 (11th Cir. 1991) (relevant market is the "provision of in-patient services by acute-care hospitals"); United States v. Rockford Mem'l Corp., 898 F.2d 1278, 1284 (7th Cir. 1990) (concluding that inpatient care, rather than both inpatient and outpatient care, was the relevant market because inpatient care provided a unique cluster of services); FTC v. Tenet Health Care Corp., 17 F. Supp. 2d 937, 942 (E.D. Mo. 1998) (relevant product market is "general acute care in-patient hospital services"), *rev'd on other grounds,* 186 F.3d 1045 (8th Cir. 1999); United States v. Long Island Jewish Med. Ctr., 983 F. Supp. 121, 137-40 (E.D.N.Y. 1997) (relevant product market is "general acute inpatient services," not the even narrower cluster "bundle of services provided by anchor hospitals to managed care plans" offered by the government); FTC v. Butterworth Health Corp., 946 F. Supp. 1285, 1290-91 (W.D. Mich. 1996) (relevant product markets are "general acute care inpatient hospital services" and "primary care inpatient services"), *aff'd*, 121 F.3d 708 (6th Cir. 1997); United States v. Mercy Health Serv., 902 F. Supp. 968, 976 (N.D. Iowa 1995) (relevant product market is "acute care inpatient services"), *vacated as moot*, 107 F.3d 632 (8th Cir. 1997); Adventist Health Sys./West, 117 F.T.C. 224, 288 (1994) (relevant market is the provision of inpatient acute care hospital services). *But see* United States v. Carilion Health Sys., 707 F. Supp. 840 (W.D. Va.), *aff'd mem.*, 892 F.2d 1042 (4th Cir. 1989) (including outpatient services that could be substituted for inpatient services in the relevant market).

84. *See, e.g.*, United States v. Von's Grocery Co., 384 U.S. 270 (1966) (clustering grocery stores); JBL Enters., Inc. v. Jhirmack, Inc., 698 F.2d 1011, 1016-17 (9th Cir. 1983) (clustering beauty products); FTC v. Staples, Inc., 970 F. Supp. 1066 (D.D.C. 1997) (clustering consumable office supplies sold through office supply superstores); FTC v. Alliant Techsystems, Inc., 808 F. Supp. 9 (D.D.C. 1992) (clustering products and services involved in the manufacture and related servicing of certain ammunition and tactical rounds); United States v. Hughes Tool Co., 415 F. Supp. 637, 640-41 (C.D. Cal. 1976) (clustering specialized surface rotary

The 1992 *Merger Guidelines* do not employ the concept of cluster markets. Instead, the *Merger Guidelines* address the implications of (demand and supply) complementarity in several alternative ways. First, if "products" are such strong complements that consumers usually purchase them together, they may be grouped together and considered a relevant "product" for market definition purposes. Second, when supply substitutability is such that the proper measure of market shares would be the same in a large number of product markets (for example, when fungible capacity properly measures market shares), the *Merger Guidelines* may make "use [of] an aggregate description of those markets as a matter of convenience."[86]

---

drilling tools); Brunswick Corp., 94 F.T.C. 1174, 1259 (1979) (clustering marine engines); British Oxygen Co., 86 F.T.C. 1241, 1346 (1975) (clustering industrial gases), *rev'd on other grounds sub nom.* BOC Int'l, Ltd. v. FTC, 557 F.2d 24 (2d Cir. 1977); *see also* William Blumenthal & David A. Cohen, *Channels of Distribution as Merger "Markets": Interpreting Staples and Cardinal,* ANTITRUST REPORT, Nov. 1998, at 10-14 (arguing that findings of distribution markets can be harmonized with cluster market analysis).

85. *See, e.g.*, Forsyth v. Humana, Inc., 99 F.3d 1504, 1513-14 (9th Cir. 1996) ("[S]pecialty shops which offer only a limited range of goods are generally considered in the same market with larger, more diverse, 'one-stop shopping' centers"); Thurman Indus. v. Pay N' Pak Stores, 875 F.2d 1369 (9th Cir. 1989) ("[T]he record is inadequate to support a finding that consumers . . . are lured to home centers and away from specialty vendors and department stores solely because of the home center product and service package."); Equifax, Inc. v. FTC, 618 F.2d 63, 67 (9th Cir. 1980) (rejecting cluster market of credit reports and mortgage reports because of product differences and lack of demonstrated cross-elasticity of production); United States v. Ivaco, Inc., 704 F. Supp. 1409 (W.D. Mich. 1989) (rejecting cluster market of all equipment used to maintain railroad rights-of-way because the different pieces of equipment were not functional substitutes and the manufacturers could not easily switch from one piece of equipment to another).

86. 1992 MERGER GUIDELINES, *supra* note 31, § 1.321 n.14. "The one difference between the Guidelines' approach on this point and that of the prior case law is that, technically at least, the Guidelines' approach would refer to an aggregate description of the relevant markets, rather than to a single aggregated market. For example, in delineating the relevant market for hospital services, one might refer to many markets in an aggregate description like 'markets for inpatient, acute care services,' which typically is loosely referred to as 'the market for inpatient, acute care services.'" Gregory J. Werden, *The History of Antitrust Market Delineation*, 76 MARQ. L. REV. 123, 197 n.471 (1992) (citation omitted).

e. The Submarket Debate

In some cases, popular perceptions may lead people to argue that a broader product market exists than is provable by economic evidence. For example, using the "reasonable substitutability" test for defining a product market, one might conclude that orange juice is part of a broad market for all beverages, all cold beverages, or all juices. But a broad definition, while appropriate in some circumstances, does not necessarily translate into the appropriate relevant market for antitrust purposes. Consequently, some courts have referred generally to a broad market, recognized by popular or industry perceptions, but then moved on to analyze narrower segments of the market, called submarkets, that are more appropriately tailored to measuring the competitive effects of the market.

The distinction between relevant markets and submarkets has caused some confusion and sparked significant debate.[87] On the one hand, the definition of the relevant market is theoretically defined with reference to the "areas of effective competition"; and therefore, the definition of a relevant submarket is neither necessary nor appropriate. Indeed, submarket analysis makes no sense whatsoever when using the *Merger Guidelines* approach to defining a market, because the *Merger Guidelines* already attempt to define the smallest possible market for which anticompetitive effects are possible.[88] By definition, any smaller submarket is too small to raise anticompetitive concerns. On the other hand, the factors—often called "practical indicia"—used by courts to determine whether a submarket exists are useful in determining what are the true "areas of effective competition."[89] And in that sense, submarket analysis has survived and proven useful in merger analysis.[90]

---

87. *See* Allen-Myland, Inc. v. IBM, 33 F.3d 194, 208 n.16 (3d Cir. 1994) ("The use of the term 'submarket' is somewhat confusing, and tends to obscure the true inquiry. . ."); Satellite Television & Associated Resources, Inc. v. Continental Cablevision of Va., Inc., 714 F.2d 351, 355 n.5 (4th Cir. 1983) ("The use of the term submarket is to be avoided; it adds only confusion to an already imprecise and complex endeavor. For antitrust purposes a product or group or geographic area either meets the listed criteria, in which case it is a relevant market; or it does not, in which case it is irrelevant for purposes of analysis").

88. *See, e.g.*, United States v. Dairy Farmers of America, 2001-1 Trade Cas. (CCH) ¶ 73,136 (E.D. Pa. 2000) (relevant product markets defined as branded stick butter and branded whipped butter).

89. *See* Community Publishers v. Donrey Corp., 892 F. Supp. 1146, 1154 n.9 (W.D. Ark. 1995) ("One approach, adopted by the Eighth Circuit, and

Submarket analysis begins with the *Brown Shoe* decision. There, the U.S. Supreme Court recognized that "well-defined submarkets may exist which, in themselves, constitute product markets for antitrust purposes."[91] The Court articulated a number of "practical indicia"[92] of submarkets which are similar to those used in defining relevant product markets; indicia of submarkets include industry or public recognition of the submarket as a separate economic unit,[93] the product's peculiar characteristics and uses,[94] unique production facilities,[95] distinct

---

described above, would simply do away with the term 'submarket' and treat the 'practical indicia' of *Brown Shoe* as types of evidence that establish the relevant market, whether it be a submarket or a broad product market."), *aff'd*, 139 F.3d 1180 (8th Cir. 1998).

90. *See* Geneva Pharmaceuticals Tech. Corp. v. Barr Labs., Inc., 201 F. Supp. 2d 236 (S.D.N.Y. 2002) (based on *Brown Shoe's* practical indicia, no submarket within the relevant pharmaceutical product market of generic and branded warfarin sodium, an oral anti-coagulant medication); FTC v. Cardinal Health, Inc., 12 F. Supp. 2d 34 (D.D.C. 1998) (noting that market existed for all prescription drug distribution but defining submarket limited to the wholesale distribution of prescription drugs); FTC v. Staples, Inc., 970 F. Supp. 1066 (D.D.C. 1997) (finding, based on *Brown Shoe's* practical indicia, a submarket consisting of consumable office supplies sold through office superstores); PepsiCo, Inc. v. Coca-Cola Co., Inc., 1998-2 Trade Cas. (CCH) ¶ 72,257 (S.D.N.Y. 1998) (noting that use of the submarket lexicon is superfluous, but using *Brown Shoe's* practical indicia to define a market consisting of fountain-dispensed soft drinks distributed through independent food service distributors).

91. Brown Shoe Co. v. United States, 370 U.S. 294, 325 (1962).

92. *Id.*

93. *See, e.g.*, *id.* (men's, women's, and children's shoes); FTC v. Warner Communs., 742 F.2d 1156 (9th Cir. 1984) (prerecorded music); Beatrice Foods Co. v. FTC, 540 F.2d 303 (7th Cir. 1976) (paint brushes and rollers); RSR Corp. v. FTC, 602 F.2d 1317 (9th Cir. 1979) (secondary lead); Reynolds Metals Co. v. FTC, 309 F.2d 223 (D.C. Cir. 1962) (florist foil); FTC v. Swedish Match, 131 F. Supp. 2d 151 (D.D.C. 2000) (loose leaf tobacco); United States v. Gillette Co., 828 F. Supp. 78, 82 (D.D.C. 1993) (manufacturers, retailers, and purchasers of premium pens priced in the range of $40-$400 view these pens as different from pens priced above or below such range).

94. *See, e.g.*, Lucas Auto. Eng'g, Inc. v. Bridgestone/Firestone, Inc., 275 F.3d 762 (9th Cir. 2001) (remanded to consider whether the peculiar characteristics and uses of original equipment major brand vintage tires result in a distinct submarket from private brand vintage tires); Olin Corp. v. FTC, 986 F.2d 1295 (9th Cir. 1993) (accepting a submarket of dry,

customers,[96] distinct prices,[97] sensitivity to price changes,[98] and specialized vendors.[99] The existence of a larger relevant product market

---

sanitizing agents to clean swimming pools over broader product market of all sanitizing agents, including liquid ones); RSR Corp. v. FTC, 602 F.2d 1317 (9th Cir. 1979), (accepting submarket of recycled or "secondary" lead because secondary lead contains impurities that limit its potential end uses); *Beatrice Foods Co.*, 540 F.2d at 303 (distinguishing paint brushes and rollers from aerosol paint dispensers based on their advantages and disadvantages for certain tasks); General Foods Corp. v. FTC, 386 F.2d 936 (3d Cir. 1967) (differentiating steel wool pads from non-steel wool alternatives by their superior scouring ability on pots and pans); Electronic Data Sys. Corp. v. Computer Assoc. Int'l, 802 F. Supp. 1463, 1467-68 (N.D. Tex. 1992) (relevant market consisted of software used on IBM and IBM compatible mainframe computers, with several discrete submarkets consisting of types of software performing various different functions).

95. *See, e.g.*, *Beatrice Foods Co.*, 540 F.2d at 308 (paint brushes and rollers found to be manufactured from "raw materials" utilizing a technology vastly different from those employed in the manufacture of aerosols and sprayers); Crown Zellerbach Corp. v. FTC, 296 F.2d 800, 812 & n.8 (9th Cir. 1961) (insufficient production flexibility in paper markets); Ansell Inc. v. Schmid Labs., Inc., 757 F. Supp. 467, 473 (D.N.J.) (difference in packaging equipment between wholesale and retail condoms), *aff'd*, 941 F.2d 1200 (3d Cir. 1991); Gearhart Indus. v. Smith Int'l, Inc., 592 F. Supp. 203, 212 (N.D. Tex.) ("Measurement-While-Drilling" is a distinct technology used in specific oil drilling processes), *aff'd in part, modified in part and vacated in part*, 741 F.2d 707 (5th Cir. 1984).

96. *See, e.g.*, *Brown Shoe Co.*, 370 U.S. at 326 (distinct customers supported finding of separate submarkets); Monfort of Colo., Inc. v. Cargill, Inc., 761 F.2d 570, 579 (10th Cir. 1985) (limiting market to fed cattle based in part on distinct customer group), *rev'd on other grounds*, 479 U.S. 104 (1986); United States v. Waste Mgmt., Inc., 743 F.2d 976, 980 (2d Cir. 1984) (consumer preferences for different types of trash removal service subdivided market); Avnet, Inc. v. FTC, 511 F.2d 70,78 (7th Cir. 1975) (separate customer groups for automotive electrical units as distinct from rebuilt units); FTC v. Cardinal Health, Inc., 12 F. Supp. 2d 34, 48 (D.D.C. 1998) (limiting market to wholesale distribution of prescription drugs in large part because of existence of distinct customer class); *Ansell Inc.*, 757 F. Supp. at 472 (condoms sold at retail in different market from condoms sold wholesale in part because "industry participants view their sales to the retail trade as a separate economic entity"); United States v. Black & Decker Mfg. Co., 430 F. Supp. 729 (D. Md. 1976) (occasional user chain saws are designed differently than those used by the professional logger to suit their distinct requirements).

97. *See, e.g.*, *Warner Communs.*, 742 F.2d at 1163 (prerecorded music,

and one or more submarkets or additional markets is not mutually exclusive.

A court need not find all of the *Brown Shoe* factors to find an appropriate submarket. They are practical indicia only;[100] the ultimate

---

excluding home tapes, found to be separate market based on 300% price difference); *Swedish Match*, 131 F. Supp. 2d at 165 (independent movement of prices of loose leaf and moist snuff support finding of separate loose leaf tobacco market); *Ansell Inc.*, 757 F. Supp. at 474 (price discrepancy between wholesale and retail condoms supported finding of separate market); *Black & Decker Mfg. Co.*, 430 F. Supp. at 738-40 (professional and occasional user chain saws distinguished based on price differential); Elco Corp. v. Microdot, Inc., 360 F. Supp. 741, 747-49 (D. Del. 1973) (metal plate back panel connectors and printed circuit connectors distinguished based on price differential); RSR Corp., 88 F.T.C. 800 (1976) (distinguishing secondary lead market from primary lead market based on 10% price differential), *aff'd*, 602 F.2d 1317 (9th Cir. 1979).

98. *See* United States v. Aluminum Co. of Am., 377 U.S. 271, 275-76 (1964) (finding separate aluminum and copper cable submarkets based on significant price differentials and independence of price movements); *Swedish Match*, 131 F. Supp. 2d at 164 (finding small price change for either tobacco product unlikely to induce switching); FTC v. Owens-Illinois, Inc., 681 F. Supp. 27, 47 (D.D.C. 1988) (inability to price discriminate against group of buyers with limited ability to substitute other products evidence that no submarket exists); B.A.T. Indus., 104 F.T.C. 852, 931-32 (1984) ("a substantially and persistently higher price [for one of two products at issue] . . . indicates that a small price change for either product would be unlikely to induce [switching]."); United States v. American Technical Indus., Inc., 1974-1 Trade Cas. (CCH) ¶ 74,873, at 95,873 (M.D. Pa. 1974) (comparing prices of products, industry pricing practices, and price fluctuations in industries when assessing cross-elasticity of demand between artificial and real Christmas trees).

99. *See, e.g.*, RSR Corp. v. FTC, 602 F.2d 1317 (9th Cir. 1979) (primary lead producers generally produced only soft lead while secondary producers chiefly produced hard lead); Bendix Corp. v. FTC, 450 F.2d 534, 537 (6th Cir. 1971) (original automotive filters are distinguished from replacement automotive filters by sales techniques, distributor channels, product outlets, and vendors); Reynolds Metals Co. v. FTC, 309 F.2d 223 (D.C. Cir. 1962) (specialized florist foil vendors supported submarket of florist foil); United States v. Healthco, Inc., 387 F. Supp. 258 (S.D.N.Y.) (dental equipment sold through dealers who employed special sales force), *aff'd mem.*, 525 F.2d 1243 (2d Cir. 1975).

100. *See, e.g.*, International Tel. & Tel. Corp. v. General Tel. & Elec. Corp.,

issue is whether the alleged submarket is economically significant and an appropriate tool for measuring the effects of the merger.[101]

In *Bon-Ton Stores v. May Department Stores Co.*,[102] a district court applied a *Brown Shoe* submarket analysis to find a "traditional department stores" (plus J.C. Penney) "submarket" within the "general merchandise, apparel and furniture" market. The court paraphrased Justice Stewart's often-quoted comment (in another context), finding "customers know a department store when they see it."[103] The court also focused on industry perception of a separate traditional department store market.[104]

Similarly, in *FTC v. Staples, Inc.*,[105] the court applied the *Brown Shoe* factors to find a "broad market encompassing the sale of consumable office supplies by all sellers of such supplies," and, within that market, a narrower submarket of consumable office supplies sold through office supply superstores. The court's findings were based primarily on evidence suggesting that office superstores were able to price higher where they faced little or no competition from other office superstores, regardless of competition from other sellers.

Finally, in *FTC v. Cardinal Health, Inc.*,[106] the court applied a *Brown Shoe* submarket analysis to find a submarket for wholesale prescription drug distribution. Although the court noted that a "broader market encompassing the delivery of prescriptions by all forms of distribution" existed,[107] the court found that the wholesale prescription drug distribution market was the relevant product market in which to assess the competitive effects of the acquisition.[108] The court based this decision on evidence that the wholesalers provided "centralized warehousing, delivery, and billing services" that were not offered by other distribution channels.[109] Further, the court was persuaded by

---

518 F.2d 913, 932 (9th Cir. 1975) (submarket indicia of *Brown Shoe* "were listed with the intention of furnishing practical aids in identifying zones of actual or potential competition rather than with the view that their presence or absence would dispose, in talisman fashion, of the submarket issue").

101. *See id.*; *see also Brown Shoe Co.*, 370 U.S. at 294, 325 (1962).
102. 881 F. Supp. 860 (W.D.N.Y. 1994).
103. *Id.* at 869-70 (citing Jacobellis v. Ohio, 378 U.S. 184, 197 (1964)).
104. *See id.* at 870-72.
105. 970 F. Supp. 1066 (D.D.C. 1997).
106. 12 F. Supp. 2d 34 (D.D.C. 1998).
107. *Id.* at 47.
108. *See id.* at 49.
109. *Id.* at 47.

internal documents that revealed that "the merging parties clearly viewed their economic competition to be from their fellow drug wholesalers," and not from other sources.[110]

As mentioned, the analytical framework for market delineation set out in the 1992 *Merger Guidelines* does not make use of the submarket concept. Instead, the *Merger Guidelines* define relevant antitrust markets based on the pricing hypothetical described above, and generally consider the smallest group of products that satisfy the pricing test to comprise the relevant product market. There are, however, two respects in which the *Merger Guidelines'* approach yields results that seem compatible with the concept of submarkets found in the case law.[111]

First, the *Merger Guidelines* generally assume that the hypothetical price increase will be uniform to all buyers and define market boundaries accordingly. If, however, there is reason to believe that price discrimination may be possible, the *Merger Guidelines* ask if there is some group of customers that could be discriminated against in price, i.e., a group for which prices could profitably be raised by 5 percent while prices to other buyers remained the same. If such a group could be identified, the relevant markets would be comprised only of that group of customers under the *Merger Guidelines*' approach. The basis for discrimination could be customer characteristics or geographic location. Generally, the markets defined assuming price discrimination will be included within broader markets defined assuming no price discrimination. Consistent with the *Brown Shoe* notion of submarkets, the price discrimination markets could be thought of as submarkets of broader markets that are defined assuming no price discrimination.

Second, the *Merger Guidelines* generally assume that the price of all the products in the posited hypothetical markets is raised uniformly by 5 percent, and market boundaries are defined accordingly. The *Merger Guidelines* do, however, consider the possibility that a merger could lead to a 5 percent increase in price only on a subset of products in a broader product market. In differentiated product markets, this approach

---

110. *Id.* at 49.

111. *But see* William Blumenthal & David A. Cohen, *Channels of Distribution as Merger "Markets": Interpreting Staples and Cardinal,* ANTITRUST REPORT, Nov. 1998, at 3 ("The *Staples* and *Cardinal* decisions are consistent with *Brown Shoe* in identifying substantial evidence of the uniqueness of the distribution channels at issue and of the existence of customers for whom other channels would not suffice, but neither their logic nor the facts they relate are adequate to support the conclusion that their markets are well-defined within the meaning of the *Merger Guidelines*").

recognizes the possibility that a monopolist might need to gain control of a broad set of substitutable products to raise prices 5 percent on all of them, but might need to control a narrower set of substitutes in order to raise price 5 percent only on some of them. Again, the *Merger Guidelines*' approach would generally result in defining different market boundaries under the differing pricing assumptions. Although the *Merger Guidelines* would define each as a relevant market (based on different pricing assumptions), and would not call one a submarket of the other, the result seems consistent with the notion of submarkets reflected in some of the case law.

f. Innovation Markets

In 1995, the DOJ and the FTC jointly issued the *Antitrust Guidelines for the Licensing of Intellectual Property*, in which they state explicitly that they will examine licensing behavior and mergers on the basis of their impact on "innovation markets." According to the *Intellectual Property Guidelines:*

> An innovation market consists of the research and development directed to particular new or improved goods or processes, and the close substitutes for that research and development. The close substitutes are research and development efforts, technologies, and goods that significantly constrain the exercise of market power with respect to the relevant research and development. The agencies will delineate an innovation market only when the capabilities to engage in the relevant research and development can be associated with specialized assets or characteristics of specific firms.[112]

In sum, the agencies will separately consider the impact of a transaction on competition in an "innovation market" if doing so would

---

112. U.S. DEP'T OF JUSTICE & FEDERAL TRADE COMM'N, ANTITRUST GUIDELINES FOR THE LICENSING OF INTELLECTUAL PROPERTY (1995), *reprinted in* 4 Trade Reg. Rep. (CCH) ¶ 13,132, at 20,738 [hereinafter INTELLECTUAL PROPERTY GUIDELINES]; *see also* FTC Staff Report, *Anticipating the 21st Century: Competition Policy in the New High-Tech, Global Marketplace,* 70 Antitrust & Trade Reg. Rep. (BNA) No. 1765, S-1, S-7 (June 6, 1996) (noting that, in the merger context, innovation markets will only be defined where "the innovation is directed toward a particular good and where the innovation can be associated with specialized assets or characteristics of specific firms"); Dennis A. Yao, *Innovation Issues Under the 1992 Merger Guidelines*, 61 ANTITRUST L.J. 505 (1993).

aid in assessing whether an arrangement would be likely substantially to reduce investment in research and development that may result in new or improved products or processes.[113] The analysis of anticompetitive effects in innovation markets has generated considerable debate among commentators, however.[114]

The Division and the FTC have filed complaints alleging anticompetitive concentration in "innovation markets."[115] For instance, in the Division's suit against the proposed acquisition of General Motors' Allison Division by ZF Friedrichshafen, the Division expressed concerns that the combined firm would have controlled most of the worldwide assets necessary for innovation in the design and production of automatic transmissions for medium and heavy duty commercial and military

---

113. *See* INTELLECTUAL PROPERTY GUIDELINES, *supra* note 112, § 3.2.3; *see also* FTC Staff Report, *Anticipating the 21st Century: Competition Policy in the New High-Tech, Global Marketplace*, 70 Antitrust & Trade Reg. Rep. (BNA) No. 1765, S-1, S-7 (June 6, 1996) ("[t]o analyze a merger's likely competitive effects on current innovation competition itself, one must ask whether a proposed merger would likely change the merged firms' abilities or incentives to engage in innovation competition post-merger").

114. *See, e.g.*, Ilene K. Gotts, *The "Innovation Market:" Competitive Fact or Regulatory Fantasy?*, THE PRACTICAL LAWYER, 79-87 (Jan. 1998); Terry Calvani, *Appendix to Book Reviews: A Brief Note on "Markets for Innovation,"* 42 ANTITRUST BULL. 215, 224-36 (1997); Thomas N. Dahdouh & James F. Mongoven, *The Shape of Things to Come: Innovation Market Analysis in Merger Cases*, 64 ANTITRUST L.J. 405 (1996); Richard J. Gilbert & Steven C. Sunshine, *The Use of Innovation Markets: A Reply to Hay, Rapp, and Hoerner*, 64 ANTITRUST L.J. 75 (1995); Richard T. Rapp, *The Misapplication of the Innovation Market Approach to Merger Analysis*, 64 ANTITRUST L.J. 19 (1995); Richard J. Gilbert & Steven C. Sunshine, *Incorporating Dynamic Efficiency Concerns in Merger Analysis: The Use of Innovation Markets*, 63 ANTITRUST L.J. 569 (1995); Dennis W. Carlton, Antitrust Policy Toward Mergers When Firms Innovate: Should Antitrust Recognize the Doctrine of Innovation Markets?, before FTC Hearings on Global and Innovation-based Competition (Oct. 25, 1995) *in* 28 J. REPRINTS FOR ANTITRUST L. & ECON. 517 (1998).

115. *See, e.g.*, Ciba-Geigy Ltd., 123 F.T.C. 842 (1997); Hoechst AG, 120 F.T.C. 1010 (1995); Glaxo plc, 119 F.T.C. 815 (1995); United States v. Flow Int'l Corp., 6 Trade Reg. Rep. (CCH) ¶ 45,094 (Aug. 9, 1994); United States v. General Motors Corp., 6 Trade Reg. Rep. (CCH) ¶ 45,093 (Nov. 16, 1993). The agencies rarely file complaints in which anticompetitive effects are alleged only in innovation markets, however. *See* Ilene Knable Gotts, *supra* note 114 at 79, 85.

vehicles.[116] The Division believed that innovation was closely linked to the possession of the productive capacity necessary to carry out research and development activities. GM and ZF were allegedly the only two firms with the necessary production capacity. The only other competitor focused solely on bus transmissions. The Division alleged that ZF would control 89 percent of the innovation market it defined. The parties abandoned the transaction in the face of the Division's challenge.

Similarly, Flow International abandoned its attempt to acquire Ingersoll-Rand's Waterjet Cutting Systems division after the Division sued to enjoin the transaction using innovation market analysis.[117] The Division alleged the transaction would eliminate competition in innovation for waterjet pumps and related components, as well as in the manufacture and sale of waterjet pumps. The combined companies' share of that product market would have been 90 percent.

Of particular concern to agencies is acquisition of patented technology in ways that stifle research and development. "The clearest case [of exclusionary conduct] would be the acquisition of an equivalent patent covering the only known economic alternative to the monopolist's product or process. Such an acquisition forecloses potential competition by rivals who might otherwise have access to that patent. Even the acquisition of one out of several patents might have exclusionary effects."[118]

Where the agencies oppose consolidation in innovation markets, they may require divestiture of certain assets[119] or they may require the parties

---

116. *See General Motors Corp.*, 6 Trade Reg. Rep. (CCH) ¶ 45,093 (Case 4027) (Nov. 16, 1993).

117. *See* United States v. Flow Int'l Corp., 6 Trade Reg. Rep. (CCH) ¶45,094 (Case 4051) (Aug. 9, 1994); *see also* United States v. Lockheed Martin Corporation and Northrop Grumman Corporation (No. 1:98CV00731) (DOJ filed March 23, 1998) (D.D.C.) (parties abandoned acquisition after the Division sued to enjoin claiming a likely reduction in innovation in military aircraft, including stealth technology).

118. William J. Baer, Antitrust Enforcement and High Technology Markets, Speech Before the ABA, Sections of Business Law, Litigation, and Tort and Insurance Practice (Nov. 12, 1998) *at* www.ftc.gov/speeches/other/ipat6.htm.

119. *See* United States v. Allied Signal Inc. and Honeywell Inc., 2000-2 Trade Cas. (CCH) ¶ 73,023 (D.D.C. 2000) (consent order required the parties, two leading competitors in the development of certain aerospace products, to divest businesses and assets relating to those products); Baxter Int'l Inc., 62 Fed. Reg. 65,706 (Dec. 15, 1997) (consent order) (FTC dropped its opposition to Baxter International Inc.'s acquisition of Immuno International, two of the leading commercial developers of Factor VIII

to license the acquired innovative technology to competitors.[120] For example, in *Summit Technology, Inc.*,[121] the FTC opposed the creation of

inhibitor treatments used to treat antibodies in hemophiliacs, but it required Baxter, among other things, to divest the Factor VIII inhibitor treatment assets); Glaxo plc., 60 Fed. Reg. 39,396 (Aug. 2, 1995) (consent order) (FTC dropped its opposition to Glaxo plc's acquisition of Wellcome plc., two leading commercial developers of migraine headache medicines, but required Glaxo to divest Wellcome's development assets for migraine headache medicines).

120. *See* United States v. 3D Sys. Corp., 2002-2 Trade Cas. (CCH) ¶ 73,738 (D.D.C. 2002) (the Division dropped its opposition to 3D Systems' acquisition of DTM, combining two of three US suppliers of industrial rapid prototyping systems and holders of extensive related patent portfolios, but it required the merged firm to grant a license under those portfolios); United States v. Miller Indus., 2001-1 Trade Cas. (CCH) ¶ 73,132 (D.D.C. 2000) (the Division dropped its challenge to the December 1997 acquisition of Chevron by Miller, which increased Miller's ownership of valuable patent rights related to improvements in light-duty tow trucks and light-duty car carriers, but required Miller to offer to any third-party non-exclusive licenses); Ciba-Geigy Ltd., 62 Fed. Reg. 65,706 (1997) (consent order) (the FTC dropped its opposition to the merger of Ciba-Geigy and Sandoz, the two leading commercial developers of gene therapy products, but it required the combined firm, among other things, to license the specified gene therapy technology and patent rights to Rhône-Poulenc in order to put Rhône-Poulenc in a position to compete against the combined firm); Baxter Int'l Inc., 62 Fed. Reg. 65,706 (Dec. 15, 1997) (consent order) (the FTC dropped its opposition to Baxter's acquisition of Immuno International, which combined two of the leading commercial developers of fibrin sealants which are used to control bleeding or to seal together tissues, but it required Baxter, among other things, to grant a nonexclusive royalty free license of its fibrin sealant assets to Haemacure Corp.); Wright Med. Tech., Inc., 60 Fed. Reg. 18,414 (Apr. 11, 1995) (consent order) (FTC dropped its opposition to the acquisition by Wright Medical Technology, the leader in the market for orthopedic implants for use in fingers, of Orthomet, the licensee of orthopedic implant technology developed by the Mayo Clinic, but it required Wright Medical to transfer the innovative technology assets back to the Mayo Clinic and assist the Mayo Clinic in securing a new nonexclusive licensee). Also noteworthy is the Division's consent order relating to Northrop Grumman's acquisition of TRW, a vertical combination alleged to result in diminishing innovation in defense satellite technologies. The consent order requires the combined firm to adhere to a competitive and non-discriminatory process when acting as a prime contractor or payload provider. United States v. Northrop Grumman Corp., No. 1:02CV02432 (filed December 11, 2002)

a partnership between Summit Technologies and VISX, Inc. Summit and VISX were the only two firms with U.S. Food and Drug Administration approval to market the laser equipment and technology employed in photorefractive keratectomy (PRK), a form of eye surgery that uses lasers to correct vision. VISX and Summit pooled most of their existing patents related to PRK (as well as certain future ones) in a newly created partnership called Pillar Point Partners (PPP). According to the Commission, this pooling arrangement eliminated competition between VISX and Summit in two ways. First, the firms no longer competed on price. The pool established a $250 licensing fee to be paid to the pool each time a laser produced by either firm was used to perform PRK. The proceeds from these license fees were then split between the two firms according to a predetermined formula, The effect of this per-procedure fee was to fix and raise the price that doctors paid for PRK equipment and technology. Second, the firms no longer had any incentive or ability to compete in the licensing of PRK technology that facilitated competitive research and development; neither firm could license its own technology without the approval of the other.

Under the consent decree, Summit and VISX were prohibited from agreeing in any way to fix the prices they would charge for the use of their PRK lasers and patents, including the per-procedure fee charged to a doctor each time he or she used one of the firms' PRK lasers, and from agreeing in any way to restrict each other's sale or licensing of their PRK lasers and patents. The companies were also required to license to each other, on a royalty-free and nonexclusive basis, the patents each firm contributed to PPP. The grant of the nonexclusive licenses recreated the competition, and the incentive to conduct research and development, that existed between the two parties before the pooling arrangement.

g. Production Substitutability as a Means of Defining a Market

In a footnote, the *Brown Shoe* Court noted the potential relevance of "cross elasticity of production facilities,"[122] or cross-elasticity of supply, when defining the product market. Prior to the widespread acceptance of the *Merger Guidelines*' hypothetical monopolist test to define a relevant product market, greater reliance was placed by courts on production flexibility as an important factor in product market definition.[123] *Merger*

(D.D.C.) (consent decree).

121. Summit Tech., Inc., No. 9286 (FTC filed Feb. 23, 1999) (consent order).

122. Brown Shoe Co. v. United States, 370 U.S. 294, 325 n.42 (1962).

123. However, production flexibility alone may be inadequate to support a

Guidelines analysis, however, treats production substitutability as a means of identifying uncommitted entrants to the relevant product market, or as a factor in the analysis of barriers to entry. Although the analytical framework used by courts is sometimes not apparent, where producers can easily switch from producing one product to another in response to a price increase, some courts have found those two products to be in the same market.[124] Where switching production capabilities

broad market definition. *See, e.g.*, Kaiser Aluminum & Chem. Corp. v. FTC, 652 F.2d 1324, 1330 (7th Cir. 1981) (questioning the reasonableness of economic theory in defining a market solely on the basis of cross-elasticity of supply).

124. *See, e.g.*, Blue Cross & Blue Shield United v. Marshfield Clinic, 65 F.3d 1406, 1410-11 (7th Cir. 1995) (although HMOs and various fee-for-service medical plans were not viewed by consumers as substitutable, the court found them to be in the same product market because the services offered by these plans were provided by the same physicians who could likely switch from one to the other); Calnetics Corp. v. Volkswagen of Am., 532 F.2d 674, 691 (9th Cir. 1976) (lower court erred by neglecting to consider cross-elasticity of production facilities or capacity in defining product market); Independent Ink, Inc. v. Trident, Inc., 210 F. Supp. 2d 1155 (C.D. Cal. 2002) (product market definition turns on evidence of cross-elasticities of supply and demand); Bepco, Inc. v. Allied-Signal, Inc., 106 F. Supp. 2d 814 (M.D.N.C. 2000) (same); New York v. Kraft Gen. Foods, Inc., 926 F. Supp. 321, 361 (S.D.N.Y. 1995) (all ready-to-eat cereals in same broad market partly because supply substitution "could be swift"); FTC v. Illinois Cereal Mills, Inc., 691 F. Supp. 1131, 1135 (N.D. Ill. 1988) (including all industrial dry corn mills in relevant market because, with minimal reconfiguration, mills could produce products acceptable to food processors), *aff'd*, 868 F.2d 901 (7th Cir. 1989); United States v. Calmar Inc., 612 F. Supp. 1298, 1304 (D.N.J. 1985) (including several different types of sprayers and dispensers made with identical procedures in a broad market definition); Carter Hawley Hale Stores v. Limited, Inc., 587 F. Supp. 246, 253 (C.D. Cal. 1984) (noting that apparel manufacturers can easily switch styles of clothing as can retailers); FTC v. Occidental Petroleum Corp., 1986-1 Trade Cas. (CCH) ¶ 67,071, at 65,517 (D.D.C. 1986) (positing that an attempted price increase by copolymer producers would cause homopolymer producers to switch production); Frank Saltz & Sons, Inc. v. Hart Schaffner & Marx, 1985-2 Trade Cas. (CCH) ¶ 66,768, at 63,721 (S.D.N.Y. 1985) (rejecting narrow market of "better quality" mens' suits in part because of supply side substitution potential); Heublein, Inc., 96 F.T.C. 385, 576 (1980) (supporting "all wine" market by the "supply-side interchangeability of productive facilities"); Coca-Cola Bottling Co., 93 F.T.C. 110, 204-05 (1979) (including all wines in relevant market because of the

would be difficult or infeasible, courts have declined to find products to be in the same market.[125]

In *New York v. Kraft General Foods,*[126] the court set out to define the relevant market for "adult" cereals. Although the plaintiff argued that adult cereals alone constituted the relevant market, the court held that the proper market was all ready-to-eat cereals. The court adopted the expanded definition of the relevant market based in part on the ease with which cereal manufacturers can switch from producing one kind of cereal to another. The court noted the ease with which a cereal manufacturer could switch from producing Frosted Flakes, a "kids" cereal, to producing Corn Flakes, an adult cereal.[127] These supply side considerations supported the court's finding, based largely on demand side analysis, that the relevant product market was all ready-to-eat cereals.

As indicated, the *Merger Guidelines* differ from the case law in the treatment of production substitution. In the *Merger Guidelines*' approach, product markets are defined, as an initial matter, solely in terms of demand-side substitution possibilities. Production substitution is taken into account either in identifying market participants (i.e., in treating "uncommitted" entrants as current participants and attributing market share to them) or in the analysis of entry conditions.

---

interchangeability of necessary equipment).

125. *See, e.g.*, Ansell Inc. v. Schmid Labs., Inc., 757 F. Supp. 467, 475-76 (D.N.J.) (limiting product market to brand name condoms despite production substitutability where switch would likely prove unprofitable), *aff'd*, 941 F.2d 1200 (3d Cir. 1991); United States v. Ivaco, Inc., 704 F. Supp. 1409, 1416-17 (W.D. Mich. 1989) (restricting product market to automatic tampers because manufacturers of maintenance of way equipment could not easily switch production due to differences in technology and engineering); B.A.T. Indus., 104 F.T.C. 852, 932 (1984) (finding separate markets based on "unique facilities, custom-designed equipment, specialized raw materials, specially trained personnel, extensive research efforts, and rigorous quality control and testing procedures"); Tenneco, Inc., 98 F.T.C. 464, 580-81 (1981) (finding separate markets for original and replacement shock absorbers despite production flexibility because of differences in marketing and distribution), *rev'd on other grounds*, 689 F.2d 346 (2d Cir. 1982); RSR Corp., 88 F.T.C. 800, 876-77 (1976) (finding submarket of secondary lead in part because of the lack of supply side interchangeability with primary lead producers), *aff'd*, 602 F.2d 1317 (9th Cir. 1979).

126. 926 F. Supp. at 361.

127. *Id.*

Despite the ostensible differences between the production substitution formulation in *Kraft* and the *Merger Guidelines*' approach, in the end, the analysis under the case law and under the *Merger Guidelines* should not differ in outcome. In ready-to-eat cereals, for example, production substitutability would initially not be a factor, and the market would probably be defined as adult cereals instead of ready-to-eat. But the producers of adult cereals would include those "uncommitted entrants" who do not manufacture adult cereals but could quickly do so in response to an increase in price. And those uncommitted entrants would include producers of other kinds of ready-to-eat cereals, such as Frosted Flakes. So the market definition would effectively be the same as in *Kraft*—manufacturers of adult cereals would be included in the same market as producers of other kinds of ready-to-eat cereals. The court in *Kraft* recognized that these two analytical approaches, production substitutability or market participants, reach similar results. "Whether assessed as part of market definition (as is suggested by decisional law) or as a separate exercise in identifying market participants (as is directed by the *Merger Guidelines*), evidence of supply substitutability supports a conclusion that the relevant market is all ready-to-eat cereals, rather than some sub-group of ready-to-eat cereals."[128]

2. *The Geographic Market*

Section 7's stricture against a "substantial lessening of competition . . . in any section of the country"[129] requires a determination of the relevant geographic market. Firms that compete in different geographic markets—even if they offer identical products—are not competitors, just as firms that offer different products in the same geographic area are not competitors. The U.S. Supreme Court has described the relevant geographic market as "the 'area of effective competition . . . in which the seller operates, and to which the purchaser can practicably turn for supplies.'"[130]

---

128. *Id.*

129. 15 U.S.C. § 18.

130. United States v. Philadelphia Nat'l Bank, 374 U.S. 321, 359 (1963) (quoting Tampa Elec. Co. v. Nashville Coal Co., 365 U.S. 320, 327 (1961)) (emphasis omitted); *see also* United States v. Phillipsburg Nat'l Bank & Trust Co., 399 U.S. 350, 364-65 (1970); Standard Oil Co. v. United States, 337 U.S. 293, 299 n.5 (1949); United States v. Eastman Kodak Co., 63 F.3d 95, 104 (2d Cir. 1995); Morgenstern v. Wilson, 29 F.3d 1291, 1296 (8th Cir. 1994) ("the geographic area to which

Geographic markets, like product markets, are typically defined according to the guidance of the *Brown Shoe* Court:

> The criteria to be used in determining the appropriate geographic market are essentially similar to those used to determine the relevant product market .. . Congress prescribed a pragmatic, factual approach to the definition of the relevant market and not a formal, legalistic one. The geographic market selected must, therefore, both "correspond to the commercial realities" of the industry and be economically significant. Thus, although the geographic market in some instances may encompass the entire Nation, under other circumstances it may be as small as a single metropolitan area.[131]

The geographic market can be local,[132] regional,[133] national,[134] or international[135] in scope. The geographic boundaries are determined by

---

consumers can practicably turn for alternative sources of the product and in which the antitrust defendants face competition"); Morgan, Strand, Wheeler & Biggs v. Radiology, Ltd., 924 F.2d 1484, 1490 (9th Cir. 1991) ("'area of effective competition' . . . where buyers can turn for alternate sources of supply") (citations omitted); A.A. Poultry Farms v. Rose Acre Farms, 881 F.2d 1396, 1403 (7th Cir. 1989) ("the set of sellers to which a set of buyers can turn for supplies at existing or slightly higher prices"); American Key Corp. v. Cole Nat'l Corp., 762 F.2d 1569, 1580 (11th Cir. 1985); Pennsylvania Dental Ass'n v. Medical Serv. Ass'n, 745 F.2d 248, 260 (3d Cir. 1984) (the area in which "a potential buyer may rationally look for . . . goods and services"); Town of Concord v. Boston Edison Co., 721 F. Supp. 1456, 1459 (D. Mass. 1989) (area served by defendant utility), *rev'd on other grounds*, 915 F.2d 17 (1st Cir. 1990); City of Chanute v. Williams Natural Gas Co., 678 F. Supp. 1517, 1532 (D. Kan. 1988) (area to which plaintiff could practicably turn for supplies, rather than all areas served by defendant); Laidlaw Acquisition Corp. v. Mayflower Group, 636 F. Supp. 1513, 1519 (S.D. Ind. 1986); Island Tobacco Co. v. R.J. Reynolds Indus., 513 F. Supp. 726, 743 (D. Haw. 1981) (the service area of tobacco service jobber); United States v. First Nat'l State Bancorp., 499 F. Supp. 793, 801 (D.N.J. 1980) (analyzing where banks' customers may turn for services); United States v. Kimberly-Clark Corp., 264 F. Supp. 439, 455 (N.D. Cal. 1967); United States v. Bethlehem Steel Corp., 168 F. Supp. 576, 599 (S.D.N.Y. 1958) ("where buyers could reasonably turn to them as alternative substantial sources of supply").

131. 370 U.S. 294, 336-37 (1962) (citations omitted); *see also Morgan, Strand*, 924 F.2d at 1490 (submarket must be "sufficiently insulated from the larger market so that supply and demand are inelastic with the larger market"; rejected submarket limited to Northwest Tucson).

132. *See, e.g.*, United States v. Rockford Mem'l Corp., 898 F.2d 1278 (7th Cir.

1990) (local market for hospitals); United States v. Waste Mgmt., Inc., 743 F.2d 976, 980-81 (2d Cir. 1984) (haulers operated almost exclusively in their respective cities); United States v. Long Island Jewish Med. Ctr., 983 F. Supp. 121, 141-42 (E.D.N.Y. 1997) (Queens and Nassau Counties, New York, are the relevant geographic market for primary and secondary acute inpatient hospital care and Manhattan, Queens, Nassau, and western Suffolk County are the relevant geographic market for tertiary care); Hospital Corp. of Am., 106 F.T.C. 361, 466-72 (1985) (metropolitan Chattanooga is relevant geographic market for analyzing hospital merger); American Med. Int'l, Inc., 104 F.T.C. 1, 194-98 (1984) (finding San Luis Obispo County and City of San Luis Obispo the relevant geographic market for acute care hospital services); United States v. Waste Mgmt., Inc., No. 1:03CV01409, 68 Fed. Reg. 47930, 47941 (Aug. 12, 2003) (proposed final judgment and competitive impact statement) (relevant geographic market was Pitkin County, CO; Garfield County, CO; Augusta, GA; Myrtle Beach, SC: Morris County, NY; and Bergen and Passaic Counties, NJ); *In re* Kroger, Dkt. No. C-3917 (FTC Jan. 10, 2000) (geographic market was Prescott, Sierra Vista, and Yuma, AZ; Cheyenne, Green River, and Rock Springs, WY; and Price, UT); *United* States v. Central Parking Corp., No. 1-99CV00652, 64 Fed. Reg. 15795, 15801 (Apr. 1, 1999) (proposed final judgment and competitive impact statement) (relevant geographic markets "no larger than the central business districts . . . of the cities identified in the Complaint").

133. *See, e.g.*, Tampa Elec. Co. v. Nashville Coal Co., 365 U.S. 320, 331-33 (1961) (relevant market comprised at least seven states from which coal is shipped); Tasty Baking Co. v. Ralston Purina, Inc., 653 F. Supp. 1250, 1260-62 (E.D. Pa. 1987) (finding separate geographic markets in Boston, New York, Philadelphia, Washington, D.C., New England, and the mid-Atlantic region); Laidlaw Acquisition Corp. v. Mayflower Group, Inc., 636 F. Supp. 1513, 1519 (S.D. Ind. 1986) (finding separate geographic markets in California, Alaska, and Pacific Northwest); Christian Schmidt Brewing Co. v. G. Heileman Brewing Co., 600 F. Supp. 1326, 1328 (finding upper Midwest region consisting of 12 states to be relevant geographic market), *aff'd*, 753 F.2d 1354 (6th Cir. 1985); Monfort of Colo., Inc. v. Cargill, Inc., 591 F. Supp. 683, 699-700 (D. Colo. 1983) (finding 12 Midwestern and Western states made up the market for cattle feed), *aff'd*, 761 F.2d 570 (10th Cir. 1985), *rev'd on other grounds*, 479 U.S. 104 (1986); United States v. Rice Growers Ass'n of Cal., 1986-2 Trade Cas. (CCH) ¶ 67,288, 61,463-64 (E.D. Cal. 1986) (finding California the relevant market); Exxon Corp., Dkt. No. C-3907, 65 Fed. Reg. 2618, 2619 (Jan. 18, 2000) (analysis to aid public comment and commissioner statements) (relevant geographic markets included the Northwestern and Mid-Atlantic United States; the West Coast of the U.S., and the "Inland Southeast" United States).

134. *See, e.g.*, United States v. Marine Bancorp., 418 U.S. 602, 620 (1974);

trade practice, not political divisions, and some inexactness in the definition of a geographic market is inevitable.[136]

a. The Pragmatic, Factual Approach

Courts have looked at a number of indicators to determine whether a particular area should be included in the relevant geographic market. For example, a close correlation between competitors' pricing patterns can lead to inclusion in the same geographic market, while uncorrelated prices have led to a finding of separate geographic markets.[137] As in

---

United States v. Continental Can Co., 378 U.S. 441, 447 (1964) (geographic market for containers determined to be entire United States); FTC v. Elders Grain, Inc., 868 F.2d 901, 906-07 (7th Cir. 1989) (national market for industrial dry corn); R.C. Bigelow, Inc. v. Unilever N.V., 867 F.2d 102 (2d Cir. 1989) (national market for herbal teas); Republic Tobacco, L.P. v. North Atlantic Trading Co., 254 F. Supp. 2d 985, 1004-05 (N.D. Ill. 2002) (national market for premium roll-your-own cigarette papers); FTC v. Cardinal Health, Inc., 12 F. Supp. 2d 34, 49-50 (D.D.C. 1988) (national market for drug wholesale industry); White Consol. Indus. v. Whirlpool Corp., 612 F. Supp. 1009, 1031 (N.D. Ohio) (United States the relevant market for dishwashers), *injunction vacated*, 619 F. Supp. 1022 (N.D. Ohio 1985), *aff'd*, 781 F.2d 1224 (6th Cir. 1986); Pennsylvania v. Russell Stover Candies, Inc., 1993-1 Trade Cas. ¶ 70,224, at 70,091 (E.D. Pa. 1993) (national market for boxed chocolates); FTC v. Bass Bros. Enters., Inc., 1984-1 Trade Cas. (CCH) ¶ 66,041, at 68,620 (N.D. Ohio 1984) (nationwide market for carbon black).

135. *See, e.g.*, United States v. Eastman Kodak, 63 F.3d 95, 104 (2d Cir. 1995) ("film sellers operate on a world-wide scale"); Consolidated Gold Fields PLC v. Minorco, S.A., 871 F.2d 252 (2d Cir. 1989) (worldwide market for gold); Gearhart Indus. v. Smith Int'l, Inc., 592 F. Supp. 203, 212 (N.D. Tex.) (worldwide market for drilling equipment), *aff'd in part, modified in part and vacated in part*, 741 F.2d 707 (5th Cir. 1984).

136. *See, e.g.*, United States v. Bethlehem Steel Corp., 168 F. Supp. 576, 602 (S.D.N.Y. 1958) ("An economically significant area in an industry cannot be determined with the precision of a surveyor").

137. *See, e.g.*, United States v. Pabst Brewing Co., 384 U.S. 546 (1962) (regional markets defined because "brewers are able to sell the same beer in different states for different prices"); Jim Walter Corp. v. FTC, 625 F.2d 676, 682 (5th Cir. 1980) (looking at the "area in which the acquired firm's marketing activities have perceptible competitive impact on the activities of other firms in the same area"); RSR Corp. v. FTC, 602 F.2d 1317, 1323 (9th Cir. 1979) (finding regional pricing patterns interrelated); Tasty Baking Co. v. Ralston Purina, Inc., 653 F. Supp. 1250, 1261 (E.D.

defining the relevant product market, however, such evidence may be difficult to interpret given that parallel price movements may be attributable to common economic or marketing conditions unrelated to supplier substitutability.[138]

Actual sales patterns can be used to include or exclude an area from the relevant geographic market.[139] Courts will also consider where

---

Pa. 1987) (finding that pricing policies recognized distinct urban and regional markets); Monfort of Colo., Inc. v. Cargill, Inc., 591 F. Supp. 683, 700 (D. Colo. 1983) (noting national price correlation between fed cattle suppliers, but nonetheless finding a regional market), *aff'd,* 761 F.2d 570 (10th Cir. 1985), *rev'd on other grounds,* 479 U.S. 104 (1986); Foremost Davies, Inc., 60 F.T.C. 944, 1061 (1962) (local markets defined due to price differences); *cf.* FTC v. Staples, Inc., 970 F. Supp. 1066 (D.D.C. 1997) (finding product submarket based in part on evidence of pricing differences between regional geographic markets); United States v. Eastman Kodak Co., 63 F.3d 95, 108 (2d Cir. 1995) (finding worldwide market where "the difference in price [in the United States] between Kodak film and that of its competitors is small and declining"); Rothery Storage & Van Co. v. Atlas Van Lines, 792 F.2d 210, 219 (D.C. Cir. 1986) (absence of evidence that prices in two areas move independently undercuts claim that there are separate geographic markets), *cert. denied*, 479 U.S. 1033 (1987); Horst v. Laidlaw Waste Sys., 917 F. Supp. 739, 744 (D. Colo. 1996) ("four landfills were sensitive to price changes charged by one another, a signal that they are part of the same geographic market"); Marathon Oil Co. v. Mobil Corp., 530 F. Supp. 315, 321-22 (N.D. Ohio) (price differentials in petroleum industry), *aff'd*, 699 F.2d 378 (6th Cir. 1981), *cert. denied*, 455 U.S. 982 (1982); United States v. Bethlehem Steel Corp., 168 F. Supp. 576, 600 (S.D.N.Y. 1958) ("if a change in price in one area has an effect on price in another area both areas may be included in one geographic market"); Coca Cola Bottling Co., 118 F.T.C. 452, 582-83 (1994) (parallel price movements suggest areas are in the same market, but only weak evidence in this case).

138. *Cf.* Coca-Cola Co., 117 F.T.C. 795, 936 n.67, 940 (1994) (finding separate product markets for branded and nonbranded carbonated soft drink concentrate despite evidence that prices "have trended together over time," noting that the parallel price trends could be attributable to other factors such as "changes in the costs of common ingredients").

139. *See, e.g.*, Republic Tobacco, L.P. v. North Atlantic Trading, Co., 254 F. Supp. 2d 985, 1004-05 (N.D. Ill. 2002) (rejecting plaintiff's proposed regional market as too narrow because manufacturers sell to sophisticated wholesalers who can and do purchase on a nationwide basis); *see also* United States v. Waste Mgmt., Inc., 743 F.2d 976, 980-81 (2d Cir. 1984) (finding that haulers operate almost exclusively in their own city).

customers are located,[140] as well as the perceptions of the merging firms and other industry members.[141] Where consumers in a given area purchase overwhelmingly from suppliers in that area, or where a substantial majority of a supplier's or suppliers' sales are to consumers in a particular area, the relevant geographic market may include only that area.[142] Conversely, where firms are based in different locations but tend

---

140. *See, e.g.*, Marathon Oil Co. v. Mobil Corp., 669 F.2d 378, 381 (6th Cir. 1981) (geographic market does not include 28 state area where no competition exists); Jim Walter Corp. v. FTC, 625 F.2d 676, 681 (5th Cir. 1980) (defining geographic market, in part, by "the points at which the acquired firm makes significant sales"); *RSR Corp.*, 602 F.2d at 1323-24 (using location of customers as a proxy for determining relevant market); Gearhart Indus. v. Smith Int'l, Inc., 592 F. Supp. at 212 (finding a worldwide market based on supplier and customer locations); United States v. Waste Mgmt., Inc., 588 F. Supp. 498, 503-04 (S.D.N.Y. 1983) (supporting geographic market which excluded Fort Worth because the merging companies had few customers in that market), *rev'd on other grounds,* 743 F.2d 976 (2d Cir. 1984).

141. *See, e.g.*, United States v. Phillipsburg Nat'l Bank & Trust Co., 399 U.S. 350, 364-65 (1970); F. & M. Schaefer Corp. v. Schmidt & Sons, Inc., 597 F.2d 814, 817 (2d Cir. 1979).

142. *See, e.g.*, United States v. Marine Bancorp., 418 U.S. 602, 619 (1973); United States v. Pabst Brewing Co., 384 U.S. 546, 559 (1966) (fact that 90% of beer sold in state came from brewers in Wisconsin or Minnesota supported limitation of geographic market to Wisconsin); Houser v. Fox Theatres Mgmt. Corp., 845 F.2d 1225, 1230 & n.10 (3d Cir. 1988) (relevant market is Lebanon, Pennsylvania, because theater patrons in Lebanon primarily attend Lebanon theaters); *Waste Mgmt.*, 743 F.2d at 980 (market for solid waste hauling limited to portion of Dallas/Fort Worth metropolitan area in light of small overlap in service of each area and high cost of travel between the cities for daily waste hauling); F. & M. Schaefer Corp. v. C. Schmidt & Sons, 597 F.2d 814 (2d Cir. 1979) (per curiam) (upholding preliminary injunction; specific metropolitan areas were relevant markets for purposes of analyzing merger of two brewers, despite fact that they competed throughout 12-state region); Town of Concord v. Boston Edison Co., 721 F. Supp. 1456, 1459-60 (D. Mass 1989) (relevant market is utility's service area because that was area in which utility competed for customers); United States v. Rice Growers Ass'n, 1986-2 Trade Cas. (CCH) ¶ 67,288, at 61,463-64 (E.D. Cal. 1986) (in light of transportation costs and low level of purchases from or sales to other areas, California is a relevant geographic market for purchase of paddy rice for milling); United States v. Central State Bank, 621 F. Supp. 1276, 1293-94 (W.D. Mich. 1985) (market limited to two-county area where nearly 95% of total deposits of residents of two

to compete in many of the same geographic areas, the relevant market may include all of the firms' sales areas.[143] For example, in *FTC v. Freeman Hospital*,[144] the Eighth Circuit held that the Commission had failed to establish that the relevant geographic market for acute care inpatient hospital services in Joplin, Missouri, should be limited to areas within twenty-seven miles of Joplin. The court criticized the Commission for presenting "a static, rather than a dynamic, picture of the acute care market" that failed to answer "the decisive question of where consumers could practicably go for alternative sources of acute care . . . services."[145] Similarly, in *Bathke v. Casey's General Stores*,[146] the

---

counties were held in banks within those two counties), *aff'd per curiam*, 817 F.2d 22 (6th Cir. 1987); Hospital Corp. of Am., 106 F.T.C. 361, 467 (1985), *aff'd*, 807 F.2d 1381 (7th Cir. 1986); *cf.* Drabbant Enters. v. Great Atl. & Pac. Tea Co., 688 F. Supp. 1567, 1579-80 (D. Del. 1988) (on motion for preliminary injunction, plaintiff failed to show that market is limited to one shopping mall given that customers regularly used practical alternatives to that mall).

143. *See, e.g.*, RSR Corp. v. FTC, 602 F.2d 1317, 1322-24 (9th Cir. 1979) (relevant geographic market is national despite high cost of transport where shipping radius around plants served by firm accounts for a majority of national consumption and where regional prices are interrelated); Weeks Dredging & Contracting v. American Dredging Co., 451 F. Supp. 468, 491-92 (E.D. Pa. 1978) (fact that same leading companies tended to bid on projects in various harbors along East Coast supported finding that market consisted of entire East Coast and not each local harbor).

144. 69 F.3d 260 (8th Cir. 1995).

145. *Id.* at 269; *accord* Morgenstern v. Wilson, 29 F.3d 1291, 1296 (8th Cir. 1994) (declining to exclude Omaha from the market of heart surgery for residents of Lincoln, Nebraska, because plaintiff proved only that Lincoln residents did not go to Omaha, not that they could not practicably do so); Tunis Bros. Co. v. Ford Motor Co., 952 F.2d 715, 726-27 (3d Cir. 1991) (rejecting plaintiffs' narrow geographic market because evidence showed that farmers did not limit themselves to this area when purchasing or servicing tractors); California v. Sutter Health Sys., 130 F. Supp. 2d 1109, 1120-32 (N.D. Cal. 2001) (rejecting plaintiff's proposed market because plaintiff "failed to show that enough patients that currently seek inpatient services at hospitals located within plaintiff's proposed . . . market would not seek such services outside the market to defeat an anticompetitive price increase"); *see also* 42nd Parallel North v. E Street Denim Co., 286 F.3d 401, 406 (7th Cir. 2002) (rejecting geographic market for designer jeans limited to a suburban shopping district as contrary to "any sensible definition of commercial reality"); A.A. Poultry Farms v. Rose Acre Farms, 881 F.2d 1396, 1403 (7th Cir. 1989) (relevant

Eighth Circuit rejected the plaintiffs' argument that the relevant geographic markets were the sixty-seven separate small towns in which they operated gas stations because they failed to show that these were the only areas where the relevant consumers could practicably purchase gasoline. More specifically, the court credited the defendant's evidence that more than forty percent of the residents of these towns commuted to work elsewhere, making it "entirely possible, if not likely, that those consumers have alternatives to purchase gas beyond their town of residence."[147]

Courts also have recognized that the relevant product market and geographic market may sometimes be closely related concepts. For example, in *United States v. Long Island Jewish Medical Center*,[148] the DOJ alleged that the relevant hospital services geographic market was limited to Queens and Nassau Counties, while the defendants argued that the relevant market also included western Suffolk County and Manhattan.[149] The court found that a health care network built around Manhattan hospitals would be impracticable because, as a general matter, patients prefer to receive medical treatment relatively close to home.[150] However, the defendants were able to show that one managed care group's enrollees would travel to Manhattan for certain services (presumably tertiary care); that 50,000 patients from Queens, Nassau, and Suffolk traveled to Manhattan for treatment; and that fifteen percent

---

market is area within about 500 miles of customer because that is area within which customer could turn for supplies); *cf.* Illinois *ex rel.* Hartigan v. Panhandle E. Pipe Line Co., 730 F. Supp. 826, 901 (C.D. Ill. 1990) (market defined narrowly because pipeline's captive customers could not switch readily), *aff'd sub nom.* Illinois *ex rel.* Burris v. Panhandle E. Pipe Line Co., 935 F.2d 1469 (7th Cir. 1991); City of Chanute v. Williams Natural Gas Co., 678 F. Supp. 1517, 1532 (D. Kan. 1988) (relevant market is area encompassing plaintiff cities because those cities have no practical alternative suppliers for natural gas).

146. 64 F.3d 340 (8th Cir. 1995).

147. *Id.* at 346; *see also* Re/Max Int'l, Inc. v. Realty One, Inc., 173 F.3d 995 (6th Cir. 1999).

148. 1997-2 Trade Cas. (CCH) ¶ 71,960, at 80,700 (E.D.N.Y. 1997).

149. *Id.*

150. *Id.* at 80,701. *But see* Urdinaran v. Aarons, 115 F. Supp. 2d 484, 490 (D.N.J. 2000) (rejecting geographic market confined to Atlantic County, New Jersey, commenting that, "[v]iewed from the patient's perspective rather than the physician's, general surgery patients might well take advantage of the various medical facilities in Philadelphia an hour or so away, and, as plaintiff conceded, he himself has referred patients to surgeons in Philadelphia").

of tertiary care patients from Queens, Nassau, and Suffolk went to Manhattan hospitals.[151] Based on this evidence, the court held that two distinct relevant geographic markets existed: (1) a market for primary and secondary care, which included hospitals only in Queens and Nassau;[152] and (2) a market for tertiary care comprising hospitals in Manhattan, Queens, Nassau, and western Suffolk County.[153] Of course, a proposed market is not deficient merely because there is evidence that some customers look beyond its boundaries to purchase the relevant product or service. In *Houser v. Fox Theatres Management Corp.*,[154] for example, the court determined that the relevant geographic market was Lebanon, Pennsylvania, the primary place of film attendance by Lebanon patrons, despite evidence that some customers would travel to theaters in other towns.[155]

Transportation costs, particularly as a percentage of the cost of the good, can also be an important consideration in determining the relevant geographic area.[156] If transportation costs are prohibitively high, courts

---

151. *Long Island Jewish Med. Ctr.*, 1997-2 Trade Cas. (CCH) ¶ 71,960, at 80,701.
152. *Id.*
153. *Id.*
154. 845 F.2d 1225, 1230 n.10 (3d Cir. 1988).
155. *See also* United States v. Archer-Daniels-Midland Co., 781 F. Supp. 1400, 1413 (S.D. Iowa 1991) (observing that "given geographic area may be a relevant market notwithstanding . . . sales by firms producing outside that area to customers within that area").
156. *See, e.g.*, United States v. General Dynamics Corp., 415 U.S. 486, 491-92 & n.3 (1974) ("a realistic geographic market should be defined in terms of transportation arteries and freight charges that determined the cost of the delivered coal"); FTC v. Proctor & Gamble Co., 386 U.S. 568, 571 (1967) (finding that most bleach manufacturers are regional because high transportation costs limits their sales area to within 300 miles of the plant); *Waste Mgmt., Inc.*, 743 F.2d at 979 (trash collectors would not travel between two counties because too costly); Hornsby Oil Co. v. Champion Spark Plug Co., 714 F.2d 1384,1394 (5th Cir. 1983) (when "ascertaining the scope of geographic market .. . transportation costs, delivery limitations, and customer convenience . . . must be considered"); Crown Zellerbach Corp. v. FTC, 296 F.2d 800, 820 (9th Cir. 1961) (discussing impact of freight charges on paper market); Monfort of Colo., Inc. v. Cargill, Inc., 591 F. Supp. 683, 699 (D. Colo. 1983) (supporting regional market by noting that all purchases of fed cattle occurred within 200 miles of the slaughter plants), *aff'd*, 761 F.2d 570 (10th Cir. 1985), *rev'd on other grounds*, 479 U.S. 104 (1986); United States v. M.P.M., Inc., 397 F. Supp. 78, 89 (D. Colo. 1975) ("Transportation expenses

are more likely to find separate markets.[157] Conversely, low transportation costs argue for more expansive geographic boundaries,

---

present a formidable barrier to delivery of ready-mix concrete outside a relatively short distance from production plants"); United States v. General Dynamics Corp., 341 F. Supp. 534, 556 (N.D. Ill. 1972) (transportation costs a "critical factor" determining geographic reach of competition between coal mines, since transport costs comprise a large portion of the delivered cost); United States v. Rice Growers Ass'n, 1986-2 Trade Cas. (CCH) ¶ 67,288, at 61,463 (E.D. Cal. 1986) (excluding the possibility of milling California grown rice in the Southern United States because of the high transportation costs).

157. *See, e.g.*, FTC v. Procter & Gamble Co., 386 U.S. 568, 571 (1967) (finding both a national market although only one manufacturer sold nationally, and a series of regional markets because most manufacturers of bleach are limited to a single region since they have only one plant and high transportation costs limit them to sales within 300 miles of the plant); United States v. Pabst Brewing Co., 384 U.S. 546, 559 (1966) ("high transportation costs .. . would, of course be highly persuasive evidence supporting the local-market theory"); United States v. Waste Mgmt., Inc., 743 F.2d 976, 980 (2d Cir. 1984) (service between Dallas and Fort Worth costly); *RSR Corp.*, 602 F.2d at 1322-23 (national market found despite limitations imposed by high trucking costs); FTC v. Owens-Illinois, Inc., 681 F. Supp. 27, 51 (D.D.C. 1988) (high freight costs, quality issues, reliability of supply, and breakage make foreign suppliers unlikely substitute sources of supply for glass containers), *vacated as moot*, 850 F.2d 694 (D.C. Cir. 1988); Tasty Baking Co. v. Ralston Purina, Inc., 653 F. Supp. 1250, 1262 (E.D. Pa. 1987) ("competitive advantages clearly accrue to bakers with bakeries relatively nearer to any given market"); Monfort of Colo., Inc. v. Cargill, Inc., 591 F. Supp. 683, 699 (D. Colo. 1983) (all purchases of fed cattle occurred within 200 miles of slaughter plant), *aff'd*, 761 F.2d 570 (10th Cir. 1985), *rev'd on other grounds,* 479 U.S. 104 (1986); United States v. M.P.M., Inc., 397 F. Supp. 78, 89 (D. Colo. 1975) (Denver area a relevant market because "[t]ransportation expenses present a formidable barrier to delivery of ready-mix concrete outside a relatively short distance from production plants"); United States v. General Dynamics Corp., 341 F. Supp. 534, 556 (N.D. Ill. 1972) (transportation costs a "critical factor" determining geographic reach of competition between coal mines because transport costs comprise a large portion of delivered cost), *aff'd*, 415 U.S. 486 (1974); United States v. Rice Growers Ass'n, 1986-2 Trade Cas. (CCH) ¶ 67,288, at 61,463 (E.D. Cal. 1986) (because of high transportation costs, shipment of rice for milling in the southern United States is not a viable alternative for California rice growers); Foremost Dairies, Inc., 60 F.T.C. 944, 1061 (1962) (markets for dairy products properly restricted to metropolitan areas due to the limited area which can

and may indicate that separate areas are within the same market.[158] Thus, the area in which supplies and services may be "'feasibly furnished, consistently with cost and functional efficiency'"[159] is an important consideration. Transportation may also impact courts' analyses of practical alternatives available to consumers. More specifically, the quality of roads, the significance of travel times, and the presence of

---

be covered by delivery trucks, despite evidence that improvements in refrigeration reduced perishability and increased the area over which dairy products could be feasibly delivered), *modified*, 67 F.T.C. 282 (1965).

158. *See, e.g.*, Apani Southwest, Inc. v. Coca-Cola Enterprises, Inc., 300 F.3d 620, 628 (5th Cir. 2002) (rejecting plaintiff's proposed geographic market for bottled water as too narrow because transportation costs were insufficient to justify limiting the market to the twenty-seven city-owned facilities covered by an exclusive agreement); FTC v. Illinois Cereal Mills, Inc., 691 F. Supp. 1131, 1136-37, 1141-44 (N.D. Ill. 1988) (relevant geographic market includes entire United States because freight costs are not high enough to prevent mills on one side of the Mississippi from effectively competing with those on the other), *aff'd sub nom.* FTC v. Elders Grain, Inc., 868 F.2d 901 (7th Cir. 1989); TCA Bldg. Co. v. Northwestern Resources Co., 873 F. Supp. 29, 35-36 (S.D. Tex. 1995) (plaintiff failed to meet burden of demonstrating that high transportation costs for lignite coal limit the geographic market to the area surrounding a single mine); United States v. Hammermill Paper Co., 429 F. Supp. 1271, 1278 (W.D. Pa. 1977) ("no freight rate barriers" isolating New England); United States v. Aluminum Co. of Am., 91 F. Supp. 333, 395 (S.D.N.Y. 1950) (United States a logical market for Canadian aluminum producer given low transportation costs); *cf.* Morgenstern v. Wilson, 29 F.3d 1291, 1296 (8th Cir. 1994) (hospitals in different cities in the same market where patients need travel only 58 miles to get from one city to the other), *cert. denied*, 513 U.S. 1150 (1995).

159. *See* Case-Swayne Co. v. Sunkist Growers, 369 F.2d 449, 458 (9th Cir. 1966) (quoting United States v. Grinnell Corp., 384 U.S. 563, 589 (1966) (Fortas, J., dissenting)), *rev'd on other grounds*, 389 U.S. 384 (1967); *see also* A.A. Poultry Farms v. Rose Acre Farms, 881 F.2d 1396, 1403 (7th Cir. 1989) (finding that customers could turn to egg processors within 500 miles); Hecht v. Pro-Football, Inc., 570 F.2d 982, 988-89 (D.C. Cir. 1977) (relevant market limited to metropolitan Washington, D.C., where "Hecht and the Redskins would have effectively competed for customers"); Cackling Acres, Inc. v. Olson Farms, 541 F.2d 242, 245 (10th Cir. 1976) (relevant market was where defendant purchased eggs); United States v. Empire Gas Corp., 537 F.2d 296, 304-05 (8th Cir. 1976) (relevant geographic market for distribution of liquefied petroleum was area within 20 miles of plant).

natural boundaries may affect consumers' willingness to access alternative suppliers and, in turn, the size and shape of the relevant geographic market.[160]

Where government regulations—such as licenses, tariffs, or quotas—serve to limit trade between areas, separate geographic markets will be found.[161] The FTC also considers such government regulations to be "especially probative" of the relevant geographic market.[162]

---

160. In *HTI Health Services v. Quorum Health Group*, 960 F. Supp. 1104 (S.D. Miss. 1997), "simple reasons such as highway conditions" might account for what appeared to be an oddly shaped geographic market. *Id.* at 1122-23 & n.14. Similarly, in *Doctor's Hospital v. Southeast Medical Alliance*, 123 F.3d 301 (5th Cir. 1997), the court rejected the plaintiff's proposed geographic market that included only the east bank of Jefferson Parish, in part, because Jefferson Parish and neighboring Orleans Parish were "not separated by any natural boundaries and [were] connected by numerous roadways." *Id.* at 311-12. And in *California v. Sutter Health System*, 130 F. Supp. 2d 1109, 1126 (N.D. Cal. 2001), the court rejected the plaintiff's proposed market, in part, because "in many instances, it took less time to travel to hospitals outside the proposed geographic market . . . than to hospitals within the proposed market." As a general matter, consumers' willingness to travel is often an important factor in defining geographic markets in service industries, particularly in hospital cases. *See, e.g.*, FTC v. Tenet Health Care Corp., 186 F.3d 1045, 1052 (8th Cir. 1999); Brokerage Concepts, Inc. v. U.S. Healthcare, Inc., 140 F.3d 494, 515 (3d Cir. 1998); *Sutter Health System*, 130 F. Supp. 2d at 1126; Minnesota Ass'n of Nurse Anesthetists v. Unity Hosp., 5 F. Supp. 2d 694, 707 (D. Minn. 1998), *aff'd*, 208 F.3d 655 (8th Cir. 2000). In the context of the airline industry, the relevant geographic market may be defined as a "city pair"—that is, all flights originating and terminating in the same pair of cities. *See, e.g.*, United States v. AMR Corp., 335 F.3d 1109, 1111 (10th Cir. 2003); *In re* Northwest Airlines Corp. Antitrust Litig., 197 F. Supp. 2d 908, 911-18 (E.D. Mich. 2002); Continental Airlines, Inc. v. United Air Lines, Inc., 120 F. Supp. 2d 556, 567-68 (E.D. Va. 2000).

161. *See, e.g.*, United States v. Marine Bancorp., 418 U.S. 602, 628 (1973); United States v. Philadelphia Nat'l Bank, 374 U.S. 321, 367 & n.44 (1963) ("Entry [in the banking industry] is wholly a matter of governmental grace."); United States v. 3D Systems Corp., 2002-2 Trade Cas. (CCH) ¶ 73,738 (D.D.C. 2002) (appropriate geographic market defined as United States because patent barriers prevented foreign entry); *see also* Foremost Dairies, 60 F.T.C. 944, 1061 (1962) (noting that differing local health and other regulations must be considered when defining relevant geographic market); United States v. LTV Corp., 1984-2 Trade Cas. (CCH) ¶ 66,133, at 66,336 (D.D.C.) (noting that DOJ

Courts have also cited industry practices, such as separate distribution territories or pricing zones,[163] the existence of nationwide planning, nationwide contracts, or a national schedule of prices, rates, and terms,[164] and industry recognition of separate markets[165] to limit the relevant geographic market. However, industry practices or views are not determinative if they do not accurately reflect commercial and economic reality.[166]

---

had included in the relevant market all imports except those from Japan and the European Communities that were subject to quotas or voluntary limitations on shipments), *appeal dismissed*, 746 F.2d 51 (D.C. Cir. 1984). In *Delaware Health Care v. MCD Holding Co.*, 957 F. Supp. 535 (D. Del. 1997), the court found that the plaintiff's alleged geographic market for hospital inpatient services, New Castle County, withstood summary judgment based in part on account licensure requirements. The court granted summary judgment, however, based on other issues.

162. *See, e.g.*, General Foods Corp., 103 F.T.C. 204, 348 (1984). The FTC considered transportation costs, shipping patterns, evidence of price differentials among regions, product differentiation among individual sales districts, and especially the history of actual entry by existing firms into new regions.

163. *See, e.g.*, Lynch Bus. Machs., Inc. v. A.B. Dick Co., 594 F. Supp. 59, 68 (N.D. Ohio 1984) (separate distribution territories); United States v. Hammermill Paper Co., 429 F. Supp. 1271, 1278 (W.D. Pa. 1977) ("no separate delivered pricing zone"); Coca Cola Bottling Co., 118 F.T.C. 452, 583 (1994) (national and regional retailers viewed San Antonio as a separate retail market and accordingly ran localized advertising and marketing campaigns).

164. *See, e.g.*, United States v. Grinnell Corp., 384 U.S. 563, 575 (1966). *Compare* Kaiser Aluminum & Chem. Corp., 93 F.T.C. 764, 814-15 (1979) (national market), *vacated and remanded on other grounds,* 652 F.2d 1324, 1329 (7th Cir. 1981), *and* United States v. Mrs. Smith's Pie Co., 440 F. Supp. 220, 230 (E.D. Pa. 1976) (national market), *with* Jim Walter Corp. v. FTC, 625 F.2d 676, 683 (5th Cir. 1980) (evidence insufficient to establish national market), *and* United States v. Bethlehem Steel Corp., 168 F. Supp. 576, 599-603 (S.D.N.Y. 1958) (national and regional markets).

165. *See, e.g.*, United States v. Phillipsburg Nat'l Bank & Trust Co., 399 U.S. 350, 364-65 (1970); Morgenstern v. Wilson, 29 F.3d 1291, 1297 (8th Cir. 1994); F. & M. Schaefer Corp. v. Schmidt & Sons, 597 F.2d 814, 817 (2d Cir. 1979); *Ralston Purina, Inc.*, 653 F. Supp. at 1262 (companies generally perceive "markets defined by metropolitan areas"); United States v. Kimberly-Clark Corp., 264 F. Supp. 439, 458 (N.D. Cal. 1967).

166. *See, e.g.*, FTC v. Freeman Hosp., 69 F.3d 260, 270 (8th Cir. 1995) ("[t]estimony of market participants is relevant to a determination of a

The reach of the geographic market tends to be less when services or retail goods, as opposed to manufactured goods, are involved.[167] Although geographic market issues are highly fact-specific and generalizations should be made cautiously, manufacturing markets tend to be regional,[168] national,[169] or international,[170] while retailing and service markets are more likely to be local.[171] However, a single case

---

proper geographic market, . . . [but] the views of market participants are not always sufficient to establish a relevant market, especially when their testimony fails to specifically address the practicable choices available to consumers").

167. *See Philadelphia Nat'l Bank*, 374 U.S. at 358 ("[i]n banking, as in most service industries, convenience of location is essential to effective competition" resulting in a localized market); *Phillipsburg Nat'l Bank & Trust Co.*, 399 U.S. at 362-63 (same); United States v. Central State Bank, 621 F. Supp. 1276, 1293 (W.D. Mich. 1985) (same), *aff'd per curiam*, 817 F.2d 22 (6th Cir. 1987).

168. *See, e.g.,* Bacchus Indus., Inc. v. Arvin Indus., Inc., 939 F.2d 887, 893 (10th Cir. 1991) (market for evaporative coolers consists of "the twelve western states").

169. *See, e.g.*, United States v. E.I. du Pont de Nemours & Co., 351 U.S. 377, 395 (1956) (market for flexible packaging material is nationwide); Republic Tobacco, L.P. v. North Atlantic Trading, Co., 254 F. Supp. 2d 985, 1004-05 (N.D. Ill. 2002) (market for premium roll-your-own cigarette paper is nationwide); Murrow Furniture Galleries v. Thomasville Furniture Indus., 889 F.2d 524, 529 (4th Cir. 1989) (furniture market is nationwide).

170. *See, e.g.*, United States v. Eastman Kodak Co., 63 F.3d 95, 104 (2d Cir. 1995) (film market is worldwide).

171. *See, e.g.*, United States v. Phillipsburg Nat'l Bank & Trust Co., 399 U.S. 350, 362-63 (1970); United States v. Philadelphia Nat'l Bank, 374 U.S. 321, 358 (1963) ("[i]n banking, as in most service industries, convenience of location is essential to effective competition" and localizes banking competition); United States v. Central State Bank, 621 F. Supp. 1276, 1293 (W.D. Mich. 1985) (single city market for banking services), *aff'd per curiam*, 817 F.2d 22 (6th Cir. 1987). *But see* Total Benefit Servs. v. Group Ins. Admin., Inc., 875 F. Supp. 1228, 1237 (E.D. La. 1995) (evidence indicated that "customers looked to suppliers from all over the country"); Tasty Baking Co. v. Ralston Purina, Inc., 653 F. Supp. 1250, 1260-62 (E.D. Pa. 1987) (four cities and two regions are each separate geographic markets for snack cakes and pies); Adventist Health Sys., 117 F.T.C. 224, 297 (1994) (complaint counsel failed to carry burden of proof that Ukiah-Willits-Lakeport or Ukiah-Willits constituted a relevant geographic market for the provision of inpatient acute care hospital services); Coca Cola Bottling Co., 118 F.T.C. 452, 584 (1994) (relevant geographic market for branded carbonated soft drinks was 10-county area centered around San Antonio, Texas); Exxon Corp., Dkt. No. C-3907 (Nov.

may involve more than one type of market. For example, in *Brown Shoe* the Court found that the relevant geographic market for retail shoes was limited to metropolitan areas, while the geographic market for wholesale shoes was nationwide.[172]

Courts may also consider the anticompetitive harm alleged in determining the relevant geographic market. For example, if the merger is challenged on the grounds that actual competition will be reduced, the relevant geographic market will likely be the area where the merging firms are direct competitors.[173] If the alleged injury is that sellers (or purchasers) of products will be shut off from the market for these products, the inquiry will likely focus on the area where the sellers (or purchasers) operate.[174] If the challenged combination is not a merger, but a joint venture, the court will likely look to the area where the joint venture plans to market its goods or services in defining the relevant geographic market.[175] Finally, if the merger is challenged on a potential competition argument, the relevant geographic market will likely be the area where the acquired firm operates and competes.[176] A merger

---

30, 1999) (complaint), *at* www.ftc.gov/us/1999/11/exxonmobilecmp.pdf (relevant geographic markets are regional areas, states, and "smaller areas contained therein," including metropolitan areas); United States v. Central Parking Corp., No. 1-99CV00652 (D.D.C. filed Mar. 16, 1999) (complaint), 64 Fed. Reg. 15795, 15801 (Apr. 1, 1999) (proposed final judgment and competitive impact statement) (relevant geographic markets are "no larger than the central business districts . . . of the cities identified in the Complaint").

172. *See* Brown Shoe Co. v. United States, 370 U.S. 294, 337-39 (1962); *see also* FTC v. Staples, Inc., 970 F. Supp. 1066, 1073 (D.D.C. 1997) (relevant geographic markets for sale of consumable office supplies through office supply superstores are each of 42 metropolitan areas).

173. *See, e.g.*, Laidlaw Acquisition Corp. v. Mayflower Group, Inc., 636 F. Supp. 1513, 1519 (S.D. Ind. 1986) (analyzing relevant geographic market based on areas of competitive overlap, including potential market entry); Carter Hawley Hale Stores, Inc. v. Limited, Inc., 587 F. Supp. 246, 250-52 (C.D. Cal. 1984).

174. *See, e.g.*, *Philadelphia Nat'l Bank*, 374 U.S. at 359.

175. *See* United States v. Marine Bancorp., 418 U.S. 602, 621 n.19 (1974); United States v. Penn-Olin Chem. Co., 378 U.S. 158, 160-61 (1964) (joint venture to enter sodium chlorate market in southeastern United States where neither had manufacturing facility).

176. *See, e.g.*, *Marine Bancorp.*, 418 U.S. at 622; Laidlaw Acquisition Corp. v. Mayflower Group, 636 F. Supp. at 1519 (analyzing relevant geographic market based on areas of competitive overlap, including potential market entry); Cable Holdings v. Home Video, Inc., 572 F. Supp. 482, 493 (N.D. Ga. 1983), *aff'd*, 825 F.2d 1559 (11th Cir. 1987); United States v. First

challenged under actual and potential competition theories could thus be analyzed within two distinct geographic markets.[177]

Imports can present special problems in defining the relevant geographic market. For example, in *Occidental Petroleum Corp.*,[178] the Commission rejected Occidental's assertion that the relevant geographic market was "at a minimum, North America" and should include several other foreign countries as well, because imports would prevent noncompetitive domestic price increases.[179] The FTC found that future imports were unlikely to constrain domestic prices, in part because of the small increase in imports likely to be triggered by a 10 percent domestic price increase; the need for timely and frequent deliveries, consistent quality and technical support; and the effect of various tariff restrictions.[180]

For the purpose of determining market shares, however, most decisions have looked to actual sales by foreign producers within the United States.[181]

As with product markets, geographic markets can be broken down into submarkets to assess localized effects.[182] Courts use the same

---

Nat'l State Bancorp., 499 F. Supp. 793, 801 (D.N.J. 1980) (area of effective competition was relevant geographic market under plaintiff's direct competition theory and area where acquired firm operated was relevant market under potential competition theory).

177. *See, e.g., First Nat'l State Bancorp.*, 499 F. Supp. at 801.

178. 115 F.T.C. 1010 (1993).

179. *Id.* at 1230.

180. *See id.* at 1229-41; *cf.* Mustad Int'l Group NV, 120 F.T.C. 865 (1995) (consent decree in which FTC included in the market all foreign and domestic suppliers based on a past instance where a foreign producer successfully established a U.S. distribution system and caused a significant reduction in U.S. prices); FTC Staff Report, *Anticipating the 21st Century: Competition Policy in the New High-Tech, Global Marketplace*, 70 Antitrust & Trade Reg. Rep. (BNA) No. 1765, S-1, S-7 (Vol. 1) (June 6, 1996) ("In today's increasingly interconnected world, merger analysis should take care to define relevant geographic markets to include foreign supply responses as appropriate, giving due regard both to actual barriers to trade and to the increasing trend toward the globalization of trade and services").

181. *See, e.g.*, United States v. Aluminum Co. of Am., 148 F.2d 416 (2d Cir. 1945); Whitaker Corp. v. Edgar, 1982-1 Trade Cas. (CCH) ¶ 64,608 (N.D. Ill. 1982); FTC v. Great Lakes Chem. Corp., 1981-2 Trade Cas. (CCH) ¶ 64,175 (N.D. Ill. 1981).

182. *See, e.g.*, United States v. Pabst Brewing Co., 384 U.S. 546, 549 (1966) (permitting the government to demonstrate a lessening of competition

factors to define geographic submarkets as they use in defining geographic markets.

b. Analytical Approaches

There are two primary analytical approaches courts have used to define the geographic market. The first is embodied in the *Merger Guidelines*' hypothetical monopolist approach, and the second is commonly referred to as the Elzinga-Hogarty test. The *Merger Guidelines*' approach has been increasingly relied upon by most courts.

1. The **Merger Guidelines***' Hypothetical Monopolist Approach*

The *Merger Guidelines*' approach to defining the geographic market is identical to its approach to defining the product market.[183] Starting with the locations of the merging firms, the agency questions the effect of a hypothetical monopolist of the relevant product imposing a small but significant and nontransitory price increase (usually 5 percent for the foreseeable future) while keeping the terms of sale of the relevant product the same in all other locations. If the price increase would prove unprofitable to the hypothetical monopolist because customers would turn to nearby locations for supply, the agency adds the next-best location for the relevant product to the equation and reevaluates the potential for supracompetitive profits. The process continues until the agency has identified a geographic market in which a hypothetical monopolist could profitably impose a small but significant and nontransitory price increase.[184] As with the product market, the smallest market that can satisfy the test will be used.

---

nationwide, within a three-state region, and in Wisconsin from the merger of two beer manufacturers).

183. *See* 1992 MERGER GUIDELINES, *supra* note 31, § 1.21; *cf.* NAAG MERGER GUIDELINES, *supra* note 50, § 3.2 (focusing on customers and the areas they turn to for suppliers instead of the hypothetical price increase test of the federal guidelines).

184. *See, e.g.*, R.R. Donnelly & Sons Co., 120 F.T.C. 36, 152 (1995) (affirming ALJ's application of the *Merger Guidelines* in finding a western U.S. market for high-speed printing); Coca-Cola Bottling Co. of the Southwest, 118 F.T.C. 452, 574-84 (1994) (applying the *Merger Guidelines* to find San Antonio market for branded carbonated soft drinks because outside suppliers would not likely enter market in response to price increase); Adventist Health Sys./West, 117 F.T.C. 224, 289 (1994) (applying the *Merger Guidelines* to find relevant geographic market for

The notion that the smallest market is necessarily the relevant one was challenged in *FTC v. H.J. Heinz Co.*[185] The Commission sued to enjoin a merger of baby food manufacturers, alleging alternative metropolitan, regional, and national geographic markets.[186] The district court found a nationwide market only, noting that the merging firms sold nationwide from single production facilities.[187] On appeal, the D.C. Circuit affirmed the district court's finding that the geographic market is nationwide, although it reversed the district court's order refusing to enjoin the merger.[188]

As a general matter, the 1992 *Merger Guidelines* state that the government will first identify firms that currently produce and sell the relevant product.[189] Then, as in defining the relevant product market, the government may include "uncommitted entrants" as part of the geographic market in certain circumstances.

Although not referring to geographic submarkets, the *Merger Guidelines* do consider the ability to engage in price discrimination to targeted buyers as a relevant factor in defining the geographic market, which may result in recognition of a narrower market.[190]

The *Merger Guidelines* state that "[m]arket shares will be assigned to foreign competitors in the same way in which they are assigned to domestic competitors."[191] However, as one commentator has observed, "U.S. enforcement agencies have, by and large, eschewed . . . presumption-based extremes in favor of a more fact-specific inquiry."[192]

---

hospital services and dismissing the complaint).

185. 116 F. Supp. 2d 190 (D.D.C. 2000), *rev'd*, 246 F.3d 708 (D.C. Cir. 2001).

186. *Id.* at 195.

187. *Id.*

188. FTC v. H.J. Heinz Co., 246 F.3d 708, 718 (D.C. Cir. 2001).

189. 1992 MERGER GUIDELINES, *supra* note 31, § 1.31. This group includes (1) "vertically integrated firms to the extent that such inclusion accurately reflects their competitive significance in the relevant market prior to the merger," and (2) firms that produce or sell used, recycled, or reconditioned products within the relevant product market.

190. 1992 MERGER GUIDELINES, *supra* note 31, § 1.22 ("The Agency will consider additional geographic markets consisting of particular locations of buyers for which a hypothetical monopolist would profitably and separately impose at least a 'small but significant and non-transitory' increase in price").

191. *Id.* § 1.43.

192. Joseph F. Winterscheid, *Foreign Competition and U.S. Merger Analysis*, 65 ANTITRUST L.J. 241, 243 (1996) (noting the difficulty in acquiring accurate information regarding foreign competitors and "real-world limitations" on foreign competitors' ability to devote capacity to the U.S.

The *Merger Guidelines*, accordingly, also suggest that the competitive significance of imports might be overstated by the current market shares of foreign firms due to quotas, tariffs, and changes in exchange rates.[193] Foreign firms may face particular strategic dilemmas.[194] If a foreign firm were to increase its sales to a single export destination, the importing country might impose additional tariffs or quotas to protect local producers.[195] Similarly, a foreign government might be unwilling to continue or extend subsidies if that future support were to flow to foreign consumers instead of its own citizens.[196]

As in the case of product market definition, courts have increasingly relied on the approach articulated in the 1984 *Merger Guidelines*, and now in the 1992 *Merger Guidelines*, to define relevant geographic markets.[197]

---

market, such as obligations to "existing customers and home market").

193. *See also* U.S. DEP'T OF JUSTICE & FEDERAL TRADE COMM'N, ANTITRUST ENFORCEMENT GUIDELINES FOR INTERNATIONAL OPERATIONS (1995), *reprinted in* 4 Trade Reg. Rep. ¶ 13,107, which similarly acknowledge the potential impact of trade barriers.

194. *See* FTC Staff Report, *Anticipating the 21st Century: Competition Policy in the New High-Tech, Global Marketplace*, 70 Antitrust & Trade Reg. Rep. (BNA) No. 1765, at S-50 (June 6, 1996).

195. *See id.*

196. *See id.*

197. *See, e.g.*, Coastal Fuels of Puerto Rico, Inc. v. Caribbean Petroleum Corp., 79 F.3d 182, 198 (1st Cir. 1996) ("The touchstone of [relevant geographic] market definition is whether a hypothetical monopolist could raise prices"); California v. Sutter Health Sys., 130 F. Supp. 2d 1109, 1128-32 (N.D. Cal. 2001) (applying a hypothetical monopolist test to determine the relevant geographic market); United States v. Mercy Health Servs., 902 F. Supp. 968, 980-83 (N.D. Iowa 1995) (applying critical loss analysis to determine the relevant geographic market), *vacated as moot*, 107 F.3d 632 (8th Cir. 1997); United States v. Country Lake Foods, Inc., 754 F. Supp. 669, 677-78 (D. Minn. 1990) (relevant geographic market includes distant dairies, which could effectively compete against merging parties in response to 5% price increase); FTC v. Illinois Cereal Mills, Inc., 691 F. Supp. 1131, 1136-37, 1143 (N.D. Ill. 1988) (national geographic market found where eastern customers would turn to western producers "in the force of a sustained ten-percent price increase" by eastern producers), *aff'd sub nom.* FTC v. Elders Grain, Inc., 868 F.2d 901 (7th Cir. 1989).

2. *The Elzinga-Hogarty Test*

Some courts have employed the Elzinga-Hogarty test for determining the geographic market.[198] This test focuses on the respective locations of buyers and sellers to draw a geographical market that captures the majority of both groups. The test first looks at sellers: to which sellers do buyers in a proposed geographic market turn, and where are those sellers located? Next, the attention turns to buyers: where are buyers in a potential geographic market located? The Elzinga-Hogarty test attempts to find a geographic market in which there is "little in from outside" (LIFO) and "little out from inside" (LOFI). In simple terms, the LIFO looks to how much of the product is "imported" and the LOFI examines the extent to which local producers are "exporting." Originally, Elzinga and Hogarty argued that a geographic market in which at least 75 percent of the goods are produced and sold locally is a weak, but recognizable, market.[199] Subsequently, the authors focused on a 90 percent test, stating that if the average for LIFO and LOFI was equal to or greater than 90 percent, the geographic market was a strong one.[200]

The Elzinga-Hogarty test, however, can only provide an initial point of reference because it communicates only present market conditions and does not predict what would happen if a firm were to attempt to exercise market power in the future.[201] Thus, courts have recognized that if

---

198. *See* Kenneth G. Elzinga & Thomas F. Hogarty, *The Problem of Geographic Market Delineation Revisited: The Case of Coal,* 23 ANTITRUST BULL. 1 (1978); Kenneth G. Elzinga & Thomas F. Hogarty, *The Problem of Geographic Market Delineation in Antitrust Suits,* 18 ANTITRUST BULL. 45 (1973); *see also* White & White, Inc. v. American Hosp. Supply Corp., 723 F.2d 495, 503 (6th Cir. 1983); Lone Star Indus. v. FTC, 1984-1 Trade Cas. (CCH) ¶ 65,922, at 67,977 (D.D.C. 1984).

199. *See* Elzinga & Hogarty, *The Problem of Geographic Market Deliniation in Antitrust Suits*, *supra* note 198, at 73-74. The *NAAG Merger Guidelines* include within the geographic market the firms supplying 75% of the purchases by customers of the merging firms and closely proximate buyers. NAAG MERGER GUIDELINES *supra* note 50, at § 3.1.

200. *See* Elzinga & Hogarty, *supra* note 198.

201. *See* Minnesota Ass'n of Nurse Anesthetists v. Unity Hosp., 208 F.3d 655, 662 (8th Cir. 2000); FTC v. Freeman Hosp., 69 F.3d 260, 269 (8th Cir. 1995); California v. Sutter Health Sys., 130 F. Supp. 2d 1109, 1120-24 (N.D. Cal. 2001); United States v. Mercy Health Servs., 902 F. Supp. 968, 978 (N.D. Iowa 1995), *vacated as moot*, 107 F.3d 632 (8th Cir. 1997); s*ee also Rockford Mem'l Corp.*, 898 F.2d at 1285 (court of appeals characterized lower court's market based on Elzinga-Hogarty methodology as "imperfect" but adopted it as the "less imperfect"

customers can easily look to more remote suppliers in response to a price increase by local suppliers, the relevant market might be broader than current sales patterns suggest.[202]

The FTC rejected the Elzinga-Hogarty test as an analytical tool in *Adventist Health System/West*,[203] in which the Commission affirmed the dismissal by an administrative law judge of an FTC complaint against a 1988 hospital merger in the Ukiah, California area. The FTC staff had placed "heavy reliance" on expert testimony employing the Elzinga-Hogarty test for geographic market definition.[204] The Commission found no "basis for definitive reliance on that Elzinga-Hogarty test as the appropriate method under the Clayton Act to establish a geographic market," noting that it provides "static" analysis and "there is no empirical evidence" to support the use of the test.[205] The Commission stated that it "has not, and does not now, endorse" any of the Elzinga-Hogarty tests as the basis for establishing a relevant market.[206] The Commission concluded that, while "patient flow analysis employing the Elzinga-Hogarty methodology" and other statistical techniques remain relevant to geographic market analysis, other evidence was "equally relevant."[207]

B. Measuring Market Shares within a Defined Market

After the relevant product and geographic markets have been determined, the percentage of the market controlled by the acquiring and the acquired firms can be calculated. This inquiry is important because

---

alternative under the "clearly erroneous" review standard); Coca Cola Bottling Co., 118 F.T.C. 452, 581-82 (1994) (Elzinga-Hogarty test provides relevant information but is not dispositive).

202. The relevant geographic market also might be narrower than existing trade patterns if customers are currently forced to purchase from distant sources because of monopolistic prices charged by nearby sellers. *See generally* Santa Cruz Med. Clinic v. Dominican Santa Cruz Hosp., 1995-2 Trade Cas. (CCH) ¶ 71,254, at 76,096-97 & n.10 (N.D. Cal. 1995).

203. 117 F.T.C. 224 (1994).

204. *Id.* at 291-92.

205. *Id.*

206. *Id.* at 293.

207. *Id.* at 292; *cf.* FTC v. Tenet Health Care Corp., 17 F. Supp. 2d 937, 944 (E.D. Mo. 1998) (recognizing that while Elzinga-Hogarty statistical analysis "provide[s] only a static picture," it is "a proper first step in the determination of the relevant geographic market"), *rev'd on other grounds*, 186 F.3d 1045 (8th Cir. 1999).

courts and agencies traditionally have viewed higher shares as suggestive of market power. Thus, the likelihood that a merger will cause anticompetitive effects is gauged in large part by determining whether it creates a firm with sufficient market share to control output and prices, or oligopolies that can distort the market through collusion.[208] Some case law suggests that the size of the merged firm alone can create a presumption of illegality.[209] In vertical cases, the concern has been increased barriers to entry created by the size of the merged firm and possible foreclosure of other competitors at the acquired firm's level to business with the acquiring firm.[210] Accurate and meaningful measurement of market shares within the defined relevant market is therefore very important.[211]

---

208. *See* United States v. General Dynamics Corp., 415 U.S. 486 (1974); Brown Shoe Co. v. United States, 370 U.S. 294 (1962).

209. *See, e.g.*, United States v. Philadelphia Nat'l Bank, 374 U.S. 321, 326 (1963) (merger producing firm with "undue percentage of the relevant market" and resulting in "a significant increase in the concentration of firms in that market" is inherently likely to lessen competition, absent clear evidence that the merger is not likely to have anticompetitive effects); *Brown Shoe Co.*, 370 U.S. at 322 n.38 ("Statistics reflecting the shares of the market controlled by the industry leaders and the parties to the merger are .. . the primary index of market power"). *But see* HTI Health Servs., Inc. v. Quorum Health Group, Inc., 960 F. Supp. 1104, 1132 n.26 (S.D. Miss. 1997) ("Notably, since the U.S. Supreme Court rendered its decision in *United States v. General Dynamics Corp.*, . . . the emphasis in Section 7 merger cases has been to analyze carefully the likely harm to consumers, instead of accepting a firm's postmerger market share as conclusive proof of its market power." (citation omitted)).

210. *See, e.g.*, *Brown Shoe Co.*, 370 U.S. at 294 (concluding that other shoe manufacturers might find it difficult to find other outlets for their shoes after Brown Shoe, a manufacturer, acquired Kinney, a retailer). *But see* *HTI Health Servs., Inc.*, 960 F. Supp. at 1112 n.4 ("[F]irms that merge vertically are engaged in different product markets; thus, a simple vertical merger neither combines market concentrations nor increases the market power of the merging entities. Courts therefore evaluate the anticompetitive effects of a vertical merger in terms of other structural consequences or economic barriers such as whether the merger 'forecloses' competitors of the merging entities from a source of supply that would otherwise be open to them." (citations omitted)).

211. *See* Gregory J. Werden, *Assigning Market Shares,* 70 ANTITRUST L.J. 67 (2002) (analyzes appropriate method for assigning market shares in various industries).

Market shares can be measured in a variety of ways. Typically, a court begins by looking at the annual sales of the firms in the relevant market.[212] The U.S. Supreme Court has stated that the "amount of annual sales is relevant as a prediction of future competitive strength,"[213] and "the primary index of market power."[214] Annual dollar sales figures are usually used as the measure of market share, but unit sales figures have on occasion been used as well.[215] Current sales figures (from the past year) are generally used, but where they do not accurately reflect the market, data from earlier periods may be used.[216]

Courts have also used production or capacity to measure competitive strength.[217] Future production capacity has also been employed as a predictor of market share where changes in the market made prior production shares unreliable.[218] Where necessary, courts have fashioned market share measurements to suit the industry's peculiarities.[219]

---

212. *See, e.g.*, United States v. Pabst Brewing Co., 384 U.S. 546, 550-51 (1966); United States v. Von's Grocery Co., 384 U.S. 270, 272 (1966); United States v. Continental Can Co., 378 U.S. 441, 458-59 (1964); United States v. Waste Mgmt., Inc., 743 F.2d 976, 980-81 (2d Cir. 1984).
213. *General Dynamics Corp.*, 415 U.S. at 501.
214. *Brown Shoe Co.*, 370 U.S. at 322 n.38.
215. *See id.* at 341 n.69 (using units sold rather than dollars because the merging firms sold in the lower price ranges, and thus dollar sales would have understated the merging parties' market shares).
216. *See, e.g.*, American Smelting & Refining Co. v. Penzoil United, Inc., 295 F. Supp. 149, 154 n.7 (D. Del. 1969) (using data from earlier period where the most recent data was distorted by the effects of an industry-wide strike).
217. *See* Olin Corp. v. FTC, 986 F.2d 1295 (9th Cir. 1993) (FTC justified in including capacity of shut down pre-acquisition facility in determining possibility of anticompetitive effects stemming from the merger); R.J. Reynolds Tobacco Co. v. Philip Morris Inc., 199 F. Supp. 2d 362, 385-86 (M.D.N.C. 2002) (plaintiff failed to demonstrate market power in industry with substantial excess capacity), *aff'd*, 2003-1 Trade Cas. (CCH) ¶ 74,068 (4th Cir. 2003).
218. *See, e.g.*, United States v. General Dynamics Corp., 415 U.S. 486, 501-04 (1974). The *General Dynamics* Court upheld the merger of two coal companies despite the strength of their combined market share as measured by sales. The Court looked instead at the companies' shortage of uncommitted reserves and concluded that their potential for future market domination was limited. *See also* Gearhart Indus. v. Smith Int'l, Inc., 592 F. Supp. 203, 213 (N.D. Tex.) ("capacity of the equipment is the most accurate measure of market share"), *aff'd in part, modified in part and vacated in part,* 741 F.2d 707 (5th Cir. 1984); Monfort of Colo., Inc.

1. *Identifying Market Participants*

Before market shares can be assigned, the *Merger Guidelines* require the agency to identify each firm that currently produces or sells in the relevant market,[220] including foreign firms[221] and "uncommitted entrants." In allocating market shares to foreign firms, the *Merger Guidelines* take into account business practices (e.g., coordination among firms), exchange rates, and the constraining effects of any quotas limiting the sales of foreign competitors.[222] Uncommitted entrants are firms that could easily enter the market "within one year and without the expenditures of significant sunk costs of entry and exit."[223] "Sunk costs"

---

v. Cargill, Inc., 591 F. Supp. 683, 706 (D. Colo. 1983) ("an effective measure of market share . . . is a firm's capacity compared to the total capacity of all firms"), *aff'd*, 761 F.2d 570 (10th Cir. 1985), *rev'd on other grounds*, 479 U.S. 104 (1986); FTC v. Bass Bros. Enters., 1984-1 Trade Cas. (CCH) ¶ 66,041, at 68,610 (N.D. Ohio 1984) (using productive capacity to determine future industry competitive structure).

219. *See, e.g.*, United States v. Phillipsburg Nat'l Bank & Trust Co., 399 U.S. 350, 354-58, 366-67 (1970) (using total assets, total deposits, and net loans to calculate market share and concentration); United States v. Rockford Mem'l Corp., 717 F. Supp. 1251, 1280 (N.D. Ill. 1989) (measuring market share based on "state inventoried beds, in-patient admissions and inpatient hospitals"), *aff'd*, 898 F.2d 1278 (7th Cir. 1990); United States v. Hospital Affiliates Int'l, Inc., 1980-1 Trade Cas. (CCH) ¶ 63,721, at 77,853 (E.D. La. 1980) (market share based on capacity ("licensed beds") and unit sales ("patient days")).

220. 1992 MERGER GUIDELINES, *supra* note 31, § 1.31.

221. *Id.* § 1.43. The relevant inquiry is to what extent will a firm's (foreign or domestic) capacity enter the market in response to a price increase. *See* Werden, *Assigning Market Shares, supra* notes 80-82.

222. 1992 MERGER GUIDELINES, *supra* note 31, § 1.31.

223. *Id.* § 1.32. In evaluating the viability of an uncommitted entrant, courts will consider the firm's financial strength. *See* United States v. Franklin Elec. Co., 130 F. Supp. 2d 1025, 1033-34 (W.D. Wis. 2000) (finding purported entrant "will have no incentive to stay in the market" due to a lack of financial resources). Courts will also discount the possibility of entry where historically firms have failed to enter the relevant market. *See* FTC v. H.J. Heinz Co., 246 F.3d 708, 717 (D.C. Cir. 2001); FTC v. Swedish Match, 131 F. Supp. 151, 170 (D.D.C. 2000) (uncommitted entry unlikely where relevant market subject to "falling sales volume, increased government regulation, shrinking shelf space and brand loyalty" and where proposed entrant historically has refused to re-enter market). *But see* United States v. Baker Hughes Inc., 908 F.2d 981, 988 (D.C. Cir. 1990) ("If barriers to entry are insignificant, the *threat* of entry

are defined as those expenditures necessary to serve the relevant market which cannot be recouped elsewhere. If the sunk costs cannot be recouped within one year,[224] they are considered "significant." The *Merger Guidelines* recognize that uncommitted entrants may enter the market quickly by switching or adapting existing productive capability, or by acquiring or constructing new productive capability.[225] Significantly, uncommitted entrants are assigned market shares based on "the best indicator of [the] firms' future competitive significance."[226]

The *Merger Guidelines* also account for another class of potential competitors, "committed entrants" or "new competition that requires expenditure of significant sunk costs of entry and exit."[227] Because the barriers to their entry are greater than for uncommitted entrants, committed entrants are not included as market participants even where there is some supply-substitution capability. They are nonetheless valued on a subjective level for their potential to "deter an anticompetitive merger in its incipiency, or deter or counteract the competitive effects of concern"[228] by entering the market.

Under the *Merger Guidelines*, committed entry must be "timely, likely and sufficient" to have the desired, procompetitive effect.[229] "Timely" means within two years from "initial planning to significant market impact."[230] "Likely" means profitable in real (not accounting) terms, taking into account the opportunity cost of the capital invested in sunk costs.[231] And "sufficient" means that there will be enough

---

can stimulate competition in a concentrated market, regardless of whether entry ever occurs.").

224. In assessing whether the sunk costs can be recouped within one year, the analysis can be based on sales at a supracompetitive level of at least 5% above the then prevailing level. *See* 1992 MERGER GUIDELINES, *supra* note 31, §§ 0.2, 1.32-1.322.

225. *Id.* § 1.321.

226. *Id.* § 1.41; *see Franklin Elec. Co.*, 130 F. Supp. 2d at 1033-34 (court finds premium price paid by acquirer for competitor demonstrated acquisition of market power and belied argument that new entrant would maintain competition in industry).

227. 1992 MERGER GUIDELINES, *supra* note 31, § 3.0.

228. *Id.*

229. *Id.*

230. *Id.* § 3.2.

231. *Id.* § 3.3. The profitability analysis is made based on premerger prices, rather than the supracompetitive level used for uncommitted entrant analysis.

profitable sales to offset the output restraint.[232] If ease of entry can be demonstrated through these criteria, the agency is less likely to challenge the merger because the potential for collusive behavior is limited.[233]

Firms that deal in recycled or reconditioned goods may be included in the relevant market if it can be shown that they would be likely competitors.[234]

2. *Calculating Market Concentration*

For each firm identified as a market participant, the agency calculates market shares "expressed either in dollar terms through measurement of sales, shipments, or production, or in physical terms through measurement of sales, shipments, production, capacity, or reserves."[235] The market shares represent the "total sales or capacity currently devoted to the relevant market"[236] plus whatever sales or capacity would be devoted to the market in response to a small but significant and nontransitory price increase. The *Merger Guidelines* recognize the speculative element of this exercise, promising that "[m]arket shares will be calculated using the best indicator of firms' *future competitive significance*."[237]

The *Merger Guidelines* recognize that bidding markets require separate analysis. For those markets "[w]here all firms have on a forward-looking basis, an equal likelihood of securing sales," the *Merger Guidelines* indicate the agency will assign equal shares to all firms.[238]

---

232. *Id.* § 3.4; *cf.* Laurence J. Gordon, Inc. v. Brandt, Inc., 554 F. Supp. 1144, 1155 n.8 (W.D. Wash. 1983) (used and reconditioned money handling equipment included in relevant market for § 2 monopolization analysis).
233. *See generally* Jonathan B. Baker, *The Problem with Baker Hughes and Syufy: On the Role of Entry in Merger Analysis*, 65 ANTITRUST L.J. 353 (1997).
234. *See* 1992 MERGER GUIDELINES, *supra* note 31, § 1.31.
235. *Id.* § 1.41.
236. *Id*.
237. *Id*. (emphasis added).
238. *Id.* § 1.41 n.15; *see* United States v. Ingersoll-Dresser Pump Co., 65 Fed. Reg. 55271 (Sept. 13, 2000) (government complaint alleged number of competitors instead of market shares where relevant products sold through bidding mechanism); United States v. Dairy Farmers of Am., Inc., Civ. Action No.: 6:03-206 (E.D. Ky. Filed Apr. 24, 2003) (complaint alleges number of competitors in school bidding market); *see also* William E. Kovacic, *Merger Policy in a Declining Defense Industry*, 36 ANTITRUST BULL. 543, 573-74 (1991) (discussing bidding models and the assignment of equal shares to potential bidders).

The U.S. Supreme Court has noted that "unsuccessful bidders are no less competitors than the successful one,"[239] and courts have accepted that the competitive significance of potential bidders for future contracts must be considered.[240]

Specialized industries may pose special problems in measuring market shares. For example, a 1994 Defense Industry Report[241] notes that, in measuring market shares in defense industry mergers, "historical market data may be an unreliable predictor of future competitive conditions . . . due to the rapidly changing, high technology nature of many defense products."[242] More important considerations may be "(1) the cost position of the merging firms relative to each other and to the remaining competition and (2) the technological capabilities of the merging firms and each of their competitors."[243] Thus, it may be inappropriate to attempt to calculate precise market shares for defense industry mergers.[244]

Once calculated, the firm's share of the market is then compared to that of the total industry to arrive at a ratio that can be used to assess the market impact of the merger.[245] The U.S. Supreme Court has used from two to ten firms in an industry to establish a concentration ratio.[246]

---

239. United States v. El Paso Natural Gas Co., 376 U.S. 651, 661 (1964).
240. *See* United States v. Thomson Corp., 949 F. Supp. 907, 919 (D.D.C. 1996) (approving a provision in a consent decree based on the existence of potential bidders that would ensure vigorous competition); Grumman Corp. v. LTV Corp., 665 F.2d 10, 12-13 (2d Cir. 1981) (manufacturer of carrier-based planes properly deemed to be of competitive significance for future contract orders from the Department of Defense); *cf.* Seeburg Corp. v. FTC, 425 F.2d 124 (6th Cir. 1970) (vending machine manufacturer, though currently not a supplier of Coca-Cola Company, considered a competitor of current supplier because of repeated efforts to become supplier and possibility of future success).
241. April 1994 Defense Industry Report, issued by the Defense Science Board Task Force on Antitrust Aspects of Defense Industry Consolidation. The Report set forth analytical principles to be used by agencies and the Department of Defense in analyzing defense mergers.
242. *Id.* at S-14-15.
243. *Id.*
244. Indeed, complaints challenging acquisitions in the defense industry seldom allege specific market shares. *See, e.g.*, United States v. Northrop Grumman Corp., Case No. 1:02CV02432 (filed Dec. 11, 2002), 68 Fed. Reg. 1861 (Jan 14, 2003) (proposed final judgment and competitive impact statement); United States v. Lockheed Martin, CV No. 1:98CV007311 (D.D.C. filed Mar. 23, 1998).
245. "The 'market' is the denominator of the fraction the numerator of which

The agency calculates the Herfindahl-Hirschman Index (HHI) of market concentration, from which rough initial judgments of the competitive impact of the merger can be drawn.[247] The HHI is "calculated by summing the squares of the individual market shares" of all the firms included in the market.[248] This calculation results in a number somewhere between a number approaching zero (for a market where no firm has more than a de minimis share) and 10,000 (a one-firm monopoly). Generally, the more firms that are included in the index and

---

is the output of the defendants or some other select group of firms; the denominator is given by the output of the suppliers to which a group of customers can turn for their requirements of a particular product. Market share is the fraction of that output that is controlled by a particular supplier or particular suppliers whose market power we wish to assess. The higher the aggregate market share of a small number of suppliers, the easier it is for them to increase price above the competitive level without losing so much business to other suppliers as to make the price increase unprofitable; this is the power we call market power." United States v. Rockford Mem'l Corp., 898 F.2d 1278, 1283 (7th Cir. 1990) (Posner, J.); *see also* United States v. Pabst Brewing Co., 384 U.S. 546, 550-51 (1966); United States v. Von's Grocery Co., 384 U.S. 270, 272 (1966); United States v. Waste Mgmt., Inc., 743 F.2d 976, 980-81 (2d Cir. 1984). Courts also will accept evidence of actual detrimental competitive effects in lieu of a specific market share analysis. *See e.g.*, FTC v. Indiana Fed'n of Dentists, 476 U.S. 447, 461 (1986); Toys "R" Us, Inc, v. FTC, 221 F.3d 928, 936 (7th Cir. 2000); FTC v. Libbey, Inc., 211 F. Supp. 2d 34, 48-50 (D.D.C. 2002) (FTC demonstrated likelihood that amended merger agreement could result in the elimination of competitor from market).

246. *See, e.g.*, United States v. General Dynamics Corp., 415 U.S. 486, 494-96 (1974) (using market shares of top two, four, and eight firms); United States v. Phillipsburg Nat'l Bank & Trust Co., 399 U.S. 350, 366-67 (1970) (top two and three firms); United States v. Pabst Brewing Co., 384 U.S. 546, 550-51 (1966) (top four, eight, and ten firms).

247. The 1968 *Merger Guidelines* used another measure of market concentration—the four-firm concentration ratio. U.S. DEP'T OF JUSTICE, MERGER GUIDELINES (1968), *reprinted in* 4 Trade Reg. Rep. (CCH) ¶ 13,101. The four-firm concentration ratio measures the portion of the market accounted for by the top four firms, and was used by the agencies like the HHI is now used, to specify threshold concentration levels likely to result in enforcement action. Under the 1968 *Merger Guidelines*, markets in which the top four firms accounted for 75% or more of sales or capacity are "highly concentrated." *Id*. at 20,523. The concentration ratio method has been utilized by courts, looking at two-firm, four-firm, eight-firm and/or 10-firm concentration ratios.

248. 1992 MERGER GUIDELINES, *supra* note 31, § 1.5.

the more evenly the market is divided among them, the lower the HHI and likelihood of competitive harm.

The HHI assigns a greater proportionate weight to larger firms than to smaller firms, thereby highlighting the greater collusive threat posed by larger firms. To illustrate, imagine a market with four participants each having a market share of 25 percent. The premerger HHI would be $25^2 + 25^2 + 25^2 + 25^2$, or 2,500. If, instead of equal market shares, one firm controlled 50 percent of the market and the other three had 20 percent, 20 percent and 10 percent respectively, the premerger HHI would be 3,400 ($50^2 + 20^2 + 20^2 + 10^2$). The 900-point difference reflects the added potential for the 50 percent market share firm to facilitate collusion or exercise unilateral market power.

The *Merger Guidelines* use the HHI for measuring pre- and post-acquisition concentration in a relevant market as a key tool in assessing the likely anticompetitive effects of a merger, and therefore in deciding whether or not to investigate and ultimately challenge a proposed merger.[249] In part reflecting the *Merger Guidelines*' reliance on the HHI, courts are increasingly adopting HHI analysis to support their own decisions.[250]

---

249. The agency application of the HHI test in reviewing mergers is discussed in Chapter 4. Note "[t]here is no automatic threshold of market concentration that will always result in a determination that a merger would violate Section 7 of the Clayton Act." Douglas Ross, Antitrust Enforcement on Agriculture, Address Before American Farm Bureau Policy Development Meeting (Aug. 20, 2002). The agency will consider other factors including the industry structure and the ease or difficulty of entry. *Id.* Market concentration, however, is the first inquiry "because as a market becomes highly concentrated not only are price fixing and other collusion easier to coordinate there is also a dampening on competitive rivalry, even in the absence of collusion." *Id.*

250. *See, e.g.*, FTC v. H.J. Heinz Co., 246 F.3d 708, 716 (D.C. Cir. 2001) (finding that an HHI increase of 510 points "creates, by a wide margin, a presumption that the merger will lessen competition"); FTC v. PPG Indus., Inc., 798 F.2d 1500, 1503 (D.C. Cir. 1986) (declaring the HHI to be a superior measurement of market concentration because it increases "as the disparity in size between firms increases and the number of firms outside of the first four or eight decreases"); *Libbey*, 211 F. Supp. 2d at 47 (relying on FTC's HHI calculations to find a "highly concentrated pre-merger market"); *Swedish Match*, 131 F. Supp. 2d at 167 (utilizing HHI to measure market concentration); FTC v. Staples, Inc., 970 F. Supp. 1066, 1082 (D.D.C. 1997) ("The *Merger Guidelines*, of course, are not binding on the court, but, as this Circuit has stated, they do provide 'a useful illustration of the application of the HHI,' and the court will use

that guidance here." (citation omitted)); United States v. United Tote, Inc., 768 F. Supp. 1064, 1069-70 (D. Del. 1991) (relying on HHI in assessing totalizator market concentration); United States v. Ivaco, Inc., 704 F. Supp. 1409, 1419 (W.D. Mich. 1989) (relying on HHI in finding joint venture in railroad tamper market illegal); FTC v. Illinois Cereal Mills, Inc., 691 F. Supp. 1131, 1137-38, 1144 (N.D. Ill. 1988), *aff'd*, 868 F.2d 901 (7th Cir. 1989); FTC v. Owens-Illinois, Inc., 681 F. Supp. 27, 47-48 & n.61 (D.D.C. 1988) (relying on HHI, but noting that the *Merger Guidelines'* analytical approach is not binding on the court), *vacated as moot*, 850 F.2d 694 (D.C. Cir. 1988); United States v. Archer-Daniels-Midland Co., 695 F. Supp. 1000, 1008 (S.D. Iowa 1987) (relying on HHI in assessing sweetener market concentration), *rev'd on other grounds*, 866 F.2d 242 (8th Cir. 1988); White Consol. Indus. v. Whirlpool Corp., 612 F. Supp. 1009, 1020 (N.D. Ohio) (stating that the HHI "gives a more accurate reading of the extent to which market share is being spread among firms in the market or is being held by a small number of firms"), *vacated*, 619 F. Supp. 1022 (N.D. Ohio 1985), *aff'd*, 781 F.2d 1224 (6th Cir. 1986); United States v. Calmar Inc., 612 F. Supp. 1298, 1305 (D.N.J. 1985); Frank Saltz & Sons, Inc. v. Hart Schaffner & Marx, 1985-2 Trade Cas. (CCH) ¶ 66,768, at 63,724 (S.D.N.Y. 1985) (applying both the HHI as well as other market concentration tests).

CHAPTER 4

HORIZONTAL MERGERS: PROVING LIKELY ANTICOMPETITIVE EFFECTS

In order to determine whether a merger or acquisition may violate the federal antitrust laws, i.e., to determine whether "the effect of such acquisition may be substantially to lessen competition, or to tend to create a monopoly,"[1] the combination must be examined to ascertain its likely competitive effects in the relevant product (or service) and geographic markets. Horizontal mergers or acquisitions are those that involve firms that compete in the same market prior to the merger, and are generally analyzed for two types of potential anticompetitive effects: the facilitation of coordinated interaction and unilateral effects.

A merger may diminish competition by enabling the firms in the relevant market to engage in successful coordinated interaction that harms consumers.[2] A merger may also substantially lessen competition by changing the pricing calculus facing the new integrated firm in a way that favors a unilateral price increase for one or more of the products or brands sold by the merged firm.[3]

Generally, the greater the homogeneity of the products offered by sellers in the relevant market, the more likely a merger between participants in that market will facilitate coordinated interaction among the remaining competitors. Conversely, the greater the differentiation

1. 15 U.S.C. § 18.
2. *See* UNITED STATES DEP'T OF JUSTICE & FEDERAL TRADE COMM'N, HORIZONTAL MERGER GUIDELINES § 2.1 (1992) [hereinafter 1992 MERGER GUIDELINES], *reprinted in* 4 Trade Reg. Rep. (CCH) ¶13,104. "Coordinated interaction is comprised of actions by a group of firms that are profitable for each of them only as a result of the accommodating reactions of the others." *Id.*
3. *See id.* § 2.2. For example, if, prior to a merger between firms A and B, firm A sets its price equal to its marginal revenue, any unilateral price increase by firm A will result in a loss of profit, because the lost profit resulting from the demand side substitution outweighs any increased profitability on the remaining products sold. However, after the merger, some of the lost profit resulting from the demand side substitution will be internalized and recaptured by firm B which could, depending on B's profit margin, result in a sufficient benefit to justify an increase in the price charged by firm A.

among products in the relevant market, the less likely the merger will facilitate tacit or express cooperation among market participants because competing sellers must constantly assess the relative value of the differing products.[4] Although coordinated interaction in markets involving differentiated products is more difficult to maintain and less likely to occur, the more the differentiated products sold by the merging firms are viewed as close substitutes for each other, relative to other competing products, the greater the likelihood that the combined firm will be able to engage in unilateral behavior affecting competition after the merger.[5]

A. Market Share as a Measure of Anticompetitive Effects

1. U.S. Supreme Court Precedent

Once the product and geographic markets have been defined properly, U.S. Supreme Court jurisprudence teaches that the government may establish its prima facie case that a merger is unlawful by relying upon market shares and market concentration in the postmerger market.[6] Increases in market concentration above certain thresholds give rise to a presumption that the combination will have anticompetitive effects and is thus unlawful. This presumption may be overcome, however, by demonstrating that market conditions make it unlikely that the presumed anticompetitive effects in fact will occur.

In the period following enactment of the Celler-Kefauver amendments in 1950,[7] courts interpreted the legislative history of those amendments as condemning most horizontal mergers. During the 1960s, the U.S. Supreme Court issued a series of opinions that emphasized that Section 7 was enacted to arrest incipient losses of competition. Mergers

---

4. *See* 1992 MERGER GUIDELINES, *supra* note 2, §2.1 ("the extent of information available to firms in the market, or the extent of homogeneity, may be relevant to both the ability to reach terms of coordination and to detect or punish deviations from those terms").
5. *See* Carl Shapiro, *Mergers with Differentiated Products*, ANTITRUST, Spring 1996, at 23 ("When products are highly differentiated, concerns about coordinated effects may be secondary to concerns about unilateral effects").
6. The courts use models that serve as indicia of market concentration, e.g., the Herfindahl-Hirschman Index or the earlier four-firm concentration ratio. *See generally* Chapter 3.
7. Act of Dec. 29, 1950, Pub. L. No. 81-899, 64 Stat. 1225 (codified as amended at 15 U.S.C. § 18).

that resulted in firms with relatively small market shares were found to violate the law, particularly where there was evidence of a trend toward increasing concentration in the relevant market.[8]

The U.S. Supreme Court's first major horizontal merger decision under the 1950 amendments to Section 7 was *Brown Shoe Co. v. United States*.[9] In *Brown Shoe*, the Court opined that market share was "one of the most important factors to be considered when determining the probable effects of the combination on effective competition in the relevant market."[10] Noting the congressional desire to "arrest[] mergers at a time when the trend to a lessening of competition . . . was still in its incipiency,"[11] the Court then condemned the merger of the Brown Shoe Company and G.R. Kinney Company, even though the two companies collectively accounted for only 5 percent of the relevant market.[12]

A year later, in *United States v. Philadelphia National Bank*,[13] the U.S. Supreme Court announced a rule of presumptive illegality in the context of heavily concentrated markets. In that case, the acquiring firm held a 30 percent market share and, while the acquired firm's market share was only 3 percent, the combined firm and the market's second largest firm shared approximately 59 percent of the relevant market.[14] The Court found that the merged firm's market share and the increased concentration resulting from the merger were sufficient to find the merger presumptively illegal.[15]

The *Philadelphia National Bank* case spawned the "leading firm" doctrine, in which acquisitions by firms with significant market shares (15 percent or greater) of firms with trivial shares (often no greater than 1 percent) were condemned.[16] Under the "leading firm" doctrine, once

---

8. *See, e.g.*, United States v. Von's Grocery Co., 384 U.S. 270 (1966) (combined shares totaled 7.5%); United States v. Pabst Brewing Co., 384 U.S. 546 (1966) (combined shares totaled 4.49% nationwide, 11.32% in a three-state area, and 23.95% in Wisconsin); United States v. Aluminum Co. of Am., 377 U.S. 271 (1964); Brown Shoe Co. v. United States, 370 U.S. 294 (1962).
9. 370 U.S. 294 (1962).
10. *Id.* at 343 (footnote omitted).
11. *Id.* at 317.
12. *See id.* at 343-44.
13. 374 U.S. 321 (1963).
14. *See id.* at 331, 365.
15. *See id.* at 363-64.
16. *See, e.g.*, *Aluminum Co. of Am.*, 377 U.S. at 277-79 (acquisition by firm with 27.8% of the market of firm with 1.3% condemned); FTC v. PepsiCo, 477 F.2d 24, 25-27 (2d Cir. 1973) (merger where acquiring firm

the government had defined the relevant market and showed an appropriate increase in concentration, the government had all but prevailed and the merger would in all likelihood be enjoined.

The U.S. Supreme Court refined its market concentration analysis in *United States v. General Dynamics Corp.*[17] and held that a prima facie case that a merger would violate Section 7 (based on current market shares) could be overcome by a showing that market share figures overstated the merged company's "future ability to compete."[18] The *General Dynamics* Court placed its imprimatur on forward-looking analysis of market concentration and market share, and the focus of merger analysis turned to the likely future impact of the merging firms on the market rather than looking solely at their historical market positions.[19]

Under this more refined approach, if competitive factors indicate that market shares (which typically rely on past performance) overstate a firm's future competitive position, the courts may give controlling weight to those factors to permit consummation of the merger.[20] Conversely, if competitive factors indicate that market shares understate

---

with 16.3% of market acquired smaller firm with 0.3% and top four firms accounted for 70.6% of the market); Stanley Works v. FTC, 469 F.2d 498, 500-01, 504 & n.13 (2d Cir. 1972) (merger of firm with 1% of the market with leading firm with 23% and top four firms accounted for 50% of market); FTC v. Coca-Cola Co., 641 F. Supp. 1128, 1134, 1138-39 (D.D.C. 1986), *vacated and remanded mem.*, 829 F.2d 191 (D.C. Cir. 1987).

17. 415 U.S. 486 (1974).

18. *Id.* at 501.

19. *See* Hospital Corp. of Am. v. FTC, 807 F.2d 1381, 1386 (7th Cir. 1986); *see also* Olin Corp. v. FTC, 986 F.2d 1295, 1304-06 (9th Cir. 1993); United States v. Baker Hughes, Inc., 908 F.2d 981 (D.C. Cir. 1990); United States v. Waste Mgmt., Inc., 743 F.2d 976 (2d Cir. 1984). *See generally* Chapter 5.

20. *See* United States v. Baker Hughes, Inc., 908 F.2d 981, 990-91 (D.C. Cir. 1990); United States v. Waste Mgmt., Inc., 743 F.2d 976, 982 (2d Cir. 1984); Lektro-Vend Corp. v. Vendo Co., 660 F.2d 255, 274-77 (7th Cir. 1981); HTI Health Serv., Inc. v. Quorum Health Group, Inc., 960 F. Supp. 1104, 1126-31 (S.D. Miss. 1997); United States v. Calmar Inc., 612 F. Supp. 1298, 1306-07 (D.N.J. 1985); United States v. Amax, Inc., 402 F. Supp. 956, 965 (D. Conn. 1975); United States v. Country Lake Foods, Inc., 1990-2 Trade Cas. (CCH) ¶ 69,113, at 64,221-22 (D. Minn. 1990); Robinson v. Intergraph Corp., 1988-2 Trade Cas. (CCH) ¶ 68,138, at 58,943 (E.D. Mich. 1988).

the proposed merger's anticompetitive effects, the courts may enjoin the merger despite low market shares and concentration levels.[21]

2. *The 1992* Merger Guidelines *and Lower Court Precedent*

The *Merger Guidelines* adopted by the Antitrust Division of the Department of Justice (DOJ or the Division) and the Federal Trade Commission (FTC or the Commission) utilize the Herfindahl-Hirschman Index (HHI) to measure the degree of concentration in the relevant market in which the effects of a particular merger are to be evaluated.[22] The 1992 *Merger Guidelines* classify mergers by their HHI concentration levels into three categories: those with postmerger HHIs below 1000 points, those with postmerger HHIs between 1000 and 1800 points, and those with postmerger HHIs above 1800 points.

A relevant market in which the postmerger HHI is less than 1000 points is considered unconcentrated. Because a merger in such a market is "unlikely to have adverse competitive effects," the government ordinarily will not challenge such a merger.[23]

A relevant market with a postmerger HHI of between 1000 and 1800 points is considered moderately concentrated.[24] A merger resulting in an increase in the HHI of less than 100 points in such a moderately concentrated market generally will not be challenged.[25] Such a merger is "unlikely to have adverse competitive consequences and ordinarily requires no further analysis."[26] A merger resulting in an increase in the HHI of more than 100 points in such a moderately concentrated postmerger market, however, "potentially raises significant competitive

---

21. *See, e.g.*, SCFC ILC, Inc. v. Visa USA, Inc., 819 F. Supp. 956, 993-94 (D. Utah 1993), *aff'd in part and rev'd in part*, 36 F.3d 958 (10th Cir. 1994).
22. *See* 1992 MERGER GUIDELINES, *supra* note 2, § 1.51; *see also* part B.2 of Chapter 3; HORIZONTAL MERGER GUIDELINES OF THE NATIONAL ASSOCIATION OF ATTORNEYS GENERAL (1993) [hereinafter NAAG MERGER GUIDELINES], §4, *reprinted in* 4 Trade Reg. Rep. (CCH) ¶ 13,406 and in Appendix M.
23. *See* 1992 MERGER GUIDELINES, *supra* note 2, § 1.51(a).
24. *Id.* § 1.51(b).
25. *Id.* The 1984 *Guidelines* stated that a postmerger HHI in this range following an increase of less than 100 points was "unlikely" to be challenged. U.S. DEP'T OF JUSTICE, MERGER GUIDELINES (1984) § 3.11, *reprinted in* 4 Trade Reg. Rep. (CCH) ¶ 13,103 [hereinafter 1984 MERGER GUIDELINES].
26. 1992 MERGER GUIDELINES, *supra* note 2, § 1.51(b).

concerns."[27] Consequently, the 1992 *Merger Guidelines* require that the merger be further scrutinized in light of entry conditions, the likelihood of coordinated interaction or unilateral competitive effects, efficiencies made possible by the combination, and the possibility that one of the merging firms may fail and its assets exit the market.[28]

Lastly, a relevant market with a postmerger HHI of greater than 1800 points is considered highly concentrated.[29] In this category, a merger resulting in an HHI increase of less than 50 points ordinarily does not require further analysis and will not be challenged because it is unlikely to have adverse competitive consequences.[30] A merger resulting in an HHI increase of between 50 and 100 points is scrutinized in light of entry conditions, the likelihood of coordinated interaction or unilateral competitive effects, efficiencies made possible by the combination, and the possibility that one of the merging firms may fail and its assets exit the market to determine whether the merger presents significant competitive concerns.[31] Finally, in a highly concentrated market, "it will be presumed that mergers producing an increase in the HHI of more than 100 points are likely to create or enhance market power or facilitate its exercise."[32] Such a merger is likely to be challenged unless that presumption can be overcome.[33]

---

27. *Id.* The 1984 *Merger Guidelines* stated that such a merger was "likely" to be challenged. 1984 MERGER GUIDELINES, *supra* note 25, § 3.11 However, this statement simply did not reflect actual enforcement during the period in which the 1984 *Merger Guidelines* were in effect. *See, e.g.*, Kevin J. Arquit, *Perspectives on the 1992 U.S. Government Horizontal Merger Guidelines*, 61 ANTITRUST L.J. 121, 126-27 (1992) ("The 1984 *Merger Guidelines* arguably did not reflect current enforcement standards in stating that mergers producing an HHI increase of more than 100 in moderately concentrated ... post-merger markets were likely to be challenged."); Charles A. James, *Overview of the 1992 Horizontal Merger Guidelines*, 61 ANTITRUST L.J. 447, 449 (1993) (arguing that the concentration standards in the 1984 *Merger Guidelines* "did not reflect actual enforcement practice .. . [T]he agencies challenged very few mergers in moderately concentrated markets and only some of the mergers in markets that were highly concentrated").
28. *See* 1992 MERGER GUIDELINES, *supra* note 2, § 1.51(b); *see also* Occidental Petroleum Corp., 115 F.T.C. 1010, 1279 (1992) (Owen, Comm'r, concurring in part and dissenting in part).
29. *See* 1992 MERGER GUIDELINES, *supra* note 2, § 1.51(c).
30. *See id.*
31. *See id.*
32. *Id.*
33. *See id.*

Unlike the 1984 *Merger Guidelines*, the 1992 *Merger Guidelines* state that, although a relevant market may be highly concentrated and the merger may lead to an HHI increase of 100 points or more, an analysis of the competitive effects of the merger may result in the merger not being challenged. As the chairman of the FTC observed:

> The *Guidelines* do *not* state . . . that a high HHI plus a significant delta is *dispositive* evidence of anticompetitive effects. Rather, a high HHI and significant change in HHI in a properly defined market, and the presence of barriers-to-entry, provides a *prima facie* case. This *prima facie* case can be rebutted by the absence of a viable factually supported theory of anticompetitive effects.[34]

The enforcement agencies have thus disavowed exclusive reliance on market shares in favor of a more "reasoned analysis of likely competitive effect of the particular transaction."[35] Consistent with *General Dynamics*, the 1992 *Merger Guidelines* make clear that the competitive effects of a merger cannot be determined based solely on levels of market concentration.[36] The 1992 *Merger Guidelines* recognize that, in certain circumstances, market share and concentration data may understate or overstate the likely future competitive significance of firms in the market or the impact of the merger.[37] Changing market conditions may suggest that market concentration calculations do not accurately

---

34. Timothy J. Muris, Chairman, FTC, Opening Remarks Before the FTC Roundtable, Understanding Mergers: Strategy and Planning, Implementation, and Outcomes (Dec. 9, 2002), *at* www.ftc.gov/speeches/muris/mergers021209.htm; *see also* Lawrence R. Fullerton, Deputy Ass't Att'y Gen., Antitrust Div., Recent Developments in Merger Enforcement, Remarks Before the Conference Board Council of Chief Legal Officers (Feb. 9, 1996), *at* www.usdoj.gov/atr/public/speeches/fullerton.htm ("[M]arket definition, the assignment of market shares, and the assessment of concentration in the market are only the starting points in our analysis").
35. *60 Minutes with The Honorable James F. Rill, Assistant Attorney General, Antitrust Division, U.S. Department of Justice*, 61 ANTITRUST L.J. 229, 235 (1992) (emphasis omitted); *see also* Timothy J. Muris, Chairman, FTC, Improving the Economic Foundations of Competition Policy, Remarks Before George Mason Univ. Law Review's Winter Antitrust Symposium (Jan. 15, 2003), *at* www.ftc.gov/speeches/muris/improveconfoundatio.htm (arguing that antitrust enforcement should be predicated on careful, fact-based analyses that properly account for the specific determinants of competition in the relevant market, not just on market structure and market power theories).
36. 1992 MERGER GUIDELINES, *supra* note 2, § 1.52.
37. *Id.*

state the competitive significance of certain firms in the market.[38] Furthermore, the 1992 *Merger Guidelines*' HHI thresholds may understate a merger's significance if market conditions, such as the absence of close substitutes outside the relevant market, make it possible for a hypothetical monopolist to raise prices by substantially more than the "small but significant and nontransitory" touchstone.[39]

The market concentration thresholds for challenging a proposed merger under the 1992 *Merger Guidelines* are arguably higher than the thresholds imposed by the courts for finding a proposed merger unlawful. Moreover, whereas U.S. Supreme Court merger jurisprudence has focused almost exclusively upon market concentration, there "is growing recognition" in the agencies "that it is *conduct*, not structure, that causes anticompetitive effects. . . . Accordingly, the [1992] Guidelines treat concentration not as an end in itself, but as an indicator that needs to be interpreted and considered along with other market factors."[40] Consistent with this methodology, the 1992 *Merger*

---

38. *See id.* § 1.521. The 1992 *Merger Guidelines* provide the example that a firm's likely future competitive significance may be overstated if a new technology that is important to the firm's ability to compete over the long term is not available to the firm, but is available to other firms in the market. *See id.*

39. *Id.* § 1.522.

40. *60 Minutes with The Honorable James F. Rill, Assistant Attorney General, Antitrust Division, U.S. Department of Justice*, 61 ANTITRUST L.J. 229, 236 (1992); *see also* Statement of the FTC Concerning Royal Caribbean Cruises, Ltd./P&O Princess Cruises plc and Carnival Corp./P&O Princess Cruises plc ("The Department of Justice and Federal Trade Commission Horizontal Merger Guidelines make it clear that 'market share and concentration data provide only the starting point for analyzing the competitive impact of a merger.'") (citing 1992 MERGER GUIDELINES, § 2.0); Jonathan B. Baker, *Mavericks, Mergers, and Exclusion: Proving Coordinated Competitive Effects under the Antitrust Laws*, 77 N.Y.U. L. REV. 135, 154 (2002) ("[T]he contemporary economic learning on the relationship between market concentration and price suggests employing concentration in much the way that the Merger Guidelines do today: as an important factor in competitive effects analysis, appropriately considered in conjunction with other factors suggested by the competitive effects theory, but far from the only factor relevant to understanding firm conduct and market performance."); Gregory J. Werden, *Assigning Market Shares*, 70 ANTITRUST L.J. 67, 67 (2002) ("[B]ecause market shares never come close to telling the whole market power story, the goal in assigning them should be merely to accurately and usefully indicate the relative sizes of competitors in the

Guidelines invite the antitrust practitioner to "tell a story about why the merger will or will not have adverse effects."[41]

Generally most of the merger cases challenged by the agencies, whether they resulted in a consent decree[42] or were litigated,[43] have been

---

market").

41. Paul T. Denis, *Practical Approaches: An Insider's Look at the New Horizontal Merger Guidelines*, ANTITRUST, Summer 1992, at 6; *Interview: Steven Newborn, Director for Litigation, Bureau of Competition, Federal Trade Commission*, ANTITRUST, Summer 1992, at 20, 21.

42. *See, e.g.,* United States v. General Elec. Co., No. 1:03CV01923 (D.D.C. filed Sept. 16, 2003) (complaint) (challenging merger with an increase in HHI of 1134, from 2661 to 3795, in the critical care monitor market); In the Matter of Nestlé Holdings, Inc. and Dreyer's Grand Ice Cream Holdings, Inc., No. C-4082 (FTC June 25, 2003) (complaint) (challenging a merger with an increase in HHI of 1396 points, from 3501 to 4897, in superpremium ice cream); In the Matter of Solvay S.A., No. C-4046 (FTC Apr. 29, 2002) (complaint) (challenging a merger with an increase in HHI of more than 1000 points, to over 4300, in polyvinylidene fluoride); United States v. Alcoa, Inc., No. 00CV954 (RMU) (D.D.C. filed May 3, 2000) (complaint) (challenging a merger with an increase in HHI of 1500, from 2722 to 4222, in the North American market for chemical grade alumina); United States v. Earthgrains Co., No. 00C1687 (N.D. Ill. filed Mar. 20, 2000) (complaint) (challenging a merger with an increase in HHI of 875, from 2925 to 3800, in the Omaha, Nebraska, market for white pan bread; an increase in HHI of 1378 points, from 2022 to 3400, in the Kansas City, Missouri, market for white pan bread; and an increase of 1530 points, from 1970 to 3500, in the Des Moines, Iowa, market for white pan bread).

43. *See, e.g.,* FTC v. H.J. Heinz Co., 246 F.3d 708, 716 (D.C. Cir. 2001) (upholding challenge to merger with an increase in the HHI of 510, from 4775 to 5285); FTC v. University Health, Inc., 938 F.2d 1206, 1211 n.12, 1225-26 (11th Cir. 1991) (upholding challenge to merger with an increase in the HHI of 630, from 2630 to 3260); Hospital Corp. of Am. v. FTC, 807 F.2d 1381 (7th Cir. 1986) (upholding challenge to merger with an increase in the HHI of 174, from 2242 to 2416); United States v. UPM-Kymmene Oyj, 2003-2 Trade Cas. ¶ 74,101 (N.D. Ill. 2003) (memorandum opinion and order) (upholding challenge to merger with an increase in the HHI of 290, from 2960 to 3250); FTC v. Swedish Match, 131 F. Supp. 2d 151, 167 (D.D.C. 2000) (upholding challenge to merger with an increase in the HHI of 1514, from 3219 to 4733); FTC v. Staples, Inc., 970 F. Supp. 1066, 1081 (D.D.C. 1997) (upholding challenge to merger with an average increase in the HHI of 2,715); United States v. United Tote, Inc., 768 F. Supp. 1064, 1069, 1087 (D. Del. 1991)

in "highly concentrated" markets where the change in the HHI is more than 100 points. The presumptions and the HHI thresholds of the 1992 *Merger Guidelines* are not binding on the courts,[44] however, and the agencies have not always prevailed.[45]

B. Coordinated Anticompetitive Effects

Both the courts and the 1992 *Merger Guidelines* eschew pure market concentration analysis and, instead, seek to analyze whether a merger or acquisition will have anticompetitive results. Although the courts and 1992 *Merger Guidelines* recognize two sources of potential adverse effects of a proposed merger—(1) increased coordinated interaction[46] and (2) unilateral anticompetitive conduct[47]—these effects are not

---

(upholding challenge to merger with an increase in the HHI of 800, from 3840 to 4640); United States v. Rockford Mem'l Corp., 717 F. Supp. 1251, 1279-80, 1291-92 (N.D. Ill. 1989) (upholding challenge to merger with an increase in the HHI of 2048, from 2555 to 4603), *aff'd*, 898 F.2d 1278 (7th Cir. 1990); United States v. Ivaco, Inc., 704 F. Supp. 1409, 1419, 1428-29 (W.D. Mich. 1989) (upholding challenge to merger with an increase in the HHI of 2260, from 3549 to 5809).

44. *See H.J. Heinz Co.*, 246 F.3d at 716 n.9; FTC v. PPG Indus., 798 F.2d 1500, 1503 n.4 (D.C. Cir. 1986). Although the 1992 *Merger Guidelines* are not binding on the courts, they have been found to provide useful guidance. *See, e.g.*, *H.J. Heinz Co.*, 246 F.3d at 716 n.9; *Swedish Match*, 131 F. Supp. 2d at 167 n.12; *Staples, Inc.*, 970 F. Supp. at 1081-82.

45. *See* United States v. Baker Hughes, Inc., 908 F.2d 981, 983 n.3, 992 (D.C. Cir. 1990) (rejecting challenge to merger with an increase in the HHI of 1425, from 2878 to 4303); United States v. SunGard Data Sys., Inc., 172 F. Supp. 2d 172, 193 n. 25 (D.D.C. 2001) (rejecting merger challenge); United States v. Engelhard Corp., 970 F. Supp. 1463 (N.D. Ga. 1997) (rejecting challenge to merger), *aff'd,* 126 F.3d 1302 (11th Cir. 1997); FTC v. Butterworth Health Corp., 946 F. Supp. 1285, 1294, 1302-03 (W.D. Mich. 1996) (rejecting challenge to merger with an increase in the HHI of between 1064 and 1889 in one relevant market and an increase in the HHI of between 1675 and 2001 in the other relevant market).

46. *See* 1992 MERGER GUIDELINES, *supra* note 2, § 2.1; *H.J. Heinz Co.*, 246 F.3d at 724-25; Hospital Corp. of Am. v. FTC, 807 F.2d 1381, 1386 (7th Cir. 1986); *Swedish Match*, 131 F. Supp. 2d at 168; FTC v. Cardinal Health, Inc., 12 F. Supp. 2d 34, 65 (D.D.C. 1998) (after merger defendants "would likely have an increased ability to coordinate their pricing practices.")

47. *See* 1992 MERGER GUIDELINES, *supra* note 2, § 2.21; *Swedish Match*, 131 F. Supp. 2d at 169; *Staples, Inc.*, 970 F. Supp. at 1066.

mutually exclusive; a transaction can raise concerns as to both adverse effects.[48]

The 1992 *Merger Guidelines* define coordinated interaction as "actions by a group of firms that are profitable for each of them only as a result of the accommodating reactions of others."[49] The behavior "includes tacit or express collusion, and may or may not be lawful in and of itself."[50] "[W]here only a few firms account for most of the sales of the product, those firms can exercise market power, perhaps even approximating the performance of a monopolist, by either explicitly or implicitly coordinating their actions."[51]

The 1992 *Merger Guidelines* ask whether the market conditions in the relevant product market "on the whole" are conducive to reaching terms of coordination profitable to all market participants and whether those in the market are able to detect and punish deviations from the collusive arrangement.[52] A merger that increases market concentration may foster conditions leading to such a diminished level of competition. A merger may make it easier to "reach[] terms of coordination that are profitable" and leave market participants with an enhanced "ability to detect and punish deviations that would undermine the coordinated interaction."[53] The issue is whether the merger will make it "easier for firms in the market to collude, expressly or tacitly, and thereby force price above or farther above the competitive level. . . . [T]he worry is that [the merger] may enable the acquiring firm to cooperate (or cooperate better) with other leading competitors on reducing or limiting output, thereby pushing up the market price."[54]

---

48. *See Swedish Match*, 131 F. Supp. 2d at 168-69; *see also* United States v. Alcoa, Inc., No. 00CV954 (RMU) (D.D.C. filed May 3, 2000) (complaint) (alleging both coordinated and unilateral effects); United States v. Earthgrains Co., No. 00C1687 (N.D. Ill. filed Mar. 20, 2000) (same); In the Matter of Phillips Petroleum Co. and Conoco Inc., No. C-4058 (FTC Aug. 30, 2002) (same); In the Matter of Deutsche Gelatine-Fabriken Stoess AG and Goodman Fielder Ltd., C-4045 (FTC Apr. 17, 2002) (same); Koninklijke Ahold NV, No. C-3861 (FTC Apr. 5, 1999) (same).
49. 1992 MERGER GUIDELINES, *supra* note 2, § 2.1.
50. *Id.*
51. *Id.* § 0.1.
52. *Id.* § 2.1.
53. *Id.*
54. Hospital Corp. of Am. v. FTC, 807 F.2d 1381, 1386 (7th Cir. 1986); *see also* United States v. Rockford Mem'l Corp., 898 F.2d 1278, 1282-83 (7th Cir. 1990) (quoting Hospital Corp. of Am. v. FTC, 807 F.2d at

In general, the agencies are more likely to challenge a transaction based on concerns about coordinated effects when the market HHI is well over 2000 and the change precipitated by the transaction is significant.[55] They are also, however, willing to challenge transactions with more modest levels of concentration. For instance, in challenging Diageo's proposed acquisition of the Seagram's spirits and wine business from Vivendi Universal, the FTC's complaint included a market with a postmerger HHI of 2000.[56]

In considering the likelihood of coordinated interaction, the agencies first ask whether there is any history in the relevant market of express collusion.[57] For example, the DOJ challenged the combination of two

---

1386); Olin Corp., 113 F.T.C. 400, 610 (1990) ("The fewer the competitors in a market, the easier it becomes for the firms to coordinate price and output decisions."). Competitors may seek to coordinate their activities in a number of ways. They may seek to fix prices (whether by actually agreeing upon price levels or by limiting the degree to which they compete on price), or to eliminate competition amongst themselves in certain geographic markets or for the business of certain customers. *See* R. Hewitt Pate, Vigorous and Principled Antitrust Enforcement: Priorities and Goals, Remarks Before Antitrust Section of the ABA Annual Meeting (Aug. 12, 2003) ("Coordinated effects analysis focuses on whether, following a merger, firms will have a greater incentive and ability to coordinate"), *at* www.usdoj.gov/atr/public/speeches/201241.htm.

55. *See, e.g.*, United States v. UPM-Kymmene Oyj, No. 03C2528 (N.D. Ill. filed Apr. 15, 2003) (verified complaint) (in two relevant markets, alleging postmerger HHIs of 3250 and 2990, and increases in the HHI of 290 and 190, respectively); Baxter Int'l, Inc., 68 Fed. Reg. 1,062, 1,064 (FTC Jan. 8, 2003) (analysis to aid public comment) (in two relevant markets, alleging postmerger HHIs of 6152 and 3852, and increases in the HHI of 2496 and 936, respectively); In the Matter of Solvay S.A., C-4046 (FTC Apr. 29, 2002) (complaint) (alleging postmerger HHIs of 4300 and 5100 in two relevant markets); United States v. Alcoa, Inc., No. 00CV954 (RMU) (D.D.C. filed May 3, 2000) (complaint) (alleging a postmerger HHI of 4222 and an increase in the HHI of 1500); United States v. Earthgrains Co., No. 00C1687 (N.D. Ill. filed Mar. 20, 2000) (complaint) (alleging a series of local white pan bread markets with postmerger HHIs over 3000).

56. *See* In the Matter of Diageo plc and Vivendi Universal S.A., No. C-4032 (FTC Dec. 19, 2001) (complaint); *see also* Shell Oil Co., No. C-3803 (FTC Dec. 19, 1997) (complaint) (asserting the increased likelihood of coordinated interaction in a market with a postmerger HHI of 1635).

57. *See* 1992 MERGER GUIDELINES, *supra* note 2, § 2.1; FTC v. Elders Grain, Inc., 868 F.2d 901, 905 (7th Cir. 1989); *Hospital Corp. of Am.*, 807 F.2d at 1388-89.

dairies that had competed for school milk contracts based in part on a clear history of industry collusion.[58] Similarly, the FTC challenged Degussa's proposed acquisition of DuPont's hydrogen peroxide plants, relying at least in part on a documented history of collusion among hydrogen peroxide producers in Europe decades earlier; those found to have colluded in Europe include "producers that after the acquisition would be the leading producers in North America."[59]

Such a history gives rise to an adverse inference, which can be overcome through an analysis of "the other market factors that pertain to competitive effects, as well as entry, efficiencies and failure."[60] Among the other factors to be considered in determining whether conditions in the postmerger market in fact will be conducive to reaching profitable terms of coordination and to detecting and punishing deviations from these terms are "the availability of key information concerning market conditions, transactions and individual competitors; the extent of firm and product heterogeneity; pricing or marketing practices typically employed by firms in the market; the characteristics of buyers and sellers; and the characteristics of typical transactions."[61]

The increased coordinated interaction occasioned by a merger need not involve express collusion,[62] but may also be evidenced by tacit

---

58. *See* United States v. Suiza Foods Corp., No. 99-CV-130 (E.D. Ky. filed Mar. 18, 1999) (complaint) (detailing history of bid-rigging guilty pleas and fines); *see also* United States v. UPM-Kymmene Oyj, No. 03C2528 (N.D. Ill. filed Apr. 15, 2003) (verified complaint) (citing past attempts to collude by the only two significant competitors that would remain postmerger); United States v. Browning-Ferris Industries, Inc., No. 94-CV-2588 (D.D.C. Dec. 1, 1994) (complaint) (alleging overt industry collusion documented in more than a dozen criminal and civil antitrust cases in previous 15 years).
59. *See* Degussa A.G., No. C-3813 (FTC June 10, 1998) (complaint).
60. 1992 MERGER GUIDELINES, *supra* note 2, § 2.0.
61. *Id.* § 2.1; *see also* Hospital Corp. of Am. v. FTC, 807 F.2d at 1389-91; United States v. Ivaco, Inc., 704 F. Supp. 1409, 1423-26 (W.D. Mich. 1989); B.F. Goodrich Co., 110 F.T.C. 207, 338-39 (1988); *cf.* Brooke Group v. Brown & Williamson Tobacco Corp., 509 U.S. 209, 238-39 (1993); FTC v. Elders Grain, Inc., 868 F.2d 901, 905-06 (7th Cir. 1989); FTC v. Owens-Illinois, Inc., 681 F. Supp. 27, 51-52 (D.D.C. 1988), *vacated as moot*, 850 F.2d 694 (D.C. Cir. 1988); FTC v. Bass Bros. Enters., 1984-1 Trade Cas. (CCH) ¶ 66,041, at 68,621 (N.D. Ohio 1984).
62. *See* 1992 MERGER GUIDELINES, *supra* note 2, § 2.1. *See, e.g.*, FTC v. H.J. Heinz Co., 246 F.3d 708, 724-25 (D.C. Cir. 2001); *Elders Grain, Inc.*, 868 F.2d at 906; Hospital Corp. of Am. v. FTC, 807 F.2d 1381, 1389 (7th Cir. 1986).

collusion, where the agreement that is a necessary predicate for a Sherman Act Section 1 violation is lacking, not detectable, or not provable.[63] Both the courts and the 1992 *Merger Guidelines* recognize facilitating practices and accommodating behavior (where market participants accept higher prices) as forms of tacit collusion.[64]

The 1992 *Merger Guidelines* also recognize that a merger that eliminates a "maverick firm" may make coordination more likely.[65] A maverick firm is a firm that has a greater economic incentive than other firms in the market to deviate from terms of coordination.[66] Thus, a competitor may seek to merge with a maverick firm in an effort to enhance the chances that any attempt at coordinated interaction will be more likely to achieve the desired (anticompetitive) results.[67]

---

63. *See* 1992 MERGER GUIDELINES, *supra* note 2, § 2.1. *See, e.g.*, *Brown & Williamson Tobacco Corp.*, 509 U.S. at 238; *H.J. Heinz Co.*, 246 F.3d at 724-25; FTC v. Swedish Match, 131 F. Supp. 2d 151, 168 (D.D.C. 2000); FTC v. Cardinal Health, 12 F. Supp. 2d 34, 65 (D.D.C. 1998) ("Although the Court is not convinced from the record that the Defendants actually engaged in wrongdoing, it is persuaded that in the event of a merger, the Defendants would likely have an increased ability to coordinate their pricing practices").

64. Included among what may be termed "facilitating" practices or "industry" practices that make coordinated interaction easier are: replicating a direct dialog among market participants by means of seriatim, public speeches addressing competitive issues in which the participants "discuss" matters as to which they might wish to agree in ever more specific terms, and thereby suggest the terms of noncompetition; announcing price increases in advance; guaranteeing buyers they will not be charged a price higher than that charged to the seller's most favored customer, or guaranteeing buyers a rebate if the seller charges any purchaser a lower price within a specified period; using delivered pricing; and using pricing manuals or using pricing formula derived from a prior conspiracy or custom. *See* 6 PHILLIP E. AREEDA & HERBERT HOVENKAMP, ANTITRUST LAW ¶ 1435 (2d ed. 2003); *see also Brown & Williamson Tobacco Corp.*, 509 U.S. at 238.

65. 1992 MERGER GUIDELINES, *supra* note 2, § 2.12.

66. *See id.* According to the 1992 *Merger Guidelines*, a firm is more likely to be a maverick firm "the greater is its excess or divertable capacity in relation to its sales or its total capacity and the lower are its direct and opportunity costs of expanding sales in the relevant market." *Id.* (footnote omitted).

67. *See id.*; *see also* William J. Kolasky, Deputy Ass't Att'y Gen., Antitrust Div., Coordinated Effects in Merger Review: From Dead Frenchmen to Beautiful Minds and Mavericks, Remarks Before the ABA Section of Antitrust Law Spring Meeting (Apr. 24, 2002), *at*

The FTC's opinion in *B.F. Goodrich Co.*[68] provides a comprehensive discussion of coordinated interaction and the conditions that are required to achieve successful coordination:

> The effective coordination of price and output strategies requires developing a consensus concerning price and output levels, and a means of enforcing its terms. The first step requires harmonizing the incentives of participating firms and mitigating firm uncertainty concerning rival firms, so that they can effectively coordinate their behavior. The second step requires creating circumstances in which the prospective value to each participating firm of cheating on the consensus does not exceed the prospective loss from rival firm retaliation. In order to create and maintain these circumstances, participating firms must be able to monitor rival firm conduct; that is, they must be able to detect cheating on the consensus. They must also be able to retaliate effectively if and when cheating occurs.[69]

In the Commission's view, the structural aspects of the market are "crucially important" in determining whether collusion is feasible in a postmerger market.[70] Collusion is most likely in a market with the following characteristics:

> (1) relatively high barriers or impediments to entry; (2) a relatively high level of concentration; (3) a low level of product differentiation, and a low level of geographic differentiation occasioned by transportation cost differences; (4) a relatively inelastic demand for industry output at competitive price levels; (5) insignificant intra-industry differences in cost functions; (6) a large number of small buyers; (7) a high degree of transaction frequency and visibility; and (8) relatively stable and predictable demand and supply conditions.[71]

---

www.usdoj.gov/atr/public/speeches/11050.htm (explaining that the Antitrust Division's challenge to the Alcoa/Reynolds merger was predicated, in part, on evidence that Reynolds was a potential maverick in the relevant markets), *see generally* Baker, *supra* note 40.

68. 110 F.T.C. 207 (1988).

69. *Id.* at 294-95 (footnotes omitted).

70. *Id.* at 295; *see also*, Pate, *supra* note 54 ("At the Division, [an inquiry into the potential for coordinated effects] involves a fact-intensive inquiry in which we ask first, what constraints exist pre-merger on the incentive and ability of suppliers to coordinate; and second, how will the proposed merger change those constraints?").

71. *B.F. Goodrich Co.*, 110 F.T.C. at 295 (footnote omitted). Some commentators, however, have questioned the reliability of using the so-called "check list" approach to evaluate whether a proposed merger would increase the likelihood of coordinated anticompetitive effects. *See*

The courts and the federal enforcement agencies both recognize the importance of entry barriers to the likelihood of increased coordinated interaction following consummation of a proposed merger.[72] Decisions addressing entry barriers in the analysis of the likelihood of collusion have considered such evidence as delays that are likely to occur as a result of the need to build or expand necessary facilities,[73] the need to obtain permits,[74] the presence or lack of actual entry,[75] the prevalence of

---

David T. Scheffman and Mary Coleman, *Quantitative Analyses of Potential Competitive Effects from a Merger* (2003) (to be published in GEO. MASON U. L. REV.), *at* www.ftc.gov/be/quartmergeranalysis.pdf. (arguing that the check list approach – including that employed by the 1992 *Merge Guidelines* – is "too crude to provide much assistance in determining whether a coordinated interaction theory is relevant"); Andrew R. Dick, Acting Chief, Competition Policy Section, Economic Analysis Group, Antitrust Div., Coordinated Interaction: Pre-Merger Constraints and Post-Merger Effects, Remarks Before the Charles River Associates Conference, Current Topics in Merger and Antitrust Enforcement, (Dec. 11, 2002).

72. *See, e.g., H.J. Heinz Co.*, 246 F.3d at 724 ("The combination of a concentrated market and barriers to entry is a recipe for price coordination."); FTC v. Occidental Petroleum Corp., 1986-1 Trade Cas. (CCH) ¶ 67,071, at 62,513 (D.D.C. 1986) (where entry is easy, "collusive behavior will not be possible"); s*ee also* Statement of the FTC Concerning Royal Caribbean Cruises, Ltd./P&O Princess Cruises plc and Carnival Corp./P&O Princess Cruises plc (basing its rejection of a theory of coordinated reduction in industry capacity, in part, on evidence indicating the likelihood of entry or expansion postmerger).

73. *See* FTC v. Elders Grain, Inc., 868 F.2d 901, 905 (7th Cir. 1989) ("[S]ince .. . it takes three to nine years to design, build, and start operating a new mill ... colluding sellers need not fear that any attempt to restrict output in order to drive up price will be promptly nullified by new production"); FTC v. Owens-Illinois, Inc., 681 F. Supp. 27, 51 (D.D.C. 1988), *vacated as moot*, 850 F.2d 694 (D.C. Cir. 1988); B.F. Goodrich, 110 F.T.C. 207, 297, 301-03 (1988); United States v. UPM-Kymmene Oyj, No. 03C2528 (N.D. Ill. filed Apr. 15, 2003) (verified complaint); United States v. Alcoa, Inc., No. 00CV954 (RMU) (D.D.C. filed May 3, 2000) (complaint).

74. *See* FTC v. University Health, Inc., 938 F.2d 1206, 1219 (11th Cir. 1991) ("certificate of need law would facilitate an illegal cartel"); United States v. Rockford Mem'l Corp., 717 F. Supp. 1251, 1281 (N.D. Ill. 1989) (hospitals required to obtain certificate of need from state regulatory body before adding beds), *aff'd*, 898 F.2d 1278 (7th Cir. 1990); FTC v. Bass Bros. Enters., 1984-1 Trade Cas. (CCH) ¶ 66,041, at 68,613 (environmental regulations); *B.F. Goodrich*, 110 F.T.C. at 297, 298-99,

long-term supply contracts,[76] and the need to reach minimum scales of production in order to be profitable.[77]

Both the 1992 *Merger Guidelines* and the courts also acknowledge that product heterogeneity is a factor that affects whether a given market is conducive to coordination. Collusion among firms in a market is easier and more likely to the extent that the products sold by competitors are similar or homogeneous.[78] The level of product differentiation may be established by demonstrating the extent to which the product is a commodity (i.e., where consumers view the products of different sellers as interchangeable and select the product of a particular seller on the basis of price);[79] the presence or absence of different grades of the product;[80] and the potential for transportation costs to undermine the ability for postmerger producers to reach a consensus on price.[81]

To gauge whether demand is relatively inelastic and therefore collusion more likely, courts and the FTC have looked to the availability

---

301 (environmental permits).

75. *See H.J. Heinz Co.*, 246 F.3d at 717 (citing the lack of entry into the domestic jarred baby food market); FTC v. Swedish Match, 131 F. Supp. 2d at 171 (citing an unsuccessful attempt to enter the U.S. loose leaf tobacco market); *B.F. Goodrich*, 110 F.T.C. at 300.

76. *See Owens-Illinois, Inc.*, 681 F. Supp. at 51.

77. *See id.*

78. *See* Hospital Corp. of Am. v. FTC, 807 F.2d 1381, 1390 (7th Cir. 1986) ("[C]ollusion is more difficult the more heterogeneous the output of the colluding firms"); *B.F. Goodrich*, 110 F.T.C. at 315; Textron, Inc., Docket No. 9226, 1991 FTC LEXIS 459 (Oct. 4, 1991) (ALJ found that aerospace blind rivets were not fungible products as to which collusion is regarded as feasible); United States v. Alcoa, Inc., No. 00CV954 (RMU) (D.D.C. filed May 3, 2000) (complaint) (homogeneous smelter and chemical grade alumina); United States v. Imetal, No. 99-1018 (D.D.C. filed Apr. 26, 1999) (certain relevant products "are only slightly differentiated"); In the Matter of Degussa A.G. and Degussa Corporation, No. C-3813 (FTC June 10, 1998) (homogeneous hydrogen peroxide).

79. *See B.F. Goodrich*, 110 F.T.C. at 315.

80. *See* FTC v. Elders Grain, Inc., 868 F.2d 901, 905 (7th Cir. 1989) ("The varieties of industrial dry corn . . . appear to be largely standardized and homogenous, making it easier for sellers to agree on a common price to charge for them."); FTC v. Bass Bros. Enters., 1984-1 Trade Cas. (CCH) ¶ 66,041 at 68,612 ("nearly all of the producers produce basically the same grades and types" of the relevant product); B.F. Goodrich, Co. 110 F.T.C. 207, 315 (1988).

81. *See B.F. Goodrich*, 110 F.T.C. at 316-17.

of substitute products[82] and, if the product at issue is not an end product, the significance of the cost of the input product in relation to the cost of the end product.[83]

Collusion is also more likely where competitors face similar costs, including both production costs and transportation costs.[84]

Evidence that a small number of buyers purchase most of the product in the market indicates that sellers may not have a great deal of freedom in establishing prices[85] and thus may be less likely to adhere to a collusive agreement. Likewise, evidence that the sellers make only a few sales each year suggests that the incentive to "cheat" on an agreement with competitors is high.[86] By contrast, evidence that sellers engage in numerous transactions in the product over the year indicates a lesser

---

82. *See Elders Grain, Inc.*, 868 F.2d at 905; *B.F. Goodrich*, 110 F.T.C. at 319-20; United States v. Alcoa, Inc., No. 00CV954 (RMU) (D.D.C. filed May 3, 2000) (complaint) ("There are no products that are substitutes for [smelter grade alumina]").

83. *See B.F. Goodrich*, 110 F.T.C. at 319, 320.

84. *See* United States v. Baker Hughes, Inc., 908 F.2d, 981, 986 (D.C. Cir. 1990); United States v. Archer-Daniels-Midland Co., 781 F. Supp. 1400, 1423 (S.D. Iowa 1991) ("The record reflects that there are significant differences in production costs .. . among firms in the industry" which "would make agreement on a single collusive price difficult to achieve"); FTC v. Bass Bros. Enters., 1984-1 Trade Cas. (CCH) ¶ 66,041, at 68,612 (producers' "costs of production appear to be quite similar").

85. *See Baker Hughes, Inc.*, 908 F.2d at 986; *Elders Grain, Inc.*, 868 F.2d at 905 (sophisticated buyers may be able to persuade sellers to cheat on any collusive agreement); *Archer-Daniels-Midland Co.*, 781 F. Supp. at 1422; FTC v. R.R. Donnelley & Sons Co., 1990-2 Trade Cas. (CCH) ¶ 69,239, at 64,855 (D.D.C. 1990) ("[T]he sophistication and bargaining power of buyers play a significant role in assessing the effects of a proposed transaction."); FTC v. Owens-Illinois, Inc., 681 F. Supp. 27, 49 (D.D.C. 1988); Owens-Illinois, 115 F.T.C. 179, 326-27 (1992) (noting that "[a]s buyer concentration within a product market increases, the benefits from cheating to capture a customer's business increase relative to the magnitude of gains from collusion," and considering testimony of large buyer that indicated it had sufficient leverage to negotiate long-term requirements contracts "which specifically tie price increases to cost changes" and permitted the purchaser to audit the seller's costs and that its considerable purchases of items with respect to which its demand was elastic would permit it to defeat a price increase targeted at its inelastic consumption); *B.F. Goodrich*, 110 F.T.C. at 323-24.

86. *See Archer-Daniels-Midland Co.*, 781 F. Supp. at 1422; *Owens-Illinois, Inc.*, 681 F. Supp. at 49; *B.F. Goodrich*, 110 F.T.C. at 325.

incentive to cheat on any given transaction.[87] The extent to which transactions are made openly or through private negotiations also affects the degree to which cheating can be detected.[88] For example, in the Conoco/Phillips transaction, the FTC based its coordinated effects allegation pertaining to one relevant market, in part, on price transparency.[89] The federal enforcement agencies have also cited sales between competitors as a factor facilitating collusion.[90]

Lastly, the greater the stability and predictability of demand conditions, the more likely that coordination will be successful.[91]

---

87. *See B.F. Goodrich*, 110 F.T.C. at 325; Solvay S.A., 67 Fed. Reg. 30,929, 30,930 (FTC May 8, 2002) (analysis to aid public comment) ("[T]he large number of customers in the industry would make cheating on any coordination easy to detect").
88. *See Baker Hughes, Inc.*, 908 F.2d at 986 (the powerful purchasers "typically insist on receiving multiple, confidential bids for each order"); FTC v. Swedish Match, 131 F. Supp. 2d 151, 168 n.13 (D.D.C. 2000) ("[T]he merger will only increase the likelihood of coordinated action because it creates a duopoly, the monitoring of prices is easy, and firms can punish price cutters."); *Archer-Daniels-Midland Co.*, 781 F. Supp. at 1422, 1423; *Owens-Illinois, Inc.*, 681 F. Supp. at 51; ("Owens-Illinois and Brockway could readily 'police' the cartel because . . . purchasers do not use sealed bids, but instead discuss competitive bids with potential suppliers."); B.F. Goodrich, Co. 110 F.T.C. 207, 325 (1988).
89. *See* Conoco Inc., 67 Fed. Reg. 30,929, 30,930 (FTC May 8, 2002) (analysis to aid public comment); *see also* In the Matter of Solvay S.A., No. C-4046 (FTC Apr. 29, 2002) (complaint) (alleging increased potential for collusion in light of readily available pricing information); United States v. Alcoa, Inc., No. 00CV954 (RMU) (D.D.C. filed May 3, 2000) (complaint) (alleging an increased likelihood of anticompetitive coordination, in part, because of transparent actions by suppliers and customers).
90. *See* United States v. UPM-Kymmene Oyj, No. 03C2528 (N.D. Ill. filed Apr. 15, 2003) (verified complaint) (alleging that an existing supply arrangement between the only two postmerger competitors provides them "with the motivations, opportunities, and means to coordinate on price, monitor adherence, [and] punish cheating"); Degussa AG, 63 Fed. Reg. 16,552, 16,553 (FTC Apr. 3, 1998) (analysis to aid public comment); *see also* Shell Oil Co., 62 Fed. Reg. 67,868, 67,870 (FTC Dec. 30, 1997) (analysis to aid public comment) (citing exchange agreements between petroleum marketers as enhancing ability to collude).
91. *See Owens-Illinois, Inc.*, 681 F. Supp. at 51 (stable prices, making price fluctuations detectable); *B.F. Goodrich*, 110 F.T.C. at 326-27; United States v. Alcoa, Inc., No. 00CV954 (RMU) (D.D.C. filed May 3, 2000)

Collusion is more difficult in a market in which supply or demand conditions are unpredictable and where producers may have excess capacity and, therefore, greater incentive to cheat.[92] Relevant evidence includes market growth and the degree of producers' excess capacity.[93] Courts and the agencies also will consider evidence of past efforts at collusion.[94]

C. Unilateral Anticompetitive Effects

A merger can raise competitive concerns if it creates the opportunity for the unilateral exercise of market power.[95] The most obvious concern (and one that for obvious reasons is subsumed by market concentration analysis) is that a merger will give rise to a monopoly. A monopoly is the state that "exists when one firm controls all or the bulk of a product's output, and no other firm can enter the market or expand output at comparable costs."[96] The "monopolist has the power to raise price above

---

(complaint) (citing "stable, predictable and inelastic demand and supply" as facilitating anticompetitive coordination).

92. *See Owens-Illinois, Inc.*, 681 F. Supp. at 49 (considering lack of excess capacity as factor "favor[ing] collusive behavior"); *B.F. Goodrich*, 110 F.T.C. at 326-27. *But see* Kolasky, *supra* note 67 ("[E]xcess capacity in the hands of leading firms can be an effective tool for punishing cheating and thereby enforcing collusive agreements").

93. *See* FTC v. Elders Grain, Inc., 868 F.2d 901, 905-06 (7th Cir. 1989) (excess capacity suggested that there would be an incentive to cheat on any agreement); *B.F. Goodrich*, 110 F.T.C. at 326-27.

94. *See* FTC v. H.J. Heinz Co., 246 F.3d 708, 724 (D.C. Cir. 2001) (citing evidence of price leadership in the baby food industry); *Elders Grain, Inc.*, 868 F.2d at 905; *Swedish Match*, 131 F. Supp. 2d at 168; United States v. Archer-Daniels-Midland Co., 781 F. Supp. 1400, 1421 (S.D. Iowa 1991) ("There is no evidence of a pattern of disciplined or coordinated pricing."); Conoco Inc., 67 Fed. Reg. 57,235, 57,236 (FTC Sept. 9, 2002) (analysis to aid public comment).

95. *See* 1992 MERGER GUIDELINES, *supra* note 2, § 2.21; Timothy J. Muris, Chairman, FTC, Antitrust Enforcement at the Federal Trade Commission: In a Word--Continuity, Remarks Before the ABA Antitrust Section (Aug. 7, 2001), *at* www.ftc.gov/speeches/muris/murisaba.htm ("although we have always had what could be called 'unilateral effects' theories, they have evolved, and they have been more widely applied since the 1992 revision of the Guidelines").

96. 2A PHILLIP E. AREEDA, HERBERT HOVENKAMP & JOHN L. SOLOW, ANTITRUST LAW ¶ 403a (2d ed. 2002). This is also known as the "dominant firm" unilateral effects model. *See* David T. Scheffman and

competitive levels by restricting its output, because the output reduction cannot be offset by expanded output of others."[97]

Another possible concern, although far less frequently encountered, is the possibility for a merger to give rise to monopsony power, that is the power of a buyer to control price or output.[98] For example, in *United States v. Cargill, Inc.*,[99] the government challenged the proposed acquisition by Cargill of Continental Grain Company's Commodity Marketing Group. The government concluded that the acquisition would have eliminated an important competitor for the purchase of crops from U.S. farmers and other grain and soybean suppliers at port, river, and rail elevators in several markets around the country. Rather than a concern about the ability of the combining firms to raise prices after the merger, the concern here was the ability of the combining firms to artificially depress the price they paid suppliers after the merger. Consequently, the

---

Mary Coleman, *Quantitative Analyses of Potential Competitive Effects from a Merger* (2003) (to be published in GEO. MASON U.L. REV.), *at* www.ftc.gov/be/quartmergeranalysis.pdf (explaining that "a merger might result in higher prices either because the merger creates a dominant firm or significantly enhances the ability of an existing firm to raise prices"); Jeffrey Church and Roger Ware, INDUSTRIAL ORGANIZATION: A STRATEGIC APPROACH § 4.2 (2000).

97. *Id. See also* Chicago Bridge & Iron Co., Dkt. No. 9300, 2003 FTC LEXIS 96 (June 18, 2003) (upholding challenge to transaction where merger of two strongest suppliers enabled CB&I to increase prices up until the point where the other less strong suppliers begin to constrain it, and CB&I has the ability to exercise market power as a result of the acquisition of the only other competitor that had constrained CB&I). As of March 1, 2004, an appeal was pending before the full Commission.

98. *See, e.g.*, United States v. Syufy Enters., 903 F.2d 659, 663 (9th Cir. 1990); United States v. Rice Growers Ass'n, 1986-2 Trade Cas. ¶ 67,288 (E.D. Cal. 1986); United States v. Penzoil Co., 252 F. Supp. 962 (W.D. Pa. 1965). *See generally* Roger Blair & Jeffrey Harrison, MONOPSONY 81-84 (1993).

99. No. 99-CV-1875 (D.D.C. filed July 8, 1999) (complaint); 2000 WL 1475752 (D.D.C.) (final judgment) (holding that "The proposed Final Judgment addresses competitive concerns that arose from the way the original acquisition was structured. The divestiture would preserve competition in the nine relevant markets, and allow new entrants into the industry an opportunity to compete with the existing companies. In addition, shortening the non-compete provision in the acquisition from five to three years ensures that Continental may re-enter the grain business sooner, giving it a fair opportunity to regain the loyalty of former Continental suppliers and customers").

government required the parties to divest four of Continental's six port elevators, four of its twenty-seven river elevators, and one of its fourteen rail terminals.[100]

In *United States v. Aetna, Inc.*,[101] the government contended that the transaction would restrict competition for the sale of health maintenance organization (HMO) and HMO-based point-of-service (HMO-POS) health plans in Houston and Dallas, Texas. The complaint alleged that this reduction in competition would enable Aetna to unduly depress physicians' reimbursement rates in addition to giving Aetna market power to increase prices or reduce quality of HMO and HMO-POS plans in the area.[102]

The potential for unilateral anticompetitive effects is analyzed most frequently in markets in which products are differentiated—that is, the products sold by market participants are not perfect substitutes for one another.[103] Where products in a market are somewhat differentiated, market participants may compete most directly with the firms selling the closest substitutes for their own products.[104] Thus, in such a market, if two competitors producing differentiated products merge, the merged firm may reduce competition by raising the price of either or both

---

100. *See id.*
101. No. 3-99-CV-1398-H (N.D. Tex. filed Aug. 3, 1999) (revised competitive impact statement).
102. *See id.* at 9.
103. *See* 1992 MERGER GUIDELINES, *supra* note 2, § 2.21. In the Bertrand model of competition among differentiated products, the merged entity raises one or more of its prices. *See* David T. Scheffman and Mary Coleman, *Quantitative Analyses of Potential Competitive Effects from a Merger* (2003) (to be published in GEO. MASON U.L. REV.) (explaining that if the merged entity raises one or more of its prices, "the result is that the demand faced by other competitors is increased, and those competitors react unilaterally to the increase in demand, which will generally involve an increase in their (unit) sales (generally at somewhat higher prices)"); *see also* Dennis W. Carlton & Jeffrey M. Perloff, MODERN INDUSTRIAL ORGANIZATION § 6 (2000).
104. *See* 1992 MERGER GUIDELINES, *supra* note 2, § 2.21. The 1992 MERGER GUIDELINES state that this analysis also will be applied in markets where "sellers are primarily distinguished by their relative advantages in serving different customers or groups of buyers, and buyers negotiate individually with sellers." *Id*. § 2.21 n.21. A market participant's closest competitor, in such a market, is a seller with "similar relative advantages in serving particular buyers or groups of buyers." *Id.* This may, of course, include advantages in serving certain customers conferred by geography.

products to a level above the premerger prices.[105] Some of the sales lost on the product for which the price has been increased will merely be diverted to the other product.[106] The price increase may be profitable postmerger even if it would not have been profitable premerger, provided that the profit margin for the product from which sales are diverted is narrower than the profit margin for the product to which sales are diverted.[107]

FTC v. Swedish Match[108] was one of the first cases to validate the differentiated product diversion theory. This acquisition would have combined the nation's largest and third-largest makers and sellers of loose leaf chewing tobacco, giving Swedish Match approximately 60 percent of sales and creating a market where two firms would control 90 percent of sales. The parties abandoned the transaction after the district court issued a preliminary injunction. The court found that "the weight of the evidence demonstrates that a unilateral price increase by Swedish Match is likely after the acquisition because it will eliminate one of Swedish Match's primary direct competitors."[109] The FTC argued that the acquisition was likely to result in significant anticompetitive effects based on relatively high diversion ratios between the merging firms and the sizable existing price-cost margins.[110] The court, agreeing with the

---

105. *See id.* § 2.21; *see also* Jonathan B. Baker, Director, Bureau of Economics, FTC, Product Differentiation Through Space and Time: Some Antitrust Policy Issues, Remarks Before the Antitrust & Trade Regulation Comm. of the Ass'n of the Bar of the City of New York (Feb. 6, 1996), *at* www.ftc.gov/speeches/other/elec1029.htm. Carl Shapiro, *Mergers with Differentiated Products*, ANTITRUST, Spring 1996, at 23; Charles E. Biggio, Senior Counsel, Antitrust Div., Antitrust for High Tech Companies, Remarks Before the Corporate Counsel Institute and Business Developers Associates (Feb. 2, 1996), *at* www.usdoj.gov/atr/public/speeches/biggiospc.htm. *See generally,* Timothy J. Muris, *Product Differentiation: Economics and Antitrust,* 5 GEO. MASON L. REV. 303 (1997).
106. *See* 1992 MERGER GUIDELINES, *supra* note 2, § 2.21.
107. *See id.*
108. 131 F. Supp 2d 151 (D.D.C. 2000).
109. *Id.* at 169; *see also* Molly S. Boast, Acting Director, Bureau of Competition, FTC, Prepared Remarks Before the American Bar Association Antitrust Section Spring Meeting (Mar. 29, 2001), *at* www.ftc.gov/speeches/boast.htm.
110. *See* 131 F. Supp. 2d at 169 (agreeing with the FTC, the court noted: "Two factors are of particular concern in determining this likelihood. First, the price –cost margin for National is important because it determines the profit that will be retained by Swedish Match by users

FTC's diversion theory, explained, "Swedish Match will raise prices as long as the profit gained by the higher prices of Swedish Match products in addition to the profits diverted to National's brands is greater than the profits lost through diversion to non-Swedish Match brands."[111] The court found that any postmerger efficiencies asserted by the parties were insufficient to mitigate the resulting post-acquisition high market share and increased concentration of the merged firm.

In challenging a ski resort merger under the unilateral effects theory, the Division explained its mode of analysis:

> Economists have developed an analytical framework to explain how a merger can allow a firm to charge higher prices after acquiring a competitor, even if firms do not coordinate their behavior (such as by explicitly colluding with one another). ... This framework has been called a ["]unilateral effects" model. It is particularly useful in markets that have differentiated products, that is, where products of different firms are not identical. . . . This unilateral effects model is an additional tool to examine the accepted, common-sense notion that a merger is more likely to have a harmful effect if the merging firms are close competitors.
>
> Before a merger, increases in price by two independent resorts are deterred by the loss of customers that would result from a price increase. If resorts are put under common ownership by a merger, however, they no longer constrain each other's prices in the same way. A merger can make a price increase profitable. In particular, before a merger, if two resorts are significant competitors to each other and one of these resorts increases its prices, a significant proportion of this resort's customers would be "lost" to the other resort. After merger between these two resorts, however, some customers who switch away from the resort that raises its price would no longer be lost, but rather would be "recaptured" at the newly-acquired resort. Price increases that would have been unprofitable to either firm alone, therefore, would become profitable to the merged entity.
>
> As a result of this recapture phenomenon, a merged firm, acting independently to earn the most profits it can, will choose higher prices than its two component firms did before the merger, if those firms were significant competitors to each other before the merger. The loss of competition that arises as a result of this

---

who switch from Swedish Match's brands to National's brands. ... Second, the diversion ratio is important because it calculates the percentage of lost sales that go to National. High margins and high diversion ratios support large price increases, a tenet endorsed by most economists").

111. *Id*. at 169-170.

> effect is what is meant by a "unilateral" anticompetitive effect, that is, an effect that does not depend on the firms in the market acting interdependently. This unilateral effect will be larger as the recapture rate (which is sometimes called the "diversion ratio," . . .) is larger, as the margin earned on recaptured customers is higher, and as the customers who leave the merging firms in response to a price increase are fewer (in technical terms, the lower the "own price elasticity").[112]

The government also employed a unilateral effects analysis in challenging the merger of Gillette and Parker pen companies. In *United States v. Gillette Co.*,[113] the court, however, rejected the government's allegation of a premium fountain pen market in favor of a premium writing instrument product market. Moreover, the court found that any price increase on premium fountain pens would cause Gillette to lose customers to other pen types. Finally, the court determined that market entry was relatively easy, making it unlikely that Gillette could unilaterally raise prices on its premium fountain pens without fostering entry into the wider premium writing instrument market.[114]

Anticompetitive effects in a market of differentiated products are most likely to materialize (and a merger may make possible "substantial unilateral price elevation"[115]) in a market in which "a significant share of

---

112. United States v. Vail Resorts, Inc., 1997-2 Trade Cas. (CCH) ¶ 72,030, at 81,142-43 (D. Colo. 1997) (competitive impact statement).
113. 828 F. Supp. 78 (D.D.C. 1993).
114. *See id.* at 84-85. Several cases have found that the existence of significant barriers to entry can be a reliable indicator that the merger may result in illegal anticompetitive effects. *See* FTC v. H.J. Heinz, 246 F.3d 708, 717 (D.C. Cir. 2001) (finding "the anticompetitive effect of the merger is further enhanced by high barriers to entry"); FTC v. Libbey, 211 F. Supp. 2d 34, 48-49 (D.D.C. 2002) (stating "The FTC presented convincing evidence that there are many barriers to entry into the food service glassware market. . . . It is therefore the Court's opinion that if RCP were unable to effectively replace Anchor as a viable competitor in the market, it is unlikely to be replaced by new entrants. If this occurs, the amended acquisition agreement would obviously have an anti-competitive impact on the market").
115. 1992 MERGER GUIDELINES, *supra* note 2, § 2.21. Areeda and Hovenkamp point out that the "substantial unilateral price elevation" must be a lower threshold than the "small but significant and nontransitory price increase" posited in market definition, because if the two merging competitors could impose the small but significant and nontransitory price increase, then those two firms would constitute the only participants in the relevant market, resulting in a merged firm with a 100% market share and an HHI of 10,000. PHILLIP E. AREEDA &

sales" in the market are made to buyers who "regard the products of the merging firms as their first and second choices"[116] and where it is unlikely that nonmerging firms in the market will reposition their product lines to replace the competition between the merging parties.[117] For

---

HERBERT HOVENKAMP, ANTITRUST LAW ¶ 901 (Supp. 1998); Timothy J. Muris, Chairman, FTC, Opening Remarks Before the FTC's Roundtable on Understanding Mergers: Strategy and Planning, Implementation, and Outcomes (Dec. 9, 2002), *at* www.ftc.gov/speeches/muris/mergers021209.htm.

116. 1992 MERGER GUIDELINES, *supra* note 2, § 2.21; *see also Heinz Co.*, 246 F.3d at 716-17 (establishing prima facie case that merger of second and third largest jarred baby food manufacturers in three firm market, with 17.4% and 15.4% market shares, respectively, would be anticompetitive resulting in an increase in the Herfindahl-Hirschman Index (HHI) of 510 points); *Libbey, Inc.*, 211 F. Supp. 2d at 38-39 (finding "The food service glassware market . . . is a 'highly concentrated' market. . . . Libby currently has a market share in excess of 65 percent. .. . Anchor is Libbey's most formidable competitor in the foodservice glassware market."); FTC v. Swedish Match, 131 F. Supp. 2d 151, 153-55 (D.D.C. 2000) (upholding challenge to merger of the largest and third largest producers of loose leaf tobacco in the United States; United States v. General Dynamics Corp., No. 1-01-CV-02200 (D.D.C. filed October 23, 2001) (verified complaint) (alleging that General Dynamics and Newport News were the only two nuclear-capable shipyards and the only designers and producers of nuclear submarines for the U.S. Navy); United States v. SunGard Data Sys., Inc., 172 F. Supp. 2d 172 (D.D.C. 2001) (declining to enjoin the transaction, the court found that the DOJ failed to prove that shared hotsite services were a relevant product market despite plaintiff's argument that SunGard and Comdisco are two of only three large providers of shared hotsite computer disaster recovery services.); *Justice Department Requires Suiza Foods and Dean Foods to Divest 11 Dairy Processing Plants*, (press release Dec. 18, 2001) (finding that many fluid milk customers regarded Suiza and Dean as their next best substitutes to supply milk).

117. *See, e.g.*, United States v. Kimberly-Clark Corp., 1996-1 Trade Cas. (CCH) ¶ 71,405, at 77,053 (N.D. Tex. 1996) (consent decree requiring divestiture in facial tissues and baby wipes markets); United States v. Interstate Bakeries Corp., 1996-1 Trade Cas. (CCH) ¶ 71,271, at 76,190 (N.D. Ill. 1996) (consent decree requiring divestiture in white pan bread market); Timothy J. Muris, Chairman, FTC, Opening Remarks Before the FTC's Roundtable on Understanding Mergers: Strategy and Planning, Implementation, and Outcomes (Dec. 9, 2002), *at* www.ftc.gov/speeches/muris/merger021209.htm ("The strength of the affirmative case matters – i.e., a 2-to-1 or 3-to-2 mergers in well defined

example, the Division has challenged mergers in the radio industry because of the potential for unilateral effects when an advertiser's first and second choice radio stations merge.[118] Although both radio stations may generally compete with others in the same relevant market, varying consumer preferences mean different radio formats reach different audiences.[119] If the owner of a rock station purchases the only other rock station and no other radio format can reach the same audience, an advertiser's options are limited substantially by the merger.[120] The advertiser's ability to negotiate price is diminished if his or her third choice is too remote a substitute.[121] The merged firm is now able to raise prices unilaterally.[122]

The 1992 *Merger Guidelines* presume "that a significant share of sales are accounted for by consumers who regard the products of the merging firms as their first and second choices" where (1) each product's market share reflects not only its relative appeal as the first choice of the consumers of the products of the merging firms, but also its relative appeal as a second choice,[123] (2) market concentration figures "fall

---

markets protected from entry are likely to pass the anticompetitive theory test simply because of very low numbers of competitors").

118. *See* Joel I. Klein, Ass't Att'y Gen., Antitrust Div., DOJ Analysis of Radio Mergers, Remarks Presented at the ANA Hotel (Feb. 19, 1997), *at* www.usdoj.gov/atr/public/speeches/jik97219.htm; *see also* United States v. Capstar Broad., 64 Fed. Reg. 31,612, 31,622 (June 11, 1999) (competitive impact statement) (requiring divestiture of Wichita radio stations because the acquisition would likely give the merged firm the unilateral power to raise advertising rates and reduce the level of service); United States v. CBS Corp., 63 Fed. Reg. 18,036, 18,045 (Apr. 13, 1998) (proposed final judgment and competitive impact statement) (requiring divestiture of radio stations in Boston, St. Louis, and Baltimore because of their strength in delivering access to certain audiences the transaction is likely to give the postmerger firm the unilateral power to raise prices and reduce the level of service).

119. *See* Joel I. Klein, Ass't Att'y Gen., Antitrust Div., DOJ Analysis of Radio Mergers, Remarks Presented at the ANA Hotel (Feb. 19, 1997), *at* www.usdoj.gov/atr/public/speeches/jik97219.htm.

120. *See id.*

121. *See id.*

122. *See id.*

123. The 1992 *Merger Guidelines* indicate that these consumer preferences may be determined from "marketing surveys, information from bidding structures, or normal course of business documents from industry participants." 1992 MERGER GUIDELINES, *supra* note 2, § 2.211 n.22. The 1992 *Merger Guidelines* recognize that market shares may either

outside the safeharbor regions" of the 1992 *Merger Guidelines*, and (3) the "merging firms have a combined market share of at least thirty-five percent."[124]

Officials at both the Division and the FTC have stated that for mergers in industries with highly differentiated products problems arise in relying on the traditional methods of market definition and market shares to assess the competitive consequences.[125] If a clear break in the

---

overstate or understate the anticompetitive effect at issue in such a market. The effect may be understated where the products of the merging firms are closest and overstated where the products are more dissimilar. *See id.* § 2.211; Steven C. Salop, *The First Principles Approach to Antitrust: Kodak, and Antitrust at the Millennium*, 68 ANTITRUST L.J. 187 (2000); Jonathan B. Baker and Steven C. Salop, *Symposium in the Antitrust Analysis of Mergers: Merger Guidelines vs. Five Forces*, 33 U. WEST L.A. L. REV. (2001); Gregory J. Werden, *Assigning Market Shares*, 70 ANTITRUST L.J. 67 (2002).

124. 1992 MERGER GUIDELINES, *supra* note 2, § 2.211. This does not necessarily mean that a safe harbor exists if there is evidence that the merging firms are each other's closest competitors. *See* Charles E. Biggio, Merger Enforcement at the Antitrust Division, Remarks Before the Antitrust Law Committee Chicago Bar Association (May 15, 1996) at 3, *at* www.usdoj.gov/atr/speeches/chibar.htm (stating that the threshold amounts are not a guarantee that the Division will not pursue a unilateral effects case where the combined market share is less than 35%); Gregory J. Werden, *Assigning Market Shares*, 70 ANTITRUST L.J. 67 (2002).

125. *See* Jonathan B. Baker, Director, Bureau of Economics, FTC, Product Differentiation Through Space and Time: Some Antitrust Policy Issues, Remarks Before the Antitrust & Trade Regulation Comm. of the Ass'n of the Bar of the City of New York (Feb. 6, 1996), *at* www.ftc.gov/speeches/other/bakst.htm; Jonathan B. Baker, Director, Bureau of Economics, FTC, Contemporary Empirical Merger Analysis, Remarks Before the George Mason University Law Symposium (Oct. 11, 1996) *at* www.ftc.gov/speeches/other/gmu5.htm; Carl Shapiro, *Mergers with Differentiated Products*, ANTITRUST, Spring 1996; Daniel L. Rubinfeld, Antitrust Enforcement at DOJ: An Economist's Perspective, Remarks Before the Ass'n of the Bar of the City of New York (Nov. 17, 1997); Steven C. Salop, *The First Principles Approach to Antitrust, Kodak, and Antitrust at the Millennium*, 68 ANTITRUST L.J. 187 (2000); Jonathan B. Baker and Steven C. Salop, *Symposium in the Antitrust Analysis of Mergers: Merger Guidelines vs. Five Forces*, 33 U. WEST LA. L. REV. 3 (2001); Gregory J. Werden, Assigning Market Shares, 70 ANTITRUST L.J. 67 (2002); Timothy J. Muris, Chairman, FTC, Improving the Economic Foundations of Competitive Policy, Remarks Before George Mason Univ. Law Review's Winter Antitrust Symposium (Jan.

chain of substitutes does not exist, they argue that differentiation within a relevant market can lead to localized competitive problems that depend little on the precise definition of market boundaries.[126] Some enforcement officials have even argued that if a merger can be shown to harm competition directly, a market must exist in which the harm occurred and the precise boundaries of the market are not necessary for finding an antitrust violation.[127] This appears to run counter, however, to Section 7's language regarding effect on a line of commerce.

Despite the closeness of the merging firms' products to one another, however, there should be no competitive concerns where the competitors of the merged firm have the capability and capacity to reposition their product lines to replace lost competition.[128] The focus is on whether competitors of the merged firm are likely to increase their own output (given contractual commitments or other binding capacity restraints and the expense of increased capacity) to the level necessary to make a price increase by the merged firms unprofitable. Competing firms might not be able to do so, for example, because they face "binding capacity

---

15, 2003), *at* www.ftc.gov/speeches/muris/improveconfoundatio.htm.

126. *See* Jonathan B. Baker, Director, Bureau of Economics, FTC, Product Differentiation Through Space and Time: Some Antitrust Policy Issues, Remarks Before the Antitrust & Trade Regulation Comm. of the Ass'n of the Bar of the City of New York (Feb. 6, 1996), *at* www.ftc.gov/speeches/other/bakst.htm; Jonathan B. Baker, Director, Bureau of Economics, FTC, Contemporary Empirical Merger Analysis, Remarks Before the George Mason University Law Symposium (Oct. 11, 1996), *at* www.ftc.gov/speeches/other/gmu5.htm; Carl Shapiro, *Mergers with Differentiated Products*, ANTITRUST, Spring 1996, at 23, 28-29; Steven C. Salop, *The First Principles Approach to Antitrust: Kodak, and Antitrust at the Millennium*, 68 ANTITRUST L.J. 187 (2000); Jonathan B. Baker and Steven C. Salop, *Symposium in the Antitrust Analysis of Mergers: Merger Guidelines vs. Five Forces*, 33 (2001); Gregory J. Werden, Assigning Market Shares, 70 ANTITRUST L.J. 67 (2002); Muris, *supra* note 125.

127. *See* Jonathan B. Baker, Director, Bureau of Economics, FTC, Product Differentiation Through Space and Time: Some Antitrust Policy Issues, Remarks Before the Antitrust & Trade Regulation Comm. of the Ass'n of the Bar of the City of New York (Feb. 6, 1996), *at* www.ftc.gov/speeches/other/bakst.htm (arguing that a "res ipsa loquitur" market definition should be used in antitrust law).

128. *See* Jonathan B. Baker and Steven C. Salop, *Symposium in the Antitrust Analysis of Mergers: Merger Guidelines vs. Five Forces*, 33 U. WEST L.A. L. REV. 3 (2001); Carl Shapiro, *Mergers with Differentiated Products*, ANTITRUST, Spring 1996, at 23.

constraints that could not be economically relaxed within two years" or because the cost of using currently excess capacity is significantly higher than the cost of operating current capacity.[129]

Application of unilateral effects analysis sometimes has led the government enforcement agencies not to challenge transactions.[130] In investigating the proposed merger of Van de Kamp and Mrs. Paul's, two of the three major suppliers of branded prepared fish products, the Division inquired as to whether the merged firm could profitably sustain a unilateral price increase after the merger.[131] Initially, the evidence suggested that Mrs. Paul's, Van de Kamp, and Gorton competed head-to-head without any substitution from other types of fish or nonfish frozen products.[132] Detailed scanner data provided price and quantity information which enabled the Division to estimate demand elasticities at both the market and individual firm level.[133] The data indicated mixed

---

129. 1992 MERGER GUIDELINES, *supra* note 2, § 2.21; *see, e.g.*, United States v. Gillette Co., 828 F. Supp. 78, 84-85 (D.D.C. 1993) (producers of fountain pens could not unilaterally raise prices because other producers could reposition their products).

130. *See* Constance K. Robinson, Director of Operations, Antitrust Div., Quantifying Unilateral Effects in Investigations and Cases, Remarks Before the Health Care Antitrust Forum (May 12, 1997); Jonathan B. Baker, *Unilateral Competitive Effects Theories in Merger Analysis*, ANTITRUST, Spring 1997, at 21; Jonathan B. Baker, Director, Bureau of Economics, FTC, Product Differentiation Through Space and Time: Some Antitrust Policy Issues, Remarks Before the Antitrust & Trade Regulation Comm. of the Ass'n of the Bar of the City of New York (Feb. 6, 1996); Carl Shapiro, *Mergers with Differentiated Products*, ANTITRUST, Spring 1996, at 23. *See generally* ANTITRUST, Spring 1997 (collecting a number of articles on unilateral effects).

131. *See* Robinson, *supra* note 130.

132. *See id*. at 3.

133. *See id*; *see also* Timothy J. Muris, Chairman, FTC, Improving the Economic Foundations of Competitive Policy, Remarks Before George Mason Univ. Law Review's Winter Antitrust Symposium (Jan. 15, 2003) (contending that the scanner data approach does not incorporate New Institutional Economics. "Econometric analyses of retail scanner data and highly simple simulation models are used based on what economists call a 'one-shot Bertrand' model. This approach has at least two major problems that proper attention to NIE would have identified. . . . the data are at the retail level while the mergers are between manufacturers. . . . the Bertrand model is imposed with virtually no analysis of its actual ability to explain competition in the market"); Dan Hosken et al., *Demand System Estimation and its Application to Horizontal Merger*

results as to whether a postmerger price increase would be profitable.[134] Although there appeared to be some substitutability between Mrs. Paul's and Van de Kamp, consumers seemed very sensitive to price increases and data indicated that other frozen seafood products besides frozen prepared seafood were viewed as substitutes.[135] This inconsistent data assisted the agency in deciding not to challenge the proposed merger.[136]

In *FTC v. Staples, Inc.*,[137] the Commission obtained a preliminary injunction against the consummation of a merger between Staples and Office Depot by convincing the court that in light of the parties' own pricing practices, including evidence of lower prices in markets where Staples competed with Office Depot and Office Max, and highest prices in markets where only one chain competed, the merger would allow the combined entity to increase prices or maintain them at anticompetitive levels in the highly concentrated submarket of superstores selling consumable office supplies—as distinguished from smaller stationery stores.[138]

In contrast to the successful government challenge in *Staples*, the government failed to block a hospital merger in *United States v. Long Island Jewish Medical Center.*[139] The government had argued that the merger would combine the only two "anchor hospitals" (full service hospitals necessary to the formation of a managed care network) in Queens and Nassau counties, thereby allowing the resulting entity to raise its prices unilaterally. The court was persuaded not only that the anchor hospital product market definition was too narrow but that prices charged by a nearby single anchor hospital were not supracompetitive as the government's theory indicated they should be.[140] Moreover, the court was impressed with the parties' commitment to pass along to consumers

---

Analysis (Apr. 2002) (FTC Bureau of Economics Working Paper #246), *at* www.ftc.gov/be/workpapers/wp246.pdf; Federal Trade Commission, Bureau of Economics, Best Practices for Data and Economic and Financial Analyses in Antitrust Investigations (Nov. 7, 2002), *at* www.ftc.gov/be/ftcbebp.pdf ; David Sheffman, Malcom Coate, and Louis Silvia, 20 Years of Merger Guidelines Enforcement at the FTC: An Economic Perspective (June 2002), *at* www.usdoj.gov/atr/hmerger/11255.htm.

134. *See Robinson, supra* note 130 at 4.
135. *See id.*
136. *See id.*
137. 970 F. Supp. 1066 (D.D.C. 1997).
138. *Id.* at 1082, 1083.
139. 983 F. Supp. 121 (E.D. N.Y. 1997).
140. *See id.* at 138.

a predicted $25 to $30 million in annual cost savings from merger-specific efficiencies and to guarantee an additional $50 million to local community programs and services.[141]

In *United States v. Interstate Bakeries Corp.*,[142] the DOJ challenged a proposed merger of Continental, the largest baker of fresh bread in the United States and the maker of two brands, with Interstate, the third largest baker and maker of at least four brands. The DOJ alleged that the relevant product market was "white pan bread baked by wholesale and captive bakeries sold through retail food stores," and that the merger "would likely cause Interstate to raise its prices for white pan bread sold under its brands and the brands it is acquiring from Continental."[143] According to the DOJ, consumers have a strong preference for white pan bread over other varieties of bread, and for premium over other types of white pan bread. They also have strong preferences for particular brands. Thus, the DOJ asserted, if the price of a particular premium brand were increased slightly, few customers would shift away, and of those who did shift, most would switch to other premium brands of white pan bread.[144]

---

141. *See id.* at 148-49; *see also* FTC v. H.J. Heinz Co., 246 F.3d 708 (D.C. Cir. 2001). Commentators have argued that the *Heinz* court ignored important efficiencies that would have occurred post-merger. *See* Timothy J. Muris, Chairman, FTC, Opening Remarks Before the FTC's Roundtable on "Understanding Mergers: Strategy and Planning Implementation, and Outcomes" (Dec. 9, 2002) ("The critical issue in that case was whether the merger was a 3-to-2 merger of head-to-head competitors (or a 2-to-1 merger of competitors competing vigorously for shelf space) or instead, a transaction that would actually enhance competition by combining two weak brands into one that could at last challenge the dominance of Gerber. If the evidence supported the 3-to-2 head-to-head competitor characterization (or the 2-to-1 competitors for shelf space characterization. . . .), the structural presumptions, rightfully, would have likely trumped, at the preliminary injunction stage, what was a solid and substantial efficiency claim. The parties lost, in part, because the district court judge ignored both antitrust economics and relevant precedent, and did not even allow the substantial customer testimony supporting the merger, let alone give that testimony proper weight."); Timothy J. Muris, *The Government and Merger Efficiencies: Still Hostile After All These Years*, 7 GEO. MASON L. REV. 729 (1999).

142. 1996-1 Trade Cas. (CCH) ¶ 71,271 (N.D. Ill. 1996) (consent decree).

143. *Id.*

144. The government also alleged that entry was unlikely due to the cost of establishing a premium brand. *Id.*

Similarly, in *United States v. Vail Resorts, Inc.*,[145] the Division challenged the proposed acquisition by Vail Resorts of three ski resorts owned by Ralston Resorts. The DoJ calculated that in a Front Range, Colorado skier market, the postmerger HHI would be approximately 2228, with an increase of approximately 643 points.[146] The DOJ concluded that the Vail and Ralston Resorts were "close competitive alternatives for a number of Front Range skiers" and that each would lose customers to the other if they raised their respective prices.[147] The Division conducted its unilateral effects analysis by collecting information on elasticities, margins, and recapture ratios, and then estimated that "if the merger were allowed to take place without any divestiture, there would be an overall average increase in Front Range discounted lift ticket prices on the order of 4%, or about $1 per lift ticket on average to all Front Range customers, with higher price increases at the merging firms' resorts."[148] Accordingly, the DOJ required the divestiture of one of the three ski resorts, bringing the postmerger HHI for the Colorado Front Range skiing market to below 1800 and the postmerger market share for the combined firm to less than 32 percent.[149]

In *Chicago Bridge and Iron Co., Inc.*,[150] an FTC Administrative Law Judge upheld FTC allegations that the effect of CB&I's acquisition of PDM assets might be substantially to lessen competition in four relevant product markets in the United States in which both CB&I and PDM competed. The ALJ stated that the acquisition "is likely to increase CB&I's ability to raise prices unilaterally in the relevant markets because the acquisition eliminates competition form PDM, CB&I's closest competitor."[151] He determined that the acquisition violated Section 7 of

---

145. 1997-2 Trade Cas. (CCH) ¶ 72,030 (D. Colo. 1997) (consent decree).

146. *See id.* at 81,142.

147. *Id.* at 81,143.

148. *Id.*

149. *See id.* at 81,144. The Division continues to pursue vigorously unilateral effects theories in challenging transactions. *See, e.g.*, United States v. Pearson plc, No. 1:98CV02836 (D.D.C. filed Nov. 23, 1998) (complaint) (basal elementary school science programs); United States v. Aluminum Co. of Am., No. 98-CV-1497 (D.D.C. filed June 15, 1998) (complaint) (aluminum cast plate); United States v. Sony Corp., No. 98-CIV-2716 (S.D.N.Y. filed Apr. 16, 1998) (complaint) (exhibition of first-run films).

150. FTC File 0015, Docket No. 9300 (filed June 12, 2003). This matter is currently on appeal.

151. *Id.* (noting that "The acquisition is a merger involving the first and second lowest cost sellers which could cause prices to rise to the constraining level of the next lowest–cost seller").

the Clayton Act and Section 5 of the FTC Act and held that a complete divestiture of all assets acquired postmerger was necessary to restore competition as it existed prior to the acquisition.[152]

152. *Id. See also* Coca Cola Bottling Co. of the Southwest, 118 F.T.C. 452 (1994). (Commission concluded that acquisition resulted in adverse unilateral effects in carbonated soft drinks market.) In *Coca Cola Bottling Co. of the Southwest*, the FTC challenged an acquisition by the Coca Cola Bottling Company of the Southwest (CCSW) of the franchises to produce and distribute Dr Pepper products in the area of San Antonio, Texas. The product market at issue consisted of branded carbonated soft drinks. The Commission concluded that "there [was] some evidence of unilateral effects that [had] occurred since the acquisition" in the form of decreased competition between CCSW's "Mr. PiBB" brand and Dr Pepper, both of which are "pepper"-flavored drinks. The Commission thus required CCSW to divest the acquired Dr Pepper assets.

CHAPTER 5

REBUTTING THE STRUCTURAL INFERENCE

Assuming, in the context of a merger or acquisition analysis, that (1) the relevant market has been defined, (2) market shares have been calculated for the parties to the transaction, (3) the resulting market concentration has been ascertained, and (4) the market shares and concentration resulting from the transaction establish a prima facie violation of Section 7 of the Clayton Act, the parties defending the transaction must rebut that structural inference. They must explain why the market shares and the resulting concentration level do not establish a violation of Section 7.

A. The *General Dynamics* Defense: Attacking the Significance of Market Shares, Market Structure, and Concentration

Since 1974, defendants have relied upon the U.S. Supreme Court's decision in *United States v. General Dynamics Corp.*[1] to rebut inferences that arise from market shares. In *General Dynamics*, the Antitrust Division of the U.S. Department of Justice (DOJ or the Division) challenged the combination of two major coal producers that resulted in "undue concentration."[2] The U.S. Supreme Court held that "other pertinent factors" affecting the market "mandated a conclusion that no substantial lessening of competition occurred or was threatened" as a result of the transaction.[3]

The U.S. Supreme Court also held that "[e]vidence of past production does not, as a matter of logic, necessarily give a proper picture of a company's future ability to compete."[4] Unlike markets involved in earlier U.S. Supreme Court merger decisions, production statistics (in this instance relating to coal) were not evidence of competitive strength.[5] Instead, the Court implicitly endorsed the district

1. 415 U.S. 486 (1974).
2. *Id.* at 497-98.
3. *Id.* at 498.
4. *Id.* at 501.
5. For example, the Court noted that annual sales in the markets in *United States v. Von's Grocery Co.*, 384 U.S. 270 (1966) (grocery stores), and *United States v. Pabst Brewing Co.*, 384 U.S. 546 (1966) (breweries), were much more likely to indicate future competitive abilities. Current

court's decision to analyze evidence of the "structure, history and probable future" of the relevant product market. For example, because the major customer of the coal industry (electric utilities) bought the product pursuant to long-term contracts, the better measure of a coal company's ability to compete was the size of its uncommitted reserves, not its past production.[6] Relying upon testimony that the acquired company's reserves were "unpromising," if not "relatively depleted," the district court found, and the U.S. Supreme Court affirmed, that the acquired company was a "far less significant factor in the coal market than the Government contended or the production statistics seemed to indicate."[7] The Court concluded that the parties' current market position and overall concentration did not show the true competitive effects likely to result from the transaction.[8]

The application and implications of *General Dynamics* have been debated vigorously. Its holding, its analysis, and its very name have been cited to support a broad variety of arguments in opposition to a plaintiff's prima facie case under Section 7 of the Clayton Act.[9] *General Dynamics* opened the door for merging parties to rebut a presumption of anticompetitive effect by showing why the prima facie case inaccurately predicts the relevant transaction's probable effect on future competition.[10]

---

sales in those markets were largely attributable to factors such as market distribution systems and brand recognition, so that competitive strength could reasonably be predicted to continue. *See General Dynamics Corp.*, 415 U.S. at 501.

6. *General Dynamics*, 415 U.S. at 501-02.
7. *Id.* at 503.
8. In so holding, the Court cited its analysis in *Brown Shoe Co. v. United States*, 370 U.S. 294 (1962), which "cautioned that statistics concerning market share and concentration, while of great significance, were not conclusive indicators of anticompetitive effects." United States v. General Dynamics Corp., 415 U.S. 486, 498 (1974).
9. *See* Kaiser Aluminum & Chem. Corp. v. FTC, 652 F.2d 1324, 1336-37 (7th Cir. 1981).
10. The ultimate burden of proof in the case remains, however, on the plaintiff. *See, e.g.*, United States v. Baker Hughes, Inc., 908 F.2d 981, 991 (D.C. Cir. 1990) ("If the burden of production imposed on a defendant is unduly onerous, the distinction between that burden and the ultimate burden of persuasion – always an elusive distinction in practice – disintegrates completely"); *Kaiser Aluminum & Chem. Corp.*, 652 F.2d at 1340 (although '*General Dynamics* requires the defendant to come forward with evidence to rebut the government's prima facie case of substantial lessening of competition through statistics showing increase in

The U.S. Supreme Court's holding that market share statistics do not necessarily end the inquiry under Section 7 led hopeful merger defendants to claim that they were actually insignificant or weak competitors notwithstanding their substantial market shares. Subsequent lower court decisions, however, have declined to interpret *General Dynamics* as a general exemption for high market share and concentration just because an explanation of some type could be provided. In *FTC v. University Health, Inc.*,[11] for example, the Eleventh Circuit, reversing the district court's denial of a preliminary injunction, stated its unwillingness to interpret *General Dynamics* as granting absolute immunity from Section 7 review:

> Rather, we view *General Dynamics* as standing for the unremarkable proposition that a defendant may rebut the government's prima facie case by showing that the government's market share statistics overstate the acquired firm's ability to compete in the future and that, discounting the acquired firm's market share to take this into account, the merger would not substantially lessen competition. The weakness of the acquired firm is only relevant if the defendant demonstrates that this weakness undermines the predictive value of the government's market share statistics.[12]

In 1997, the Federal Trade Commission (FTC or the Commission) determined that the weakness of the acquired firm was relevant to its decision not to challenge the merger of the Boeing Company and McDonnell Douglas Corporation. The proposed merger raised serious antitrust issues in the market for large commercial aircraft because the merging parties were two of three competitors, Boeing had over half the market, and there were high barriers to entry.[13] Nonetheless, a majority of the Commissioners voted not to challenge the merger because,

---

market share and concentration in relevant product markets, [t]he government continues to bear the burden of persuasion even after it has made out a prima facie case through statistical evidence").

11. 938 F.2d 1206 (11th Cir. 1991).

12. *Id*. at 1221 (citations omitted). The appellee hospital had successfully argued in the district court that the competing hospital it proposed to acquire offered limited services and, therefore, its likelihood of future success as a meaningful competitor, notwithstanding its present market share, was "dim."

13. *See* Statement of Chairman Robert Pitofsky and Commissioners Janet D. Steiger, Roscoe B. Starek III, and Christine A. Varney, Boeing Co., File No. 971-0051 (July 1, 1997), *reprinted in* 5 Trade Reg. Rep. (CCH) ¶ 24,295.

although the failing company or failing division defense was not applicable,

> . . . the vast majority of airlines will no longer consider purchasing Douglas aircraft and [as a result] the company is no longer in a position to influence significantly the competitive dynamics of the commercial aircraft market. . . . [T]he absence of any prospect of significant commercial sales, combined with a dismal financial forecast, indicate that Douglas Aircraft is no longer an effective competitor, and there is no prospect that position could be reversed.[14]

The 1992 *Merger Guidelines* follow the teaching of *General Dynamics* by expressly stating that "market share and market concentration data may either understate or overstate the likely future competitive significance of a firm or firms in the market or the impact of a merger."[15] The *Merger Guidelines* give specific examples of circumstances in which market shares may not be an accurate predictor of future competitive significance, such as the availability or absence of a new technology that is critical to the long-term viability of market competitors, or changes in market conditions leading to growth in the size of the market.[16] The *Merger Guidelines* and the antitrust

---

14. *See id.* at 4-5. Commissioner Mary L. Azcuenaga filed a separate statement in which she concluded that a challenge to the merger in the commercial aircraft market was warranted.

15. U.S. DEP'T OF JUSTICE & FEDERAL TRADE COMM'N, HORIZONTAL MERGER GUIDELINES (1992) § 1.52 [hereinafter 1992 MERGER GUIDELINES], *reprinted in* 4 Trade Reg. Rep. (CCH) ¶ 13,104 and in Appendix I. The 1992 *Merger Guidelines* eliminated the section of the 1984 *Merger Guidelines* entitled "Financial Condition of Firms in the Relevant Market." *See* U.S. DEP'T OF JUSTICE, MERGER GUIDELINES § 3.22 (1984) [hereinafter 1984 MERGER GUIDELINES], 49 Fed. Reg. 26,823 (1984), *reprinted in* 4 Trade Reg. Rep. (CCH) ¶ 13,103. The 1984 drafters had intended this section to apply the holding of *General Dynamics*, but subsequent experience demonstrated that merger proponents attempting to diminish the significance of merging firms' market shares often inappropriately cited the alleged weak financial position of one of the parties as justification for the transaction. *See* Kevin J. Arquit, *Perspectives on the 1992 U.S. Governmental Horizontal Merger Guidelines*, 61 ANTITRUST L.J. 121 (1992).

16. *See* 1992 MERGER GUIDELINES, *supra* note 15, § 1.521; *see also, e.g.*, United States v. Borland Int'l Inc., 56 Fed. Reg. 56,096, 56,100 (Oct. 31, 1991) (competitive impact statement) (rejecting argument that new technology would make past market shares unreliable to predict competitive effects because "market changes resulting from these

enforcement agencies also have recognized that a company's position as a product innovator may not be necessarily reflected in market share, but may be appropriately considered a critical competitive effect, and have directed enforcement and relief accordingly.[17]

---

technological advances are likely to be evolutionary rather than revolutionary"). Cases pre-dating the 1992 *Merger Guidelines* that discuss the "technological change" argument are few in number and generally conclude that the evidence offered was not sufficient to discredit the market share data. *See, e.g.*, FTC v. PPG Indus., 798 F.2d 1500, 1504-07 (D.C. Cir. 1986) (rejecting aircraft window manufacturers' argument that, "because of rapid and continuing technological changes in the industry, statistics reflecting past market shares do not accurately indicate future market shares"); United States v. Ivaco, Inc., 704 F. Supp. 1409, 1428-29 (W.D. Mich. 1989) (rejecting argument that, because "technological innovation will soon make their existing products obsolete . . . their past dominance of the tamper market does not suggest an ability to continue that dominance in the future"); United States v. Black & Decker Mfg. Co., 430 F. Supp. 729, 750 (D. Md. 1976) (defendants in a civil antitrust action presented evidence of product innovation to prove that the market concentration ratios submitted by the government do not accurately reflect the competitive nature of the gasoline powered chain saw market); United States v. Falstaff Brewing Corp., 383 F. Supp. 1020, 1022-23 (D.R.I. 1974) (in attempting to prove that an acquisition of another beer company would not substantially lessen competition, defendant produced evidence of technological innovations being studied by his company before and after the acquisition as evidence of the existence of vigorous competition among the sellers in the New England beer market); Echlin Mfg. Co., 105 F.T.C. 410, 469 (1985) (finding that "rapid technological change" is another market factor relevant to the assessment of market power effects of a merger for market power may be harder to exercise or less likely to endure in the face of such a change); Brunswick Corp., 94 F.T.C. 1174, 1238 (1979) (commenting that proof of product improvement in the boat power motor market offered by defendant was proper in rebutting the evidence of high concentration ratios submitted by the government as unreliable indicators of actual market behavior), *aff'd in part and modified in part sub nom*; Yamaha Motor Co. v. FTC, 657 F.2d 971 (8th Cir. 1981).

17. *See* Constance K. Robinson, Director of Operations and Merger Enforcement, Antitrust Div., Leap-Frog and Other Forms of Innovation: Protecting the Future for High-Tech and Emerging Industries Through Merger Enforcement, Remarks Before the ABA (June 10, 1999) (citing United States v. Halliburton, 63 Fed. Reg. 58,770 (1998) (consent agreement requiring divestiture of competitive assets in logging-while-drilling market including specialized assets necessary for innovation));

The way in which market shares are calculated may also affect their accuracy as a proxy for predicting the merging firms' future competitive significance.[18] In certain markets, annual sales or production in the market in any given year are so small that they distort the firms' relative competitive significance. In *Baker Hughes*, for example, the D.C. Circuit affirmed the district court's characterization of the relevant market shares as "volatile and shifting," and "easily skewed."[19] Only a few units of the high-cost relevant product were sold each year and, as a result, substantial year-to-year shifts in market share occurred that were attributable to the sale of one unit.[20]

Other product markets may lend themselves to a measure of share based upon a firm's capability to bid on new consumer demand, particularly those in which long-term contracts are typical. Calculation of shares under a bidding model would assign equal shares of the market to all qualified bidders for the relevant product without consideration to historical performance, either in terms of units of production or sales revenues. The 1992 *Merger Guidelines* recognize this methodology in appropriate circumstances.[21] Market performance and idiosyncrasies will dictate whether the manner in which market share is calculated should diminish or explain its relative significance.

United States v. Lockheed Martin Corp., No. 1:98CV00731 (D.D.C. filed Mar. 23, 1998) (complaint), *at* www.usdoj.gov/atr/cases/f1600/1609.htm (reduction in innovation of aircraft design, manufacture and in various technology markets asserted as resulting anticompetitive effect).

18. In *General Dynamics*, the U.S. Supreme Court endorsed the district court's rejection of historic production statistics as a measure of market share and competitive strength in a market where product reserves more accurately predicted future competitive abilities. United States v. General Dynamics Corp., 415 U.S. 486, 510-11 (1974).

19. United States v. Baker Hughes, 908 F.2d 981, 986 (D.C. Cir. 1990) (citation omitted).

20. In *Baker Hughes*, the relevant product market was the manufacture and sale of hardrock hydraulic underground drilling rigs (HHUDRs), of which only 38 were sold in the calendar year prior to the merger's announcement. *Id.* at 986. The district court had found that obtaining a single contract to provide multiple HHUDRs could move a competitor from last to first place in the market. *See id.*

21. "Where all firms have, on a forward-looking basis, an equal likelihood of securing sales, the Agency will assign firms equal shares." 1992 MERGER GUIDELINES, *supra* note 15, § 1.41 n.15; *see also* part B.2 of Chapter 3.

B. Proving Ease of Entry

Merger proponents frequently argue that the entry of new market participants would eliminate or at least discipline the ability of the merged entity to exercise market power or facilitate collusion. In the event that the combined entity raised prices or decreased output, the market would attract new competitors such that the merged entity would be forced to return to premerger conduct in both price and output. Such a position requires demonstrating that the barriers to entry into the market do not prevent the anticipated disciplinary effect.

1. Types of Entry Barriers

Economists and antitrust analysts vary substantially in their view as to what constitutes a barrier to entry. At one extreme, entry barriers have been broadly defined as "any factor that permits firms already in the market to earn returns above the competitive level while deterring outsiders from entering."[22] Under this theory, if prices are above the competitive level, new entry will be attracted until total market output is restored to a competitive level.[23] A narrower definition of an entry barrier is a cost "that must be borne by a firm which seeks to enter an industry but is not borne by firms already in the industry."[24] This narrower view has been criticized as failing to consider adequately the reason why antitrust law is concerned with the existence of entry barriers, i.e., whether entry into a market is likely to occur and limit or eliminate supracompetitive pricing.[25] Entry barriers such as regulatory requirements and economies of scale can restrict entry and protect supracompetitive pricing although those very same impediments had to be confronted by firms already in the market.

---

22. 2A PHILLIP E. AREEDA, HERBERT HOVENKAMP & JOHN L. SOLOW, ANTITRUST LAW ¶ 420 (1995) (citing J. S. BAIN, BARRIERS TO NEW COMPETITION: THEIR CHARACTER AND CONSEQUENCES IN MANUFACTURING INDUSTRIES (1962)).
23. *See id.*
24. GEORGE STIGLER, THE ORGANIZATION OF INDUSTRY 67 (1968).
25. 2A PHILLIP E. AREEDA, HERBERT HOVENKAMP & JOHN L. SOLOW, ANTITRUST LAW ¶ 420 (1995).

a. Financial

Courts have frequently addressed claims that extensive capital requirements and "sunk costs" required for entry constitute barriers.[26] For example, in *Laidlaw Acquisition Corp. v. Mayflower Group*,[27] the district court cited as barriers to entry high capitalization costs, a performance bond requirement, and the cost of insurance required merely to submit a bid on school bus transportation contracts.[28] Similarly, in *United States v. United Tote, Inc.*,[29] the court cited the defendant's evidence that entry into the market for totalisator systems, the computerized betting equipment for pari-mutuel wagering, would require almost two years and $5 million.[30]

When entering Final Judgment on consent decrees entered into by parties to an investigated merger, courts also look to whether divestitures alleviate financial barriers to entry. For example, in *United States v. Worldcom, Inc.*,[31] the district court cited as a barrier to entry in the Tier 1 Internet backbone services market "substantial time and enormous sums of capital," and entered Final Judgment on the merger in part because it required divestitures in that market to alleviate that barrier.[32] Similarly, in *United States v. Alcoa, Inc.*,[33] the court cited approvingly divestitures in certain alumina markets in order to reduce the "time delay and significant start-up costs" of entry.[34]

Antitrust enforcement agencies, in explaining the basis for negotiated consent agreements, share the view that extensive sunk costs constitute

---

26. The 1992 *Merger Guidelines* define "sunk costs" as "acquisition costs . . . that cannot be recovered through the redeployment of these assets outside the relevant market, *i.e.*, costs uniquely incurred to supply the relevant product and geographic market." 1992 MERGER GUIDELINES, *supra* note 15, § 1.32.
27. 636 F. Supp. 1513 (S.D. Ind. 1986).
28. *Id*. at 1513; *see also* FTC v. Bass Bros. Enters., 1984-1 Trade Cas. (CCH) ¶ 66,041, at 68,613 (N.D. Ohio 1984) (requirement for new environmental protection equipment resulted in permanent cost disadvantage to potential entrants but not to market incumbents).
29. 768 F. Supp. 1064 (D. Del. 1991).
30. *Id*. at 1075; *see also* FTC v. Swedish Match, 131 F. Supp. 2d 151, 171 (D.D.C. 2000) (citing sunk costs as a barrier to entry, and granting preliminary injunction barring acquisition).
31. 2001 WL 1188484 (D.D.C. 2001).
32. *Id.* at * 13.
33. 152 F. Supp. 2d 37 (D.D.C. 2001).
34. *Id.* at 40-41.

an entry barrier. In the proposed acquisition of Digital Equipment Corporation by Intel, for example, the FTC identified "large sunk costs to build a [microprocessor production facility] . . . [and] design a microprocessor" as a significant barrier to entry in the microprocessor market.[35] Similarly, in its challenge of a merger of competing airport fixed-based operator businesses, the Division asserted that the prospect of new entry was not likely due to the "significant sunk costs involved in building an FBO, including the cost of building hangar and ramp facilities."[36]

However, courts have not always accepted the argument that entry into a particular market requires such significant expenditures as to rise to the level of an entry barrier. For example, in *United States v. Syufy Enterprises*,[37] the Ninth Circuit upheld the district court's rejection of the government's challenge of several acquisitions by Syufy Enterprises in the Las Vegas first-run movie exhibition market, describing the market as devoid of any significant barriers to entry, including financial entry barriers:

> Nor is this the type of industry, like heavy manufacturing or mining, which requires onerous front-end investments that might deter competition from all but the hardiest and most financially secure investors. . . . Nor do we have here a business dependent on a scarce commodity, control over which might give the incumbent a substantial structural advantage. Nor is there a network of exclusive contracts or distribution arrangements designed to lock out potential competitors. To the contrary, the record discloses a rough-and-tumble industry, marked by easy market access, fluid relationships with distributors, an ample and

---

35. Digital Equip. Corp., 63 Fed. Reg. 24,544, 24,545 (May 4, 1998) (analysis to aid public comment); *see also* Pfizer, 65 Fed. Reg. 39,407, 39,408 (June 26, 2000) (analysis to aid public comment) (identifying large sunk costs to research, develop, manufacture, and sell the pharmaceuticals at issue as a significant barrier to entry); Hoechst AG, 64 Fed. Reg. 71,141 (December 20, 1999) (analysis to aid public comment) (identifying substantial sunk costs to build a dedicated production facility in the relevant market as a significant barrier to entry).
36. United States v. Signature Flight Support Corp., 64 Fed. Reg. 14,758, 14,766 (Mar. 26, 1999) (proposed final judgment and competitive impact statement). *See also* The Williams Companies, 63 Fed. Reg. 16,553 (Apr. 3, 1998) (analysis to aid public comment) (new entry into the market for pipeline transportation of propane would entail substantial sunk costs and, therefore, would not be timely and sufficient to defeat an anticompetitive price increase).
37. 903 F.2d 659 (9th Cir. 1990).

> continuous supply of product, and a healthy and growing demand.[38]

Similarly, in *FTC v. Cardinal Health Inc.*,[39] the district court found that, based upon the evidence presented during trial, capital requirements were not a major barrier to entry into the wholesale prescription drug market.[40]

b. Technical

In addition to financial entry barriers, technical barriers to entry can defeat a defendant's efforts to demonstrate a lack of anticompetitive effects from a challenged transaction. In *United Tote*, for example, the district court found that totalisator systems needed a high processing speed, because most bets were placed shortly before the beginning of the race. During this period, bets were sold, odds were calculated and displayed, and the total wagered amounts were displayed in each different pool. In the district court's view, the need to meet these high-performance requirements, combined with a customer demand for 100 percent system reliability, was an additional barrier to entry.[41] The FTC and the Division also have recognized the existence of technical and scientific barriers to entry in their negotiation of consent agreements to resolve challenged transactions. In objecting to Northrop Grumman's proposed acquisition of TRW, the Division asserted that entry into the "complex, high technology markets" at issue would not be timely, likely or sufficient because "it would be extremely difficult for a new entrant to establish the technological expertise required to compete successfully."[42]

---

38. *Id*. at 666-67.
39. 12 F. Supp. 2d 34 (D.D.C. 1998).
40. *Id*. at 77.
41. *See* United States v. United Tote, Inc., 768 F. Supp. 1064, 1072-73 (D. Del. 1991).
42. United States v. Northrop Grumman Corp., 68 Fed. Reg. 1,861 (Jan. 14, 2003) (competitive impact statement); *see also* Baxter International, Inc., 68 Fed. Reg. 1,062 (Jan. 8, 2003) (analysis to aid public comment) (entry into the Propofol market unlikely due to complexity of the development process); Bayer AG, 67 Fed. Reg. 39,395 (June 7, 2002) (analysis to aid public comment) (entry into the market for New Generation Chemical Insecticide Active Ingredients would require years of research, development, testing, registration and commercial scale production synthesis); Glaxco Wellcome plc, 65 Fed. Reg. 82,374 (Dec. 28, 2000) (analysis to aid public comment) (production of ceftazidime requires an aseptic facility for both the manufacture and sterile filling processes,

c. Government Regulation

Governmental regulation, most typically licensing or certificate requirements, constitute another frequently cited category of entry barriers. In *University Health*, for example, the Eleventh Circuit found that Georgia's certificate of need law, which regulated the addition of hospital services based upon the need of the public, was a substantial barrier to entry not only to new competitors but also to expansion by existing ones.[43] Such a requirement provides advance notice to existing competitors that they will face competition in the future; the requirement of need also permits a group of colluding hospitals (i.e., a cartel) to oppose the government's issuance of the certificate with evidence of excess capacity artificially created by the diminished use of hospital services, due to the increased prices of the cartel.[44] Also, in *Swedish Match*, the district court pointed to government regulation of sales of loose leaf tobacco as a significant barrier to entry in that market, supporting its conclusion that the acquisition at issue should be enjoined.[45]

Similarly, in a consent decree obtained by the DOJ in the proposed merger of a California natural gas utility and a California electric utility, regulations such as safety requirements, environmental rules, and zoning approvals were found to function as barriers to entry in the electricity market.[46] Barriers to entry also may exist when new entrants are denied access to critical access or inputs.[47] In radio mergers, for example, the Division frequently alleges that the lack of spectrum availability makes entry into the relevant local radio market unlikely.[48]

---

greatly increasing the costs and complexities of manufacturing the product).

43. *See* FTC v. University Health Inc., 938 F.2d 1206, 1219 (11th Cir. 1991).
44. *See id.*
45. *See* FTC v. Swedish Match, 131 F. Supp. 2d 151, 170 (D.D.C. 2000).
46. *See* United States v. Enova Corp., 63 Fed. Reg. 33,396 (June 18, 1998) (proposed final judgment and competitive impact statement).
47. *See generally* Robert Pitofsky, Chairman, FTC, Competition Policy in Communications Industries: New Antitrust Approaches, Remarks Before the Glasser LegalWorks Seminar on Competitive Policy in Communications Industries: New Antitrust Approaches (Mar. 10, 1997), *at* www.ftc.gov/speeches/pitofsky/newcomm.htm (the self-correcting cycle in the communications industry—constant entry of new firms and new technology that tends to dissipate market power—is most at risk when existing firms deny new entrants access to critical inputs).
48. *See, e.g.*, United States v. American Radio Sys. Corp., 62 Fed. Reg. 15,920,

d. Brand Loyalty and Reputational Effects

Consumer loyalty to existing brands of products has sometimes been cited, particularly by the enforcement agencies, as an impediment to new entry.[49] Courts, however, sometimes view consumer brand loyalty simply as evidence of well-organized or effective distribution systems or superior products.[50]

Courts have debated whether the requirements of certain qualifications or reputation constitute a barrier to entry or merely reflect one competitor's superior ability to compete.[51] Although some courts have considered a competitor's reputation as a barrier to entry,[52] others have concluded that a firm's reputation or goodwill acquired through quality service constitutes evidence of competition, not an impediment to competition.[53]

15,927 (Apr. 3, 1997), *at* www.usdoj.gov/atr/public/speeches/jik97219.htm (proposed final judgment and competitive impact statement); *see also* Joel I. Klein, Assistant Att'y Gen., Antitrust Div., DOJ Analysis of Radio Mergers, Remarks Presented at the ANA Hotel (Feb. 19, 1997) (the possibility of new entrants has had "little impact" in radio mergers).

49. *See, e.g.*, United States v. Pabst Brewing Co., 384 U.S. 546, 559-60 (1966) (heavy emphasis upon consumer recognition and promotional techniques in the marketing of beer supported the conclusion that a substantial barrier to entry existed); United States v. Microsoft Corp., No. C95-1393 (N.D. Cal. filed Apr. 27, 1995) (complaint) (most personal computer OEMs and retail customers will only purchase personal finance/checkbook software that has an established reputation for reliability, performance, and customer support); Precision Castparts Corp., 64 Fed. Reg. 62,676, 62,678 (Nov. 17, 1999) (analysis to aid public comment) (customers of aerospace investment cast structural components are generally reluctant to contract with suppliers without a proven reputation as a barrier to entry); Pfizer, Inc., 65 Fed. Reg. 39,407, 39,409 (July 22, 1999) (analysis to aid public comment) (brand loyalty in pharmaceutical markets is a barrier to entry).

50. *See, e.g.*, United States v. Consolidated Foods Corp., 455 F. Supp. 108, 137-38 (E.D. Pa. 1978).

51. This discussion frequently is blurred with notions of customer or brand loyalty. *See, e.g.*, Southern Pac. Communs. Co. v. AT&T, 740 F.2d 980, 1002 (D.C. Cir. 1984).

52. *See, e.g.*, FTC v. Swedish Match, 131 F. Supp. 2d 151 (D.D.C. 2000); United States v. Crowell, Collier & MacMillan, Inc., 361 F. Supp. 983 (S.D.N.Y. 1973).

53. *See, e.g.*, United States v. Waste Mgmt., Inc., 743 F.2d 976, 984 (2d Cir. 1984). *But see* FTC v. Cardinal Health, Inc., 12 F. Supp. 2d 34, 82 (D.D.C. 1998) ("the sheer economies of scale and strength of reputation

e. Network Externalities

Finally, network externalities—consumers' preference for one type of technology because it is more widely adopted than other technologies—may function as a barrier to entry.[54] Network externalities are a particular concern in high-tech industry.[55] For example, in Intel's acquisition of certain microprocessor assets of Digital Equipment Corporation,[56] the FTC viewed Digital's "Alpha" microprocessor as the only non-Intel microprocessor capable of running the Windows operating system in a "native," or optimal, mode. The acquisition by Intel of certain "Alpha" technology threatened competition in this market, which new entrants could not have remedied due to the barrier of network externalities.[57]

---

that the Defendants already have over these wholesalers serve as barriers to competitors as they attempt to grow significantly in size" (citations omitted)).

54. *See* United States v. Worldcom, Inc., 66 Fed. Reg. 2,929 (Jan. 12, 2001) ("[a]s is true in network industries generally, the value of internet access to end users becomes greater as more and more users can easily be reached through the internet"); *see also* Gregory J. Werden, *Network Effects and Conditions of Entry: Lessons from the Microsoft Case*, 69 ANTITRUST L.J. 87 (2001) (discussing antitrust issues raised by network externalities); David A. Balto, Assistant Director, Office of Policy and Evaluation, Bureau of Competition, FTC, Standard Setting in a Network Economy, Remarks as part of Cutting Edge Antitrust Seminars International (Feb. 17, 2000), *at* www.ftc.gov/speeches/other/standardsetting.htm (discussing network industries).

55. *See generally* William J. Kolasky, *Network Effects: A Contrarian View*, 7 GEO. MASON L. REV. 577 (1999) (discussing network effects in the context of high-tech industries); *see also* Max Schanzenbach, *Network Effects and Antitrust Law: Predation, Affirmative Defenses, and the Case of U.S. v. Microsoft*, 2002 STAN. TECH. L. REV. 4 (2002).

56. *See* Digital Equip. Corp., 63 Fed. Reg. 24,544 (May 4, 1998) (analysis to aid public comment).

57. *See id.* The Commission found that would-be entrants into the microprocessor market faced a significant catch-22: a successful entrant would need to convince computer system manufacturers to design their systems around the new microprocessor; however, manufacturers were unwilling to support new microprocessor technology unless it enjoyed consumer support, and consumers placed little value on new technology because of network externalities. *See id.* at 24,545.

Critics of WorldCom's acquisition of MCI also pointed to network effects theories in voicing their concerns over the merger.[58] Both MCI and WorldCom were leading Internet backbone providers (IBPs). IBPs, coupled with Internet service providers (ISPs) and end users, comprise the "network of networks" that is the Internet. Critics of the merger argued that the merged firm, with the largest IBP network, would be able to exploit the size of that network vis-a-vis IBPs and ISPs by increasing connection costs to rival IBPs and also increasing costs to other ISPs and, ultimately, to end users.[59]

Following investigations by both the Division and the European Commission, the parties agreed to sell the MCI IBP to Cable & Wireless plc, satisfying the two agencies' concerns with the transaction.[60] Analysis of the merger's anticompetitive effects was scant in the agencies' respective press releases, but the European Commission noted that "'network externalities' (i.e., the phenomenon whereby the attraction of a network to its customers is a function of the number of other customers connected to the same network) would have enabled the merged entity to behave independently of its competitors, and to degrade the quality of Internet related services offering of its competitors."[61]

2. *Pre-1992 Cases and* Merger Guidelines

During the 1980s and early 1990s, the courts generally analyzed the capability—rather than the likelihood—of entry by outside firms. In *United States v. Waste Management, Inc.*,[62] for example, the Second

58. *See* WorldCom, Inc., 13 F.C.C.R. 18025, ¶¶ 142-49 (1998); *see generally* William J. Kolasky, *Network Effects: A Contrarian View*, 7 GEO. MASON L. REV. 577 (1999) (discussing the opposition to the merger); Constance K. Robinson, Director of Operations and Merger Enforcement, Antitrust Div., Network Effects in Telecommunications Mergers, Remarks Before the Practicing Law Institute (Aug. 23, 1999), *at* www.usdoj.gov/atr/public/speeches/3889.htm.
59. *See WorldCom, Inc.*, at ¶ 149.
60. *See* U.S. Dep't of Justice, Antitrust Div., Justice Department Clears WorldCom/MCI Merger after MCI Agrees to Sell Its Internet Business, Press Release (July 15, 1998), *at* www.usdoj.gov/atr/public/press_releases/1998/1829.htm; European Comm'n, Commission Clears WorldCom and MCI Merger Subject to Conditions, Press Release (July 8, 1998).
61. European Comm'n, Commission Clears WorldCom and MCI Merger Subject to Conditions, Press Release (July 8, 1998).
62. 743 F.2d 976 (2d Cir. 1984).

Circuit reversed a district court order enjoining the acquisition of the second largest waste hauler in the Dallas market by the largest hauler, notwithstanding a combined postmerger share of almost 50 percent. The court reasoned that entry was "relatively easy, and the barriers to entry not great."[63] Specifically, the court opined that a new entrant into the trash collection business "can acquire a truck, a few containers, drive the truck himself, and operate out of his home."[64] Similarly, in *United States v. Calmar Inc.*,[65] the district court refused to grant an injunction against a transaction that would result in the leader of the plastic sprayer and dispenser market having 50 percent of the market and a 738-point increase in the HHI to 2302.[66] In addition to the lack of any patents or proprietary designs, the court cited the short time and low costs required to enter the manufacturing market. Moreover, some existing manufacturers contracted out much of their work and, according to the court, were little more than sales corporations. The court concluded that "[n]ew entrants could do the same."[67] No evidence was discussed, or apparently presented, that such new entry actually would occur.[68] Like the courts, the Division's 1982 and 1984 *Merger Guidelines* analyzed entry by asking whether new entry theoretically *could* occur, not whether it *would* occur. The enforcement agencies also focused upon whether structural impediments to entry existed that would somehow thwart new entrants from preventing the exercise of market power by those already in the market.[69]

---

63. *Id.* at 982.
64. *Id.*
65. 612 F. Supp. 1298 (D.N.J. 1985).
66. *Id.*
67. *Id.* at 1306.
68. But see *United States v. Country Lake Foods, Inc.*, 754 F. Supp. 669, 676 (D. Minn. 1990), where the DOJ sought to enjoin the merger of the second and third largest dairies in the Minneapolis metropolitan market, a combination which would have substantially increased concentration. The court relied upon declarations from five dairies outside the geographic market that stated they would probably enter the market if customers were to approach them in the wake of a fluid milk price increase and make firm commitments for the purchase of sufficient quantities so as to make such new entry profitable.
69. *See* 1984 MERGER GUIDELINES, *supra* note 15, § 3.3 ("If entry into a market is so easy that existing competitors could not succeed in raising price for any significant period of time, the Division is unlikely to challenge mergers in that market. . . ");U.S. DEP'T OF JUSTICE, MERGER GUIDELINES, 47 Fed. Reg. 28,493 (1982); §III(B) [hereinafter 1982 MERGER GUIDELINES], *reprinted in* 4 Trade Reg. Rep. (CCH) ¶13,102.

In late 1989 and early 1990, the enforcement agencies' entry barriers analysis underwent a metamorphosis as a result of the Division's position on appeal, and the court of appeals' analysis, in *Baker Hughes*. The lower court had denied the Division's motion for a permanent injunction against the merger of two market leaders based in part upon the likelihood of actual and potential entry. On appeal, the Division argued that the district court had applied the wrong legal standard, and claimed that only a showing by the defendant that new entry was likely to be "quick and effective" could overcome a prima facie case under Section 7.[70]

The court of appeals disagreed, finding the standard proposed by the Division "devoid of support in the statute, in the case law, and in the government's own Merger Guidelines."[71] Further, the D.C. Circuit wrote, the Division's quick and effective entry standard would impose "a degree of clairvoyance alien to Section 7" and a burden of producing evidence of competitors' intentions that is not only rarely available, but is generally downplayed.[72] Moreover, the court found, the Division's standard ignored the fact that threatened entry by a firm that never actually enters the market can also exert meaningful competitive pressure. By requiring the defendant to demonstrate that new entry will be quick and effective, the Division implicitly rejected any procompetitive effects attributable to potential competitors.[73]

3. *1992* Merger Guidelines *and Subsequent Cases*

The 1992 *Merger Guidelines* expressly require entry to be "timely, likely and sufficient";[74] they also reconfirm that "if entry into the market is so easy that market participants, after the merger, either collectively or

---

In assessing the ease of entry into a market, the Division considered the likelihood and probable magnitude of entry in response to a "small but significant and non-transitory" increase in price. *Id.*

70. *See* United States v. Baker Hughes, Inc., 908 F.2d at 981, 983 (D.C. Cir. 1990).
71. *See id.* at 987.
72. *See id.*
73. *See id.* at 988.
74. 1992 MERGER GUIDELINES, *supra* note 15, § 3.1; *see also* HORIZONTAL MERGER GUIDELINES OF THE NATIONAL ASSOCIATION OF ATTORNEYS GENERAL (1993) [hereinafter NAAG MERGER GUIDELINES] § 5.1, *reprinted in* 4 Trade Reg. Rep. (CCH) ¶ 13,406 and in Appendix M (following the federal guidelines in requiring entry to be timely, likely, and sufficient).

unilaterally could not profitably maintain a price increase above premerger levels," a merger would not likely create, enhance, or facilitate the exercise of market power.[75]

Before the agencies will conclude that committed entry would deter or counteract anticompetitive effects,[76] the proponent of the transaction must demonstrate that entry (1) is achievable in two years, (2) will achieve a significant impact on price in the relevant market within two years from initial planning,[77] (3) will be profitable to the new entrant at premerger prices,[78] and (4) will cause prices to fall to their premerger levels.[79] Moreover, the 1992 *Merger Guidelines* expressly state that committed entrants do not include firms that intended to enter prior to the merger's announcement but have not yet done so; like the uncommitted entrant, they already are counted as being "in" the market because the merger did not induce their entry.

Commentary by FTC and DOJ officials on entry issues since the release of the 1992 *Merger Guidelines* has stressed the enforcement agencies' views that all three prongs of the "timely, likely and sufficient" standard must be satisfied. These statements suggest the increased difficulty of effectively arguing in support of a transaction by citing the lack of barriers to entry.[80] "[T]he FTC routinely asks the right questions

---

75. 1992 MERGER GUIDELINES, *supra* note 15, § 3.0.

76. *See id.* The 1992 *Merger Guidelines* divide entrants into those that are "uncommitted" and those that are "committed." Only the procompetitive effects of entry by committed entrants are analyzed by this section of the 1992 *Merger Guidelines*, because the uncommitted entrant would likely enter the market without incurring significant sunk costs. Under the 1992 *Guidelines*, uncommitted entrants are already considered to be market participants and, therefore, the procompetitive effect of their entry has already been considered in the market concentration analysis.

77. *See id.* § 3.2.

78. *See id.* § 3.3.

79. *See id.* § 3.4. For a further discussion of the meaning behind the timely, likely, and sufficient standard, see Kevin J. Arquit, *Perspectives on the 1992 U.S. Governmental Horizontal Merger Guidelines*, 61 ANTITRUST L.J. 121 (1992).

80. Thomas B. Leary, *The Essential Stability of Merger Policy in the United States*, 70 ANTITRUST L.J. 105, 119 (2002) ("[I]t is true that the 1992 Guidelines were overtly intended to shift the entry analysis from 'whether effective entry *could* occur given the conditions of entry to whether would occur given the alternative profit opportunities facing possible potential entrants.' This shift in emphasis is further articulated by the requirements that potential 'entry would be timely, likely, and sufficient in its magnitude, character and scope to deter or counteract the

when analyzing committed entry—examining whether such entry would cure the competitive problem, and considering whether the scale needed for low cost entry would make it unprofitable."[81]

However, FTC officials also have recognized that the *Merger Guidelines*' entry analysis may differ slightly when applied to mergers in unique markets, such as the defense industry.[82] In that market, the typical two-year timeliness period for entry analysis may be shortened or lengthened depending on scheduled procurements.[83] In addition, the Department of Defense may be uniquely positioned to provide information relevant to an antitrust inquiry about entry conditions and potential participants in the defense industry.[84]

Although the enforcement agencies' application of the entry standard in the context of consent decrees is faithful to the timely, likely, and sufficient standard of the *Merger Guidelines*, courts have not wholeheartedly applied it, generally relying instead upon a restatement of

---

competitive effects of concern,' with further refinements that amplify on these terms"); *see also* William J. Baer, Director, Bureau of Competition, FTC, Report from the Bureau of Competition, Remarks Before the American Bar Association Antitrust Section, Spring Meeting 1999 (Apr. 15, 1999), *at* www.ftc.gov/speeches/other/bawerspaba99.htm; Richard G. Parker, Senior Deputy Director, Bureau of Competition, FTC, Trends in Merger Enforcement and Litigation, Remarks Before the Annual Briefing for Corporate Counsel (Sept. 16, 1998); Charles E. Biggio, Senior Counsel to the AAG, Antitrust Div., Merger Enforcement at the Antitrust Division, Remarks Before the Antitrust Law Committee Chicago Bar Association (May 15, 1996); Jonathan B. Baker, Director, Bureau of Economics, FTC, The Problem with *Baker Hughes* and *Syufy:* On the Role of Entry in Merger Analysis, Remarks Before Charles River Associates, Inc. Conference on Economists' Perspective on Antitrust Today (Apr. 25, 1996), *at* www.ftc.gov/speeches/other/entry2.htm.

81. Baker, *supra* note 80, at 31 (citations omitted).

82. *See* Robert Pitofsky, Chairman, FTC, Prepared Statement of the Federal Trade Commission, Remarks Before the Armed Services Committee Subcommittee on Acquisitions and Technology, United States Senate (Apr. 15, 1997), *at* www.ftc.gov/os/1997/04/defenmer.htm

83. For example, if the merging parties competed to build fighter aircraft and the next major fighter procurement was scheduled to take place in six months, potential entrants would probably be limited to those companies planning or capable of bidding in six months' time. *See id.*

84. This unique knowledge stems from the Defense Department's practice of influencing entry by providing financial or other assistance to encourage entry by private firms, or by entering into the supply of defense-related products itself.

the *Baker Hughes* entry analysis.[85] However, in *FTC v. Staples, Inc.*,[86] the district court enjoined the proposed merger of two of the three players in the office supply superstore market, rejecting the defendants' arguments under *Baker Hughes* that new entry into the market was likely and would avert the merger's anticompetitive effects.[87]

By contrast, in *FTC v. Cardinal Health, Inc.*,[88] the district court precisely applied the *Merger Guidelines*' analysis to examine the claim that entry into the wholesale prescription drug distribution market would counteract any competitive effects from the merger.[89] Finding that a leased distribution center could be opened in as little as ninety days and that capital requirements are not a major barrier to entry in the wholesale prescription drug distribution market, the court was satisfied that "new entry or expansion within the market could plausibly occur within a short enough period of time."[90] After finding that entry could be timely, however, the court found little evidence of past entry to consider the prospect of future entry likely, and concluded that possible entry by regional wholesalers was "far more suggestive."[91] Finally, looking at sufficiency of entry, the court found that any expansion or entry that would occur "would not be sufficient to offset any post-merger pricing practices that would result from the lack of competition."[92] Therefore, the court found that the defendants' entry claims were insufficient to rebut the government's prima facie case.[93]

---

85. *See, e.g.*, HTI Health Servs. v. Quorum Health Group, 960 F. Supp. 1104 (S.D. Miss. 1997) ("It is important to note that the Guidelines are not binding on the courts or the agencies") (citing Olin Corp v. FTC, 986 F.2d 1295, 1300 (9th Cir. 1993)).
86. 970 F. Supp. 1066 (D.D.C. 1997).
87. *Id.* at 1086-87.
88. 12 F. Supp. 2d 34 (D.D.C. 1998).
89. *Id.* at 54-58; *see also* United States v. Long Island Jewish Med. Ctr., 983 F. Supp. 121, 149 (E.D.N.Y. 1997) (holding that the likely expansion of the services offered by a new hospital located seven miles from the acquiring hospital "fulfills all the merger guidelines entry criteria, namely, the likelihood of its entry; the timeliness of its entry; and the sufficiency of its entry"); *cf.* Rebel Oil Co., Inc. v. Atlantic Richfield Co., 51 F.3d 1421, 1440 (9th Cir. 1995) (pointing to the *Merger Guidelines* timely, likely, and sufficient requirement in discussing entry argument in an attempted monopolization claim under Section 2 of the Sherman Act).
90. *Cardinal Health, Inc.*, 12 F. Supp. 2d at 56.
91. *Id.* at 56-58.
92. *Id.* at 58.
93. *See id.*

C. Rebutting Market Power: The Power Buyer/Sophisticated Purchaser Debate

Merging parties have successfully argued that, due to size, sophistication, the long-term nature of their buying arrangements, or some combination of these or similar attributes, their customers actually wield sufficient market power to counter any possible anticompetitive effects of the merger. The "power buyer" argument is an application of *General Dynamics'* holding that "other factors" besides market share actually determine a seller's ability to exert market power. In power buyer cases, market share data are not dispositive, and courts analyze whether the merging parties' customers wield decision-making power affecting conditions of competition in the relevant market.

Powerful purchasers can prevent collusive behavior by switching their purchases from those sellers perceived to be participating in a cartel-like arrangement to those sellers who are outside the cartel or who are willing to deviate from the cartel's collusive activity. In a market with few purchasers, and particularly one in which there are few transactions for which to compete, the influence of a buyer's decision making increases dramatically.[94] Large or sophisticated buyers also can counteract potential anticompetitive effects by encouraging or subsidizing new entry in order to provide a competitive alternative to those sellers perceived to be engaged in collusion. Sometimes this new entry actually can come in the form of the vertical integration by the buyer itself.[95]

Power buyers also can attempt to discipline their suppliers by playing suppliers against one another. For example, buyers can shift their purchases frequently among suppliers, insist upon and maintain secrecy in transaction prices, act aggressively to cut off suppliers, and demand multiyear contracts that diminish the number of transactions each year and increase their relative importance.[96]

Courts confronted with the power buyer defense have tended to view it favorably, and defendants have successfully asserted the power buyer defense to rebut the claim that market share means market power. For

---

94. *See, e.g.*, United States v. Syufy Enters., 903 F.2d 659, 670 (9th Cir. 1990).

95. *See, e.g.*, United States v. Country Lake Foods, Inc., 754 F. Supp. 669, 680 (D. Minn. 1990).

96. *See, e.g.*, United States v. Archer-Daniels-Midland Co., 781 F. Supp. 1400, 1422 (S.D. Iowa 1991).

example, in *FTC v. R.R. Donnelley & Sons Co.*,[97] the district court found that the publication printing product market comprised a few large, sophisticated customers who could "drive hard bargains because of the large print volume they control and typically enter into long-term contracts which guarantee their pricing; and they can provide a printer with financing to enable the installation or expansion of printing facilities, thereby drawing new capacity into the market."[98]

Defendants who develop the factual predicate to support the assertion that market power resides in the hands of a few large or sophisticated purchasers can be successful in rebutting an inference of market power from market share.[99] Markets are rarely so uncomplicated in their constituency, however, and frequently the existence of smaller buyers, who will not be protected by the actions of the larger, more powerful buyers, threatens the viability of the power buyer defense.[100]

---

97. 1990-2 Trade Cas. (CCH) ¶ 69,239 (D.D.C. 1990).

98. *Id.* at 64,855.

99. *See, e.g.*, United States v. Baker Hughes, Inc., 908 F.2d 981, 986 (D.C. Cir. 1990) (court of appeals affirms district court's finding that competition was promoted even in a highly concentrated market where the buyers were sophisticated customers spending millions of dollars on infrequent purchases and were insistent upon receiving multiple confidential bids for each of their orders); *Country Lake Foods, Inc.*, 754 F. Supp. at 679 (most buyers of fluid milk in the Minneapolis metropolitan statistical area are primarily food distributors which account for over 90% of market purchases; no dairy could afford to lose any of the business represented by these purchasers, meaning that market power resides with the buyers, not the sellers); *Archer-Daniels-Midland Co.*, 781 F. Supp. at 1422-23; *see also* FTC v. Tenet Health Care Corp., 186 F.3d 1045, 1054 (8th Cir. 1999) (relevant geographic market in hospital merger case was larger than what FTC proposed, in part, because managed care companies were large, sophisticated third-party buyers that would not "unhesitatingly accept a price increase rather than steer their subscribers to hospitals" in surrounding towns). *But see* In re Chicago Bridge & Iron Co., N.V., FTC Docket No. 9300, at 108-09 (June 18, 2003), *at* www.ftc.gov/os/caselist/d9300.htm (rejecting power buyer defense even where plaintiffs proved customers were large and generally sophisticated companies, because in three of the four contested product markets, the companies purchased very few products, and confidentiality provisions prevented past pricing information from being disseminated; hence, the buyers lacked sophistication with regard to purchases of the relevant products and thus were not power buyers).

100. *See, e.g.*, United States v. United Tote, Inc., 768 F. Supp. 1064 (D. Del. 1991) (where less than 50% of the purchases in a market were attributed

The power buyer defense, even when asserted in a concentrated buyers' market, is not always successful when the court views the sellers' market as historically prone to collusion.[101] Moreover, the defense may prove too much in circumstances where the buyers' market power would allow them to pass along any price increases downstream, thereby removing the incentive to constrain prices.[102]

The 1992 *Merger Guidelines* confirm the legitimacy of the power buyer defense but limit its applicability. In describing those conditions that assist in detecting (and encouraging) deviations from coordinated behavior, the *Merger Guidelines* include as an example "buyer characteristics and the nature of the procurement process."[103] The *Merger Guidelines* expressly state, however, that the size of the buyer does not exclusively determine whether such a departure from

---

to 39 customers, with the remainder accounted for by more than approximately 100 other smaller buyers, the larger customers could not exert the requisite market power to prevent the smaller buyers from suffering from increased prices); FTC v. Bass Bros. Enters., 1984-1 Trade Cas. (CCH) ¶ 66,041 (N.D. Ohio 1984) (buyers representing approximately 70% of the market's purchasers, even though they were large automotive tire manufacturers, could not protect the remainder of the purchasers in the carbon black market from price discrimination); *see also* FTC v. Cardinal Health, Inc., 12 F. Supp. 2d 34, 58-61 (D.D.C. 1998) (finding fragmented power buyer market insufficient to rebut the government's prima facie case).

101. *See, e.g.*, FTC v. Elders Grain, Inc., 868 F.2d 901, 905-06 (7th Cir. 1989) (a merger of two principal manufacturers of industrial dry corn, a highly concentrated market as geographically defined by the court, was not defensible because of the sophistication and small number of major food manufacturer customer; the relevant market was already highly concentrated and historically prone to collusion); *see also* FTC v. University Health, Inc., 938 F.2d 1206, 1213 n.13 (11th Cir. 1991) (court of appeals found that certain health insurance companies were actually not large power buyers and were incapable of preventing collusion on prices).

102. *See* Allied Signal, Inc. v. Goodrich Co., 183 F.3d 568, 575 (7th Cir. 1999) ("The buying power of the large airplane manufacturers might in fact be sufficient to prevent B.F. Goodrich-Coltec from charging uncompetitive prices. However, if airplane manufacturers have market power relative to the purchasers of the fully-assembled airplanes, the airplane manufacturers would simply pass along the increased landing gear costs and hence would have no incentive to prevent B.F. Goodrich-Coltec from charging uncompetitive prices.").

103. 1992 MERGER GUIDELINES, *supra* note 15, § 2.12; *see also* NAAG MERGER GUIDELINES, *supra* note 76, § 5.4.

coordinated behavior is likely to occur.[104] Rather, the *Merger Guidelines* provide that some additional circumstances must exist, such as purchases made pursuant to long-term contracts, as evidence that firms may have adequate incentive to deviate from coordinated market behavior.[105]

D. Proving the Difficulty of Collusion

1. Market Conditions That Are Not Conducive to Coordinated Interaction

Merger proponents may claim a variety of market characteristics or behavior as contributing to a competitive climate that is not conducive to collusion. These characteristics, like the power buyer defense and entry barrier analysis, are the types of "other factors" to which *General Dynamics* speaks.

The 1992 *Merger Guidelines* define "coordinated interaction" as "actions by a group of firms that are profitable for each of them only as a result of the accommodating reactions of the others. This behavior includes tacit or explicit collusion, and may or may not be lawful in and of itself."[106] Such coordinated interaction or collusion must involve the firms not only agreeing to profitable terms of coordinated behavior, but also establishing a mechanism to detect and punish those who deviate from the negotiated terms.[107]

Various market conditions are not conducive to agreement upon such a coordinated system and, instead, demonstrate the difficulty of successful collusion.[108] In *R.R. Donnelley & Sons Co.*, for example, the Commission found that "significant obstacles" to collusion existed in the high-volume publication printing market alleged by complaint counsel. First, the evidence demonstrated that potentially colluding printers could not likely agree upon the margin they would enjoy as a result of their pricing. Second, the commercial printers had various cost structures that

---

104. *See* 1992 MERGER GUIDELINES, *supra* note 15, § 2.12.
105. *See id.*
106. *Id.* § 2.1.
107. *See id; see also* R.R. Donnelley & Sons Co., 120 F.T.C. 36, 183 (1995).
108. "Collusion is easier to establish . . . in a market that is concentrated on the seller side and in which the products are homogeneous, demand is inelastic, conditions are stable, sellers have similar costs, buyers are unable to contain prices, transactions are numerous and frequent and information about price and other competitive variables is readily available." Occidental Petroleum Corp., 115 F.T.C. 1010, 1250 (1992) (citations omitted), *order mod.*, 117 F.T.C. 45 (1994).

would frustrate coordination. Third, the printing business involved a great many variables, each of which could provide an opportunity for a participant to cheat and deviate from the terms of coordination. Therefore, the Commission concluded that successful coordination of terms could not be achieved in a fashion that would promote collusion.[109]

After an agreement is reached upon terms, the other critical component of coordinated interaction or collusion is the cartel's ability to detect and punish deviations.[110] In some markets, the very existence and nature of a company's plans for expanding capacity are a matter of public record, which is a severe disincentive for any participant in coordinated interaction to deviate or cheat from the terms agreed upon by its competitors in the cartel.[111] In contrast, the transaction characteristics

---

109. *See R.R. Donnelley & Sons Co.*, 120 F.T.C. at 183-93. In contrast, where a product is largely standardized or homogeneous, sellers attempting to coordinate prices are more likely to agree upon a common price. *See, e.g.*, FTC v. Elders Grain, Inc., 868 F.2d 901, 905 (7th Cir. 1989). *See generally* Brooke Group v. Brown & Williamson Tobacco Corp., 509 U.S. 209, 239 (1993). *But see* Degussa AG, 63 Fed. Reg. 16,552 (Apr. 3, 1998) (analysis to aid public comment) (high concentration and restrictive entry conditions into hydrogen peroxide market along with various historical industry conditions made coordinated interaction a serious threat).

110. *See* FTC v. Swedish Match, 131 F. Supp. 2d 151, 168 n.13 (D.D.C. 2000) (finding that a proposed merger between the first and third largest loose leaf tobacco producers would increase the likelihood of coordinated action because "it creates a duopoly, the monitoring of prices is easy, and firms can punish price cutters"); FTC v. Cardinal Health, Inc. 12 F. Supp. 2d 34, 65 (D.D.C. 1998) (group purchasing organization contract with three of the four merging drug wholesaler defendants contained provisions guaranteeing members a favorable price, thereby encouraging price coordination and policing the defendants from attempts to cheat on one another); In re Solvay, S.A., 67 Fed. Reg. 30,929 (May 8, 2002) (analysis to aid public comment) (consent agreement negotiated, in part, because proposed acquisition would leave only two significant producers of chemical product, and reliable pricing information along with a large number of customers in the industry would make cheating on any coordination easy to detect).

111. *See, e.g.*, Hospital Corp. of Am. v. FTC, 807 F.2d 1381, 1387 (7th Cir. 1986) (a state statute which requires that hospitals obtain a certificate of need prior to expansion or new construction provides competing hospitals in the geographic market not only notice of any deviation from established terms of output, but also the means by which to punish the hospital departing from the coordinated terms, i.e., by opposing the grant of the certificate).

of other markets (including some that are marked by high concentration on the buying side) discourage the successful administration of price collusion or coordination by maintaining a high degree of secrecy regarding price quotations and by limiting purchases to a few relatively infrequent, but large, transactions.[112]

Cheaters or mavericks are more likely to deviate from coordinated prices or output schedules when the economic incentives are greater, such as, for example, in capital intensive product markets.[113] The impetus to maintain full production in order to cover high fixed costs encourages cheating or deviation from the terms of coordination.[114] Excess capacity, whether on a seasonal basis or because of the general economic conditions of the market, also encourages maverick behavior.[115]

Similarly, a strong incentive also exists to divert capacity (whether or not excess) to portions of the market with inelastic demand because they are likely to be more profitable.[116] Although cheating on cartel behavior with respect to large, single, or infrequent transactions (as opposed to a series of smaller transactions) is difficult to detect, such large transactions also provide a significant incentive to cheat on the cartel: a large order from a single buyer may present such an opportunity for profit that the cheater is willing to risk discipline by the cartel if caught.[117]

---

112. *See* United States v. Archer-Daniels-Midland Co., 781 F. Supp. 1400, 1423 (S.D. Iowa 1991); FTC v. Owens-Illinois, Inc., 681 F. Supp. 27, 48-49 (D.D.C. 1988).
113. *See Archer-Daniels-Midland Co.*, 781 F. Supp. at 1423; *Owens-Illinois, Inc.*, 681 F. Supp. at 48-49; *see also* Shell Oil Co., 62 Fed. Reg. 67,868 (Dec. 30, 1997) (analysis to and public comment) (exchange agreements between refiners could facilitate identification and punishment of participants deviating from a coordinated price).
114. *See Archer-Daniels-Midland Co.*, 781 F. Supp. at 1423; *Owens-Illinois, Inc.*, 681 F. Supp. at 48-49.
115. *See* William J. Kolasky, Coordinated Effects in Merger Review: From Dead Frenchmen to Beautiful Minds and Mavericks, Address Before the ABA Section of Antitrust Law Spring Meeting (Apr. 24, 2002) [hereinafter Coordinated Effects in Merger Review] (discussing the ability of mavericks to constrain coordinated interaction); *see also* Jonathan B. Baker, *Mavericks, Mergers and Exclusion: Proving Coordinated Competitive Effects Under the Antitrust Laws*, 77 N.Y.U. L. REV. 135 (2002).
116. *See, e.g.*, R.R. Donnelley & Sons Co., 120 F.T.C. 36, 184-90 (1995).
117. *See, e.g.*, *Hospital Corp. of Am.*, 807 F.2d at 1391.

Finally, it should be noted that in *FTC v. H.J. Heinz Co.*,[118] the D.C. Circuit Court of Appeals held that the second and third largest baby food manufacturers failed to rebut the "ordinary presumption of collusion in a merger to duopoly," noting that "[t]he combination of a concentrated market and barriers to entry is a recipe for price coordination" and that "[t]he creation of a durable duopoly affords both the opportunity and incentive for both firms to coordinate to increase prices."[119] Rebutting the presumption of coordinated interaction in a 3-2 merger is likely to be especially difficult regardless of what other countervailing factors may exist.

2. *Recent Developments before the Agencies*

Recently, the agencies have stated publicly their view that coordinated interaction analysis should play an important role in merger review,[120] and they have undertaken efforts to study the economics of coordinated interaction to better gauge when collusion among merged entities is most likely to occur.[121] Agency action over the past few years also reveals that coordinated interaction has become more prominent in merger review.[122]

---

118. 246 F.3d 708 (D.C. Cir. 2001).

119. *Id.* at 724-25.

120. *See, e.g.*, Coordinated Effects in Merger Review, *supra* n.115, (the Division has not lost confidence in its ability to predict coordinated interaction in mergers other than 3-2 mergers, and it "will bring coordinated effects cases where we think that potential is likely to be fulfilled").

121. *See, e.g.*, Deborah Platt Majoras, Deputy Ass't. Att'y Gen., Antitrust Div., A Review of Recent Antitrust Division Actions, distributed at the ABA, Section of Business Law 2003 Conference for Corporate Counsel, at 26 (June 12, 2003) ("We have now rolled out internally an approximately 200-page Coordinated Effects policy manual designed to serve as a resource for Division Staff attorneys and economists"); *see also* David T. Scheffman and Mary Coleman, *Quantitative Analyses of Potential Competitive Effects From a Merger,* (2003) (to be published in GEO. MASON U.L. REV.), *at* www.ftc.gov/be/quartmergeranalysis.pdf.

122. *See, e.g.*, FTC v. H.J. Heinz Co., 246 F.3d 708, 724-25 (D.C. Cir. 2001). In *Heinz*, the court agreed that the FTC had established a prima facie case that the merger between the second and third largest baby food manufacturers (Heinz and Beech-Nut, respectively) was anticompetitive, and that the manufacturers failed to rebut this prima facie case. The court noted that "[t]he combination of a concentrated market and barriers to entry is a recipe for price coordination," and that the failure of the

The FTC, for example, carefully considered the possibility of increased coordinated interaction in its "Cruise Line" merger investigation, ultimately concluding that the parties had rebutted a prima facie case. This investigation concerned two alternative proposed transactions: the creation of a dual-list company combining Royal Caribbean Cruises, Ltd. ("Royal") and P&O Princess Cruises plc ("Princess"), and a competing hostile tender offer by Carnival Corporation ("Carnival") for Princess. Carnival was the largest cruise line, Royal the second-largest, and Princess the third-largest. Importantly, however, the Commission found there were other significant cruise lines, in particular, Star Cruises, whose Norwegian Cruise Lines was the fourth-largest.[123] By a 3-2 vote, the FTC allowed both transactions to proceed.

The statements issued by the majority and dissent reveal, in particular, a disagreement over the likelihood of coordination on pricing and capacity reductions. On price coordination, the majority concluded that the industry was too complex and heterogeneous in its price, itinerary, and entertainment options to allow for successful coordination. The dissent disagreed, citing, in part, the cruise lines' past efforts to monitor each other's prices, adjustments in prices in response to competitors' price changes, and the ability of travel agents, who book the vast majority of cruises, to facilitate price competition by communicating competing offers to rival cruise lines. Significantly, the *relevance* of these factors—heterogeneous pricing on the one hand, a history of price monitoring and adjustment on the other—were not subject to debate so much as whether the evidence demonstrated the presence or absence of these factors. Indeed, the majority statement emphasized several times that the ultimate resolution depended on a close analysis of industry-specific facts.

---

manufacturers' expert and the district court to identify structural market barriers to collusion meant that the "ordinary presumption of collusion in a merger to duopoly" controlled.

123. Statement of the Federal Trade Commission concerning Royal Caribbean Cruises, Ltd./P&O Princess Cruises plc and Carnival Corporation/P&O Princess Cruises plc, FTC File No. 021 0041, *at* www.ftc.gov/os/2002/10/cruisestatement.htm; *see also* Joseph J. Simons, Director, FTC Bureau of Competition, Merger Enforcement at the FTC, Keynote Address to the Tenth Annual Golden State Antitrust and Unfair Competition Law Institute (Oct. 24, 2002), *at* www.ftc.gov/speeches/other/02102mergeenforcement.htm (providing a detailed discussion of the Cruise Lines case and coordinated interaction).

The same industry-specific factual analysis led to disagreement over coordination on capacity reductions. The majority concluded that redeploying ships to non-North American markets to affect North American prices would be too costly, and that reducing the number of ships would be too risky in light of pre-existing contractual commitments for a large expansion over the next four years. Coordination was therefore unlikely. The dissent acknowledged that the industry would grow in the short term, but concluded that either of the proposed transactions would create a market leader that could set a slower pace for future growth, which its nearest competitors could be expected to follow.

The agencies will continue to pay close attention to mergers in industries with a history of collusion.[124]

E. Creating a Stronger Competitor

Although not as well-grounded in case law or economic theory as the other means of rebuttal discussed in this chapter, an additional defensive argument is that the merger will make the merging parties better able to compete against the market leader. For purposes of rebutting the inference created by increased market shares in a highly concentrated market, arguments that increased market share will improve competition in the market are, however, rarely successful or publicly endorsed by courts or the enforcement agencies.[125]

---

124. *See, e.g.*, U.S. Department of Justice Files Suit to Stop SGL Carbon from Acquiring Carbide/Graphite Group's Graphite Electrode Assets, Press Release (Apr. 15, 2003), *at* www.usdoj.gov/atr/public/press_releases/2003/200954.htm ("This market is one in which competitors have a history of colluding rather than competing. This acquisition would increase the incentive and ability of the remaining producers to revert to collusive behavior"); U.S. Department of Justice Intends to File Suit to Stop UPM Kymmene Oyj from Acquiring Bemis Corporation's MACtac Division, Press Release, (Apr. 14, 2003), *at* www.usdoj.gov/atr/public/press_releases/2003/200932.htm ("Our investigation has revealed that this marked [sic] is already one in which competitors have sought to coordinate rather than compete. This merger would increase the likelihood that UPM and others will coordinate on bulk paper labelstock prices").

125. Commentators, however, have debated the role of the stronger competitor theory. *See, e.g.*, C. Paul Rogers, *The Limited Case for an Efficiency Defense in Horizontal Mergers*, 58 TUL. L. REV. 503, 533 (Nov. 1983); David J. Clanton, *Recent Merger Developments: Coming of Age Under the Guidelines*, 53 ANTITRUST L.J. 345, 347 (1984).

Early U.S. Supreme Court cases implicitly recognized the apparent validity of protecting two small companies that merged in order to compete more effectively against the larger corporation(s) dominating the market.[126] For example, in *United States v. Philadelphia National Bank*,[127] the Court appeared to endorse the hypothetical transaction where two small firms in a market propose a merger to compete more successfully against the market leader but nonetheless rejected the countervailing power argument actually presented in that case, i.e., that the merger of local banks would permit more effective competition with larger, out-of-market New York banks.[128]

Although the argument for permitting small firms to join forces against their larger competitors in an already concentrated market may seem logical, courts generally have accepted the argument only if other persuasive factors are present. For example, when considering the merger of the market's second- and third-ranked dairies in *United States v. Country Lake Foods, Inc.*, the district court accepted as additional justification the evidence from customers that the creation of a second large dairy would benefit competition.[129] The court made this finding only after expressly characterizing these arguments as efficiencies that provided relevant evidence as to the lack of anticompetitive effect, but not independent justification for the transaction.[130]

Not surprisingly, the DOJ and the FTC do not generally agree with the assertion that a merger arguably creating a larger, more effective competitor against the market leader successfully rebuts statistical evidence of market power in the form of market share.[131] For example,

---

126. *See, e.g.*, Brown Shoe Co. v. United States, 370 U.S. 294, 319 (1962) (quoting the legislative history of Section 7 of the Clayton Act to permit such a transaction).
127. 374 U.S. 321 (1963).
128. *See id.* at 370-71.
129. *See* United States v. Country Lake Foods, Inc., 754 F. Supp. 669, 680 (D. Minn. 1990) (the merger of the second and third largest dairies in the market with 18.2% and 17.8%, respectively, justified in part on the ground that the resulting competitor would enjoy the same economies of scale as the current market leader with 36% of the market and, therefore, would be able to compete more directly).
130. *See id.*; *see also* Kaiser Aluminum & Chem. Corp. v. FTC, 652 F.2d 1324, 1341 (7th Cir. 1981) ("unique economic circumstances might make other factors significant, *e.g.*, . . . the merger of two small firms to survive competitively in a market, or the demand of a market for large producers").
131. *See, e.g.*, RSR Corp. v. FTC, 602 F.2d 1317, 1325 (9th Cir. 1979);

the FTC rejected this assertion in *FTC v. H.J. Heinz Co.*,[132] where Heinz and Beech-Nut (the second and third largest baby food manufacturers) argued that their proposed merger was necessary to enable Heinz to innovate and compete against Gerber, the market leader.[133] The parties claimed that without the merger the two firms could not launch new products because they lacked a sufficient shelf presence; cost-effective new product launches, they argued, required a shelf space of 70% or greater. The FTC was not persuaded that the economic evidence supported this proposition nor was the D.C. Circuit, which held: "In the absence of reliable and significant evidence that the merger will permit innovation that otherwise could not be accomplished, the district court had no basis to conclude that the FTC's showing was rebutted by an innovation defense."[134]

Commentators have suggested that there is little economic justification in support of the "countervailing power" argument. For example, these commentators note that affording greater latitude to the merger of two smaller firms in a market dominated by one or more large firms may ignore that the larger firms obtained their market share by superior performance, historical accident, or past mergers that led to the current concentration level.[135] Furthermore, absent demonstrated efficiencies, reducing the disparities in market shares does not necessarily mean that competition will be increased:

> When one starts with large disparities in an already concentrated market, however, reducing the number of firms and increasing the size of the market's smaller firms makes non-competitive pricing more likely. Unless there are scale economies, the merged firm is less likely to compete on price than the unmerged firms previously were. ... Mutually beneficial coordination of pricing is much easier in a four-firm market. ... [M]ere reduction of size disparities is not a persuasive reason for treating mergers in highly concentrated industries more liberally.[136]

In reality, the "stronger number two" theory is a form of the argument that the merger will result in efficiencies and, as the district

---

Country Lake Foods, Inc., 754 F. Supp. at 680; United States v. Provident Nat'l Bank, 280 F. Supp. 1, 16-20 (E.D. Pa. 1968).

132. 246 F.3d 708 (D.C. Cir. 2001).

133. *Id.* at 722-23.

134. *Id.* at 723.

135. *See* 4 PHILLIP E. AREEDA, HERBERT HOVENKAMP & JOHN L. SOLOW, ANTITRUST LAW ¶ 927(d)(4) (rev. ed. 1998).

136. *Id.*

court in *Country Lake Foods* suggested, is appropriately dealt with in that fashion.[137]

F. The Significance of Declining Industries

Merging companies in a declining industry often claim that, because of decreasing demand, the industry as a whole suffers from overcapacity. Efficiencies within the industry will result, they assert, if a merger of market competitors is permitted. These arguments have arisen often in the defense industry. Proponents of defense mergers argue that overcapacity and the resulting industry decline, together with the need to protect the national defense, should be considered as among the "other factors" to which the U.S. Supreme Court referred in *General Dynamics* as justification for overcoming statistical market share evidence indicating the presence of market power.

Significantly, in four defense industry mergers,[138] neither the asserted decline of the industry nor the protection of national security convinced the courts to depart from the principles of traditional merger analysis in the context of a highly concentrated market.[139] Rather, the courts generally have assumed that the protection of competition through enforcement of the antitrust laws was even more necessary because of the Defense Department's position as keeper of the national security.[140]

---

137. *See* United States v. Country Lake Foods, 754 F. Supp. 669, 680 (D. Minn. 1990); *see also* Chapter 6.

138. *See* FTC v. Alliant Techsystems Inc., 808 F. Supp. 9 (D.D.C. 1992); FTC v. PPG Indus., 628 F. Supp. 881 (D.D.C.), *modified*, 1986-1 Trade Cas. (CCH) ¶ 67,119 (D.D.C.), *aff'd in part*, 798 F.2d 1500 (D.C. Cir. 1986); Grumman Corp. v. LTV Corp., 527 F. Supp. 86 (E.D.N.Y.) (injunction action originally brought by the target of a hostile tender offer in which the FTC intervened on the side of the plaintiff in support of its antitrust claims), *aff'd*, 665 F.2d 10 (2d Cir. 1981); FTC v. Imo Indus., 1992-2 Trade Cas. (CCH) ¶ 69,943 (D.D.C. 1989).

139. *See, e.g.*, *Alliant Techsystems Inc.*, 808 F. Supp. at 21 ("The anticompetitive effects of the merger, however, are not counterbalanced by the competing efficiency considerations alleged by defendants. Defendants' concerns regarding the risks of transferring technology to cost, delay, and quality are speculative at best"); *Imo Indus.*, 1992-2 Trade Cas. (CCH) ¶ 69,943, at 68,560 ("a merger could be in the interest of a strong national defense," but these alleged benefits could not overcome the "strong public interest in the preservation of competition").

140. *See, e.g.*, *Grumman Corp.*, 527 F. Supp. at 106 ("the interest of the public here is greater than in the ordinary case since a lessening of competition might very well affect the quality and price of weapons sold to the United

Largely as a result of the downsizing of the defense industry in the 1990s and the FTC's successful challenge in *Alliant Techsystems Inc.*, the Under Secretary of Defense (Acquisition and Technology) and the General Counsel of the Department of Defense established a task force to inform the Department of Defense about antitrust analysis of mergers and joint ventures so that it can play a more constructive role in the antitrust review process of the enforcement agencies.[141] The Department of Defense task force conducted a thorough review of the military procurement process, the status and likely future of the defense industry, and the role of the antitrust review and enforcement function in the context of defense mergers, and concluded that:

> [c]ompetition among firms in the defense industry is significantly different from competition among firms in other sectors of the economy, but .. . the Antitrust Merger Guidelines are flexible enough to take into consideration the special circumstances of downsizing in the defense industry.[142]

When specifically addressing the argument that, as a distressed industry, the defense industry deserved special treatment under the antitrust laws, the task force report stated:

> In some instances, mergers in distressed industries can be defended on grounds they produce substantial efficiencies. But there is nothing in the Clayton Act case law or Merger Guidelines that would adjust antitrust enforcement—absent efficiency claims—when all or most firms in an industry are barely breaking even and are subject to long-term overcapacity.[143]

The Department of Defense has expressed the view that the defense industry is transforming, not declining, and that current industry consolidation will not prevent the spawning of "dozens of new entrants to the global defense industrial base."[144] Where defense mergers and

---

States Navy"); *see also Lockheed Martin, Northrop Grumman Cancel Merger Plans Due to Government Opposition,* 75 Antitrust & Trade Reg. Rep. (BNA) 94 (1998) (noting that the Division and the Department of Defense opposed the merger on competition grounds while the latter voiced support for consolidations consistent with competition).

141. *See* Report of the Defense Science Board Task Force on Antitrust Aspects of Defense Industry Consolidation, at 1 (Apr. 1994), *at* www.acq.osd.mil/dsb/antitrust.pdf.

142. Memorandum for Under Secretary of Defense (Acquisition & Technology), dated Apr. 4, 1994 (forwarding task force report).

143. *Id.* at 34.

144. Annual Industrial Capabilities Report to Congress, Department of Defense, at 6 (Feb. 2003); *see also* Transforming the Defense Industrial

acquisitions raise anticompetitive concerns, the "declining industry" rebuttal may be more difficult to prove than in the past.[145]

Base: A Roadmap, Department of Defense (Feb. 2003), *at* www.acq.osd.mil/ip/docs/ind-cap-annual-report-to-congress_2003.pdf.

145. The "declining industry" argument does not appear to have been raised in connection with the two largest proposed defense industry mergers in the past few years. *See* Justice Department Requires Northrop Grumman to Adopt Non-Discrimination Terms in order to Consummate its Acquisition of TRW, Inc., Press Release (Dec. 11, 2002), *at* www.usdoj.gov/atr/public/press_releases/2002/200543.htm; United States v. Northrop Grumman Corp., 68 Fed. Reg. 1861 (Jan. 14, 2002) (competitive impact statement); United States v. General Dynamics Corp., Civ. No. 1:01CV02200 (D.D.C. filed Oct. 23, 2001) (complaint), *at* www.usdoj.gov/atr/cases/f9300/9373.htm.; U.S. Dep't of Justice, Antitrust Div., Justice Department Files Suit to Block General Dynamics' Purchase of Newport News, Press Release (Oct. 23, 2001).

CHAPTER 6

EFFICIENCIES

The debate over the appropriate role of efficiencies in merger analysis has endured at least since Oliver Williamson first proposed that the cost savings generated by a merger could justify otherwise anticompetitive combinations.[1] Despite general acceptance among scholars, both the judiciary and enforcement agencies have traditionally been less receptive, even hostile, to efficiency claims presented by merging firms. Nonetheless, the 1997 amendment to the efficiencies section of the Antitrust Division of the U.S. Department of Justice (DOJ or the Division) and Federal Trade Commission (FTC or the Commission) 1992 *Merger Guidelines*, recent speeches by senior officials, as well as subsequent lower court decisions, indicate that efficiencies are beginning to achieve heightened recognition by both courts and agencies analyzing the anticompetitive effects of mergers. Yet there remains a fundamental debate regarding the extent to which efficiencies should be considered in merger analysis, and, if so, how they should be considered.[2]

A. Efficiencies Defined

Generally, "economic efficiency" describes an event that increases the total value of all economically measurable assets in society.[3] In the context of a merger, efficiencies grow out of the ability of the combining firms to "better utilize existing assets" through integration.[4]

---

1. *See* Oliver Williamson, *Economies and an Antitrust Defense: The Welfare Tradeoffs*, 58 AMER. ECON. REV. 18 (1968).
2. For an extensive discussion, see Ilene Knable Gotts and Calvin S. Goldman, *The Role of Efficiencies in M & A Global Antitrust Review: Still in Flux?*, *in* 2002 FORDHAM CORPORATE LAW INSTITUTE: INTERNATIONAL ANTITRUST LAW AND POLICY 201 (Barry Hawk, ed. 2003).
3. *See, e.g.*, Joseph F. Brodley, *The Economic Goals of Antitrust: Efficiency, Consumer Welfare, and Technological Progress*, 62 N.Y.U. L. REV. 1020, 1025 (1987).
4. U.S. DEP'T OF JUSTICE & FEDERAL TRADE COMM'N, HORIZONTAL MERGER GUIDELINES (1992) [hereinafter 1992 MERGER GUIDELINES] § 4 (revised Apr. 8, 1997), *reprinted in* 4 Trade Reg. Rep. (CCH) ¶13,104

The two types of efficiencies most commonly recognized in merger analysis are productive efficiencies and innovative efficiencies.[5] Productive efficiencies are achieved when the merged firms are able to reduce long-run average costs through a more cost-effective combination of resources. Examples of productive efficiencies include achieving economies of scale and economies of scope, superior integration of production facilities, plant specialization, and lower transportation costs.[6] The cost savings associated with productive efficiencies are generally more susceptible to quantification than other types of efficiencies because cost savings may be estimated reliably from available information.

Innovative efficiencies arise when, for example, merging firms lower costs by eliminating duplicative research and development operations or by combining to expand the benefits of a superior technology.[7] Although the long-term benefits to consumers of innovative efficiencies may be significant, the evidentiary problems of projecting such cost savings may be substantial.[8]

Mergers also generate other savings, including managerial and pecuniary efficiencies, such as tax and other fixed cost reductions, that are generally treated less favorably because reductions in fixed costs are less likely to result in lower prices to consumers and frequently may be obtained without a merger. Managerial and pecuniary cost reductions also are generally not considered by the agencies in evaluating the procompetitive effects of a merger.[9]

---

and in Appendix I.

5. *See*, *e.g.*, Joseph F. Brodley, *Proof of Efficiencies in Mergers and Joint Ventures*, 64 ANTITRUST L.J. 575 (1996).

6. *See* 1992 MERGER GUIDELINES, *supra* note 4, § 4.

7. *See* Joseph Kattan, *Efficiencies and Merger Analysis*, 62 ANTITRUST L.J. 513, 522-23 (1994).

8. *See* Joseph F. Brodley, *Proof of Efficiencies in Mergers and Joint Ventures*, 64 ANTITRUST L.J. 575, 581 (1996).

9. *See* Joseph Kattan, *Efficiencies and Merger Analysis*, 62 ANTITRUST L.J. 513 (1994). *But see* Thomas B. Leary, Commissioner, FTC, Efficiencies and Antitrust: A Story of Ongoing Evolution, Remarks at ABA Section of Antitrust Law 2002 Fall Forum, Washington, D.C. (Nov. 8, 2002) [hereinafter Leary Remarks] ("whether they are called innovation or managerial economies . . . we do not overtly take them into account when deciding merger cases"), *at* www.ftc.gov/speeches/leary.htm.

B. Efficiencies and the Goals of Antitrust Laws

Most commentators believe that the extent to which efficiencies are cognizable in assessing the legality of a merger is dependent on the intent of Congress in formulating antitrust policy. Neither the statutory language nor the legislative history of Section 7 of the Clayton Act,[10] however, makes explicit reference to efficiencies. In the absence of any clearly expressed congressional intent, scholars have debated the extent to which Congress sought to measure the effects of a merger on competition. Thus, determining the appropriate role of efficiencies depends in large part on whether Congress sought only to promote allocative efficiency or whether the statute embodies a consumer welfare approach, thereby accounting for the distributive effects of a merger.

Allocative efficiency is achieved by maximizing overall societal welfare,[11] without accounting for the distributive consequences of a merger. Thus, allocative efficiency leads to the placement of resources where consumers most value their output, which is achieved where a good is priced at marginal cost.[12] Proponents of the view originally expounded by Oliver Williamson would condone any merger where the reduced costs of the merged firm (ranging from 5 to 10 percent), spread over the entire output of the firm, outweigh the value of goods lost to society due to monopolistic pricing.[13] Under this standard, a merger to monopoly creating substantial efficiencies could survive antitrust scrutiny even where the monopolist obtained the benefit of all the cost savings.

Advocates of the consumer welfare approach argue that Congress intended that distributive goals take precedence, and that antitrust laws

---

10. 15 U.S.C. § 18.
11. This is also referred to as "total surplus," which is equal to the sum of consumer surplus and profits. Consumer surplus is the difference between the amount consumers would have paid for the quantity consumed and the amount actually paid.
12. *See* Mark N. Berry, *Efficiencies and Horizontal Mergers: In Search of a Defense*, 33 SAN DIEGO L. REV. 515, 529-32 (1996).
13. In economic parlance, this is called the "deadweight loss"—the total value of the goods that are lost to society as a result of monopolistic pricing. *See* Oliver Williamson, *Economies and an Antitrust Defense: The Welfare Tradeoffs*, 58 AMER. ECON. REV. 18 (1968). For the argument that economic efficiency should be the sole relevant consideration and that proof of cost saving should not receive consideration, see Robert H. Bork & Ward S. Bowman, *The Crisis in Antitrust*, 65 COLUM. L. REV. 363 (1965).

are aimed at "preventing 'unfair' transfers of wealth from consumers to firms with market power."[14] Under this approach, consumer surplus is viewed as the entitlement of consumers. Thus, efficiencies are a relevant consideration in merger analysis only where consumers benefit directly from the resulting cost savings. Many efficiencies arising from a merger, however, especially fixed cost savings, will not necessarily affect consumer surplus. Scholars favoring this view have been unable to create an applicable test for determining when efficiencies justify a merger that also ensures that consumer surplus is passed on to consumers.[15]

While the debate continues among scholars, the judiciary and enforcement agencies traditionally have sought to bar mergers that would result in the unfair distribution of wealth away from consumers. This concern is incorporated into the 1992 *Merger Guidelines*, which appear to invoke a consumer welfare standard by requiring that the cost savings be passed on to consumers.[16] The difficulty lies in resolving the conflict between adopting a consumer welfare standard of merger analysis while distinguishing between those efficiencies that promote consumer welfare and those that may inure only to the benefit of the monopolist.

C. U.S. Supreme Court Treatment of Efficiencies

Beginning with *Brown Shoe Co. v. United States*,[17] the U.S. Supreme Court has passed on efficiencies claims in only three Section 7 horizontal merger cases, each time taking a different, and somewhat conflicting, approach.

---

14. Joseph Kattan, *Efficiencies and Merger Analysis*, 62 ANTITRUST L.J., 513, 520 (1994); Robert H. Lande, *Wealth Transfers as the Original and Primary Concern of Antitrust: The Efficiency Interpretation Challenged*, 34 HASTINGS L.J. 65, 68 (1982).
15. *See* William J. Kolasky, Conglomerate Mergers and Range Effects: It's A Long Way From Chicago To Brussels, Prepared Remarks Before the George Mason University Symposium (Nov. 9, 2001), at 5-7, *at* www.usdoj.gov/atr/public/speeches/speech_kolasky.htm (arguing that agency officials have very limited ability to determine when efficiencies will or will not benefit consumers); Mark N. Berry, *Efficiencies and Horizontal Mergers: In Search of a Defense*, 33 SAN DIEGO L. REV. 515, 535-38 (1996).
16. *See* Deborah A. Garza, *The New Efficiencies Guidelines: The Same Old Transparent Wine in a More Transparent Bottle*, ANTITRUST, Summer 1997, at 6.
17. 370 U.S. 294 (1962).

In *Brown Shoe*, the Court considered the merger of competing retail shoe stores, noting that because the merged retail outlets would be vertically integrated with Brown's substantial shoe manufacturing operations, the combined entity, "by eliminating wholesalers and by increasing the volume of purchases from the manufacturing division of the enterprise," would be able to "market [its] own brands at prices below those of competing independent retailers."[18] This expansion would benefit consumers and was "not rendered unlawful by the mere fact that small independent stores [might] be adversely affected."[19] Nevertheless, while recognizing the potential benefits to consumers, the Court felt constrained not to accord great weight to this efficiency given the perceived congressional determination to promote competition by protecting small competitors: "Congress appreciated that occasional higher costs and prices might result from the maintenance of fragmented industries and markets. It resolved these competing considerations in favor of decentralization. We must give effect to that decision."[20] Adhering to the notion that antitrust laws were designed to promote fragmentation and low concentration, the Court thus disregarded efficiencies claims regardless of the recognized cost savings that would benefit consumers.

In *United States v. Philadelphia National Bank*,[21] the Court rejected a series of "affirmative justifications" proffered by the merging firms to save their transaction, which had been judged likely substantially to lessen competition.[22] The Court stated that

> a merger the effect of which "may be substantially to lessen competition" is not saved because, on some ultimate reckoning of social or economic debits and credits, it may be deemed beneficial. A value choice of such magnitude is beyond the ordinary limits of judicial competence, and in any event has been made for us already, by Congress when it enacted the amended § 7. Congress determined to preserve our traditionally competitive economy. It therefore proscribed anticompetitive mergers, the benign and the malignant alike, fully aware, we must assume, that some price might have to be paid.[23]

The Court, however, was not responding to an argument that the merger would lower the costs of the combined firm. Rather, the Court

---

18. *Id*. at 344.
19. *Id*.
20. *Id*.
21. 374 U.S. 321 (1963).
22. *Id*. at 370-71.
23. *Id*. at 371.

was rejecting the argument that the merger of two banks in Philadelphia could be justified on the grounds that "Philadelphia needs a bank larger than it now has in order to bring business to the area and stimulate its economic development."[24] As articulated, the defendants' claims did not qualify as cost-saving efficiencies, making application of the Court's statement to a true efficiencies claim questionable.

Elsewhere in the *Philadelphia National Bank* opinion, the Court signaled its willingness to consider efficiency arguments. At one point the Court rejected the argument that "the merger would enable certain economies of scale, specifically, that it would enable the formation of a more elaborate foreign department than either bank is presently able to maintain."[25] The Court did not suggest that efficiency arguments could not be made; instead, it merely pointed out that the issue had been abandoned below.[26] Later in the opinion, the Court rejected the claim that the merger would enable the combined firm "to compete with large out-of-state (particularly New York banks)" for very large loans.[27] The Court noted that procompetitive effects in one market could not justify anticompetitive effects in another, but was careful to distinguish the case where two small firms in a market propose to merge in order to compete more effectively with the leading firms in that market.[28]

In *FTC v. Proctor & Gamble Co.*,[29] the Court appeared to reject definitively all efficiencies claims, declaring that "[p]ossible economies cannot be used as a defense to illegality."[30] The absence of any context for this statement makes it difficult to assess. Scholars have suggested that, as opposed to economies that are merely "possible," those that are more certain to materialize could succeed as a defense.[31] Alternatively, it is not clear if the Court would be more receptive to efficiency claims in assessing the anticompetitive effects of a merger, rather than as an affirmative defense to a merger already found to be illegal, as was the case in *Proctor & Gamble*. Nonetheless, the U.S. Supreme Court's

---

24. *Id*.
25. *Id*. at 334-35 n.10.
26. *See* id.
27. *Id*. at 334.
28. *See id*. at 371.
29. 386 U.S. 568 (1967).
30. *Id*. at 580 (citing Brown Shoe Co. v. United States, 370 U.S. 294, 344 (1962)).
31. *See, e.g.*, Alan A. Fisher & Robert H. Lande, *Efficiency Considerations in Merger Enforcement*, 71 CALIF. L. REV. 1582, 1594-95, 1595 n. 66 (1983).

statement in *Proctor* initiated confusion as to whether efficiencies claims were completely precluded from consideration.[32]

D. *Guidelines* Treatment of Efficiencies

1. Federal Merger Guidelines

In 1984, the federal antitrust enforcement agencies expanded the role of efficiencies in merger analysis.[33] For example, pursuant to the 1984 *Merger Guidelines*,[34] rather than only considering efficiency claims in "extraordinary circumstances," as did the 1982 *Merger Guidelines*,[35] the agencies determined to consider efficiency claims whenever "they are established by clear and convincing evidence."[36] The 1984 *Merger Guidelines* also indicated that efficiencies are not a defense to an otherwise anticompetitive merger; instead, they are one of many factors that the agencies consider in determining whether to challenge a merger. Thus, the agencies considered such efficiencies as "economies of scale, better integration of production facilities, plant specialization, and lower transportation costs."[37] Under the 1984 *Merger Guidelines*, the agencies also considered "general selling, administrative and overhead expenses."[38] According to the 1984 *Merger Guidelines*, however, the

---

32. In contrast to the U.S. Supreme Court's reluctance to consider efficiencies in the horizontal merger context, the court has repeatedly credited efficiencies with justifying potentially anticompetitive vertical restraints, including tying arrangements and exclusive dealing arrangements. *See*, *e.g.*, Aspen Skiing Co. v. Aspen Highlands Skiing Corp., 472 U.S. 585 (1985) (cost savings may justify otherwise anticompetitive conduct); United States v. United States Gypsum Co., 438 U.S. 422 (1978) (recognizing procompetitive effect of efficiencies); Northern Pac. Ry. Co. v. United States, 356 U.S. 1 (1958) (recognizing efficiency as goal of antitrust).
33. *See* Janusz A. Ordover, *The Role of Efficiencies in Merger Assessment: The 1997 Guidelines*, ANTITRUST REPORT, Sept. 1997 at 10.
34. U.S. DEP'T OF JUSTICE, MERGER GUIDELINES (1984) [hereinafter 1984 MERGER GUIDELINES], 49 Fed. Reg. 26,823 (1984), *reprinted in* 4 Trade Reg. Rep. (CCH) ¶ 13,103.
35. *See* U.S. DEP'T OF JUSTICE, MERGER GUIDELINES (1982) [hereinafter 1982 GUIDELINES], 47 Fed. Reg. 28,493, *reprinted in* 4 Trade Reg. Rep. (CCH) ¶ 13,102.
36. *Id*. § 4.
37. *Id*.
38. *Id*.

agencies would reject claimed efficiencies if they could be achieved through comparable yet less restrictive means.

As originally promulgated, the 1992 *Merger Guidelines* generally preserved the 1984 *Merger Guidelines*' approach to efficiencies in merger analysis. The efficiencies section of the 1992 *Merger Guidelines* was revised in 1997, however, a product of pressure on the agencies to clarify the role efficiencies play in merger analysis and to broaden the range of circumstances in which merger-related efficiencies may overcome possible anticompetitive effects of the merger.[39]

As revised, the 1992 *Merger Guidelines* make efficiencies a direct part of competitive effects analysis.[40] The agencies examine whether efficiencies might reduce the likelihood of coordinated interaction among firms or the incentive of a firm to raise price unilaterally.[41] Efficiencies that do so are considered likely to benefit consumers. In addition, the agencies only consider "merger-specific" efficiencies. Merger-specific efficiencies are efficiencies that are attributable to the merger and unachievable through less anticompetitive means.[42] Moreover, in addition to being merger specific, any claimed efficiencies must also be "cognizable." Cognizable efficiencies are those that are verifiable by reasonable means and that do not arise from anticompetitive reductions

---

39. *See* 1992 MERGER GUIDELINES, *supra* note 4, § 4 (revised Apr. 8, 1997); *see also* Janusz A. Ordover, *The Role of Efficiencies in Merger Assessment: The 1997 Guidelines*, ANTITRUST REPORT Sept. 1997.

40. *See* Robert Pitofsky, Chairman, FTC, Efficiencies in Defense Mergers: 18 Months After, Speech at the George Mason Law Review, Antitrust Symposium (Oct. 16, 1998), *at* www.ftc.gov/speeches/pitofsky/pitofeff.htm In addition to being a direct part of the analysis of a merger's competitive effects, efficiency considerations still influence the agencies' prosecutorial discretion. For example, early presentation of efficiencies evidence in the Chrysler-Daimler Benz merger influenced the decision not to issue a Second Request. *See id.*

41. *See* 1992 MERGER GUIDELINES, *supra* note 4, § 4 (revised Apr. 8, 1997); *see also* Robert Pitofsky, Chairman, FTC, Efficiencies in Defense Mergers: 18 Months After, Speech at the George Mason Law Review, Antitrust Symposium (Oct. 16, 1998) ("The [1997] revisions recognized that cost reductions may reduce the likelihood of coordinated interaction or the incentive to raise price unilaterally").

42. *See* 1992 MERGER GUIDELINES, *supra* note 4, § 4 (revised Apr. 8, 1997) ("The Agency will only consider those efficiencies likely to be accomplished with the proposed merger and unlikely to be accomplished in the absence of either the proposed merger or another means having comparable anticompetitive effects").

in output, service, or innovation.[43] Finally, the 1992 *Merger Guidelines*, as revised, expressly incorporate a sliding scale approach, stating that "[t]he greater the potential adverse competitive effect of a merger . . . the greater must be cognizable efficiencies in order for the Agency to conclude that the merger will not have an anticompetitive effect in the relevant market."[44]

2. *Federal* Health Care Statements

The enforcement agencies have also affirmed the relevance of efficiencies, at least as a matter of prosecutorial discretion, in the *Health Care Statements* jointly released by the Division and the FTC.[45] The 1993 and 1994 *Health Care Statements* note that:

> Applying the analytical framework of the Merger Guidelines to particular facts of hospital mergers, the Agencies often have concluded that an investigated hospital merger will not result in a substantial lessening of competition in situations where market concentration might otherwise raise an inference of anticompetitive effects. Such situations include transactions where the Agencies found that . . . the merger would allow the hospitals to realize significant cost savings that could not otherwise be realized . . .[46]

The 1993 and 1994 *Health Care Statements* are silent, however, on what efficiencies were cognizable in these situations.

The 1996 *Health Care Statements* refer to and incorporate the 1992 *Merger Guidelines* provisions, adding only that "the Agencies have often concluded that an investigated hospital merger will not result in a substantial lessening of competition in situations . . . where the merger

---

43. *See id.*; *see also* Robert Pitofsky, Chairman, FTC, Efficiencies in Defense Mergers: 18 Months After, Speech at the George Mason Law Review, Antitrust Symposium (Oct. 16, 1998), *at* www.ftc.gov/speeches/pitofsky/pitofeff.htm.

44. 1992 MERGER GUIDELINES, *supra* note 4, § 4 (revised Apr. 8, 1997).

45. *See* U.S. DEP'T OF JUSTICE & FEDERAL TRADE COMM'N, ANTITRUST ENFORCEMENT POLICY STATEMENTS IN THE HEALTH CARE AREA (1994) [hereinafter 1994 HEALTH CARE STATEMENTS], *reprinted in* 4 Trade Reg. Rep. (CCH) ¶ 13,152; U.S. DEP'T OF JUSTICE & FEDERAL TRADE COMM'N, ANTITRUST ENFORCEMENT POLICY STATEMENTS IN THE HEALTH CARE AREA (1993) [hereinafter 1993 HEALTH CARE STATEMENTS], *reprinted in* 4 Trade Reg. Rep. (CCH) ¶ 13,151.

46. 1994 HEALTH CARE STATEMENTS, *supra* note 45, 4 Trade Reg. Rep. (CCH) ¶ 13,152, at 20,774; 1993 HEALTH CARE STATEMENTS, *supra* note 45, 4 Trade Reg. Rep. (CCH) ¶ 13,151, at 20,758.

would allow the hospitals to realize significant cost savings that could not otherwise be realized."[47]

3. *State Enforcement Guidelines*

States have taken smaller steps to incorporate efficiencies into merger analysis. The 1993 *Horizontal Merger Guidelines*[48] issued by the National Association of Attorneys General (NAAG) explain the general enforcement policy of the state attorneys general concerning horizontal mergers. The *NAAG Merger Guidelines* contain a more skeptical view of the relevance of efficiencies in merger analysis than is reflected in the 1992 *Merger Guidelines*.

Unlike the 1992 *Merger Guidelines*, the 1993 *NAAG Merger Guidelines* explicitly reject the notion of efficiency claims as an affirmative defense.[49] In addition, the 1993 *NAAG Merger Guidelines* state that the attorneys general will consider efficiencies only when the claimed efficiencies meet four requirements. First, the efficiencies must be "significant" as demonstrated by "clear and convincing evidence."[50] Second, the efficiencies must "ensure that consumer prices will not increase despite any increase in market power due to the merger."[51] Third, the merging parties must show that comparable cost savings cannot be achieved through other means,[52] and fourth, the parties must demonstrate that the cost savings "will persist over the long run."[53]

E. Role of Efficiencies in Merger Analysis

The courts and federal antitrust agencies have examined whether efficiencies should be considered in assessing the likely anticompetitive effects of a merger or as an affirmative defense to an illegal merger.

---

47. U.S. DEP'T OF JUSTICE & FEDERAL TRADE COMM'N, STATEMENTS OF ANTITRUST ENFORCEMENT POLICY IN HEALTH CARE (1996), *reprinted in* 4 Trade Reg. Rep. (CCH) ¶ 13,153 and in Appendix L.
48. NATIONAL ASS'N OF ATTORNEYS GENERAL, HORIZONTAL MERGER GUIDELINES (1993) [hereinafter 1993 NAAG MERGER GUIDELINES], *reprinted in* 4 Trade Reg. Rep. (CCH) ¶ 13,406 and in Appendix M.
49. *See id.* § 5.3.
50. *Id.*
51. *Id.* Thus, the *NAAG Merger Guidelines* impose a type of modified "pass-on" requirement.
52. *See id.*
53. *Id.*

1. *Judicial Approach*

The majority of courts have considered efficiencies as a means to rebut the government's prima facie case that a merger will lead to restricted output or increased prices.[54] These courts, however, generally have found inadequate proof of efficiencies to sustain a rebuttal of the government's case.[55]

In *FTC v. H.J. Heinz, Co.*,[56] the D.C. Circuit considered whether substantial efficiencies could overcome the structural presumption that a three-to-two merger between Heinz and Beech-Nut would have anticompetitive effects.[57] The asserted relevant market, baby food, was allegedly dominated by Gerber (approximately 65 percent market share), with Heinz and Beech-Nut controlling most of the remaining market. The merging parties claimed that a merger between Heinz and Beech-Nut would result in a combined entity that would be better positioned to compete with Gerber than either individual party had managed; Heinz had a less attractive brand and excess manufacturing capacity, while Beech-Nut had high production costs. The merger would allow the Beech-Nut brand to be produced in Heinz plants, in theory producing a potent combination potentially capable of competing more effectively with Gerber.

The district court accepted these arguments, but the D.C. Circuit reversed and remanded for entry of a preliminary injunction. In theory, the appellate court acknowledged efficiencies as a "defense" that could

---

54. See *infra* notes 73-75 and accompanying text.
55. *Id. But cf.* FTC v. Butterworth Health Corp., 946 F. Supp. 1285, 1302 (W.D. Mich. 1996) (finding evidence of $100 million in efficiencies that rebutted government's prima facie case).
56. 246 F.3d 708 (D.C. Cir. 2001). For a detailed analysis of this case, see Jonathan B. Baker, *Efficiencies and High Concentration: Heinz Proposes to Acquire Beech-Nut, in* THE ANTITRUST REVOLUTION 150 (John E. Kwoka, Jr. and Lawrence J. White, eds., 4th ed., Oxford Press 2003).
57. Previous D.C. district court opinions had offered largely similar analyses, though in far less depth and with less authority. *See, e.g.*, FTC v. Swedish Match, 131 F. Supp. 2d. 151, 171-72 (D.D.C. 2000) (efficiency defense denied because claimed efficiencies were speculative and insufficient to overcome presumption of illegality derived from market share analysis); FTC v. Cardinal Health, 1998-2 Trade Case. (CCH) ¶ 72,226 (D.D.C. 1998) (anticipated efficiencies were not sufficiently merger-specific to outweigh the costs of reduced competition resulting from the merger).

rebut the government's *prima facie* case, but held that such efficiencies would have to be "extraordinary" given the high concentration levels in the baby food market. The court also emphasized that the claimed efficiencies must be merger-specific—a requirement that the court concluded had not been met during the district court proceedings because Heinz had failed to demonstrate that it was impossible to improve its product internally by spending a sum equivalent to the acquisition price on product development. The court did not consider, however, whether the premerger market structure—specifically, Heinz's difficulties in securing nationwide grocery store shelf space—rendered such internal expansion impractical.[58] Rather, the court treated the shelf space issue separately, as a speculative "innovation efficiency" that would make *future* innovation less costly, leaving aside its relevance to Heinz's argument that *current* innovations were far less efficient than the merger.[59]

The exact impact of the *Heinz* decision on future transactions may be difficult to gauge. In the view of FTC Chairman Muris, the "parties lost, in part, because the district court judge ignored both antitrust economics and relevant precedent, and did not even allow the substantial customer testimony supporting the merger"—factual errors that alone made it difficult to affirm the district court.[60] Nonetheless, in requiring an effective rebuttal to be composed of concrete evidence of "extraordinary" and highly merger-specific efficiencies—a very high bar for any party to meet—the *Heinz* opinion was not inconsistent with earlier precedents.

For instance, in *FTC v. University Health, Inc.*, the Eleventh Circuit acknowledge that "an efficiency defense . . . may be used in certain cases to rebut the government's *prima facie* case showing in a section 7 challenge," but found that the merging parties' efficiency claims were too speculative to counter the presumption drawn from the market share

---

58. Specifically, Heinz relied on a study by an outside consulting company showing that expansion of its product line would be profitable only if Heinz could have shelf space in at least 70% of the nation's supermarkets—a market penetration level it did not approach premerger. *See* William J. Kolasky, *Lessons from Baby Food: The Role of Efficiencies in Merger Review*, ANTITRUST, Fall 2001, at 82.

59. *H.J. Heinz*, 246 F.3d at 722.

60. Timothy J. Muris, Understanding Mergers: Strategy, Planning, Implementation and Outcomes, Opening Remarks, FTC Bureau of Economics Roundtable on Understanding Mergers, Washington, D.C. (Dec. 9, 2002), *at* www.ftc.gov/speeches/muris.htm ("Muris FTC Roundtable Remarks").

data.[61] The court reasoned that "evidence that a proposed acquisition would create significant efficiencies benefiting consumers is useful in evaluating the ultimate issue—the acquisition's overall effect on competition."[62] But to make such a showing, merging parties must "specifically explain .. . how these efficiencies would be created and maintained" so that a district court can draw conclusions grounded in fact; in addition, the parties must show that the efficiencies benefit consumers, by (at a minimum) comparing the benefits of the transaction with the costs it may exact on competition.[63] Finally, the court rejected the notion that efficiencies somehow constituted a defense to an anticompetitive merger, stating that "[o]f course, once it is determined that a merger would substantially lessen competition, expected economies, however, great, will not insulate a merger from a section 7 challenge."[64]

In *United States v. Country Lake Foods, Inc.,*[65] the district court concluded that the government was not likely to succeed on the merits of its challenge to the proposed transaction, given "the lack of entry barriers, the potential entry by distant dairies, the power of the fluid milk buyers in the area, the possibility of vertical integration, and efficiencies enabling [the merged firm] to compete with the market leader in the [relevant market]."[66] The court stated that it found the "efficiencies relevant, not so much as an independent factor justifying the proposed acquisition, but as further evidence that the proposed acquisition will enhance competition."[67] The district court noted that the claimed efficiencies would enable the merged firm to "have similar resources [to that of the market leader] derived from the benefits of economies of scale."[68]

Rather than integrate efficiencies into the initial assessment of a merger's anticompetitive effects, some courts appear to consider the possibility that efficiencies claims function as an affirmative defense to a merger already found to be anticompetitive rather than as a means of

---

61. 938 F.2d 1206, 1223-24 (11th Cir. 1991).
62. *Id.* at 1222. The court apparently equated "effect on competition" with "effect on price."
63. *Id.* at 1222 n.30.
64. *Id.* n.29 (emphasis omitted) (*citing* FTC v. Proctor & Gamble Co., 386 U.S. 568, 579 (1967) *and* United States v. Philadelphia Nat'l Bank, 374 U.S. 321, 371 (1963)).
65. 754 F. Supp. 669 (D. Minn. 1990).
66. *Id.* at 675.
67. *Id.* at 680.
68. *Id.*

rebutting the government's prima facie case. In no case, however, has a court approved an otherwise anticompetitive merger based on proffered efficiencies. In *United States v. Mercy Health Services*,[69] the court rejected the defendants' "affirmative" defense that the efficiencies generated by the merger of two hospitals would justify the otherwise illegal combination. The court, however, had already found that the government had failed to establish that the merger was likely to result in anticompetitive effects, and merely decided the issue for the record.[70]

In *United States v. Rockford Memorial Corp.*,[71] the district court rejected as a matter of law the defendants' "qualitative" efficiencies defense to the finding that the merger was anticompetitive.[72] In *FTC v. Staples, Inc.*,[73] the district court noted the treatment of efficiencies under the amended *Merger Guidelines* and observed that "[w]hether an efficiencies defense showing that the intended merger would create significant efficiencies in the relevant market, thereby offsetting any anticompetitive effects, may be used to rebut the government's prima facie case is not entirely clear."[74] The court went on to assume that it was a viable defense, although ultimately held that the defendants' evidence of the claimed efficiencies did not sufficiently rebut the government's prima facie showing that the merger would lead to increased prices.[75]

---

69. 902 F. Supp. 968 (N.D. Iowa 1995).
70. *See id.* at 987.
71. 717 F. Supp. 1251 (N.D. Ill. 1989), *aff'd*, 898 F.2d 1278 (7th Cir. 1990).
72. *See id.* at 1287-91; *see also* United States v. Archer-Daniels-Midland Co., 866 F.2d 242, 248 (8th Cir. 1988) (refusing to consider "special defense" of efficiencies in light of holding that government failed to make out prima facie case).
73. 970 F. Supp. 1066 (D.D.C. 1997).
74. *Id.* at 1088.
75. *See id.* at 1088-90. Although the court's use of the phrase "affirmative defense" may suggest otherwise, the *Staples* court resolved the issue in favor of evaluating efficiencies as part of the defendant's effort "to rebut the government's prima facie case." *Id.* Courts have held that efficiencies are relevant to the balancing of the equities in a preliminary injunction proceeding. In *FTC v. Warner Communs.*, 742 F.2d 1156 (9th Cir. 1984), the Ninth Circuit held that the "public equities" weighing against the grant of a preliminary injunction included any "beneficial economic effects and pro-competitive advantages for consumers" arising from the transaction. *Id.* at 1165 (*citing* FTC v. Pharmtech Research, Inc., 576 F. Supp. 294, 299 (D.D.C. 1983)). Similarly, in *FTC v. Weyerhaeuser Co.*, 665 F.2d 1072 (D.C. Cir. 1981), the D.C. Circuit held that projected procompetitive benefits

The increasingly important role that efficiencies arguments play in courts' analyses of Section 7 mergers, particularly hospital mergers, is further evidenced in *FTC v. Tenet Health Care Corp.*[76] In *Tenet Health Care*, the Eighth Circuit reversed the district court's judgment that the proposed merger of two hospitals in Poplar Bluff, Missouri was anticompetitive and dissolved the order enjoining the merger, ruling that the FTC failed to prove its relevant geographic market. Concomitantly, the court ruled that the FTC did not show that the merged entity would possess market power, finding that "although Tenet's efficiencies defense may have been properly rejected by the district court, the district court should nonetheless have considered evidence of enhanced efficiency in the context of the competitive effects of the merger."[77] The court further opined that the merged entity would provide better medical care than either hospital could on its own, be able to attract higher quality doctors, and offer integrated delivery and some tertiary care.[78]

2. *Agency Approach*

Because mergers are infrequently challenged in court, the *Merger Guidelines* and agency precedent largely define the approach of the U.S. antitrust authorities. Although the *Merger Guidelines* do not directly state an approach, they suggest that the agencies will consider efficiencies as part of the overall evaluation of the anticompetitive nature of the merger. For example, the *Merger Guidelines* state "the Agency will not simply compare the magnitude of the cognizable efficiencies with the magnitude of the likely harm to competition absent the efficiencies."[79]

As a matter of their prosecutorial discretion, the antitrust authorities will consider efficiencies in close cases.[80] The extent to which

---

could be weighed by the court among the benefits that might be lost due to issuance of the injunction, "whether or not those benefits could be asserted defensively in a proceeding for permanent relief." *Id.* at 1083. *But see* FTC v. Alliant Techsystems, Inc., 808 F. Supp. 9 (D.D.C. 1992) (rejecting defendants' efforts to introduce efficiencies into weighing of the equities).

76. 186 F.3d 1045 (8th Cir. 1999).

77. *Id*. at 1054.

78. *Id*.

79 1992 MERGER GUIDELINES, *supra* note 4, § 4 (revised Apr. 8, 1997).

80. *See, e.g.*, Press Release, FTC, Federal Trade Commission Votes to Close Investigation of Proposed Merger of Amerisource Health Corporation and Bergen Brunswig Corporation, Aug. 24, 2001, *at*

efficiencies are considered depends on the postmerger concentration levels: the lower the postmerger concentration, the more likely the agencies will take efficiencies into account.[81]

In addition, as FTC Commissioner Leary noted, the agencies treat efficiency claims less as an affirmative defense and more as part of the initial assessment of a transaction's competitive effects.[82] Typically, efficiencies are considered as part of the rebuttal to the *prima facie* case; in close cases, informal, less quantitative evidence of a broad range of efficiencies may act as a tipping factor to rebut a presumption of illegality drawn from the market share data.

The agencies have also taken a more liberal approach than the courts both to recognizing efficiencies and to the merger specificity requirements. As Commissioner Leary observed, few efficiencies are truly merger-specific, in the sense of being unrealizable without the merger; but often an efficiency can be achieved more quickly and at lower cost than through alternative means.[83] Therefore, it could make sense in some cases to treat the transaction cost savings associated with the cheaper solution as "merger-specific" efficiencies. In addition, agency personnel have publicly expressed a willingness to treat a wide range of merger benefits as efficiencies relevant to antitrust analysis. Commission Leary has mentioned the benefits of knowledge transfer among merging parties, as well as the innovation or managerial economies that will allow the surviving firm to be more efficiently and effectively managed. FTC Chairman Muris has also described the timing advantage of a merger as a cognizable efficiency.[84]

---

www.ftc.gov/opa/2001/amerisourcebergen.htm (four-to-three merger permitted to proceed, at least in part due to efficiencies); *see also* Ilene Knable Gotts, *FY 2002—All Quiet on the Antitrust Front in M&A Review?* ANTITRUST REPORT, Jan. 2003 at 3.

81. *See, e.g.*, William J. Kolasky, Conglomerate Mergers and Range Effects: It's A Long Way From Chicago to Brussels, Prepared Remarks Before the George Mason University Symposium (Nov. 9, 2001) *at* www.usdoj.gov/atr/public/speeches/9536.htm; Gary L. Roberts and Steven C. Salop, *Efficiencies in Dynamic Merger Analysis*, 19 WORLD COM. 5, 15 (June 1996); Robert Pitofsky, *Proposals for Revised United States Merger Enforcement in a Global Economy*, 81 GEO. L.J. 195, 198 (1992).

82. Leary Remarks, *supra* note 9, at 7-8.

83. Thomas B. Leary, *An Inside Look at the Heinz Case*, ANTITRUST, Spring 2002 at 32.

84. *Id.*; Muris, FTC Roundtable Remarks, *supra* note 60, at 2-3.

F. Proving Efficiencies

The lower courts have been reluctant to credit efficiency claims due in large part to the difficult issues of proof inherent in such claims. Alleged cost savings resulting from a merger are difficult to prove because the alleged efficiencies are purely prospective and cannot be evaluated by reference to existing conditions.[85] Whereas ascertaining the anticompetitive effects of a merger is somewhat tractable, determining the effects of claimed efficiencies arising from a combination is more elusive.[86] Courts are therefore hesitant to justify an otherwise anticompetitive merger based on claimed cost savings that cannot be established with certainty.[87]

1. Pass-On Requirement

Courts and agencies have required proof that the cost savings associated with proffered efficiencies be passed on to consumers in the form of decreased prices or improved quality.

a. Judicial Approach

Courts have often rejected efficiencies claims on the basis of inadequate proof that consumers would enjoy the benefits. Although a number of courts have rejected efficiencies claims where defendants did not demonstrate that consumers would benefit,[88] the district court in *United States v. United Tote, Inc.* articulated the requirement with no

---

85. *See* Joseph F. Brodley, *Proof of Efficiencies in Mergers and Joint Ventures*, 64 ANTITRUST L.J. 576 (1996).
86. *Id.*
87. *See, e.g.*, Joseph P. Griffin & Leeanne T. Sharp, *Efficiency Issues in Competition Analysis in Australia, the European Union, and the United States*, 64 ANTITRUST L.J. 649 (1996).
88. *See, e.g.*, FTC v. University Health, Inc., 938 F.2d 1206, 1223 (11th Cir. 1991) ("a defendant who seeks to overcome a presumption that a proposed acquisition would substantially lessen competition must demonstrate that the intended acquisition would result in significant economies and that these economies ultimately would benefit competition and, hence, consumers"); United States v. Rockford Mem'l Corp., 717 F. Supp. 1251, 1291 (N.D. Ill. 1989), *aff'd*, 898 F.2d 1278 (7th Cir. 1990) (defendants must demonstrate that efficiencies will lead to consumer benefits in order to receive consideration).

ambiguity.[89] In rejecting the defendants' proffered efficiencies justification, the court in *United Tote* held that "even if the merger resulted in efficiency gains, there are no guarantees that these savings would be passed on to the consuming public."[90]

The district court in *California v. American Stores Co.*,[91] a proposed merger involving two grocery store chains, was similarly wary of claimed benefits actually being passed on to consumers. While opining that the U.S. Supreme Court in *Philadelphia National Bank*[92] "has already clearly rejected this efficiency argument,"[93] the court considered but rejected the defendants' efficiencies argument because it did not see any projected benefits actually inuring to consumers. "Moreover, even assuming these efficiency savings do result, the court is not convinced that defendants will invariably pass these savings on to consumers."[94] The court had serious reservations about the merged entity's ability to achieve the projected $50 million in savings after servicing the assumed debt in leveraging the $2.5 billion buyout.[95]

Similarly, the district court in *FTC v. Staples, Inc.* rejected the defendants' claims in part due to inadequate proof that the cost savings of the combined entity would be sufficiently passed on to consumers. Although the court had "no doubt that a portion of any efficiencies achieved through a merger of the defendants would be passed on to customers," the fact that Staples had a history of passing on a significantly lower percentage (15 percent to 17 percent) of savings than the two-thirds alleged by the defendants led the court to find that the defendants had not rebutted the presumption that the merger would substantially lessen competition.[96]

Efficiencies claims have been successfully advanced in defense of mergers of nonprofit hospitals. Relying on the Eleventh Circuit Court's

---

89. *See* United States v. United Tote, Inc., 768 F. Supp 1064, 1074 (D. Del. 1991).
90. *Id.* at 1084-85.
91. 697 F. Supp. 1125 (C.D. Cal. 1988), *aff'd in part and rev'd in part on other grounds*, 872 F.2d 837 (9th Cir. 1989), *rev'd on other grounds*, 495 U.S. 271 (1990).
92. *See* United States v. Philadelphia National Bank, 374 U.S. 321, 370 (1945).
93. State of California v. American Stores Co., 697 F. Supp. 1125, 1133 (C.D. Cal. 1988).
94. *Id.*
95. *Id.*
96. FTC v. Staples, Inc., 970 F. Supp. 1066, 1090 (D.D.C. 1997).

opinion in *FTC v. University Health, Inc.*[97] the district court in *FTC v. Butterworth Health Corp.*[98] recognized the viability of an efficiencies claim as long as defendants demonstrate that significant economies result from the transaction and that the economies ultimately benefit consumers.[99] The court in *Butterworth* was persuaded by the defendants' arguments that more than $100 million in efficiencies would result from the merger of two nonprofit hospitals in the form of capital expenditure avoidance and operating costs. "This is, by any account, a substantial amount, and represents savings that would, in view of defendants' nonprofit status and the Community Commitment, invariably be passed on to consumers."[100]

The FTC appealed to the Sixth Circuit Court of Appeals. In an unpublished per curiam opinion, the Sixth Circuit ruled that the district court did not commit reversible error by considering the defendants' efficiencies arguments (consumer cost savings) to rebut the FTC's prima facie case.[101] By virtue of this ruling, the Sixth Circuit effectively joined the Seventh[102] and Eleventh[103] Circuits in integrating consumer benefits considerations into an analysis of the likely competitive effects of a hospital merger.

Defendants in *United States v. Long Island Jewish Medical Center*[104] also successfully asserted an efficiencies defense in support of the proposed merger of two nonprofit hospitals. The district court opined that such a defense was a difficult one to pursue due to the often speculative nature of alleged efficiencies which are vigorously disputed by opposing experts.[105] The court also pointed out the difficulty in measuring the extent to which efficiencies might inure to the benefit of consumers, holding that for the efficiencies defense to be viable, "the defendants must clearly demonstrate that the proposed merger itself will, in fact, create a net economic benefit for the health care consumer."[106]

---

97. 938 F.2d 1206, 1222-23 (11th Cir. 1991).
98. 946 F. Supp. 1285 (W.D. Mich. 1996), *aff'd*, 121 F.3d 708 (6th Cir. 1997) (per curiam) (table decision).
99. *Id.* at 1300.
100. *Id.* at 1301.
101. FTC v. Butterworth Health Corp., 121 F.3d 708 (6th Cir. 1997) (per curiam) (table decision).
102. *See* United States v. Rockford Mem'l Corp., 898 F.2d 1278 (7th Cir. 1990).
103. *See* FTC v. University Health Inc., 938 F.2d 1206 (11th Cir. 1991).
104. 983 F. Supp. 121 (E.D.N.Y. 1997).
105. *Id.* at 147.
106. *Id.*

Nevertheless, the court was convinced by defendants' efficiencies arguments, finding that, "with reasonable certainty, the 'efficiencies' gained in this merger will ultimately result in benefits to the consumers."[107] Such merger-related savings included a reduction in personnel in various departments of both hospitals, a reduction in the cost of laboratory services and medical supplies, and some capital avoidance savings.[108] The court also was likely swayed by the existence of an agreement between the merged hospitals and the Attorney General of the State of New York which provided, in part, that the merged hospitals would pass on to the community cost savings equal to $100 million over five years, with up to $50 million earmarked to provide care to the economically disadvantaged and the elderly.[109]

In both *Butterworth* and *Long Island Jewish Medical Center,* the fact that the merging hospitals were nonprofit was important to the court's analysis, though not dispositive. In *Butterworth*, the court agreed with the FTC that the merged entity would have substantial market power in two relevant markets with an "undue percentage share" of those markets, but allowed the merger to proceed, due, in part, to the nonprofit status of the merging hospitals. "The nonprofit status of the hospitals is not a dispositive consideration, but it is material, as evidenced by Dr. Lynk's undisputed empirical findings. These findings suggest that a substantial increase in market concentration among nonprofit hospitals is not likely to result in price increases."[110] The court further opined, "[i]n addition, the involvement of prominent community and business leaders on the boards of these hospitals can be expected to bring real accountability to price structuring . . . ."[111]

The court in *Long Island Jewish Medical Center* also deemed the nonprofit status of the merging hospitals to be worthy of consideration in its analysis. "[T]he Court deduces that while the not-for-profit status of the merging hospitals does not provide an exemption from the antitrust laws, this factor may be considered if supported by other evidence that such status would inhibit anti-competitive effects."[112] Further, analyzing whether the savings generated by the hospitals' efficiencies would be passed on to consumers, the court noted, "[b]oth hospitals are not-for-

107. *Id*.

108. *See id*. at 148.

109. *See id*. at 149.

110. FTC v. Butterworth Health Corp., 946 F. Supp. 1285, 1297 (W.D. Mich. 1996).

111. *Id*. at 1297.

112. *Long Island Jewish Med. Ctr.*, 983 F. Supp. at 146.

profit organizations, and the court finds that both have a genuine commitment to help their communities. This finding would be some circumstantial evidence that the cost savings would ultimately inure to the benefit of the consumers."[113]

Other courts have refrained from treating nonprofits differently when analyzing a potential merger's anticompetitive effects, dismissing the view that they are less likely to act anticompetitively.[114]

b. Agency Approach

The FTC and the DOJ have incorporated the "pass-on" requirement into their efficiencies analysis as well. The FTC first imposed the requirement in *American Medical International, Inc.*[115] Although apparently willing to consider efficiencies arising from the reduction of operating expenses that the parties alleged would result from their merger, the FTC ultimately rejected the defendant's claims in part because of inadequate evidence that consumers would benefit through lower prices.[116]

A 1996 FTC staff report endorses the pass-on requirement, but with certain modifications. Recognizing that a requirement that cost savings be passed on immediately postmerger would necessitate a perfectly competitive market,[117] the FTC staff report states an intention to "employ a sufficiently flexible time frame in its analysis in order to capture adequately the dynamic effect of efficiencies that likely contribute to more (or no less) competitive market behavior post-merger and likely

---

113. *Id*. at 149.

114. *See, e.g.*, FTC v. University Health, Inc. 938 F.2d 1206, 1224 (11th Cir. 1991); United States v. Rockford Mem'l Corp., 898 F.2d 1278 1285 (7th Cir. 1990).

115. 104 F.T.C. 1 (1984).

116. *See id*. at 213-20; *see* Olin Corp., 113 F.T.C. 400, 580 (1985); Hospital Corp. of Am., 106 F.T.C. 361, 513 (1985).

117. A strict pass-on requirement creates a significant barrier to merging firms in markets that are not perfectly competitive and where efficiencies could have a significant impact. *See* Michael G. Vita & Paul L. Yde, *Merger Efficiencies: Reconsidering the "Passing-On" Requirement*, 64 ANTITRUST L.J. 735, 739 (1996). *But see* Gregory J. Werden, Luke Froeb, & Steven Tschantz, "The Effects of Merger Synergies on Consumers of Differentiated Products," (Nov. 15, 2001) (arguing that pass-through depends less on competition than on demand properties, and that pass-through is likely only in markets where a merger can be expected to increase price).

result over time in a downward pressure on price or improved quality goods."[118] As a result, those efficiencies that would not result in immediate benefit to consumers may still be included in the evaluation.

The amended 1992 *Merger Guidelines* adopt a consumer welfare standard, stating that "the agency [will consider] whether cognizable efficiencies likely would be sufficient to reverse the merger's potential harm to consumers in the relevant market, e.g., by preventing price increases in that market."[119] Although the *Merger Guidelines* are thus preoccupied with the potential impact on consumers, there is no clearly articulated requirement that cost savings generated by a merger be passed on to consumers. Instead, the *Merger Guidelines* seem to devise a flexible approach, stating that "[d]elayed benefits from efficiencies (due to delay in the achievement of, or the realization of consumer benefits from the efficiencies) will be given less weight because they are less proximate and more difficult to predict."[120] The position taken by the *Merger Guidelines* coincides with the approach outlined in the FTC staff report, reflecting the agencies' recognition that certain cost savings, such as those derived from innovative efficiencies, may have long-term procompetitive benefits that directly benefit consumers, and should not be discounted.[121]

The *NAAG Merger Guidelines* suggest that the merging parties must demonstrate that efficiencies claims are of such a character and magnitude as to "ensure that consumer prices will not increase despite any increase in market power due to the merger."[122] The *NAAG Merger Guidelines* thus impose a type of modified pass-on requirement.

---

118. FTC Staff Report, "Anticipating the 21st Century: Competition Policy in the New High-Tech, Global Marketplace," *reprinted in* 70 Antitrust & Trade Reg. Rep. (BNA) No. 1765, at S-34 (June 6, 1996).

119. 1992 MERGER GUIDELINES, *supra* note 4, § 4 (revised Apr. 8, 1997).

120. *Id.* § 4 n.37.

121. *See* James R. Loftis III & Christine S. Chambers, *The New Efficiencies Guidelines: Transparency or Peek-A-Boo?*, FTC: WATCH, Apr. 21, 1997 at 9. In addition, Commissioner Leary's endorsement of managerial efficiencies—efficiencies that typically affect fixed costs and are therefore unlikely to be passed on—further evidences that pass-through is not a rigid requirement. *See* Thomas B. Leary, *An Inside Look at the Heinz Case*, ANTITRUST, Spring 2002, at 32; Joseph Kattan, *Efficiencies and Merger Analysis*, 62 ANTITRUST L.J., 513, 520 (1994).

122. 1993 NAAG MERGER GUIDELINES, *supra* note 48, § 5.3.

2. *Merger-Specific Requirement*

For the claimed efficiencies to be credited in the merger analysis, it is generally required that they be "merger specific," which necessitates proof that the claimed efficiencies could not be achieved through other less anticompetitive means. Thus, in the absence of a merger, if the firms could independently realize similar cost savings through, for example, internal expansion or reorganization, such efficiencies claims would not be cognizable. Critics have argued that ignoring nonmerger-specific efficiencies in competitive effects analysis thwarts the purpose of the analysis: determining whether the merger is anticompetitive.[123]

a. Judicial Approach

Courts have often discounted efficiencies claims if the alleged cost savings are achievable through less anticompetitive means than the proposed merger. For example, in *United States v. Rockford Memorial Corp.*,[124] the district court refused to give any consideration to "[e]fficiencies benefiting the merged entity, but obtainable by means independent of merger."[125] The court applied a strict standard, stating that efficiencies "made possible only through the merger and in no other manner" would receive consideration.[126]

The court in *United States v. Ivaco, Inc.*[127] likewise rejected the defendants' claims that operating efficiencies resulting from improved utilization of resources and elimination of duplicative resources sufficiently rebutted the government's prima facie case, stating that "a merger is not required to achieve many of the efficiencies [claimed by defendants]."[128] The court went on to state that "if the efficiencies may be obtained through a method which would not limit competition, then they may not be used as a valid defense."[129]

The court in *FTC v. Staples, Inc.* similarly discredited efficiencies claims that were not merger specific, stating that "defendants did not accurately calculate which projected cost savings were merger specific

---

123. *See, e.g.*, Deborah A. Garza, *The New Efficiencies Guidelines: The Same Old Transparent Wine in a More Transparent Bottle*, ANTITRUST, Summer 1997, at 7.
124. 717 F. Supp. 1251 (N.D. Ill. 1989), *aff'd*, 898 F.2d 1278 (7th Cir. 1990).
125. *Id*. at 1289.
126. *Id*.
127. 704 F. Supp. 1409 (W.D. Mich. 1989).
128. *Id*. at 1425-27.
129. *Id*.

and which were not, in fact, related to the merger."[130] The defendants had calculated cost savings "in relation to the cost savings enjoyed by Staples at the end of [the previous year] without considering the additional cost savings that Staples would have received in the future as a stand alone company."[131]

Finally, the court in *FTC v. Cardinal Health, Inc.*[132] also rejected substantial efficiencies that could be achieved absent the merger. While the court conceded that the merger would produce the cost savings "more immediately,"[133] the court held that the defendants had not demonstrated that "the projected savings from the mergers are enough to overcome the evidence that tends to show that possibly greater benefits can be achieved by the public through existing, continued competition."[134]

b. Agency Approach

A 1996 FTC staff report declines to embrace a strict merger-specific requirement, stating that "[s]uch a strict requirement might make sense if the underlying analysis involved comparing a pile of likely adverse effects or costs from a merger with another pile of probable efficiencies or cost savings."[135] Rather, the FTC staff report manifests a willingness to apply a more flexible standard in accordance with the perceived mandate of Section 7 to consider the future with and without the combination.[136] Efficiencies that would occur absent the combination are not cognizable.[137] Efficiencies that could theoretically be achieved through "internal growth, a joint venture, a specialization agreement, or a licensing, lease, or other contractual agreement," are not automatically excluded from consideration, however, because "it is not for antitrust enforcers to require some imagined alternative business arrangement."[138]

The *Merger Guidelines* similarly embrace a more flexible merger-specific requirement. Those efficiencies that are likely to be accomplished with the proposed merger and unlikely to be accomplished

130. 970 F. Supp. 1066, 1090 (D.D.C. 1997).
131. *Id.*
132. 12 F. Supp. 2d 34 (D.D.C. 1998).
133. *See id.* at 63.
134. *Id.*
135. FTC Staff Report, "Anticipating the 21st Century: Competition Policy in the New High-Tech, Global Marketplace," *reprinted in* 70 Antitrust & Trade Reg. Rep. (BNA), No. 1765, at S-34 (June 6, 1996).
136. *See id.* at S-35.
137. *See id.*
138. *Id.*

in the absence of the proposed merger or another means having comparable anticompetitive effects are recognized in assessing the anticompetitive effects of a merger.[139] Consequently, those efficiencies that "could be preserved by practical alternatives that mitigate competitive concerns" are denied consideration.[140] To diminish the evidentiary burden on merging firms, the agencies do not consider theoretical alternatives, only alternatives that are "practical in the business situation faced by the merging firms."[141]

In addition, some agency officials have suggested a continuing commitment to a more relaxed interpretation of the merger specificity requirement. In an article written before his appointment to the FTC, Chairman Muris favored a test focused on whether efficiencies are likely to occur absent the merger, rather than the possibility of alternate means of realizing the efficiencies.[142] Commissioner Leary has noted that mergers are often cheaper and quicker to realize than the alternative means, which could imply that those transaction cost savings ought to be considered a merger-specific efficiency even if the entire package of benefits is not.[143]

3. *Standard of Proof*

Courts and agencies have struggled over the appropriate standard of proof applicable to efficiencies claims. Specifically, the conflict has focused on whether the courts should apply the same standard imposed on the government in establishing its prima facie case or whether a higher standard should be imposed due to the uncertainty inherent in efficiency claims.

a. Judicial Approach

Some courts have imposed the rigorous "clear and convincing" standard on defendants presenting efficiencies claims. Not surprisingly, no defendant has met that standard.

In *Rockford Memorial,* the court adhered to the clear and convincing standard employed by the efficiencies section of the unrevised 1992

---

139. *See* 1992 MERGER GUIDELINES, *supra* note 4, § 4 n.35 (revised Apr. 8, 1997).

140. *Id*.

141. *Id*.

142. Timothy J. Muris, *The Government and Merger Efficiencies: Still Hostile After All These Years*, 7 GEO. MASON L. REV. 729, 732 (1999).

143. Leary Remarks, *supra* note 9, at 12.

Merger Guidelines. Before evaluating the claims themselves, the court stated "[i]n order for [defendant's qualitative efficiencies argument] to prove successful the defendants must establish by clear and convincing evidence that the efficiencies provided by the merger produce a significant economic benefit to consumers, even in light of the possible anticompetitive effects of the merger."[144] The court then proceeded to consider the specific argument proffered by the defendants, ultimately holding that "much of the savings cited . . . were not clearly and convincingly generated by the merger."[145]

The court in *FTC v. Staples, Inc.* expressly rejected the clear and convincing standard, however, stating:

> the Court [does not] believe that the defendants must prove their efficiencies by "clear and convincing evidence" in order for those efficiencies to be considered by the Court. That would saddle Section 7 defendants with the nearly impossible task of rebutting a possibility with a certainty.[146]

The appropriate inquiry, the *Staples* court held, was whether the defendants' evidence offered showed that the government's evidence "gave an inaccurate prediction of the proposed acquisition's probable effect."[147] Like other courts that have embraced the less stringent standard,[148] the *Staples* Court nonetheless found the efficiencies claims insufficient.

b. Agency Approach

The 1996 FTC staff report states that, although the burden of proof is on the defendant, the appropriate standard should not be one as insurmountable as clear and convincing.[149] Imposing the stringent standard solely to efficiencies claims would not comport with the

---

144. United States v. Rockford Mem'l Corp., 717 F. Supp. 1251, 1289 (N.D. Ill. 1989), *aff'd*, 898 F.2d 1278 (7th Cir. 1990); *see also* United States v. Baker Hughes, Inc., 908 F.2d 981, 991 (D.C. Cir. 1990); United States v. Country Lake Foods, Inc., 754 F. Supp. 669, 680 (D. Minn. 1990).
145. *Rockford Mem'l Corp.*, 717 F. Supp. at 1291.
146. 970 F. Supp. 1066, 1089 (D.D.C. 1997).
147. *Id.* at 1090.
148. *See, e.g.*, FTC v. University Health, Inc., 938 F.2d 1206, 1222 (11th Cir. 1991).
149. *See* FTC Staff Report, "Anticipating the 21st Century: Competition Policy in the New High-Tech, Global Marketplace," *reprinted in* 70 Antitrust & Trade Reg. Rep. (BNA) No. 1765, at S-37 (June 6, 1996).

standard required of other rebuttal claims, such as ease of entry.[150] Additionally, the FTC staff report recognizes that, because efficiencies claims necessarily deal with projecting probabilities, a clear and convincing standard would be almost impossible to meet.[151] Still, agency officials occasionally acknowledge that the proffered evidence of efficiencies must overcome a substantial skepticism that such claims are exaggerated—a skepticism that stems from the fact that the merging parties usually control the evidence required to evaluate the efficiency claims.[152]

The *Merger Guidelines* do not set forth any particular standard of proof. The *Merger Guidelines* simply state that "merging firms must substantiate efficiency claims so that the Agency can verify by reasonable means the likelihood and magnitude of each asserted efficiency."[153] The *Merger Guidelines* further state that an agency will not consider claims that are "vague or speculative or otherwise cannot be verified by reasonable means."[154]

---

150. *See id*.
151. *See id*.
152. *See, e.g.*, Craig W. Conrath and Nicholas A. Widnell, *Efficiency Claims in Merger Analysis: Hostility or Humility?* 7 GEO. MASON L. REV. 685, 696-97 (Spring 1999).
153. 1992 MERGER GUIDELINES, *supra* note 4, § 4 (revised Apr. 8, 1997).
154. *Id*.

CHAPTER 7

POSSIBLE DEFENSES

There are several possible defenses to transactions that may otherwise violate Section 7. Some defenses are matters of federal statutes, while others have been created by the courts. The statutory defenses, such as those for railroads, are absolute and based on the extensive regulatory scheme for the industry. In contrast, judicially created exemptions, such as the failing company doctrine or the state action doctrine, require detailed analyses of the facts and potential effects of the transaction.

A. The Failing Company Doctrine

The "failing company doctrine" is a judicially created defense, sanctioned by Congress,[1] to actions challenging otherwise unlawful mergers or acquisitions.[2] The U.S. Supreme Court first articulated the

---

1. The Senate Report on the 1950 amendments to Section 7 stated:

> The argument has been made that the proposed bill, if passed, would have the effect of preventing a company which is in a failing or bankrupt condition from selling out. The committee are [sic] in full accord with the proposition that any firm in such a condition should be free to dispose of its stock or assets. The committee however, do [sic] not believe that the proposed bill will prevent sales of this type. The judicial interpretation on this point goes back many years and is abundantly clear. According to decisions of the U.S. Supreme Court, the Clayton Act does not apply in bankruptcy or receivership cases. Moreover, the court has held, with respect to this specific section, that a company does not have to be actually in a state of bankruptcy to be exempt from its provisions; it is sufficient that it is heading in that direction with the probability that bankruptcy will ensue.

S. REP. NO. 81-1775, at 7 (1950), *reprinted in* 1950 U.S.C.C.A.N. 4293, 4299; *accord* H.R. REP. NO. 81-1191, at 6 (1949).

2. The failing company doctrine is applicable to mergers challenged under either Section 7 or Section 5. *See, e.g.*, Citizen Publ'g Co. v. United States, 394 U.S. 131 (1969); United States Steel Corp. v. FTC, 426 F.2d 592 (6th Cir. 1970). Some dispute has arisen, however, concerning the extent to which the doctrine is applicable to mergers challenged under Section 1 of the Sherman Act. *Compare* American Press Ass'n v. United

doctrine in *International Shoe Co. v. FTC*,[3] which involved a horizontal merger between two shoe manufacturers. The Federal Trade Commission (FTC or the Commission) had found that the merger violated Section 7 of the Clayton Act, but the U.S. Supreme Court reversed on two grounds. First, the Court found that the parties to the merger competed in separate markets and, thus, the merger would not substantially lessen competition.[4] Second, the Court found that Section 7 was not violated because the acquired company faced "financial ruin."[5] The Court postulated two rationales for the creation of the failing company doctrine. The first rationale emphasized the social consequences of business failure, noting the adverse impact on stockholders, creditors, employees, and others. The second rationale assumed that there would be less of an anticompetitive effect if a

---

States, 245 F. 91, 93-94 (7th Cir. 1917) (acquisition of failing company does not violate Section 1 of Sherman Act), *with* Bowl Am., Inc. v. Fair Lanes, Inc., 299 F. Supp. 1080, 1092-93 (D. Md. 1969) (doctrine inapplicable to mergers challenged under Section 1). *See also* Ilene K. Gotts et al., *Transactions with Financially Distressed Entities*, ANTITRUST , Summer 2002, 64-70; Janet L. McDavid, *Failing Companies and the Antitrust Laws,* 14 MICH. J. L. REFORM 229, 231-48 (1981).

3. 280 U.S. 291 (1930). An earlier version of the failing company doctrine was the basis for a 1917 circuit court decision permitting the acquisition of a failing company in an action under Section 1 of the Sherman Act. *See American Press Ass'n*, 245 F. 91.

4. *International Shoe Co.*, 280 U.S. at 298-99.

5. The court stated:

> In the light of the case thus disclosed of a corporation with resources so depleted and the prospect of rehabilitation so remote that it faced the grave probability of a business failure with resulting loss to its stockholders and injury to the communities where its plants were operated, we hold that the purchase of its capital stock by a competitor (there being no other prospective purchaser), not with a purpose to lessen competition, but to facilitate the accumulated business of the purchaser and with the effect of mitigating seriously injurious consequences otherwise probable, is not in contemplation of law prejudicial to the public and does not substantially lessen competition or restrain commerce within the intent of the Clayton Act.

Id. at 302-03. For a discussion of the financial condition of the acquired company in *International Shoe*, see Marc P. Blum, *The Failing Company Doctrine,* 16 B.C. INDUS. & COM. L. REV. 75, 76-81 (1974).

corporation that otherwise would fail were acquired, even by a competitor, than if its assets were allowed to exit the market.[6]

1. Judicial Interpretation of the Failing Company Doctrine: Elements of the Defense

Because the doctrine is an exception to the general rules governing acquisitions, the courts have construed the requirements of the defense narrowly. Under the traditional formulation of the failing company doctrine, the acquiring company must prove two elements: the probability of imminent business failure of the target company and the unavailability of other purchasers with less anticompetitive impact.[7] Some courts have also added a third element—that the failing firm could not be reorganized successfully. The failing company doctrine is an affirmative defense, and the parties to the acquisition bear the burden of proving that these conditions have been satisfied.[8] It is notable that, although there are many cases involving acquisitions of bankrupt firms, the failing firm defense is rarely applicable and thus, parties typically must defend such transactions on the merits.[9]

---

6. *See International Shoe*, 280 U.S. at 302.
7. *See, e.g.*, United States v. Greater Buffalo Press, Inc., 402 U.S. 549, 555 (1971) (acquisition by newspaper of printing company that was profitable, but which owners chose to sell rather than modernize).
8. *See* Citizen Publ'g Co. v. United States, 394 U.S. 131, 138-39 (1969); United States v. Third Nat'l Bank, 390 U.S. 171, 192 (1968); F. & M. Schaefer Corp. v. C. Schmidt & Sons, Inc., 597 F.2d 814, 817-18 (2d Cir. 1979); FTC v. Harbour Group Invs., L.P., 1990-2 Trade Cas. (CCH) ¶ 69,247, at 64,914-15 (D.D.C. 1990); *see also* 4 PHILLIP AREEDA, HERBERT HOVENKAMP & JOHN L. SOLOW, ANTITRUST LAW ¶ 951c (rev. ed. 1998).
9. For example, in *United States v. SunGard Data Sys., Inc.*, 172 F. Supp. 2d 172 (D.D.C. 2001), the defendants successfully defended against the Division's antitrust challenge to a proposed acquisition of a bankrupt firm without asserting the failing firm defense. In *SunGard*, the Division alleged that SunGard's proposed acquisition of Comdisco would have substantially reduced competition in the market for hotsite disaster recovery services. At the time of the case, Comdisco had filed for bankruptcy and its assets were being sold at auction pursuant to an order of the bankruptcy court. At auction, Comdisco received bids from SunGard and another firm, though SunGard's bid was the highest. Following the auction, the Division sued to enjoin the transaction. As part of their defense, the parties did not assert that they were entitled to the "failing firm" defense, presumably because another bid had been

a. Imminent Business Failure

The requirement of imminent business failure has been the subject of extensive judicial interpretation. The courts have interpreted strictly the *International Shoe* requirement of "grave probability of a business failure." Courts have been unwilling to find that business failure is imminent when a company continues to be profitable,[10] is solvent,[11] or has prospects of showing a profit.[12] Likewise, a showing that management of a viable company intends to go out of business or liquidate,[13] or that a company has either declining profits or large losses,[14] is badly managed,[15] lacks capital for modernization,[16] or has

---

received. *See* J. Mark Gidley & David A. Balto, *Leveling the Playing Field in Antitrust Merger Litigation: The SunGard Decision*, THE M&A LAWYER, Jan. 2002 at 16, 20 (noting that the failing firm doctrine was arguably not applicable in *SunGard* because of the presence of the other bid). *Id.* at 20. The court held that the proposed acquisition did not violate Section 7 because the Division had relied on an overly narrow, and thus improper, definition of the relevant market. *See United States v. SunGard Sys.*, 172 F. Supp. 2d at 183-93.

10. *See Greater Buffalo Press, Inc.*, 402 U.S. at 555; FTC v. University Health, Inc., 938 F.2d 1206, 1221 (11th Cir. 1991).

11. *See* FTC v. Food Town Stores, Inc., 539 F.2d 1339, 1345 (4th Cir. 1976) (company had substantial short-term liabilities, but was solvent and operated at a profit); United States v. Pabst Brewing Co., 296 F. Supp. 994, 999-1000 (E.D. Wis. 1969) (company with large losses was solvent and could obtain credit).

12. *See* Papercraft Corp., 78 F.T.C. 1352, 1406-08 (1971) (company had operating losses and management problems, but had significant sales and assets).

13. *See, e.g.*, Erie Sand & Gravel Co. v. FTC, 291 F.2d 279, 280 (3d Cir. 1961) (owners of profitable sand company, which was a going concern, wanted to liquidate); United States v. Phillips Petroleum Co., 367 F. Supp. 1226, 1258-60 (C.D. Cal. 1973), *aff'd per curiam,* 418 U.S. 906 (1974) (parts of acquired company were profitable; intention to go out of business irrelevant).

14. *See, e.g., Citizen Publ'g Co.*, 394 U.S. at 133, 137; *F. & M. Schaefer Corp.*, 597 F.2d at 817 (large losses and declining sales, but company was rebuilding with support of creditors); *Pabst Brewing Co.*, 296 F. Supp. at 999-1000 (declining market share and sales, but company had substantial assets and sound credit rating); FTC v. H. J. Heinz Co., 246 F.3d 708, 726 (D.C. Cir. 2001) (affirming district court's rejection of failing firm defense because the acquired firm was at present a "profitable and ongoing enterprise," notwithstanding the defendants' argument that the acquired firm would become increasingly unprofitable over time due to

obsolete facilities has been held to be insufficient to prove this element of the defense.[17] Thus, the courts have required that defendants show a strong likelihood of business failure.[18]

b. No Other Available Purchasers

The requirement that there be no other available purchasers has been the subject of less judicial interpretation than the imminent business failure requirement. Presumably the requirement is imposed to satisfy the court that less anticompetitive alternatives to the otherwise unlawful acquisition are unavailable. Thus, courts have required that the failing company actively seek alternative purchasers.[19] A putative failing firm

---

its outdated production methods and ultimately exit the market), *rev'g on other grounds*, 116 F. Supp. 2d 190 (D.D.C. 2000); *cf.* Dean Foods Co., 70 F.T.C. 1146, 1272-84 (1966) (company with declining sales, but that was able to meet its short-term debts and had operating profit, was not failing), *modified*, 71 F.T.C. 731 (1967).

15. *See* United States v. American Technical Indus., Inc., 1974-1 Trade Cas. (CCH) ¶ 74,873 (M.D. Pa. 1974) (negative cash balance and liabilities exceeded assets, but company operated at a profit in most years); *cf.* Crown Zellerbach Corp. v. FTC, 296 F.2d 800, 831 (9th Cir. 1961) (death of key officer involved in attempt to rehabilitate company).

16. United States v. Greater Buffalo Press, Inc., 402 U.S. 549, 555 (1971).

17. *See Pabst Brewing Co.*, 296 F. Supp. at 1001; *Dean Foods*, 70 F.T.C. at 1280-81; *H.J. Heinz,* 246 F.3d at 726.

18. *See* California v. Sutter Health Sys., 130 F. Supp. 2d 1109, 1133-35 (N.D. Cal. 2001) (acquired hospital demonstrated strong likelihood of business failure by showing inability to meet trade debt, inability to assume more debt to meet financial obligations as they come due, and fair market value of its assets less than the value of its liabilities); Reilly v. Hearst Corp., 107 F. Supp. 2d 1192, 1203-05 (N.D. Cal. 2000) (holding that San Francisco newspaper qualified as a "failing company" where its projected annual net losses were substantial, its "prospect of recovering such losses through future profits [were] extremely remote," and, in addition, the newspaper would not be "economically viable" as part of its existing joint operating agreement (JOA) enterprise with another newspaper). For a further discussion of JOAs under the antitrust laws, see Section D.3., *infra*.

19. *See, e.g., Greater Buffalo Press, Inc.*, 402 U.S. at 556; Golden Grain Macaroni Co. v. FTC, 472 F.2d 882, 887 (9th Cir. 1972); *Sutter Health Sys.*, 130 F. Supp. 2d at 1136 (failing firm demonstrated lack of alternative purchaser where it had retained an investment banker to seek proposals from potential acquirers); *Hearst Corp.*, 107 F. Supp. 2d at 1205 (failing firm demonstrated lack of alternative purchaser where

must demonstrate that there are no viable alternative purchasers at the time that the defense is asserted.[20] Furthermore, some courts have found that a "generalized expression of interest" from a possible alternative purchaser is not sufficient to preclude a party from asserting a failing firm defense.[21] As one court stated, the failing company must show that it "undertook a well-conceived and thorough canvass of the industry such as to ferret out viable alternative partners for merger."[22]

c. Dim Prospects of Reorganization

In 1969, in *Citizen Publishing Co. v. United States*,[23] the U.S. Supreme Court implied that inability to reorganize a failing company under the bankruptcy laws might be a third requirement of the failing company doctrine.[24] Later U.S. Supreme Court decisions, however, omit

---

failing firm's broker had conducted two major, but unsuccessful, sales efforts to attract prospective purchasers); United States v. Black & Decker Mfg. Co., 430 F. Supp. 729, 781-82 (D. Md. 1976); United States v. M.P.M., Inc., 397 F. Supp. 78, 101-02 (D. Colo. 1975); Retail Credit Co., 92 F.T.C. 1 (1978). *But see,* United States v. Culbro Corp., 504 F. Supp. 661, 669 (S.D.N.Y. 1981) (financial difficulties well known, but no other offer was made).

20. *See Sutter Health Sys.*, 130 F. Supp. 2d at 1136-37. In *Sutter Health*, the court concluded that no viable alternative existed even though the acquired hospital had received an offer from a possible purchaser eighteen months previously. The court found that the failing company had received the offer when it was in substantially better financial condition, and there was no evidence that the offeror would have been interested in making a similar offer again. *Id.*

21. *Id.* (fact that a possible alternative purchaser indicated that it would "take a look" at the company, but was not in a position to make an offer was not sufficient to elevate that firm to the status of viable alternative purchaser); *accord Culbro Corp.*, 504 F. Supp. at 669.

22. United States v. Pabst Brewing Co., 296 F. Supp. 994, 1002 (E.D. Wis. 1969); *see also* Calnetics Corp. v. Volkswagen of Am., Inc., 348 F. Supp. 606, 622 (C.D. Cal. 1972) (failing company held not to have made an adequate effort where it failed to utilize the services of a broker to attempt to locate other potential purchasers), *rev'd on other grounds*, 532 F.2d 674 (9th Cir. 1976).

23. 394 U.S. 131 (1969).

24. *See id.* at 138. *Citizen Publishing* involved an unlawful joint operating agreement between two newspapers. Following the U.S. Supreme Court's decision, Congress passed the Newspaper Preservation Act of 1970, 15 U.S.C. §§ 1801-1804, which was designed to overrule *Citizen Publishing.* The act created an antitrust exemption for other existing joint

any reference to the reorganization possibility as a third requirement,[25] and the few lower courts that have considered the issue are divided.[26]

2. *Federal Agency Interpretation of the Failing Company Doctrine*

The doctrine was expressly recognized in the 1992 *Merger Guidelines* issued jointly by the Antitrust Division of the U.S. Department of Justice (DOJ or the Division) and the FTC.[27] Section 5.1 of the *Merger Guidelines* outlines the essential elements of the defense, largely based on the traditional judicial formulation of the defense. As

---

operating agreements. It also permits future joint operating agreements if one of the newspapers is "in probable danger of financial failure" and the Attorney General determines that such an arrangement would effectuate the policy and purpose of the act. 15 U.S.C. §§ 1802(5), 1803(b).

25. *See, e.g.*, United States v. General Dynamics Corp., 415 U.S. 486, 507 (1974); United States v. Greater Buffalo Press, Inc., 402 U.S. 549, 555 (1971)

26. *Compare* United States Steel Corp. v. FTC, 426 F.2d 592, 606 n.30 (6th Cir. 1970) *and* United States v. Phillips Petroleum Co., 367 F. Supp. 1226, 1259 (C.D. Cal. 1973) case remanded because no determination was made concerning how the "failing company" would have fared under bankruptcy or reorganization *aff'd per curiam,* 418 U.S. 906 (1974) (dictum), *with Black & Decker Mfg. Co.*, 430 F. Supp. at 778 (dictum), *and M.P.M., Inc.*, 397 F. Supp. at 96-97 (reorganization is an alternative to the "no other prospective purchaser" requirement). In one case, *United States v. Culbro Corp.*, 504 F. Supp. at 661, unsuccessful attempts had been made to reorganize the failing company under Chapter 11, and unless the acquisition took place it would be liquidated. In *Sutter Health Sys.*, 130 F. Supp. 2d at 1136, the court stated that a showing that a firm's prospects for reorganization under Chapter 11 are dim or nonexistent because the causes of financial distress were systematic and likely to increase over time satisfied this requirement.

27. U.S. DEP'T OF JUSTICE & FEDERAL TRADE COMM'N, HORIZONTAL MERGER GUIDELINES (1992) [hereinafter 1992 MERGER GUIDELINES], *reprinted in* 4 Trade Reg. Rep. (CCH) ¶ 13,104 and in Appendix I. In addition, the failing firm doctrine was acknowledged in the UNITED STATES DEP'T OF JUSTICE MERGER GUIDELINES, 49 Fed. Reg. 21,823 (1984) [hereinafter 1984 MERGER GUIDELINES], *reprinted in* 4 Trade Reg. Rep. (CCH) ¶ 13,103, the 1982 STATEMENT OF THE FEDERAL TRADE COMMISSION CONCERNING HORIZONTAL MERGERS (1982), *reprinted in* 4 Trade Reg. Rep. (CCH) ¶ 13,200, and the NATIONAL ASSOCIATION OF ATTORNEYS GENERAL MERGER GUIDELINES (1993) [hereinafter NAAG MERGER GUIDELINES], *reprinted in* 4 Trade Reg. Rep. (CCH) ¶13,406 and in Appendix M. In its 1982 *Statement*, the FTC stated that it imposes a "rigorous requirement" on defendants to meet its requirements.

outlined in the 1992 *Merger Guidelines*, the failing firm defense has four elements.[28]

First, the acquired firm must be failing, which is defined to mean that it is unable to meet its financial obligations in the near future.[29] Second, the acquired firm must be unable to reorganize under Chapter 11 of the Bankruptcy Code. The FTC has applied this requirement in several decisions.[30] Third, the failing firm must have made an unsuccessful good faith effort to attract a purchaser that would keep the assets in the market and that would pose less of a competitive threat than the proposed purchaser.[31] Such efforts typically include use of an investment banker or broker to locate alternative buyers.[32] A less anticompetitive purchaser

---

28. *Cf.* NAAG MERGER GUIDELINES, *supra* note 27, § 6 (delineating the three elements of a somewhat more hospitable failing firm defense: (1) the resources of the failing firm must be so depleted that the potential for rehabilitation is so remote that it faces a great likelihood of business failure, (2) the failing firm made reasonable good faith efforts to find another prospective purchaser, and (3) no other less anticompetitive alternative is available).
29. *See* DAVID SCHEFFMAN, MALCOLM COATE & LOUIS SILVIA, 20 YEARS OF MERGER GUIDELINES ENFORCEMENT AT THE FTC: AN ECONOMIC PERSPECTIVE, *at* www.usdoj.gov/atr/hmerger/12881.pdf 38 (June 2002) (noting that the FTC has "undertaken a variety of accounting and economic analyses to determine the financial health of" an allegedly failing firm, including "reviewing cash flow forecasts to determine whether financial obligations will be met in short term, analyzing operating statements to render an opinion on what impact exiting a market has on corporate cash flow and profitability post exit, evaluating cost allocation methods to assure appropriate costs have been allocated to failing assets, performing standard financial statement analyses of a firm or division which is anticipating exit, and assessing alternative buyers or other financing opportunities").
30. *See, e.g.*, Pillsbury Co., 93 F.T.C. 966, 1031-33 (1979); Reichold Chems., Inc., 91 F.T.C. 246, 289-91 (1978), *aff'd mem.,* 598 F.2d 616 (4th Cir. 1979); Retail Credit Co., 92 F.T.C. 1, 156-57 (1978) (inability to reorganize is a critical third element); United States Steel Corp., 81 F.T.C. 629, 653 (1972); Papercraft Corp., 78 F.T.C. 1352, 1406-08 (1971).
31. *See, e.g.*, FTC v. Harbour Group Invs. L.P., 1990-2 Trade Cas. (CCH) ¶ 69,247 (D.D.C. 1990); *Pillsbury Co.*, 93 F.T.C. at 1032.
32. *See, e.g.,* California v. Sutter Health Sys., 130 F. Supp. 2d 1109, 1136 (N.D. Cal. 2001) (failing hospital conducted an "extensive good faith search" for three years during which time it retained an investment banker to seek proposals from potential acquirers); Reilly v. Hearst Corp., 107 F. Supp. 2d 1192, 1205 (N.D. Cal. 2000) (failing newspaper used

is preferred, even if it will pay a lower price than another buyer.[33] It is notable that, in a recent settlement agreement, the Division initially required that parties asserting failing-firm type defenses in a nonmerger case conduct a good faith effort to sell assets in order to demonstrate the unavailability of an alternative purchaser.[34]

The 1992 *Merger Guidelines* added a fourth element not contained in the traditional judicial formulation: absent the acquisition, the assets of the failing firm will soon exit the relevant market. The Ninth Circuit has upheld the FTC's determination that the failing firm defense was not satisfied when the acquired firm planned to exit a market and close

---

investment bank in "two major sales efforts" to contact 97 prospective purchasers).

33. For example, in one case, the DOJ required that the failing company consider "any good faith offer from any company capable of operating . . . [the failing firm] as a viable competitive entity regardless of how that offer compares to the present offer." United States Dep't of Justice, Business Review Letter to Motorola, Inc., [1969-1983 Transfer Binder] Trade Reg. Rep. (CCH) ¶ 50,209 (Apr. 23, 1974). The Division subsequently approved the acquisition after an investment banker contacted 38 alternative purchasers, none of whom expressed an interest. United States Dep't of Justice, Business Review Letter to Motorola, Inc., [1969-1983 Transfer Binder] Trade Reg. Rep. (CCH) ¶ 50,212 (May 20, 1974). *See generally* Thomas Kauper, *The 1982 Horizontal Merger Guidelines: Of Collusion, Efficiency, and Failure,* 71 CAL. L. REV. 497, 529-31 (1983).

34. United States v. The MathWorks Inc., 2003 WL 1922140 (E.D. Va. Mar. 6, 2003) (final judgment containing competitive impact statement). In *MathWorks*, the Division alleged that MathWorks and Wind River, two head–to-head competitors in the market for "dynamic control system design software" tools, violated Section 1 by entering into a *per se* unlawful market allocation agreement. *Id.* at *7. Pursuant to an exclusive distribution and licensing agreement, MathWorks had obtained control over the pricing and marketing of WindRiver's dynamic control software products. As part of its defense, MathWorks asserted that WindRiver had a "genuine desire to exit the market" and no competitive buyer would be interested in purchasing WindRiver's assets. *Id.* at *11. In order to settle the case, the parties initially agreed to test their failing assets argument by making a good faith effort to "shop" the WindRiver assets in exchange for the Division closing the investigation if another viable purchaser was not found. *Id.* However, the parties did not comply with the terms of the "shop" agreement and the Division filed suit seeking to force a sale of the assets. *Id.* The parties ultimately agreed to settle with the Division and the assets were sold pursuant to a consent decree. *Id.*

plants.[35] The court concluded that there was evidence to support the FTC's view that the assets would not have exited the market absent the acquisition.

The failing company doctrine was addressed in the FTC's Hearings on the Changing Nature of Competition in 1995.[36] Testimony during the FTC hearings supported the view that the defense was rarely applicable, and that the weak financial state of the acquired firm is generally best addressed as part of the competitive effects analysis.[37] As a result, the FTC staff report did not recommend any changes in the defense. In particular, the staff report concluded that it would not be appropriate to consider the social costs of business failure as an element of the defense.

3. The Failing Division or Subsidiary

The extent to which the failing firm doctrine applies to a failing division or subsidiary of an otherwise profitable, viable corporation is quite controversial. The few judicial decisions on the issue are divided.[38]

---

35. *See* Olin Corp. v. FTC, 986 F.2d 1295, 1307 (9th Cir. 1993).
36. The FTC hearings resulted in the FTC Staff Report, *Anticipating the 21st Century: Competition Policy in the New High-Tech, Global Marketplace*, 70 Antitrust & Trade Reg. Rep. (BNA) No. 1765, S-1 (June 6, 1996).
37. *See id*. at S-43 to S-44.
38. *Compare* FTC v. Great Lakes Chem. Corp., 528 F. Supp. 84, 96 (N.D. Ill. 1981) ("failing company defense applies to a failing business . . . whether or not it is a division of a larger corporation which is successful in other areas"), *and* United States v. Reed Roller Bit Co., 274 F. Supp. 573, 584 n.1 (W.D. Okla. 1967) (dictum suggesting the doctrine applies to failing subsidiaries), *with* United States v. Blue Bell, Inc., 395 F. Supp. 538, 550 (M.D. Tenn. 1975) (failing division not a defense), and United States v. Phillips Petroleum Co., 367 F. Supp. at 1226, 1260 (C.D. Cal. 1973) (noting that firm had significant net income even though division had some financial difficulties), *aff'd per curiam,* 418 U.S. 906 (1974). In *United States v. Lever Bros. Co.*, 216 F. Supp. 887 (S.D.N.Y. 1963), the court permitted the sale of a failing detergent brand to a competitor. In *Chicago Bridge*, a case involving an FTC challenge to a previously consummated acquisition of two distinct divisions of a diversified company (the "assets"), an Administrative Law Judge concluded that even if the "exiting assets" defense were "legally recognizable," the parties had failed to present sufficient evidence to establish the elements of the defense: (1) that the assets would have been closed in the near future, and (2) an exhaustive effort to sell the assets had been conducted. *In re* Chicago Bridge & Iron Co. N.V., 2003 F.T.C. LEXIS 96, 263 (June

Section 5.2 of the 1992 *Merger Guidelines* recognizes that the defense may be available to a failing division or subsidiary, but imposes a high standard of proof:[39] (1) upon applying appropriate cost allocation rules, the division must have a negative cash flow on an operating basis; (2) absent the acquisition, the assets would exit the relevant market if not sold; and (3) the owner of the failing division or subsidiary must have complied with the competitively preferable purchaser requirement imposed by Section 5.1.

Because the parent firm may be able to allocate costs, revenues, and intracompany transactions among itself and its divisions and subsidiaries, the Division and the FTC require evidence of the first two elements other than evidence that could be prepared solely to demonstrate negative cash flow or the prospect of exit.

4. *Weakened Firm and* **General Dynamics** *Defenses*

At times, some courts have evaluated and labeled as a separate merger defense arguments regarding the weakness of the target company on a going forward basis.[40] In *United States v. General Dynamics*

18, 2003). At the same time, the ALJ acknowledged that the viability of the "exiting assets" defense is uncertain. *Id.* at *260-64. Three prominent commentators recognize the difficulty of applying the doctrine to a division or subsidiary, but would allow the parent company to attempt to demonstrate that the division is failing. *See also* 4 PHILLIP E. AREEDA, HERBERT HOVENKAMP & JOHN L. SOLOW, ANTITRUST LAW ¶ 953e (rev. ed. 1998).

39. In a pre-*Merger Guidelines* case, the FTC challenged the sale of a division of Federal Paperboard Company to a competitor. *See* FTC v. Lancaster Colony Corp., 434 F. Supp. 1088 (S.D.N.Y. 1977). Later, the FTC allowed the sale after the plant had closed and alternative buyers had rejected proposed acquisitions. *See* Lancaster Colony Corp., 93 F.T.C. 318, 322 (1979); *see also* NAAG MERGER GUIDELINES, *supra* note 27, § 6 (claims of a failing division defense are recognized as a matter of prosecutorial discretion and require proof of all elements by clear and convincing evidence).

40. A possible variant of the quasi-failing company defense (or weakened company defense) is the "distressed industry defense" under which an otherwise anticompetitive merger might be allowed in an industry that, as a whole, has experienced substantial reduction in demand and sales, an emerging pattern of overcapacity, a significant increase in production costs, and/or inflated unit costs. A distressed industry defense or exception has never been expressly recognized by any court, the Division, or the FTC. *See* Bernard A. Nigro, Jr. & Jonathan S. Kanter, *The Effect*

Corp.,[41] the U.S. Supreme Court concluded that the acquisition of a coal company did not violate Section 7, despite the fact that the acquisition produced a company with a large market share in a concentrated industry. One of the factors the Court emphasized was that the acquired company's large market share did not accurately reflect its competitive condition because its coal reserves were either depleted or committed under long-term contracts.[42] The acquired company's future competitive weakness undermined the government's prima facie statistical case. The Court made it clear that mere competitive weakness was not sufficient to prove the failing company defense because the acquired company was both profitable and efficient. Rather, the Court determined that the acquisition would not substantially lessen competition.[43] The Court believed that present combined market shares did not accurately reflect future competitive weakness.[44]

Some lower courts expanded the *General Dynamics* defense by creating a quasi-failing company defense for companies that are merely faltering. In *United States v. International Harvester Co.*,[45] for example, the court held that the acquisition did not violate Section 7 because the acquired company did not have sufficient financial resources to compete effectively.[46] A similar conclusion was reached in *United States v.*

---

of Market Conditions on Merger Review: Distressed Industries, Failing Firms, and Mergers with Bankrupt Companies, 2 ABA SECTION OF ANTITRUST LAW, 51ST ANNUAL SPRING MEETING COURSE MATERIALS, 736, 737 (2003). However, it has been considered appropriate to consider distressed industry conditions in evaluating the competitive effects of a proposed merger. *Id.*

41. 415 U.S. 486 (1974). *General Dynamics* is also discussed in part A of Chapter 5, in the context of challenging the significance of market shares, market structure, and concentration.

42. *See id.* at 503-04.

43. *See id.* at 510-11.

44. *See id.* at 501-04. In contrast, in *FTC v. Bass Bros. Enters., Inc.*, 1984-1 Trade Cas. (CCH) ¶ 66,041 (N.D. Ohio 1984), the court concluded that the supposedly failing firm had neither depleted its mineral resources nor made bona fide efforts to seek less anticompetitive purchasers, and that, unlike *General Dynamics,* its market share reflected its future competitive significance.

45. 564 F.2d 769 (7th Cir. 1977).

46. *See id.* at 774. In *F. & M. Schaefer Corp. v. C. Schmidt & Sons, Inc.*, 597 F.2d 814, 817-18 (2d Cir. 1979), the Second Circuit avoided deciding whether to follow *International Harvester* by concluding that the acquired company was an effective competitor. *International Harvester* was cited favorably in a district court decision, *Lektro-Vend Corp. v.*

Consolidated Foods Corp.,[47] where technological difficulties and limited product variety had resulted in a decline in sales and an impaired ability to compete on the part of the acquired company.[48]

Not all decisions, however, followed the trend begun in *International Harvester.* Some lower courts have faithfully applied *General Dynamics* only in evaluating competitive strengths and weaknesses.[49] Thus, in *FTC v. University Health, Inc.*,[50] the court rejected the merging hospitals' claim that one was a "weak company," concluding that it would recognize such a defense only if the hospital could show that its market share was likely to decline sufficiently to undermine the FTC's prima facie case.[51] In *FTC v. National Tea Co.*,[52] the Eighth Circuit applied *General Dynamics* in concluding that, because the acquired company was such an ineffective competitor and so likely to depart from the market, its present market share inaccurately reflected its future competitive position, and the merger should not be enjoined.[53] The FTC has expressly refused to follow *International Harvester.*[54]

Vendo Co., 500 F. Supp. 332, 360-61 (N.D. Ill. 1980), *aff'd*, 660 F.2d 255 (7th Cir. 1981), where the court found that management problems undermined a company's competitive position.

47. 455 F. Supp. 108 (E.D. Pa. 1978).

48. *See id*. at 136.

49. *See, e.g.*, United States v. Amax, Inc., 402 F. Supp. 956 (D. Conn. 1975) (recognizing the validity of the *General Dynamics* analysis, but holding that the test was not met in this instance); *cf.* United States v. UPM-Kymmene Oyj, 2003-2 Trade Cas. (CCH) ¶ 74,101 (N.D. Ill. 2003), (finding that although a consideration of the weakness of a competitor might make sense in the abstract, it does not justify an otherwise anticompetitive merger where the firm is viable and its noncompetitiveness is simply the result of its parent deciding not to compete because its return on investment is lower than from its other operations).

50. 938 F.2d 1206 (11th Cir. 1991).

51. *See id. at* 1220-21. *Accord* Olin Corp. v. FTC, 986 F.2d 1295, 1306-07 (9th Cir. 1993).

52. FTC v. National Tea Co., 603 F.2d 694 (8th Cir. 1979).

53. *See id*. at 700.

54. *See* Pillsbury Co., 93 F.T.C. 966 (1979). FTC Commissioner Pitofsky wrote:

> Inclusion of financial weakness as a separate factor or defense—other than in a failing company situation, of course—raises serious antitrust policy problems. First, there may be a sort of double counting in that financial weaknesses may already be reflected in a market share of the troubled company that is

The Division's 1984 *Merger Guidelines* explicitly recognized in Section 3.21, as the U.S. Supreme Court had in 1974 in *General Dynamics,* that current market conditions may not accurately reflect future competition in an industry. Section 3.22 also explicitly recognized that weakened financial conditions could affect a firm's future competitive significance. In the wake of *General Dynamics,* and to an even greater extent after the 1984 *Merger Guidelines* discussed financial weakness in Section 3.22, merging firms argued that virtually any kind of financial weakness created a "flailing firm" defense, as it was termed by Division and the FTC.[55]

This overuse or abuse led to the elimination of the "financial weakness" language when the Division and the FTC issued the 1992

> lower than it would have been but for the financial problems. Second, the issue of financial weakness is extremely difficult to handle in court, and susceptible to invented claims and vague expert testimony generating factual issues that the courts are not well equipped to measure. Third, if all sorts of company "weaknesses" or structural market changes operating to the disadvantage of particular companies . . . can overcome a *prima facie* case of illegality, then the whole valuable trend in merger enforcement toward streamlining cases by concentrating on properly measured market shares and concentration ratios will be undermined. This is not to say that in a close case, financial weakness cannot be taken into account along with many other factors in predicting the market consequences of a merger, but rather that there ought not be a broad "*General Dynamics*" defense that may be relied upon to overcome clear instances of illegality based on market shares and concentration ratios.

Id. at 1038; *accord* Reichold Chems., Inc., 91 F.T.C. 246, 289-91 (1978), *aff'd mem.,* 598 F.2d at 616 (1978); Kaiser Aluminum & Chemical Corp., [1976-1979 FTC Complaints & Orders Transfer Binder] Trade Reg. Rep. (CCH) ¶ 21,578 (May 17, 1979).

55. *See, e.g., 60 Minutes with the Honorable Janet D. Steiger, Chairman, Federal Trade Commission,* 61 ANTITRUST L.J. 187, 194 (1992); Kevin J. Arquit, *Perspectives on the 1992 U.S. Government Horizontal Merger Guidelines,* 61 ANTITRUST L.J. 121 (1992). Cases in which a weakened firm defense under Section 3.21 of the 1984 *Merger Guidelines* was rejected include *FTC v. University Health, Inc.*, 938 F.2d 1206, 1221 (11th Cir. 1991) (rejecting weak company defense); *FTC v. Warner Communs.*, 742 F.2d 1156, 1164 (9th Cir. 1984) (allowing defense for a firm that is not failing would undermine strict requirements of defense); and *United States v. Rice Growers Ass'n of Cal.*, 1986-2 Trade Cas. (CCH) ¶ 67,287 (E.D. Cal. 1986) (plan to exit business is not sufficient absent business failure).

Merger Guidelines. However, the 1992 *Merger Guidelines* retain the basic *General Dynamics* concept by recognizing that "recent or ongoing changes in the market may indicate that the current market share of a particular firm either understates or overstates the firm's competitive significance. . . . The Agency will consider reasonably predictable effects of recent or ongoing changes in market conditions in interpreting market concentration and market share data."[56]

The FTC hearings and FTC staff report also addressed the continued viability of the *General Dynamics* defense and concluded that it was appropriate to evaluate special competitive conditions of failing firms and distressed industries as part of a competitive effects analysis.[57] As a result, under the 1992 *Merger Guidelines* and the FTC staff report, it is still possible to argue that a firm's current market share does not reflect its future competitive significance as a means of defending a proposed merger.[58]

B. State Action Doctrine

In *Parker v. Brown*,[59] the U.S. Supreme Court held that when a state requires or regulates a practice, principles of federalism prevent the federal laws from overriding the state laws. Over the years the U.S. Supreme Court has further refined the state action doctrine.[60]

---

56. 1992 MERGER GUIDELINES, *supra* note 27, § 1.521. The FTC relied on this proposition and on *General Dynamics* in approving the Boeing-McDonnell Douglas merger, finding that McDonnell Douglas' past sales were not a valid indication of its future competitive strength. Robert Pitofsky, Mergers and Corporate Consolidation in the New Economy, Statement Before the Senate Judiciary Committee (June 16, 1998), *at* www.ftc.gov/os/1998/oldmerger98.tes.htm.
57. FTC Staff Report, *Anticipating the 21st Century: Competition Policy in the New High-Tech, Global Marketplace*, 70 Antitrust & Trade Reg. Rep. (BNA) No. 1765, S-1, S-45 (June 6, 1996).
58. *See, e.g.*, FTC v. Tenet Health Care Corp., 17 F. Supp. 2d 937, 947 (E.D. Mo. 1998), *rev'd on other grounds*, 186 F.3d 1045 (8th Cir. 1999). The defendants in *Tenet* conceded that the failing firm defense did not apply, *see id.* at 947 n.7, arguing instead that the acquired party was a failing firm with a weakened financial position that "limits its effectiveness as a competitor." *Id*. at 947. The court rejected this defense, emphasizing the need to show that the acquired firm's weakness would cause its market share to reduce "to a level that would undermine the government's prima facie case. . . ." *Id*.
59. 317 U.S. 341 (1943).
60. *See* FTC v. Ticor Title Ins. Co., 504 U.S. 621 (1992); Patrick v. Burget,

Under the state action doctrine, a state must clearly articulate an affirmative policy to allow private parties to act anticompetitively.[61] In addition, the state must actively supervise the anticompetitive activity of the private parties.[62] It must substitute an "adequate system of regulation" and exercise "significant control" over the anticompetitive behavior.[63] "Active supervision" includes a review on the merits of a decision, not just on the procedures.[64] In *FTC v. Ticor Title Insurance Co.*,[65] the U.S. Supreme Court held that state action immunity "is disfavored" and that the state must *in fact* exercise its authority to supervise.[66] Staffing and funding a state regulatory board is not sufficient if the board is inactive. "Negative option" schemes must show that state officials in fact take the necessary steps to supervise any price-fixing schemes.[67]

FTC Chairman Timothy J. Muris has expressed concerns about an "overbroad" application of state action immunity.[68] In 2001, the FTC formed a State Action Task Force to evaluate and consider, among other issues, the "clear articulation" and "active supervision" prongs to ensure that the requirements for state action immunity have "teeth."[69] In 2003 the Director of the FTC's Bureau of Competition, addressed the active supervision issue in *Indiana Movers*, a nonmerger case.[70] In *Indiana*

---

486 U.S. 94 (1988); Southern Motor Carriers Rate Conference v. United States, 471 U.S. 48 (1985); California Retail Liquor Dealers Ass'n v. Midcal Aluminum, Inc., 445 U.S. 97 (1980).

61. *See Southern Motor Carriers Rate Conference*, 471 U.S. at 63. In *University Health, Inc.*, 938 F.2d at 1213 n.13, the court concluded that this element of the state action doctrine was not satisfied and enjoined a hospital merger.
62. *See California Retail Liquor Dealers Ass'n*, 445 U.S. at 105-06; *Patrick*, 486 U.S. at 100-01; Town of Hallie v. City of Eau Claire, 471 U.S. 34, 46-47 (1985).
63. 324 Liquor Corp. v. Duffy, 479 U.S. 335, 344-345, 345 n.7 (1987).
64. *See Patrick*, 486 U.S. at 104-05.
65. 504 U.S. 621 (1992).
66. *Id.* at 636-38.
67. *Id.* at 639.
68. *See* Timothy J. Muris, FTC Chairman, Looking Forward: The Federal Trade Commission and the Future Development of U.S. Competition Policy (Dec. 10, 2002), *at* www.ftc.gov/speeches/muris/handler.htm.
69. *See id.*
70. *See* Joseph J. Simons, Report From the Bureau of Competition (Apr. 4, 2003), *at* www.ftc.gov/speeches/other/030404simonsaba.htm (discussing Indiana Household Movers & Warehousemen, Inc., No. C-4077, 2003 F.T.C. LEXIS 71 (Mar. 18, 2003)); *see also* Timothy J. Muris, FTC

Movers, a case in which the FTC alleged that an association of household goods moving services and its members engaged in price fixing through the collective filing of rate tariffs, the FTC described three factors as relevant to the "active supervision" analysis: "(1) the development of an actual factual record, including notice and opportunity to be heard; (2) a written decision on the merits; and (3) a specific assessment – both qualitative and quantitative – of how the private action comports with the substantive standards supported by the state."[71]

The issue whether state action immunity may preclude an antitrust challenge to a merger has been addressed by a number of courts.[72] In *FTC v. Hospital Board of Directors*, a case brought by the FTC attacking the proposed merger of hospitals in Lee County, Florida, the district court held that the state action doctrine precluded the FTC's challenge, and the FTC appealed.[73] The Eleventh Circuit affirmed on the ground

---

Chairman, Before the Committee on the Judiciary Antitrust Task Force United States House of Representatives, An Overview of Federal Trade Commission Antitrust Activities, 2003 WL 21721118 (F.T.C. July 24, 2003) (discussing the State Action Task Force and *Indiana Movers* standard).

71. Ind. Household Movers & Warehousemen, Inc., No. 021-0115, 68 Fed. Reg. 14234 (FTC Apr. 25, 2003) (proposed consent decree and aid to public comment), *at* www.ftc.gov/os/2003/03/indianahouseholdmoversanalysis.pdf; *accord* Iowa Movers & Warehousemen's Ass'n, No. 021-0115 (FTC filed Aug. 1, 2003), *at* www.ftc.gov/os/2003/08/imwaanlysis.htm; Minn. Transport Svcs. Assoc., No. 021-0115 (FTC Aug. 1, 2003), *at* www.ftc.gov/os/2003/08/mtsanalysis.htm.

72. FTC v. Hospital Bd. of Dirs., 38 F.3d 1184 (11th Cir. 1994) (granting state action immunity); Cine 42nd St. Theater Corp. v. Nederlander Org., 790 F.2d 1032 (2d Cir. 1986) (granting state action immunity); North Carolina *ex rel.* Edmisten v. PIA Asheville, Inc., 740 F.2d 274 (4th Cir. 1984) (denying state action immunity); California *ex rel.* Lockyer v. Mirant Corp., C-02-1787-VRW, 2003 U.S. Dist. LEXIS 10005 (N.D. Cal. 2003) (denying state action immunity); *cf.* New York v. St. Francis Hosp., 94 F. Supp. 2d 399, 408-411 (S.D.N.Y. 2000). In *St. Francis*, the district court rejected defendants' state action immunity argument for antitrust claims brought against participants in a hospital joint venture that had been formed with the consent of the New York Department of Health ("DOH") because there was no "continuing state involvement" by DOH in supervising the allegedly unlawful practices. New York alleged that the parties had engaged in a *per se* unlawful scheme of price fixing and market allocation for various hospital services in violation of Section 1, though the state did not challenge the formation of the joint venture itself.

73. 38 F.3d at 1184.

that the state action doctrine immunized the transaction from antitrust challenge because the Florida legislature foresaw possible anticompetitive effects when it authorized the public hospitals to make acquisitions.[74] The merger was abandoned at the time despite the ruling, although a new transaction between the parties was announced two years later.[75]

In *California ex rel. Lockyer v. Mirant Corp*., however, the district court rejected a claim of state action immunity in a case involving an antitrust challenge to certain acquisitions of power generation plants that were being divested as part of California's overall efforts to restructure the state's power industry. Among other claims, *Mirant* involved allegations that two firms' power generation plant acquisitions violated Section 7 because the transactions enabled each firm to obtain market power and substantially increase electricity prices, thereby violating Section 7. Notwithstanding the fact that the acquisitions had been approved by the state regulatory agency, the court rejected the defendants' state action immunity claims because the defendants had not satisfied the first element of the state action immunity defense – "clear articulation" – which requires a demonstration that the state "intend[ed] to displace competition." The court did not address the "active supervision" element.[76]

---

74. Many states have enacted legislation to provide antitrust immunity to certain collaborative agreements among health care providers, including hospital mergers. *See, e.g.*, N.Y. Laws of 1993, ch. 731, amending N.Y. PUB. HEALTH LAW §§ 2950 & 2955; N.C. Sess. L. ch. 529 § 5.2 (July 24, 1993); Health Care Cooperation Act, S.C. CODE ANN. title 44, ch. 7; Health Care Facility-Provider Cooperation Act, NEB. REV. STAT. § 71-7709; Idaho Health Planning Act, IDAHO CODE § 39-4903; ABA, HEALTHCARE MERGERS & ACQUISITIONS HANDBOOK 136-40 (2003) (discussing state statutes); Sarah S. Vance, *Immunity for State-Sanctioned Provider Collaboration After Ticor,* 62 ANTITRUST L.J. 409, 420 (1993) (discussing statutes in 13 states).
75. Elizabeth Bryant, *Cape Picks Lee-Memorial*, Fort Myers News-Press, Apr. 2, 1996, at A1.
76. California *ex rel*. Lockyer v. Mirant Corp., 2003 U.S. Dist LEXIS 10005 at *19; *see also* North Carolina *ex rel.* Edmisten v. PIA Asheville Inc., 740 F.2d at 278-79 (denying state action immunity in challenge to hospital merger because of the absence of ongoing post-acquisition supervision).

C. Antitrust Exemptions through Regulation

1. Banking

Bank mergers are generally subject not only to the antitrust laws,[77] but also to federal banking statutes. The Bank Merger Act[78] allows federal bank regulators (the Comptroller of the Currency, the Federal Reserve Board, and the Federal Deposit Insurance Corporation) to approve transactions, even if they are anticompetitive, if they find that the "anticompetitive effects of the proposed transaction are clearly outweighed in the public interest by the probable effect of the transaction in meeting the convenience and needs of the community to be served."[79] The burden of proving the "convenience and needs" defense rests on the parties to the transaction.[80] The defense cannot be satisfied if a less anticompetitive alternative would have been available.[81]

It should be noted that, even if regulators approve a transaction, the Division may still challenge that transaction as long as it does so within the statutory time period. A transaction is immune only if the statutory period has run and the Division has taken no action.[82]

---

77. *See, e.g.*, United States v. Philadelphia Nat'l Bank, 374 U.S. 321 (1963).
78. 12 U.S.C. § 1828.
79. *Id*. The defense has also been applied in bank mergers challenged under Section 1 of the Sherman Act. *See* United States v. Central State Bank, 564 F. Supp. 1478, 1482-83 (W.D. Mich. 1983).
80. *See* United States v. First City Nat'l Bank, 386 U.S. 361, 366 (1967).
81. *See* United States v. Third Nat'l Bank of Nashville, 390 U.S. 171, 189 (1968).
82. The time period is defined in 12 U.S.C. § 1828(c)(6) & (7). Transactions subject to the Bank Merger Act are exempt from the requirements of the HSR Act. *See* 15 U.S.C. § 18a(c)(7). To the extent that some portion of a proposed bank transaction does not require approval under the Bank Merger Act, that portion of the transaction will be subject to the reporting requirements of the HSR Act. *Id.* An antitrust action by the Division must be brought prior to the expiration of the time allotted to it by the statute to review the transaction. The length of time depends upon the action taken by the banking regulators. If the regulating agency approves the transaction, finds that it must act immediately to prevent the probable failure of one of the financial institutions involved in the merger, and reports on competitive factors have been dispensed with, the transaction may be consummated immediately upon approval of the agency. If the agency has notified the Attorney General of an emergency requiring expeditious action and has requested reports on competitive factors within 10 days, the transaction may not be consummated before the fifth

2. *Energy*

a. Natural Gas

The Federal Energy Regulatory Commission (FERC) has no regulatory authority over acquisitions of voting securities of natural gas companies, some of which have been challenged by the DOJ or the FTC.[83] FERC has authority over acquisitions under Section 7(c) of the Natural Gas Act,[84] which prohibits the operation of acquired assets

---

calendar day after approval by the agency. In all other cases, the transaction may not be completed before the thirtieth day after approval by the agency, or if there is no adverse comment by the Attorney General regarding competitive factors, whatever shorter time period is agreed upon by the Attorney General and the regulating agency (but in no event will the time period be shorter than 15 days after agency approval). *See* 12 U.S.C. § 1828(c)(7)(C) (providing that a merger consummated in compliance with these rules may not be attacked judicially for any antitrust violation except a violation of Section 2 of the Sherman Act if litigation is not commenced prior to the expiration of the statutory time period).

83. The government has challenged several mergers involving natural gas companies. *See, e.g.*, *In re* Conoco Inc., C-4058, 2002 F.T.C. LEXIS 49 (Aug. 30, 2002) (consent decree requiring divestiture); *In re* Chevron Corp., C-4023, 2001 F.T.C. LEXIS 135 (Sept. 7, 2001) (consent order requiring divestiture); *In re* El Paso Energy Corp., C-3996, 2001 F.T.C. LEXIS 17 (Feb. 7, 2001) (consent decree requiring divestiture); *In re* Exxon Corp., C-3907, 2001 F.T.C. LEXIS 16 (Jan. 26, 2001) (consent order required divestiture); *In re* El Paso Energy Corp., File No. 001-0121, 2000 F.T.C. LEXIS 174 (Dec. 19, 2000) (consent decree requiring divestiture); *In re* BP Amoco PLC., File No. 001-0086, 2000 F.T.C. LEXIS 100 (Aug. 25, 2000) (consent decree requiring divestiture); *In re* Duke Energy Corp, C-3932, 2000 F.T.C. LEXIS 62 (March 30, 2000) (consent decree requiring divestiture); *In re* El Paso Corp., C-3915, 2000 F.T.C. LEXIS 7 (Jan. 16, 2000) (consent decree requiring divestiture); *In re* Shell Oil Co., File No. 981-0166, 1998 F.T.C. LEXIS 110 (Oct. 1, 1998) (consent decree requiring divestiture); *In re* NGC Corp., 122 F.T.C. 472 (1996) (consent decree requiring divestiture); *In re* Phillips Petroleum Co., File No. 951-0037, 1995 F.T.C. LEXIS 252 No. 951-0037 (1995); *In re* Arkla, Inc., 112 F.T.C. 509 (1989) (consent decree requiring divestiture); *In re* Midcon Corp., 107 F.T.C. 48 (1986) (complaint dismissed because staff failed to prove that competition would be affected in a relevant geographic market); United States v. El Paso Natural Gas Co., 376 U.S. 651 (1964) (merger enjoined under Section 7).

84. 15 U.S.C. § 717(c).

without a certificate of public convenience and necessity. However, the U.S. Supreme Court has held that Section 7(c) does not deprive the federal courts of jurisdiction to enforce the antitrust laws with respect to the natural gas industry.[85] As a result, the Division and the FTC may challenge transactions approved by FERC.

b. Electric Power

Under Section 203 of the Federal Power Act,[86] FERC may authorize proposed mergers of electric utilities subject to its jurisdiction. FERC may approve mergers "consistent with the public interest," which requires analysis of competitive effects.[87] The Securities and Exchange Commission (SEC) has jurisdiction over stock acquisitions by registered public utility holding companies and must consider possible anticompetitive effects of such acquisitions.[88] There are no antitrust exemptions for transactions subject to FERC or SEC review, and such mergers are regularly reviewed by either the FTC or the Division.[89]

---

85. *See* California v. FPC, 369 U.S. 482 (1962).
86. 16 U.S.C. § 824b.
87. *See* Wabash Valley Power Ass'n v. FERC, 268 F.3d 1105, 1115 (D.C. Cir. 2001) (noting that the proper standard for reviewing a FERC merger order is whether the merger is consistent with the "public interest," which encompasses both "the preservation of economic cooperation, as expressed in the antitrust laws" and the policies of energy regulation, but not necessarily whether the merger fully eliminates market inefficiencies); Revised Filing Requirements Under Part 33 of the Commission's Regulations: Final Rule, Order No. 642, 65 Fed. Reg. 70,984 (2000) (establishing framework for analyzing vertical mergers and affirming approach to horizontal mergers); Inquiry Concerning the Commission's Merger Policy Under the Federal Power Act Policy Statement, 61 Fed. Reg. 68,595 (1996) (endorsing analytical framework used in 1992 *Merger Guidelines*).
88. *See* Public Utility Holding Company Act of 1935, 15 U.S.C. §§ 79i, 79j. In *Municipal Elec. Ass'n v. SEC*, 413 F.2d 1052, 1053 (D.C. Cir. 1969), the D.C. Circuit concluded that the SEC must consider antitrust issues in approving such transactions.
89. *See In re* United States v. Enova Corp., 107 F. Supp. 2d 10 (D.D.C. 2000); DTE Energy Co., C-4008, 2001 F.T.C. LEXIS 81 (Mar. 15, 2001) (consent agreement requiring divestiture of certain assets in merger of distributor of electricity and distributor of natural gas); Public Comments and Response of the United States, 64 Fed. Reg. 3551 (Jan. 22, 1999) (DOJ consent agreement regarding Enova Corp.'s proposed merger with Pacific Enterprises in which Enova agreed to sell its two largest low-cost

3. *Transportation*

a. Rail Transportation

Until late 1995, the Interstate Commerce Commission (ICC) had authority to approve and immunize from antitrust challenge railroad mergers that it found "consistent with the public interest."[90] In 1995, the ICC was abolished and its regulatory authority was transferred to the new Surface Transportation Board within the Department of Transportation (DOT).[91] The Surface Transportation Board (STB) has the same regulatory functions as the ICC with respect to railroad mergers, and approval confers antitrust immunity. The DOJ has no jurisdiction to enjoin a railroad merger but has a statutory right to be a part of the proceedings if it so chooses, and may file comments after the

---

electric power plants and provide notice to and get approval of DOJ should it wish to acquire or manage certain California electric power facilities); *In re* PacifiCorp, File No. 971-0091 (Feb. 18, 1998) (consent agreement between the parties and the FTC that would have required both divestment and segregation of confidential information as a condition of PacifiCorp.'s proposed acquisition of the Energy Group PLC; this transaction was later abandoned in the face of a competing tender offer).

90. 49 U.S.C. § 11344(c) (current version at 49 U.S.C. §11324). In one of its last acts, the ICC approved the merger of the Burlington Northern and Santa Fe, concluding that "trackage rights" that allowed third-party railroads independent access to certain routes in which there might be insufficient competition postmerger solved concerns about possible competitive harms. *See* Burlington Northern Inc., No. 32549, 1995 WL 528184 (I.C.C. Aug. 16, 1995). In 2000, the Division filed comments in support of a petition by a shipper to reexamine the ICC's order in the Burlington Northern-Santa Fe railroad merger. U.S. DEP'T OF JUSTICE, ANTITRUST DIVISION, RESPONSE OF THE UNITED STATES DEPARTMENT OF JUSTICE TO PETITION OF ROQUETTE AMERICA, INC. TO REOPEN (2000) *at* www.usdoj.gov/atr/public/comments/4282.htm. The petition sought remedies to replace the loss of competition that had occurred when one of the third-party railroads that had been granted independent access to the merged company's routes in 1995 eliminated service on certain routes in southeast Iowa. *Id.* The petition was withdrawn pursuant to a settlement between the parties. *See* Surface Transportation Board Summarizes Private Sector Dispute Resolution of Pending Proceedings, U.S. Dep't of Transp. Press Release (Mar. 1, 2001), *at* www.transource.org/news/news.htm?news_ID=151.

91. *See* 49 U.S.C. §§ 11323-11325.

proponent and opponent have done so.[92] Soon after the creation of the STB, it approved the merger of two western railroads, the Union Pacific and the Southern Pacific, over the objections of the DOJ.[93]

In 2000, following its approval of a merger between two of the largest North American railroads, Canadian National and Burlington Northern, the STB imposed a fifteen-month moratorium on all Class I railroad transactions because it was concerned that the industry had reached the point where another round of mergers could possibly result in a duopoly of North American Class I railroads.[94] Thereafter, in 2001, the STB implemented new rules for Class I railroad mergers.[95] Under the new rules, parties have a higher burden in demonstrating that a proposed combination is consistent with the public interest.[96] The STB now requires that a proposed merger "enhance, not merely preserve, competition, in order to secure approval."[97] Examples of "competitive enhancements" include reciprocal switching arrangements, trackage rights, and new connections for smaller railroads.[98] Furthermore, the STB has broad discretion to impose remedies, such as conditioning approval of a merger on the implementation of competitive enhancements.

b. Air Transportation

Until January 1, 1989, the Civil Aeronautics Board, and later the DOT, had broad authority to approve mergers and acquisitions of air carriers.[99] After that date, however, the DOT lost its authority to approve

---

92. *See* 49 U.S.C. § 11325(b)(1), (c)(1), (d)(1).

93. *See* Union Pacific Corp., Decision No. 44 (Surf. Transp. Bd. Aug. 12, 1996); *Transportation Board Flashes Green Light to Union Pacific-Southern Pacific Merger*; 71 Antitrust & Trade Reg. Rep. (BNA) 35 (July 11, 1996); *DOJ Expresses Competitive Concerns over Proposed Merger of Rail Carriers,* 70 Antitrust & Trade Reg. Rep. (BNA) 430 (Apr. 18, 1996) (summarizing DOJ competitive concerns).

94. Ex Parte No. 582 (Sub-No. 1), Major Rail Consolidation Procedures, 2001, 2001 S.T.B. LEXIS 546, *29 (June 11, 2001).

95. *Id.*

96. *Id.* at *13.

97. *Id.* at *14.

98. *Id.*

99. From 1938 to 1978, air carriers were subject to regulation under the Civil Aeronautics Act of 1938 and the Federal Aviation Act of 1958. *See* Civil Aeronautics Act of 1938, 49 U.S.C. §§ 401-403, *repealed and replaced by* Federal Aviation Act of 1958, 49 U.S.C. app. §§ 1301-1387 (1988).

aviation mergers.[100] The DOJ now analyzes such transactions under the antitrust laws using the same standards it applies to other industries.[101] However, the DOT has retained express statutory authority to approve and grant antitrust immunity to agreements between U.S. and foreign carriers.[102] The DOT has granted antitrust immunity to many international alliances, particularly where the United States and a foreign nation have entered into an "Open Skies" agreement,[103] which DOT has

---

The regulatory scheme set forth in these acts was administered by the Civil Aeronautics Board (CAB) until 1978. The passage of the Airline Deregulation Act of 1978, however, reduced the powers of the CAB, ultimately resulting in the termination of the CAB in 1985. *See* Airline Deregulation Act of 1978, Pub. L. No. 95-504, 92 Stat. 1705 (1978) (amending the Federal Aviation Act); CAB Sunset Act of 1984, Pub. L. No. 98-443, 98 Stat. 1703 (1984). At that point, the DOT assumed regulatory responsibility.

100. *See* 49 U.S.C. app. § 1551 (1988) (terminating DOT authority held under §§ 408 and 409 of Federal Aviation Act (49 U.S.C. app. §§ 1378, 1379 (1988))).

101. The Division has challenged a number of airline transactions. In July 2001, the Division announced its intention to block the proposed merger between United Airlines and US Airways; thereafter, the parties abandoned the transaction. *See* Department of Justice and Several States Will Sue to Stop United Airlines from Acquiring US Airways, U.S. Dep't of Justice Press Release (July 27, 2001), *at* www.usdoj.gov/atr/public/press_releases/2001/8701.htm. In 1998, the Division filed a complaint challenging Northwest Airlines' proposed acquisition of Continental Airlines and code-sharing arrangement. *See United States v. Northwest Airlines Corp.*, Civ. No. 98-74611 (E.D. Mich. filed Oct. 23, 1998) (complaint), *at* www.usdoj.gov/atr/cases/f2100/2158.htm; Department Announces Tentative Settlement in Northwest-Continental Lawsuit; Dep't of Justice Press Release (Nov. 6, 2000) *at* www.usdoj.gov/atr/public/press_release/1998/2024.htm. Thereafter, pursuant to a settlement agreement, Northwest agreed to divest all but 7% of its interest in Continental, but the parties were permitted to retain their code-sharing arrangement. *Id.*; United States v. USAir Group, 1993-2 Trade Cas. (CCH) ¶ 70,416 (D.D.C. 1993) (consent decree).

102. *See* 49 U.S.C. §§ 41308-41309.

103. *See, e.g., In re* Joint Application of Alitalia-Linee Aeree Italia-S.p.A., KLM Royal Dutch Airlines and Northwest Airlines, Inc. Pursuant to 49 U.S.C. §§ 41308-09, for Approval of, and Antitrust Immunity for, Alliance Agreements, DOT Docket No. OST-1999-5674 (Dec. 3, 1999) (final order); Delta-Austrian, Swissair Antitrust Immunity Exemption Approved, U.S. Dep't of Transp. Press Release (June 14, 1996); DOT

defined as an agreement that contains, among other provisions, open entry on all routes, unrestricted capacity and frequency on all routes, unrestricted route and traffic rights, and open code-sharing opportunities.[104] Although the Division opposed some of the DOT's first grants of immunity in 1996,[105] since then it generally has not opposed such grants where an "Open Skies" agreement has existed.[106] However, according to Assistant Attorney General R. Hewett Pate, it has been the Division's policy to seek to "carve out" from the grant of immunity certain routes where the proposed alliance partners are "two of very few current or likely future competitors."[107] Finally, for a very limited period

---

Grants Antitrust Immunity to United Lufthansa Alliance, U.S. Dep't of Transp. Press Release (Apr. 4, 2002), *at* www.dot.gov/affairs/dot03502.htm. In some cases, the DOT has limited the grant of immunity to certain activities. *See, e.g.*, American Airlines, Swissair, and Sabena, Order 2000-5-13, 2000 DOT Av. LEXIS 244 (2000) (excluding from the grant of immunity full fare coach, business class, and first class fares for U.S. point-of-sale passengers flying nonstop between Chicago and Brussels, and between Chicago and Zurich).

104. Order 92-8-13, 1992 DOT Av. LEXIS 568 (1992).

105. Anne K. Bingaman, Ass't Att'y Gen., Antitrust Div., Consolidation and Code Sharing: Antitrust Enforcement in the Airline Industry, Remarks Before the ABA Forum on Air and Space Law (Jan. 25, 1996), *at* www.usdoj.gov/atr/public/speeches/speech.akb.htm (stating that "[i]t is not necessary for code share partners to receive antitrust immunity for any agreement that would not violate the antitrust laws; and conduct that would violate the antirust laws should not be permitted, much less immunized").

106. *See* R. Hewitt Pate, Dep. Ass't. Att'y Gen. Antitrust Div., U.S. Dep't of Justice, International Aviation Alliances: Market Turmoil and the Future of Airline Competition, Statement before the Committee on the Judiciary, Subcommittee on Antitrust, Competition, and Business Rights, U.S. Senate (Nov. 7, 2001), *at* www.usdoj.gov/atr/public/testimony/9508.htm (discussing how the Division evaluates international code share agreements).

107. *Id.* In 2001, the Division recommended that immunity not be granted to a proposed international alliance between American Airlines and British Airways unless the DOT required, among other conditions, divestitures of slots and related facilities on certain concentrated routes and the exclusion of certain routes entirely from immunity. US-UK Alliance Case, No. OST 2001-11029, Public Comments of the Department of Justice (Dec. 17, 2001), *at* www.usdoj.gov/atr/public/comments/9712.htm In its decision, DOT conditioned a grant of immunity on, among other requirements, divestitures of slots and facilities that were greater than those recommended by the Division and the exclusion of certain routes

of time after September 11, 2001, Congress granted DOT the ability to grant antitrust immunity to agreements among airlines concerning domestic intrastate flights that might otherwise have been anticompetitive.[108]

4. Communications

Under the Telecommunications Act of 1996 (TA),[109] mergers in the telecommunications industry are subject to dual review by the DOJ and the Federal Communications Commission (FCC). This dual merger review is meant to further the TA's stated goal of a "procompetitive, deregulatory national policy framework for the U.S. communications

---

from immunity. Order to Show Cause, Order 2001-011029-69 (Jan. 25, 2002). The parties ultimately abandoned their proposed alliance and withdrew their applications. Final Order, Order 2001-11029-125 (Apr. 4, 2002).

108. Aviation and Transportation Security Act of 2001, Pub. L. 107-71, 115 Stat. 264 (2001) (providing that DOT may grant antitrust immunity to an agreement among airlines to coordinate intrastate flight operations upon a declaration by the governor of the affected state that the agreement is necessary to ensure the continuing availability of air transportation within the state and DOT finds that "(1) the State to which it relates has extraordinary air transportation needs and concerns; and (2) approval is in the public interest"). The statute provided that immunity could be granted until October 1, 2002 and, upon a public interest finding, extended up to October 1, 2003, but it was repealed in November 2002. *See* Pub. L. 107-273, 116 Stat. 1921 (2002). In 2002, however, DOT granted antitrust immunity and approved a one-year agreement between Aloha Airlines and Hawaiian Airlines to jointly set capacity levels in the Hawaii inter-island market over the Division's opposition. Order Approving Agreement and Granting Antitrust Immunity 2002-13002-14 (Sept. 30, 2002) (granting immunity with conditions); *see also* Public Comments of the Department of Justice on Joint Application of Aloha Airlines Inc. and Hawaiian Airlines Inc., for Approval of and Antitrust Immunity for a Joint Operating Agreement Pursuant to § 116 of the Aviation and Transportation Act, DOT Docket No. OST-2002-13002 (Aug. 30, 2002) (opposing grant of immunity because (1) the cooperation agreement would have anticompetitive effects (increased incentives to raise prices and powerful disincentives to improve service) and (2) based on the Division's interpretation of the statute, immunity should not be available unless both firms are "failing firms" that would otherwise exit the market).

109. Telecommunications Act of 1996, Pub. L. No. 104-104, 110 Stat. 56 (1996).

industry . . . and the opening of all telecommunications markets to competition."[110]

The TA explicitly provides that the Division retains its traditional role in review of mergers of telecommunications companies under the Hart-Scott-Rodino Antitrust Improvements Act.[111] The TA also removes the FCC's ability to immunize a merger of "telephone companies" from the antitrust laws.[112] The Division reviews mergers in the telecommunications industry using the *Merger Guidelines* to determine whether the proposed merger would eliminate current competition or future potential competition in a way that harms consumers.[113]

---

110. Commentators and observers have criticized dual merger review for several reasons, including that it is duplicative, unnecessarily lengthy, and the FCC lacks the expertise and resources to properly conduct merger reviews. *See, e.g.*, Opening Statement of Michael K. Powell, FCC Commissioner, Before the Subcommittee on Telecommunications, Trade and Consumer Protection of the House Committee on Commerce on The Telecommunications Merger Act of 2000 (Mar. 14, 2000) (discussing criticism of FCC merger review process); Maurice E. Stucke & Allen P. Grunes, *Antitrust and the Marketplace of Ideas*, 69 ANTITRUST L.J. 249 (2001). In response to criticism, the FCC has adopted a new streamlined approach to merger review under which it will "process even the most complex transactions" within 180 days. FCC, PROPOSED TIMELINE FOR CONSIDERATION OF APPLICATIONS FOR TRANSFERS OR ASSIGNMENTS OF LICENSES OR REQUESTS FOR AUTHORIZATION RELATING TO COMPLEX MERGERS (Mar. 1, 2000), *at* www.fcc.gov/transaction/timeline.html; *see also* U.S. Dep't of Justice, Press Release, Justice Department Will Not Challenge News Corp.'s Acquisition of Hughes Corp., (Dec. 19, 2003), *at* www.usdoj.gov/atr/public/press_release/2003/201918.htm.

111. See Telecommunications Act, *supra* note 109 at § 601.

112. *Id.*

113. *See* Joel I. Klein, Ass't Att'y Gen., Antitrust Div., U.S. Dep't of Justice, Statement Before the House Committee of the Judiciary Concerning Consolidation in the Telecommunications Industry (June 24, 1998), *at* www.usdoj.gov/atr/public/testimony/1806.htm. Since the passage of the Telecommunications Act of 1996, the Division has investigated and challenged a number of telecommunications mergers. *See, e.g.*, United States v. AT&T Corp. No. 1: 00CV01176 (RCL) (Sept. 20, 2000) (consent decree and competitive impact statement), *at* www.usdoj.gov/atr/cases/indx4468.htm; United States v. WorldCom, Inc. (June 7, 2000) (complaint) *at* www.usdoj.gov/atv/cases/F5000/5051.htm. (Division suit seeking to enjoin WorldCom's proposed acquisition of Sprint, alleging that the transaction would substantially lessen competition in several telecommunications markets; after the complaint was filed, the parties abandoned the transaction).

The FCC also independently reviews mergers that involve the transfer of FCC licenses to determine whether the transfer would be "in the public interest." In analyzinga merger, the FCC examines how the proposed transaction will affect the development of competition in all communications markets, and balances the potential procompetitive effects of a transaction with its anticompetitive effects.[114] If the merger, on balance, will enhance competition, the FCC will deem it in the public interest.[115]

There are a few significant differences between DOJ and FCC review of telecommunications mergers. First, the agencies' burdens of proof are different. When reviewing a merger, the Division bears the burden of proving that the effect of the merger may be substantially to lessen competition or to tend to create a monopoly.[116] By contrast, during FCC merger review, the parties bear the burden of proving that the merger would advance the public interest.[117] Thus, if a proposed telecommunications merger has a neutral impact on competition, the Division could not successfully block the merger, but the FCC could.[118] Second, the FCC's public interest standard allows the FCC to challenge mergers on grounds unrelated to competition, such as the impact the merger might have on universal access to telecommunications service or how the merger might impact other communications markets.[119]

Finally, it is notable that the FCC has established ownership caps that might affect FCC merger reviews in certain telecommunications

---

114. *See* Gloria Tristani, Comm'r, FCC, Remarks Before the National Association of Regulatory Utility Commissioners (Nov. 8, 1998), *at* www.fcc.gov/speeches/tristani/spgt813.html.

115. *Id.*

116. 15 U.S.C. § 18.

117. *See* Gloria Tristani, Comm'r, FCC, Remarks Before the National Association of Regulatory Utility Commissioners (Nov. 8, 1998), *at* www.fcc.gov/speeches/tristani/spgt813.html.

118. *Id.*

119. *Id.*; *see also* Harvey I. Saferstein, Antitrust Issues For Telecom Mergers and Acquisitions, Practicing Law Institute (Mar.-Apr. 2003) (discussing the implications of FCC merger review); Statement of Commissioner Susan Ness, Federal Communications Commission on Mergers and Consolidation in the Telecommunications Industry before the Committee on the Judiciary, U.S. House of Representatives (June 24, 1998), *at* www.fcc.gov/speeches/ness/states/stsn820.html.

markets such as wireless services,[120] cable and satellite television,[121] and radio and television broadcasting.[122]

---

120. Until December 2001, the FCC prohibited wireless providers from owning more than 45 MHz (or 55 MHz in rural areas) in any geographic area, but these spectrum caps were eliminated effective January 1, 2003. *See* FCC, *In Re* 2000 Biennial Regulatory Review Spectrum Aggregation Limits or Commercial Mobile Radio Services (2001) (report and order), *at* ftp.fcc.gov/Bureaus/Wireless?orders/2001/fcc01328.txt.

121. In 1999, pursuant to the 1992 Cable Act, the FCC adopted cable horizontal ownership rules under which one entity could not reach more than 30% of all multichannel video programming distribution ("MVPD") (i.e.. cable television and satellite) customers nationwide, but these rules were vacated by the D.C. Circuit in *Time Warner Entm't Co. v. FCC*, 240 F.3d 1126, 1139 (D.C. Cir. 2001) (finding, among other grounds, that the FCC had exceeded its statutory authority). Although the FCC initiated proceedings in 2001 to reexamine the horizontal cable ownership rules in light of *Time Warner*, it has not implemented new rules. Further Notice of Proposed Rulemaking, Implementation of Section 11 of the Cable Television Consumer Protection and Competition Act of 1992, 2001 FCC LEXIS 5025 (Sept. 21, 2001). Cable mergers are thus analyzed on a case-by-case basis. *See, e.g.*, *In re* Comcast 17 F.C.C.R. 23,246, 17 FCC Rcd. 23,246 (2002). In comments filed by the Division in connection with the FCC rulemaking proceeding, the Division did not oppose horizontal ownership caps, but noted that it would "continue to review, on a case-by-case basis, mergers in the MVPD industry to determine whether they will have anticompetitive consequences in violation of Section 7." In the Matter of Implementation of Section 11 of the Cable Television Consumer Protection and Competition Act of 1992, Reply Comments of the U.S. Dep't of Justice, No. 98-82 (Feb. 19, 2002), *at* www.usdoj.gov/atr/public/comments/10086.htm.

122. In 2003, the FCC established new media-ownership rules for television and radio broadcasting. In the Matter of 2002 Biennial Regulatory Review-Review of the Commission's Broadcast Ownership Rules and Other Rules Adopted Pursuant to Section 202 of the Telecommunications Act of 1996, Docket No. 02-277 (June 2, 2003) (report and order), *at* www.hraunfoss.fcc.gov/edoc_public/attachmatch/FCC-03-127A1.doc. The new rules prohibit one entity from owning television stations reaching more than 45% of all households nationwide. Previously, the cap was set at 35%. *Id.* The new rules also increase limits for ownership of local television stations, ease restrictions on newspapers-television station and radio-television cross-ownership, and increase restrictions on local radio station ownership. *Id.* However, the fate of the new FCC rules were put in doubt when the House has passed a bill repealing the 45% ownership rule. *See* Christopher Stern & Jonathan Krim, *House Votes to Prevent Change in Media Rule*, Washington Post, July 24, 2003 at A1, and the Senate passed

D. Specific Industries

Mergers may be allowed in some industries based on particular conditions in those industries.

1. Health Care

Despite some doubts in the past, it is now clear that the antitrust laws apply to the health care industry generally[123] and hospital mergers in particular.[124] The fact that some hospitals may be nonprofit institutions does not exempt their mergers from antitrust scrutiny,[125] but it is a factor that courts have considered.[126] State certificate-of-need statutes do not protect hospital mergers from antitrust scrutiny.[127] The federal agencies' *Statements of Antitrust Enforcement Policy and Analytical Principles Relating to Health Care and Antitrust*[128] establish a "safe harbor" for

---

a joint resolution of disapproval on September 16, 2003, *at* www.hraunfoss.fcc.gov/edocs_public/attachmatch/FCC-03-127A1.doc.

123. *See, e.g.*, Arizona v. Maricopa County Med. Soc'y, 457 U.S. 332 (1982).

124. *See, e.g.*, Hospital Bldg. Co. v. Trustees of the Rex Hosp., 425 U.S. 738 (1976); FTC v. University Health, Inc., 938 F.2d 1206 (11th Cir. 1991); United States v. Rockford Mem'l Corp., 898 F.2d 1278 (7th Cir. 1990). *But see,* California v. Sutter Health Sys., 130 F. Supp. 2d 1109 (N.D. Cal. 2001) (failing firm defense precluded challenge to hospital merger).

125. *See, e.g.*, *University Health, Inc.*, 938 F.2d at 1221; *Rockford Mem'l Corp.*, 898 F.2d at 1281; United States v. Long Island Jewish Med. Ctr., 983 F. Supp. 121, 145-46 (E.D.N.Y. 1997); FTC v. Butterworth Health Corp., 946 F. Supp. 1285, 1296 (W.D. Mich. 1996), *aff'd*, 121 F.3d 708 (6th Cir. 1997); FTC v. Freeman Hosp., 911 F. Supp. 1213, 1227 (W.D. Mo.), *aff'd*, 69 F.3d 260 (8th Cir. 1995); *see also* CAL. CORP. CODE § 5914 (West 2000) (requiring notice to and approval of state attorney general before non-profit health facility may sell its assets or transfer operational control to a for-profit entity).

126. *See, e.g.*, *Long Island Jewish Med. Ctr.*, 983 F. Supp. at 146 (nonprofit status has limited and nondeterminative effect); *Butterworth Health Corp.*, 946 F. Supp. at 1296 (nonprofit status is material but not dispositive); *Freeman Hosp.*, 911 F. Supp. at 1227 (nonprofit status must be considered by the court).

127. *See* North Carolina *ex rel.* Edmisten v. PIA Asheville Inc., 740 F.2d 274 (4th Cir. 1984). State statutes may provide a basis for asserting a state action defense. *See supra* notes 72-74, and accompanying text; *cf.* New York v. St. Francis Hosp., 94 F. Supp. 2d 399 (S.D.N.Y. 2000) (rejecting state action claim for joint venture alleged to violate Section 1).

128. U.S. DEP'T OF JUSTICE & FEDERAL TRADE COMM'N, STATEMENTS OF ANTITRUST ENFORCEMENT POLICY IN HEALTH CARE (1996), *reprinted in*

mergers in which one of the hospitals is not less than five years old, has had fewer than one hundred licensed beds over the three most recent years, and has had an average daily inpatient census of fewer than forty patients over the three most recent years. If a merger falls within this "safety zone," it will not be challenged "absent extraordinary circumstances."

Between February and October 2003, the Division and the FTC conducted a series of joint hearings, the Health Care and Competition Law and Policy hearings, to examine a wide range of issues concerning antitrust policy in the health care industry, including hospital mergers, the significance of the hospitals' nonprofit status, vertical arrangements, quality and efficiency, the *Noerr-Pennington* and state action doctrines, and the adequacy of existing remedies for anticompetitive conduct.[129] A formal report is expected to be released in 2004.[130] In addition, in 2002, the FTC established a merger litigation task force to investigate and potentially challenge previously consummated hospital mergers that may have resulted in anticompetitive price increases.[131]

2. *Defense*

Although the Department of Defense is the only U.S. purchaser of defense products, mergers of defense contractors are subject to the federal antitrust laws.[132] In its 1994 report, the Defense Science Board Task Force on the Antitrust Aspects of Defense Industry Consolidation concluded that it did not recommend any antitrust exemption for mergers in the defense industry[133] and that, with certain modest modifications and

---

4 Trade Reg. Rep. (CCH) ¶ 13,153 (Aug. 28, 1996).

129. Press Release, Antitrust Division to Co-Host Hearings on Health Care Competition Law and Policy (Nov. 7, 2002), *at* www.usdoj.gov/atr/public/press_releases/2002/200443.htm.

130. Statement of R. Hewitt Pate, Ass't Att'y General, Antitrust Div., Before the Committee on the Judiciary United States House of Representatives Concerning Antitrust Enforcement Oversight (July 24, 2003), *at* www.usdoj.gov/atr/public/testimoney/201190.htm.

131. Federal Trade Commission Announces Formation of Merger Litigation Task Force, Federal Trade Commission Press Release (Aug. 28, 2002), *at* www.ftc.gov/opa/2002/08/mergerlitigation.htm.

132. *See, e.g.,* FTC v. Alliant Techsystems Inc., 808 F. Supp. 9 (D.D.C. 1992); FTC v. Imo Indus., 1992-2 Trade Cas. (CCH) ¶ 69,943 (D.D.C. 1989).

133. Task Force Report Finds No Need For Defense Industry Antitrust Exemption, *reprinted in* 66 Antitrust & Trade Reg. Rep. (BNA) S-1, S-12 (Apr. 14, 1994).

the prudent exercise of prosecutorial discretion, analysis under the 1992 *Merger Guidelines* was sufficiently flexible to accommodate any special national security concerns related to defense industry mergers.[134] In a more recent report, the Defense Science Board Task Force on Vertical Integration and Supplier Decisions confirmed that the merger review process established after the 1994 task force is working well, that it has identified and resolved issues posed by both horizontal mergers and vertical transactions, and that antitrust agency and Department of Defense reviews are complementary.[135] The task force also identified possible concerns about vertical integration of defense contractors and recommended that the Department of Defense take certain actions to identify and minimize possible concerns.[136]

The Department of Defense also has raised concerns about exclusive "teaming arrangements" (generally, collaborations among government contractors to jointly bid and/or provide services) and has stated that such agreements should be closely scrutinized.[137] Under an exclusive

---

134. *See id.* at S-5, S-19 to S-24. After the task force report was issued, the Department of Defense established an internal review process in DOD Directive 5000.62 (Oct. 21, 1996).

135. *See* Report of the Defense Science Board Task Force on Vertical Integration and Supplier Decisions 29-33 (May 1997). For example, opposition from both the Department of Defense and the DOJ to the proposed Lockheed Martin-Northrop Grumman merger prompted the parties to abandon the deal. *See* Lockheed Martin, Northrop Grumman Cancel Merger Plans Due to Government Opposition, 75 Antitrust & Trade Reg. Rep. (BNA) 94 (July 23, 1998). In 2001, the DOJ and the Department of Defense raised significant competitive concerns about the proposed acquisition of Newport News by General Dynamics, and the DOJ filed suit seeking to enjoin the transaction because it would have created a monopoly in nuclear submarines. *See, e.g.*, United States v. Gen. Dynamics Corp., No: 1:01CV02200 (D.D.C. 2001), *at* www.usdoj.gov/atr/cases/f9300/9373.htm; Justice Department Files Suit to Block General Dynamics' Purchase of Newport News Shipbuilding, U.S. Dep't of Justice Press Release (Oct. 23, 2002). The parties ultimately abandoned the transaction and Newport News was acquired by Northrop Grumman in a separate transaction.

136. Report of the Defense Science Board Task Force on Vertical Integration and Supplier Decisions at 15-28, viii-xvi (May 1997).

137. Department of Defense, DCAA Contract Audit Manual § 4-705(c) (Jan. 2000). *But see* Federal Acquisition Regulations, 48 C.F.R. § 9.602 (noting that teaming arrangements are generally desirable). In 2001, the Department of Defense proposed a new policy under which any exclusive teaming arrangements would be considered as evidence of a potential

teaming agreement, parties might agree either not to compete independently or team with other competitors. The Division and FTC would evaluate any potentially anticompetitive teaming arrangement under the *Competitor Collaborations Guidelines*.[138]

3. *Newspapers*

The Newspaper Preservation Act[139] (NPA) provides the Attorney General of the United States with authority to approve, and thereby grant limited antitrust immunity to, joint operating arrangements (JOAs) between competing newspapers in the same geographic area.[140] A JOA generally allows for the merger of the business functions of the two newspapers (advertising, circulation, and publishing), while each of the two newspapers remains independent in its editorial and reporting product. Antitrust immunity is only available for those arrangements entered into with the prior consent of the Attorney General (assuming that the JOA was not in effect at the time the statute was enacted).[141] Newspapers that were functioning under JOAs at the time the statute was enacted were permitted to continue joint operations without DOJ approval.[142] To put a JOA into effect does not require consent of the

---

antitrust violation, but the proposed policy was withdrawn in 2002. *See* Defense Federal Acquisition Regulation Supplement; Anticompetitive Teaming, 66 Fed. Reg. 55,157 (proposed Nov. 1, 2001) (withdrawn 67 Fed. Reg. 18160, Apr. 15, 2002).

138. *See infra* Chapter 8; *cf.* United States v. Alliant Sys., 1994 WL 362247 (C.D. Ill. filed May 13, 1994) (consent decree prohibiting parties from entering teaming arrangements without advance approval from DOJ).

139. 15 U.S.C. §§ 1801-1804.

140. The NPA does not exempt parties to the JOA from the antitrust laws generally. *See* 15 U.S.C. § 1803(c).

141. *See id.* § 1803(b); Newspaper Operating Arrangement, Times Printing Co., and the Chattanooga News-Free Press Co., 45 Fed. Reg. 58,733 (1980) (approving only those arrangements that were not yet implemented).

142. *See* 15 U.S.C. § 1803(a). Modifications to JOAs in existence prior to the act may be amended simply by filing the amendment with the DOJ (except in cases where a newspaper is added to the agreement). *See id.* The statute is silent on amendments to JOAs approved by the Attorney General. One court has found that unapproved amendments to previously approved JOAs do not strip the entire agreement of the protections provided by the statute. *See* Mahaffey v. Detroit Newspaper Agency, 969 F. Supp. 446, 448-49 (E.D. Mich. 1997), *aff'd,* 1998-2 Trade Cas. (CCH) ¶ 72,324 (6th Cir. 1998).

Attorney General; however, absent approval, the arrangement remains fully subject to the antitrust laws.[143] The mere lack of approval by the Attorney General does not make the JOA unlawful under the antitrust laws.[144]

The requirements for approval of a JOA under the NPA are defined in the statute itself. First, the Attorney General must find that a newspaper "is in probable danger of financial failure."[145] Early on, Attorneys General interpreting the NPA found that a newspaper was failing where it was in a "downward spiral."[146] The downward spiral test has been broadened to include situations where a paper is "poised on the brink of the spiral"[147] and where "a paper is suffering losses which more than likely cannot be reversed."[148] Second, the Attorney General must find that the arrangement would "effectuate the policy and purpose of [the act.]."[149] The applicants have the burden of proving that the proposed arrangement will satisfy the requirements of the act.[150] One

143. *See* Newspaper Guild v. Levi, 539 F.2d 755 (D.C. Cir. 1976); 28 C.F.R. § 48.1.

144. *See* News Weekly-Systems v. Chattanooga News-Free Press, 1993-1 Trade Cas. (CCH) ¶ 70,150 (6th Cir. 1993) (citing with approval the comments of the Attorney General in Newspaper Operating Arrangement, Times Printing Co., and the Chattanooga News-Free Press Co., 45 Fed. Reg. 58,733 (1980)).

145. 15 U.S.C. § 1802(5).

146. *See, e.g.*, Opinion and Order Regarding Application of Seattle Times Co. and Hearst Corp. for Approval of Joint Operating Arrangement, 47 Fed. Reg. 26,472 (1982); Newspaper Operating Arrangement, Times Printing Co., and the Chattanooga News-Free Press Co., 45 Fed. Reg. 58,733 (1980). Although the statute has not changed, the Attorney General has appeared to take a more pragmatic stance regarding whether conditions are sufficient to find that a newspaper is a "failing newspaper." *See, e.g.*, *In re* Application by York Daily Record, Inc. and York Newspapers, Inc., for Approval of a Joint Operating Agreement Pursuant to the Newspaper Preservation Act, 1990-1 Trade Cas. (CCH) ¶ 68,935 (Office of the Att'y Gen. Feb. 21, 1990); *In re* Application by Las Vegas Sun, Inc., and Donrey of Nevada, Inc., for Approval of a Joint Newspaper Operating Arrangement Pursuant to the Newspaper Preservation Act, 1990-1 Trade Cas. (CCH) ¶ 69,047 (Office of the Att'y Gen. June 1, 1990).

147. Michigan Citizens for an Indep. Press v. Thornburgh, 868 F.2d 1285, 1292 (D.C. Cir.), *aff'd*, 493 U.S. 38 (1989).

148. Committee for an Indep. PI v. Hearst Corp., 704 F.2d 467, 478 (9th Cir. 1983).

149. 15 U.S.C. § 1803(b).

150. *Hearst Corp.*, 704 F.2d at 479.

court has found that "Congress has preempted the field of regulations based on a newspaper's involvement in a JOA."[151]

Pursuant to DOJ regulations, the Attorney General will refer the JOA application to the Assistant Attorney General in charge of the Antitrust Division. The Assistant Attorney General then recommends either approval of the JOA or that a hearing be held before an administrative law judge (ALJ).[152] If a hearing is held, the Division becomes a party to the proceedings and other interested parties may intervene.[153] The Attorney General must base his or her decision on the hearing record, the ALJ's recommendation, and any exceptions filed.[154] The Attorney General need not follow the recommendation of the Division or the ALJ.[155] The Attorney General's decision is subject to judicial review.

The Division has established standards for analyzing the merger of newspapers that were previously operated pursuant to a JOA. In conjunction with its review of a merger of two St. Louis newspapers, the Division announced that, for proposed mergers of JOA newspapers, the Division will "insist upon a rigorous application of the more demanding, traditional failing firm test whenever the parties . . . propose to discontinue one of the two newspapers" rather than the standard for approving JOAs under the NPA.[156] In other words, the Division will challenge such mergers unless: (1) one of the JOA newspapers would be a failing company if operated outside the JOA and (2) there were no alternative purchasers who were willing to operate the newspaper outside the JOA.[157] In *Reilly v. Hearst Corp.*, the court followed this approach, stating that "in an antitrust challenge to a proposed merger of JOA

---

151. Haw. Newspaper Agency v. Bronster, 103 F.3d 742, 749 (9th Cir. 1996).
152. *See* 28 C.F.R. § 48.7. *See also, e.g., In re* Application by E.W. Scripps and MediaNews Group, Inc. for Approval of a Joint Newspaper Operating Arrangement Pursuant to the Newspaper Preservation Act, (Office of the Att'y Gen. Sep. 8, 2000), *at* www.usdoj.gov/atr/public/press_releases/2000/6449.htm. (Antitrust Division recommending to the Attorney General that the JOA application submitted by the publisher of the Denver Rocky Mountain News and the publisher of The Denver Post, be approved).
153. *See* 28 C.F.R. § 48.10(b), § 48.11.
154. *See id.* § 48.13(b).
155. *Hearst Corp.*, 704 F.2d at 471; *In re* Application by Detroit Free Press, Inc., and The Detroit News for Approval of a Joint Newspaper Operating Arrangement Pursuant to the Newspaper Preservation Act, 1990-1 Trade Cas. (CCH) ¶ 68,929 (Office of the Att'y Gen. Aug. 8, 1988).
156. U.S. Dep't of Justice Press Release (Nov. 8, 1983).
157. *Id.*

newspapers, the defendants may avoid liability by proving the traditional failing company defense . . . ."[158]

158. 107 F. Supp. 2d 1192, 1203 (N.D. Cal. 2000) (dismissing private antitrust suit challenging newspaper acquisitions); *see* discussion of the failing firm defense generally, *supra*, at Section A.1; *cf.* Hawaii *ex rel.* Anzai v. Gannett Pac. Corp., 99 F. Supp. 2d 1241 (D. Haw.) (NPA does not exempt agreement among JOA newspapers to terminate JOA early, which would result in one newspaper closing, from scrutiny under Section 1 and 2 of the Sherman Act), *aff'd*, 203 F.3d 832 (9th Cir. 1999); Brief Amicus Curiae of the United States of America in Support of Appellee State Of Hawaii and Affirmance, Hawaii v. Gannett Pac. Corp., No. 99-17201, 1999 U.S. App. LEXIS 30030 (9th Cir. Nov. 3, 1999) (arguing that the district court's holding in *Gannett* should be affirmed by Ninth Circuit).

CHAPTER 8

JOINT VENTURES

In a typical acquisition, the buyer obtains complete ownership of the acquired business, whether it be a company, an unincorporated division, a line of business, or some collection of assets. Upon closing, the seller transfers dominion over the acquired properties to the buyer. The buyer then employs the properties as directed by its management and its owners' best interests. The seller may continue to exist and retain its pre-transaction identity, but it no longer has any post-transaction control, either directly or indirectly, over the acquired properties. Similarly, the combining firms in a merger lose their independent identities to become a single firm under the control of a unified management. The management and shareholders of both firms may continue their involvement in the business.

Joint ventures differ from the transactions just described. In a joint venture, rather than one firm assuming dominion over the properties to the exclusion of all other contributors, two or more of the contributors continue their independent existence, but share some direct or indirect control over the properties. To the extent that such transactions involve actual or potential competitors, they may be referred to as "competitor collaborations."[1]

Joint ventures are inherently difficult to categorize, and there is no single, well-accepted definition of the term under the antitrust laws.[2] In its broadest sense, a joint venture can embrace any collaborative activity

---

1. The U.S. Department of Justice and the Federal Trade Commission use this term in describing antitrust implications of joint ventures. *See* U.S. DEP'T OF JUSTICE & FEDERAL TRADE COMM'N, ANTITRUST GUIDELINES FOR COLLABORATIONS AMONG COMPETITORS (2000) [hereinafter COMPETITOR COLLABORATIONS GUIDELINES], *reprinted in* 4 Trade Reg. Rep. (CCH) ¶ 13,161, *at* www.ftc.gov/os/2000/04/ftcdojguidelines.pdf *and* in Appendix N. These guidelines arose out of the Joint Venture Project initiated by the agencies in 1997. *See* FTC Comment and Hearings on Joint Venture Project, 62 Fed. Reg. 22,945 (1997).
2. *See* COMPACT v. Metropolitan Gov't, 594 F. Supp. 1567, 1574 (M.D. Tenn. 1984) ("Joint ventures present a difficult concept for antitrust analysis, defying neat classification and precise definition and, by extension, well established rules for evaluating their competitive impact").

among multiple firms, accompanied by some degree of integration of resources, management, and risk, and designed to produce or procure some product or service.[3] The *Competitor Collaborations Guidelines* issued by the Federal Trade Commission (FTC or Commission) and the Antitrust Division of the U.S. Department of Justice (DOJ or the Division) define competitor collaborations as comprising "a set of one or more agreements, other than merger agreements, between or among competitors to engage in economic activity, and the economic activity resulting therefrom."[4]

As in the case of mergers and acquisitions, integrations through joint ventures can have a wide variety of competitive effects. Depending on their structure, the applicable technology and the market environment, joint ventures can create additional productive capacity through the formation of a new operating unit, engage in research and development for a new product or technology, lower costs through economies of scale and scope, achieve synergies from the pooling of complementary resources, create entry into new markets, and share or diversify risk.[5]

---

3. *See* Joseph F. Brodley, *Joint Ventures and Antitrust Policy*, 95 HARV. L. REV. 1521, 1574 (1982) (defining joint venture as "a separate enterprise characterized by an integration of operations between and subject to control by its parent firms which results in the creation of significant new enterprise capability in terms of new productive capacity, new technology, a new product, or entry into a new market"); *see also* Robert Pitofsky, *Joint Ventures Under the Antitrust Laws: Some Reflections on the Significance of Penn-Olin*, 82 HARV. L. REV. 1007 (1969) (explaining that "joint venture" refers to almost any collaboration by competitors that is not a merger).
4. COMPETITOR COLLABORATIONS GUIDELINES, *supra* note 1, § 1.1.
5. *See, e.g.*, Northwest Wholesale Stationers v. Pacific Stationery & Printing Co., 472 U.S. 284, 295 (1985) (economies of scale from joint purchasing joint venture); Broadcast Music, Inc. v. CBS, 441 U.S. 1, 20-23 (1979) (economies of scale and reduced transaction costs from blanket licenses); SCFC ILC, Inc. v. Visa USA, Inc., 36 F.3d 958, 963 (10th Cir. 1994) (recognizing that "efficiencies created by joint ventures are similar to those resulting from mergers—risk-sharing, economies of scale, access to complementary resources and the elimination of duplication and waste"); Brunswick Corp., 94 F.T.C. 1174, 1265 (1979) ("The combined capital, assets, or know-how of two companies may facilitate entry into new markets and thereby enhance competition, or may create efficiencies or new productive capacity unachievable by either alone"), *aff'd in part and modified in part sub nom.*, Yamaha Motor Co. v. FTC, 657 F.2d 971 (8th Cir. 1981); *cf. In re* Warner Communs. Inc., 66 Fed. Reg. 41,238, 41,240 (FTC Aug. 7, 2001) (aid to public comment) ("joint ventures can enable

But joint ventures also may provide a venue for collusion among the venture parents, facilitate anticompetitive coordination among the venture parents and third parties, create or enhance market power in the hands of the venture or its parents, foreclose competitors from access to a competitively advantageous resource, or eliminate potential competition.[6]

The mission of antitrust law is to distinguish those joint ventures that on balance are procompetitive or competitively neutral from those that are anticompetitive and reduce consumer welfare. To do this, the law must assess the overall competitive effect of a joint venture in its formation and in its operation by carefully considering all of the potential positive and negative effects of the joint venture on price, aggregate output, product quality, and the rate and direction of technological innovation.

A. Antitrust Statutes Applicable to Joint Ventures

Because joint ventures involve an agreement of separate and independent parties, Section 1 of the Sherman Act[7] applies to the venture's formation. After formation, the venture's operation and any collateral agreements among the venture's parents also are subject to Section 1 unless the venture participants embody such unity of interest that the *Copperweld* doctrine prevents the parties from being deemed separate persons for Section 1 purposes.[8] In addition, where the joint

---

companies to expand into foreign markets, fund expensive innovation and research efforts, and lower costs to the benefit of industry and consumers alike") (Statement of Commissioner Thompson).

6. *See* COMPETITOR COLLABORATIONS GUIDELINES, *supra* note 1, § 2.2 (listing potential anticompetitive effects of joint ventures); *see also* Citizen Publ'g Co. v. United States, 394 U.S. 131 (1969) (joint venture gave participants monopoly power in relevant market); United States v. Penn-Olin Chem. Co., 378 U.S. 158 (1964) (joint venture unlawful because of lessening of potential competition); Timken Roller Bearing Co. v. United States, 341 U.S. 593 (1951) (agreement styled as joint venture found to be a per se unlawful naked agreement to divide territories and fix prices); Associated Press v. United States, 326 U.S. 1 (1945) (joint venture news gathering association unlawfully denied access to competing newspapers).

7. 15 U.S.C. § 1.

8. *See* Copperweld Corp. v. Independence Tube Corp., 467 U.S. 752 (1984). Similarly, courts will treat a joint venture as a single actor if the purpose of its organization is to pursue a common interest, even if the participants remain independent companies. *See* Siegel Transfer, Inc. v. Carrier

venture competes with its parents, the prohibition found in Section 8 of the Clayton Act[9] on interlocking officers or directors may be implicated. After considerable controversy, in 1964 the U.S. Supreme Court in *United States v. Penn-Olin Chemical Co.*[10] held that Section 7 of the Clayton Act[11] applies to joint ventures, including situations where two corporations form a joint venture corporation to engage in an entirely new enterprise. The formation of a joint venture also may be subject to the premerger notification requirements of the Hart-Scott-Rodino Antitrust Improvements Act of 1976 (HSR Act).[12] Section 2 of the Sherman Act[13] applies if the venture's formation, operation or any ancillary agreement is used to monopolize, attempt to monopolize or engage in a conspiracy to monopolize a relevant market.[14] Finally, Section 5 of the Federal Trade Commission Act[15] applies to both the formation and the operation of a joint venture as well as any side agreements among the joint venture participants.[16]

To address specifically research and development joint ventures, Congress enacted the National Cooperative Research Act of 1984,[17] which provides certain protections and procedural advantages to notified research and development joint ventures. Congress subsequently expanded the National Cooperative Research Act to include certain production joint ventures and retitled the amended act the National Cooperative Research and Production Act of 1993 (NCRPA).[18]

B. Antitrust Agency Guidelines Applicable to Joint Ventures

The enforcement standards and policies of the FTC and the DOJ with respect to joint ventures are collected in the *Competitor Collaborations*

Express, Inc., 54 F.3d 1125, 1127 (3d Cir. 1995).

9. 15 U.S.C. § 19.
10. 378 U.S. 158 (1964).
11. 15 U.S.C. § 18.
12. *Id.* § 18a.
13. *Id.* § 2.
14. *See, e.g.*, United States v. Pan Am World Airways, 193 F. Supp. 18, 36 (S.D.N.Y. 1961), *rev'd on other grounds*, 371 U.S. 296 (1963).
15. 15 U.S.C. § 45.
16. *See, e.g.*, Brunswick Corp., 94 F.T.C. 1174 (1979), *aff'd in part and modified in part sub nom.* Yamaha Motor Co. v. FTC, 657 F.2d 971 (8th Cir. 1981).
17. 15 U.S.C. §§ 4301-4305.
18. *Id.* §§ 4301-4306.

Guidelines issued jointly by the two agencies.[19] The 1992 *Merger Guidelines*,[20] the *Intellectual Property Guidelines*,[21] and the *Health Care Statements*[22] also provide guidance on the antitrust analysis of joint ventures in certain circumstances.

The *Competitor Collaborations Guidelines* provide a general outline of the analytical framework for evaluating collaboration among competitors, except to the extent that such collaboration involves such a high degree of integration among the competitors that it should be analyzed as a merger between the parties.[23] The 1992 *Merger Guidelines*

---

19. *See* COMPETITOR COLLABORATIONS GUIDELINES, *supra* note 1.
20. UNITED STATES DEP'T OF JUSTICE & FEDERAL TRADE COMM'N, HORIZONTAL MERGER GUIDELINES (1992) [hereinafter 1992 MERGER GUIDELINES], *reprinted in* 4 Trade Reg. Rep. (CCH) ¶13,104 *and* in Appendix I.
21. UNITED STATES DEP'T OF JUSTICE & FEDERAL TRADE COMM'N, ANTITRUST GUIDELINES FOR THE LICENSING OF INTELLECTUAL PROPERTY (1995) [hereinafter INTELLECTUAL PROPERTY GUIDELINES], *reprinted in* 4 Trade Reg. Rep. (CCH) ¶ 13,132 and in Appendix K. The *Intellectual Property Guidelines* note that a licensing arrangement between horizontal competitors is not necessarily anticompetitive: "As in the case of joint ventures among horizontal competitors, licensing arrangements among such competitors may promote rather than hinder competition if they result in integrative efficiencies." *Id.* § 5.1. The *Intellectual Property Guidelines* also contain antitrust "safety zones" applicable to licensing arrangements, including horizontal arrangements between competitors. *Id.* § 4.3.
22. UNITED STATES DEP'T OF JUSTICE & FEDERAL TRADE COMM'N, STATEMENTS OF ANTITRUST ENFORCEMENT POLICY IN HEALTH CARE (1996) [hereinafter HEALTH CARE STATEMENTS], *reprinted in* 4 Trade Reg. Rep. (CCH) ¶ 13,153 and in Appendix L. The *Health Care Statements* specifically apply to hospital joint ventures involving high technology or other expensive health care equipment, *see id.* at Statement 2; hospital joint ventures involving specialized clinical or other expensive health care services, *see id.* at Statement 3; physician network joint ventures, *see id.* at Statement 8; and multiprovider networks, *see id.* at Statement 9. But the approach outlined in the *Health Care Statements* may be applied by the DOJ and the FTC in a broader context. In the *Health Care Statements* themselves, "[t]he Agencies emphasize that it is not their intent to treat [health care joint ventures] either more strictly or more leniently than joint ventures in other industries." *Id.* Introduction.
23. The *Competitor Collaborations Guidelines* provide that a collaborative venture will be analyzed as a merger under the 1992 *Merger Guidelines* if: "(a) the participants are competitors in a relevant market; (b) the formation of the collaboration involves an efficiency-enhancing

outline the enforcement policy of the federal enforcement agencies concerning horizontal combinations subject to Section 7 of the Clayton Act, Section 1 of the Sherman Act, and Section 5 of the FTC Act. The *Intellectual Property Guidelines* articulate the agencies' enforcement policy concerning the licensing of intellectual property protected by patent, copyright or trade secret law, and know-how, and also set forth the agencies' approach to research and development joint ventures. The *Health Care Statements* provide the health care industry with guidance on how the agencies will analyze joint activity by health care providers.

As described in the *Competitor Collaborations Guidelines*, the application of the antitrust laws to putative joint ventures involves two separate inquiries. First, the agencies consider whether the collaborative activity is of the type that is so likely to be harmful to competition and to have no significant benefits that it does not warrant the time and expense required for rule of reason analysis. Such agreements will be condemned per se.[24] If, however, participants in an efficiency-enhancing integration of economic activity enter into an agreement that is reasonably related to the integration and reasonably necessary to achieve its procompetitive benefits, then the agencies will analyze the agreement under the rule of reason, even if it is of a type that might otherwise be considered per se illegal.[25] The *Competitor Collaborations Guidelines* caution that "[t]he mere coordination of decisions on price, output, customers, territories, and the like is not integration, and cost savings without integration are not a basis for avoiding per se condemnation."[26]

---

integration of economic activity in the relevant market; (c) the integration eliminates all competition between the participants in the relevant market; and (d) the collaboration does not terminate within a sufficiently limited period by its own specific and express terms." *See* COMPETITOR COLLABORATIONS GUIDELINES, *supra* note 1, § 1.3.

24. *See* COMPETITOR COLLABORATIONS GUIDELINES, *supra* note 1, § 3.2.

25. *Id.* Similarly, the *Health Care Statements* indicate that the agencies will generally apply the rule of reason to joint ventures where there is sufficient integration "to produce significant efficiencies, [and] any agreements on price [are] reasonably necessary to accomplish the venture's procompetitive benefits." HEALTH CARE STATEMENTS, *supra* note 22, Introduction.

26. COMPETITOR COLLABORATIONS GUIDELINES, *supra* note 1, § 3.2. A number of recent consent orders obtained by the FTC dealing with physician associations formed to standardize prices without significant integration specify that the associations are permitted to form qualified risk-sharing joint agreements or qualified clinically-integrated joint arrangements. *See, e.g.,* Obstetrics and Gynecology Med. Corp. of Napa

Second, assuming that the agreement is not of the type condemned as per se illegal, the agencies consider whether the agreement will likely harm competition by increasing the ability or incentive of participants to raise prices above or reduce output, quality, service, or innovation below what likely would prevail in the absence of the agreement. The rule of reason analysis involves a flexible inquiry into the nature of the agreement, including its business purpose, whether the participants have market power, and whether an agreement in operation actually has caused harm to competition. If the nature of the agreement and the absence of market power together demonstrate the absence of anticompetitive harm, the agencies will investigate no further and will not challenge the agreement. Alternatively, where the likelihood of anticompetitive harm is evident from the nature of the agreement, or anticompetitive harm has resulted from an agreement already in operation, then, absent overriding benefits that could offset the anticompetitive harm, the agencies will challenge the agreement without a detailed market analysis—i.e., they will apply a "quick look" analysis.[27]

If the initial examination of the nature of the agreement indicates possible competitive concerns but the agreement is not one that would be challenged without a detailed market analysis, the agencies will analyze the agreement in greater depth. They will typically define a relevant market—including, where appropriate, product markets, research and development markets, and "innovation" markets—and calculate market shares and concentration.[28] They will then examine factors relevant to the competitive effects of the collaboration, including the ability and

---

Valley, Docket No. C-4048 (May 14, 2002) (consent order); Professionals in Women's Care, Docket No. C-4063 (October 8, 2002) (consent order).

27. COMPETITOR COLLABORATIONS GUIDELINES, *supra* note 1, § 3.3. *See* California Dental Ass'n v. FTC, 526 U.S. 756, 770 (1999) (court of appeal erred in applying a quick look analysis when the dental association's advertising restrictions did not have obvious anticompetitive effects); FTC v. Indiana Fed'n of Dentists, 476 U.S. 447, 460-61 (1986) ("Since the purpose of the inquiries into market definition and market power is to determine whether an arrangement has the potential for genuine adverse effects on competition, 'proof of actual detrimental effects, such as a reduction of output,' can obviate the need for an inquiry into market power, which is but a 'surrogate for detrimental effects'" (quoting 7 Phillip E. Areeda, ANTITRUST LAW ¶ 1511 at 424 (1986))).

28. COMPETITOR COLLABORATIONS GUIDELINES, *supra* note 1, §§ 3.32, 3.33.

incentives for the participants to continue to compete independently[29] and the likelihood, timeliness, and sufficiency of entry by other firms into the relevant market.[30]

In addition to assessing the competitive effects of a competitor collaboration on relevant product and geographic markets, the agencies may also directly evaluate the competitive effects outside of the relevant market in which the joint venture operates.[31] In other words, the agencies may consider the "spill over" effects of the proposed joint venture on any other market in which the joint venture integration does not occur and in which the joint venture members are actual or potential competitors.[32] For example, if two hospitals form a joint venture for the purpose of operating a magnetic resonance imaging clinic, it may be improper to exchange information related to other product markets where the venture participants are competitors, like physician services.[33] The primary concern is that collaboration in one market may "spill over" into a second market in which there is existing competition between the joint venturers.[34]

If this more detailed rule of reason analysis indicates that no potential for anticompetitive harm will result from the agreement, the agencies will discontinue their investigation. If a potential for anticompetitive harm is revealed, however, the agencies will weigh the harm against procompetitive benefits that would likely flow from the

---

29. *Id.* § 3.34. Factors relevant to the ability and incentive of the participants and the venture to compete include the following: (1) whether the collaboration is exclusive or nonexclusive; (2) whether the participants are required to contribute specialized assets that cannot be readily replaced, thereby eliminating the participants' ability to compete against each other and their collaboration; (3) whether the collaboration requires financial contribution so significant that incentives to compete are reduced or eliminated; (4) whether the joint venture can act independently from its participants or whether the participants control joint venture decision making; (5) the extent to which the collaboration enables participants to share competitively sensitive information; and (6) the duration of the venture.

30. *Id.* § 3.35.

31. *See id.* § 3.32.

32. *See id.*

33. *See* Janet L. McDavid, *Antitrust Issues in Health Care Reform*, 43 DEPAUL L. REV. 1045, 1065 (1994).

34. *See* COMPETITOR COLLABORATIONS GUIDELINES, *supra* note 1, §3.32 n.41; *see also* Ilene K. Gotts, *Health Care Joint Ventures and Antitrust Laws: A Guardedly Optimistic Prognosis*, 10 J. CONTEMP. HEALTH L. & POL'Y 169 (1994).

joint venture. Efficiency claims are "not considered [in this process] if they are vague or speculative or otherwise cannot be verified by reasonable means."[35] Moreover, the relevant agreement is not "reasonably necessary" to achieve these benefits if "the participants could have achieved or could achieve similar efficiencies by practical, significantly less restrictive means."[36]

Finally, like the *Health Care Statements* and the *Intellectual Property Guidelines*, the *Competitor Collaborations Guidelines* set forth antitrust safety zones to provide participants in collaborations "a degree of certainty in those situations in which anticompetitive effects are so unlikely that the Agencies presume the arrangements to be lawful without inquiring further into particular circumstances."[37] In particular, the *Competitor Collaborations Guidelines* establish a safety zone for all bona fide collaborations where the market shares of the collaboration and its participants collectively account for no more than 20 percent of each relevant market.[38] In addition, the *Competitor Collaborations Guidelines* provide a "safety zone" for research and development joint ventures when "three or more independently controlled research efforts in addition to those of the collaboration possess the required specialized assets or characteristics and the incentive to engage in a research and development effort that is a close substitute for the research and development activity of the venture."[39] These safety zones are inapplicable, however, to agreements that are per se illegal, or that could be challenged without a detailed market analysis (i.e., a "quick look"), or to competitor collaborations to which a merger analysis is applied. The *Merger Guidelines* emphasize that competitor collaborations are not

---

35. *See* COMPETITOR COLLABORATIONS GUIDELINES, *supra* note 1, § 3.36(a).
36. *Id.* § 3.36(b).
37. *Id.* § 4.1.
38. *Id.* § 4.2. *See* U.S. Dep't of Justice, Business Review Letter to Olympus Am. Inc. and C.R. Bard Inc. (Sept. 28, 2000) (no intention to challenge a joint selling arrangement involving endoscopy accessory products, because the combined market share was not "significantly above" 20%). The *Health Care Statements* provide a safety zone to nonexclusive physician networks that do not have 30% market share in a given geographic area. HEALTH CARE STATEMENTS, *supra* note 22, Statement 8.A.1; *see* U.S. Dep't of Justice, Business Review Letter to Rio Grande Eye Associates, P.A. (August 29, 2001) (clearing a nonexclusive network of ophthalmologists that would provide reduced-price opthalmologic services to managed care plans and other third-party purchasers provided that the network did not exceed its proposed 31% market share).
39. COMPETITOR COLLABORATIONS GUIDELINES, *supra* note 1, § 4.3.

anticompetitive merely because they fall outside of the safety zones and that many competitor collaborations falling outside of the safety zones are procompetitive or competitively neutral.[40]

C. Per Se or Rule of Reason Treatment

The threshold issue with respect to a joint venture involving actual or potential competitors is whether it involves a sufficient integration of the economic resources of the parties to escape scrutiny for possible per se illegal restraints of trade under Section 1 of the Sherman Act. In *Timken Roller Bearing Co. v. United States*,[41] the U.S. Supreme Court held that simply characterizing an agreement among competitors as a joint venture will not save it from condemnation as an otherwise per se unlawful agreement in restraint of trade where the only purpose and effect of the agreement is to suppress competition.[42] The lower courts and enforcement agencies have likewise found so-called joint venture arrangements per se unlawful where there was no meaningful integration and the arrangement served merely as a device to fix prices or allocate customers.[43] Where, on the other hand, joint ventures involve the

---

40. *Id.* § 4.1.
41. 341 U.S. 593 (1951).
42. *See id.* at 598 ("Nor do we find any support in reason or authority for the proposition that agreements between legally separate persons and companies to suppress competition among themselves and others can be justified by labeling a project a 'joint venture.' Perhaps every agreement and combination to restrain trade could be so labeled"); *see also* Perma Life Mufflers, Inc. v. International Parts Corp., 392 U.S. 134, 141-42 (1968); Silver v. New York Stock Exch., 373 U.S. 341, 347 (1963); Radovich v. NFL, 352 U.S. 445, 449-52 (1957).
43. *See, e.g.*, Freeman v. San Diego Ass'n of Realtors, 322 F.3d 1133, 1144-47 (9th Cir. 2003) (a joint venture comprised of realtor associations providing multi-listing services committed a per se violation of Section 1 by agreeing to fix prices charged for services related to the multiple listing services); Engine Specialties, Inc. v. Bombardier Ltd., 605 F.2d 1, 11 (1st Cir. 1979) ("[t]he talisman of 'joint venture' cannot save an agreement otherwise inherently illegal"); New York v. St. Francis Hosp., 94 F. Supp. 2d 399, 417 (S.D.N.Y. 2000) (holding that joint venture between two hospitals organized for the purpose of joint negotiations with insurers, allocation of services, and implementation of noncompete agreements, and not creating any new product, constituted a per se violation of the Sherman Act); United States v. Columbia Pictures Indus., 507 F. Supp. 412, 430 (S.D.N.Y. 1980) (holding joint venture agreement facially unreasonable because restraints "appear to be the heart of the

integration of the parties' productive assets in a manner that "hold[s] the promise of increasing a firm's efficiency and enabling it to compete more effectively,"[44] the U.S. Supreme Court has held that they should be subject to the rule of reason under Section 1.[45]

In effect, the existence of integrative efficiencies qualifies a joint venture for rule of reason analysis. U.S. Supreme Court precedent identifies two factors, either of which independently can support a finding that the requisite integrative efficiencies exist: (1) the joint venture involves some pooling of the parents' resources and sharing of risks by the parents of the joint activity, and (2) the joint venture leads to the creation of a new product or, expressed slightly differently, is reasonably necessary to the development, manufacture, marketing, or distribution of some product.[46] The *Competitor Collaborations Guidelines* similarly provide that an otherwise per se illegal restraint will

---

joint venture and its reason for being"), *aff'd mem.*, 659 F.2d 1063 (2d Cir. 1981); Brunswick Corp., 94 F.T.C. 1174, 1266 (1979) ("A price-fixing scheme or other cartel-like behavior cannot be insulated from review simply by fixing the 'joint venture' label to a device used to engage in behavior inherently pernicious to competition"), *aff'd in part and modified in part sub nom.*, Yamaha Motor Co. v. FTC, 657 F.2d 971 (8th Cir. 1981); *cf.* United States v. Dynalectric Co., 859 F.2d 1559, 1562 (11th Cir. 1988) (defendants convicted of per se violation of Sherman Act notwithstanding defense of establishing a "silent joint venture"); COMPETITOR COLLABORATIONS GUIDELINES, *supra* note 1, § 3.2 ("The mere coordination of decisions on price, output, customers, territories, and the like is not integration, and cost savings without integration are not a basis for avoiding per se condemnation").

44. Copperweld Corp. v. Independence Tube Corp., 467 U.S. 752, 768 (1984).

45. *See* Northwest Wholesale Stationers, Inc. v. Pacific Stationery & Printing Co., 472 U.S. 284 (1985) (applying rule of reason to purchasing cooperative because of potential for economies of scale); NCAA v. Board of Regents, 468 U.S. 85, 103 (1984) (applying rule of reason to sports league, noting that "*Broadcast Music* squarely holds that a joint selling arrangement may be so efficient that it will increase sellers' aggregate output and thus be procompetitive"); Broadcast Music, Inc. v. CBS, 441 U.S. 1, 23 (1979) ("Joint ventures and other cooperative arrangements are . . . not usually unlawful, at least not as price fixing schemes, where the agreement on price is necessary to market the product at all"). For a description of rule of reason review generally, see ABA SECTION OF ANTITRUST LAW, ANTITRUST LAW DEVELOPMENTS 58-79 (5th ed. 2002).

46. *See* Arizona v. Maricopa County Med. Soc'y, 457 U.S. 332, 355-56 (1982); *Broadcast Music*, 441 U.S. at 21-23.

be evaluated under the rule of reason if it is part of "an efficiency-enhancing integration of economic activity and is reasonably related to the integration and reasonably necessary to achieve [the venture's] procompetitive benefits."[47]

Whether the sharing of risks alone by the venture parents, without any pooling of their resources, is sufficient to support a finding of integrative efficiencies is an open question. Certainly a pooling arrangement whereby horizontal competitors share risks by pooling the revenues they earn and distributing the pooled income according to a set fixed formula would be treated, as it always has been, as a naked cartel arrangement.[48] At the same time, it is equally clear that a financial syndicate underwriting arrangement, whereby competing distributors combine to underwrite the securities of an issuer without any pooling of resources, will be treated under the rule of reason.[49] The difference in treatment in these two examples, however, may lie in the second integrative efficiencies factor: the pooling arrangement in no way aids the delivery of a product or service to consumers, whereas in the absence of underwriting syndicates few if any public securities would ever reach the market.

Three cases illustrate the U.S. Supreme Court's approach to distinguishing per se unlawful cartel activity from legitimate joint ventures subject to review under the rule of reason.

In *Broadcast Music, Inc. v. CBS*,[50] forty thousand authors and composers granted nonexclusive rights to the American Society of Composers, Authors, and Publishers (ASCAP) and Broadcast Music, Inc. (BMI) to allow ASCAP and BMI to offer a blanket license to all their musical compositions. Reversing the Second Circuit's determination that the blanket license constituted a per se illegal price-fixing agreement, the Court remanded for review under the rule of reason. The Court noted that the blanket license was "not a 'naked restraint of trade with no purpose except stifling of competition,' but rather accompanie[d] the integration of sales, monitoring, and enforcement against unauthorized copyright use,"[51] thereby offering substantial efficiencies

---

47. COMPETITOR COLLABORATIONS GUIDELINES, *supra* note 1, § 3.2.
48. *See, e.g.*, Chicago Prof'l Sports Ltd. Partnership v. NBA, 961 F.2d 667, 675 (7th Cir. 1992) ("Revenue pooling and pass-over payments are the usual tools of cartels").
49. *See* United States v. Morgan, 118 F. Supp. 621, 687-89 (S.D.N.Y. 1953).
50. 441 U.S. 1 (1979).
51. *Id.* at 20 (quoting White Motor Co. v. United States, 372 U.S. 253, 263 (1963)).

"potentially beneficial to both sellers and buyers."[52] The Court also stressed that the blanket license was "to some extent, a different product" from what the artists could offer individually[53] and that the artists remained free to license their individual works outside the licensing organizations.[54]

In *NCAA v. Board of Regents*,[55] the National Collegiate Athletic Association ("NCAA"), a membership organization governing intercollegiate athletics, limited the number of college football telecasts by individual member schools. The Court held that per se treatment of the NCAA's restrictions on the marketing of televised college football was inappropriate—despite the obvious restraint on output—because the "case involves an industry in which horizontal restraints on competition

---

52. *Id.* at 21.
53. *Id.* at 22-23 ("[T]o the extent the blanket license is a different product, ASCAP is not really a joint sales agency offering the individual goods of many sellers, but is a separate seller offering its blanket license, of which the individual compositions are raw material. ASCAP, in short, made a market in which individual composers are inherently unable to compete fully effectively") (footnote omitted); *see also* NFL v. North Am. Soccer League, 459 U.S. 1074, 1077 (1982) (Rehnquist, J., dissenting) ("NFL football is a different product from what the NFL teams could offer independently"), *denying cert. to* 670 F.2d 1249 (2d Cir. 1981).
54. *See Broadcast Music,* 441 U.S. at 23-24; *see also* Arizona v. Maricopa County Med. Soc'y, 457 U.S. 332, 355 (1982) (holding that "the blanket license arrangement [in *Broadcast Music*] did not place any restraint on the right of any individual copyright owner to sell his own compositions separately to any buyer at any price"); NCAA v. Board of Regents, 468 U.S. 85, 114 n.54 (1984) (freedom of individual participants to increase output was central to analysis of competitive effect of the venture); Buffalo Broad. Co. v. American Soc'y of Composers, Authors & Publishers, 744 F.2d 917, 926-33 (2d Cir. 1984) (holding that blanket license is not an unreasonable restraint of trade where a realistic alternative opportunity to acquire individual rights is available); National Cable Television Ass'n v. Broadcast Music, Inc., 772 F. Supp. 614, 627-36 (D.D.C. 1991) (same); United States v. American Soc'y of Composers, Authors & Publishers, 586 F. Supp. 727, 729-32 (S.D.N.Y. 1984) (refusing to modify consent decree to eliminate requirement that per-program license be offered as alternative to blanket license); National Bancard Corp. v. VISA USA, Inc., 596 F. Supp. 1231, 1254-55 (S.D. Fla. 1984) ("A practice is not unlawful per se where as in this case, there is no legal, practical or conspiratorial impediment to making alternate arrangements"), *aff'd*, 779 F.2d 592 (11th Cir. 1986).
55. 468 U.S. 85 (1984).

are essential if the product is to be available at all."[56] The Court nonetheless found that the NCAA's television plan violated Section 1 of the Sherman Act under a rule of reason analysis because the plan directly restrained output and did not serve any legitimate procompetitive purpose.[57]

In *Arizona v. Maricopa County Medical Society*,[58] the Court struck down as per se illegal a price-fixing agreement among competing medical doctors creating a maximum fee schedule for services provided under health plans. In reaching this conclusion, the Court noted the absence of any integrative efficiencies:

> The foundations [in this case] are not analogous to partnerships or other joint arrangements in which persons who would otherwise be competitors *pool their capital and share the risks of loss* as well as the opportunities for profit. . . . If a clinic [had] offered complete medical coverage for a flat fee, the cooperating doctors would have the type of partnership arrangement in which a price-fixing agreement among the doctors would be perfectly proper. But *the fee arrangements disclosed by the record in this case are among independent competing entrepreneurs*.[59]

Based on these U.S. Supreme Court decisions, lower courts have held, more generally, that an arrangement qualifies for rule of reason analysis as a joint venture only when it involves some potential for an efficiency-generating integration of the parties' resources.[60] When that is

56. *Id.* at 101 ("[S]ome activities can only be carried out jointly. Perhaps the leading example is league sports. When a league of professional lacrosse teams is formed, it would be pointless to declare their cooperation illegal on the ground that there are no other professional lacrosse teams") (quoting ROBERT H. BORK, THE ANTITRUST PARADOX 278 (1978)).
57. *See NCAA*, 468 U.S. at 120 ("[W]e hold only that the record supports the District Court's conclusion that by curtailing output and blunting the ability of member institutions to respond to consumer preference, the NCAA has restricted rather than enhanced the place of intercollegiate athletics in the Nation's life").
58. 457 U.S. 332 (1982).
59. *Id.* at 356-57 (emphasis added).
60. *See, e.g.*, Augusta News Co. v. Hudson News Co., 269 F.3d 41 (1st Cir. 2001) (analyzing under rule of reason joint venture among distributors to provide one stop service for large buyers that none could as easily provide for itself); SCFC ILC, Inc. v. Visa USA, Inc., 36 F.3d 958, 963-65 (10th Cir. 1994) (rejecting per se treatment of credit card association's decision to exclude applicant due to potential efficiency justifications); Sullivan v. NFL, 34 F.3d 1091, 1102 (1st Cir. 1994) (accepting *Broadcast Music* proposition that certain restraints created by joint ventures may not

not the case, characterizing an agreement as a joint venture will not save it from per se illegality.[61]

---

violate antitrust laws because they render the joint activity more efficient and remanding case for determination by jury); United States Healthcare, Inc. v. Healthsource, Inc., 986 F.2d 589, 594 (1st Cir. 1993) (exclusive dealing arrangement warranted rule of reason treatment because it was not a horizontal agreement "devoid of joint venture efficiencies"); Rothery Storage & Van Co. v. Atlas Van Lines, 792 F.2d 210, 226-30 (D.C. Cir. 1986) (per se rules inapplicable to joint venture's membership policies because of economic integration of participants); National Bancard Corp. v. VISA USA, Inc., 779 F.2d 592, 599 (11th Cir. 1986) ("BMI's underlying teaching therefore appears to be that courts should look to whether the restraint at issue [in the joint venture] potentially could create an efficiency enhancing integration to which the restraint is ancillary"); Northrop Corp. v. McDonnell Douglas Corp., 705 F.2d 1030, 1050-53 (9th Cir. 1983) (cooperative production agreement which restricted Northrop to selling one type of aircraft and McDonnell Douglas to selling another found to be procompetitive); United States v. Realty Multi-List, Inc., 629 F.2d 1351, 1367 (5th Cir. 1980) ("[W]ith group boycotts, we must be cautious to determine whether conduct whose apparent purposes, standing alone, might warrant per se treatment are reasonably connected to an integration of productive activities or other efficiency-creating activity in such a manner as to require an inquiry into the net competitive effect under the rule of reason"); Addamax Corp. v. Open Software Found., Inc., 888 F. Supp. 274, 281 (D. Mass. 1995) ("[I]f . . . the joint venture is based on a lawful attempt to integrate resources, the agreement is measured according to the standard 'rule of reason' analysis." (citation omitted)); *see also* Continental Airlines, Inc. v. United Air Lines, Inc., 126 F. Supp. 2d 962, 976 (E.D. Va. 2001) (employing abbreviated rule of reason to analyze airline association's efforts to restrict the size of carry-on baggage because there was no showing that restriction would achieve procompetitive benefits such as on-time performance, safety or passenger comfort).

61. *See, e.g.*, Freeman v. San Diego Ass'n of Realtors, 322 F.3d 1133, 1152-53 (9th Cir. 2003) (rejecting defendants' argument that fixing prices at supracompetitive levels was necessary to induce smaller, less efficient associations to join the county-wide multiple listing service venture); Premier Elec. Constr. Co. v. National Elec. Contractors Ass'n, 814 F.2d 358, 370-71 (7th Cir. 1987) (holding 1% surcharge on all contracts to benefit union served no purpose but to increase non-union contractor's costs, and stating "there [must] be some productive cooperation as a condition of the application of the Rule of Reason, at least when producers with a high market share agree on price"); New York v. St. Francis Hosp., 94 F. Supp. 2d 399, 417 (S.D.N.Y. 2000) (holding that joint venture between two hospitals organized for the purpose of joint

D. Types of Joint Ventures

Although the principles governing the formation of a joint venture are the familiar Section 7 and Section 1 precepts, the content of the analysis may vary dramatically from one joint venture to another. The structure of the venture, and hence the antitrust analysis of the joint venture's formation, depends on the purpose of the joint activity. Although in every case the purpose of the antitrust analysis is to determine whether the venture is likely to result in a substantial lessening of competition, the content of the analysis can be tailored to the venture's structure and the competitive effects such a structure is likely (or unlikely) to produce. Specialized analytical frameworks have emerged in which to analyze the formation of each of the five most common types of joint ventures: (1) fully integrated joint ventures, (2) research and development joint ventures, (3) production joint ventures, (4) joint marketing, selling and buying arrangements, and (5) network joint ventures.

1. Fully Integrated Joint Ventures

A fully integrated joint venture encompasses all aspects of a line of business (or at least each of the levels at which the pre-joint venture activities were conducted), including manufacturing, distribution, marketing, and sales. As a partial merger of the venture parents, the formation of a fully integrated joint venture is reviewed by antitrust enforcement agencies and the courts under the same standard applicable to mergers or acquisitions under Section 7 of the Clayton Act[62]—that is,

---

negotiations with insurers, allocation of services, and implementation of noncompete agreements, and not creating any new product, constituted a per se violation of the Sherman Act); Bascom Food Prods. Corp. v. Reese Finer Foods, Inc., 715 F. Supp. 616, 629-32 (D.N.J. 1989) (granting preliminary injunction under per se rule where there was sufficient evidence to establish that horizontal agreement to divide territories was in place and where no new product was being offered); COMPACT v. Metropolitan Gov't, 594 F. Supp. 1567, 1575-79 (M.D. Tenn. 1984) (joint venture that divided markets among the participants and interfered with bidding structure for public contractors per se illegal because horizontal restraints lacked any possible procompetitive efficiency).

62. *See, e.g.*, United States v. Ivaco, Inc., 704 F. Supp. 1409, 1414 (W.D. Mich. 1989); FTC v. Harbour Group Invs., L.P., 1990-2 Trade Cas. (CCH) ¶ 69,247 (D.D.C. 1990) (merger analysis used in granting preliminary injunction against a joint venture involving competing

the analysis requires an examination and evaluation of whether the parties are competitors, the relevant markets in which the parties compete, market shares, competitive effects, entry, and other relevant factors.[63] Accordingly, the *Competitor Collaborations Guidelines* provide that, when a bona fide collaboration eliminates all competition between the participants and does not terminate within a sufficiently limited time, the collaboration is evaluated as a horizontal merger under the 1992 *Merger Guidelines*.[64]

United States v. Ivaco, Inc.[65] illustrates how a fully integrated joint venture may be found unlawful where the parties are horizontal competitors and the venture is likely substantially to lessen actual competition. In *Ivaco*, the Division sought to enjoin a proposed joint venture between Jackson Jordan, Inc. and Tamper Corporation, two manufacturers of automatic tampers used in laying railroad tracks.[66] The Division alleged that automatic tampers were the relevant product market and introduced evidence to show that only three firms, Jackson Jordan, Tamper, and Plasser American, produced and marketed automatic tampers in the United States. The government's evidence, which the court accepted, also showed that Ivaco, through Tamper, controlled 45 percent of all sales of tampers in the United States while Jackson Jordan controlled 25.1 percent. The joint venture, therefore, would create a firm controlling 70.1 percent of the automatic tamper market and would result

---

subsidiaries of the parties); *see also* Citizen Publ'g Co. v. United States, 394 U.S. 131, 134-35 (1969); United States v. Penn-Olin Chem. Co., 378 U.S. 158, 169 (1964).

63. In instances where the government challenges a full-function joint venture, it generally will allege that the arrangement violates Section 7. *See, e.g.*, Citizen Publ'g Co. v. United States, 394 U.S. 131 (1969) (challenge to newspaper joint operating agreement under Section 7 of the Clayton Act and Sections 1 and 2 of the Sherman Act).

64. *See* COMPETITOR COLLABORATIONS GUIDELINES, *supra* note 1, § 1.3.

65. 704 F. Supp. 1409 (W.D. Mich. 1989); *cf.* United States v. FCC, 652 F.2d 72, 96-101 (D.C. Cir. 1980) (en banc) (joint venture to construct a communications satellite network does not violate antitrust laws if parents were not actual or potential competitors in the relevant market).

66. Tamper was a wholly owned subsidiary of Canron Industries, 79% of which was owned by Ivaco, Inc. The joint venture would have been equally owned by Jackson Jordan and Canron, and Jackson Jordan and Canron had agreed not to compete with the venture in the maintenance of way industry. The venture would have been managed by an owner's committee consisting of representatives from Jackson Jordan and Canron. *See Ivaco*, 704 F. Supp. at 1411-12.

in two firms controlling 100 percent of the relevant market, with high barriers to entry.[67]

The defendants attempted to rebut the government's prima facie case under Section 7 with a *General Dynamics* defense.[68] The defendants claimed that the market for the tampers that Canron and Jackson Jordan manufactured was shrinking and that customers were demanding a more technologically advanced product that only Plasser produced. According to their argument, absent the creation of the joint venture, neither Jackson Jordan nor Canron would be able or willing to finance the development of a high-technology product and therefore without the joint venture at least one of them would be forced to exit the market.[69]

The court found that the procompetitive justifications advanced by the defendants were insufficient to rebut the presumption of illegality created by the venture's high market shares.[70] The court rejected the defendants' assertion that the market conditions justified "the clear anticompetitive effects of the joint venture."[71] The court found no evidence to indicate that either Jackson Jordan or Canron would have exited the market absent the creation of the joint venture, nor was it persuaded that the joint venture was necessary for the development of a high technology tamper. Although the joint venture might have been the most financially attractive alternative for the two companies, the court found there were several alternative transactions that would allow for the same technological advances without the anticompetitive effects. The court interpreted the parties' failure to consider a more limited transaction for the express purpose of developing a high-technology product as circumstantial evidence of an anticompetitive intent (and presumably a likely anticompetitive effect).[72] Finally, the court found that supportive customer testimony, although significant, was insufficient to offset the evidence of anticompetitive effects.[73]

---

67. *See id.* at 1415, 1420.
68. *See* United States v. General Dynamics Corp., 415 U.S. 486 (1974) (finding that acquisition that significantly increased market concentration nevertheless caused no substantial lessening of competition due to unique industry conditions). For a discussion of *General Dynamics*, see Chapter 5.
69. *See Ivaco*, 704 F. Supp. at 1424.
70. *See id.* at 1428.
71. *Id.* at 1424.
72. *See id.* at 1426 ("The parties appear to have carefully chosen a transaction which will completely eliminate price competition between them . . . .").
73. *See id.* at 1428.

United States v. Penn-Olin Chem. Co.[74] illustrates how a fully integrated joint venture may be found unlawful for eliminating potential competition.[75] The district court had dismissed the government's complaint against Pennsalt Chemical Corporation and Olin Mathieson Chemical Corporation, two major chemical companies that had created a joint venture for the purpose of setting up a chlorate plant in the southeastern United States.[76] The U.S. Supreme Court vacated the district court's ruling and held that the lower court should have considered not only the probability that, in the absence of the joint venture, *both* companies would have independently entered the market and thus have become actual competitors,[77] but also the probability that one of the corporations would have entered the market by building a plant while the other would have remained a "significant potential competitor"[78] which, by "[remaining] at the edge of the market, continually threatening to enter," would restrain other market participants from overcharging those to whom they sell or underpaying those from whom they buy.[79]

Yamaha Motor Co. v. FTC[80] also involved a fully-integrated joint venture agreement held to violate Section 7 of the Clayton Act by eliminating potential competition in a highly concentrated, oligopolistic, market. The Eighth Circuit found that Yamaha Motor Company, Ltd. had "available feasible means for entering the [United States] outboard-motor market" other than entering into a joint venture with Brunswick Corporation. The court established Yamaha's probable entry by ascertaining the firm's ability to enter the market and its subjective intent to enter the market independently.[81] In addition, the court found that Yamaha's independent entry into the United States market likely would

---

74. 378 U.S. 158 (1964).
75. For a discussion of potential competition analysis, see Chapter 9, *infra*.
76. *See* United States v. Penn-Olin Chem. Co., 217 F. Supp. 110, 129 (D. Del. 1963), *vacated*, 378 U.S. 158 (1964).
77. *See Penn-Olin*, 378 U.S. at 172-73.
78. *Id.* at 175-76.
79. *Id.* at 173-74 (citation omitted). On remand, the district court again upheld the joint venture on the grounds that the government had failed to prove that without the joint venture there was a reasonable probability that either of the corporations would have constructed a plant and thereby entered the relevant market independently. *See* United States v. Penn-Olin Chem. Co., 246 F. Supp. 917, 928, 934 (D. Del. 1965), *aff'd per curiam*, 389 U.S. 308 (1967).
80. 657 F.2d 971 (8th Cir. 1981).
81. *See id.* at 978-79.

"'produce deconcentration of . . . [the] market or other significant procompetitive effects.'"[82] Thus, applying reasoning similar to *Penn-Olin*, the court found that the combination of Yamaha's probable independent entry and the procompetitive benefits likely resulting from that entry into a concentrated market comprised a Section 7 violation by possibly substantially lessening competition in the U.S. outboard motor market.[83]

Finally, fully integrated joint ventures between firms having a vertical relationship may be found to violate Section 7 for the same reasons as vertical mergers. Two Division enforcement actions illustrate the use of this theory of anticompetitive harm as applied to joint ventures.[84] In *United States v. MCI Communications Corp.*,[85] the Division challenged the proposed formation of a joint venture between MCI Communications Corporation and British Telecommunications plc (BT) to provide international enhanced telecommunications services.[86] The Division explained in its competitive impact statement[87] that a vertical affiliation between the dominant telecommunications carrier in the United Kingdom and the second largest long distance provider in the United States would be likely substantially to lessen competition in the U.S. market for seamless global telecommunications services, because it would give BT the incentive and ability to favor the joint venture and MCI and to disfavor their competitors with respect to the interconnections necessary to provide such service.[88] The Division also alleged that the joint venture would give MCI access, through BT, to competitively sensitive business information about its rivals that would increase the risk of price collusion. Similarly, in *United States v. Sprint*

---

82. *Id.* at 979 (citing United States v. Marine Bancorp., 418 U.S. 602, 633 (1974)).
83. *Id.* at 977.
84. For a general discussion of the circumstances in which a vertical merger may be found to violate Section 7, see Chapter 10.
85. 1994-2 Trade Cas. (CCH) ¶ 70,730 (D.D.C. 1994) (consent decree).
86. In addition to forming a joint venture with MCI, BT also proposed to acquire 20% of MCI's outstanding voting securities, thus forming what is commonly called a "strategic alliance" between BT and MCI. *See* United States v. Sprint Corp., 1996-1 Trade Cas. (CCH) ¶71,300, at 76,392 (D.D.C. 1996). The Division also challenged BT's acquisition of MCI's voting securities. *See* United States v. MCI Communs., 59 Fed. Reg. 33,009, 33,014-15 (June 27, 1994) (proposed final judgment).
87. *See MCI Communs.*, 59 Fed. Reg. at 33,014-24.
88. *See id.* at 33,015, 33,017-18.

Corp.,[89] the Division challenged the proposed formation of a joint venture between Sprint Corporation and the principal telecommunications carriers in France and Germany, France Telecom and Deutsche Telekom AG, each of which the Division alleged possessed a monopoly in its home market. The Division's theories of competitive harm were largely the same as the theories set forth in the *MCI* case.[90]

Both challenges were resolved with consent decrees that imposed restrictions and obligations on the parties designed to assure competitors of the joint ventures equal access to interconnections with the foreign carriers and to deny MCI and Sprint access to competitively sensitive information about their long distance rivals. First, the decrees imposed transparency requirements that required the joint ventures and the foreign carriers to disclose the terms of their interconnection agreements. Second, the decrees required that the foreign carriers provide the joint ventures' rivals nondiscriminatory access to their systems. Third, the decrees included confidentiality requirements aimed at preventing spillover effects, which prohibited the joint ventures (and MCI and Sprint) from receiving, or seeking to receive, from the foreign carriers specified types of confidential information about their U.S. competitors. Both decrees provided for these restrictions and obligations to remain in effect for five years, with procedures that gave the Division an opportunity to seek further relief at the end of that term.

2. *Research and Development Joint Ventures*

Research and development joint ventures can provide procompetitive benefits while maintaining competition between the joint venture parents. These benefits include sharing the substantial economic risks involved in research and development, increasing economies of scale beyond those which individual firms could realize, pooling important research and development information or complementary skills, and overcoming the free-rider disincentive to invest in research and development by including likely end users of the research and development in undertaking the research efforts and sharing the costs. At the same time, the formation of joint research and development ventures typically pose few of the anticompetitive risks associated with full integrations or mergers. For this reason, the courts and antitrust enforcement authorities have long viewed joint research and

---

89. 1996-1 Trade Cas. (CCH) ¶ 71,300 (D.D.C. 1996) (consent decree).
90. *See id.* at 76,392.

development ventures more favorably than many other types of joint ventures.[91]

For example, in 1998 the First Circuit considered an antitrust challenge to a research and development joint venture in the computer industry, *Addamax Corp. v. Open Software Foundation, Inc.*[92] The Open Software Foundation (OSF), a joint venture of computer manufacturers, was founded to develop, among other things, a version of the popular Unix operating system to compete with a Unix version being developed jointly by AT&T and Sun Microsystems. The plaintiff, Addamax, was a producer of security software for Unix operating systems. OSF awarded its bid for security software to another company. Subsequently, Addamax sued OSF and several of its member computer companies alleging horizontal price fixing, a group boycott, and unlawful joint venture conduct under the Sherman and Clayton Acts.

The trial court held that the joint venture was properly examined under the rule of reason, not the per se rule.[93] After a bench trial, the court found for the defendants primarily on the ground that the defendants' alleged illegal conduct (forcing down the price of security

---

91. *See* COMPETITOR COLLABORATIONS GUIDELINES, *supra* note 1, § 3.31(a) ("Most [R&D collaborations] are procompetitive, and they typically are analyzed under the rule of reason"). FTC Chairman Robert Pitofsky, noted in discussing collaborations in the high-tech sector that "antitrust traditionally has taken a very lenient view of research and development cooperation and standard setting across the economy, and, in almost all cases, production cooperation as well." Robert Pitofsky, Chairman, FTC, Antitrust Analysis in High-Tech Industries, Remarks Before the ABA Section of Antitrust Law Workshop on Antitrust Issues in High-Tech Industries (Feb. 25-26, 1999); *see also* U.S. Dep't of Justice, Business Review Letter to the American Heart Ass'n (Mar. 20, 1998) ("Legitimate research joint ventures are not usually on balance anticompetitive, particularly in the case of joint ventures to perform basic, non-appropriable research"); U.S. Dep't of Justice, Business Review Letter to Computer Aided Manufacturing-International, Inc. (June 25, 1985) ("Joint Research and development ventures generally are procompetitive, and are condemned by the antitrust laws when they have a net negative effect on competition. Generally Research and development joint ventures rarely will raise competitive concerns . . . ."); S. REP. NO. 98-427, at 3, *reprinted in* 1984 U.S.C.C.A.N. 3105, 3107 (the Division has never challenged a pure research and development joint venture without ancillary restraints).

92. 152 F.3d 48 (1st Cir. 1998).

93. Addamax v. Open Software Found., 888 F. Supp. 274, 281-83 (D. Mass. 1995).

software) was not a substantial cause of the plaintiff's failure to succeed in the sale of security software.[94] On appeal, the First Circuit affirmed.[95] The court rejected the plaintiff's argument that the per se rule should have applied to the joint venture, explaining:

> Joint Venture enterprises like [OSF], unless they amount to complete sham [of which there was no evidence], are rarely susceptible to per se treatment. Where the venture is producing a new product—here, the [OSF-1] software package—there is patently a potential for a productive contribution to the economy, and the conduct that is strictly ancillary to this productive effort (*e.g.*, the joint venture's decision as to the price at which it will purchase inputs) is evaluated under the rule of reason.[96]

The court also held that there was sufficient evidence to conclude that the failure of Addamax in the security software business was caused not by the allegedly illegal conduct of the defendants, but by other factors such as Addamax's late entry into the business, the high price of its product, and the strong competitive position of its competitors.[97]

The enforcement agencies' approach to research and development joint ventures is set forth in their joint *Competitor Collaborations Guidelines* and *Intellectual Property Guidelines*.[98] The *Competitor Collaborations Guidelines* note that most research and development joint ventures are procompetitive and are typically analyzed under the rule of reason because of their potential to enable participants to develop more quickly or efficiently new or improved goods, services, or production processes.[99] The *Competitor Collaborations Guidelines* also note, however, that such collaborations may create or increase market power or facilitate its exercise by limiting independent decision making or by combining in the collaboration, or in certain participants, control over competitively significant assets or all or a portion of participants' individual competitive research and development efforts.[100]

---

94. Addamax v. Open Software Found., 964 F. Supp. 549 (D. Mass. 1997).
95. *See Addamax*, 152 F.3d at 48.
96. *Id.* at 52 (citation and footnote omitted).
97. *Id.* at 54-55.
98. For a discussion of the *Intellectual Property Guidelines generally,* see ABA Section of Antitrust Law, The 1995 Federal Antitrust Guidelines for the Licensing of Intellectual Property (1996). *See generally* ABA SECTION OF ANTITRUST LAW, ANTITRUST LAW DEVELOPMENTS 1052-1054 (5th ed. 2002).
99. *See* COMPETITOR COLLABORATIONS GUIDELINES, *supra* note 1, § 3.31(a).
100. *Id.*

As with other joint ventures, the agencies initially consider whether the competitive effect of a research and development collaboration can be determined without a detailed market analysis. Assuming that such an analysis is necessary, the agencies begin by defining the relevant markets in which the venture is likely to affect competition, including what they term "innovation markets."[101] An innovation market consists of the research and development directed to particular new or improved goods or processes, and the close substitutes for that research and development.[102] In the *Competitor Collaborations Guidelines*, the agencies indicate that they will not ordinarily challenge a research venture when there are three or more other independently controlled firms with comparable research capabilities and incentives.[103] If there are fewer than three such firms, the agencies consider whether the venture is likely to give the parties an incentive or ability collectively to retard the pace or scope of research and development efforts.[104] They also consider the potential efficiency justifications for the venture, such as combining complementary research and development assets in a way that makes successful innovation more likely, more rapid, or less costly. The agencies also assess the likelihood that the venture may adversely affect competition in other relevant markets by, for example, facilitating the exchange of competitively sensitive information. Finally, the agencies examine any collateral restraints that might significantly restrict competition among the participants.[105]

In the last two decades, the Division has issued a number of business review letters indicating that it did not intend to challenge research and development joint ventures.[106] The joint ventures analyzed in these

---

101. *Id.* § 3.32(c).
102. *See* INTELLECTUAL PROPERTY GUIDELINES, *supra* note 21, § 3.2.3.
103. *See* COMPETITOR COLLABORATIONS GUIDELINES, *supra* note 1, § 4.3.
104. This safety zone appears to be slightly more lenient than that included in the *Intellectual Property Guidelines*, which provides that the agencies generally will not challenge a bona fide intellectual property licensing restraint affecting competition (1) in a technology market, if there are *four* or more independent technologies that may substitute for the licensed technology; or (2) in an innovation market, if there are *four* or more independently controlled research and development efforts that may substitute for the research and development activities of the parties to the licensing arrangement. *See* INTELLECTUAL PROPERTY GUIDELINES, *supra* note 21, § 3.2.3.
105. *See* COMPETITOR COLLABORATIONS GUIDELINES, *supra* note 1, § 3.31(b).
106. *See, e.g.*, U.S. Dep't of Justice, Business Review Letter to the American Heart Ass'n (Mar. 20, 1998) (no intention to challenge modifications to

letters were similar in that all created various structural safeguards concerning the exchange of competitively sensitive information so as not to facilitate collusion among members.[107] To varying degrees, each joint venture left oversight of the projects in the hands of independent researchers, had a generally open membership, and was committed to dissemination of the accrued knowledge.[108]

A research and development joint venture might also present antitrust concerns if the effect of the venture would be to reduce the pace of innovation in a given market.[109] Important in this analysis would be

---

research and development joint venture composed of pharmaceuticals manufacturers which would permit joint venture to engage in "targeted research" in the cardiovascular field); U.S. Dep't of Justice, Business Review Letter to the Pump Research and Development Committee (July 5, 1985) (no intention to challenge research and development joint venture formed by the four U.S. manufacturers of centrifugal pumps used by electric utilities with the purpose of conducting basic research into the reliability and performance of such pumps); U.S. Dep't of Justice, Business Review Letter to Computer Aided Manufacturing-International, Inc. (June 25, 1985) (no intention to challenge bylaw changes for joint venture formed to conduct research and development relating to computer aided design and manufacturing).

107. U.S. Dep't of Justice, Business Review Letter to the Pump Research and Development Committee (July 5, 1995) (noting that "the projects' structural safeguards concerning exchange of competitively sensitive information, should insure that [the venture] will not serve to facilitate collusion among the parties").

108. U.S. Dep't of Justice, Business Review Letter to the American Heart Ass'n (Mar. 20, 1998) ("[T]he knowledge obtained from the research funded by the [joint venture] will be published and otherwise made public, rather than used privately by the [venture members]").

109. *Id.*; *see also* United States v. Motor Vehicles Mfrs. Ass'n, 1982-83 Trade Cas. (CCH) ¶ 65,088 (C.D. Cal. 1982) (alleging conspiracy to eliminate competitors in the research, development, manufacture, and installation of pollution control devices). Antitrust enforcement officials and commentators have increasingly emphasized the importance of innovation to consumer welfare. *See, e.g.*, Robert Pitofsky, Chairman, FTC, Antitrust and Intellectual Property: Unresolved Issues at the Heart of the New Economy, Remarks Before the Antitrust, Technology and Intellectual Property Conference (March 2, 2001) ("With respect to antitrust's overall reaction to consumer welfare consequences of innovation, antitrust historically has often if not always been sensitive to the value of innovation. Research and development joint ventures are a classic example of innovative arrangements, but since the passage of the Sherman Act in 1890, there has been only one federal government

any agreement among the participants that could delay any member's use of the results of the collaboration. Joint venture participants also should analyze carefully any agreements that go beyond the scope of the research to be conducted in the venture.

To help assure that fear of antitrust liability does not unduly discourage firms from forming research and development joint ventures, Congress enacted the National Cooperative Research Act of 1984 (NCRA),[110] which was amended to include production joint ventures and renamed the National Cooperative Research and Production Act of 1993 (NCRPA).[111] The NCRPA provides that a covered joint venture will not be illegal per se but will "be judged on the basis of its reasonableness, taking into account all relevant factors affecting competition."[112] The NCRPA also provides that, by filing a prescribed notification of the venture with the DOJ and the FTC in accordance with the act's terms, joint ventures and their parents will be subject in federal and state antitrust actions only to actual damages plus costs and attorneys' fees with respect to activities within the scope of the act and identified in the notification.[113] Finally, the NCRPA includes a fee-shifting provision so

---

challenge to a research joint venture. It would be difficult to imagine a more lenient policy"), *at* www.ftc.gov/speeches/pitofsky/ipf301.htm; Richard J. Gilbert & Steven C. Sunshine, *Incorporating Dynamic Efficiency Concerns in Merger Analysis: The Use of Innovation Markets*, 63 ANTITRUST L.J. 569 (1995) ("Economic progress depends upon a steady stream of innovation"); Thomas M. Jorde & David J. Teece, *Rule of Reason Analysis of Horizontal Arrangements: Agreements Designed to Advance Innovation and Commercialized Technology*, 61 ANTITRUST L.J. 579 (1993) ("The development, commercialization, and diffusion of product and process technologies have long been the most fundamental competitive forces in advanced industrialized economies, generating economic growth, [and] enhancing consumer welfare"); Joseph F. Brodley, *The Economic Goals of Antitrust, Efficiency, Consumer Welfare, and Technological Progress*, 62 N.Y.U. L. REV. 1020, 1026 (1987) ("[T]echnological progress is the single most important factor in the growth of real output in the United States and the rest of the industrialized world").

110. 15 U.S.C. §§ 4301-05.

111. *Id.* §§ 4301-06.

112. *Id.* § 4302.

113. No protection from treble damages is available if the conduct in question is a violation of an antitrust decree or order entered or issued after October 11, 1984. 15 U.S.C. § 4303(e). *See generally*, Charles D. Weller, *New Antitrust Relief for Health Care Joint Ventures: The National Cooperative Research and Production Act of 1993*, 9 No. 5

that prevailing defendants may recover costs and attorneys' fees if an action is found to be "frivolous, unreasonable, without foundation, or in bad faith."[114] Filing notification under the act is not necessary, however, to assure rule of reason treatment for a research or production joint venture.[115]

The key to the NCRPA lies in its definition of a joint venture subject to the act's coverage. The NCRPA defines a joint venture to be:

> any group of activities, including attempting to make, making, or performing a contract, by two or more persons for the purpose of—
>
> (A) theoretical analysis, experimentation, or systematic study of phenomena or observable facts,
>
> (B) the development or testing of basic engineering techniques,
>
> (C) the extension of investigative findings or theory of a scientific or technical nature into practical application for experimental and demonstration purposes, including the experimental production and testing of models, prototypes, equipment, materials, and processes,
>
> (D) the production of a product, process, or service,
>
> (E) the testing in connection with the production of a product, process, or service by such venture,
>
> (F) the collection, exchange, and analysis of research or production information, or
>
> (G) any combination of the purposes specified in subparagraphs (A), (B), (C), (D), (E), and (F).[116]

Covered joint ventures may include the establishment and operation of facilities for the conducting of the venture, the conducting of the venture on a protected and proprietary basis, the prosecuting of applications for patents, and the granting of licenses for the results of the

---

HEALTH LAW. 1 (1997); John A. Maher, *National Cooperative Production Amendments of 1993: Limited Cartelism Invited!*, 12 DICK. J. INT'L L. 195 (1994); Drake D. McKenney, *New Antitrust Treatment of Production Joint Ventures*, 66 N.Y. ST. B.J. 46 (Oct. 1994).

114. 15 U.S.C. § 4304(a)(2).

115. *See id.* § 4302.

116. *Id.* § 4301(a)(6).

venture.[117] With the amendment of the act in 1993 to include production, the act became even more seamless in encompassing activity helpful to developing new technologies and products and bringing them to market.

The NCRPA excludes from its coverage joint ventures that engage in any of the following activities:

> (1) exchanging information among competitors relating to costs, sales, profitability, prices, marketing, or distribution of any product, process, or service if such information is not reasonably required to carry out the purpose of such venture,
>
> (2) entering into any agreement or engaging in any other conduct restricting, requiring, or otherwise involving the marketing, distribution, or provision by any person who is a party to such venture of any product, process, or service, other than—
>
> (A) the distribution among the parties to such venture, in accordance with such venture, of a product, process, or service produced by such venture,
>
> (B) the marketing of proprietary information, such as patents and trade secrets, developed through such venture formed under a written agreement entered into before June 10, 1993, or
>
> (C) the licensing, conveying, or transferring of intellectual property, such as patents and trade secrets, developed through such venture formed under a written agreement entered into on or after June 10, 1993,
>
> (3) entering into any agreement or engaging in any other conduct—
>
> (A) to restrict or require the sale, licensing, or sharing of inventions, developments, products, processes, or services not developed through, or produced by, such venture, or
>
> (B) to restrict or require participation by any person who is a party to such venture in other research and development activities, that is not reasonably required to prevent misappropriation of proprietary information contributed by any person who is a party to such venture or of the results of such venture,
>
> (4) entering into any agreement or engaging in any other conduct allocating a market with a competitor,

117. *See id.*

(5) exchanging information among competitors relating to production (other than production by such venture) of a product, process, or service if such information is not reasonably required to carry out the purpose of such venture,

(6) entering into any agreement or engaging in any other conduct restricting, requiring, or otherwise involving the production (other than the production by such venture) of a product, process, or service,

(7) using existing facilities for the production of a product, process, or service by such venture unless such use involves the production of a new product or technology, and

(8) except as provided in paragraphs (2), (3), and (6), entering into any agreement or engaging in any other conduct to restrict or require participation by any person who is a party to such venture, in any unilateral or joint activity that is not reasonably required to carry out the purpose of such venture.[118]

The protections afforded production joint ventures under the NCRPA[119] apply only to ventures the principal facilities of which are located within the United States and both parents of which are U.S. persons or "foreign person[s] from a country whose law accords antitrust treatment no less favorable to U.S. persons than to such country's domestic persons with respect to participation in joint ventures for production."[120]

3. *Production Joint Ventures*

Production joint ventures involve the integration or creation of production facilities, usually but not always for the purpose of manufacturing a new product. Once manufactured, the product is distributed to the venture's parents, who then typically compete with each other in the marketing and sale of the product. Production joint ventures allow for an increase in capacity while maintaining competition between or among the independent parent entities. As a result, courts and federal enforcement agencies have looked favorably at true production joint ventures and generally have upheld them as lawful.[121]

---

118. *Id.* § 4301(b).
119. *Id.* §§ 4301-05.
120. *Id.* § 4306.
121. *See,* COMPETITOR COLLABORATIONS GUIDELINES, *supra* note 1, § 3.31(a), n.37 ("The NCRPA accords rules of reason treatment to certain production collaborations. However, the statute permits per se

As noted in the *Competitor Collaborations Guidelines*, however, production joint ventures may involve agreements on the level of output and the use of assets, or the price at which the joint product will be marketed or on other competitively significant variables. Such agreements may create or enhance market power or facilitate its exercise, thus damaging competition.[122] Such agreements may also reduce individual participants' control over assets necessary to compete and thereby reduce their ability to compete independently, combine financial interests in ways that undermine incentives to compete, or both.[123]

A striking example of a production joint venture was the 1984 Toyota-GM joint venture,[124] pursuant to which the first and fourth largest automobile manufacturers in the United States and Canada agreed to produce jointly a small car in a factory in California. The venture was narrowly tailored to achieve its distinct purpose: it was confined to car assembly and sheet metal stamping, limited the number of cars supplied to GM, and had a limited duration. After an investigation by the FTC, the parties agreed to a consent order mandating the limited structure of the joint venture that had been proposed by the parties.[125] The FTC based its eventual approval in part on its finding that the joint venture would create substantial efficiencies: it would increase the number of

---

challenges, in appropriate circumstances, to a variety of activities, including agreements to jointly market the goods or services produced or to limit the participants' independent sale of goods or services produced outside the collaborations"); *see also* United States v. Alcan Aluminum Ltd., 605 F. Supp. 619, 621-22 (W.D. Ky. 1985) (DOJ challenged sale of production facility but approved production joint venture owned 60% by seller and 40% by buyer in light of facts that procompetitive effects outweighed anticompetitive effects, no consumer voiced any objections to the proposed decree, and only objections came from companies that had a higher share of the market than the parties to the decree); *In re* General Motors Corp., 103 F.T.C. 374, 386 (1984) (statement of Chairman James C. Miller III) (production joint venture between two of the largest automobile manufacturers in the world upheld because it was a limited enterprise rather than a merger of two parents). *But see* FTC v. Harbour Group Invs., L.P., 1990-2 Trade Cas. (CCH) ¶69,247 (D.D.C. 1990) (successful challenge to joint venture which involved the complete integration of the parties' production assets).

122. *See* COMPETITOR COLLABORATIONS GUIDELINES, *supra* note 1, § 3.31(a).

123. *Id.*

124. *In re* General Motors Corp., 103 F.T.C. 374 (1984) (consent decree).

125. The consent decree also added a limitation on information exchange, added record keeping requirements, and provided for FTC compliance inspection. *See id.* at 384-85.

small cars available to U.S. consumers, the cars would cost less to produce than if GM had to rely on some other production source, and the joint venture would give GM management the opportunity to learn more efficient Japanese manufacturing and management methods.[126]

Significant competitors wishing to capture efficiencies made possible by the creation of a production joint venture may decrease their antitrust risk by the use of a joint venture structure referred to by the Division as a competitive rules joint venture (CRJV). The CRJV is designed to mimic two independent firms with access to a single plant. The joint venture parties become the owners of the CRJV, have common production, and both receive the benefits of economies of scale, yet remain two separate competitors in sales and marketing, making their own output and pricing decisions. Because of the cost and capacity utilization structure imposed by the CRJV, its owners have the incentive to increase production efficiency and utilize production capacity.

The basic features of a CRJV are reflected in the terms of the Alcan-ARCO consent decree.[127] In 1984, Atlantic Richfield Company (ARCO) was completing a new state-of-the-art aluminum rolling mill devoted to the production of aluminum can body stock. ARCO had not previously been engaged in the production of aluminum can body stock. Prior to the mill coming on line, ARCO agreed to sell the mill to Alcan Aluminum Limited (Alcan), the largest producer of aluminum in the world. The Division brought an action under Section 7 of the Clayton Act to block the transaction.

Although the acquisition was perceived as having severe competition problems, in particular the elimination of ARCO as a soon-to-be competitor in a highly concentrated market, it was also viewed as presenting significant efficiencies. In particular, the participation of

---

126. *See* Thomas B. Leary, Commissioner, FTC, Efficiencies and Antitrust: A Story of Ongoing Evolution, before the ABA Section of Antitrust Law 2002 Fall Forum (Nov. 8, 2002), at www.ftc.gov/speeches/leary/efficienciesandantitrust.htm; ("Since GM-Toyota, the antitrust agencies have not only issued increasingly pro-efficiency merger guidelines but they also have expressed support for expanded recognition of efficiencies"), Timothy J. Muris, Chairman of the FTC, cited *General Motors* as an example of a case in which "the managerial expertise of one company had substantial positive impact on another firm." Timothy J. Muris, *The Government and Merger Efficiencies: Still Hostile After All These Years*, 7 GEO. MASON L. REV. 729, 734 (1999).

127. United States v. Alcan Aluminum Ltd., 605 F. Supp. 619 (W.D. Ky. 1985).

Alcan would bring expertise and technology to the operation of the mill, thus allowing the mill to come on line more quickly and operate more efficiently.

The parties and the Division executed a consent decree which restructured the acquisition into a 60/40 joint venture. The plant would be operated by an independent management company owned in the same percentages as the mill. The production capacity of the mill was also split 60/40, and each party was given the right to use the other's unused capacity and to initiate and participate in capacity expansions. Each firm was made responsible for fixed costs based upon its percentage of capacity rights, and fixed costs were to be paid according to that percentage, even if all of the capacity was not actually used. Variable costs would be allocated based on actual production taken by each parent. The firms could not exchange competitively sensitive information or share employees with the management company and, importantly, were solely responsible for their own pricing and output decisions.

A production joint venture may raise concerns that it could be used as a vehicle for sharing competitively sensitive information. For example, in *General Motors Corp.*, the FTC identified the creation of a structure enabling information exchange as one of the two primary anticompetitive effects that could result from the joint production venture.[128] The consent decree, therefore, prohibited the transfer of any information among GM, Toyota, and the joint venture that was not necessary to operate the joint venture. The Commission-imposed limitations on the exchange of nonpublic information left "the parents free to compete in the marketing of automobiles generally, and greatly reduced the danger of collusion."[129]

The *Health Care Statements* address production joint ventures among hospitals for purposes of operating high technology or other expensive health care equipment or for providing specialized clinical or other expensive health care services.[130] Recognizing that such collaborative activities create procompetitive efficiencies that benefit consumers, the agencies note that they have never challenged a hospital

---

128. *See General Motors Corp.*, 103 F.T.C. at 376. For a discussion of another possible concern, a decrease in the incentive to compete, see Edmund W. Kitch, *The Antitrust Economics of Joint Ventures*, 54 ANTITRUST L.J. 957, 962 (1987).

129. *General Motors Corp.*, 103 F.T.C. at 376.

130. *See* HEALTH CARE STATEMENTS, *supra* note 22, Statements 2 and 3.

joint venture created for these purposes.[131] The agencies further indicate that, absent extraordinary circumstances, they will not challenge "any joint venture among hospitals to purchase or otherwise share the ownership cost of, operate, and market the related services of, high technology or other expensive health care equipment if the joint venture includes only the number of hospitals whose participation is needed to support the agreement."[132] For specialized care joint ventures and for high-technology joint ventures that fall outside the safety zone, the agencies apply a rule of reason analysis.[133]

4. *Joint Selling Arrangements*

A joint venture may be specifically designed to achieve an integration of the venturers' selling or marketing activities for a particular product or service. As noted in the *Competitor Collaborations Guidelines*, such an arrangement may be procompetitive if it combines complementary assets and permits products or services to more quickly or efficiently reach the marketplace.[134]

Such an arrangement potentially raises significant antitrust issues, however, because its activities go to the core of the competitive process: pricing and marketing to customers. A joint selling or marketing arrangement may create or increase market power or facilitate its exercise by limiting independent decision making; by combining in the collaboration, or in certain participants, control over competitively significant assets or decisions about competitively significant variables that otherwise would be controlled independently; or by combining financial interests in ways that undermine incentives to compete independently.[135] A joint selling or marketing arrangement may also provide an opportunity for improper information exchanges between competitors. For example, the FTC's advisory opinion on the joint marketing venture, Partlinx, LLC, expressed some concern about the requirement that the members would disclose forward-looking marketing and strategic plans, including plans that speak to future prices. The exchange of such information could facilitate coordinated efforts to reduce or eliminate price differences among members as a way of

131. *See id.* at Statements 2 and 3.
132. *Id.* at Statement 2.
133. *See id.* at Statements 2 and 3.
134. *See* COMPETITOR COLLABORATIONS GUIDELINES, *supra* note 1, § 3.31(a).
135. *Id.*

increasing price levels.[136] Thus, in the absence of real integration and substantial efficiencies, the courts have held exclusive joint marketing agreements among competitors to be per se unlawful.[137] For these reasons, any proposed joint selling arrangement must be analyzed with considerable care to determine whether the venture is viable at all.[138]

The courts and enforcement agencies also recognize, however, that joint marketing arrangements that involve a true integration of their members' resources may generate substantial efficiencies and should therefore be evaluated under the rule of reason.[139] This is most obviously

---

136. FTC Advisory Opinion in Partlinx, LLC B2B Joint Venture (Oct. 10, 2003), *at* www.ftc.gov/os/2003/10/031010partlinx.htm.

137. *See, e.g.*, Freeman v. San Diego Ass'n of Realtors, 322 F.3d 1133, 1144-47 (9th Cir. 2003) (finding that a joint venture comprised of realtor associations providing multi-listing services ("MLS") had committed a per se violation of Section 1 by agreeing to fix prices charged to real estate firms); Virginia Excelsior Mills, Inc. v. FTC, 256 F.2d 538 (4th Cir. 1958) (creation of jointly owned, exclusive marketing organization to sell collective output of participating competitors at agreed-upon prices constitutes per se illegal price fixing); New York v. St. Francis Hosp., 94 F. Supp. 2d 399, 417 (S.D.N.Y. 2000) (holding that joint venture between two hospitals organized for the purpose of joint negotiations with insurers, allocation of services, and implementation of noncompete agreements, and not creating any new product, constituted a per se violation of the Sherman Act); COMPACT v. Metropolitan Gov't, 594 F. Supp. 1567 (M.D. Tenn. 1984) (coalition of minority-owned architectural firms whose members agreed to refrain from bidding against each other on construction contracts and to pursue contracts only on terms negotiated exclusively by coalition was illegal per se, despite compelling motive to overcome racial discrimination); United States v. American Smelting & Ref. Co., 182 F. Supp. 834 (S.D.N.Y. 1960) (joint selling arrangement between two largest miners of lead whereby one acted as the exclusive seller of a portion of the production of the other in a designated territory held to constitute illegal price fixing and horizontal market division); *cf.* United States v. American Radio Sys. Corp., 1997-1 Trade Cas. (CCH) ¶ 71,747 (D.D.C. 1996) (proposed consent decree requiring parties to terminate joint sales agreement between two competing radio stations).

138. It should also be noted that selling and marketing joint ventures explicitly are not included within the protections of the NCRPA. 15 U.S.C. § 4301(b).

139. *See, e.g.*, California Dental Ass'n v. FTC, 526 U.S. 756, 757 (1999) (rule of reason analysis applies to dental trade association's restrictions on price and discount advertising when restrictions may promote competition by reducing unverifiable and misleading advertising); NCAA

the case where the integration of the parties' resources enables them to market a product that the individual members could not have sold on their own.[140] Short of this, rule of reason treatment may still be

---

v. Board of Regents, 468 U.S. 85, 113 (1984) (per se treatment inappropriate for college athletic association's limitations on live television broadcasts of college football even though plan restrained price and output; recognizing that "a joint selling agreement may mak[e] possible a new product by reaping otherwise unattainable efficiencies") (quoting Arizona v. Maricopa County Med. Soc'y, 457 U.S. 332, 365 (1982) (Powell, J., dissenting)); Broadcast Music, Inc. v. CBS, 441 U.S. 1, 20-24 (1979) (blanket licenses permitting licensees to perform any and all musical compositions of the licensing agencies' members was not a naked restraint subject to per se condemnation; rather, the blanket license "accompanies the integration of sales, monitoring, and enforcement against unauthorized copyright use" and therefore "should be subjected to a more discriminating examination under the rule of reason"); Appalachian Coals, Inc. v. United States, 288 U.S. 344, 361 (1933) (emphasizing the necessity of "consider[ing] economic conditions peculiar to the coal industry, [and] its practices," and refusing to condemn as illegal a joint marketing arrangement among 137 coal producers); Association of Indep. Television Stations v. College Football Ass'n, 637 F. Supp. 1289, 1296 (W.D. Okla. 1986) (intercollegiate football association acting as joint selling agency with respect to sales of telecasts of its members' football games could not be condemned as per se unlawful because some cooperation in college football is necessary in order for the televised product to be available, and cooperation may "foster[] production and efficiency"); Polygram Holdings, Inc., Docket No. 9298 (July 24, 2003) (FTC Opinion at 35-49) (applying the rule of reason to a "moratorium" on price discounting and advertising reached by companies jointly distributing recordings of the 1998 "Three Tenors" concert); U.S. Dep't of Justice, Business Review Letter to Arkansas Elec. Coop. Corp. (Jan. 10, 2001) (applying the rule of reason where electric companies could enter markets via the joint venture that they could not enter independently); U.S. Dep't of Justice, Business Review Letter to Olympus Am. Inc. and C.R. Bard Inc. (Sept. 28, 2000) (applying rule of reason analysis to joint selling venture because proposed venture would generate procompetitive efficiencies that members of the joint venture could not produce independently); U.S. Dep't of Justice, Business Review Letter to the Heritage Alliance (Sept. 15, 1998) (no intention to challenge physician network joint venture that provided all member physicians with joint marketing, based on rule of reason analysis).

140. *See, e.g.*, *NCAA*, 468 U.S. at 101 (recognizing that horizontal restraints on competition were essential to make the product, college football, available at all); *Broadcast Music*, 441 U.S. at 23 ("Joint ventures and other cooperative arrangements are also not usually unlawful, at least not

warranted if the parties can show that the arrangement, while eliminating competition among the members, provides efficiencies in distribution, advertising, and other marketing-related activities that enable them to compete more effectively and thereby expand their aggregate output.[141]

In applying the rule of reason, the courts consider the market share of the participating sellers and the actual or expected effect on output and price.[142] They also examine the scope and importance of the alleged efficiencies and whether the joint marketing arrangement enables the participating sellers to offer a product they could not offer individually or to compete more effectively.[143] Especially where the participating sellers

---

as price-fixing schemes, where the agreement on price is necessary to market the product at all"); Augusta News Co. v. Hudson News Co., 269 F.3d 41 (1st Cir. 2001) (analyzing joint venture among distributors to provide one stop service for large buyers that none could as easily provide for itself under rule of reason); SCFC ILC, Inc. v. Visa USA, Inc., 36 F.3d 958, 964 (10th Cir. 1994) (citing *NCAA* and noting that "[k]ey to the analysis of the 'competitive significance of the restraint,' is the Court's appreciation that the horizontal restraint may be essential to create the product in the first instance"); U.S. Dep't of Justice, Business Review Letter to Armored Transp. (Mar. 12, 1998) (no intention to challenge joint selling arrangement involving small armored car companies because venture "would enable its small armored transport service provider members to, in effect, provide a new service—to serve customers they currently can not service efficiently").

141. *See, e.g., NCAA,* 468 U.S. at 103 (certain joint selling arrangements "may be so efficient that [they] will increase the sellers' aggregate output and thus be procompetitive"); *Broadcast Music*, 441 U.S. at 18-23 (same); *SCFC ILC*, 36 F.3d at 963 ("In the case of a joint venture, present here in the Visa USA association, competitive incentives between independent firms are intentionally restrained and their functions and operations integrated to achieve efficiencies and increase output."); *Association of Indep. Television Stations*, 637 F. Supp. at 1304 (exclusive licenses in the television industry "hold[] the potential to increase the number of available programs").

142. *See, e.g., NCAA*, 468 U.S. at 105-13 (accepting district court's findings that there is a separate market for telecasts of college football, that NCAA possesses market power in that market, and that NCAA's television plan reduced the volume of television rights sold and had the effect of raising the price the networks pay for television rights); *Association of Indep. Television Stations*, 637 F. Supp. at 1298-1302 (examining whether college football is a separate market and whether defendant had power to raise prices above a competitive level).

143. *See, e.g., Appalachian Coals*, 288 U.S. at 372-75 (in light of economically distressed condition of coal industry, establishment of

represent a substantial share of the market, the courts also take into account whether the arrangement is exclusive or nonexclusive.[144]

The formation of a legitimate joint selling arrangement may have a structural impact on the market in which it operates. For example, in *United States v. Columbia Pictures Industries*,[145] the district court enjoined pending trial a joint venture (Premiere) among competing motion picture companies to establish and operate a pay television network. The joint venture agreement provided that Premiere was to have certain films distributed by the movie company venturers available

---

exclusive selling agent for 137 coal producers held legal because it "better . . . enable[d] the producers in this region, through the larger and more economic facilities of such selling agency, more equally to compete in the general market"); Hudson's Bay Co. Fur Sales v. American Legend Coop., 651 F. Supp. 819, 839 (D.N.J. 1986) (creation of own auction house by trade association of mink producers was designed to effect efficiencies and to respond to competition from world markets); *Association of Indep. Television Stations*, 637 F. Supp. at 1297-98 (summary judgment for plaintiffs denied where association of college football teams was asserted to be a joint selling agency permitting "the packaging and sale of an otherwise impossible national series of games"); U.S. Dep't of Justice, Business Review Letter to Delta Airlines, Inc. and Societe Air France (March 6, 2001) (approving a joint marketing venture where the individual members could not offer independently the combined cargo services network that they could offer operating under the joint venture agreement). *But cf.* Association of Retail Travel Agents v. Air Transp. Ass'n, 1987-1 Trade Cas. (CCH) ¶ 67,449, at 59,885 (D.D.C. 1987) (denying summary judgment to joint venture of air carriers that imposed on travel agents various requirements relating to payment schedules, posting of a bond or letter of credit, and the like; asserted "efficiencies" defense fell far short of *Broadcast Music*, noting that the antitrust laws were designed to "protect competition, not efficiency").

144. *See* COMPETITOR COLLABORATIONS GUIDELINES, *supra* note 1, § 3.34(a); *see also Broadcast Music*, 441 U.S. at 23-24 (blanket licenses at issue were nonexclusive—nearly all radio and television broadcasters held blanket licenses from the licensing agencies; noting in upholding the arrangement that "the blanket license cannot be wholly equated with a simple horizontal arrangement among competitors" because the composers had not agreed to refrain from selling individually and direct negotiation with the composers was available and feasible); *Association of Indep. Television Stations*, 637 F. Supp. at 1302 (members of sports league must be viewed as competitors in judging the league's market power where they are free to sell individual games outside the venture).

145. 507 F. Supp. 412 (S.D.N.Y. 1980), *aff'd mem.*, 659 F.2d 1063 (2d Cir. 1981).

to it exclusively for a nine-month period before these films could be shown on other networks.[146] Under the joint venture agreement, the four motion picture producers would contribute films to the venture and their contributions would be valued according to a complex allocation formula. The allocation formula precluded a movie company from negotiating with Premiere for a higher allocation than it would have received under the formula, even if in its own judgment the film's value was not properly reflected in the allocation.[147] The Division argued that this pricing system constituted price fixing and that the nine-month exclusivity window was a group boycott, both of which were unlawful per se.

The district court analyzed the transaction under the rule of reason, although it found it "probable" that the per se rule applied to at least part of the venture agreement,[148] and held that "the Government would probably be able to demonstrate the unreasonableness of the Premiere agreement at trial."[149] The court found Premiere's pricing system to be anticompetitive and unreasonable given the broader context of the pay television market:

> Since the movie company venturers in recent years have received approximately one-half of the motion picture licensing fees paid by the network programming services, they seem likely to have sufficient economic power in the future to control the market by setting the price and conditions of sale of motion pictures licensed to pay television. The ultimate effect of Premiere's pricing mechanism could thus be not only to raise the prices of films licensed to pay television, but also to eliminate competition in the network program service market through the manipulation of the price of Premiere's product.[150]

The court also held the exclusivity provision to be anticompetitive and therefore unreasonable. It found the nine-month restraint to be "drastic" in light of the fact that the movie company venturers were "responsible for approximately one-third of the movies and one-half of the revenues paid for movies in the . . . industry."[151]

The agencies' *Health Care Statements* take a similar approach in discussing joint marketing of health care services by physicians and other health care providers. The agencies' revised statements on physician and

---

146. *See id.* at 420.
147. *See id.*
148. *See id.* at 430.
149. *Id.* at 431.
150. *Id.*
151. *Id.*

multiprovider network joint ventures explain that where integration through the network is likely to produce significant efficiencies, any agreements on price reasonably necessary to accomplish the venture's procompetitive benefits will be analyzed under the rule of reason.[152]

Certain types of physician networks fall within antitrust safety zones designated by the agencies. For exclusive physician networks, where the network's physician participants are restricted in their ability to, or do not in practice, individually contract or affiliate with other network joint ventures or health plans, the agencies will not challenge, absent extraordinary circumstances, a joint venture whose physician participants share substantial financial risk and constitute 20 percent or less of the physicians in each physician specialty with active hospital staff privileges who practice in the relevant geographic market.[153] The agencies explain that the safety zones are limited to networks involving substantial financial risk sharing because risk sharing "normally is a clear and reliable indicator that a physician network involves sufficient integration by its physician participants to achieve significant efficiencies . . . [and] provide[] incentives for the physicians to cooperate in controlling costs and improving quality."[154] For nonexclusive physician networks, where the physician participants do, or are available to, affiliate with other networks or contract individually with health plans, the safety zone is 30 percent.[155] The DOJ and the FTC indicate that the same general antitrust principles used to analyze health care provider networks are applicable to similar joint marketing ventures in other professions and industries,[156] and the DOJ has taken a similar approach in its business review letters.[157]

---

152. *See* HEALTH CARE STATEMENTS, *supra* note 22, Statements 8 and 9.

153. *See id*. at Statements 8.A.2 and 8.A.3.

154. *Id.* at Statement 8.A.4.

155. *See id.* at Statement 8.A.3; *see also* U.S. Dep't of Justice, Business Review Letter to Rio Grande Eye Associates, P.A. (Aug. 29, 2001) (clearing a nonexclusive network of ophthalmologists that would provide reduced-price opthalmologic services to managed care plans and other third-party purchasers. The venture's 31% market share was deemed permissible because it did not substantially exceed 30%).

156. *See* HEALTH CARE STATEMENTS, *supra* note 22, at Introduction and Statement 8.B.

157. *See, e.g.*, U.S. Dep't of Justice, Business Review Letter to Newspaper Ass'n of Am. (Dec. 10, 1993) (no intention to challenge a joint venture in which newspapers would market advertising space jointly at a single price to national advertisers because joint venture would increase the ability of newspapers to compete with other media and because the

5. Joint Buying Arrangements

Joint buying arrangements have generally posed less significant problems and thus have enjoyed more lenient treatment than joint selling arrangements.[158] Purchasing arrangements among competitors often provide for economies of scale in both the purchase and warehousing of supplies and also ensure access to a stock of goods that might otherwise

---

efficient delivery of advertising through a central sales and billing service could not be offered by any individual newspaper).

158. *See, e.g.*, Northwest Wholesale Stationers, Inc. v. Pacific Stationery & Printing Co., 472 U.S. 284, 295 (1985) ("[W]holesale purchasing cooperatives [are] .. . 'designed to increase economic efficiency and render markets more, rather than less, competitive'") (quoting Broadcast Music, Inc. v. CBS, 441 U.S. 1, 20 (1979))). In *United States v. Topco Associates*, 405 U.S. 596, 601-04 (1972), the government challenged as a horizontal division of markets territorial restrictions imposed on the sale of Topco private label products by a cooperative association of 25 regional supermarket chains, and the U.S. Supreme Court found such restrictions to be per se unlawful. The "basic function" of Topco, which the court described as being a "purchasing agent for its members" of more than 1,000 different food and related nonfood items distributed to members under Topco brand names was, however, upheld. *Id.* at 598; *see also* Webster County Mem'l Hosp., Inc. v. United Mine Workers of Am. Welfare & Retirement Fund of 1950, 536 F.2d 419, 420 (D.C. Cir. 1976) (per curiam) (treating concerted action to negotiate with a hospital on behalf of union welfare fund beneficiaries as equivalent to that of a group buying agent and finding that joint negotiation with supplier, without more, did not amount to an unreasonable restraint of trade); Sewell Plastics, Inc. v. Coca-Cola Co., 720 F. Supp. 1186, 1217-19 (W.D.N.C. 1988), *aff'd mem.*, 912 F.2d 463 (4th Cir. 1990); Langston Corp. v. Standard Register Co., 553 F. Supp. 632, 639 (N.D. Ga. 1982) (group purchasing agreements and selection of one supplier over another not per se illegal); Instant Delivery Corp. v. City Stores Co., 284 F. Supp. 941, 948 (E.D. Pa. 1968) (joint purchasing to reduce costs upheld); Parmelee Transp. Co. v. Keeshin, 186 F. Supp. 533, 538-39 (N.D. Ill. 1960) (same), *aff'd*, 292 F.2d 794 (7th Cir. 1961). *But cf.* Vogel v. American Soc'y of Appraisers, 744 F.2d 598, 601 (7th Cir. 1984) (Posner J.) (dictum that "buyer cartels, the object of which is to force the prices that suppliers charge the members of the cartel below the competitive level, are illegal per se"); U.S. Dep't of Justice, Business Review Letter to Baker Hughes Inteq (May 13, 1996) (no intention to challenge a joint venture in which oil well-drilling suppliers would jointly purchase Chinese produced barite because the three buyers account for less than 35% of world barite production and venture likely to be procompetitive by lowering costs).

be unavailable on short notice. For this reason, such arrangements are commonly found to be legitimate joint ventures and are upheld under the rule of reason.[159]

The leading case in the area of joint purchasing, *Northwest Wholesale Stationers, Inc. v. Pacific Stationery & Printing Co.*,[160] upheld, under the rule of reason, the legality of a purchasing cooperative among competing stationery retailers on the ground that such purchasing cooperatives are "designed to increase economic efficiency and render markets more, rather than less, competitive."[161] The Court also explained that the cooperative was beneficial to the competitive process, inasmuch as it allowed "participating retailers to achieve economies of scale in both the purchase and warehousing of wholesale supplies, and also ensured ready access to a stock of goods that might otherwise be unavailable at short notice."[162]

The decision in *Northwest Wholesale*, while obviously indicating a favorable attitude to many joint purchasing arrangements, does not mean that all such arrangements are per se legal. The court specifically noted that if the joint arrangement possessed "market power" or "exclusive access to an element essential to effective competition," the rule of reason approach might no longer be appropriate.[163] Joint purchasing arrangements have been invalidated in extreme circumstances where the arrangement did pose a structural problem: it included essentially all companies in the market and apparently had no redeeming virtues.[164] In addition, naked agreements among purchasers as to the quantity or price

---

159. *See, e.g.*, White & White, Inc. v. American Hosp. Supply Corp., 723 F.2d 495 (6th Cir. 1983); Webster County Mem'l Hosp. v. United Mine Workers of Am. Welfare & Retirement Fund of 1950, 536 F.2d 419 (D.C. Cir. 1976); *Sewell Plastics, Inc.*, 720 F. Supp. at 1217-19; *Langston Corp.*, 553 F. Supp. at 639; Medical Arts Pharmacy v. Blue Cross & Blue Shield, 518 F. Supp. 1100, 1107-08 (D. Conn. 1981), *aff'd*, 675 F.2d 502 (2d Cir. 1982).
160. 472 U.S. 284 (1985).
161. *Id.* at 295.
162. *Id.* at 286-87.
163. *Id.* at 296.
164. *See, e.g.*, Mandeville Island Farms v. American Crystal Sugar Co., 334 U.S. 219 (1948) (conspiracy among three sugar refiners, collectively controlling 100% of the market, to purchase sugar beets at agreed-upon prices); National Macaroni Mfrs. Ass'n v. FTC, 345 F.2d 421 (7th Cir. 1965) (agreement among largest macaroni producers to limit amount of premium-priced durum wheat purchased and to substitute specified percentage of inferior wheat in finished macaroni).

at which they will purchase needed supplies remain per se unlawful under Section 1[165] and may be prosecuted criminally.[166]

For example, in *United States v. Socony Vacuum Oil Co.*,[167] the U.S. Supreme Court considered an arrangement among a group of large oil companies which involved the joint purchasing of surplus gasoline from independent refiners. While the defendants argued that their purchasing of this gasoline was necessary to avoid "ruinous competition," the court applied the per se rule and found the arrangement to be unlawful.[168]

Consistent with the case law described above, the *Competitor Collaborations Guidelines* explain that many joint buying arrangements do not raise antitrust concerns and may be procompetitive, especially to the extent that they permit participants to centralize ordering, to combine warehousing or distribution facilities, or to achieve other efficiencies. Such arrangements may, however, create or facilitate the exercise of market power among buyers ("monopsony" power). They may also facilitate collusion among buyers by standardizing participants' costs or by enhancing the ability to project or monitor a participant's output level through knowledge of its input purchases.[169] Despite these potential

---

165. *See, e.g., Mandeville Island Farms*, 334 U.S. 219; *American Soc'y of Appraisers*, 744 F.2d at 601 (dictum that "buyer cartels, the object of which is to force the prices that suppliers charge the members of the cartel below the competitive level, are illegal per se"); *cf. National Macaroni Mfrs. Ass'n*, 345 F.2d 421.

166. The Division has prosecuted several "buyers cartels" in which buyers have allocated among themselves the right to bid at public auctions. *See, e.g.*, United States v. Seville Indus. Mach. Corp., 696 F. Supp. 986 (D.N.J. 1988); United States v. Kempler Indus., [1988-1996 Transfer Binder, U.S. Antitrust Cases] ¶ 45,089, at 44,469 (N.D. Ill. July 24, 1989) (felony information); United States v. McCarraher, [1980-1988 Transfer Binder, U.S. Antitrust Cases] Trade Reg. Rep. (CCH) ¶ 45,087, at 53,795 (E.D. Pa. Jan. 7, 1987) (indictment); *see also* HEALTH CARE STATEMENTS, *supra* note 22, Statement 7 ("An agreement among purchasers that simply fixes the price that each purchaser will pay or offer to pay for a product or service is not a legitimate joint purchasing arrangement and is a per se antitrust violation").

167. 310 U.S. 150 (1940).

168. *Id*. at 221.

169. *See* COMPETITOR COLLABORATIONS GUIDELINES, *supra* note 1, § 3.31(a). The *Health Care Statements* state that the agencies will not challenge, absent extraordinary circumstances, any joint purchasing arrangement among health care providers where two conditions are present: (1) the joint purchases account for less than 35% of the total sales of the purchased product or service in the relevant market and (2) the cost of the

anticompetitive effects, in the last decade the U.S. Department of Justice has issued a number of business review letters approving joint purchasing arrangements.[170]

6. *Network Joint Ventures*

Network industries are those in which consumers attach themselves to a physical network.[171] Traditional examples include the computer,

---

jointly purchased products or services accounts for less than 20% of the total revenues from all products or services sold by each competing participant in the joint purchasing arrangement. *See* HEALTH CARE STATEMENTS, *supra* note 22, Statement 7. The safety zone adopted in the *Competitor Collaborations Guidelines* appears more stringent and provides that, as a general matter, bona fide competitor collaborations will not be challenged if the participants (including the venture itself) account for no more than 20% of any relevant market(s). *See* COMPETITOR COLLABORATIONS GUIDELINES, *supra* note 1, § 4.2. It is not clear how the agencies will reconcile these two sets of Guidelines.

170. *See, e.g.*, U.S. Dep't of Justice, Business Review Letter to NSM Purchasing Ass'n (Jan. 13, 1999) (no intention to challenge joint purchasing entity to aggregate casket purchases for association of 865 privately-owned funeral homes); U.S. Dep't of Justice, Business Review Letter to Textile Energy Ass'n (Sept. 4, 1998) (no intention to challenge joint electricity purchasing arrangement among textile manufacturers); U.S. Dep't of Justice, Business Review Letter to California Large Electric Power Purchasing Ass'n (Nov. 20, 1997) (no intention to challenge joint purchasing electricity arrangement among cement and steel manufacturers); U.S. Dep't of Justice, Business Review Letter to Nickel User's Purchasing Ass'n, Inc. (June 2, 1993) (no intention to challenge formation of association to negotiate and purchase primary nickel where membership will be open to all U.S. purchasers); U.S. Dep't of Justice, Business Review Letter to FRA Shipper's Ass'n (June 17, 1988) (no intention to challenge nonprofit corporation formed by trade association of 25 footwear retailers open to any qualified footwear retailer to negotiate transportation services for its members for goods shipped between foreign countries and the United States).

171. *See* A. Douglas Melamed, Principal Deputy Ass't Att'y Gen., Antitrust Div., Network Industries and Antitrust, Address Before the Federalist Society (Apr. 10, 1999), *at* www.usdoj.gov/atr/public/speeches/2428.htm; Carl Shapiro, Deputy Ass't Att'y Gen., Antitrust Div., Antitrust in Network Industries, Address to the American Law Inst. and ABA Conference on Antitrust/Intellectual Property Claims in High Technology Markets (Jan. 25, 1996), *at* www.usdoj.gov/atr/public/speeches/shair.mar.htm The *Health Care Statements* discuss a very different type of network joint

telecommunications, transportation, and electric power industries. More recently, electronic finance has become a network industry as credit card issuers and banks have made increasing use of large regional and national networks to process credit card transactions and to provide consumers twenty-four-hour access to their deposits through automated teller machines (ATMs).[172]

Broadly speaking, a network industry can be defined as any industry in which "consumers attach themselves to one or more networks,"[173] and in which "each individual's demand for a product is positively related to the usage of other individuals."[174] Networks frequently exhibit a type of demand-side scale economy: the larger the network, the more valuable the network is to individual buyers of the network product or service. In other words, large networks are attractive to consumers, and thus the large networks tend to get larger. Where network scale economies exist, companies often form joint ventures to create and operate the networks to provide products or services that are essential to the industry's functions.[175]

---

venture—physician and multi-provider network joint ventures—in which physicians and other health care providers join together to contract as a group with health care insurers to provide health care services to plan subscribers at predetermined prices, subject to controls aimed at containing costs and assuring efficient provision of high-quality health care services. *See* HEALTH CARE STATEMENTS, *supra* note 22, Statements 8 and 9.

172. *See, e.g.*, SCFC ILC, Inc. v. Visa USA, Inc., 36 F.3d 958 (10th Cir. 1994) (credit card network); United States v. VISA USA Inc. and MasterCard Int'l Inc., 163 F. Supp. 2d 322 (S.D.N.Y. 2001) (same); United States v. Electronic Payment Servs., 1994-2 Trade Cas. (CCH) ¶ 70,796 (D. Del. 1994) (ATM network).

173. *See* Shapiro, *supra* note 171.

174. Daniel Rubinfeld, Deputy Ass't Att'y Gen., Antitrust Div., Competition, Innovation, and Antitrust Enforcement in Dynamic Network Industries, Address to Software Publishers Ass'n (Mar. 24, 1998), *at* www.usdoj.gov/atr/public/speeches/1611.htm. Put another way, network industries exhibit what has been termed "positive feedback due to demand-side scale-economies." Shapiro, *supra* note 171; *see also* Melamed, *supra* note 171 (the "defining characteristic" of network industries "is that they involve products that are more valuable to purchasers or consumers to the extent that they are widely used").

175. Examples include the VISA and MasterCard credit card networks, e.g., *SCFC ILC, Inc.*, 36 F.3d at 960; *VISA USA Inc. and MasterCard Int'l Inc.*, 163 F. Supp. 2d at 322; ATM networks, e.g., United States v. Electronic Payment Servs., 1994-2 Trade Cas. (CCH) ¶ 70,796 (D. Del.

The nature of network industries also results in extensive cooperation and coordination among firms that participate in the network.[176] Networks may require cooperation among firms in a vertical relationship or among firms that are horizontal competitors. Such cooperation, particularly among horizontal competitors, may raise antitrust concerns. It is generally recognized, however, that such cooperation may be essential to the proper functioning of the network and may generate valuable efficiencies; on the other hand, it may facilitate the acquisition or maintenance of market power.[177] This possibility of a network gaining or retaining market power brings with it at least two issues that are relevant to antitrust enforcement: first, a network may "increase the incentive for, and thus the likelihood of, anticompetitive conduct" (as a result of the creation of entry barriers that may be difficult for rivals to overcome), and second, firms may deny rivals access to the network, thereby threatening the rivals' competitive viability.[178]

The courts and enforcement agencies recognize that there are substantial efficiencies associated with these network joint ventures and therefore generally apply the rule of reason to them when analyzing them under Section 1.[179] In *SCFC ILC, Inc. v. Sears, Roebuck & Co.*,[180] for example, the Tenth Circuit held that a bylaw adopted by the VISA/MasterCard credit card network which prohibited certain

---

1994); news gathering networks, e.g., Associated Press v. United States, 326 U.S. 1 (1945); and floral delivery networks, e.g., United States v. Florists' Tel. Delivery Ass'n, 1996-1 Trade Cas. (CCH) ¶71,394 (E.D. Mich. 1990).

176. *See* Shapiro, *supra* note 171 ("Cooperation among participants in network industries is the norm, not the exception, and serves a variety of beneficial purposes").

177. Robert Pitofsky, Chairman, FTC, Antitrust Analysis in High-Tech Industries: A 19th Century Discipline Addresses 21st Century Problems, Address Before ABA Section of Antitrust Law, Antitrust Issues in High-Tech Industries Workshop (Feb. 25-26, 1999), *at* www.ftc.gov/speeches/pitofsky/hitch.htm.

178. *See* Melamed, *supra* note 171.

179. *See, e.g.*, *SCFC ILC, Inc.*, 36 F.3d at 962-64; National Bancard Corp. v. VISA USA, Inc., 779 F.2d 592, 601 (11th Cir. 1986); Worthen Bank & Trust Co. v. National BankAmericard Inc., 485 F.2d 119, 124-29 (8th Cir. 1973); United States v. VISA USA Inc. and Mastercard Int'l Inc., 163 F. Supp. 2d 322 (S.D.N.Y. 2001), *aff'd*, 344 F.3d 229 (2d Cir. 2003); United States Dep't of Justice, Business Review Letter to National Telecommuns. Network (June 17, 1986) (no intention to challenge joint venture to build and operate fiber-optic transmission facilities).

180. 36 F.3d 958 (10th Cir. 1994).

competitors from joining the network should be evaluated under the rule of reason.[181] The court then went on to reverse a jury verdict for the plaintiff and uphold the legality of the bylaw under the rule of reason.[182] More recently, the U.S. District Court for the Southern District of New York utilized the rule of reason in analyzing two Section 1 claims brought by the DOJ against the Visa and MasterCard credit card associations.[183] The first claim challenged the associations' "dual governance" structure, which allowed a bank that issued the majority of its cards on one association's network to sit on the board of the other association.[184] The government's second claim challenged bylaws adopted by the two associations that allowed issuers to issue cards of either network but not of American Express or Discover.[185] The court ultimately found against the government on the "dual governance" issue, but concluded that the exclusionary by-laws weakened competition and harmed consumers, and thus violate Section 1.[186]

The enforcement agencies, however, have challenged network ventures under Section 2 where they have a dominant market share and impose restrictions on their members that prevent them from joining competing networks, thereby limiting internetwork competition. In *United States v. Electronic Payment Services*,[187] for example, the DOJ filed a civil complaint against Electronic Payment Services, Inc. (EPS), the owner of the MAC regional ATM network, alleging that EPS's refusal to allow MAC network banks to obtain ATM processing services from providers other than EPS violated Sections 1 and 2 of the Sherman Act.[188] The Division characterized this as a per se unlawful tying arrangement that unnecessarily excluded third-party processor competition from the network and enabled MAC, which had a dominant market share in the region it served, to exact very high profits from small

---

181. *Id.* at 964-65.
182. *Id.* at 968-69.
183. *VISA USA Inc. and Mastercard Int'l Inc.*, 163 F. Supp. 2d at 322.
184. *Id.*
185. *Id.*
186. *Id.*
187. 1994-2 Trade Cas. (CCH) ¶ 70,796 (D. Del. 1994); *see also* United States v. First Data Corp., No. 1:03CV02169 (RMC) (D.D.C. Dec. 15, 2003).
188. *See* United States v. Electronic Payment Servs., 59 Fed. Reg. 24,711, 24,718-19 (May 12, 1994) (complaint); *see also* United States v. FTD Corp., 60 Fed. Reg. 40,859 (Aug. 10, 1995) (challenging "FTD Only" policy designed to induce florists not to join competing floral wire associations).

banks, thrifts, and credit unions.[189] The case was resolved through a consent decree in which EPS agreed to terminate its restrictions on the use of third-party processors by MAC members. Network joint ventures can raise serious issues with respect to access.

The ability to limit membership may be procompetitive in that it encourages nonmembers to set up competing networks and creates "incentives [to develop] innovative networks by letting the initial venturers keep their gains rather than forcing them to share their bounty with free riders."[190] A denial of access may, however, have anticompetitive effects where the network has market power and intrasystem rivalry is, therefore, the principal source of competition.[191]

Anticompetitive conduct may also take the form of "restricted access to network standards."[192] For example, the FTC filed an administrative complaint against Rambus Incorporated alleging that Rambus failed to inform JEDEC, an organization that sets standards for a common type of computer memory, that Rambus possessed patents, or pending applications, for several technologies that were proposed for, and ultimately adopted in, JEDEC standards.[193] According to the FTC's complaint, Rambus' conduct threatened to cause substantial harm to competition and consumers because it placed Rambus in a position to assert patent rights over the relevant standards, and obtain royalties from manufacturers complying with those standards.[194] The FTC Administrative Law Judge subsequently ruled against the agency.[195] Previously, the FTC alleged that Dell Computer misled a standard-setting group by denying that it had any patent rights that might have given it exclusive or preferred ability to exploit a proposed standard. Dell and the FTC entered into a consent decree pursuant to which Dell agreed not to enforce the patent rights at issue.[196] In addition, attempts by

---

189. *See* United States v. Electronic Payment Servs., 59 Fed. Reg. at 24,718-19.

190. FTC Staff Report, *Anticipating the 21st Century: Competition Policy in the New High-Tech, Global Marketplace*, 70 Antitrust & Trade Reg. Rep. (BNA) No. 1765, S-1, S-84 (June 6, 1996) (citation omitted).

191. *See id.*

192. Melamed, *supra* note 171.

193. Rambus Inc., No. 011-0017 (filed June 19, 2002).

194. *Id.*

195. *See In re* Rambus, Inc., Docket No. 9302 (FTC Feb. 23, 2004), *at* www.ftc.gov/os/adjpro/d9302/040223initialdecision.pdf.

196. Dell Computer Corp., No. 931-0097, 60 Fed. Reg. 57,870 (FTC Nov. 22, 1995) (proposed consent and aid to public comment), 121 F.T.C. 616 (1996) (decision and order).

competitors to have standard-setting organizations adopt their proposed standards so as to exclude rivals have also been struck down.[197]

E. Operation of a Joint Venture

Joint venture agreements often include restraints on pricing and output or on the territories or customers to which the venture will sell. In addition, joint venture agreements often include restraints on competition between the parents and the joint venture or between the parents themselves. Most cases in which joint ventures have been challenged under Section 1 of the Sherman Act have involved challenges not to the joint venture itself, but to these collateral restraints.

The application of Section 1 to the collateral restraints of joint venture activity in the course of the venture's operation raises two important questions. First, does the restraint involve the requisite plurality of actors with the capability of combining within the meaning of Section 1 or are the interests of the joint venturers sufficiently unified to make them a single entity under the *Copperweld* doctrine?[198] Second, under what circumstances are restraints otherwise subject to per se condemnation analyzed under the rule of reason because of their connection with the joint venture? Ever since *United States v. Addyston Pipe & Steel Co.*,[199] agreements that are truly ancillary to a legitimate joint activity have been judged under the rule of reason.[200] The central issue in evaluating collateral restrictive agreements is often whether the collateral restraints in question are reasonably related to the operation of the joint venture and no broader than necessary to achieve their legitimate purpose.[201]

---

197. *See, e.g.*, Indian Head, Inc. v. Allied Tube & Conduit Corp., 486 U.S. 492 (1988); American Society of Mech. Eng'rs v. Hydrolevel Corp., 456 U.S. 556 (1982).

198. *See* Copperweld Corp. v. Independence Tube Corp., 467 U.S. 752 (1984).

199. 85 F. 271 (6th Cir. 1898) (Taft, C.J.), *aff'd*, 175 U.S. 211 (1899).

200. *See id* at 280; *see also* Business Elecs. Corp. v. Sharp Elecs. Corp., 485 U.S. 717, 729 n.3 (1988); National Soc'y of Prof'l Eng'rs v. United States, 435 U.S. 679, 689 (1978); Chicago Bd. of Trade v. United States, 246 U.S. 231, 239-40 (1918). The rule of reason is discussed in detail in ABA SECTION OF ANTITRUST LAW, ANTITRUST LAW DEVELOPMENTS 58-79 (5th ed. 2002).

201. *See, e.g.*, Rothery Storage & Van Co. v. Atlas Van Lines, 792 F.2d 210, 224 (D.C. Cir. 1986) (Bork, J.). The court in *Rothery* explained the application of the ancillary restraint rule:

> To be ancillary, and hence exempt from the per se rule, an

1. Applicability of Section 1

Applying Section 1 to a joint venture's pricing and output decisions, or to collateral restraints in the joint venture agreement, raises the threshold question of whether the joint venture represents the plurality of actors necessary for a finding of liability under Section 1. In *Copperweld Corp. v. Independence Tube Corp*,[202] the U.S. Supreme Court held that a parent and its wholly owned subsidiary were legally incapable of conspiring in violation of the Sherman Act.[203] The Court relied essentially on two related justifications: (1) that a parent and wholly owned subsidiary have a "unity of interest,"[204] and (2) that coordination between a corporation and a wholly owned subsidiary does not represent a "sudden joining of two independent sources of economic power previously pursuing separate interests."[205] Companies have invoked the *Copperweld* decision to argue that a joint venture is a single economic entity, thereby negating the capacity of the venture partners to combine with one another with respect to the subject matter of the venture.[206]

> agreement eliminating competition must be subordinate and collateral to a separate, legitimate transaction. . . . If [the restraint] is so broad that part of the restraint suppresses competition without creating efficiency, the restraint is, to that extent, not ancillary.

Id. at 224; *see also* United States v. Columbia Pictures Corp., 189 F. Supp. 153, 178 (S.D.N.Y. 1960); Brunswick Corp., 94 F.T.C. 1174, 1275 (1979) ("[T]o be legitimately ancillary to a joint venture [such agreements] must be limited to those inevitably arising out of dealings between partners, or necessary (and of no broader scope than necessary) to make the joint venture work") (citation omitted), *aff'd in part and modified in part sub nom.*, Yamaha Motor Co. v. FTC, 657 F.2d 971 (8th Cir. 1981).

202. 467 U.S. 752 (1984).

203. *See id.* at 771-77.

204. *Id.* at 771.

205. *Id.* at 769-71; *see also id.* at 772-74. *Copperweld* and its application to allegations of intracorporate conspiracies are discussed more fully in ABA SECTION OF ANTITRUST LAW, ANTITRUST LAW DEVELOPMENTS 25-34 (5th ed. 2002) and Steven Calkins, *Copperweld in the Courts: The Road to Caribe*, 63 ANTITRUST L.J. 345 (1995).

206. *See e.g.*, Freeman v. San Diego Ass'n of Realtors, 322 F.3d 1133, 1148-50 (9th Cir. 2003) (analyzing and rejecting defendants' argument that the venture was immune from Section 1 condemnation because its members constituted a "single entity"). Of course, even if a joint venture were determined to be a single entity such that Section 1 does not apply to it,

The Eighth Circuit's decision in *City of Mt. Pleasant v. Associated Electric Cooperative, Inc.*,[207] in which the court held that a rural electric cooperative organization consisting of some fifty separate cooperatives organized in three tiers constituted a single entity, illustrates the *Copperweld* analysis in the joint venture context. In addressing whether the member cooperatives were capable of conspiring with each other, the court of appeals explained that, under *Copperweld*, "a conglomeration of two or more legally distinct entities cannot conspire among themselves if they 'pursue[] the common interests of the whole rather than interests separate from those of the [group] itself.'"[208] Focusing on the fundamental purpose of Section 1, the Eighth Circuit applied the following *Copperweld* reasoning: "'Because [such] coordination . . . does not represent a sudden joining of two independent sources of economic power previously pursuing separate interests, it is not activity that warrants § 1 scrutiny.'"[209] The *Mt. Pleasant* court found that the defendants had provided sufficient evidence that the cooperative organization was "a single enterprise pursuing a common goal—the provision of low-cost electricity to its consumer-members."[210]

Generally, however, where the members of a joint venture are actual or potential competitors, they are typically found to be capable of conspiring under Section 1. In *Rothery Storage & Van Co. v. Atlas Van Lines*,[211] for example, the D.C. Circuit held that the *Copperweld* doctrine had no application to a nationwide common carrier operating through a

---

its conduct would still be subject to Section 2 of the Sherman Act. *See* Chicago Prof'l Sports Ltd. P'ship v. NBA, 95 F.3d 593, 599 (7th Cir. 1996).

207. 838 F.2d 268 (8th Cir. 1988).

208. *Id.* at 274 (quoting *Copperweld Corp.*, 467 U.S. at 770-71).

209. *Id.* at 274-75 (quoting *Copperweld Corp.*, 467 U.S. at 770-71).

210. *Id.* at 276; *see also In re* Appraiser Found. Antitrust Litig., 867 F. Supp. 1407 (D. Minn. 1994) (holding joint venture which consisted of eight associations of appraisers to be a single enterprise because its members were interdependent and shared a common purpose of establishing industry standards); Greensboro Lumber Co. v. Georgia Power Co., 643 F. Supp. 1345, 1367 and n.26 (N.D. Ga. 1986) (holding rural electric cooperative to be a single entity because it is "a permanent ongoing organization structure created and controlled by its members to serve as a conduit in order to generate electricity for their own resale needs"), *aff'd*, 844 F.2d 1538, 1541-42 (11th Cir. 1988) (but questioning the applicability of the "single entity theory," and declining to reach the issue).

211. 792 F.2d 210 (D.C. Cir. 1986).

network of independent moving companies acting as the carrier's agents.[212] Because the venture consisted of actual or potential competitors, the court held that the van line had the plurality of actors necessary for Section 1 liability.[213] Similarly, courts have generally found physician peer review committees to be combinations of independent competitors who are capable of conspiring with each other.[214] In contrast, however, some (though not all) courts have found that peer review committees are unable to conspire with the hospital itself, due either to the absence of competition between the hospital and its attending physicians or to a unity of interest between the hospital and its staff.[215]

---

212. *See id.* at 214-15.
213. *See id.*
214. *See, e.g.*, Capital Imaging Assocs. v. Mohawk Valley Med. Assocs., 996 F.2d 537, 544 (2d Cir. 1993) (analyzing the capacity of physicians to conspire and stating "[t]he first question is—are member physicians of an independent practice association legally capable of conspiring among themselves? We think the answer is 'yes' . . . ."); Oksanen v. Page Mem'l Hosp., 945 F.2d 696, 706 (4th Cir. 1991) (en banc) (medical staff members may have "independent and at times competing economic interests," and therefore have the capacity to conspire when they join together to take action among themselves); Nurse Midwifery Assocs. v. Hibbett, 918 F.2d 605, 614 (6th Cir. 1990) (individual members of the medical staff may have the capacity to conspire among themselves); Bolt v. Halifax Hosp. Med. Ctr., 891 F.2d 810, 819 (11th Cir. 1990) (members of medical staff have capacity to conspire with one another because each member "is a separate economic entity potentially in competition with other physicians"); Weiss v. York Hosp., 745 F.2d 786, 814 (3d Cir. 1984) ("as a matter of law, the medical staff is a combination of individual doctors and therefore . . . any action taken by the medical staff satisfies the 'contract, combination, or conspiracy' requirement of Section 1").
215. *See, e.g.*, American Council of Certified Podiatric Physicians & Surgeons v. American Bd. of Podiatric Surgery, Inc., 185 F.3d 606, 620 (6th Cir. 1999) (holding that, as a matter of law, podiatrist certification board could not conspire with its members because they were not independent legal entities); Okusami v. Psychiatric Inst. of Wash., 959 F.2d 1062 (D.C. Cir. 1992) (hospital and medical staff incapable of conspiracy if they have unity of interest); *Page Mem'l Hosp.*, 945 F.2d at 703-05 (hospital board and medical staff members were incapable of conspiring under Section 1 in the peer review process because both implemented a single, unitary policy regarding the provision of hospital privileges; "[f]ar from being a competitor with the hospital, the medical staff was in fact a natural component of the hospital's management structure"); *Nurse*

Both before and after *Copperweld*, most courts generally have found or assumed that member franchises of sports leagues can conspire with each other under Section 1.[216] Competition among member teams for

---

Midwifery Assocs., 918 F.2d at 614 (hospital and its medical staff are incapable of conspiring because "hospital and the medical staff are not competitors"); *Weiss*, 745 F.2d at 813-17 (the "[medical] staff as an entity had no interest in competition with the hospital. Accordingly, . . . there could not be a conspiracy between the hospital and the medical staff."). *But see Bolt*, 891 F.2d at 819 ("we perceive no basis . . . for holding that a hospital is legally incapable of conspiring with the members of its medical staff" because "[a] hospital and the members of its medical staff . . . are legally separate entities, and consequently no . . . danger exists that what is in fact unilateral activity will be bootstrapped into a 'conspiracy.'"); Oltz v. St. Peter's Community Hosp., 861 F.2d 1440, 1450 (9th Cir. 1988) (following *Bolt* in a case outside the peer review context and holding that "the collaborated conduct between the [doctors] and [the hospital] coalesced economic power previously directed at disparate goals").

216. *See* Fraser v. Major League Soccer, L.L.C., 284 F.3d 47, 55-60 (1st Cir. 2002) (discussing *Copperweld* analysis as applied to sports leagues); Sullivan v. NFL, 34 F.3d 1091, 1099 (1st Cir. 1994); Volvo N. Am. Corp. v. Men's Int'l Prof'l Tennis Council, 857 F.2d 55, 71 (2d Cir. 1986); Los Angeles Mem'l Coliseum Comm'n v. NFL, 726 F.2d 1381, 1387-90 (9th Cir. 1984); North Am. Soccer League v. NFL, 670 F.2d 1249, 1257-58 (2d Cir. 1982); Smith v. Pro Football, Inc., 593 F.2d 1173, 1177, 1181-89 (D.C. Cir. 1978); Mackey v. NFL, 543 F.2d 606, 616-18 (8th Cir. 1976); NBA v. Williams, 857 F. Supp. 1069, 1078-79 (S.D.N.Y. 1994), *aff'd*, 45 F.3d 684 (2d Cir. 1995); McNeil v. NFL, 790 F. Supp. 871, 878-80 (D. Minn. 1992); *cf.* Seattle Totems Hockey Club v. NHL, 783 F.2d 1347, 1350 (9th Cir. 1986) (finding an absence of injury to competition when a potential franchisee failed to obtain an NHL franchise in part because the potential franchisee was seeking to join the NHL, not compete with it); Levin v. NBA, 385 F. Supp. 149, 152-53 (S.D.N.Y. 1974) (acknowledging that joint action by members of a league can have antitrust implications, but finding that, because potential owners of NBA franchise wished to "join with" NBA franchises, "not to compete with them," rejection of potential owners did not have anticompetitive effect). *But see* Seabury Mgmt., Inc. v. PGA, 878 F. Supp. 771, 777-79 (D. Md. 1994) (finding that the PGA could not conspire with the regional section of the PGA), *aff'd in part and rev'd in part*, 52 F.3d 322 (4th Cir. 1995) (unpublished table decision); San Francisco Seals, Ltd. v. NHL, 379 F. Supp. 966, 969-70 (C.D. Cal. 1974) (finding that the NHL and one of its franchise teams were "acting together as one single business enterprise" for the purposes of Section 1).

players, coaches, managers, fan support, ticket sales, and overall revenues has been a primary basis for finding that league members can conspire in violation of Section 1.[217] Courts have also considered the extent to which teams compete in the sale of ownership interests[218] and the separate ownership, administration, and operation of the league members.[219] In *Chicago Professional Sports Limited Partnership v. NBA*,[220] however, the Seventh Circuit rejected a district court's determination that a sports league should not be treated as a single firm unless the member teams have a complete unity of interest, and remanded for further consideration of that issue.[221] The Seventh Circuit

---

217. *See Sullivan*, 34 F.3d at 1098 (noting that teams compete for "fan support, players, coaches, ticket sales, local broadcast revenues, and the sale of team paraphernalia"); *Los Angeles Mem'l Coliseum Comm'n*, 726 F.2d at 1389-90 (finding that teams compete for players, coaches, and management personnel, and "where two teams operate in close proximity, there is also competition for fan support, local television and local radio revenues, and media space"); *Mackey*, 543 F.2d at 619 (finding competition for players' services); *cf.* Mid-South Grizzlies v. NFL, 720 F.2d 772, 787 (3d Cir. 1983) (two teams that are geographically close to each other conceivably compete for "ticket buyers, for local broadcast revenue, and for sale of the concession items like food and beverages and team paraphernalia").

218. *See Sullivan*, 34 F.3d at 1100; *cf.* Piazza v. Major League Baseball, 831 F. Supp. 420, 429-31, 440 (E.D. Pa. 1993) (finding a market in the sale of "ownership interests in existing baseball teams").

219. *See Los Angeles Mem'l Coliseum Comm'n*, 726 F.2d at 1389-90 (finding a capacity to conspire in part because "[t]he member clubs are all independently owned" with "independent management policies").

220. 95 F.3d 593 (7th Cir. 1996).

221. *See id.* at 605-06. In *San Francisco Seals, Ltd. v. NHL*, 379 F. Supp. 966 (C.D. Cal. 1974), the court found that member franchises of the NHL are "all members of a single unit competing as such with other similar professional leagues. Consequently, the organizational scheme of the NHL, by which all its members are bound, imposes no restraint upon trade or commerce ..., but rather makes possible a segment of commercial activity which could hardly exist without it." *Id.* at 970. In *Los Angeles Mem. Coliseum Comm'n v. NFL*, 726 F.2d at 1381, the Ninth Circuit considered, but declined to follow, the reasoning of the district court in *San Francisco Seals*. *See id.* at 1390 n.4 ("Although [*San Francisco Seals*] and [a cited law review article] offer persuasive reasons for recognizing the NFL as a single entity, we do not find these reasons so compelling that existing precedent can be ignored or that we should grant this association of 28 independent businesses blanket immunity from attack under § 1 of the Sherman Act").

instructed the district court to base its further review primarily on the "functional" test articulated in *Copperweld:* Does the conduct at issue "deprive[] the marketplace of the independent centers of decisionmaking that competition assumes"?[222] The Seventh Circuit suggested that under this test a sports league might act as a single entity for some purposes but not others.[223]

---

222. Chicago Prof'l Sports Ltd. P'ship v. NBA, 95 F.3d 593, 606 (7th Cir. 1996) (quoting Copperweld Corp. v. Independence Tube Corp., 467 U.S. 752, 769 (1984)). The Seventh Circuit added that it saw "no reason why a sports league cannot be treated as a single firm in this typology. It produces a single product; cooperation is essential . . . and a league need not deprive the market of independent centers of decision-making." *Id.* at 598. In *Brown v. Pro Football, Inc.*, 518 U.S. 231 (1996), a case involving the application of the nonstatutory labor exemption to professional football, the U.S. Supreme Court in dicta observed similarly that the clubs that make up a professional sports league are not "completely independent economic competitors, as they depend upon a degree of cooperation for economic survival." *Id.* at 248 (citations omitted).

223. *See* Fraser v. Major League Soccer, L.L.C., 284 F.3d 47, 55-60 (1st Cir. 2002) (characterizing MLS as "a hybrid arrangement, somewhere between a single company (with or without wholly owned subsidiaries) and a cooperative arrangement between existing competitors"); *Chicago Prof'l Sports Ltd P'ship*, 95 F.3d at 600 ("[W]e do not rule out the possibility that an organization such as the NBA is best understood as one firm when selling broadcast rights to a network in competition with a thousand other producers of entertainment, but is best understood as a joint venture when curtailing competition for players who have few other market opportunities"). Other courts have found no antitrust violation by league activities, though relying more on the absence of antitrust injury than on the presence of a single entity. *See, e.g.*, *Seattle Totems Hockey Club*, 783 F.2d at 1350 (finding an absence of injury to competition when a potential franchisee failed to obtain an NHL franchise in part because the potential franchisee was seeking to join the NHL, not compete with it); *Levin*, 385 F. Supp. at 150-53 (dismissing complaint because bidders for franchise sought to join NBA rather than compete with it, and noting that the NBA teams "are dependent upon one another as partners in the league format to make [the league] possible" and suggesting that there cannot be competition among league members). A number of cases have declined expressly to follow *Levin*'s analysis. *See, e.g.*, *Sullivan*, 34 F.3d at 1098 ("*Levin* simply presumed, incorrectly, that there could never be any competition among league members.") (citations omitted); *Mid-South Grizzlies*, 720 F.2d at 787 n.9 (not approving, and perhaps questioning, *Levin*'s suggestion "that there can never be competition among league

2. *General Principles Governing Collateral Restraints*

When evaluating collateral restraints, courts often distinguish between "naked restraints"—restraints "lacking any redeeming virtue"—and "ancillary" restraints—restraints that are "an essential or at least important part of the same arrangement that has potentially redeeming virtues."[224] The former category of restraints may be condemned under the per se rule or under an abbreviated or quick look analysis under the rule of reason, while the latter are typically subject to a more complete rule of reason review.[225] The categorization of a restraint as either ancillary or naked substantially influences the subsequent antitrust analysis of the restraint and, in many cases, may determine the outcome of a challenge to the legality of the restraint.

The distinction between naked and ancillary restraints has its roots in the *Addyston Pipe* decision,[226] a price-fixing case decided outside of the joint venture context. There, Judge (later Chief Justice and President) Taft condemned a complex bid-rigging scheme as constituting a naked restraint on competition and distinguished various other ancillary

---

members"); *cf. Piazza*, 831 F. Supp. at 431 n.16 (distinguishing *Levin* because it "gives no indication that either the plaintiffs asserted or that the court considered a claim that competition had been restrained in the market for professional basketball teams or for participation in professional basketball").

224. XI PHILLIP E. AREEDA & HERBERT HOVENKAMP, ANTITRUST LAW ¶ 1905, at 203 (1998). It is possible that a given horizontal restraint may be neither ancillary nor naked—i.e., the restraint may not be related to a joint venture, but may not be completely lacking in redeeming social value. Such a restraint is analyzed under the rule of reason, but without reference to the procompetitive benefits of the joint venture. *See id.* ¶ 1912c3, at 289 ("While the most frequent application of the rule of reason involves restraints that are 'ancillary' to some underlying productive joint venture, a significant number of challenged agreements qualify for rule of reason treatment even though they are not realistically ancillary to anything"); Gregory J. Werden, *Antitrust Analysis of Joint Ventures: An Overview*, 66 ANTITRUST L.J. 701, 707 (1998) ("Nonancillary restraints are not necessarily unlawful, but the competitive benefits of a joint venture are irrelevant to the analysis of its nonancillary restraints . . . .").

225. AREEDA & HOVENKAMP, *supra* note 224, ¶ 1905, at 202.

226. United States v. Addyston Pipe & Steel Co., 85 F. 271 (6th Cir. 1898), *modified and aff'd*, 175 U.S. 211 (1899). *Addyston Pipe* is discussed in detail in AREEDA & HOVENKAMP, *supra* note 224, ¶ 1905. *See also* Werden, *supra* note 224, at 707.

restraints: "[N]o conventional restraint of trade can be enforced unless the covenant embodying it is merely ancillary to the main purpose of a lawful contract, and necessary to protect the covenantee in the full enjoyment of the legitimate fruits of the contract, or to protect him from the dangers of unjust use of those fruits by the other party."[227] Judge Taft cited several examples of lawful ancillary restraints, including restraints among partners who join together to create a new business:

> [W]hen two men became partners in a business, although their union might reduce competition, this effect was only an incident to the main purpose of a union of their capital, enterprise, and energy to carry on a successful business, and one useful to the community. Restrictions in the articles of partnership upon the business activity of the members, with a view of securing their entire effort in the common enterprise, were, of course, only ancillary to the main end of the union and were to be encouraged.[228]

Following *Addyston Pipe*, courts and commentators have proposed a variety of different formulae for distinguishing between ancillary and nonancillary restraints in the context of joint ventures. A restraint is ancillary if it "contributes to" or is "subordinate and collateral to" the efficiency-enhancing purposes of a joint venture.[229] The basic goal is to determine "whether the challenged restraint is an inherent feature of the joint venture at all, or simply an unnecessary, output-limiting appendage."[230]

Courts have differed, however, with respect to the relationship they require between the restraint and the venture's procompetitive purposes.

---

227. *Addyston Pipe & Steel Co.*, 85 F. at 282.

228. *Id.* at 280.

229. *See* Sullivan v. NFL, 34 F.3d 1091, 1102 (1st Cir. 1994) (an ancillary restraint is "one that is required to make the joint activity more efficient"); Rothery Storage & Van Co. v. Atlas Van Lines, 792 F.2d 210, 244 (D.C. Cir. 1986) ("To be ancillary, and hence exempt from the per se rule, an agreement eliminating competition must be subordinate and collateral to a separate, legitimate transaction. The ancillary restraint is subordinate and collateral in the sense that it serves to make the main transaction more effective in accomplishing its purpose"); Polk Bros. v. Forest City Enters., 776 F.2d 185, 189 (7th Cir. 1985) ("A restraint is ancillary when it may contribute to the success of a cooperative venture that promises greater productivity and output").

230. AREEDA & HOVENKAMP, *supra* note 224, ¶ 1908, at 227-28; *see also Polk Bros.*, 776 F.2d at 190 ("The reason for distinguishing between 'ancillary' and 'naked' restraints is to determine whether the agreement is part of a cooperative venture with the prospects for increasing output").

Most courts have required that the restraint be "reasonably related to . . . and no broader than necessary to effectuate" the venture's procompetitive business purposes and will consider whether there are substantially less restrictive alternatives available to achieve those objectives.[231] Other courts have criticized this less restrictive alternatives test and have required only that the restraint be "fairly necessary" to

---

231. Freeman v. San Diego Ass'n of Realtors, 322 F.3d 1133, 1157 (9th Cir. 2003); SCFC ILC, Inc. v. Visa USA, Inc. 36 F.3d 958, 970 (10th Cir. 1994); *accord* Law v. NCAA, 134 F.3d 1010, 1019 (10th Cir. 1998); *Sullivan*, 34 F.3d at 1103 (stating that "a given restriction is not reasonable, that is, its benefits cannot outweigh its harm to competition, if a reasonable, less restrictive alternative . . . exists"); Chicago Prof'l Sports Ltd. P'ship v. NBA, 961 F.2d 667, 675-76 (7th Cir. 1996) (apparently adopting a less restrictive alternative analysis in reviewing the NBA's free-rider defense); Los Angeles Mem'l Coliseum Comm'n v. NFL, 726 F.2d 1381, 1395-98 (8th Cir. 1984) (stating that under the ancillary restraint doctrine "some agreements which restrain competition may be valid if they are . . . necessary to make that transaction effective" (quoting Robert H. Bork, *The Rule of Reason and the Per se Concept: Price Fixing and Market Division*, 74 YALE L.J. 775, 797-98 (1965))); North Am. Soccer League v. NFL, 670 F.2d 1249, 1261 (2d Cir. 1982) (stating that "the NFL was required to come forward with proof that any legitimate purpose could not be achieved through less restrictive means. This it has failed to do"); Union Carbide Corp. v. Montell N.V., 27 F. Supp. 2d 414, 417 (S.D.N.Y. 1998) (simply because one agreement can be considered ancillary to a more legitimate one does not end the inquiry into whether the ancillary agreement restrains trade); Brunswick Corp., 94 F.T.C. 1174, 1275 (1979) ("[T]o be legitimately ancillary to a joint venture [such agreements] must be limited to those inevitably arising out of dealings between partners, and necessary (and of no broader scope than necessary) to make the joint venture work"), *aff'd in part and modified in part sub nom.*, Yamaha Motor Co. v. FTC, 657 F.2d 971 (8th Cir. 1981); *cf.* K.M.B. Warehouse Distribs., Inc. v. Walker Mfg. Co., 61 F.3d 123, 128-29 (2d Cir. 1995) (requiring under rule of reason generally that a plaintiff prove that a procompetitive effect established by the defendant could not be achieved through "an alternative means that is less restrictive of competition"); Image Tech. Servs., Inc. v. Eastman Kodak Co., 903 F.2d 612, 618 (9th Cir. 1990) (under § 1 a tying arrangement supported by market power must constitute the least restrictive alternative in achieving a legitimate business purpose), *aff'd on other grounds*, 504 U.S. 451 (1992); Copper Liquor, Inc. v. Adolph Coors Co., 506 F.2d 934, 944-45 (5th Cir. 1975) (applying "less restrictive means" test to territorial restrictions on distributors).

achieve the venture's objectives.[232] Still other courts require that the restraint be "reasonably necessary" to achieve the procompetitive objectives, without specifying whether they will examine less restrictive alternatives.[233]

The *Competitor Collaborations Guidelines* require that a restraint adopted in connection with a joint venture be "reasonably related to the integration and reasonably necessary to achieve its procompetitive benefits."[234] To be "reasonably necessary," a restraint need not be "essential." However, if the participants could achieve "an equivalent or comparable efficiency-enhancing integration through practical, significantly less restrictive means," then the agencies will conclude that the restraint is not reasonably necessary. In making this assessment, the agencies consider whether "practical, significantly less restrictive means"

---

232. *See* Fleer Corp. v. Topps Chewing Gum, Inc., 658 F.2d 139, 151 n.18 (3d Cir. 1981) ("In a rule of reason case, the test is not whether the defendant displayed the least restrictive alternative. Rather the issue is whether the restriction actually implemented is 'fairly necessary' in the circumstances of the particular case"); American Motor Inns v. Holiday Inns, 521 F.2d 1230, 1249 (3d Cir. 1975) (criticizing the use of the least restrictive alternative test in a rule of reason analysis in the franchise context as requiring "[e]ntrepreneurs [to be] guarantors that the imaginations of lawyers could not conjure up some method of achieving the business purpose in question that would result in a somewhat lesser restriction of trade"); Anderson v. American Auto. Assoc., 454 F.2d 1240, 1246 (9th Cir. 1972) ("To sustain the restraint, it must be . . . fairly necessary in the circumstances of the particular case"); National Bancard Corp. v. VISA USA Inc., 596 F. Supp. 1231, 1256-57 (S.D. Fla. 1984) ("[i]t should be stressed . . . that . . . the relevant question is not whether the challenged practice is the . . . 'least restrictive,' but simply whether it is reasonable"), *aff'd*, 779 F.2d 592 (11th Cir. 1986).

233. *See, e.g.*, United States v. Realty Multi-List, Inc., 629 F.2d 1351, 1375 (5th Cir. 1980) ("the [restraints] themselves must be reasonably necessary to the accomplishment of the legitimate goals"); *see also* COMPETITOR COLLABORATIONS GUIDELINES, *supra* note 1, § 3.3 (adopting "reasonably necessary" standard); HEALTH CARE STATEMENTS, *supra* note 22, Statement 7.B.2 (requiring that collateral agreements contained in certain joint ventures be "reasonably necessary" to achieve stated efficiencies); INTELLECTUAL PROPERTY GUIDELINES, *supra* note 21, § 4.2 (examining whether restraint in a licensing arrangement is "reasonably necessary to achieve procompetitive benefits").

234. COMPETITOR COLLABORATIONS GUIDELINES, *supra* note 1, § 3.2.

were reasonably available and do not search for a "theoretically less restrictive alternative."[235]

It should be noted that the initial inquiry into whether a restraint is ancillary is different from the analysis of whether, as part of the rule of reason analysis, there are less restrictive alternatives available to achieve the goals of the restraint. The two inquiries may sometimes be formulated in similar language, but the ancillarity inquiry occurs at the threshold of the antitrust review, while the less restrictive alternative inquiry occurs, if at all, only as part of the rule of reason analysis and "only after power and a potential threat to competition have been established, making it necessary to determine whether an activity or function that is essential to the venture can be carried out by less harmful means."[236] Thus, in *Sullivan v. NFL*,[237] the First Circuit accepted that an NFL rule restricting the public sale of shares of professional football teams might be ancillary to legitimate joint activity, but noted that there was evidence that the rule was not reasonable because there was a less restrictive alternative to this policy "that would yield the same benefits as the current policy."[238]

The classification of a collateral restraint as ancillary or naked substantially influences the substantive antitrust analysis of the restraint. Ancillary restraints are analyzed under the rule of reason. A plaintiff bringing a rule of reason challenge typically bears the burden of coming forward with evidence that the restraint has or is likely to have a substantial anticompetitive effect. In most cases, this requires some showing that the defendants possess market power in a relevant product and geographic market.[239] "Proof of market power . . . is a critical first

---

235. *Id.*
236. AREEDA & HOVENKAMP, *supra* note 224, ¶ 1908, at 227-28.
237. 34 F.3d 1091 (1st Cir. 1994).
238. *Id.* at 1102.
239. *See* SCFC ILC, Inc. v. Visa USA, Inc. 36 F.3d 958, 965 (10th Cir. 1994) ("Rule of reason analysis first asks whether the offending competitor . . . possesses market power in the relevant market where the alleged anticompetitive activity occurs."); Polk Bros. v. Forest City Enters., Inc., 776 F.2d 185, 191 (7th Cir. 1985) ("The first step in any Rule of Reason case is an assessment of market power."); AREEDA & HOVENKAMP, *supra* note 224, ¶ 1912c4, at 290 ("[T]he plaintiff must show that the defendants collectively wield sufficient market power to warrant a conclusion that their restraint threatens to reduce marketwide output . . . ."). The *Health Care Statements* use a version of the market power screen by adopting various safe harbors based on the market shares of the entities involved in the joint venture. *See* HEALTH CARE STATEMENTS,

step, or 'screen,' or 'filter' which is often dispositive of the case."[240] Assuming that market power can be demonstrated, the critical question in the rule of reason analysis is whether the restraint at issue will likely have the effect of increasing prices or decreasing output.[241]

In contrast, naked restraints are analyzed under the per se rule or an abbreviated or quick look version of the rule of reason. Courts often state that naked restraints, even in the context of joint ventures, are per se illegal.[242] For example, in *Freeman v. San Diego Ass'n of Realtors*, the Ninth Circuit held that a joint venture comprised of real estate associations providing multi-listing services (MLS) had committed a per se violation of Section 1 by agreeing to fix prices charged to realtors necessary in supporting the MLS system.[243] In reaching this conclusion, the court rejected the defendants' assertion that fixing the support fees charged by the joint venture was necessary to realize the benefits of the joint venture, and thus should be analyzed under the rule of reason.[244] Likewise, the *Competitor Collaborations Guidelines* suggest that a restraint on price or output will be condemned as per se illegal, even if adopted as part of a joint venture, to the extent that the restraint is not reasonably necessary to achieve the procompetitive goals of the venture.[245]

---

supra note 22, Statement 7.A (joint purchasing arrangements); Statement 8.A (physician network joint venture).

240. *SCFC ILC*, 36 F.3d at 965 (quoting Easterbrook, *The Limits of Antitrust*, 63 TEX. L. REV. 1, 17 (1984)).

241. AREEDA & HOVENKAMP, *supra* note 224, ¶ 1912d, at 291 (defining unreasonable restraint of trade as "an agreement tending to result in reduced output or higher prices in the market or markets affected by the restraint").

242. *See e.g.*, Freeman v. San Diego Ass'n of Realtors, 322 F.3d 1133, 1144 (9th Cir. 2003)("No antitrust violation is more abominated than the agreement to fix prices. With few exceptions, price-fixing agreements are unlawful per se under the Sherman Act . . . . The dispositive question generally is not whether any price fixing was justified, but simply whether it occurred"); Rothery Storage & Van Co. v. Atlas Van Lines, 792 F.2d 210, 229 (D.C. Cir. 1986) ("[A] naked horizontal restraint . . .is illegal per se"); *Polk Bros.*, 776 F.2d at 188 ("[T]he per se rule is designed for 'naked' restraints . . . ."); Werden, *supra* note 224, at 707 (nonancillary restraints "may fall within the scope of the per se rule").

243. 322 F.3d 1133, 1144-47 (9th Cir. 2003).

244. *Id.* at 1150-52.

245. COMPETITOR COLLABORATIONS GUIDELINES, *supra* note 1, § 3.2.

In *NCAA v. Board of Regents*,[246] however, the U.S. Supreme Court declined to apply the per se rule to an NCAA plan for televising college football despite the conclusion that the plan included a "naked restriction on price and output."[247] The Court instead held that the rule of reason was applicable because "this case involves an industry in which horizontal restraints on competition are essential if the product is to be available at all."[248] The Court ultimately applied an abbreviated rule of reason analysis which examined the proffered justification for the restraint but did not require proof of market power; based upon this analysis, the Court ruled that the restraint was unlawful.[249] Certain courts and commentators have interpreted *NCAA v. Board of Regents* to stand for the proposition that *every* restraint created by a joint venture qualifies for rule of reason treatment, even naked price-fixing agreements.[250] Application of the rule of reason, even in abbreviated form, to naked restraints has been criticized as "unnecessarily complicat[ing] litigation against obviously unnecessary and harmful restraints."[251]

The abbreviated or quick look version of the rule of reason described in *NCAA v. Board of Regents* has also been applied to restraints that are

---

246. 468 U.S. 85 (1984).

247. *Id.* at 109.

248. *Id.* at 101.

249. *Id.* at 109-10 ("This naked restraint on price and output requires some competitive justification even in the absence of a detailed market analysis"). The result was similar in *Law v. NCAA*, 134 F.3d 1010 (10th Cir. 1998), where the court addressed an NCAA rule which limited the compensation paid to entry-level coaches. The court held that, because this restraint "is a horizontal price restraint on its face," a quick look analysis was appropriate and no proof of market power was required. *Id.* at 1020. After examining and rejecting the proffered procompetitive rationales for the rule, the court affirmed the district court's grant of a permanent injunction barring the NCAA from reenacting the compensation limits. *Id.* at 1024.

250. *See Law*, 134 F.3d 1010, 1018-19 ("Board of Regents more generally concluded that because horizontal agreements are necessary for sports competition, all horizontal agreements among NCAA members, even those as egregious as price fixing, should be subject to a rule of reason analysis"); AREEDA & HOVENKAMP, *supra* note 224, ¶ 1910d, at 263 ("In sum, in a situation involving a complex network joint venture in which horizontal restraints are necessary if the product is to be marketed 'at all,' *every* restraint created by that venture qualifies for rule of reason treatment").

251. AREEDA & HOVENKAMP, *supra* note 224, ¶ 1910d, at 263-64.

not necessarily naked but which have "obvious anticompetitive effects."[252] Such restraints have been described as "nearly naked."[253] For example, in *FTC v. Indiana Federation of Dentists*,[254] the U.S. Supreme Court addressed an agreement among members of a professional association of dentists to withhold X rays from an insurer seeking to verify claims. While this restraint resembled a per se illegal group boycott or concerted refusal to deal, the Court held that it could not be characterized as a naked restraint and would be evaluated under the rule of reason.[255] Nevertheless, the Court held that "no elaborate industry analysis is required to demonstrate the anticompetitive character of such an agreement."[256] Since the defendants advanced no credible argument that the restraint produced a "countervailing procompetitive virtue," the Court condemned the restraint as unlawful under the rule of reason.[257] In contrast, the Court in *California Dental Ass'n v. FTC*,[258] held that it was inappropriate to apply the abbreviated rule of reason in evaluating limitations on price and quality advertising imposed by a professional dental association on its members. The Court explained that the case failed "to present a situation in which the likelihood of anticompetitive effects [was] comparably obvious"[259] and remanded for a "less quick look" and a "fuller consideration of the issue."[260]

---

252. *Law*, 134 F.3d at 1020; *see also* California Dental Ass'n v. FTC, 526 U.S. 756, 770 (1999) ("[Q]uick look analysis carries the day when the great likelihood of anticompetitive effects can easily be ascertained.") (citation omitted).
253. AREEDA & HOVENKAMP, *supra* note 224, ¶ 1911, at 265.
254. 476 U.S. 447 (1986).
255. The Court explained that "we have been slow to condemn rules adopted by professional associations as unreasonable per se [citing Nat'l Soc. of Prof'l Engineers v. United States, 435 U.S. 679 (1978)] and, in general, to extend per se analysis to restraints imposed in the context of business relationships where the economic impact of certain practices is not immediately obvious [citing Broadcast Music, Inc. v. CBS, 441 U.S. 1 (1979)]." *Indiana Federation*, 476 U.S. at 458-59.
256. *Id.* at 459 (quoting *Professional Engineers*, 435 U.S. at 692).
257. *Id.*; *see also* Chicago Prof'l Sports Ltd. P'ship v. NBA, 961 F.2d 667 (7th Cir. 1992) (applying quick look to affirm preliminary injunction against NBA rule limiting number of games televised on "superstations").
258. 526 U.S. 756 (1999).
259. *Id.* at 770.
260. *Id.* at 781.

3. *Restraints on Competition among the Joint Venture and Its Parents*

Agreements among the parents not to compete with the joint venture in the market in which the joint venture operates generally have been upheld as reasonable ancillary restraints under Section 1, at least where the joint venture and its parents do not have market power in that market.[261] In *Rothery Storage & Van Co. v. Atlas Van Lines*,[262] for

---

261. *See, e.g.*, Polk Bros. v. Forest City Enters., 776 F.2d 185, 190 (7th Cir. 1985) (building products dealer's covenant not to sell items sold by appliance dealer housed in the same building upheld because restraints ancillary to their "productive cooperation"); Engine Specialties, Inc. v. Bombardier Ltd., 605 F.2d 1, 11 (1st Cir. 1979) (an alleged restraint imposed by a joint venture "is not offensive in and of itself: it purports to state merely that neither of the parties to the joint venture will compete with it"); Brunswick Corp., 94 F.T.C. 1174, 1275 (1979) ("Certain reductions in competition between the parents are an inevitable consequence of a joint venture agreement"), *aff'd in part and modified in part sub nom.*, Yamaha Motor Corp. v. FTC, 657 F.2d 971 (8th Cir. 1981); Worthen Bank & Trust Co. v. National BankAmericard, Inc., 485 F.2d 119, 130 (8th Cir. 1973) (holding that a joint venture restricting member banks from affiliating with any other national bank card was not a per se unlawful group boycott); United States v. Addyston Pipe & Steel Co., 85 F. 271, 280 (6th Cir. 1898) (agreements by joint venture parents not to compete with the venture should be upheld as ancillary restraints because they are made "with a view of securing [each partner's] entire effort in the common enterprise"), *aff'd as modified*, 175 U.S. 211 (1899); Hudson's Bay Co. Fur Sales v. American Legend Coop., 651 F. Supp. 819, 838-39 (D.N.J. 1986) (trademark restrictions imposed by association of mink producers were restraints ancillary to attempt to improve efficiency of marketing fur products); American Floral Servs. v. Florists' Transworld Delivery Ass'n, 633 F. Supp. 201, 212-13 (N.D. Ill. 1986) (joint venture "pirate order rules" upheld as legitimate response to threat of free-riding); United States v. Pan Am. World Airways, 193 F. Supp. 18, 33-36 (S.D.N.Y. 1961) (finding valid monopolization claim, but upholding agreement by parent not to compete with joint venture), *rev'd on other grounds*, 371 U.S. 296 (1963); *cf.* United States v. Penn-Olin Chem. Co., 378 U.S. 158, 168 (1964) ("Realistically, the parents would not compete with their progeny."). *But see* Regents of Univ. of Cal. v. American Broad. Cos., 747 F.2d 511, 516-18 (9th Cir. 1984) (upholding preliminary injunction against "crossover restriction" preventing joint venture teams from participating with non-joint venture teams in broadcasts on other networks); Pennsylvania Water & Power Co. v. Consolidated Gas Elec. Light & Power Co., 97 F. Supp. 952, 955-

example, the D.C. Circuit upheld a joint venture's policy of terminating participating agents that engaged in moving and storage operations for their own account rather than through specified subsidiaries. The court reasoned that the policy, although eliminating competition among the participating agents, enhanced efficiency by eliminating the problem of free-riding[263] and could not lessen competition in the market for moving and storage, because Atlas and its agents accounted for only 6 percent of sales in that market. Eliminating free-riding was procompetitive, the court found, because "the van line's incentive to spend for reputation, equipment, facilities, and services declines as it receives less of the benefit from them. That produces a deterioration of the system's efficiency because the things consumers desire are not provided in the amounts they are willing to pay for."[264]

Agreements among parents not to compete in markets other than the joint venture market, however, generally have been invalidated as naked restraints of trade.[265] The FTC sued Polygram Music Group and Warner

---

56 (D.Md. 1951) (invalidating agreement precluding competition between parents and joint venture in electrical generation market), *aff'd*, 194 F.2d 89 (4th Cir. 1952); Nippon Sheet Glass Co., 113 F.T.C. 715, 717, 720 (1990) (requiring joint venturers to abolish the portion of their agreement that prevented venturers from expanding production capacity outside the venture).

262. 792 F.2d 210 (D.C. Cir. 1986).

263. *See id.* at 221, 222-23; *see also American Floral Servs.*, 633 F. Supp. at 219-20.

264. *Rothery Storage & Van Co.*, 792 F.2d at 222-23. Not all restrictions aimed at eliminating the free-rider phenomenon have been upheld by the courts. *See, e.g.*, Chicago Prof'l Sports Ltd. P'ship v. NBA, 961 F.2d 667, 674-76 (7th Cir. 1992) (affirming grant of preliminary injunction against league rule limiting number of broadcasts by teams over superstations and rejecting free-rider justification because of availability of less restrictive alternatives); Premier Elec. Constr. Co. v. National Elec. Contractors Ass'n, 814 F.2d 358, 370 (7th Cir. 1987) ("From the perspective of the cartel, the price cutting by individual firms is a form of 'free-riding.' . . . A group of firms trying to extract a supra-competitive price therefore hardly can turn around and try to squelch lower prices . . . by branding the lower prices 'free riding'!"); General Leaseways, Inc. v. National Truck Leasing Ass'n, 744 F.2d 588, 592 (7th Cir. 1984) (affirming grant of preliminary injunction against association of firms engaged in full-service, over-the-road commercial truck leasing based on finding that location and nonaffiliation restrictions imposed on members were not reasonable measures to prevent free-riding).

265. *See, e.g.*, Timken Roller Bearing Co. v. United States, 341 U.S. 593, 597-

Communications, Inc. over their agreements with respect to the "Three Tenors" performances. Polygram held the distribution rights to the 1990 "Three Tenors" performance, and Warner held the rights to the 1994 performance.[266] The two companies agreed to distribute the 1998 performance jointly.[267] According to the complaint, in order to reduce competition for products resulting from the 1998 performance, the companies adopted a "moratorium" agreement in which each company agreed not to discount or advertise the 1990 or 1994 album or video for a specified period of time.[268] The FTC unanimously concluded that the restrictions contained in the "moratorium" constituted "naked restraints on competition", lacking any "cognizable justification."[269] To prevent the recurrence of such conduct, which the FTC described as "antithetical to the fundamental policies of our antitrust laws,"[270] Polygram and its subsidiaries were ordered to cease and desist from entering into "any combination, conspiracy, or agreement to fix, raise, or stabilize prices or price levels" in connection with the sale of audio or video products.[271]

Joint ventures allowing for competition among the joint venture and its parents in the joint venture market can raise complex issues. On the one hand, the U.S. Supreme Court appears to have recognized in *Broadcast Music, Inc. v. CBS*,[272] that such competition can increase the

---

98 (1951) (allocation of territories outside joint venture market struck down); *Brunswick Corp.*, 94 F.T.C. at 1276 (invalidating agreement foreclosing one party from continuing "pre-existing competitive efforts" with other parent "outside the ambit of the joint venture"); *see also* United States v. Addyston Pipe & Steel Co., 85 F. at 282 ("[I]f the restraint exceeds the necessity presented by the main purpose of the contract, it is void for two reasons: First, because it oppresses the covenantor, without any corresponding benefit to the covenantee; and, second, because it tends to a monopoly").

266. Polygram Holdings, Inc., Docket No. 9298 (July 31, 2001) (administrative complaint).
267. *Id.*
268. *Id.*
269. Polygram Holdings, Inc., Docket No. 9298, 2003 FTC LEXIS 120 (July 24, 2003) (Opinion at 49).
270. *Id.* at 61.
271. Polygram Holdings, Inc., Docket No. 9298, (July 24, 2003) (Final Order). Warner Communications and the FTC settled the matter by consent agreement. Warner Communications, Inc., Docket No. C-4025 (Sept. 17, 2001) (Final Order). Polygram chose instead to litigate the matter at the FTC.
272. 441 U.S. 1, 23-24 (1979); *see also* Association of Indep. Television Stations v. College Football Ass'n, 637 F. Supp. 1289, 1297-98 (W.D.

number of output channels in the joint venture market and thus enhance competition. On the other hand, depending on the circumstances, such competition could also be found to lead to unlawful coordination among the parents and the venture.

To avoid improper coordination, the enforcement agencies or courts may require, in these circumstances, that the parents continue to act independently in making decisions concerning the output of the venture and that the transfer prices from the venture to the parents not exceed the venture's production costs.[273] In addition, the parents and the venture may be required to restrict the flow of confidential and competitively sensitive information between and among themselves so that all decisions by the parents and the venture as to their respective terms of trade and competitive strategies in the joint venture market are made unilaterally and independently.[274]

Okla. 1986).

273. *See, e.g.*, United States v. Alcan Aluminum Ltd., 605 F. Supp. 619 (W.D. Ky. 1985) (consent decree prohibiting parents from communicating with each other either directly or through the management company with regard to competitively sensitive matters, including future production schedules, present or future terms or conditions of sale, sales forecasts, marketing plans, and sales or proposed sales to specific customers; the consent decree further provided that each partner would independently determine its own product mix and level of output and be assured of the independent right to expand plant capacity); *cf.* General Motors Corp., 103 F.T.C. 374 (1984) (limiting production of small cars by GM-Toyota joint venture in order "to ensure that GM would retain incentives to fill remainder of its small car needs from other sources"). Concerns under Section 8 of the Clayton Act (interlocking directorates) may also be implicated where the joint venture competes with the parents. Section 8 is discussed in ABA SECTION OF ANTITRUST LAW, ANTITRUST LAW DEVELOPMENTS 401-407 (5th ed. 2002).

274. *See, e.g.*, *General Motors Corp.*, 103 F.T.C. at 384-85 (consent order restricting transfer of information between joint venture parents concerning current or future prices of new automobiles or parts, sales or production forecasts or plans for any product not produced by the venture, marketing plans for any product, and development and engineering activities relating to the joint venture's product); COMPETITOR COLLABORATIONS GUIDELINES, *supra* note 1, § 3.34(e) ("The Agencies evaluate the extent to which competitively sensitive information concerning markets affected by the collaboration likely would be disclosed."); HEALTH CARE STATEMENTS, *supra* note 23, Statement 6 (providing that information exchanges between health care providers require appropriate safeguards); U.S. Dep't of Justice, Business

4. *Restraints on Prices and Output*

In determining the legality of price and output restrictions imposed by collateral agreements under the rule of reason, the U.S. Supreme Court has focused on two factors: (1) the extent of integration between the participants in the venture and (2) the importance of the challenged restrictions in achieving the venture's legitimate objectives.[275] In

---

Review Letter to the Securities Industry Ass'n, (Sept. 23, 1999) (no intention to challenge information exchange designed to facilitate the conversion of equity securities and options trading from a fractional-based to decimal-based system because of limited nature of information to be exchanged and restrictions placed on dissemination of competitively sensitive information); U.S. Dep't of Justice, Business Review Letter to NSM Purchasing Ass'n, (Jan. 13, 1999) (no intention to challenge joint purchasing entity provided independent buying agent would keep all competitively sensitive information confidential and would not disseminate such information among members); U.S. Dep't of Justice, Business Review Letter to Apparel Industry P'ship, (Oct. 31, 1996) (no intention to challenge implementation of joint venture's code of industry conduct provided that steps were taken to avoid exchange of competitively sensitive information among rivals); U.S. Dep't of Justice, Business Review Letter to Auto. Transp. Fleet Affiliation (Apr. 19, 1994) (continuing competition between joint venture and its members and safeguards with respect to competitively sensitive information suggests joint venture will result in no anticompetitive effects); U.S. Dep't of Justice, Business Review Letter to Recording Indus. Ass'n of Am. (Mar. 14, 1991) (no intention to challenge venture to develop digital audio technology where structure of venture safeguarded against exchange of competitively sensitive information); U.S. Dep't of Justice, Business Review Letter to Petroleum Indeps. Coop. (Mar. 9, 1988) (no intention to challenge proposed association of natural gas producers where safeguards including confidentiality guidelines are in place); U.S. Dep't of Justice, Business Review Letter to Pump Research & Dev. Comm. (July 5, 1985) (no intention to challenge joint research venture in which nature of competition in industry and structural safeguards concerning exchange of competitively sensitive information insured against collusion among parties).

275. *Compare* Arizona v. Maricopa County Med. Soc'y, 457 U.S. 332, 356-57 (1982) (invalidating horizontal arrangement as per se unlawful where unintegrated "independent competing entrepreneurs" set maximum fees for health services provided under health plans) *with* Broadcast Music, Inc. v. CBS, 441 U.S. 1, 20, 21-24 (1979) (agreement on price was valid where accompanied by "integration of sales" and essential to offering new product).

Broadcast Music, for example, the Court upheld the price restraints accompanying the blanket licenses after having determined that "the agreement on price [was] necessary to market the product at all."[276] In *NCAA*, however, the Court invalidated the output restrictions imposed by the NCAA on televised college football games once it had decided that the restraints did not advance the association's goals of enhancing the competitiveness of televising college football and maintaining the integrity of college football as a distinctive and attractive product.[277]

Based on these U.S. Supreme Court decisions, lower courts have applied these two factors to collateral restraints in a variety of contexts.[278] In a case involving the allocation of costs of the joint

---

276. *Broadcast Music*, 441 U.S. at 23.

277. *See* NCAA v. Board of Regents, 468 U.S. 85, 114-17, 133-34 (1984). The Court found that the restraints imposed by the NCAA prevented the colleges and networks from bargaining for television broadcasts in a noncompetitive market.

278. *See, e.g.*, Fraser v. Major League Soccer, L.L.C., 7 F. Supp. 2d 73 (D. Mass. 1998) (applying rule of reason to soccer league's rule requiring soccer clubs hiring new players to pay a transfer fee because transfer fee had potential to reduce costs to consumers and enhance competition in the market for soccer matches); Fran Welch Real Estate Sales, Inc. v. Seabrook Island Co., 809 F.2d 1030, 1032-33 (4th Cir. 1987) (covenants between development company and landowners barring "for sale" and other commercial signs had reasonable business purpose based on aesthetics); Worthen Bank & Trust Co. v. National BankAmericard, Inc., 485 F.2d 119, 127-129 (8th Cir. 1973) (a joint venture restricting member banks from affiliating with any other national bank card was not a per se unlawful group boycott); Hassan v. Independent Practice Assocs., 698 F. Supp. 679, 688 (E.D. Mich. 1988) ("Price fixing agreements can be lawful if they are a necessary part of an integration of resources—a joint venture."); Hudson's Bay Co. Fur Sales v. American Legend Coop., 651 F. Supp. 819, 838-39 (D.N.J. 1986) (trademark restriction imposed by association of mink producers ancillary to attempt to improve efficiency of marketing fur products); American Floral Servs. v. Florists' Transworld Delivery Ass'n, 633 F. Supp. 201, 212-13 (N.D. Ill. 1986) (upholding joint venture "pirate order rules" which prevented florists from sending orders through wire service other than those requested by customers); National Bank of Can. v. Interbank Card Ass'n, 507 F. Supp. 1113, 1123 (S.D.N.Y. 1980) (upholding exclusivity provisions in bank credit card license under the rule of reason), *aff'd*, 666 F.2d 6 (2d Cir. 1981); Van Dyk Research Corp. v. Xerox Corp., 478 F. Supp. 1268, 1304 (D.N.J. 1979) (upholding a joint venture for xerography which divided world markets for output since the restraints "were reasonable and ancillary to the formation of speculative business ventures"), *aff'd*, 631

venture, for example, the Eleventh Circuit, in *National Bancard Corp. v. VISA U.S.A., Inc.*,[279] upheld a bank credit card's interchange fee system, reasoning that the fee established a necessary term without which the system could not function.[280] The Eleventh Circuit also relied on the district court's finding that nothing impeded members of the joint venture from making alternative arrangements outside the interchange fee system.[281] However, in a similar case involving credit card networks, the U.S. District Court for the Southern District of New York, also employing the rule of reason, held that bylaws adopted by the Visa and MasterCard which allowed issuers to issue cards of either association, but not those of American Express or Discovery, violated Section 1 because the restrictions weakened competition between networks and harmed consumers.[282]

F.2d 251 (3d Cir. 1980); United States v. E.I. du Pont de Nemours & Co., 118 F. Supp. 41, 219 (D. Del. 1953) (territorial restrictions incident to the licensing of the right to manufacture cellophane granted by a French company to a U.S. company upheld as ancillary to the establishment of a new business), *aff'd*, 351 U.S. 377 (1956); Brown v. Pro Football, Inc., 1992-1 Trade Cas. (CCH) ¶ 69,747, at 67,405-06 (D.D.C. 1992) (NFL unable sufficiently to demonstrate necessity of salary restraint).

279. 779 F.2d 592 (11th Cir. 1986).

280. *But see In re* Arbitration Between First Tex. Sav. Ass'n and Financial Interchange, Inc., 55 Antitrust & Trade Reg. Rep. (BNA) No. 1380, at 340, 350-51, 374 (Aug. 25, 1988) (Kauper, Arb.) (automated teller machine network's practice of establishing a uniform interchange fee for ATM transactions without a provision for charging a surcharge and granting rebate by the owner/operator of the machine which could be settled through the network's system—although not per se illegal—constitutes an unreasonable restraint of trade).

281. *See* National Bancard Corp. v. VISA USA Inc., 596 F. Supp. 1231, 1254-55 (S.D. Fla. 1984), *aff'd*, 779 F.2d 592 (11th Cir. 1986); *see also* Stratmore v. Goodbody, 866 F.2d 189, 193 (6th Cir. 1989) (restriction on auctions were not considered a restraint since seller had alternative means to reach customers); Buffalo Broad. Co. v. American Soc'y of Composers, Authors & Publishers, 744 F.2d 917, 924-28 (2d Cir. 1984) (restraint of trade depends in part on whether joint venture members offer realistic alternative to blanket copyright license); CBS v. American Soc'y of Composers, Authors, and Publishers, 620 F.2d 930, 936-39 (2d Cir. 1980) (blanket licensing was not restraint of trade in part because composers retained right to license compositions independently); *cf. Board of Regents*, 468 U.S. at 114 n.54 (freedom of individual schools to increase output central to evaluation of joint venture) (citation omitted).

282. United States v. VISA USA Inc. and Mastercard Int'l Inc., 163 F. Supp. 2d 322 (S.D.N.Y. 2001), *aff'd*, 344 F.3d 229 (2d Cir. 2003).

The licensing of intellectual property and the creation of so-called "patent pools" may present unique challenges to courts or enforcement agencies analyzing joint ventures. The *Intellectual Property Guidelines* recognize that intellectual property licensing arrangements are "typically welfare-enhancing and procompetitive."[283] However, "antitrust concerns may arise when a licensing arrangement harms competition among entities that would have been actual or likely potential competitors in a relevant market in the absence of the license."[284] With respect to pooling arrangements, the *Merger Guidelines* repeat the same analytical principles. The *Intellectual Property Guidelines* note that pooling arrangements "may provide procompetitive benefits by integrating complementary technologies, reducing transaction costs, clearing blocking positions, and avoiding costly infringement litigation."[285] However, where pooling arrangements "are mechanisms to accomplish naked price fixing or market division," or where they "diminish competition among entities that would have been actual or likely potential competitors in a relevant market in the absence of the cross-license," they are subject to challenge.[286] Applying this distraction, the FTC brought complaints against VISX, and Summit Technology, the only competitors in the market for photorefractive keratectomy ("PRK"), also known as "laser eye surgery," alleging that the companies had agreed to fix prices and eliminate competition between them by forming a patent pool and establishing a fixed fee system for licensing the pooled

283. INTELLECTUAL PROPERTY GUIDELINES, *supra* note 21, § 3.1.

284. *Id.*

285. *Id.* § 5.5.

286. *Id.* The DOJ has generally applied a rule of reason approach in analyzing patent pools or other intellectual property collaborations between competitors, focusing on factors that ensure continued competition between members of the pool. Among the factors considered by the DOJ are: whether the pool is essential to developing or implementing a standard; the royalty rate relative to the cost of manufacturing downstream products; whether licenses are granted in a nondiscriminatory manner; whether patent holders are allowed to license patents outside of the pool; whether competitively sensitive information will be shared between the members of the pool, and; whether pool members retain the economic incentive to compete and innovate. *See e.g.*, U.S. Dep't of Justice Business Review Letter to 3G Patent Platform Partnership (Nov. 12, 2002); U.S. Dep't of Justice Business Review Letter to DVD 6C (June 10, 1999); U.S. Dep't of Justice Business Review Letter to DVD 3C (Dec. 16, 1998); U.S. Dep't of Justice Business Review Letter to MPEG LA (June 26, 1997).

patents.[287] In order to resolve the FTC's concerns, the two firms entered into a consent agreement with the FTC in which they agreed to dissolve the patent pool and refrain from future efforts to fix prices.[288]

Courts have been particularly wary of price or output restraints that preclude the joint venture members from competing with the venture. For example, in *United States v. Columbia Pictures Industries*,[289] the court found that the Premiere allocation formula was a substitute for competitive negotiations over the value of individual films and that the restraints amounting to price fixing in the Premiere agreement were "hardly ancillary," but rather, were the "heart of the joint venture and its reason for being."[290] Although the fact that the network was the creation of the alleged coconspirators made it an "unusual price fixing situation,"[291] the court nonetheless found that the pricing mechanisms, if not illegal per se, were likely facially unreasonable.[292] More recently, in *Freeman v. San Diego Ass'n of Realtors*, the Ninth Circuit rejected the defendants' argument that fixing prices at supracompetitive levels was necessary to induce smaller, less efficient associations to join the venture.[293] According to the court, this argument failed because: "Inefficiency is precisely what the market aims to weed out. The Sherman Act, to put it bluntly, contemplates some roadkill on the turnpike to Efficiencyville."[294]

---

287. Summit Technology, Inc. and VISX, Inc., Docket No. 9286 (Mar. 24, 1998) (Administrative Complaint).
288. Summit Technology, Inc. and VISX, Inc., Docket No. 9286 (Mar. 5, 1999) (Decision and Order).
289. 507 F. Supp. 412 (S.D.N.Y. 1980).
290. *Id*. at 430.
291. *Id*. at 427.
292. *See id*. at 433; *see also* Premier Elec. Constr. Co. v. National Elec. Contractors Ass'n, 814 F.2d 358, 368-71 (7th Cir. 1987) (mandatory fee assessment on contractors per se illegal); Chicago Prof'l Sports Ltd. Partnership v. NBA, 754 F. Supp. 1336, 1359-62 (N.D. Ill. 1991) (sports league restriction on number of games televised illegal under rule of reason); COMPACT v. Metropolitan Gov't, 594 F. Supp. 1567, 1577-79 (M.D. Tenn. 1984) (agreement by minority-owned architectural firms not to bid individually on projects on which they were bidding jointly was akin to price fixing); Nippon Sheet Glass Co., 113 F.T.C. 715 (1990) (consent order terminating provision in joint venture agreement which prohibited joint venturers from acquiring productive capacity outside the joint venture).
293. Freeman v. San Diego Ass'n of Realtors, 322 F.3d 1133, 1152-53 (9th Cir. 2003).
294. *Id*. at 1154.

5. *Territorial and Customer Restraints*

The analysis of restraints on territorial and customer allocation in connection with a joint venture has been the subject of some debate.[295] In *United States v. Topco Associates*,[296] the U.S. Supreme Court held that horizontal territorial limitations, standing alone, were per se illegal.[297] In that case, twenty-five small to medium sized supermarkets set up a purchasing cooperative association in connection with which the parties agreed to divide resale territories and grant the original assignee a complete veto over new entrants. Although the exclusive territorial restrictions were struck down as unlawful, the establishment of a purchasing cooperative (that acted as a joint purchasing agent) and the creation of a private Topco label by the cooperative were not overturned. The trial court found that collaboration between the chains and supermarkets created economies of scale which in turn led to lower prices and greater competition with the national chains.[298] After remand, the district court entered a final judgment permitting Topco to utilize areas of primary responsibility, designate warehouse locations, determine the locations of places of business for trademark licensees, terminate the membership of businesses not adequately promoting Topco products, and formulate and implement profit pass overs, unless such practices directly or indirectly achieved or maintained territorial exclusivity.[299]

In *Rothery Storage & Van Co. v. Atlas Van Lines*,[300] the D.C. Circuit questioned the continuing validity of *Topco* to the extent that it stands for the proposition that horizontal territorial restrictions that are ancillary to a legitimate joint venture are per se illegal.[301] The court opined that post-*Topco* decisions such as *Broadcast Music* and *NCAA* have limited the per se treatment to restraints that "'would always or almost always tend to

---

295. *See generally* Rothery Storage & Van Co. v. Atlas Van Lines, 792 F.2d 210 (D.C. Cir. 1986).
296. 405 U.S. 596, 608 (1972).
297. *See* United States v. Sealy, Inc., 388 U.S. 350 (1967) (horizontal territorial restraints per se illegal); Timken Roller Bearing Co. v. United States, 341 U.S. 593 (1951) (same).
298. *Topco*, 405 U.S. at 606 (citing United States v. Topco Assocs., 319 F. Supp. 1031, 1043 (N.D. Ill. 1970)).
299. *See* United States v. Topco Assocs., 1973-1 Trade Cas. (CCH) ¶ 74,391 (N.D. Ill. 1972), *as amended*, 1973-1 Trade Cas. (CCH) ¶ 74,485 (N.D. Ill.), *aff'd*, 414 U.S. 801 (1973).
300. 792 F.2d 210 (D.C. Cir. 1986).
301. *See id.* at 226.

restrict competition and decrease output,'"[302] and that horizontal territorial restraints that are ancillary to a legitimate joint activity must be analyzed under the rule of reason.[303] The *Topco* decision, however, has never been overruled, and it was cited by the U.S. Supreme Court after the D.C. Circuit's *Rothery* decision for the proposition that "agreements between competitors to allocate territories to minimize competition are illegal."[304]

The FTC and the Eighth Circuit in *Brunswick Corp.*[305] distinguished territorial restrictions imposed by a legitimate joint venture from a horizontal territorial division of markets having no purpose other than to restrain competition. The FTC held that the rule of *Topco* was inapplicable to the former and proceeded to evaluate the three collateral agreements imposed by a joint venture between the respondents Yamaha and Brunswick under the rule of reason.[306] Nevertheless, all three agreements were found to be illegal under the rule of reason because they were not "limited to those inevitably arising out of the dealings between partners, or necessary (and of no broader scope than necessary) to make

302. *Id.* at 228 (quoting Broadcast Music, Inc. v. CBS, 441 U.S. 1, 19-20 (1979) (emphasis removed)).

303. *See id.* at 229; *see also* Polk Bros. v. Forest City Enters., 776 F.2d 185, 188-89 (7th Cir. 1985) (distinguishing between "naked" restraints and "ancillary" restraints and explaining why ancillary restraints should be tested under the rule of reason).

304. Palmer v. BRG of Ga., Inc., 498 U.S. 46, 49 (1990) (per curiam); *see also* Business Elecs. Corp. v. Sharp Elecs. Corp., 485 U.S. 717, 734 (1988). In the amicus brief filed by the United States in *Palmer*, the DOJ noted that some lower courts have read subsequent decisions of the U.S. Supreme Court as effectively overruling *Topco* "to the extent *Topco* can be said to hold ancillary market allocations per se unlawful." Brief for the United States as Amicus Curiae at 10 n.9, Palmer v. BRG of Ga., Inc., 498 U.S. 46 (1990) (No. 89-1667). The Division argued that the Court need not reach that aspect of *Topco* for the purposes of deciding *Palmer*. One district court relied on *Topco* in finding that horizontal territorial restraints imposed by a food distribution cooperative were per se illegal. *See* Bascom Food Prods. Corp. v. Reese Finer Foods, Inc., 715 F. Supp. 616, 632 (D.N.J. 1989). The district court noted that the U.S. Supreme Court has never indicated an intent to overrule *Topco* and that the per se treatment of horizontal territorial restraints was acknowledged in *Business Electronics*. *See id.*

305. 94 F.T.C. 1174, 1251-52 (1979), *aff'd in part and modified in part sub nom.*, Yamaha Motor Co. v. FTC, 657 F.2d 971 (8th Cir. 1981).

306. *See* 94 F.T.C. at 1251-53.

the joint venture work."[307] The agreements thus held illegal included (1) a territorial limitation imposed upon Yamaha by Brunswick,[308] (2) an agreement to limit competition between the joint venturers in certain parts of the world,[309] and (3) a "technical assistance agreement" that effectively barred Brunswick from manufacturing products that might compete with Yamaha products, including products not involved in the joint venture.[310]

Following this reasoning, many lower courts have now held that territorial and customer restraints ancillary to a joint venture are not per se unlawful.[311] Those decisions striking down attempts by joint venture

---

307. *Id.* at 1275 (citing United States v. Columbia Pictures Corp., 189 F. Supp. 153, 178 (S.D.N.Y. 1960)).

308. *See id.* at 1276. Under this agreement, Brunswick was permitted to market its products in competition with the joint venture worldwide (including Japan), but Yamaha was prohibited from selling non-joint venture products anywhere but in Japan. The FTC determined that foreclosing Yamaha from continuing its competitive efforts in the United States amounted to a division of markets outside the ambit of the joint venture. The elimination of Yamaha as an actual potential competitor in the U.S. market only served the anticompetitive goal of insulating Brunswick from Yamaha in the United States. As such, the FTC found the agreement to be an impermissible collateral restriction. *See id.*

309. This agreement limited competition between the defendants in the "non-exclusive markets," principally Europe and South America. The FTC determined that the agreement was wholly unrelated to the legitimate ends of the joint venture and that "it [was], on its face, a naked agreement between horizontal competitors to direct their competitive efforts away from each other." *Id.* at 1277; *see also Yamaha Motor Co. v. FTC*, 657 F.2d at 981.

310. The Technical Assistance Agreement went beyond the outboard motors produced by the joint venture to foreclose Brunswick from manufacturing any product competitive with Yamaha except snowmobiles. Thus, the agreement was deemed to be impermissibly broad and lacking in any offsetting procompetitive benefits. *See Brunswick Corp.*, 94 F.T.C. at 1277-78; *see also Yamaha Motor Co.*, 657 F.2d at 981.

311. *See, e.g.*, Northrop Corp. v. McDonnell Douglas Corp., 705 F.2d 1030, 1050-54 (9th Cir. 1983) ("teaming arrangement" by which one joint venturer would be prime contractor for land-based aircraft and the other would be prime contractor for carrier-based aircraft should be judged under rule of reason); Hudson's Bay Co. Fur Sales Inc. v. American Legend Coop., 651 F. Supp. 819, 838-39 (D.N.J. 1986) (trademark restrictions imposed by association of mink producers were restraints ancillary to attempt to improve efficiency of marketing fur products); American Floral Servs. v. Florists' Transworld Delivery Ass'n, 633 F.

participants to divide markets or allocate customers among themselves have generally done so only after determining that the restraint was not reasonably ancillary to the venture.[312]

6. Restraints on Access to the Joint Venture

A joint venture may also affect competition by excluding rivals to the venture. Courts examine a number of criteria in evaluating the legality of a venture's refusal to deal with a horizontal competitor, including (1) the degree to which access is essential to effective competition;[313] (2) the nature and scope of the joint venture's power in the relevant market;[314] (3) the degree to which the benefits of the venture

---

Supp. 201, 212-13 (N.D. Ill. 1986) (joint venture "pirate order rules" upheld as legitimate response to threat of free-riding); Van Dyk Research Corp. v. Xerox Corp., 478 F. Supp. 1268, 1304 (D.N.J. 1979) (upholding a joint venture which divided world markets for output since the restraints "were reasonable and ancillary to the formation of speculative business ventures"), *aff'd*, 631 F.2d 251 (3d Cir. 1980); United States v. E.I. du Pont de Nemours & Co., 118 F. Supp. 41, 219 (D. Del. 1953) (territorial restrictions incident to the licensing of the right to manufacture cellophane granted by a French company to a U.S. company upheld as ancillary to the establishment of a new business), *aff'd*, 351 U.S. 377 (1956). *But see* Panache Broad. v. Richardson Elecs., 1993-1 Trade Cas. (CCH) ¶ 70,169, at 69,817-18 (N.D. Ill. 1993) (granting leave to replead where a joint venture between horizontal competitors might be construed to contain an illegal agreement to allocate customers).

312. *See, e.g.*, Blackburn v. Sweeney, 53 F.3d 825, 828 (7th Cir. 1995) (geographic restriction on advertising held not ancillary to dissolution agreement between partners); General Leaseways, Inc. v. National Truck Leasing Ass'n, 744 F.2d 588, 592-95 (7th Cir. 1984) (market division not likely to be justified by needs of reciprocal arrangement for servicing of trucks); Los Angeles Mem'l Coliseum Comm'n v. NFL, 726 F.2d 1381, 1395-98 (9th Cir. 1984) (rule effecting territorial allocation not justified where less restrictive alternative was available); Engine Specialties, Inc. v. Bombardier Ltd., 605 F.2d 1, 11 (1st Cir. 1979) (holding unlawful provisions prohibiting the foreign participant from manufacturing in North America and the U.S. participant from manufacturing outside North America); COMPACT v. Metropolitan Gov't, 594 F. Supp. 1567, 1574-77 (M.D. Tenn. 1984) (agreement to bid only as joint venture for certain contracts was per se unlawful horizontal allocation of markets because of absence of integration efficiencies).

313. *See, e.g.*, United States v. Terminal R.R. Ass'n, 224 U.S. 383 (1912).

314. *See, e.g.*, Northwest Wholesale Stationers, Inc. v. Pacific Stationery & Printing Co., 472 U.S. 284 (1985).

can be duplicated by non-participants in some other fashion, such as the formation of a similar joint enterprise;[315] and (4) the business reasons for the refusal to grant access.[316]

In *United States v. Terminal Railroad Ass'n*,[317] fourteen railroad companies formed a joint venture to acquire and operate terminal companies and limited the use of these facilities to member companies. The U.S. Supreme Court held that the denial of access to nonmembers violated Section 1 of the Sherman Act because the geographical conditions were such that no competition was possible without the use of the facilities that were wholly owned by the joint venture.[318] In so holding, the Court noted that it dealt with "extraordinary" circumstances, and that:

> [I]n ordinary circumstances, a number of independent companies [may lawfully] combine for the purpose of controlling or acquiring terminals for their common but exclusive use. In such cases other companies [may] be admitted upon terms or excluded altogether. If such terms were too onerous, there would ordinarily remain the right and power to construct their own terminals.[319]

In *Associated Press v. United States*,[320] over twelve hundred newspapers had formed a cooperative joint venture news gathering association which did not allow dissemination of the news it gathered to nonmembers and provided members with a competitive veto over membership decisions. The Court held this restraint on membership to be unlawful, finding that the effect of the inability to buy news from the "largest news agency"[321] or any of its members was "seriously to limit the opportunity of any new paper to enter these cities."[322] In both cases, the Court, rather than invalidating the whole joint venture, required that

---

315. *See, e.g.*, SCFC ILC, Inc. v. Visa USA, Inc., 36 F.3d 958, 971 (10th Cir. 1994) (citing Associated Press v. United States, 326 U.S. 1 (1945)).
316. *See Northwest Wholesale Stationers*, 472 U.S. at 296.
317. 224 U.S. 383 (1912).
318. *See id.* at 397-405.
319. *Id.* at 405. *See also* Dennis W. Carlton & Steven C. Salop, *You Keep Knocking But You Can't Come In: Evaluating Restrictions on Access to Joint Ventures*, 9 HARV. J.L. & TECH. 319, 330 (1996) (discussing the potential harm of a joint venture access rule).
320. 326 U.S. 1 (1945).
321. *Id.* at 13.
322. *Id.*

the venture be modified to provide reasonable access to the excluded firms.[323]

The U.S. Supreme Court more recently addressed the exclusion of companies seeking membership in a joint venture in *Northwest Wholesale Stationers, Inc. v. Pacific Stationery & Printing Co.*,[324] in which a wholesale buying cooperative had expelled a member that had refused to abide by the cooperative's rules. Finding that the "act of expulsion from a wholesale cooperative does not necessarily imply anticompetitive animus and thereby raise a probability of anticompetitive effect," the U.S. Supreme Court declined to apply the per se rule to all limitations on access to joint buying cooperatives.[325] The Court held that "[u]nless the cooperative possesses market power or exclusive access to an element essential to effective competition, the conclusion that expulsion is virtually always likely to have an anticompetitive effect is not warranted."[326] The Court further held that "[w]hen the plaintiff challenges expulsion from a joint buying cooperative [under the per se rule], some showing must be made that the cooperative possesses market power or unique access to a business element necessary for effective competition."[327] In all other cases, the reasons for the exclusion and its effects are analyzed under the rule of reason.[328]

Based on these U.S. Supreme Court decisions, lower federal courts and the enforcement agencies have generally applied the rule of reason and upheld denials of access to or membership in a joint venture.[329]

---

323. In *Terminal Railroad*, 224 U.S. at 411-12, the Court held that the joint venture must allow any railroad joint ownership or the use of the terminal facilities on reasonable and nondiscriminatory terms and abolish its discriminatory charges and billing practices. In *Associated Press*, 326 U.S. at 21, the Court upheld the establishment of the venture and any objective membership criteria, but rejected arbitrary competitive vetoes on the admission of nonmembers.

324. 472 U.S. 284 (1985); *see also* Radiant Burners, Inc. v. People's Gas Light & Coke Co., 364 U.S. 656 (1961) (discussing a claim by excluded outsiders).

325. 472 U.S. at 296; *see id.* at 295-98.

326. *Id*. at 296.

327. *Id*. at 298.

328. *See id*. at 296-97.

329. *See, e.g.*, Foundation for Interior Design Educ. Research v. Savannah Coll. of Art and Design, 244 F.3d 521, 531 (6th Cir. 2001) (applying rule of reason to accrediting body's denial of accreditation to college's interior design program because no evidence of market power); Big Bear Lodging Ass'n v. Snow Summit, Inc., 182 F.3d 1096, 1103-04 (9th Cir. 1999) (reversing district court's dismissal of plaintiff's claim that defendants

Most courts that have done so have found that market power or exclusive access to an essential element of competition did not exist.[330]

---

participated in a group boycott in violation of the Sherman Act when joint venture of ski resorts refused to sell discount lift tickets to nonmembers); Retina Assocs. v. Southern Baptist Hosp. of Fla., 105 F.3d 1376, 1381-82 (10th Cir. 1997) (applying rule of reason to eye care network's refusal to deal with nonaffiliated retina specialists); SCFC ILC, Inc. v. Visa USA, Inc., 36 F.3d 958, 969-70 (10th Cir. 1994) (exclusion of issuers of competitive credit cards from Visa joint venture not unlawful where relevant market of general purpose credit card issuers was unconcentrated, evidence was insufficient to establish that venture had market power, and the restraint was reasonably related to the venture's operation); Charley's Taxi Radio Dispatch Corp. v. SIDA of Haw., Inc., 810 F.2d 869, 878 (9th Cir. 1987) (exclusion of taxi fleet from association of taxi drivers was not unlawful since association did not possess market power); Rothery Storage & Van Co. v. Atlas Van Lines, 792 F.2d 210, 221, 229-30 (D.C. Cir. 1986) (applying rule of reason and noting that the "evidence . . . demonstrates the absence of market power in any van line, much less Atlas"); Futurevision Cable Sys. v. Multivision Cable TV Corp., 789 F. Supp. 760, 774-75 (S.D. Miss. 1992) (applying the rule of reason after noting that "[n]owhere in the complaint does [the plaintiff] allege that [the defendant] possesses market power"), *aff'd mem.*, 986 F.2d 1418 (5th Cir. 1993); Hassan v. Independent Practice Assocs., 698 F. Supp. 679, 694-95 (E.D. Mich. 1988) (20% market share insufficient); National Bank of Can. v. Interbank Card Ass'n, 507 F. Supp. 1113, 1122-23 (S.D.N.Y. 1980) (joint venture membership restrictions were not unlawful group boycott), *aff'd*, 666 F.2d 6 (2d Cir. 1981); *cf.* United States v. Realty Multi-List, Inc., 629 F.2d 1351, 1372-74 (5th Cir. 1980) (pre-*Northwest Wholesale Stationers* case holding that threshold inquiry into market power needed to determine if denial of access foreclosed opportunity to compete effectively on equal terms). *But see* Bascom Food Prods. Corp. v. Reese Finer Foods, Inc., 715 F. Supp. 616, 632-34 (D.N.J. 1989) (granting preliminary injunction where there was sufficient evidence to establish that there was a horizontal group boycott and that plaintiffs would be unable to compete in the relevant market without access to defendants' products); United States v. Columbia Pictures Indus., 507 F. Supp. 412, 432-33 (S.D.N.Y. 1980) (agreement among motion picture companies forming pay television network joint venture to make movies available to the venture nine months before making them available to competing networks held likely facially unreasonable), *aff'd mem.*, 659 F.2d 1063 (2d Cir. 1981).

330. *See, e.g.*, *Charley's Taxi Radio Dispatch Corp., Inc.*, 810 F.2d at 878 (exclusion of taxi fleet from association of taxi drivers was not unlawful since association did not possess market power); *Rothery Storage*, 792 F.2d at 229 (restrictions imposed by defendant with only 6% of the

Some courts have commented, primarily in dicta and reaching apparently inconsistent conclusions, on whether a finding of market power or exclusive access to an essential element of competition is itself sufficient to mandate per se treatment of membership restrictions or expulsions. One court, for example, has noted that "*Northwest Stationers* says only that 'market power or exclusive access' is a necessary precondition before expulsion from a cooperative should be deemed per se unreasonable. Neither market power nor exclusive access is a sufficient condition . . . ."[331] A few decisions, however, seem to imply that under *Northwest Wholesale Stationers* a finding of either market power or exclusive access to an essential element of competition is both necessary and sufficient to mandate per se treatment of access restraints to, or expulsions from, a joint venture.[332]

---

market lacked the ability to reduce output or increase price); *Realty Multi-List.*, 629 F.2d at 1372-74 (threshold inquiry into market power needed to determine if denial of access foreclosed opportunity to compete effectively on equal terms); *Hassan*, 698 F. Supp. at 694-95 (20% market share insufficient).

331. Carleton v. Vermont Dairy Herd Improvement Ass'n, 782 F. Supp. 926, 933 (D. Vt. 1991); *see also SCFC ILC*, 36 F.3d at 965 (finding that market power did not exist but noting that, "[i]f market power is found, the court may then proceed under rule of reason analysis to assess the procompetitive justifications of the alleged anticompetitive conduct"); *cf.* Wilk v. American Med. Ass'n, 895 F.2d 352, 359 (7th Cir. 1990) (noting that in the context of a learned profession and the facts there at issue, the nature and extent of the restraint's anticompetitive effect were too uncertain to warrant per se treatment); Hahn v. Oregon Physicians' Serv., 868 F.2d 1022, 1030 n.9 (9th Cir. 1988) (*Northwest Wholesale Stationers* "seems to suggest that the facts be developed as in a rule of reason case . . . in order to determine whether the conduct is per se illegal").

332. *See, e.g.*, Carpet Group Int'l v. Oriental Rug Importers Ass'n, 227 F.3d 62, 74 (3d Cir. 2000) (applying per se rule to association of importers/wholesalers of oriental rugs who refused to deal with manufacturers that sold directly to U.S. retailers because a strong inference of market power could be drawn and there was no procompetitive justification for the challenged conduct); Wigod v. Chicago Mercantile Exch., 981 F.2d 1510, 1517 (7th Cir. 1992) (holding that a per se claim had been alleged because the defendant Mercantile Exchange "is a monopolistic market that wields great control over who may be a member"); All Care Nursing Serv. v. Bethesda Mem'l Hosp., 887 F.2d 1535, 1540 (11th Cir. 1989) (Tjoflat, C.J., concurring) (reviewing *Northwest Wholesale Stationers* and concluding that, "[i]f the court finds either .. . market power *or* . . . control over access to an essential element of competition, then the court should apply the per se

In addition to undertaking a threshold inquiry into market power, lower courts have resorted to a rule of reason analysis in order to determine whether access restraints are reasonably necessary to the accomplishment of the joint venture's legitimate goals.[333] Here, courts have generally recognized that requiring a joint venture to open its facilities to competitors who did not share the costs and risks inherent in creating the joint venture would undermine the incentives companies have to create efficiency-enhancing joint ventures.[334] They have held, therefore, at least where a joint venture lacks market power, that it is a valid business justification that the venture believes a competitor is seeking a "free ride" by taking advantage of facilities it had "done nothing to create but had chosen to compete against."[335] In such circumstances, some courts have held that so long as the refusal "is not objectively anticompetitive the fact that it was motivated by hostility to competitors . . . is irrelevant."[336]

The *Health Care Statements* likewise provide generally for a rule of reason analysis of arrangements excluding others from health care joint ventures, such as providers from physician or multiprovider networks.[337] The *Health Care Statements* focus not on whether a particular provider has been harmed by the exclusion but on whether the exclusion reduces competition among providers in the market and thereby harms consumers. That analysis requires an assessment and balancing of potential procompetitive and anticompetitive effects, which in turn requires an evaluation of the market structure, the basis for the exclusion,

---

rule"); *Bascom Food Prods. Corp.*, 715 F. Supp. at 633-34 (noting that per se treatment likely would be appropriate because of the substantial allegations that the defendant possessed exclusive access to an element essential to competition and related market power).

333. *See Realty Multi-List*, 629 F.2d at 1362-64; *see also Rothery Storage & Van Co.*, 792 F.2d at 224.

334. *See, e.g.*, SCFC ILC, Inc. v. Visa USA, Inc., 36 F.3d at 968-71 and n.20 ("[S]electivity in the membership of a joint venture often enhances a joint venture's procompetitive potential. Forcing joint ventures to open membership to all competitors . . . would decrease the incentives to form joint ventures . . . ." (citing U.S. DEP'T OF JUSTICE, ANTITRUST ENFORCEMENT GUIDELINES FOR INTERNATIONAL OPERATIONS § 3.42 (1988))).

335. *Id.* at 970.

336. *Id.* (quoting Olympia Equip. Leasing Corp. v. Western Union Tel. Co., 797 F.2d 370, 379 (7th Cir. 1986)).

337. *See* HEALTH CARE STATEMENTS, *supra* note 22.

and the resulting competitive incentives, all of which are integral to a rule of reason analysis.

CHAPTER 9

POTENTIAL COMPETITION DOCTRINE

The potential competition doctrine addresses the question of whether a firm that is not currently competing in a market still has a procompetitive influence on the market because of the firm's potential for entry. Underlying the doctrine is the belief that a market exhibiting high prices and profits will attract entry by additional firms, causing production to increase and prices and profits to fall toward a competitive level. The presence of firms outside the market with the potential to enter provides a present and/or future constraint on incumbent firms in a noncompetitive market, as the incumbents seek to prevent or delay new entry and respond to entry as it occurs.

In potential competition mergers, the potential entrant acquires (or is acquired by) a significant market participant. Such entry by acquisition eliminates the potential entrant as an independent entity that influences or could influence the competitive performance of the market. As a theory for challenging a merger, the potential competition doctrine considers whether the elimination of the potential competitor as a separate entity violates Section 7 of the Clayton Act by removing the entity's procompetitive influence. The potential competition doctrine consists of two different theories: the "actual potential competition" theory and the "perceived potential competition" theory.

The "actual potential competition" theory reasons that, but for the merger with the significant market participant, the acquiring firm actually would have entered the market either de novo or by acquiring a very small or "toehold" incumbent firm, thereby creating additional competition that would have deconcentrated the market or produced other long-run procompetitive benefits.[1] The merger with a significant

---

1. Though the maximum size of a toehold firm is the subject of some debate, the Federal Trade Commission has stated that it is "desirable to observe a general rule in potential competition cases that firms possessing no more than 10 percent in a target market (where, as here, the 4-firm concentration is approximately 60 percent or more) should ordinarily be presumed to be toehold or foothold firms." Budd Co., 86 F.T.C. 518, 582 (1975). Lower courts likewise have generally established the threshold at or near 10% of the market. *See* United States v. Black & Decker Mfg. Co., 430 F. Supp. 729, 767-68 (D. Md. 1976) (10% presumed a toehold, firm with more than 10% not a toehold). *But see* Missouri Portland

market participant eliminates the possibility of de novo or toehold entry by the potential entrant, and thus eliminates the possibility that the market in the future will become as competitive as it otherwise might have become if the potential competitor entered independently.[2] Under the actual potential competition theory, therefore, the injury to competition is the loss of the procompetitive *future* effect that the potential entrant would have had on the relevant market if the independent entry had not been preempted by the merger.[3]

The perceived potential competition theory is based on the premise that, if the current market participants perceive the presence of a potential entrant on the fringe of the market, they will limit their prices

---

Cement Co. v. Cargill, Inc., 498 F.2d 851, 865 n.29 (2d Cir. 1974) (firm with 10% of market is "probably too substantial" to be toehold candidate); United States v. Phillips Petroleum Co., 367 F. Supp. 1226, 1258 (C.D. Cal. 1973) ("acquisition of a company which ranks seventh in a concentrated market, holding a 6-7% share of the market, is simply not small enough to constitute a mere foothold acquisition"), *aff'd mem.*, 418 U.S. 906 (1974). The 1982 and 1984 *Merger Guidelines*, however, establish the threshold at 5%. *See* U.S. DEP'T OF JUSTICE, MERGER GUIDELINES, 47 Fed. Reg. 28,493 (1982) § IV(A)(3)(d), *reprinted in* 4 Trade Reg. Rep. (CCH) ¶13,102; U.S. DEP'T OF JUSTICE, MERGER GUIDELINES, 49 Fed. Reg. 26,823 (1984) § 4.134 [hereinafter 1984 MERGER GUIDELINES], *reprinted in* 4 Trade Reg. Rep. (CCH) ¶ 13,103.

2. Underlying the actual potential competition theory is the assumption that the addition of one more competitor to a concentrated market will increase output and reduce prices. There is, however, only conflicting empirical proof that market share and concentration are accurate indicators of the likely competitive conditions in an industry. Nonetheless, they remain the foundation of most merger analysis. There has been significant debate in economics literature concerning the empirical support for the existence of a relationship between the structure, conduct, and performance of industries. For discussions and summaries of the literature, *see* F. M. SCHERER & DAVID ROSS, INDUSTRIAL MARKET STRUCTURE AND ECONOMIC PERFORMANCE 57-96 (3d ed. 1990); Richard Schmalensee, *Inter-Industry Studies of Structure and Performance*, *in* 2 HANDBOOK OF INDUSTRIAL ORGANIZATION 952-1009 (Richard Schmalensee & Robert D. Willig, eds., 1989).

3. *See, e.g.*, William J. Baer, Director, Bureau of Competition, FTC, Report from the Bureau of Competition, Remarks Before the ABA Antitrust Section, Spring Meeting 1999 (Apr. 15, 1999), *at* www.ftcgov/speeches/other/baerspaba99.htm ("where the Commission is trying to protect future competition, potential competition doctrine and the use of innovation markets may be necessary for effective enforcement").

and refrain from engaging in anticompetitive behavior to deter de novo or toehold entry by the additional competitor.[4] But for the merger with the significant market participant, the acquiring firm that is a perceived potential entrant would have continued to exert a competitive influence on the conduct of the existing market participants simply by remaining as a potential competitor, poised to enter the market in the event market prices were to rise above competitive levels. The merger with a significant market participant reduces competition by eliminating the constraining influence on incumbents' behavior provided by the presence of the potential entrant on the fringe of the market. Under the perceived potential competition theory, therefore, the injury to competition is the loss of the *present* procompetitive influence exerted by the possible entrant on the relevant market. Thus, it matters little whether the

---

4. Underlying the perceived potential competition doctrine is the economic theory of limit pricing, i.e., that the incumbent firms will price below the level at which they otherwise could price to make entry appear unattractive and prevent entry by the potential entrant. *See* Joseph Bain, *A Note on Pricing in Monopoly and Oligopoly*, 39 AM. ECON. REV. 448 (1949). *See generally* DENNIS W. CARLTON & JEFFREY M. PERLOFF, MODERN INDUSTRIAL ORGANIZATION 343-47 (3d ed. 2000); F. M. SCHERER & DAVID ROSS, INDUSTRIAL MARKET STRUCTURE AND ECONOMIC PERFORMANCE 356-66 (3d ed. 1990). In related economic models, the current market participants may not attempt to deter all entry, but only slow the rate of entry into the industry. In these models, incumbent firms price the product at a level that is lower than the monopoly price, but higher than the price which deters all entry. *See, e.g., id.*; Darius W. Gaskins, Jr., *Dynamic Limit Pricing: Optimal Pricing under Threat of Entry,* 3 J. ECON. THEORY 306 (1971). Limit pricing models have been criticized, however, because entering firms are concerned with the post-entry price that will be encountered, and the pre-entry price need not demonstrate a commitment by incumbents regarding prices following entry. *See generally* JEAN TIROLE, THEORY OF INDUSTRIAL ORGANIZATION 367-74 (1988).

The threat of entry leads to lower prices under the economic theory of contestable markets. In contestable markets, firms can enter and exit sufficiently, quickly, and without cost so that incumbent firms cannot raise and maintain prices above a competitive level. *See* WILLIAM J. BAUMOL, ET AL., CONTESTABLE MARKETS AND THE THEORY OF INDUSTRY STRUCTURE (rev'd ed. 1988). The assumption about the ease and cost of entry and exit is typically counterfactual. *See* Marius Schwartz, *The Nature and Scope of Contestability Theory*, 38 OXFORD ECON. PAPERS 37 (1986); Marius Schwartz & Robert J. Reynolds, *Contestable Markets: An Uprising in the Theory of Industry Structure: Comment*, 73 AM. ECON. REV. 488-89 (1983).

perceived entrant would in fact have entered the market as long as the market participants believe such entry would be a reasonable possibility.

A. Origins of the Potential Competition Doctrine

The U.S. Supreme Court first addressed the potential competition doctrine in *United States v. Penn-Olin Chemical Co.*[5] In *Penn-Olin*, the government challenged the formation of a joint venture between Pennsalt and Olin Mathieson to market sodium chlorate in the southeastern United States. The district court had dismissed the government's complaint, finding that, although both Pennsalt and Olin Mathieson produced sodium chlorate and although expansion into sodium chlorate production in the southeastern United States (the relevant geographic market) would be natural for both companies, the two companies would not have both entered the southeastern market independently.[6]

The U.S. Supreme Court reversed, holding that even if only one of the companies would have entered on its own, the joint venture eliminated the potential competition that might have continued from the presence of the other firm on the fringe of the market.[7] Although the Court did not distinguish between the present and future effects on competition corresponding to the perceived and actual potential competition theories, the Court established the principle that the potential competition doctrine is applicable in Section 7 cases.[8]

---

5. 378 U.S. 158 (1964). There were issues that implicated the potential competition doctrine in *United States v. El Paso Natural Gas Co.*, 376 U.S. 651 (1964), but the U.S. Supreme Court did not apply a potential competition analysis in that case. El Paso, the major out-of-state natural gas supplier to the California market, acquired another supplier, which did not supply out-of-state gas to California but had submitted unsuccessful bids to the California market. *Id.* at 655. Thus, the merger involved an actual as well as potential competitor. *See* 5 PHILLIP AREEDA & DONALD F. TURNER, ANTITRUST LAW ¶ 1117a (1980); *see also* Missouri Portland Cement Co. v. Cargill, Inc., 498 F.2d 851, 861 n.15 (2d Cir. 1974) (for unsuccessful bidders, "the line between potential and actual competition loses much of its significance").
6. *See* United States v. Penn-Olin Chem. Co., 217 F. Supp. 110 (D. Del. 1963), *vacated*, 378 U.S. 158 (1964).
7. *See* United States v. Penn-Olin Chem. Co., 378 U.S. 158, 173 (1964).
8. *See id.*

The current potential competition doctrine was largely written by the U.S. Supreme Court in *United States v. Marine Bancorporation.*[9] In *Marine Bancorp.*, the United States challenged the acquisition of a Spokane bank by a bank headquartered in Seattle. Neither bank operated in the other's market, and thus the two banks were not actual competitors. The government argued that the acquisition would violate Section 7, however, because it would (1) eliminate the possibility that the Seattle bank would enter the Spokane market by other means and thus deconcentrate the market over the long run (actual potential competition) and (2) eliminate the present procompetitive effects resulting from the perception of current Spokane banks that the acquiring bank was operating just outside the market and could enter the Spokane market if the existing market participants engaged in anticompetitive behavior (perceived potential competition).[10] Following a trial, the district court entered judgment for the defendants, finding that there was (1) no reasonable probability that, absent the merger, the Seattle bank would enter the Spokane market in the foreseeable future and (2) no perceptible procompetitive effect from the Seattle bank's presence outside the market.[11]

The U.S. Supreme Court affirmed the district court articulating the necessary preconditions for the application of both the actual potential competition and the perceived potential competition theories. The Court explained that the potential competition doctrine (whether actual or perceived) is meaningful only as applied in concentrated target markets. If the target market is not concentrated, the existing market participants are unlikely to engage in anticompetitive behavior because of the existence of actual competition (without regard to *potential* competition) and the theories underlying the potential competition doctrine are inapplicable.[12]

---

9. 418 U.S. 602 (1974).
10. *See id.* at 614-15.
11. *See id.* at 616-17.
12. The Court elaborated, stating that:

> [T]he doctrine comes into play only where there are dominant participants in the target market engaging in interdependent or parallel behavior and with the capacity effectively to determine price and total output of goods or services. If the target market performs as a competitive market in traditional antitrust terms, the participants in the market will have no occasion to fashion their behavior to take into account the presence of a potential entrant. The present procompetitive effects that a perceived potential entrant may produce in an oligopolistic market will

The Court acknowledged its prior recognition of the perceived potential competition theory of illegality, stating that:

> [A] market extension merger may be unlawful if the target market is substantially concentrated, if the acquiring firm has the characteristics, capabilities, and economic incentive to render it a perceived, potential de novo entrant, and if the acquiring firm's pre-merger presence on the fringe of the target market in fact tempered oligopolistic behavior on the part of existing participants in the market.[13]

But, the Court continued, "[a]lthough the concept of perceived potential entry has been accepted in the Court's prior § 7 cases, the [actual] potential-competition theory upon which the government places principal reliance in the instant case has not."[14] The Court set forth two "essential preconditions" that must be found to exist before a court could apply the actual potential competition theory to invalidate an acquisition. According to the Court, "[i]t must be determined: (1) that in fact [the acquiring firm] has available means for entering the [target] market other than by acquiring [the target firm]; and (2) that those means offer a substantial likelihood of ultimately producing deconcentration of that market or other significant procompetitive effects."[15]

The Court ultimately determined that state banking regulations rendered it unlikely that the Seattle bank would be able to enter the Spokane market either de novo or through a toehold acquisition.[16] Accordingly, the government could not establish the existence of the two "essential preconditions" to the application of the actual potential competition theory and the Court therefore did not need to express any

---

> already have been accomplished if the target market is performing competitively. Likewise, there would be no need for concern about the prospects of long-term deconcentration [from an actual potential entrant] of a market which is in fact genuinely competitive.

Id. at 630-31.

13. *Id.* at 624-25. "In other words," the Court wrote, "[this] Court has interpreted § 7 as encompassing what is commonly known as the 'wings effect'—the probability that the acquiring firm prompted pre-merger procompetitive effects within the target market by being perceived by the existing firms in that market as likely to enter de novo. The elimination of such present pro-competitive effects may render a merger unlawful under § 7." *Id.* at 625 (citation omitted).
14. *Id.*
15. *Id.* at 633.
16. *See id.* at 633-39.

view as to the viability of that theory as a tool to challenge acquisitions under Section 7.[17] Moreover, the Court rejected the government's perceived potential competition theory, holding that because "[r]ational commercial bankers in Spokane . . . are aware of the regulatory barriers that render [the Seattle bank] an unlikely or an insignificant potential entrant . . .[,] it is improbable that [the Seattle bank] exerts any meaningful procompetitive influence over Spokane banks by 'standing in the wings.'"[18]

B. General Requirements of the Potential Competition Doctrine

In the years since the U.S. Supreme Court's decision in *Marine Bancorporation*, the potential competition doctrine has been infrequently used in litigation, and rarely successfully.[19] Nevertheless, the theory is still employed as a tool in the government's antitrust enforcement arsenal.[20] Indeed, since the mid-to-late 1990s the enforcement agencies' use of the potential competition doctrine has been somewhat

---

17. *Id.* at 639.
18. *Id.* at 639-40.
19. *See, e.g.*, Tenneco, Inc. v. FTC, 689 F.2d 346, 355 (2d Cir. 1982) (reversing FTC decision finding § 7 violation based on potential competition doctrine); Fraser v. Major League Soccer, 97 F. Supp. 2d 130, 141 (D. Mass. 2000) (finding that there is no potential competition where there was no market prior to the league's formation); United States v. Phillips Petroleum, 367 F. Supp. 1226, 1254-56 (C.D. Cal. 1973) (acquired firm viewed acquiring firm as potential entrant that may have placed downward pressure on prices), *aff'd mem.*, 418 U.S. 906 (1974); Brunswick Corp., 94 F.T.C. 1174, 1222 (1979) (manufacturer improved product on threat of entry by acquiring firm), *aff'd in part and modified in part sub nom.* Yamaha Motor Co. v. FTC, 657 F.2d 971 (8th Cir. 1981). In *Antitrust Law*, Judge Posner explains that the potential competition doctrine "remains pretty much where the Court left it in [1973]." RICHARD A. POSNER, ANTITRUST LAW 143 (2d ed. 2001).
20. *See, e.g.*, Grand Union Co., 102 F.T.C. 812, 1050-51 (1983); Tenneco, Inc., 98 F.T.C. 464, 577 n.3 (1981), *rev'd on other grounds*, 689 F.2d 346 (2d Cir. 1982); Heublein, Inc., 96 F.T.C. 385, 583 n.22 (1980); Brunswick Corp., 94 F.T.C. 1174, 1267 n.25 (1979) (Commission "confident" doctrine "eventually will receive the U.S. Supreme Court's approval"), *aff'd in part and modified in part sub nom.*, Yamaha Motor Co. v. FTC, 657 F.2d 971 (8th Cir. 1981); British Oxygen Co., 86 F.T.C. 1241, 1261-63 (1975), *rev'd sub nom.*, BOC Int'l, Ltd. v. FTC, 557 F.2d 24 (2d Cir. 1977); Beatrice Foods Co., 86 F.T.C. 1, 63 (1975), *aff'd,* 540 F.2d 303 (7th Cir. 1976).

reinvigorated, with the Federal Trade Commission (FTC or the Commission) employing the doctrine to challenge several acquisitions,[21] and the Antitrust Division of the U.S. Department of Justice (DOJ or the Division) utilizing the doctrine as well.[22] In fact, the theory appears to be particularly important in the area of innovation markets.[23]

---

21. *See* GenCorp Inc., Docket No. C-4099 (FTC Dec. 19, 2003) (decision and order) *at* www.ftc.gov/03/caselist/0310152/03123do031/0152.pdf; Pfizer Inc., 68 Fed. Reg. 19,827 (FTC Apr. 22, 2003); Baxter Int'l, Inc., 68 Fed. Reg. 1062 (FTC Jan. 8, 2003); Amgen Inc. & Immunex Corp., 67 Fed. Reg. 48,475 (FTC July 24, 2002); Bayer AG, 67 Fed. Reg. 39,395 (FTC June 7, 2002); Dow Chem. Co., Docket No. C-3999, 2001 FTC Lexis 27 (Mar. 15, 2001); Hoechst AG, Docket No. C-3919, 2000 FTC Lexis 3 (Jan. 18, 2000); Kroger Co., Docket No. C-3917, 2000 FTC Lexis 5 (Jan. 10, 2000); El Paso Energy Corp., Docket No. C-3915, 2000 FTC Lexis 7 (Jan. 6, 2000); Zeneca Group plc, 127 F.T.C. 874 (June 7, 1999) (consent order requiring Zeneca to transfer all rights and assets regarding one facet of the company); ABB AB, 127 F.T.C. 494 (Apr. 14, 1999) (consent decree requiring divestitures based on potential competition theory); Koninklijke Ahold NV, 127 F.T.C. 404 (Apr. 5, 1999); Institut Merieux, SA, [1987-1993 FTC Complaints & Orders Transfer Binder] Trade Reg. Rep. (CCH) ¶ 22,779 (Aug. 6, 1990); Atlantic Richfield Co., [1987-1993 FTC Complaints & Orders Transfer Binder] Trade Reg. Rep. (CCH) ¶ 22,878 (Nov. 26, 1990); Roche Holding Ltd., [1987-1993 FTC Complaints & Orders Transfer Binder] Trade Reg. Rep. (CCH) ¶ 22,879 (Nov. 28, 1990); William J. Baer, Director, Bureau of Competition, FTC, Report from the Bureau of Competition, Remarks Before the ABA Antitrust Section, Spring Meeting 1999, FTC Committee (Apr. 15, 1999), *at* www.ftc.gov/speeches/other/baerspaba99.htm; William J. Baer, Director, Bureau of Competition, FTC, FTC Perspectives on Competition Policy and Enforcement Initiatives in Electric Power, Remarks Before the Conference on The New Rules of the Game for Electric Power: Antitrust & Anticompetitive Behavior (Dec. 4, 1997), *at* www.ftc.gov/speeches/other/elec1204.htm (discussing the proposed Questar/Kern River merger, where the FTC challenged the transaction using a potential competition theory and the deal was abandoned).
22. *See* United States v. Bell Atl. Corp., Civ. No. 1:99CV01119 (filed May 7, 1999) (complaint), *at* www.usdoj.gov/atr/cases/f2400/2435.htm (in its complaint filed with the consent decree, the DOJ alleged that the merger would eliminate actual and potential competition in cellular mobile wireless telephone business); United States v. Allied Waste Indus., Inc., Civ. No. 1:99CV0192 (filed July 20, 1999) (complaint) (as part of consent decree proceedings, complaint alleged that merger would substantially lessen actual and potential competition in small container waste hauling in the St. Louis market), *at*

Certain general requirements must be established to prevail on a Section 7 challenge under the potential competition doctrine, regardless of whether the plaintiff seeks to demonstrate that the challenged acquisition will likely reduce competition by eliminating actual potential competition or perceived potential competition. First, as the U.S. Supreme Court in *Marine Bancorporation* pointed out, the target market must be concentrated. Second, as subsequent lower court and FTC decisions have recognized, the acquiring firm must be one of only a few equally likely potential entrants, because the elimination of one of many potential competitors would not substantially lessen either present or

---

www.usdoj.gov/atr/cases/f2500/2579.htm; United States v. Signature Flight Support Corp., Civ. No. 1:99CV 00537 (filed Mar. 1, 1999) (complaint), *at* www.usdoj.gov/atr/cases/f2200/2268.htm; (as more fully explained by the complaint accompanying the consent decree, DOJ required divestiture of flight services by flight support company because the proposed acquisition was likely to lessen potential competition in the market for FBO services at APA Airport); United States v. Imetal, Civ. No. 1:99CV01018 (filed Apr. 26, 1999) (complaint), *at* www.usdoj.gov/atr/cases/f2400/2472.htm (as explained more fully by the complaint, incident to a consent decree DOJ prevented proposed acquisition by producer of kaolin because "actual and potential competition between Imetal and ECC in the markets for water-washed kaolin, calcined kaolin, paper-grade GCC and fused silica [would] be eliminated"); United States v. Waste Mgmt., Inc., Civ. No. 98 CV 7168 (filed Dec. 2, 1998), *at* www.usdoj.gov/atr/cases/f2500/2508.htm; United States v. Halliburton Co., Civ. Action No. 98-CV-2340 (filed Sept. 29, 1998) (complaint), *at* www.usdoj.gov/atr/cases/f1900/1964.htm; United States v. Primestar, Inc., Civ. No. 1:98CV01193 (filed May 12, 1998) (complaint), *at* www.usdoj.gov/atr/cases/f1700/1757.htm. *But cf.* United States v. Rank Org. plc, 1990-2 Trade Cas. (CCH) ¶ 69,257 (C.D. Cal. 1990).

23. *See, e.g.*, William J. Baer, Director, Bureau of Competition, FTC, Report from the Bureau of Competition, Remarks Before the American Bar Association Antitrust Section, Spring Meeting 1999 (Apr. 15, 1999), *at* www.ftc.gov/speeches/other/baerspaba99.htm; Joel I. Klein, Assistant Att'y Gen., Antitrust Div., Before the House Committee on the Judiciary Concerning Consolidation in the Telecommunications Industry (June 24, 1998), *at* www.usdoj.gov/atr/public/testimony/1806.htm; *see also generally* Hearings on Global and Innovation-Based Competition, FTC (1995); Richard J. Gilbert & Willard K. Tom, *Is Innovation King at the Antitrust Agencies? The Intellectual Property Guidelines Five Years Later*, 69 ANTITRUST L.J. 43 (2001).

future competition arising from the acquiring firm's presence in the wings.[24]

1. A Concentrated, Oligopolistic Target Market

As the *Marine Bancorporation* Court succinctly stated, "[t]he potential-competition doctrine has meaning only as applied to concentrated markets."[25] A target market that displays evidence of high levels of concentration is thus "a candidate for the potential-competition doctrine."[26] And while no particular threshold of concentration has been

---

24. *See, e.g.*, Mercantile Tex. Corp. v. Board of Governors, 638 F.2d 1255, 1267 (5th Cir. 1981); FTC v. Atlantic Richfield Co., 549 F.2d 289, 300 (4th Cir. 1977); B.A.T. Indus., 104 F.T.C. 852, 924 (1984); Grand Union Co., 102 F.T.C. 812, 1051 (1983); Heublein, Inc., 96 F.T.C. 385, 588 (1980); United States v. Bell Atlantic Corp., Civ. No. 1:99CV01119 (filed May 7, 1999) (complaint), *at* www.usdoj.gov/atr/cases/f2400/2435.htm; United States v. Allied Waste Indus., Inc., Civ. No. 1:99CV0192 (filed Apr. 8, 1999) (complaint), *at* www.usdoj.gov/atr/cases/f2500/2579.htm; United States v. Signature Flight Support Corp., Civ. No. 1:99CV00537 (filed Mar. 1, 1999) (complaint), at www.usdoj.gov/atr/cases/f2200/2268.htm.
25. United States v. Marine Bancorp., 418 U.S. 602, 630 (1974); *see also* 1984 MERGER GUIDELINES, *supra* note 1, § 4.133 (adverse competitive effects likely only if overall industry concentration is high).
26. *Marine Bancorp.*, 418 U.S. at 631. *See, e.g.*, Baxter Int'l, Inc., 68 Fed. Reg. 1062 (FTC Jan. 8, 2003); Amgen Inc. & Immunex Corp., 67 Fed. Reg. 48,475 (FTC July 24, 2003); United States v. Bell Atl. Corp., Civ. No. 1:99CV01119 (May 7, 1999) (complaint), *at* www.usdoj.gov/atr/cases/f2400/2435.htm (market for wireless mobile telephone services is highly concentrated with an HHI in excess of 2800 before the merger); United States v. Allied Waste Indus., Inc., Civ. No. 1:99CV0192 (filed Apr. 8, 1999) (complaint), *at* www.usdoj.gov/atr/cases/f2500/2579.htm; (as part of consent decree proceedings, complaint alleged merger would reduce the number of significant firms competing in small container waste hauling in the St. Louis market from three to two); United States v. SBC Communs. Inc., Civ. No. 99-0715 (filed Mar. 23, 1999) (competitive impact statement) (merger would cause level of concentration among wireless mobile telephone service providers to increase significantly and market is already highly concentrated), *at* www.usdoj.gov/atr/cases/f2300/2347.htm; United States v. Signature Flight Support Corp., Civ. No. 1:99CV00537 (filed Mar. 1, 1999) (complaint alleged market highly concentrated with only two providers), *at* www.usdoj.gov/atr/cases/f2200/2268.htm; United States v. Imetal, Civ. No. 1:99CV01018 (filed Apr. 26, 1999) (complaint), *at* www.usdoj.gov/atr/cases/f2400/2472.htm (incident to a

adopted as sufficient to trigger the potential competition doctrine, the FTC years ago expressed its view that "[f]our-firm market shares in the range of 50 percent are sufficient to raise concern over the loss of potential competition."[27] Today, the agencies are likely to refer to the *Merger Guidelines* in defining concentrated markets.

Obviously, the merging parties may rebut a prima facie structural case of market concentration with evidence that the market is nevertheless operating competitively.[28] As the U.S. Supreme Court in *Marine Bancorporation* acknowledged, market concentration figures may be "unreliable indicators of actual market behavior, [and may] not accurately depict the economic characteristics of the . . . market."[29] Courts and the FTC have thus declined to find a violation of Section 7 on the basis of the potential competition doctrine when there is sufficient evidence of competitive market performance.[30]

---

consent decree, complaint alleged proposed merger would substantially increase the highly concentrated water-washed kaolin market; HHI would increase from 2130 to 2940).

27. *Heublein*, 96 F.T.C. at 584-85 (four-firm concentration ratio of 47.9%).

28. *See generally* Chapter 5. *See also* Joel I. Klein, Assistant Att'y Gen., Antitrust Div., Remarks Before the New York State Bar Association Antitrust Law Section Program (Jan. 29, 1998), *at* www.usdoj.gov/atr/public/speeches/1338.htm (discussing how DOJ declined to challenge the Bell Atlantic/NYNEX merger, despite the fact that it was one of the largest mergers in history, because it determined that, "while it was a difficult case, on balance the merger was likely to benefit consumers in that the resulting efficiencies would lead to improved services").

29. *Marine Bancorp.*, 418 U.S. at 631 (citations omitted).

30. *See* United States v. Siemens Corp., 621 F.2d 499, 506 (2d Cir. 1980) (market relatively new, volatile, and competitive as evidenced by new entry); Gearhart Indus. v. Smith Int'l, Inc., 592 F. Supp. 203, 213-14 (N.D. Tex. 1984) (frequent introductions of new technology and new entrants), *aff'd in part, modified in part, and vacated in part*, 741 F.2d 707 (5th Cir. 1984); United States v. Hughes Tool Co., 415 F. Supp. 637, 643 (C.D. Cal. 1976) (91 firms competing for sales with trend toward deconcentration among top firms); United States v. Falstaff Brewing Corp., 383 F. Supp. 1020, 1022-23 (D.R.I. 1974); B.A.T. Indus., 104 F.T.C. 852, 920-21 (1984) (requiring an affirmative showing that the target market is "characterized by prices substantially in excess of marginal cost"); *cf.* Grand Union Co., 102 F.T.C. 812, 1055 (1983) ("more pervasive rebuttal evidence will generally be required" for higher levels of concentration in prima facie showing).

2. *The Acquiring Firm as One of Only a Few Potential Entrants*

In addition to a concentrated, oligopolistic target market, the potential competition doctrine requires that there be only a few other equally situated potential competitors that could enter the market.[31] Whether the theory of the challenge is the reduction of actual potential competition or the lessening of perceived potential competition, if there are several firms equally positioned for entry, then the loss of the acquiring firm as a potential entrant would be insignificant to the competitive operation of the market. The remaining potential competitors would likely provide the competitive constraint in the target market that the acquiring firm is claimed to exert.[32]

There is no threshold number of other potential entrants that would provide a safe harbor with respect to the potential competition doctrine.

---

31. *See, e.g.*, United States v. Falstaff Brewing Corp., 410 U.S. 526, 534 n.13 (1973); FTC v. Procter & Gamble Co., 386 U.S. 568, 580-81 (1967); Mercantile Tex. Corp. v. Board of Governors, 638 F.2d 1255, 1267 (5th Cir. 1981); United States v. Black & Decker Mfg. Co., 430 F. Supp. 729, 771-72 (D. Md. 1976); United States v. Hughes Tool Co., 415 F. Supp. 637, 645 (C.D. Cal. 1976); Heublein, Inc., 96 F.T.C. 385, 588-89 (1980); Beatrice Foods Co., 86 F.T.C. 1, 63 (1975), *aff'd,* 540 F.2d 303 (7th Cir. 1976); United States v. Signature Flight Support Corp., Civ. Action No. 1:99CV00537 (filed Mar. 1, 1999) (complaint), *at* www.usdoj.gov/atr/cases/f2200/2268.htm (complaint alleged "Signature's acquisition of Combs significantly lessens the potential for competition among three FBOs at APA Airport. Entry by a different firm to become the third independent FBO is not likely because Signature is one of only a few firms positioned to make the necessary commitment for a start-up operation on the scale desired by the airport's board").
32. *See* United States v. Falstaff Brewing Corp., 410 U.S. 526, 534 n.13 (1973); United States v. Black & Decker Mfg. Co., 430 F. Supp. 729, 743 n.23 (D. Md. 1976). Refinements on the evaluation of other potential competitors might include the issue of which potential entrants are actually or perceived to be the most likely entrants. This is because the firm believed to be the most likely entrant will likely be the marginal firm whose entry current participants are attempting to deter, and whose presence creates the most significant constraint on current market behavior. Thus, one court was unwilling to find that the presence of the acquiring firm on the edge of the market produced procompetitive benefits where there were several significant potential entrants and where objective economic factors, such as the lack of a technological base and the dissimilar nature of the product to the acquiring firm's current product line, led it to conclude that the acquiring firm was not the most likely entrant. *See Black & Decker Mfg. Co.*, 430 F. Supp. at 772.

Where there has been a large number of potential entrants, courts have found that the proposed transaction will not likely cause a substantial lessening of competition in violation of Section 7.[33] Professors Areeda and Turner have suggested "that a universe exceeding three similarly well-qualified potential entrants should be presumptively sufficient to obviate concern for the elimination of potential competition . . . [and] a universe of four or five or more entrants removes any plausible basis for attacking a merger eliminating a potential entrant and should create a conclusive presumption of legality."[34] The federal enforcement agencies appear to apply a similar standard.[35]

The substantiality of the entry barriers in the relevant market bears directly on the requirement that there be few other potential entrants. "All other things equal (including the competitive vigor of each potential entrant), the lower the entry barriers, the greater the likelihood of a larger pool of potential entrants."[36] If entry barriers are low, a large number of firms would be able to enter the market under approximately the same conditions, so that the merger of one potential competitor with an existing market participant would not likely result in a substantial lessening of competition. In such a case, the potential for new entry would remain essentially unchanged.[37]

---

33. *See* United States v. Crowell, Collier & MacMillan, Inc., 361 F. Supp. 983 (S.D.N.Y. 1973) (finding that divestiture was unwarranted when there was a "mammoth industry" on the fringe of the relevant product market, capable of easy entry into the market); Champion Spark Plug Co., 103 F.T.C. 546, 631 (1984) (no lessening of competition where 12 other firms were interested in entering market); Heublein, Inc., 96 F.T.C. 385, 591-92 (1980) (no § 7 violation where at least 21 companies with entry possibilities comparable to acquiring firm).
34. 5 PHILLIP AREEDA & DONALD F. TURNER, ANTITRUST LAW ¶ 1130b, at 116-17 (2d ed. 2003).
35. *See* 1984 MERGER GUIDELINES, *supra* note 1, §4.133 (challenge to merger unlikely if three or more similarly situated firms exist). *Compare* British Oxygen Co., 86 F.T.C. 1241, 1351 (1975) (violation of Heublein, Inc., 96 F.T.C. 385, 588-89 (1980) § 7 found when there were only possibly two or three large international firms as other potential entrants), *rev'd sub nom.* BOC Int'l, Ltd. v. FTC, 557 F.2d 24 (2d Cir. 1977) (no discussion of number of other possible entrants)), *with* United States v. Hughes Tool Co., 415 F. Supp. 637, 646 (C.D. Cal. 1976) (six other potential entrants made loss of acquiring firm insignificant).
36. Grand Union Co., 102 F.T.C. 812, 1063 (1983).
37. *See, e.g.*, *id.* at 1066 (relatively low entry barriers in markets assure minimum number of other potential entrants is exceeded); Budd Co., 86 F.T.C. 518, 577 (1975); Beatrice Foods Co., 81 F.T.C. 481, 530 (1972).

The entry barriers cannot be so high, however, that they would prevent alternative entry by the acquiring firm.[38] Thus, the entry barriers must be such that they preclude most, but not all, entry, leaving the acquiring firm uniquely positioned to overcome those not insubstantial entry barriers as one of a very few actual or perceived potential entrants into the target market.[39]

C. The Essential Preconditions of the Actual Potential Competition Theory

Without expressing any view as to the viability of the actual potential competition theory, the U.S. Supreme Court in *United States v. Marine Bancorporation* articulated two "essential preconditions" that, in addition to a concentrated target market and few other potential competitors, must exist before the actual potential competition theory may be applied to invalidate a transaction under Section 7. First, before a market extension merger may be condemned as eliminating an actual potential competitor, the plaintiff must demonstrate that the acquiring firm "has available feasible means for entering the [target] market other than by acquiring [the significant market participant]."[40] Second, those "available feasible means" must "offer a substantial likelihood of ultimately producing deconcentration of that market or other significant procompetitive effects."[41]

1. The Likelihood of Entry by Alternative Feasible Means

The first essential precondition established by the U.S. Supreme Court in *Marine Bancorporation* for the application of the actual potential competition theory is proof of the existence of alternative

---

38. As the U.S. Supreme Court explained in *Marine Bancorp.*, high entry barriers "often significantly reduce, if they do not eliminate, the likelihood that the acquiring [firm] is either a perceived potential de novo entrant or a source of future competitive benefit through de novo or foothold entry." United States v. Marine Bancorp., 418 U.S. 602, 630 (1974).

39. *See* United States v. Signature Flight Support Corp., Civ. Action No. 1:99CV00537 (filed Mar. 1, 1999) (complaint), *at* www.usdoj.gov/atr/cases/f2200/2268.htm; Mercantile Tex. Corp. v. Board of Governors, 638 F.2d 1255, 1267 (5th Cir. 1981); Grand Union Co., 102 F.T.C. 812, 1062-64 (1963).

40. *Marine Bancorp.*, 418 U.S. at 633.

41. *Id.*

feasible means for entering the target market either de novo or through a toehold acquisition. To determine whether alternative feasible means of entry exist, courts must examine the acquiring firm's interest, economic incentive, and capability to enter the target market either de novo or through a toehold acquisition. The object of such an examination is the determination of whether, absent the acquisition of the significant market participant, the acquiring firm would likely otherwise enter the market.[42]

---

42. Because, as the U.S. Supreme Court in *Marine Bancorp.* stated, "[u]nequivocal proof that an acquiring firm actually would have entered de novo but for a merger is rarely available," *id.* at 624, courts have adopted different articulations of the standard of proof necessary to satisfy this first essential precondition. *See, e.g.*, Tenneco, Inc. v. FTC, 689 F.2d 346, 352 (2d Cir. 1982) (requiring proof that the acquiring firm "would likely have entered the market in the near future"); Yamaha Motor Co. v. FTC, 657 F.2d 971, 977 (8th Cir. 1981) (affirming FTC finding of likely entry as "reasonable"); Republic of Tex. Corp. v. Board of Governors, 649 F.2d 1026, 1047 (5th Cir. 1981) ("reasonable probability"); Mercantile Tex. Corp. v. Board of Governors, 638 F.2d 1255, 1268-69 (5th Cir. 1981) ("reasonable probability"); United States v. Siemens Corp., 621 F.2d 499, 506-07 (2d Cir. 1980) ("there must . . . be at least a 'reasonable probability' that the acquiring firm would enter the market, . . . and preferably clear proof that entry would occur"); BOC Int'l, Ltd. v. FTC, 557 F.2d 24, 28-29 n.7. (2d Cir. 1977) (reasonable probability); FTC v. Atlantic Richfield Co., 549 F.2d 289, 294-95 (4th Cir. 1977) ("clear proof" with "little evidence . . . required to prove that there would not be de novo entry"). There has been considerable debate regarding the standard the FTC requires for likelihood of entry in an actual potential competition case. In *B.A.T. Industries, Ltd.*, 104 F.T.C. 852 (1984), the Commission held that in order to establish an antitrust violation under this theory, there must be "clear proof" that the firm in question would have entered the relevant market independently if the acquisition did not occur. This is contrary to the position taken by most federal courts—that there be a "reasonable probability" that independent entry would have occurred without the acquisition. In fact, certain FTC officials have questioned the "clear proof" standard. As FTC Commissioner Mary L. Azcuenaga commented, when discussing the fact that the Commission's "clear proof" standard appeared to create a chilling effect for lawyers bringing a potential competition case, "I think the case is easily overread, if one focuses too much on the phrase 'clear proof.' Clear proof may mean nothing more nor less than the preponderance of the evidence, the greater weight of the evidence. This is the 'touchstone of judicial decisions across the Nation,' and it seems doubtful that the Commission in *B.A.T.* intended to create a different standard for assessing liability." *See* Mary L. Azcuenaga, Comm'r, FTC, FTC Enforcement:

The acquiring firm's interest in entering the market de novo or by a toehold acquisition may be evidenced by internal studies or planning documents showing an evaluation of the market,[43] discussions with other acquisition candidates,[44] or earlier attempts to enter.[45] The expression of the firm's interest must be made by senior management with decision-making capability,[46] and the expression of interest must reveal an interest in independent entry, particularly where independent entry involves a greater risk and higher cost than the acquisition of a significant incumbent firm.[47]

The acquiring firm's economic incentive to enter the target market de novo or through a toehold acquisition may be established by objective evidence such as the competitiveness of the market and the profit levels of existing market participants.[48] The incentive for entry must be

---

An Idiosyncratic Journey, Remarks Before the National Economic Research Associates, Inc., 15th Annual Antitrust and Trade Regulation Seminar (July 7, 1994); *see also* Mary Lou Steptoe, Acting Director, Bureau of Competition, FTC, Potential Competition and Vertical Mergers: Theories and Law Enforcement Action at the Federal Trade Commission, Remarks Before the American Bar Association Section of Antitrust Law, Annual Meeting (Aug. 9, 1994) ("the time may be ripe to reexamine what the phrase 'clear proof' really means").

43. *See, e.g.*, FTC v. Atlantic Richfield Co., 549 F.2d 289, 296 (4th Cir. 1977); United States v. Black & Decker Mfg. Co., 430 F. Supp. 729, 756-58 (D. Md. 1976); Grand Union Co., 102 F.T.C. 812, 1059-61 (1983); British Oxygen Co., 86 F.T.C. 1241, 1354-56 (1975), *rev'd sub nom.* BOC Int'l, Ltd. v. FTC, 557 F.2d 24 (2d Cir. 1977).

44. *See* Tenneco, Inc. v. FTC, 689 F.2d 346 (2d Cir. 1982); *British Oxygen Co.*, 86 F.T.C. at 1354; Bendix Corp., 77 F.T.C. 731, 816 (talks with candidates, even though no offers made), *rev'd on other grounds and remanded*, 450 F.2d 534 (6th Cir. 1971), *consent order entered*, 84 F.T.C. 1291 (1974).

45. *See* Heublein, Inc., 96 F.T.C. 385, 586 (1980) (previous unsuccessful bid for firms on market); Brunswick Corp., 94 F.T.C. 1174, 1269 (1979), *aff'd in part and modified in part sub nom.*, Yamaha Motor Co. v. FTC, 657 F.2d 971 (8th Cir. 1981).

46. *See* United States v. Penn-Olin Chem. Co., 378 U.S. 158 (1964); United States v. Siemens Corp., 621 F.2d 499, 508 (2d Cir. 1980); FTC v. Atlantic Richfield Co., 549 F.2d 289, 297 n.9 (4th Cir. 1977); B.A.T. Indus., 104 F.T.C. 852, 928 (1984).

47. *See, e.g.*, BOC Int'l, Ltd. v. FTC, 557 F.2d 24, 28 (2d Cir. 1977); *B.A.T. Indus.*, 104 F.T.C. at 927; Grand Union Co., 102 F.T.C. 812, 1061 (1983) (internal documents only demonstrate interest in expansion by acquisition).

48. *See, e.g.*, *Tenneco, Inc.*, 689 F.2d at 353 (industry highly profitable and

sufficiently strong for the acquiring firm both to choose this expansion option over other areas of opportunity for expansion or investment[49] and to cause the firm to choose independent entry if the challenged acquisition is blocked.[50]

The third factor for assessing the likelihood of independent entry—the acquiring firm's capability for de novo or toehold entry—may be demonstrated by such objective factors as the acquiring firm's financial, technological, and business abilities, and its reputation and experience.[51] Prior unilateral expansions by the acquiring firm into other geographic or related product markets may provide evidence of a firm's capability of independent entry.[52] Conversely, regulatory restrictions or other high entry barriers may render a firm incapable of independently entering the target market.[53] Similarly, the unavailability of attractive toehold candidates offering resources or products that would enable the acquiring firm to compete effectively in the target market may also render an acquiring firm incapable of independent entry.[54]

---

industry experts foresee a bright future); *Yamaha Motor Co.*, 657 F.2d at 978; *Black & Decker Mfg. Co.*, 430 F. Supp. at 748.

49. *See* Mercantile Tex. Corp. v. Board of Governors, 638 F.2d 1255, 1269 (5th Cir. 1981); Republic of Tex. Corp. v. Board of Governors, 649 F.2d 1026, 1047 (5th Cir. 1981).

50. *See B.A.T. Indus.*, 104 F.T.C. at 939 (the acquiring firm must have "sufficiently strong economic incentives to enter the . . . market independently, rather than through the acquisition of a leading firm, so that if the acquisition had been prevented, it *clearly* would have entered the market in some other fashion"); *see also* Grand Union Co., 102 F.T.C. 812, 1060 (1983) (grocery chain had incentive to enter region because of economic and population growth, but Commission assumed without deciding that there was sufficient incentive for each market, noting "closer scrutiny might have led us to conclude that the evidence here falls short in some of the 13 markets").

51. *See, e.g.*, United States v. Phillips Petroleum Co., 367 F. Supp. 1226, 1239-42 (C.D. Cal. 1973), *aff'd mem.*, 418 U.S. 906 (1974); Heublein, Inc., 96 F.T.C. 385, 585-86 (1980); British Oxygen Co., 86 F.T.C. 1241, 1353 (1975), *rev'd sub nom.*, BOC Int'l, Ltd. v. FTC, 557 F.2d 24 (2d Cir. 1977); *see also* United States v. Black & Decker Mfg. Co., 430 F. Supp. 729, 760 (D. Md. 1976) (acquiring firm deemed unable to enter target market de novo where firm did not possess the technological expertise to design and develop the product and product development would take several years even if the firm attempted to hire the expertise).

52. *See Heublein, Inc.*, 96 F.T.C. at 585-86.

53. *See* United States v. Marine Bancorp., 418 U.S. 602, 633 (1974).

54. In *British Oxygen Co.*, the FTC specifically rejected the notion that

In addition to the acquiring firm's interest, incentive, and capability for independent entry, some courts have required evidence that the independent entry would likely occur in the near future.[55] Because the actual potential competition doctrine is based on the future benefits of entry by the acquiring firm and because "remote possibilities are not sufficient to satisfy the test set forth in § 7,"[56] these courts reason that the finding of probable entry should "contain some reasonable temporal estimate related to the near future, with 'near' defined in terms of the entry barriers and lead time necessary for entry in the particular

---

"before toehold entry can be considered as a procompetitive means of entry it must be shown that any of these firms was available at a reasonable price as of the time of the acquisition." 86 F.T.C. at 1357. The Second and Fourth Circuits, however, have required proof that a toehold candidate is available to the acquiring firm at a reasonable price. *See, e.g.*, Tenneco, Inc. v. FTC, 689 F.2d 346, 354 (2d Cir. 1982) (unsuccessful negotiations with other candidates where toehold candidates demanded 100% premium over market price of stock and selling price of 100 times earnings indicated acquiring firm would not use candidates as means of entry and Commission could not negate evidence with prediction that situation might change in future); FTC v. Atlantic Richfield Co., 549 F.2d 289, 297 n.10 (4th Cir. 1977) (acquiring company's overtures to candidates rejected). Moreover, the toehold candidates must offer resources or products that would enable the acquiring firm to compete effectively in the market. *See Tenneco*, 689 F.2d at 354-55 (candidate not viable means of entry where candidate is deteriorating firm with "poorly accepted product and run-down equipment in which . . . [no] company had shown significant interest"); *Atlantic Richfield*, 549 F.2d at 297 n.10 (company so small that "there is not substantial difference between toehold acquisition and de novo entry"); Missouri Portland Cement Co. v. Cargill, Inc., 498 F.2d 851, 864-65 (2d Cir. 1974) (small firms with technological problems, offering limited resources, or located at significant distance from market inadequate to qualify as toehold candidates).

55. *See Mercantile Tex. Corp.*, 638 F.2d at 1271-72; *Republic of Tex. Corp.*, 649 F.2d at 1047 (more definite finding than "reasonably foreseeable future," specifying a range of months or years, is necessary); *BOC Int'l, Ltd.*, 557 F.2d at 28-29 (near future); Raybestos-Manhattan, Inc. v. Hi-Shear Indus., 503 F. Supp. 1122, 1135-36 (E.D.N.Y. 1980) (plant construction, announcing plan to enter market, and hiring experienced employee is not enough to overcome the arduous quality control proceedings and sophisticated performance testing required to win certification into aerospace fasteners industry in near future); B.A.T. Indus., 104 F.T.C. 852, 925 (1984) (near future).

56. United States v. Marine Bancorp., 418 U.S. 602, 623 n.22 (1974).

industry."[57] Entry within the near future "is necessary in order . . . to predict with any degree of accuracy whether the target market will still be performing oligopolistically at the time of entry, which in turn is a necessary finding en route to the ultimate conclusion that independent entry would result in a substantial likelihood of significant procompetitive effects."[58] This timeliness requirement has been called into question in areas such as the pharmaceutical industry, based on patent protection and FDA approval, both of which would require enforcers to look far into the future to determine whether a merger presents antitrust risks.[59]

2. *The Likelihood of Deconcentration or Other Procompetitive Effects*

Application of the actual potential competition theory also requires that the likely de novo or toehold entry offer a substantial likelihood of ultimately producing deconcentration or other significant procompetitive effects in the target market. Such deconcentration or other procompetitive effects were found to be likely where the financial strength and brand familiarity of the potential entrant would make the product immediately acceptable to consumers.[60] Procompetitive effects were deemed unlikely, however, where industry regulations precluded a small new entrant from causing long-term structural improvement in the target market,[61] where industry conditions were such that new entry would be neither timely nor sufficient to mitigate the competitive harm that would be caused by the merger,[62] and where past toehold entry into

---

57. *BOC Int'l*, 557 F.2d at 29 (rejecting a standard of proof based on "reasonable probability of eventual entry").
58. *Republic of Tex. Corp.*, 649 F.2d at 1047.
59. *See* William J. Baer, Director, Bureau of Competition, FTC, Report from the Bureau of Competition, Remarks Before the American Bar Association Antitrust Section, Spring Meeting 1999 (Apr. 15, 1999), *at* www.ftc.gov/speeches/other/baerspaba99.htm; *see also* Ciba-Geigy Ltd., 62 Fed. Reg. 409 (Jan. 3, 1997) (analysis to aid public comment) (regulatory approvals needed to begin selling relevant products not expected until at least three years after consent decree).
60. *See* Brunswick Corp., 94 F.T.C. 1174, 1271 (1979), *aff'd in part and modified in part sub nom.* Yamaha Motor Co. v. FTC, 657 F.2d 971 (8th Cir. 1981).
61. *See Marine Bancorp.*, 418 U.S. at 638-39.
62. *See* United States v. Bell Atl. Corp., Civ. No. 1:99CV01119 (filed May 7, 1999), *at* www.usdoj.gov/atr/cases/2400/2435.htm.

the market had not produced procompetitive effects, and any past gains in market share by new entrants and small companies had been accompanied by increases in the market shares of the leading firms.[63]

Some courts have questioned the importance of this second precondition, because "typically in an oligopolistic situation the entry of a large firm as a new competitor necessarily has significant procompetitive effects, at least to the extent of 'shak[ing] things up.'"[64] In *United States v. Phillips Petroleum Co.*,[65] for instance, the district court simply inferred that new entry to the concentrated California oil market would likely lead to possible procompetitive effects, including increased industry capacity and price competition, improved service and quality, and the "impact on the market caused by the entering firm's struggle to obtain a market share at the expense of the other firms in the market."[66] In *Mercantile Texas Corp. v. Board of Governors*,[67] however, the Fifth Circuit required proof of greater likely procompetitive effects than a temporary disruption of market patterns; the effects should be significant and lasting, although the potential entry "need not single-handedly deconcentrate" the market.[68]

D. The Necessary Elements of the Perceived Potential Competition Theory

Unlike the actual potential competition theory, the U.S. Supreme Court has acknowledged the validity of the perceived potential competition theory.[69] The Court has recognized that a market extension merger may be unlawful if (1) existing participants in the target market

---

63. *See* United States v. Black & Decker Mfg. Co., 430 F. Supp. 729, 768 (D. Md. 1976).

64. BOC Int'l, Ltd. v. FTC, 557 F.2d 24, 27 (2d Cir. 1977) (citing Ford Motor Co. v. United States, 405 U.S. 562, 587 (1972)); *accord* Yamaha Motor Co. v. FTC, 657 F.2d 971 (8th Cir. 1981); Heublein, Inc., 96 F.T.C. 385, 588 n.43 (1980) (precondition does not require elaborate factual proof). *But cf.* United States v. Siemens Corp., 621 F.2d 499, 505 n.5 (2d Cir. 1980) (FTC study shows that toehold acquisitions do not challenge entrenched market leaders).

65. 367 F. Supp. 1226 (C.D. Cal. 1973), *aff'd mem.*, 418 U.S. 906 (1974).

66. *Id.* at 1257.

67. 638 F.2d 1255 (5th Cir. 1981).

68. *Id.* at 1270 (expressing doubt that shaking things up "is sufficient in itself, as it may have no lasting impact").

69. *See* United States v. Marine Bancorp., 418 U.S. 602, 625 (1974); United States v. Falstaff Brewing Corp., 410 U.S. 526, 531-37 (1973).

perceive the acquiring firm as a potential de novo entrant, and (2) the acquiring firm's premerger presence on the fringe of the target market in fact tempered oligopolistic behavior on the part of existing market participants.[70]

Despite the Court's recognition of the theory's validity as a tool for the enforcement of Section 7, the practical difficulties associated with mustering the proof necessary to show that existing market participants truly perceive the acquiring firm as a potential entrant constraining their market behavior has prevented the perceived potential competition theory from having much judicial success. One commentator has noted that, although "[e]vidence showing that competitors of the acquired company thought the acquiring company was likely to enter certainly is relevant and may be highly probative,"[71] the collection of such evidence directly from existing market participants may present two problems. First, for business reasons, the acquiring firm may not want its interest in the target market known and the inquiry may create a perception of possible entry where one did not previously exist.[72] Second, the testimony of existing market participants may be self-interested and, motivated by a desire to block the transaction, may exaggerate the extent to which the existing participants view the acquiring firm as a potential entrant.[73]

Given the practical difficulties of obtaining reliable direct evidence of the existing market participants' perception of the acquiring firm, courts generally examine objective, circumstantial evidence, such as the public perception of the acquiring firm's interest, economic incentive and capability to enter the target market, as a proxy for a perception of the acquiring firm as a potential entrant. Where objective evidence, such as public information about the acquiring firm's financial strength and prior acquisition efforts, demonstrate likely interest and capability to enter the target market, courts may infer that the acquiring firm is perceived as a potential entrant.[74]

---

70. *See Marine Bancorp.*, 418 U.S. at 624-25.
71. Lewis A. Kaplan, *Potential Competition and Section 7 of the Clayton Act*, 25 ANTITRUST BULL. 297, 307 (1980).
72. *See id.*
73. *See id.*
74. *See, e.g.*, *Falstaff Brewing Corp.*, 410 U.S. at 533 (acquiring firm's general interest in market known and "if it would appear to rational beer merchants in New England that Falstaff might well build a new brewery . . . then its entry by merger becomes suspect under § 7"); Tenneco, Inc. v. FTC, 689 F.2d 346, 355 (2d Cir. 1982) (acquiring firm deemed perceived potential entrant where its financial strength and compatibility

The perceived potential entrant theory also requires proof that the perception of the acquiring firm as a potential market entrant has tempered the oligopolistic conduct of existing market participants. Although direct evidence of the existing market participants' reactions to the acquiring firm's presence on the fringe of the market will obviously satisfy this element,[75] such an effect in the target market may also be inferred from circumstantial evidence if objective factors demonstrate a procompetitive effect.[76] Where, however, the circumstantial evidence of objective factors suggests that the acquiring firm's presence on the edge of the target market has not had a procompetitive effect, the effect will not be inferred.[77]

---

of existing product lines, together with its previous negotiations with market participants and the fact that an independent broker approached the acquiring firm with an earlier entry opportunity, were publicly known); United States v. Phillips Petroleum Co., 367 F. Supp. 1226, 1255-56 (C.D. Cal. 1973) (industry recognition of possible entry from capability and motivation for entry and previous attempts to enter placed industry on notice), *aff'd mem.,* 418 U.S. 906 (1974); *cf.* Missouri Portland Cement Co. v. Cargill, Inc. 498 F.2d 851, 863 (2d Cir. 1974) (salt company diversifying into cement industry was never viewed as likely entrant and unlikely to be perceived as entrant if acquisition blocked); United States v. Black & Decker Mfg. Co., 430 F. Supp. 729, 770-71 (D. Md. 1976) (acquiring firm not perceived as potential entrant where leading market participant did not perceive the acquiring firm as one of many likely entrants, even though other market participants believed the acquiring firm was either the most likely entrant or one of several likely entrants).

75. *See Phillips Petroleum*, 367 F. Supp. at 1254-56 (acquiring firm viewed as potential entrant that might contribute to downward pressure on price by acquired firm); Brunswick Corp., 94 F.T.C. 1174 (1979) (competitor improved product due to threat of acquiring firm), *aff'd in part and modified in part sub nom.*, Yamaha Motor Co. v. FTC, 657 F.2d 971 (8th Cir. 1981); Kennecott Copper Corp., 78 F.T.C. 744, 919, 934 (1971) (incumbent offered to supply potential entrant's product requirements), *aff'd,* 467 F.2d 67 (10th Cir. 1972).

76. *See Falstaff Brewing Corp.*, 410 U.S. at 534 n.13 (circumstantial evidence sufficient if perceived potential entrant intends to enter and is capable of such entry); United States v. First Nat'l State Bancorporation, 499 F. Supp. 793, 816 (D.N.J. 1980); *Black & Decker Mfg. Co.*, 430 F. Supp. at 747 n.34; *see also* Ford Motor Co. v. United States, 405 U.S. 562, 567-68 (1972).

77. *See, e.g.*, Tenneco, Inc. v. FTC, 689 F.2d 346, 356 (2d Cir. 1982) (testimony indicated source of competitive performance of market was growth of firm already present in market); Lektro-Vend Corp. v. Vendo

E. The Treatment of Potential Competition Mergers under the *Merger Guidelines*

The 1984 *Merger Guidelines* explicitly recognize the possible harm to competition arising from the loss of an actual or perceived potential competitor and convert the underlying conditions of the potential competition theories to a structural analysis to determine applicability of the theories. The 1984 *Merger Guidelines* state that the Division is likely to challenge a merger using the potential competition doctrine if certain quantitative and qualitative factors are present.[78] For example, under the 1984 *Merger Guidelines*, the Division will likely challenge a potential competition merger if, among other things, the target market is highly concentrated, meaning that the Herfindahl-Hirschmann Index is above 1800.[79] Entry to the market must be difficult and the acquiring

---

Co., 660 F.2d 255 (7th Cir. 1981); United States v. Siemens Corp., 621 F.2d 499, 509-10 (2d Cir. 1980); Raybestos-Manhattan, Inc. v. Hi-Shear Indus., 503 F. Supp. 1122, 1135 (E.D.N.Y. 1980); United States v. Amax, Inc., 402 F. Supp. 956 (D. Conn. 1975); *see also Missouri Portland Cement Co.*, 498 F.2d at 863; *Black & Decker Mfg. Co.*, 430 F. Supp. at 772-73; United States v. Hughes Tool Co., 415 F. Supp. 637, 645-46 (C.D. Cal. 1976); British Oxygen Co., 86 F.T.C. 1241, 1351 n.8 (1975), *rev'd sub nom.*, BOC Int'l, Ltd. v. FTC, 557 F.2d 24 (2d Cir. 1977); Budd Co., 86 F.T.C. 518, 579-80 (1975); General Mills, Inc., 83 F.T.C. 696, 732-33 (1973). *But see* Copperweld Corp. v. Imetal, 403 F. Supp. 579, 592 (W.D. Pa. 1975) (preliminary injunction denied based on balance of equities, but insufficient evidence to assess market impact creates serious question going to merits); *Phillips Petroleum*, 367 F. Supp. at 1257 ("it must be assumed that such influence exists where the market is concentrated" although direct evidence existed in case).

78. Although the 1992 *Merger Guidelines* were issued jointly by the DOJ and the FTC, the 1984 *Merger Guidelines* were issued by the DOJ alone. The 1992 *Merger Guidelines*, however, address only horizontal mergers, leaving in place the 1984 *Merger Guidelines'* discussion of nonhorizontal mergers, to be read "in the context of the [1992] revisions to the treatment of horizontal mergers." U.S. DEP'T OF JUSTICE & FEDERAL TRADE COMM'N, STATEMENT ACCOMPANYING RELEASE OF REVISED MERGER GUIDELINES (Apr. 2, 1992) [hereinafter 1992 STATEMENT], *reprinted in* 4 Trade Reg. Rep. (CCH) ¶ 13,104 and in Appendix I. The discussion of the theory of potential competition in the 1984 *Merger Guidelines*, *see* 1984 MERGER GUIDELINES, *supra* note 1, § 4.1, remains in effect.

79. *See* 1984 MERGER GUIDELINES, *supra* note 1, § 4.131. *See, e.g.*, United States v. Bell Atl. Corp., Civ. No. 1:99CV01119 (filed May 7, 1999) (complaint), *at* www.usdoj.gov/atr/cases/2400/2435.htm (divestiture

firm must have some entry advantage not possessed by many firms.[80] The Division is more likely to challenge the transaction as the entry advantage of the acquiring firm over similarly situated firms increases and the number of comparably advantaged potential entrants falls to three.[81] If the target firm has a market share of 5 percent or less, the 1984 *Merger Guidelines* view the merger as a toehold acquisition and a challenge is unlikely.[82] The likelihood of a challenge increases as the market share of the target firm increases; a challenge is likely if the target firm possesses 20 percent of the market.[83] Finally, if there is particularly strong evidence, such as significant prior investments in the target market, to demonstrate that independent de novo or toehold entry by the acquiring firm is likely, the Division will likely evaluate the transaction using the 1984 *Merger Guidelines*' horizontal merger criteria.[84]

In adopting the structural factors to identify cases where a challenge will be based on the loss of a potential entrant, the 1984 *Merger Guidelines* treat actual and perceived potential competition under a unified analytical approach. The 1984 *Merger Guidelines* explain that only perceived potential competition would exist if information and coordination were perfect, because existing firms would be able to set price to deter all entry if entry deterrence was a profit-maximizing strategy for the industry.[85] The 1984 *Merger Guidelines* recognize, however, that perfect information and perfect coordination are unlikely so that actual potential competition has its own significance.[86] Although the 1984 *Merger Guidelines* acknowledge the difference in the underlying assumptions of the two theories, the 1984 *Merger Guidelines* recognize the close relationship between the necessary conditions for actual and perceived potential competition.

---

required in highly concentrated wireless mobile telephone services market with a pre-merger HHI of over 2800); United States v. Allied Waste Indus., Inc., Civ. No. 1:99CV0894 (filed Apr. 8, 1999) (merger disallowed because premerger HHI was 2500 and postmerger HHI would be over 3900).

80. *See* 1984 MERGER GUIDELINES, *supra* note 1, §§ 4.132, 4.133.
81. *See id.* § 4.133.
82. *See id.* § 4.134.
83. *See id.*
84. *See id.* § 4.133.
85. *See id.* § 4.12.
86. *See id.*

The 1992 *Merger Guidelines* do not address the potential competition doctrine directly.[87] However, the 1992 *Merger Guidelines* modify the approach for the identification of firms that are included in a particular relevant market from the case law and 1984 *Merger Guidelines* with the result that some mergers that might previously have been evaluated under the potential competition doctrine may be treated under the 1992 *Merger Guidelines* as horizontal mergers.

Unlike the 1984 *Merger Guidelines*, the 1992 *Merger Guidelines* include "uncommitted" entrants as participants within the relevant market.[88] A firm is considered to be an uncommitted entrant if "it likely would enter rapidly into production or sale of a market product in the market's area, without incurring significant sunk costs of entry and exit."[89] By including these uncommitted entrants among the firms that participate in the market, the 1992 *Merger Guidelines* consider many actual potential competitors to be existing market participants. If one of these uncommitted entrants were the acquiring or acquired firm, the merger would be considered under the horizontal framework of the 1992 *Merer Guidelines* rather than under the actual potential competition analysis.

Moreover, uncommitted entrants are also described as "capable of making such quick and uncommitted supply responses that they likely influenced the market premerger, [and] would influence it post-merger."[90] Thus, some perceived potential competitors that influence the

87. The statement by the DOJ and the FTC accompanying the release of the 1992 *Guidelines* indicated that guidance on nonhorizontal mergers was provided by the 1984 *Guidelines*, read in the context of the changes to *Guidelines* concerning horizontal mergers. *See* 1992 STATEMENT, *supra* note 78; *see also generally* Chapter 3.

88. *See* 1984 MERGER GUIDELINES, *supra* note 1, § 1.0; *see also generally* Chapter 3.

89. *Id.*

90. *Id.*

target market from its fringes are also among the uncommitted entrants and, under the 1992 *Merger Guidelines*, are deemed to be existing market participants.

CHAPTER 10

VERTICAL MERGERS

Certain mergers between firms participating in different but related markets are termed "vertical mergers." Historically, vertical merger challenges have mostly involved firms at different levels of production or distribution of a good or service,[1] and vertical merger case law accordingly tends to involve fact patterns in which there is a potential customer-supplier relationship between the parties to the transaction at issue. That relationship may involve two producers (one of which supplies an input used in the production of the other's product), a producer and a distributor, or a combination of firms at different stages of the distribution process.

The "vertical merger" moniker and analytical framework also have been applied to a limited number of transactions in which the merging firms supply products or services that are used by a single pool of customers and potential customers. As discussed below, such complementary-product mergers may present issues similar to those presented by customer-supplier mergers.

Firms undertaking vertical mergers may happen to be direct horizontal competitors in other markets, competing directly as alternative suppliers of the same product or service. The competition issues arising from the firms' participation in markets that are adjacent to each other, however, are the issues that give rise to the characterization of a merger as vertical.[2] By contrast, the "conglomerate" mergers discussed in the

---

1. *See* Brown Shoe Co. v. United States, 370 U.S. 294 (1962) ("Economic arrangements between companies standing in a customer-supplier relationship are characterized as 'vertical'").
2. *See, e.g.*, *Brown Shoe*, 370 U.S. at 323 (horizontal in shoe manufacturing and vertical in shoe retailing); HTI Health Servs. v. Quorum Health Group, 960 F. Supp. 1104, 1112 (S.D. Miss. 1997) (horizontal in certain physician services and managed care markets and vertical in the acute inpatient hospital services market); Harnischfeger Corp. v. Paccar, Inc., 474 F. Supp. 1151, 1158 (E.D. Wis.) (horizontal in mine excavating loaders and vertical in hydraulic crane winches), *aff'd mem.*, 624 F.2d 1103 (7th Cir. 1979). *See generally* James R. Loftis III, *How to Analyze Dual Distribution Problems*, *in* 2 ANTITRUST COUNSELING AND LITIGATION TECHNIQUES § 11.02[3] (Julian O. von Kalinowski ed., 1992).

next chapter involve firms that are neither direct competitors nor competitors in adjacent markets.

When describing the firms involved in the customer-supplier type of merger, the firm that provides inputs or operates at the earlier stage in the production process is referred to as the "upstream" firm and the firm that uses the input to make a product or is closer to the ultimate consumer is called the "downstream" firm. A vertical merger may involve a supplier's integration "forward" toward the ultimate consumer, such as a shoe manufacturer's acquisition of a shoe retail chain[3] or a Portland cement producer's acquisition of a ready-mix concrete company.[4] Alternatively, the merger may involve a downstream firm's integration "backward" toward the supplier of an input, such as an automobile manufacturer's acquisition of a spark plug producer.[5]

In the complementary-product type of vertical merger, the two firms' products are used in tandem, in either variable or fixed proportion. In one example, the merging firms supplied electronic design automation software used at different stages in the design of integrated circuits. Although the products themselves were not substitutable, and neither product was an input for the other, the firms' software had to be compatible so that customers could use the data output from one firm's software as data input for the other firm's software.[6]

A. Historical Perceptions of Vertical Mergers

The antitrust treatment of vertical mergers tends to be fact specific, with emphasis on whether a likelihood of harm to competition can be demonstrated in the particular transaction at hand. Because the analytical framework applied to vertical mergers has changed over time, an understanding of the historical development of the legislative, jurisprudential, and economic underpinnings of vertical merger law is essential.

---

3. *Brown Shoe*, 370 U.S. at 323 (both parties were integrated manufacturers and retailers, but Brown Shoe was primarily a manufacturer while Kinney was primarily a retailer).
4. *See* Mississippi River Corp. v. FTC, 454 F.2d 1083 (8th Cir. 1972).
5. *See* Ford Motor Co. v. United States, 405 U.S. 562 (1972).
6. *See* Cadence Design Sys., 124 F.T.C. 131 (1997).

1. *Early Cases*

At first, vertical mergers were thought to be immune from challenge under Section 7 of the Clayton Act. The original Clayton Act as it was enacted in 1914, prohibited acquisitions of stock that would tend substantially to lessen competition between the acquiring and the acquired companies in any line of commerce.[7] The prevailing view of this language was that the original Section 7 did not "preclude the acquisition of stock in any corporation other than a direct competitor."[8] Consequently, during the period from 1914 to 1950, the Antitrust Division of the U.S. Department of Justice (DOJ or the Division)[9] and the Federal Trade Commission (FTC or the Commission)[10] brought only a limited number of vertical merger cases.

Prior to 1950, the case law relied upon the Sherman Act and the common law regarding restraints of trade as bases for challenging vertical mergers. Under Section 1 of the Sherman Act, a vertical merger may be unlawful when combined with a plan to monopolize a business through many stages of the production of a good or service.[11] An illegal

---

7. Section 7 originally read, in part, that a corporation shall not acquire the stock of another corporation "where the effect of such acquisition may be to substantially lessen competition between the corporation whose stock is so acquired and the corporation making the acquisition, or to restrain such commerce in any section or community, or tend to create a monopoly of any line of commerce." Ch. 323, § 7, 38 Stat 731 (1914).
8. Brown Shoe v. United States, 370 U.S. 294, 313, 314 n.25, 317 (1962); *see also* United States v. E.I. du Pont de Nemours & Co., 353 U.S. 586, 615-17 (1957) (Burton, J., dissenting); FEDERAL TRADE COMM'N, REPORT ON CORPORATE MERGERS AND ACQUISITIONS 168 (1955) (citing legislative history of 1950 amendments to Section 7).
9. *See E.I. du Pont de Nemours & Co.*, 353 U.S. at 586; United States v. General Motors Corp., 1952 Trade Cas. (CCH) ¶ 67,324 (N.D. Ill 1952) (consent decree); United States v. Swiss Bank Corp., 1940-43 Trade Cas. (CCH) ¶ 56,188 (D.N.J. 1941) (consent decree).
10. *See* Aluminum Co. v. FTC, 284 F. 401 (3d Cir. 1922); Austin, Nichols & Co., 9 F.T.C. 170 (1925).
11. *See* United States v. Yellow Cab Co., 332 U.S. 218 (1947) (plan or intent to monopolize cab business from manufacture through operation in four large cities by acquiring operating companies and requiring operating companies to purchase cabs from manufacturer); United States v. American Tobacco Co., 221 U.S. 106, 182-83 (1911) ("[c]onclusion of wrongful purpose and illegal combination is overwhelmingly established" by defendants' acts, which include creating trade conflicts to injure smaller competitors, vertical integration to control essential inputs for

restraint of trade under Section 1 of the Sherman Act may also be established in part by the foreclosure of a significant portion of the market for competitors. In *United States v. Yellow Cab Co.*,[12] the U.S. Supreme Court found a violation of Section 1 when there was an attempt to merge a cab manufacturing company with the companies holding the majority of cab licenses in four major cities.[13] The Section 1 violation was based, in part, on the exclusion of unaffiliated taxi manufacturers "from that part of the market represented by the cab operating companies under [the integrated cab company's] control" and the higher price paid by the controlled operating companies for the cab purchases.[14] By contrast, the U.S. Supreme Court upheld a vertical merger under Section 1 where only 3 percent of market demand for rolled steel products was foreclosed.[15]

2. *The 1950 Amendments to the Clayton Act*

The Clayton Act was amended in 1950 to make clear that Section 7 applied to vertical and conglomerate mergers.[16] The intent of Congress was to make Section 7 applicable "to all types of mergers and acquisitions, vertical and conglomerate as well as horizontal, which have the specified effects of substantially lessening competition . . . or tending to create a monopoly."[17] The number of challenges to vertical mergers by the government, however, did not increase dramatically[18] even after the 1950 amendments and a confirmation by the U.S. Supreme Court that the Clayton Act applied to vertical mergers.[19]

---

production of tobacco products, and buying plants with intent to close them).

12. 332 U.S. 218 (1947).
13. The companies held 86% of the cab licenses in Chicago, 15% of the licenses in New York City, 100% in Pittsburgh, and 58% of the licenses in Minneapolis.
14. *Yellow Cab Co.*, 332 U.S. at 226.
15. *See* United States v. Columbia Steel Co., 334 U.S. 495, 527 (1948).
16. As amended, Section 7 reads, "That no corporation . . . shall acquire . . . the whole or any part of the stock . . . [or] any part of the assets of another corporation .. . where in any line of commerce in any section of the country, the effect of such acquisition may be substantially to lessen competition, or to tend to create a monopoly." 15 U.S.C. § 18.
17. H.R. REP. NO. 1191, 81st Cong., 1st Sess. 11 (1949).
18. ABA SECTION OF ANTITRUST LAW: MONOGRAPH NO. 14, NON-HORIZONTAL MERGER LAW AND POLICY 7 (1988).
19. *See* United States v. E.I. du Pont de Nemours & Co., 353 U.S. 586, 590-

B. *Brown Shoe* and Vertical Foreclosure

Judicial analysis of vertical mergers under the amended Section 7 of the Clayton Act begins (and arguably ends) with *Brown Shoe Co. v. United States*.[20] The Division challenged the merger of the Brown Shoe Company with the G.R. Kinney Company. Although each company was integrated into both manufacturing and retailing of men's, women's, and children's shoes, Brown Shoe was primarily a manufacturer and Kinney was primarily a retailer.[21]

The U.S. Supreme Court affirmed the district court's finding that the merger violated amended Section 7. The Court identified the *foreclosure* of a portion of the market to competitors as the "primary vice of a vertical merger or other arrangement tying a customer to a supplier . . . which deprive[s] . . . rivals of a fair opportunity to compete."[22] In addition, the Court's analysis stated that where the fraction of the market foreclosed to competitors does not approach either monopoly proportions or a de minimis share of the market, other non-market share factors must be considered in the analysis of the merger.[23] These other factors include "the nature and purpose of the arrangement"[24] and any trend toward concentration arising from vertical integration in the industry.[25] The Court also cautioned, however, in the language of Section 7, that only those mergers whose effect may be substantially to lessen competition or tend to create a monopoly are unlawful under the Clayton Act.[26]

The approach to vertical merger analysis described in *Brown Shoe* became the method of analysis for subsequent lower court decisions for the next twenty years. Most courts adopted a mechanical approach to vertical merger analysis in which the facts of the particular case were analogized to those in *Brown Shoe*. In particular, courts examined the percentage of the market foreclosed to competitors, the purpose of the acquisition, the concentration in the relevant markets, and whether there was a trend toward vertical integration in the industry.[27]

---

92 (1957).

20. 370 U.S. 294 (1962).
21. Analysis of the transaction involved horizontal as well as vertical aspects because both companies operated at both levels of production and distribution. *See id.* at 334.
22. 370 U.S. at 324.
23. *See id.* at 328-29.
24. *Id.* at 329.
25. *See id.* at 332.
26. *See id.* at 324.
27. *See, e.g.*, Ash Grove Cement Co. v. FTC, 577 F.2d 1368 (9th Cir. 1978)

This approach was also incorporated into the 1968 *Merger Guidelines*.[28] The 1968 *Merger Guidelines* stated that the Division would ordinarily challenge a merger between an upstream firm accounting for 10 percent or more of sales in its market and a downstream firm accounting for 6 percent or more of the total purchases in its market.[29] The underlying theory was the same as that articulated by the U.S. Supreme Court in *Brown Shoe*, the perceived harms resulting from foreclosure.[30]

(upholding FTC finding that acquisition of two purchasers with 14% and 4.3% of downstream market foreclosed competitors and violated §7); Heatransfer Corp. v. Volkswagenwerk, AG, 553 F.2d 964, 982 (5th Cir. 1977) (manufacturer's acquisition of company supplying automobile air conditioners to franchisees foreclosed sales opportunities to independent air conditioner suppliers); Mississippi River Corp. v. FTC, 454 F.2d 1083, 1090-92 (8th Cir. 1972) (FTC order affirmed where merger foreclosed 20% of downstream market from competitors, purpose of acquisition was to insure captive market, there was trend toward vertical integration and concentration in industry, and merger raised barriers to entry); United States Steel Corp. v. FTC, 426 F.2d 592, 599-601 (6th Cir. 1970) (§ 7 violated where acquisition potentially foreclosed of 9.8% of purchases of upstream input, purpose of acquisition was to secure captive market, trends existed toward concentration and vertical integration in industry, and merger raised barriers to entry); Reynolds Metal Co. v. FTC, 309 F.2d 223, 229 (D.C. Cir. 1962) (§ 7 violated where merger foreclosed downstream purchaser controlling 33% of florist foil); Harnischfeger Corp. v. Paccar, Inc., 474 F. Supp. 1151, 1157-59 (E.D. Wis.) (preliminary injunction granted where prior to merger acquired firm purchased 55% of hydraulic crane winches from acquiring firm and merger would foreclose remaining 45% of purchases), *aff'd mem.*, 624 F.2d 1103 (7th Cir. 1979); United States v. Sybron Corp., 329 F. Supp. 919 (E.D. Pa. 1971) (§ 7 violated where competing manufacturers would be foreclosed from 8% of downstream market, competing retailers would be foreclosed from supply by manufacturer which accounted for 18% of market, and market was concentrated and barriers to entry were significant); United States v. Kimberly-Clark Corp., 264 F. Supp. 439 (N.D. Cal. 1967) (§7 violated where 14% of market foreclosed for some products in six states and purpose of acquisition was to secure captive outlet for products).

28. U.S. DEP'T OF JUSTICE, MERGER GUIDELINES (1968) [hereinafter 1968 MERGER GUIDELINES], *reprinted in* 4 Trade Reg. Rep. (CCH) ¶ 13,101.

29. *See id.* §§ 12-13.

30. *See id.* § 11.

C. Chicago School Criticism of *Brown Shoe*

The theory of foreclosure articulated by the U.S. Supreme Court in *Brown Shoe* became the subject of considerable criticism as part of a broader law and economics challenge to fundamental assumptions underlying antitrust law. Because much of the criticism emanated from the University of Chicago, the critics came to be referred to as the "Chicago School." The critics argued that foreclosure, as articulated in *Brown Shoe*, is nothing more than a conclusory label.

First, according to the Chicago School critique, a monopolist will set output at the level that maximizes its profits, or "rents," given a firm-specific cost structure and product-specific demand conditions. Because of the firm- and product-specific nature of the monopolist's economic calculus, a firm cannot simultaneously exploit monopolies in two products that are used in fixed proportion to each other.[31] The monopolist may achieve its profit-maximizing output for one product or the other but not both, because differences in cost and demand conditions between the two markets will result in a different profit-maximizing output for each market.[32] Thus, it was argued, there is a "single monopoly rent" which can be taken at either monopolized level of the vertical chain, but not both. Given this analysis, Chicago School adherents reasoned that motivations for vertical mergers should not be assumed to lie in the desire to leverage a monopoly from one market to another, but instead in the desire to create significant, potentially procompetitive, integrative efficiencies.

Second, even in cases in which vertically-related products are used in variable proportion to each other, Chicago School critics saw the competitive effects of complete vertical foreclosure by a monopolist as indeterminate.[33] It was argued that given the difficulty of predicting

---

31. The Chicago School critics recognized that this explanation applies only where one unit (or some fixed fraction thereof) of the input is needed to produce one unit of output. For example, for each can of soda sold by a store owner, the retailer must purchase one can from the manufacturer. *See* Robert H. Bork, THE ANTITRUST PARADOX 228-30 (1978).
32. *See id.*
33. *See, e.g.*, Parthasaradhi Mallela & Babu Nahata, *Theory of Vertical Control with Variable Proportions*, 88 J. POL. ECON. 1009 (1980); M. L. Greenhut & H. Ohta, *Vertical Integration of Successive Oligopolists*, 69 AM. ECON. REV. 137 (1979); M. L. Greenhut & H. Ohta, *Related Market Conditions and Interindustrial Mergers*, 66 AM. ECON. REV. 267-77 (1976); Frederick R. Warren-Boulton, *Vertical Control with Variable Proportions*, 82 J. POL. ECON. 783 (1974); John M. Vernon & Daniel A.

whether the price would go up or down, or remain unchanged, there should be no intervention in the marketplace under these circumstances.[34]

Third, the justification for judicial intervention was seen as even less compelling where market power was not found at either relevant level of the vertical chain. In that situation, a vertical merger would result only in a temporary foreclosure at worst, because suppliers and customers would simply realign their relationships after the merger to match the remaining unforeclosed supply to the unforeclosed demand.[35]

Fourth, Chicago School critics argued that vertical integration through merger is typically efficient and should not be discouraged. Vertical mergers, for example, were viewed as tending to reduce transaction costs associated with the transfer of the product to the downstream division; for example, it may be more costly to buy, sell, and monitor quality through vertical contracts than to do so internally.[36]

Graham, *Profitability of Monopolization by Vertical Integration*, 79 J. POL. ECON. 924 (1971); *See generally* Martin K. Perry, *Vertical Integration: Determinants and Effects*, *in* 1 HANDBOOK OF INDUSTRIAL ORGANIZATION 190-92 (Richard Schmalensee & Robert D. Willig eds., 1989); Alan A. Fisher & Richard Sciacca, *An Economic Analysis of Vertical Merger Enforcement Policy*, 6 RES. IN L. & ECON. 17-21 (1984).

34. Variable proportion defines a production process in which the fabricator can substitute one input for another as the prices of the two inputs vary. Thus, the fabricator may be able to substitute more labor in order to use less equipment for the production of a product. As the price of a piece of equipment rises to monopoly levels, the fabricator will use labor more intensively and purchase fewer pieces of equipment, which results in an inefficient combination of equipment and labor in the production process. Vertical integration by the equipment monopolist will eliminate the inefficiency because the vertically integrated monopolist will transfer the equipment to itself at cost. The effect of such a merger on the downstream price depends to a significant degree on whether elasticity of substitution between the equipment and labor was greater than the elasticity of demand facing the fabricated product downstream. That is, are there more substitution possibilities for the fabricator than for the fabricator's customers? If so, then the retail price would be likely to rise. *See* Mallela & Nahata and Warren-Boulton, *supra* note 33.

35. *See, e.g.*, ROBERT H. BORK, THE ANTITRUST PARADOX 232 (1978).

36. *See, e.g.*, Oliver E. Williamson, *Transaction Cost Economics*, *in* 1 HANDBOOK OF INDUSTRIAL ORGANIZATION 136-82 (Richard Schmalensee & Robert D. Willig eds., 1989); Oliver E. Williamson, *Vertical Integration and Related Variations on a Transaction-Cost Economics Theme*, *in* NEW DEVELOPMENTS IN THE ANALYSIS OF MARKET

Similarly, coordination in design may be achieved more readily in a vertically integrated firm than when arm's length negotiations are required. There may also be complementarities in the production stage that serve to reduce inventories and eliminate the incremental cost of transportation or successive processing. A vertical merger can also increase efficient investment by internalizing incentives to eliminate opportunism and assuring the supply of inputs when there is market risk.[37]

One type of risk, which has been viewed as a transaction cost relevant to the analysis of vertical integration, occurs when a firm is called on to make a specialized sunk investment in the business of another firm. For example, a firm may have an opportunity to develop a product that can be used only as an input by another firm or to construct dedicated facilities near a customer's place of business. In evaluating such an opportunity, it is necessary to weigh the risk of sudden cancellation, or other opportunistic behavior, by the firm that is not making the investment. Credible assurances against opportunism may be achieved by contract in many cases. In other cases, however, the difficulty of making credible assurances contractually may lead to vertical mergers that are not principally motivated by anticompetitive objectives.[38]

Finally, it has been argued that a vertical merger may create efficiencies by eliminating the price distortion caused by double

---

STRUCTURE 149-77 (Joseph E. Stiglitz & G. Frank Matthewson eds., 1986).

37. *See, e.g.*, Martin K. Perry, *Vertical Integration: Determinants and Effects*, 1 HANDBOOK OF INDUSTRIAL ORGANIZATION 213-15 (Richard Schmalensee & Robert D. Willig eds., 1989); MICHAEL WATERSON, ECONOMIC THEORY OF THE INDUSTRY 96-98 (1984); Dennis W. Carlton, *Vertical Integration in Competitive Markets Under Uncertainty*, 27 J. INDUS. ECON. 189 (1979); Benjamin Klein et al., *Vertical Integration, Appropriable Rents, and the Competitive Contracting Process*, 21 J.L. & ECON. 297 (1978); Roger G. Blair & David L. Kaserman, *Uncertainty and the Incentive for Vertical Integration*, 45 SOUTHERN ECON. J. 266 (1978); Kenneth J. Arrow, *Vertical Integration and Communication*, 6 BELL J. ECON. 173 (1975).

38. *See, e.g.,* Oliver E. Williamson, THE ECONOMIC INSTITUTIONS OF CAPITALISM 94 (1984) ("Internal organization enjoys the advantage where optimal asset specificity is substantial"); Timothy J. Muris, *The Efficiency Defense under Section 7 of the Clayton Act*, 30 CASE WESTERN L. REV. 381, 423 (1980) (discussing vertical integration as a means of avoiding post-contractual opportunistic behavior).

monopoly markup where there is market power in both the upstream and downstream markets.[39]

D. Effect of Criticism on Vertical Merger Enforcement Policy

The criticisms leveled by the Chicago School against foreclosure theory had a dramatic impact, both on judicial treatment of vertical merger cases, and on federal vertical merger enforcement activity.

1. Changes in Judicial Treatment

The Chicago School critique of the *Brown Shoe* foreclosure analysis had an impact on the judiciary. Although the formal legal standard remained the one articulated in *Brown Shoe*, courts sometimes acknowledged economic criticism of foreclosure theory, vertical mergers were more routinely upheld, and courts more frequently distinguished the facts of the cases before them from the facts of *Brown Shoe*.[40]

In *Fruehauf Corp. v. FTC*,[41] for example, the Second Circuit reversed the FTC's order blocking a vertical merger on the grounds that the FTC's finding of foreclosure was not supported by the evidence. The Commission had found, among other things, that Fruehauf's acquisition of Kelsey-Hayes foreclosed suppliers of heavy duty wheels (HDW) from selling to Fruehauf's trailer business. The Second Circuit determined, however, that even "if Fruehauf were to switch its purchase of its entire HDW wheel needs, amounting to 5.8% of the market, from others to Kelsey . . ., there would merely be a realignment of the existing market sales without any likelihood of a diminution in competition."[42] The

---

39. *See, e.g.*, John M. Vernon & Daniel A. Graham, *Profitability of Monopolization by Vertical Integration*, 79 J. POL. ECON. 924 (1971).
40. *See, e.g.*, Alberta Gas Chems. Ltd. v. E.I. du Pont de Nemours & Co., 826 F.2d 1235 (3d Cir. 1987); Fruehauf Corp. v. FTC, 603 F.2d 345 (2d Cir. 1979); HTI Health Servs., Inc. v. Quorum Health Group, 960 F. Supp. 1104, 1135-37 (S.D. Miss. 1997); Crane Co. v. Harsco Corp., 509 F. Supp. 115 (D. Del. 1981); Crouse-Hinds Co. v. Internorth, Inc., 518 F. Supp. 416 (N.D.N.Y. 1980); Carrier Corp. v. United Techs. Corp. 1978-2 Trade Cas. (CCH) ¶ 62,393 (N.D.N.Y.), *aff'd*, 1978-2 Trade Cas. ¶ 62,405 (2d Cir. 1978) (substantial foreclosure not established); United States v. Hammermill Paper Co., 429 F. Supp. 1271, 1293-94 (W.D. Pa. 1977) (discounting share of market foreclosed because of prior sales relationship with acquired purchasers).
41. 603 F.2d 345 (2d Cir. 1979).
42. *Id.* at 360.

Commission had also found that the acquisition of Kelsey-Hayes would eliminate certain procompetitive effects that Fruehauf had on the market through collaborative efforts with HDW suppliers to develop new types of wheels and to draw new entrants into the market through the promise of its patronage. The court concluded that the evidence did not support the conclusions that Fruehauf was unique in this regard or that other firms would not draw new entry if Fruehauf stopped doing so.[43] The court also rejected the Commission's finding that Fruehauf would obtain an anticompetitive advantage over other truck trailer suppliers because it could divert Kelsey's HDW output to itself in times of shortage. The Second Circuit's rejection of the finding as having "no appreciable evidentiary support"[44] demonstrates how vertical merger enforcement may be affected when careful judicial scrutiny is applied to a proposition that might not have been seriously questioned a decade earlier.

In *Alberta Gas Chemicals Ltd. v. E.I. du Pont de Nemours & Co.*,[45] the Third Circuit expressed a strong skepticism of foreclosure concerns, noting specifically that "respected antitrust scholars question the anticompetitive effects of vertical mergers in general."[46] Alberta had argued that du Pont's purchase of Conoco foreclosed Alberta's sales of methanol to Conoco. The court noted that Alberta's sales had increased dramatically following the merger and distinguished the case from others where a vertical merger virtually precluded the plaintiff from selling any of its products.[47] The court found that the case more closely resembled the *Fruehauf* case, in which a mere realignment of existing market sales was likely without any diminution in competition.[48]

2. *Changes in Enforcement Policy and Agency Case Selection*

The *Merger Guidelines* issued by the Division in 1982 and revised in 1984[49] eschewed all references to "foreclosure" and articulated three

---

43. *See id.* at 361.
44. *See id.* at 354.
45. 826 F.2d 1235 (3d Cir. 1987).
46. *Id.* at 1244 (citing ROBERT H. BORK, THE ANTITRUST PARADOX 226, 237 (1978)) ("Antitrust's concern with vertical mergers is mistaken. Vertical mergers are a means of creating efficiency, not of injuring competition. [The] foreclosure theory is not merely wrong, it is irrelevant").
47. *See id.* at 1246.
48. *See id.*
49. U.S. DEP'T OF JUSTICE, MERGER GUIDELINES (1982) [hereinafter 1982 MERGER GUIDELINES], *reprinted in* 4 Trade Reg. Rep. (CCH) ¶13,102. The analysis of vertical mergers is similar under the amended DOJ

potential theories of harm to competition from vertical mergers: (1) raising barriers to entry by making it necessary for new competitors to enter two markets simultaneously, (2) facilitating collusion by making it easier to monitor price or by eliminating a disruptive buyer, and (3) evading rate regulation by enabling the combined firm to manipulate the internal prices of inputs used to determine the level of regulated rates.

There were few challenges to vertical mergers during the 1980s, and most such challenges involved evasion of rate regulation as the theory of harm to competition.[50] The 1980s-era vertical merger challenges brought by the antitrust enforcement agencies only rarely alleged harm to competition as a result of increased barriers to entry, such as by making it necessary for new competitors to enter two markets simultaneously, or enhanced ease of collusion.[51]

In 1983, GTE reached an agreement to acquire Southern Pacific Communications Company (now known as Sprint).[52] The Division was concerned that GTE, as a regulated monopoly provider of local telephone

---

Merger Guidelines issued in 1984. U.S. DEP'T OF JUSTICE, MERGER GUIDELINES (1984) [hereinafter 1984 MERGER GUIDELINES], *reprinted in* 4 Trade Reg. Rep. (CCH) ¶ 13,103. The *Merger Guidelines* issued by the National Association of Attorneys General do not address vertical mergers. *See* NATIONAL ASSOCIATION OF ATTORNEYS GENERAL, MERGER GUIDELINES (1993), *reprinted in* 4 Trade Reg. Rep. (CCH) ¶ 13,406 and in Appendix M.

50. The 1982 *Merger Guidelines* introduced the concept of evasion of rate regulation into merger law. The clearest example is when a regulated utility subject to rate-of-return regulation merges with one of its suppliers. The potential harm articulated in this circumstance is that the merger will enable the utility to shift costs from the regulated portion of the combined business and thereby evade capped rate of return regulation on the regulated assets. *See* 1982 MERGER GUIDELINES, *supra* note 49, § IV(B)(3).

51. Although the *Merger Guidelines* state that the Division will challenge vertical mergers that raise barriers to entry or facilitate collusion, there appears to have been agency action in only one or two such cases. *See* Lawrence J. White, *Antitrust and Video Markets: The Merger of Showtime and The Movie Channel as a Case Study*, *in* VIDEO MEDIA COMPETITION: REGULATION, ECONOMICS, AND TECHNOLOGY 338 (Eli M. Noam ed., 1985); B.F. Goodrich Co., 110 F.T.C. 207, 330-38 (1988) (merger primarily challenged for horizontal effects in concentrated market from merger of two integrated firms, but the Commission also found that vertical integration of both acquiring and acquired firms facilitated monitoring of collusion in upstream market).

52. *See* United States v. GTE Corp., 603 F. Supp. 730 (D.D.C. 1984).

service, would have the incentive and ability to evade rate regulation due to the vertical integration into long-distance service. Specifically, the Division was concerned that the combined firm would misallocate the cost of providing long-distance service to its local telephone service and to discriminate against other long-distance providers if the acquisition were consummated. This was the same theory supporting the government's case against AT&T, which ultimately resulted in the modified final judgment.[53] The parties to the transaction and the Division agreed to a consent decree that permitted the acquisition to proceed subject to separate subsidiary and equal access requirements.

Similarly, in 1986, the FTC challenged the acquisition of MidCon by Occidental Petroleum.[54] MidCon was the owner of several natural gas pipelines that were subject to rate-of-return regulation and Occidental's subsidiary, Cities Service, was a significant producer of natural gas. The Commission was concerned that the merger would allow Occidental to cause MidCon to take Cities Service natural gas at a high price and pass on the cost through the rate regulation mechanism to its customers. The case was settled when Occidental agreed to divest the MidCon pipeline that was in closest proximity to Occidental's natural gas fields.

It is also reported that the combination of Showtime and The Movie Channel (TMC) was restructured in 1983 to eliminate certain vertical aspects to the transaction because of concerns it would significantly increase the incentives for collusion among distributors of theatrical motion pictures upstream. Showtime was owned by Viacom and TMC was owned by Warner Brothers. The transaction was originally proposed as a merger of Showtime and TMC, with the combined entity owned by Paramount Pictures, Universal Studios, Warner Brothers, and Viacom. The Division was concerned that the joint venture would facilitate collusion among the motion picture distributors and raise barriers to entry into movie-driven pay services by tying up critical inputs.[55]

---

53. *See* United States v. AT&T, 552 F. Supp. 131 (D.D.C. 1982), *aff'd sub nom.*, Maryland v. United States, 460 U.S. 1001 (1983).
54. *See* Occidental Petroleum Corp., 109 F.T.C. 167 (1986).
55. *See* White, *supra* note 51. White reports that the market was defined as pay programming services for cable television that relied heavily on theatrically released motion pictures (movie-driven pay services). The providers of these services were thus dependent on the distributors of theatrical motion pictures for their inputs and the firms involved in the proposed joint venture accounted for approximately 40 to 50% of theatrical film rentals. The market for movie-driven pay services was highly concentrated, with HBO accounting for 60%, followed by

E. Post-Chicago Treatment of Foreclosure

As one commentator has observed, "the Chicago School contribution to antitrust did two things. First, it gave us much that was useful. Second, it was oversold."[56] Over time, empiricists found opportunities to test the theoretical approach of the Chicago School, which sometimes included simplifying assumptions inconsistent with the facts of particular cases.[57]

New economic research led to a more complex and textured "post-Chicago" view of vertical mergers and vertical restraints, which may be more likely than the Chicago School approach to support challenges under certain circumstances. At the same time, however, it has also been observed that the more convoluted post-Chicago approach is more difficult to apply and more likely to lead to ambiguous results.[58]

Based on economic studies of strategic behavior and game theory, post-Chicago merger enforcement continued the Chicago School's focus on economic analysis and recognized the efficiency-enhancing potential of many vertical mergers. At the same time, however, post-Chicagoans rejected the view of vertical mergers as almost per se benign and instead emphasized whether intervention was warranted in particular types of cases.[59] The relationship between the post-Chicagoans and the Chicago School is, however, evolutionary rather than revolutionary.

The post-Chicago view focuses vertical merger concerns on vertical integration into markets that do not behave competitively. "Th[e] post-Chicago approach is similar to the traditional 'foreclosure' theory of

---

Showtime with 20% and TMC with 10%.

56. Herbert Hovenkamp, *Post-Chicago Antitrust: A Review and Critique*, 2001 COLUM. BUS. L. REV. 257, 267 (2001).

57. This approach has been called a "post-Chicago" view of antitrust analysis. Michael H. Riordan & Steven C. Salop, *Evaluating Vertical Mergers: A Post-Chicago Approach*, 63 ANTITRUST L.J. 513 (1995).

58. *See* Herbert Hovenkamp, *Post-Chicago Antitrust: A Review and Critique*, 2001 COLUM. BUS. L. REV. 257, 271 (2001) ("[A] constant complaint about post-Chicago economic theories is that they are not testable in the conventional positivist sense").

59. *See, e.g.*, Michael H. Riordan & Steven C. Salop, *Evaluating Vertical Mergers: A Post-Chicago Approach*, 63 ANTITRUST L.J. 513 (1995); Janusz A. Ordover, et al., *Equilibrium Vertical Foreclosure*, 80 AM. ECON. REV. 127 (1990); Patrick Bolton & Michael D. Whinston, *The "Foreclosure" Effects of Vertical Mergers*, 147 J. INST. & THEORETICAL ECON. 207 (1991); Michael A. Salinger, *Vertical Mergers and Market Foreclosure*, 77 Q.J. ECON. 345 (1988).

vertical mergers, except for refinements that control the excesses of the traditional foreclosure approach."[60] At the same time, the foreclosure discussed in post-Chicago literature is not necessarily the foreclosure of *Brown Shoe*. "In the post-Chicago literature, 'foreclosure' generally means raising rivals' costs, not outright market exclusion."[61]

F. Examples of Recent Vertical Merger Enforcement Activity

Antitrust enforcement authorities have incorporated much of the new thinking into their enforcement policies and have stepped up enforcement activity against vertical mergers,[62] leading to a number of enforcement actions based at least in part on various permutations of the raising rivals' costs theory.[63]

---

60. Herbert Hovenkamp, *Post-Chicago Antitrust: A Review and Critique*, 2001 COLUM. BUS. L. REV. 257, 323 (2001).

61. *Id.* at 324.

62. *See* M. Howard Morse, *Vertical Mergers: Recent Learning*, 53 BUS. LAW. 1217 (1998) (discussing 20 post-1992 enforcement actions); Scott A. Stempel, *Government Shows Increasing Concern with Vertical Mergers*, ANTITRUST, Fall 1994, at 17; Richard G. Parker, Trends in Merger Enforcement and Litigation, Remarks Before the Annual Briefing for Corporate Counsel (Sept. 16, 1998), *at* www.ftc.gov/speeches/other/parker.htm (reviewing four 1998 FTC enforcement actions); Steven C. Sunshine, Vertical Merger Enforcement Policy, Remarks at the ABA Section of Antitrust Law Spring Meeting (Apr. 5, 1995), *at* www.usdoj.gov/atr/public/speeches/2215.htm; Christine A. Varney, Competition Policy in Vertical Mergers and Innovation Markets, Remarks Before the Conference of Nat'l Health Lawyers Ass'n (Feb. 16, 1995).

63. *See, e.g.*, United States v. Enova Corp., 63 Fed. Reg. 33,396 (June 18, 1998) (competitive impact statement); PacifiCorp, 5 Trade Reg. Rep. (CCH) ¶24,384 (Feb. 18, 1998) (analysis to aid public comment); Lockheed Martin Corp., 122 F.T.C. 161 (1996); Hughes Danbury Optical Sys., 121 F.T.C. 495 (1996); Silicon Graphics, Inc., 120 F.T.C. 928 (1995); United States v. Sprint Corp., 60 Fed. Reg. 44,049, 44,058 (D.D.C. Aug. 24, 1995) (competitive impact statement); Eli Lilly & Co., 120 F.T.C. 243 (1995); United States v. AT&T, 59 Fed. Reg. 44,158, 44,166 (D.D.C. Aug. 26, 1994) (competitive impact statement); United States v. Tele-Communications, Inc., 1996-2 Trade Cas. (CCH) ¶ 71,496 (D.D.C. 1994); Martin Marietta Corp., 117 F.T.C. 1039 (1994); *see also, e.g.*, Richard G. Parker, Global Merger Enforcement, Remarks Before the Int'l Bar Ass'n (Sept. 28, 1999), *at* www.ftc.gov/speeches/other/barcelona.htm (discussing FTC's application of the raising rivals' cost theory to proposed acquisition of Ingram Group

1. Raising Rivals' Costs and Two-Level Entry

The post-Chicago work began largely as a result of research dealing with possible anticompetitive effects of vertical integration generally.[64] For example, mergers may anticompetitively "raise rivals' costs" in cases in which a downstream firm (the unexcluded firm) is able to purchase exclusionary rights through vertical contract or merger from multiple upstream suppliers, in essence to facilitate a tacit cartel of the upstream suppliers against disadvantaged downstream competitors. Subsequently, the interest of post-Chicago vertical analysis has also been directed to "network externalities," a peculiarity of certain highly networked industries, especially computers and telecommunications, in which access to a network may become increasingly more valuable each time a user is added to the network because a larger network can be employed to reach more users.[65]

In certain circumstances, a cost-raising strategy can cause disadvantaged downstream rivals (whose costs are increased) to follow, or even to lead, a price increase. Disadvantaged rivals may thus be brought into a system of coordinated interaction, or tacit collusion. Their profits can be squeezed by increases in the cost of inputs from the vertically integrated firm, while the conspicuous cost advantage of a vertically integrated competitor-supplier discourages the disadvantaged firms from cutting price to increase sales volume.

The FTC thus entered into a consent decree to resolve its competitive concerns regarding Eli Lilly and Company's acquisition of PCS Health Systems.[66] Eli Lilly was a significant pharmaceutical manufacturer and PCS was a pharmacy benefit manager that managed the pharmacy benefits of health insurance companies and other third-party payors. The complaint alleged that, after the acquisition, Lilly would be likely to foreclose other pharmaceutical manufacturers from the pharmacy plans managed by PCS and that the likelihood of tacit collusion or interdependent conduct between Lilly and the other vertically integrated

by Barnes & Noble, Inc.).

64. *See* Thomas G. Krattenmaker & Steven C. Salop, *Anticompetitive Exclusion: Raising Rivals' Cost to Achieve Power Over Price*, 96 YALE L.J. 209 (1986); Steven C. Salop & David T. Scheffman, *Recent Advances in the Theory of Industrial Structure, Raising Rivals' Costs*, 73 AM. ECON. REV. 267 (1983). *But see* Bruce H. Kobayashi, *Game Theory and Antitrust: A Post Mortem*, 5 GEO. MASON L. REV. 411 (1997).

65. *See, e.g.,* Carl Shapiro, *Exclusivity in Network Industries*, 7 GEO. MASON L. REV 673 (1999).

66. Eli Lilly & Co., 120 F.T.C. 243 (1995).

pharmaceutical manufacturers would be enhanced. The FTC was concerned in part because the Lilly/PCS transaction had been preceded by two other similar transactions involving pharmaceutical companies and pharmacy benefits managers. In the FTC's view, the integrated firms could collectively foreclose unintegrated pharmaceutical companies from an important distribution channel and raise costs significantly. By thus raising their rivals' costs, the integrated firms might be able to raise their own prices collusively or through enhanced interdependent conduct without fear of any competitive response from their unintegrated rivals. To remedy the situation, the consent order prohibited the combined firm from favoring Lilly products distributed through PCS over those of Lilly's competitors.[67]

In 1997, the FTC opposed a vertical merger involving complementary software products, relying on the theory of two-level entry expressed in the 1984 *Merger Guidelines*. According to the first of the 1984 *Merger Guidelines*' three vertical effects theories, a vertical merger may produce anticompetitive effects by requiring new entry to occur in multiple markets simultaneously. The FTC challenged the acquisition by Cadence Design Systems, Inc. of Cooper and Chyan Technology, Inc. (CCT).[68] According to the complaint, Cadence supplied the dominant software environment for the automated design of integrated circuits while CCT sold a particular software tool, known as a "router," which must be able to interface with the software environment in order to plot, or route, the interconnections between transistors and other elements on an integrated circuit. The complaint alleged that, as a result of the merger, Cadence would have the incentive and ability to impede entry attempts by companies developing competing routing technology by denying the competing router an interface to the Cadence integrated circuit layout environment. It was alleged that one likely effect would be to make it necessary for an entrant into the routing tool market to enter simultaneously the market for integrated circuit layout environments.

Thus, according to a statement accompanying the consent agreement that was issued by a majority of the Commission, the complaint alleged "a well-established vertical theory of competitive harm, laid out in the

---

67. The consent order was subsequently set aside following Lilly's sale of PCS to Rite Aid Corporation. *See* Eli Lilly & Co., Order Reopening and Setting Aside Order, Docket No. C-3594, 1999 FTC LEXIS 86 (May 13, 1999).

68. *See* Cadence Design Sys., 124 F.T.C. 131 (1997).

1984 *Merger Guidelines*"[69] that anticompetitive effects can result if entry is less likely because firms must simultaneously enter two or more markets. The statement, however, identified the loss of innovation generated by entrants to the market as the competitive harm resulting from the barrier to entry[70] rather than the effect of the entry barrier on collusion. The Commission allowed the transaction to proceed but required Cadence to permit developers of integrated circuit routing tools to participate in a Cadence licensing program to enable them to create and sell competing routers.

In 1999, the FTC investigated the proposed acquisition by Barnes & Noble, the largest book retailer in the United States, of Ingram Book Group, the largest wholesaler of books in the United States. The FTC was concerned that the acquisition of an important upstream supplier such as Ingram might enable Barnes & Noble to raise the costs of its bookselling rivals, such as independent book retailers or Internet retailers, by foreclosing access to Ingram's books and services or denying access on competitive terms. The rivals would be less able to compete, and Barnes & Nobel could increase its profits at the retail level or prevent its profits from being eroded as a result of competition from new business forms such as Internet retailing. The FTC was concerned that the combined Barnes & Noble/Ingram could do that in a number of ways, including strategies short of an outright refusal to sell to the non-Barnes & Noble bookstores. For example, Barnes & Noble/Ingram could choose to (1) sell to non-Barnes & Noble bookstores at higher prices, (2) slow down book shipments to rivals, (3) restrict access to hot titles, (4) restrict access to Ingram's extended inventory or back list, or (5) price services higher or discontinue or reduce these services.[71] The parties abandoned the acquisition following press reports that the FTC would seek an injunction.

2. *Facilitating Coordinated Interaction*

Another vertical merger issue involves certain information exchanges alleged to increase the likelihood of coordinated interaction, a

---

69. *Id.* at 142.
70. *See id.* at 143.
71. Sheila F. Anthony, Vertical Issues; The Federal View, Remarks Before The American Law Institute-American Bar Association (Mar. 9, 2000), *at* www.ftc.gov/speeches/anthony/verticalspeech/other/barcelona.htm; Richard G. Parker, Global Merger Enforcement, Remarks Before the International Bar Association (Sept. 28, 1999), *at* www.ftc.gov/speeches/other/barcelona.htm.

type of problem that has often been addressed by allowing the transaction to proceed subject to some form of information firewall.[72] Such firewalls often were used when there is already some regulatory scheme in place, such as in the military procurement context. Martin Marietta's acquisition of the Space Systems Division of General Dynamics, which manufactured Atlas class expendable satellite launch vehicles, is an example of a vertical merger raising concerns that it would enable information exchanges that could facilitate coordinated interaction.[73]

Martin Marietta was a significant producer of satellites that use such launch vehicles. The complaint alleged that the acquisition could increase the ability of Martin Marietta to gain access to competitively significant and nonpublic information concerning other satellite manufacturers using Atlas class expendable launch vehicles. The Commission, with one dissent, accepted a consent decree that permitted that acquisition to go forward but prohibited the merged firm's launch vehicle business from transferring nonpublic information to the satellite division regarding other satellite manufacturers.

Northrop Grumman's acquisition of TRW raised similar vertical merger concerns in connection with satellite payloads, as opposed to satellite launch vehicles, and produced a similar firewall along with related open access requirements as a solution.[74] Northrop Grumman was one of two companies supplying the U.S. Government with certain reconnaissance satellite payloads, including radar sensors and electro-optical/infrared sensors. TRW was one of only a few companies with the capability to act as a prime contractor on the reconnaissance satellite programs that used the Northrop Grumman payloads. The Antitrust

---

72. *See, e.g.*, Raytheon Co., 122 F.T.C. 94 (1996); Hughes Danbury Optical Sys., 121 F.T.C. 495 (1996); Eli Lilly & Co., 120 F.T.C. 243 (1995); Alliant Techsystems Inc., 119 F.T.C. 440 (1995) (consent decree prohibiting Alliant from disclosing any nonpublic information received from competing ammunition manufacturers in its capacity as a supplier of propellant to them); United States v. MCI Communs. Corp., 59 Fed. Reg. 33,009 (D.D.C. June 15, 1994) (competitive impact statement) (consent decree imposing strict confidentiality requirements on the formation of a joint venture with British Telecommunications plc to provide international telecommunications services). *But see* TRW Inc., 125 F.T.C. 496 (1998) (divestiture of service contract and related assets required as a condition of proceeding with the transaction).

73. *See* Martin Marietta Corp., 117 F.T.C. 1039 (1994).

74. *See* United States v. Northrop Grumman Corp., 68 Fed. Reg. 1861 (Jan. 14, 2003) (competitive impact statement).

Division alleged that the acquisition would give Northrop Grumman the incentive and ability to favor its captive payload and/or prime contractor capabilities to the detriment or foreclosure of rivals, or enable Northrop Grumman to raise rivals' costs anticompetitively.

The consent agreement required Northrop Grumman to maintain its satellite payload and satellite prime contractor businesses as separate entities, establish firewalls, and take other actions to protect the information provided by other payload providers or prime contractors. The consent agreement also required Northrop Grumman's payload operations to supply other satellite prime contractors on terms comparable to the intra-company terms.

3. *Media Mergers*

During the 1990s, three media mergers demonstrated vertical merger concerns that may arise as a result of the combination of a firm that produces media content with a firm that distributes the content: TCI/Liberty, Time Warner/Turner, and AOL/Time Warner. In 1994, the Division entered into a consent decree directed at the merger of Tele-Communications, Inc. (TCI) and Liberty Media Corporation.[75] TCI was the largest cable system operator in the United States and Liberty also owned a significant number of cable systems. Together, the two companies accounted for approximately one-quarter of the nation's cable subscribers. In addition, both companies had substantial interests in video programming providers (e.g., TBS, CNN, Home Shopping Network, Prime Sports Network). The complaint alleged that the merger would decrease competition among video programming services because the combined firm would have the ability and incentive to foreclose independent video programmers from the combined firm's cable systems. Such exclusion would likely subject independent programming services to serious cost disadvantages due to the size of the merged firm's cable operations from which these independent programmers would be foreclosed. The complaint also alleged that the combined firm, with its substantial share of the video programming providers market, could similarly discriminate against direct broadcast and other program delivery systems, thereby raising their costs of obtaining video programming. The consent judgment mandated open access to prevent such foreclosure.

---

75. *See* United States v. Tele-Communications, Inc., 1996-2 Trade Cas. (CCH) ¶ 71,496 (D.D.C. 1994).

The FTC, in 1997, challenged another media merger involving Time Warner's acquisition of Turner Broadcasting.[76] Because Tele-Communications, Inc. owned a large share of Turner Broadcasting, the combination of Turner Broadcasting and Time Warner would have resulted in Tele-Communications, Inc., the nation's largest cable operator, owning a significant percentage of Time Warner, the nation's second largest cable system. In addition, the three companies—Tele-Communications, Inc., Turner Broadcasting and Time Warner—were also significant providers of video programming services. The Commission alleged that Time Warner and TCI would have the collective ability to foreclose unaffiliated program services from their cable systems and that their programming services could disadvantage competing multichannel distribution systems (e.g., direct broadcast satellite, wireless cable) by price discriminating against them. The Commission also feared that the acquisition could block future entry into all-news networks, a segment then dominated by Turner-owned CNN. By controlling access to 44 percent of the nation's cable subscribers, it was alleged, the postmerger Time Warner would have the power and the incentive to prevent competing all-news networks from accessing the Time Warner distribution system.

The Commission allowed the transaction to proceed subject to the provisions of a consent decree prohibiting Time Warner from discriminating against providers of programming services in its cable operations, from discriminating against competing multi-channel distribution systems in its programming service business, and requiring Time Warner cable operations to carry all-news networks that competed with CNN. The consent decree also imposed limitations on TCI's exercise of the minority ownership position it would have acquired in Time Warner as a result of the exchange of Turner shares for Time Warner shares, plus eventual disposition of the shares.

A few years later, the world's leading provider of online access and related services, AOL, announced that it would acquire Time Warner, by then the world's largest media company.[77] In addition to its other information and entertainment operations, Time Warner's CNN and Time Magazine distributed news content through Internet web sites, and Time Warner's cable television operations offered broadband Internet

---

76. Time Warner Inc., 123 F.T.C. 171 (1997).

77. *See* America Online, Inc., 2001 F.T.C. LEXIS 44 (2001); FTC Docket No. C-3989 (Apr. 18, 2001), *at* www.ftc.gov/os/2001/04/aoltwdo.pdf.

hardware connection service bundled with Time Warner's internet service provider (ISP), Roadrunner.[78]

Shortly before the public announcement of the AOL/Time Warner acquisition, the Chairman of the FTC had cited his agency's Time Warner/Turner consent decree in testimony before the Senate Commerce Committee to illustrate the anticompetitive effects that might result from telecommunications mergers. As discussed above, vertical effects of concern in Time Warner/Turner included limitations on access to content by distribution systems and on access to distribution by content providers. Meanwhile, senior staff of the FTC Bureau of Competition opined that the FTC's analysis of the Time Warner/Turner merger would be applicable to a merger involving an ISP and a broadband Internet connection service.[79]

Following a year-long investigation, the FTC found the possibility of harm to competition as a result of vertical foreclosure in three product markets: residential broadband Internet hardware connection service, broadband ISP service, and interactive television service, which was viewed as requiring a broadband connection to be commercially viable. To remedy this harm, the FTC required AOL to agree to guarantees of open access along the lines of what AOL itself had advocated prior to the announcement of the Time Warner investigation.[80]

---

78. *See* Daniel L. Rubinfeld and Hal J. Singer, *Open Access to Broadband Networks: A Case Study of the AOL/Time Warner Merger*, 16 BERKELEY TECH. L.J. 631 (Spring 2001).

79. *See* Robert N. Cook, *AOL/Time Warner: The Close Antitrust Call and the Changing of the Guard at the FTC*, ANTITRUST REPORT, May 2001 at 2, 11.

80. For more than a year before the announcement of the Time Warner merger, AOL had been lobbying for government action to impose open access requirements on cable companies with broadband modem service. AOL was frequently prevented from providing ISP service to consumers trading up from dial-in Internet access over conventional telephone lines to broadband cable modem access, because cable companies generally required cable modem customers to use a captive, or otherwise exclusive, ISP. That left ISPs that did not own cable systems, such as AOL, unable to reach customers trading up to cable modem service. At about the time it was becoming evident that AOL would not be able to obtain access to broadband Internet users through government regulation, AOL announced its proposed acquisition of Time Warner, which operated the second largest cable television system in the United States. *See id.* at 9. *See also* Federal Communications Commission's approval of the Hughes Electronics Corp. and News Corp. transaction in December 2003. 2003 FCC LEXIS 7056 (As a result of the transaction, News Corp. obtained a controlling interest over Hughes and its subsidiary Direct TV). In light of restrictions imposed by the

In areas where Time Warner operated cable systems, AOL was required to offer broadband ISP service via non-cable DSL connection, in addition to Time Warner's cable modem service. The FTC also required the combined AOL/Time Warner to permit Earthlink, a competing ISP, to offer broadband Internet access to Time Warner cable modem service subscribers. Finally, the consent agreement prohibited the combined AOL/Time Warner from discriminating against interactive television services provided by other companies.

FCC, the Division declined to challenge the transaction. *See* U.S. Dep't of Justice, Press Release, Justice Department Will Not Challenge News Corp.'s Acquisition of Hughes Electronics Corp. (Dec. 19, 2003), *at* www.usdoj.gov/atr/public_releases/2003/201918.htm.

CHAPTER 11

CONGLOMERATE MERGERS

The U.S. Supreme Court has described a conglomerate merger as "one in which there are no economic relationships between the acquiring and the acquired firm."[1] Lower courts and commentators have categorized a merger as conglomerate more generally, calling any merger conglomerate if the relationship between the parties is neither horizontal nor vertical.[2]

Historically, courts classified nonhorizontal mergers as either "vertical" or "conglomerate" and developed separate analytical approaches and criteria to evaluate the likely competitive effects of particular transactions in each of these categories.[3] But, as the U.S. Supreme Court said in another context, "easy labels do not always supply ready answers."[4] Some nonhorizontal mergers do not fit neatly into this dichotomy and the analysis identified for a single category of

---

1. FTC v. Procter & Gamble Co., 386 U.S. 568, 577 n.2 (1967). The description is similar to the definition used when the Clayton Act was amended. Conglomerate mergers were defined as "those in which there is no discernible relationship in the nature of the business between the acquiring and acquired firms." H.R. REP. NO. 1191, 81st Cong., 1st Sess. 11 (1949).
2. *See, e.g.*, Babcock & Wilcox Co. v. United Techs. Corp., 435 F. Supp. 1249, 1284 (N.D. Ohio 1977) (conglomerate merger occurs where firms "each operate in markets that are not horizontally or vertically related to those in which the other functions"). Professor Turner defines conglomerate mergers as "all acquisitions other than (1) acquisition by a producer of the stock or assets of a firm producing an identical product or close substitute and selling it in the same geographical market—the simple horizontal merger; and (2) acquisition of the stock or assets of a firm that buys the product sold by the acquirer or sells a product bought by the acquirer—the simple vertical merger." Donald F. Turner, *Conglomerate Mergers and Section 7 of the Clayton Act,* 78 HARV. L. REV. 1313, 1315 (1965).
3. *See, e.g.*, Brown Shoe Co. v. United States, 370 U.S. 294, 317 (1962); *see also* 5 PHILLIP E. AREEDA & DONALD F. TURNER, ANTITRUST LAW ¶¶ 1100-1164 (2003); LAWRENCE ANTHONY SULLIVAN, HANDBOOK OF THE LAW OF ANTITRUST 653-69 (1977).
4. Broadcast Music, Inc. v. CBS, 441 U.S. 1, 8 (1979); *see also* NCAA v. Board of Regents, 468 U.S. 85, 109 n.39 (1984).

nonhorizontal mergers does not always provide the full analysis of a transaction. For instance, in some cases, the analysis of a single merger may require the application of vertical merger analysis in some markets, conglomerate analysis in other markets, and horizontal analysis in still others.[5] In other cases, such as mergers between producers of imperfect substitutes, the transaction may not fit easily into any of the horizontal, vertical, or conglomerate classifications.

In its 1982 *Merger Guidelines*, the Antitrust Division of the U.S. Department of Justice (DOJ or the Division) departed from this historical classification of nonhorizontal mergers.[6] The 1982 *Merger Guidelines* state that the characterization of nonhorizontal mergers as either vertical or conglomerate "adds nothing to the analysis."[7] Without regard to the traditional classifications, the 1982 *Merger Guidelines* and their revision in 1984[8] focus on the ability of the nonhorizontal merger to reduce competition by permitting the creation or exercise of market power. The *Merger Guidelines* still organize the theories that the Division is likely to use to challenge nonhorizontal mergers according to

---

5. *See, e.g.*, United States v. Aluminum Co. of Am., 377 U.S. 271 (1964) (acquisition of aluminum and copper wire manufacturer by integrated producer of aluminum and aluminum products was vertical in the supply of aluminum for aluminum wire and in the supply of an intermediate aluminum wire product, conglomerate in the acquisition of copper products because aluminum and copper wire were found to be separate lines of commerce, and horizontal in the manufacture and sale of aluminum wire and cable).
6. U.S. DEP'T OF JUSTICE, MERGER GUIDELINES (1982) [hereinafter 1982 MERGER GUIDELINES], *reprinted in* 4 Trade Reg. Rep. (CCH) ¶ 13,102.
7. *Id.* § IV.A.1, n.39.
8. U.S. DEP'T OF JUSTICE, MERGER GUIDELINES (1984) § 4.1 n.25 [hereinafter 1984 MERGER GUIDELINES], *reprinted in* 4 Trade Reg. Rep. (CCH) ¶ 13,103. The 1992 *Horizontal Merger Guidelines* do not specifically address nonhorizontal mergers. U.S. DEP'T OF JUSTICE & FEDERAL TRADE COMM'N, HORIZONTAL MERGER GUIDELINES (1992) [hereinafter 1992 MERGER GUIDELINES], *reprinted in* 4 Trade Reg. Rep. ¶ 13,104 and in Appendix I. A statement accompanying the release of the 1992 *Merger Guidelines* said that the policy regarding nonhorizontal mergers was unchanged and that guidance is provided by the 1984 *Merger Guidelines* read in the context of the changes regarding the treatment of horizontal mergers provided by the 1992 *Merger Guidelines*. U.S. DEP'T OF JUSTICE & FEDERAL TRADE COMM'N, STATEMENT ACCOMPANYING RELEASE OF REVISED MERGER GUIDELINES 3 (Apr. 2, 1992), *reprinted in* 4 Trade Reg. Rep. (CCH) ¶ 13,104.

the traditional vertical and conglomerate classifications, but do not restrict the application of the theories to those labels.

Within the group of mergers that are neither horizontal nor vertical, the U.S. Supreme Court has distinguished between pure conglomerate mergers (no economic relationship) and mergers which are "neither horizontal, vertical, nor conglomerate."[9] Within the latter classification are product extension mergers and market extension mergers. An acquisition has been termed a "product extension merger" because "the products of the acquired company are complementary to those of the acquiring company and may be produced with similar facilities, marketed through the same channels and in the same manner, and advertised by the same media."[10] In addition, the products of the acquiring and acquired firms may be marketed to the same ultimate consumer.[11] A merger is termed a "market extension merger" when the merger occurs between firms that sell the same product but in different geographic markets.[12]

The 1982 and 1984 *Merger Guidelines* do not identify any theories on which to challenge conglomerate mergers, except the elimination of potential competition.[13] Given the economic focus of merger analysis, there has been little interest in conglomerate mergers since the 1970s.[14] Nevertheless, there are a number of competitive concerns, including the entrenchment of dominant firms, the prospect of increasing reciprocal dealing arrangements, and the potential for increased tying, that could arise in the context of conglomerate mergers.

---

9. FTC v. Procter & Gamble Co., 386 U.S. 568, 578 (1967).
10. *Id.*
11. *Id.* at 577-78.
12. *See, e.g.*, United States v. Marine Bancorp., 418 U.S. 602 (1974); United States v. Connecticut Nat'l Bank, 418 U.S. 656 (1974); United States v. Falstaff Brewing Corp., 410 U.S. 526 (1973); United States v. Phillips Petroleum Co., 367 F. Supp. 1226 (C.D. Cal. 1973), *aff'd mem.*, 418 U.S. 906 (1974).
13. *See generally* Chapter 9.
14. Indeed, one court has suggested that theories of anticompetitive effects from conglomerate mergers are not persuasive. *See* T. N. Dickinson Co. v. LL Corp., 1985-2 Trade Cas. (CCH) ¶ 66,777 (D. Conn. 1985) ("[n]o allegations suggest that [successor company] was either a competitor, a supplier or customer, or potential competitor" on face of complaint so that, according to complaint, acquisition had no effect on structure of competition).

A. Evaluative Criteria for Judging Conglomerate Mergers

The legislative history of the 1950 amendments to Section 7 makes clear that Section 7 was intended to apply to all mergers—horizontal, vertical, and conglomerate.[15] As the U.S. Supreme Court acknowledged in *FTC v. Procter & Gamble Co.*,[16] "[a]ll mergers are within the reach of § 7, and all must be tested by the same standard, whether they are classified as horizontal, vertical, conglomerate or other."[17] Thus, like any other merger, conglomerate mergers violate Section 7 if they are likely substantially to lessen competition or to tend to create a monopoly.[18]

Although the evaluation of conglomerate mergers under Section 7 is primarily an economic evaluation, conglomerate mergers have been publicly condemned for other perceived social and political effects. Conglomerate mergers have been criticized, for example, for contributing to aggregate increases in economic power and possible noneconomic effects that could result from an increase in general economic concentration.[19] Critics have feared that the economic concentration would lead to a corresponding aggregation in political power by the fewer but more powerful conglomerate firms, placing major decisions, both political and economic, in the hands of a few individuals or firms that have no direct accountability to the general public.[20] Moreover, opponents have expressed the fear that the

---

15. H.R. REP. NO. 1191, 81st Cong. 1st Sess. 11 (1949). *See* Brown Shoe Co. v. United States, 370 U.S. 294, 317 (1962); FTC v. Procter & Gamble Co., 386 U.S. at 577.
16. 386 U.S. 568 (1967).
17. *Id.* at 577.
18. *See* United States v. Northwest Indus., 301 F. Supp. 1066, 1096 (N.D. Ill. 1969) ("the law as it now stands ... makes the adverse effect on competition the test of validity and until Congress broadens the criteria, the Court must judge proposed transactions on that standard"); United States v. Times Mirror Co., 274 F. Supp. 606, 613-14 (C.D. Cal. 1967), *aff'd*, 390 U.S. 712 (1967).
19. *See, e.g.*, Staff of Federal Trade Comm'n, Economic Report on Corporate Mergers: Hearings on Economic Concentration Before the Subcomm. on Antitrust and Monopoly of the Senate Comm. on the Judiciary, 91st Cong., 1st Sess. (1969); White House Task Force, Report on Antitrust Policy (July 5, 1968) (Neal Report), *reprinted in* Antitrust & Trade Reg. Rep. (BNA) No. 411, Special Supplement—Part II (May 27, 1969); Robert Pitofsky, *The Political Content of Antitrust*, 127 U. PA. L. REV. 1051 (1979).
20. *Hearings on Acquisitions and Mergers by Conglomerates of Unrelated*

aggregation of economic power would lead to the loss of local control of businesses and economic decisions. Finally, there has been apprehension that the loss of local control and accountability would lead to demands by the public for a greater role of government to control industry.[21]

These concerns about economic concentration and conglomerate mergers led to congressional hearings during the conglomerate merger wave of the 1970s to determine whether legislation was needed to reduce the number of mergers and slow the rate of economic concentration.[22] Legislative proposals were introduced to require fuller disclosure of the financial operations of corporations, to change the tax laws to remove incentives for acquisitions, and to prohibit mergers involving firms over particular dollar thresholds and leading firms in concentrated industries.[23] None of the proposals has been enacted.[24] Currently, economic analysis

---

Businesses Before the Subcomm. on Antitrust and Monopoly of the Senate Comm. on the Judiciary, 95th Cong., 2d Sess. (1978) (Statement of John H. Shenefield, Ass't Att'y Gen., for Antitrust); *Hearings on Small and Independent Business Protection Act of 1979 Before the Subcomm. on Antitrust, Monopoly and Business Rights of the Senate Comm. on the Judiciary*, 96th Cong., 1st Sess. 14-15 (1979) (Statement of Michael Pertschuk, Chairman, FTC).

21. *Hearings on Small and Independent Business Protection Act of 1979 Before the Subcomm. on Antitrust, Monopoly and Business Rights of the Senate Comm. on the Judiciary*, 96th Cong., 1st Sess. 14 (1979) (Statement of Michael Pertschuk, Chairman, FTC).

22. *See, e.g.*, *Hearings on Acquisitions and Mergers by Conglomerates of Unrelated Businesses Before the Subcomm. on Antitrust and Monopoly of the Comm. on the Judiciary*, 95th Cong., 2d Sess. (1978); *Hearings on Small and Independent Business Protection Act of 1979 Before the Subcomm. on Antitrust, Monopoly and Business Rights of the Comm. on the Judiciary*, 96th Cong., 1st Sess. (1979).

23. *See, e.g.*, Staff of Federal Trade Comm'n, Economic Report on Corporate Mergers: Hearings on Economic Concentration Before the Subcomm. on Antitrust and Monopoly of the Senate Comm. on the Judiciary, 91st Cong., 1st Sess. 19 (1969); White House Task Force, Report on Antitrust Policy 7-9 (July 5, 1968) (Neal Report), *reprinted in* Antitrust & Trade Reg. Rep. (BNA) No. 411, Special Supplement—Part II (May 27, 1969); Julian O. von Kalinowski & Kenneth W. Starr, *Congress and the Conglomerate Merger Phenomenon: The Introduction of Antitrust Proposals to Address Non-Antitrust Concerns*, 17 HARV. J. ON LEGIS. 209 (1980).

24. Critics and commentators too have proposed that noneconomic and political considerations be incorporated into antitrust decisions. *See, e.g.*, Robert Pitofsky, *The Political Content of Antitrust*, 127 U. PA. L. REV. 1051 (1979); Louis B. Schwartz, *"Justice" and Other Non-Economic*

dominates the legal evaluation of conglomerate mergers.[25] Indeed, in the wake of sharp disagreement between U.S. and EU competition authorities over the European Commission's decision to block the proposed GE/Honeywell merger, U.S. antitrust officials have issued broad criticisms of conglomerate merger analysis, stating that, "[a]fter fifteen years of painful experience with these now long-abandoned theories, the U.S. antitrust agencies concluded that antitrust should rarely, if ever, interfere with any conglomerate merger."[26]

B. Competitive Concerns

1. Entrenchment

Conglomerate mergers have been found substantially to lessen competition and therefore to violate Section 7 where a dominant firm in an oligopolistic market is acquired by an even stronger and larger company with resources that entrench the existing dominant position of the acquired firm.[27] In *FTC v. Procter & Gamble Co.*,[28] the seminal entrenchment case under Section 7, the U.S. Supreme Court found that "the substitution of the powerful acquiring firm for the smaller, but already dominant, firm may substantially reduce the competitive structure of the industry by raising entry barriers and by dissuading the

---

Goals of Antitrust, 127 U. PA. L. REV. 1076 (1979); Willard F. Mueller, *The Rising Economic Concentration in America: Reciprocity, Conglomeration, and the New American "Zaibatsu" System*, 4 ANTITRUST L. & ECON. REV. 15 (1971).

25. Courts have rejected arguments regarding general economic concentration as a basis to challenge conglomerate mergers under § 7 of the Clayton Act. *See* United States v. ITT Corp., 324 F. Supp. 19, 52-54 (D. Conn. 1970), *cert. dismissed*, 404 U.S. 801 (1971).

26. Conglomerate Mergers and Range Effects: It's a Long Way from Chicago to Brussels, Address by William J. Kolasky, Deputy Ass't Att'y Gen., Antitrust Div., U.S. Dept. of Justice, Before the George Mason Univ. Symposium, (Nov. 9, 2001), *at* www.usdoj.gov/atr/public/speeches/9536.htm.

27. Most mergers which have been challenged for entrenching the dominant firm in the industry also challenge the merger for the elimination of potential competition because the plaintiff alleges that the resources that the acquiring firm provides also made the acquiring firm a likely de novo entrant. For a discussion of the potential competition doctrine, see Chapter 9.

28. 386 U.S. 568 (1967).

smaller firms from aggressively competing."[29] Thus, the substitution of the larger firm is thought to make the existing oligopoly in the market more rigid because the acquiring firm provides some cost advantage that reinforces the dominant position of the acquired firm.

Early cases concluded that the mere substitution of the dominant firm in the industry with a larger firm, with its financial "deep pocket," would entrench the position of the acquired firm. These cases concluded that the deep pocket alone would discourage competition and entry because the company could obtain financial or other backing to better withstand narrow profit margins.[30] They do not necessarily identify a specific relative advantage arising from a deep pocket or large size.[31]

Generally, however, the entrenchment theory requires that the acquiring firm provide the acquired firm some competitive advantage that secures the existing dominant position in the industry. Under this theory, the large size of the acquiring firm alone is insufficient to violate Section 7.[32] To prevail on an entrenchment theory, a Section 7 plaintiff

---

29. *Id.* at 578.

30. *See* United States Steel Corp. v. FTC, 426 F.2d 592 (6th Cir. 1970) ("sheer size and financial resources of U.S. Steel visit non-competitive stabilizing forces upon the competitors"); Reynolds Metals Co. v. FTC, 309 F.2d 223, 229-30 (D.C. Cir. 1962) (deep pocket provides ability to price below cost, but court does not "intimate that the mere intrusion of 'bigness' into a competitive economic community otherwise populated by commercial 'pygmies' will per se invoke the Clayton Act"); United States v. Wilson Sporting Goods Co., 288 F. Supp. 543, 556-57 (N.D. Ill. 1968) (greater likelihood that "competition in the industry will be lessened because of the adverse psychological effects the merger will engender among Nissen's smaller rivals, and upon potential new entrants into the market").

31. *See* Kennecott Copper Corp. v. FTC, 467 F.2d 67 (10th Cir. 1972) (funds will enable firm to purchase coal reserves); Ekco Prods. Co. v. FTC, 347 F.2d 745 (7th Cir. 1965) (resources provide ability to overcome financial distress of acquired monopolist); United States v. Ingersoll-Rand Co., 218 F. Supp. 530, 554 (W.D. Pa.) (economy of scale is advantage), *aff'd,* 320 F.2d 509 (3d Cir. 1963).

32. *See, e.g.*, Emhart Corp. v. USM Corp., 527 F.2d 177, 181 (1st Cir. 1975); NBO Indus. Treadway Cos. v. Brunswick Corp., 523 F.2d 262, 274 (3d Cir. 1975), *vacated and remanded sub nom.* Brunswick Corp. v. Pueblo Bowl-O-Mat, Inc., 429 U.S. 477 (1977); Missouri Portland Cement Co. v. Cargill, Inc., 498 F.2d 851, 865 & n.32 (2d Cir. 1974) ("the 'deep pocket' claim seems more metaphorical than real"); Reynolds Metals Co. v. FTC, 309 F.2d 223, 230 (D.C. Cir. 1962); *Wilson Sporting Goods Co.*, 288 F. Supp. at 554; Smith-Victor Corp. v. Sylvania Elec. Prods., Inc., 242 F.

must do "more than simply showing that the acquiring firm has a deep pocket."[33] "The likelihood of specific, anticompetitive advantages must be established."[34]

The 1982 and 1984 *Merger Guidelines* do not include entrenchment as a possible basis to challenge conglomerate mergers.[35] Furthermore, the Federal Trade Commission (FTC or the Commission) has required rigorous proof of the elements before the theory will block an acquisition.[36] In *Beatrice Foods*,[37] for example, the FTC found that Beatrice Foods' acquisition of Tropicana would not entrench Tropicana in the market because "the record proves no *unique* advertising efficiencies to the merged firm that are a direct consequence of the acquisition."[38] The FTC found that it was "at least questionable whether" the integration of Beatrice Foods' distribution system "would

---

Supp. 315, 319-20 (N.D. Ill. 1965) (summary judgment for defendant granted on other grounds); United States v. FMC Corp., 218 F. Supp. 817 (N.D. Cal. 1963) (preliminary injunction denied because no anticompetitive effects shown where bigness is only basis for challenge). *But see* Allis-Chalmers Mfg. Co. v. White Consol. Indus., 414 F.2d 506, 521 (3d Cir. 1969) (preliminary injunction should be granted where acquired firm is dominant competitor for complementary products of acquiring firm).

33. *Missouri Portland Cement Co.*, 498 F.2d at 865; FTC v. Atlantic Richfield Co., 549 F.2d 289, 298 n.12 (4th Cir. 1977) (deep pocket unpersuasive); *accord* United States v. Consolidated Foods Corp., 1978-1 Trade Cas. (CCH) ¶ 62,063, at 74,617 (E.D. Pa. 1978); *Emhart Corp.*, 527 F.2d at 181; *NBO Indus. Treadway Co.*, 523 F.2d at 274 (practical limitations on extent to which capital may be utilized for competitive advantage); Nov. 9, 2001 Kolasky Address, *supra* note 26 (criticizing European Commission use of "deep pockets" analysis in blocking GE/Honeywell merger). *But see* Monfort of Colo., Inc. v. Cargill, Inc., 761 F.2d 570, 581 (10th Cir. 1985) (deep pocket relevant where wealthy parent company would facilitate sustained predation), *rev'd on other grounds*, 479 U.S. 104 (1986).

34. *Emhart Corp.*, 527 F.2d at 181; *accord Missouri Portland Cement Co.*, 498 F.2d at 865-66.

35. *See* 1984 MERGER GUIDELINES, *supra* note 8; 1982 MERGER GUIDELINES, *supra* note 6.

36. *See* Beatrice Foods Co., 101 F.T.C. 733, 829 (1983); Heublein, Inc., 96 F.T.C. 385, 593 (1980) ("because adverse competitive effects from 'entrenchment' can be rather elusive, it is particularly important that a factual basis be carefully constructed").

37. 101 F.T.C. 733 (1983).

38. *Id.* at 828.

have the effect of significantly raising barriers to entry or expansion or otherwise substantially decreasing competition."[39]

Many commentators argue that the entrenchment theory encounters important theoretical and practical problems that discourage its application. It is difficult to determine, for example, whether the competitive advantages bestowed on an acquired firm by a merger are actually anticompetitive. Frequently, the mechanism that confers the advantage on the merged firm produces reductions in cost and increases in economic efficiency.[40] Thus, on a fundamental level, the doctrine may be inconsistent with the first principle of antitrust: promoting economic efficiency and consumer welfare.[41]

Other commentators have challenged the underlying premise of the theory that rival firms will compete less aggressively following the creation of the more efficient firm.[42] These commentators argue that rivals are more likely to try to match the competitive efforts of the larger firm to keep from falling behind the merged firm. Consequently, smaller firms in the industry may reduce their costs and improve their products to compete with the more efficient firm.[43]

Proponents of the entrenchment theory argue that the doctrine promotes deconcentration and furthers one of the social goals underlying congressional enactment of the antitrust laws.[44] Under this view, the antitrust laws were enacted to deconcentrate economic power and encourage decentralization, not to promote economic efficiency. Use of

---

39. *Id.* at 829.
40. *See* Emhart Corp. v. USM Corp., 527 F.2d 177, 182 (1st Cir. 1975) (sharing technological capabilities and rationalization of machinery are "gains in straightforward efficiency, and not unfair advantages").
41. 5 PHILLIP AREEDA & DONALD F. TURNER, ANTITRUST LAW ¶ 1102 (2003).
42. *See, e.g.*, ROBERT H. BORK, THE ANTITRUST PARADOX 256-57 (1978). This position was advocated in the concurring opinion of Justice Harlan in *FTC v. Procter & Gamble Co.*, 386 U.S. 568, 584 (1967) (Harlan, J., concurring); *accord* Butler Aviation Co. v. Civil Aeronautics Bd., 389 F.2d 517, 520 (2d Cir. 1968).
43. *Cf.* Jonathan B. Baker, *Promoting Innovation Competition through the Aspen/Kodak Rule*, 7 GEO. MASON L. REV. 495 (1999) (discussing the debate over whether competition or monopoly best promotes innovation).
44. Lawrence K. Hellman, *"Entrenchment" under Section 7 of the Clayton Act: An Approach for Analyzing Conglomerate Mergers*, 13 LOY. L. REV. 225 (1982).

the entrenchment theory as a tool to challenge conglomerate mergers is consistent with this view of the purposes of antitrust law.

2. *Reciprocity*

In conglomerate merger cases, reciprocity refers "to a seller's practice of utilizing the volume or potential volume of its purchases to induce others to purchase its goods or services."[45] The essence of the reciprocal arrangement is that each company is willing to buy from the other on the expectation that the other company will reciprocate. The products that are purchased are generally dissimilar and may be in wholly unrelated markets.

The 1982, 1984 and 1992 *Merger Guidelines* do not make any reference to reciprocal dealing.[46] Moreover, neither the Division nor the FTC has brought a Section 7 case based on the reciprocity theory in recent years.

Nonetheless, the creation of a structure that permits reciprocal dealing by merger has in the past been considered a violation of Section 7. In *FTC v. Consolidated Foods Corp.*,[47] the U.S. Supreme Court held that

> [R]eciprocity made possible by such an acquisition is one of the congeries of anticompetitive practices at which the antitrust laws

---

45. Crouse-Hinds Co. v. Internorth, Inc., 518 F. Supp. 416, 434 (N.D.N.Y. 1980); *see also* FTC v. Consolidated Foods Corp., 380 U.S. 592, 594 (1965); Southern Concrete Co. v. United States Steel Corp., 535 F.2d 313, 317 (5th Cir. 1976); Gulf & W. Indus. v. Great Atl. & Pac. Tea Co., 476 F.2d 687, 694 (2d Cir. 1973); Allis-Chalmers Mfg. Co. v. White Consol. Indus., 414 F.2d 506, 518-19 (3d Cir. 1969); Carrier Corp. v. United Techs. Corp., 1978-2 Trade Cas. (CCH) ¶62,393 (N.D.N.Y.), *aff'd*, 1978-2 Trade Cas. (CCH) ¶ 62,405 (2d Cir. 1978); United States v. ITT Corp., 306 F. Supp. 766, 781 (S.D.N.Y. 1969), *appeal dismissed*, 404 U.S. 801 (1971); United States v. General Dynamics Corp., 258 F. Supp. 36, 57 (S.D.N.Y. 1966).

46. The Division's 1968 *Merger Guidelines* listed reciprocal buying as a competitive effect from a conglomerate merger that would lead the Division to challenge the merger. U.S. DEP'T OF JUSTICE, MERGER GUIDELINES § 19 (1968), *reprinted in* 4 Trade Reg. Rep. (CCH) ¶ 13,101. The 1968 *Merger Guidelines* also stated that the Division would likely challenge a conglomerate merger where the purpose of the merger was to create reciprocal buying arrangements and the merging firms have a history of directly or indirectly attempting to induce firms to engage in reciprocal buying. *See id.* § 19(b).

47. 380 U.S. 592 (1965).

> are aimed. The practice results in an irrelevant and alien factor intruding into the choice among competing products, creating at the least a priority on the business at equal prices. . . . A threatened withdrawal of orders if products of an affiliate cease being bought, as well as a conditioning of future purchases on the receipt of orders for products of that affiliate, is an anti-competitive practice. . . . Reciprocity in trading as a result of an acquisition violates § 7, if the probability of a lessening of competition is shown.[48]

In *Consolidated Foods*, the Court agreed with the FTC[49] that the acquisition of Gentry, a manufacturer of dehydrated onions and garlic, by Consolidated, which owned food processing plants and a network of wholesale and retail food stores, violated Section 7. Consolidated was a substantial purchaser from food processors that were purchasers of dehydrated onion and garlic. The FTC had found that, even though the post-acquisition market share of Gentry was not improved, the connection between Gentry and Consolidated would provide Gentry with an "unfair advantage over competitors enabling it to make sales that otherwise might not have been made."[50] The U.S. Supreme Court agreed, though it acknowledged that an acquisition that created the probability of reciprocal dealing for only a de minimis share of the market would not violate Section 7.[51]

Generally, subsequent lower court cases have established three prerequisites to a finding that the merger violates Section 7 based on reciprocity. First, the merger must create a market structure that is conducive to a significant increase in the opportunities for reciprocity. Second, there must be a reasonable probability that those opportunities for reciprocity will be exploited. Finally, the resulting reciprocal dealing must have a tendency substantially to lessen competition.[52]

---

48. *Id.* at 594 (citations, internal quotation marks, and footnote omitted); *accord* United States v. General Dynamics Corp., 258 F. Supp. 36, 59 (S.D.N.Y. 1966).
49. The U.S. Supreme Court reversed the decision of the Seventh Circuit, 329 F.2d 623 (7th Cir. 1964), which had set aside the Commission's order for divestiture, 62 F.T.C. 929 (1963).
50. *Consolidated Foods*, 380 U.S. at 597.
51. *See id.* at 600.
52. *See, e.g.*, Crouse-Hinds Co. v. Internorth, Inc., 518 F. Supp. 416, 435-36 (N.D.N.Y. 1981); United States v. Northwest Indus., 301 F. Supp. 1066, 1088 (N.D. Ill. 1969); *General Dynamics Corp.*, 258 F. Supp. at 60-65; Carrier Corp. v. United Techs. Corp., 1978-2 Trade Cas. (CCH) ¶ 62,393, at 76,371 (N.D.N.Y.), *aff'd*, 1978-2 Trade Cas. (CCH) ¶ 62,405 (2d Cir. 1978); United States v. ITT Corp., 1971 Trade Cas. (CCH) ¶ 73,619, at

The theory that reciprocal dealing creates an anticompetitive effect has been subject to significant criticism, much of it the same as the criticism addressed to other theories of monopoly leveraging and foreclosure.[53] Moreover, in the absence of market power, a supplier cannot be coerced into reciprocal dealing unless the transaction is beneficial to that supplier and other possible transactions are inferior to the transaction with the merged firm.[54] In cases where the reciprocal arrangements are not coerced but have been entered into voluntarily, such reciprocity may enhance economic efficiency by, for example, reducing transaction costs[55] or potential opportunism problems when both parties have specialized assets at risk.[56]

Because reciprocal dealing is not generally harmful to competition, commentators have suggested that it should be addressed when it actually occurs, rather than challenging a merger under Section 7 when the mere potential for reciprocity is created.[57]

90,545 (N.D. Ill. 1971). Although most cases require a showing of all three prerequisites, several cases in the Second and Third Circuits have found a violation of § 7 based solely on the first prerequisite. *See* Gulf & W. Indus. v. Great Atl. & Pac. Tea Co., 476 F.2d 687 (2d Cir. 1973) (preliminary injunction granted); Allis-Chalmers Mfg. Co. v. White Consol. Indus., 414 F.2d 506, 518-19 (3d Cir. 1969) (preliminary injunction granted); United States v. White Consol. Indus., 323 F. Supp. 1397 (N.D. Ohio 1971) (preliminary injunction granted); United States v. Ingersoll-Rand Co., 218 F. Supp. 530, 533 (W.D. Pa.) (preliminary injunction granted where mere existence of purchasing power may lead sophisticated businessmen to see advantages in securing goodwill of firm), *aff'd*, 320 F.2d 509 (3d Cir. 1963). *But see* United States v. International Tel. & Tel. Corp., 306 F. Supp. 766, 783-86 (D. Conn. 1969) (court rejected position that opportunity alone is sufficient to violate § 7 of Clayton Act where opportunities unlikely to be exploited because company policy opposes reciprocity and profits determined by divisions), *appeal dismissed*, 404 U.S. 801 (1971).

53. *See generally* Chapter 10.

54. *See* Crouse-Hinds Co. v. Internorth, Inc., 518 F. Supp. 416, 435 (N.D.N.Y. 1981).

55. *See* 10 PHILLIP AREEDA & DONALD F. TURNER, ANTITRUST LAW ¶ 1777a (2003).

56. *See* Stephen J. K. Walters, *Reciprocity Reexamined: The Consolidated Foods Case*, 29 J.L. & ECON. 423 (1986).

57. *See, e.g.*, 10 PHILLIP AREEDA & DONALD F. TURNER, ANTITRUST LAW ¶ 1777a (2003).

3. *Tying*

Tying occurs when a seller conditions the sale of one product or service on the requirement that the customer purchase an additional product or service.[58] When a firm with market power in one product or service (the tying product) forces the purchaser of that product or service to buy a second product or service (the tied product) as a condition of purchasing the first, competition is arguably unreasonably restrained.[59] Buyers wishing to purchase the first, or tying, product or service are deprived of the choice concerning the purchase of the second product. And rival producers of the second, or tied, product or service are foreclosed from that part of the market accounted for by buyers forced to accept the tying arrangement in order to purchase the tying product.[60]

The anticompetitive effects of tying are comparable to the effects of coerced reciprocal dealing. Conglomerate mergers that create the possibility of tying arrangements resemble those that create the possibility of reciprocal dealing. Like mergers that provide an opportunity for reciprocity, a merger which violates Section 7 under a tying theory must significantly increase the opportunities for tying and create a reasonable likelihood that the opportunities will be exploited, the result of which must have a tendency substantially to lessen competition.[61]

The prospect of anticompetitive tying arrangements as a basis to challenge a conglomerate merger under Section 7 raises several theoretical difficulties. First, tying arrangements do not add to the acquiring firm's existing power in the market. The acquiring firm is not able to achieve any incremental increase in market power because the acquiring firm could have exploited the full power it possesses in the

---

58. *See, e.g.*, Fortner Enters. v. United States Steel Corp., 394 U.S. 495 (1969).

59. *See* Betaseed, Inc. v. U & I Inc., 681 F.2d 1203, 1216 (9th Cir. 1982); Spartan Grain & Mill Co. v. Ayers, 581 F.2d 419, 425 (5th Cir. 1978).

60. *See, e.g.*, Times-Picayune Publ'g Co. v. United States, 345 U.S. 594, 606 (1953). For a complete analysis of tying arrangements, see ABA SECTION OF ANTITRUST LAW, ANTITRUST LAW DEVELOPMENTS 175-213 (5th ed. 2002).

61. *See* Crouse-Hinds Co. v. Internorth, Inc., 518 F. Supp. 416, 442 (N.D.N.Y. 1981); United States v. Wachovia Corp., 313 F. Supp. 632, 637 (W.D.N.C. 1970) (customers will patronize one portion of lender's operation to gain favored position for other loans); Heublein, Inc., 96 F.T.C. 385, 596-99 (1980) (wine sales will be tied to sale of branded vodka).

prices of its existing products.[62] Second, the antitrust laws other than Section 7 can be used to combat the practice of tying if it arises so that it is unnecessary to challenge the underlying merger, which only creates the potential conditions that permit tying.[63]

Perhaps in view of these difficulties, the FTC has concluded that possible leverage or tying "should be ground for barring a merger only when the evidence shows that it will probably produce significant adverse competitive effects."[64]

4. *Multiple Market Strategies*

Finally, a conglomerate merger could create an industry structure that facilitates price agreements by linking oligopolies in two or more markets. The presence of common participants in each market may discourage competitive behavior in one market for fear of retaliation in the other by other common participants.[65]

Three preconditions must exist for this anticompetitive effect to arise. First, both markets must be oligopolistic to create a pricing opportunity that can be exploited and to make possible a retaliatory move in one market if the competitor does not cooperate in the second market. Second, while potentially oligopolistic, at least one of the markets must currently be performing competitively so that the change in industry structure would change market performance. Third, following the merger, each market must contain at least two firms that operate in each market. These firms must be sufficiently important in each market to be able to impose a sufficient penalty on a noncooperating firm.[66]

This theory was the basis, in part, of Section 7 challenges to two banking mergers that were ultimately reviewed by the U.S. Supreme Court in 1974.[67] In each case, a commercial bank attempted to enter a

62. *See* 5 PHILLIP AREEDA & DONALD F. TURNER, ANTITRUST LAW ¶ 1134b, at 204 (1980).

63. *See id.* ¶ 1134c, at 206; THOMAS W. BRUNNER ET AL., MERGERS IN THE NEW ANTITRUST ERA 63 (1985).

64. *Heublein, Inc.*, 96 F.T.C. at 597-98.

65. *See* United States v. Marine Bancorp., 418 U.S. 602 (1974); United States v. Connecticut Nat'l Bank, 418 U.S. 656 (1974); Allis-Chalmers Mfg. Co. v. White Consol. Indus., 414 F.2d 506, 523 (3d Cir. 1969); United States v. Northwest Indus., 301 F. Supp. 1066, 1094 (N.D. Ill. 1969) (preliminary injunction denied).

66. *See* 5 PHILLIP AREEDA & DONALD F. TURNER, ANTITRUST LAW ¶ 1146b, at 51-55 (1980).

67. *See Marine Bancorp.*, 418 U.S. 602; *Connecticut Nat'l Bank*, 418 U.S.

new local geographic market through the acquisition of an existing bank operating in another part of the same state. There was a limited number of banks operating in each local market. The government challenged the mergers, claiming that the consolidations would permit a linkage of statewide oligopolistic banking markets as large banks across the state engaged in standardized behavior.[68]

The U.S. Supreme Court rejected the government's theory as too speculative, finding that the allegations did not have evidentiary support.[69] The theory has not resurfaced in the years since, although the European Commission has pursued a multiple market theory dubbed "portfolio effects" or "portfolio power."[70] That theory holds that a company's strength across a range of individual but related product markets enhances that supplier's market power in each of the product categories.[71]

The European Commission used portfolio effects analysis in blocking a proposed $45 billion merger between General Electric and Honeywell.[72] The European Commission was primarily concerned with the merged entity's ability to offer packages of products that had previously only been sold individually in distinct markets.[73] The European Commission cited two ways in which such packaging tactics could be employed to create anticompetitive effects. First, the merged entity would be able to "cross-subsidize discounts across the products composing the packaged deal," enabling it to offer the package at a lower price than if the components were sold separately, a practice it termed "mixed bundling."[74] This rationale most closely resembles the "portfolio

---

656.

68. *See Marine Bancorp.*, 418 U.S. at 620; *Connecticut Nat'l Bank*, 418 U.S. at 672.

69. *See Marine Bancorp.*, 418 U.S. at 623; *Connecticut Nat'l Bank*, 418 U.S. at 672.

70. Commission Decision 98/602/EC of 15 Oct. 1997 Declaring a Concentration to Be Compatible With the Common Market and the Functioning of the EEA Agreement, (Case No. IV/M.938 - Guinness/Grand Metropolitan) 1997 O.J.C.D. 1, 19.

71. *See id.* at 20.

72. Commission Decision of 3/07/2001 Declaring a Concentration to Be Incompatible With the Common Market and the EEA Agreement, (Case No. COMP/M.2220-General Electric/Honeywell), p.3, ¶ 8. As of the date of publication, the decision is on appeal to the European Court of First Instance had not been decided. A decision is expected sometime in 2004.

73. *Id.* at p.84, ¶ 350.

74. *Id.* ¶ 353. In the decision itself, however, the Euorpean Commission

effects" theory as set forth in the Euorpean Commission's 1997 Guinness/Grand Metropolitan decision.[75] Second, the European Commission opined that the merged entity would be able to engage in more coercive forms of bundling which would effectively deprive the customer of choice,[76] an analysis similar to the concept of "tying" in U.S. antitrust law.[77]

The European Commission forecast that these bundling tactics would have multiple detrimental effects on GE/Honeywell's competitors in the markets for aerospace equipment and jet engines. Competitors' market share would be eroded by their inability to compete with the merged entity's package deals, which in turn would reduce profitability and "likely . . . lead to market exit of existing competitors and market foreclosure."[78]

The Division had previously approved the GE/Honeywell deal, and the DOJ harshly criticized the European Commission's decision in a series of speeches. In a speech to the OECD, for example, the Assistant Attorney Genral for Antitrust he declared that the "difference in

---

qualified its reliance on the mixed bundling model, stating that the submissions of the parties had brought its validity into question. *Id.* ¶ 352. The Euorpean Commission argued, however, that other anticompetitive effects were sufficient to block the merger and thus that mixed bundling was not essential to its holding.

75. Commission Decision of 15 Oct. 1997 Declaring a Concentration to be Compatible With the Common Market and the Functioning of the EEA Agreement, (Case No. IV/M.938—Guinness/Grand Metropolitan) 1997 O.J.C.D. 1, 16-17, ¶¶ 99-100 (the Commission argued that "a deep portfolio" of brands across multiple product categories gave the firm "considerable price flexibility" and "major marketing advantages").

76. The European Commission identified two forms of this more coercive type of bundling: "pure bundling, whereby the entity sells only the bundle but does not make the individual components available on a stand-alone basis" and "technical bundling, whereby the individual components only function effectively as part of the bundled system." *GE/Honeywell*, *supra* note 72, at 85, ¶ 351.

77. *See* notes 58 and 59, *supra,* and accompanying text. As a second conglomerate effect, distinct from portfolio effects analysis, the European Commission argued that GE Capital's financial resources would enable Honeywell to invest more in research and development than its competitors and offer customers deeply discounted prices that competitors could not match. Such a theory most closely resembles the "entrenchment" argument against a conglomerate merger, described in section B.1 above.

78. *GE/Honeywell*, *supra* note 72, at 94, ¶ 398.

approach to analyzing mergers under U.S. and EU antitrust law is significant. Under U.S. law, we believe that the purpose of the antitrust laws is not to protect business from the working of the market; it is to protect the public from failure of the market."[79] Another DOJ official specifically criticized "portfolio effects" analysis, declaring that it "is neither soundly grounded in economic theory nor supported by empirical evidence, but rather, is antithetical to the goals of sound antitrust enforcement."[80]

The European Commission's decision is currently being reviewed by the European Court of First Instance. The Court recently overturned two Commission decisions to block mergers, partly on the basis that insufficient evidence was cited in support of the European Commission's portfolio effects analysis.[81]

In the wake of the GE/Honeywell furor, EU and U.S. enforcement authorities have been speaking publicly about the need for "convergence" and "harmonization" of merger standards so that future conflicts are avoided.[82] Several international bodies have been set up to promote greater dialogue on this issue.[83] In addition, at a recent European Commission meeting in which new horizontal merger

---

79. Charles A. James, Ass't. Att'y Gen., Antitrust Div., U.S. Dept. of Justice, International Antitrust in the 21st Century: Cooperation and Convergence, Address Before the OECD Global Forum on Competition, (Oct. 17, 2001), *at* www.usdoj.gov/atr/public/speeches/9330.htm.

80. William J. Kolasky, Deputy Ass't. Att'y Gen., Antitrust Div., U.S. Dept. of Justice, U.S. and EU Competition Policy: Cartels, Mergers, and Beyond, Address Before the Council for the United States and Italy Bi-Annual Conf., (Jan. 25, 2002), *at* www.usdoj.gov/atr/public/speeches/9848.htm. *See also* Barry Nalebuff & David Majerus, *Bundling, Tying, and Portfolio Effects*, DTI Economic Paper No. 1 (discussing the *Tetra Pak, GE/Honeywell,* and *Guinness* cases, as well as other cases involving bundling).

81. *Tetra Laval BV v. Commission*, EC Ct. 1st Inst., No. T-5/02, 10/25/02; *Schneider Electric SA v. Commission*, EC Ct. 1st Inst., Nos. T-310/01, T-77/02, 10/22/02.

82. *See, e.g.,* Kolasky address, *supra* note 80; *Anniversary Conference Focuses on Different Facets of Enforcement,* 82 Antitrust and Trade Reg. Rep. (BNA), No. 2044, *at* 144 (Feb. 15, 2002) (European Union and French competition officials address need for harmonization of standards).

83. Two of these groups are the International Competition Network (ICN) and the U.S.-EU Merger Working Group.

guidelines were adopted, the European Commission discussed the possibility of adopting guidelines for conglomerate mergers.[84]

84. *See Commission Adopts Comprehensive Reform of European Union Merger Control Regime,* 83 Antitrust and Trade Reg. Rep. (BNA), No. 2086, at 585, (Dec. 13, 2002); see *infra*, part e of Chapter 12.

CHAPTER 12

APPLICATION OF MERGER LAWS TO MULTINATIONAL TRANSACTIONS

Multinational transactions may implicate the merger control laws and premerger notification systems of numerous countries, and the number of states with such notification and enforcement regimes has increased in recent years to over sixty.[1] Enforcement cooperation, both formal and informal, among national competition authorities is also on the rise.[2] In the United States, the same substantive standards that apply to transactions between U.S. firms also apply to transactions involving non-U.S. firms, provided that the requisite effect on U.S. commerce is present.[3] Mergers and acquisitions involving foreign firms, however, can raise special issues of jurisdiction, international comity, and enforcement policy. In addition, in what are likely to be rare instances, foreign firms may be able to raise the defenses of foreign sovereign immunity, act of state, or foreign sovereign compulsion.

A. Jurisdictional Issues Raised by Transactions Involving Non-U.S. Firms

Courts and federal enforcement agencies have applied the jurisdictional limits of the Sherman Act in interpreting the jurisdictional bounds of merger challenges under the Clayton Act and the FTC Act.[4]

---

1. *See generally* THE GLOBAL MERGER NOTIFICATION HANDBOOK (Howard Adler, Jr. et al. eds., 2001).
2. *See* R. Hewitt Pate, Ass't. Att'y Gen., Antitrust Div., U.S. Dept. of Justice, The DOJ International Antitrust Program – Maintaining Momentum (Feb. 6, 2003), *at* www.usdoj.gov/atr/public/speeches/200736.htm; John J. Parisi, Counsel for European Union Affairs, International Antitrust Div., FTC, Enforcement Cooperation Among Antitrust Authorities, § III.b (May 19, 1999 *updated* Oct. 2000), *at* www.ftc.gov/speeches/other/ibc990599 11update.htm; *see generally* part D of this Chapter.
3. *See* FTC Staff Report, *Anticipating the 21st Century: Competition Policy in the New High-Tech, Global Marketplace*, 70 Antitrust & Trade Reg. Rep. (BNA) No. 1765, at S-47-S-53 (June 6, 1996).
4. *But see* Hartford Fire Ins. Co. v. California, 509 U.S. 764, 812-15 (1993)

1. Sherman Act

The Sherman Act by its express terms prohibits agreements in restraint of trade "with foreign nations."[5] Originally, the Sherman Act was held to apply solely to transactions occurring on U.S. soil.[6] In 1945, however, this narrow view was rejected in favor of a much broader effects test that extends Sherman Act coverage to any anticompetitive foreign conduct that is intended to affect and does affect U.S. commerce, regardless of where that conduct occurs.[7] Courts continued to refine the effects test over the next several decades, clarifying the magnitude and type of effect on U.S. commerce required to justify the extraterritorial application of U.S. antitrust law. Most courts required the effect to be "substantial,"[8] some required the effect to be "foreseeable,"[9] and others required it to be "direct."[10] The Antitrust Division of the U.S.

(Scalia, J., dissenting) (distinguishing subject matter jurisdiction under 28 U.S.C. § 1331 from congressional intent to reach foreign conduct in enacting the Sherman Act).

5. Section 1 prohibits agreements "in restraint of trade or commerce among the several States, or with foreign nations." 15 U.S.C. § 1. Section 2 prohibits actual or attempted monopolization of commerce "among the several States, or with foreign nations." 15 U.S.C. § 2.

6. *See* American Banana Co. v. United Fruit Co., 213 U.S. 347, 356 (1909) ("[T]he general and almost universal rule is that the character of an act as lawful or unlawful must be determined wholly by the law of the country where the act is done").

7. *See* United States v. Aluminum Co. of Am., 148 F.2d 416, 443 (2d Cir. 1945) (Hand, J.) ("[I]t is settled law . . . that any state may impose liabilities, even upon persons not within its allegiance, for conduct outside its borders that has consequences within its borders which the state reprehends"). The Second Circuit acted as the court of last resort, having had the case certified to it for decision by the U.S. Supreme Court. *Id.* at 421. *See also* Matsushita Elec. Indus. Co. v. Zenith Radio Corp., 475 U.S. 574, 582 n.6 (1986); Continental Ore Co. v. Union Carbide & Carbon Corp., 370 U.S. 690, 704 (1962) ("A conspiracy to monopolize or restrain the domestic or foreign commerce of the United States is not outside the reach of the Sherman Act just because part of the conduct complained of occurs in foreign countries").

8. *See* Mannington Mills, Inc. v. Congoleum Corp., 595 F.2d 1287 (3d Cir. 1979).

9. *See* Southeastern Hose, Inc. v. Imperial-Eastman Corp., 1973-1 Trade Cas. (CCH) ¶ 74,479 (N.D. Ga. 1973).

10. *See* Spears Free Clinic & Hosp. for Poor Children v. Cleere, 197 F.2d 125 (10th Cir. 1952).

Department of Justice (DOJ or the Division) adopted an enforcement policy requiring the effect on U.S. commerce to be both "substantial and foreseeable."[11]

Congress amended the Sherman Act by enacting the Foreign Trade Antitrust Improvements Act of 1982 (FTAIA),[12] which codifies a version of the effects test[13] and establishes a general framework for Sherman Act enforcement actions when foreign trade is involved.[14] The FTAIA is

---

11. *See* U.S. DEP'T OF JUSTICE, ANTITRUST GUIDE FOR INTERNATIONAL OPERATIONS (1977) [hereinafter 1977 INTERNATIONAL GUIDELINES], *reprinted in* 4 Trade Reg. Rep. (CCH) ¶ 13,110, at 20,645. The U.S. Department of Justice replaced the 1977 *International Guidelines* with the 1988 *International Guidelines*. *See* U.S. DEP'T OF JUSTICE, ANTITRUST ENFORCEMENT GUIDELINES FOR INTERNATIONAL OPERATIONS (1988) [hereinafter 1988 INTERNATIONAL GUIDELINES], *reprinted in* 4 Trade Reg. Rep. (CCH) ¶ 13,109. These were in turn replaced with the jointly issued 1995 *International Guidelines*. *See* U.S. DEP'T OF JUSTICE & FEDERAL TRADE COMM'N, ANTITRUST ENFORCEMENT GUIDELINES FOR INTERNATIONAL OPERATIONS (1995) § 3.11 [hereinafter 1995 INTERNATIONAL GUIDELINES], *reprinted in* 4 Trade Reg. Rep. (CCH) ¶ 13,107 and in Appendix J.

12. 15 U.S.C. § 6(a). This section provides that the Sherman Act:

> [S]hall not apply to conduct involving trade or commerce (other than import trade or import commerce) with foreign nations unless –
>
> (1) such conduct has a direct, substantial, and reasonably foreseeable effect –
>
> (A) on trade or commerce which is not trade or commerce with foreign nations, or on import trade or import commerce with foreign nations; or
>
> (B) on export trade or export commerce with foreign nations, of a person engaged in such trade or commerce in the United States; and
>
> (2) such effect gives rise to a claim under the provisions of this Act, other than this section.
>
> If this Act applies to such conduct only because of the operation of paragraph (1)(B), then this Act shall apply to such conduct only for injury to export business in the United States.

13. *Cf.* Hartford Fire Ins. Co v. California, 509 U.S. 764, 796 n.23 (1993) (stating that it is unclear whether the FTAIA's "direct, substantial, and reasonably foreseeable" standard amends existing law or merely codifies it).

14. Although the FTAIA formula focuses on whether activity is import trade or nonimport commerce, recent case law suggests that it is sometimes difficult to determine whether challenged conduct fits into the FTAIA's specified categories. There is particular uncertainty about whether the FTAIA permits foreign plaintiffs to bring antitrust claims against

"inelegantly phrased"[15] and case law in this area is not particularly coherent.[16] However, the FTAIA basically provides that the Sherman Act shall not apply to conduct involving trade or commerce with foreign nations *other than import trade* unless the conduct has a "direct, substantial, and reasonably foreseeable effect" (1) on U.S. domestic or import commerce, or (2) on the export business of a firm engaged in export trade in the United States.[17]

Whether the FTAIA operates to limit the reach of the Sherman Act thus depends as a threshold issue on whether the foreign conduct in question involves import or nonimport trade.

a. Import Trade

The jurisdictional test applicable to foreign conduct involving imports is the common law effects test, which the U.S. Supreme Court

---

international cartels combining foreign and domestic conduct. For a general discussion, see Ronald W. Davis, *The Mystery Deepens: U.S. Antitrust Treatment of International Cartels*, 17 ANTITRUST 31 (Summer 2003); Ronald W. Davis, *Developments: International Cartel and Monopolization Cases Expose a Gap in Foreign Trade Antitrust Improvements Act*, 15 ANTITRUST 53 (Summer 2001). *See* Dee-K Enters., Inc. v. Heveafil Sdn. Bhd., 299 F.3d 281, 286-87 (4th Cir. 2002) (observing that conspiracies with both foreign and domestic elements make analysis particularly challenging and that "neither the statutory scheme nor the case law provide clear guidance"); *see also* Empagram S.A. v. F. Hoffman-Laroche, Ltd., 315 F.3d 338 (D.C. Cir.), *petition for cert. granted*, 72 U.S.L.W. 3406 (2003).

15. United States v. Nippon Paper Indus. Co., Ltd., 109 F.3d 1, 4 (1st Cir. 1997).

16. For example, while most courts invoke § 6(a) in a threshold "jurisdictional" inquiry, there is currently some disagreement over whether the domestic commercial "effects" nexus required by § 6(a) is actually an issue of subject matter jurisdiction or an element of the substantive claim. For debate on this issue, see Hartford Fire Ins. Co. v. California, 509 U.S. 764 (1993); United Phosphorus, Ltd. v. Angus Chem. Co., 322 F.3d 942 (7th Cir.), *cert. denied*, 72 U.S.L.W. 3327 (2003).

17. *See* 15 U.S.C. § 6(a)(1). Congress enacted the FTAIA for the purpose of facilitating the export of domestic goods by exempting export transactions that do not injure the U.S. economy from the Sherman Act and relieving U.S. exporters from a perceived competitive disadvantage in foreign trade. Carpet Group Int'l v. Oriental Rug Importers Ass'n, 227 F.3d 69, 71 (3d Cir. 2000) (citations omitted).

most recently articulated in *Hartford Fire Insurance Co. v. California*[18] as being whether the conduct "was meant to produce and did in fact produce some substantial effect in the United States."[19] The Division and Federal Trade Commission (FTC or the Commission) have taken the position that foreign conduct involving U.S. imports "by definition affect[s] the U.S. domestic market directly."[20] It therefore will "almost invariably satisfy the intent part of the Hartford Fire test," leaving for a case-by-case determination on the facts whether the effect is "substantial."[21]

b. Nonimport Trade

Jurisdiction with respect to conduct involving nonimport foreign commerce is as delineated in the FTAIA: such conduct must have a "direct, substantial, and reasonably foreseeable effect" on either U.S. domestic or import commerce or the export business of a person engaged in that business in the United States. This test is thus more stringent than the test for foreign conduct involving imports. In addition to being "substantial," the U.S. effect of nonimport foreign conduct must be both "direct" and "reasonably foreseeable."[22] Currently, there is some

---

18. 509 U.S. 764 (1993).
19. *See id.* at 795-96 ("Although the proposition was perhaps not always free from doubt, . . . it is well established by now that the Sherman Act applies to foreign conduct that was meant to produce and did in fact produce some substantial effect in the United States"). *See also* United States v. Nippon Paper Indus. Co., 109 F.3d 1 (1st Cir. 1997) (holding that the *Hartford Fire* standard applies to criminal as well as civil Sherman Act enforcement actions); Eskofot A/S v. E.I. du Pont de Nemours & Co., 872 F. Supp. 81, 85 (S.D.N.Y. 1995) (applying the common law effects test, rather than the FTAIA, to conduct precluding plaintiff from "exporting goods into the United States").
20. *See* 1995 INTERNATIONAL GUIDELINES, *supra* note 11, § 3.11. Because the Sherman Act prohibits agreements, rather than acts performed in furtherance of an agreement, the DOJ and FTC consider the potential harm that a conspiracy could have on U.S. domestic or import commerce rather than whether conduct in furtherance of the agreement has actually had such an effect. *Id.* § 3.12 (Illustrative Example B).
21. *See id.* at § 3.11.
22. The FTAIA direct, substantial, and reasonably foreseeable standard has been applied in a number of Sherman Act cases. *See, e.g.*, Metallgesellschaft AG v. Sumitomo Corp. of Am., 325 F.3d 836, 841-42 (7th Cir. 2003); Turicentro, S.A. v. American Airlines, Inc., 303 F.3d 293, 304-06 (3d Cir. 2002); Carpet Group Int'l v. Oriental Rug Importers

uncertainty as to whether Section 2 of the FTAIA imposes an additional requirement that the direct, substantial, and reasonably foreseeable domestic effect on which jurisdiction is based must be the same effect that gives rise to the plaintiff's injury. [23]

2. *Clayton Act*

Section 7 of the Clayton Act prohibits mergers or acquisitions that would have an anticompetitive effect "in any line of commerce or in any activity affecting commerce in any section of the country," provided that both parties to the transaction are "engaged in commerce or in any activity affecting commerce."[24] "Commerce" is defined in Section 1 of

---

Ass'n, 227 F.3d 62, 75 (3d Cir. 2000); McGlinchy v. Shell Chem. Co., 845 F.2d 802, 813 (9th Cir. 1988); *In re* Microsoft Corp. Antitrust Litig., 127 F. Supp. 2d 702, 714-15 (D. Md. 2001); United Phosphorus, Ltd. v. Angus Chem. Co., 131 F. Supp. 2d 1003, 1009-13 (N.D. Ill. 2001); Sniado v. Bank Austria AG, 174 F. Supp. 2d 159, 163-66 (S.D.N.Y. 2001); Coors Brewing Co. v. Miller Brewing Co., 889 F. Supp. 1394, 1398 (D. Colo. 1995); The "IN" Porters, S.A. v. Hanes Printables, Inc., 663 F. Supp. 494, 498-99 (M.D.N.C. 1987); Liamuiga Tours v. Travel Impressions, Ltd., 617 F. Supp. 920, 922-23 (E.D.N.Y. 1985); Eurim-Phann GmbH v. Pfizer Inc., 593 F. Supp. 1102, 1106 (S.D.N.Y. 1984). For an analysis, see Richard W. Beckler & Matthew H. Kirtland, *Extraterritorial Application of U.S. Antitrust Law: What Is a "Direct, Substantial, and Reasonably Forseeable Effect" under the Foreign Trade Antitrust Improvements Act?*, 38 TEX. INT'L L.J. 11 (2003)

23. There is significant disagreement in the federal courts on this issue. *Compare* Den Norske Stats Oljeselskap AS v. Heeremac VOF, 241 F.3d 420, 428 (5th Cir. 2001) ("[P]lain language of the FTAIA precludes subject matter jurisdiction over claims by foreign plaintiffs against defendants where the situs of the injury is overseas and the injury arises from effects in a non-domestic market"); *and* Ferromin Int'l Trade Corp. v. UCAR Int'l, Inc., 153 F. Supp. 2d 700, 705 (E.D. Pa. 2001) (FTAIA permits jurisdiction over the antitrust claims of foreign plaintiffs only when injuries arise from effects of illegal conduct in the U.S. market), *with* Empagran S.A. v. F. Hoffman-Laroche, Ltd., 315 F.3d 338, 341 (D.C. Cir.) ("anticompetitive conduct itself must violate the Sherman Act and the conduct's harmful effect on United States commerce must give rise to 'a claim' by someone, even if not the foreign plaintiff who is before the court"), *petition for cert. granted*, 72 U.S.L.W. 3406 (2003); Kruman v. Christie's Int'l, PLC, 284 F.3d 384, 399-400 (2d Cir. 2002) (FTAIA does not require plaintiffs to prove that alleged U.S. effect gives rise to their claimed injury).

24. 15 U.S.C. § 18.

the Clayton Act to include trade or commerce with foreign nations.[25] "Person" is defined to include corporations existing under or authorized by the laws of the United States or of any foreign country.[26]

Section 7 originally applied only to mergers involving persons engaged in commerce. In 1980, the act was amended to expand its coverage to mergers of persons engaged in activities affecting commerce, as well as those engaged in commerce.[27] Even prior to its amendment in 1980, however, the Clayton Act was held to apply to acquisitions by U.S. firms of foreign companies having U.S. subsidiaries[28] and acquisitions by foreign companies of U.S. firms.[29]

More recently, the courts and federal enforcement agencies have applied the direct, substantial, and reasonably foreseeable standard of the FTAIA to merger challenges under the Clayton Act.[30] The DOJ/FTC 1995 *International Guidelines* state that "[i]t is appropriate to do so because the FTAIA sheds light on the type of effects Congress considered necessary for foreign commerce cases, even though the FTAIA did not amend the Clayton Act."[31]

Illustrative Example H of the *International Guidelines* presents a hypothetical merger of two foreign firms that have sales offices (but no production facilities) in the United States and account for a "substantial percentage of U.S. sales" of the relevant product through direct imports.

---

25. *See id.* § 12.
26. *See id.*
27. *See* Antitrust Procedural Improvements Act of 1980, Pub. L. No. 96-349, 94 Stat. 1154.
28. *See* Brunswick Corp., 94 F.T.C. 1174, 1264-65 (1979), *aff'd in part and modified in part sub nom.* Yamaha Motor Co. v. FTC, 657 F.2d 971 (8th Cir. 1981) (challenge to acquisition by U.S. corporation of Japanese corporation that distributed products in the United States through a subsidiary); United States v. Jos. Schlitz Brewing Co., 253 F. Supp. 129 (N.D. Cal.), *aff'd*, 385 U.S. 37 (1966) (defendant ordered to divest a controlling stock interest in a Canadian brewer that itself held a controlling interest in a U.S. brewer).
29. *See* British Oxygen Co., 86 F.T.C. 1241 (1975), *rev'd on other grounds sub nom.* BOC Int'l, Ltd. v. FTC, 557 F.2d 24 (2d Cir. 1977).
30. *See* The "IN" Porters, S.A. v. Hanes Printables, Inc., 663 F. Supp. 494, 498 n.4 (M.D.N.C. 1987) ("Given the evident purpose of the [FTAIA] . . . a court would find it difficult to take jurisdiction under Clayton Act § 7 over a venture that the new statute immunizes from the Sherman Act") (quoting PHILLIP AREEDA & HERBERT HOVENKAMP, ANTITRUST LAW 171-76 (Supp. 1986)).
31. 1995 INTERNATIONAL GUIDELINES, *supra* note 11, § 3.14 (Illustrative Example H).

In such a case, the FTC and DOJ would argue that jurisdiction was established based on the merger's likely effect on U.S. imports.[32] Under the assumed facts of Example H, the effect on U.S. domestic commerce would be direct (because the merging companies directly import into the United States), substantial (because the merging parties account for a "substantial percentage of U.S. sales" of the relevant product), and reasonably foreseeable.

If the facts were changed so that the merger's main effect would instead be on U.S. export commerce, the DOJ and FTC would have to consider whether there were also direct, substantial, and reasonably foreseeable effects on U.S. domestic or import commerce.[33] (The *International Guidelines* offer no example of when such an "export effect" merger would have sufficient effects on U.S. domestic or import commerce to support a finding of jurisdiction under FTAIA provisions.)

According to the *International Guidelines*, in either instance the DOJ and the FTC would have to consider the likelihood of achieving effective relief. Effective relief would be difficult to obtain, for example, if neither of the merging firms has assets in the United States relating to production or distribution of the relevant product. In such a case, the DOJ or FTC might refrain from taking enforcement action and instead request foreign competition authorities to take action, as an exercise of "positive comity."[34]

---

32. *See id.*
33. *See id.*
34. For a discussion of the various cooperation agreements currently in place between the United States and other countries under which such positive comity might be exercised, see part D of this Chapter. Illustrative Example H represents a slightly different formulation of DOJ policy than what was stated in the now-superseded 1988 *International Guidelines*. See 1988 INTERNATIONAL GUIDELINES, *supra* note 11. Case 4 of the 1988 *International Guidelines* assumed a hypothetical merger of two foreign firms that together supply about 60% of the relevant product consumed in the United States. The relevant market was already highly concentrated, and it was determined that the merger could have an anticompetitive effect in the United States. But neither firm had any production or distribution assets in the United States. The 1988 *International Guidelines* stated that the Division would not challenge such a merger because "it would be difficult, if not practically impossible, to obtain effective relief that would preserve competition in the United States." However, if either of the merging firms did have production facilities or substantial related distribution assets in the United States, the Division might require a divestiture of assets located in the United States, possibly after consulting with involved foreign sovereigns about

3. *FTC Act*

Section 5 of the FTC Act prohibits "[u]nfair methods of competition in or affecting commerce."[35] Like the Sherman Act, however, Section 5 does not apply to conduct involving nonimport foreign commerce, unless that conduct has a direct, substantial, and reasonably foreseeable effect on U.S. domestic or import commerce, or on the export commerce of a person engaged in such commerce in the United States.[36] With respect to conduct involving import trade, the FTC has taken the position that the FTC Act should be construed identically to the Sherman Act.[37]

B. Comity

Even if a merger or acquisition has the requisite effect to permit the exercise of jurisdiction under the FTAIA, an enforcement agency or court may still decline to exercise jurisdiction due to international comity concerns. International comity comes into play when more than one sovereign has jurisdiction to regulate a merger or acquisition. It has been described as the recognition and respect that one sovereign gives to another sovereign's significant interests before taking action that would affect those interests.[38] However, the appropriate role of comity as a rule

---

the impact of alternative remedies on their national interests.

Importantly, the FTC has reached consent agreements in matters where the parties were without productive assets in the United States. *See, e.g.*, Institut Merieux, 113 F.T.C. 742 (1990); Oerikon-Buhrle, 59 Fed. Reg. 59,780 (Nov. 18, 1994).

35. *See* 15 U.S.C. § 45(a)(1).
36. *See id.* § 45(a)(3).
37. *See* Massachusetts Bd. of Registration in Optometry, 110 F.T.C. 549, 609 (1988); *see also* 1995 INTERNATIONAL GUIDELINES, *supra* note 11, § 3.1.
38. *See* Hilton v. Guyot, 159 U.S. 113, 163-64 (1895) ("'Comity', in the legal sense, is neither a matter of absolute obligation, on the one hand, nor of mere courtesy and good will, upon the other. But it is the recognition which one nation allows within its territory to the legislative, executive or judicial acts of another nation, having due regard both to the international duty and convenience, and to the rights of its own citizens . . . ."); United States v. Nippon Paper Indus. Co., 109 F.3d 1, 8 (1st Cir. 1997) ("International comity is a doctrine that counsels voluntary forbearance when a sovereign which has a legitimate claim to jurisdiction concludes that a second sovereign also has a legitimate claim to jurisdiction under principles of international law. Comity is more an aspiration than a fixed rule, more a matter of grace than a matter of obligation") (citation omitted); Laker Airways Ltd. v. Sabena, Belgian World Airlines, 731

of decision by courts in antitrust actions continues to evolve, and there is uncertainty and disagreement on such issues as whether comity applies in the absence of a "true" conflict of laws, and whether a court may refuse to apply the Sherman Act for reasons of international comity in an action brought by the U.S. government.

Prior to enactment of the FTAIA, some courts had applied a jurisdictional "rule of reason," or balancing test, in addition to the *Alcoa* effects test, to take into account considerations of international comity. The leading jurisdictional rule of reason case is *Timberlane Lumber Co. v. Bank of America National Trust & Savings Ass'n*.[39] In *Timberlane*, the Ninth Circuit added a requirement to the *Alcoa* effects test that the exercise of jurisdiction must be appropriate "as a matter of international comity and fairness."[40] In making this determination, a court was to consider factors such as:

> (1) whether (and the extent to which) applying U.S. law would conflict with foreign law or policy;
>
> (2) the citizenship of the parties involved and the location or principal places of their business;
>
> (3) whether (and the extent to which) a foreign state's own enforcement efforts can be expected to achieve compliance with U.S. law;
>
> (4) the relative significance of effects in the United States as compared to effects in foreign jurisdictions;
>
> (5) whether (and the extent to which) the parties committing the alleged violation had an explicit purpose to harm or affect U.S. commerce;

F.2d 909, 937-39, 943-55 (D.C. Cir. 1984) (containing extensive discussion of international comity and ultimately rejecting argument that comity compelled recognition of a British judicial ruling that a U.S. court shall not apply U.S. law to a British corporation doing business in the United States); Virgin Atlantic Airways v. British Airways, 872 F. Supp. 52, 60-61 (S.D.N.Y. 1994) (discussing the concerns that underlie international comity and rejecting defendant's appeal to comity considerations where the remedy for alleged harms to competition would not be "disproportionate" to those alleged harms); 1995 INTERNATIONAL GUIDELINES, *supra* note 11, § 3.2.

39. 549 F.2d 597 (9th Cir. 1976) (*Timberlane I*), *on remand*, 574 F. Supp. 1453 (N.D. Cal. 1983), *aff'd*, 749 F.2d 1378 (9th Cir. 1984) (*Timberlane II*).

40. 549 F.2d at 613.

(6) the extent to which such an effect was foreseeable; and

(7) the relative importance to the alleged violation of conduct within the United States as compared with conduct in foreign jurisdictions.[41]

The *Timberlane* approach or a similar approach was adopted in the Second, Third, Fifth, Seventh, and Tenth Circuits,[42] but rejected by the D.C. Circuit.[43]

In enacting the FTAIA, Congress declined to clarify when, if ever, a court with jurisdiction under the Sherman Act should abstain from exercising that jurisdiction on the basis of international comity.[44] Citing *Timberlane*, however, the House Report states that "[i]f a court determines that the requirements for subject matter jurisdiction are met, this bill would have no effect on the court's ability to employ notions of comity . . . or otherwise to take account of the international character of the transaction."[45] This statement supports an argument that Congress intended to leave courts free to continue to apply a *Timberlane*-like comity analysis.

The appropriate role of international comity as a rule of decision in a Sherman Act case was most recently considered by the U.S. Supreme Court in *Hartford Fire Insurance Co. v. California*.[46] Plaintiffs in the

---

41. 749 F.2d at 1384-86.

42. *See* O.N.E. Shipping Ltd. v. Flota Mercante Grancolombiana, S.A., 830 F.2d 449, 451 (2d Cir. 1987) (implicitly approving district court's application of *Timberlane* factors); Industrial Inv. Dev. Corp. v. Mitsui & Co., 671 F.2d 876, 884-85 (5th Cir. 1982); Montreal Trading Ltd. v. Amax, Inc., 661 F.2d 864 (10th Cir. 1981); *In re* Uranium Antitrust Litig., 617 F.2d 1248, 1255 (7th Cir. 1980) (endorsing factors such as those set forth in *Mannington Mills*); Mannington Mills, Inc. v. Congoleum Corp., 595 F.2d 1287, 1297-99 (3d Cir. 1979) (also considering the existence of any relevant treaties, the effect on U.S. foreign policy, and difficulties that might be created by any relief granted); Filetech S.A.R.L. v. France Telecom, 978 F. Supp. 464, 473 (S.D.N.Y. 1997) ("Second Circuit authority is in accord with the Ninth Circuit's *Timberlane* comity principles"); National Bank of Can. v. Interbank Card Ass'n, 507 F. Supp. 1113, 1119-21 (S.D.N.Y. 1980), *aff'd*, 666 F.2d 6 (2d Cir. 1981).

43. *See* Laker Airways Ltd. v. Sabena, Belgian World Airlines, 731 F.2d 909 (D.C. Cir. 1980).

44. *See* Hartford Fire Ins. Co. v. California, 509 U.S. 764, 798 (1993).

45. *See* H.R. REP. NO. 686, 97th Cong., 2d Sess. 9, 13 (1982), *reprinted in* 1982 U.S.C.C.A.N. 2487 (citing *Timberlane I*).

46. 509 U.S. 764 (1993).

consolidated cases below had sued a number of United States and British insurance companies for conspiring to set the terms of insurance policies and limit the availability of certain types of coverage available in the United States.[47] The British defendants moved for dismissal on the ground that the Sherman Act should not apply to conduct by non-U.S. citizens occurring entirely outside the United States that is legal in the territory in which it occurred.[48] The district court dismissed the case against the British defendants on comity grounds,[49] but the Ninth Circuit reversed.[50]

A 5-4 majority of the U.S. Supreme Court affirmed the Ninth Circuit's reversal, but applied different reasoning. Writing for the majority,[51] Justice Souter reaffirmed that "the Sherman Act applies to foreign conduct that was meant to produce and did in fact produce some substantial effect in the United States."[52] Justice Souter declined to say whether international comity is ever a proper basis for abstaining from the exercise of such jurisdiction.[53] Assuming—without ruling—that it is, the majority found that there was no comity basis for judicial abstention

---

47. The plaintiffs alleged that groups of London-based reinsurers and brokers had conspired, in some instances with domestic firms, to coerce primary insurers in the United States to offer commercial general liability insurance only on a claims-made basis and to withhold certain types of reinsurance for pollution risks in the United States. *See Hartford Fire Ins. Co.*, 509 U.S. at 776-77, 796.

48. *See In re* Insurance Antitrust Litig., 723 F. Supp. 464, 468, 470-71, 484 (N.D. Cal. 1989), *rev'd*, 938 F.2d 919 (9th Cir. 1991), *aff'd in relevant part and rev'd in part sub nom. Hartford Fire Ins. Co.*, 509 U.S. 764 (1993).

49. *See In re Insurance Antitrust Litig.*, 723 F. Supp. at 490.

50. *See In re Insurance Antitrust Litig.*, 938 F.2d at 932-34.

51. *See* Hartford Fire Ins. Co. v. California, 509 U.S. 764 (1993). Justice Souter was joined by Chief Justice Rehnquist and Justices Blackmun, Stevens, and White.

52. *See id.* at 796. In a footnote, Justice Souter stated that it is "unclear" how the FTAIA "might apply" to the alleged conspiracies or whether the FTAIA standard differs from established case law. Nevertheless, "[a]ssuming that the FTAIA's standard" affected the case and that the FTAIA standard "differs from prior law," the alleged conduct of the London reinsurers "plainly meets its requirements." *Id.* at 796-97 n.23.

53. *See id.* at 798 ("We need not decide that question here, however, for even assuming that in a proper case a court may decline to exercise Sherman Act jurisdiction over foreign conduct . . . international comity would not counsel against exercising jurisdiction in the circumstances alleged here").

in the circumstances alleged in *Hartford Fire* because the conspiracies alleged in *Hartford Fire* were not compelled by British law, and there thus was no "true conflict" between U.S. and British law.[54]

The *Hartford Fire* majority thus appears to have strictly limited the circumstances in which courts may decline to exercise Sherman Act jurisdiction based on international comity to those where the challenged conduct was actually compelled by the foreign sovereign (i.e., those instances in which the merging parties would have available to them the defense of sovereign compulsion).[55] As the Court explained, "[t]he only substantial question" in *Hartford Fire* was whether there was a "true conflict" between foreign and U.S. antitrust law.[56] Citing the *Restatement*, Justice Souter noted that the simple legality of challenged conduct in a foreign jurisdiction is not a bar to the application of U.S. antitrust law "*even where* the foreign state has a strong policy to permit or encourage such conduct."[57] Because the London reinsurers were not required by British law to engage in the alleged conspiracies, finding that

---

54. *See id.* (citing Societe Nationale Industrielle Aerospatiale v. United States District Court, 482 U.S. 522, 555 (1987)).

55. *See* United States v. Nippon Paper Indus. Co., 109 F.3d 1, 8 (1st Cir. 1997) (comity's "growth in the antitrust sphere has been stunted by Hartford Fire, in which the Court suggested that comity concerns would operate to defeat the exercise of jurisdiction only in those few cases in which the law of the foreign sovereign required a defendant to act in a manner incompatible with the Sherman Act or in which full compliance with both statutory schemes was impossible"); *In re* Maxwell Communs. Corp., 93 F.3d 1036, 1049 (2d Cir. 1996) (noting that "[i]nternational comity comes into play only when there is a true conflict between American law and that of a foreign jurisdiction," but finding such a conflict in the bankruptcy context even where English law did not compel conduct violative of U.S. law); Trugman-Nash, Inc. v. New Zealand Dairy Bd., 942 F. Supp. 905, 909 (S.D.N.Y. 1996) (following *Hartford Fire*, the only relevant comity-related question was whether defendants' anticompetitive conduct was compelled by New Zealand law); *cf.* Metro Indus., Inc. v. Sammi Corp., 82 F.3d 839, 846 n.5 (9th Cir. 1996) ("While *Hartford Fire Ins.* overruled our holding in *Timberlane II* that a foreign government's encouragement of conduct which the United States prohibits would amount to a conflict of law, it did not question the propriety of the jurisdictional rule of reason or the seven comity factors set forth in *Timberlane I*").

56. *See* 509 U.S. at 798.

57. *See id.* (emphasis added).

the conspiracies were prohibited by U.S. law would not give rise to any conflict.[58]

Under *Hartford Fire*, considerations of international comity may almost never compel a U.S. court to refuse to enjoin a merger involving foreign firms that otherwise meets the jurisdictional requirements of the FTAIA, given that sovereigns ordinarily do not compel private companies to merge. Even under this strict standard, however, international comity might still be implicated where a remedy sought by the United States would frustrate the ability of a foreign sovereign with concurrent jurisdiction to effectuate a remedy essential to promoting its significant national interests. In addition, the Ninth Circuit has held that the *Timberlane* jurisdictional rule of reason and seven comity factors were left intact by *Hartford Fire*.[59] A court thus might find application of the Sherman or Clayton Act to a foreign merger to be unreasonable based on other factors unrelated to the issue of a true conflict of laws—for example, where the effect on U.S. domestic or import commerce would be relatively insignificant as compared to the effect on other markets, or where neither of the merging firms are U.S. companies or have significant related assets in the United States.

C. Justice Department and FTC Enforcement Policy

1. Whether to Investigate or Challenge a Transaction

Implementing regulations under the Hart-Scott-Rodino Antitrust Improvements Act of 1976 (the HSR Act)[60] exempt certain foreign transactions having an insignificant direct relationship to U.S. commerce.[61] Nevertheless, about one-quarter of the transactions notified under the HSR Act have involved foreign persons as either parties or ultimate parent entities.[62] In addition, the Division has vigorously

58. *See id. But see* Andreas F. Lowenfeld, *Conflict, Balancing of Interests and the Exercise of Jurisdiction to Prescribe: Reflections on the Insurance Antitrust Case*, 89 AM. J. INT'L L. 42, 53 (1995) (arguing that the *Hartford Fire* majority "misunderstood" the approach of the *Restatement (Third)* on which it relied).

59. *See Metro Indus.*, 82 F.3d at 846 n.5.

60. 15 U.S.C. § 18a.

61. *See* 16 C.F.R. §§ 802.50-802.52. For example, an acquisition of foreign assets by a U.S. or foreign person is exempt if the sales in or into the United States attributable to the foreign assets to be acquired are less than $50 million. *See id.* at § 802.50.

62. *See* Christine A. Varney, Remarks Before Fordham Corporate Law

enforced compliance with the HSR Act notification requirements by foreign firms.[63] Of course, the DOJ and FTC are free to investigate and challenge any foreign transaction as to which they have jurisdiction, regardless of whether the transaction is subject to prenotification under the HSR Act.[64]

According to the 1995 *International Guidelines*, the Division and FTC both will consider the significant interests of any foreign sovereign

---

Institute 23rd Annual Conference on International Antitrust Law and Policy (Oct. 17, 1996). By 1998, half of the mergers being notified to the FTC involved a foreign party, information located abroad, or foreign assets critical to the remedy. *See* Robert Pitofsky, Merger and Competition Policy—The Way Ahead, Remarks Before the ABA Annual Meeting (Aug. 4, 1998). Similarly, half of the FTC's second-stage merger investigations have an important international component. *See* William J. Baer, Report from the Bureau of Competition, FTC, Remarks Before the ABA Antitrust Section Spring Meeting (Apr. 15, 1999). *See also* Debra A. Valentine, General Counsel, Federal Trade Comm'n, Global Mergers: Trade Issues and Alliances in the New Millennium, Remarks Before the Tenth Annual Organization of Women in International Trade Conference, Washington, D.C. (Oct. 4-5, 1999) *at* www.ftc.gov/speeches/other/dvwiitmerger.htm (discussion of mergers resulting from trade liberalization enabling foreign firms to provide meaningful competition).

63. *See, e.g.*, United States v. Mahle GmbH, 1997-2 Trade Cas. (CCH) ¶ 71,868 (D.D.C. 1997) (German and Brazilian piston manufacturers fined $5.6 million for failure to report the acquisition by one of the firms of a controlling interest in the other); United States v. Anova Holding AG, 1993-2 Trade Cas. (CCH) ¶ 70,383 (D.D.C. 1993) (Swiss citizen and two Swiss investment companies controlled by him fined $414,650 for failing to report transaction involving the acquisition of two Swiss companies that each made sales in the United States exceeding HSR Act reporting thresholds); United States v. Beazer PLC, 1992-2 Trade Cas. (CCH) ¶ 69,923 (D.D.C. 1992) ($760,000 fine); United States v. Baker Hughes, Inc., 1990-1 Trade Cas. (CCH) ¶ 68,976 (D.D.C. 1990) ($275,000 fine for failure to include "4(c)" document with filing); United States v. Tengelmann Warenhandelsgesellschaft, 1989-1 Trade Cas. (CCH) ¶ 68,623 (D.D.C. 1989) ($3 million fine); United States v. Lonrho PLC, 1988-2 Trade Cas. (CCH) ¶ 68,232 (D.D.C. 1988) ($122,000 fine); United States v. Bell Resources, Ltd., 1986-2 Trade Cas. (CCH) ¶ 67,321 (S.D.N.Y. 1986) ($450,000 fine).

64. *See, e.g.*, Aspen Tech., Inc., Docket No. 9310 (F.T.C. Aug. 7, 2003) (complaint), *at* www.ftc.gov/os/2003/08/aspencmp.pdf (FTC post-merger investigation of Aspen Tech acquisition of Hyprotech despite its exemption from the reporting obligations of the HSR Act).

in deciding whether to investigate or challenge conduct affecting significant interests of the sovereign or its nationals.[65] The agencies will consider "all relevant factors," including (1) the relative significance to the alleged violation of conduct within the United States as compared to conduct abroad; (2) the nationality of the persons involved in or affected by the conduct; (3) the presence or absence of a purpose to affect U.S. consumers, markets, or exporters; (4) the relative significance and foreseeability of the effects of the conduct on the United States as compared to the effects abroad; (5) the existence of reasonable expectations that would be furthered or defeated by the action; (6) the degree of conflict with foreign law or articulated foreign economic policies; (7) the extent to which enforcement activities of another country with respect to the same persons, including remedies resulting from those actions, may be affected; and (8) the effectiveness of foreign enforcement as compared to U.S. enforcement.[66]

With respect to the sixth factor—conflict with foreign law—the agencies have adopted the *Hartford Fire* majority's holding that a true conflict exists only where it is impossible for a person to comply with both U.S. and foreign law.[67] Unlike the *Hartford Fire* majority, however, the DOJ and FTC will also consider factors in addition to conflict with foreign law. In lieu of bringing an enforcement action, the

---

65. *See* 1995 INTERNATIONAL GUIDELINES, *supra* note 11, § 3.2.

66. *See id.* The first six factors were also stated in the Division's 1988 *International Guidelines*. The seventh and eighth factors are based on the terms of the Agreement Between the Government of the United States of America and the Commission of the European Communities Regarding the Application of Their Competition Laws, Sept. 23, 1991, 30 I.L.M. 1491 [hereinafter US-EU Agreement], *reprinted in* 4 Trade Reg. Rep. (CCH) ¶ 13,504.

67. *See* 1995 INTERNATIONAL GUIDELINES, *supra* note 11, § 3.2. The *International Guidelines* state:

> [T]he Agencies first ask what laws or policies of the arguably interested foreign jurisdictions are implicated by the conduct in question. There may be no actual conflict between the antitrust enforcement interests of the United States and the laws or policies of a foreign sovereign. This is increasingly true as more countries adopt antitrust or competition laws that are compatible with those of the United States. In these cases, the anticompetitive conduct in question may also be prohibited under the pertinent foreign laws, and thus the possible conflict would relate to enforcement practices or remedy. If the laws or policies of a foreign nation are neutral, it is again possible for the parties in question to comply with the U.S. prohibition without violating foreign law.

DOJ or FTC may attempt to persuade foreign competition authorities to take steps that will address competition concerns in the United States.[68]

The *International Guidelines* state that pursuant to a 1986 Organization for Economic Cooperation and Development (OECD) Recommendation,[69] the DOJ and FTC would notify any affected OECD country that a merger review had been commenced, and the two countries might attempt to coordinate the processing of their respective merger reviews, subject to the limitations of national confidentiality laws limiting the disclosure of nonpublic information acquired from the merging parties. For example, the United States might solicit or provide publicly available information relevant to the investigation, agree to inform the other interested country or countries when it had made a decision whether to challenge the transaction, and consult with foreign competition authorities about proposed remedies and investigatory methods. In addition, the DOJ or FTC might urge the merging parties to cooperate in a joint investigation of their merger by waiving confidentiality protection afforded under U.S. and foreign law.[70]

Significantly, in Illustrative Example J, the *International Guidelines* treat international comity as a matter requiring consultation with affected foreign sovereigns, particularly in regard to the crafting of an effective remedy that will not unreasonably conflict with the foreign sovereign's significant interests in the matter. The *International Guidelines* assume without discussion that applying the Sherman Act would be appropriate, regardless of where the hypothetical merging companies are incorporated or organized.[71]

---

68. *See id.*

69. The DOJ and FTC have agreed to consider the legitimate interests of other OECD nations in accordance with relevant OECD recommendations. Under a 1986 recommendation, the DOJ or FTC is to notify another OECD country whenever a U.S. antitrust enforcement action might affect important interests of that country or its citizens. *See Revised Recommendation of the OECD Council Concerning Cooperation Between Member Countries on Restrictive Business Practices Affecting International Trade*, OECD Doc. No. C(86)44 (May 21, 1986).

70. *See* 1995 INTERNATIONAL GUIDELINES, *supra* note 11 (Illustrative Example J).

71. Implicit in the illustrative example, however, is an assumption that most, if not all, of the affected countries recognize the importance and validity of antitrust merger regulation. In addition, given that the merging companies manufacture the relevant product in the United States, they obviously have related assets in the United States which would facilitate the crafting of a remedy that would not unduly affect the interests of other affected

The Division followed principles of comity in deciding not to challenge an acquisition by John Deere & Co. of the North American agricultural equipment operations of the Canadian company, Versatile Corporation.[72] The parties contended that the acquisition should be permitted to proceed because Versatile qualified as a "failing firm" under U.S. antitrust law and would be forced to shut down its Canadian agricultural equipment operations if the acquisition were blocked.[73] The Canadian competition authorities accepted this argument, while the Division, at least initially, did not.[74] After extensive discussions between Canadian and DOJ competition officials, however, the DOJ decided to defer to the "substantial Canadian interests" in the matter and did not challenge the transaction.[75]

The DOJ and FTC also believe a court should not question their determination to challenge foreign conduct. According to the *International Guidelines*, "[i]n cases where the United States decides to prosecute an antitrust action, such a decision represents a determination by the executive branch that the importance of antitrust enforcement outweighs any relevant foreign policy concerns."[76] One court has agreed with this position with respect to a merger challenge by the Division.[77] But the position has not been tested with regard to the FTC, which is not

---

sovereigns.

72. *See* James F. Rill, *Antitrust in a Global Environment: Conflict and Resolutions,* 60 ANTITRUST L.J. 557, 558 (1992).

73. *See* Donald I. Baker & David A. Balto, *Foreign Competition and the Market Power Inquiry*, 60 ANTITRUST L.J. 945, 949 (1992).

74. *See id.*

75. *See id.* at 950. *See also* U.S. Dep't of Justice Press Release (June 20, 1986) ("Having in mind, therefore, the substantial Canadian interests in this matter, and consistent with our obligation under the 1984 Memorandum of Understanding on antitrust cooperation entered into between the U.S. and the Canadian governments, the Division has determined to treat Versatile as satisfying the first criterion of the failing firm doctrine").

76. *See* 1995 INTERNATIONAL GUIDELINES, *supra* note 11, § 3.2.

77. *See* United States v. Baker Hughes, Inc., 731 F. Supp. 3, 6 n.5 (D.D.C.), *aff'd*, 908 F.2d 981 (D.C. Cir. 1990). The defendants argued that the court should decline to exercise jurisdiction on the basis of comity, relying on a diplomatic note from the Embassy of Finland opposing U.S. intervention in the transaction. The court rejected the defendants' comity argument, holding that it is not the court's role to second-guess the executive branch's judgment as to the proper role of comity concerns under these circumstances. *See id.*; *accord* United States v. Time Warner, 1997-1 Trade Cas. (CCH) ¶ 71,702 (D.D.C. 1997).

part of the executive branch. In addition, the American Bar Association has criticized this *Guidelines* position.[78]

2. *What Kind of Remedy Will Be Sought*

Comity considerations may also shape the type of relief the government will seek or obtain in a merger case. In the matter of *Institut Merieux S.A.*,[79] for example, the Canadian government objected to the terms of an FTC consent decree that required a Canadian firm to lease certain of its assets in Canada for at least twenty-five years to an FTC-approved lessor. The case involved the acquisition of a Canadian firm by a French competitor. In response to the Canadian government's objection, the consent decree was modified to require the concurrence of Canadian authorities in any disposition of the Canadian company's assets in Canada.[80]

In *United States v. MCI Communications Corp.*,[81] which involved the sale of 20 percent of the voting shares of MCI Communications Corporation (MCI) to British Telecommunications PLC (BT), and the formation of a joint venture by MCI and BT to provide international telecommunications services, the Division's complaint alleged that the proposed acquisition and joint venture would violate Section 7 of the Clayton Act by lessening competition in the markets for international telecommunications services between the United States and the United Kingdom and for international seamless telecommunications services. The competitive impact statement accompanying the proposed consent decree stated that the relief sought by the Division was evaluated against considerations of international comity:

---

78. *See Report to the House of Delegates by ABA Section of Antitrust Law and Section of International Trade and Practice*, 57 ANTITRUST L.J. 651, 658-59 (1988); *see also* Joseph P. Griffin, *EC and U.S. Extraterritoriality: Activism and Cooperation*, 17 FORDHAM INT'L L.J. 353, 382-84 (1994). For an explanation of the Division's position, see Charles F. Rule, Ass't Att'y Gen., Antitrust Division, U.S. Dep't of Justice, Remarks Before the International Trade Section and Antitrust Committee of the District of Columbia Bar (Nov. 29, 1988) (explaining the identical position taken in 1988 *International Guidelines*).
79. 5 Trade Reg. Rep. (CCH) ¶ 22,779 (Aug. 6, 1990) (consent decree).
80. *See* Debra K. Owen & John J. Parisi, *International Mergers and Joint Ventures: A Federal Trade Commission Perspective*, 1990 FORDHAM L. INST. 1, 11 (B. Hawk ed. 1991).
81. Civ. Action No. 94-CV1317 (proposed final judgment and competitive impact statement), 59 Fed. Reg. 33,009 (June 27, 1994).

> Consistently with its longstanding enforcement policy, the United States sought in the substantive provisions of the Final Judgment to avoid situations that could give rise to international conflicts between sovereign governments and their agencies. The substantive requirements imposed on MCI and NewCo have been tailored so as to avoid direct United States involvement in BT's operation of its telecommunications network in the United Kingdom on an ongoing basis, minimizing the potential for conflict with the United Kingdom authorities.[82]

A similar example is found in *United States v. Sprint Corp.*,[83] which involved a sale of 20 percent of the voting shares of Sprint Corporation (Sprint) to French government-owned France Telecom (FT) and German government-owned Deutsche Telekom AG (DT).[84] The complaint alleged that the proposed acquisition and formation of a joint venture among Sprint, FT, and DT to provide international telecommunications services would violate Section 7 of the Clayton Act by lessening competition in the markets for international telecommunications services between the United States and France and Germany. DOJ approval of the transaction was conditioned on the consummation of a planned divestiture by FT and DT of a part of their shareholdings in a competitor to Sprint (Infonet) and agreement by the joint venture to submit to the jurisdiction of the U.S. courts.[85] Although the partly foreign-government controlled joint venture would be subject to significant ongoing and close regulation by the Division, the competitive impact statement states that the decree was written "to avoid situations that could give rise to international conflicts between sovereign governments and their agencies," and that the Division is aware of no such conflict that would arise from enforcement of the decree. Specifically, the competitive impact statement notes that neither FT nor DT were named as defendants, "so that the United States is not imposing direct obligations on any foreign government-owned entity."[86] In addition, to the extent that the decree indirectly affected the conduct of FT and DT, it would be with regard to practices as to which regulation by the French and German

82. *Id.* at 33,023.
83. Civ. Action No. 95-CV1304 (consent decree), 60 Fed. Reg. 44,049 (Aug. 24, 1995).
84. *See id.* DT became a private corporation in January 1995, but the German government was at the time DT's sole shareholder, and it was expected to hold a majority of DT's shares through 1999.
85. *See id.* at 44,049-50 (listing stipulations).
86. *Id.*

governments is either nonexistent, "insubstantial," or consistent with the decree requirements.[87]

D. International Cooperation Agreements

In speeches on international antitrust, federal enforcers invariably discuss the practical benefits associated with cooperation among national enforcement agencies.[88] Much of this cooperation occurs at an informal

---

87. *See id.* The CIS states:

> [T]he substantive obligations [of the decree], to the extent that they may indirectly affect the conduct of FT and DT, apply to practices over which either foreign regulation is insubstantial or nonexistent, or, to the extent that regulation exists it also condemns in a general sense the practices that the proposed Final Judgment seeks to prevent.

88. *See, e.g.*, John Parisi, Enforcement Cooperation Among Antitrust Authorities, Remarks Before the IBC UK Conferences Sixth Annual London Conference on EC Competition Law (May 19, 1999, *updated* Oct. 2000), *at* www.ftc.gov/speeches/other/ibc9905991lupdate.htm; Robert Pitofsky, EU and U.S. Approaches to International Mergers, Remarks Before the EC Merger Control 10th Anniversary Conference (Sept. 14-15, 2000), *at* www.ftc.gov/speeches/pitofsky/pitintermergers.htm; Debra A. Valentine, Merger Enforcement: Multijurisdictional Review and Restructuring Remedies, Remarks Before the International Bar Ass'n (Mar. 24, 2000) *at* www.ftc.gov/speeches/other/dvmergerenforcement.htm, Joel I. Klein, Remarks Before the Subcommittee on Antitrust, Business Rights, and Competition, Committee on the Judiciary, United States Senate (May 4, 1999), *at* www.usdoj.gov/atr/public/testimony/2413.htm. Orson Swindle, Enforcement of Consumer Protection and Competition Laws in the Global Marketplace: The North American Experience, Remarks Before the Sydney Global Commerce Conference 1998 (Nov. 10, 1998), *at* www.ftc.gov/speeches/swindle/austspch.htm; Robert Pitofsky, Competition Policy in a Global Economy—Today and Tomorrow, Remarks Before the European Institute's Eighth Annual Transatlantic Seminar on Trade and Investment (Nov. 4, 1998), *at* www.ftc.gov/speeches/pitofsky/global.htm; A. Douglas Melamed, Antitrust Enforcement in a Global Economy, Remarks Before the Fordham Corporate Law Institute (Oct. 22, 1998), *at* www.usdoj.gov/atr/public/speeches/2043.htm; Roscoe B. Starek, III, International Cooperation in Antitrust Enforcement, Remarks Before the Annual Conference of the American Corporate Counsel Association European Chapter (Sept. 29, 1997), *at* www.ftc.gov/speeches/starek/londspch.htm.

level, with U.S. officials conferring on an ad hoc, yet effective, basis with officials from foreign agencies.[89] In addition, the United States has negotiated several bilateral cooperation agreements with foreign countries.[90] These agreements establish formal mechanisms whereby one nation's international enforcement efforts can be bolstered by assistance from agencies overseas. While some differences exist, these agreements generally provide for: (1) notification to the other party of an

89. *See* Robert Pitofsky, Competition Policy in a Global Economy—Today and Tomorrow, Remarks Before the European Institute's Eighth Annual Transatlantic Seminar on Trade and Investment (Nov. 4, 1998), *at* www.ftc.gov/speeches/pitofsky/global.htm.

90. *See* Agreement between the Government of the United States of America and the Government of the United Mexican States Regarding the Application of Their Competition Laws, July 11, 2000, *reprinted in* 4 Trade Reg. Rep. (CCH) ¶ 13,509; Agreement between the Government of the United States of America and the Government of the Federative Republic of Brazil Regarding Cooperation between Their Competition Authorities in the Enforcement of Their Competition Laws, Oct. 26, 1999, *reprinted in* 4 Trade Reg. Rep. (CCH) ¶ 13,508; Agreement between the Government of the United States of America and the Government of Japan Concerning Cooperation on Anticompetitive Activities, Oct. 7, 1999, *reprinted in* 4 Trade Reg. Rep. (CCH) ¶ 13,507; Agreement between the Government of the United States of America and the Government of Australia on Mutual Antitrust Enforcement Assistance, Apr. 27, 1999, *reprinted in* 4 Trade Reg. Rep. (CCH) ¶ 13,502A; Agreement between the Government of the United States of America and the Government of the State of Israel Regarding the Application of Their Competition Laws, Mar. 15, 1999, *reprinted in* 4 Trade Reg. Rep. (CCH) ¶ 13,506; Agreement between the Government of the United States of America and the European Communities on the Application of Positive Comity Principles in the Enforcement of Their Competition Laws, June 4, 1998, 37 I.L.M. 1070, *reprinted in* 4 Trade Reg. Rep. (CCH) ¶ 13,504A; Agreement between the Government of the United States of America and the Government of Canada Regarding the Application of Their Competition and Deceptive Marketing Practices Laws, Aug. 3, 1995, 35 I.L.M. 1487, *reprinted in* 4 Trade Reg. Rep. (CCH) ¶ 13,503; Agreement between the Government of the United States of America and the Government of Australia Relating to Cooperation on Antitrust Matters, June 29, 1982, 34 U.S.T. 388, *reprinted in* 4 Trade Reg. Rep. (CCH) ¶ 13,502; Agreement between the Government of the United States of America and the Government of the Federal Republic of Germany Relating to Mutual Cooperation Regarding Restrictive Business Practices, June 23, 1976, 27 U.S.T. 1956, *reprinted in* 4 Trade Reg. Rep. (CCH) ¶ 13,501.

enforcement investigation or proceedings that may affect its important interest, (2) sharing information relevant to each other's investigation or proceedings to the extent permitted by domestic law, (3) coordination of parallel investigations, and (4) consultation to resolve issues arising from enforcement activities.[91]

The U.S.'s agreements with the European Union and Canada, as well as the IAEAA-based agreement with Australia, are considered second-generation cooperation agreements and will likely serve as models for cooperation agreements negotiated henceforth.[92]

1. *The 1991 US-EU Cooperation Agreement*

On September 23, 1991, the United States entered into an agreement with the Commission of the European Communities (US-EU Agreement)[93] requiring both parties to consult concerning their

---

91. *See, e.g.*, Agreement between the Government of the United States of America and the Government of the United Mexican States Regarding the Application of their Competition Laws, July 11, 2000, *reprinted in* 4 Trade Reg. Rep. (CCH) ¶ 13,509; Agreement between the Government of the United States of America and the Government of Australia Relating to Cooperation on Antitrust Matters, June 29, 1982, 34 U.S.T. 388, *reprinted in* 4 Trade Reg. Rep. (CCH) ¶ 13,502.
92. *See, e.g.*, U.S. Dep't of Justice, Press Release, Attorney General Signs Antitrust Assistance Agreement with Australia, 99-157 (Apr. 27, 1999) ("[Assistant Attorney General] Klein said that today's agreement will serve as a model for similar bilateral agreements with major U.S. trading partners around the world"); U.S. Dep't of Justice, Press Release, Attorney General Signs Antitrust Cooperation Agreement with Israel, 99-093 (Mar. 15, 1999) ("The new agreement, which is similar to existing U.S. agreements with Canada and the European Union, contains provisions for enforcement cooperation and coordination, notification of enforcement actions that may affect the other country, conflict avoidance with respect to enforcement actions, and effective confidentiality provisions"); FTC, Press Release, FTC, Justice Department Sign Cooperation Agreement with Canada (Aug. 3, 1995) (noting that the 1995 agreement with Canada replaced the outdated 1984 memorandum of understanding with Canada and followed the pattern laid out in the successful 1991 agreement with the EC). For information on the IAEAA see Diane P. Wood, Dep. Ass't Att'y Gen., Antitrust Div., International Enforcement at the Antitrust Division (Jan. 17, 1995), *at* www.usdoj.gov/atr/public/speeches/intern.txt.
93. *See* Agreement between the Government of the United States of America and the Commission of the European Communities Regarding the

investigations of mergers involving U.S. and European Community companies and establishing a general framework for cooperation in such investigations. Articles II and III of the US-EU Agreement are of particular potential relevance to merger investigations.[94] Article II of the Agreement requires each party to notify the other "whenever its competition authorities become aware that their enforcement activities may affect important interests" of the other party. Notification is presumed to be appropriate with regard to the investigation of any merger or acquisition in which one or more of the companies involved are incorporated or organized under the laws of one of the parties or their

---

Application of Their Competition Laws, Sept. 23, 1991, 30 I.L.M. 1491, *reprinted in* 4 Trade Reg. Rep. (CCH) ¶ 13,504. In August 1994, the European Court of Justice held that the European Commission lacked authority to conclude the Agreement. 1995 INTERNATIONAL GUIDELINES, *supra* note 11, § 2.91 & n.46. *See* Case C-327/91, French Republic v. Commission, I E.C.R. 3641 (1994); But the Agreement ultimately was approved by the European Union (EU) Council of Ministers on April 10, 1995, effective from the date of its signing in 1991. *See* Commission Report to the Council and the European Parliament on the Application of the Agreement Between the European Communities and the Government of the United States of America Regarding the Application of Their Competition Laws, COM(96)479 final. The "positive comity" provisions of Article V of the 1991 US-EU Agreement were expanded and elaborated on in a subsequent agreement between the United States and the European Communities; *see* Agreement Between The Government of the United States of America and the European Communities on the Application of Positive Comity Principles in the Enforcement of Their Competition Laws, June 4, 1998, 37 I.L.M. 1070, *reprinted in* 4 Trade Reg. Rep. (CCH) ¶ 13,504A, but this agreement is inapplicable in the merger context. *See* U.S. Dep't of Justice, Press Release, U.S. and European Communities Sign Antitrust Cooperation Agreement, 98-255 (June 4, 1998).

94. Article IV provides that the United States and another party to the Agreement may agree to coordinate their enforcement activities with regard to anticompetitive conduct. Article V—the positive comity provision—provides that one party may request the other to initiate an enforcement action in regard to conduct occurring within its territory having an anticompetitive effect in the requesting party's territory. Article VI of the US-EU Agreement provides that each party will take account of the other's "important interests" when deciding on enforcement activities. Finally, Article VII provides that the parties agree to consult with one another regarding any matter under the Agreement. *See* US-EU Agreement arts. IV, V, VII.

states or member states.[95] Notification by the United States must be made at several points in a merger investigation: (1) when a request for additional information or documentary material (Second Request) is issued by the DOJ or FTC, (2) when the DOJ or FTC decides to file a complaint challenging the transaction, and (3) sufficiently in advance of the entry of a consent decree to enable the views of the EU to be taken into account.[96] Because the DOJ and FTC are prohibited by the HSR Act from disclosing that an HSR filing has been made,[97] the EU is notified about a reported transaction only when the DOJ or FTC has decided to open an investigation of the transaction.[98] The EU Commission in turn sends copies of that notification to interested EU member states.[99]

Article III of the US-EU Agreement provides that, within the limits of national confidentiality laws, each party must honor the other party's request for information relevant to an enforcement action.[100] Because neither party is required to disclose information in contravention of national law, however, the United States will not turn over confidential information received from merging parties pursuant to the HSR Act or civil investigative demand (CID) process without the merging company's permission. Similarly, the EU is not required to turn over confidential information that it may have obtained from companies operating within its jurisdiction if such disclosure is prohibited by legislation in force in the EU or is deemed to be incompatible with important EU interests.[101] In addition, any proprietary information of a merging company that is exchanged pursuant to Article III must be treated as confidential and should not be disclosed to third persons (e.g., pursuant to a FOIA or

---

95. *See id.* art. II § 2(c).
96. *See id.* art. II § 3(a). There are similar requirements applicable to the EU.
97. *See* 15 U.S.C. § 18a(h).
98. In contrast, all merger notifications to the EU Commission are published in the *EU Official Journal*, so that the fact of the proposed merger is immediately made public.
99. *See* Commission Report to the Council and the European Parliament on the Application of the Agreement Between the European Communities and the Government of the United States of America Regarding the Application of Their Competition Laws § 3.3, COM(96)479 final. The DOJ and FTC also themselves typically notify affected EU member states directly, pursuant to the July 1995 Revised Recommendation of the OECD Council concerning cooperation between member countries.
100. Because the US-EU Agreement is not a treaty, it does not supersede the domestic law of the United States or any other party to the Agreement. *See* US-EU Agreement, *supra* note 94, art. IX.
101. *See id.* art. VIII.

similar request) without the permission of the party supplying the information.[102]

In the fall of 2002, the US/EU Merger Working Group announced a set of Best Practices for coordinating merger investigations in an effort to avoid divergent enforcement decisions, facilitate coherence and compatible remedies, and reduce burdens on those subject to multiple antitrust reviews.[103]

2. *The 1995 US-Canada Cooperation Agreement*

Terms substantially similar to the US-EU Agreement are found in an agreement between the United States and Canada signed in 1995.[104] Like the US-EU Agreement, the US-Canada Agreement requires the DOJ or FTC to notify Canada's competition authorities (specifically, Canada's Commissioner of Competition) of any merger investigation involving a Canadian corporation no later than when a Second Request is issued.[105] Further notifications are required whenever one party's competition authorities request documents or information located in the other party's territory and prior to the issuance of a complaint or application for a temporary restraining order or preliminary injunction, the filing of a proposed consent decree, or the issuance of a publicly available business review or advisory opinion.[106] In addition, upon request, each party will assist the other in securing information and witnesses and the voluntary compliance of companies with information requests.[107] The US-Canada

---

102. Section 2 of Article VIII provides:

> Each Party agrees to maintain, to the fullest extent possible, the confidentiality of any information provided to it in confidence by the other Party under this Agreement and to oppose, to the fullest extent possible, any application for disclosure of such information by a third party that is not authorized by the Party that supplied the information.

103. Working Group, Best Practices on Cooperation in Merger Investigations (Oct. 30, 2002), *at* www.usdoj.gov/atr/public/international/docs/200405.htm (emphasizing general cooperation and coordination between reviewing agencies).

104. Agreement Between the Government of the United States of America and the Government of Canada Regarding the Application of Their Competition and Deceptive Marketing Practices Laws, Aug. 3, 1995, 35 I.L.M. 1487 [hereinafter US-Canada Agreement], *reprinted in* 4 Trade Reg. Rep. (CCH) ¶ 13,503.

105. *See* US-Canada Agreement, *supra* note 104, art. II § 2.

106. *See id.* art. II §§ 5, 7.

107. *See id.* art. III § 3. *See also* Debra A. Valentine, Cross-Border Canada/U.S. Cooperation in Investigation and Enforcement Action,

Agreement also includes three additional factors a party must consider before taking enforcement action that would significantly affect the other party's interests that are not expressly stated in either the US-EU Agreement or the DOJ/FTC *International Guidelines*: (1) whether private persons will be placed under conflicting requirements by the two parties, (2) the location of relevant assets, and (3) the degree to which a remedy, in order to be effective, must be carried out within the other party's territory.[108]

3. *The 1994 International Antitrust Enforcement Assistance Act*

The 1994 International Antitrust Enforcement Assistance Act (IAEAA)[109] authorizes the DOJ and FTC to enter into mutual assistance agreements with foreign competition authorities under which one party may request the other to provide confidential information in its possession or to go out and obtain such information by use of compulsory process. Confidential information obtained pursuant to the HSR Act is exempted, though HSR Act-type information obtained through other forms of compulsory process may be covered.[110]

The first IAEAA agreement was signed with Australia in 1999.[111] Under the terms of the agreement, the parties will assist one another in obtaining or providing evidence in antitrust matters, regardless of whether the conduct to which the evidence relates would violate the laws of the country producing the evidence.[112] Further, this evidence is to be used only for antitrust enforcement purposes, except in certain

---

Remarks Before the Canda/United States Law Institute, Apr. 15, 2000, *at* www.ftc.gov/speeches/other/dvcrossborder.htm (discussing cooperation between U.S. and Canadian enforcement agency in various transactions).

108. *See* US-Canada Agreement, *supra* note 104 § 5.

109. 15 U.S.C. §§ 6201-6212.

110. *See* Nina L. Hachigan, *An Overview: International Antitrust Enforcement*, ANTITRUST, Fall 1997, at 26 n.17 (citing H.R. REP. NO. 772, 103d Cong., 2d Sess., pt. 2 (1994)). *See* Request for Comments on Proposed Agreement Between the Government of the United States of America and the Government of Australia on Mutual Antitrust Enforcement Assistance, 62 Fed. Reg. 20,022 (1997).

111. *See* Agreement between the Government of the United States of America and the Government of Australia on Mutual Antitrust Enforcement Assistance, *reprinted in* 4 Trade Reg. Rep. (CCH) ¶ 13,502A (Apr. 27, 1999).

112. *See id.* art. II §§ E, F.

circumstances.[113] The party providing such information must determine whether the provision of information is consistent with the public interest,[114] and the agreement contains strict confidentiality requirements designed to protect sensitive business information.[115]

E. Investigations of Transnational Mergers

Investigation of the merger of Guinness plc and Grand Metropolitan plc illustrates how closely U.S. and foreign competition authorities can coordinate their investigations of a transnational merger under the current legal regime. Guinness and GrandMet (both British companies) competed in the sale of distilled spirits, including premium brands of scotch and gin.[116] Premerger, Guinness had about 68 percent, and GrandMet about 24 percent, of the U.S. premium scotch market.[117] Market share figures for the premium gin market were nearly as high, with Guinness controlling about 58 percent of the market and GrandMet about 15 percent of the market.[118] Anticipating likely price increases resulting from the increased concentration, the FTC required the parties to divest worldwide rights and assets relating to the Dewars scotch and Bombay gin brands.[119] Similarly, the EU had required the parties, inter alia, to divest of Guinness' interests in the Dewars and Ainslies scotch whiskey brands in Europe.

According to FTC Chairman Pitofsky, the FTC (for the first time) "sat in on the actual investigative process in Brussels."[120] The FTC "was

---

113. *See id.* art. II § H. Such evidence may be used for nonantitrust purposes "only if (1) such use or disclosure is essential to a significant law enforcement objective and (2) the Executing Authority that provided such antitrust evidence has given its prior written consent to the proposed use or disclosure." *Id.* art VII § C. Once such evidence has been made public in this manner, it "may thereafter be used by the Requesting Party for any purpose consistent with the Parties' mutual assistance legislation." *Id.* art VII § D.

114. *See id.* art. II §§ B, C.

115. *See id.* art. VI.

116. *See* Guinness plc, 62 Fed. Reg. 66,867 (Dec. 22, 1997) (analysis to aid public comment).

117. *See id.* The merger would have increased the HHI for the premium scotch market by over 3000 points, producing a merged firm HHI of over 8000 points. *See id.*

118. *See id.* The HHI for the premium gin market would have increased by over 1700 points, resulting in a market concentration of over 6000 points.

119. *See id.*

120. *See* Lawsky, *US-EU Show Unprecedented Cooperation on Guinness*,

there" when the companies explained why the EU should not challenge the merger and when the EU notified the companies what competition concerns it had. In addition, the FTC also worked closely with Canadian, Australian, and Mexican authorities "to achieve the necessary remedies and to assure that its settlement would be complementary to the enforcement actions already taken by the EC and contemplated by others."[121]

Substantial cooperation also occurred in the investigations by the Division and the European Commission of the 1998 merger between MCI and WorldCom. The parties to the $44 billion transaction agreed to implement a $1.75 billion divestiture of the MCI Internet business to Cable & Wireless plc. This divestiture assuaged Division concerns that the merged firm would have combined the two leading nationwide Internet backbone service providers.[122]

The simultaneous investigations of the merger by the Division and the European Commission were conducted separately, but with much cooperation. The two agencies held joint meetings with the parties and, after receiving the parties' consent, the Division and the European Commission exchanged information obtained during their respective investigations.[123] In addition, pursuant to the 1991 U.S.-EU cooperation

---

REUTERS, Sept. 15, 1997.

121. *See* FTC Press Release, Dewar's Scotch, Bombay Gin and Bombay Sapphire Gin to Find New Corporate Homes Under FTC Agreement (Dec. 15, 1997). Guinness/GrandMet is not the only matter in which the FTC has cooperated with several foreign authorities simultaneously. In its investigation of the Federal Mogul/T&N merger, the FTC cooperated simultaneously with the U.K., French, German, and Italian competition authorities. *See* Robert Pitofsky, Merger and Competition Policy—The Way Ahead, Remarks Before the ABA Annual Meeting (Aug. 4, 1998) ("Extensive consultation among staff of all involved agencies led to mutual conclusions that there were competition problems . . . [t]he parties responded with a proposal to all of the involved authorities...[t]he achievement of [the remedy eventually reached] was closely coordinated with the European authorities, particularly the German Federal Cartel Office whose desired relief we were able to incorporate into our consent order") (footnote omitted).

122. *See* Pitofsky, *supra* note 121.

123. *See id.* Confidentiality waivers have been used in other matters to allow U.S. agencies to share information with foreign competition authorities. For example, in its investigation of the Zeneca/Astra merger, confidentiality waivers allowed the FTC to discuss documents relevant to a settlement proposal with the European Commission, facilitating the development of remedies that were acceptable to both authorities. *See*

agreement, the Commission formally requested the Division's assistance in "evaluating and implementing" the proposed divestiture.[124]

In yet another example of close cooperation, the European Commission adopted a remedy that had been negotiated by the Division in the Halliburton-Dresser merger. Halliburton and Dresser were two of only four participants in the worldwide logging-while-drilling (LWD) oilfield services market.[125] In addition, these same four firms were the only participants in the LWD tool manufacturing market.[126] In its consent decree with the parties, the Division advanced actual and potential competition theories in the LWD oilfield services market, as well as an innovation market theory in LWD tools.[127] The consent decree resolved these concerns by requiring the divestiture of Halliburton's entire LWD business, including its research and development capacity in LWD tools.[128]

In addition, though, during the negotiations that led to the final consent decree, the parties agreed to divest Halliburton's 36 percent stake in M-I Drilling to Smith International.[129] Dresser's Baroid Division was a direct competitor with M-I Drilling in the drilling fluids market, and it was this pre-consent decree divestiture that resolved the European Commission's concerns with the transaction and allowed it to clear the deal.[130]

William J. Baer, Director, Bureau of Competition, FTC, Report from the Competition Bureau, Remarks Before the ABA Antitrust Section Spring Meeting (Apr. 15, 1999). Similarly, waivers allowed the FTC to share documents with the Canadian Competition Bureau in the investigation of the Lafarge/Holnam merger, easing the burden on the parties of compliance with the investigation. *See id.*

124. *See* Pitofsky, *supra* note 121.

125. *See* United States v. Halliburton Co., 63 Fed. Reg. 58,770, 58,778 (1998) (competitive impact statement).

126. *See id.*

127. *See id.*

128. *See id.* at 58,772 (proposed final judgment); U.S. Dep't of Justice, Press Release, Halliburton Co. Agrees to Sell Part of Its Worldwide Oil Field Services Business and Its Drilling Fluids Business in order to Proceed with Dresser Industries Merger, 98-450 (Sept. 29, 1998).

129. *See* U.S. Dep't of Justice, Press Release, Halliburton Co. Agrees to Sell Part of Its Worldwide Oil Field Services Business and Its Drilling Fluids Business in order to Proceed with Dresser Industries Merger, 98-450 (Sept. 29, 1998).

130. *See* European Comm'n, Press Release, Commission Clears the Merger of Halliburton and Dresser in the Area of Oilfield Services, IP/98/643 (July 8, 1998).

The lack of common international merger review standards and procedures can lead, and has led, to outright conflicts, an example of which is the 1997 merger of Boeing and McDonnell Douglas. This merger left only two large commercial aircraft manufacturers in the world: Boeing/McDonnell Douglas, with well over 60 percent of the market, and Airbus Industries, which is owned by a group of EU companies and member states. The merger was subject to review by both U.S. and EU competition authorities. The FTC concluded that the merger would not significantly lessen competition because McDonnell Douglas was a weak competitor "no longer in a position to influence significantly the competitive dynamics of the commercial aircraft model."[131]

The EU, however, concluded that the transaction would violate the EC Merger Regulation by giving the merged company a dominant position. The EU ultimately refused to approve the merger without significant conditions, including that Boeing (1) would not enforce exclusive supply contracts it had negotiated with a number of U.S. airlines, (2) would license to Airbus and other competitors all technology benefits gained from contracts with the U.S. Department of Defense and NASA, (3) would create a firewall between its civil aircraft business and that of McDonnell Douglas, and (4) would not abuse its relationship with customers and suppliers. The highest officials on both sides (including the U.S. President and Secretary of State) were involved in negotiations concerning the EU's decision and, during these negotiations, there were threats of trade war retaliation by both sides.[132]

Gaps in existing mechanisms for coordinating multijurisdictional transaction review also led in 2001 to an acrimonious public confrontation between U.S. and EU authorities in connection with the EU's rejection of the proposed acquisition of Honeywell International Inc. by General Electric Co.[133] The Division had cleared the proposed $42 billion acquisition subject to the parties' commitments to divest

---

131. *See* Statement of Chairman Robert Pitofsky and Commissioners Janet D. Steiger, Roscoe B. Starek III, and Christine A. Varney, Boeing Co., File No. 971-0051 (July 1, 1997), *reprinted in* 5 Trade Reg. Rep. (CCH) ¶ 24,295.

132. *See* Robert Pitofsky, Remarks Before the Business Development Associates, Staples & Boeing: What They Say About Merger Enforcement at the FTC (Sept. 23, 1997), *at* www.ftc.gov/opa/1997/09/pitmerg.htm.

133. *General Electric/Honeywell*, Case COMP/M.2220 (July 3, 2001), on appeal Cases T-209/01 and T-210/01 *Honeywell v. Commission* (grounds of appeal OJ [2001] C 331/23, judgment pending).

Honeywell's helicopter engine business and to authorize a new entity to service "auxiliary power units" and certain aircraft engines manufactured by Honeywell.[134] The two authorities traded blunt public criticisms. The EU Commissioner for Competition "deplore[d] attempts to misinform the public and to trigger political intervention."[135] When the EU issued its order of disapproval the Assistant Attorney General announced that the apparent EU emphasis on protecting "competitors" rather than "competition" was a "significant point of divergence" between the standards and policies of the United States and those of the EU.[136]

These open public confrontations contributed to the redoubling of longstanding efforts to achieve better coordination of procedures and convergence of policies between the U.S. and EU competition authorities, and among a wider community of antitrust and competition enforcement agencies around the world.

Even before the *GE/Honeywell* imbroglio the EU had adopted a policy statement on definition of relevant markets influenced strongly by the comparable methodology employed by the U.S. antitrust agencies.[137] Following the *GE/Honeywell* confrontation the U.S. and EU established a bilateral Merger Working Group, which published a series of "Best Practices on Cooperation in Merger Investigations" in 2002, setting forth a framework for coordination with regard to transactions investigated by both jurisdictions.[138]

The International Competition Network ("ICN") was launched in October, 2001.[139] It operates through dialogue and research leading to

---

134. *See* U.S. Dep't of Justice, Press Release, Justice Department Requires Divestitures in Merger Between General Electric and Honeywell (May 2, 2001), *at* www.usdoj.gov/atr/public/press_releases/2001/8140.htm.

135. E.U. Press Release, Monti Dismisses Criticism of GE/Honeywell Merger Deplores Politicization of the Case (June 18, 2001), *at* www.eurunion.org/news/press/2001/2001047.htm.

136. U.S. Dep't of Justice, Press Release, Statement by Ass't. Att'y Gen. Charles A. James on the EU's Decision Regarding the GE/Honeywell Acquisition (July 3, 2001), *at* www.usdoj.gov/atr/public/press_releases/2001/8510.htm.

137. Commission Notice on the Definition of the Relevant Market for the Purposes Of Community Competition Law, OJ C 372 (Sept. 12, 1997).

138. See U.S. Dep't of Justice, Press Release, US-EU Merger Working Group: Best Practices on Cooperation in Merger Investigations, *at* www.usdoj.gov/atr/public/international/docs/200405.htm (Oct. 30, 2002).

139. *See* U.S. Dep't of Justice, Press Release, U.S. and Foreign Antitrust Officials Launch International Competition Network (Oct. 12, 2001), *at* www.usdoj.gov/atr/public/press_releases/2001/9400.htm.

consensus adoption of "guiding principles" and "recommended practices" for voluntary consideration by member jurisdictions.[140] The ICN quickly established a "Mergers Working Group" that has carried forward an active work program intended to facilitate both procedural coordination and substantive convergence in the antitrust review of structural transactions.

In January of 2004, the European Union revealed a variety of reforms under its Merger Regulation.[141] This package, consisting of the new Merger Control Regulations, a Notice of the appraisal of horizontal mergers, and new "best practices guidelines" makes a number of important changes to the substantive test, EU jurisdiction, investigative powers, timing of review and monetary penalities.[142]

F. Special Defenses

1. Foreign Sovereign Immunities Act

Under the Foreign Sovereign Immunities Act (FSIA), foreign governments and their instrumentalities are immune from suit in U.S. courts except under certain specified circumstances.[143] State-owned enterprises and corporations in which a state (or one of its political subdivisions) owns a majority interest are considered to be "instrumentalities" of the foreign government.[144]

---

140. Direct membership in the ICN is open only to competition authorities, although private sector input and participation has been a significant element of many of the ICN Mergers Working Group activities. Detailed descriptions of the activities of the ICN and the past and pending activities of the Mergers Working Group are available at www.internationalcompetitionnetwork.org. Founded by thirteen original member agencies, membership of the ICN now includes every known operational competition authority (at national and supranational level) in the world.
141. *See* EU Press Release; *EU Gives Itself New Merger Control Rules for 21st Century* (Jan. 20, 2004), *at* www.europa.eu.int/rapid/start/cgi/guesten.ksh?p_action.gettxt=gt&doc=IP/04/70|0|RAPID&lg=EN&display=).
142. *Id.*
143. *See* 28 U.S.C. §§ 1602-11; *see also* Argentine Republic v. Amerada Hess Shipping Corp., 488 U.S. 428 (1989).
144. *See* 28 U.S.C. § 1603(b); *see also* Dole Food Co. v. Patrickson, 538 U.S. 468 (2003) (actual, direct ownership interest required for corporation to be state instrumentality); Corporacion Mexicana de Servicios Maritimos, S.A. de C.V. v. M/T Respect, 89 F.3d 650 (9th Cir. 1996) (elaborating on

The most important exception to FSIA immunity for purposes of merger law is the exception for commercial activities.[145] FSIA immunity does not apply to the commercial activities of a foreign sovereign or its instrumentality (1) in the United States or (2) outside the United States if those activities cause a "direct effect" in the United States.[146] Whether an activity is "commercial" depends on the nature of the activity, rather than its purpose, and on whether the activity is of a type that ordinarily would be carried on by private concerns for profit.[147] An effect is "direct" if it "follows as an immediate consequence" of the alleged anticompetitive commercial activity.[148] Plaintiffs whose alleged harms rely upon the occurrence of intermediate events fail the "immediate consequence" test.[149]

Mergers and acquisitions typically would involve entities selling goods and services that would most likely be considered as commercial activities.[150] In addition, it seems clear that a foreign government's

---

analysis of whether an enterprise is a state instrumentality); 1995 INTERNATIONAL GUIDELINES, *supra* note 11, § 3.31 n.81. ("not uncommon in antitrust cases to see state-owned enterprises meeting this definition" of "agency or instrumentality of a foreign state").

145. 28 U.S.C. §§ 1605(a)(2) reads:

> A foreign state shall not be immune from the jurisdiction of courts of the United States or of the States in any case—in which the action is based . . . upon an act outside the territory of the United States in connection with a commercial activity of the foreign state elsewhere and that act causes a direct effect in the United States.

146. *See id.*

147. *See* 28 U.S.C. § 1603(d); *see also* Argentina v. Weltover, Inc., 504 U.S. 607 (1992); Millicom Int'l Cellular, S.A. v. Republic of Costa Rica, 995 F. Supp. 14, 21 (D.D.C. 1998) ("state engages in 'commercial activity' when it exercises only those powers that can also be exercised by private citizens, as distinct from those powers peculiar to sovereigns").

148. *See Weltover,* 504 U.S. at 618; *see also* General Elec. Capital Corp. v. Grossman, 991 F.2d 1376 (8th Cir. 1993) (Canada's operation of a commercial airline did not destroy immunity where underlying suit was unrelated to the airline's operations).

149. *See, e.g.*, Virtual Countries, Inc. v. Republic of South Africa, 300 F.3d 230, 237-38 (2d Cir. 2002) (holding press release that allegedly hampered plaintiff's business was legally insufficient because press must publish press release and investors must learn of press release and make independent decision).

150. *See Weltover,* 504 U.S. at 614 ("[W]hen a foreign government acts, not as a regulator of a market, but in the manner of a private player within it, the foreign sovereign's actions are 'commercial' within the meaning of the

agreement to acquire assets in the United States would be subject to challenge in U.S. courts. The more difficult issue is likely to be whether a merger or acquisition that occurs wholly outside the United States has a sufficiently direct effect in the United States as to be exempt from the FSIA. It could be argued that, if the merger meets the jurisdictional hurdle of the FTAIA—because it would have a direct, substantial, and reasonably foreseeable effect in the United States—it will also satisfy the lesser "direct effect" standard of the FSIA.[151] However, several circuits have interpreted the FSIA direct effect standard to require that "something legally significant actually happened in the United States" in connection with the foreign state's commercial activity.[152] In addition, the U.S. Supreme Court in *Weltover* warned that the FSIA standard is distinct from other jurisdictional standards.[153] The FTC itself has recognized the complexity of this issue.[154]

The *International Guidelines* state that, in the government's view of the FTC and DOJ, "[a]s a practical matter, most activities of foreign government-owned corporations operating in the commercial

---

FSIA"); *General Elec. Capital Corp.*, 991 F.2d at 1383 ("There is little doubt that acquiring a commercial business constitutes commercial activity").

151. Prior to *Weltover*, several circuits had interpreted § 1605(a)(2) of the FSIA as requiring that direct effects also be substantial and foreseeable. *See* McKesson Corp v. Iran, 52 F.3d 346 (D.C. Cir. 1995); America West Airlines, Inc. v. GPA Group, Ltd., 877 F.2d 793, 798-800 (9th Cir. 1989); Zemicek v. Brown & Root, Inc., 826 F.2d 415, 417-19 (5th Cir. 1987); Ohntrup v. Firearms Ctr. Inc., 516 F. Supp. 1281, 1286 (E.D. Pa. 1981), *aff'd*, 760 F.2d 259 (3d Cir. 1985). *But see* Texas Trading & Milling Corp. v. Nigeria, 647 F.2d 300, 311 (2d Cir. 1981).

152. *See* Adler v. Nigeria, 107 F.3d 720, 726 (9th Cir. 1997); United World Trade, Inc. v. Mangyshlakneft Oil Production Ass'n, 33 F.3d 1232, 1239 (10th Cir. 1994); Antares Aircraft, L.P. v. Nigeria, 999 F.2d 33, 36 (2d Cir. 1993); General Elec. Capital Corp. v. Grossman, 991 F.2d at 1385; Rush-Presbyterian-St. Luke's Medical Ctr. v. Greece, 877 F.2d 574, 581 (7th Cir. 1989). *But see* Voest-Alpine Trading USA Corp. v. Bank of China, 142 F.3d 887, 894 (5th Cir. 1998) ("The Fifth Circuit, however, has not adopted this requirement and, we think, for good reasons").

153. *See* 504 U.S. at 617.

154. Richard G. Parker, Director of the Bureau of Competition, FTC, Solutions to Competitive Problems in the Oil Industry, Prepared Statement of the Federal Trade Commission Before the House Judiciary Committee (Mar. 29, 2000), *at* www.ftc.gov/os/2000/03/opectestimony.htm (discussing FSIA and act of state doctrine).

marketplace will be subject to U.S. antitrust laws to the same extent as the activities of foreign privately-owned firms."[155] The *International Guidelines* characterize the FSIA's direct effect test as being "similar to proximate cause formulations adopted by other courts."[156]

2. *Act of State*

The act of state doctrine is a common law rule of decision based on considerations of international comity and deference to the role of the executive branch in conducting the foreign relations of the United States. Under this doctrine, the official acts of a foreign sovereign within its own territory are presumed to be valid and lawful.[157] A court may decline to invoke the doctrine, however, where judicial inquiry into the validity of a foreign state act would not compromise principles of international comity and the separation of powers.[158]

The act of state doctrine conceivably would be relevant to the merger of foreign firms in two instances: (1) where one of the parties to the transaction is the instrumentality of a foreign state and the merger occurs wholly within the territory of that state, and (2) where a foreign state has officially reviewed and approved a merger occurring wholly within its sovereign territory. In neither instance, however, would the doctrine likely preclude a U.S. enforcement action, although considerations of international comity ultimately might cause the enforcement agencies or courts to stay their hands.

In regard to the first instance, numerous courts have held that the act of state doctrine does not apply to the commercial actions of a foreign

---

155. *See* 1995 INTERNATIONAL GUIDELINES, *supra* note 11, § 3.3.

156. *See id.* (citing Martin v. South Africa, 836 F.2d 91, 95 (2d Cir. 1987) (a direct effect is one with no intervening element which flows in a straight line)). A foreign state's sale or acquisition of assets located within its territory or of voting securities of an issuer organized under its laws is exempt from HSR Act reporting requirements. *See* 16 C.F.R. § 802.52.

157. *See* W.S. Kirkpatrick & Co. v. Environmental Tectonics Corp., 493 U.S. 400 (1990).

158. *See id.* at 408-09. In *W.S. Kirkpatrick*, the U.S. Supreme Court declined to address whether there is a "Bernstein letter" exception, see Bernstein v. NV Nederlandsche-Amerikaansche StoomvaartMaatschappij, 210 F.2d 375 (2d Cir. 1954) (per curiam), to the act of state doctrine. But the Court's adoption of a "balancing approach" leaves it open to a court to decline to invoke the doctrine based on advice from the U.S. State Department. *See W.S. Kirkpatrick & Co.*, 493 U.S. at 408-09.

sovereign.[159] The DOJ and FTC also have taken that position. The *International Guidelines* state that the act of state doctrine "applies only if the specific conduct complained of is a public act of the foreign sovereign within its territorial jurisdiction on matters pertaining to its governmental sovereignty."[160] The *International Guidelines* further explain that the DOJ and FTC will not challenge foreign acts of state if allegedly anticompetitive conduct is the public act of the sovereign taken within its territorial jurisdiction and "the matter is governmental, rather than commercial."[161]

In regard to the second instance, a foreign government's approval of a merger would constitute a noncommercial, public governmental act. However, a challenge to the merger itself, which is the act of private parties, would not necessarily require condemnation of a public act of state. In act of state cases, the courts have looked to see whether the private conduct was actually compelled by the state, so that the private parties could not comply with both U.S. and foreign law.[162] For example, in *Trugman-Nash, Inc. v. New Zealand Dairy Board*, U.S. importers of New Zealand cheese sued the New Zealand Dairy Board and two U.S. corporations created by it to act as the Board's agent in the distribution and sale of New Zealand dairy products in the United States. The plaintiffs alleged that the Board and the two U.S. corporations had conspired to restrain and monopolize trade in New Zealand dairy products. The trial court found that the act of state doctrine did not apply

---

159. *See* Alfred Dunhill of London, Inc. v. Cuba, 425 U.S. 682, 695-706 (1976); Northrop Corp. v. McDonnell Douglas Corp., 705 F.2d 1030, 1048 n.25 (9th Cir. 1983); Hunt v. Mobil Oil Corp., 550 F.2d 68, 73 (2d Cir. 1977); Sampson v. Germany, 975 F. Supp. 1108, 1116-17 (N.D. Ill. 1997), *aff'd*, 250 F.3d 1145 (7th Cir. 2001); Eckert Int'l, Inc. v. Fiji, 834 F. Supp, 167 (E.D. Va. 1993), *aff'd*, 32 F.3d 77 (4th Cir. 1994). *But see* Honduras Aircraft Registry, Ltd. v. Honduras, 129 F.3d 543 (11th Cir. 1997); International Ass'n of Machinists & Aerospace Workers v. OPEC, 649 F.2d 1354, 1360 & n.8 (9th Cir. 1981). Although the parties "argued at length" in *W.S. Kirkpatrick* about the existence of a commercial activity exception to the act of state doctrine, the Court declined to reach the issue. *See W.S. Kirkpatrick & Co.*, 493 U.S. at 405.

160. *See* 1995 INTERNATIONAL GUIDELINES, *supra* note 11, § 3.33.

161. *See id.*

162. *See, e.g.*, *Trugman-Nash, Inc.*, 942 F. Supp. 905 (S.D.N.Y. 1996); Alomang v. Freeport-McMoRan, No. 96-2139, 1996 U.S. Dist. LEXIS 15908, at *15 (E.D. La. Oct. 18, 1996) (although the regulations of a foreign state formed "part of the background of the activities alleged, neither the validity of those regulations nor the legality of the behavior of the Indonesian government [was] in question").

because the court was not required to judge the validity of the New Zealand Dairy Board Act. The New Zealand Dairy Board Act did not compel the particular commercial arrangement pursued by the Board, which was owned by cooperatives of private New Zealand dairy farmers.[163]

3. *Webb-Pomerene Act*

The Webb-Pomerene Act[164] provides a limited exemption from the Sherman Act for the formation and operation of associations engaged solely in U.S. export trade. The exemption does not apply to conduct by an export association that has an anticompetitive effect in the United States or on the export trade of firms that compete with the export association.[165]

To obtain an exemption under the Webb-Pomerene Act, an association must register with the FTC and file annual reports of its activities.[166] Activities of the association that fall outside the scope of the exemption—for example, because they restrain U.S. domestic or import trade—remain fully subject to challenge by the federal enforcement agencies and private parties.[167]

4. *Export Trading Company Act*

Title III of the Export Trading Company Act[168] establishes a procedure by which any U.S. person proposing export trade activities

---

163. *See* Trugman-Nash, Inc. v. New Zealand Dairy Bd., 942 F. Supp. at 914.
164. 15 U.S.C. §§ 61-65.
165. *Cf.* United States v. Minnesota Mining & Mfg. Co., 92 F. Supp. 947, 965 (D. Mass. 1950) ("Now it may very well be that every successful export company does inevitably affect adversely the foreign commerce of those not in the joint enterprise and does bring the members of the enterprise so closely together as to affect adversely the members' competition in domestic commerce. . . But if there are only these inevitable consequences an export association is not an unlawful restraint")
166. For a description of how to file and a list of filings, see Webb-Pomerene Act filings, *at* www.ftc.gov/os/statutes/webbpomerene/index.htm.
167. *See* United States v. United States Alkali Export Ass'n, 58 F. Supp. 785 (S.D.N.Y. 1994), *aff'd*, 325 U.S. 196 (1945).
168. 15 U.S.C. §§ 4011-22. Unlike the Webb-Pomerene Act, the Export Trading Company Act covers the export of both goods and services. Moreover, unlike the Webb-Pomerene Act those covered by Title III of the Export Trading Company Act need not be exclusively engaged in exporting. However, the immunity provided by the Certificate of Review

may obtain an antitrust certificate of review granting immunity from federal and state antitrust laws. The certificate is issued, in advance, by the Department of Commerce with the concurrence of the DOJ.[169] The certificate immunizes its holder and identified members[170] from both government enforcement of federal and state antitrust laws and private treble damage actions.[171]

Any U.S. individual, partnership, or corporation (including trade associations and joint ventures) may apply for a certificate. Identified members of the certificate need not be U.S. persons. To obtain a certificate, the proposed export trade activities must not have an anticompetitive effect in the United States or on the trade of an export competitor of the applicant.

---

covers only export conduct.

169. For a discussion of how the certificate is issued see www.ita.doc.gov/fd/oetca/TitleIII.htm.

170. "Members" of a certificate might include, for example, the shareholders of the certificate holder, trade association members that elect to be covered by a certificate obtained by the association, and joint venture partners. While members of the certificate need not be U.S. persons, only exports from the United States will be covered by the certificate. Members receive the same antitrust protections as the actual certificate holder.

171. The certificate does not immunize its holder and members from private actions for single damages. The certificate provides, however, significant disincentives to private party actions. For example, the statute of limitations is shortened from four to two years, and a certificate holder that successfully defends itself is entitled to collect attorneys' fees.

CHAPTER 13

JUDICIAL RELIEF AND REMEDIES

Private parties can often resolve the investigating agency's concerns about their merger short of litigation.[1] Through "fix-it-first" restructuring of their transaction, or through the negotiation of a consent decree, the parties to a contested merger can address the agency's concerns and avoid the need for litigation.[2] These prelitigation remedies are employed in the majority of mergers that raise anticompetitive concerns.[3] In cases where the investigating agency or the parties to a

---

1. For a thorough discussion of those administrative procedures and remedies, see ABA SECTION OF ANTITRUST LAW, THE MERGER REVIEW PROCESS: A STEP-BY-STEP GUIDE (2d ed. 2001).
2. *See also*, R. Hewitt Pate, Ass't Att'y Gen., Antitrust Div., Concerning Antitrust Enforcement Oversight, Statement Before the House Committee on the Judiciary (July 24, 2003), *at* www.usdoj.gov/atr/public/testimony/201190.htm. The Antitrust Div. has initiated a similar review of its practices and policies regarding remedies. *See* Charles A. James, Ass't Att'y Gen., Antitrust Div., Recent Developments and Future Challenges at the Antitrust Division, Remarks Before the Dallas Bar Ass'n (Sept. 17, 2002); *at* www.usdoj.gov/atr/public/speeches/200239.htm; BUREAU OF COMPETITION, FTC, A STUDY OF THE COMMISSION'S DIVESTITURE PROCESS 10-11 (1999) (FTC's study of divestiture orders from 1990 to 1994 indicates that divestiture of an entire business is more likely to result in a viable operation than divestiture of selected assets of the business); Richard G. Parker, Senior Deputy Director, Bureau of Competition, FTC, Global Merger Enforcement, Remarks Before the International Bar Association (Sept. 28, 1999) (discussing the FTC Divestiture Study in the context of cases during the mid-1990s), *at* www.ftc.gov/speeches/other/barcelona.htm.
3. *See, e.g.*, A Positive Agenda for Consumers: The FTC Year in Review (Apr. 2003), *at* www.ftc.gov/reports/aba/gpra2003.pdf (indicating that in 2002, 31 antitrust enforcement actions were taken and 19 consent decrees entered into); Deborah D. Marjoras, Dep. Ass't Att'y Gen., Antitrust Div., Merger Enforcement at the Antitrust Division (Sept. 27, 2002), *at* www.usdjo.gov/atr/public/speeches/200285.htm (noting that 2001 the DOJ opened 131 preliminary investigations and challenged 21 mergers); John M. Nannes, Deputy Ass't Att'y Gen., Antitrust Div., Last Year and This Year: The View from the Antitrust Trenches, Remarks Before the New York State Bar Ass'n (Jan. 27, 2000), *at*

transaction cannot reach a negotiated settlement, however, litigation seeking preliminary or permanent relief may be initiated by the agency, by state attorneys general, or by private parties.[4] With the statutory increase in the Hart-Scott-Rodino Antitrust Improvements Act of 1976 (HSR Act) "size of transaction" filing threshold in 2001 from $15 million to $50 million, there is now a greater likelihood of litigation involving non-HSR reportable transactions.[5]

---

www.usdoj.gov/atr/public/speeches/4086.htm (noting that in FY 1999 the DOJ challenged or advised parties of its intention to challenge 46 transactions, most of which were resolved by consent decrees); Richard G. Parker, Senior Deputy Director, Bureau of Competition, FTC, Trends in Merger Enforcement and Litigation, Remarks Before the Annual Briefing for Corporate Counsel (Sept. 16, 1998), *at* www.ftc.gov/speeches/other/parker.htm (pointing out that, as the FTC neared the close of FY 1998, over 4,400 HSR filings had been received and 23 enforcement actions had been initiated, resulting in 20 consent agreements); *see also* Appendix O for selected merger enforcement statistics.

4. *See, e.g.*, Richard G. Parker, Senior Deputy Director, Bureau of Competition, FTC, Trends in Merger Enforcement and Litigation, Remarks Before the Annual Briefing for Corporate Counsel (Sept. 16, 1998), *at* www.ftc.gov/speeches/other/parker.htm (discussing FTC merger litigation).

5. *See, e.g.*, Aspen Tech. Inc., Docket No. 9310 (F.T.C. Aug. 7, 2003) (complaint), *at* www.ftc.gov/os/2003/08/aspencmp.pdf (FTC post-merger investigation of transaction despite exemption from the reporting obligations of the HSR Act); Chicago Bridge & Iron Co., Docket No. 9300 (F.T.C. Oct. 5, 2001) (complaint), *at* www.ftc.gov/os/2001/chicagobridgeadmincmp.htm (same); *see also* Joseph J. Simons, Director, Bureau of Competition, FTC, Report from the Bureau of Competition, Remarks Before The 51st Annual ABA Antitrust Section Spring Meeting (Apr. 4, 2003), *at* www.ftc.gov/speeches/other/030404simonaba.htm ("The number of investigations of mergers not reported under HSR is up sharply since the change in reporting thresholds"); *see also* FTC v. Hearst Trust, No. 1:01CV00734 (D.D.C. Nov. 9, 2001) (requiring Hearst to divest acquired party and to disgorge $19 million in illegal profits); United States v. 3D Systems Corp., No. 1:01CV01237 (D.D.C. Aug. 16, 2001) (DOJ blocking 3D's $45 million acquisition of DTM until certain patents were licensed to a third party competitor); FTC v. MSC Software, Docket No. 9299 (F.T.C. Aug. 14, 2002) (requiring MSC to divest two companies it had acquired).

A. Preliminary Relief

1. Preliminary Injunctions

Preliminary injunction actions, which seek to preserve the status quo by preventing the consummation of a merger, are a powerful and frequently used tool in Section 7 enforcement. They are particularly important because many Section 7 cases do not survive beyond the preliminary injunction stage. An unsuccessful effort to obtain a preliminary injunction can be the plaintiff's final battle in an effort to block a merger (although the Federal Trade Commission (FTC or Commission) may pursue administrative litigation against a merger even after losing an action for preliminary injunction),[6] and an unsuccessful effort to defend against a preliminary injunction very often means the proposed deal will be scuttled, given the costs, delay, and uncertainty of a full-blown Section 7 trial.[7]

---

6. *See* FTC, *Statement of Federal Trade Commission Policy Regarding Administrative Merger Litigation Following the Denial of a Preliminary Injunction*, 1995 WL 369485 (F.T.C. June 21, 1995). The FTC has adopted "fast-track" procedures for certain cases, 16 C.F.R. § 3.11A, to respond to concerns about the "glacial place" of FTC administrative proceedings; *see, e.g.*, FTC v. Occidental Petroleum Corp., 1986-1 Trade Cas. (CCH) ¶ 67, 071 (D.D.C.).
7. *See, e.g.*, Missouri Portland Cement Co. v. Cargill, Inc., 498 F.2d 851, 870 (2d Cir. 1994) ("Experience seems to demonstrate that . . . the grant of a temporary injunction in a Government antitrust suit is likely to spell the doom of an agreed merger"); FTC v. Exxon Corp., 636 F.2d 1336, 1343 (D.C. Cir. 1980) ("[T]he issuance of a preliminary injunction blocking an acquisition or merger may prevent the transaction from ever being consummated"). Even the announcement of a government challenge can end a planned acquisition. In fiscal years 1989 to 1994, the FTC "voted to seek a preliminary injunction to block 32 transactions," and in 23 of those cases, "the parties either entered into a negotiated settlement or withdrew from the transaction before a court decision on the complaint." FTC, Mergers: A View from the Federal Trade Commission, 1995 WL 122744, at *3 (F.T.C. Mar. 15, 1995) (Remarks of Commissioner Azcuenaga); FTC v. Staples, 970 F. Supp. 1066, 1093 (D.D.C. 1997) ("This decision [to grant a preliminary injunction] will most likely kill the merger").

a. Statutory Authority

Preliminary injunctions to block a proposed merger on Section 7 grounds may be sought by the federal government, private plaintiffs, and by state attorneys general suing on behalf of state citizens.

Section 15 of the Clayton Act[8] empowers the Antitrust Division of the U.S. Department of Justice (DOJ or the Division) to institute proceedings "to prevent and restrain" Section 7 violations. Pending determination of the case, "the court may at any time make such temporary restraining order or prohibition as shall be deemed just."[9] The district court may, in the interests of justice, order the trial on the merits to be consolidated with the preliminary injunction motion.[10] Orders granting or denying preliminary relief are appealable to the court of appeals[11] except where direct review lies with the U.S. Supreme Court.[12]

Section 13(b) of the Federal Trade Commission Act[13] authorizes the Federal Trade Commission (FTC or the Commission) to bring suit to preliminarily enjoin the violations of "any provision of law enforced by the Federal Trade Commission" (e.g., the Clayton Act and Section 5 of the FTC Act) "pending the issuance of a complaint by the Commission and until such complaint is dismissed by the Commission or set aside by the court on review," where such action would be "in the interest of the public."[14] FTC requests for preliminary injunctions granted by the

---

8. 15 U.S.C. § 25.
9. *Id.*
10. FED. R. CIV. P. 65(a)(2); *see also* United States v. Long Island Jewish Med. Ctr., 983 F. Supp. 121, 125 (E.D.N.Y. 1997).
11. 28 U.S.C. § 1292(a)(1).
12. The 1974 amendments to the Expediting Act, 15 U.S.C. § 29, now restrict direct review by the U.S. Supreme Court to cases where "immediate consideration of the appeal .. . is of general public importance in the administration of justice." *Id.*
13. 15 U.S.C. § 53(b).
14. *Id.* ("Upon a proper showing that, weighing the equities and considering the Commission's likelihood of ultimate success, such action would be in the public interest, and after notice to the defendant, a temporary restraining order or preliminary injunction may be granted . . . ."). *See* FTC v. Cardinal Health, Inc., 12 F. Supp. 2d 34, 45 (1998) (to be awarded preliminary injunctive relief, FTC does not need to prove that merger would in fact violate § 7, only that the FTC is likely to succeed on the merits of the case in a full administrative hearing); *see also* FTC v. H.J. Heinz, 246 F.3d 708, 719 (D.C. Cir. 2001) ("All that is necessary [to prove] is that the merger create[s] an appreciable danger of [collusive practices] in the future").

district court are not consolidated with hearings on the merits, and an injunction remains in place until the FTC completes its administrative proceedings.[15]

The merger review process instituted under the HSR Act[16] has allowed the federal government to act more effectively by providing it with the relevant information prior to the consummation of most mergers.[17] Where the information thus supplied raises competitive concerns, the FTC or DOJ may seek a preliminary injunction to stop the transaction rather than having to attempt to undo it after it has been consummated.[18] However, recent FTC cases underscore that HSR Act clearance does not preclude the agencies from subsequently challenging a merger.[19]

Section 16 of the Clayton Act[20] authorizes private parties and state attorneys general in parens patriae actions to sue for injunctive relief from "threatened loss or damage by a violation of the antitrust laws," including Section 7 violations.[21] Such actions are expressly subject to

---

15. The court may, however, ask the FTC to expedite proceedings. *See* FTC v. Warner Communs., 742 F.2d 1156, 1165 (9th Cir. 1984).
16. 15 U.S.C. § 18a.
17. For a detailed discussion of the premerger notification process, see ABA SECTION OF ANTITRUST LAW: THE MERGER REVIEW PROCESS: A STEP-BY-STEP GUIDE (2d ed. 2001). *See also* Marian R. Bruno, Ass't Dir., Premerger Notification Office, Bureau of Competition, FTC, Hart-Scott-Rodino at 25, Remarks Before the American Bar Association Mergers and Acquisitions: Getting Your Deal Through the New Antitrust Climate (June 13, 2002), *at* www.ftc.gov/speeches/other/brunohsr25.htm.
18. 15 U.S.C. § 18a. In addition to strengthening the agencies' hand, the HSR Act process helps private parties by "making it easier for businesses and unions to predict the consequences of mergers and to conform their economic strategies in accordance with the probable outcome." California v. American Stores Co., 495 U.S. 271, 297 (1990) (Kennedy, J., concurring).
19. *See, e.g., In re* Chicago Bridge & Iron Co.. No. 9300, (F.T.C. June 18, 2003); FTC v. The Hearst Trust, The Hearst Corporation, and First DataBank, Civil Action No. 1:01CV00734 (D.D.C. Apr. 6, 2001); *see also In re* Coca-Cola Co., 117 F.T.C. 795, 911 (1994) (FTC jurisdiction includes adjudicating the lawfulness of acquisitions that have already been consummated).
20. 15 U.S.C. § 26.
21. *Id.* ("Any person, firm, corporation, or association shall be entitled to sue for and have injunctive relief, in any court of the United States having jurisdiction over the parties, against threatened loss or damage by a violation of the antitrust laws").

the "same conditions and principles" applied to injunctions "by courts of equity."[22] In the past, state governments deferred to the federal authorities' enforcement of the antitrust laws and rarely challenged a transaction approved by the FTC or DOJ. However, since the U.S. Supreme Court's decision in *California v. American Stores Co.*,[23] which held that divestiture was one of the forms of equitable relief available to state attorneys general even after a settlement between the merging parties and the FTC, states have begun to challenge mergers approved by the federal government[24] and there is a continuing trend towards more

---

22. *Id*.
23. 495 U.S. 271 (1990).
24. *See, e.g., Wal-Mart Stores, Inc. v. Rodriguez*, 238 F. Supp. 2d 395 (D.P.R. 2002). Puerto Rico's antitrust challenge to a merger was blocked on Commerce Clause and selective enforcement grounds. The Puerto Rico Department of Justice objected to a proposed acquisition by Wal-Mart and attempted to extract allegedly unrelated concessions from the parties by securing a preliminary injunction from a Puerto Rico state court. Wal-Mart successfully brought suit in U.S. district court seeking an injunction preventing further interference by the PRDOJ. The court opined that Puerto Rico should have deferred to the FTC's investigation, which ended with a consent order in November 2002, citing the federal government's resources and credibility. *Id.* at 421. Furthermore, the court labeled Puerto Rico's antitrust arguments "fabricated," "pretextual" and "bogus," (*id.* at 410-11) calling the lawsuit a "sham which seeks to further harass [Wal-Mart] and finds no support in any of the provisions of the local anti-monopolistic laws." *Id.* at 420. The Puerto Rico Attorney General settled with Wal-Mart on February 27, 2003, effectively preventing any further action by the Puerto Rican authorities). *See also* Bon-Ton Stores v. May Dep't Stores Co., 881 F. Supp. 860 (W.D.N.Y. 1994) (granting preliminary injunction to state of New York and competitor of May against May's acquisition of Rochester department stores); New York v. Kraft Gen. Foods, Inc., 862 F. Supp. 1030 (S.D.N.Y.) (denying New York's motion for preliminary injunction to prevent Kraft from integrating cereal assets purchased from Nabisco), *aff'd mem.*, 14 F.3d 590 (2d Cir. 1993); Alaska v. Suburban Propane Gas Corp., 1995-1 Trade Cas. (CCH) ¶ 71,042 (D. Alaska 1995) (denying class certification motion by plaintiffs, including state of Alaska, in action challenging merger in the propane industry); Pennsylvania v. Russell Stover Candies, Inc., 1993-1 Trade Cas. (CCH) ¶ 70,224 (E.D. Pa. 1993) (denying Pennsylvania's motion for preliminary injunction against sale of Whitman's to Russell Stover-controlled company); Washington v. Texaco Ref. & Mktg. Inc., 1991-1 Trade Cas. (CCH) ¶¶ 69,345, 69,346 (W.D. Wash. 1991) (Washington obtained a preliminary injunction in case involving acquisition of service stations); Connecticut v. Wyco New

active state participation in merger review.[25] In other cases, particularly those involving consolidation of the oil & gas[26] and supermarket industries,[27] state attorneys general have cooperated with the FTC in investigating transactions.

b. Private Party Standing

Private parties face certain standing issues not faced by government plaintiffs in seeking antitrust relief. Despite the broad remedial language of Sections 4 and 16 of the Clayton Act, which authorize private antitrust suits against mergers, the U.S. Supreme Court's decisions in *Brunswick Corporation v. Pueblo Bowl-O-Mat, Inc.*[28] and *Cargill, Inc. v. Monfort of Colorado, Inc.*[29] have imposed a standing requirement that significantly

---

Haven, Inc., 1990-1 Trade Cas. (CCH) ¶ 69,024 (D. Conn. 1990) (Connecticut and Massachusetts obtained divestiture in case involving heating oil facilities).

25. *See* Rebecca Fisher, States' Merger Enforcement Continues in Many Form, Clayton Act Newsletter, Vol. III: No. 2, Spring 2003; *see also* Press Release, Connecticut Attorney General's Office, State Files Antitrust Lawsuit Against Oracle to Block Hostile Takeover of Software Rival (June 18, 2003) (Connecticut filed suit to enjoin Oracle/PeopeSoft transaction during pendency of DOJ review).
26. *See, e.g*., Texas v. Conoco Inc., No. H-02-3266 (S.D. Tex. 2002); Utah v. Phillips Petroleum Comp., No. 202CV-0982-TS (D. Utah 2002); Oregon v. Valero Energy Corp., No. 01CV1830 (D. Or. 2001); California v. Chevron Corp., No. 01-07746 (C.D. Cal. 2001); California v. BP Amoco, PLC, No. C00420 (N.D. Cal. 2000); Alaska v. Exxon Corp., No. A99-0618-CV (D. Alaska 1999); Washington v. Texaco Inc., No. C97-1980WD (W.D. Wash. 1997).
27. *See, e.g*., California v. Albertson's, Inc., No. CV-99-825 (C.D. Cal. June 24, 1999).
28. 429 U.S. 477 (1977). The Court held that the plaintiffs were not entitled to any damages where their claimed injury was the loss of the market share they would have gained but for the defendant's acquisition of certain companies that otherwise would have failed. The plaintiffs' "injury" was not "antitrust injury," inasmuch as it stemmed from preserved competition rather than from "the anticompetitive effects either of the violation or of anticompetitive acts made possible by the violation." *Id*. at 489.
29. 479 U.S. 104 (1986). The plaintiff sought to enjoin a merger on the ground that, after its consummation, the defendant would institute a price cut designed to drive competitors out of business and increase market share. The Court held that a plaintiff seeking an injunction must make the same antitrust injury showing as a plaintiff seeking treble damages (as

curtails the ability of private parties to sue for violations of the Clayton Act.[30] Essentially, a private plaintiff may only enforce Section 7 through a preliminary injunction (or otherwise) if it can show it has suffered or will suffer "antitrust injury," meaning "injury of the type the antitrust laws were intended to prevent and that flows from that which makes the defendants' acts unlawful."[31] Standing to obtain injunctive relief under Section 16 is broader than standing to obtain treble damages under Section 4 because the nature of the treble damages remedy raises dangers not relevant where equitable relief is concerned.[32] Thus, in addition to antitrust injury,[33] courts consider additional factors "such as the potential for duplicative recovery, the complexity of apportioning damages, and the existence of other parties that have been more directly harmed, to determine whether a party is a proper plaintiff under § 4."[34] In contrast,

---

in *Brunswick*) and that the plaintiff in *Cargill* had failed to establish antitrust injury, since the price competition it feared was merely "vigorous competition" which "is not activity forbidden by the antitrust laws." *Id.* at 116.

30. *See* Serpa Corp. v. McWane, Inc., 199 F.3d 6, 10 (1st Cir. 1999) ("Standing is restricted in antitrust cases to avoid overdeterrence. By limiting the availability of private antitrust actions to certain parties, federal courts 'ensure that suits inapposite to the goals of the antitrust laws are not litigated and that persons operating in the market do not restrict procompetitive behavior because of a fear of antitrust liability'") (quoting Todorov v. DCH Healthcare Auth., 921 F.2d 1438, 1449 (11th Cir. 1991)); Greater Rockford Energy & Tech. Corp. v. Shell Oil Co., 998 F.2d 391, 394 (7th Cir. 1993) ("Given the potential scope of antitrust violations and the availability of treble damages, an over-broad reading of § 4 could result in 'overdeterrence,' imposing ruinous costs on antitrust defendants, severely burdening the judicial system, and possibly chilling economically efficient behavior").

31. *Pueblo Bowl-O-Mat, Inc.*, 429 U.S. at 489.

32. "The treble damages remedy, if afforded to 'every person tangentially affected by an antitrust violation,' Blue Shield v. McCready, 457 U.S. 465, 476-77 (1982), or for 'all injuries that might be conceivably traced to an antitrust violation,' Hawaii v. Standard Oil Co., 405 U.S. 251, 264 n.14 (1972), would 'open the door to duplicative recoveries,' *id.* at 264, and to multiple lawsuits." *Cargill, Inc.*, 479 U.S. at 111 n.6.

33. Although many cases speak of "standing" and "antitrust injury" as if they were interchangeable, in fact "[a] showing of antitrust injury is necessary, but not always sufficient, to establish standing under § 4." *Cargill, Inc.*, 479 U.S. at 110 n.5.

34. *Cargill, Inc.*, 479 U.S. at 111 n.6. In *Associated General Contractors, Inc. v. California State Council of Carpenters*, 459 U.S. 519 (1983) (which was not a merger case), the Court held that the plaintiff had no

since "one injunction is as effective as 100,"[35] standing under Section 16 raises no threat of multiple lawsuits or duplicative recoveries and, therefore, "some of the factors other than antitrust injury that are appropriate to a determination of standing under § 4 are not relevant under § 16."[36]

The analysis varies according to the type of plaintiff involved.

(1) Competitor Standing

Since *Brunswick* and *Cargill*, competitor plaintiffs have had great difficulty surmounting the obstacle of antitrust injury.[37] Mindful of the

---

standing to collect damages because its claimed injury was "tenuous[ly] and speculative[ly]" related to the antitrust violation, there was a danger of duplicative recoveries or complex apportionment of damages, and there were "more direct victims of the alleged conspiracy." *Id.* at 545. The Tenth Circuit synthesized the U.S. Supreme Court's standing decisions into the following set of "factors to be considered:" "the causal connection between the antitrust violations and [the] plaintiff's injury; the defendant's intent; the nature of the plaintiff's injury; the directness or indirectness of the connection between the plaintiff's injury and the allegedly unlawful market restraint; the speculativeness of the plaintiff's damages; and the 'risk of duplicative recoveries .. . or the danger of complex apportionment of damages.'" Reazin v. Blue Cross & Blue Shield of Am., Inc., 899 F.2d 951, 962 n.15 (10th Cir.) (quoting *Associated Gen. Contractors, Inc.*, 459 U.S. at 544); *see also* Alberta Gas Chems. Ltd. v. E.I. du Pont de Nemours & Co., 826 F.2d 1235, 1240 (3d Cir. 1987) ("The statutory sanctions do not constitute a broad restitutionary scheme for injuries not closely related to the violation but caused by other effects, desirable or not, of the illegal conduct").

35. Hawaii v. Standard Oil Co., 405 U.S. 251, 261 (1972).

36. *Cargill, Inc.*, 479 U.S. at 111 n.6. According to one court, indirect purchasers have standing under § 7 for equitable relief but not damages. *See* Lucas Automotive Eng'g, Inc. v. Bridgestone/Firestone, Inc., 140 F.3d 1228, 1237 (9th Cir. 1998) ("We conclude that [appellant], as a . . . customer in a market controlled by a monopolist, has standing to assert a § 7 claim for equitable relief, including divestiture, under § 16").

37. For pre-*Cargill* cases finding competitors had standing, see, for example, Cia. Petrolera Caribe, Inc. v. Arco Caribbean, Inc., 754 F.2d 404 (1st Cir. 1985); Christian Schmidt Brewing Co. v. G. Heileman Brewing Co., 753 F.2d 1354 (6th Cir. 1985); McCaw Personal Communs. v. Pacific Telesis Group, 645 F. Supp. 1166 (N.D. Cal. 1986); Parrish's Cake Decorating Supplies, Inc. v. Wilton Enters., 1984-1 Trade Cas. (CCH) ¶65,917 (N.D. Ill. 1984), *modified*, 1985-1 Trade Cas. (CCH) ¶ 66,630 (N.D. Ill. 1985).

divergence of interests between competitors and consumers (the intended beneficiaries of the antitrust laws), courts have regarded competitor challenges with suspicion[38] and have largely adhered to the U.S. Supreme Court's famous admonition that the purpose of the antitrust laws is "the protection of competition, not competitors."[39] Like the U.S. Supreme Court in *Brunswick*, many lower courts have held competitor plaintiffs' claimed injuries to be the result of increased or preserved competition rather than of competition suppressed in violation of the antitrust laws,[40] or have found the injuries to be so indirectly related to or

---

38. *See, e.g.*, Alberta Gas Chems. Ltd. v. E.I. du Pont de Nemours & Co., 826 F.2d 1235, 1239 (3d Cir. 1987) ("Courts have carefully scrutinized enforcement efforts by competitors because their interests are not necessarily congruent with the consumer's stake in competition"); Ball Mem'l Hosp., Inc. v. Mutual Hosp. Ins., Inc., 784 F.2d 1325, 1334 (7th Cir. 1986) (competitor "gains from higher prices and loses from lower prices—just the opposite of the consumers' interest"); Community Publishers, Inc. v. Donrey Corp., 892 F. Supp. 1146, 1166 (W.D. Ark. 1995) ("Many mergers have valuable pro-competitive effects, and a rival has every incentive to challenge such pro-competitive mergers simply because they are pro-competitive"), *aff'd*, 139 F.3d 1180 (8th Cir. 1998); William J. Baumol & Janusz A. Ordover, *Use of Antitrust to Subvert Competition*, 28 J.L. & ECON. 247, 256-67 (1985) (if acquisition will introduce economies or improve product quality, "then, and only then, when the [transaction] is really beneficial, can those rivals be relied on to denounce the undertaking as 'anticompetitive'").
39. Brown Shoe Co. v. United States, 370 U.S. 294, 320 (1962); *see also* Atlantic Richfield Co. v. USA Petroleum Co., 495 U.S. 328, 340 (1990) ("Low prices benefit consumers regardless of how those prices are set, and so long as they are above predatory levels, they do not threaten competition").
40. *See* Pool Water Prods. v. Olin Corp., 258 F.3d 1024, 1035 (9th Cir. 2001) ("The Supreme Court has made clear . . . that a decrease in profits from a reduction in a competitor's prices, so long as the prices are not predatory, is not an antitrust injury"); Balaklaw v. Lovell, 14 F.3d 793 (2d Cir. 1994) (Sherman Act case); Phototron Corp. v. Eastman Kodak Co., 842 F.2d 95, 99 (5th Cir. 1988) (plaintiff's proof demonstrated only that defendant was "pricing in a competitive manner"); Ansell Inc. v. Schmid Labs., 757 F. Supp. 467, 485 (D.N.J.) (condom manufacturer's feared injury merely "a demonstration of threatened loss from continued competition" after competitor acquired "a popular brand"), *aff'd*, 941 F.2d 1200 (3d Cir. 1991); Remington Prods., Inc. v. North Am. Philips Corp., 755 F. Supp. 52, 57 (D. Conn. 1991) ("Remington's alleged injury is decreased sales due to increased competition" after merger producing market share of 55%); Pearl Brewing Co. v. Miller Brewing Co., 1993-2

remote from the antitrust violation as to fail to "flo[w] from that which makes defendants' acts unlawful."[41]

Even where the merger arguably lessens competition by facilitating oligopolistic collusion (as by reducing the number of firms and increasing market concentration),[42] competitors likely benefit from the cartelistic behavior made possible by the merger. If they join the cartel, they benefit by charging its supracompetitive price. If they decline to participate in the collusion, competitors may be able to do even better, by undercutting the cartel and thereby increasing their own volume. In either case, the violation of the antitrust laws—the tendency of the merger substantially to lessen competition by facilitating oligopolistic practices—actually helps competitors of the merging parties.

Thus, where the would-be plaintiff is a competitor,[43] the touchstone of the antitrust injury analysis is predation.[44] Competitors have no

---

Trade Cas. (CCH) ¶ 70,370, at 70,958 (W.D. Tex. 1993) ("What plaintiffs apparently fear is the loss of profits due to price competition . . ."), *aff'd mem.*, 52 F.3d 1066 (5th Cir. 1995).

41. Brunswick Corp. v. Pueblo Bowl-O-Mat, Inc., 429 U.S. 477 489 (1977); *see also* Lucas Automotive Eng'g, Inc. v. Bridgestone/Firestone, Inc., 140 F.3d 1228, 1233 (9th Cir. 1998) (denying standing to competing distributor); Lovett v. General Motors Corp., 975 F.2d 518 (8th Cir. 1992); Axis S.P.A. v. Micafil, Inc., 870 F.2d 1105, 1111 (6th Cir. 1989) (machine manufacturer's lost sales were not antitrust injury because they were not caused by the merger and elimination of a competitor); *E.I. du Pont de Nemours & Co.*, 826 F.2d at 1241 (alleged losses from lost sales "were neither connected with, nor resulted from, du Pont's market power in the methanol-producing industry"); Go-Video, Inc. v. Matsushita Elec. Indus. Co., 1992-2 Trade Cas. (CCH) ¶ 69,972, at 68,725 (D. Ariz. 1992) (VCR manufacturer's allegations of injury from competitor's post-acquisition change in video software format "insufficiently connected to any anticompetitive conduct to satisfy the requirements of antitrust standing"), *aff'd*, 15 F.3d 1085 (9th Cir. 1994).

42. *See, e.g.*, Hospital Corp. of Am. v. FTC, 807 F.2d 1381, 1386 (7th Cir. 1986) ("the ultimate issue is whether the challenged acquisition is likely to facilitate collusion").

43. A company that has not yet entered the market may show antitrust injury, but courts require that a "potential" competitor show both intention to enter the market and preparedness to do so. *See* Hecht v. Pro Football, Inc., 570 F.2d 982, 994 (D.C. Cir. 1977) ("[i]ndicia of preparedness include adequate background and experience in the new field, sufficient financial capability to enter it, and the taking of actual and substantial affirmative steps toward entry, 'such as the consummation of relevant contracts and procurement of necessary facilities and equipment'").

standing to challenge the merger unless they can present a credible claim of predation resulting from the merger, demonstrating that the merger will produce a firm so dominant that it can price below cost in order to drive its competitors out of the market and reap monopoly profits.[45] Because "predatory pricing schemes are rarely tried, and even more rarely successful,"[46] "[c]laims of threatened injury from predatory pricing must, of course, be evaluated with care."[47] Competitors have succeeded in demonstrating antitrust injury where they have shown that the merger would so concentrate market power in the merged entity as to

---

44. The U.S. Supreme Court has defined predatory pricing as "pricing below an appropriate measure of cost for the purpose of eliminating competitors in the short run and reducing competition in the long run." Cargill, Inc. v. Monfort, Inc., 479 U.S. 104, 117 (1986); *see also id.* at 118 n.12 (discussing courts' and commentators' treatment of the issue of the "appropriate" measure of cost). In *Atlantic Richfield Co. v. USA Petroleum Co.*, 495 U.S. 328 (1990), the Court held that the rule announced in *Brunswick* and *Cargill* was a general principle, applicable as well to a vertical, maximum price-fixing claim per se unlawful under § 1 of the Sherman Act: "When prices are not predatory, any losses flowing from them cannot be said to stem from an anticompetitive aspect of the defendant's conduct." *Id.* at 340-41; *see also Eastman Kodak Co.*, 842 F.2d at 102 ("To obtain a preliminary injunction, competitors must now supply evidence of predatory behavior demonstrating a substantial likelihood that the plaintiff will be injured").

45. In *Atlantic Richfield*, the Court again emphasized that "in the context of pricing practices, only predatory pricing has the requisite anticompetitive effect" to give rise to antitrust injury. 495 U.S. at 339.

46. *Cargill, Inc.*, 479 U.S. at 122 n.17 (quoting Matsushita Elec. Indus. Co. v. Zenith Radio Corp., 475 U.S. 574, 587 (1986)). Indeed, the Court noted that "the commentators disagree as to whether it is ever rational for a firm to engage in such conduct." *Id.* The Court acknowledged, however, that, "[w]hile firms may engage in the practice only infrequently, there is ample evidence suggesting that the practice does occur." *Id.* at 121; *see also* United States v. AMR Corp., 335 F.3d 1109, 1115 (10th Cir. 2003) (rejecting DOJ predatory pricing case against American Airlines and holding "although this court approaches [the plausibility of predation] with caution, we do not do so with the incredulity that once prevailed").

47. *Cargill, Inc.*, 479 U.S. at 122 n. 17. In particular, the uncertain boundary between predatory pricing and procompetitive price cutting, which "often is the very essence of competition," counsels caution in finding predation; "mistaken inferences" of predatory pricing "are especially costly, because they chill the very conduct the antitrust laws are designed to protect"—cutting prices. *Id.* (quoting Matsushita Elec. Indus. Co. v. Zenith Radio Corp., 475 U.S. at 594).

enable it to sustain a campaign of predation,[48] or would create a monopolist capable of excluding others from the market.[49]

---

48. Some post-*Cargill* decisions have found antitrust injury on the basis of predatory pricing. The Second Circuit held that proof of a postmerger market share of 84% was sufficient to enable plaintiff to survive summary judgment by "demonstrat[ing] a substantial likelihood of sustaining 'antitrust injury'" from predatory pricing. R.C. Bigelow, Inc. v. Unilever N.V., 867 F.2d 102, 111 (2d Cir. 1989); *see also* Tasty Baking Co. v. Ralston Purina, Inc., 653 F. Supp. 1250, 1275-76 (E.D. Pa. 1987) (permitting maker of Tastykake products to enjoin merger of makers of Hostess and Drake products, on the ground that merged entity would be monopolist in some markets, thus enabling it to subsidize predatory pricing in markets in which it competed with Tasty, and would be able to leverage monopolist status into preferential treatment from retailers and exclusion of plaintiff). In both cases, the court noted that the antitrust injury showing needed to withstand summary judgment or to seek a preliminary injunction is less demanding than that needed to prevail on the merits. *R.C. Bigelow, Inc.*, 867 F.2d at 111; *Tasty Baking Co.*, 653 F. Supp. at 1256; *contra* Phototron Corp. v. Eastman Kodak Co., 842, F.2d 95, 100 (5th Cir. 1988) ("merely facing the specter of a monopoly" is not sufficient to establish antitrust injury).

These cases stand in contrast to *Cargill*, where "[w]ith only a 28.4% share of market capacity and lacking a plan to collude, Excel would harm only itself by embarking on a sustained campaign of predatory pricing," 479 U.S. at 119 n.15, prompting the Court to caution that "[c]ourts should not find allegations of predatory pricing credible when the alleged predator is incapable of successfully pursuing a predatory scheme." *Id.*; *cf.* Coors Brewing Co. v. Miller Brewing Co., 889 F. Supp. 1394, 1401 (D. Colo. 1995) (denying motion to dismiss for lack of standing even though plaintiff alleged no predation and none was possible given the market share of the merging companies; while plaintiff's antitrust injury theory was "less than clear," court would not dismiss case but would revisit issue at summary judgment stage).

49. The concept of predation includes nonprice predatory conduct as well as below-cost pricing. *Eastman Kodak Co.*, 842 F.2d at 100 ("Advertising that creates barriers to entry in a market constitutes predatory behavior of the type the antitrust laws are designed to prevent"); Community Publishers, Inc. v. Donrey Corp., 892 F. Supp. 1146, 1166 (W.D. Ark. 1995) (permitting competitor to obtain injunction forbidding one family from owning both major northwest Arkansas newspapers, on the ground that in the "unique circumstances of the newspaper industry," a "monopolistic price increase" by the two papers "would harm not only readers and advertisers, but also competitors" like plaintiff because the supracompetitive advertising prices extracted by the monopolist would cut into the advertising funds available to competitor papers), *aff'd*, 139 F.3d

(2) Target Standing

Where the would-be plaintiff is the target of the acquisition, most courts today hold that the plaintiff cannot establish antitrust injury.[50] A merger that unduly increases concentration may be illegal, but the illegal lessening of competition does not injure the target; on the contrary, "once the takeover is complete, [the target] and its shareholders are likely to benefit from any increased prices or decreased competition that might result."[51] Courts have characterized the injury suffered by targets as a "loss of independence"[52] and have concluded that such injury is not related to competition and thus is outside the scope of the antitrust laws.[53] The Second Circuit, however, has held that a target suffers

---

1180 (8th Cir. 1998); Bon-Ton Stores v. May Dep't Stores Co., 881 F. Supp. 860, 878 (W.D.N.Y. 1994) (granting preliminary injunction to state of New York and competitor to prevent May Co. from obtaining a monopoly in retail space suitable for department stores in Rochester area; since there was "direct nexus" between May's § 7 violation—obtaining a monopoly—and Bon-Ton's injury—exclusion from the market—the antitrust injury requirement was met); *Tasty Baking Co.*, 653 F. Supp. at 1275-76 ("Plaintiffs are even more likely to suffer the injury of disadvantageous treatment by retailers" and exclusion from the market than that of predatory pricing).

50. Before *Brunswick* and *Cargill* focused courts' attention on the requirement of antitrust injury, targets were often held to have standing. *See, e.g.*, Marathon Oil Co. v. Mobil Corp., 530 F. Supp. 315 (N.D. Ohio), *aff'd*, 669 F.2d 378 (6th Cir. 1981); Hamilton Watch Co. v. Benrus Watch Co., 114 F. Supp. 307 (D. Conn.), *aff'd*, 206 F.2d 738 (2d Cir. 1953); *see also* Grumman Corp. v. LTV Corp., 665 F.2d 10, 11 (2d Cir. 1981) (finding target standing without mentioning antitrust injury; "[I]f the effect of a proposed takeover may be substantially to lessen competition, the target company is entitled to fend off its suitor").

51. Anago, Inc. v. Tecnol Med. Prods., Inc., 976 F.2d 248, 251 (5th Cir. 1992); *see also* Burnup & Sims, Inc. v. Posner, 688 F. Supp. 1532, 1534 (S.D. Fla. 1988) ("Here, even assuming a lessening of competition in violation of the Federal anti-trust laws would occur, the target company does not suffer from any such injury, but rather is benefitted by it").

52. *Tecnol Med. Prods., Inc.*, 976 F.2d at 251.

53. *Id.* ("Anago will suffer a loss of independence whether or not its takeover violates antitrust principles"); *see also* Central Nat'l Bank v. H.E. Rainbolt, 720 F.2d 1183, 1186 (10th Cir. 1983) ("ouster" of chairman of acquired company "is not a result of any anticompetitive act, it is the consequence of his loss of majority control" and "is not cognizable injury under the antitrust laws . . . [because] [i]t is not the result of any lessening in competition"); A.D.M. Corp. v. Sigma Instruments, Inc., 628 F.2d 753,

antitrust injury because it "los[es] one of the vital components of competition—the power of independent decision-making as to price and output."[54]

---

754 (1st Cir. 1980) ("If the sale of assets had an effect on competition, it would have occurred whether or not appellant was harmed. There is thus lacking the essential connection between injury and the aims of the antitrust laws necessary to give appellant standing."); *Burnup & Sims, Inc.*, 688 F. Supp. at 1534 ("The suit must be understood in its true sense, an attempt by incumbent management to defend their own positions, not as an attempt to vindicate any public interest."); Carter Hawley Hale Stores v. Limited, Inc., 587 F. Supp. 246, 250 (C.D. Cal. 1984) (claimed injuries do not "result from the possibility of substantially lessened competition, but rather deriv[e] from the fact that after a successful, albeit unfriendly, merger, two corporate entities become one"); Burlington Indus. v. Edelman, 666 F. Supp. 799, 805 (M.D.N.C.) ("The type of injuries about which a target such as Burlington complains—potential loss of employees, possible diversion of customers to other businesses, and loss of trade secrets and financial information—are not injuries that occur because of the potential lessening of competition attending the merger. Rather, these injuries occur because of a change in corporate control."), *aff'd*, [1987 Transfer Binder] Fed. Sec. L. Rep. (CCH) ¶ 93,339 (4th Cir. 1987).

54. Consolidated Gold Fields PLC v. Minorco, S.A., 871 F.2d 252, 258 (2d Cir. 1989). The court went on to declare that "[i]t is hard to imagine an injury to competition more clearly 'of the type the antitrust laws were intended to prevent' than the elimination of a major competitor's power to determine its prices and output." *Id.* (quoting Brunswick Corp. v. Pueblo Bowl-O-Mat, Inc., 429 U.S. 477, 489 (1977)). Thus, although *Gold Fields* might "ultimately derive some economic benefit from the enhanced power of its corporate parent," it "is entitled to prefer to take its chances on its capacity to prosper as an independent entity. . . . The antitrust laws ensure the right to compete. That is what *Gold Fields* wishes to do, and that is what it will not be able to do if the threatened takeover succeeds." *Id.* at 258-59. In *Square D Co. v. Schneider S.A.*, 760 F. Supp. 362 (S.D.N.Y. 1991), the district court followed *Gold Fields* as "the law of the Second Circuit," but acknowledged its "unfavorable reception in some of the secondary literature" and other circuits' differing approaches to target standing. *Id.* at 365. In *Anago*, the Fifth Circuit expressly questioned *Gold Fields.* 976 F.2d at 250-51; *see also* A. Copeland Enters. v. Guste, 1989-2 Trade Cas. (CCH) ¶ 68,712 (E.D. La. 1988) (finding target standing); *cf.* First & First, Inc. v. Dunkin' Donuts, Inc., 1990-1 Trade Cas. (CCH) ¶ 68,989, at 63,419 (E.D. Pa. 1990) (franchisees of target have standing) (denying injunction).

Occasionally, the target (or a supportive state or local government agency) has asserted that the merger will result in lost jobs or other injury to the local economy. These arguments, however, generally do not establish antitrust injury. In *Pennsylvania v. Russell Stover Candies, Inc.*,[55] for example, Pennsylvania sought divestiture, on antitrust grounds, of the Pennsylvania assets of a candy manufacturer that had been acquired by a competitor, in part because the acquiring firm planned to shut down the acquired plant as soon as raw materials and packaging were exhausted. The state argued in part that the resulting loss of jobs and harm to Pennsylvania's economy constituted the type of injury the antitrust laws were intended to prevent. The district court rejected the plaintiff's position and denied its motion stating:

> Although I recognize the likely detrimental effect of the plant closing, it is clear that any potential "anticompetitive effect" of [the] acquisition cannot be causally linked to the plant closing. Unfortunately, the antitrust laws are not designed to prevent the effects likely to occur after Whitman's ceases operations in Philadelphia. . . . Nothing in the Clayton Act or other federal antitrust laws addresses Pennsylvania's concern about the plant closing.[56]

Because such lawsuits frequently are part of a joint effort by the target and the state or local government agency to thwart an unwanted takeover, these lawsuits are generally dismissed or settled, either because the private plaintiff no longer opposes the transaction or because the defendant acquiring company, anxious to eliminate any roadblocks in its hostile takeover attempt, agrees to a settlement providing for relief that is not very significant in the context of the entire transaction. As a result, courts rarely have the opportunity, as the district court did in *Russell Stover*, to adjudicate the scope of the antitrust laws as applied to the special considerations that merger opponents claim for issues relating to the state's economy.

(3) Consumer Standing

Because the antitrust laws are designed to protect consumers by preserving competition among sellers, a plaintiff that is a consumer with respect to the upstream market in which the merging entities compete may establish antitrust injury.[57] Unlike competitors or targets,

---

55. 1993-1 Trade Cas. (CCH) ¶ 70,224 (E.D. Pa. 1993).
56. *Id.* at 70,094.
57. *See* Reilly v. Hearst Corp., 107 F. Supp. 2d 1192, 1195 (N.D. Cal. 2000) (newspaper subscriber has standing to challenge acquisition by competing

consumers are injured by the supracompetitive prices resulting from a merger that substantially lessens competition, so the Section 7 violation itself causes antitrust injury to consumers.[58] An indirect purchaser has also been found to have standing to seek equitable relief under Section 16 but not to seek damages under Section 4.[59]

---

paper); Blue Cross & Blue Shield United v. Marshfield Clinic, 883 F. Supp. 1247, 1255-56, 1263 (W.D. Wis.) (monopolization case) (health insurer had standing as consumer to recover damages and obtain injunctive relief against a clinic and its wholly-owned HMO where jury could find that plaintiffs paid supracompetitive prices in purchasing defendants' physician services), *aff'd in part and rev'd in part*, 65 F.3d 1406 (7th Cir. 1995); Santa Cruz Med. Clinic v. Dominican Santa Cruz Hosp., No. 1995-2 Trade Cas. (CCH) ¶ 71,254 (N.D. Cal. 1995) (granting physicians standing to challenge hospital acquisition because they are consumers of hospital services; despite fact that physician referrals cannot be bought or sold, "there is nothing fundamentally flawed with the idea of a market among competing hospitals to attract physicians by offering superior services").

58. *See Santa Cruz Med. Clinic*, 1995-2 Trade Cas. (CCH) ¶ 71,254 (N.D. Cal. 1995) (plaintiff physicians sufficiently alleged antitrust injury by "stat[ing] that reduced competition among hospitals would directly injure them by causing 'a deterioration in the quality or quantity of hospital services to physicians'"). Plaintiffs who are not competitors, targets, or consumers generally do not have standing to attack a merger. *See, e.g.*, Alberta Gas Chems. Ltd. v. E.I. du Pont de Nemours & Co., 826 F.2d 1235, 1241 (3d Cir. 1987) (Alberta Gas potential supplier to acquired firm was hurt by acquirer's decision to abandon acquired company's methanol production, not by loss of competition between du Pont and acquired company; same harm would have occurred had any acquirer made same decision, whether or not acquisition had any effect on competition); Turner v. Johnson & Johnson, 809 F.2d 90, 102 (1st Cir. 1986) "The alleged injury to plaintiffs here unquestionably flowed from the alleged fraud and not from suppressed competition . . .").

59. *See* Lucas Automotive Eng'g, Inc. v. Bridgestone/Firestone, Inc., 140 F.3d 1228, 1237 (9th Cir. 1998).

c. The Requirements for Preliminary Injunctive Relief

(1) General Considerations

(a) THE COMMON-LAW STANDARD AND ITS MODIFICATION IN SECTION 7 ACTIONS BY THE FTC OR DOJ

At common law, a court will only grant a preliminary injunction upon a finding that (1) the plaintiff will suffer irreparable harm if the injunction does not issue, (2) this injury to the plaintiff outweighs the harm to the defendant if the injunction is granted, (3) the plaintiff has a substantial likelihood of success on the merits, and (4) the injunction comports with the public interest.[60]

The most important modification of the traditional test for preliminary injunctive relief in the context of enforcement of Section 7 concerns the burden borne by governmental plaintiffs. Under the FTC Act, the Commission may obtain a preliminary injunction "[u]pon a proper showing that, weighing the equities and considering the Commission's likelihood of ultimate success, such action would be in the public interest."[61] It is well settled that this statutory standard eliminates the traditional requirement of proof of irreparable harm, based on Congress' intent "that equitable relief be broadly available to the FTC."[62]

---

60. *See, e.g.*, Wisconsin Music Network, Inc. v. Muzak Ltd. Partnership, 5 F.3d 218 (7th Cir. 1993); Consolidated Gold Fields PLC v. Minorco, S.A., 871 F.2d 252 (2d Cir. 1989); Christian Schmidt Brewing Co. v. G. Heileman Brewing Co., 753 F.2d 1354, 1356 (6th Cir. 1985); Tate v. Frey, 735 F.2d 986, 990 (6th Cir. 1984); United States v. Gillette Co., 828 F. Supp. 78, 80 (D.D.C. 1993); United States v. Country Lake Foods, Inc., 754 F. Supp. 669, 674 (D. Minn. 1990) (applying traditional standard and denying motion for preliminary injunction because there were no "questions 'so serious and difficult as to call for more deliberate investigation'" (quoting Dataphase Sys. v. C.L. Sys., 640 F.2d 109, 113 (8th Cir. 1981))); United States v. Ivaco, Inc., 704 F. Supp. 1409, 1414 (W.D. Mich. 1989); USG Corp. v. Wagner & Brown, 689 F. Supp. 1483, 1487 (N.D. Ill. 1988); Laidlaw Acquisition Corp. v. Mayflower Group, 636 F. Supp. 1513, 1517 (S.D. Ind. 1986) (applying traditional factors as proper test in Seventh Circuit); Sun Newspapers, Inc. v. Omaha World-Herald Co., 1983-2 Trade Cas. (CCH) ¶ 65,522, at 68,585 (D. Neb.) (applying factors to acquisition challenged by competitor), *aff'd in part and modified in part*, 713 F.2d 428 (8th Cir. 1983).
61. 15 U.S.C. § 53(b).
62. FTC v. Exxon Corp., 636 F.2d 1336, 1343 (D.C. Cir. 1980); *see also* FTC v. H.J. Heinz, 246 F.3d 708, 714 (D.C. Cir. 2001); FTC v. University

Consequently, the FTC usually has a lower burden of proof than the DOJ in seeking preliminary relief.[63] Some courts, however, have also held that actions brought by the DOJ do not require proof of irreparable harm.[64]

(b) ALTERNATIVE FORMULATIONS

In practice, the criteria for obtaining a preliminary injunction are often not treated as distinct requirements, but rather as factors to be balanced by the court in determining what is equitable in the particular case at bar.[65] It is unclear whether or to what extent the different

---

Health, Inc., 938 F.2d 1206, 1218 (11th Cir. 1991) ("the FTC need not prove irreparable harm"); FTC v. Staples, Inc., 970 F. Supp. 1066, 1071 n.2 (D.D.C. 1997); FTC v. Butterworth Health Corp., 1997-2 Trade Cas. (CCH) ¶ 71,863, at 80,063 (6th Cir. 1997); S. REP. NO. 93-207 (1973), *reprinted in* 1973 U.S.C.C.A.N. 2533.

63. As one FTC official has noted, "[t]he FTC has had tremendous success at winning P.I. cases." David Scheffman, Director, & Mary Coleman, Deputy Director, Bureau of Economics, FTC, The Role of Economic and Financial Analyst Experts in Merger Litigation, Remarks Before the Litigating a Merger Program at the American Bar Association Spring Meeting (Apr. 12, 2003), *at* www.ftc.gov/be/ftcperspectivesoneconometrics.pdf.

64. *See, e.g.*, United States v. Siemens Corp., 621 F.2d 499, 506 (2d Cir. 1980) ("once the Government demonstrates a reasonable probability that § 7 has been violated, irreparable harm to the public should be presumed"); United States v. Ingersoll-Rand Co., 320 F.2d 509, 523 (3d Cir. 1963); United States v. Ivaco, Inc., 704 F. Supp. 1409, 1429 (W.D. Mich. 1989); United States v. Culbro Corp., 436 F. Supp. 746, 750 (S.D.N.Y. 1977); *but see Gillette Co.*, 828 F. Supp. at 80 (discussing standard applicable in FTC actions but stating, "[t]his case, however, is not brought pursuant to § 53(b) and therefore the court must apply this circuit's fundamental four-part preliminary injunction standard").

65. In *Lawson Products, Inc. v. Avnet, Inc.*, 782 F.2d 1429 (7th Cir. 1986), the Seventh Circuit acknowledged that "[o]nce all the equitable factors are before the judge, [notwithstanding the impulse to quantify or formalize the determination], a classic discretionary decision must be made" that is "in a real sense intuitive," *id.* at 1436, and inevitably involves "subjective, impressionistic weighing." *Id.* at 1435. *See also Christian Schmidt Brewing Co.*, 753 F.2d at 1356 (all four factors must be considered, but they "do not establish a rigid and comprehensive test"); Dataphase Sys. v. C.L. Sys., 640 F.2d 109, 112-14 (8th Cir. 1981) (arguing against "wooden application" of a formalistic test requiring greater than 50% probability of success). *But see* Friendship Materials,

formulations of the preliminary injunction test articulated in the cases represent different tests. The Second Circuit introduced an alternative to the traditional standard under which the movant must show "(a) irreparable harm and (b) either (1) likelihood of success on the merits or (2) sufficiently serious questions going to the merits to make them a fair ground for litigation and a balance of the hardships tipping decidedly" in the movant's favor.[66] In *Dataphase Systems, Inc. v. C.L. Systems*,[67] the Eighth Circuit, en banc, held that despite the use of the Second Circuit's version in some opinions and the traditional test in others, "there is a

---

Inc. v. Michigan Brick, Inc., 679 F.2d 100, 105 (6th Cir. 1982) (vacating injunction for failure to make explicit finding of irreparable harm; factors are not rigid and comprehensive test, but private plaintiff must always show irreparable injury); HTI Health Servs., Inc. v. Quorum Health Group, 960 F. Supp. 1104, 1110 (S.D. Miss. 1997) ("The precedent in [the Fifth Circuit] clearly warns that a preliminary injunction is an extraordinary remedy that can be granted only if the movant has clearly shown all four prerequisites"); White Consol. Indus. v. Whirlpool Corp., 612 F. Supp. 1009, 1030 (N.D. Ohio) (all four factors must be considered by court), *vacated*, 619 F. Supp. 1022 (N.D. Ohio 1985), *aff'd*, 781 F.2d 1224 (6th Cir. 1986).

66. Consolidated Gold Fields plc v. Minorco, S.A., 871 F.2d 252, 256 (2d Cir. 1989) (quoting Jackson Dairy, Inc. v. H.P. Hood & Sons, 596 F.2d 70, 72 (2d Cir. 1979)); *see also* Bon-Ton Stores v. May Dep't Stores Co., 881 F. Supp. 860, 866 (W.D.N.Y. 1994); Hamilton Watch Co. v. Benrus Watch Co., 206 F.2d 738, 740 (2d Cir. 1953). The Ninth Circuit has adopted the Second Circuit's version. *See* FTC v. Warner Communs., 742 F.2d 1156, 1162 (9th Cir. 1984); William Inglis & Sons Baking Co. v. ITT Continental Baking Co., 526 F.2d 86, 88 (9th Cir. 1976) (remanding for application of alternative test); *see also* Atari Games Corp. v. Nintendo of Am., Inc., 897 F.2d 1572, 1575 (Fed. Cir. 1990) (applying alternative test as the law of the Ninth Circuit); Washington v. Texaco Ref. & Mktg. Inc., 1991-1 Trade Cas. (CCH) ¶¶ 69,345, 69,346 (W.D. Wash. 1991).

In a case brought by the FTC, the Eleventh Circuit also appeared to adopt a test similar to the Second Circuit's. FTC v. University Health, Inc., 938 F.2d 1206, 1218 (11th Cir. 1991) ("To show a likelihood of ultimate success, the FTC must 'raise[ ] questions going to the merits so serious, substantial, difficult and doubtful as to make them fair ground for thorough investigation, study, deliberation and determination by the FTC in the first instance and ultimately by the Court of Appeals.'" (quoting *Warner Communs.*, 742 F.2d at 1162)); *see also* FTC v. Freeman Hosp., 69 F.3d 260, 268 (8th Cir. 1995) (FTC must raise serious, substantial, and difficult questions going to the merits).

67. 640 F.2d 109 (8th Cir. 1981).

single 'test' or list of considerations to be used in every case" to evaluate an application for preliminary injunction, with the ultimate question being "whether the balance of equities so favors the movant that justice requires the court to intervene to preserve the status quo until the merits are determined."[68] The Seventh and Fourth Circuits employ a "sliding scale approach" under which "[t]he greater the plaintiff's likelihood of success on the merits . . . the less harm from denial of the preliminary injunction the plaintiff need show in relation to the harm that the defendant will suffer if the preliminary injunction is granted."[69]

---

68. *Id.* at 112, 113. A concurring judge denied that the two formulations represent the same test and characterized the opinion as "adopt[ing] a third test which seems to include most of the elements of both of the previously existing tests." *Id.* at 115 (Ross, J., concurring). In *Friendship Materials, Inc. v. Michigan Brick, Inc.*, 679 F.2d 100 (6th Cir. 1982), the Sixth Circuit appeared to accept the Second Circuit's test (and appeared to accept that it was different than the traditional test), but reversed the trial court for mistakenly believing that the test did not include a requirement that plaintiff prove irreparable harm. *Id.* at 104-05. "Whatever the merits of the alternate, or 'balance of hardships' test may be," the court said, "the purpose of the test is surely not to eliminate the irreparable harm requirement. . . . Instead, it merely demonstrates that 'in general, the likelihood of success that need be shown .. . will vary inversely with the degree of injury the plaintiff will suffer absent an injunction.'" *Id.* at 105 (quoting Metropolitan Detroit Plumbing & Mech. Contractors Ass'n v. H.E.W., 418 F. Supp. 585, 586 (E.D. Mich. 1976)).

69. *See* FTC v. Elders Grain, Inc., 868 F.2d 901, 903 (7th Cir. 1989) ("So, for example, if the balance of harms is even, the plaintiff is entitled to the injunction upon a showing that he has a better than 50 percent chance of winning") *see also In re* Microsoft Corp. Antitrust Litig., 333 F.3d 517, 526 (4th Cir. 2003) ("demands less of a showing of likelihood of success on the merits when the balance of hardships weighs strongly in favor of the plaintiff, and vice versa"); Allied Signal, Inc. v. B.F. Goodrich Co., 183 F.3d 568, 573-74 (7th Cir. 1999). This approach was developed by Judge Posner in *Roland Machinery Co. v. Dresser Indus., Inc.*, 749 F.2d 380, 387-88 (7th Cir. 1984), and was expressed as an error-cost minimization equation in *American Hospital Supply Corp. v. Hospital Products Ltd.*, 780 F.2d 589, 593 (7th Cir. 1986) (Posner, J.) (injunction should be granted "only if the harm to the plaintiff if the injunction is denied, multiplied by the probability that the denial would be an error (that the plaintiff, in other words, will win at trial), exceeds the harm to the defendant if the injunction is granted, multiplied by the probability that granting the injunction would be an error"). The Seventh Circuit has held that *Roland* and *American Hospital* "provide important insights into the theoretical underpinnings of injunctive relief and a valuable source of

(2) Factors

(a) IRREPARABLE HARM

Although the FTC and the DOJ generally need not make such a showing,[70] private plaintiffs and state attorneys general must establish the threat of irreparable injury under every version of the preliminary injunction test.[71] Courts usually justify the application of a lower

---

guidance for district judges," but Judge Posner's formulation works "no change in the substantive law." Lawson Prods., Inc. v. Avnet, Inc., 782 F.2d 1429, 1432, 1434 (7th Cir. 1986); *see also* Ball Mem'l Hosp., Inc. v. Mutual Hosp. Ins., Inc., 784 F.2d 1325, 1333 (7th Cir. 1986); *American Hosp. Supply Corp.*, 780 F.2d at 594 ("The formula is new; the analysis it capsulizes is standard."); *but see Ball Mem'l Hosp. Inc.*, 784 F.2d at 1346-47 (Will, J., concurring in the judgment) (noting that *Roland* and *American Hospital* were "wide-ranging revisions" to the law, and *Ball Memorial Hospital*, like *Lawson*, should be seen as "attempt to 'bury [them] with kindness'"); Safety-Kleen, Inc. v. Wyche, 274 F.3d 846, 868 (4th Cir. 2001) (Luttig, J. concurring) (criticizing the "sliding scale" approach because the "Supreme Court has consistently applied the four-part test governing the decision on an injunction . . . without ever distinguishing among the four parts as to analytical order, priority, or weight"); *American Hosp. Supply Corp.*, 780 F.2d at 602-10 (Swygert, J., dissenting) (criticizing formula as "wholesale revision of the law of preliminary injunctions," that threatens "potentially far-reaching and baneful consequences").

70. Courts presume irreparable harm to the public when the FTC satisfies the likelihood of success criterion and some courts afford the DOJ similar treatment. *See supra* notes 64-68 and accompanying text. *But see* United States v. Gillette Co., 828 F. Supp. 78, 80 (D.D.C. 1993) (distinguishing between cases brought by FTC and by the DOJ); United States v. Culbro Corp., 436 F. Supp. 746, 751-54 (S.D.N.Y. 1977) (holding that the government failed to show reasonable probability of interim harm to the public).

71. *See In re Microsoft Corp. Antitrust Litig.*, 333 F.3d at 527 (a "condition precedent to the entry of any preliminary injunction [is] that it be entered to prevent harm that is both irreparable and immediate"). DFW Metro Line Servs. v. Southwestern Bell Tel. Co., 901 F.2d 1267, 1269 (5th Cir. 1990) (because plaintiff "failed to make the threshhold [sic] showing of irreparable injury," court affirmed district court's denial of injunction); Dataphase Sys., Inc. v. C.L. Sys., 640 F.2d 109, 114 n.9 (8th Cir. 1981) (irreparable harm required under any test, and "absence of a finding of irreparable injury is alone sufficient ground for vacating the preliminary injunction"); Triebwasser & Katz v. AT&T, 535 F.2d 1356, 1359 (2d Cir.

standard to the federal agencies than to private plaintiffs[72] on the ground that the common-law standard is not "appropriate for the implementation

1976) (alternative test "does not eliminate the basic obligation of the plaintiff to make a clear showing of the threat of irreparable harm. That is a fundamental and traditional requirement of all preliminary injunctive relief"); Consolidated Gold Fields PLC v. Minorco, S.A., 871 F.2d 252, 256 (2d Cir. 1989) (irreparable harm is part of alternative test); Advocacy Org. for Patients & Providers v. Mercy Health Servs., 987 F. Supp. 967, 971 (E.D. Mich. 1997) ("A showing of irreparable harm . . . is fundamental to obtaining injunctive relief"); Pine Ridge Recycling, Inc. v. Butts County, 864 F. Supp. 1338, 1342 (M.D. Ga. 1994); Bon-Ton Stores v. May Dep't Stores Co., 881 F. Supp. 860, 866 (W.D.N.Y. 1994) ("possible irreparable injury" is requirement of all injunctions); Tasty Baking Co. v. Ralston Purina, Inc., 653 F. Supp. 1250, 1276-77 (E.D. Pa. 1987); Sun-Drop Bottling Co. v. Coca-Cola Bottling Co. Consol., 604 F. Supp. 1197, 1198 (W.D.N.C. 1985) (two most important factors to consider in grant of preliminary injunction are probability of irreparable harm to plaintiff and likelihood of harm to defendant); Pearl Brewing Co. v. Miller Brewing Co., 1993-2 Trade Cas. (CCH) ¶ 70,370, at 70,957 (W.D. Tex. 1993) (plaintiff must show all four factors), *aff'd mem.*, 52 F.3d 1066 (5th Cir. 1995); *Friendship Materials, Inc.*, 679 F.2d at 104-05 (alternative test retains traditional irreparable harm requirement); Anti-Monopoly, Inc. v. Hasbro Inc., No. 94 Civ 2120, 1994 WL 202730, at *1 (S.D.N.Y. May 23, 1994) ("[A] showing of probable irreparable harm is 'the single most important prerequisite' for the issuance of a preliminary injunction" (quoting Reuters Ltd. v. United Press Int'l, Inc., 903 F.2d 904, 907 (2d Cir. 1990)). The states are considered private parties for Section 7 purposes. California v. American Stores Co., 495 U.S. 271, 295-96 (1990); New York v. Kraft Gen. Foods, Inc., 862 F. Supp. 1030, 1033 (S.D.N.Y.) ("Although the State of New York is a governmental actor, it is considered a private party when seeking an injunction pursuant to the Clayton Act"), *aff'd mem.*, 14 F.3d 590 (2d Cir. 1993); *accord* Pennsylvania v. Russell Stover Candies, Inc., 1993-1 Trade Cas. (CCH) ¶ 70,224, at 70,094 (E.D. Pa. 1993).

72. *See* Kinney v. International Union of Operating Eng'rs, 994 F.2d 1271, 1277 (7th Cir. 1993) ("The public interest test is easier to meet than the traditional test because the petitioner need not demonstrate either irreparable injury or that an injunction would serve the public interest"); FTC v. Alliant Techsystems Inc., 808 F. Supp. 9, 19 (D.D.C. 1992) ("[T]he agency is 'not held to the high thresholds applicable where private parties seek interim restraining orders. Most importantly, the [statute] lightened the agency's burden by eliminating the need to show irreparable harm.'" (quoting FTC v. Weyerhaeuser Co., 665 F.2d 1072, 1082 (D.C. Cir. 1981))); United States v. Atlantic Richfield Co., 297 F. Supp. 1061, 1074 n.21 (S.D.N.Y. 1969) ("The failure of Congress to

of a Federal statute by an independent regulatory agency where the standards of the public interest measure the propriety and the need for injunctive relief."[73]

Irreparable harm means injury that will occur before the court can order a final disposition on the merits and that is insufficiently quantifiable, ascertainable, or reversible to be remedied adequately by an award of damages.[74] The difficulty inherent in attempting to "unscramble the eggs" once an acquisition has been consummated is often recited as irreparable harm supporting the grant of a preliminary injunction.[75]

---

require that the Government show irreparable loss ... indicates the Congressional desire to lighten the burden generally imposed on an applicant for preliminary injunctive relief"), *aff'd sub nom.*, Bartlett v. United States, 401 U.S. 986 (1971).

73. S. REP. NO. 93-207 (1973), *reprinted in* 1973 U.S.C.C.A.N. 2417, 2533. *See also Weyerhaeuser Co.*, 665 F.2d at 1080-81; United States v. Siemens Corp., 621 F.2d 499, 506 (2d Cir. 1980) ("Because the Government in seeking to enjoin a merger under § 7 represents the public's interest in a competitive marketplace, the standards governing the granting of preliminary relief in private litigation are inappropriate").

74. *See Roland Mach. Co.*, 749 F.2d at 386 (grant preliminary injunction only if movant "will suffer irreparable harm in the interim—that is, harm that cannot be prevented or fully rectified by the final judgment after trial"; damages must be "seriously deficient as a remedy for the harm suffered," but need not be "wholly ineffectual"). In *Roland*, the Seventh Circuit said that "[a] damages remedy can be inadequate for any of four reasons: (a) The damage award may come too late to save the plaintiff's business. . . . (b) The plaintiff may not be able to finance his lawsuit against the defendant without the revenues from his business that the defendant is threatening to destroy. . . . (c) Damages may be unobtainable from the defendant because he may become insolvent before a final judgment can be entered and collected. . . . (d) The nature of the plaintiff's loss may make damages very difficult to calculate." *Id.*; *see also* Bon-Ton Stores v. May Dep't Stores Co., 881 F. Supp. 860, 866 (W.D.N.Y. 1994) ("The applicant for such an injunction must show 'injury for which a monetary award cannot be adequate compensation'" (quoting Jackson Dairy v. H.P. Hood & Sons, 596 F.2d 70, 72 (2d Cir. 1979))).

75. *Consolidated Gold Fields PLC*, 871 F.2d at 261 ("Since it will be well nigh impossible for the District Court to undo the takeover after the fact, we cannot say that Judge Mukasey exceeded his discretion in determining that the harm threatened here was irreparable."); FTC v. Elders Grain, Inc., 868 F.2d 901, 904 (7th Cir. 1989); Sonesta Int'l Hotels Corp. v. Wellington Assocs., 483 F.2d 247, 250 (2d Cir. 1973) ("once the tender

offer has been consummated it becomes difficult, and sometimes virtually impossible, for a court to 'unscramble the eggs'"); *Bon-Ton Stores*, 881 F. Supp. at 878; Laidlaw Acquisition Corp. v. Mayflower Group, 636 F. Supp. 1513, 1517 (S.D. Ind. 1986); Midcon Corp. v. Freeport-McMoran, Inc., 625 F. Supp. 1475, 1479 (N.D. Ill. 1986); Marathon Oil Co. v. Mobil Corp., 530 F. Supp. 315 (N.D. Ohio), *aff'd*, 669 F.2d 378 (6th Cir. 1981); FTC v. OKC Corp., 1970 Trade Cas. (CCH) ¶ 73,288 (5th Cir. 1970); Chemetron Corp. v. Crane Co., 1977-2 Trade Cas. (CCH) ¶ 61,717, at 72,932 (N.D. Ill. 1977) (preliminary injunction is necessary because of "[t]he difficulty, if not the impossibility," of divestiture if the merger is consummated).

Other cases have also found irreparable harm. *See* Grumman Corp. v. LTV Corp., 665 F.2d 10, 15-16 (2d Cir. 1981) (irreparable harm prong satisfied by danger that acquirer would liquidate part of plaintiff target company's business, fact that integration "would seriously disrupt Grumman's business," and inevitability that acquirer would gain access to target's confidential information); Pine Ridge Recycling, Inc. v. Butts County, Ga., 864 F. Supp. 1338, 1342 (M.D. Ga. 1994) (defendant municipality's immunity from damages made whatever harm plaintiff suffered irreparable); Tasty Baking Co. v. Ralston Purina, Inc., 653 F. Supp. 1250, 1277 (E.D. Pa. 1987) (irreparable harm satisfied because "any lost business cannot be reestablished easily and money damages cannot be calculated readily"); Washington v. Texaco Ref. & Mktg., Inc., 1991-1 Trade Cas. (CCH) ¶¶ 69,345, 69,346 (W.D. Wash. 1991).

Meanwhile, many cases have not found irreparable harm. *See* Lawson Prods., Inc. v. Avnet, Inc., 782 F.2d 1429, 1440-41 (7th Cir. 1986) (claims of loss of goodwill and confidential information did not support finding of irreparable harm because losses adequately compensable by damages for lost profits and information lost was not confidential trade secrets); Pearl Brewing Co. v. Miller Brewing Co., 1993-2 Trade Cas. (CCH) ¶ 70,370, at 70,959 (W.D. Tex. 1993) (finding no irreparable harm where plaintiff alleged threat of loss of distributors but plaintiff was not "in such a precarious financial position that to allow the acquisition to go forward at this point would push them over the edge" and plaintiff alleged "merely a potential injury, not an immediate, irreparable injury"), *aff'd mem.*, 52 F.3d 1066 (5th Cir. 1995); *see also* DFW Metro Line Servs. v. Southwestern Bell Tel. Co., 901 F.2d 1267, 1269 (5th Cir. 1990) (Sherman Act case) ("The district court correctly observed that, because any potential injury suffered by DFW (including its going out of business) could be calculated and recompensed in the form of damages, DFW did not prove a likelihood of irreparable injury."); Triebwasser & Katz v. AT&T, 535 F.2d 1356, 1360 (2d Cir. 1976) (Sherman Act case) ("whatever reasonable costs are undertaken to secure comparable advertising in media not averse to accepting the advertisement rejected here are obviously capable of proof and are

In *Tasty Baking Co. v. Ralston Purina, Inc.*,[76] the court concluded that if Hostess' acquisition of Drake were not enjoined pending trial, Drake would be injured irreparably because "defendants will bleed Drake of substantial assets and restructure Drake so that it could not easily survive on its own after divestiture."[77] By substituting its own management personnel and integrating the production, distribution, promotion, and administration functions of the acquired company into its own, Hostess would obtain much information about Drake and transform Drake from an independent going concern into part of Hostess. Merely ordering Hostess to divest Drake after trial would give Hostess "an unfair advantage" because "the viability of a divested Drake organization would be difficult to assure."[78] Therefore, a preliminary injunction was necessary to safeguard Drake in the event the acquisition was ultimately held to be unlawful, for "[a] contrary conclusion would leave defendants free to swallow up a competitor, to digest it in part, and, upon a court order, to regurgitate insubstantial remains."[79]

In contrast, in *New York v. Kraft General Foods, Inc.*[80] the court denied New York's application for a preliminary injunction forbidding Kraft from altering the status quo in its acquisition of Nabisco's ready-to-eat cereal assets because it held the state had failed to show irreparable harm.[81] At the time the state moved for a preliminary injunction, the

---

therefore reparable"); Advocacy Org. for Patients & Providers v. Mercy Health Servs., 987 F. Supp. 967, 971-72 (E.D. Mich. 1997) (claim that acquired hospital would no longer provide late term abortions and fertility testing services did not constitute irreparable injury).

76. 653 F. Supp. 1250 (E.D. Pa. 1987).

77. *Id.* at 1277 ("Any diminution in Drake's post-divestiture competitive power clearly will harm consumers irreparably and, plaintiffs claim and I agree, will harm Tasty irreparably" by facilitating predatory, monopolistic practices. "Simply put, Tasty is better positioned to compete with Hostess in some markets if Hostess faces strong competition (keeping prices fair) in others").

78. *Id.*

79. *Id.*

80. 862 F. Supp. 1030 (S.D.N.Y.), *aff'd mem.*, 14 F.3d 590 (2d Cir. 1993); *see also* New York v. Kraft Gen. Foods, Inc., 862 F. Supp. 1030, 1035 (S.D.N.Y.) (denying state's renewed motion for preliminary injunction), *aff'd mem.*, 14 F.3d 590 (2d Cir. 1993); New York *ex rel.* Abrams v. Kraft Gen. Foods, Inc., No. 93 Civ. 0811, 1993 WL 302644 (S.D.N.Y. July 30, 1993) (denying state's motion for injunction pending appeal).

81. 862 F. Supp. at 1033-34 (injunction must be denied unless "plaintiff, or here the consumers of RTE cereal, will be irreparably harmed prior to the conclusion of the trial of plaintiff's claims").

acquisition had already been consummated, and Kraft had "thoroughly integrated" Nabisco's assets into its own operations "with respect to production, marketing, pricing and promotion."[82] New York sought to enjoin Kraft from "plac[ing] the integrity of [Nabisco's] brand identity, and consequently the availability of any effective relief in this action, in jeopardy" by changing the trade dress of its cereals or displaying Kraft's trademark in addition to Nabisco's on the cereal box, alleging that consumers were threatened with irreparable harm because they "will be confused by (1) the simultaneous association of two brands with a product, and (2) a later un-coupling of the brands if the court orders divestiture."[83] Nonetheless, evidence that Kraft's Post cereal trademark "is a good name in the cereal business," and that Kraft had stepped up promotion and lowered the price of the Nabisco cereals it acquired prompted the court to comment that, contrary to the state's argument, "association with Post may enhance the value of the former Nabisco cereals."[84] The court thus rejected New York's contentions as "too speculative to support a finding of irreparable harm" and denied the motion for preliminary injunctive relief.[85]

(b) LIKELIHOOD OF SUCCESS

Every plaintiff, private or governmental, seeking a preliminary injunction to block a merger must show a likelihood of success on the merits of the Section 7 challenge.[86] As discussed above, courts have offered different articulations of the standard that the plaintiff must meet and of the relationship among the factors to be considered in deciding

---

82. *Id.* at 1033.
83. *Id.* at 1035.
84. *Id.* at 1034 & n.5.
85. *Id.* at 1035.
86. 15 U.S.C. § 53(b) ("[u]pon a proper showing that, weighing the equities and considering the Commission's likelihood of ultimate success, such action would be in the public interest"); *see also* FTC v. Freeman Hosp., 69 F.3d 260, 267 (8th Cir. 1995) (district court is "charged with making two separate inquiries"); FTC v. Libbey, Inc., 211 F. Supp. 2d 34, 44 (D.D.C. 2002), citing FTC v. H.J. Heinz Co., 246 F.3d 708 (D.C. Cir. 2001) ("the Court must assess whether the FTC has established a prima facie case of a Section 7 violation"); FTC v. Cardinal Health, Inc., 12 F. Supp. 2d 34, 45 (D.D.C. 1998) ("To prevail, the FTC needs to prove only that it is likely to succeed on the merits of its case in a full administrative proceeding"); FTC v. Staples, Inc., 970 F. Supp. 1066, 1071 (D.D.C. 1997).

whether to grant a preliminary injunction.[87] But whether the court expresses the standard as "sufficiently serious questions going to the merits to make them a fair ground for litigation," or "substantial likelihood of success," or in some other manner, the plaintiff must always satisfy certain thresholds in order to demonstrate the required likelihood of success.[88] The plaintiff must show that it has standing to attack the transaction, it must define the relevant market, and it must show that the transaction will "produce[] a firm controlling an undue percentage share of the relevant market, and result[] in a significant increase in the concentration of firms in that market."[89]

"'Determination of the relevant product and geographic markets is a necessary predicate to deciding whether an acquisition contravenes the Clayton Act.'"[90] The relevant market includes both product and

---

87. *See supra* notes 60-73 and accompanying text.

88. A few courts have applied still another standard, requiring the government to demonstrate a "fair and tenable" chance of success on the merits. FTC v. Beatrice Foods Co., 587 F.2d 1225, 1229 (D.C. Cir. 1978) (the Commission meets its burden "'if it shows preliminarily, by affidavits or other proof, that it has a fair and tenable chance of ultimate success on the merits'" (quoting FTC v. Lancaster Colony Corp., Inc., 434 F. Supp. 1088, 1090 (S.D.N.Y. 1977)); FTC v. Southland Corp., 471 F. Supp. 1, 3 (D.D.C. 1979). But this standard appears to have been rejected and to have fallen into disfavor. *See* FTC v. Tenet Health Care Corp., 186 F.3d 1045, 1051 (8th Cir. 1999) ("A showing of a fair or tenable chance of success on the merits will not suffice for injunctive relief"); United States v. Siemens Corp., 621 F.2d 499, 506 (2d Cir. 1980) ("To warrant [the presumption of irreparable harm to the public], the Government must do far more than merely raise sufficiently serious question with respect to the merits to make them a fair ground for litigation. A preliminary injunction remains a drastic form of relief"); FTC v. National Tea Co., 603 F.2d 694, 698 (8th Cir. 1979) (rejecting the "fair and tenable" chance standard in favor of the tougher standard requiring "questions going to the merits so serious, substantial, difficult and doubtful as to make them fair ground for thorough investigation, study, deliberation and determination by the FTC in the first instance and ultimately by the Court of Appeals"); *Staples, Inc.*, 970 F. Supp. at 1072 ("It is not enough for the FTC to show merely that it has a 'fair and tenable chance' of ultimate success on the merits as has been argued and rejected in other cases").

89. United States v. Philadelphia Nat'l Bank, 374 U.S. 321, 363 (1963).

90. *Libbey*, 211 F. Supp. 2d. 45; U.S. v. SunGard Data Systems, Inc. 172 F. Supp. 2d 172, 181 (D.D.C. 2001); Tasty Baking Co. v. Ralston Purina, Inc., 653 F. Supp. 1250, 1257 (E.D. Pa. 1987) (quoting United States v. Marine Bancorp., 418 U.S. 602, 618 (1974) (internal citations omitted));

geographical dimensions. The defendant may of course contest plaintiff's market definition, and the fight over the proper definition may be critical in the assessment of the plaintiff's likelihood of success.[91] If the court is unable to define a relevant market, it may hold that the plaintiff cannot succeed on the merits.[92]

---

see also Consolidated Gold Fields PLC v. Minorco, S.A., 871 F.2d 252, 260 (2d Cir. 1989); *Cardinal Health, Inc.*, 12 F. Supp. 2d at 45 ("Defining the relevant market is the starting point for any merger analysis."); HTI Health Servs. v. Quorum Health Group, 960 F. Supp. 1104, 1114 (S.D. Miss. 1997) (plaintiff "must show that the merger ... will substantially lessen competition within an established 'area of effective competition,' or relevant market"); Bon-Ton Stores v. May Dep't Stores Co., 881 F. Supp. 860, 867 (W.D.N.Y. 1994) ("A necessary first step in the evaluation of an antitrust claim is a determination of the relevant product market and geographical market." (citing *Marine Bancorp.*, 418 U.S. at 618)); United States v. Gillette Co., 828 F. Supp. 78, 81 (D.D.C. 1993). *See generally* part A of Chapter 3. Of course, the plaintiff's standing is also a threshold component of the likelihood of success criterion, since a plaintiff cannot succeed on the merits if the court will not permit the plaintiff to bring suit. For a discussion of private party standing to enforce § 7, see *supra* notes 25-63 and accompanying text.

91. *See, e.g.*, *Staples, Inc.*, 970 F. Supp. at 1073 ("As with many antitrust cases, the definition of the relevant product market in this case is crucial. In fact, to a great extent, this case hinges on the proper definition of the relevant product market."); *Bon-Ton Stores*, 881 F. Supp. at 867 ("The definition of relevant product market is the fundamental point of dispute among the parties. As is the case in many antitrust cases, this definitional question is crucial"); *Gillette Co.*, 828 F. Supp. at 83-84 (rejecting plaintiff's proposed product market and holding that as to the "significantly broader" correctly defined market, "[p]laintiff has not made its prima facie case").

92. *See* FTC v. Tenet Health Care Corp., 186 F.3d 1045, 1051 (8th Cir. 1999) (reversing district court decision granting preliminary injunction because FTC failed to produce sufficient evidence of a well-defined relevant geographic market); United States v. Long Island Jewish Med. Ctr., 983 F. Supp. 121, 140 (E.D.N.Y. 1997) (preliminary injunction denied where "the Government failed to establish its definition of the relevant product market"); Carter Hawley Hale Stores v. Limited, Inc., 587 F. Supp. 246, 253 (C.D. Cal. 1984) (rejecting plaintiff's proposed product and geographic markets, and holding that "[w]here, as here, proof (and an adequate definition) of the relevant product and geographic markets is absent, it is impossible to assess whether" the acquisition violates § 7); Pennsylvania v. Russell Stover Candies, Inc., 1993-1 Trade Cas. (CCH) ¶ 70,224, at 70,091 (E.D. Pa. 1993) ("Without a clear showing of the relevant market, plaintiff

Once the relevant market is defined, the plaintiff establishes a prima facie case of illegality by showing that the acquisition "would significantly increase the concentration of an already highly concentrated market."[93] The plaintiff need not stop there, but can go on to seek to prove additional factors that make unilateral or coordinated anticompetitive effects likely.[94] If the plaintiff raises a presumption of illegality, the defendant must rebut it with evidence showing that "the market-share statistics g[i]ve an inaccurate account of the acquisition['s] probable effects on competition."[95]

---

is not entitled to the requested preliminary relief."); First & First, Inc. v. Dunkin' Donuts, Inc., 1990-1 Trade Cas. (CCH) ¶ 68,989 (E.D. Pa. 1990) (plaintiff failed to prove product market); *cf.* Pearl Brewing Co. v. Miller Brewing Co., 1993-2 Trade Cas. (CCH) ¶ 70,370, at 70,957 n.3 (W.D. Tex. 1993) ("a finding as to the relevant market is not essential to a determination of plaintiffs' likelihood of success on the merits" where acquired company's share of U.S. market was only 0.8% and acquisition increased HHI by only 34 or 35 points); FTC v. PPG Indus., 798 F.2d 1500, 1502 (D.C. Cir. 1986) (district court defined product market as "aircraft transparencies requiring, for want of a better term, 'high technology' to produce, without regard to the materials of which they are fabricated").

93. FTC v. University Health, Inc., 938 F.2d 1206, 1219 (11th Cir. 1991); *see also* Baker Hughes, Inc., 908 F.2d 981, 983 (D.C. Cir. 1990); *Consolidated Gold Fields PLC*, 871 F.2d at 260; FTC v. Elders Grain, Inc., 868 F.2d 901, 905 (7th Cir. 1989); United States v. Siemens Corp., 621 F.2d 499, 506 (2d Cir. 1980); FTC v. Food Town Stores, Inc., 539 F.2d 1339, 1344-45 (4th Cir. 1976); United States v. Franklin Elec. Co., 130 F. Supp. 2d 1025, 1032 (W.D. Wis. 2000); *Gillette Co.*, 828 F. Supp. at 84; United States v. United Tote, Inc., 768 F. Supp. 1064, 1068 (D. Del. 1991); United States v. Ivaco, Inc., 704 F. Supp. 1409, 1428 (W.D. Mich. 1989); *Tasty Baking Co.*, 653 F. Supp. at 1262-65; Pennsylvania v. Russell Stover Candies, Inc., 1993-1 Trade Cas. (CCH) ¶ 70,224, at 70,091 (E.D. Pa. 1993). *See generally* part A of Chapter 4.

94. *See generally* Chapter 4.

95. United States. v. Citizens & Southern Nat'l Bank, 422 U.S. 86, 120 (1975); *see also Baker Hughes, Inc.*, 908 F.2d at 984-92 (canvassing cases and commentary on proper rebuttal evidence); Ball Mem'l Hosp., Inc. v. Mutual Hosp. Ins., Inc., 784 F.2d 1325, 1336 (7th Cir. 1986) ("Market share is just a way of estimating market power, which is the ultimate consideration. When there are better ways to estimate market power, the court should use them"); FTC v. Butterworth Health Corp., 946 F. Supp. 1285, 1294 (W.D. Mich. 1996), *aff'd mem.*, 121 F.3d 708 (6th Cir. 1997).

Rebuttal evidence need not be statistical and may be directed at a variety of propositions.[96] Perhaps the most significant non-market share evidence concerns barriers to entry, but defendants are free to introduce whatever evidence "casts doubt on the persuasive quality of the [plaintiff's] statistics to predict future anticompetitive consequences"[97] or "demonstrate[s] unique economic circumstances that undermine the predictive value of the [plaintiff's] statistics."[98]

In many instances, courts have relied on the absence of entry barriers when determining that the defendants have successfully rebutted the plaintiff's prima facie case, recognizing that, without "significant barriers, a company probably cannot maintain supracompetitive pricing for any length of time."[99] In other cases, the existence of high barriers to entry has persuaded a court to grant preliminary injunctive relief.[100]

---

96. *See generally* Chapter 5.

97. *University Health, Inc.*, 938 F.2d at 1218 (quoting Kaiser Aluminum & Chem. Corp. v. FTC, 652 F.2d 1324, 1341 (7th Cir. 1981)).

98. *Id.* In *Baker Hughes, Inc.*, the court emphatically rejected the government's contention that "section 7 defendants can rebut a prima facie case only by a clear showing that entry into the market by competitors would be quick and effective," 908 F.2d at 983, and held that "evidence on a variety of factors can rebut a prima facie case," *id.* at 984. The court noted:

> [T]he Department of Justice's own Merger Guidelines contain a detailed discussion of non-entry factors that can overcome a presumption of illegality established by market share statistics. *See* United States Dep't of Justice, Merger Guidelines (June 14, 1984), *reprinted in* 4 Trade Reg. Rep. (CCH) ¶ 13,103, at 20,561-64 (1988). According to the Guidelines, these factors include changing market conditions (§ 3.21), the financial condition of firms in the relevant market (§ 3.22), special factors affecting foreign firms (§ 3.23), the nature of the product and the terms of sale (§ 3.41), information about specific transactions and buyer market characteristics (§ 3.42), the conduct of firms in the market (§ 3.44), market performance (§ 3.45), and efficiencies (§ 3.5).

Id. at 985-86.

99. *Baker Hughes, Inc.*, 908 F.2d at 987 (citing United States v. Falstaff Brewing Corp., 410 U.S. 526, 532-33 (1973)). For cases relying on the lack of entry barriers in denying preliminary relief, see *Baker Hughes, Inc.*, 908 F.2d at 988 (entry barriers "not high enough to impede future entry should [the acquisition] lead to supracompetitive pricing"); Phototron Corp. v. Eastman Kodak Co., 842 F.2d 95, 101 (5th Cir. 1988) ("Without evidence of how advertising in the wholesale photofinishing industry can act as a barrier to Phototron's participation in the industry, we cannot conclude that Phototron is likely to succeed on this theory of predation"); United States v.

Siemens Corp., 621 F.2d 499, 509 (2d Cir. 1980) ("In view of the large number of potential entrants, the elimination of Siemens does not appear to pose a significant threat to competition"); United States v. Gillette Co., 828 F. Supp. 78, 84-85 (D.D.C. 1993) no legal, regulatory, or technological barriers; given "ease with which manufacturers may enter this wider market, Gillette will not be able to raise prices unilaterally on its premium fountain pens"); United States v. Calmar Inc., 612 F. Supp. 1298, 1305-07 (D.N.J. 1985) (ease of entry shown); Pennsylvania v. Russell Stover Candies, Inc., 1993-1 Trade Cas. (CCH) ¶ 70,224, at 70,094 (E.D. Pa. 1993) ("the barriers to entry in the boxed chocolate market are not significant"); Pearl Brewing Co. v. Miller Brewing Co., 1993-2 Trade Cas. (CCH) ¶ 70,370, at 70,959 (W.D. Tex. 1993) (no evidence that defendants' advertising functions as barrier to entry), *aff'd mem.*, 52 F.3d 1066 (5th Cir. 1995); *cf.* FTC v. Freeman Hosp., 911 F. Supp 1213, 1223 (W.D. Mo.) (denying injunction despite existence of "some substantial barriers" to entry), *aff'd*, 69 F.3d 260 (8th Cir. 1995); United States v. Culbro Corp., 436 F. Supp. 746, 752 (S.D.N.Y. 1977) (denying injunction but granting hold separate order; because of existing barriers, increasing unprofitability, and excess capacity of cigar industry, "there are no potential entrants anyway," rendering heightening of barriers "irrelevant").

100. *See, e.g.*, FTC v. University Health, Inc., 938 F.2d 1206, 1219 (11th Cir. 1991) (because of certificate of need law, barriers "are as substantial as they could be, barring outright statutory prohibition"); *Elders Grain, Inc.*, 868 F.2d at 905 ("since entry into the industry is slow .. . colluding sellers need not fear that any attempt to restrict output in order to drive up price will be promptly nullified by new production"); FTC v. PepsiCo, 477 F.2d 24, 28 (2d Cir. 1973) (anticompetitive effect probable in light of "difficulty of new entry which requires bottling facilities and huge advertising outlays"); FTC v. Cardinal Health, Inc., 12 F. Supp. 2d 34, 57-58 (D.D.C. 1998) (entry by regional wholesale distributors is not adequate to offset lack of entry by new and existing competitors at the national level); FTC v. Staples, Inc., 970 F. Supp. 1066, 1087 (D.D.C. 1997) (entry extremely unlikely where "a new office superstore would need to open a large number of stores nationally in order to achieve the purchasing and distributing economies of scale enjoyed by the three existing firms"); Bon-Ton Stores v. May Dep't Stores Co., 881 F. Supp. 860, 876-77 (W.D.N.Y. 1994) ("even a monopolist will not be able to exercise power over price in a market that is easily entered"; in this case, while new entry not "impossible," "it is obvious that a significant and substantial barrier to entry would exist if May obtained all of the present space in the four major regional shopping malls"); United States v. Ivaco, Inc., 704 F. Supp. 1409, 1429 (W.D. Mich. 1989) ("entry into the market is not so easy that it could pose a significant restraint to price increases"); Tasty Baking Co. v. Ralston Purina, Inc., 653 F. Supp. 1250, 1263 (E.D. Pa. 1987) (snack cake and pie business plagued by "substantial barriers to

Courts have also cited a number of other factors as sufficient to rebut a plaintiff's prima facie case, including evidence of a dwindling supply of irreplaceable raw materials,[101] the weak or deteriorating market position of one or both of the merging parties,[102] the level of competition

---

entry," reflecting the "high costs to build bakeries, to develop brand recognition, and to establish routes with favorable retailer participation").

101. *See* United States v. General Dynamics Corp., 415 U.S. 486, 503-04 (1974) (firm was weak future competitor because of its low supply of coal reserves and fact that its production was already largely committed in long-term contracts).

102. *See* FTC v. National Tea Co., 603 F.2d 694, 700-01 (8th Cir. 1979) (firm was "weak competitor" and "would probably be forced out of the relevant market" if merger was blocked); Lektro-Vend Corp. v. Vendo Co., 660 F.2d 255, 276 (7th Cir. 1981) (deteriorating market position); United States v. International Harvester Co., 564 F.2d 769, 773-74 (7th Cir. 1977) ("weakness as a competitor" was properly considered); *Freeman Hosp.*, 911 F. Supp. at 1224-25 ("Oak Hill's competitive significance is diminished by the fact that . . . it has the lowest percentage of privately insured ('private-pay') patients" in the relevant market and its "continuing decline in patient volume [and] financial sustainability"); *cf. University Health, Inc.*, 938 F.2d at 1220-21 (rejecting defendant's argument that "St. Joseph's, despite its present market share, is not, and will not be, a meaningful competitor in the relevant market," since, inter alia, St. Joseph's "is presently enjoying the most profitable year in its history"); FTC v. Warner Communs., 742 F.2d 1156, 1164-65 (9th Cir. 1984) ("a company's stated intention to leave the market or its financial weakness does not in itself justify a merger"); Grumman Corp. v. LTV Corp., 665 F.2d 10, 12 (2d Cir. 1981) (rejecting defendant's argument that firm will not be "competitive factor in the future"); Kaiser Aluminum & Chem. Corp. v. FTC, 652 F.2d 1324, 1339 (7th Cir. 1981) (weakness of acquired firm is relevant rebuttal evidence, but is "probably the weakest ground of all for justifying a merger"); FTC v. Food Town Stores, Inc., 539 F.2d 1339, 1345 (4th Cir. 1976) (rejecting argument that "Lowe's is in such poor financial condition that absent the merger it will cease to be an effective competitor anyway" on ground that Lowe's was "solvent and profit-making"); *Ivaco, Inc.*, 704 F. Supp. at 1428-29 (court unpersuaded by defendants' argument that "because technological innovations will soon make their existing products obsolete, and because they have been unable to match Plassers' innovative products, their past dominance of the tamper market does not suggest an ability to continue that dominance in the future").

Rebuttal evidence of a firm's weakness is designed to "undermine[ ] the predictive value of the [plaintiff's] market share statistics," *University Health*, 938 F.2d at 1220, and should be distinguished from the "failing

in the relevant market,[103] competitive trends in the relevant market,[104] the independence of the acquired firm from the acquirer,[105] efficiencies or procompetitive results created by the acquisition,[106] buyer

---

company" defense, under which the acquired firm's impending bankruptcy saves the merger if the bankruptcy cannot be averted by any less anticompetitive means. *Id.* at 1220 n.28; *see* Citizen Publ'g Co. v. United States, 394 U.S. 131, 136-39 (1969).

103. United States v. Baker Hughes, Inc., 908 F.2d 981, 989 (D.C. Cir. 1980) ("there had been tremendous turnover in the [relevant] market in the 1980s"); *National Tea Co.*, 603 F.2d at 701 (market is "relatively competitive one" compared to food retailing markets in other cities); *See International Harvester Co.*, 564 F.2d at 778 (strong present competition in relevant market).

104. *See Baker Hughes, Inc.*, 908 F.2d at 986 ("High concentration has long been the norm in this market . . . 'there is no proof of overpricing, excessive profit or any decline in quality, service or diminishing innovation,'" and high concentration is not "surprising where, as here, a product is esoteric and its market small," so no evidence of any troublesome competitive trend) (citation omitted); *International Harvester Co.*, 564 F.2d at 778-79 (tendency of market toward even stronger competition); *cf. Grumman Corp.*, 665 F.2d at 15 ("In a concentrated market expected to see total volume grow and the share of the dominant firm decrease, the District Court was properly concerned with maintaining small aggressive competitors in the market").

105. *See International Harvester Co.*, 564 F.2d at 777-78 (de facto independence of acquired company from acquiring company made lessening of competition less likely); *Culbro Corp.*, 436 F. Supp. at 753 ("Since Havatampa and Culbro will continue to operate as separate entities, it is clear that Havatampa will not be eliminated as a competitor. Thus, there will not be the loss of one competitor and concomitant increase in market share of another competitor as classically results when one company is merged into another"); *cf.* Consolidated Gold Fields PLC v. Minorco, S.A., 871 F.2d 256, 261 (2d Cir. 1989) ("the evidence in the record adequately supports Judge Mukasey's conclusion that the intertwined relationships among Anglo, De Beers, Minorco, and the Oppenheimer family warrant attribution of aggregate market power to Minorco").

106. *See Freeman Hosp.*, 911 F. Supp. at 1224 (merged entity will be more able to compete with market leader, and merger will eliminate inefficient administrative duplication and reduce overhead expenses); FTC v. Freeman Hosp., 1995-1 Trade Cas. (CCH) ¶ 70,929, at 74,143-44 (W.D. Mo. 1995) (same); *cf.* FTC v. H.J. Heinz, 246 F.3d 708, 721-22 (D.C. Cir. 2001) (to be recognized, efficiencies must be "merger specific"); *University Health, Inc.*, 938 F.2d at 1222-24 (rejecting FTC's contention that efficiencies of a merger are never a defense to its illegality, but defendants failed to prove

sophistication,[107] the unreliability of market share evidence,[108] and other considerations.[109] If the defendant successfully rebuts the presumption of

---

significant efficiencies benefiting consumers); FTC v. PPG Indus., 798 F.2d 1500, 1507-08 (D.C. Cir. 1986) (holding that purported benefits of maintaining domestic ownership of acquired firm and facilitation of innovation did not rebut FTC's prima facie case); Christian Schmidt Brewing Co. v. G. Heileman Brewing Co., 753 F.2d 1354, 1357-58 (6th Cir. 1985) (affirming as not abuse of discretion trial court's grant of preliminary injunction despite defendants' claim that merger was procompetitive because it would allow the merged entity to compete with the dominant national brewers); *id.* at 720-21 (efficiencies must be "extraordinary" to counteract a merger to duopoly); *see also Franklin Elec. Co.*, 130 F. Supp. 2d at 1033 (rejecting defendant's argument that a remedy that included a licensing and supply agreement with a third party created a viable competitor because licensee did not appear to have incentive to develop product and compete); United States v. UPM-Kymmene Oyj, No. 2003-2 Trade Cas. (CCH) ¶ 74,101 (N.D. Ill. July 25, 2003) (rejecting weakened competitor argument and argument that combining smaller competitors would allow them to compete against industry leader).

107. *See Baker Hughes, Inc.*, 908 F.2d at 986 ("These products are hardly trinkets sold to small consumers who may possess imperfect information and limited bargaining power. [These] buyers closely examine available options and typically insist on receiving multiple, confidential bids for each order," which "promote[s] competition even in a highly concentrated market"); FTC v. Freeman Hosp., 911 F. Supp. 1213, 1223 (W.D. Mo.), *aff'd*, 69 F.3d 260 (8th Cir. 1995) (relevant market "is dominated by large, sophisticated payors," none of whom objected to the acquisition); *cf.* FTC v. Elders Grain, Inc., 868 F.2d 901, 905 (7th Cir. 1989) (noting that "[a] concentrated and knowledgeable buying side makes collusion by sellers more difficult," but affirming grant of injunction to FTC).

108. *See Baker Hughes, Inc.*, 908 F.2d at 986 (market share evidence was misleading because the relevant market is "minuscule," rendering the statistics "volatile and shifting" and "easily skewed"); *cf.* FTC v. University Health, Inc., 938 F.2d 1206, 1218 (11th Cir. 1991) (rebuttal evidence may "cast [ ] doubt on the persuasive quality of the [plaintiff's] statistics").

109. *See* United States v. Citizens & Southern Nat'l Bank, 422 U.S. 86, 121-23 (1975) (since the acquiring and acquired banks were already associated, the acquisition did not substantially lessen competition); *Elders Grain, Inc.*, 868 F.2d at 905-06 (existence of excess capacity provides incentive to cheat on cartel, since it allows "additional sales [to be] made at little additional cost, making them disproportionately profitable". . . "But of course excess capacity may be a symptom of cartelization rather than a cure for it"); FTC v. Butterworth Health Corp., 946 F. Supp. 1285, 1296-97

illegality, the burden of producing additional evidence of anticompetitive effect shifts to the plaintiff, and merges with the ultimate burden of persuasion, which remains with the plaintiff at all times.[110]

(c) BALANCE OF THE EQUITIES

If a court determines that the plaintiff has made the required showing of irreparable harm and likelihood of success, it must balance the respective equities, or hardships, which will result from the grant or denial of the requested injunction.[111] The strength of the plaintiff's showing with respect to its likelihood of success relates inversely to the balance of the equities showing that will be required.[112] The alternative

---

(W.D. Mich. 1996) (relying on study showing that market concentration among nonprofit hospitals appeared to be positively correlated with lower prices rather than with higher prices), *aff'd mem.*, 121 F.3d 708 (6th Cir. 1997); *Freeman Hosp.*, 911 F. Supp. at 1223 (since hospitals were nonprofit and controlled by their communities, they were less likely to engage in supracompetitive pricing); *see also* FTC v. Freeman Hosp., 1995-1 Trade Cas. (CCH) ¶ 70,929, at 74,143 (some deference appropriate to fact that nonprofit hospitals are dedicated to the public interest). *But see University Health, Inc.*, 938 F.2d at 1224 (reversing district court's holding that hospital's nonprofit status militates against finding a violation of § 7).

110. *See Baker Hughes, Inc.*, 908 F.2d at 983; *see also H.J. Heinz*, 246 F.3d at 715.

111. 15 U.S.C. § 53(b)(2) provides that the FTC is entitled to a preliminary injunction "[u]pon a proper showing that, weighing the equities and considering the Commission's likelihood of ultimate success, such action would be in the public interest . . ." 15 U.S.C. § 26, however, holds private plaintiffs to the same standard as the common law required for injunctive relief, including the traditional criterion of the balance of the hardships.

112. Friendship Materials, Inc. v. Michigan Brick, Inc., 679 F.2d 100, 105 (6th Cir. 1982); *see also In re* Microsoft Antitrust Litig., 333 F.3d 517, 526 (4th Cir. 2003) (employing a sliding scale approach, the greater the risk of competitive harm, the greater the justification burden); Roland Mach. Co. v. Dresser Indus., 749 F.2d 380, 387 (7th Cir. 1984) ("the more likely the plaintiff is to win, the less heavily need the balance of harms weigh in his favor; the less likely he is to win, the more it need weigh in his favor"); Dataphase Sys., Inc. v. C.L. Sys., 640 F.2d 109, 113 (8th Cir. 1981) (if balance of harms favors defendant, plaintiff "faces a heavy burden of demonstrating that he is likely to prevail on the merits," and conversely, provided plaintiff meets minimum threshold of raising a substantial question going to the merits, "the showing of success on the merits can be less" if the balance favors plaintiff); *cf.* Dynamics Corp. v. CTS Corp., 805 F.2d 705, 709 (7th Cir. 1986) (noting that, where the balance of harms is

test expresses this relationship as obligating the plaintiff to show "sufficiently serious questions going to the merits to make them a fair ground for litigation"—rather than a likelihood of actual success on the merits—"and a balance of hardships tipping decidedly"—rather than merely slightly—in its favor.[113]

There are two types of equities to be balanced: public and private. Generally, public equities receive greater weight than private equities, or put differently, private equities alone cannot outweigh conflicting public equities.[114] In some cases, however, the presence of private equities has

---

equal, the only issue is the plaintiff's likelihood of success).

113. *See, e.g.*, Sonesta Int'l Hotels Corp. v. Wellington Assocs., 483 F.2d 247, 250 (2d Cir. 1973). *But see* United States v. Siemens Corp., 621 F.2d 499, 505 (2d Cir. 1980) (government not entitled to its usual presumption of irreparable harm if it meets only the alternative test; proper test is "whether the Government has shown a reasonable likelihood of success on the merits and whether the balance of equities tips in its favor").

114. *See, e.g.*, FTC v. H.J. Heinz, 246 F.2d 708, 726 (D.C. Cir. 2001) (citing *University Health, Inc.*, 938 F.2d at 1225); *Elders Grain, Inc.*, 868 F.2d at 903 (same); FTC v. PPG Indus., 798 F.2d 1500, 1506 (D.C. Cir. 1986) (same); FTC v. Warner Communs., 742 F.2d 1156, 1165 (9th Cir. 1984) ("Although private equities may be considered, public equities receive far greater weight."); FTC v. Weyerhaeuser Co., 665 F.2d 1072, 1083 (D.C. Cir. 1981) ("Private equities do not outweigh effective enforcement of the antitrust laws. When the Commission demonstrates a likelihood of ultimate success, a countershowing of private equities alone would not suffice to justify denial of a preliminary injunction."); *Siemens Corp.*, 621 F.2d at 506 ("once the Government has shown a reasonable likelihood of success on the merits, the equities will usually tip in its favor, since private interests must be subordinated to public ones"); FTC v. National Tea Co., 603 F.2d 694, 697 (8th Cir. 1979) ("public equities are to be given the greater weight"); FTC v. Cardinal Health, Inc., 12 F. Supp. 2d 34, 66 (D.D.C. 1998) ("In balancing the public and private equities, benefits to the public are entitled to substantially more deference than the benefits to the private Defendants."); FTC v. Staples, Inc., 970 F. Supp. 1066, 1091 (D.D.C. 1997) (noting that while private equities are important, they cannot overcome showing of likely success on the merits); United States v. Ivaco, Inc., 704 F. Supp. 1409, 1430 (W.D. Mich. 1989) ("the private interest in obtaining increased profits from such a transaction 'cannot outweigh the public interest in preventing this merger from taking effect pending trial'" (quoting United States v. Atlantic Richfield Co., 297 F. Supp. 1061, 1074 (S.D.N.Y. 1969)); *cf.* FTC v. Food Town Stores, Inc., 539 F.2d 1339, 1346 (4th Cir. 1976) (Winter, J., sitting alone) (private equities "are not proper considerations for granting or withholding injunctive relief"); FTC v. Bass Bros. Enters., Inc., 1984-1 Trade Cas. (CCH) ¶ 66,041 (N.D. Ohio 1984)

led courts to deny relief when the other factors did not strongly weigh in favor of granting the injunction, especially where divestiture would still be possible after trial or where less drastic relief would be appropriate.[115]

(same). This holding has been criticized as "go[ing] too far." *National Tea Co.*, 603 F.2d at 697 n.4 (contrary to legislative intent to exclude private equities entirely); *see also Weyerhaeuser Co.*, 665 F.2d at 1083 (same).

115. *Weyerhaeuser Co.*, 665 F.2d at 264-65 (interest of shareholders of acquired firm in realizing value of their stock and advantage to that firm of continuing operations weighed against granting preliminary injunction when hold separate order would preserve feasibility of eventual relief; also, only part of the acquisition raised Section 7 problems); *Siemens Corp.*, 621 F.2d at 506 ("surely where the harm to defendants is great and there is little likelihood that consummation of the merger would jeopardize ultimate relief, the court clearly may deny injunctive relief or fashion prophylactic measures to obviate the threat of harm" such as hold separate order"); *see National Tea Co.*, 603 F.2d at 696-97 (acquired firm run by family who had invested most of their lives in the firm and were reluctant to turn it over to outsiders and were unlikely to have other opportunities to sell; acquirer agreed to divest without objection to FTC-approved purchaser if so ordered by final judgment); FTC v. PepsiCo, 477 F.2d 24, 30 (2d Cir. 1973) (PepsiCo invested $57 million to obtain 83% stake and control over management; "in view of the fait accompli of 83% control and the staggering investment made, we are not persuaded that we should deprive PepsiCo of its corporate managerial responsibilities particularly when incumbent management has divested itself of its stock interests"; hold separate order granted in lieu of preliminary injunction); FTC v. Freeman Hosp., 911 F. Supp. 1213, 1227-28 (W.D. Mo.) (injunction would likely shut down acquired hospital, which would not further public interest in maintaining competition), *aff'd*, 69 F.3d 260 (8th Cir. 1995); United States v. Gillette Co., 828 F. Supp. 78, 85-86 (D.D.C. 1993) (discounting defendants' self-serving claims of private equities, but still finding that "forestall[ing]" a transaction "valued at in excess of $400 million" because of Section 7 problems involving $5 million in each party's sales supported denial of injunction); United States v. Culbro Corp., 436 F. Supp. 746, 757-58 (S.D.N.Y. 1977) (risk that acquisition will fall through, resulting in loss of $500,000 expended in preparation for closing and loss of opportunity for shareholders to make substantial profit, militated against enjoining transaction when hold separate order was feasible); Pearl Brewing Co. v. Miller Brewing Co., 1993-2 Trade Cas. (CCH) ¶ 70,370, at 70,959 (W.D. Tex. 1993) ("[i]n contrast to plaintiffs' speculative injury, defendants have come forward with evidence that enjoining the closing would have serious adverse effects upon defendants" such as "threaten[ing] the implementation of marketing plans [for] the crucial summer season" and possibly scuttling the acquisition), *aff'd mem.*, 52 F.3d 1066 (5th Cir. 1995).

Courts frequently recite "the public's interest in the effective enforcement of the antitrust laws" as the public equity supporting a grant of preliminary injunctive relief[116] (and relatedly, the problems inherent in fashioning subsequent permanent relief such as divestiture if a preliminary injunction is denied),[117] but some cases have also recognized public equities on the defendants' side.[118]

---

116. FTC v. University Health, Inc., 938 F.2d 1206, 1225 (11th Cir. 1991) (antitrust laws "are intended to safeguard competition, and, hence, consumers," so denying the injunction "would frustrate the FTC's ability to protect the public from anticompetitive behavior"); *see also* FTC v. Elders Grain, Inc., 868 F.2d 901, 908 (7th Cir. 1989) (Ripple, J., concurring) ("A strong showing by the government that a violation of law has occurred necessarily produces 'public equities' that must 'receive far greater weight' than 'private equities.' . . . When the government's case is weak, the 'public equities' will be less clear. Consequently, in such a case, 'private equities' often will play a more dominant role in the analysis." (quoting FTC v. Warner Communications Inc., 742 F.2d 1156, 1165 (9th Cir. 1984))); *Freeman Hosp.*, 911 F. Supp. at 1228 (recognizing "public equities favoring the FTC's enforcement of the antitrust laws"); *cf.* Ball Mem'l Hosp., Inc. v. Mutual Hosp. Ins., Inc., 784 F.2d 1325, 1334 (7th Cir. 1986) ("[g]iven the risk that business rivals may seek to use antitrust to stifle rather than promote competition, district courts should pay particular attention to the public interest" in cases brought by private parties); *Weyerhaeuser Co.*, 665 F.2d at 1081 (rejecting FTC's contention that the only equity to be weighed is "the one it advances—the public interest in effective antitrust enforcement").

117. *See University Health, Inc.*, 938 F.2d at 1225 (citing *Warner Communs.*, 742 F.2d at 1165); *Warner Communs. Inc.*, 742 F.2d at 1165 ("because the record contains conflicting evidence on the anticompetitive effects of the merger, it is unclear whether [public equity of FTC's effective enforcement of antitrust laws] support[s] the grant or denial of injunctive relief. A different public equity, however, supports the grant of injunctive relief. A denial of preliminary injunctive relief would preclude effective relief if the Commission ultimately prevails and divestiture is ordered"); *National Tea Co.*, 603 F.2d at 696 ("the principal public equity was that an after-the-fact remedy of divestiture would be inadequate"); *Ivaco, Inc.*, 704 F. Supp. at 1429 ("post-judgment relief, such as divestiture, would not effectively remedy the injury to competition threatened by this transaction"); Grumman Corp. v. LTV Corp., 665 F.2d 10, 16 (2d Cir. 1981) (merger "not likely to be undone by a divestiture in the event the acquisition is found to be unlawful after it has occurred"); FTC v. Libbey, Inc., 211 F. Supp. 2d 34, 54 (D.D.C. 2002) (citing *Staples*, 970 F. Supp. at 1091).

118. *See Weyerhaeuser Co.*, 665 F.2d at 1082 (increase in linerboard supply and alleviation of unemployment in depressed area counted as public equities

Courts have recognized a number of private equities (or harms to defendants), including the shareholders' interest in realizing the value of their stock,[119] the likelihood that the acquired firm would not be acquired by another firm if the transaction were disallowed,[120] an improvement in the acquired firm's competitiveness and financial condition,[121] the alleviation of uncertainty associated with the pending challenge to the merger,[122] and the avoidance of costs to the merging parties.[123]

---

favoring defendants); *Freeman Hosp.*, 911 F. Supp. at 1227 ("primary public interest in this case is the interest in maintaining competitive hospital prices," which would be furthered by the acquisition). *But see University Health, Inc.*, 938 F.2d at 1225 (defendants' "attempt to convert [their] private injuries into public costs is of no avail"); *PPG Indus.*, 798 F.2d at 1507-08 (rejecting district court's analysis of public equities; ability of acquired firm to obtain needed capital rejected because the challenged merger was not necessary for it to do so; keeping acquired firm "out of foreign corporate hands" insufficient because foreign ownership not inevitable; facilitation of innovation dismissed because hold-separate order entered by district court prohibited exchange of information).

119. *See Warner Communs.*, 742 F.2d at 1165 ("although th[is] asserted private injur[y] [is] entitled to serious consideration, private equities alone do not outweigh the Commission's showing of likelihood of success"); *Weyerhaeuser Co.*, 665 F.2d at 1082 (appearing to recognize this interest; affirming hold separate order in lieu of injunction); *Culbro Corp.*, 436 F. Supp. at 757-58 (recognizing shareholders' interest; issuing hold separate order in lieu of injunction).

120. *See National Tea Co.*, 603 F.2d at 696-97 (recognizing as private equity militating in favor of denying injunction fact that acquired company's management was very old and unlikely to receive another offer; denying relief); *Culbro Corp.*, 436 F. Supp. at 757-58 (injunction likely to abort acquisition and deprive shareholders of "a good opportunity which might have no counterpart on the immediate horizon"; issuing hold separate order in lieu of injunction). *But see PPG Indus.*, 798 F.2d at 1507 (rejecting claimed public equity of age and failing health of acquired firm's founder and his desire to sell his firm as going concern as "mere expectation of private gain"; other offers had been made to acquire the firm).

121. *See Warner Communs.*, 742 F.2d at 1165 (claimed equity of "allowing Polygram to escape its troubled financial condition by merging with Warner" was "entitled to serious consideration," but did not outweigh FTC's public equities); *Weyerhaeuser Co.*, 665 F.2d at 1082 (recognizing "advantage to Menasha of continued operations on a more centralized basis" and affirming hold separate order in lieu of injunction).

122. *See* FTC v. Warner Communs., 742 F.2d 1156, 1165 (9th Cir. 1984) (Polygram's claim that uncertainty led employees to leave and made more difficult to sign artists "entitled to serious consideration," but outweighed

(d) PUBLIC INTEREST

Few cases analyze the public interest as a separate component of the preliminary injunction standard.[124] Instead, the court's finding with

---

by FTC's public equities); United States v. Siemens Corp., 621 F.2d 499, 510 (2d Cir. 1980) ("Because of the uncertainty of SD's future after two years of substantial losses and the importance of continued future service, customers began to shy away from SD as a supplier and the morale of SD's employees declined. This trend was temporarily reversed by the news that Siemens, a strong company with a good reputation, would acquire SD. The apprehension regarding SD's future, however, resumed when the Government commenced its suit . . . with marketplace rumors to the effect that if the acquisition were not approved SD would go out of business"; denying relief); Pearl Brewing Co. v. Miller Brewing Co., 1993-2 Trade Cas. (CCH) ¶ 70,370, at 70,959 (W.D. Tex. 1993) (Molson unable to implement "crucial summer selling season" promotion because of delay in closing; denying relief), *aff'd*, 52 F.3d 1066 (5th Cir. 1995).

123. *See* United States v. Gillette Co., 828 F. Supp. 78, 86 (D.D.C. 1993) ("the court cannot ignore that a transaction valued at in excess of $400 million would be forestalled because each party sells approximately $5 million (at wholesale) in premium fountain pens"; denying relief); United States v. Culbro Corp., 436 F. Supp. 746, 757-58 (S.D.N.Y. 1977) ($500,000 spent in preparation for closing by acquired company's president would be lost; issuing hold separate order in lieu of injunction). *But see University Health, Inc.*, 938 F.2d at 1225 (rejecting defendants' asserted equity of "the cost that delaying this transaction would exact" on the ground that private injuries alone "do not outweigh the injury the public suffers from anticompetitive practices").

124. FTC v. Freeman Hosp., 911 F. Supp. 1213, 1227 (W.D. Mo) ("The primary public interest in this case is the interest in maintaining competitive hospital prices," and since the acquisition had not been shown to pose a threat to this interest, enjoining it would not have been in the public interest), *aff'd*, 69 F.3d 260 (8th Cir. 1995). For cases formally analyzing the public interest separately from the other factors comprising the preliminary injunction standard, see United States v. Ivaco, Inc., 704 F. Supp. 1409, 1429-30 (W.D. Mich. 1989) (because injunction would preserve competition between defendants, injunction was in public interest); Tasty Baking Co. v. Ralston Purina, Inc., 653 F. Supp. 1250, 1276 (E.D. Pa. 1987) (because acquisition would increase concentration and permit monopolistic practices, "[t]he public has good reason to fear the consequences" if it were not enjoined); FTC v. Freeman Hosp., 1995-1 Trade Cas. (CCH) ¶ 70,929, at 74,144 ("[t]he public's interest in having access to the most efficient and effective medical care is of paramount importance"; since the acquisition would not lessen competition but would strengthen a weak competitor, the public interest compelled allowing the

respect to the plaintiff's likelihood of success on the merits is frequently piggybacked into a finding with respect to the injunction's effect on the public interest by means of one simple and well-established step: "By enacting Section 7, Congress declared that the preservation of competition is always in the public interest,"[125] so if a transaction may substantially lessen competition, it follows that it is always in the public interest to enjoin it.[126] Conversely, if a transaction is not anticompetitive, there is no reason to condemn it under the antitrust laws.[127]

(3) Standard of Review

The standard of review for grants and denials of preliminary injunctions is usually held to be abuse of discretion,[128] but courts often

---

acquisition to proceed); Pearl Brewing Co. v. Miller Brewing Co., 1993-2 Trade Cas. (CCH) ¶ 70,370, at 70,959 (Miller intended to lower Molson's prices after the acquisition, so enjoining the acquisition would "inhibit a procompetitive result").

125. *Ivaco, Inc.*, 704 F. Supp. at 1430; *see also* National Soc'y of Prof'l Eng'rs v. United States, 435 U.S. 679, 692, 695 (1978) (statutory policy is that competition is always good, so defendant cannot be heard to argue that challenged restraint is lawful under the rule of reason on ground that unfettered competition would be dangerous).

126. *See Ivaco, Inc.*, 704 F. Supp. at 1430.

127. In *FTC v. Elders Grain, Inc.*, Judge Posner issued the following critique of a strict dichotomy between public and private interests: "First of all, public and private interests are not altogether distinct, since in many situations the public interest is merely the aggregation of private interests. Ours is not a society in which the state is normally assumed to have interests distinct from those of its citizens. The public interest in enforcing the antitrust laws is, in the main, the sum of the private interests of consumers in being able to buy goods and services at a competitive price." 868 F.2d 901, 904 (7th Cir. 1989); *see also* Ball Mem'l Hosp., Inc. v. Mutual Hosp. Ins., Inc., 784 F.2d 1325, 1333-34 (7th Cir. 1986) ("The Hospitals insist that the public interest is on their side and that they are likely to prevail on the merits. These are related considerations"; sometimes, though, "the plaintiff's interests do not coincide with those of consumers," in which case "a court must be especially careful not to grant relief that may undercut the proper functions of antitrust"); *Gillette Co.*, 828 F. Supp. at 86 ("The interests of the public are not necessarily coextensive with the irreparable harm criterion . . . even though the case is brought by the United States to enforce federal anti-trust laws").

128. *See* United States v. Microsoft, 253 F.3d 34, 104 (D.C. Cir. 2001) ("[T]he standard of appellate review is simply whether the issuance of the injunction, in the light of the applicable standard, constituted an abuse of

engage in review that is more searching than that standard generally implies.[129]

---

discretion") (citing Doran v. Salem Inn, Inc., 422 U.S. 922, 931-32 (1975))); FTC v. H.J. Heinz Co., 246 F.3d 708, 713 (D.C. Cir. 2001); *see also* Consolidated Gold Fields PLC v. Minorco, S.A., 871 F.2d 252, 256, 261 (2d Cir. 1989) (affirming grant of injunction); Christian Schmidt Brewing Co. v. G. Heileman Brewing Co., 753 F.2d 1354, 1358 (6th Cir. 1985) (affirming grant of injunction and emphasizing limited scope of review and "tentative nature of any holdings which must necessarily be made, albeit with great care, at this stage of the proceedings"); Friendship Materials, Inc. v. Michigan Brick, Inc., 679 F.2d 100, 102-03 (6th Cir. 1982) (vacating injunction for failure to find irreparable harm); FTC v. Weyerhaeuser Co., 665 F.2d 1072, 1088, 1090 (D.C. Cir. 1981) (affirming district court's decision to enter hold separate order rather than injunction as not abuse of discretion); Dataphase Sys., Inc. v. C.L. Sys., Inc., 640 F.2d 109, 114 & n.8 (8th Cir. 1981) (reversing grant of injunction for failure to find irreparable harm); FTC v. National Tea Co., 603 F.2d 694 (8th Cir. 1979) (affirming denial of injunction where district court considered relevant factors and findings not clearly erroneous); William Inglis & Sons Baking Co. v. ITT Continental Baking Co., 526 F.2d 86, 88 (9th Cir. 1975) (applying abuse of discretion standard but remanding for consideration of alternative test); FTC v. Butterworth Health Corp., 1997-2 Trade Cas. (CCH) ¶ 71,863, at 80,062 (6th Cir. 1997); *cf.* Atari Games Corp. v. Nintendo of Am., Inc., 897 F.2d 1572, 1575 (Fed. Cir. 1990) ("This court may reverse the district court's decision only if the district court has committed an abuse of discretion, if the decision is based upon an error of law or if the court misapplied the law to particular facts").

129. *See, e.g.*, FTC v. Tenet Health Care Corp., 186 F.3d 1045 (8th Cir. 1999) (reversing grant of injunction based on district court's improper determination of geographic markets); *Atari Games Corp.*, 897 F.2d at 1577 (reversing grant of injunction for insufficient factual basis where district court relied solely on plaintiff's uncontradicted affidavits and did not find that plaintiff could actually prove its allegations); FTC v. PPG Indus., 798 F.2d 1500 (D.C. Cir. 1986) (reversing district court's issuance of hold separate order in lieu of injunction, and ordering court to grant injunction); *cf.* Lawson Prods., Inc. v. Avnet, Inc., 782 F.2d 1429, 1438 (7th Cir. 1986) (calling question of how to articulate standard of review "somewhat unimportant" since "reviewing courts have never appeared to be stymied in reaching results in preliminary injunction cases" regardless of how the standard was framed); Roland Mach. Co. v. Dresser Indus., 749 F.2d 380, 396-97 (7th Cir. 1984) (Swygert, J., dissenting) ("the actual scrutiny with which appellate courts have reviewed preliminary injunction decisions by the lower courts has differed markedly irrespective of the seeming concensus [sic] on the applicable standard of review," provoking criticism of "formulation of the standard of review" as "a purely verbal

2. *Hold Separate Orders*

As an alternative to issuing a preliminary injunction, a court may issue a "hold separate" order with respect to the assets raising competitive concerns. Hold separate orders are seen as less drastic than preliminary injunctions. They allow the transaction to be consummated, so long as there are mechanisms in place that separate the assets at issue from the rest of the acquiring company pending final resolution of the Section 7 case.[130] At a minimum, a hold separate order will mean that the acquiring company cannot exercise control over the pricing, output and marketing decisions affecting the assets involved. Separate management is typically required and the order usually contains prohibitions on the exchange of information. From the plaintiff's perspective, the purpose of hold separate orders, like preliminary injunctions, is to keep the businesses separate to make it easier to implement permanent relief.[131]

Hold separate orders have been used as an alternative to a preliminary injunction[132] and may be particularly appropriate where only

---

exercise" masking standardless, result-oriented decision making).

130. *See, e.g.*, Marathon Oil Co. v. Mobil Corp., 669 F.2d 378 (6th Cir. 1981), *reaff'd on petition for injunction*, 669 F.2d 384 (6th Cir. 1982).

131. *See, e.g.*, United States v. United Techs. Corp., 466 F. Supp. 196, 200 (N.D.N.Y. 1979).

132. *See, e.g.*, *Weyerhaeuser Co.*, 665 F.2d at 1085, 1090-91 (granting hold separate order where merger had been consummated); United States v. Coca-Cola Bottling Co., 575 F.2d 222 (9th Cir. 1978); FTC v. PepsiCo, 477 F.2d 24, 30-31 (2d Cir. 1973); FTC v. Southland Corp., 471 F. Supp. 1, 4-5 (D.D.C. 1979) (granting hold separate order); United States v. Culbro Corp., 436 F. Supp. 746, 754-56 (S.D.N.Y. 1977); United States v. Northwest Indus., Inc., 301 F. Supp. 1066, 1097 (N.D. Ill. 1969); United States v. Cities Serv. Co., 289 F. Supp. 133, 134, 136 (D. Mass. 1968); United States v. United Tote, Inc., 1991-1 Trade Cas. (CCH) ¶ 69,300 (D. Del. 1991) (denying modification of hold separate order voluntarily entered into by the parties); United States v. Acorn Eng'g Co., 1981-2 Trade Cas. (CCH) ¶ 64,197, at 73,711 (N.D. Cal. 1981) (granting hold separate order where merger had been consummated); FTC v. Exxon Corp., 1979-2 Trade Cas. (CCH) ¶ 62,972, at 79,537-39 (D.D.C. 1979) (allowing merger to be consummated subject to hold separate order); FTC v. Pillsbury Co., 1976-2 Trade Cas. (CCH) ¶ 61,200, at 70,471-72 (N.D. Ill. 1976) (requiring formation of new company to operate acquired company's business pending resolution on the merits); United States v. Brown Shoe Co., 1956 Trade Cas. (CCH) ¶ 68,244, at 71,117 (E.D. Mo. 1956); *cf.* FTC v. Occidental Petroleum Corp., 1986-1 Trade Cas. (CCH)

part of the assets to be acquired raise competitive concerns.[133] Several lower courts also have indicated that a hold separate order may be appropriate when the plaintiff cannot meet the requirements for a preliminary injunction.[134] Hold separate orders may be adopted voluntarily by the parties to a transaction[135] or they may be imposed pursuant to a court's equitable powers.[136] Some early decisions set aside challenges on the strength of commitments for future divestiture without hold separate orders.[137]

¶ 67,071, at 62,515-19 (D.D.C. 1986) (denying injunction and noting that divestiture remains available).

133. *See* United States v. BNS Inc., 848 F.2d 945 (9th Cir.), *modified*, 858 F.2d 456 (9th Cir. 1988) (upholding preliminary injunction barring tender offer, but only until trustee could be appointed to operate acquired firm's subsidiary operating in the only market which raised competitive concern, who would then manage assets separately and independently from the acquiring firm and maintain the confidentiality of business plans); *PepsiCo.*, 477 F.2d at 25 (where ultimate divestiture need cover only a portion of the acquired assets, such relief can be preserved through a hold separate order).

134. *See* United States v. Acorn Eng'g Co., 1981-2 Trade Cas. (CCH) ¶ 64,197, at 73,711; United States v. Hospital Affiliates Int'l, Inc., 1980-1 Trade Cas. (CCH) ¶ 63,721, at 77,854 (E.D. La. 1980) (dictum); *Southland Corp.*, 471 F. Supp. at 4-5 (granting hold separate order absent showing of likelihood of success, but with defendant's consent); *United Techs. Corp.*, 466 F. Supp. at 205 (stating that failure to show likelihood of success did not preclude issuance of hold separate order; granting order with defendant's consent).

135. *See, e.g., Southland Corp.*, 471 F. Supp. at 6; United States v. Black & Decker Mfg. Co., 430 F. Supp. 729, 733 (D. Md. 1976) (requiring acquired company to be maintained as a "separate, identifiable business entity").

136. *See* FTC v. Weyerhaeuser Co., 665 F.2d 1072, 1083-84, 1090 (D.C. Cir. 1981) (rejecting FTC contention that hold separate orders not authorized by Congress); *cf. id.* at 1091 (Mikva, J., dissenting) (plain words of statute mandate only two forms of relief: temporary restraining orders and preliminary injunctions); FTC v. Exxon Corp., 636 F.2d 1336, 1344 (D.C. Cir. 1980) (acknowledging the less drastic nature of hold separate orders as compared to preliminary injunctions).

137. In *United States v. Atlantic Richfield Co.*, 297 F. Supp. 1061, 1075 (S.D.N.Y. 1969), *aff'd sub nom., Bartlett v. United States* 401 U.S. 986 (1971), an injunction was vacated in reliance on the defendant's promise to divest to an identified seller, while in *United States v. First National State Bancorp.*, 499 F. Supp. 793, 804 (D.N.J. 1980), a merger was allowed on the basis of a commitment to future divestiture. *But see* FTC

Courts have been reluctant to issue a hold separate order where the order would make subsequent divestiture difficult,[138] or where the acquiring company can still gain some anticompetitive advantage in the interim,[139] although hold separate orders can be structured to address this latter problem.[140] By contrast, a court may be more willing to issue such an order where the defendant can demonstrate equitable considerations in its favor, such as its own good faith and the harm to it from a preliminary injunction.[141] Finally, the ease of administering the order also will play a role in the likelihood of its issuance.[142]

---

v. Food Town Stores, 539 F.2d 1339, 1345 (4th Cir. 1976).

138. *See Exxon Corp.*, 636 F.2d at 1343 (subsidiary's restoration as effective and viable competitor frequently impossible because FTC unable to unscramble merged assets); *United Techs. Corp.*, 466 F. Supp. at 203 (certain government-proposed hold separate provisions rejected as unnecessary to preserve target corporation's independence if divestiture ultimately decreed); FTC v. Tenneco, Inc., 433 F. Supp. 105, 107 (D.D.C. 1977) (FTC argued preliminary injunction necessary to preserve target as viable and independent entity); United States v. Wilson Sporting Goods Co., 288 F. Supp. 543, 569-70 (N.D. Ill. 1968) (preliminary injunction necessary because hold separate order would not assure adequate eventual relief); United States v. Foremost-McKesson, Inc., 1976-2 Trade Cas. (CCH) ¶ 61,165, at 70,254-55 (D. Nev. 1976) (preliminary injunction necessary because divestiture could not re-create corporations' premerger status quo); *cf. Weyerhaeuser Co.*, 665 F.2d at 1087 (hold separate order may not issue unless eventual divestiture safeguarded).

139. *See Weyerhaeuser Co.*, 665 F.2d at 1085-86 & nn.32-33 (hold separate orders run risk of transfer of sensitive information and fruits of research and development efforts).

140. *See, e.g.*, United States v. Acorn Eng'g Co., 1981-2 Trade Cas. (CCH) ¶ 64,197, at 73,713 (hold separate order requiring that acquired firm's facilities be kept operating and in good repair). Many hold separate orders require the maintenance of separate sales forces. *See, e.g.*, FTC v. Southland Corp., 471 F. Supp. 1, 4-5 (D.D.C. 1979); FTC v. Exxon Corp., 1979-2 Trade Cas. (CCH) ¶ 62,972, at 79,538-39 (D.D.C. 1979) (concluding that a hold separate order adequately protects both public and private equities, particularly where the merger is not between horizontal competitors and the acquiring company does not plan to dispose of the acquired company's assets), *modified,* 1980-2 Trade Cas. (CCH) ¶ 63,478 (D.D.C.), *aff'd in part and rev'd in part on other grounds,* 636 F.2d 1336 (D.C. Cir. 1980); United States v. United Techs. Corp., 466 F. Supp. at 205.

141. *See* FTC v. PepsiCo, 477 F.2d 24, 30 (2d Cir. 1973) (citing good faith of acquirer and harm to defendants).

142. *See Weyerhaeuser Co.*, 665 F.2d at 1089 & n.46 (hold separate order

The standard for issuing a hold separate order has not always been clear. In 1981, the D.C. Circuit identified three conditions for issuing a hold separate order once the plaintiff has established a likelihood of success on the merits: (1) strong equities favoring consummation of the transaction, (2) the order will check interim competitive harm, and (3) the order will permit adequate ultimate relief.[143] None of these criteria seemed to hinge on the strength of the plaintiff's case. Five years later, however, in 1986, the same appellate court held that there is a "presumption in favor of a preliminary injunction" when a plaintiff "establishes a strong likelihood of success on the merits."[144]

Once a voluntary hold separate order has been entered, it is often difficult to modify or dissolve. In *United States v. United Tote, Inc.*,[145] the defendant voluntarily agreed to a hold separate order in lieu of litigating a motion for preliminary injunction. Later, the defendant sought to dissolve the order. The court required that the defendant make a showing of "changed circumstances" to discontinue the order, and the defendant was unable to persuade the judge that the order should be dissolved.[146]

---

acceptable when district court has means to check any blatant attempts to circumvent order); FTC v. Lancaster Colony Corp., 434 F. Supp. 1088 (S.D.N.Y. 1977) (hold separate order unacceptable when court constantly would have to supervise compliance).

143. FTC v. Weyerhaeuser Co., 665 F.2d 1072, 1087 (D.C. Cir. 1981).

144. FTC v. PPG Indus., 798 F.2d 1500, 1506-07 (D.C. Cir. 1986). By contrast, one district court has held that there should be a reverse presumption in favor of effective relief short of a preliminary injunction. *See* United States v. Culbro Corp., 436 F. Supp. 746, 750 (S.D.N.Y. 1977) (prior to issuing a preliminary injunction, a court should determine whether "an effective but less drastic preliminary remedy, such as a hold separate order . . . will prevent th[e] probable interim harm to the public").

145. 1991-1 Trade Cas. (CCH) ¶ 69,300 (D. Del. 1991).

146. Specifically, the defendant argued that financial difficulties induced by the hold separate agreement constituted changed circumstances. The court rejected this argument, noting that such difficulties were foreseeable when the agreement was reached. *See id.*

B. Permanent Relief

1. Permanent Injunctions

A permanent injunction is a final adjudication on the merits. The DOJ and the FTC may seek permanent injunctive relief[147] where it is in the public interest.[148] Private parties may also seek permanent injunctive relief under Section 16 of the Clayton Act.[149]

The purpose of permanent injunctive relief is to restore competition.[150] Courts have the discretion to fashion the kind of permanent relief best able to protect the plaintiff from future harms, regardless of the burden on the acquirer. The court may consider the economic hardship to the defendants in fashioning the equitable relief it ultimately orders.[151]

2. Divestiture

Divestiture is the primary postconsummation remedy for a Section 7 violation.[152] The alleged harm from an acquisition claimed to violate Section 7 is typically that the increased concentration in the industry will create a structure more conducive to anticompetitive pricing. The logical

---

147. The DOJ may seek permanent injunctive relief under Section 15 of the Clayton Act, 15 U.S.C. § 25; the FTC may seek permanent injunctive relief under § 13(b) of the FTC Act, 15 U.S.C. § 53(b).
148. *See* Ford Motor Co. v. United States, 405 U.S. 562, 573 & n.8 (1972); United States v. Coca-Cola Bottling Co., 575 F.2d 222 (9th Cir. 1978).
149. *See* 15 U.S.C. § 26.
150. *See* United States v. E.I. du Pont de Nemours & Co., 366 U.S. 316, 325-26 (1961) ("But the primary focus of inquiry . . . is upon the question of the relief required effectively to eliminate the tendency of the acquisition condemned by § 7. For it will be remembered that the violation was not actual monopoly but only a tendency towards monopoly. The required relief therefore is a remedy which reasonably assures the elimination of that tendency").
151. *Id.* at 327 ("Economic hardship can influence choice only as among two or more effective remedies").
152. *See* Consolidated Gold Fields PLC v. Anglo Am. Corp., 713 F. Supp. 1457 (S.D.N.Y. 1989); United States v. Phillips Petroleum Co., 367 F. Supp. 1226, 1262 (C.D. Cal. 1973), *aff'd mem.*, 418 U.S. 906 (1974); *see also* United States v. Spectra-Physics, Inc., 46 Fed. Reg. 31,095, 31,098 (1981) (competitive impact statement) ("total divestiture has been, and will continue to be, the principal relief sought by the Government in Section 7 cases").

solution is thus to reduce the resulting concentration by requiring the acquiring party to shed the assets which are causing the excessive concentration.[153]

Postconsummation divestiture often requires the court to "unscramble the eggs," a process that can do more harm than good. However, in *United States v. E.I. du Pont de Nemours & Co.*,[154] the U.S. Supreme Court stated that, even though divestiture may be a "drastic" approach, it is nevertheless "appropriate," since "[t]he very words of § 7 suggest that an undoing of the acquisition is a natural remedy."[155] The Court thus instructed lower courts to proceed "whatever the adverse effect of such a decree on private interests."[156] The U.S. Supreme Court has bluntly stated that those "who violate the Act may not reap the

---

153. *See* William J. Baer, Director, Bureau of Competition, FTC, Reflections on 20 Years of Merger Enforcement under the Hart-Scott-Rodino Act, Remarks Before the Conference Board (Oct. 29, 1996), *at* www.ftc.gov/speeches/other/hsrspeec.htm (discussing FTC efforts to make the divestiture process better and faster); *see also* Federal Trade Comm'n, Statement of the Federal Trade Commission's Bureau of Competition on Negotiating Merger Remedies (Apr. 2, 2003).

154. 366 U.S. 316 (1961).

155. *Id*. at 326, 328-29; *see* Schine Chain Theatres, Inc. v. United States, 334 U.S. 110, 128-29 (1948) (divestiture serves three remedial functions: (1) ending illegal combinations or conspiracies, (2) depriving antitrust violators of the benefits of their unlawful action, and (3) breaking up or neutralizing monopoly power. Merely enjoining future violations of § 7 may fail to protect the public interest).

156. *E.I. du Pont de Nemours & Co.*, 366 U.S. at 326; *see also* United States v. United Tote, Inc., 768 F. Supp. 1064, 1085-87 (D. Del. 1991) (rejecting financial hardship as a rationale for avoiding divestiture); The passage of time or the intermingling of assets, management, and business does not necessarily preclude an order of divestiture. *See* United States v. Greater Buffalo Press, Inc., 402 U.S. 549, 556 (1971); Ash Grove Cement Co. v. FTC, 577 F.2d 1368, 1379-80 (9th Cir. 1978); Crown Zellerbach Corp., 54 F.T.C. 769, 807 (1957) (divestiture order entered four years after acquisition was consummated and FTC noted that "the broad purpose of [§ 7] cannot be thwarted merely because [the acquiring firm] has commingled its own assets with those of the acquired firm"), *aff'd.,* 296 F.2d 800 (9th Cir. 1961); *In re* Chicago Bridge & Iron Co. N.V. No. 9300 (F.T.C. June 18, 2003) (divestiture ordered by administrative law judge more than two years after acquisition consummated). Proof of the existence of vigorous competition following an illegal merger or acquisition does not necessarily preclude a divestiture order, "because it does not show what kind of competition might have remained had there been no illegal acquisitions."

benefits of their violations and avoid an undoing of their unlawful project on the plea of hardship or inconvenience."[157]

At the same time, courts are not authorized to impose "punitive" relief for Section 7 violations.[158] Restoring competition is the goal, and no more harm to the defendant is warranted than that which is required to achieve this goal. Therefore, while total divestiture may be appropriate in some circumstances,[159] if a court were convinced that a less disruptive but equally effective remedy were available, it might decline to order complete divestiture.[160] For example, where only a portion of the

---

157. United States v. Crescent Amusement Co., 323 U.S. 173, 189 (1944).

158. United States v. E.I. du Pont de Nemours & Co., 366 U.S. 316, 326 (1961).

159. In 2003, an FTC administrative law judge ordered total divestiture to reestablish the acquired company as a competitor. Press Release, FTC, Administrative Law Judge Upholds Allegations of Anticompetitive Acquisition by Chicago Bridge & Iron Company (June 27, 2003) (complete "divesti[ture] of all assets acquired in the Acquisition is required to restore competition as it existed prior to the Acquisition"). *See also* R.R. Donnelley & Sons Co., [1993-1997 FTC Complaints & Orders Transfer Binder] Trade Reg. Rep. (CCH) ¶23,523, at 23,201 (Dec. 30, 1993) (requiring defendant to divest all assets it had acquired, including all rights, privileges, customer agreements, and technology necessary to reestablish acquired company's pre-acquisition status). Total divestiture may in some circumstances be appropriate, however, even where the violation relates to less than the whole acquisition. *See, e.g.*, OKC Corp. v. FTC, 455 F.2d 1159, 1163 (10th Cir. 1972).

160. *See* Kennecott Copper Corp. v. Curtiss-Wright Corp., 449 F. Supp. 951, 968 (S.D.N.Y.) ("Divestiture . . . is a harsh remedy which should not be ordered without an opportunity for the presentation and consideration of less drastic alternative forms of relief appropriate to remedy the antitrust violation."), *aff'd in part and rev'd in part,* 584 F.2d 1195 (2d Cir. 1978); International Travel Arrangers v. NWA, Inc., 1990-2 Trade Cas. (CCH) ¶ 69,112, at 64,113 (D. Minn. 1990) ("[D]ivestiture is a severe remedy that is to be avoided when other forms of injunctive relief can adequately protect against further anticompetitive conduct without the same degree of economic dislocation"); *see also* Community Publishers, Inc. v. Donrey Corp., 892 F. Supp. 1146, 1175 (W.D. Ark. 1995) ("[t]he court need not resort to either rescission or divestiture if some other equitable relief suffices to provide an effective means of eliminating the illegal effects of the acquisition and is in the public interest. The court's equitable power are to be exercised to restore as nearly as possible the competitive situation that existed before the asset acquisition."), *aff'd sub nom.*, Community Publishers, Inc. v. DR Partners, 139 F.3d 1180 (8th Cir. 1998).

merged assets overlap in the same relevant market, a remedial divestiture may be confined to the overlapping assets,[161] and courts have resolved litigated cases by requiring only partial divestiture even in cases where the government enforcement agencies have sought total divestiture.[162]

Because the goal of divestiture is enhanced competition, courts look to fashion divestitures in a manner in which the divested assets can be used to form an independent and viable competitor.[163] Consequently, courts give plaintiffs leeway to seek divestiture of assets not necessarily connected to the antitrust problem but nevertheless necessary to ensure the viability of the divested entity.[164]

In some circumstances, even after-acquired assets may be included in the divestiture decree. In *Cascade Natural Gas Corp. v. El Paso Natural Gas Co.*,[165] for example, the U.S. Supreme Court required that new gas reserves developed since the challenged merger be divided equitably between El Paso and the divested company because the merged company that had discovered them represented the interests of both.[166]

---

161. *See, e.g.*, RSR Corp. v. FTC, 602 F.2d 1317, 1325-26 (9th Cir. 1979); United States v. Reed Roller Bit Co., 274 F. Supp. 573, 585-92 (W.D. Okla. 1967), *modified,* 1969 Trade Cas. (CCH) ¶ 72,755 (W.D. Okla. 1969); United States v. Stroh Brewery Co., 1982-83 Trade Cas. (CCH) ¶ 65,037, at 70,782 (D.D.C. 1982), *modified,* 1983-2 Trade Cas. (CCH) ¶ 65,627 (D.D.C. 1983); Brillo Mfg. Co., 64 F.T.C. 245, 261-64 (1964), *modified,* 75 F.T.C. 811 (1969); Union Carbide Corp., 59 F.T.C. 614, 657-59 (1961). The DOJ and the FTC often seek partial divestitures in settlement of § 7 claims.
162. *See RSR Corp.*, 602 F.2d at 1325 (requiring sale of three of four acquired lead recycling plants); United States v. Waste Mgmt., Inc., 588 F. Supp. 498, 514 (S.D.N.Y. 1983) (rejecting request for total divestiture and ordering only partial divestiture), *rev'd on other grounds,* 743 F.2d 976 (2d Cir. 1984).
163. *See* United States v. Atlantic Richfield Co., 297 F. Supp. 1061, 1068-69 (S.D.N.Y. 1969), *aff'd sub nom.*, Bartlett v. United States, 401 U.S. 986 (1971); *see also* United States v. Jos. Schlitz Brewing Co., 253 F. Supp. 129, 147-48 (N.D. Cal.), *aff'd*, 385 U.S. 37 (1966).
164. *See* Olin Corp. v. FTC, 986 F.2d 1295 (9th Cir. 1993) (accepting FTC's argument that additional assets needed to be divested in order to ensure the viability of the divested assets).
165. 386 U.S. 129 (1967).
166. *Id.* at 136-42 (divestiture guidelines set down by court also addressed specific financial management procedures in company to be created under divestiture decree); *see* United States v. Aluminum Co. of Am., 247 F. Supp. 308, 316 (E.D. Mo. 1964) (Alcoa required to divest itself of operational control and products manufactured in the facility but not the

Where, however, there is no connection between the after-acquired property and the Section 7 violation and where the after-acquired property is not necessary to restore the status quo or create a viable competitor, divestiture of after-acquired property has not been required.[167]

Moreover, like consent decrees, divestiture decrees may include provisions ancillary to the divestiture. For example, a court may order relief not only against the buyer but also against the seller, if such relief is necessary to eliminate the effects of the acquisition offensive to the statute.[168]

The courts historically have considered evidence of the parties' interest to divest overlapping businesses in deciding whether a transaction substantially lessens competition.[169] In recent years, courts have increasingly considered remedies offered by the parties, including divestiture proposals presented subsequent to HSR review. In *United States v. Franklin Electric Co.*,[170] the court held that evidence relating to a divestiture or other fix, including facts presented after a complaint has been filed, should be considered when determining whether a merger

---

title of a plant it had built after the acquisition), *aff'd*, 382 U.S. 12 (1965); United States v. Combustion Eng'g, Inc., 1971 Trade Cas. (CCH) ¶ 73,648, at 90,694-95 (D. Conn. 1971) (consent decree requiring sale of all improvements made after acquisition); Gates Rubber Co., [1970-1973 FTC Complaints & Orders Transfer Binder] Trade Reg. Rep. (CCH) ¶ 19,657 (June 18, 1971) (consent order requiring divestiture of acquired assets plus subsequent additions and improvements); Proctor & Gamble Co., 63 F.T.C. 1465, 1585-86 (1963), *rev'd,* 358 F.2d 74 (6th Cir. 1966), *rev'd,* 386 U.S. 568 (1967).

167. *See* Reynolds Metals Co. v. FTC, 309 F.2d 223, 231 (D.C. Cir. 1962); United States v. Carrols Dev. Corp., 454 F. Supp. 1215, 1222-23 (N.D.N.Y. 1978); United States v. Ford Motor Co., 315 F. Supp. 372, 379-80 (E.D. Mich. 1970), *aff'd*, 405 U.S. 562 (1972); Union Carbide Corp., 59 F.T.C. 614, 657 (1961) (reversing hearing examiner order that acquiring company divest plant built after the illegal acquisition on theory that order exceeded the return to status quo mandate of divestiture).

168. *See* 15 U.S.C. § 26; United States v. Coca-Cola Bottling Co., 575 F.2d 222, 229-30 (9th Cir. 1978); United States v. Phillips Petroleum Co., 367 F. Supp. 1226, 1261-62 (C.D. Cal. 1973), *aff'd mem.,* 418 U.S. 906 (1974); United States v. Reed Roller Bit Co., 274 F. Supp. 573, 590 (W.D. Okla. 1967), *modified,* 1969 Trade Cas. (CCH) ¶ 72,755 (W.D. Okla. 1969); United States v. Pabst Brewing Co., 183 F. Supp. 220, 221 (E.D. Wis. 1960).

169. *See Atlantic Richfield Co.*, 279 F. Supp. at 1068.

170. 130 F. Supp. 2d 1025 (W.D. Wis. 2000).

violates Section 7 of the Clayton Act.[171] In *FTC v. Libbey, Inc.*,[172] the D.C. District Court came to a similar conclusion when it considered both the defendant's original and amended divestiture proposals.[173] In both cases, however, the courts concluded that the proposed divestiture was insufficeint to cure the transactions potential anticompetitive effects.[174]

Traditionally, divestiture has been viewed as a government remedy. Until 1990, there was a split among the circuits as to whether divestiture was even available to private plaintiffs.[175] In *California v. American Stores Co.*,[176] however, the U.S. Supreme Court held that Section 16 of the Clayton Act authorizes private plaintiffs (including, in that case, the state of California) to seek divestiture decrees to remedy Section 7 violations.[177] By construing Section 16 to include a private divestiture remedy, the Court sought more closely to harmonize Section 16 with the

---

171. In *Franklin Electric,* the DOJ sought to exclude evidence relating to a third-party fix that was amended the day before the DOJ filed its complaint and effectuated after the complaint had been filed. The DOJ argued that the licensing and enabling agreements with the third party (1) had already been rejected by the DOJ as an inadequate remedy; (2) constituted evidence that was part of "settlement discussion"; and (3) should only be considered as part of the remedy once liability had been found. The court rejected the DOJ's arguments, and held that the third party licensing and enabling agreements could have an effect upon the issue of liability and whether the transaction substantially lessens competition.

172. 211 F. Supp. 2d 34 (D.D.C. 2002).

173. In *Libbey,* the FTC argued that the court should consider only the original merger agreement because the parties amended the agreement to "evade FTC and judicial review." *Id.* at 46. The court rejected the FTC's arguments and concluded that [the] "the parties to a merger agreement that is being challenged by the government can abandon that agreement and propose a new one in an effort to address the government's concerns. And when they do so under circumstances as occurred in this case, it becomes the new agreement that the Court must evaluate in deciding whether an injunction should be issued." *Id.*

174 *See Libbey, Inc.*, 211 F. Supp. 2d 34; *Franklin Elec. Co.*, 130 F. Supp. 2d 1025.

175. *Compare, e.g.*, International Tel. & Tel. Corp. v. General Tel. & Elec. Corp., 518 F.2d 913 (9th Cir. 1975) (§ 16 of Clayton Act does not contemplate private remedy of divestiture) *with* Cia. Petrolera Caribe, Inc. v. Arco Caribbean, Inc., 754 F.2d 404 (1st Cir. 1985) (divestiture a form of injunctive relief authorized by § 16).

176. 495 U.S. 271 (1990).

177. *Id.* at 278-85.

Clayton Act's "clear intent to encourage vigorous private litigation against anticompetitive mergers."[178]

Among other things, the *American Stores* decision opens the door to litigation by private parties (particularly state attorneys general) that are dissatisfied with a DOJ or FTC consent decree with respect to a particular merger. The *American Stores* Court noted, however, that "equitable defenses such as laches, or perhaps 'unclean hands,' may protect unconsummated transactions from belated attacks by private parties when it would not be too late for the Government to vindicate the public interest."[179] In addition, the Court cautioned that a private litigant must meet the requirements for antitrust injury and standing.[180]

3. *Rescission*

One alternative to divestiture is rescission. Unlike divestiture, where the acquiring company is required to sell the offending assets to a third party, rescission forces the seller to reacquire the assets at the price at which it sold them. For a number of reasons, rescission is rarely sought as a remedy.[181]

First, the seller already has expressed its preference to sell the assets and rescission will likely be followed by a subsequent sale to a third party. Because the federal antitrust enforcement agencies will likely

---

178. *Id.* at 284; *see also* SCFC ILC, Inc. v. Visa USA, Inc., 801 F. Supp. 517 (D. Utah 1992) (Visa properly pled claim for potential divestiture under § 7). *But see* Town of Norwood v. New England Power Co., 202 F.3d 408, 424 (1st Cir. 2000) (noting that divestiture may not be an appropriate remedy for private parties).

179. 495 U.S. at 296; *see also* Antoine L. Garabet, M.D., Inc. v. Autonomous Tech. Corp., 116 F. Supp. 2d 1159, 1171 (C.D. Cal. 2000) (barring plaintiffs' remedies under the doctrine of laches).

180. *Id.* *See supra,* notes 25-59, and accompanying text. In the context of objecting to a proposed consent decree, a private party may be able to circumvent the standing and antitrust injury requirements by becoming a "participant" under the Tunney Act. 15 U.S.C. § 16(f)(3) (a district court may hear the arguments of a "participant" if those arguments are "appropriate" and it "serves the public interest").

181. In affirming the district court's granting of an injunction rescinding a merger, Judge Posner noted that, at least with respect to the FTC, "[a]pparently a district court has never ordered rescission in a proceeding under section 13(b)." FTC v. Elders Grain, Inc., 868 F.2d 901, 907 (7th Cir. 1989). Rescission, as an interim remedy, is not appropriate when a less onerous alternative exists. *See* FTC v. Weyerhaeuser Co., 665 F.2d 1072, 1085-90 (D.C. Cir. 1981).

have to review the subsequent sale under Section 7 anyway, divestiture directly to a third party seems a more straightforward approach than rescission.

Second, while Section 7 is, by its terms, directed at buyers, rescission imposes the burden of the remedy upon the seller. Although several courts have stated in dicta that the equitable power to grant a preliminary injunction "carries with it the power to issue whatever ancillary equitable relief is necessary to the effective exercise of the granted power,"[182] the good faith conduct of the seller, including for example whether the seller conspired with the buyer to accelerate the closing date to prevent the government from enjoining the transaction, will greatly influence the decision as to whether to exercise that discretionary power.[183] In most cases, the court has acknowledged the availability of the rescission remedy but has granted divestiture as the relief.[184]

4. Damages

Section 4 of the Clayton Act authorizes recovery of treble damages for injuries to a plaintiff's business or property arising from the violation of antitrust laws, as well as recovery of reasonable attorneys' fees and costs.[185] In *Brunswick Corp. v. Pueblo Bowl-O-Mat, Inc.*,[186] the U.S. Supreme Court recognized that a private party may recover treble damages for injuries to its business or property arising from a violation of Section 7. Because a private plaintiff seeking treble damages must first establish "antitrust injury" and standing to bring the suit, however, the relationship of the plaintiff to the defendant in a Section 7 case (i.e., competitor, acquisition target, or customer) will dictate the allegations of harm necessary to establish such antitrust injury and standing. These hurdles combined with the fact that most merger challenges occur preconsummation result in damages rarely being obtained.[187]

---

182. *Elders Grain, Inc.*, 868 F.2d at 907; *see also* FTC v. H.N. Singer, Inc., 668 F.2d 1107, 1113 (9th Cir. 1982); FTC v. Southwest Sunsites, Inc., 665 F.2d 711, 718 (5th Cir. 1982).
183. *See Elders Grain, Inc.*, 868 F.2d at 907.
184. *See, e.g.*, United States v. Reed Roller Bit Co., 274 F. Supp. 573, 590 (W.D. Okla. 1967) (finding that divestiture would best restore competition to the relevant market); United States v. Rice Growers Ass'n, 1986-2 Trade Cas. (CCH) ¶ 67,288, at 61,467 (E.D. Cal. 1986).
185. *See* 15 U.S.C. § 15.
186. 429 U.S. 477 (1977).
187. *But see* Heatransfer Corp. v. Volkswagonwerk, A.G., 553 F.2d 964 (5th Cir. 1977) (affirming a $5 million damage award stemming from an

5. *Disgorgement*

Companies that consummate mergers in violation of the antitrust laws may be subject to disgorgement of profits gained as a result of their illegal actions. Depriving a violator of ill-gotten gains has long been accepted as a necessary element of antitrust remedies.[188] The FTC has the right to seek disgorgement pursuant to Section 13(b).[189] *In FTC v. Hearst Trust.*,[190] the FTC sought disgorgement of profits for a consummated merger for the first time, in addition to requiring divestiture. The FTC charged that the Hearst Corporation made an unlawful acquisition and illegally omitted in its pre-merger filing several high-level corporate documents prepared to evaluate the acquisition and its competitive effects. As a result, the FTC alleged that it was unable to fully analyze the competitive effects of the transaction prior to consummation and that the transaction resulted in an anticompetitive acquisition. In order to resolve these charges, Hearst agreed to divest the acquired business and pay $19 million as disgorgement of unlawful profits.[191]

The FTC has issued a policy statement that endorses the use, in certain circumstances, of monetary remedies including disgorgement and restitution in competition cases.[192] The FTC identified three factors that will be considered to determine whether to seek disgorgement or restitution: (1) when the underlying violation is clear, (2) when there is a reasonable basis for calculating the amount of remedial payment, and (3) when there is value added by the monetary remedy because other remedies are likely to fail to accomplish complete relief.[193]

---

illegal vertical acquisition that precluded competition in the downstream market).

188. *See, e.g.,* United States v. Grinnell Corp., 384 U.S. 563, 577 (1966); Schine Chain Theatres, Inc. v. United States, 334 U.S. 110, 128 (1948).
189 FTC v. Mylan Labs., Inc., 62 F. Supp. 2d 25, 37 (D.D.C. 1999).
190. No. 1:01CV00734 (D.D.C. Nov. 9, 2001).
191. Press Release, FTC, Hearst Corp. to Disgorge $19 Million and Divest Business to Facts and Comparisons to Settle FTC Complaint (Dec. 14, 2001), *at* www.ftc.gov/opa/2001/12/hearst.htm.
192. *See* Federal Trade Comm'n, Policy Statement on Monetary Equitable Remedies in Competition Cases, (July 25, 2003), *at* www.ftc.gov/os/2003/07/disgorementfrn.htm.
193. *Id*.

APPENDIX A

SHERMAN ACT

Section 1

Every contract, combination in the form of trust or otherwise, or conspiracy, in restraint of trade or commerce among the several States, or with foreign nations, is hereby declared to be illegal. Every person who shall make any contract or engage in any combination or conspiracy hereby declared to be illegal shall be deemed guilty of a felony and, on conviction thereof, shall be punished by fine not exceeding $10,000,000 if a corporation, or, if any other person, $350,000, or by imprisonment not exceeding three years, or by both said punishments, in the discretion of the court. [15 U.S.C. § 1]

Section 2

Every person who shall monopolize, or attempt to monopolize, or combine or conspire with any other person or persons, to monopolize any part of the trade or commerce among the several States, or with foreign nations, shall be deemed guilty of a felony, and, on conviction thereof, shall be punished by fine not exceeding $10,000,000 if a corporation, or, if any other person, $350,000, or by imprisonment not exceeding three years, or by both said punishments, in the discretion of the court. [15 U.S.C. § 2]

APPENDIX B

CLAYTON ACT

Section 7

No person engaged in commerce or in any activity affecting commerce shall acquire, directly or indirectly, the whole or any part of the stock or other share capital and no person subject to the jurisdiction of the Federal Trade Commission shall acquire the whole or any part of the assets of another person engaged also in commerce or in any activity affecting commerce, where in any line of commerce or in any activity affecting commerce in any section of the country, the effect of such acquisition may be substantially to lessen competition, or to tend to create a monopoly.

No person shall acquire, directly or indirectly, the whole or any part of the stock or other share capital and no person subject to the jurisdiction of the Federal Trade Commission shall acquire the whole or any part of the assets of one or more persons engaged in commerce or in any activity affecting commerce, where in any line of commerce or in any activity affecting commerce in any section of the country, the effect of such acquisition, of such stocks or assets, or of the use of such stock by the voting or granting of proxies or otherwise, may be substantially to lessen competition, or to tend to create a monopoly.

This section shall not apply to persons purchasing such stock solely for investment and not using the same by voting or otherwise to bring about, or in attempting to bring about, the substantial lessening of competition. Nor shall anything contained in this section prevent a corporation engaged in commerce or in any activity affecting commerce from causing the formation of subsidiary corporations for the actual carrying on of their immediate lawful business, or the natural and legitimate branches or extensions thereof, or from owning and holding all or a part of the stock of such subsidiary corporations, when the effect of such formation is not to substantially lessen competition.

Nor shall anything herein contained be construed to prohibit any common carrier subject to the laws to regulate commerce from aiding in the construction of branches or short lines so located as to become feeders to the main line of the company so aiding in such construction or from acquiring or owning all or any part of the stock of such branch lines, nor to prevent any such common carrier from acquiring and owning all or any part of the stock of a branch or short line constructed by an independent company where there is no substantial competition between the company owning the branch line so constructed and the company owning the main line acquiring the property or an interest therein, nor to prevent such common carrier from extending any of its lines through the medium of the acquisition of stock or otherwise of any other common carrier where there is no substantial competition between the company extending its lines and the company whose stock, property, or an interest therein is so acquired.

Nothing contained in this section shall be held to affect or impair any right heretofore legally acquired: *Provided,* That nothing in this section shall be held or construed to authorize or make lawful anything heretofore prohibited or made illegal by the antitrust laws, nor to exempt any person from the penal provisions thereof or the civil remedies therein provided.

Nothing contained in this section shall apply to transactions duly consummated pursuant to authority given by the Secretary of Transportation, Federal Power Commission, Surface Transportation Board, the Securities and Exchange Commission in the exercise of its jurisdiction under section 79j of this title, the United States Maritime Commission or the Secretary of Agriculture under any statutory provision vesting such power in such Commission, Board, or Secretary. [15 U.S.C. § 18].

Section 7A

(a) Filing

Except as exempted pursuant to subsection (c), no person shall acquire, directly or indirectly, any voting securities or assets of any other person, unless both persons (or in the case of a tender offer, the acquiring person) file notification pursuant to rules under subsection (d)(1) and the waiting period described in subsection (b)(1) has expired, if--

(1) the acquiring person, or the person whose voting securities or assets are being acquired, is engaged in commerce or in any activity affecting commerce; and

(2) as a result of such acquisition, the acquiring person would hold an aggregate total amount of the voting securities and assets of the acquired person--

(A) in excess of $200,000,000 (as adjusted and published for each fiscal year beginning after September 30, 2004, in the same manner as provided in section 8(a)(5) to reflect the percentage change in the gross national product for such fiscal year compared to the gross national product for the year ending September 30, 2003); or

(B) (i) in excess of $50,000,000 (as so adjusted and published) but not in excess of $200,000,000 (as so adjusted and published); and

(ii)(I) any voting securities or assets of a person engaged in manufacturing which has annual net sales or total assets of $10,000,000 (as so adjusted and published) or more are being acquired by any person which has total assets or annual net sales of $100,000,000 (as so adjusted and published) or more;

(II) any voting securities or assets of a person not engaged in manufacturing which has total assets of $10,000,000 (as so adjusted and published) or more are being acquired by any person which has total assets or annual net sales of $100,000,000 (as so adjusted and published) or more; or

(III) any voting securities or assets of a person with annual net sales or total assets of $100,000,000 (as so adjusted and published) or more are being acquired by any person with total assets or annual net sales of $10,000,000 (as so adjusted and published) or more. In the case of a tender offer, the person whose voting securities are sought to be acquired by a person required to file notification under this subsection shall file notification pursuant to rules under subsection (d).

(b) Waiting period; publication; voting securities

(1) The waiting period required under subsection (a) of this section shall -

(A) begin on the date of the receipt by the Federal Trade Commission and the Assistant Attorney General in charge of the Antitrust Division of the Department of Justice (hereinafter referred to in this section as the "Assistant Attorney General") of -

(i) the completed notification required under subsection (a) of this section, or

(ii) if such notification is not completed, the notification to the extent completed and a statement of the reasons for such noncompliance, from both persons, or, in the case of a tender offer, the acquiring person; and

(B) end on the thirtieth day after the date of such receipt (or in the case of a cash tender offer, the fifteenth day), or on such later date as may be set under subsection (e)(2) or (g)(2) of this section.

(2) The Federal Trade Commission and the Assistant Attorney General may, in individual cases, terminate the waiting period specified in paragraph (1) and allow any person to proceed with any acquisition subject to this section, and promptly shall cause to be published in the Federal Register a notice that neither intends to take any action within such period with respect to such acquisition.

(3) As used in this section -

(A) The term "voting securities" means any securities which at present or upon conversion entitle the owner or holder thereof to vote for the election of directors of the issuer or, with respect to unincorporated issuers, persons exercising similar functions.

(B) The amount or percentage of voting securities or assets of a person which are acquired or held by another person shall be determined by aggregating the amount or percentage of such voting securities or assets held or acquired by such other person and each affiliate thereof.

(c) Exempt transactions

The following classes of transactions are exempt from the requirements of this section –

(1) acquisitions of goods or realty transferred in the ordinary course of business;

(2) acquisitions of bonds, mortgages, deeds of trust, or other obligations which are not voting securities;

(3) acquisitions of voting securities of an issuer at least 50 per centum of the voting securities of which are owned by the acquiring person prior to such acquisition;

(4) transfers to or from a Federal agency or a State or political subdivision thereof;

(5) transactions specifically exempted from the antitrust laws by Federal statute;

(6) transactions specifically exempted from the antitrust laws by Federal statute if approved by a Federal agency, if copies of all information and documentary material filed with such agency are contemporaneously filed with the Federal Trade Commission and the Assistant Attorney General;

(7) transactions which require agency approval under section 1467a(e) of title 12, section 1828(c) of title 12, or section 1842 of title 12, except that a portion of a transaction is not exempt under this paragraph if such portion of the transaction (A) is subject to section 1843(k) of title 12; and (B) does not require agency approval under section 1842 of title 12;

(8) transactions which require agency approval under section 1843 of title 12 or section 1464 of title 12, except that a portion of a transaction is not exempt under this paragraph if such portion of the transaction (A) is subject to section 1843(k) of title 12; and (B) does not require agency approval under section 1843 of title 12, if copies of all information and documentary material filed with any such agency are contemporaneously filed with the Federal Trade Commission and the Assistant Attorney General at least 30 days prior to consummation of the proposed transaction;

(9) acquisitions, solely for the purpose of investment, of voting securities, if, as a result of such acquisition, the securities acquired or held do not exceed 10 per centum of the outstanding voting securities of the issuer;

(10) acquisitions of voting securities, if, as a result of such acquisition, the voting securities acquired do not increase, directly or indirectly, the acquiring person's per centum share of outstanding voting securities of the issuer;

(11) acquisitions, solely for the purpose of investment, by any bank, banking association, trust company, investment company, or insurance company, of (A) voting securities pursuant to a plan of reorganization or dissolution; or (B) assets in the ordinary course of its business; and

(12) such other acquisitions, transfers, or transactions, as may be exempted under subsection (d)(2)(B) of this section.

(d) Commission rules

The Federal Trade Commission, with the concurrence of the Assistant Attorney General and by rule in accordance with section 553 of title 5, consistent with the purposes of this section -

(1) shall require that the notification required under subsection (a) of this section be in such form and contain such documentary material and information relevant to a proposed acquisition as is necessary and appropriate to enable the Federal Trade Commission and the Assistant Attorney General to determine whether such acquisition may, if consummated, violate the antitrust laws; and (2) may -

(A) define the terms used in this section;

(B) exempt, from the requirements of this section, classes of persons, acquisitions, transfers, or transactions which are not likely to violate the antitrust laws; and

(C) prescribe such other rules as may be necessary and appropriate to carry out the

purposes of this section.

(e) Additional information; waiting period extensions

(1)(A) The Federal Trade Commission or the Assistant Attorney General may, prior to the expiration of the 30-day waiting period (or in the case of a cash tender offer, the 15-day waiting period) specified in subsection (b)(1) of this section, require the submission of additional information or documentary material relevant to the proposed acquisition, from a person required to file notification with respect to such acquisition under subsection (a) of this section prior to the expiration of the waiting period specified in subsection (b)(1) of this section, or from any officer, director, partner, agent, or employee of such person.

(B)(i) The Assistant Attorney General and the Federal Trade Commission shall each designate a senior official who does not have direct responsibility for the review of any enforcement recommendation under this section concerning the transaction at issue, to hear any petition filed by such person to determine--

(I) whether the request for additional information or documentary material is unreasonably cumulative, unduly burdensome, or duplicative; or

(II) whether the request for additional information or documentary material has been substantially complied with by the petitioning person.

(ii) Internal review procedures for petitions filed pursuant to clause (i) shall include reasonable deadlines for expedited review of such petitions, after reasonable negotiations with investigative staff, in order to avoid undue delay of the merger review process.

(iii) Not later than 90 days after the date of the enactment of this Act, the Assistant Attorney General and the Federal Trade Commission shall conduct an internal review and implement reforms of the merger review process in order to eliminate unnecessary burden, remove costly duplication, and eliminate undue delay, in order to achieve a more effective and more efficient merger review process.

(iv) Not later than 120 days after the date of enactment of this Act, the Assistant Attorney General and the Federal Trade Commission shall issue or amend their respective industry guidance, regulations, operating manuals and relevant policy documents, to the extent appropriate, to implement each reform in this subparagraph.

(v) Not later than 180 days after the date the of enactment of this Act, the Assistant Attorney General and the Federal Trade Commission shall each report to Congress—

(I) which reforms each agency has adopted under this subparagraph;

(II) which steps each has taken to implement such internal reforms; and

(III) the effects of such reforms.

(2) The Federal Trade Commission or the Assistant Attorney General, in its or his discretion, may extend the 30-day waiting period (or in the case of a cash tender offer, the 15-day waiting period) specified in subsection (b)(1) of this section for an additional period of not more than 30 days (or in the case of a cash tender offer, 10 days) after the date on which the Federal Trade Commission or the Assistant Attorney General, as the case may be, receives from any person to whom a request is made under paragraph (1), or in the case of tender offers, the acquiring person, (A) all the information and documentary material required to be submitted pursuant to such a request, or (B) if such request is not fully complied with, the information and documentary material submitted and a statement of the reasons for such noncompliance. Such additional period may be further extended only by the United States district court, upon an application by the Federal Trade Commission or the Assistant Attorney General pursuant to subsection (g)(2) of this section.

(f) Preliminary injunctions; hearings

If a proceeding is instituted or an action is filed by the Federal Trade Commission, alleging that a proposed acquisition violates section 18 of this title, or section 45 of this title, or an action is filed by the United States, alleging that a proposed acquisition violates such section 18 of this title, or section 1 or 2 of this title, and the Federal Trade Commission or the Assistant Attorney General (1) files a motion for a preliminary injunction against consummation of such acquisition pendente lite, and (2) certifies the United States district court for the judicial district within which the respondent resides or carries on business, or in which the action is brought, that it or he believes that the public interest requires relief pendente lite pursuant to this subsection, then upon the filing of such motion and certification, the chief judge of such district court shall immediately notify the chief judge of the United States court of appeals for the circuit in which such district court is located, who shall designate a United States district judge to whom such action shall be assigned for all purposes.

(g) Civil penalty; compliance; power of court

(1) Any person, or any officer, director, or partner thereof, who fails to comply with any provision of this section shall be liable to the United States for a civil penalty of not more than $10,000 for each day during which such person is in violation of this section. Such penalty may be recovered in a civil action brought by the United States. (NOTE: $10,000 changed to $11,000 pursuant to the Debt Collections Improvement Act of 1996, Pub. L. 104-134, Section 31001(s) (amending the Federal Civil Penalties Inflation Adjustment Act of 1990, 28 U.S.C. Section 2461 note), and Federal Trade Commission Rule 1.98, 16 C.F.R. Section 1.98, 61 Fed. Reg. 54548 (Oct. 21, 1996))

(2) If any person, or any officer, director, partner, agent, or employee thereof, fails substantially to comply with the notification requirement under subsection (a) of this section or any request for the submission of additional information or documentary material under subsection (e)(1) of this section within the waiting period specified in subsection (b)(1) of this section and as may be extended under subsection (e)(2) of this section, the United States district court -

(A) may order compliance;

(B) shall extend the waiting period specified in subsection (b)(1) of this section and as may have been extended under subsection (e)(2) of this section until there has been substantial compliance, except that, in the case of a tender offer, the court may not extend such waiting period on the basis of a failure, by the person whose stock is sought to be acquired, to comply substantially with such notification requirement or any such request; and

(C) may grant such other equitable relief as the court in its discretion determines necessary or appropriate, upon application of the Federal Trade Commission or the Assistant Attorney General.

(h) Disclosure exemption

Any information or documentary material filed with the Assistant Attorney General or the Federal Trade Commission pursuant to this section shall be exempt from disclosure under section 552 of title 5, and no such information or documentary material may be made public, except as may be relevant to any administrative or judicial action or proceeding. Nothing in this section is intended to prevent disclosure to either body of Congress or to any duly authorized committee or subcommittee of the Congress.

(i) Construction with other laws

(1) Any action taken by the Federal Trade Commission or the Assistant Attorney General or any failure of the Federal Trade Commission or the Assistant Attorney General to take any action under this section shall not bar any proceeding or any action with respect to such acquisition at any time under any other section of this Act or any other provision of law.

(2) Nothing contained in this section shall limit the authority of the Assistant Attorney General or the Federal Trade Commission to secure at any time from any person documentary material, oral testimony, or other information under the Antitrust Civil Process Act (15 U.S.C. 1311 et seq.), the Federal Trade Commission Act (15 U.S.C. 41 et seq.), or any other provision of law.

(j) Report to Congress; legislative recommendations

Beginning not later than January 1, 1978, the Federal Trade Commission, with the concurrence of the Assistant Attorney General, shall annually report to the Congress on the operation of this section. Such report shall include an assessment of the effects of this section, of the effects, purpose, and need for any rules promulgated pursuant thereto, and any recommendations for revisions of this section.

(k) If the end of any period of time provided in this section falls on a Saturday, Sunday, or legal public holiday (as defined in section 6103(a) of title 5 of the United States Code), then such period shall be extended to the end of the next day that is not a Saturday, Sunday, or legal public holiday.

[15 U.S.C. §18a.]

APPENDIX C

FEDERAL TRADE COMMISSION ACT

Section 5

(a) (1) Unfair methods of competition in or affecting commerce, and unfair or deceptive acts or practices in or affecting commerce, are hereby declared unlawful.

(2) The Commission is hereby empowered and directed to prevent persons, partnerships, or corporations, except banks, savings and loan institutions described in section 57a(f)(3) of this title, Federal credit unions described in section 57a(f)(4) of this title, common carriers subject to the Acts to regulate commerce, air carriers and foreign air carriers subject to part A of subtitle VII of title 49, and persons, partnerships, or corporations insofar as they are subject to the Packers and Stockyards Act, 1921, as amended [7 U.S.C. 181 et seq.], except as provided in section 406(b) of said Act [7 U.S.C. 227(b)], from using unfair methods of competition in or affecting commerce and unfair or deceptive acts or practices in or affecting commerce.

(3) This subsection shall not apply to unfair methods of competition involving commerce with foreign nations (other than import commerce) unless—

(A) such methods of competition have a direct, substantial, and reasonably foreseeable effect—

(i) on commerce which is not commerce with foreign nations, or on import commerce with foreign nations; or

(ii) on export commerce with foreign nations, of a person engaged in such commerce in the United States; and

(B) such effect gives rise to a claim under the provisions of this subsection, other than this paragraph.

If this subsection applies to such methods of competition only because of the operation of subparagraph (A)(ii), this subsection shall apply to such conduct only for injury to export business in the United States.

(b) Whenever the Commission shall have reason to believe that any such person, partnership, or corporation has been or is using any unfair method of competition or unfair or deceptive act or practice in or affecting commerce, and if it shall appear to the Commission that a proceeding by it in respect thereof would be to the interest of the public, it shall issue and serve upon such person, partnership, or corporation a complaint stating its charges in that respect and containing a notice of a hearing upon a day and at a place therein fixed at least thirty days after the service of said complaint. The person, partnership, or corporation so complained of shall have the right to appear at the place and time so fixed and show cause why an order should not be entered by the Commission requiring such person, partnership, or corporation to cease and desist from the violation of the law so charged in said complaint. Any person, partnership, or corporation may make application, and upon good cause shown may be allowed by the Commission to intervene and appear in said proceeding by counsel or in person. The testimony in any such proceeding shall be reduced to writing and filed in the office of the Commission. If upon such hearing the Commission shall be of the opinion that the method of competition or the act or practice in question is prohibited by this Act, it shall make a report in writing in which it shall state its findings as to the facts and shall issue and cause to be served on such person, partnership, or corporation an order requiring such person, partnership, or corporation to cease and desist from using such method of competition or such act or practice. Until the expiration of the time allowed for filing a petition for review, if no such petition has been duly filed within such time, or, if a petition for review has been filed within such time then until the record in the proceeding has been filed in a court of appeals of the United States, as hereinafter provided, the Commission may at any time, upon such notice and in such manner as it shall deem proper, modify or set aside, in whole or in part, any report or any order made or issued by it under this section. After the expiration of the time allowed for filing a petition for review, if no such petition has been duly filed within such time, the Commission may at any time, after notice and opportunity for hearing, reopen and alter, modify, or set aside, in whole or in part, any report or order made or issued by it under this section, whenever in the opinion of the Commission conditions of fact or of law have so changed as to require such action or if the public interest shall so require, except that (1) the said person, partnership, or corporation may, within sixty days after service upon him or it of said report or order entered after such a reopening, obtain a review thereof in the appropriate court of appeals of the United States, in the manner provided in subsection (c) of this section; and (2) in the case of an order, the Commission shall reopen any such order to consider whether such order (including any affirmative relief provision contained in such order) should be altered, modified, or set aside, in whole or in part, if the person, partnership, or corporation involved files a request with the Commission which makes a satisfactory showing that changed conditions of law or fact require such order to be altered, modified, or set aside, in whole or in part. The Commission shall determine whether to alter, modify, or set aside any order of the Commission in response to a request made by a person, partnership, or corporation under paragraph (2) not later than 120 days after the date of the filing of such request.

(c) Any person, partnership, or corporation required by an order of the Commission to cease and desist from using any method of competition or act or practice may obtain a review of such order in the court of appeals of the United States, within any circuit where the method of competition or the act or practice in question was used or where such person, partnership, or corporation resides or carries on business, by filing in the court, within sixty days from the date of the service of such order, a written petition praying that the order of the Commission be set aside. A copy of such petition shall be forthwith transmitted by the clerk of the court to the Commission, and thereupon the Commission shall file in the court the record in the proceeding, as provided in section 2112 of title 28. Upon such filing of the petition the court shall have jurisdiction of the proceeding and of the question determined therein concurrently with the Commission until the filing of the record and shall have power to make and enter a decree affirming, modifying, or setting aside the order of the Commission, and enforcing the same to the extent that such order is affirmed and to issue such writs as are ancillary to its jurisdiction or are necessary in its judgment to prevent injury to the public or to competitors pendente lite. The findings of the Commission as to the facts, if supported by evidence, shall be conclusive. To the extent that the order of the Commission is affirmed, the court shall thereupon issue its own order commanding obedience to the terms of such order of the Commission. If either party shall apply to the court for leave to adduce additional evidence, and shall show to the satisfaction of the court that such additional evidence is material and that there were reasonable grounds for the failure to adduce such evidence in the proceeding before the Commission, the court may order such additional evidence to be taken before the Commission and to be adduced upon the hearing in such manner and upon such terms and conditions as to the court may seem proper. The Commission may modify its findings as to the facts, or make new findings, by reason of the additional evidence so taken, and it shall file such modified or new findings, which, if supported by evidence, shall be conclusive, and its recommendation, if any, for the modification or setting aside of its original order, with the return of such additional evidence. The judgment and decree of the court shall be final, except that the same shall be subject to review by the Supreme Court upon certiorari, as provided in section 1254 of title 28.

(d) Upon the filing of the record with it the jurisdiction of the court of appeals of the United States to affirm, enforce, modify, or set aside orders of the Commission shall be exclusive.

(e) No order of the Commission or judgment of court to enforce the same shall in anywise relieve or absolve any person, partnership, or corporation from any liability under the Antitrust Acts.

(f) Complaints, orders, and other processes of the Commission under this section may be served by anyone duly authorized by the Commission, either (a) by delivering a copy thereof to the person to be served, or to a member of the partnership to be served, or the president, secretary, or other executive officer or a director of the corporation to be served; or (b) by leaving a copy thereof at the residence or the principal office or place of business of such person, partnership, or corporation; or (c) by mailing a copy thereof by registered mail or by certified mail addressed to such person, partnership, or corporation at his or its residence or principal office or place of business. The verified return by the person so serving said complaint, order, or other process setting forth the manner of said service shall be proof of the same, and the return post office receipt for said complaint, order, or other process mailed by registered mail or by certified mail as aforesaid shall be proof of the service of the same.

(g) An order of the Commission to cease and desist shall become final—

(1) Upon the expiration of the time allowed for filing a petition for review, if no such petition has been duly filed within such time; but the Commission may thereafter modify or set aside its order to the extent provided in the last sentence of subsection (b).

(2) Except as to any order provision subject to paragraph (4), upon the sixtieth day after such order is served, if a petition for review has been duly filed; except that any such order may be stayed, in whole or in part and subject to such conditions as may be appropriate, by—

(A) the Commission;

(B) an appropriate court of appeals of the United States, if (i) a petition for review of such order is pending in such court, and (ii) an application for such a stay was previously submitted to the Commission and the Commission, within the 30-day period beginning on the date the application was received by the Commission, either denied the application or did not grant or deny the application; or

(C) the Supreme Court, if an applicable petition for certiorari is pending.

(3) For purposes of subsection (m)(1)(B) of this section and of section 57b(a)(2) of this title, if a petition for review of the order of the Commission has been filed—

(A) upon the expiration of the time allowed for filing a petition for certiorari, if the order of the Commission has been affirmed or the petition for review has been dismissed by the court of appeals and no petition for certiorari has been duly filed;

(B) upon the denial of a petition for certiorari, if the order of the Commission has been affirmed or the petition for review has been dismissed by the court of appeals; or

(C) upon the expiration of 30 days from the date of issuance of a mandate of the Supreme Court directing that the order of the Commission be affirmed or the petition for review be dismissed.

(4) In the case of an order provision requir ing a person, partnership, or corporation to divest itself of stock, other share capital, or assets, if a petition for review of such order of the Commission has been filed—

(A) upon the expiration of the time allowed for filing a petition for certiorari, if the order of the Commission has been affirmed or the petition for review has been dismissed by the court of appeals and no petition for certiorari has been duly filed;

(B) upon the denial of a petition for certiorari, if the order of the Commission has been affirmed or the petition for review has been dismissed by the court of appeals; or

(C) upon the expiration of 30 days from the date of issuance of a mandate of the Supreme Court directing that the order of the Commission be affirmed or the petition for review be dismissed.

(h) If the Supreme Court directs that the order of the Commission be modified or set aside, the order of the Commission rendered in accordance with the mandate of the Supreme Court shall become final upon the expiration of thirty days from the time it was rendered, unless within such thirty days either party has instituted proceedings to have such order corrected to accord with the mandate, in which event the order of the Commission shall become final when so corrected.

(i) If the order of the Commission is modified or set aside by the court of appeals, and if (1) the time allowed for filing a petition for certiorari has expired and no such petition has been duly filed, or (2) the petition for certiorari has been denied, or (3) the decision of the court has been affirmed by the Supreme Court, then the order of the Commission rendered in accordance with the mandate of the court of appeals shall become final on the expiration of thirty days from the time such order of the Commission was rendered, unless within such thirty days either party has instituted proceedings to have such order corrected so that it will accord with the mandate, in which event the order of the Commission shall become final when so corrected.

(j) If the Supreme Court orders a rehearing; or if the case is remanded by the court of appeals to the Commission for a rehearing, and if (1) the time allowed for filing a petition for certiorari has expired, and no such petition has been duly filed, or (2) the petition for certiorari has been denied, or (3) the decision of the court has been affirmed by the Supreme Court, then the order of the Commission rendered upon such rehearing shall become final in the same manner as though no prior order of the Commission had been rendered.

(k) As used in this section the term "mandate," in case a mandate has been recalled prior to the expiration of thirty days from the date of issuance thereof, means the final mandate.

(l) Any person, partnership, or corporation who violates an order of the Commission after it has become final, and while such order is in effect, shall forfeit and pay to the United States a civil penalty of not more than $10,000 for each violation, which shall accrue to the United States and may be recovered in a civil action brought by the Attorney General of the United States. Each separate violation of such an order shall be a separate offense, except that in the case of a violation through continuing failure to obey or neglect to obey a final order of the Commission, each day of continuance of such failure or neglect shall be deemed a separate offense. In such actions, the United States district courts are empowered to grant mandatory injunctions and such other and further equitable relief as they deem appropriate in the enforcement of such final orders of the Commission.

(m) (1) (A) The Commission may commence a civil action to recover a civil penalty in a district court of the United States against any person, partnership, or corporation which violates any rule under this Act respecting unfair or deceptive acts or practices (other than an interpretive rule or a rule violation of which the Commission has provided is not an unfair or deceptive act or practice in violation of subsection (a)(1)) of this section with actual knowledge or knowledge fairly implied on the basis of objective circumstances that such act is unfair or deceptive and is prohibited by such rule. In such action, such person, partnership, or corporation shall be liable for a civil penalty of not more than $10,000 for each violation.

(B) If the Commission determines in a proceeding under subsection (b) of this section that any act or practice is unfair or deceptive, and issues a final cease and desist order, other than a consent order, with respect to such act or practice, then the Commission may commence a civil action to obtain a civil penalty in a district court of the United States against any person, partnership, or corporation which engages in such act or practice—

(1) after such cease and desist order becomes final (whether or not such person, partnership, or corporation was subject to such cease and desist order), and

(2) with actual knowledge that such act or practice is unfair or deceptive and is unlawful under subsection (a)(1) of this section.

In such action, such person, partnership, or corporation shall be liable for a civil penalty of not more than $10,000 for each violation.

(C) In the case of a violation through continuing failure to comply with a rule or with section 5(a)(1) of this section, each day of continuance of such failure shall be treated as a separate violation, for purposes of subparagraphs (A) and (B). In determining the amount of such a civil penalty, the court shall take into account the degree of culpability, any history of prior such conduct, ability to pay, effect on ability to continue to do business, and such other matters as justice may require.

(2) If the cease and desist order establishing that the act or practice is unfair or deceptive was not issued against the defendant in a civil penalty action under paragraph (1)(B) the issues of fact in such action against such defendant shall be tried de novo. Upon request of any party to such an action against such defendant, the court shall also review the determination of law made by the Commission in the proceeding under

subsection (b) of this section that the act or practice which was the subject of such proceeding constituted an unfair or deceptive act or practice in violation of subsection (a) of this section.

(3) The Commission may compromise or settle any action for a civil penalty if such compromise or settlement is accompanied by a public statement of its reasons and is approved by the court.

(n) The Commission shall have no authority under this section or section 57a of this title to declare unlawful an act or practice on the grounds that such act or practice is unfair unless the act or practice causes or is likely to cause substantial injury to consumers which is not reasonably avoidable by consumers themselves and not outweighed by countervailing benefits to consumers or to competition. In determining whether an act or practice is unfair, the Commission may consider established public policies as evidence to be considered with all other evidence. Such public policy considerations may not serve as a primary basis for such determination. [15 U.S.C. § 45]

APPENDIX D

NATIONAL COOPERATIVE RESEARCH AND PRODUCTION ACT OF 1993

Section 1

(a) For purposes of this chapter:

(1) The term "antitrust laws" has the meaning given it in subsection (a) of section 12 of this title, except that such term includes [section 5 of the FTC Act] to the extent that such [section 5 of the FTC Act] applies to unfair methods of competition.

(2) The term "Attorney General" means the Attorney General of the United States.

(3) The term "Commission" means the Federal Trade Commission.

(4) The term "person" has the meaning given it in subsection (a) of section 12 of this title.

(5) The term "State" has the meaning given it in section 15g(2) of this title.

(6) The term "joint venture" means any group of activities, including attempting to make, making, or performing a contract, by two or more persons for the purpose of—

(A) theoretical analysis, experimentation, or systematic study of phenomena or observable facts,

(B) the development or testing of basic engineering techniques,

(C) the extension of investigative findings or theory of a scientific or technical nature into practical application for experimental and demonstration purposes, including the experimental production and testing of models, prototypes, equipment, materials, and processes,

(D) the production of a product, process, or service,

(E) the testing in connection with the production of a product, process, or service by such venture,

(F) the collection, exchange, and analysis of research or production information, or

(G) any combination of the purposes specified in subparagraphs (A), (B), (C), (D), (E), and (F), and may include the establishment and operation of facilities for the conducting of such venture, the conducting of such venture on a protected and proprietary basis, and the prosecuting of applications for patents and the granting of licenses for the results of such venture, but does not include any activity specified in subsection (b) of this section.

(b) The term "joint venture" excludes the following activities involving two or more persons:

(1) exchanging information among competitors relating to costs, sales, profitability, prices, marketing, or distribution of any product, process, or service if such information is not reasonably required to carry out the purpose of such venture,

(2) entering into any agreement or engaging in any other conduct restricting, requiring, or otherwise involving the marketing, distribution, or provision by any person who is a party to such venture of any product, process, or service, other than—

(A) the distribution among the parties to such venture, in accordance with such venture, of a product, process, or service produced by such venture,

(B) the marketing of proprietary information, such as patents and trade secrets, developed through such venture formed under a written agreement entered into before June 10, 1993, or

(C) the licensing, conveying, or transferring of intellectual property, such as patents and trade secrets, developed through such venture formed under a written agreement entered into on or after June 10, 1993,

(3) entering into any agreement or engaging in any other conduct—

(A) to restrict or require the sale, licensing, or sharing of inventions, developments, products, processes or services not developed through, or produced by, such venture, or

(B) to restrict or require participation by any person who is a party to such venture in other research and development activities, that is not reasonably required to prevent misappropriation of proprietary information contributed by any person who is a party to such venture or of the results of such venture,

(4) entering into any agreement or engaging in any other conduct allocating a market with a competitor,

(5) exchanging information among competitors relating to production (other than production by such venture) of a product, process, or service if such information is not reasonably required to carry out the purpose of such venture,

(6) entering into any agreement or engaging in any other conduct restricting, requiring, or otherwise involving the production (other than the production by such venture) of a product, process, or service,

(7) using existing facilities for the production of a product, process, or service by such venture unless such use involves the production of a new product or technology, and

(8) except as provided in paragraphs (2), (3), and (6), entering into any agreement or engaging in any other conduct to restrict or require participation by any person who is a party to such venture, in any unilateral or joint activity that is not reasonably required to carry out the purpose of such venture. [15 U.S.C. § 4301].

Section 2

In any action under the antitrust laws, or under any State law similar to the antitrust laws, the conduct of any person in making or performing a contract to carry out a joint venture shall not be deemed illegal per se; such conduct shall be judged on the basis of its reasonableness, taking into account all relevant factors affecting competition, including, but not limited to, effects on competition in properly defined, relevant research, development, product, process, and service markets. For the purpose of determining a properly defined, relevant market, worldwide capacity shall be considered to the extent that it may be appropriate in the circumstances. [15 U.S.C. § 4302].

Section 3

(a) Notwithstanding section 15 of this title and in lieu of the relief specified in such section, any person who is entitled to recovery on a claim under such section shall recover the actual damages sustained by such person, interest calculated at the rate specified in section 1961 of title 28 on such actual damages as specified in subsection (d) of this section, and the cost of suit attributable to such claim, including a reasonable attorney's fee pursuant to [section 4 of this Act] if such claim—

(1) results from conduct that is within the scope of a notification that has been filed under [section 5(a) of this Act] for a joint venture, and

(2) is filed after such notification becomes effective pursuant to [section 5(c) of this Act].

(b) Notwithstanding section 15c of this title, and in lieu of the relief specified in such section, any State that is entitled to monetary relief on a claim under such section shall recover the total damage sustained as described in subsection (a)(1) of such section, interest calculated at the rate specified in section 1961 of title 28 on such total damage as specified in subsection (d) of this section, and the cost of suit attributable to such claim, including a reasonable attorney's fee pursuant to section 15c of this title if such claim—

(1) results from conduct that is within the scope of a notification that has been filed under [section 5(a) of this Act] for a joint venture, and

(2) is filed after such notification becomes effective pursuant to [section 5(c) of this Act].

(c) Notwithstanding any provision of any State law providing damages for conduct similar to that forbidden by the antitrust laws, any person who is entitled to recovery on a claim under such provision shall not recover in excess of the actual damages sustained by such person, interest calculated at the rate specified in section 1961 of title 28 on such actual damages as specified in subsection (d) of this section, and the cost of suit attributable to such claim, including a reasonable attorney's fee pursuant to [section 4 of this Act] if such claim—

(1) results from conduct that is within the scope of a notification that has been filed under [section 5(a) of this Act] for a joint venture, and

(2) is filed after notification has become effective pursuant to [section 5(c) of this Act].

(d) Interest shall be awarded on the damages involved for the period beginning on the earliest date for which injury can be established and ending on the date of judgment, unless the court finds that the award of all or part of such interest is unjust in the circumstances.

(e) This section shall be applicable only if the challenged conduct of a person defending against a claim is not in violation of any decree or order, entered or issued after October 11, 1984, in any case or proceeding under the antitrust laws or any State law similar to the antitrust laws challenging such conduct as part of a joint venture. [15 U.S.C. § 4303].

Section 4

(a) Notwithstanding sections 15 and 26 of this title, in any claim under the antitrust laws, or any State law similar to the antitrust laws, based on the conducting of a joint venture, the court shall, at the conclusion of the action—

(1) award to a substantially prevailing claimant the cost of suit attributable to such claim, including a reasonable attorney's fee, or

(2) award to a substantially prevailing party defending against any such claim the cost of suit attributable to such claim, including a reasonable attorney's fee, if the claim, or the claimant's conduct during the litigation of the claim, was frivolous, unreasonable, without foundation, or in bad faith.

(b) The award made under subsection (a) of this section may be offset in whole or in part by an award in favor of any other party for any part of the cost of suit, including a reasonable attorney's fee, attributable to conduct during the litigation by any prevailing party that the court finds to be frivolous, unreasonable, without foundation, or in bad faith. [15 U.S.C. § 4304].

Section 5

(a) Any party to a joint venture, acting on such venture's behalf, may, not later than 90 days after entering into a written agreement to form such venture or not later than 90 days after October 11, 1984, whichever is later, file simultaneously with the Attorney General and the Commission a written notification disclosing—

(1) the identities of the parties to such venture,

(2) the nature and objectives of such venture.

(3) if a purpose of such venture is the production of a product, process, or service, as referred to in [section 1(a)(6)(D) of this Act], the identity and nationality of any person who is a party to such venture, or who controls any party to such venture whether separately or with one or more persons acting as a group for the purpose of controlling such party.

Any party to such venture, acting on such venture's behalf, may file additional disclosure notifications pursuant to this section as are appropriate to extend the protections of [section 3 of this Act]. In order to maintain the protections of [section 3 of this Act], such venture shall, not later than 90 days after a change in its membership, file simultaneously with the Attorney General and the Commission a written notification disclosing such change, and

(b) Except as provided in subsection (e) of this section, not later than 30 days after receiving a notification filed under subsection (a) of this section, the Attorney General or the Commission shall publish in the Federal Register a notice with respect to such venture that identifies the parties to such venture and that describes in general terms the area of planned activity of such venture. Prior to its publication, the contents of such notice shall be made available to the parties to such venture.

(c) If with respect to a notification filed under subsection (a) of this section, notice is published in the Federal Register, then such notification shall operate to convey the protections of [section 3 of this Act] as of the earlier of—

(1) the date of publication of notice under subsection (b) of this section, or

(2) if such notice is not so published within the time required by subsection (b) of this section, after the expiration of the 30-day period beginning on the date the Attorney General or the Commission receives the applicable information described in subsection (a) of this section.

(d) Except with respect to the information published pursuant to subsection (b) of this section—

(1) all information and documentary material submitted as part of a notification filed pursuant to this section, and

(2) all other information obtained by the Attorney General or the Commission in the course of any investigation, administrative proceeding, or case, with respect to a potential violation of the antitrust laws by the joint venture with respect to which such notification was filed, shall be exempt from disclosure under section 552 of title 5, and shall not be made publicly available by any agency of the United States to which such section applies except in a judicial or administrative proceeding in which such information and material is subject to any protective order.

(e) Any person who files a notification pursuant to this section may withdraw such notification before notice of the joint venture involved is published under subsection (b) of this section. Any notification so withdrawn shall not be subject to subsection (b) of this section and shall not confer the protections of [section 3 of this Act] on any person with respect to whom such notification was filed.

(f) Any action taken or not taken by the Attorney General or the Commission with respect to notifications filed pursuant to this section shall not be subject to judicial review.

(g) (1) Except as provided in paragraph (2), for the sole purpose of establishing that a person is entitled to the protections of [section 3 of this Act], the fact of disclosure of conduct under subsection (a) of this section and the fact of publication of a notice under subsection (b) of this section shall be admissible into evidence in any judicial or administrative proceeding.

(2) No action by the Attorney General or the Commission taken pursuant to this section shall be admissible into evidence in any such proceeding for the purpose of supporting or answering any claim under the antitrust laws or under any State law similar to the antitrust laws. [15 U.S.C. § 4305].

Section 6

Notwithstanding [sections 3 and 5 of this Act], the protections of [section 3 of this Act] shall not apply with respect to a joint venture's production of a product, process, or service, as referred to in [section 1(a)(6)(D) of this Act] unless—

(1) the principal facilities for such production are located in the United States or its territories, and

(2) each person who controls any party to such venture (including such party itself) is a United States person, or a foreign person from a country whose law accords antitrust treatment no less favorable to United States persons than to such country's domestic persons with respect to participation in joint ventures for production. [15 U.S.C. § 4306].

APPENDIX E

NEWSPAPER PRESERVATION ACT

Section 1

In the public interest of maintaining a newspaper press editorially and reportorially independent and competitive in all parts of the United States, it is hereby declared to be the policy of the United States to preserve the publication of newspapers in any city, community, or metropolitan area where a joint operating arrangement has been heretofore entered into because of economic distress or is hereafter effected in accordance with the provisions of this chapter. [15 U.S.C. § 1801].

Section 2

As used in this Act—

(1) The term "antitrust law" means the Federal Trade Commission Act [15 U.S.C. 41 et seq.] and each statute defined by section 4 thereof [15 U.S.C. 44] as "Antitrust Acts" and all amendments to such Act and such statutes and any other Acts in pari materia.

(2) The term "joint newspaper operating arrangement" means any contract, agreement, joint venture (whether or not incorporated), or other arrangement entered into by two or more newspaper owners for the publication of two or more newspaper publications, pursuant to which joint or common production facilities are established or operated and joint or unified action is taken or agreed to be taken with respect to any one or more of the following: printing; time, method, and field of publication; allocation of production facilities; distribution; advertising solicitation; circulation solicitation; business department; establishment of advertising rates; establishment of circulation rates and revenue distribution: *Provided,* That there is no merger, combination, or amalgamation of editorial or reportorial staffs, and that editorial policies be independently determined.

(3) The term "newspaper owner" means any person who owns or controls directly, or indirectly through separate or subsidiary corporations, one or more newspaper publications.

(4) The term "newspaper publication" means a publication produced on newsprint paper which is published in one or more issues weekly (including as one publication any daily newspaper and any Sunday newspaper published by the same owner in the same city, community, or metropolitan area), and in which a substantial portion of the content is devoted to the dissemination of news and editorial opinion.

(5) The term "failing newspaper" means a newspaper publication which, regardless of its ownership or affiliations, is in probable danger of financial failure.

(6) The term "person" means any individual, and any partnership, corporation, association, or other legal entity existing under or authorized by the law of the United States, any State or possession of the United States, the District of Columbia, the Commonwealth of Puerto Rico, or any foreign country. [15 U.S.C. § 1802].

Section 3

(a) It shall not be unlawful under any antitrust law for any person to perform, enforce, renew, or amend any joint newspaper operating arrangement entered into prior to July 24, 1970, if at the time at which such arrangement was first entered into, regardless of ownership or affiliations, not more than one of the newspaper publications involved in the performance of such arrangement was likely to remain or become a financially sound publication: *Provided,* That the terms of a renewal or amendment to a joint operating arrangement must be filed with the Department of Justice and that the amendment does not add a newspaper publication or newspaper publications to such arrangement.

(b) It shall be unlawful for any person to enter into, perform, or enforce a joint operating arrangement, not already in effect, except with the prior written consent of the Attorney General of the United States. Prior to granting such approval, the Attorney General shall determine that not more than one of the newspaper publications involved in the arrangement is a publication other than a failing newspaper, and that approval of such arrangement would effectuate the policy and purpose of this [Act].

(c) Nothing contained in this Act shall be construed to exempt from any antitrust law any predatory pricing, any predatory practice, or any other conduct in the otherwise lawful operations of a joint newspaper operating arrangement which would be unlawful under any antitrust law if engaged in by a single entity. Except as provided in this Act, no joint newspaper operating arrangement or any party thereto shall be exempt from any antitrust law. [15 U.S.C. § 1803]

Section 4

(a) Notwithstanding any final judgment rendered in any action brought by the United States under which a joint operating arrangement has been held to be unlawful under any antitrust law, any party to such final judgment may reinstitute said joint newspaper operating arrangement to the extent permissible under [section 3(a) of this Act].

(b) The provisions of [section 3(a) of this Act] shall apply to the determination of any civil or criminal action pending in any district court of the United States on July 24, 1970, in which it is alleged that any such joint operating agreement is unlawful under any antitrust law. [15 U.S.C. § 1804]

APPENDIX F

EXPORT TRADING COMPANY ACT

Section 301

To promote and encourage export trade, the Secretary [of Commerce] may issue certificates of review and advise and assist any person with respect to applying for certificates of review. [15 U.S.C. § 4011]

Section 302

(a) To apply for a certificate of review, a person shall submit to the Secretary a written application which—

(1) specifies conduct limited to export trade, and

(2) is in a form and contains any information, including information pertaining to the overall market in which the applicant operates, required by rule or regulation promulgated under [section 310 of this Act].

(b) (1) Within ten days after an application submitted under subsection (a) of this section is received by the Secretary, the Secretary shall publish in the Federal Register a notice that announces that an application for a certificate of review has been submitted, identifies each person submitting the application, and describes the conduct for which the application is submitted.

(2) Not later than seven days after an application submitted under subsection (a) is received by the Secretary, the Secretary shall transmit to the Attorney General—

(A) a copy of the application,

(B) any information submitted to the Secretary in connection with the application, and

(C) any other relevant information (as determined by the Secretary) in the possession of the Secretary, including information regarding the market share of the applicant in the line of commerce to which the conduct specified in the application relates. [15 U.S.C. § 4012]

Section 303

(a) A certificate of review shall be issued to any applicant that establishes that its specified export trade, export trade activities, and methods of operation will—

(1) result in neither a substantial lessening of competition or restraint of trade within the United States nor a substantial restraint of the export trade of any competitor of the applicant,

(2) not unreasonably enhance, stabilize, or depress prices within the United States of the goods, wares, merchandise, or services of the class exported by the applicant,

(3) not constitute unfair methods of competition against competitors engaged in the export of goods, wares, merchandise, or services of the class exported by the applicant, and

(4) not include any act that may reasonably be expected to result in the sale for consumption or resale within the United States of the goods, wares, merchandise, or services exported by the applicant.

(b) Within ninety days after the Secretary receives an application for a certificate of review, the Secretary shall determine whether the applicant's export trade, export trade activities, and methods of operation meet the standards of subsection (a) of this section. If the Secretary, with the concurrence of the Attorney General, determines that such standards are met, the Secretary shall issue to the applicant a certificate of review. The certificate of review shall specify—

(1) the export trade, export trade activities, and methods of operation to which the certificate applies,

(2) the person to whom the certificate of review is issued, and

(3) any terms and conditions the Secretary or the Attorney General deems necessary to assure compliance with the standards of subsection (a) of this section.

(c) If the applicant indicates a special need for prompt disposition, the Secretary and the Attorney General may expedite action on the application, except that no certificate of review may be issued within thirty days of publication of notice in the Federal Register under [section 302(b)(1) of this Act].

(d) (1) If the Secretary denies in whole or in part an application for a certificate, he shall notify the applicant of his determination and the reasons for it.

(2) An applicant may, within thirty days of receipt of notification that the application has been denied in whole or in part, request the

Secretary to reconsider the determination. The Secretary, with the concurrence of the Attorney General, shall notify the applicant of the determination upon reconsideration within thirty days of receipt of the request.

(e) If the Secretary denies an application for the issuance of a certificate of review and thereafter receives from the applicant a request for the return of documents submitted by the applicant in connection with the application for the certificate, the Secretary and the Attorney General shall return to the applicant, not later than thirty days after receipt of the request, the documents and all copies of the documents available to the Secretary and the Attorney General, except to the extent that the information contained in a document has been made available to the public.

(f) A certificate shall be void ab initio with respect to any export trade, export trade activities, or methods of operation for which a certificate was procured by fraud. [15 U.S.C. § 4013]

Section 304

(a) (1) Any applicant who receives a certificate of review—

(A) shall promptly report to the Secretary any change relevant to the matters specified in the certificate, and

(B) may submit to the Secretary an application to amend the certificate to reflect the effect of the change on the conduct specified in the certificate.

(2) An application for an amendment to a certificate of review shall be treated as an application for the issuance of a certificate. The effective date of an amendment shall be the date on which the application for the amendment is submitted to the Secretary.

(b) (1) If the Secretary or the Attorney General has reason to believe that the export trade, export trade activities, or methods of operation of a person holding a certificate of review no longer comply with the standards of [section 303(a) of this Act], the Secretary shall request such information from such person as the Secretary or the Attorney General deems necessary to resolve the matter of compliance. Failure to comply with such request shall be grounds for revocation of the certificate under paragraph (2).

(2) If the Secretary or the Attorney General determines that the export trade, export trade activities, or methods of operation of a person holding a certificate no longer comply with the standards of [section 303(a) of this Act], or that such person has failed to comply with a request made under paragraph (1), the Secretary shall give written notice of the determination to such person. The notice shall include a statement of the circumstances underlying, and the reasons in support of, the determination. In the 60-day period beginning 30 days after the notice is given, the Secretary shall revoke the certificate or modify it as the Secretary or the Attorney General deems necessary to cause the certificate to apply only to the export trade, export trade activities, or methods of operation which are in compliance with the standards of [section 303(a) of this Act].

(3) For purposes of carrying out this subsection, the Attorney General, and the Assistant Attorney General in charge of the antitrust division of the Department of Justice, may conduct investigations in the same manner as the Attorney General and the Assistant Attorney General conduct investigations under section 1312 of this title, except that no civil investigative demand may be issued to a person to whom a certificate of review is issued if such person is the target of such investigation. [15 U.S.C. § 4014]

Section 305

(a) If the Secretary grants or denies, in whole or in part, an application for a certificate of review or for an amendment to a certificate, or revokes or modifies a certificate pursuant to [section 304(b) of this Act], any person aggrieved by such determination may, within 30 days of the determination, bring an action in any appropriate district court of the United States to set aside the determination on the ground that such determination is erroneous.

(b) Except as provided in subsection (a) of this section, no action by the Secretary or the Attorney General pursuant to this title shall be subject to judicial review.

(c) If the Secretary denies, in whole or in part, an application for a certificate of review or for an amendment to a certificate, or revokes or amends a certificate, neither the negative determination nor the statement of reasons therefore shall be admissible in evidence, in any administrative or judicial proceeding, in support of any claim under the antitrust laws. [15 U.S.C. § 4015]

Section 306

(a) Except as provided in subsection (b) of this section, no criminal or civil action may be brought under the antitrust laws against a person to whom a certificate of review is issued which is based on conduct which is specified in, and complies with the terms of, a certificate issued under [section 303 of this Act] which certificate was in effect when the conduct occurred.

(b) (1) Any person who has been injured as a result of conduct engaged in under a certificate of review may bring a civil action for injunctive relief, actual damages, the loss of interest on actual damages, and the cost of suit (including a reasonable attorney's fee) for the failure to comply with the standards of [section 303(a) of this Act]. Any action commenced under this subchapter shall proceed as if it were an action commenced under section 15 or section 26 of this title, except that the standards of [section 303(a) of this Act] and the remedies provided in this paragraph shall be the exclusive standards and remedies applicable to such action.

(2) Any action brought under paragraph (1) shall be filed within two years of the date the plaintiff has notice of the failure to comply with the standards of [section 303(a) of this Act] but in any event within four years after the cause of action accrues.

(3) In any action brought under paragraph (1), there shall be a presumption that conduct which is specified in and complies with a certificate of review does comply with the standards of [section 303(a) of this Act].

(4) In any action brought under paragraph (1), if the court finds that the conduct does comply with the standards of [section 303(a) of this Act], the court shall award to the person against whom the claim is brought the cost of suit attributable to defending against the claim (including a reasonable attorney's fee).

(5) The Attorney General may file suit pursuant to section 25 of this title to enjoin conduct threatening clear and irreparable harm to the national interest. [15 U.S.C. § 4016]

Section 307

(a) To promote greater certainty regarding the application of the antitrust laws to export trade, the Secretary, with the concurrence of the Attorney General, may issue guidelines—

(1) describing specific types of conduct with respect to which the Secretary, with the concurrence of the Attorney General, has made or would make, determinations under [sections 303 and 304 of this Act], and

(2) summarizing the factual and legal bases in support of the determinations.

(b) Section 553 of title 5, United States Code, shall not apply to the issuance of guidelines under subsection (a). [15 U.S.C. § 4017]

Section 308

Every person to whom a certificate of review is issued shall submit to the Secretary an annual report, in such form and at such time as the Secretary may require, that updates where necessary the information required by [section 302(a) of this Act]. [15 U.S.C. § 4018]

Section 309

(a) Information submitted by any person in connection with the issuance, amendment, or revocation of a certificate of review shall be exempt from disclosure under section 552 of title 5.

(b) (1) Except as provided in paragraph (2), no officer or employee of the United States shall disclose commercial or financial information submitted in connection with the issuance, amendment, or revocation of a certificate of review if the information is privileged or confidential and if disclosure of the information would cause harm to the person who submitted the information.

(2) Paragraph (1) shall not apply with respect to information disclosed—

(A) upon a request made by the Congress or any committee of the Congress,

(B) in a judicial or administrative proceeding, subject to appropriate protective orders,

(C) with the consent of the person who submitted the information,

(D) in the course of making a determination with respect to the issuance, amendment, or revocation of a certificate of review, if the Secretary deems disclosure of the information to be necessary in connection with making the determination,

(E) in accordance with any requirement imposed by a statute of the United States, or

(F) in accordance with any rule or regulation promulgated under [section 310 of this Act] permitting the disclosure of the information to an agency of the United States or of a State on the condition that the agency will disclose the information only under the circumstances specified in subparagraphs (A) through (E). [15 U.S.C. § 4019]

Section 310

The Secretary, with the concurrence of the Attorney General, shall promulgate such rules and regulations as are necessary to carry out the purposes of this [Act]. [15 U.S.C. § 4020]

Section 311

As used in this title—

(1) the term "export trade" means trade or commerce in goods, wares, merchandise, or services exported, or in the course of being exported, from the United States or any territory thereof to any foreign nation,

(2) the term "service" means intangible economic output, including, but not limited to—

(A) business, repair, and amusement services,

(B) management, legal, engineering, architectural, and other professional services, and

(C) financial, insurance, transportation, informational and any other data-based services, and communication services,

(3) the term "export trade activities" means activities or agreements in the course of export trade,

(4) the term "methods of operation" means any method by which a person conducts or proposes to conduct export trade,

(5) the term "person" means an individual who is a resident of the United States; a partnership that is created under and exists pursuant to

the laws of any State or of the United States; a State or local government entity; a corporation, whether organized as a profit or nonprofit corporation, that is created under and exists pursuant to the laws of any State or of the United States; or any association or combination, by contract or other arrangement, between or among such persons,

(6) the term "antitrust laws" means the antitrust laws, as such term is defined in section 12 of this title and [section 5 of the FTC Act] (to the extent that [section 5 of the FTC Act] prohibits unfair methods of competition), and any State antitrust or unfair competition law,

(7) the term "Secretary" means the Secretary of Commerce or his designee, and

(8) the term "Attorney General" means the Attorney General of the United States or his designee. [15 U.S.C. § 4021]

APPENDIX G

WEBB-POMERENE ACT

Section 1

The words "export trade" wherever used in this subchapter mean solely trade or commerce in goods, wares, or merchandise exported, or in the course of being exported from the United States or any Territory thereof to any foreign nation; but the words "export trade" shall not be deemed to include the production, manufacture, or selling for consumption or for resale, within the United States or any Territory thereof, of such goods, wares, or merchandise, or any act in the course of such production, manufacture, or selling for consumption or resale.

The words "trade within the United States" wherever used in this Act mean trade or commerce among the several States or in any Territory of the United States, or in the District of Columbia, or between any such Territory and another, or between any such Territory or Territories and any State or States or the District of Columbia, or between the District of Columbia and any State or States.

The word "association" wherever used in this Act means any corporation or combination, by contract or otherwise, or two or more persons, partnerships, or corporations. [15 U.S.C. § 61]

Section 2

Nothing contained in the Sherman Act [15 U.S.C. 1 et seq.] shall be construed as declaring to be illegal an association entered into for the sole purpose of engaging in export trade and actually engaged solely in such export trade, or an agreement made or act done in the course of export trade by such association, provided such association, agreement, or act is not in restraint of trade within the United States, and is not in restraint of the export trade of any domestic competitor of such association: *Provided*, That such association does not, either in the United States or elsewhere, enter into any agreement, understanding, or conspiracy, or do any act which artificially or intentionally enhances or depresses prices within the United States of commodities of the class exported by such association or which substantially lessens competition within the United States or otherwise restrains trade therein. [15 U.S.C. § 62]

Section 3

Nothing contained in [section 7 of the Clayton Act] shall be construed to forbid the acquisition or ownership by any corporation of the whole or any part of the stock or other capital of any corporation organized solely for the purpose of engaging in export trade, and actually engaged solely in such export trade, unless the effect of such acquisition or ownership may be to restrain trade or substantially lessen competition within the United States. [15 U.S.C. § 63]

Section 4

The prohibition against "unfair methods of competition" and the remedies provided for enforcing said prohibition contained in the Federal Trade Commission Act [15 U.S.C. 41 et seq.] shall be construed as extending to unfair methods of competition used in export trade against competitors engaged in export trade, even though the acts constituting such unfair methods are done without the territorial jurisdiction of the United States. [15 U.S.C. § 64]

Section 5

Every association which engages solely in export trade, within thirty days after its creation, shall file with the Federal Trade Commission a verified written statement setting forth the location of its offices or places of business and the names and addresses of all its officers and of all its stockholders or members, and if a corporation, a copy of its certificate or articles of incorporation and by-laws, and if unincorporated, a copy of its articles or contract of association, and on the first day of January of each year thereafter it shall make a like statement of the location of its offices or places of business and the names and addresses of all its officers and of all its stockholders or members and of all amendments to and changes in its articles or certificate of incorporation or in its articles or contract of association. It shall also furnish to the commission such information as the commission may require as to its organization, business, conduct, practices, management and relation to other associations, corporations, partnerships, and individuals. Any association which shall fail so to do shall not have the benefit of the provisions of section two and section three of this Act, and it shall also forfeit to the United States the sum of $100 for each and every day of the continuance of such failure, which forfeiture shall be payable into the Treasury of the United States, and shall be recoverable in a civil suit in the name of the United States brought in the district where the association has its principal office, or in any district in which it shall do business. It shall be the duty of the various district attorneys, under the direction of the Attorney General of the United States, to prosecute for the recovery of the forfeiture. The costs and expenses of such prosecution shall be paid out of the appropriation for the expenses of the courts of the United States.

Whenever the Federal Trade Commission shall have reason to believe that an association or any agreement made or act done by such association is in restraint of trade within the United States or in restraint of the export trade of any domestic competitor of such association, or that an association either in the United States or elsewhere has entered into any agreement, understanding, or conspiracy, or done any act which artificially or intentionally enhances or depresses prices within the United States of commodities of the class exported by such association, or which substantially lessens competition within the United States or otherwise restrains trade therein, it shall summon such association, its officers, and agents to appear before it, and thereafter conduct an investigation into the alleged violations of law. Upon investigation, if it shall conclude that the law has been violated, it may make to such association recommendations for the readjustment of its business, in order that it may thereafter maintain its organization and management and conduct its business in accordance with law. If such association fails to comply with the recommendations of the Federal Trade Commission, said commission shall refer its findings and recommendations to the Attorney General of the United States for such action thereon as he may deem proper.

For the purpose of enforcing these provisions the Federal Trade Commission shall have all the powers, so far as applicable, given it in the Federal Trade Commission Act [15 U.S.C. 41 et seq.]. [15 U.S.C. § 65]

Section 6

This subchapter may be cited as the "Webb-Pomerene Act." [15 U.S.C. § 66]

APPENDIX H

1984 DEPARTMENT OF JUSTICE MERGER GUIDELINES*

1. Purpose and Underlying Policy Assumptions

1.0 These Guidelines state in outline form the present enforcement policy of the U.S. Department of Justice ("Department") concerning acquisition and mergers ("mergers") subject to section 7 of the Clayton Act[1] or to section 1 of the Sherman Act.[2] They describe the general principles and specific standards normally used by the Department in analyzing mergers.[3] By stating its policy as simply and clearly as possible, the Department hopes to reduce the uncertainty associated with enforcement of the antitrust laws in this area.

Although the Guidelines should improve the predictability of the Department's merger enforcement policy, it is not possible to remove the exercise of judgment from the evaluation of mergers under the antitrust laws. Because the specific standards set forth in the Guidelines must be applied to a broad range of possible factual circumstances, strict

---

* *Editors' Note*: The 1992 *Merger Guidelines*, reprinted in Appendix I hereto, superseded the discussion of horizontal mergers in the 1984 *Merger Guidelines*. The 1992 *Merger Guidelines*, however, do not discuss horizontal effects from nonhorizontal mergers. The discussion in the 1984 *Merger Guidelines* of horizontal effects from nonhorizontal mergers, therefore, remains applicable.

1. 15 U.S.C. § 18 (1982). Mergers subject to section 7 are prohibited if their effect "may be substantially to lessen competition, or to tend to create a monopoly."

2. 15 U.S.C. § 1 (1982). Mergers subject to section 1 are prohibited if they constitute a "contract, combination . . . , or conspiracy in restraint of trade."

3. They update the Guidelines issued by the Department in 1982. The Department may from time to time revise the Merger Guidelines as necessary to reflect any significant changes in enforcement policy or to clarify aspects of existing policy.

application of those standards may provide misleading answers to the economic questions raised under the antitrust laws. Moreover, the picture of competitive conditions that develops from historical evidence may provide an incomplete answer to the forward-looking inquiry of the Guidelines. Therefore, the Department will apply the standards of the Guidelines reasonably and flexibly to the particular facts and circumstances of each proposed merger.

The Guidelines are designed primarily to indicate when the Department is likely to challenge mergers, not how it will conduct the litigation of cases that it decides to bring. Although relevant in the latter context, the factors contemplated in the standards do not exhaust the range of evidence that the Department may introduce in court.[4]

The unifying theme of the Guidelines is that mergers should not be permitted to create or enhance "market power" or to facilitate its exercise. A sole seller (a "monopolist") of a product with no good substitutes can maintain a selling price that is above the level that would prevail if the market were competitive. Where only a few firms account for most of the sales of a product, those firms can in some circumstances either explicitly or implicitly coordinate their actions in order to approximate the performance of a monopolist. This ability of one or more firms profitably to maintain prices above competitive levels for a significant period of time is termed "market power." Sellers with market power also may eliminate rivalry on variables other than price. In either case, the result is a transfer of wealth from buyers to sellers and a misallocation of resources.

"Market power" also encompasses the ability of a single buyer or group of buyers to depress the price paid for a product to a level that is below the competitive price. The exercise of market power by buyers has wealth transfer and resource misallocation effects analogous to those associated with the exercise of market power by sellers.

Although they sometimes harm competition, mergers generally play an important role in a free enterprise economy. They can penalize ineffective management and facilitate the efficient flow of investment

---

4. Parties seeking more specific advance guidance concerning the Department's enforcement intentions with respect to any particular merger should consider using the Business Review Procedure. 28 CFR § 50.6.

capital and the redeployment of existing productive assets. While challenging competitively harmful mergers, the Department seeks to avoid unnecessary interference with that larger universe of mergers that are either competitively beneficial or neutral. In attempting to mediate between these dual concerns, however, the Guidelines reflect the congressional intent that merger enforcement should interdict competitive problems in their incipiency.

* * *

4. Horizontal Effect from Non-Horizontal Mergers

4.0 By definition, non-horizontal mergers involve firms that do not operate in the same market. It necessarily follows that such mergers produce no immediate change in the level of concentration in any relevant market as defined in Section 2 of these Guidelines. Although non-horizontal mergers are less likely than horizontal mergers to create competitive problems, they are not invariably innocuous. This section describes the principal theories under which the Department is likely to challenge non-horizontal mergers.

4.1 Elimination of Specific Potential Entrants

4.11 The Theory of Potential Competition

In some circumstances, the non-horizontal merger[5] of a firm already in a market (the "acquired firm") with a potential entrant to that market (the "acquiring firm")[6] may adversely affect competition in the market. If the merger effectively removes the acquiring firm from the edge of the market, it could have either of the following effects:

---

5. Under traditional usage, such a merger could be characterized as either "vertical" or "conglomerate," but the label adds nothing to the analysis.
6. The terms "acquired" and "acquiring" refer to the relationship of the firms to the market of interest, not to the way the particular transaction is formally structured.

4.111 Harm to "Perceived Potential Competition"

By eliminating a significant present competitive threat that constrains the behavior of the firms already in the market, the merger could result in an immediate deterioration in market performance. The economic theory of limiting pricing suggests that monopolists and groups of colluding firms may find it profitable to restrain their pricing in order to deter new entry that is likely to push prices even lower by adding capacity to the market. If the acquiring firm had unique advantages in entering the market, the firms in the market might be able to set a new and higher price after the threat of entry by the acquiring firm was eliminated by the merger.

4.112 Harm to "Actual Potential Competition"

By eliminating the possibility of entry by the acquiring firm in a more procompetitive manner, the merger could result in a lost opportunity for improvement in market performance resulting from the addition of a significant competitor. The more procompetitive alternatives include both new entry and entry through a "toehold" acquisition of a present small competitor.

4.12 Relation Between Perceived and Actual Potential Competition

If it were always profit-maximizing for incumbent firms to set price in such a way that all entry was deterred and if information and coordination were sufficient to implement this strategy, harm to perceived potential competition would be the only competitive problem to address. In practice, however, actual potential competition has independent importance. Firms already in the market may not find it optimal to set price low enough to deter all entry; moreover, those firms may misjudge the entry advantages of a particular firm and, therefore, the price necessary to deter its entry.[7]

---

7. When collusion is only tacit, the problem of arriving at and enforcing the correct limit price is likely to be particularly difficult.

4.13 Enforcement Standards

Because of the close relationship between perceived potential competition and actual potential competition, the Department will evaluate mergers that raise either type of potential competition concern under a single structural analysis analogous to that applied to horizontal mergers. The Department first will consider a set of objective factors designed to identify cases in which harmful effects are plausible. In such cases, the Department then will conduct a more focused inquiry to determine whether the likelihood and magnitude of the possible harm justify a challenge to the merger. In this context, the Department will consider any specific evidence presented by the merging parties to show that the inferences of competitive harm drawn from the objective factors are unreliable.

The factors that the Department will consider are as follows:

4.131 Market Concentration

Barriers to entry are unlikely to affect market performance if the structure of the market is otherwise not conducive to monopolization or collusion. Adverse competitive effects are likely only if overall concentration, or the largest firm's market share, is high. The Department is unlikely to challenge a potential competition merger unless overall concentration of the acquired firm's market is above 1800 HHI (a somewhat lower concentration will suffice if one or more of the factors discussed in Section 3.4 indicate that effective collusion in the market is particularly likely). Other things being equal, the Department is increasingly likely to challenge a merger as this threshold is exceeded.

4.132 Conditions of Entry Generally

If entry to the market is generally easy, the fact that entry is marginally easier for one or more firms is unlikely to affect the behavior of the firms in the market. The Department is unlikely to challenge a potential competition merger when new entry into the acquired firm's market can be accomplished by firms without any specific entry advantages under the conditions stated in Section 3.3. Other things being equal, the Department is increasingly likely to challenge a merger as the difficulty of entry increases above that threshold.

4.133 The Acquiring Firm's Entry Advantage

If more than a few firms have the same or a comparable advantage in entering the acquired firm's market, the elimination of one firm is unlikely to have any adverse competitive effect. The other similarly situated firm(s) would continue to exert a present restraining influence, or, if entry would be profitable, would recognize the opportunity and enter. The Department is unlikely to challenge a potential competition merger if the entry advantage ascribed to the acquiring firm (or another advantage of comparable importance) is also possessed by three or more other firms. Other things being equal, the Department is increasingly likely to challenge a merger as the number of other similarly situated firms decreases below three and as the extent of the entry advantage over nonadvantaged firms increases.

If the evidence of likely actual entry by the acquiring firm is particularly strong,[8] however, the Department may challenge a potential competition merger, notwithstanding the presence of three or more firms that are objectively similarly situated. In such cases, the Department will determine the likely scale of entry, using either the firm's own documents or the minimum efficient scale in the industry. The Department will then evaluate the merger much as it would a horizontal merger between a firm the size of the likely scale of entry and the acquired firm.

4.134 The Market Share of the Acquired Firm

Entry through the acquisition of a relatively small firm in the market may have a competitive effect comparable to new entry. Small firms frequently play peripheral roles in collusive interactions, and the particular advantages of the acquiring firm may convert a fringe firm into a significant factor in the market.[9] The Department is unlikely to

---

8. For example, the firm already may have moved beyond the stage of consideration and have made significant investments demonstrating an actual decision to enter.

9. Although a similar effect is possible with the acquisition of larger firms, there is an increased danger that the acquiring firm will choose to acquiesce in monopolization or collusion because of the enhanced profits that would result from its own disappearance from the edge of the market.

challenge a potential competition merger when the acquired firm has a market share of five percent or less. Other things being equal, the Department is increasingly likely to challenge a merger as the market share of the acquired firm increases above that threshold. The Department is likely to challenge any merger satisfying the other conditions in which the acquired firm has market share of 20 percent or more.

4.135 Efficiencies

As in the case of horizontal mergers, the Department will consider expected efficiencies in determining whether to challenge a potential competition merger. See Section 3.5 [Efficiencies].

4.2 Competitive Problems from Vertical Mergers

4.21 Barriers to Entry from Vertical Mergers

In certain circumstances, the vertical integration resulting from vertical mergers could create competitively objectionable barriers to entry. Stated generally, three conditions are necessary (but not sufficient) for this problem to exist. First, the degree of vertical integration between the two markets must be so extensive that entrants to one market (the "primary market") also would have to enter the other market (the "secondary market")[10] simultaneously. Second, the requirement of entry at the secondary level must make entry at the primary level significantly more difficult and less likely to occur. Finally, the structure and other characteristics of the primary market must be otherwise so conducive to non-competitive performance that the increased difficulty of entry is likely to affect its performance. The following standards state the criteria

---

10. This competitive problem could result from either upstream or downstream integration, and could affect competition in either the upstream market or the downstream market. In the text, the term "primary market" refers to the market in which the competitive concerns are being considered, and the term "secondary market" refers to the adjacent market.

by which the Department will determine whether these conditions are satisfied.

4.211 Need for Two-Level Entry

If there is sufficient unintegrated capacity[11] in the secondary market, new entrants to the primary market would not have to enter both markets simultaneously. The Department is unlikely to challenge a merger on this ground where post-merger sales (purchases) by unintegrated firms in the secondary market would be sufficient to service two minimum- efficient-scale plants in the primary market. When the other conditions are satisfied, the Department is increasingly likely to challenge a merger as the unintegrated capacity declines below this level.

4.212 Increased Difficulty of Simultaneous Entry to Both Markets

The relevant question is whether the need for simultaneous entry to the secondary market gives rise to a substantial incremental difficulty as compared to entry into the primary market alone. If entry at the secondary level is easy in absolute terms, the requirement of simultaneous entry to that market is unlikely adversely to affect entry to the primary market, whatever the difficulties of entry into the primary market may be, the Department is unlikely to challenge a merger on this ground if new entry into the secondary market can be accomplished

---

11. Ownership integration does not necessarily mandate two-level entry by new entrants to the primary market. Such entry is most likely to be necessary where the primary and secondary markets are completely integrated by ownership and each firm in the primary market uses all of the capacity of its associated firm in the secondary market. In many cases of ownership integration, however, the functional fit between vertically integrated firms is not perfect, and an outside market exists for the sales (purchases) of the firms in the secondary market. If that market is sufficiently large and diverse, new entrants to the primary market may be able to participate without simultaneous entry to the secondary market. In considering the adequacy of this alternative, the Department will consider the likelihood of predatory price or supply "squeezes" by the integrated firms against their unintegrated rivals.

under the conditions stated in Section 3.3.[12] When entry is not possible under those conditions, the Department is increasingly concerned about vertical mergers as the difficulty of entering the secondary market increases. The Department, however, will invoke this theory only where the need for secondary market entry significantly increases the costs (which may take the form of risks) of primary market entry.

More capital is necessary to enter two markets than to enter one. Standing alone, however, this additional capital requirement does not constitute a barrier to entry to the primary market. If the necessary funds were available at a cost commensurate with the level of risk in the secondary market, there would be no adverse effect. In some cases, however, lenders may doubt that would-be entrants to the primary market have the necessary skills and knowledge to succeed in the secondary market and, therefore, in the primary market. In order to compensate for this risk of failure, lenders might charge a higher rate for the necessary capital. This problem becomes increasingly significant as a higher percentage of the capital assets in the secondary market are long-lived and specialized to that market and, therefore, difficult to recover in the event of failure. In evaluating the likelihood of increased barriers to entry resulting from increased cost of capital, therefore, the Department will consider both the degree of similarity in the essential skills in the primary and secondary markets and the economic life and degree of specialization of the capital assets in the secondary market.

Economies of scale in the secondary market may constitute an additional barrier to entry to the primary market in some situations requiring two-level entry. The problem could arise if the capacities of minimum-efficient-scale plants in the primary and secondary markets differ significantly. For example, if the capacity of a minimum-efficient-scale plant in the secondary market were significantly greater than the needs of a minimum-efficient-scale plant in the primary market, entrants would have to choose between inefficient operation at the secondary level (because of operating an efficient plant at an inefficient output or because of operating an efficiently small plant) or a larger than necessary

---

12. Entry into the secondary market may be greatly facilitated in that an assured supplier (customer) is provided by the primary market entry.

scale at the primary level. Either of these effects could cause a significant increase in the operating costs of the entering firm.[13]

4.213 Structure and Performance of the Primary Market

Barriers to entry are unlikely to affect performance if the structure of the primary market is otherwise not conducive to monopolization or collusion.[14] The Department is unlikely to challenge a merger on this ground unless overall concentration of the primary market is above 1800 HHI (a somewhat lower concentration will suffice if one or more of the factors discussed in Section 3.4 indicate that effective collusion is particularly likely). Above that threshold, the Department is increasingly likely to challenge a merger that meets the other criteria set forth above as the concentration increases.

4.22 Facilitating Collusion Through Vertical Mergers

4.221 Vertical Integration to the Retail Level

A high level of vertical integration by upstream firms into the associated retail market may facilitate collusion in the upstream market by making it easier to monitor price. Retail prices are generally more visible than prices in upstream markets, and vertical mergers may increase the level of vertical integration to the point at which the monitoring effect becomes significant. Adverse competitive consequences are unlikely unless the upstream market is generally conducive to collusion and a large percentage of the products produced there are sold through vertically integrated retail outlets.

The Department is unlikely to challenge a merger on this ground unless (1) overall concentration of the upstream market is above 1800 HHI (a somewhat lower concentration will suffice if one or more of the factors discussed in Section 3.4 indicate that effective collusion is

---

13. It is important to note, however, that this problem would not exist if a significant outside market exists at the secondary level. In that case, entrants could enter with the appropriately scaled plants at both levels, and sell or buy in the market as necessary.

14. For example, a market with 100 firms of equal size would perform competitively despite a significant increase in entry barriers.

particularly likely), and (2) a large percentage of the upstream product would be sold through vertically-integrated retail outlets after the merger. Where the stated thresholds are met or exceeded, the Department's decision whether to challenge a merger on this ground will depend upon an individual evaluation of its likely competitive effect.

4.222 Elimination of a Disruptive Buyer

The elimination by vertical merger of a particularly disruptive buyer in a downstream market may facilitate collusion in the upstream market. If upstream firms view sales to a particular buyer as sufficiently important, they may deviate from the terms of a collusive agreement in an effort to secure that business, thereby disrupting the operation of the agreement. The merger of such a buyer with an upstream firm may eliminate that rivalry, making it easier for the upstream firms to collude effectively. Adverse competitive consequences are unlikely unless the upstream market is generally conducive to collusion and the disruptive firm is significantly more attractive to sellers than the other firms in its market.

The Department is unlikely to challenge a merger on this ground unless (1) overall concentration of the upstream market is 1800 HHI or above (a somewhat lower concentration will suffice if one or more of the factors discussed in Section 3.4 indicate that effective collusion is particularly likely), and (2) the allegedly disruptive firm differs substantially in volume of purchases or other relevant characteristics from the other firms in its market. Where the stated thresholds are met or exceeded, the Department's decision whether to challenge a merger on this ground will depend upon an individual evaluation of its likely competitive effect.

4.23 Evasion of Rate Regulation

Non-horizontal mergers may be used by monopoly public utilities subject to rate regulation as a tool for circumventing that regulation. The clearest example is the acquisition by a regulated utility of a supplier of its fixed or variable inputs. After the merger, the utility would be selling to itself and might be able arbitrarily to inflate the prices of internal transactions. Regulators may have great difficulty in policing these practices, particularly if there is no independent market for the product (or service) purchased from the affiliate.[15] As a result, inflated prices could be passed along to consumers as "legitimate" costs. In extreme cases, the regulated firm may effectively preempt the adjacent market, perhaps for the purpose of suppressing observable market transactions, and may distort resources allocation in that adjacent market as well as in the regulated market. In such cases, however, the Department recognizes that genuine economies of integration may be involved. The Department will consider challenging mergers that create substantial opportunities for such abuses.[16]

4.24 Efficiencies

As in the case of horizontal mergers, the Department will consider expected efficiencies in determining whether to challenge a vertical merger. See Section 3.5 (Efficiencies). An extensive pattern of vertical integration may constitute evidence that substantial economies are afforded by vertical integration. Therefore, the Department will give relatively more weight to expected efficiencies in determining whether to challenge a vertical merger than in determining whether to challenge a horizontal merger.

---

15. A less severe, but nevertheless serious, problem can arise when a regulated utility acquires a firm that is not vertically related. The use of common facilities and managers may create an insoluble cost allocation problem and provide the opportunity to charge utility customers for non-utility costs, consequently distorting resource allocation in the adjacent as well as the regulated market.
16. Where a regulatory agency has the responsibility for approving such mergers, the Department may express its concerns to that agency in its role as competition advocate.

APPENDIX I

1992 DEPARTMENT OF JUSTICE AND FEDERAL TRADE COMMISSION HORIZONTAL MERGER GUIDELINES

U.S. Department of Justice and Federal Trade Commission Statement Accompanying Release of Revised Merger Guidelines.

April 2, 1992

The U.S. Department of Justice ("Department") and Federal Trade Commission ("Commission") today jointly issued Horizontal Merger Guidelines revising the Department's 1984 *Merger Guidelines* and the Commission's 1982 *Statement Concerning Horizontal Merger Guidelines.* The release marks the first time that the two federal agencies that share antitrust enforcement jurisdiction have issued joint guidelines.

Central to the 1992 Department of Justice and Federal Trade Commission Horizontal Merger Guidelines is a recognition that sound merger enforcement is an essential component of our free enterprise system benefiting the competitiveness of American firms and the welfare of American consumers. Sound merger enforcement must prevent anticompetitive mergers yet avoid deterring the larger universe of procompetitive or competitively neutral mergers. The 1992 Horizontal Merger Guidelines implement this objective by describing the analytical foundations of merger enforcement and providing guidance enabling the business community to avoid antitrust problems when planning mergers.

The Department first released *Merger Guidelines* in 1968 in order to inform the business community of the analysis applied by the Department to mergers under the federal antitrust laws. The 1968 *Merger Guidelines* eventually fell into disuse, both internally and externally, as they were eclipsed by developments in legal and economic thinking about mergers.

In 1982, the Department released revised *Merger Guidelines* which, reflecting those developments, departed dramatically from the 1968 version. Relative to the Department's actual practice, however, the 1982 *Merger Guidelines* represented an evolutionary not revolutionary change.

On the same date, the Commission released its *Statement Concerning Horizontal Mergers* highlighting the principal considerations guiding the Commission's horizontal merger enforcement and noting the "considerable weight" given by the Commission to the Department's 1982 *Merger Guidelines*.

The Department's current *Merger Guidelines*, released in 1984, refined and clarified the analytical framework of the 1982 *Merger Guidelines.* Although the agencies' experience with the 1982 *Merger Guidelines* reaffirmed the soundness of its underlying principles, the Department concluded that there remained room for improvement.

The revisions embodied in the 1992 Horizontal Merger Guidelines reflect the next logical step in the development of the agencies' analysis of mergers. They reflect the Department's experience in applying the 1982 and 1984 *Merger Guidelines* as well as the Commission's experience in applying those Guidelines and the Commission's 1982 *Statement.* Both the Department and the Commission believed that their respective Guidelines and Statement presented sound frameworks for antitrust analysis of mergers, but that improvements could be made to reflect advances in legal and economic thinking. The 1992 Horizontal Merger Guidelines accomplish this objective and also clarify certain aspects of the *Merger Guidelines* that proved to be ambiguous or were interpreted by observers in ways that were inconsistent with the actual policy of the agencies.

The 1992 Horizontal Merger Guidelines do not include a discussion of horizontal effects from non-horizontal mergers (e.g., elimination of specific potential entrants and competitive problems from vertical mergers). Neither agency has changed its policy with respect to non-horizontal mergers. Specific guidance on non-horizontal mergers is provided in Section 4 of the Department's 1984 *Merger Guidelines*, read in the context of today's revisions to the treatment of horizontal mergers.

A number of today's revisions are largely technical or stylistic. One major objective of the revisions is to strengthen the document as an analytical road map for the evaluation of mergers. The language, therefore, is intended to be burden-neutral, without altering the burdens of proof or burdens of coming forward as those standards have been established by the courts. In addition, the revisions principally address two areas.

The most significant revision to the *Merger Guidelines* is to explain more clearly how mergers may lead to adverse competitive effects and how particular market factors relate to the analysis of those effects. These revisions are found in Section 2 of the Horizontal Merger Guidelines. The second principal revision is to sharpen the distinction between the treatment of various types of supply responses and to articulate the framework for analyzing the timeliness, likelihood and sufficiency of entry. These revisions are found in Sections 1.3 and 3.

The new Horizontal Merger Guidelines observe, as did the *1984 Guidelines*, that because the specific standards they set out must be applied in widely varied factual circumstances, mechanical application of those standards could produce misleading results. Thus, the *Guidelines* state that the agencies will apply those standards reasonably and flexibly to the particular facts and circumstances of each proposed merger.

Department of Justice and Federal Trade Commission Horizontal Merger Guidelines, Issued April 2, 1992

5.2 Failing Division

0. Purpose, Underlying Policy Assumptions and Overview

These Guidelines outline the present enforcement policy of the Department of Justice and the Federal Trade Commission (the "Agency") concerning horizontal acquisitions and mergers ("mergers") subject to section 7 of the Clayton Act,[1] to section 1 of the Sherman Act,[2] or to section 5 of the FTC Act.[3] They describe the analytical framework and specific standards normally used by the Agency in analyzing mergers.[4] By stating its policy as simply and clearly as possible, the Agency hopes to reduce the uncertainty associated with enforcement of the antitrust laws in this area.

Although the Guidelines should improve the predictability of the Agency's merger enforcement policy, it is not possible to remove the exercise of judgment from the evaluation of mergers under the antitrust laws. Because the specific standards set forth in the Guidelines must be applied to a broad range of possible factual circumstances, mechanical application of those standards may provide misleading answers to the economic questions raised under the antitrust laws. Moreover, information is often incomplete and the picture of competitive conditions that develops from historical evidence may provide an incomplete answer to the forward-looking inquiry of the Guidelines. Therefore, the Agency will apply the standards of the Guidelines reasonably and

---

1. 15 U.S.C. § 18 (1988). Mergers subject to section 7 are prohibited if their effect "may be substantially to lessen competition, or to tend to create a monopoly."
2. 15 U.S.C. § 1 (1988). Mergers subject to section 1 are prohibited if they constitute a "contract, combination . . ., or conspiracy in restraint of trade."
3. 15 U.S.C. § 45 (1988). Mergers subject to section 5 are prohibited if they constitute an "unfair method of competition."
4. These Guidelines update the Merger Guidelines issued by the U.S. Department of Justice in 1984 and the Statement of Federal Trade Commission Concerning Horizontal Mergers issued in 1982. The Merger Guidelines may be revised from time to time as necessary to reflect any significant changes in enforcement policy or to clarify aspects of existing policy.

flexibly to the particular facts and circumstances of each proposed merger.

0.1 Purpose and Underlying Policy Assumptions of the Guidelines

The Guidelines are designed primarily to articulate the analytical framework the Agency applies in determining whether a merger is likely substantially to lessen competition, not to describe how the Agency will conduct the litigation of cases that it decides to bring. Although relevant in the latter context, the factors contemplated in the Guidelines neither dictate nor exhaust the range of evidence that the Agency must or may introduce in litigation. Consistent with their objective, the Guidelines do not attempt to assign the burden of proof, or the burden of coming forward with evidence, on any particular issue. Nor do the Guidelines attempt to adjust or reapportion burdens of proof or burdens of coming forward as those standards have been established by the courts.[5] Instead, the Guidelines set forth a methodology for analyzing issues once the necessary facts are available. The necessary facts may be derived from the documents and statements of both the merging firms and other sources.

Throughout the Guidelines, the analysis is focused on whether consumers or producers "likely would" take certain actions, that is, whether the action is in the actor's economic interest. References to the profitability of certain actions focus on economic profits rather than accounting profits. Economic profits may be defined as the excess of revenues over costs where costs include the opportunity cost of invested capital.

Mergers are motivated by the prospect of financial gains. The possible sources of the financial gains from mergers are many, and the Guidelines do not attempt to identify all possible sources of gain in every merger. Instead, the Guidelines focus on the one potential source of gain that is of concern under the antitrust laws: market power.

The unifying theme of the Guidelines is that mergers should not be permitted to create or enhance market power or to facilitate its exercise. Market power to a seller is the ability profitably to maintain prices above

---

5. For example, the burden with respect to efficiency and failure continues to reside with the proponents of the merger.

competitive levels for a significant period of time.[6] In some circumstances, a sole seller (a "monopolist") of a product with no good substitutes can maintain a selling price that is above the level that would prevail if the market were competitive. Similarly, in some circumstances, where only a few firms account for most of the sales of a product, those firms can exercise market power, perhaps even approximating the performance of a monopolist, by either explicitly or implicitly coordinating their actions. Circumstances also may permit a single firm, not a monopolist, to exercise market power through unilateral or non-coordinated conduct—conduct the success of which does not rely on the concurrence of other firms in the market or on coordinated responses by those firms. In any case, the result of the exercise of market power is a transfer of wealth from buyers to sellers or a misallocation of resources.

Market power also encompasses the ability of a single buyer (a "monopsonist"), a coordinating group of buyers, or a single buyer, not a monopsonist, to depress the price paid for a product to a level that is below the competitive price and thereby depress output. The exercise of market power by buyers ("monopsony power") has adverse effects comparable to those associated with the exercise of market power by sellers. In order to assess potential monopsony concerns, the Agency will apply an analytical framework analogous to the framework of these Guidelines.

While challenging competitively harmful mergers, the Agency seeks to avoid unnecessary interference with the larger universe of mergers that are either competitively beneficial or neutral. In implementing this objective, however, the Guidelines reflect the congressional intent that merger enforcement should interdict competitive problems in their incipiency.

0.2 Overview

The Guidelines describe the analytical process that the Agency will employ in determining whether to challenge a horizontal merger. First, the Agency assesses whether the merger would significantly increase

6. Sellers with market power also may lessen competition on dimensions other than price, such as product quality, service, or innovation.

concentration and result in a concentrated market, properly defined and measured. Second, the Agency assesses whether the merger, in light of market concentration and other factors that characterize the market, raises concern about potential adverse competitive effects. Third, the Agency assesses whether entry would be timely, likely and sufficient either to deter or to counteract the competitive effects of concern. Fourth, the Agency assesses any efficiency gains that reasonably cannot be achieved by the parties through other means. Finally the Agency assesses whether, but for the merger, either party to the transaction would be likely to fail, causing its assets to exit the market. The process of assessing market concentration, potential adverse competitive effects, entry, efficiency and failure is a tool that allows the Agency to answer the ultimate inquiry in merger analysis: whether the merger is likely to create or enhance market power or to facilitate its exercise.

1. Market Definition, Measurement and Concentration

1.0 Overview

A merger is unlikely to create or enhance market power or to facilitate its exercise unless it significantly increases concentration and results in a concentrated market, properly defined and measured. Mergers that either do not significantly increase concentration or do not result in a concentrated market ordinarily require no further analysis.

The analytic process described in this section ensures that the Agency evaluates the likely competitive impact of a merger within the context of economically meaningful markets—i.e., markets that could be subject to the exercise of market power. Accordingly, for each product or service (hereafter "product") of each merging firm, the Agency seeks to define a market in which firms could effectively exercise market power if they were able to coordinate their actions.

Market definition focuses solely on demand substitution factors—i.e., possible consumer responses. Supply substitution factors—i.e., possible production responses—are considered elsewhere in the Guidelines in the identification of firms that participate in the relevant market and the analysis of entry. See Sections 1.3 and 3. A market is defined as a product or group of products and a geographic area in which it is produced or sold such that a hypothetical profit-maximizing firm, not subject to price regulation, that was the only present and future producer or seller of those products in that area likely would impose at least a "small but significant and nontransitory" increase in price, assuming the terms of sale of all other products are held constant. A relevant market is a group of products and a geographic area that is no bigger than necessary to satisfy this test. The "small but significant and non-transitory" increase in price is employed solely as a methodological tool for the analysis of mergers: it is not a tolerance level for price increases.

Absent price discrimination, a relevant market is described by a product or group of products and a geographic area. In determining whether a hypothetical monopolist would be in a position to exercise market power, it is necessary to evaluate the likely demand responses of consumers to a price increase. A price increase could be made unprofitable by consumers either switching to other products or switching to the same product produced by firms at other locations. The nature and magnitude of these two types of demand responses respectively determine the scope of the product market and the geographic market.

In contrast, where a hypothetical monopolist likely would discriminate in prices charged to different groups of buyers, distinguished, for example, by their uses or locations, the Agency may delineate different relevant markets corresponding to each such buyer group. Competition for sales to each such group may be affected differently by a particular merger and markets are delineated by evaluating the demand response of each such buyer group. A relevant market of this kind is described by a collection of products for sale to a given group of buyers.

Once defined, a relevant market must be measured in terms of its participants and concentration. Participants include firms currently producing or selling the market's products in the market's geographic area. In addition, participants may include other firms depending on their likely supply responses to a "small but significant and nontransitory" price increase. A firm is viewed as a participant if, in response to a "small but significant and nontransitory" price increase, it likely would enter rapidly into production or sale of a market product in the market's area, without incurring significant sunk costs of entry and exit. Firms likely to make any of these supply responses are considered to be "uncommitted" entrants because their supply response would create new production or sale in the relevant market and because that production or sale could be quickly terminated without significant loss.[7] Uncommitted entrants are capable of making such quick and uncommitted supply responses that they likely influenced the market premerger, would influence it post-merger, and accordingly are considered as market participants at both times. This analysis of market definition and market measurement applies equally to foreign and domestic firms.

If the process of market definition and market measurement identifies one or more relevant markets in which the merging firms are both participants, then the merger is considered to be horizontal. Sections 1.1 through 1.5 describe in greater detail how product and geographic markets will be defined, how market shares will be calculated and how market concentration will be assessed.

1.1 Product Market Definition

The Agency will first define the relevant product market with respect to each of the products of each of the merging firms.[8]

1.11 General Standards

Absent price discrimination, the Agency will delineate the product market to be a product or group of products such that a hypothetical profit-maximizing firm that was the only present and future seller of those products ("monopolist") likely would impose at least a "small but significant and nontransitory" increase in price. That is, assuming that buyers likely would respond to an increase in price for a tentatively

---

7. Probable supply responses that require the entrant to incur significant sunk costs of entry and exit are not part of market measurement, but are included in the analysis of the significance of entry. *See* Section 3. Entrants that must commit substantial sunk costs are regarded as "committed" entrants because those sunk costs make entry irreversible in the short term without foregoing that investment; thus the likelihood of their entry must be evaluated with regard to their long-term profitability.
8. Although discussed separately, product market definition and geographic market definition are interrelated. In particular, the extent to which buyers of a particular product would shift to other products in the event of a "small but significant and nontransitory" increase in price must be evaluated in the context of the relevant geographic market.

identified product group only by shifting to other products, what would happen? If the alternatives were, in the aggregate, sufficiently attractive at their existing terms of sale, an attempt to raise prices would result in a reduction of sales large enough that the price increase would not prove profitable, and the tentatively identified product group would prove to be too narrow.

Specifically, the Agency will begin with each product (narrowly defined) produced or sold by each merging firm and ask what would happen if a hypothetical monopolist of that product imposed at least a "small but significant and nontransitory" increase in price, but the terms of sale of all other products remained constant. If, in response to the price increase, the reduction in sales of the product would be large enough that a hypothetical monopolist would not find it profitable to impose such an increase in price, then the Agency will add to the product group the product that is the next-best substitute for the merging firm's product.[9]

In considering the likely reaction of buyers to a price increase, the Agency will take into account all relevant evidence, including, but not limited to, the following:

(1) evidence that buyers have shifted or have considered shifting purchases between products in response to relative changes in price or other competitive variables;
(2) evidence that sellers base business decisions on the prospect of buyer substitution between products in response to relative changes in price or other competitive variables;
(3) The influence of downstream competition faced by buyers in their output markets; and
(4) the timing and costs of switching products.

The price increase question is then asked for a hypothetical monopolist controlling the expanded product group. In performing successive iterations of the price increase test, the hypothetical monopolist will be assumed to pursue maximum profits in deciding whether to raise the prices of any or all of the additional products under its control. This process will continue until a group of products is

---

9. Throughout the Guidelines, the term "next best substitute" refers to the alternative which, if available in unlimited quantities at constant prices, would account for the greatest value of diversion of demand in response to a "small but significant and nontransitory" price increase.

identified such that a hypothetical monopolist over that group of products would profitably impose at least a "small but significant and nontransitory" increase, including the price of a product of one of the merging firms. The Agency generally will consider the relevant product market to be the smallest group of products that satisfies this test.

In the above analysis, the Agency will use prevailing prices of the products of the merging firms and possible substitutes for such products, unless premerger circumstances are strongly suggestive of coordinated interaction, in which case the Agency will use a price more reflective of the competitive price.[10] However, the Agency may use likely future prices, absent the merger, when changes in the prevailing prices can be predicted with reasonable reliability. Changes in price may be predicted on the basis of, for example, changes in regulation which affect price either directly or indirectly by affecting costs or demand.

In general, the price for which an increase will be postulated will be whatever is considered to be the price of the product at the stage of the industry being examined.[11] In attempting to determine objectively the effect of a "small but significant and nontransitory" increase in price, the Agency, in most contexts, will use a price increase of five percent lasting for the foreseeable future. However, what constitutes a "small but significant and nontransitory" increase in price will depend on the nature of the industry, and the Agency at times may use a price increase that is larger or smaller than five percent.

1.12 Product Market Definition in the Presence of Price Discrimination

The analysis of product market definition to this point has assumed that price discrimination—charging different buyers different prices for

---

10. The terms of sale of all other products are held constant in order to focus market definition on the behavior of consumers. Movements in the terms of sale for other products, as may result from the behavior of producers of those products, are accounted for in the analysis of competitive effects and entry. *See* Sections 2 and 3.

11. For example, in a merger between retailers, the relevant price would be the retail price of a product to consumers. In the case of a merger among oil pipelines, the relevant price would be the tariff—the price of the transportation service.

the same product, for example—would not be profitable for a hypothetical monopolist. A different analysis applies where price discrimination would be profitable for a hypothetical monopolist.

Existing buyers sometimes will differ significantly in their likelihood of switching to other products in response to a "small but significant and nontransitory" price increase. If a hypothetical monopolist can identify and price differently to those buyers ("targeted buyers") who would not defeat the targeted price increase by substituting to other products in response to a "small but significant and nontransitory" price increase for the relevant product, and if other buyers likely would not purchase the relevant product and resell to targeted buyers, then a hypothetical monopolist would profitably impose a discriminatory price increase on sales to targeted buyers. This is true regardless of whether a general increase in price would cause such significant substitution that the price increase would not be profitable. The Agency will consider additional relevant product markets consisting of a particular use or uses by groups of buyers of the product for which a hypothetical monopolist would profitably and separately impose at least a "small but significant and nontransitory" increase in price.

1.2 Geographic Market Definition

For each product market in which both merging firms participate, the Agency will determine the geographic market or markets in which the firms produce or sell. A single firm may operate in a number of different geographic markets.

1.21 General Standards

Absent price discrimination, the Agency will delineate the geographic market to be a region such that a hypothetical monopolist that was the only present or future producer of the relevant product at locations in that region would profitably impose at least a "small but significant and nontransitory" increase in price, holding constant the terms of sale for all products produced elsewhere. That is, assuming that buyers likely would respond to a price increase on products produced within the tentatively identified region only by shifting to products produced at locations of production outside the region, what would happen? If those locations of production outside the region were, in the aggregate, sufficiently attractive at their existing terms of sale, an attempt to raise price would result in a reduction in sales large enough that the price increase would not prove profitable, and the tentatively identified geographic area would prove to be too narrow.

In defining the geographic market or markets affected by a merger, the Agency will begin with the location of each merging firm (or each plant of a multiplant firm) and ask what would happen if a hypothetical monopolist of the relevant product at that point imposed at least a "small but significant and nontransitory" increase in price, but the terms of sale at all other locations remained constant. If, in response to the price increase, the reduction in sales of the product at that location would be large enough that a hypothetical monopolist producing or selling the relevant product at the merging firm's location would not find it profitable to impose such an increase in price, then the Agency will add the location from which production is the next-best substitute for production at the merging firm's location.

In considering the likely reaction of buyers to a price increase, the Agency will take into account all relevant evidence, including, but not limited to, the following:

(1) evidence that buyers have shifted or have considered shifting purchases between different geographic locations in response to relative changes in price or other competitive variables;
(2) evidence that sellers base business decisions on the prospect of buyer substitution between geographic locations in response to relative changes in price or other competitive variables;
(3) the influence of downstream competition faced by buyers in their output markets; and
(4) the timing and costs of switching suppliers.

The price increase question is then asked for a hypothetical monopolist controlling the expanded group of locations. In performing successive iterations of the price increase test, the hypothetical monopolist will be assumed to pursue maximum profits in deciding whether to raise the price at any or all of the additional locations under its control. This process will continue until a group of locations is identified such that a hypothetical monopolist over that group of locations would profitably impose at least a "small but significant and nontransitory" increase, including the price charged at a location of one of the merging firms.

The "smallest market" principle will be applied as it is in product market definition. The price for which an increase will be postulated, what constitutes a "small but significant and nontransitory" increase in price, and the substitution decisions of consumers all will be determined in the same way in which they are determined in product market definition.

1.22 Geographic Market Definition in the Presence of Price Discrimination

The analysis of geographic market definition to this point has assumed that geographic price discrimination—charging different prices net of transportation costs for the same product to buyers in different areas, for example—would not be profitable for a hypothetical monopolist. However, if a hypothetical monopolist can identify and price differently to buyers in certain areas ("targeted buyers") who would not defeat the targeted price increase by substituting to more distant sellers in response to a "small but significant and nontransitory" price increase for the relevant product, and if other buyers likely would not purchase the relevant product and resell to targeted buyers,[12] then a hypothetical monopolist would profitably impose a discriminatory price increase. This is true even where a general price increase would cause such significant substitution that the price increase would not be profitable. The Agency will consider additional geographic markets consisting of particular locations of buyers for which a hypothetical monopolist would profitably and separately impose at least a "small but significant and nontransitory" increase in price.

1.3 Identification of Firms That Participate in the Relevant Market

1.31 Current Producers or Sellers

The Agency's identification of firms that participate in the relevant market begins with all firms that currently produce or sell in the relevant market. This includes vertically integrated firms to the extent that such inclusion accurately reflects their competitive significance in the relevant market prior to the merger. To the extent that the analysis under Section

---

12. This arbitrage is inherently impossible for many services and is particularly difficult where the product is sold on a delivered basis and where transportation costs are a significant percentage of the final cost.

1.1 indicates that used, reconditioned or recycled goods are included in the relevant market, market participants will include firms that produce or sell such goods and that likely would offer those goods in competition with other relevant products.

1.32 Firms That Participate Through Supply Response

In addition, the Agency will identify other firms not currently producing or selling the relevant product in the relevant area as participating in the relevant market if their inclusion would more accurately reflect probable supply responses. These firms are termed "uncommitted entrants." These supply responses must be likely to occur within one year and without the expenditure of significant sunk costs of entry and exit, in response to a "small but significant and nontransitory" price increase. If a firm has the technological capability to achieve such an uncommitted supply response, but likely would not (e.g., because difficulties in achieving product acceptance, distribution, or production would render such a response unprofitable), that firm will not be considered to be a market participant. The competitive significance of supply responses that require more time or that require firms to incur significant sunk costs of entry and exit will be considered in entry analysis. See Section 3.[13]

Sunk costs are the acquisition costs of tangible and intangible assets that cannot be recovered through the redeployment of these assets outside the relevant market, i.e., costs uniquely incurred to supply the relevant product and geographic market. Examples of sunk costs may include market-specific investments in production facilities, technologies, marketing (including product acceptance), research and development, regulatory approvals, and testing. A significant sunk cost is one which would not be recouped within one year of the commencement of the supply response, assuming a "small but significant and nontransitory" price increase in the relevant market. In this context, a "small but significant and nontransitory" price increase will be

13. If uncommitted entrants likely would also remain in the market and would meet the entry tests of timeliness, likelihood and sufficiency, and thus would likely deter anticompetitive mergers or deter or counteract the competitive effects of concern (*see* Section 3, infra), the Agency will consider the impact of those firms in the entry analysis.

determined in the same way in which it is determined in product market definition, except the price increase will be assumed to last one year. In some instances, it may be difficult to calculate sunk costs with precision. Accordingly, when necessary, the Agency will make an overall assessment of the extent of sunk costs for firms likely to participate through supply responses.

These supply responses may give rise to new production of products in the relevant product market or new sources of supply in the relevant geographic market. Alternatively, where price discrimination is likely so that the relevant market is defined in terms of a targeted group of buyers, these supply responses serve to identify new sellers to the targeted buyers. Uncommitted supply responses may occur in several different ways: by the switching or extension of existing assets to production or sale in the relevant market; or by the construction or acquisition of assets that enable production or sale in the relevant market.

1.321 Production Substitution and Extension: The Switching or Extension of Existing Assets to Production or Sale in the Relevant Market

The productive and distributive assets of a firm sometimes can be used to produce and sell either the relevant products or products that buyers do not regard as good substitutes. Production substitution refers to the shift by a firm in the use of assets from producing and selling one product to producing and selling another. Production extension refers to the use of those assets, for example, existing brand names and reputation, both for their current production and for production of the relevant product. Depending upon the speed of that shift and the extent of sunk costs incurred in the shift or extension, the potential for production substitution or extension may necessitate treating as market participants firms that do not currently produce the relevant product.[14] If a firm has

14. Under other analytical approaches, production substitution sometimes has been reflected in the description of the product market. For example, the product market for stamped metal products such as automobile hub caps might be described as "light metal stamping," a production process rather than a product. The Agency believes that the approach described in the text provides a more clearly focused method of incorporating this factor in merger analysis. If production substitution among a group of products

existing assets that likely would be shifted or extended into production and sale of the relevant product within one year, and without incurring significant sunk costs of entry and exit, in response to a "small but significant and nontransitory" increase in price for only the relevant product, the Agency will treat that firm as a market participant. In assessing whether a firm is such a market participant, the Agency will take into account the costs of substitution or extension relative to the profitability of sales at the elevated price, and whether the firm's capacity is elsewhere committed or elsewhere so profitably employed that such capacity likely would not be available to respond to an increase in price in the market.

1.322 Obtaining New Assets for Production or Sale of the Relevant Product

A firm may also be able to enter into production or sale in the relevant market within one year and without the expenditure of significant sunk costs of entry and exit, in response to a "small but significant and nontransitory" increase in price for only the relevant product, even if the firm is newly organized or is an existing firm without products or productive assets closely related to the relevant market. If new firms, or existing firms without closely related products or productive assets, likely would enter into production or sale in the relevant market within one year without the expenditure of significant sunk costs of entry and exit, the Agency will treat those firms as market participants.

1.4 Calculating Market Shares

1.41 General Approach

The Agency normally will calculate market shares for all firms (or plants) identified as market participants in Section 1.3 based on the total sales or capacity currently devoted to the relevant market together with that which likely would be devoted to the relevant market in response to

---

is nearly universal among the firms selling one or more of those products, however, the Agency may use an aggregate description of those markets as a matter of convenience.

a "small but significant and nontransitory" price increase. Market shares can be expressed either in dollar terms through measurement of sales, shipments, or production, or in physical terms through measurement of sales, shipments, production, capacity, or reserves.

Market shares will be calculated using the best indicator of firms' future competitive significance. Dollar sales or shipments generally will be used if firms are distinguished primarily by differentiation of their products. Unit sales generally will be used if firms are distinguished primarily on the basis of their relative advantages in serving different buyers or groups of buyers. Physical capacity or reserves generally will be used if it is these measures that most effectively distinguish firms.[15] Typically, annual data are used, but where individual sales are large and infrequent so that annual data may be unrepresentative, the Agency may measure market shares over a longer period of time.

In measuring a firm's market share, the Agency will not include its sales or capacity to the extent that the firm's capacity is committed or so profitably employed outside the relevant market that it would not be available to respond to an increase in price in the market.

1.42 Price Discrimination Markets

When markets are defined on the basis of price discrimination (Sections 1.12 and 1.22), the Agency will include only sales likely to be made into, or capacity likely to be used to supply, the relevant market in response to a "small but significant and nontransitory" price increase.

1.43 Special Factors Affecting Foreign Firms

Market shares will be assigned to foreign competitors in the same way in which they are assigned to domestic competitors. However, if exchange rates fluctuate significantly, so that comparable dollar calculations on an annual basis may be unrepresentative, the Agency may measure market shares over a period longer than one year.

If shipments from a particular country to the United States are subject to a quota, the market shares assigned to firms in that country

---

15. Where all firms have, on a forward-looking basis, an equal likelihood of securing sales, the Agency will assign firms equal shares.

will not exceed the amount of shipments by such firms allowed under the quota.[16] In the case of restraints that limit imports to some percentage of the total amount of the product sold in the United States (i.e., percentage quotas), a domestic price increase that reduced domestic consumption also would reduce the volume of imports into the United States. Accordingly, actual import sales and capacity data will be reduced for purposes of calculating market shares. Finally, a single market share may be assigned to a country or group of countries if firms in that country or group of countries act in coordination.

1.5 Concentration and Market Shares

Market concentration is a function of the number of firms in a market and their respective market shares. As an aid to the interpretation of market data, the Agency will use the Herfindahl-Hirschman Index ("HHI") of market concentration. The HHI is calculated by summing the squares of the individual market shares of all the participants.[17] Unlike the four-firm concentration ratio, the HHI reflects both the distribution of the market shares of the top four firms and the composition of the market outside the top four firms. It also gives proportionately greater weight to the market shares of the larger firms, in accord with their relative importance in competitive interactions.

The Agency divides the spectrum of market concentration as measured by the HHI into three regions that can be broadly characterized as unconcentrated (HHI below 1000), moderately concentrated (HHI between 1000 and 1800), and highly concentrated (HHI above 1800). Although the resulting regions provide a useful framework for merger analysis, the numerical divisions suggest greater precision than is

---

16. The constraining effect of the quota on the importer's ability to expand sales is relevant to the evaluation of potential adverse competitive effects. *See* Section 2.
17. For example, a market consisting of four firms with market shares of 30 percent, 30 percent, 20 percent and 20 percent has an HHI of 2600 ($30^2 + 30^2 + 20^2 + 20^{2+} = 2600$). The HHI ranges from 10,000 (in the case of a pure monopoly) to a number approaching zero (in the case of an atomistic market). Although it is desirable to include all firms in the calculation, lack of information about small firms is not critical because such firms do not affect the HHI significantly.

possible with the available economic tools and information. Other things being equal, cases falling just above and just below a threshold present comparable competitive issues.

1.51 General Standards

In evaluating horizontal mergers, the Agency will consider both the post-merger market concentration and the increase in concentration resulting from the merger.[18] Market concentration is a useful indicator of the likely potential competitive effect of a merger. The general standards for horizontal mergers are as follows:

a) *Post-Merger HHI Below 1000.* The Agency regards markets in this region to be unconcentrated. Mergers resulting in unconcentrated markets are unlikely to have adverse competitive effects and ordinarily require no further analysis.
b) *Post-Merger HHI Between 1000 and 1800.* The Agency regards markets in this region to be moderately concentrated. Mergers producing an increase in the HHI of less than 100 points in moderately concentrated markets post-merger are unlikely to have adverse competitive consequences and ordinarily require no further analysis. Mergers producing an increase in the HHI of more than 100 points in moderately concentrated markets post-merger potentially raise significant competitive concerns depending on the factors set forth in Sections 2-5 of the Guidelines.
c) *Post-Merger HHI Above 1800.* The Agency regards markets in this region to be highly concentrated. Mergers producing an increase in the HHI of less than 50 points, even in highly concentrated markets post-merger, are unlikely to have adverse

---

18. The increase in concentration as measured by the HHI can be calculated independently of the overall market concentration by doubling the product of the market shares of the merging firms. For example, the merger of firms with shares of 5 percent and 10 percent of the market would increase the HHI by 100 (5 x 10 x 2 = 100). The explanation for this technique is as follows: In calculating the HHI before the merger, the market shares of the merging firms are squared individually: $a^2 + b^2$. After the merger, the sum of those shares would be squared: $(a + b)^2$, which equals $a^2 + 2ab + b^2$. The increase in the HHI therefore is represented by 2ab.

competitive consequences and ordinarily require no further analysis. Mergers producing an increase in the HHI of more than 50 points in highly concentrated markets post-merger potentially raise significant competitive concerns, depending on the factors set forth in Sections 2-5 of the Guidelines.

1.52 Factors Affecting the Significance of Market Shares and Concentration

The post-merger level of market concentration and the change in concentration resulting from a merger affect the degree to which a merger raises competitive concerns. However, in some situations, market share and market concentration data may either understate or overstate the likely future competitive significance of a firm or firms in the market or the impact of a merger. The following are examples of such situations.

1.521 Changing Market Conditions

Market concentration and market share data of necessity are based on historical evidence. However, recent or ongoing changes in the market may indicate that the current market share of a particular firm either understates or overstates the firm's future competitive significance. For example, if a new technology that is important to long-term competitive viability is available to other firms in the market, but is not available to a particular firm, the Agency may conclude that the historical market share of that firm overstates its future competitive significance. The Agency will consider reasonably predictable effects of recent or ongoing changes in market conditions in interpreting market concentration and market share data.

1.522 Degree of Difference Between the Products and Locations in the Market and Substitutes Outside the Market

All else equal, the magnitude of potential competitive harm from a merger is greater if a hypothetical monopolist would raise price within the relevant market by substantially more than a "small but significant and nontransitory" amount. This may occur when the demand substitutes outside the relevant market, as a group, are not close substitutes for the products and locations within the relevant market. There thus may be a wide gap in the chain of demand substitutes at the edge of the product and geographic market. Under such circumstances, more market power is at stake in the relevant market than in a market in which a hypothetical monopolist would raise price by exactly five percent.

2. The Potential Adverse Competitive Effects of Mergers

2.0 Overview

Other things being equal, market concentration affects the likelihood that one firm, or a small group of firms, could successfully exercise market power. The smaller the percentage of total supply that a firm controls, the more severely it must restrict its own output in order to produce a given price increase, and the less likely it is that an output restriction will be profitable. If collective action is necessary for the exercise of market power, as the number of firms necessary to control a given percentage of total supply decreases, the difficulties and costs of reaching and enforcing an understanding with respect to the control of that supply might be reduced. However, market share and concentration data provide only the starting point for analyzing the competitive impact of a merger. Before determining whether to challenge a merger, the Agency also will assess the other market factors that pertain to competitive effects, as well as entry, efficiencies and failure.

This section considers some of the potential adverse competitive effects of mergers and the factors in addition to market concentration relevant to each. Because an individual merger may threaten to harm competition through more than one of these effects, mergers will be analyzed in terms of as many potential adverse competitive effects as are appropriate. Entry, efficiencies, and failure are treated in Sections 3-5.

2.1 Lessening of Competition Through Coordinated Interaction

A merger may diminish competition by enabling the firms selling in the relevant market more likely, more successfully, or more completely to engage in coordinated interaction that harms consumers. Coordinated interaction is comprised of actions by a group of firms that are profitable for each of them only as a result of the accommodating reactions of the others. This behavior includes tacit or express collusion, and may or may not be lawful in and of itself.

Successful coordinated interaction entails reaching terms of coordination that are profitable to the firms involved and an ability to detect and punish deviations that would undermine the coordinated interaction. Detection and punishment of deviations ensure that coordinating firms will find it more profitable to adhere to the terms of coordination than to pursue short-term profits from deviating, given the costs of reprisal. In this phase of the analysis, the Agency will examine the extent to which post-merger market conditions are conducive to reaching terms of coordination, detecting deviations from those terms, and punishing such deviations. Depending upon the circumstances, the following market factors, among others, may be relevant: the availability of key information concerning market conditions, transactions and individual competitors; the extent of firm and product heterogeneity; pricing or marketing practices typically employed by firms in the market; the characteristics of buyers and sellers; and the characteristics of typical transactions.

Certain market conditions that are conducive to reaching terms of coordination also may be conducive to detecting or punishing deviations from those terms. For example, the extent of information available to firms in the market, or the extent of homogeneity, may be relevant to both the ability to reach terms of coordination and to detect or punish deviations from those terms. The extent to which any specific market condition will be relevant to one or more of the conditions necessary to coordinated interaction will depend on the circumstances of the particular case.

It is likely that market conditions are conducive to coordinated interaction when the firms in the market previously have engaged in express collusion and when the salient characteristics of the market have not changed appreciably since the most recent such incident. Previous express collusion in another geographic market will have the same weight when the salient characteristics of that other market at the time of the collusion are comparable to those in the relevant market.

In analyzing the effect of a particular merger on coordinated interaction, the Agency is mindful of the difficulties of predicting likely future behavior based on the types of incomplete and sometimes contradictory information typically generated in merger investigations. Whether a merger is likely to diminish competition by enabling firms more likely, more successfully or more completely to engage in coordinated interaction depends on whether market conditions, on the whole, are conducive to reaching terms of coordination and detecting and punishing deviations from those terms.

2.11 Conditions Conducive to Reaching Terms of Coordination

Firms coordinating their interactions need not reach complex terms concerning the allocation of the market output across firms or the level of the market prices but may, instead, follow simple terms such as a common price, fixed price differentials, stable market shares, or customer or territorial restrictions. Terms of coordination need not perfectly achieve the monopoly outcome in order to be harmful to consumers. Instead, the terms of coordination may be imperfect and incomplete—inasmuch as they omit some market participants, omit some dimensions of competition, omit some customers, yield elevated prices short of monopoly levels, or lapse into episodic price wars—and still result insignificant competitive harm. At some point, however, imperfections cause the profitability of abiding by the terms of coordination to decrease and, depending on their extent, may make coordinated interaction unlikely in the first instance.

Market conditions may be conducive to or hinder reaching terms of coordination. For example, reaching terms of coordination may be facilitated by product or firm homogeneity and by existing practices among firms, practices not necessarily themselves antitrust violations, such as standardization of pricing or product variables on which firms could compete. Key information about rival firms and the market may also facilitate reaching terms of coordination. Conversely, reaching terms of coordination may be limited or impeded by product heterogeneity or by firms having substantially incomplete information about the conditions and prospects of their rivals' businesses, perhaps because of important differences among their current business operations. In addition, reaching terms of coordination may be limited or impeded by firm heterogeneity, for example, differences in vertical integration or the production of another product that tends to be used together with the relevant product.

2.12 Conditions Conducive to Detecting and Punishing Deviations

Where market conditions are conducive to timely detection and punishment of significant deviations, a firm will find it more profitable to abide by the terms of coordination than to deviate from them. Deviation from the terms of coordination will be deterred where the threat of punishment is credible. Credible punishment, however, may not need to be any more complex than temporary abandonment of the terms of coordination by other firms in the market.

Where detection and punishment likely would be rapid, incentives to deviate are diminished and coordination is likely to be successful. The detection and punishment of deviations may be facilitated by existing practices among firms, themselves not necessarily antitrust violations, and by the characteristics of typical transactions. For example, if key information about specific transactions or individual price or output levels is available routinely to competitors, it may be difficult for a firm to deviate secretly. If orders for the relevant product are frequent, regular and small relative to the total output of a firm in a market, it may be difficult for the firm to deviate in a substantial way without the knowledge of rivals and without the opportunity for rivals to react. If demand or cost fluctuations are relatively infrequent and small, deviations may be relatively easy to deter.

By contrast, where detection or punishment is likely to be slow, incentives to deviate are enhanced and coordinated interaction is unlikely to be successful. If demand or cost fluctuations are relatively frequent and large, deviations may be relatively difficult to distinguish from these other sources of market price fluctuations, and, in consequence, deviations may be relatively difficult to deter.

In certain circumstances, buyer characteristics and the nature of the procurement process may affect the incentives to deviate from terms of coordination. Buyer size alone is not the determining characteristic. Where large buyers likely would engage in long-term contracting, so that the sales covered by such contracts can be large relative to the total output of a firm in the market, firms may have the incentive to deviate. However, this only can be accomplished where the duration, volume and profitability of the business covered by such contracts are sufficiently large as to make deviation more profitable in the long term than honoring the terms of coordination, and buyers likely would switch suppliers.

In some circumstances, coordinated interaction can be effectively prevented or limited by maverick firms—firms that have a greater economic incentive to deviate from the terms of coordination than do most of their rivals (e.g., firms that are unusually disruptive and competitive influences in the market). Consequently, acquisition of a maverick firm is one way in which a merger may make coordinated interaction more likely, more successful, or more complete. For example, in a market where capacity constraints are significant for many competitors, a firm is more likely to be a maverick the greater is its excess or divertable capacity in relation to its sales or its total capacity, and the lower are its direct and opportunity costs of expanding sales in the relevant market.[19] This is so because a firm's incentive to deviate from price-elevating and output-limiting terms of coordination is greater the more the firm is able profitably to expand its output as a proportion of the sales it would obtain if it adhered to the terms of coordination and the smaller is the base of sales on which it enjoys elevated profits prior to the price cutting deviation.[20] A firm also may be a maverick if it has an unusual ability secretly to expand its sales in relation to the sales it would obtain if it adhered to the terms of coordination. This ability might arise from opportunities to expand captive production for a downstream affiliate.

2.2 Lessening of Competition Through Unilateral Effects

A merger may diminish competition even if it does not lead to increased likelihood of successful coordinated interaction, because merging firms may find it profitable to alter their behavior unilaterally following the acquisition by elevating price and suppressing output. Unilateral competitive effects can arise in a variety of different settings. In each setting, particular other factors describing the relevant market affect the likelihood of unilateral competitive effects. The settings differ by the primary characteristics that distinguish firms and shape the nature of their competition.

---

19. But excess capacity in the hands of non-maverick firms may be a potent weapon with which to punish deviations from the terms of coordination.
20. Similarly, in a market where product design or quality is significant, a firm is more likely to be an effective maverick the greater is the sales potential of its products among customers of its rivals, in relation to the sales it would obtain if it adhered to the terms of coordination. The likelihood of expansion responses by a maverick will be analyzed in the same fashion as uncommitted entry or committed entry (*see* Sections 1.3 and 3) depending on the significance of the sunk costs entailed in expansion.

2.21 Firms Distinguished Primarily by Differentiated Products

In some markets the products are differentiated, so that products sold by different participants in the market are not perfect substitutes for one another. Moreover, different products in the market may vary in the degree of their substitutability for one another. In this setting, competition may be non-uniform (i.e., localized), so that individual sellers compete more directly with those rivals selling closer substitutes.[21]

A merger between firms in a market for differentiated products may diminish competition by enabling the merged firm to profit by unilaterally raising the price of one or both products above the premerger level. Some of the sales loss due to the price rise merely will be diverted to the product of the merger partner and, depending on relative margins, capturing such sales loss through merger may make the price increase profitable even though it would not have been profitable premerger. Substantial unilateral price elevation in a market for differentiated products requires that there be a significant share of sales in the market accounted for by consumers who regard the products of the merging firms as their first and second choices, and that repositioning of the non-parties' product lines to replace the localized competition lost through the merger be unlikely. The price rise will be greater the closer substitutes are the products of the merging firms, i.e., the more the buyers of one product consider the other product to be their next choice.

---

21. Similarly, in some markets sellers are primarily distinguished by their relative advantages in serving different buyers or groups of buyers, and buyers negotiate individually with sellers. Here, for example, sellers may formally bid against one another for the business of a buyer, or each buyer may elicit individual price quotes from multiple sellers. A seller may find it relatively inexpensive to meet the demands of particular buyers or types of buyers, and relatively expensive to meet others' demands. Competition, again, may be localized: sellers compete more directly with those rivals having similar relative advantages in serving particular buyers or groups of buyers. For example, in open outcry auctions, price is determined by the cost of the second lowest-cost seller. A merger involving the first and second lowest-cost sellers could cause prices to rise to the constraining level of the next lowest-cost seller.

2.211 Closeness of the Products of the Merging Firms

The market concentration measures articulated in Section 1 may help assess the extent of the likely competitive effect from a unilateral price elevation by the merged firm notwithstanding the fact that the affected products are differentiated. The market concentration measures provide a measure of this effect if each product's market share is reflective of not only its relative appeal as a first choice to consumers of the merging firms' products but also its relative appeal as a second choice, and hence as a competitive constraint to the first choice.[22] Where this circumstance holds, market concentration data fall outside the safe harbor regions of Section 1.5, and the merging firms have a combined market share of at least thirty-five percent, the Agency will presume that a significant share of sales in the market are accounted for by consumers who regard the products of the merging firms as their first and second choices.

Purchasers of one of the merging firms' products may be more or less likely to make the other their second choice than market shares alone would indicate. The market shares of the merging firms' products may understate the competitive effect of concern, when, for example, the products of the merging firms are relatively more similar in their various attributes to one another than to other products in the relevant market. On the other hand, the market shares alone may overstate the competitive effects of concern when, for example, the relevant products are less similar in their attributes to one another than to other products in the relevant market.

Where market concentration data fall outside the safe harbor regions of Section 1.5, the merging firms have a combined market share of at least thirty-five percent, and where data on product attributes and relative product appeal show that a significant share of purchasers of one merging firm's product regard the other as their second choice, then market share data may be relied upon to demonstrate that there is a significant share of sales in the market accounted for by consumers who would be adversely affected by the merger.

---

22. Information about consumers' actual first and second product choices may be provided by marketing surveys, information from bidding structures, or normal course of business documents from industry participants.

2.212 *Ability of Rival Sellers to Replace Lost Competition*

A merger is not likely to lead to unilateral elevation of prices of differentiated products if, in response to such an effect, rival sellers likely would replace any localized competition lost through the merger by repositioning their product lines.[23]

In markets where it is costly for buyers to evaluate product quality, buyers who consider purchasing from both merging parties may limit the total number of sellers they consider. If either of the merging firms would be replaced in such buyers' consideration by an equally competitive seller not formerly considered, then the merger is not likely to lead to a unilateral elevation of prices.

2.22 Firm Distinguished Primarily By Their Capacities

Where products are relatively undifferentiated and capacity primarily distinguishes firms and shapes the nature of their competition, the merged firm may find it profitable unilaterally to raise price and suppress output. The merger provides the merged firm a larger base of sales on which to enjoy the resulting price rise and also eliminates a competitor to which customers otherwise would have diverted their sales. Where the merging firms have a combined market share of at least thirty-five percent, merged firms may find it profitable to raise price and reduce joint output below the sum of their premerger outputs because the lost markups on the foregone sales may be outweighed by the resulting price increase on the merged base of sales.

This unilateral effect is unlikely unless a sufficiently large number of the merged firm's customers would not be able to find economical alternative sources of supply, i.e., competitors of the merged firm likely would not respond to the price increase and output reduction by the merged firm with increases in their own outputs sufficient in the aggregate to make the unilateral action of the merged firm unprofitable. Such non-party expansion is unlikely if those firms face binding capacity constraints that could not be economically relaxed within two years or if

23. The timeliness and likelihood of repositioning responses will be analyzed using the same methodology as used in analyzing uncommitted entry or committed entry (*see* Sections 1.3 and 3), depending on the significance of the sunk costs entailed in repositioning.

existing excess capacity is significantly more costly to operate than capacity currently in use.[24]

3. Entry Analysis

3.0 Overview

A merger is not likely to create or enhance market power or to facilitate its exercise, if entry into the market is so easy that market participants, after the merger, either collectively or unilaterally could not profitably maintain a price increase above premerger levels. Such entry likely will deter an anticompetitive merger in its incipiency, or deter or counteract the competitive effects of concern.

Entry is that easy if entry would be timely, likely, and sufficient in its magnitude, character and scope to deter or counteract the competitive effects of concern. In markets where entry is that easy (i.e., where entry passes these tests of timeliness, likelihood, and sufficiency), the merger raises no antitrust concern and ordinarily requires no further analysis.

The committed entry treated in this Section is defined as new competition that requires expenditure of significant sunk costs of entry and exit.[25] The Agency employs a three step methodology to assess whether committed entry would deter or counteract a competitive effect of concern.

The first step assesses whether entry can achieve significant market impact within a timely period. If significant market impact would require a longer period, entry will not deter or counteract the competitive effect of concern.

The second step assesses whether committed entry would be a profitable and, hence, a likely response to a merger having competitive effects of concern. Firms considering entry that requires significant sunk costs must evaluate the profitability of the entry on the basis of long term participation in the market, because the underlying assets will be

---

24. The timeliness and likelihood of non-party expansion will be analyzed using the same methodology as used in analyzing uncommitted or committed entry (*see* Sections 1.3 and 3) depending on the significance of the sunk costs entailed in expansion.

25. Supply responses that require less than one year and insignificant sunk costs to effectuate are analyzed as uncommitted entry in Section 1.3.

committed to the market until they are economically depreciated. Entry that is sufficient to counteract the competitive effects of concern will cause prices to fall to their premerger levels or lower. Thus, the profitability of such committed entry must be determined on the basis of premerger market prices over the long-term.

A merger having anticompetitive effects can attract committed entry, profitable at premerger prices, that would not have occurred premerger at these same prices. But following the merger, the reduction in industry output and increase in prices associated with the competitive effect of concern may allow the same entry to occur without driving market prices below premerger levels. After a merger that results in decreased output and increased prices, the likely sales opportunities available to entrants at premerger prices will be larger than they were premerger, larger by the output reduction caused by the merger. If entry could be profitable at premerger prices without exceeding the likely sales opportunities—opportunities that include pre-existing pertinent factors as well as the merger-induced output reduction—then such entry is likely in response to the merger.

The third step assesses whether timely and likely entry would be sufficient to return market prices to their premerger levels. This end may be accomplished either through multiple entry or individual entry at a sufficient scale. Entry may not be sufficient, even though timely and likely, where the constraints on availability of essential assets, due to incumbent control, make it impossible for entry profitably to achieve the necessary level of sales. Also, the character and scope of entrants' products might not be fully responsive to the localized sales opportunities created by the removal of direct competition among sellers of differentiated products. In assessing whether entry will be timely, likely, and sufficient, the Agency recognizes that precise and detailed information may be difficult or impossible to obtain. In such instances, the Agency will rely on all available evidence bearing on whether entry will satisfy the conditions of timeliness, likelihood, and sufficiency.

3.1 Entry Alternatives

The Agency will examine the timeliness, likelihood, and sufficiency of the means of entry (entry alternatives) a potential entrant might practically employ, without attempting to identify who might be potential entrants. An entry alternative is defined by the actions the firm must take in order to produce and sell in the market. All phases of the entry effort will be considered, including, where relevant, planning, design, and management; permitting, licensing, and other approvals; construction, debugging, and operation of production facilities; and promotion (including necessary introductory discounts), marketing, distribution, and satisfaction of customer testing and qualification requirements.[26] Recent examples of entry, whether successful or unsuccessful, may provide a useful starting point for identifying the necessary actions, time requirements, and characteristics of possible entry alternatives.

3.2 Timeliness of Entry

In order to deter or counteract the competitive effects of concern, entrants quickly must achieve a significant impact on price in the relevant market. The Agency generally will consider timely only those committed entry alternatives that can be achieved within two years from initial planning to significant market impact.[27] Where the relevant product is a durable good, consumers, in response to a significant commitment to entry, may defer purchases by making additional investments to extend the useful life of previously purchased goods and in this way deter or counteract for a time the competitive effects of concern. In these circumstances, if entry only can occur outside of the two year period, the Agency will consider entry to be timely so long as it would deter or counteract the competitive effects of concern within the two year period and subsequently.

3.3 Likelihood of Entry

An entry alternative is likely if it would be profitable at premerger prices, and if such prices could be secured by the entrant.[28] The

26. Many of these phases may be undertaken simultaneously.
27. Firms which have committed to entering the market prior to the merger generally will be included in the measurement of the market. Only committed entry or adjustments to pre-existing entry plans that are induced by the merger will be considered as possibly deterring or counteracting the competitive effects of concern.
28. Where conditions indicate that entry may be profitable at prices below premerger levels, the Agency will assess the likelihood of entry at the

committed entrant will be unable to secure prices at premerger levels if its output is too large for the market to absorb without depressing prices further. Thus, entry is unlikely if the minimum viable scale is larger than the likely sales opportunity available to entrants.

Minimum viable scale is the smallest average annual level of sales that the committed entrant must persistently achieve for profitability at premerger prices.[29] Minimum viable scale is a function of expected revenues, based upon premerger prices,[30] and all categories of costs associated with the entry alternative, including an appropriate rate of return on invested capital given that entry could fail and sunk costs, if any, will be lost.[31]

Sources of sales opportunities available to entrants include: (a) the output reduction associated with the competitive effect of concern,[32] (b) entrants' ability to capture a share of reasonably expected growth in market demand,[33] (c) entrants' ability securely to divert sales from incumbents, for example, through vertical integration or through forward contracting, and (d) any additional anticipated contraction in incumbents' output in response to entry.[34] Factors that reduce the sales opportunities

---

lowest price at which such entry would be profitable.

29. The concept of minimum viable scale ("MVS") differs from the concept of minimum efficient scale ("MES"). While MES is the smallest scale at which average costs are minimized, MVS is the smallest scale at which average costs equal the premerger price.

30. The expected path of future prices, absent the merger, may be used if future price changes can be predicted with reasonable reliability.

31. The minimum viable scale of an entry alternative will be relatively large when the fixed costs of entry are large, when the fixed costs of entry are largely sunk, when the marginal costs of production are high at low levels of output, and when a plant is underutilized for a long time because of delays in achieving market acceptance.

32. Five percent of total market sales typically is used because where a monopolist profitably would raise price by five percent or more across the entire relevant market, it is likely that the accompanying reduction in sales would be no less than five percent.

33. Entrants' anticipated share of growth in demand depends on incumbents' capacity constraints and irreversible investments in capacity expansion, as well as on the relative appeal, acceptability and reputation of incumbents' and entrants' products to the new demand.

34. For example, in a bidding market where all bidders are on equal footing,

available to entrants include: (a) the prospect that an entrant will share in a reasonably expected decline in market demand, (b) the exclusion of an entrant from a portion of the market over the long term because of vertical integration or forward contracting by incumbents, and (c) any anticipated sales expansion by incumbents in reaction to entry, either generalized or targeted at customers approached by the entrant, that utilizes prior irreversible investments in excess production capacity. Demand growth or decline will be viewed as relevant only if total market demand is projected to experience long-lasting change during at least the two year period following the competitive effect of concern.

3.4 Sufficiency of Entry

Inasmuch as multiple entry generally is possible and individual entrants may flexibly choose their scale, committed entry generally will be sufficient to deter or counteract the competitive effects of concern whenever entry is likely under the analysis of Section 3.3. However, entry, although likely, will not be sufficient if, as a result of incumbent control, the tangible and intangible assets required for entry are not adequately available for entrants to respond fully to their sales opportunities. In addition, where the competitive effect of concern is not uniform across the relevant market, in order for entry to be sufficient, the character and scope of entrants' products must be responsive to the localized sales opportunities that include the output reduction associated with the competitive effect of concern. For example, where the concern is unilateral price elevation as a result of a merger between producers of differentiated products, entry, in order to be sufficient, must involve a product so close to the products of the merging firms that the merged firm will be unable to internalize enough of the sales loss due to the price rise, rendering the price increase unprofitable.

4. Efficiencies (as revised April 8, 1997)

Competition usually spurs firms to achieve efficiencies internally. Nevertheless, mergers have the potential to generate significant efficiencies by permitting a better utilization of existing assets, enabling

---

the market share of incumbents will contract as a result of entry.

the combined firm to achieve lower costs in producing a given quantity and quality than either firm could have achieved without the proposed transaction. Indeed, the primary benefit of mergers to the economy is their potential to generate such efficiencies.

Efficiencies generated through merger can enhance the merged firm's ability and incentive to compete, which may result in lower prices, improved quality, enhanced service, or new products. For example, merger-generated efficiencies may enhance competition by permitting two ineffective (e.g., high cost) competitors to become one effective (e.g., lower cost) competitor. In a coordinated interaction context (see Section 2.1), marginal cost reductions may make coordination less likely or effective by enhancing the incentive of a maverick to lower price or by creating a new maverick firm. In a unilateral effects context (see Section 2.2), marginal cost reductions may reduce the merged firm's incentive to elevate price. Efficiencies also may result in benefits in the form of new or improved products, and efficiencies may result in benefits even when price is not immediately and directly affected. Even when efficiencies generated through merger enhance a firm's ability to compete, however, a merger may have other effects that may lessen competition and ultimately may make the merger anticompetitive.

The Agency will consider only those efficiencies likely to be accomplished with the proposed merger and unlikely to be accomplished in the absence of either the proposed merger or another means having comparable anticompetitive effects. These are termed merger-specific efficiencies.[35] Only alternatives that are practical in the business situation faced by the merging firms will be considered in making this determination; the Agency will not insist upon a less restrictive alternative that is merely theoretical.

Efficiencies are difficult to verify and quantify, in part because much of the information relating to efficiencies is uniquely in the possession of the merging firms. Moreover, efficiencies projected reasonably and in good faith by the merging firms may not be realized. Therefore, the

---

35. The Agency will not deem efficiencies to be merger-specific if they could be preserved by practical alternatives that mitigate competitive concerns, such as divestiture or licensing. If a merger affects not whether but only when an efficiency would be achieved, only the timing advantage is a merger-specific efficiency.

merging firms must substantiate efficiency claims so that the Agency can verify by reasonable means the likelihood and magnitude of each asserted efficiency, how and when each would be achieved (and any costs of doing so), how each would enhance the merged firm's ability and incentive to compete, and why each would be merger-specific. Efficiency claims will not be considered if they are vague or speculative or otherwise cannot be verified by reasonable means.

Cognizable efficiencies are merger-specific efficiencies that have been verified and do not arise from anticompetitive reductions in output or service. Cognizable efficiencies are assessed net of costs produced by the merger or incurred in achieving those efficiencies.

The Agency will not challenge a merger if cognizable efficiencies are of a character and magnitude such that the merger is not likely to be anticompetitive in any relevant market.[36] To make the requisite determination, the Agency considers whether cognizable efficiencies likely would be sufficient to reverse the merger's potential to harm consumers in the relevant market, e.g., by preventing price increases in that market. In conducting this analysis,[37] the Agency will not simply

---

36. Section 7 of the Clayton Act prohibits mergers that may substantially lessen competition "in any line of commerce . . . in any section of the country." Accordingly, the Agency normally assesses competition in each relevant market affected by a merger independently and normally will challenge the merger if it is likely to be anticompetitive in any relevant market. In some cases, however, the Agency in its prosecutorial discretion will consider efficiencies not strictly in the relevant market, but so inextricably linked with it that a partial divestiture or other remedy could not feasibly eliminate the anticompetitive effect in the relevant market without sacrificing the efficiencies in the other market(s). Inextricably linked efficiencies rarely are a significant factor in the Agency's determination not to challenge a merger. They are most likely to make a difference when they are great and the likely anticompetitive effect in the relevant market(s) is small.
37. The result of this analysis over the short term will determine the Agency's enforcement decision in most cases. The Agency also will consider the effects of cognizable efficiencies with no short-term, direct effect on prices in the relevant market. Delayed benefits from efficiencies (due to delay in the achievement of, or the realization of consumer benefits from, the efficiencies) will be given less weight because they are less proximate and more difficult to predict.

compare the magnitude of the cognizable efficiencies with the magnitude of the likely harm to competition absent the efficiencies. The greater the potential adverse competitive effect of a merger—as indicated by the increase in the HHI and post-merger HHI from Section 1, the analysis of potential adverse competitive effects from Section 2, and the timeliness, likelihood, and sufficiency of entry from Section 3—the greater must be cognizable efficiencies in order for the Agency to conclude that the merger will not have an anticompetitive effect in the relevant market. When the potential adverse competitive effect of a merger is likely to be particularly large, extraordinarily great cognizable efficiencies would be necessary to prevent the merger from being anticompetitive.

In the Agency's experience, efficiencies are most likely to make a difference in merger analysis when the likely adverse competitive effects, absent the efficiencies, are not great. Efficiencies almost never justify a merger to monopoly or near-monopoly.

The Agency has found that certain types of efficiencies are more likely to be cognizable and substantial than others. For example, efficiencies resulting from shifting production among facilities formerly owned separately, which enable the merging firms to reduce the marginal cost of production, are more likely to be susceptible to verification, merger-specific, and substantial, and are less likely to result from anticompetitive reductions in output. Other efficiencies, such as those relating to research and development, are potentially substantial but are generally less susceptible to verification and may be the result of anticompetitive output reductions. Yet others, such as those relating to procurement, management, or capital cost are less likely to be merger-specific or substantial, or may not be cognizable for other reasons.

5. Failure and Exiting Assets

5.0 Overview

Notwithstanding the analysis of Sections 1-4 of the Guidelines, a merger is not likely to create or enhance market power or to facilitate its exercise, if imminent failure, as defined below, of one of the merging firms would cause the assets of that firm to exit the relevant market. In such circumstances, post-merger performance in the relevant market may be no worse than market performance had the merger been blocked and the assets left the market.

5.1 Failing Firm

A merger is not likely to create or enhance market power or facilitate its exercise if the following circumstances are met: (1) the allegedly failing firm would be unable to meet its financial obligations in the near future; (2) it would not be able to reorganize successfully under Chapter 11 of the Bankruptcy Act;[38] (3) it has made unsuccessful good-faith efforts to elicit reasonable alternative offers of acquisition of the assets of the failing firm[39] that would both keep its tangible and intangible assets in the relevant market and pose a less severe danger to competition than does the proposed merger; and (4) absent the acquisition, the assets of the failing firm would exit the relevant market.

5.2 Failing Division

A similar argument can be made for "failing" divisions as for failing firms. First, upon applying appropriate cost allocation rules, the division must have a negative cash flow on an operating basis. Second, absent the acquisition, it must be that the assets of the division would exit the relevant market in the near future if not sold. Due to the ability of the parent firm to allocate costs, revenues, and intracompany transactions among itself and its subsidiaries and divisions, the Agency will require evidence, not based solely on management plans that could be prepared solely for the purpose of demonstrating negative cash flow or the prospect of exit from the relevant market. Third, the owner of the failing division also must have complied with the competitively-preferable purchaser requirement of Section 5.1.

---

38. 11 U.S.C. §§ 1101-1174 (1988).

39. Any offer to purchase the assets of the failing firm for a price above the liquidation value of those assets—the highest valued use outside the relevant market or equivalent offer to purchase the stock of the failing firm—will be regarded as a reasonable alternative offer.

APPENDIX J

1995 DEPARTMENT OF JUSTICE AND FEDERAL TRADE COMMISSION ANTITRUST ENFORCEMENT GUIDELINES FOR INTERNATIONAL OPERATIONS

April 1995

1. Introduction

For more than a century, the U.S. antitrust laws have stood as the ultimate protector of the competitive process that underlies our free market economy. Through this process, which enhances consumer choice and promotes competitive prices, society as a whole benefits from the best possible allocation of resources.

Although the federal antitrust laws have always applied to foreign commerce, that application is particularly important today. Throughout the world, the importance of antitrust law as a means to ensure open and free markets, protect consumers, and prevent conduct that impedes competition is becoming more apparent. The Department of Justice ("the Department") and the Federal Trade Commission ("the Commission" or "FTC") (when referred to collectively, "the Agencies"), as the federal agencies charged with the responsibility of enforcing the antitrust laws, thus have made it a high priority to enforce the antitrust laws with respect to international operations and to cooperate wherever appropriate with foreign authorities regarding such enforcement. In furtherance of this priority, the Agencies have revised and updated the Department's 1988 Antitrust Enforcement Guidelines for International Operations, which are hereby withdrawn.[1]

The 1995 Antitrust Enforcement Guidelines for International Operations (hereinafter "Guidelines") are intended to provide antitrust guidance to businesses engaged in international operations on questions that relate specifically to the Agencies' international enforcement policy.[2] They do not, therefore, provide a complete statement of the Agencies' general enforcement policies. The topics covered include the Agencies' subject matter jurisdiction over conduct and entities outside the United States and the considerations, issues, policies, and processes that govern their decision to exercise that jurisdiction; comity; mutual assistance in international antitrust enforcement; and the effects of foreign governmental involvement on the antitrust liability of private entities. In addition, the Guidelines discuss the relationship between antitrust and international trade initiatives. Finally, to illustrate how these principles may operate in certain contexts, the Guidelines include a number of examples.

---

1. The U.S. Department of Justice and Federal Trade Commission Antitrust Guidelines for the Licensing of Intellectual Property (1995), the U.S. Department of Justice and Federal Trade Commission Horizontal Merger Guidelines (1992), and the Statements of Antitrust Enforcement Policy and Analytical Principles Relating to Health Care and Antitrust, Jointly Issued by the U.S. Department of Justice and Federal Trade Commission (1994), are not qualified, modified, or otherwise amended by the issuance of these Guidelines.
2. Readers should separately evaluate the risk of private litigation by competitors, consumers and suppliers, as well as the risk of enforcement by state prosecutors under state and federal antitrust laws.

As is the case with all guidelines, users should rely on qualified counsel to assist them in evaluating the antitrust risk associated with any contemplated transaction or activity. No set of guidelines can possibly indicate how the Agencies will assess the particular facts of every case. Persons seeking more specific advance statements of enforcement intentions with respect to the matters treated in these Guidelines should use the Department's Business Review procedure,[3] the Commission's Advisory Opinion procedure,[4] or one of the more specific procedures described below for particular types of transactions.

2. Antitrust Laws Enforced By The Agencies

Foreign commerce cases can involve almost any provision of the antitrust laws. The Agencies do not discriminate in the enforcement of the antitrust laws on the basis of the nationality of the parties. Nor do the Agencies employ their statutory authority to further non-antitrust goals. Once jurisdictional requirements, comity, and doctrines of foreign governmental involvement have been considered and satisfied, the same substantive rules apply to all cases.

The following is a brief summary of the laws enforced by the Agencies that are likely to have the greatest significance for international transactions.

2.1 Sherman Act

Section 1 of the Sherman Act, 15 U.S.C. § 1, sets forth the basic antitrust prohibition against contracts, combinations, and conspiracies "in restraint of trade or commerce among the several States or with foreign nations." Section 2 of the Act, 15 U.S.C. § 2, prohibits monopolization, attempts to monopolize, and conspiracies to monopolize "any part of trade or commerce among the several States or with foreign nations." Section 6a of the Sherman Act, 15 U.S.C. § 6a, defines the jurisdictional reach of the Act with respect to non-import foreign commerce.

Violations of the Sherman Act may be prosecuted as civil or criminal offenses. Conduct that the Department prosecutes criminally is limited to

---

3. 28 C.F.R. § 50.6 (1994).
4. 16 C.F.R. §§ 1.1-1.4 (1994).

traditional per se offenses of the law, which typically involve price-fixing, customer allocation, bid-rigging or other cartel activities that would also be violations of the law in many countries. Criminal violations of the Act are punishable by fines and imprisonment. The Sherman Act provides that corporate defendants may be fined up to $10 million, other defendants may be fined up to $350,000, and individuals may be sentenced to up to 3 years imprisonment.[5] The Department has sole responsibility for the criminal enforcement of the Sherman Act. In a civil proceeding, the Department may obtain injunctive relief against prohibited practices. It may also obtain treble damages if the U.S. government is the purchaser of affected goods or services.[6] Private plaintiffs may also obtain injunctive and treble damage relief for violations of the Sherman Act.[7] Before the Commission, conduct that violates the Sherman Act may be challenged pursuant to the Commission's power under Section 5 of the Federal Trade Commission Act, described below.

2.2 Clayton Act

The Clayton Act, 15 U.S.C. § 12 et seq., expands on the general prohibitions of the Sherman Act and addresses anticompetitive problems in their incipiency.[8] Section 7 of the Clayton Act, 15 U.S.C. § 18, prohibits any merger or acquisition of stock or assets "where in any line of commerce or in any activity affecting commerce in any section of the

---

5. Defendants may be fined up to twice the gross pecuniary gain or loss caused by their offense in lieu of the Sherman Act fines, pursuant to 18 U.S.C. § 3571(d) (1988 & Supp. 1993). In addition, the U.S. Sentencing Commission Guidelines provide further information about possible criminal sanctions for individual antitrust defendants in § 2R1.1 and for organizational defendants in Chapter 8.
6. *See* 15 U.S.C. § 4 (1988) (injunctive relief); 15 U.S.C. § 15(a) (1988 & Supp. 1993) (damages).
7. *See* 15 U.S.C. §§ 16, 26 (1988).
8. Under the Clayton Act, "commerce" includes "trade or commerce among the several States and with foreign nations." "Persons" include corporations or associations existing under or authorized either by the laws of the United States or any of its states or territories, or by the laws of any foreign country. 15 U.S.C. § 12 (1988 & Supp. 1993).

country, the effect of such acquisition may be substantially to lessen competition, or to tend to create a monopoly."[9] Section 15 of the Clayton Act empowers the Attorney General, and Section 13(b) of the FTC Act empowers the Commission, to seek a court order enjoining consummation of a merger that would violate Section 7. In addition, the Commission may seek a cease and desist order in an administrative proceeding against a merger under Section 11 of the Clayton Act, Section 5 of the FTC Act, or both. Private parties may also seek injunctive relief under 15 U.S.C. § 26.

Section 3 of the Clayton Act prohibits any person engaged in commerce from conditioning the lease or sale of goods or commodities upon the purchaser's agreement not to use the products of a competitor, if the effect may be "to substantially lessen competition or to tend to create a monopoly in any line of commerce."[10] In evaluating transactions, the trend of recent authority is to use the same analysis employed in the evaluation of tying under Section 1 of the Sherman Act to assess a defendant's liability under Section 3 of the Clayton Act.[11] Section 2 of the Clayton Act, known as the Robinson-Patman Act,[12] prohibits price discrimination in certain circumstances. In practice, the Commission has exercised primary enforcement responsibility for this provision.

2.3 Federal Trade Commission Act

---

9. 15 U.S.C. § 18 (1988). The asset acquisition clause applies to "person[s] subject to the jurisdiction of the Federal Trade Commission" under the Clayton Act.
10. 15 U.S.C. § 14 (1988).
11. *See, e.g.,* Mozart Co. v. Mercedes-Benz of N. Am., Inc., 833 F.2d 1342, 1352 (9th Cir. 1987), *cert. denied,* 488 U.S. 870 (1988).
12. 15 U.S.C. §§ 13-13b, 21a (1988). The Robinson-Patman Act applies only to purchases involving commodities "for use, consumption, or resale within the United States." Id. at § 13. It has been construed not to apply to sales for export. *See, e.g.,* General Chem., Inc. v. Exxon Chem. Co., 625 F.2d 1231, 1234 (5th Cir. 1980). Intervening domestic sales, however, would be subject to the Act. *See* Raul Int'l Corp. v. Sealed Power Corp., 586 F. Supp. 349, 351-55 (D.N.J. 1984).

Section 5 of the Federal Trade Commission Act ("FTC Act") declares unlawful "unfair methods of competition in or affecting commerce, and unfair or deceptive acts or practices in or affecting commerce."[13] Pursuant to its authority over unfair methods of competition, the Commission may take administrative action against conduct that violates the Sherman Act and the Clayton Act, as well as anticompetitive practices that do not fall within the scope of the Sherman or Clayton Acts. The Commission may also seek injunctive relief in federal court against any such conduct under Section 13(b) of the FTC Act. Although enforcement at the Commission relating to international deceptive practices has become increasingly important over time, these Guidelines are limited to the Commission's antitrust authority under the unfair methods of competition language of Section 5.

2.4 Hart-Scott-Rodino Antitrust Improvements Act of 1976

Title II of the Hart-Scott-Rodino Antitrust Improvements Act of 1976 ("HSR Act"), 15 U.S.C. § 18a, provides the Department and the Commission with several procedural devices to facilitate enforcement of the antitrust laws with respect to anticompetitive mergers and acquisitions.[14] The HSR Act requires persons engaged in commerce or

---

13. 15 U.S.C. § 45 (1988 & Supp. 1993).
14. The scope of the Agencies' jurisdiction under Clayton § 7 exceeds the scope of those transactions subject to the premerger notification requirements of the HSR Act. Whether or not the HSR Act premerger notification thresholds are satisfied, either Agency may request the parties to a merger affecting U.S. commerce to provide information voluntarily concerning the transaction. In addition, the Department may issue Civil Investigative Demands ("CIDs") pursuant to the Antitrust Civil Process Act, 15 U.S.C. §§ 1311-1314 (1988), and the Commission may issue administrative CIDs pursuant to the Act of Aug. 26, 1994, Pub. L. No. 103-312, § 7; 108 Stat. 1691 (1994). The Commission may also issue administrative subpoenas and orders to file special reports under Sections 9 and 6(b) of the FTC Act, respectively. 15 U.S.C. §§ 49, 46(b) (1988). Authority in particular cases is allocated to either the Department or the Commission pursuant to a voluntary clearance protocol. *See* Antitrust & Trade Reg. Daily (BNA), Dec. 6, 1993, and U.S. Department of Justice and Federal Trade Commission, Hart-Scott-Rodino Premerger Program Improvements (March 23, 1995).

in any activity affecting commerce to notify the Agencies of proposed mergers or acquisitions that would exceed statutory size-of-party and size-of-transaction thresholds,[15] to provide certain information relating to reportable transactions, and to wait for a prescribed period—15 days for cash tender offers and 30 days for most other transactions-before consummating the transaction.[16] The Agency may, before the end of the waiting period, request additional information concerning a transaction (make a "Second Request") and thereby extend the waiting period beyond the initial one prescribed, to a specified number of days after the receipt of the material required by the Second Request—10 days for cash tender offers and 20 days for most other transactions.[17]

---

15. Unless exempted pursuant to the HSR Act, the parties must provide premerger notification to the Agencies if (1) the acquiring person, or the person whose voting securities or assets are being acquired, is engaged in commerce or any activity affecting commerce; and (2)(a) any voting securities or assets of a person engaged in manufacturing which has annual net sales or total assets of $10 million or more are being acquired by any person which has total assets or annual net sales of $100 million or more, or (b) any voting securities or assets of a person not engaged in manufacturing which has total assets of $10 million or more are being acquired by any person which has total assets or annual sales of $100 million or more; or (c) any voting securities or assets of a person with annual net sales or total assets of $100 million or more are being acquired by any person with total assets or annual net sales of $ 10 million or more; and (3) as a result of such acquisition, the acquiring person would hold (a) 15 percent or more of the voting securities or assets of the acquired person, or (b) an aggregate total amount of the voting securities and assets of the acquired person of $15 million. 15 U.S.C. § 18a(a) (1988). The size of the transaction test set forth in (3) must be read in conjunction with 16 C.F.R. § 802.20 (1994). This Section exempts asset acquisitions valued at $15 million or less. It also exempts voting securities acquisitions of $15 million or less unless, if as a result of the acquisition, the acquiring person would hold 50 percent or more of the voting securities of an issuer that has annual net sales or total assets of $25 million or more. The HSR rules are necessarily technical, contain other exemptions, and should be consulted, rather than relying on this summary.
16. 15 U.S.C. § 18a(b) (1988 & Supp. 1993); 16 C.F.R. § 803.1 (1994); *See also* 11 U.S.C. § 363(b)(2).
17. 15 U.S.C. § 18a(e) (1988).

The HSR Act and the FTC rules implementing the HSR Act[18] exempt from the premerger notification requirements certain international transactions (typically those having little nexus to U.S. commerce) that otherwise meet the statutory thresholds.[19] Failure to comply with the HSR Act is punishable by court-imposed civil penalties of up to $10,000 for each day a violation continues. The court may also order injunctive relief to remedy a failure substantially to comply with the HSR Act. Businesses may seek an interpretation of their obligations under the HSR Act from the Commission.[20]

2.5 National Cooperative Research and Production Act

The National Cooperative Research and Production Act ("NCRPA"), 15 U.S.C. §§ 4301-06, clarifies the substantive application of the U.S. antitrust laws to joint research and development ("R&D") activities and joint production activities. Originally drafted to encourage research and development by providing a special antitrust regime for research and development joint ventures, the NCRPA requires U.S. courts to judge the competitive effects of a challenged joint R&D or joint production venture, or a combination of the two, in properly defined relevant markets and under a rule-of-reason standard. The statute specifies that the conduct "shall be judged on the basis of its reasonableness, taking into account all relevant factors affecting competition, including, but not limited to, effects on competition in properly defined, relevant research, development, product, process, and service markets."[21] This approach is consistent with the Agencies' general analysis of joint ventures.[22]

---

18. 16 C.F.R. §§ 801-803 (1994).
19. 16 C.F.R. §§ 801.1(e), (k), 802.50-52 (1994). *See infra* at Section 4.22.
20. *See* 16 C.F.R. § 803.30 (1994).
21. 15 U.S.C. § 4302 (1988 & Supp. 1993).
22. *See, e.g.,* U.S. Department of Justice and Federal Trade Commission Antitrust Guidelines for the Licensing of Intellectual Property, § 4 (1995); Statements of Antitrust Enforcement Policy and Analytical Principles Relating to Health Care and Antitrust, Jointly Issued by the U.S. Department of Justice and the Federal Trade Commission (1994), Statement 2 (outlining a four-step approach for joint venture analysis). *See* generally National Collegiate Athletic Ass'n v. Board of Regents of Univ. of Okla., 468 U.S. 85 (1984); Federal Trade Comm'n v. Indiana

The NCRPA also establishes a voluntary procedure pursuant to which the Attorney General and the FTC may be notified of a joint R&D or production venture. The statute limits the monetary relief that may be obtained in private civil suits against the participants in a notified venture to actual rather than treble damages, if the challenged conduct is within the scope of the notification. With respect to joint production ventures, the National Cooperative Production Amendments of 1993[23] provide that the benefits of the limitation on recoverable damages for claims resulting from conduct within the scope of a notification are not available unless (1) the principal facilities for the production are located within the United States or its territories, and (2) "each person who controls any party to such venture (including such party itself) is a United States person, or a foreign person from a country whose law accords antitrust treatment no less favorable to United States persons than to such country's domestic persons with respect to participation in joint ventures for production."[24]

2.6 Webb-Pomerene Act

The Webb-Pomerene Act, 15 U.S.C. §§ 61-65, provides a limited antitrust exemption for the formation and operation of associations of otherwise competing businesses to engage in collective export sales. The exemption applies only to the export of "goods, wares, or merchandise."[25] It does not apply to conduct that has an anticompetitive effect in the United States or that injures domestic competitors of the members of an export association. Nor does it provide any immunity from prosecution under foreign antitrust laws.[26] Associations seeking an exemption under the Webb-Pomerene Act must file their articles of agreement and annual reports with the Commission, but pre-formation approval from the Commission is not required.

Fed'n of Dentists, 476 U.S. 447 (1986). *See also* Massachusetts Board of Registration in Optometry, 110 F.T.C. 549 (1988).

23. Pub. L. No. 103-42, 107 Stat. 117, 119 (1993).
24. 15 U.S.C. § 4306(2) (Supp. 1993).
25. 15 U.S.C. § 61 (1988).
26. *See, e.g.,* Cases 89/85, etc., A. Ahlstrom Osakeyhtio v. Commission ("Wood Pulp"), 1988 E.C.R. 5193, Common Mkt. Rep. (CCH) ¶ 14,491 (1988).

2.7 Export Trading Company Act of 1982

The Export Trading Company Act of 1982 (the "ETC Act"), Pub. L. No. 97-290, 96 Stat. 1234, is designed to increase U.S. exports of goods and services. It addresses that goal in several ways. First, in Title II, it encourages more efficient provision of export trade services to U.S. producers and suppliers by reducing restrictions on trade financing provided by financial institutions.[27] Second, in Title III, it reduces uncertainty concerning the application of the U.S. antitrust laws to export trade through the creation of a procedure by which persons engaged in U.S. export trade may obtain an export trade certificate of review ("ETCR").[28] Third, in Title IV, it clarifies the jurisdictional rules applicable to non-import cases brought under the Sherman Act and the FTC Act.[29] The Title III certificates are discussed briefly here; the jurisdictional rules are treated below in Section 3.1.

Export trade certificates of review are issued by the Secretary of Commerce with the concurrence of the Attorney General. Persons named in the ETCR obtain limited immunity from suit under both state and federal antitrust laws for activities that are specified in the certificate and that comply with the terms of the certificate. To obtain an ETCR, an applicant must show that proposed export conduct will:

(1) result in neither a substantial lessening of competition or restraint of trade within the United States nor a substantial restraint of the export trade of any competitor of the applicant;

(2) not unreasonably enhance, stabilize, or depress prices in the United States of the class of goods or services covered by the application;

(3) not constitute unfair methods of competition against competitors engaged in the export of the class of goods or services exported by the applicant; and

27. *See* 12 U.S.C. §§ 372, 635 a-4, 1841, 1843 (1988 & Supp. 1993) (Because Title II does not implicate the antitrust laws, it is not discussed further in these Guidelines.)
28. 15 U.S.C. §§ 4011-21 (1988 & Supp. 1993).
29. 15 U.S.C. § 6a (1988); 15 U.S.C. § 45(a)(3) (1988).

(4) not include any act that may reasonably be expected to result in the sale for consumption or resale in the United States of such goods or services.[30]

Congress intended that these standards "encompass the full range of the antitrust laws," as defined in the ETC Act.[31]

Although an ETCR provides significant protection under the antitrust laws, it has certain limitations. First, conduct that falls outside the scope of a certificate remains fully subject to private and governmental enforcement actions. Second, an ETCR that is obtained by fraud is void from the outset and thus offers no protection under the antitrust laws. Third, any person that has been injured by certified conduct may recover actual (though not treble) damages if that conduct is found to violate any of the statutory criteria described above. In any such action, certified conduct enjoys a presumption of legality, and the prevailing party is entitled to recover costs and attorneys' fees.[32] Fourth, an ETCR does not constitute, explicitly or implicitly, an endorsement or opinion by the Secretary of Commerce or by the Attorney General concerning the legality of such business plans under the laws of any foreign country.

The Secretary of Commerce may revoke or modify an ETCR if the Secretary or the Attorney General determines that the applicant's export activities have ceased to comply with the statutory criteria for obtaining a certificate. The Attorney General may also bring suit under Section 15 of the Clayton Act to enjoin conduct that threatens "a clear and irreparable harm to the national interest,"[33] even if the conduct has been pre-approved as part of an ETCR.

The Commerce Department, in consultation with the Department, has issued guidelines setting forth the standards used in reviewing ETCR applications.[34] The ETC Guidelines contain several examples illustrating application of the certification standards to specific export trade conduct,

---

30. 15 U.S.C. § 4013(a) (1988).

31. H.R. Rep. No. 924, 97th Cong., 2d Sess. 26 (1982). *See* 15 U.S.C. § 4021(6).

32. *See* 15 U.S.C. § 4016(b)(1) (1988) (injured party) and § 4016(b)(4) (1988) (party against whom claim is brought).

33. 15 U.S.C. § 4016(b)(5) (1988); *See* 15 U.S.C. § 25 (1988).

34. *See* Department of Commerce, International Trade Administration, Guidelines for the Issuance of Export Trade Certificates of Review (2d ed.), 50 Fed. Reg. 1786 (1985) (hereinafter "ETC Guidelines").

including the use of vertical and horizontal restraints and technology licensing arrangements. In addition, the Commerce Department's Export Trading Company Guidebook[35] provides information on the functions and advantages of establishing or using an export trading company, including factors to consider in applying for an ETCR. The Commerce Department's Office of Export Trading Company Affairs provides advice and information on the formation of export trading companies and facilitates contacts between producers of exportable goods and services and firms offering export trade services.

2.8 Other Pertinent Legislation

2.81 Wilson Tariff Act

The Wilson Tariff Act, 15 U.S.C. §§ 8-11, prohibits "every combination, conspiracy, trust, agreement, or contract" made by or between two or more persons or corporations, either of whom is engaged in importing any article from a foreign country into the United States, where the agreement is intended to restrain trade or increase the market price in any part of the United States of the imported articles, or of "any manufacture into which such imported article enters or is intended to enter." Violation of the Act is a misdemeanor, punishable by a maximum fine of $5,000 or one year in prison. The Act also provides for seizure of the imported articles.[36]

2.82 Antidumping Act of 1916

The Revenue Act of 1916, better known as the Antidumping Act, 15 U.S.C. §§ 71-74, is not an antitrust statute, but its subject matter is closely related to the antitrust rules regarding predation. It is a trade statute that creates a private claim against importers who sell goods into the United States at prices substantially below the prices charged for the same goods in their home market. In order to state a claim, a plaintiff must show both that such lower prices were commonly and systematically charged, and that the importer had the specific intent to

---

35. U.S. Department of Commerce, International Trade Administration, The Export Trading Company Guidebook (1984).
36. 15 U.S.C. § 11 (1988).

injure or destroy an industry in the United States, or to prevent the establishment of an industry. Dumping cases are more commonly brought using the administrative procedures of the Tariff Act of 1930, discussed below.

2.83 Tariff Act of 1930

A comprehensive discussion of the trade remedies available under the Tariff Act is beyond the scope of these Guidelines. However, because antitrust questions sometimes arise in the context of trade actions, it is appropriate to describe these laws briefly.

2.831 Countervailing Duties

Pursuant to Title VII.A of the Tariff Act,[37] U.S. manufacturers, producers, wholesalers, unions, and trade associations may petition for the imposition of offsetting duties on subsidized foreign imports.[38] The Department of Commerce's International Trade Administration ("ITA") must make a determination that the foreign government in question is subsidizing the imports, and in almost all cases the International Trade Commission ("ITC") must determine that a domestic industry is materially injured or threatened with material injury by reason of these imports.

2.832 Antidumping Duties

Pursuant to Title VII.B of the Tariff Act,[39] parties designated in the statute (the same parties as in the countervailing duties provision) may petition for antidumping duties, which must be imposed on foreign

---

37. *See* 19 U.S.C. §§ 1671 et seq. (1988 & Supp. 1993), *amended by* Uruguay Round Agreements Act, Pub. L. No. 103-465, 108 Stat. 4809 (1994).
38. Some alternative procedures exist under Tariff Act § 701(c) for countries that have not subscribed to the World Trade Organization ("WTO") Agreement on Subsidies and Countervailing Measures or measures equivalent to it. 19 U.S.C. § 1671(c) (1988 & Supp. 1993), *amended by* the Uruguay Round Agreements Act, Pub. L. No. 103-465, 108 Stat. 4809 (1994).
39. *See* 19 U.S.C. §§ 1673 et seq. (1988).

merchandise that is being, or is likely to be, sold in the United States at "less than fair value" ("LTFV"), if the U.S. industry is materially injured or threatened with material injury by imports of the foreign merchandise. The ITA makes the LTFV determination, and the ITC is responsible for the injury decision.

2.833 Section 337

Section 337 of the Tariff Act, 19 U.S.C. § 1337, prohibits "unfair methods of competition and unfair acts in the importation of articles into the United States," if the effect is to destroy or substantially injure a U.S. industry, or where the acts relate to importation of articles infringing U.S. patents, copyrights, trademarks, or registered mask works.[40] Complaints are filed with the ITC. The principal remedies under Section 337 are an exclusion order directing that any offending goods be excluded from entry into the United States, and a cease and desist order directed toward any offending U.S. firms and individuals.[41] The ITC is required to give the Agencies an opportunity to comment before making a final determination.[42] In addition, the Department participates in the interagency group that prepares recommendations for the President to approve, disapprove, or allow to take effect the import relief proposed by the ITC.

2.84 Trade Act of 1974

2.841 Section 201

Section 201 of the Trade Act of 1974, 19 U.S.C. §§ 2251 et seq., provides that American businesses claiming serious injury due to significant increases in imports may petition the ITC for relief or modification under the so-called "escape clause." If the ITC makes a determination that "an article is being imported into the United States in such increased quantities as to be a substantial cause of serious injury, or the threat thereof, to the domestic industry producing an article like or

---

40. 19 U.S.C. § 1337 (1988), *amended by* the Uruguay Round Agreements Act, Pub. L. No. 103-465, 108 Stat. 4809 (1994).
41. 19 U.S.C. §§ 1337(d), (f) (1988).
42. 19 U.S.C. § 1337(b)(2) (1988).

directly competitive with the imported article," and formulates its recommendation for appropriate relief, the Department participates in the interagency committee that conducts the investigations and advises the President whether to adopt, modify, or reject the import relief recommended by the ITC.

2.842 Section 301

Section 301 of the Trade Act of 1974, 19 U.S.C. § 2411, provides that the U.S. Trade Representative ("USTR"), subject to the specific direction, if any, of the President, may take action, including restricting imports, to enforce rights of the United States under any trade agreement, to address acts inconsistent with the international legal rights of the United States, or to respond to unjustifiable, unreasonable or discriminatory practices of foreign governments that burden or restrict U.S. commerce. Interested parties may initiate such actions through petitions to the USTR, or the USTR may itself initiate proceedings.[43] Of particular interest to antitrust enforcement is Section 301(d)(3)(B)(i)(IV), which includes among the "unreasonable" practices of foreign governments that might justify a proceeding the "toleration by a foreign government of systematic anticompetitive activities by enterprises or among enterprises in the foreign country that have the effect of restricting . . . access of United States goods or services to a foreign market."[44] The Department participates in the interagency committee that makes recommendations to the President on what actions, if any, should be taken.

2.9 Relevant International Agreements

To further the twin goals of promoting enforcement cooperation between the United States and foreign governments and of reducing any tensions that may arise in particular proceedings, the Agencies have

43. 19 U.S.C. § 2412(a), (b) (1988), *amended by* the Uruguay Round Agreements Act, Pub. L. No. 103-465, 108 Stat. 4809 (1994); *See also* Identification of Trade Expansion Priorities, Exec. Order No. 12,901, 59 Fed. Reg. 10,727 (1994).
44. 19 U.S.C. § 2411(d)(3)(B)(i)(IV) (1988), *amended by* the Uruguay Round Agreements Act, Pub. L. No. 103-465, 108 Stat. 4809 (1994), § 314(c).

developed close relationships with antitrust and competition policy officials of many different countries. In some instances, understandings have been reached with respect to notifications, consultations, and cooperation in antitrust matters.[45] In other instances, more general rules endorsed by multilateral organizations such as the Organization for Economic Cooperation and Development ("OECD") provide the basis for the Agencies' cooperative policies. Finally, even in the absence of specific or general international understandings or recommendations, the Agencies often seek cooperation with foreign authorities.

2.91 Bilateral Cooperation Agreements

Formal written bilateral arrangements exist between the United States and the Federal Republic of Germany, Australia, and Canada.[46]

---

45. Chapter 15 of the North American Free Trade Agreement ("NAFTA") addresses competition policy matters and commits the Parties to cooperate on antitrust matters. North American Free Trade Agreement Between the Government of the United States of America, the Government of Canada and the Government of the United Mexican States, 32 I.L.M. 605, 663 (1993), *reprinted in* H.R. Doc. No. 159, 103d Cong., 1st Sess. 712, 1170-1174 (1993).
46. *See* Agreement Relating to Mutual Cooperation Regarding Restrictive Business Practices, June 23, 1976, U.S.-Federal Republic of Germany, 27 U.S.T. 1956, T.I.S. No. 8291, *reprinted in* 4 Trade Reg. Rep. (CCH) ¶ 13,501; Agreement Between the Government of the United States of America and the Government of Australia Relating to Cooperation on Antitrust Matters, June 29, 1982, U.S.-Australia, T.I.A.S. No. 10365, *reprinted in* 4 Trade Reg. Rep. (CCH) ¶ 13,502; and Memorandum of Understanding as to Notification, Consultation, and Cooperation with Respect to the Application of National Antitrust Laws, March 9, 1984, U.S.-Canada, *reprinted in* 4 Trade Reg. Rep. (CCH) ¶ 13,503. The Agencies *also* signed a similar agreement with the Commission of the European Communities in 1991. *See* Agreement Between the Government of the United States of America and the Commission of the European Communities Regarding the Application of Their Competition Laws, Sept. 23, 1991, 30 I.L.M. 1491 (Nov. 1991), *reprinted in* 4 Trade Reg. Rep. (CCH) ¶ 13,504. However, on August 9, 1994, the European Court of Justice ruled that the conclusion of the Agreement did not comply with institutional requirements of the law of the European Union

International antitrust cooperation can also occur through mutual legal assistance treaties ("MLATs"), which are treaties of general application pursuant to which the United States and a foreign country agree to assist one another in criminal law enforcement matters. MLATs currently are in force with over one dozen countries, and many more are in the process of ratification or negotiation. However, only the MLAT with Canada has been used to date to obtain assistance in antitrust investigations.[47] The Agencies also hold regular consultations with the antitrust officials of Canada, the European Commission, and Japan, and have close, informal ties with the antitrust authorities of many other countries. Since 1990, the Agencies have cooperated closely with countries in the process of establishing competition agencies, assisted by funding provided by the Agency for International Development.

On November 2, 1994, President Clinton signed into law the International Antitrust Enforcement Assistance Act of 1994,[48] which authorizes the Agencies to enter into antitrust mutual assistance agreements in accordance with the legislation.

2.92 International Guidelines and Recommendations

The Agencies have agreed with respect to member countries of the OECD to consider the legitimate interests of other nations in accordance with relevant OECD recommendations.[49] Under the terms of a 1986 recommendation, the United States agency with responsibility for a particular case notifies a member country whenever an antitrust enforcement action may affect important interests of that country or its

---

("). Under the Court's decision, action by the EU Council of Ministers is necessary for this type of agreement. *See* French Republic v. Commission of European Communities (No. C-327/91) (Aug. 9, 1994).

47. Treaty with Canada on Mutual Legal Assistance in Criminal Matters, S. Treaty Doc. No. 28, 100th Cong., 2d Sess. (1988).

48. Pub. L. No. 103-438, 108 Stat. 4597 (1994).

49. *See* Revised Recommendation of the OECD Council Concerning Cooperation Between Member Countries on Restrictive Business Practices Affecting International Trade, OECD Doc. No. C(86)44 (Final) (May 21, 1986). The Recommendation also calls for countries to consult with each other in appropriate situations, with the aim of promoting enforcement cooperation and minimizing differences that may arise.

nationals.[50] Examples of potentially notifiable actions include requests for documents located outside the United States, attempts to obtain information from potential witnesses located outside the United States, and cases or investigations with significant foreign conduct or involvement of foreign persons.

3. Threshold International Enforcement Issues

3.1 Jurisdiction

Just as the acts of U.S. citizens in a foreign nation ordinarily are subject to the law of the country in which they occur, the acts of foreign citizens in the United States ordinarily are subject to U.S. law. The reach of the U.S. antitrust laws is not limited, however, to conduct and transactions that occur within the boundaries of the United States. Anticompetitive conduct that affects U.S. domestic or foreign commerce may violate the U.S. antitrust laws regardless of where such conduct occurs or the nationality of the parties involved.

Under the Sherman Act and the FTC Act, there are two principal tests for subject matter jurisdiction in foreign commerce cases. With respect to foreign import commerce, the Supreme Court has recently stated in Hartford Fire Insurance Co. v. California that "the Sherman Act applies to foreign conduct that was meant to produce and did in fact produce some substantial effect in the United States."[51] There has been

---

50. The OECD has 25 member countries and the European Commission takes part in its work. The OECD's membership includes many of the most advanced market economies in the world. The OECD also has several observer nations, which have made rapid progress toward open market economies. The Agencies follow recommended OECD practices with respect to all member countries.

51. 113 S. Ct. 2891, 2909 (1993). In a world in which economic transactions observe no boundaries, international recognition of the "effects doctrine" of jurisdiction has become more widespread. In the context of import trade, the "implementation" test adopted in the European Court of Justice usually produces the same outcome as the "effects" test employed in the United States. *See* Cases 89/85, etc., Ahlstrom v. Commission, *supra* at note 26. The merger laws of the European Union, Canada, Germany, France, Australia, and the Czech and Slovak Republics, among others, take a similar approach.

no such authoritative ruling on the scope of the FTC Act, but both Acts apply to commerce "with foreign nations" and the Commission has held that terms used by both Acts should be construed together.[52] Second, with respect to foreign commerce other than imports, the Foreign Trade Antitrust Improvements Act of 1982 ("FTAIA") applies to foreign conduct that has a direct, substantial, and reasonably foreseeable effect on U.S. commerce.[53]

3.11 Jurisdiction Over Conduct Involving Import Commerce

Imports into the United States by definition affect the U.S. domestic market directly, and will, therefore, almost invariably satisfy the intent part of the Hartford Fire test. Whether they in fact produce the requisite substantial effects will depend on the facts of each case.

ILLUSTRATIVE EXAMPLE A[54]

Situation: A, B, C, and D are foreign companies that produce a product in various foreign countries. None has any U.S. production, nor any U.S. subsidiaries. They organize a cartel for the purpose of raising the price for the product in question. Collectively, the cartel members make substantial sales into the United States, both in absolute terms and relative to total U.S. consumption.

Discussion: These facts present the straightforward case of cartel participants selling products directly into the United States. In this situation, the transaction is unambiguously an import into the U.S.

---

52. In re Massachusetts Bd. of Registration in Optometry, 110 F.T.C. 598, 609 (1988).
53. 15 U.S.C. § 6a (1988) (Sherman Act) and § 45(a)(3) (1988) (FTC Act).
54. The examples incorporated into the text are intended solely to illustrate how the Agencies would apply the principles articulated in the Guidelines in differing fact situations. In each case, of course, the ultimate outcome of the analysis, i.e. whether or not a violation of the antitrust laws has occurred, would depend on the specific facts and circumstances of the case. These examples, therefore, do not address many of the factual and economic questions the Agencies would ask in analyzing particular conduct or transactions under the antitrust laws. Therefore, certain hypothetical situations presented here may, when fully analyzed, not violate any provision of the antitrust laws.

market, and the sale is not complete until the goods reach the United States. Thus, U.S. subject matter jurisdiction is clear under the general principles of antitrust law expressed most recently in *Hartford Fire*. The facts presented here demonstrate actual and intended participation in U.S. commerce.[55] The separate question of personal jurisdiction under the facts presented here would be analyzed using the principles discussed *infra* in Section 4.1.

3.12 Jurisdiction Over Conduct Involving Other Foreign Commerce

With respect to foreign commerce other than imports, the jurisdictional limits of the Sherman Act and the FTC Act are delineated in the FTAIA. The FTAIA amended the Sherman Act to provide that it: shall not apply to conduct involving trade or commerce (other than import trade or commerce) with foreign nations unless (1) such conduct has a direct, substantial, and reasonably foreseeable effect:

(A) on trade or commerce which is not trade or commerce with foreign nations, or on import trade or import commerce with foreign nations; or

(B) on export trade or export commerce with foreign nations, of a person engaged in such trade or commerce in the United States;[56] (2) such effect gives rise to a claim under the provisions of [the Sherman Act], other than this section.

The FTAIA uses slightly different statutory language for the FTC Act,[57] but produces the same jurisdictional outcomes.

3.121 Jurisdiction in Cases Under Subsection 1(A) of the FTAIA

To the extent that conduct in foreign countries does not "involve" import commerce but does have an "effect" on either import transactions or commerce within the United States, the Agencies apply the "direct, substantial, and reasonably foreseeable" standard of the FTAIA. That standard is applied, for example, in cases in which a cartel of foreign

---

55. *See infra* at Section 3.12.
56. If the Sherman Act applies to such conduct only because of the operation of paragraph (1)(B), then that Act shall apply to such conduct only for injury to export business in the United States. 15 U.S.C. § 6a (1988).
57. *See* 15 U.S.C. § 45(a)(3) (1988).

enterprises, or a foreign monopolist, reaches the U.S. market through any mechanism that goes beyond direct sales, such as the use of an unrelated intermediary, as well as in cases in which foreign vertical restrictions or intellectual property licensing arrangements have an anticompetitive effect on U.S. commerce.

ILLUSTRATIVE EXAMPLE B

Situation: As in Illustrative Example A, the foreign cartel produces a product in several foreign countries. None of its members has any U.S. production, nor do any of them have U.S. subsidiaries. They organize a cartel for the purpose of raising the price for the product in question. Rather than selling directly into the United States, however, the cartel sells to an intermediary outside the United States, which they know will resell the product in the United States. The intermediary is not part of the cartel.

Discussion: The jurisdictional analysis would change slightly from the one presented in Example A, because not only is the conduct being challenged entered into by cartelists in a foreign country, but it is also initially implemented through a sale made in a foreign country. Despite the different test, however, the outcome on these facts would in all likelihood remain the same. The fact that the illegal conduct occurs prior to the import would trigger the application of the FTAIA. The Agencies would have to determine whether the challenged conduct had "direct, substantial and reasonably foreseeable effects" on U.S. domestic or import commerce. Furthermore, since "the essence of any violation of Section 1 [of the Sherman Act] is the illegal agreement itself—rather than the overt acts performed in furtherance of it,"[58] the Agencies would focus on the potential harm that would ensue if the conspiracy were successful, not on whether the actual conduct in furtherance of the conspiracy had in fact the prohibited effect upon interstate or foreign commerce.

ILLUSTRATIVE EXAMPLE C

Situation: Variant (1): Widgets are manufactured in both the United States and various other countries around the world. The non-U.S.

58. Summit Health, Ltd. v. Pinhas, 500 U.S. 322, 330-31 (1991).

manufacturers meet privately outside the United States and agree among themselves to raise prices to specified levels. Their agreement clearly indicates that sales in or into the United States are not within the scope of the agreement, and thus that each participant is free independently to set its prices for the U.S. market. Over time, the cartel members begin to sell excess production into the United States. These sales have the effect of stabilizing the cartel for the foreign markets. In the U.S. market, these "excess" sales are priced at levels below those that would have prevailed in the U.S. market but for the cartel, but there is no evidence that the prices are predatory. As a result of these events, several U.S. widget manufacturers curtail their production, overall domestic output falls, and remaining manufacturers fail to invest in new or improved capacity.

Variant (2): Assume now that the cartel agreement specifically provides that cartel members will set agreed prices for the U.S. market at levels designed to soak up excess quantities that arise as a result of price increases in foreign markets. The U.S. price level is set at periodic meetings where each participant indicates how much it must off-load in this way. Thus, the cartel members sell goods in the U.S. market at fixed prices that undercut prevailing U.S. price levels, with consequences similar to those in Variant 1. Discussion: Variant (1): The jurisdictional issue is whether the predictable economic consequences of the original cartel agreement and the independent sales into the United States are sufficient to support jurisdiction. The mere fact that the existence of U.S. sales or the level of U.S. prices may ultimately be affected by the cartel agreement is not enough for either Hartford Fire jurisdiction or the FTAIA.[59] Furthermore, in the absence of an agreement with respect to the U.S. market, sales into the U.S. market at non-predatory levels do not raise antitrust concerns.[60]

---

59. If the Agencies lack jurisdiction under the FTAIA to challenge the cartel, the facts of this example would nonetheless lend themselves well to cooperative enforcement action among antitrust agencies. Virtually every country with an antitrust law prohibits horizontal cartels and the Agencies would willingly cooperate with foreign authorities taking direct action against the cartel in the countries where the agreement has raised the price of widgets to the extent such cooperation is allowed under U.S. law and any agreement executed pursuant to U.S. law with foreign agencies or governments.

60. *Cf.* Matsushita Elec. Indus. Co. v. Zenith Radio Corp., 475 U.S. 574 (1986).

Variant (2): The critical element of a foreign price-fixing agreement with direct, intended effects in the United States is now present. The fact that the cartel believes its U.S. prices are "reasonable," or that it may be exerting downward pressure on U.S. price levels, does not exonerate it.[61] Variant 2 presents a case where the Agencies would need clear evidence of the prohibited agreement before they would consider moving forward. They would be particularly cautious if the apparent effects in the U.S. market appeared to be beneficial to consumers.]

3.122 Jurisdiction in Cases Under Subsection 1(B) of the FTAIA

Two categories of "export cases" fall within the FTAIA's jurisdictional test. First, the Agencies may, in appropriate cases, take enforcement action against anticompetitive conduct, wherever occurring, that restrains U.S. exports, if (1) the conduct has a direct, substantial, and reasonably foreseeable effect on exports of goods or services from the United States, and (2) the U.S. courts can obtain jurisdiction over persons or corporations engaged in such conduct.[62] As Section 3.2 below explains more fully, if the conduct is unlawful under the importing country's antitrust laws as well, the Agencies are also prepared to work with that country's authorities if they are better situated to remedy the conduct, and if they are prepared to take action that will address the U.S. concerns, pursuant to their antitrust laws.

Second, the Agencies may in appropriate cases take enforcement action against conduct by U.S. exporters that has a direct, substantial, and reasonably foreseeable effect on trade or commerce within the United States, or on import trade or commerce. This can arise in two principal ways. First, if U.S. supply and demand were not particularly elastic, an agreement among U.S. firms accounting for a substantial share of the relevant market, regarding the level of their exports, could reduce

---

61. *Cf.* Arizona v. Maricopa County Medical Soc'y, 457 U.S. 332 (1982); United States v. Socony-Vacuum Oil Co., 310 U.S. 150 (1940); United States v. Trenton Potteries Co., 273 U.S. 392 (1927).

62. *See* U.S. Department of Justice Press Release dated April 3, 1992 (announcing enforcement policy that would permit the Department to challenge foreign business conduct that harms U.S. exports when the conduct would have violated U.S. antitrust laws if it occurred in the United States).

supply and raise prices in the United States.[63] Second, conduct ostensibly export-related could affect the price of products sold or resold in the United States. This kind of effect could occur if, for example, U.S. firms fixed the price of an input used to manufacture a product overseas for ultimate resale in the United States.

ILLUSTRATIVE EXAMPLE D

Situation: Companies E and F are the only producers of product Q in country Epsilon, one of the biggest markets for sales of Q in the world. E and F together account for 99 percent of the sales of product Q in Epsilon.[64] In order to prevent a competing U.S. producer from entering the market in Epsilon, E and F agree that neither one of them will purchase or distribute the U.S. product, and that they will take "all feasible" measures to keep the U.S. company out of their market. Without specifically discussing what other measures they will take to carry out this plan, E and F meet with their distributors and, through a variety of threats and inducements, obtain agreement of all of the distributors not to carry the U.S. product. There are no commercially feasible substitute distribution channels available to the U.S. producer. Because of the actions of E and F, the U.S. producer cannot find any distributors to carry its product and is unable to make any sales in Epsilon.

Discussion: The agreement between E and F not to purchase or distribute the U.S. product would clearly have a direct and reasonably foreseeable effect on U.S. export commerce, since it is aimed at a U.S. exporter. The substantiality of the effects on U.S. exports would depend on the significance of E and F as purchasers and distributors of Q, although on these facts the virtually total foreclosure from Epsilon would almost certainly qualify as a substantial effect for jurisdictional purposes.

---

63. One would need to show more than indirect price effects resulting from legitimate export efforts to support an antitrust challenge. *See* ETC Guidelines, *supra* at note 34, 50 Fed. Reg. at 1791.

64. That E and F together have an overwhelmingly dominant share in Epsilon may or may not, depending on the market conditions for Q, satisfy the requirement of "substantial effect on U.S. exports" as required by the FTAIA. Foreclosure of exports to a single country, such as Epsilon, may satisfy the statutory threshold if that country's market accounts for a significant part of the export opportunities for U.S. firms.

However, if the Agencies believe that they may encounter difficulties in establishing personal jurisdiction or in obtaining effective relief, the case may be one in which the Agencies would seek to resolve their concerns by working with other authorities who are examining the transaction.

ILLUSTRATIVE EXAMPLE E

Situation: Companies P, Q, R, and S, organized under the laws of country Alpha, all manufacture and distribute construction equipment. Much of that equipment is protected by patents in the various countries where it is sold, including Alpha. The companies all belong to a private trade association, which develops industry standards that are often (although not always) adopted by Alpha's regulatory authorities. Feeling threatened by competition from the United States, the companies agree at a trade association meeting (1) to refuse to adopt any U.S. company technology as an industry standard, and (2) to boycott the distribution of U.S. construction equipment. The U.S. companies have taken all necessary steps to protect their intellectual property under the law of Alpha.

Discussion: In this example, the collective activity impedes U.S. companies in two ways: their technology is boycotted (even if U.S. companies are willing to license their intellectual property) and they are foreclosed from access to distribution channels. The jurisdictional question is whether these actions create a direct, substantial, and reasonably foreseeable effect on the exports of U.S. companies. The mere fact that only the market of Alpha appears to be foreclosed is not enough to defeat such an effect. Only if exclusion from Alpha as a quantitative measure were so de minimis in terms of actual volume of trade that there would not be a substantial effect on U.S. export commerce would jurisdiction be lacking. Given that this example involves construction equipment, a generally highly priced capital good, the exclusion from Alpha would probably satisfy the substantiality requirement for FTAIA jurisdiction. This arrangement appears to have been created with particular reference to competition from the United States, which indicates that the effects on U.S. exports are both direct and foreseeable.

3.13 Jurisdiction When U.S. Government Finances or Purchases

The Agencies may, in appropriate cases, take enforcement action when the U.S. Government is a purchaser, or substantially funds the purchase, of goods or services for consumption or use abroad. Cases in which the effect of anticompetitive conduct with respect to the sale of these goods or services falls primarily on U.S. taxpayers may qualify for redress under the federal antitrust laws.[65] As a general matter, the Agencies consider there to be a sufficient effect on U.S. commerce to support the assertion of jurisdiction if, as a result of its payment or financing, the U.S. Government bears more than half the cost of the transaction. For purposes of this determination, the Agencies apply the standards used in certifying export conduct under the ETC Act of 1982, 15 U.S.C. §§ 4011-21(1982).[66]

ILLUSTRATIVE EXAMPLE F

---

65. *Cf.* United States v. Concentrated Phosphate Export Ass'n, 393 U.S. 199, 208 (1968) ("[A]lthough the fertilizer shipments were consigned to Korea and although in most cases Korea formally let the contracts, American participation was the overwhelmingly dominant feature. The burden of noncompetitive pricing fell, not on any foreign purchaser, but on the American taxpayer. The United States was, in essence, furnishing fertilizer to Korea. . . . The foreign elements in the transaction were, by comparison, insignificant."); United States v. Standard Tallow Corp., 1988-1 Trade Cas. (CCH) ¶ 67,913 (S.D.N.Y. 1988) (consent decree) (barring suppliers from fixing prices or rigging bids for the sale of tallow financed in whole or in part through grants or loans by the U.S. Government); Unites States v. Anthracite Export Ass'n, 1970 Trade Cas. (CCH) ¶ 73,348 (M.D. Pa. 1970) (consent decree) (barring price-fixing, bid-rigging, and market allocation in Army foreign aid program).
66. *See* ETC Guidelines, *supra* at note 34, 50 Fed. Reg. at 1799-1800. The requisite U.S. Government involvement could include the actual purchase of goods by the U.S. Government for shipment abroad, a U.S. Government grant to a foreign government that is specifically earmarked for the transaction, or a U.S. Government loan specifically earmarked for the transaction that is made on such generous terms that it amounts to a grant. U.S. Government interests would not be considered to be sufficiently implicated with respect to a transaction that is funded by an international agency, or a transaction in which the foreign government received non-earmarked funds from the United States as part of a general government-to-government aid program.

Situation: A combination of U.S. firms and local firms in country Beta create a U.S.-based joint venture for the purpose of building a major pollution control facility for Beta's Environmental Control Agency ("BECA"). The venture has received preferential funding from the U.S. Government, which has the effect of making the present value of expected future repayment of the principal and interest on the loan less than half its face value. Once the venture has begun work, it appears that its members secretly have agreed to inflate the price quoted to BECA, in order to secure more funding.

Discussion: The fact that the U.S. Government bears more than half the financial risk of the transaction is sufficient for jurisdiction. With jurisdiction established, the Agencies would proceed to investigate whether the apparent bid-rigging actually occurred.[67]

ILLUSTRATIVE EXAMPLE G

Situation: The United States has many military bases and other facilities located in other countries. These facilities procure substantial goods and services from suppliers in the host country. In country X, it comes to the attention of the local U.S. military base commander that bids to supply certain construction services have been rigged.

Discussion: Sales made by a foreign party to the U.S. Government, including to a U.S. facility located in a foreign country, are within U.S. antitrust jurisdiction when they fall within the rule of Section 3.13. Bid-rigging of sales to the U.S. Government represents the kind of conduct that can lead to an antitrust action. Indeed, in the United States this type of behavior is normally prosecuted by the Department as a criminal offense. In practice, the Department has whenever possible worked closely with the host country antitrust authorities to explore remedies under local law. This has been successful in a number of instances.[68]

3.14 Jurisdiction Under Section 7 of the Clayton Act

---

67. Such conduct might also violate the False Claims Act, 31 U.S.C. §§ 3729-3733 (1988 & Supp. 1993).

68. If, however, local law does not provide adequate remedies, or the local authorities are not prepared to take action, the Department will weigh the comity factors, discussed *infra* at Section 3.2, and take such action as is appropriate.

Section 7 of the Clayton Act applies to mergers and acquisitions between firms that are engaged in commerce or in any activity affecting commerce. The Agencies would apply the same principles regarding their foreign commerce jurisdiction to Clayton Section 7 cases as they would apply in Sherman Act cases.

ILLUSTRATIVE EXAMPLE H

Situation: Two foreign firms, one in Europe and the other in Canada, account together for a substantial percentage of U.S. sales of a particular product through direct imports. Both firms have sales offices and are subject to personal jurisdiction in the United States, although neither has productive assets in the United States. They enter into an agreement to merge.

Discussion: The express language of Section 7 of the Clayton Act reaches the stock and asset acquisitions of persons engaged in trade and commerce "with foreign nations".[69] Thus, in assessing jurisdiction for this merger outside the United States the Agencies could establish U.S. subject matter jurisdiction based on its effect on U.S. imports.

If the facts stated above were modified to show that the proposed merger would have effects on U.S. export commerce, as opposed to import trade, then in assessing jurisdiction under the Clayton Act the Agencies would analyze the question of effects on commerce in a manner consistent with the FTAIA: that is, they would look to *See* whether the effects on U.S. domestic or import commerce are direct, substantial, and reasonably foreseeable.[70] It is appropriate to do so because the FTAIA sheds light on the type of effects Congress considered necessary for foreign commerce cases, even though the FTAIA did not amend the Clayton Act.

In both these situations, the Agencies would conclude that Section 7 jurisdiction technically exists. However, if effective relief is difficult to obtain, the case may be one in which the Agencies would seek to coordinate their efforts with other authorities who are examining the transaction.[71]

---

69. Clayton Act § 1, 15 U.S.C. § 12 (1988).
70. See *supra* at Section 3.121.
71. Through concepts such as "positive comity," one country's authorities may ask another country to take measures that address possible harm to competition in the requesting country's market.

3.2 Comity

In enforcing the antitrust laws, the Agencies consider international comity. Comity itself reflects the broad concept of respect among co-equal sovereign nations and plays a role in determining "the recognition which one nation allows within its territory to the legislative, executive or judicial acts of another nation."[72] Thus, in determining whether to assert jurisdiction to investigate or bring an action, or to seek particular remedies in a given case, each Agency takes into account whether significant interests of any foreign sovereign would be affected.[73]

In performing a comity analysis, the Agencies take into account all relevant factors. Among others, these may include (1) the relative significance to the alleged violation of conduct within the United States, as compared to conduct abroad; (2) the nationality of the persons involved in or affected by the conduct; (3) the presence or absence of a purpose to affect U.S. consumers, markets, or exporters; (4) the relative significance and foreseeability of the effects of the conduct on the United States as compared to the effects abroad; (5) the existence of reasonable expectations that would be furthered or defeated by the action; (6) the degree of conflict with foreign law or articulated foreign economic policies; (7) the extent to which the enforcement activities of another country with respect to the same persons, including remedies resulting from those activities, may be affected; and (8) the effectiveness of foreign enforcement as compared to U.S. enforcement action.[74]

The relative weight that each factor should be given depends on the facts and circumstances of each case. With respect to the factor concerning conflict with foreign law, the Supreme Court made clear in *Hartford Fire*[75] that no conflict exists for purposes of an international comity analysis in the courts if the person subject to regulation by two

---

72. Hilton v. Guyot, 159 U.S. 113, 164 (1895).
73. The Agencies have agreed to consider the legitimate interests of other nations in accordance with the recommendations of the OECD and various bilateral agreements, see *supra* at Section 2.9.
74. The first six of these factors are based on previous Department Guidelines. The seventh and eighth factors are derived from considerations in the U.S.-EC Antitrust Cooperation Agreement. *See supra* at note 46.
75. 113 S. Ct. 2891, 2910.

states can comply with the laws of both. Bearing this in mind, the Agencies first ask what laws or policies of the arguably interested foreign jurisdictions are implicated by the conduct in question. There may be no actual conflict between the antitrust enforcement interests of the United States and the laws or policies of a foreign sovereign. This is increasingly true as more countries adopt antitrust or competition laws that are compatible with those of the United States. In these cases, the anticompetitive conduct in question may also be prohibited under the pertinent foreign laws, and thus the possible conflict would relate to enforcement practices or remedy. If the laws or policies of a foreign nation are neutral, it is again possible for the parties in question to comply with the U.S. prohibition without violating foreign law.

The Agencies also take full account of comity factors beyond whether there is a conflict with foreign law. In deciding whether or not to challenge an alleged antitrust violation, the Agencies would, as part of a comity analysis, consider whether one country encourages a certain course of conduct, leaves parties free to choose among different strategies, or prohibits some of those strategies. In addition, the Agencies take into account the effect of their enforcement activities on related enforcement activities of a foreign antitrust authority. For example, the Agencies would consider whether their activities would interfere with or reinforce the objectives of the foreign proceeding, including any remedies contemplated or obtained by the foreign antitrust authority.

The Agencies also will consider whether the objectives sought to be obtained by the assertion of U.S. law would be achieved in a particular instance by foreign enforcement. In lieu of bringing an enforcement action, the Agencies may consult with interested foreign sovereigns through appropriate diplomatic channels to attempt to eliminate anticompetitive effects in the United States. In cases where the United States decides to prosecute an antitrust action, such a decision represents a determination by the Executive Branch that the importance of antitrust enforcement outweighs any relevant foreign policy concerns.[76] The

---

76. Foreign policy concerns may also lead the United States not to prosecute a case. *See, e.g.,* U.S. Department of Justice Press Release dated Nov. 19, 1984 (announcing the termination, based on foreign policy concerns, of a grand jury investigation into passenger air travel between the United States and the United Kingdom).

Department does not believe that it is the role of the courts to "second-guess the executive branch's judgment as to the proper role of comity concerns under these circumstances."[77] To date, no Commission cases have presented the issue of the degree of deference that courts should give to the Commission's comity decisions.[78] It is important also to note that in disputes between private parties, many courts are willing to undertake a comity analysis.[79]

ILLUSTRATIVE EXAMPLE I

Situation: A group of buyers in one foreign country decide that they will agree on the price that they will offer to U.S. suppliers of a particular product. The agreement results in substantial loss of sales and capacity reductions in the United States.

Discussion: From a jurisdictional point of view, the FTAIA standard appears to be satisfied because the effects on U.S. exporters presented here are direct and the percentage of supply accounted for by the buyers' cartel is substantial given the fact that the U.S. suppliers are "major." The Agencies, however, would also take into consideration the comity aspects presented before deciding whether or not to proceed.

Consistent with their consideration of comity and its obligations under various international agreements, the Agencies would ordinarily notify the antitrust authority in the cartel's home country. If that authority were in a better position to address the competitive problem, and were prepared to take effective action to address the adverse effects on U.S. commerce, the Agencies would consider working cooperatively with the foreign authority or staying their own remedy pending enforcement efforts by the foreign country. In deciding whether to proceed, the Agencies would weigh the factors relating to comity set forth above. Factors weighing in favor of bringing such an action include the substantial and purposeful harm caused by the cartel to the United States.

---

77. United States v. Baker Hughes, Inc., 731 F. Supp. 3, 6 n.5 (D.D.C. 1990), *aff'd,* 908 F.2d 981 (D.C. Cir. 1990).

78. Like the Department, the Commission considers comity issues and consults with foreign antitrust authorities, but the Commission is not part of the Executive Branch.

79. *See, e.g.,* Timberlane Lumber Co. v. Bank of America, 549 F.2d 597 (9th Cir. 1976).

ILLUSTRATIVE EXAMPLE J

Situation: A and B manufacture a consumer product for which there are no readily available substitutes in ten different countries around the world, including the United States, Canada, Mexico, Spain, Australia, and others. When they decide to merge, it becomes necessary for them to file premerger notifications in many of these countries, and to subject themselves to the merger law of all ten.[80]

Discussion: Under the 1986 OECD Recommendation, OECD countries notify one another when a proceeding such as a merger review is underway that might affect the interests of other countries. Within the strict limits of national confidentiality laws, agencies attempt to cooperate with one another in processing these reviews. This might extend to exchanges of publicly available information, agreements to let the other agencies know when a decision to institute a proceeding is taken, and to consult for purposes of international comity with respect to proposed remedial measures and investigatory methods. The parties can facilitate faster resolution of these cases if they are willing voluntarily to waive confidentiality protections and to cooperate with a joint investigation. At present, confidentiality provisions in U.S. and foreign laws do not usually permit effective coordination of a single international investigation in the absence of such waivers.

3.3 Effects of Foreign Government Involvement

Foreign governments may be involved in a variety of ways in conduct that may have antitrust consequences. To address the implications of such foreign governmental involvement, Congress and the courts have developed four special doctrines: the doctrine of foreign sovereign immunity; the doctrine of foreign sovereign compulsion; the act of state doctrine; and the application of the Noerr-Pennington doctrine to immunize the lobbying of foreign governments. Although these doctrines are interrelated, for purposes of discussion the Guidelines discuss each one individually.

---

80. Not every country has compulsory premerger notification, and the events triggering duties to notify vary from country to country.

3.31 Foreign Sovereign Immunity

The scope of immunity of a foreign government or its agencies and instrumentalities (hereinafter foreign government)[81] from the jurisdiction of the U.S. courts for all causes of action, including antitrust, is governed by the Foreign Sovereign Immunities Act of 1976 ("FSIA").[82] Subject to the treaties in place at the time of FSIA's enactment, a foreign government is immune from suit except where designated in the FSIA.[83]

Under the FSIA, a U.S. court has jurisdiction if the foreign government has: (a) waived its immunity explicitly or by implication, (b) engaged in commercial activity as described in the statute, (c) expropriated property in violation of international law, (d) acquired rights to U.S. property, (e) committed certain torts within the United States, or agreed to arbitration of a dispute.[84]

The commercial activities exception is a frequently invoked exception to sovereign immunity under the FSIA. Under the FSIA, a foreign government is not immune in any case: in which the action is based upon a commercial activity carried on in the United States by the foreign state; or upon an act performed in the United States in connection with a commercial activity of the foreign state elsewhere; or upon an act outside the territory of the United States in connection with a commercial activity of the foreign state elsewhere and that act causes a direct effect in the United States.[85]

---

81. Section 1603(b) of the Foreign Sovereign Immunities Act of 1976 defines an "agency or instrumentality of a foreign state" to be any entity "(1) which is a separate legal person, corporate or otherwise; and (2) which is an organ of a foreign state or political subdivision thereof, or a majority of whose shares or other ownership interest is owned by a foreign state or political subdivision thereof; and (3) which is neither a citizen of a State of the United States as defined in Section 1332(c) and (d) of [Title 28, U.S. Code], nor created under the laws of any third country." 28 U.S.C. § 1603(b) (1988). It is not uncommon in antitrust cases to *See* state-owned enterprises meeting this definition.
82. 28 U.S.C. §§ 1602, et seq. (1988).
83. 28 U.S.C. § 1604 (1988 & Supp. 1993).
84. 28 U.S.C. § 1605(a)(1-6) (1988).
85. 28 U.S.C. § 1605(a)(2) (1988).

"Commercial activity of the foreign state" is not defined in the FSIA, but is to be determined by the "nature of the course of conduct or particular transaction or act, rather than by reference to its purpose."[86] In attempting to differentiate commercial from sovereign activity, courts have considered whether the conduct being challenged is customarily performed for profit[87] and whether the conduct is of a type that only a sovereign government can perform.[88] As a practical matter, most activities of foreign government- owned corporations operating in the commercial marketplace will be subject to U.S. antitrust laws to the same extent as the activities of foreign privately-owned firms.

The commercial activity also must have a substantial nexus with the United States before a foreign government is subject to suit. The FSIA sets out three different standards for meeting this requirement. First, the challenged conduct by the foreign government may occur in the United States.[89] Alternatively, the challenged commercial activity may entail an act performed in the United States in connection with a commercial activity of the foreign government elsewhere.[90] Or, finally, the

---

86. 28 U.S.C. § 1603(d) (1988).

87. *See, e.g.,* Republic of Argentina v. Weltover, Inc., 112 S. Ct. 2160 (1992); Schoenberg v. Exportadora de Sal, S.A. de C.V., 930 F.2d 777 (9th Cir. 1991); Rush-Presbyterian-St. Luke's Medical Ctr. v. Hellenic Republic, 877 F.2d 574, 578 n.4 (7th Cir.), *cert. denied,* 493 U.S. 937 (1989).

88. *See, e.g.,* Saudi Arabia v. Nelson, 113 S. Ct. 1471 (1993); de Sanchez v. Banco Central de Nicaragua, 770 F.2d 1385 (5th Cir. 1985); Letelier v. Republic of Chile, 748 F.2d 790, 797-98 (2d Cir. 1984), *cert. denied,* 471 U.S. 1125 (1985); International Ass'n of Machinists & Aerospace Workers v. Organization of Petroleum Exporting Countries, 477 F. Supp. 553 (C.D. Cal. 1979), *aff'd on other grounds,* 649 F.2d 1354 (9th Cir. 1981), *cert. denied,* 454 U.S. 1163 (1982).

89. 28 U.S.C. § 1603(e) (1988).

90. *See* H.R. Rep. No. 1487, 94th Cong., 2d Sess. 18-19 (1976), *reprinted in* 1976 U.S.C.C.A.N. 6604, 6617-18 (providing as an example the wrongful termination in the United States of an employee of a foreign state employed in connection with commercial activity in a third country.) *But* see Filus v. LOT Polish Airlines, 907 F.2d 1328, 1333 (2d Cir. 1990) (holding as too attenuated the failure to warn of a defective product sold outside of the United States in connection with an accident outside the United States.)

challenged commercial activity of a foreign government outside of the United States may produce a direct effect within the United States, i.e., an effect which follows "as an immediate consequence of the defendant's . . . activity."[91]

3.32 Foreign Sovereign Compulsion

Although U.S. antitrust jurisdiction extends to conduct and parties in foreign countries whose actions have the required effects on U.S. commerce, as discussed above, those parties may find themselves subject to conflicting requirements from the other country (or countries) where they are located.[92] Under *Hartford Fire*, if it is possible for the party to comply both with the foreign law and the U.S. antitrust laws, the existence of the foreign law does not provide any legal excuse for actions that do not comply with U.S. law. However, a direct conflict may arise when the facts demonstrate that the foreign sovereign has compelled the very conduct that the U.S. antitrust law prohibits.

In these circumstances, at least one court has recognized a defense under the U.S. antitrust laws, and the Agencies will also recognize it.[93]

---

91. Republic of Argentina, 112 S. Ct. at 2168. This test is similar to proximate cause formulations adopted by other courts. *See* Martin v. Republic of South Africa, 836 F.2d 91, 95 (2d Cir. 1987) (a direct effect is one with no intervening element which flows in a straight line without deviation or interruption), *quoting* Upton v. Empire of Iran, 459 F. Supp. 264, 266 (D.D.C. 1978), *aff'd mem.*, 607 F.2d 494 (D.C. Cir. 1979).
92. Conduct by private entities not required by law is entirely outside of the protections afforded by this defense. *See* Continental Ore Co. v. Union Carbide & Carbon Corp., 370 U.S. 690, 706 (1962); United States v. Watchmakers of Switzerland Info. Ctr., Inc., 1963 Trade Cas. (CCH) ¶ 70,600 at 77,456-57 (S.D.N.Y. 1962) ("[T]he fact that the Swiss Government may, as a practical matter, approve the effects of this private activity cannot convert what is essentially a vulnerable private conspiracy into an unassailable system resulting from a foreign government mandate.") *See supra* at Section 3.2.
93. Interamerican Refining Corp. v. Texaco Maracaibo, Inc., 307 F. Supp. 1291 (D. Del. 1970) (defendant, having been ordered by the government of Venezuela not to sell oil to a particular refiner out of favor with the current political regime, held not subject to antitrust liability under the Sherman Act for an illegal group boycott). The defense of foreign

There are two rationales underlying the defense of foreign sovereign compulsion. First, Congress enacted the U.S. antitrust laws against the background of well recognized principles of international law and comity among nations, pursuant to which U.S. authorities give due deference to the official acts of foreign governments. A defense for actions taken under the circumstances spelled out below serves to accommodate two equal sovereigns. Second, important considerations of fairness to the defendant require some mechanism that provides a predictable rule of decision for those seeking to conform their behavior to all pertinent laws.

Because of the limited scope of the defense, the Agencies will refrain from enforcement actions on the ground of foreign sovereign compulsion only when certain criteria are satisfied. First, the foreign government must have compelled the anticompetitive conduct under circumstances in which a refusal to comply with the foreign government's command would give rise to the imposition of penal or other severe sanctions. As a general matter, the Agencies regard the foreign government's formal representation that refusal to comply with its command would have such a result as being sufficient to establish that the conduct in question has been compelled, as long as that representation contains sufficient detail to enable the Agencies to see precisely how the compulsion would be accomplished under local law.[94] Foreign government measures short of compulsion do not suffice for this defense, although they can be relevant in a comity analysis.

Second, although there can be no strict territorial test for this defense, the defense normally applies only when the foreign government

---

sovereign compulsion is distinguished from the federalism-based state action doctrine. The state action doctrine applies not just to the actions of states and their subdivisions, *But* also to private anticompetitive conduct that is both undertaken pursuant to clearly articulated state policies, and is actively supervised by the state. *See* Federal Trade Comm'n v. Ticor Title Insurance Co., 112 S. Ct. 2169 (1992); California Retail Liquor Dealers Ass'n v. Midcal Aluminum, Inc., 445 U.S. 97, 105 (1980); Parker v. Brown, 317 U.S. 341 (1943).

94. For example, the Agencies may not regard as dispositive a statement that is ambiguous or that on its face appears to be internally inconsistent. The Agencies may inquire into the circumstances underlying the statement and they may also request further information if the source of the power to compel is unclear.

compels conduct which can be accomplished entirely within its own territory. If the compelled conduct occurs in the United States, the Agencies will not recognize the defense.[95] For example, no defense arises when a foreign government requires the U.S. subsidiaries of several firms to organize a cartel in the United States to fix the price at which products would be sold in the United States, or when it requires its firms to fix mandatory resale prices for their U.S. distributors to use in the United States.

Third, with reference to the discussion of foreign sovereign immunity in Section 3.31 above, the order must come from the foreign government acting in its governmental capacity. The defense does not arise from conduct that would fall within the FSIA commercial activity exception.

ILLUSTRATIVE EXAMPLE K

Situation: Greatly increased quantities of commodity X have flooded into the world market over the last two or three years, including substantial amounts indirectly coming into the United States. Because they are unsure whether they would prevail in an antidumping and countervailing duty case, U.S. industry participants have refrained from filing trade law petitions. The officials of three foreign countries meet with their respective domestic firms and urge them to "rationalize" production by cooperatively cutting back. Going one step further, one of the interested governments orders cutbacks from its firms, subject to substantial penalties for non-compliance. Producers from the other two countries agree among themselves to institute comparable cutbacks, but their governments do not require them to do so.

Discussion: Assume for the purpose of this example that the overseas production cutbacks have the necessary effects on U.S. commerce to support jurisdiction. As for the participants from the two countries that did not impose any penalty for a failure to reduce production, the Agencies would not find that sovereign compulsion precluded prosecution of this agreement.[96] As for participants from the

---

95. *See* Linseman v. World Hockey Ass'n, 439 F. Supp. 1315, 1325 (D. Conn. 1977).

96. As in all such cases, the Agencies would consider comity factors as part of their analysis. *See supra* at Section 3.2.

country that did compel production cut-backs through the imposition of severe penalties, the Agencies would acknowledge a defense of sovereign compulsion.

3.33 Acts of State

The act of state doctrine is a judge-made rule of federal common law.[97] It is a doctrine of judicial abstention based on considerations of international comity and separation of powers, and applies only if the specific conduct complained of is a public act of the foreign sovereign within its territorial jurisdiction on matters pertaining to its governmental sovereignty. The act of state doctrine arises when the validity of the acts of a foreign government is an unavoidable issue in a case.[98]

Courts have refused to adjudicate claims or issues that would require the court to judge the legality (as a matter of U.S. law or international law) of the sovereign act of a foreign state.[99] Although in some cases the sovereign act in question may compel private behavior, such compulsion is not required by the doctrine.[100] While the act of state doctrine does not compel dismissal as a matter of course, judicial abstention is appropriate in a case where the court must "declare invalid, and thus ineffective as a rule of decision in the U.S. courts, . . . the official act of a foreign sovereign."[101]

When a restraint on competition arises directly from the act of a foreign sovereign, such as the grant of a license, award of a contract, expropriation of property, or the like, the Agencies may refrain from bringing an enforcement action based on the act of state doctrine. For example, the Agencies will not challenge foreign acts of state if the facts

---

97. Banco Nacional de Cuba v. Sabbatino, 376 U.S. 398, 421-22 n.21 (1964) (noting that other countries do not adhere in any formulaic way to an act of state doctrine).

98. *See* W.S. Kirkpatrick & Co. v. Envtl. Tectonics Corp., 493 U.S. 400 (1990).

99. International Ass'n of Machinists and Aerospace Workers v. Organization of Petroleum Exporting Countries, 649 F.2d 1354, 1358 (9th Cir. 1981), cert. denied, 454 U.S. 1163 (1982).

100. *See* Timberlane, *supra* at note 79, 549 F.2d at 606-08.

101. Kirkpatrick, 493 U.S. at 405, *quoting* Ricaud v. American Metal Co., 246 U.S. 304, 310 (1918).

and circumstances indicate that: (1) the specific conduct complained of is a public act of the sovereign, (2) the act was taken within the territorial jurisdiction of the sovereign, and (3) the matter is governmental, rather than commercial.

3.34 Petitioning of Sovereigns

Under the Noerr-Pennington doctrine, a genuine effort to obtain or influence action by governmental entities in the United States is immune from application of the Sherman Act, even if the intent or effect of that effort is to restrain or monopolize trade.[102] Whatever the basis asserted for Noerr-Pennington immunity (either as an application of the First Amendment or as a limit on the statutory reach of the Sherman Act, or both), the Agencies will apply it in the same manner to the petitioning of foreign governments and the U.S. Government.

ILLUSTRATIVE EXAMPLE L

Situation: In the course of preparing an antidumping case, which requires the U.S. industry to demonstrate that it has been injured through the effects of the dumped imports, producers representing 75 percent of U.S. output exchange the information required for the adjudication. All the information is exchanged indirectly through third parties and in an aggregated form that makes the identity of any particular producer's information impossible to discern.

---

102. *See* Eastern R.R. Presidents Conference v. Noerr Motor Freight, Inc., 365 U.S. 127 (1961); United Mine Workers of Am. v. Pennington, 381 U.S. 657 (1965); California Motor Transp. Co. v. Trucking Unlimited, 404 U.S. 508 (1972) (extending protection to petitioning before "all departments of Government," including the courts); Professional Real Estate Investors, Inc. v. Columbia Pictures Indus., 113 S. Ct. 1920 (1993). However, this immunity has never applied to "sham" activities, in which petitioning "ostensibly directed toward influencing governmental action, is a mere sham to cover . . . an attempt to interfere directly with the business relationships of a competitor." Professional Real Estate Investors, 113 S. Ct. at 1926, *quoting* Noerr, 365 U.S. at 144. See *also* USS-Posco Indus. v. Contra Costa Cty. Bldg. Constr. Council, AFL-CIO, 31 F.3d 800 (9th Cir. 1994).

Discussion: Information exchanged by competitors within the context of an antidumping proceeding implicates the Noerr-Pennington petitioning immunity. To the extent that these exchanges are reasonably necessary in order for them to prepare their joint petition, which is permitted under the trade laws, Noerr is available to protect against antitrust liability that would otherwise arise. On these facts the parties are likely to be immunized by Noerr if they have taken the necessary measures to ensure that the provision of sensitive information called for by the Commerce Department and the ITC cannot be used for anticompetitive purposes. In such a situation, the information exchange is incidental to genuine petitioning and is not subject to the antitrust laws. Conversely, were the parties directly to exchange extensive information relating to their costs, the prices each has charged for the product, pricing trends, and profitability, including information about specific transactions that went beyond the scope of those facts required for the adjudication, such conduct would go beyond the contemplated protection of Noerr immunity.

3.4 Antitrust Enforcement and International Trade Regulation

There has always been a close relationship between the international application of the antitrust laws and the policies and rules governing the international trade of the United States. Restrictions such as tariffs or quotas on the free flow of goods affect market definition, consumer choice, and supply options for U.S. producers. In certain instances, the U.S. trade laws set forth specific procedures for settling disputes under those laws, which can involve price and quantity agreements by the foreign firms involved. When those procedures are followed, an implied antitrust immunity results.[103] However, agreements among competitors

---

103. *See, e.g.,* Letter from Charles F. Rule, Acting Assistant Attorney General, Antitrust Division, Department of Justice, to Mr. Makoto Kuroda, Vice-Minister for International Affairs, Japanese Ministry of International Trade and Industry, July 30, 1986 (concluding that a suspension agreement did not violate U.S. antitrust laws on the basis of factual representations that the agreement applied only to products under investigation, that it did not require pricing above levels needed to eliminate sales below foreign market value, and that assigning weighted-average foreign market values to exporters who were not respondents in the investigation was necessary to achieve the purpose of the antidumping

that do not comply with the law, or go beyond the measures authorized by the law, do not enjoy antitrust immunity. In the absence of legal authority, the fact, without more, that U.S. or foreign government officials were involved in or encouraged measures that would otherwise violate the antitrust laws does not immunize such arrangements.[104]

If a particular voluntary export restraint does not qualify for express or implied immunity from the antitrust laws, then the legality of the arrangement would depend upon the existence of the ordinary elements of an antitrust offense, such as whether or not a prohibited agreement exists or whether defenses such as foreign sovereign compulsion can be invoked.

ILLUSTRATIVE EXAMPLE M

Situation: Six U.S. producers of product Q have initiated an antidumping action alleging that imports of Q from country Sigma at less than fair value are causing material injury to the U.S. Q industry. The ITC has made a preliminary decision that there is a reasonable indication that the U.S. industry is suffering material injury from Q imported from Sigma. The Department of Commerce has preliminarily concluded that the foreign market value of Q imported into the United States by Sigma's Q producers exceeds the price at which they are selling Q in this country by margins of 10 to 40 percent. Sigma's Q producers jointly initiate discussions with the Department of Commerce that lead to suspension of the investigation in accordance with Section 734 of the Tariff Act of 1930, 19 U.S.C. § 1673c. The suspension agreement provides that each of Sigma's Q producers will sell product Q in the United States at no less than its individual foreign market value, as determined periodically by the Department of Commerce in accordance with the Tariff Act. Before determining to suspend the investigation, the Department of Commerce provides copies of the proposed agreement to the U.S. Q producers, who

---

law).

104. *Cf.* United States v. Socony-Vacuum Oil Co., 310 U.S. 150, 226 (1940) ("Though employees of the government may have known of those programs and winked at them or tacitly approved them, no immunity would have thereby been obtained. For Congress had specified the precise manner and method of securing immunity [in the National Industrial Recovery Act]. None other would suffice . . . ."); *See also* Otter Tail Power Co. v. United States, 410 U.S. 366, 378-79 (1973).

jointly advise the Department that they do not object to the suspension of the investigation on the terms proposed. The Department also determines that suspension of the investigation would be in the public interest. As a result of the suspension agreement, prices in the United States of Q imported from Sigma rise by an average of 25 percent from the prices that prevailed before the antidumping action was initiated.

Discussion: While an unsupervised agreement among foreign firms to raise their U.S. sales prices ordinarily would violate the Sherman Act, the suspension agreement outlined above qualifies for an implied immunity from the antitrust laws. As demonstrated here, the parties have engaged only in conduct contemplated by the Tariff Act and none of the participants have engaged in conduct beyond what is necessary to implement that statutory scheme.

ILLUSTRATIVE EXAMPLE N

Situation: The Export Association is a Webb-Pomerene association that has filed the appropriate certificates and reports with the Commission. The Association exports a commodity to markets around the world, and fixes the price at which all of its members sell the commodity in the foreign markets. Nearly 80 percent of all U.S. producers of the commodity belong to the Association, and on a world-wide level, the Association's members account for approximately 40 percent of annual sales.

Discussion: The Webb-Pomerene Act addresses only the question of antitrust liability under U.S. law. Although the U.S. antitrust laws confer an immunity on such associations, the Act does not purport to confer immunity under the law of any foreign country, nor does the Act compel the members of a Webb-Pomerene association to act in any particular way. Thus, a foreign government retains the ability to initiate proceedings if such an association allegedly violates that country's competition law.

4. Personal Jurisdiction And Procedural Rules

4.1 Personal Jurisdiction and Venue

The Agencies will bring suit only if they conclude that personal jurisdiction exists under the due process clause of the U.S. Constitution.[105] The Constitution requires that the defendant have affiliating or minimum contacts with the United States, such that the proceeding comports with "fair play and substantial justice."[106]

Section 12 of the Clayton Act, 15 U.S.C. § 22, provides that any suit under the antitrust laws against a corporation may be brought in the judicial district where it is an inhabitant, where it may be found, or where it transacts business. The concept of transacting business is interpreted pragmatically by the Agencies. Thus, a company may transact business in a particular district directly through an agent, or through a related corporation that is actually the "alter ego" of the foreign party.[107]

4.2 Investigatory Practice Relating to Foreign Nations

In conducting investigations that require documents that are located outside the United States, or contacts with persons located outside the United States, the Agencies first consider requests for voluntary cooperation when practical and consistent with enforcement objectives. When compulsory measures are needed, they seek whenever possible to

---

105. *See also* International Shoe Co. v. Washington, 326 U.S. 310 (1945); Asahi Metal Industry Co. Ltd. v. Superior Court, 480 U.S. 102 (1987).

106. Go-Video, Inc. v. Akai Elec. Co., Ltd. 885 F.2d 1406, 1414 (9th Cir. 1989); Wells Fargo & Co. v. Wells Fargo Express Co., 556 F.2d 406, 418 (9th Cir. 1977). To establish jurisdiction, parties must also be served in accordance with the Federal Rules of Civil Procedure or other relevant authority. Fed. R. Civ. P. 4(k); 15 U.S.C. §§ 22, 44.

107. *See, e.g.,* Letter from Donald S. Clark, Secretary of the Federal Trade Commission, to Caswell O. Hobbs, Esq., Morgan, Lewis & Bockius, Jan. 17, 1990 (Re: Petition to Quash Subpoena Nippon Sheet Glass, et al., File No. 891-0088, at page 3) ("The Commission . . . may exercise jurisdiction over and serve process on, a foreign entity that has a related company in the United States acting as its agent or alter ego."); *see also* Fed. R. Civ. P. 4; Volkswagenwerk AG v. Schlunk, 486 U.S. 694, 707-708 (1988); United States v. Scophony Corp., 333 U.S. 795, 810-818 (1948).

work with the foreign government involved. U.S. law also provides authority in some circumstances for the use of compulsory measures directed to parties over whom the courts have personal jurisdiction, which the Agencies may use when other efforts to obtain information have been exhausted or would be unavailing.[108]

Conflicts can arise, however, where foreign statutes purport to prevent persons from disclosing documents or information for use in U.S. proceedings. However, the mere existence of such statutes does not excuse noncompliance with a request for information from one of the Agencies.[109] To enable the Agencies to obtain evidence located abroad more effectively, as noted in Section 2.91 above, Congress recently has enacted legislation authorizing the Agencies to negotiate bilateral agreements with foreign governments or antitrust enforcement agencies to facilitate the exchange of documents and evidence in civil and criminal investigations.[110]

4.22 Hart-Scott-Rodino: Special Foreign Commerce Rules

As noted above in Section 2.4, qualifying mergers and acquisitions, defined both in terms of size of party and size of transaction, must be reported to the Agencies, along with certain information about the parties and the transaction, prior to their consummation, pursuant to the HSR Amendments to the Clayton Act, 15 U.S.C. § 18a.

In some instances, the HSR implementing regulations exempt otherwise reportable foreign transactions.[111] First, some acquisitions by U.S. persons are exempt. Acquisitions of foreign assets by a U.S. person are exempt when (i) no sales in or into the United States are attributable

---

108. For example, 28 U.S.C. § 1783(a) (1988) authorizes a U.S. court to order the issuance of a subpoena "requiring the appearance as a witness before it, or before a person or body designated by it, of a national or resident of the United States who is in a foreign country, or requiring the production of a specified document or other thing by him," under circumstances spelled out in the statute.

109. *See* Societe Internationale pour Participations Industrielles et Commerciales, S.A. v. Rogers, 357 U.S. 197 (1958).

110. International Antitrust Enforcement Assistance Act of 1994, Pub. L. No. 103-438, 108 Stat. 4597 (1994).

111. *See* 16 C.F.R. §§ 802.50-52 (1994).

to those assets, or (ii) some sales in or into the United States are attributable to those assets, but the acquiring person would not hold assets of the acquired person to which $25 million or more of such sales in the acquired person's most recent fiscal year were attributable.[112] Acquisitions by a U.S. person of voting securities of a foreign issuer are exempt unless the issuer holds assets in the United States having an aggregate book value of $15 million or more, or made aggregate sales in or into the United States of $25 million or more in its most recent fiscal year.[113]

Second, some acquisitions by foreign persons are exempt. An exemption exists for acquisitions by foreign persons if (i) the acquisition is of voting securities of a foreign issuer and would not confer control of a U.S. issuer having annual net sales or total assets of $25 million or more, or of any issuer with assets located in the United States having a book value of $15 million or more; or (ii) the acquired person is also a foreign person and the aggregate annual net sales of the merging firms in or into the United States is less than $110 million and their aggregate total assets in the United States are less than $110 million.[114] In addition, an acquisition by a foreign person of assets located outside the United States is exempt. Acquisitions by foreign persons of U.S. issuers or assets are not exempt.

Finally, acquisitions are exempt if the ultimate parent entity of either the acquiring or the acquired person is controlled by a foreign state, and the acquisition is of assets located within that foreign state, or of voting securities of an issuer organized under its laws.[115] The HSR rules are necessarily technical, and should be consulted rather than relying on the summary description herein.

---

112. *See* 16 C.F.R. § 802.50(a) (1994).
113. *See* 16 C.F.R. § 802.50(b) (1994).
114. *See* 16 C.F.R. § 802.51 (1994).
115. *See* 16 C.F.R. § 802.52 (1994).

APPENDIX K

1995 DEPARTMENT OF JUSTICE AND FEDERAL TRADE COMMISSION ANTITRUST GUIDELINES FOR THE LICENSING OF INTELLECTUAL PROPERTY

1. Intellectual Property Protection and the Antitrust Laws

1.0 These Guidelines state the antitrust enforcement policy of the U.S. Department of Justice and the Federal Trade Commission (individually, "the Agency," and collectively, "the Agencies") with respect to the licensing of intellectual property protected by patent, copyright, and trade secret law, and of know-how.[1] By stating their general policy, the Agencies hope to assist those who need to predict whether the Agencies will challenge a practice as anticompetitive. However, these Guidelines cannot remove judgment and discretion in antitrust law enforcement. Moreover, the standards set forth in these Guidelines must be applied in unforeseeable circumstances. Each case will be evaluated in light of its own facts, and these Guidelines will be applied reasonably and flexibly.[2]

In the United States, patents confer rights to exclude others from making, using, or selling in the United States the invention claimed by the patent for a period of seventeen years from the date of issue.[3] To gain patent protection, an invention (which may be a product, process, machine, or composition of matter) must be novel, nonobvious, and

---

1. These Guidelines do not cover the antitrust treatment of trademarks. Although the same general antitrust principles that apply to other forms of intellectual property apply to trademarks as well, these Guidelines deal with technology transfer and innovation-related issues that typically arise with respect to patents, copyrights, trade secrets, and know-how agreements, rather than with product-differentiation issues that typically arise with respect to trademarks.
2. As is the case with all guidelines, users should rely on qualified counsel to assist them in evaluating the antitrust risk associated with any contemplated transaction or activity. No set of guidelines can possibly indicate how the Agencies will assess the particular facts of every case. Parties who wish to know the Agencies' specific enforcement intentions with respect to any particular transaction should consider seeking a Department of Justice business review letter pursuant to 28 C.F.R. § 50.6 or a Federal Trade Commission Advisory Opinion pursuant to 16 C.F.R. §§ 1.1-1.4.
3. *See* 35 U.S.C. § 154 (1988). Section 532(a) of the Uruguay Round Agreements Act, Pub. L. No. 103-465, 108 Stat. 4809, 4983 (1994) would change the length of patent protection to a term beginning on the date at which the patent issues and ending twenty years from the date on which the application for the patent was filed.

useful. Copyright protection applies to original works of authorship embodied in a tangible medium of expression.[4] A copyright protects only the expression, not the underlying ideas.[5] Unlike a patent, which protects an invention not only from copying but also from independent creation, a copyright does not preclude others from independently creating similar expression. Trade secret protection applies to information whose economic value depends on its not being generally known.[6] Trade secret protection is conditioned upon efforts to maintain secrecy and has no fixed term. As with copyright protection, trade secret protection does not preclude independent creation by others.

The intellectual property laws and the antitrust laws share the common purpose of promoting innovation and enhancing consumer welfare.[7] The intellectual property laws provide incentives for innovation and its dissemination and commercialization by establishing enforceable property rights for the creators of new and useful products, more efficient processes, and original works of expression. In the absence of intellectual property rights, imitators could more rapidly exploit the efforts of innovators and investors without compensation. Rapid imitation would reduce the commercial value of innovation and erode incentives to invest, ultimately to the detriment of consumers. The antitrust laws promote innovation and consumer welfare by prohibiting certain actions that may harm competition with respect to either existing or new ways of serving consumers.

---

4. *See* 17 U.S.C. § 102 (1988 & Supp. V 1993). Copyright protection lasts for the author's life plus 50 years, or 75 years from first publication (or 100 years from creation, whichever expires first) for works made for hire. *See* 17 U.S.C. § 302 (1988). The principles stated in these Guidelines also apply to protection of mask works fixed in a semiconductor chip product (*See* 17 U.S.C. § 901 et seq. (1988)), which is analogous to copyright protection for works of authorship.
5. *See* 17 U.S.C. § 102(b) (1988).
6. Trade secret protection derives from state law. *See generally* Kewanee Oil Co. v. Bicron Corp., 416 U.S. 470 (1974).
7. "[T]he aims and objectives of patent and antitrust laws may seem, at first glance, wholly at odds. However, the two bodies of law are actually complementary, as both are aimed at encouraging innovation, industry and competition." Atari Games Corp. v. Nintendo of America, Inc., 897 F.2d 1572, 1576 (Fed. Cir. 1990).

2. General Principles

2.0 These Guidelines embody three general principles: (a) for the purpose of antitrust analysis, the Agencies regard intellectual property as being essentially comparable to any other form of property; (b) the Agencies do not presume that intellectual property creates market power in the antitrust context; and (c) the Agencies recognize that intellectual property licensing allows firms to combine complementary factors of production and is generally procompetitive.

2.1 Standard Antitrust Analysis Applies to Intellectual Property

The Agencies apply the same general antitrust principles to conduct involving intellectual property that they apply to conduct involving any other form of tangible or intangible property. That is not to say that intellectual property is in all respects the same as any other form of property. Intellectual property has important characteristics, such as ease of misappropriation, that distinguish it from many other forms of property. These characteristics can be taken into account by standard antitrust analysis, however, and do not require the application of fundamentally different principles.[8]

Although there are clear and important differences in the purpose, extent, and duration of protection provided under the intellectual property regimes of patent, copyright, and trade secret, the governing antitrust principles are the same. Antitrust analysis takes differences among these forms of intellectual property into account in evaluating the specific market circumstances in which transactions occur, just as it does with other particular market circumstances.

Intellectual property law bestows on the owners of intellectual property certain rights to exclude others. These rights help the owners to profit from the use of their property. An intellectual property owner's rights to exclude are similar to the rights enjoyed by owners of other forms of private property. As with other forms of private property,

8. As with other forms of property, the power to exclude others from the use of intellectual property may vary substantially, depending on the nature of the property and its status under federal or state law. The greater or lesser legal power of an owner to exclude others is also taken into account by standard antitrust analysis.

certain types of conduct with respect to intellectual property may have anticompetitive effects against which the antitrust laws can and do protect. Intellectual property is thus neither particularly free from scrutiny under the antitrust laws, nor particularly suspect under them.

The Agencies recognize that the licensing of intellectual property is often international. The principles of antitrust analysis described in these Guidelines apply equally to domestic and international licensing arrangements. However, as described in the 1995 Department of Justice and Federal Trade Commission Antitrust Enforcement Guidelines for International Operations, considerations particular to international operations, such as jurisdiction and comity, may affect enforcement decisions when the arrangement is in an international context.

2.2 *Intellectual Property and Market Power*

Market power is the ability profitably to maintain prices above, or output below, competitive levels for a significant period of time.[9] The Agencies will not presume that a patent, copyright, or trade secret necessarily confers market power upon its owner. Although the intellectual property right confers the power to exclude with respect to the specific product, process, or work in question, there will often be sufficient actual or potential close substitutes for such product, process, or work to prevent the exercise of market power.[10] If a patent or other

---

9. Market power can be exercised in other economic dimensions, such as quality, service, and the development of new or improved goods and processes. It is assumed in this definition that all competitive dimensions are held constant except the ones in which market power is being exercised; that a seller is able to charge higher prices for a higher-quality product does not alone indicate market power. The definition in the text is stated in terms of a seller with market power. A buyer could also exercise market power (*e.g.*, by maintaining the price below the competitive level, thereby depressing output).

10. The Agencies note that the law is unclear on this issue. *Compare* Jefferson Parish Hospital District No. 2 v. Hyde, 466 U.S. 2, 16 (1984) (expressing the view in dictum that if a product is protected by a patent, "it is fair to presume that the inability to buy the product elsewhere gives the seller market power") *with id.* at 37 n.7 (O'Connor, J., concurring) ("[A] patent holder has no market power in any relevant sense if there are close substitutes for the patented product."). *Compare also* Abbott

form of intellectual property does confer market power, that market power does not by itself offend the antitrust laws. As with any other tangible or intangible asset that enables its owner to obtain significant supracompetitive profits, market power (or even a monopoly) that is solely "a consequence of a superior product, business acumen, or historic accident" does not violate the antitrust laws.[11] Nor does such market power impose on the intellectual property owner an obligation to license the use of that property to others. As in other antitrust contexts, however, market power could be illegally acquired or maintained, or, even if lawfully acquired and maintained, would be relevant to the ability of an intellectual property owner to harm competition through unreasonable conduct in connection with such property.

2.3 Procompetitive Benefits of Licensing

Intellectual property typically is one component among many in a production process and derives value from its combination with complementary factors. Complementary factors of production include manufacturing and distribution facilities, workforces, and other items of intellectual property. The owner of intellectual property has to arrange for its combination with other necessary factors to realize its commercial value. Often, the owner finds it most efficient to contract with others for these factors, to sell rights to the intellectual property, or to enter into a joint venture arrangement for its development, rather than supplying these complementary factors itself.

Licensing, cross-licensing, or otherwise transferring intellectual property (hereinafter "licensing") can facilitate integration of the licensed property with complementary factors of production. This integration can lead to more efficient exploitation of the intellectual property, benefiting

---

Laboratories v. Brennan, 952 F.2d 1346, 1354-55 (Fed. Cir. 1991) (no presumption of market power from intellectual property right), *cert. denied*, 112 S. Ct. 2993 (1992) *with* Digidyne Corp. v. Data General Corp., 734 F.2d 1336, 1341-42 (9th Cir. 1984) (requisite economic power is presumed from copyright), *cert. denied*, 473 U.S. 908 (1985).

11. United States v. Grinnell Corp., 384 U.S. 563, 571 (1966); *see also* United States v. Aluminum Co. of America, 148 F.2d 416, 430 (2d Cir. 1945) (Sherman Act is not violated by the attainment of market power solely through "superior skill, foresight and industry").

consumers through the reduction of costs and the introduction of new products. Such arrangements increase the value of intellectual property to consumers and to the developers of the technology. By potentially increasing the expected returns from intellectual property, licensing also can increase the incentive for its creation and thus promote greater investment in research and development.

Sometimes the use of one item of intellectual property requires access to another. An item of intellectual property "blocks" another when the second cannot be practiced without using the first. For example, an improvement on a patented machine can be blocked by the patent on the machine. Licensing may promote the coordinated development of technologies that are in a blocking relationship.

Field-of-use, territorial, and other limitations on intellectual property licenses may serve procompetitive ends by allowing the licensor to exploit its property as efficiently and effectively as possible. These various forms of exclusivity can be used to give a licensee an incentive to invest in the commercialization and distribution of products embodying the licensed intellectual property and to develop additional applications for the licensed property. The restrictions may do so, for example, by protecting the licensee against free-riding on the licensee's investments by other licensees or by the licensor. They may also increase the licensor's incentive to license, for example, by protecting the licensor from competition in the licensor's own technology in a market niche that it prefers to keep to itself. These benefits of licensing restrictions apply to patent, copyright, and trade secret licenses, and to know-how agreements.

EXAMPLE 1[12]

Situation: ComputerCo develops a new, copyrighted software program for inventory management. The program has wide application in the health field. ComputerCo licenses the program in an arrangement that imposes both field of use and territorial limitations. Some of ComputerCo's licenses permit use only in hospitals; others permit use only in group medical practices. ComputerCo charges different royalties

12. The examples in these Guidelines are hypothetical and do not represent judgments about, or analysis of, any actual market circumstances of the named industries.

for the different uses. All of ComputerCo's licenses permit use only in specified portions of the United States and in specified foreign countries.[13] The licenses contain no provisions that would prevent or discourage licensees from developing, using, or selling any other program, or from competing in any other good or service other than in the use of the licensed program. None of the licensees are actual or likely potential competitors of ComputerCo in the sale of inventory management programs.

Discussion: The key competitive issue raised by the licensing arrangement is whether it harms competition among entities that would have been actual or likely potential competitors in the absence of the arrangement. Such harm could occur if, for example, the licenses anticompetitively foreclose access to competing technologies (in this case, most likely competing computer programs), prevent licensees from developing their own competing technologies (again, in this case, most likely computer programs), or facilitate market allocation or price-fixing for any product or service supplied by the licensees. (*See* section 3.1.) If the license agreements contained such provisions, the Agency evaluating the arrangement would analyze its likely competitive effects as described in parts 3-5 of these Guidelines. In this hypothetical, there are no such provisions and thus the arrangement is merely a subdivision of the licensor's intellectual property among different fields of use and territories. The licensing arrangement does not appear likely to harm competition among entities that would have been actual or likely potential competitors if ComputerCo had chosen not to license the software program. The Agency therefore would be unlikely to object to this arrangement. Based on these facts, the result of the antitrust analysis would be the same whether the technology was protected by patent, copyright, or trade secret. The Agency's conclusion as to likely competitive effects could differ if, for example, the license barred licensees from using any other inventory management program.

---

13. These Guidelines do not address the possible application of the antitrust laws of other countries to restraints such as territorial restrictions in international licensing arrangements.

3. Antitrust Concerns and Modes of Analysis

3.1 Nature of the Concerns

While intellectual property licensing arrangements are typically welfare-enhancing and procompetitive, antitrust concerns may nonetheless arise. For example, a licensing arrangement could include restraints that adversely affect competition in goods markets by dividing the markets among firms that would have competed using different technologies. *See*, *e.g.*, Example 7. An arrangement that effectively merges the research and development activities of two of only a few entities that could plausibly engage in research and development in the relevant field might harm competition for development of new goods and services. *See* section 3.2.3. An acquisition of intellectual property may lessen competition in a relevant antitrust market. *See* section 5.7. The Agencies will focus on the actual effects of an arrangement, not on its formal terms.

The Agencies will not require the owner of intellectual property to create competition in its own technology. However, antitrust concerns may arise when a licensing arrangement harms competition among entities that would have been actual or likely potential competitors[14] in a relevant market in the absence of the license (entities in a "horizontal relationship"). A restraint in a licensing arrangement may harm such competition, for example, if it facilitates market division or price-fixing. In addition, license restrictions with respect to one market may harm such competition in another market by anticompetitively foreclosing access to, or significantly raising the price of, an important input,[15] or by facilitating coordination to increase price or reduce output. When it appears that such competition may be adversely affected, the Agencies will follow the analysis set forth below. *See generally* sections 3.4 and 4.2.

---

14. A firm will be treated as a likely potential competitor if there is evidence that entry by that firm is reasonably probable in the absence of the licensing arrangement.

15. As used herein, "input" includes outlets for distribution and sales, as well as factors of production. *See*, *e.g.*, sections 4.1.1 and 5.3-5.5 for further discussion of conditions under which foreclosing access to, or raising the price of, an input may harm competition in a relevant market.

3.2 Markets Affected by Licensing Arrangements

Licensing arrangements raise concerns under the antitrust laws if they are likely to affect adversely the prices, quantities, qualities, or varieties of goods and services[16] either currently or potentially available. The competitive effects of licensing arrangements often can be adequately assessed within the relevant markets for the goods affected by the arrangements. In such instances, the Agencies will delineate and analyze only goods markets. In other cases, however, the analysis may require the delineation of markets for technology or markets for research and development (innovation markets).

3.2.1 Goods Markets

A number of different goods markets may be relevant to evaluating the effects of a licensing arrangement. A restraint in a licensing arrangement may have competitive effects in markets for final or intermediate goods made using the intellectual property, or it may have effects upstream, in markets for goods that are used as inputs, along with the intellectual property, to the production of other goods. In general, for goods markets affected by a licensing arrangement, the Agencies will approach the delineation of relevant market and the measurement of market share in the intellectual property area as in section 1 of the U.S. Department of Justice and Federal Trade Commission Horizontal Merger Guidelines.[17]

3.2.2 Technology Markets

Technology markets consist of the intellectual property that is licensed (the "licensed technology") and its close substitutes--that is, the

---

16. Hereinafter, the term "goods" also includes services.
17. U.S. Department of Justice and Federal Trade Commission, Horizontal Merger Guidelines (April 2, 1992) (hereinafter "1992 Horizontal Merger Guidelines"). As stated in section 1.41 of the 1992 Horizontal Merger Guidelines, market shares for goods markets "can be expressed either in dollar terms through measurement of sales, shipments, or production, or in physical terms through measurement of sales, shipments, production, capacity or reserves."

technologies or goods that are close enough substitutes significantly to constrain the exercise of market power with respect to the intellectual property that is licensed.[18] When rights to intellectual property are marketed separately from the products in which they are used,[19] the Agencies may rely on technology markets to analyze the competitive effects of a licensing arrangement.

EXAMPLE 2

Situation: Firms Alpha and Beta independently develop different patented process technologies to manufacture the same off-patent drug for the treatment of a particular disease. Before the firms use their technologies internally or license them to third parties, they announce plans jointly to manufacture the drug, and to assign their manufacturing processes to the new manufacturing venture. Many firms are capable of using and have the incentive to use the licensed technologies to manufacture and distribute the drug; thus, the market for drug manufacturing and distribution is competitive. One of the Agencies is evaluating the likely competitive effects of the planned venture.

Discussion: The Agency would analyze the competitive effects of the proposed joint venture by first defining the relevant markets in which competition may be affected and then evaluating the likely competitive effects of the joint venture in the identified markets. (*See* Example 4 for a discussion of the Agencies' approach to joint venture analysis.) In this example, the structural effect of the joint venture in the relevant goods market for the manufacture and distribution of the drug is unlikely to be significant, because many firms in addition to the joint venture compete in that market. The joint venture might, however, increase the prices of the drug produced using Alpha's or Beta's technology by reducing

18. For example, the owner of a process for producing a particular good may be constrained in its conduct with respect to that process not only by other processes for making that good, *but also* by other goods that compete with the downstream good and by the processes used to produce those other goods.

19. Intellectual property is often licensed, sold, or transferred as an integral part of a marketed good. An example is a patented product marketed with an implied license permitting its use. In such circumstances, there is no need for a separate analysis of technology markets to capture relevant competitive effects.

competition in the relevant market for technology to manufacture the drug.

The Agency would delineate a technology market in which to evaluate likely competitive effects of the proposed joint venture. The Agency would identify other technologies that can be used to make the drug with levels of effectiveness and cost per dose comparable to that of the technologies owned by Alpha and Beta. In addition, the Agency would consider the extent to which competition from other drugs that are substitutes for the drug produced using Alpha's or Beta's technology would limit the ability of a thetical monopolist that owned both Alpha's and Beta's technology to raise its price.

* * *

To identify a technology's close substitutes and thus to delineate the relevant technology market, the Agencies will, if the data permit, identify the smallest group of technologies and goods over which a hypothetical monopolist of those technologies and goods likely would exercise market power—for example, by imposing a small but significant and nontransitory price increase.[20] The Agencies recognize that technology often is licensed in ways that are not readily quantifiable in monetary terms.[21] In such circumstances, the Agencies will delineate the relevant market by identifying other technologies and goods which buyers would substitute at a cost comparable to that of using the licensed technology.

In assessing the competitive significance of current and likely potential participants in a technology market, the Agencies will take into account all relevant evidence. When market share data are available and accurately reflect the competitive significance of market participants, the Agencies will include market share data in this assessment. The Agencies also will seek evidence of buyers' and market participants' assessments of the competitive significance of technology market

---

20. This is conceptually analogous to the analytical approach to goods markets under the 1992 Horizontal Merger Guidelines. *Cf.* § 1.11. Of course, market power also can be exercised in other dimensions, such as quality, and these dimensions also may be relevant to the definition and analysis of technology markets.

21. For example, technology may be licensed royalty-free in exchange for the right to use other technology, or it may be licensed as part of a package license.

participants. Such evidence is particularly important when market share data are unavailable, or do not accurately represent the competitive significance of market participants. When market share data or other indicia of market power are not available, and it appears that competing technologies are comparably efficient,[22] the Agencies will assign each technology the same market share. For new technologies, the Agencies generally will use the best available information to estimate market acceptance over a two-year period, beginning with commercial introduction.

3.2.3 Research and Development: Innovation Markets

If a licensing arrangement may adversely affect competition to develop new or improved goods or processes, the Agencies will analyze such an impact either as a separate competitive effect in relevant goods or technology markets, or as a competitive effect in a separate innovation market. A licensing arrangement may have competitive effects on innovation that cannot be adequately addressed through the analysis of goods or technology markets. For example, the arrangement may affect the development of goods that do not yet exist.[23]

Alternatively, the arrangement may affect the development of new or improved goods or processes in geographic markets where there is no actual or likely potential competition in the relevant goods.[24]

An innovation market consists of the research and development directed to particular new or improved goods or processes, and the close

---

22. The Agencies will regard two technologies as "comparably efficient" if they can be used to produce close substitutes at comparable costs.

23. *E.g.*, Sensormatic, FTC Inv. No. 941-0126, 60 Fed. Reg. 5428 (accepted for comment Dec. 28, 1994); Wright Medical Technology, Inc., FTC Inv. No. 951-0015, 60 Fed. Reg. 460 (accepted for comment Dec. 8, 1994); American Home Products, FTC Inv. No. 941-0116, 59 Fed. Reg. 60,807 (accepted for comment Nov. 28, 1994); Roche Holdings Ltd., 113 F.T.C. 1086 (1990); United States v. Automobile Mfrs. Ass'n, 307 F. Supp. 617 (C.D. Cal. 1969), *appeal dismissed sub nom.* City of New York v. United States, 397 U.S. 248 (1970), *modified sub nom.* United States v. Motor Vehicles Mfrs. Ass'n, 1982-83 Trade Cas. (CCH) ¶ 65,088 (C.D. Cal. 1982).

24. *See* Complaint, United States v. General Motors Corp., Civ. No. 93-530 (D. Del., filed Nov. 16, 1993).

substitutes for that research and development. The close substitutes are research and development efforts, technologies, and goods[25] that significantly constrain the exercise of market power with respect to the relevant research and development, for example by limiting the ability and incentive of a hypothetical monopolist to retard the pace of research and development. The Agencies will delineate an innovation market only when the capabilities to engage in the relevant research and development can be associated with specialized assets or characteristics of specific firms.

In assessing the competitive significance of current and likely potential participants in an innovation market, the Agencies will take into account all relevant evidence. When market share data are available and accurately reflect the competitive significance of market participants, the Agencies will include market share data in this assessment. The Agencies also will seek evidence of buyers' and market participants' assessments of the competitive significance of innovation market participants. Such evidence is particularly important when market share data are unavailable or do not accurately represent the competitive significance of market participants. The Agencies may base the market shares of participants in an innovation market on their shares of identifiable assets or characteristics upon which innovation depends, on shares of research and development expenditures, or on shares of a related product. When entities have comparable capabilities and incentives to pursue research and development that is a close substitute for the research and development activities of the parties to a licensing arrangement, the Agencies may assign equal market shares to such entities.

EXAMPLE 3

Situation: Two companies that specialize in advanced metallurgy agree to cross-license future patents relating to the development of a new component for aircraft jet turbines. Innovation in the development of the component requires the capability to work with very high tensile strength

---

25. For example, the licensor of research and development may be constrained in its conduct not only by competing research and development efforts but also by other existing goods that would compete with the goods under development.

materials for jet turbines. Aspects of the licensing arrangement raise the possibility that competition in research and development of this and related components will be lessened. One of the Agencies is considering whether to define an innovation market in which to evaluate the competitive effects of the arrangement.

Discussion: If the firms that have the capability and incentive to work with very high tensile strength materials for jet turbines can be reasonably identified, the Agency will consider defining a relevant innovation market for development of the new component. If the number of firms with the required capability and incentive to engage in research and development of very high tensile strength materials for aircraft jet turbines is small, the Agency may employ the concept of an innovation market to analyze the likely competitive effects of the arrangement in that market, or as an aid in analyzing competitive effects in technology or goods markets. The Agency would perform its analysis as described in parts 3-5.

If the number of firms with the required capability and incentive is large (either because there are a large number of such firms in the jet turbine industry, or because there are many firms in other industries with the required capability and incentive), then the Agency will conclude that the innovation market is competitive. Under these circumstances, it is unlikely that any single firm or plausible aggregation of firms could acquire a large enough share of the assets necessary for innovation to have an adverse impact on competition.

If the Agency cannot reasonably identify the firms with the required capability and incentive, it will not attempt to define an innovation market.

EXAMPLE 4

Situation: Three of the largest producers of a plastic used in disposable bottles plan to engage in joint research and development to produce a new type of plastic that is rapidly biodegradable. The joint venture will grant to its partners (but to no one else) licenses to all patent rights and use of know-how. One of the Agencies is evaluating the likely competitive effects of the proposed joint venture.

Discussion: The Agency would analyze the proposed research and development joint venture using an analysis similar to that applied to other joint ventures.[26] The Agency would begin by defining the relevant markets in which to analyze the joint venture's likely competitive effects. In this case, a relevant market is an innovation market—research and development for biodegradable (and other environmentally friendly) containers. The Agency would seek to identify any other entities that would be actual or likely potential competitors with the joint venture in that relevant market. This would include those firms that have the capability and incentive to undertake research and development closely substitutable for the research and development proposed to be undertaken by the joint venture, taking into account such firms' existing technologies and technologies under development, R&D facilities, and other relevant assets and business circumstances. Firms possessing such capabilities and incentives would be included in the research and development market even if they are not competitors in relevant markets for related goods, such as the plastics currently produced by the joint venturers, although competitors in existing goods markets may often also compete in related innovation markets.

Having defined a relevant innovation market, the Agency would assess whether the joint venture is likely to have anticompetitive effects in that market. A starting point in this analysis is the degree of concentration in the relevant market and the market shares of the parties to the joint venture. If, in addition to the parties to the joint venture (taken collectively), there are at least four other independently controlled entities that possess comparable capabilities and incentives to undertake research and development of biodegradable plastics, or other products that would be close substitutes for such new plastics, the joint venture ordinarily would be unlikely to adversely affect competition in the relevant innovation market (*Cf.* section 4.3). If there are fewer than four other independently controlled entities with similar capabilities and incentives, the Agency would consider whether the joint venture would give the parties to the joint venture an incentive and ability collectively to reduce investment in, or otherwise to retard the pace or scope of, research and development efforts. If the joint venture creates a

26. *See*, *e.g.*, U.S. Department of Justice and Federal Trade Commission, Statements of Enforcement Policy and Analytical Principles Relating to Health Care and Antitrust 20-23, 37-40, 72-74 (September 27, 1994). This type of transaction may qualify for treatment under the National Cooperative Research and Production Act of 1993, 15 U.S.C.A §§ 4301-05.

significant risk of anticompetitive effects in the innovation market, the Agency would proceed to consider efficiency justifications for the venture, such as the potential for combining complementary R&D assets in such a way as to make successful innovation more likely, or to bring it about sooner, or to achieve cost reductions in research and development.

The Agency would also assess the likelihood that the joint venture would adversely affect competition in other relevant markets, including markets for products produced by the parties to the joint venture. The risk of such adverse competitive effects would be increased to the extent that, for example, the joint venture facilitates the exchange among the parties of competitively sensitive information relating to goods markets in which the parties currently compete or facilitates the coordination of competitive activities in such markets. The Agency would examine whether the joint venture imposes collateral restraints that might significantly restrict competition among the joint venturers in goods markets, and would examine whether such collateral restraints were reasonably necessary to achieve any efficiencies that are likely to be attained by the venture.

3.3 Horizontal and Vertical Relationships

As with other property transfers, antitrust analysis of intellectual property licensing arrangements examines whether the relationship among the parties to the arrangement is primarily horizontal or vertical in nature, or whether it has substantial aspects of both. A licensing arrangement has a vertical component when it affects activities that are in a complementary relationship, as is typically the case in a licensing arrangement. For example, the licensor's primary line of business may be in research and development, and the licensees, as manufacturers, may be buying the rights to use technology developed by the licensor. Alternatively, the licensor may be a component manufacturer owning intellectual property rights in a product that the licensee manufactures by combining the component with other inputs, or the licensor may manufacture the product, and the licensees may operate primarily in distribution and marketing.

In addition to this vertical component, the licensor and its licensees may also have a horizontal relationship. For analytical purposes, the Agencies ordinarily will treat a relationship between a licensor and its licensees, or between licensees, as horizontal when they would have been actual or likely potential competitors in a relevant market in the absence of the license.

The existence of a horizontal relationship between a licensor and its licensees does not, in itself, indicate that the arrangement is anticompetitive. Identification of such relationships is merely an aid in determining whether there may be anticompetitive effects arising from a licensing arrangement. Such a relationship need not give rise to an anticompetitive effect, nor does a purely vertical relationship assure that there are no anticompetitive effects.

The following examples illustrate different competitive relationships among a licensor and its licensees.

EXAMPLE 5

Situation: AgCo, a manufacturer of farm equipment, develops a new, patented emission control technology for its tractor engines and licenses it to FarmCo, another farm equipment manufacturer. AgCo's emission control technology is far superior to the technology currently owned and used by FarmCo, so much so that FarmCo's technology does not significantly constrain the prices that AgCo could charge for its technology. AgCo's emission control patent has a broad scope. It is likely that any improved emissions control technology that FarmCo could develop in the foreseeable future would infringe AgCo's patent.

Discussion: Because FarmCo's emission control technology does not significantly constrain AgCo's competitive conduct with respect to its emission control technology, AgCo's and FarmCo's emission control technologies are not close substitutes for each other. FarmCo is a consumer of AgCo's technology and is not an actual competitor of AgCo in the relevant market for superior emission control technology of the kind licensed by AgCo. Furthermore, FarmCo is not a likely potential competitor of AgCo in the relevant market because, even if FarmCo could develop an improved emission control technology, it is likely that it would infringe AgCo's patent. This means that the relationship between AgCo and FarmCo with regard to the supply and use of emissions control technology is vertical. Assuming that AgCo and FarmCo are actual or likely potential competitors in sales of farm equipment products, their relationship is horizontal in the relevant markets for farm equipment.

EXAMPLE 6

Situation: FarmCo develops a new valve technology for its engines and enters into a cross-licensing arrangement with AgCo, whereby AgCo licenses its emission control technology to FarmCo and FarmCo licenses its valve technology to AgCo. AgCo already owns an alternative valve technology that can be used to achieve engine performance similar to that using FarmCo's valve technology and at a comparable cost to consumers. Before adopting FarmCo's technology, AgCo was using its own valve technology in its production of engines and was licensing (and continues to license) that technology for use by others. As in Example 5, FarmCo does not own or control an emission control technology that is a close substitute for the technology licensed from AgCo. Furthermore, as in Example 5, FarmCo is not likely to develop an improved emission control technology that would be a close substitute for AgCo's technology, because of AgCo's blocking patent.

Discussion: FarmCo is a consumer and not a competitor of AgCo's emission control technology. As in Example 5, their relationship is vertical with regard to this technology. The relationship between AgCo and FarmCo in the relevant market that includes engine valve technology is vertical in part and horizontal in part. It is vertical in part because AgCo and FarmCo stand in a complementary relationship, in which AgCo is a consumer of a technology supplied by FarmCo. However, the relationship between AgCo and FarmCo in the relevant market that includes engine valve technology is also horizontal in part, because FarmCo and AgCo are actual competitors in the licensing of valve technology that can be used to achieve similar engine performance at a comparable cost. Whether the firms license their valve technologies to others is not important for the conclusion that the firms have a horizontal relationship in this relevant market. Even if AgCo's use of its valve technology were solely captive to its own production, the fact that the two valve technologies are substitutable at comparable cost means that the two firms have a horizontal relationship.

As in Example 5, the relationship between AgCo and FarmCo is horizontal in the relevant markets for farm equipment.

3.4 Framework for Evaluating Licensing Restraints

In the vast majority of cases, restraints in intellectual property licensing arrangements are evaluated under the rule of reason. The Agencies' general approach in analyzing a licensing restraint under the rule of reason is to inquire whether the restraint is likely to have anticompetitive effects and, if so, whether the restraint is reasonably necessary to achieve procompetitive benefits that outweigh those anticompetitive effects. *See Federal Trade Commission v. Indiana Federation of Dentists,* 476 U.S. 447 (1986); *NCAA v. Board of Regents of the University of Oklahoma*, 468 U.S. 85 (1984); *Broadcast Music, Inc. v. Columbia Broadcasting System, Inc.,* 441 U.S. 1 (1979); 7 Phillip E. Areeda, *Antitrust Law* ¶ 1502 (1986). *See also* part 4.

In some cases, however, the courts conclude that a restraint's "nature and necessary effect are so plainly anticompetitive" that it should be treated as unlawful per se, without an elaborate inquiry into the restraint's likely competitive effect. *Federal Trade Commission v. Superior Court Trial Lawyers Association,* 493 U.S. 411, 433 (1990); *National Society of Professional Engineers v. United States,* 435 U.S. 679, 692 (1978). Among the restraints that have been held per se unlawful are naked price-fixing, output restraints, and market division among horizontal competitors, as well as certain group boycotts and resale price maintenance.

To determine whether a particular restraint in a licensing arrangement is given per se or rule of reason treatment, the Agencies will assess whether the restraint in question can be expected to contribute to an efficiency-enhancing integration of economic activity. *See Broadcast Music*, 441 U.S. at 16-24. In general, licensing arrangements promote such integration because they facilitate the combination of the licensor's intellectual property with complementary factors of production owned by the licensee. A restraint in a licensing arrangement may further such integration by, for example, aligning the incentives of the licensor and the licensees to promote the development and marketing of the licensed technology, or by substantially reducing transactions costs. If there is no efficiency-enhancing integration of economic activity and if the type of restraint is one that has been accorded per se treatment, the Agencies will challenge the restraint under the per se rule. Otherwise, the Agencies will apply a rule of reason analysis.

Application of the rule of reason generally requires a comprehensive inquiry into market conditions. (*See* sections 4.1-4.3.) However, that inquiry may be truncated in certain circumstances. If the Agencies conclude that a restraint has no likely anticompetitive effects, they will treat it as reasonable, without an elaborate analysis of market power or the justifications for the restraint. Similarly, if a restraint facially appears to be of a kind that would always or almost always tend to reduce output or increase prices,[27] and the restraint is not reasonably related to efficiencies, the Agencies will likely challenge the restraint without an elaborate analysis of particular industry circumstances.[28] *See Indiana Federation of Dentists*, 476 U.S. at 459-60; *NCAA*, 468 U.S. at 109.

EXAMPLE 7

Situation: Gamma, which manufactures Product X using its patented process, offers a license for its process technology to every other manufacturer of Product X, each of which competes world-wide with Gamma in the manufacture and sale of X. The process technology does not represent an economic improvement over the available existing technologies. Indeed, although most manufacturers accept licenses from Gamma, none of the licensees actually uses the licensed technology. The licenses provide that each manufacturer has an exclusive right to sell Product X manufactured using the licensed technology in a designated geographic area and that no manufacturer may sell Product X, however manufactured, outside the designated territory.

Discussion: The manufacturers of Product X are in a horizontal relationship in the goods market for Product X. Any manufacturers of Product X that control technologies that are substitutable at comparable cost for Gamma's process are also horizontal competitors of Gamma in the relevant technology market. The licensees of Gamma's process technology are technically in a vertical relationship, although that is not significant in this example because they do not actually use Gamma's technology.

The licensing arrangement restricts competition in the relevant goods market among manufacturers of Product X by requiring each

---

27. Details about the Federal Trade Commission's approach are set forth in *Massachusetts Board of Registration in Optometry*, 110 F.T.C. 549, 604 (1988). In applying its truncated rule of reason inquiry, the FTC uses the analytical category of "inherently suspect" restraints to denote facially anticompetitive restraints that would always or almost always tend to decrease output or increase prices, but that may be relatively unfamiliar or may not fit neatly into traditional per se categories.

28. Under the FTC's *Mass. Board* approach, asserted efficiency justifications for inherently suspect restraints are examined to determine whether they are plausible and, if so, whether they are valid in the context of the market at issue. *Mass. Board*, 110 F.T.C. at 604.

manufacturer to limit its sales to an exclusive territory. Thus, competition among entities that would be actual competitors in the absence of the licensing arrangement is restricted. Based on the facts set forth above, the licensing arrangement does not involve a useful transfer of technology, and thus it is unlikely that the restraint on sales outside the designated territories contributes to an efficiency-enhancing integration of economic activity. Consequently, the evaluating Agency would be likely to challenge the arrangement under the per se rule as a horizontal territorial market allocation scheme and to view the intellectual property aspects of the arrangement as a sham intended to cloak its true nature.

If the licensing arrangement could be expected to contribute to an efficiency-enhancing integration of economic activity, as might be the case if the licensed technology were an advance over existing processes and used by the licensees, the Agency would analyze the arrangement under the rule of reason applying the analytical framework described in this section.

In this example, the competitive implications do not generally depend on whether the licensed technology is protected by patent, is a trade secret or other know-how, or is a computer program protected by copyright; nor do the competitive implications generally depend on whether the allocation of markets is territorial, as in this example, or functional, based on fields of use.

4. General Principles Concerning the Agencies' Evaluation of Licensing Arrangements Under the Rule of Reason

4.1 Analysis of Anticompetitive Effects

The existence of anticompetitive effects resulting from a restraint in a licensing arrangement will be evaluated on the basis of the analysis described in this section.

4.1.1 Market Structure, Coordination, and Foreclosure

When a licensing arrangement affects parties in a horizontal relationship, a restraint in that arrangement may increase the risk of coordinated pricing, output restrictions, or the acquisition or maintenance of market power. Harm to competition also may occur if the arrangement poses a significant risk of retarding or restricting the development of new or improved goods or processes. The potential for competitive harm depends in part on the degree of concentration in, the difficulty of entry into, and the responsiveness of supply and demand to changes in price in the relevant markets. *Cf.* 1992 Horizontal Merger Guidelines §§ 1.5, 3.

When the licensor and licensees are in a vertical relationship, the Agencies will analyze whether the licensing arrangement may harm competition among entities in a horizontal relationship at either the level of the licensor or the licensees, or possibly in another relevant market. Harm to competition from a restraint may occur if it anticompetitively forecloses access to, or increases competitors' costs of obtaining, important inputs, or facilitates coordination to raise price or restrict output. The risk of anticompetitively foreclosing access or increasing competitors' costs is related to the proportion of the markets affected by the licensing restraint; other characteristics of the relevant markets, such as concentration, difficulty of entry, and the responsiveness of supply and demand to changes in price in the relevant markets; and the duration of the restraint. A licensing arrangement does not foreclose competition merely because some or all of the potential licensees in an industry choose to use the licensed technology to the exclusion of other technologies. Exclusive use may be an efficient consequence of the licensed technology having the lowest cost or highest value.

Harm to competition from a restraint in a vertical licensing arrangement also may occur if a licensing restraint facilitates coordination among entities in a horizontal relationship to raise prices or reduce output in a relevant market. For example, if owners of competing technologies impose similar restraints on their licensees, the licensors may find it easier to coordinate their pricing. Similarly, licensees that are competitors may find it easier to coordinate their pricing if they are subject to common restraints in licenses with a common licensor or competing licensors. The risk of anticompetitive coordination is increased when the relevant markets are concentrated and difficult to enter. The use of similar restraints may be common and procompetitive in an industry, however, because they contribute to efficient exploitation of the licensed property.

4.1.2 Licensing Arrangements Involving Exclusivity

A licensing arrangement may involve exclusivity in two distinct respects. First, the licensor may grant one or more exclusive licenses, which restrict the right of the licensor to license others and possibly also to use the technology itself. Generally, an exclusive license may raise antitrust concerns only if the licensees themselves, or the licensor and its licensees, are in a horizontal relationship. Examples of arrangements involving exclusive licensing that may give rise to antitrust concerns include cross-licensing by parties collectively possessing market power (*See* section 5.5), Grantbacks (*See* section 5.6), and acquisitions of intellectual property rights (*See* section 5.7).

A non-exclusive license of intellectual property that does not contain any restraints on the competitive conduct of the licensor or the licensee generally does not present antitrust concerns even if the parties to the license are in a horizontal relationship, because the non-exclusive license normally does not diminish competition that would occur in its absence.

A second form of exclusivity, exclusive dealing, arises when a license prevents or restrains the licensee from licensing, selling, distributing, or using competing technologies. *See* section 5.4. Exclusivity may be achieved by an explicit exclusive dealing term in the license or by other provisions such as compensation terms or other economic incentives. Such restraints may anticompetitively foreclose access to, or increase competitors' costs of obtaining, important inputs, or facilitate coordination to raise price or reduce output, but they also may have procompetitive effects. For example, a licensing arrangement that prevents the licensee from dealing in other technologies may encourage the licensee to develop and market the licensed technology or specialized applications of that technology. *See*, *e.g.*, Example 8. The Agencies will take into account such procompetitive effects in evaluating the reasonableness of the arrangement. *See* section 4.2.

The antitrust principles that apply to a licensor's grant of various forms of exclusivity to and among its licensees are similar to those that apply to comparable vertical restraints outside the licensing context, such as exclusive territories and exclusive dealing. However, the fact that intellectual property may in some cases be misappropriated more easily than other forms of property may justify the use of some restrictions that might be anticompetitive in other contexts.

As noted earlier, the Agencies will focus on the actual practice and its effects, not on the formal terms of the arrangement. A license denominated as non-exclusive (either in the sense of exclusive licensing or in the sense of exclusive dealing) may nonetheless give rise to the same concerns posed by formal exclusivity. A non-exclusive license may have the effect of exclusive licensing if it is structured so that the licensor is unlikely to license others or to practice the technology itself. A license that does not explicitly require exclusive dealing may have the effect of exclusive dealing if it is structured to increase significantly a licensee's cost when it uses competing technologies. However, a licensing arrangement will not automatically raise these concerns merely because a party chooses to deal with a single licensee or licensor, or confines his activity to a single field of use or location, or because only a single licensee has chosen to take a license.

EXAMPLE 8

Situation: NewCo, the inventor and manufacturer of a new flat panel display technology, lacking the capability to bring a flat panel display product to market, grants BigCo an exclusive license to sell a product embodying NewCo's technology. BigCo does not currently sell, and is not developing (or likely to develop), a product that would compete with the product embodying the new technology and does not control rights to another display technology. Several firms offer competing displays, BigCo accounts for only a small proportion of the outlets for distribution of display products, and entry into the manufacture and distribution of display products is relatively easy. Demand for the new technology is uncertain and successful market penetration will require considerable promotional effort. The license contains an exclusive dealing restriction preventing BigCo from selling products that compete with the product embodying the licensed technology.

Discussion: This example illustrates both types of exclusivity in a licensing arrangement. The license is exclusive in that it restricts the right of the licensor to grant other licenses. In addition, the license has an exclusive dealing component in that it restricts the licensee from selling competing products.

The inventor of the display technology and its licensee are in a vertical relationship and are not actual or likely potential competitors in the manufacture or sale of display products or in the sale or development of technology. Hence, the grant of an exclusive license does not affect competition between the licensor and the licensee. The exclusive license may promote competition in the manufacturing and sale of display products by encouraging BigCo to develop and promote the new product in the face of uncertain demand by rewarding BigCo for its efforts if they lead to large sales. Although the license bars the licensee from selling competing products, this exclusive dealing aspect is unlikely in this example to harm competition by anticompetitively foreclosing access, raising competitors' costs of inputs, or facilitating anticompetitive pricing because the relevant product market is unconcentrated, the exclusive dealing restraint affects only a small proportion of the outlets for distribution of display products, and entry is easy. On these facts, the evaluating Agency would be unlikely to challenge the arrangement.

4.2 Efficiencies and Justifications

If the Agencies conclude, upon an evaluation of the market factors described in section 4.1, that a restraint in a licensing arrangement is unlikely to have an anticompetitive effect, they will not challenge the restraint. If the Agencies conclude that the restraint has, or is likely to have, an anticompetitive effect, they will consider whether the restraint is reasonably necessary to achieve procompetitive efficiencies. If the restraint is reasonably necessary, the Agencies will balance the procompetitive efficiencies and the anticompetitive effects to determine the probable net effect on competition in each relevant market.

The Agencies' comparison of anticompetitive harms and procompetitive efficiencies is necessarily a qualitative one. The risk of anticompetitive effects in a particular case may be insignificant compared to the expected efficiencies, or vice versa. As the expected anticompetitive effects in a particular licensing arrangement increase, the Agencies will require evidence establishing a greater level of expected efficiencies.

The existence of practical and significantly less restrictive alternatives is relevant to a determination of whether a restraint is reasonably necessary. If it is clear that the parties could have achieved similar efficiencies by means that are significantly less restrictive, then the Agencies will not give weight to the parties' efficiency claim. In making this assessment, however, the Agencies will not engage in a search for a theoretically least restrictive alternative that is not realistic in the practical prospective business situation faced by the parties.

When a restraint has, or is likely to have, an anticompetitive effect, the duration of that restraint can be an important factor in determining whether it is reasonably necessary to achieve the putative procompetitive efficiency. The effective duration of a restraint may depend on a number of factors, including the option of the affected party to terminate the arrangement unilaterally and the presence of contract terms (*e.g.*, unpaid balances on minimum purchase commitments) that encourage the licensee to renew a license arrangement. Consistent with their approach to less restrictive alternative analysis generally, the Agencies will not attempt to draw fine distinctions regarding duration; rather, their focus will be on situations in which the duration clearly exceeds the period needed to achieve the procompetitive efficiency.

The evaluation of procompetitive efficiencies, of the reasonable necessity of a restraint to achieve them, and of the duration of the restraint, may depend on the market context. A restraint that may be justified by the needs of a new entrant, for example, may not have a procompetitive efficiency justification in different market circumstances. *Cf.* United States v. Jerrold Electronics Corp., 187 F. Supp. 545 (E.D. Pa. 1960), *aff'd per curiam,* 365 U.S. 567 (1961).

4.3 Antitrust "Safety Zone"

Because licensing arrangements often promote innovation and enhance competition, the Agencies believe that an antitrust "safety zone" is useful in order to provide some degree of certainty and thus to encourage such activity.[29] Absent extraordinary circumstances, the Agencies will not challenge a restraint in an intellectual property licensing arrangement if (1) the restraint is not facially anticompetitive[30] and (2) the licensor and its licensees collectively account for no more than twenty percent of each relevant market significantly affected by the restraint. This "safety zone" does not apply to those transfers of intellectual property rights to which a merger analysis is applied. *See* section 5.7.

Whether a restraint falls within the safety zone will be determined by reference only to goods markets unless the analysis of goods markets alone would inadequately address the effects of the licensing arrangement on competition among technologies or in research and development.

If an examination of the effects on competition among technologies or in research development is required, and if market share data are

---

29. The antitrust "safety zone" does not apply to restraints that are not in a licensing arrangement, or to restraints that are in a licensing arrangement but are unrelated to the use of the licensed intellectual property.

30. "Facially anticompetitive" refers to restraints that normally warrant per se treatment, as well as other restraints of a kind that would always or almost always tend to reduce output or increase prices. *See* section 3.4.

unavailable or do not accurately represent competitive significance, the following safety zone criteria will apply. Absent extraordinary circumstances, the Agencies will not challenge a restraint in an intellectual property licensing arrangement that may affect competition in a technology market if (1) the restraint is not facially anticompetitive and (2) there are four or more independently controlled technologies in addition to the technologies controlled by the parties to the licensing arrangement that may be substitutable for the licensed technology at a comparable cost to the user. Absent extraordinary circumstances, the Agencies will not challenge a restraint in an intellectual property licensing arrangement that may affect competition in an innovation market if (1) the restraint is not facially anticompetitive and (2) four or more independently controlled entities in addition to the parties to the licensing arrangement possess the required specialized assets or characteristics and the incentive to engage in research and development that is a close substitute of the research and development activities of the parties to the licensing agreement.[31]

The Agencies emphasize that licensing arrangements are not anticompetitive merely because they do not fall within the scope of the safety zone. Indeed, it is likely that the great majority of licenses falling outside the safety zone are lawful and procompetitive. The safety zone is designed to provide owners of intellectual property with a degree of certainty in those situations in which anticompetitive effects are so unlikely that the arrangements may be presumed not to be anticompetitive without an inquiry into particular industry circumstances. It is not intended to suggest that parties should conform to the safety zone or to discourage parties falling outside the safety zone from adopting restrictions in their license arrangements that are reasonably necessary to achieve an efficiency-enhancing integration of economic activity. The Agencies will analyze arrangements falling outside the safety zone based on the considerations outlined in parts 3-5.

The status of a licensing arrangement with respect to the safety zone may change over time. A determination by the Agencies that a restraint in a licensing arrangement qualifies for inclusion in the safety zone is

---

31. This is consistent with congressional intent in enacting the National Cooperative Research Act. *See* H.R. Conf. Rpt. No. 1044, 98th Cong., 2d Sess., 10, *reprinted in* 1984 U.S.C.C.A.N. 3105, 3134-35.

based on the factual circumstances prevailing at the time of the conduct at issue.[32]

5. Application of General Principles

5.0 This section illustrates the application of the general principles discussed above to particular licensing restraints and to arrangements that involve the cross-licensing, pooling, or acquisition of intellectual property. The restraints and arrangements identified are typical of those that are likely to receive antitrust scrutiny; however, they are not intended as an exhaustive list of practices that could raise competitive concerns.

5.1 Horizontal Restraints

The existence of a restraint in a licensing arrangement that affects parties in a horizontal relationship (a "horizontal restraint") does not necessarily cause the arrangement to be anticompetitive. As in the case of joint ventures among horizontal competitors, licensing arrangements among such competitors may promote rather than hinder competition if they result in integrative efficiencies. Such efficiencies may arise, for example, from the realization of economies of scale and the integration of complementary research and development, production, and marketing capabilities.

Following the general principles outlined in section 3.4, horizontal restraints often will be evaluated under the rule of reason. In some circumstances, however, that analysis may be truncated; additionally, some restraints may merit per se treatment, including price fixing, allocation of markets or customers, agreements to reduce output, and certain group boycotts.

EXAMPLE 9

Situation: Two of the leading manufacturers of a consumer electronic product hold patents that cover alternative circuit designs for the product. The manufacturers assign their patents to a separate corporation wholly

32. The conduct at issue may be the transaction giving rise to the restraint or the subsequent implementation of the restraint.

owned by the two firms. That corporation licenses the right to use the circuit designs to other consumer product manufacturers and establishes the license royalties. None of the patents is blocking; that is, each of the patents can be used without infringing a patent owned by the other firm. The different circuit designs are substitutable in that each permits the manufacture at comparable cost to consumers of products that consumers consider to be interchangeable. One of the Agencies is analyzing the licensing arrangement.

Discussion: In this example, the manufacturers are horizontal competitors in the goods market for the consumer product and in the related technology markets. The competitive issue with regard to a joint assignment of patent rights is whether the assignment has an adverse impact on competition in technology and goods markets that is not outweighed by procompetitive efficiencies, such as benefits in the use or dissemination of the technology. Each of the patent owners has a right to exclude others from using its patent. That right does not extend, however, to the agreement to assign rights jointly. To the extent that the patent rights cover technologies that are close substitutes, the joint determination of royalties likely would result in higher royalties and higher goods prices than would result if the owners licensed or used their technologies independently. In the absence of evidence establishing efficiency-enhancing integration from the joint assignment of patent rights, the Agency may conclude that the joint marketing of competing patent rights constitutes horizontal price fixing and could be challenged as a per se unlawful horizontal restraint of trade. If the joint marketing arrangement results in an efficiency-enhancing integration, the Agency would evaluate the arrangement under the rule of reason. However, the Agency may conclude that the anticompetitive effects are sufficiently apparent, and the claimed integrative efficiencies are sufficiently weak or not reasonably related to the restraints, to warrant challenge of the arrangement without an elaborate analysis of particular industry circumstances (*See* section 3.4).

5.2 Resale Price Maintenance

Resale price maintenance is illegal when "commodities have passed into the channels of trade and are owned by dealers." *Dr. Miles Medical Co. v. John D. Park & Sons Co.*, 220 U.S. 373, 408 (1911). It has been held per se illegal for a licensor of an intellectual property right in a product to fix a licensee's resale price of that product. *United States v. Univis Lens Co.*, 316 U.S. 241 (1942); *Ethyl Gasoline Corp. v. United*

States, 309 U.S. 436 (1940).[33] Consistent with the principles set forth in section 3.4, the Agencies will enforce the per se rule against resale price maintenance in the intellectual property context.

5.3 Tying Arrangements

A "tying" or "tie-in" or "tied sale" arrangement has been defined as "an agreement by a party to sell one product . . . on the condition that the buyer also purchases a different (or tied) product, or at least agrees that he will not purchase that [tied] product from any other supplier." *Eastman Kodak Co. v. Image Technical Services, Inc.,* 112 S. Ct. 2072, 2079 (1992). Conditioning the ability of a licensee to license one or more items of intellectual property on the licensee's purchase of another item of intellectual property or a good or a service has been held in some cases to constitute illegal tying.[34] Although tying arrangements may result in anticompetitive effects, such arrangements can also result in significant efficiencies and procompetitive benefits. In the exercise of their prosecutorial discretion, the Agencies will consider both the anticompetitive effects and the efficiencies attributable to a tie-in. The Agencies would be likely to challenge a tying arrangement if: (1) the

---

33. *But cf.* United States v. General Electric Co., 272 U.S. 476 (1926) (holding that an owner of a product patent may condition a license to manufacture the product on the fixing of the first sale price of the patented product). Subsequent lower court decisions have distinguished the GE decision in various contexts. *See, e.g.,* Royal Indus. v. St. Regis Paper Co., 420 F.2d 449, 452 (9th Cir. 1969) (observing that GE involved a restriction by a patentee who also manufactured the patented product and leaving open the question whether a nonmanufacturing patentee may fix the price of the patented product); Newburgh Moire Co. v. Superior Moire Co., 237 F.2d 283, 293-94 (3d Cir. 1956) (grant of multiple licenses each containing price restrictions does not come within the GE doctrine); Cummer-Graham Co. v. Straight Side Basket Corp., 142 F.2d 646, 647 (5th Cir.) (owner of an intellectual property right in a process to manufacture an unpatented product may not fix the sale price of that product), *cert. denied*, 323 U.S. 726 (1944); Barber-Colman Co. v. National Tool Co., 136 F.2d 339, 343-44 (6th Cir. 1943) (same).

34. *See, e.g.*, United States v. Paramount Pictures, Inc., 334 U.S. 131, 156-58 (1948) (copyrights); International Salt Co. v. United States, 332 U.S. 392 (1947) (patent and related product).

seller has market power in the tying product,[35] (2) the arrangement has an adverse effect on competition in the relevant market for the tied product, and (3) efficiency justifications for the arrangement do not outweigh the anticompetitive effects.[36] The Agencies will not presume that a patent, copyright, or trade secret necessarily confers market power upon its owner.

Package licensing—the licensing of multiple items of intellectual property in a single license or in a group of related licenses—may be a form of tying arrangement if the licensing of one product is conditioned upon the acceptance of a license of another, separate product. Package licensing can be efficiency enhancing under some circumstances. When multiple licenses are needed to use any single item of intellectual property, for example, a package license may promote such efficiencies. If a package license constitutes a tying arrangement, the Agencies will evaluate its competitive effects under the same principles they apply to other tying arrangements.

5.4 Exclusive Dealing

In the intellectual property context, exclusive dealing occurs when a license prevents the licensee from licensing, selling, distributing, or using competing technologies. Exclusive dealing arrangements are evaluated under the rule of reason. *See Tampa Electric Co. v. Nashville Coal Co.,* 365 U.S. 320 (1961) (evaluating legality of exclusive dealing under section 1 of the Sherman Act and section 3 of the Clayton Act); *Beltone Electronics Corp.*, 100 F.T.C. 68 (1982) (evaluating legality of exclusive dealing under section 5 of the Federal Trade Commission Act). In determining whether an exclusive dealing arrangement is likely to reduce competition in a relevant market, the Agencies will take into account the extent to which the arrangement (1) promotes the exploitation and development of the licensor's technology and (2) anticompetitively

---

35. *Cf.* 35 U.S.C. *§* 271(d) (1988 & Supp. V 1993) (requirement of market power in patent misuse cases involving tying).

36. As is true throughout these Guidelines, the factors listed are those that guide the Agencies' internal analysis in exercising their prosecutorial discretion. They are not intended to circumscribe how the Agencies will conduct the litigation of cases that they decide to bring.

forecloses the exploitation and development of, or otherwise constrains competition among, competing technologies.

The likelihood that exclusive dealing may have anticompetitive effects is related, inter alia, to the degree of foreclosure in the relevant market, the duration of the exclusive dealing arrangement, and other characteristics of the input and output markets, such as concentration, difficulty of entry, and the responsiveness of supply and demand to changes in price in the relevant markets. (*See* sections 4.1.1 and 4.1.2.) If the Agencies determine that a particular exclusive dealing arrangement may have an anticompetitive effect, they will evaluate the extent to which the restraint encourages licensees to develop and market the licensed technology (or specialized applications of that technology), increases licensors' incentives to develop or refine the licensed technology, or otherwise increases competition and enhances output in a relevant market. (*See* section 4.2 and Example 8.)

5.5 Cross-licensing and Pooling Arrangements

Cross-licensing and pooling arrangements are agreements of two or more owners of different items of intellectual property to license one another or third parties. These arrangements may provide procompetitive benefits by integrating complementary technologies, reducing transaction costs, clearing blocking positions, and avoiding costly infringement litigation. By promoting the dissemination of technology, cross-licensing and pooling arrangements are often procompetitive.

Cross-licensing and pooling arrangements can have anticompetitive effects in certain circumstances. For example, collective price or output restraints in pooling arrangements, such as the joint marketing of pooled intellectual property rights with collective price setting or coordinated output restrictions, may be deemed unlawful if they do not contribute to an efficiency-enhancing integration of economic activity among the participants. *Compare NCAA* 468 U.S. at 114 (output restriction on college football broadcasting held unlawful because it was not reasonably related to any purported justification) *with Broadcast Music*, 441 U.S. at 23 (blanket license for music copyrights found not per se illegal because the cooperative price was necessary to the creation of a new product). When cross-licensing or pooling arrangements are mechanisms to accomplish naked price fixing or market division, they are subject to challenge under the per se rule. *See United States v. New Wrinkle, Inc.,* 342 U.S. 371 (1952) (price fixing).

Settlements involving the cross-licensing of intellectual property rights can be an efficient means to avoid litigation and, in general, courts favor such settlements. When such cross-licensing involves horizontal competitors, however, the Agencies will consider whether the effect of the settlement is to diminish competition among entities that would have been actual or likely potential competitors in a relevant market in the absence of the cross-license. In the absence of offsetting efficiencies, such settlements may be challenged as unlawful restraints of trade. *Cf. United States v. Singer Manufacturing Co.,* 374 U.S. 174 (1963) (cross-license agreement was part of broader combination to exclude competitors).

Pooling arrangements generally need not be open to all who would like to join. However, exclusion from cross-licensing and pooling arrangements among parties that collectively possess market power may, under some circumstances, harm competition. *Cf. Northwest Wholesale Stationers, Inc. v. Pacific Stationery & Printing Co.,* 472 U.S. 284 (1985) (exclusion of a competitor from a purchasing cooperative not per se unlawful absent a showing of market power). In general, exclusion from a pooling or cross-licensing arrangement among competing technologies is unlikely to have anticompetitive effects unless (1) excluded firms cannot effectively compete in the relevant market for the good incorporating the licensed technologies and (2) the pool participants collectively possess market power in the relevant market. If these circumstances exist, the Agencies will evaluate whether the arrangement's limitations on participation are reasonably related to the efficient development and exploitation of the pooled technologies and will assess the net effect of those limitations in the relevant market. *See* section 4.2.

Another possible anticompetitive effect of pooling arrangements may occur if the arrangement deters or discourages participants from engaging in research and development, thus retarding innovation. For example, a pooling arrangement that requires members to grant licenses to each other for current and future technology at minimal cost may reduce the incentives of its members to engage in research and development because members of the pool have to share their successful research and development and each of the members can free ride on the accomplishments of other pool members. *See generally United States v.*

Mfrs. Aircraft Ass'n, Inc., 1976-1 Trade Cas. (CCH) ¶ 60,810 (S.D.N.Y. 1975); *United States v. Automobile Mfrs. Ass'n*, 307 F. Supp. 617 (C.D. Cal 1969), *appeal dismissed sub nom. City of New York v. United States*, 397 U.S. 248 (1970), *modified sub nom. United States v. Motor Vehicle Mfrs. Ass'n*, 1982-83 Trade Cas. (CCH) ¶ 65,088 (C.D. Cal. 1982). However, such an arrangement can have procompetitive benefits, for example, by exploiting economies of scale and integrating complementary capabilities of the pool members, (including the clearing of blocking positions), and is likely to cause competitive problems only when the arrangement includes a large fraction of the potential research and development in an innovation market. *See* section 3.2.3 and Example 4.

EXAMPLE 10

Situation: As in Example 9, two of the leading manufacturers of a consumer electronic product hold patents that cover alternative circuit designs for the product. The manufacturers assign several of their patents to a separate corporation wholly owned by the two firms. That corporation licenses the right to use the circuit designs to other consumer product manufacturers and establishes the license royalties. In this example, however, the manufacturers assign to the separate corporation only patents that are blocking. None of the patents assigned to the corporation can be used without infringing a patent owned by the other firm.

Discussion: Unlike the previous example, the joint assignment of patent rights to the wholly owned corporation in this example does not adversely affect competition in the licensed technology among entities that would have been actual or likely potential competitors in the absence of the licensing arrangement. Moreover, the licensing arrangement is likely to have procompetitive benefits in the use of the technology. Because the manufacturers' patents are blocking, the manufacturers are not in a horizontal relationship with respect to those patents. None of the patents can be used without the right to a patent owned by the other firm, so the patents are not substitutable. As in Example 9, the firms are horizontal competitors in the relevant goods market. In the absence of collateral restraints that would likely raise price or reduce output in the relevant goods market or in any other relevant antitrust market and that are not reasonably related to an efficiency-enhancing integration of economic activity, the evaluating Agency would be unlikely to challenge this arrangement.

5.6 Grantbacks

A grantback is an arrangement under which a licensee agrees to extend to the licensor of intellectual property the right to use the licensee's improvements to the licensed technology. Grantbacks can have procompetitive effects, especially if they are nonexclusive. Such arrangements provide a means for the licensee and the licensor to share risks and reward the licensor for making possible further innovation based on or informed by the licensed technology, and both promote innovation in the first place and promote the subsequent licensing of the results of the innovation. Grantbacks may adversely affect competition, however, if they substantially reduce the licensee's incentives to engage in research and development and thereby limit rivalry in innovation markets.

A non-exclusive grantback allows the licensee to practice its technology and license it to others. Such a grantback provision may be necessary to ensure that the licensor is not prevented from effectively competing because it is denied access to improvements developed with the aid of its own technology. Compared with an exclusive grantback, a non-exclusive grantback, which leaves the licensee free to license improvements technology to others, is less likely to have anticompetitive effects.

The Agencies will evaluate a grantback provision under the rule of reason, *See generally Transparent-Wrap Machine Corp. v. Stokes & Smith* 329 U.S. 637, 645-48 (1947) (grantback provision in technology license is not per se unlawful), considering its likely effects in light of the overall structure of the licensing arrangement and conditions in the relevant markets. An important factor in the Agencies' analysis of a grantback will be whether the licensor has market power in a relevant technology or innovation market. If the Agencies determine that a particular grantback provision is likely to reduce significantly licensees' incentives to invest in improving the licensed technology, the Agencies will consider the extent to which the grantback provision has offsetting procompetitive effects, such as (1) promoting dissemination of licensees' improvements to the licensed technology, (2) increasing the licensors' incentives to disseminate the licensed technology, or (3) otherwise increasing competition and output in a relevant technology or innovation market. *See* section 4.2. In addition, the Agencies will consider the extent to which grantback provisions in the relevant markets generally increase licensors' incentives to innovate in the first place.

5.7 Acquisition of Intellectual Property Rights

Certain transfers of intellectual property rights are most appropriately analyzed by applying the principles and standards used to analyze mergers, particularly those in the 1992 Horizontal Merger Guidelines. The Agencies will apply a merger analysis to an outright sale by an intellectual property owner of all of its rights to that intellectual property and to a transaction in which a person obtains through grant, sale, or other transfer an exclusive license for intellectual property (i.e., a license that precludes all other persons, including the licensor, from using the licensed intellectual property).[37] Such transactions may be assessed under section 7 of the Clayton Act, sections 1 and 2 of the Sherman Act, and section 5 of the Federal Trade Commission Act.

EXAMPLE 11

Situation: Omega develops a new, patented pharmaceutical for the treatment of a particular disease. The only drug on the market approved for the treatment of this disease is sold by Delta. Omega's patented drug has almost completed regulatory approval by the Food and Drug Administration. Omega has invested considerable sums in product development and market testing, and initial results show that Omega's drug would be a significant competitor to Delta's. However, rather than enter the market as a direct competitor of Delta, Omega licenses to Delta the right to manufacture and sell Omega's patented drug. The license agreement with Delta is nominally nonexclusive. However, Omega has rejected all requests by other firms to obtain a license to manufacture and sell Omega's patented drug, despite offers by those firms of terms that are reasonable in relation to those in Delta's license.

Discussion: Although Omega's license to Delta is nominally nonexclusive, the circumstances indicate that it is exclusive in fact

---

37. The safety zone of section 4.3 does not apply to transfers of intellectual property such as those described in this section.

because Omega has rejected all reasonable offers by other firms for licenses to manufacture and sell Omega's patented drug. The facts of this example indicate that Omega would be a likely potential competitor of Delta in the absence of the licensing arrangement, and thus they are in a horizontal relationship in the relevant goods market that includes drugs for the treatment of this particular disease. The evaluating Agency would apply a merger analysis to this transaction, since it involves an acquisition of a likely potential competitor.

6. Enforcement of Invalid Intellectual Property Rights

The Agencies may challenge the enforcement of invalid intellectual property rights as antitrust violations. Enforcement or attempted enforcement of a patent obtained by fraud on the Patent and Trademark Office or the Copyright Office may violate section 2 of the Sherman Act, if all the elements otherwise necessary to establish a section 2 charge are proved, or section 5 of the Federal Trade Commission Act. *Walker Process Equipment, Inc. v. Food Machinery & Chemical Corp.,* 382 U.S. 172 (1965) (patents); American Cyanamid Co., 72 F.T.C. 623, 684-85 (1967), aff'd sub. nom. *Charles Pfizer & Co.*, 401 F.2d 574 (6th Cir. 1968), *cert. denied*, 394 U.S. 920 (1969) (patents); *Michael Anthony Jewelers, Inc. v. Peacock Jewelry, Inc.,* 795 F. Supp. 639, 647 (S.D.N.Y. 1992) (copyrights). Inequitable conduct before the Patent and Trademark Office will not be the basis of a section 2 claim unless the conduct also involves knowing and willful fraud and the other elements of a section 2 claim are present. *Argus Chemical Corp. v. Fibre Glass-Evercoat, Inc.*, 812 F.2d 1381, 1384-85 (Fed. Cir. 1987). Actual or attempted enforcement of patents obtained by inequitable conduct that falls short of fraud under some circumstances may violate section 5 of the Federal Trade Commission Act, American Cyanamid Co., *supra*. Objectively baseless litigation to enforce invalid intellectual property rights may also constitute an element of a violation of the Sherman Act. *See Professional Real Estate Investors, Inc. v. Columbia Pictures Industries, Inc.,* 113 S. Ct. 1920, 1928 (1993) (copyrights); *Handgards, Inc. v. Ethicon, Inc.*, 743 F.2d 1282, 1289 (9th Cir. 1984), *cert. denied*, 469 U.S. 1190 (1985) (patents); *Handgards, Inc. v. Ethicon, Inc.,* 601 F.2d 986, 992-96 (9th Cir. 1979), *cert. denied*, 444 U.S. 1025 (1980) (patents); *CVD, Inc. v. Raytheon Co.,* 769 F.2d 842 (1st Cir. 1985) (trade secrets), *cert. denied*, 475 U.S. 1016 (1986).

APPENDIX L

1996 DEPARTMENT OF JUSTICE AND FEDERAL TRADE COMMISSION STATEMENTS OF ANTITRUST ENFORCEMENT POLICY IN HEALTH CARE

Introduction

In September 1993, the Department of Justice and the Federal Trade Commission (the "Agencies") issued six statements of their antitrust enforcement policies regarding mergers and various joint activities in the health care area. The six policy statements addressed: (1) hospital mergers; (2) hospital joint ventures involving high-technology or other expensive medical equipment; (3) physicians' provision of information to purchasers of health care services; (4) hospital participation in exchanges of price and cost information; (5) health care providers' joint purchasing arrangements; and (6) physician network joint ventures. The Agencies also committed to issuing expedited Department of Justice business reviews and Federal Trade Commission advisory opinions in response to requests for antitrust guidance on specific proposed conduct involving the health care industry.

The 1993 policy statements and expedited specific Agency guidance were designed to advise the health care community in a time of tremendous change, and to address, as completely as possible, the problem of uncertainty concerning the Agencies' enforcement policy that some had said might deter mergers, joint ventures, or other activities that could lower health care costs. Sound antitrust enforcement, of course, continued to protect consumers against anticompetitive activities.

When the Agencies issued the 1993 health care antitrust enforcement policy statements, they recognized that additional guidance might be desirable in the areas covered by those statements as well as in other health care areas, and committed to issuing revised and additional policy statements as warranted. In light of the comments the Agencies received on the 1993 statements and the agencies' own experience, the Agencies revised and expanded the health care antitrust enforcement policy statements in September 1994. The 1994 statements, which superseded the 1993 statements, added new statements addressing hospital joint ventures involving specialized clinical or other expensive health care services, providers' collective provision of fee-related information to purchasers of health care services, and analytical principles relating to abroad range of health care provider networks (termed "multiprovider networks"), and expanded the antitrust "safety zones" for several other statements.

Since issuance of the 1994 statements, health care markets have continued to evolve in response to consumer demand and competition in the marketplace. New arrangements and variations on existing arrangements involving joint activity by health care providers continue to emerge to meet consumers', purchasers', and payers' desire for more efficient delivery of high quality health care services. During this period, the Agencies have gained additional experience with arrangements involving joint provider activity. As a result of these developments, the Agencies have decided to amplify the enforcement policy statement on physician network joint ventures and the more general statement on multiprovider networks.

In these revised statements, the Agencies continue to analyze all types of health care provider networks under general antitrust principles. These principles are sufficiently flexible to take into account the particular characteristics of health care markets and the rapid changes that are occurring in those markets. The Agencies emphasize that it is not their intent to treat such networks either more strictly or more leniently than joint ventures in other industries, or to favor any particular procompetitive organization or structure of health care delivery over other forms that consumers may desire. Rather, their goal is to ensure a competitive marketplace in which consumers will have the benefit of high quality, cost-effective health care and a wide range of choices, including new provider-controlled networks that expand consumer choice and increase competition.

The revisions to the statements on physician network joint ventures and multiprovider networks are summarized below. In addition to these revisions, various changes have been made to the language of both statements to improve their clarity. No revisions have been made to any of the other statements.

Physician Network Joint Ventures

The revised statement on physician network joint ventures provides an expanded discussion of the antitrust principles that apply to such ventures. The revisions focus on the analysis of networks that fall outside the safety zones contained in the existing statement, particularly those networks that do not involve the sharing of substantial financial risk by their physician participants. The revised statement explains that where physicians' integration through the network is likely to produce significant efficiencies, any agreements on price reasonably necessary to accomplish the venture's procompetitive benefits will be analyzed under the rule of reason.

The revised statement adds three hypothetical examples to further illustrate the application of these principles: (1) a physician network joint venture that does not involve the sharing of substantial financial risk, but receives rule of reason treatment due to the extensive integration among its physician participants; (2) a network that involves both risk-sharing and non-risk-sharing activities, and receives rule of reason treatment; and (3) a network that involves little or no integration among its physician participants, and is per se illegal.

The safety zones for physician network joint ventures remain unchanged, but the revised statement identifies additional types of financial risk-sharing arrangements that can qualify a network for the safety zones. It also further emphasizes two points previously made in the 1994 statements. First, the enumeration in the statements of particular examples of substantial financial risk sharing does not foreclose consideration of other arrangements through which physicians may share substantial financial risk. Second, a physician network that falls outside the safety zones is not necessarily anticompetitive.

Multiprovider Networks

In 1994, the Agencies issued a new statement on multiprovider health care networks that described the general antitrust analysis of such networks. The revised statement on multiprovider networks emphasizes that it is intended to articulate general principles relating to a wide range of health care provider networks. Many of the revisions to this statement reflect changes made to The revised statement on physician network joint ventures. In addition, four hypothetical examples involving PHOs ("physician-hospital organizations"), including one involving "messenger model" arrangements, have been added.

Safety Zones and Hypothetical Examples

Most of the nine statements give health care providers guidance in the form of antitrust safety zones, which describe conduct that the Agencies will not challenge under the antitrust laws, absent extraordinary circumstances. The agencies are aware that some parties have interpreted the safety zones as defining the limits of joint conduct that is permissible under the antitrust laws. This view is incorrect. The inclusion of certain conduct within the antitrust safety zones does not imply that conduct falling outside the safety zones is likely to be challenged by the Agencies. Antitrust analysis is inherently fact-intensive. The safety zones are designed to require consideration of only a few factors that are relatively easy to apply, and to provide the Agencies with a high degree of confidence that arrangements falling within them are unlikely to raise substantial competitive concerns. Thus, the safety zones encompass only a subset of provider arrangements that the Agencies are unlikely to challenge under the antitrust laws. The statements outline the analysis the Agencies will use to review conduct that falls outside the safety zones.

Likewise, the statements' hypothetical examples concluding that the Agencies would not challenge the particular arrangement do not mean that conduct varying from the examples is likely to be challenged by the Agencies. The hypothetical examples are designed to illustrate how the statements' general principles apply to specific situations. Interested parties should examine the business review letters issued by the Department of Justice and the advisory opinions issued by the Federal Trade Commission and its staff for additional guidance on the application and interpretation of these statements. Copies of those letters and opinions and summaries of the letters and opinions are available from the agencies at the mailing and Internet addresses listed at the end of the statements.

The statements also set forth the Department of Justice's business review procedure and the Federal Trade Commission's advisory opinion procedure under which the health care community can obtain the Agencies' antitrust enforcement intentions regarding specific proposed conduct on an expedited basis. The statements continue the commitment of the Agencies to respond to requests for business reviews or advisory opinions from the health care community no later than 90 days after all necessary information is received regarding any matter addressed in the statements, except requests relating to hospital mergers outside the antitrust safety zone and multiprovider networks. The Agencies also will respond to business review or advisory opinion requests regarding multiprovider networks or other non-merger health care matters within 120 days after all necessary information is received. The Agencies intend to work closely with persons making requests to clarify what information is necessary and to provide guidance throughout the process. The Agencies continue this commitment to expedited review in an effort to reduce antitrust uncertainty for the health care industry in what the Agencies recognize is a time of fundamental change.

The Agencies recognize the importance of antitrust guidance in evolving health care contexts. Consequently, the Agencies continue their commitment to issue additional guidance as warranted.

1. Statement of Department of Justice and Federal Trade Commission Enforcement Policy on Mergers Among Hospitals

Introduction

Most hospital mergers and acquisitions ("mergers") do not present competitive concerns. While careful analysis may be necessary to determine the likely competitive effect of a particular hospital merger, the competitive effect of many hospital mergers is relatively easy to assess. This statement sets forth an antitrust safety zone for certain mergers in light of the Agencies' extensive experience analyzing hospital mergers. Mergers that fall within the antitrust safety zone will not be challenged by the Agencies under the antitrust laws, absent extraordinary circumstances.[1] This policy statement also briefly describes the Agencies' antitrust analysis of hospital mergers that fall outside the antitrust safety zone.

A. Antitrust Safety Zone: Mergers of Hospitals That Will Not Be Challenged, Absent Extraordinary Circumstances, By The Agencies

The Agencies will not challenge any merger between two general acute-care hospitals where one of the hospitals (1) has an average of fewer than 100 licensed beds over the three most recent years, and (2) has an average daily inpatient census of fewer than 40 patients over the three most recent years, absent extraordinary circumstances. This antitrust safety zone will not apply if that hospital is less than 5 years old.

The Agencies recognize that in some cases a general acute care hospital with fewer than 100 licensed beds and an average daily inpatient census of fewer than 40 patients will be the only hospital in a relevant market. As such, the hospital does not compete in any significant way with other hospitals. Accordingly, mergers involving such hospitals are unlikely to reduce competition substantially.

---

1. The Agencies are confident that conduct falling within the antitrust safety zones contained in these policy statements is very unlikely to raise competitive concerns. Accordingly, the Agencies anticipate that extraordinary circumstances warranting a challenge to such conduct will be rare.

The Agencies also recognize that many general acute care hospitals, especially rural hospitals, with fewer than 100 licensed beds and an average daily inpatient census of fewer than 40 patients are unlikely to achieve the efficiencies that larger hospitals enjoy. Some of those cost-saving efficiencies may be realized, however, through a merger with another hospital.

B. The Agencies' Analysis of Hospital Mergers That Fall Outside the Antitrust Safety Zone

Hospital mergers that fall outside the antitrust safety zone are not necessarily anticompetitive, and may be procompetitive. The Agencies' analysis of hospital mergers follows the five steps set forth in the Department of Justice/ Federal Trade Commission 1992 Horizontal Merger Guidelines.

Applying the analytical framework of the Merger Guidelines to particular facts of specific hospital mergers, the Agencies often have concluded that an investigated hospital merger will not result in a substantial lessening of competition in situations where market concentration might otherwise raise an inference of anticompetitive effects. Such situations include transactions where the Agencies found that: (1) the merger would not increase the likelihood of the exercise of market power either because of the existence post-merger of strong competitors or because the merging hospitals were sufficiently differentiated; (2) the merger would allow the hospitals to realize significant cost savings that could not otherwise be realized; or (3) the merger would eliminate a hospital that likely would fail with its assets exiting the market.

Antitrust challenges to hospital mergers are relatively rare. Of the hundreds of hospital mergers in the United States since 1987, the Agencies have challenged only a handful, and in several cases sought relief only as to part of the transaction. Most reviews of hospital mergers conducted by the Agencies are concluded within one month.

* * *

If hospitals are considering mergers that appear to fall within the antitrust safety zone and believe they need additional certainty regarding the legality of their conduct under the antitrust laws, they can take advantage of the Department's business review procedure (28 C.F.R. § 50.6 (1992)) or the Federal Trade Commission's advisory opinion procedure (16 C.F.R. §§ 1.1-1.4 (1993)). The Agencies will respond to business review or advisory opinion requests on behalf of hospitals considering mergers that appear to fall within the antitrust safety zone within 90 days after all necessary information is submitted.

2. Statement of Department of Justice and Federal Trade Commission Enforcement Policy on Hospital Joint Ventures Involving High-Technology or Other Expensive Health Care Equipment

Introduction

Most hospital joint ventures to purchase or otherwise share the ownership cost of, operate, and market high-technology or other expensive health care equipment and related services do not create antitrust problems. In most cases, these collaborative activities create procompetitive efficiencies that benefit consumers. These efficiencies include the provision of services at a lower cost or the provision of services that would not have been provided absent the joint venture. Sound antitrust enforcement policy distinguishes those joint ventures that on balance benefit the public from those that may increase prices without providing a countervailing benefit, and seeks to prevent only those that are harmful to consumers. The Agencies have never challenged a joint venture among hospitals to purchase or otherwise share the ownership cost of, operate and market high-technology or other expensive health care equipment and related services.

This statement of enforcement policy sets forth an antitrust safety zone that describes hospital high-technology or other expensive health care equipment joint ventures that will not be challenged, absent extraordinary circumstances, by the Agencies under the antitrust laws. It then describes the Agencies' antitrust analysis of hospital high-technology or other expensive health care equipment joint ventures that fall outside the antitrust safety zone. Finally, this statement includes examples of its application to hospital high-technology or other expensive health care equipment joint ventures.

A. Antitrust Safety Zone: Hospital High-Technology Joint Ventures That Will Not Be Challenged, Absent Extraordinary Circumstances, By The Agencies

The Agencies will not challenge under the antitrust laws any joint venture among hospitals to purchase or otherwise share the ownership cost of, operate, and market the related services of, high-technology or other expensive health care equipment if the joint venture includes only the number of hospitals whose participation is needed to support the equipment, absent extraordinary circumstances.[2] This applies to joint ventures involving purchases of new equipment as well as to joint ventures involving existing equipment.[3] A joint venture that includes additional hospitals also will not be challenged if the additional hospitals could not support the equipment on their own or through the formation of a competing joint venture, absent extraordinary circumstances.

For example, if two hospitals are each unlikely to recover the cost of individually purchasing, operating, and marketing the services of a magnetic resonance imager (MRI) over its useful life, their joint venture with respect to the MRI would not be challenged by the Agencies. On the other hand, if the same two hospitals entered into a joint venture with a third hospital that independently could have purchased, operated, and marketed an MRI in a financially viable manner, the joint venture would not be in this antitrust safety zone. If, however, none of the three hospitals could have supported an MRI by itself, the Agencies would not challenge the joint venture.[4]

---

2. A hospital or group of hospitals will be considered able to support high-technology or other expensive health care equipment for purposes of this antitrust safety zone if it could recover the costs of owning, operating, and marketing the equipment over its useful life. If the joint venture is limited to ownership, only the ownership costs are relevant. If the joint venture is limited to owning and operating, only the owning and operating costs are relevant.
3. Consequently, the safety zone would apply in a situation in which one hospital had already purchased the health care equipment, but was not recovering the costs of the equipment and sought a joint venture with one or more hospitals in order to recover the costs of the equipment.
4. The antitrust safety zone described in this statement applies only to the joint venture and agreements reasonably necessary to the venture. The

Information necessary to determine whether the costs of a piece of high-technology health care equipment could be recovered over its useful life is normally available to any hospital or group of hospitals considering such a purchase. This information may include the cost of the equipment, its expected useful life, the minimum number of procedures that must be done to meet a machine's financial breakeven point, the expected number of procedures the equipment will be used for given the population served by the joint venture and the expected price to be charged for the use of the equipment. Expected prices and costs should be confirmed by objective evidence, such as experiences in similar markets for similar technologies.

B. The Agencies' Analysis of Hospital High-Technology or Other Expensive Health Care Equipment Joint Ventures That Fall Outside the Antitrust Safety Zone

The Agencies recognize that joint ventures that fall outside the antitrust safety zone do not necessarily raise significant antitrust concerns. The Agencies will apply a rule of reason analysis in their antitrust review of such joint ventures.[5] The objective of this analysis is to determine whether the joint venture may reduce competition substantially, and, if it might, whether it is likely to produce procompetitive efficiencies that outweigh its anticompetitive potential. This analysis is flexible and takes into account the nature and effect of the joint venture, the characteristics of the venture and of the hospital industry generally, and the reasons for, and purposes of, the venture. It also allows for consideration of efficiencies that will result from the

---

safety zone does not apply to or protect agreements made by participants in a joint venture that are related to a service not provided by the venture. For example, the antitrust safety zone that would apply to the MRI joint venture would not apply to protect an agreement among the hospitals with respect to charges for an overnight stay.

5. This statement assumes that the joint venture arrangement is not one that uses the joint venture label but is likely merely to restrict competition and decrease output. For example, two hospitals that independently operate profitable MRI services could not avoid charges of price fixing by labeling as a joint venture their plan to obtain higher prices through joint marketing of their existing MRI services.

venture. The steps involved in a rule of reason analysis are set forth below.[6]

Step one: Define the relevant market. The rule of reason analysis first identifies what is produced through the joint venture. The relevant product and geographic markets are then properly defined. This process seeks to identify any other provider that could offer what patients or physicians generally would consider a good substitute for that provided by the joint venture. Thus, if a joint venture were to purchase and jointly operate and market the related services of an MRI, the relevant market would include all other MRIs in the area that are reasonable alternatives for the same patients, but would not include providers with only traditional X-ray equipment.

Step two: Evaluate the competitive effects of the venture. This step begins with an analysis of the structure of the relevant market. If many providers would compete with the joint venture, competitive harm is unlikely and the analysis would continue with step four described below.

If the structural analysis of the relevant market showed that the joint venture would eliminate an existing or potentially viable competing provider and that there were few competing providers of that service, or that cooperation in the joint venture market may spill over into a market in which the parties to the joint venture are competitors, it then would be necessary to assess the extent of the potential anticompetitive effects of the joint venture. In addition to the number and size of competing providers, factors that could restrain the ability of the joint venture to raise prices either unilaterally or through collusive agreements with other providers would include: (1) characteristics of the market that make anticompetitive coordination unlikely; (2) the likelihood that other

---

6. Many joint ventures that could provide substantial efficiencies also may present little likelihood of competitive harm. Where it is clear initially that any joint venture presents little likelihood of competitive harm, the step-by-step analysis described in the text below will not be necessary. For example, when two hospitals propose to merge existing expensive health care equipment into a joint venture in a properly defined market in which many other hospitals or other health care facilities operate the same equipment, such that the market will be unconcentrated, then the combination is unlikely to be anticompetitive and further analysis ordinarily would not be required. *See* Department of Justice/Federal Trade Commission 1992 Horizontal Merger Guidelines.

providers would enter the market; and (3) the effects of government regulation.

The extent to which the joint venture restricts competition among the hospitals participating in the venture is evaluated during this step. In some cases, a joint venture to purchase or otherwise share the cost of high-technology equipment may not substantially eliminate competition among the hospitals in providing the related service made possible by the equipment. For example, two hospitals might purchase a mobile MRI jointly, but operate and market MRI services separately. In such instances, the potential impact on competition of the joint venture would be substantially reduced.[7]

Step three: Evaluate the impact of procompetitive efficiencies. This step requires an examination of the joint venture's potential to create procompetitive efficiencies, and the balancing of these efficiencies against any potential anticompetitive effects. The greater the venture's likely anticompetitive effects, the greater must be the venture's likely efficiencies. In certain circumstances, efficiencies can be substantial because of the need to spread the cost of expensive equipment over a large number of patients and the potential for improvements in quality to occur as providers gain experience and skill from performing a larger number of procedures.

Step four: Evaluate collateral agreements. This step examines whether the joint venture includes collateral agreements or conditions that unreasonably restrict competition and are unlikely to contribute significantly to the legitimate purposes of the joint venture. The Agencies will examine whether the collateral agreements are reasonably necessary to achieve the efficiencies sought by the joint venture. For example, if the participants in a joint venture formed to purchase a mobile lithotripter also agreed on the daily room rate to be charged lithotripsy patients who required overnight hospitalization, this collateral agreement as to room rates would not be necessary to achieve the benefits of the lithotripter joint venture. Although the joint venture itself would be legal, the collateral agreement on hospital room rates would not be legal and would be subject to challenge.

---

7. If steps one and two reveal no competitive concerns with the joint venture, step three is unnecessary, and the analysis continues with step four described below.

C. Examples of Hospital High-Technology Joint Ventures

The following are examples of hospital joint ventures that are unlikely to raise significant antitrust concerns. Each is intended to demonstrate an aspect of the analysis that would be used to evaluate the venture.

1. New Equipment That Can Be Offered Only by a Joint Venture

All the hospitals in a relevant market agree that they jointly will purchase, operate and market a helicopter to provide emergency transportation for patients. The community's need for the helicopter is not great enough to justify having more than one helicopter operating in the area and studies of similarly sized communities indicate that a second helicopter service could not be supported. This joint venture falls within the antitrust safety zone. It would make available a service that would not otherwise be available, and for which duplication would be inefficient.

2. Joint Venture to Purchase Expensive Equipment

All five hospitals in a relevant market agree to jointly purchase a mobile health care device that provides a service for which consumers have no reasonable alternatives. The hospitals will share equally in the cost of maintaining the equipment, and the equipment will travel from one hospital to another and be available one day each week at each hospital. The hospitals' agreement contains no provisions for joint marketing of, and protects against exchanges of competitively sensitive information regarding, the equipment.[8] There are also no limitations on the prices that each hospital will charge for use of the equipment, on the number of procedures that each hospital can perform, or on each hospital's ability to purchase the equipment on its own. Although any combination of two of the hospitals could afford to purchase the equipment and recover their costs within the equipment's useful life, patient volume from all five hospitals is required to maximize the efficient use of the equipment and lead to significant cost savings. In

8. Examples of such information include prices and marketing plans.

addition, patient demand would be satisfied by provision of the equipment one day each week at each hospital. The joint venture would result in higher use of the equipment, thus lowering the cost per patient and potentially improving quality.

This joint venture does not fall within the antitrust safety zone because smaller groups of hospitals could afford to purchase and operate the equipment and recover their costs. Therefore, the joint venture would be analyzed under the rule of reason. The first step is to define the relevant market. In this example, the relevant market consists of the services provided by the equipment, and the five hospitals all potentially compete against each other for patients requiring this service.

The second step in the analysis is to determine the competitive effects of the joint venture. Because the joint venture is likely to reduce the number of these health care devices in the market, there is a potential restraint on competition. The restraint would not be substantial, however, for several reasons. First, the joint venture is limited to the purchase of the equipment and would not eliminate competition among the hospitals in the provision of the services. The hospitals will market the services independently, and will not exchange competitively sensitive information. In addition, the venture does not preclude a hospital from purchasing another unit should the demand for these services increase.

Because the joint venture raises some competitive concerns, however, it is necessary to examine the potential efficiencies associated with the venture. As noted above, by sharing the equipment among the five hospitals significant cost savings can be achieved. The joint venture would produce substantial efficiencies while providing access to high quality care. Thus, this joint venture would on balance benefit consumers since it would not lessen competition substantially, and it would allow the hospitals to serve the community's need in a more efficient manner. Finally, in this example the joint venture does not involve any collateral agreements that raise competitive concerns. On these facts, the joint venture would not be challenged by the Agencies.

3. Joint Venture of Existing Expensive Equipment Where One of the Hospitals in the Venture Already Owns the Equipment

Metropolis has three hospitals and a population of 300,000. Mercy and University Hospitals each own and operate their own magnetic resonance imaging device ("MRI"). General Hospital does not. Three independent physician clinics also own and operate MRIs. All of the existing MRIs have similar capabilities. The acquisition of an MRI is not subject to review under a certificate of need law in the state in which Metropolis is located.

Managed care plans have told General Hospital that, unless it can provide MRI services, it will be a less attractive contracting partner than the other two hospitals in town. The five existing MRIs are slightly underutilized—that is, the average cost per scan could be reduced if utilization of the machines increased. There is insufficient demand in Metropolis for six fully-utilized MRIs.

General has considered purchasing its own MRI so that it can compete on equal terms with Mercy and University Hospitals. However, it has decided based on its analysis of demand for MRI services and the cost of acquiring and operating the equipment that it would be better to share the equipment with another hospital. General proposes forming a joint venture in which it will purchase a 50 percent share in Mercy's MRI, and the two hospitals will work out an arrangement by which each hospital has equal access to the MRI. Each hospital in the joint venture will independently market and set prices for those MRI services, and the joint venture agreement protects against exchanges of competitively sensitive information among the hospitals. There is no restriction on the ability of each hospital to purchase its own equipment.

The proposed joint venture does not fall within the antitrust safety zone because General apparently could independently support the purchase and operation of its own MRI. Accordingly, the Agencies would analyze the joint venture under a rule of reason.

The first step of the rule of reason analysis is defining the relevant product and geographic markets. Assuming there are no good substitutes for MRI services, the relevant product market in this case is MRI services. Most patients currently receiving MRI services are unwilling to travel outside of Metropolis for those services, so the relevant geographic market is Metropolis. Mercy, University, and the three physician clinics are already offering MRI services in this market. Because General intends to offer MRI services within the next year, even if there is no joint venture, it is viewed as a market participant.

The second step is determining the competitive impact of the joint venture. Absent the joint venture, there would have been six independent MRIs in the market. This raises some competitive concerns with the joint venture. The fact that the joint venture will not entail joint price setting or marketing of MRI services to purchasers reduces the venture's potential anticompetitive effect. The competitive analysis would also consider the likelihood of additional entry in the market. If, for example, another physician clinic is likely to purchase an MRI in the event that the price of MRI services were to increase, any anticompetitive effect from the joint venture becomes less likely. Entry may be more likely in Metropolis than other areas because new entrants are not required to obtain certificates of need.

The third step of the analysis is assessing the likely efficiencies associated with the joint venture. The magnitude of any likely anticompetitive effects associated with the joint venture is important; the greater the venture's likely anticompetitive effects, the greater must be the venture's likely efficiencies. In this instance, the joint venture will avoid the costly duplication associated with General purchasing an MRI, and will allow Mercy to reduce the average cost of operating its MRI by increasing the number of procedures done. The competition between the Mercy/General venture and the other MRI providers in the market will provide some incentive for the joint venture to operate the MRI in as low-cost a manner as possible. Thus, there are efficiencies associated with the joint venture that could not be achieved in a less restrictive manner.

The final step of the analysis is determining whether the joint venture has any collateral agreements or conditions that reduce competition and are not reasonably necessary to achieve the efficiencies sought by the venture. For example, if the joint venture required managed care plans desiring MRI services to contract with both joint venture participants for those services, that condition would be viewed as anticompetitive and unnecessary to achieve the legitimate procompetitive goals of the joint venture. This example does not include any unnecessary collateral restraints.

On balance, when weighing the likelihood that the joint venture will significantly reduce competition for these services against its potential to result in efficiencies, the Agencies would view this joint venture favorably under a rule of reason analysis.

4. Joint Venture of Existing Equipment Where Both Hospitals in the Venture Already Own the Equipment

Valley Town has a population of 30,000 and is located in a valley surrounded by mountains. The closest urbanized area is over 75 miles away. There are two hospitals in Valley Town: Valley Medical Center and St. Mary's. Valley Medical Center offers a full range of primary and secondary services. St. Mary's offers primary and some secondary services. Although both hospitals have a CT scanner, Valley Medical Center's scanner is more sophisticated. Because of its greater sophistication, Valley Medical Center's scanner is more expensive to operate, and can conduct fewer scans in a day. A physician clinic in Valley Town operates a third CT scanner that is comparable to St. Mary's scanner and is not fully utilized.

Valley Medical Center has found that many of the scans that it conducts do not require the sophisticated features of its scanner. Because scans on its machine take so long, and so many patients require scans, Valley Medical Center also is experiencing significant scheduling problems. St. Mary's scanner, on the other hand, is underutilized, partially because many individuals go to Valley Medical Center because they need the more sophisticated scans that only Valley Medical Center's scanner can provide. Despite the underutilization of St. Mary's scanner, and the higher costs of Valley Medical Center's scanner, neither hospital has any intention of discontinuing its CT services. Valley Medical Center and St. Mary's are proposing a joint venture that would own and operate both hospitals' CT scanners. The two hospitals will then independently market and set the prices they charge for those services, and the joint venture agreement protects against exchanges of competitively sensitive information between the hospitals. There is no restriction on the ability of each hospital to purchase its own equipment.

The proposed joint venture does not qualify under the Agencies' safety zone because the participating hospitals can independently support their own equipment. Accordingly, the Agencies would analyze the joint venture under a rule of reason. The first step of the analysis is to determine the relevant product and geographic markets. As long as other diagnostic services such as conventional X-rays or MRI scans are not viewed as a good substitute for CT scans, the relevant product market is CT scans. If patients currently receiving CT scans in Valley Town would be unlikely to switch to providers offering CT scans outside of Valley

Town in the event that the price of CT scans in Valley Town increased by a small but significant amount, the relevant geographic market is Valley Town. There are three participants in this relevant market: Valley Medical Center, St. Mary's, and the physician clinic.

The second step of the analysis is determining the competitive effect of the joint venture. Because the joint venture does not entail joint pricing or marketing of CT services, the joint venture does not effectively reduce the number of market participants. This reduces the venture's potential anticompetitive effect. In fact, by increasing the scope of the CT services that each hospital can provide, the joint venture may increase competition between Valley Medical Center and St. Mary's since now both hospitals can provide sophisticated scans. Competitive concerns with this joint venture would be further ameliorated if other health care providers were likely to acquire CT scanners in response to a price increase following the formation of the joint venture.

The third step is assessing whether the efficiencies associated with the joint venture outweigh any anticompetitive effect associated with the joint venture. This joint venture will allow both hospitals to make either the sophisticated CT scanner or the less sophisticated, but less costly, CT scanner available to patients at those hospitals.

Thus, the joint venture should increase quality of care by allowing for better utilization and scheduling of the equipment, while also reducing the cost of providing that care, thereby benefitting the community. The joint venture may also increase quality of care by making more capacity available to Valley Medical Center; while Valley Medical Center faced capacity constraints prior to the joint venture, it can now take advantage of St. Mary's underutilized CT scanner. The joint venture will also improve access by allowing patients requiring routine scans to be moved from the sophisticated scanner at Valley Medical Center to St. Mary's scanner where the scans can be performed more quickly.

The last step of the analysis is to determine whether there are any collateral agreements or conditions associated with the joint venture that reduce competition and are not reasonably necessary to achieve the efficiencies sought by the joint venture. Assuming there are no such agreements or conditions, the Agencies would view this joint venture favorably under a rule of reason analysis.

As noted in the previous example, excluding price setting and marketing from the scope of the joint venture reduces the probability and magnitude of any anticompetitive effect of the joint venture, and thus reduces the likelihood that the Agencies will find the joint venture to be anticompetitive. If joint price setting and marketing were, however, a part of that joint venture, the Agencies would have to determine whether the cost savings and quality improvements associated with the joint venture offset the loss of competition between the two hospitals.

Also, if neither of the hospitals in Valley Town had a CT scanner, and they proposed a similar joint venture for the purchase of two CT scanners, one sophisticated and one less sophisticated, the Agencies would be unlikely to view that joint venture as anticompetitive, even though each hospital could independently support the purchase of its own CT scanner. This conclusion would be based upon a rule of reason analysis that was virtually identical to the one described above.

* * *

Hospitals that are considering high-technology or other expensive equipment joint ventures and are unsure of the legality of their conduct under the antitrust laws can take advantage of the Department's expedited business review procedure for joint ventures and information exchanges announced on December 1, 1992 (58 Fed. Reg. 6132 (1993)) or the Federal Trade Commission's advisory opinion procedure contained at 16 C.F.R. §§ 1.1-1.4 (1993). The Agencies will respond to a business review or advisory opinion request on behalf of hospitals that are considering a high-technology joint venture within 90 days after all necessary information is submitted. The Department's December 1, 1992 announcement contains specific guidance as to the information that should be submitted.

3. Statement of Department of Justice and Federal Trade Commission Enforcement Policy on Hospital Joint Ventures Involving Specialized Clinical or Other Expensive Health Care Services

Introduction

Most hospital joint ventures to provide specialized clinical or other expensive health care services do not create antitrust problems. The Agencies have never challenged an integrated joint venture among hospitals to provide a specialized clinical or other expensive health care service.

Many hospitals wish to enter into joint ventures to offer these services because the development of these services involves investments—such as the recruitment and training of specialized personnel—that a single hospital may not be able to support. In many cases, these collaborative activities could create procompetitive efficiencies that benefit consumers, including the provision of services at a lower cost or the provision of a service that would not have been provided absent the joint venture. Sound antitrust enforcement policy distinguishes those joint ventures that on balance benefit the public from those that may increase prices without providing a countervailing benefit, and seeks to prevent only those that are harmful to consumers.

This statement of enforcement policy sets forth the Agencies' antitrust analysis of joint ventures between hospitals to provide specialized clinical or other expensive health care services and includes an example of its application to such ventures. It does not include a safety zone for such ventures since the Agencies believe that they must acquire more expertise in evaluating the cost of, demand for, and potential benefits from such joint ventures before they can articulate a meaningful safety zone. The absence of a safety zone for such collaborative activities does not imply that they create any greater antitrust risk than other types of collaborative activities.

A. The Agencies' Analysis of Hospital Joint Ventures Involving Specialized Clinical or Other Expensive Health Care Services

The Agencies apply a rule of reason analysis in their antitrust review of hospital joint ventures involving specialized clinical or other expensive health care services.[9] The objective of this analysis is to determine whether the joint venture may reduce competition substantially, and if it might, whether it is likely to produce

---

9. This statement assumes that the joint venture is not likely merely to restrict competition and decrease output. For example, if two hospitals that both profitably provide open heart surgery and a burn unit simply agree without entering into an integrated joint venture that in the future each of the services will be offered exclusively at only one of the hospitals, the agreement would be viewed as an illegal market allocation.

procompetitive efficiencies that outweigh its anticompetitive potential. This analysis is flexible and takes into account the nature and effect of the joint venture, the characteristics of the services involved and of the hospital industry generally, and the reasons for, and purposes of, the venture. It also allows for consideration of efficiencies that will result from the venture. The steps involved in a rule of reason analysis are set forth below.[10]

Step one: Define the relevant market. The rule of reason analysis first identifies the service that is produced through the joint venture. The relevant product and geographic markets that include the service are then properly defined. This process seeks to identify any other provider that could offer a service that patients or physicians generally would consider a good substitute for that provided by the joint venture. Thus, if a joint venture were to produce intensive care neonatology services, the relevant market would include only other neonatal intensive care nurseries that patients or physicians would view as reasonable alternatives.

Step two: Evaluate the competitive effects of the venture. This step begins with an analysis of the structure of the relevant market. If many providers compete with the joint venture, competitive harm is unlikely and the analysis would continue with step four described below.

If the structural analysis of the relevant market showed that the joint venture would eliminate an existing or potentially viable competing provider of a service and that there were few competing providers of that service, or that cooperation in the joint venture market might spill over into a market in which the parties to the joint venture are competitors, it then would be necessary to assess the extent of the potential anticompetitive effects of the joint venture. In addition to the number and size of competing providers, factors that could restrain the ability of the joint venture to act anticompetitively either unilaterally or through collusive agreements with other providers would include: (1) characteristics of the market that make anticompetitive coordination

---

10. Many joint venturers that could provide substantial efficiencies also may present little likelihood of competitive harm. Where it is clear initially that any joint venture presents little likelihood of competitive harm, it will not be necessary to complete all steps in the analysis to conclude that the joint venture should not be challenged. *See* note 7, above.

unlikely; (2) the likelihood that others would enter the market; and (3) the effects of government regulation.

The extent to which the joint venture restricts competition among the hospitals participating in the venture is evaluated during this step. In some cases, a joint venture to provide a specialized clinical or other expensive health care service may not substantially limit competition. For example, if the only two hospitals providing primary and secondary acute care inpatient services in a relevant geographic market for such services were to form a joint venture to provide a tertiary service, they would continue to compete on primary and secondary services. Because the geographic market for a tertiary service may in certain cases be larger than the geographic market for primary or secondary services, the hospitals may also face substantial competition for the joint-ventured tertiary service.[11]

Step three: Evaluate the impact of procompetitive efficiencies. This step requires an examination of the joint venture's potential to create procompetitive efficiencies, and the balancing of these efficiencies against any potential anticompetitive effects. The greater the venture's likely anticompetitive effects, the greater must be the venture's likely efficiencies. In certain circumstances, efficiencies can be substantial because of the need to spread the cost of the investment associated with the recruitment and training of personnel over a large number of patients and the potential for improvement in quality to occur as providers gain experience and skill from performing a larger number of procedures. In the case of certain specialized clinical services, such as open heart surgery, the joint venture may permit the program to generate sufficient patient volume to meet well-accepted minimum standards for assuring quality and patient safety.

Step four: Evaluate collateral agreements. This step examines whether the joint venture includes collateral agreements or conditions that unreasonably restrict competition and are unlikely to contribute significantly to the legitimate purposes of the joint venture. The Agencies will examine whether the collateral agreements are reasonably necessary to achieve the efficiencies sought by the venture. For example,

---

11. If steps one and two reveal no competitive concerns with the joint venture, step three is unnecessary, and the analysis continues with step four described below.

if the participants in a joint venture to provide highly sophisticated oncology services were to agree on the prices to be charged for all radiology services regardless of whether the services are provided to patients undergoing oncology radiation therapy, this collateral agreement as to radiology services for non-oncology patients would be unnecessary to achieve the benefits of the sophisticated oncology joint venture. Although the joint venture itself would be legal, the collateral agreement would not be legal and would be subject to challenge.

B. Example—Hospital Joint Venture for New Specialized Clinical Service Not Involving Purchase of High-Technology or Other Expensive Health Care Equipment

Midvale has a population of about 75,000, and is geographically isolated in a rural part of its state. Midvale has two general acute care hospitals, Community Hospital and Religious Hospital, each of which performs a mix of basic primary, secondary, and some tertiary care services. The two hospitals have largely non-overlapping medical staffs. Neither hospital currently offers open-heart surgery services, nor has plans to do so on its own. Local residents, physicians, employers, and hospital managers all believe that Midvale has sufficient demand to support one local open-heart surgery unit.

The two hospitals in Midvale propose a joint venture whereby they will share the costs of recruiting a cardiac surgery team and establishing an open-heart surgery program, to be located at one of the hospitals. Patients will be referred to the program from both hospitals, who will share expenses and revenues of the program. The hospitals' agreement protects against exchanges of competitively sensitive information.

As stated above, the Agencies would analyze such a joint venture under a rule of reason. The first step of the rule of reason analysis is defining the relevant product and geographic markets. The relevant product market in this case is open-heart surgery services, because there are no reasonable alternatives for patients needing such surgery. The relevant geographic market may be limited to Midvale. Although patients now travel to distant hospitals for open-heart surgery, it is significantly more costly for patients to obtain surgery from them than from a provider located in Midvale. Physicians, patients, and purchasers believe that after the open heart surgery program is operational, most Midvale residents will choose to receive these services locally.

The second step is determining the competitive impact of the joint venture. Here, the joint venture does not eliminate any existing competition, because neither of the two hospitals previously was providing open-heart surgery. Nor does the joint venture eliminate any potential competition, because there is insufficient patient volume for more than one viable open-heart surgery program. Thus, only one such program could exist in Midvale, regardless of whether it was established unilaterally or through a joint venture.

Normally, the third step in the rule of reason analysis would be to assess the procompetitive effects of, and likely efficiencies associated with, the joint venture. In this instance, this step is unnecessary, since the analysis has concluded under step two that the joint venture will not result in any significant anticompetitive effects.

The final step of the analysis is to determine whether the joint venture has any collateral agreements or conditions that reduce competition and are not reasonably necessary to achieve the efficiencies sought by the venture. The joint venture does not appear to involve any such agreements or conditions; it does not eliminate or reduce competition between the two hospitals for any other services, or impose any conditions on use of the open-heart surgery program that would affect other competition.

Because the joint venture described above is unlikely significantly to reduce competition among hospitals for open-heart surgery services, and will in fact increase the services available to consumers, the Agencies would view this joint venture favorably under a rule of reason analysis.

* * *

Hospitals that are considering specialized clinical or other expensive health care services joint ventures and are unsure of the legality of their conduct under the antitrust laws can take advantage of the Department of Justice's expedited business review procedure announced on December 1, 1992 (58 Fed. Reg. 6132 (1993)) or the Federal Trade Commission's advisory opinion procedure contained at 16 C.F.R. §§ 1.1-1.4 (1993). The Agencies will respond to a business review or advisory opinion request on behalf of hospitals that are considering jointly providing such services within 90 days after all necessary information is submitted. The Department's December 1, 1992 announcement contains specific guidance as to the information that should be submitted.

4. Statement of Department of Justice and Federal Trade Commission Enforcement Policy on Providers' Collective Provision of Non-Fee-Related Information to Purchasers of Health Care Services

Introduction

The collective provision of non-fee-related information by competing health care providers to a purchaser in an effort to influence the terms upon which the purchaser deals with the providers does not necessarily raise antitrust concerns. Generally, providers' collective provision of certain types of information to a purchaser is likely either to raise little risk of anticompetitive effects or to provide procompetitive benefits.

This statement sets forth an antitrust safety zone that describes providers' collective provision of non-fee-related information that will not be challenged by the Agencies under the antitrust laws, absent extraordinary circumstances.[12] It also describes conduct that is expressly excluded from the antitrust safety zone.

A. Antitrust Safety Zone: Providers' Collective Provision of Non-Fee-Related Information that Will Not Be Challenged, Absent Extraordinary Circumstances, by the Agencies

Providers' collective provision of underlying medical data that may improve purchasers' resolution of issues relating to the mode, quality, or efficiency of treatment is unlikely to raise any significant antitrust concern and will not be challenged by the Agencies, absent extraordinary circumstances. Thus, the Agencies will not challenge, absent extraordinary circumstances, a medical society's collection of outcome

---

12. This statement addresses only providers' collective activities. As a general proposition, providers acting individually may provide any information to any purchaser without incurring liability under federal antitrust law. This statement also does not address the collective provision of information through an integrated joint venture or the exchange of information that necessarily occurs among providers involved in legitimate joint venture activities. Those activities generally do not raise antitrust concerns.

data from its members about a particular procedure that they believe should be covered by a purchaser and the provision of such information to the purchaser. The Agencies also will not challenge, absent extraordinary circumstances, providers' development of suggested practice parameters—standards for patient management developed to assist providers in clinical decisionmaking—that also may provide useful information to patients, providers, and purchasers. Because providers' collective provision of such information poses little risk of restraining competition and may help in the development of protocols that increase quality and efficiency, the Agencies will not challenge such activity, absent extraordinary circumstances.

In the course of providing underlying medical data, providers may collectively engage in discussions with purchasers about the scientific merit of that data. However, the antitrust safety zone excludes any attempt by providers to coerce a purchaser's decisionmaking by implying or threatening a boycott of any plan that does not follow the providers' joint recommendation. Providers who collectively threaten to or actually refuse to deal with a purchaser because they object to the purchaser's administrative, clinical, or other terms governing the provision of services run a substantial antitrust risk. For example, providers' collective refusal to provide X-rays to a purchaser that seeks them before covering a particular treatment regimen would constitute an antitrust violation. Similarly, providers' collective attempt to force purchasers to adopt recommended practice parameters by threatening to or actually boycotting purchasers that refuse to accept their joint recommendation also would risk antitrust challenge.

* * *

Competing providers who are considering jointly providing non-fee-related information to a purchaser and are unsure of the legality of their conduct under the antitrust laws can take advantage of the Department of Justice's expedited business review procedure announced on December 1, 1992 (58 Fed. Reg. 6132 (1993)) or the Federal Trade Commission's advisory opinion procedure contained at 16 C.F.R. §§ 1.1-1.4 (1993). The Agencies will respond to a business review or advisory opinion request on behalf of providers who are considering jointly providing such information within 90 days after all necessary information is submitted.

The Department's December 1, 1992 announcement contains specific guidance as to the information that should be submitted.

5. Statement of Department of Justice and Federal Trade Commission on Enforcement Policy on Providers' Collective Provision of Fee-Related Information to Purchasers of Health Care Services

Introduction

The collective provision by competing health care providers to purchasers of health care services of factual information concerning the fees charged currently or in the past for the providers' services, and other factual information concerning the amounts, levels, or methods of fees or reimbursement, does not necessarily raise antitrust concerns. With reasonable safeguards, providers' collective provision of this type of factual information to a purchaser of health care services may provide procompetitive benefits and raise little risk of anticompetitive effects.

This statement sets forth an antitrust safety zone that describes collective provision of fee-related information that will not be challenged by the Agencies under the antitrust laws, absent extraordinary circumstances.[13] It also describes types of conduct that are expressly excluded from the antitrust safety zone, some clearly unlawful, and others that may be lawful depending on the circumstances.

A. Antitrust Safety Zone: Providers' Collective Provision of Fee-Related Information that Will Not Be Challenged, Absent Extraordinary Circumstances, by the Agencies

---

13. This statement addresses only providers' collective activities. As a general proposition, providers acting individually may provide any information to any purchaser without incurring liability under federal antitrust law. This statement also does not address the collective provision of information through an integrated joint venture or the exchange of information that necessarily occurs among providers involved in legitimate joint venture activities. Those activities generally do not raise antitrust concerns.

Providers' collective provision to purchasers of health care services of factual information concerning the providers' current or historical fees or other aspects of reimbursement, such as discounts or alternative reimbursement methods accepted (including capitation arrangements, risk-withhold fee arrangements, or use of all-inclusive fees), is unlikely to raise significant antitrust concern and will not be challenged by the Agencies, absent extraordinary circumstances. Such factual information can help purchasers efficiently develop reimbursement terms to be offered to providers and may be useful to a purchaser when provided in response to a request from the purchaser or at the initiative of providers.

In assembling information to be collectively provided to purchasers, providers need to be aware of the potential antitrust consequences of information exchanges among competitors. The principles expressed in the Agencies' statement on provider participation in exchanges of price and cost information are applicable in this context. Accordingly, in order to qualify for this safety zone, the collection of information to be provided to purchasers must satisfy the following conditions:

(1) the collection is managed by a third party (e.g., a purchaser, government agency, health care consultant, academic institution, or trade association);

(2) although current fee-related information may be provided to purchasers, any information that is shared among or is available to the competing providers furnishing the data must be more than three months old; and

(3) for any information that is available to the providers furnishing data, there are at least five providers reporting data upon which each disseminated statistic is based, no individual provider's data may represent more than 25 percent on a weighted basis of that statistic, and any information disseminated must be sufficiently aggregated such that it would not allow recipients to identify the prices charged by any individual provider.

The conditions that must be met for an information exchange among providers to fall within the antitrust safety zone are intended to ensure that an exchange of price or cost data is not used by competing providers for discussion or coordination of provider prices or costs. They represent a careful balancing of a provider's individual interest in obtaining information useful in adjusting the prices it charges or the wages it pays in response to changing market conditions against the risk that the exchange of such information may permit competing providers to communicate with each other regarding a mutually acceptable level of prices for health care services or compensation for employees.

B. The Agencies' Analysis of Providers' Collective Provision of Fee-Related Information that Falls Outside the Antitrust Safety Zone

The safety zone set forth in this policy statement does not apply to collective negotiations between unintegrated providers and purchasers in contemplation or in furtherance of any agreement among the providers on fees or other terms or aspects of reimbursement,[14] or to any agreement among unintegrated providers to deal with purchasers only on agreed terms. Providers also may not collectively threaten, implicitly or explicitly, to engage in a boycott or similar conduct, or actually undertake such a boycott or conduct, to coerce any purchaser to accept collectively-determined fees or other terms or aspects of reimbursement. These types of conduct likely would violate the antitrust laws and, in many instances, might be per se illegal.

Also excluded from the safety zone is providers' collective provision of information or views concerning prospective fee-related matters. In some circumstances, the collective provision of this type of fee-related information also may be helpful to a purchaser and, as long as independent decisions on whether to accept a purchaser's offer are truly preserved, may not raise antitrust concerns. However, in other circumstances, the collective provision of prospective fee-related information or views may evidence or facilitate an agreement on prices or other competitively significant terms by the competing providers. It also may exert a coercive effect on the purchaser by implying or threatening a collective refusal to deal on terms other than those proposed, or amount to an implied threat to boycott any plan that does not follow the providers' collective proposal.

The Agencies recognize the need carefully to distinguish possibly procompetitive collective provision of prospective fee-related information or views from anticompetitive situations that involve unlawful price agreements, boycott threats, refusals to deal except on

---

14. Whether communications between providers and purchasers will amount to negotiations depends on the nature and context of the communications, not solely the number of such communications.

collectively determined terms, collective negotiations, or conduct that signals or facilitates collective price terms. Therefore, the collective provision of such prospective fee-related information or views will be assessed on a case-by-case basis. In their case-by-case analysis, the Agencies will look at all the facts and circumstances surrounding the provision of the information, including, but not limited to, the nature of the information provided, the nature and extent of the communications among the providers and between the providers and the purchaser, the rationale for providing the information, and the nature of the market in which the information is provided.

In addition, because the collective provision of prospective fee-related information and views can easily lead to or accompany unlawful collective negotiations, price agreements, or the other types of collective conduct noted above, providers need to be aware of the potential antitrust consequences of information exchanges among competitors in assembling information or views concerning prospective fee-related matters. Consequently, such protections as the use of a third party to manage the collection of information and views, and the adoption of mechanisms to assure that the information is not disseminated or used in a manner that facilitates unlawful agreements or coordinated conduct by the providers, likely would reduce antitrust concerns.

* * *

Competing providers who are considering collectively providing fee-related information to purchasers, and are unsure of the legality of their conduct under the antitrust laws, can take advantage of the Department of Justice's expedited business review procedure announced on December 1, 1992 (58 Fed. Reg. 6132 (1993)) or the Federal Trade Commission's advisory opinion procedure contained at 16 C.F.R. §§ 1.1-1.4 (1993). The Agencies will respond to a business review or advisory opinion request on behalf of providers who are considering collectively providing fee-related information within 90 days after all necessary information is submitted. The Department's December 1, 1992 announcement contains specific guidance as to the information that should be submitted.

6. Statement of Department of Justice and Federal Trade Commission Enforcement Policy on Provider Participation in

Exchanges of Price and Cost Information

Introduction

Participation by competing providers in surveys of prices for health care services, or surveys of salaries, wages or benefits of personnel, does not necessarily raise antitrust concerns. In fact, such surveys can have significant benefits for health care consumers. Providers can use information derived from price and compensation surveys to price their services more competitively and to offer compensation that attracts highly qualified personnel. Purchasers can use price survey information to make more informed decisions when buying health care services. Without appropriate safeguards, however, information exchanges among competing providers may facilitate collusion or otherwise reduce competition on prices or compensation, resulting in increased prices, or reduced quality and availability of health care services. A collusive restriction on the compensation paid to health care employees, for example, could adversely affect the availability of health care personnel.

This statement sets forth an antitrust safety zone that describes exchanges of price and cost information among providers that will not be challenged by the Agencies under the antitrust laws, absent extraordinary circumstances. It also briefly describes the Agencies' antitrust analysis of information exchanges that fall outside the antitrust safety zone.

A. Antitrust Safety Zone: Exchanges of Price and Cost Information Among Providers that Will Not Be Challenged, Absent Extraordinary Circumstances, by the Agencies

The Agencies will not challenge, absent extraordinary circumstances, provider participation in written surveys of (a) prices for health care services,[15] or (b) wages, salaries, or benefits of health care personnel, if the following conditions are satisfied:

---

15. The "prices" at which providers offer their services to purchasers can take many forms, including billed charges for individual services, discounts off billed charges, or per diem, capitated, or diagnosis related group rates.

(1) the survey is managed by a third-party (e.g., a purchaser, government agency, health care consultant, academic institution, or trade association);

(2) the information provided by survey participants is based on data more than 3 months old; and

(3) there are at least five providers reporting data upon which each disseminated statistic is based, no individual provider's data represents more than 25 percent on a weighted basis of that statistic, and any information disseminated is sufficiently aggregated such that it would not allow recipients to identify the prices charged or compensation paid by any particular provider.

The conditions that must be met for an information exchange among providers to fall within the antitrust safety zone are intended to ensure that an exchange of price or cost data is not used by competing providers for discussion or coordination of provider prices or costs. They represent a careful balancing of a provider's individual interest in obtaining information useful in adjusting the prices it charges or the wages it pays in response to changing market conditions against the risk that the exchange of such information may permit competing providers to communicate with each other regarding a mutually acceptable level of prices for health care services or compensation for employees.

B. The Agencies' Analysis of Provider Exchanges of Information that Fall Outside the Antitrust Safety Zone

Exchanges of price and cost information that fall outside the antitrust safety zone generally will be evaluated to determine whether the information exchange may have an anticompetitive effect that outweighs any procompetitive justification for the exchange. Depending on the circumstances, public, non-provider initiated surveys may not raise competitive concerns. Such surveys could allow purchasers to have useful information that they can use for procompetitive purposes.

Exchanges of future prices for provider services or future compensation of employees are very likely to be considered anticompetitive. If an exchange among competing providers of price or cost information results in an agreement among competitors as to the prices for health care services or the wages to be paid to health care employees, that agreement will be considered unlawful per se.

* * *

Competing providers that are considering participating in a survey of price or cost information and are unsure of the legality of their conduct under the antitrust laws can take advantage of the Department's expedited business review procedure announced on December 1, 1992 (58 Fed. Reg. 6132 (1993)) or the Federal Trade Commission's advisory opinion procedure contained at 16 C.F.R. §§ 1.1-1.4 (1993). The Agencies will respond to a business review or advisory opinion request on behalf of providers who are considering participating in a survey of price or cost information within 90 days after all necessary information is submitted. The Department's December 1, 1992 announcement contains specific guidance as to the information that should be submitted.

7. Statement of Department of Justice and Federal Trade Commission Enforcement Policy on Joint Purchasing Arrangements Among Health Care Providers

Introduction

Most joint purchasing arrangements among hospitals or other health care providers do not raise antitrust concerns. Such collaborative activities typically allow the participants to achieve efficiencies that will benefit consumers. Joint purchasing arrangements usually involve the purchase of a product or service used in providing the ultimate package of health care services or products sold by the participants. Examples include the purchase of laundry or food services by hospitals, the purchase of computer or data processing services by hospitals or other groups of providers, and the purchase of prescription drugs and other pharmaceutical products. Through such joint purchasing arrangements, the participants frequently can obtain volume discounts, reduce transaction costs, and have access to consulting advice that may not be available to each participant on its own.

Joint purchasing arrangements are unlikely to raise antitrust concerns unless (1) the arrangement accounts for so large a portion of the purchases of a product or service that it can effectively exercise market power[16] in the purchase of the product or service, or (2) the products or services being purchased jointly account for so large a proportion of the total cost of the services being sold by the participants that the joint purchasing arrangement may facilitate price fixing or otherwise reduce competition. If neither factor is present, the joint purchasing arrangement will not present competitive concerns.[17]

This statement sets forth an antitrust safety zone that describes joint purchasing arrangements among health care providers that will not be challenged, absent extraordinary circumstances, by the Agencies under the antitrust laws. It also describes factors that mitigate any competitive concerns with joint purchasing arrangements that fall outside the antitrust safety zone.[18]

A. Antitrust Safety Zone: Joint Purchasing Arrangements Among Health Care Providers that Will Not Be Challenged, Absent Extraordinary Circumstances, by the Agencies

The Agencies will not challenge, absent extraordinary circumstances, any joint purchasing arrangement among health care providers where two conditions are present: (1) the purchases account for less than 35 percent of the total sales of the purchased product or service in the relevant market; and (2) the cost of the products and services purchased jointly accounts for less than 20 percent of the total revenues from all products or services sold by each competing participant in the joint purchasing arrangement.

---

16. In the case of a purchaser, this is the power to drive the price of goods or services purchased below competitive levels.
17. An agreement among purchasers that simply fixes the price that each purchaser will pay or offer to pay for a product or service is not a legitimate joint purchasing arrangement and is a per se antitrust violation. Legitimate joint purchasing arrangements provide some integration of purchasing functions to achieve efficiencies.
18. This statement applies to purchasing arrangements through which the participants acquire products or services for their own use, not arrangements in which the participants are jointly investing in equipment or providing a service. Joint ventures involving investment in equipment and the provision of services are discussed in separate policy statements.

The first condition compares the purchases accounted for by a joint purchasing arrangement to the total purchases of the purchased product or service in the relevant market. Its purpose is to determine whether the joint purchasing arrangement might be able to drive down the price of the product or service being purchased below competitive levels. For example, a joint purchasing arrangement may account for all or most of the purchases of laundry services by hospitals in a particular market, but represent less than 35 percent of the purchases of all commercial laundry services in that market. Unless there are special costs that cannot be easily recovered associated with providing laundry services to hospitals, such a purchasing arrangement is not likely to force prices below competitive levels. The same principle applies to joint purchasing arrangements for food services, data processing, and many other products and services.

The second condition addresses any possibility that a joint purchasing arrangement might result in standardized costs, thus facilitating price fixing or otherwise having anticompetitive effects. This condition applies only where some or all of the participants are direct competitors. For example, if a nationwide purchasing cooperative limits its membership to one hospital in each geographic area, there is not likely to be any concern about reduction of competition among its members. Even where a purchasing arrangement's membership includes hospitals or other health care providers that compete with one another, the arrangement is not likely to facilitate collusion if the goods and services being purchased jointly account for a small fraction of the final price of the services provided by the participants. In the health care field, it may be difficult to determine the specific final service in which the jointly purchased products are used, as well as the price at which that final service is sold.[19] Therefore, the Agencies will examine whether the cost of the products or services being purchased jointly accounts, in the aggregate, for less than 20 percent of the total revenues from all health care services of each competing participant.

---

19. This especially is true because some large purchasers negotiate prices with hospitals and other providers that encompass a group of services, while others pay separately for each service.

B. *Factors Mitigating Competitive Concerns with Joint Purchasing Arrangements that Fall Outside the Antitrust Safety Zone*

Joint purchasing arrangements among hospitals or other health care providers that fall outside the antitrust safety zone do not necessarily raise antitrust concerns. There are several safeguards that joint purchasing arrangements can adopt to mitigate concerns that might otherwise arise. First, antitrust concern is lessened if members are not required to use the arrangement for all their purchases of a particular product or service. Members can, however, be asked to commit to purchase a voluntarily specified amount through the arrangement so that a volume discount or other favorable contract can be negotiated. Second, where negotiations are conducted on behalf of the joint purchasing arrangement by an independent employee or agent who is not also an employee of a participant, antitrust risk is lowered. Third, the likelihood of anticompetitive communications is lessened where communications between the purchasing group and each individual participant are kept confidential, and not discussed with, or disseminated to, other participants.

These safeguards will reduce substantially, if not completely eliminate, use of the purchasing arrangement as a vehicle for discussing and coordinating the prices of health care services offered by the participants.[20] The adoption of these safeguards also will help demonstrate that the joint purchasing arrangement is intended to achieve economic efficiencies rather than to serve an anticompetitive purpose. Where there appear to be significant efficiencies from a joint purchasing arrangement, the Agencies will not challenge the arrangement absent substantial risk of anticompetitive effects.

The existence of a large number and variety of purchasing groups in the health care field suggests that entry barriers to forming new groups currently are not great. Thus, in most circumstances at present, it is not necessary to open a joint purchasing arrangement to all competitors in the market. However, if some competitors excluded from the

---

20. Obviously, if the members of a legitimate purchasing group engage in price fixing or other collusive anticompetitive conduct as to services sold by the participants, whether through the arrangement or independently, they remain subject to antitrust challenge.

arrangement are unable to compete effectively without access to the arrangement, and competition is thereby harmed, antitrust concerns will exist.

C. Example—Joint Purchasing Arrangement Involving Both Hospitals in Rural Community that the Agencies Would Not Challenge

Smalltown is the county seat of Rural County. There are two general acute care hospitals, County Hospital ("County") and Smalltown Medical Center ("SMC"), both located in Smalltown. The nearest other hospitals are located in Big City, about 100 miles from Smalltown.

County and SMC propose to join a joint venture being formed by several of the hospitals in Big City through which they will purchase various hospital supplies—such as bandages, antiseptics, surgical gowns, and masks. The joint venture will likely be the vehicle for the purchase of most such products by the Smalltown hospitals, but under the joint venture agreement, both retain the option to purchase supplies independently.

The joint venture will be an independent corporation, jointly owned by the participating hospitals. It will purchase the supplies needed by the hospitals and then resell them to the hospitals at average variable cost plus a reasonable return on capital. The joint venture will periodically solicit from each participating hospital its expected needs for various hospital supplies, and negotiate the best terms possible for the combined purchases. It will also purchase supplies for its member hospitals on an ad hoc basis.

Competitive Analysis

The first issue is whether the proposed joint purchasing arrangement would fall within the safety zone set forth in this policy statement. In order to make this determination, the Agencies would first inquire whether the joint purchases would account for less than 35 percent of the total sales of the purchased products in the relevant markets for the sales of those products. Here, the relevant hospital supply markets are likely to be national or at least regional in scope. Thus, while County and SMC might well account for more than 35 percent of the total sales of many hospital supplies in Smalltown or Rural County, they and the other hospitals in Big City that will participate in the arrangement together would likely not account for significant percentages of sales in the actual relevant markets. Thus, the first criterion for inclusion in the safety zone is likely to be satisfied.

The Agencies would then inquire whether the supplies to be purchased jointly account for less than 20 percent of the total revenues from all products and services sold by each of the competing hospitals that participate in the arrangement. In this case, County and SMC are competing hospitals, but this second criterion for inclusion in the safety zone is also likely to be satisfied, and the Agencies would not challenge the joint purchasing arrangement.

* * *

Hospitals or other health care providers that are considering joint purchasing arrangements and are unsure of the legality of their conduct under the antitrust laws can take advantage of the Department of Justice's expedited business review procedure for joint ventures and information exchanges announced on December 1, 1992 (58 Fed. Reg. 6132 (1993)) or the Federal Trade Commission's advisory opinion procedure contained at 16 C.F.R. §§ 1.1-1.4 (1993). The Agencies will respond to a business review or advisory opinion request on behalf of health care providers considering a joint purchasing arrangement within 90 days after all necessary information is submitted. The Department's December 1, 1992 announcement contains specific guidance as to the information that should be submitted.

8. Statement of Department of Justice and Federal Trade Commission Enforcement Policy on Physician Network Joint Ventures

Introduction

In recent years, health plans and other purchasers of health care services have developed a variety of managed care programs that seek to reduce the costs and assure the quality of health care services. Many physicians and physician groups have organized physician network joint ventures, such as individual practice associations ("IPAs"), preferred provider organizations ("PPOs"), and other arrangements to market their services to these plans.[21] Typically, such networks contract with the plans to provide physician services to plan subscribers at predetermined prices, and the physician participants in the networks agree to controls aimed at containing costs and assuring the appropriate and efficient provision of high quality physician services. By developing and implementing mechanisms that encourage physicians to collaborate in practicing efficiently as part of the network, many physician network joint ventures promise significant procompetitive benefits for consumers of health care services.

As used in this statement, a physician network joint venture is a physician-controlled venture in which the network's physician participants collectively agree on prices or price-related terms and jointly market their services.[22] Other types of health care network joint ventures are not directly addressed by this statement.[23]

---

21. An IPA or PPO typically provides medical services to the subscribers of health plans but does not act as their insurer. In addition, an IPA or PPO does not require complete integration of the medical practices of its physician participants. Such physicians typically continue to compete fully for patients who are enrolled in health plans not served by the IPA or PPO, or who have indemnity insurance or pay for the physician's services directly "out of pocket."

22. Although this statement refers to IPAs and PPOs as examples of physician network joint ventures, the Agencies' competitive analysis focuses on the substance of such arrangements, not on their formal titles. This policy statement applies, therefore, to all entities that are substantively equivalent to the physician network joint ventures described in this statement.

23. The physician network joint ventures discussed in this statement are one type of the multiprovider network joint ventures discussed below in the Agencies' Statement Of Enforcement Policy On Multiprovider Networks. That statement also covers other types of networks, such as networks that include both hospitals and physicians, and networks involving non-physician health professionals. In addition, that statement (*see infra* pp. 106-141), and Example 7 of this statement, address networks that do not include agreements among competitors on prices or price-related terms, through use of various "messenger model" arrangements. Many of the issues relating to physician network joint ventures are the same as those that arise and are addressed in connection with multiprovider networks generally, and the analysis often will be very similar for all such

This statement of enforcement policy describes the Agencies' antitrust analysis of physician network joint ventures, and presents several examples of its application to specific hypothetical physician network joint ventures. Before describing the general antitrust analysis, the statement sets forth antitrust safety zones that describe physician network joint ventures that are highly unlikely to raise substantial competitive concerns, and therefore will not be challenged by the Agencies under the antitrust laws, absent extraordinary circumstances.

The Agencies emphasize that merely because a physician network joint venture does not come within a safety zone in no way indicates that it is unlawful under the antitrust laws. On the contrary, such arrangements may be procompetitive and lawful, and many such arrangements have received favorable business review letters or advisory opinions from the Agencies.[24] The safety zones use a few factors that are relatively easy to apply, to define a category of ventures for which the Agencies presume no anticompetitive harm, without examining competitive conditions in the particular case. A determination about the lawfulness of physician network joint ventures that fall outside the safety zones must be made on a case-by-case basis according to general

---

arrangements.

24. For example, the Agencies have approved a number of non-exclusive physician or provider networks in which the percentage of participating physicians or providers in the market exceeded the 30% criterion of the safety zone. *See,* e.g., Letter from Anne K. Bingaman, Assistant Attorney General, Department of Justice, to John F. Fischer (Oklahoma Physicians Network, Inc.) (Jan. 17, 1996) ("substantially more" than 30% of several specialties in a number of local markets, including more than 50% in one specialty); Letter from Anne K. Bingaman to Melissa J. Fields (Dermnet, Inc.) (Dec. 5, 1995) (44% of board-certified dermatologists); Letter from Anne K. Bingaman to Dee Hartzog (International Chiropractor's Association of California) (Oct. 27, 1994) (up to 50% of chiropractors); Letter from Mark Horoschak, Assistant Director, Federal Trade Commission, to Stephen P. Nash (Eastern Ohio Physicians Organization) (Sept. 28, 1995) (safety zone's 30% criterion exceeded for primary care physicians by a small amount, and for certain subspecialty fields "to a greater extent"); Letter from Mark Horoschak to John A. Cook (Oakland Physician Network) (Mar. 28, 1995) (multispecialty network with 44% of physicians in one specialty).

antitrust principles and the more specific analysis described in this statement.

A. Antitrust Safety Zones

This section describes those physician network joint ventures that will fall within the antitrust safety zones designated by the Agencies. The antitrust safety zones differ for "exclusive" and "non-exclusive" physician network joint ventures. In an "exclusive" venture, the network's physician participants are restricted in their ability to, or do not in practice, individually contract or affiliate with other network joint ventures or health plans. In a "non-exclusive" venture, on the other hand, the physician participants in fact do, or are available to, affiliate with other networks or contract individually with health plans. This section explains how the Agencies will determine whether a physician network joint venture is exclusive or non-exclusive. It also illustrates types of arrangements that can involve the sharing of substantial financial risk among a network's physician participants, which is necessary for a network to come within the safety zones.

1. Exclusive Physician Network Joint Ventures that the Agencies Will Not Challenge, Absent Extraordinary Circumstances

The Agencies will not challenge, absent extraordinary circumstances, an exclusive physician network joint venture whose physician participants share substantial financial risk and constitute 20 percent or less of the physicians[25] in each physician specialty with active hospital staff privileges who practice in the relevant geographic market.[26] In relevant markets with fewer than five physicians in a particular specialty, an exclusive physician network joint venture otherwise qualifying for the antitrust safety zone may include one physician from that specialty, on a

---

25. For purposes of the antitrust safety zones, in calculating the number of physicians in a relevant market and the number of physician participants in a physician network joint venture, each physician ordinarily will be counted individually, whether the physician practices in a group or solo practice.

26. Generally, relevant geographic markets for the delivery of physician services are local.

non-exclusive basis, even though the inclusion of that physician results in the venture consisting of more than 20 percent of the physicians in that specialty.

2. Non-Exclusive Physician Network Joint Ventures that the Agencies Will Not Challenge, Absent Extraordinary Circumstances

The Agencies will not challenge, absent extraordinary circumstances, a non-exclusive physician network joint venture whose physician participants share substantial financial risk and constitute 30 percent or less of the physicians in each physician specialty with active hospital staff privileges who practice in the relevant geographic market. In relevant markets with fewer than four physicians in a particular specialty, a non-exclusive physician network joint venture otherwise qualifying for the antitrust safety zone may include one physician from that specialty, even though the inclusion of that physician results in the venture consisting of more than 30 percent of the physicians in that specialty.

3. Indicia of Non-Exclusivity

Because of the different market share thresholds for the safety zones for exclusive and non-exclusive physician network joint ventures, the Agencies caution physician participants in a non-exclusive physician network joint venture to be sure that the network is non-exclusive in fact and not just in name. The Agencies will determine whether a physician network joint venture is exclusive or non-exclusive by its physician participants' activities, and not simply by the terms of the contractual relationship. In making that determination, the Agencies will examine the following indicia of non-exclusivity, among others:

(1) that viable competing networks or managed care plans with adequate physician participation currently exist in the market; (2) that physicians in the network actually individually participate in, or contract with, other networks or managed care plans, or there is other evidence of their willingness and incentive to do so; (3) that physicians in the network earn substantial revenue from other networks or through individual contracts with managed care plans; (4) the absence of any indications of significant departicipation from other networks or managed care plans in the market; and (5) the absence of any indications of coordination among the physicians in the network regarding price or

other competitively significant terms of participation in other networks or managed care plans.

Networks also may limit or condition physician participants' freedom to contract outside the network in ways that fall short of a commitment of full exclusivity. If those provisions significantly restrict the ability or willingness of a network's physicians to join other networks or contract individually with managed care plans, the network will be considered exclusive for purposes of the safety zones.

4. Sharing of Substantial Financial Risk by Physicians in a Physician Network Joint Venture

To qualify for either antitrust safety zone, the participants in a physician network joint venture must share substantial financial risk in providing all the services that are jointly priced through the network.[27] The safety zones are limited to networks involving substantial financial risk sharing not because such risk sharing is a desired end in itself, but because it normally is a clear and reliable indicator that a physician network involves sufficient integration by its physician participants to achieve significant efficiencies.[28] Risk sharing provides incentives for the physicians to cooperate in controlling costs and improving quality by managing the provision of services by network physicians.

---

27. Physician network joint ventures that involve both risk-sharing and non-risk-sharing arrangements do not fall within the safety zones. For example, a network may have both risk-sharing and non-risk-sharing contracts. It also may have contracts that involve risk sharing, but not all the physicians in the network participate in risk sharing or not all of the services are paid for on a risk-sharing basis. The Agencies will consider each of the network's arrangements separately, as well as the activities of the venture as a whole, to determine whether the joint pricing with respect to the non-risk-sharing aspects of the venture is appropriately analyzed under the rule of reason. *See infra* Example 2. The mere presence of some risk-sharing arrangements, however, will not necessarily result in rule of reason analysis of the non-risk-sharing aspects of the venture.
28. The existence of financial risk sharing does not depend on whether, under applicable state law, the network is considered an insurer.

The following are examples of some types of arrangements through which participants in a physician network joint venture can share substantial financial risk:[29]

(1) agreement by the venture to provide services to a health plan at a "capitated" rate;[30]

(2) agreement by the venture to provide designated services or classes of services to a health plan for a predetermined percentage of premium or revenue from the plan; [31]

(3) use by the venture of significant financial incentives for its physician participants, as a group, to achieve specified cost-containment goals. Two methods by which the venture can accomplish this are: (a) withholding from all physician participants in the network a substantial amount of the compensation due to them, with distribution of that amount to the physician participants based on group performance in meeting the cost-containment goals of the network as a whole; or (b) establishing overall cost or utilization targets for the network as a whole, with the network's physician participants subject to subsequent substantial financial rewards or penalties based on group performance in meeting the targets; and (4) agreement by the venture to provide a complex or extended course of treatment that requires the substantial coordination of care by physicians in different specialities offering a complementary mix of services, for a fixed, predetermined payment, where the costs of that course of treatment for any individual patient can

---

29. Physician participants in a single network need not all be involved in the same risk-sharing arrangement within the network to fall within the safety zones. For example, primary care physicians may be capitated and specialists subject to a withhold, or groups of physicians may be in separate risk pools.

30. A "capitated" rate is a fixed, predetermined payment per covered life (the "capitation") from a health plan to the joint venture in exchange for the joint venture's (not merely an individual physician's) providing and guaranteeing provision of a defined set of covered services to covered individuals for a specified period, regardless of the amount of services actually provided.

31. This is similar to a capitation arrangement, except that the amount of payment to the network can vary in response to changes in the health plan's premiums or revenues.

vary greatly due to the individual patient's condition, the choice, complexity, or length of treatment, or other factors.[32]

The Agencies recognize that new types of risk-sharing arrangements may develop. The preceding examples do not foreclose consideration of other arrangements through which the participants in a physician network joint venture may share substantial financial risk in the provision of medical services through the network.[33] Organizers of physician networks who are uncertain whether their proposed arrangements constitute substantial financial risk sharing for purposes of this policy statement are encouraged to take advantage of the Agencies' expedited business review and advisory opinion procedures.

B. *The Agencies' Analysis of Physician Network Joint Ventures that Fall Outside the Antitrust Safety Zones*

Physician network joint ventures that fall outside the antitrust safety zones also may have the potential to create significant efficiencies, and do not necessarily raise substantial antitrust concerns. For example, physician network joint ventures in which the physician participants share substantial financial risk, but which involve a higher percentage of physicians in a relevant market than specified in the safety zones, may be lawful if they are not anticompetitive on balance.[34] Likewise, physician

---

32. Such arrangements are sometimes referred to as "global fees" or "all-inclusive case rates." Global fee or all-inclusive case rate arrangements that involve financial risk sharing as contemplated by this example will require that the joint venture (not merely an individual physician participant) assume the risk or benefit that the treatment provided through the network may either exceed, or cost less than, the predetermined payment.
33. The manner of dividing revenues among the network's physician participants generally does not raise antitrust issues so long as the competing physicians in a network share substantial financial risk. For example, capitated networks may distribute income among their physician participants using fee-for-service payment with a partial withhold fund to cover the risk of having to provide more services than were originally anticipated.
34. *See infra* Examples 5 and 6. Many such physician networks have received favorable business review or advisory opinion letters from the Agencies. The percentages used in the safety zones define areas in which the lack of

network joint ventures that do not involve the sharing of substantial financial risk also may be lawful if the physicians' integration through the joint venture creates significant efficiencies and the venture, on balance, is not anticompetitive.

The Agencies emphasize that it is not their intent to treat such networks either more strictly or more leniently than joint ventures in other industries, or to favor any particular procompetitive organization or structure of health care delivery over other forms that consumers may desire. Rather, their goal is to ensure a competitive marketplace in which consumers will have the benefit of high quality, cost-effective health care and a wide range of choices, including new provider-controlled networks that expand consumer choice and increase competition.

1. Determining When Agreements Among Physicians in a Physician Network Joint Venture Are Analyzed under the Rule of Reason

Antitrust law treats naked agreements among competitors that fix prices or allocate markets as per se illegal. Where competitors economically integrate in a joint venture, however, such agreements, if reasonably necessary to accomplish the procompetitive benefits of the integration, are analyzed under the rule of reason.[35] In accord with general antitrust principles, physician network joint ventures will be analyzed under the rule of reason, and will not be viewed as per se illegal, if the physicians' integration through the network is likely to produce significant efficiencies that benefit consumers, and any price agreements (or other agreements that would otherwise be per se illegal) by the network physicians are reasonably necessary to realize those efficiencies.[36]

---

anticompetitive effects ordinarily will be presumed.

35. In a network limited to providers who are not actual or potential competitors, the providers generally can agree on the prices to be charged for their services without the kinds of economic integration discussed below.

36. In some cases, the combination of the competing physicians in the network may enable them to offer what could be considered to be a new product producing substantial efficiencies, and therefore the venture will be analyzed under the rule of reason. *See* Broadcast Music, Inc. v. Columbia Broadcasting System, Inc., 441 U.S. 1, 21-22 (1979)

Where the participants in a physician network joint venture have agreed to share substantial financial risk as defined in Section A.4. of this policy statement, their risk-sharing arrangement generally establishes both an overall efficiency goal for the venture and the incentives for the physicians to meet that goal. The setting of price is integral to the venture's use of such an arrangement and therefore warrants evaluation under the rule of reason.

Physician network joint ventures that do not involve the sharing of substantial financial risk may also involve sufficient integration to demonstrate that the venture is likely to produce significant efficiencies. Such integration can be evidenced by the network implementing an active and ongoing program to evaluate and modify practice patterns by the network's physician participants and create a high degree of interdependence and cooperation among the physicians to control costs and ensure quality. This program may include: (1) establishing mechanisms to monitor and control utilization of health care services that are designed to control costs and assure quality of care; (2) selectively choosing network physicians who are likely to further these efficiency objectives; and (3) the significant investment of capital, both monetary and human, in the necessary infrastructure and capability to realize the claimed efficiencies.

The foregoing are not, however, the only types of arrangements that can evidence sufficient integration to warrant rule of reason analysis, and the Agencies will consider other arrangements that also may evidence such integration. However, in all cases, the Agencies' analysis will focus on substance, rather than form, in assessing a network's likelihood of producing significant efficiencies. To the extent that agreements on prices to be charged for the integrated provision of services are

---

(competitors' integration and creation of a blanket license for use of copyrighted compositions results in efficiencies so great as to make the blanket license a "different product" from the mere combination of individual competitors and, therefore, joint pricing of the blanket license is subject to rule of reason analysis, rather than the per se rule against price fixing). The Agencies' analysis will focus on the efficiencies likely to be produced by the venture, and the relationship of any price agreements to the achievement of those efficiencies, rather than on whether the venture creates a product that can be labeled "new" or "different."

reasonably necessary to the venture's achievement of efficiencies, they will be evaluated under the rule of reason.

In contrast to integrated physician network joint ventures, such as these discussed above, there have been arrangements among physicians that have taken the form of networks, but which in purpose or effect were little more than efforts by their participants to prevent or impede competitive forces from operating in the market. These arrangements are not likely to produce significant procompetitive efficiencies. Such arrangements have been, and will continue to be, treated as unlawful conspiracies or cartels, whose price agreements are per se illegal.

Determining that an arrangement is merely a vehicle to fix prices or engage in naked anticompetitive conduct is a factual inquiry that must be done on a case-by-case basis to determine the arrangement's true nature and likely competitive effects. However, a variety of factors may tend to corroborate a network's anticompetitive nature, including: statements evidencing anticompetitive purpose; a recent history of anticompetitive behavior or collusion in the market, including efforts to obstruct or undermine the development of managed care; obvious anticompetitive structure of the network (e.g., a network comprising a very high percentage of local area physicians, whose participation in the network is exclusive, without any plausible business or efficiency justification); the absence of any mechanisms with the potential for generating significant efficiencies or otherwise increasing competition through the network; the presence of anticompetitive collateral agreements; and the absence of mechanisms to prevent the network's operation from having anticompetitive spillover effects outside the network.

2. Applying the Rule of Reason

A rule of reason analysis determines whether the formation and operation of the joint venture may have a substantial anticompetitive effect and, if so, whether that potential effect is outweighed by any procompetitive efficiencies resulting from the joint venture. The rule of reason analysis takes into account characteristics of the particular physician network joint venture, and the competitive environment in which it operates, that bear on the venture's likely effect on competition.

A determination about the lawfulness of a network's activity under the rule of reason sometimes can be reached without an extensive inquiry under each step of the analysis. For example, a physician network joint venture that involves substantial clinical integration may include a relatively small percentage of the physicians in the relevant markets on a non-exclusive basis. In that case, the Agencies may be able to conclude expeditiously that the network is unlikely to be anticompetitive, based on the competitive environment in which it operates. In assessing the competitive environment, the Agencies would consider such market factors as the number, types, and size of managed care plans operating in the area, the extent of physician participation in those plans, and the economic importance of the managed care plans to area physicians. *See infra* Example 1. Alternatively, for example, if a restraint that facially appears to be of a kind that would always or almost always tend to reduce output or increase prices, but has not been considered per se unlawful, is not reasonably necessary to the creation of efficiencies, the Agencies will likely challenge the restraint without an elaborate analysis of market definition and market power.[37]

The steps ordinarily involved in a rule of reason analysis of physician network joint ventures are set forth below.

Step one: Define the relevant market. The Agencies evaluate the competitive effects of a physician network joint venture in each relevant market in which it operates or has substantial impact. In defining the relevant product and geographic markets, the Agencies look to what substitutes, as a practical matter, are reasonably available to consumers for the services in question.[38] The Agencies will first identify the relevant services that the physician network joint venture provides. Although all services provided by each physician specialty might be a separate relevant service market, there may be instances in which significant overlap of services provided by different physician specialties, or in some circumstances, certain nonphysician health care providers, justifies including services from more than one physician specialty or category of providers in the same market. For each relevant service market, the relevant geographic market will include all physicians (or other providers) who are good substitutes for the physician participants in the joint venture.

---

37. *See* FTC v. Indiana Federation of Dentists, 476 U.S. 447, 459-60 (1986).
38. A more extensive discussion of how the Agencies define relevant markets is contained in the Agencies' 1992 Horizontal Merger Guidelines.

Step two: Evaluate the competitive effects of the physician joint venture. The Agencies examine the structure and activities of the physician network joint venture and the nature of competition in the relevant market to determine whether the formation or operation of the venture is likely to have an anticompetitive effect. Two key areas of competitive concern are whether a physician network joint venture could raise the prices for physician services charged to health plans above competitive levels, or could prevent or impede the formation or operation of other networks or plans.

In assessing whether a particular network arrangement could raise prices or exclude competition, the Agencies will examine whether the network physicians collectively have the ability and incentive to engage in such conduct. The Agencies will consider not only the proportion of the physicians in any relevant market who are in the network, but also the incentives faced by physicians in the network, and whether different groups of physicians in a network may have significantly different incentives that would reduce the likelihood of anticompetitive conduct. The Department of Justice has entered into final judgments that permit a network to include a relatively large proportion of physicians in a relevant market where the percentage of physicians with an ownership interest in the network is strictly limited, and the network subcontracts with additional physicians under terms that create a sufficient divergence of economic interest between the subcontracting physicians and the owner physicians so that the owner physicians have an incentive to control the costs to the network of the subcontracting physicians.[39] Evaluating the incentives faced by network physicians requires an examination of the facts and circumstances of each particular case. The Agencies will assess whether different groups of physicians in the network actually have significantly divergent incentives that would override any shared interest, such as the incentive to profit from higher fees for their medical services. The Agencies will also consider whether the behavior of network physicians or other market evidence indicates

---

39. *See, e.g.,* Competitive Impact Statements in United States v. Health Choice of Northwest Missouri, Inc., Case No. 95-6171-CV-SJ-6 (W.D. Mo.; filed Sept. 13, 1995), 60 Fed. Reg. 51808, 51815 (Oct. 3, 1995); United States and State of Connecticut v. HealthCare Partners, Inc., Case No. 395-CV-01946-RNC (D. Conn.; filed Sept. 13, 1995), 60 Fed. Reg. 52018, 52020 (Oct. 4, 1995).

that the differing incentives among groups of physicians will not prevent anticompetitive conduct.

If, in the relevant market, there are many other networks or many physicians who would be available to form competing networks or to contract directly with health plans, it is unlikely that the joint venture would raise significant competitive concerns. The Agencies will analyze the availability of suitable physicians to form competing networks, including the exclusive or non-exclusive nature of the physician network joint venture.

The Agencies recognize that the competitive impact of exclusive arrangements or other limitations on the ability of a network's physician participants to contract outside the network can vary greatly. For example, in some circumstances exclusivity may help a network serve its subscribers and increase its physician participants' incentives to further the interests of the network. In other situations, however, the anticompetitive risks posed by such exclusivity may outweigh its procompetitive benefits. Accordingly, the Agencies will evaluate the actual or likely effects of particular limitations on contracting in the market situation in which they occur.

An additional area of possible anticompetitive concern involves the risk of "spillover" effects from the venture. For example, a joint venture may involve the exchange of competitively sensitive information among competing physicians and thereby become a vehicle for the network's physician participants to coordinate their activities outside the venture. Ventures that are structured to reduce the likelihood of such spillover are less likely to result in anticompetitive effects. For example, a network that uses an outside agent to collect and analyze fee data from physicians for use in developing the network's fee schedule, and avoids the sharing of such sensitive information among the network's physician participants, may reduce concerns that the information could be used by the network's physician participants to set prices for services they provide outside the network.

Step three: Evaluate the impact of procompetitive efficiencies.[40] This step requires an examination of the joint venture's likely

---

40. If steps one and two reveal no competitive concerns with the physician network joint venture, step three is unnecessary, and the analysis continues with step four, below.

procompetitive efficiencies, and the balancing of these efficiencies against any likely anticompetitive effects. The greater the venture's likely anticompetitive effects, the greater must be the venture's likely efficiencies. In assessing efficiency claims, the Agencies focus on net efficiencies that will be derived from the operation of the network and that result in lower prices or higher quality to consumers. The Agencies will not accept claims of efficiencies if the parties reasonably can achieve equivalent or comparable savings through significantly less anticompetitive means. In making this assessment, however, the Agencies will not search for a theoretically least restrictive alternative that is not practical given business realities.

Experience indicates that, in general, more significant efficiencies are likely to result from a physician network joint venture's substantial financial risk sharing or substantial clinical integration. However, the Agencies will consider a broad range of possible cost savings, including improved cost controls, case management and quality assurance, economies of scale, and reduced administrative or transaction costs.

In assessing the likelihood that efficiencies will be realized, the Agencies recognize that competition is one of the strongest motivations for firms to lower prices, reduce costs, and provide higher quality. Thus, the greater the competition facing the network, the more likely it is that the network will actually realize potential efficiencies that would benefit consumers.

Step four: Evaluation of collateral agreements. This step examines whether the physician network joint venture includes collateral agreements or conditions that unreasonably restrict competition and are unlikely to contribute significantly to the legitimate purposes of the physician network joint venture. The Agencies will examine whether the collateral agreements are reasonably necessary to achieve the efficiencies sought by the joint venture. For example, if the physician participants in a physician network joint venture agree on the prices they will charge patients who are not covered by the health plans with which their network contracts, such an agreement plainly is not reasonably necessary to the success of the joint venture and is an antitrust violation.[41] Similarly, attempts by a physician network joint venture to exclude

41. This analysis of collateral agreements also applies to physician network joint ventures that fall within the safety zones.

competitors or classes of competitors of the network's physician participants from the market could have anticompetitive effects, without advancing any legitimate, procompetitive goal of the network. This could happen, for example, if the network facilitated agreements among the physicians to refuse to deal with such competitors outside the network, or to pressure other market participants to refuse to deal with such competitors or deny them necessary access to key facilities.

C. Examples of Physician Network Joint Ventures

The following are examples of how the Agencies would apply the principles set forth in this statement to specific physician network joint ventures. The first three are new examples: 1) a network involving substantial clinical integration, that is unlikely to raise significant competitive concerns under the rule of reason; 2) a network involving both substantial financial risk-sharing and non-risk-sharing arrangements, which would be analyzed under the rule of reason; and 3) a network involving neither substantial financial risk-sharing nor substantial clinical integration, and whose price agreements likely would be challenged as per se unlawful. The last four examples involve networks that operate in a variety of market settings and with different levels of physician participants; three are networks that involve substantial financial risk-sharing and one is a network in which the physician participants do not jointly agree on, or negotiate, price.

1. Physician Network Joint Venture Involving Clinical Integration

Charlestown is a relatively isolated, medium-sized city. For the purposes of this example, the services provided by primary care physicians and those provided by the different physician specialties each constitute a relevant product market; and the relevant geographic market for each of them is Charlestown.

Several HMOs and other significant managed care plans operate in Charlestown. A substantial proportion of insured individuals are enrolled in these plans, and enrollment in managed care is expected to increase. Many physicians in each of the specialties participate in more than one of these plans. There is no significant overlap among the participants on the physician panels of many of these plans.

A group of Charlestown physicians establishes an IPA to assume greater responsibility for managing the cost and quality of care rendered to Charlestown residents who are members of health plans. They hope to reduce costs while maintaining or improving the quality of care, and thus to attract more managed care patients to their practices.

The IPA will implement systems to establish goals relating to quality and appropriate utilization of services by IPA participants, regularly evaluate both individual participants' and the network's aggregate performance with respect to those goals, and modify individual participants' actual practices, where necessary, based on those evaluations. The IPA will engage in case management, preauthorization of some services, and concurrent and retrospective review of inpatient stays. In addition, the IPA is developing practice standards and protocols to govern treatment and utilization of services, and it will actively review the care rendered by each doctor in light of these standards and protocols.

There is a significant investment of capital to purchase the information systems necessary to gather aggregate and individual data on the cost, quantity, and nature of services provided or ordered by the IPA physicians; to measure performance of the group and the individual doctors against cost and quality benchmarks; and to monitor patient satisfaction. The IPA will provide payers with detailed reports on the cost and quantity of services provided, and on the network's success in meeting its goals.

The IPA will hire a medical director and a support staff to perform the above functions and to coordinate patient care in specific cases. The doctors also have invested appreciable time in developing the practice standards and protocols, and will continue actively to monitor care provided through the IPA. Network participants who fail to adhere to the network's standards and protocols will be subject to remedial action, including the possibility of expulsion from the network.

The IPA physicians will be paid by health plans on a fee-for-service basis; the physicians will not share substantial financial risk for the cost of services rendered to covered individuals through the network. The IPA will retain an agent to develop a fee schedule, negotiate fees, and contract with payers on behalf of the venture. Information about what participating doctors charge non-network patients will not be disseminated to participants in the IPA, and the doctors will not agree on the prices they will charge patients not covered by IPA contracts.

The IPA is built around three geographically dispersed primary care group practices that together account for 25 percent of the primary care doctors in Charlestown. A number of specialists to whom the primary care doctors most often refer their patients also are invited to participate in the IPA. These specialists are selected based on their established referral relationships with the primary care doctors, the quality of care provided by the doctors, their willingness to cooperate with the goals of the IPA, and the need to provide convenient referral services to patients of the primary care doctors. Specialist services that are needed less frequently will be provided by doctors who are not IPA participants. Participating specialists constitute from 20 to 35 percent of the specialists in each relevant market, depending on the specialty. Physician participation in the IPA is non-exclusive. Many IPA participants already do and are expected to continue to participate in other managed care plans and earn substantial income from those plans.

Competitive Analysis

Although the IPA does not fall within the antitrust safety zone because the physicians do not share substantial financial risk, the Agencies would analyze the IPA under the rule of reason because it offers the potential for creating significant efficiencies and the price agreement is reasonably necessary to realize those efficiencies. Prior to contracting on behalf of competing doctors, the IPA will develop and invest in mechanisms to provide cost-effective quality care, including standards and protocols to govern treatment and utilization of services, information systems to measure and monitor individual physician and aggregate network performance, and procedures to modify physician behavior and assure adherence to network standards and protocols. The network is structured to achieve its efficiencies through a high degree of interdependence and cooperation among its physician participants. The price agreement, under these circumstances, is subordinate to and reasonably necessary to achieve these objectives.[42]

---

42. Although the physicians in this example have not directly agreed with one another on the prices to be charged for services rendered through the network, the venture's use of an agent, subject to its control, to establish fees and to negotiate and execute contracts on behalf of the venture amounts to a price agreement among competitors. However, the use of

Furthermore, the Agencies would not challenge under the rule of reason the doctors' agreement to establish and operate the IPA. In conducting the rule of reason analysis, the Agencies would evaluate the likely competitive effects of the venture in each relevant market. In this case, the IPA does not appear likely to limit competition in any relevant market either by hampering the ability of health plans to contract individually with area physicians or with other physician network joint ventures, or by enabling the physicians to raise prices above competitive levels. The IPA does not appear to be overinclusive: many primary care physicians and specialists are available to other plans, and the doctors in the IPA have been selected to achieve the network's procompetitive potential. Many IPA participants also participate in other managed care plans and are expected to continue to do so in the future. Moreover, several significant managed care plans are not dependent on the IPA participants to offer their products to consumers. Finally, the venture is structured so that physician participants do not share competitively sensitive information, thus reducing the likelihood of anticompetitive spillover effects outside the network where the physicians still compete, and the venture avoids any anticompetitive collateral agreements.

Since the venture is not likely to be anticompetitive, there is no need for further detailed evaluation of the venture's potential for generating procompetitive efficiencies. For these reasons, the Agencies would not challenge the joint venture. However, they would reexamine this conclusion and do a more complete analysis of the procompetitive efficiencies if evidence of actual anticompetitive effects were to develop.

2. Physician Network Joint Venture Involving Risk-Sharing and Non-Risk-Sharing Contracts

An IPA has capitation contracts with three insurer-developed HMOs. Under its contracts with the HMOs, the IPA receives a set fee per member per month for all covered services required by enrollees in a particular health plan. Physician participants in the IPA are paid on a fee-for-service basis, pursuant to a fee schedule developed by the IPA.

---

such an agent should reduce the risk of the network's activities having anticompetitive spillover effects on competition among the physicians for non-network patients.

Physicians participate in the IPA on a non-exclusive basis. Many of the IPA's physicians participate in managed care plans outside the IPA, and earn substantial income from those plans.

The IPA uses a variety of mechanisms to assure appropriate use of services under its capitation contracts so that it can provide contract services within its capitation budgets. In part because the IPA has managed the provision of care effectively, enrollment in the HMOs has grown to the point where HMO patients are a significant share of the IPA doctors' patients.

The three insurers that offer the HMOs also offer PPO options in response to the request of employers who want to give their employees greater choice of plans. Although the capitation contracts are a substantial majority of the IPA's business, it also contracts with the insurers to provide services to the PPO programs on a fee-for-service basis. The physicians are paid according to the same fee schedule used to pay them under the IPA's capitated contracts. The IPA uses the same panel of providers and the same utilization management mechanisms that are involved in the HMO contracts. The IPA has tracked utilization for HMO and PPO patients, which shows similar utilization patterns for both types of patients.

Competitive Analysis

Because the IPA negotiates and enters into both capitated and fee-for-service contracts on behalf on its physicians, the venture is not within a safety zone. However, the IPA's HMO contracts are analyzed under the rule of reason because they involve substantial financial risk-sharing. The PPO contracts also are analyzed under the rule of reason because there are significant efficiencies from the capitated arrangements that carry over to the fee-for-service business. The IPA's procedures for managing the provision of care under its capitation contracts and its related fee schedules produce significant efficiencies; and since those same procedures and fees are used for the PPO contracts and result in similar utilization patterns, they will likely result in significant efficiencies for the PPO arrangements as well.

3. Physician Network that is Per Se Unlawful

A group of physicians in Clarksville forms an IPA to contract with managed care plans. There is some limited managed care presence in the area, and new plans have announced their interest in entering. The physicians agree that the only way they can effectively combat the power of the plans and protect themselves from low fees and intrusive utilization review is to organize and negotiate with the plans collectively through the IPA, rather than individually.

Membership in the IPA is open to any licensed physician in Clarksville. Members contribute $2,000 each to fund the legal fees associated with incorporating the IPA and its operating expenses, including the salary of an executive director who will negotiate contracts on behalf of the IPA. The IPA will enter only into fee-for-service contracts. The doctors will not share substantial financial risk under the contracts. The Contracting Committee, in consultation with the executive director, develops a fee schedule.

The IPA establishes a Quality Assurance and Utilization Review Committee. Upon recommendation of this committee, the members vote to have the IPA adopt two basic utilization review parameters: strict limits on documentation to be provided by physicians to the payers, and arbitration of disputes regarding plan utilization review decisions by a committee of the local medical society. The IPA refuses to contract with plans that do not accept these utilization review parameters. The IPA claims to have its own utilization review/quality assurance programs in development, but has taken very few steps to create such a program. It decides to rely instead on the hospital's established peer review mechanisms.

Although there is no formal exclusivity agreement, IPA physicians who are approached by managed care plans seeking contracts refer the plans to the IPA. Except for some contracts predating the formation of the IPA, the physicians do not contract individually with managed care plans on terms other than those set by the IPA.

Competitive Analysis

This IPA is merely a vehicle for collective decisions by its physicians on price and other significant terms of dealing. The physicians' purpose in forming the IPA is to increase their bargaining power with payers. The IPA makes no effort to selectively choose physicians who are likely to further the network's achievement of efficiencies, and the IPA involves no significant integration, financial or otherwise. IPA physicians' participation in the hospital's general peer review procedures does not evidence integration by those physicians that is likely to result in significant efficiencies in the provision of services through the IPA. The IPA does not manage the provision of care or offer any substantial potential for significant procompetitive efficiencies. The physicians are merely collectively agreeing on prices they will receive for services rendered under IPA contracts and not to accept certain aspects of utilization review that they do not like.

The physicians' contribution of capital to form the IPA does not make it a legitimate joint venture. In some circumstances, capital contributions by an IPA's participants can indicate that the participants have made a significant commitment to the creation of an efficiency-producing competitive entity in the market.[43] Capital contributions, however, can also be used to fund a cartel. The key inquiry is whether the contributed capital is being used to further the network's capability to achieve substantial efficiencies. In this case, the funds are being used primarily to support the joint negotiation, and not to achieve substantial procompetitive efficiencies. Thus, the physicians' agreement to bargain through the joint venture will be treated as per se illegal price fixing.

4. Exclusive Physician Network Joint Venture with Financial Risk-Sharing and Comprising More Than Twenty Percent of Physicians with Active Admitting Privileges at a Hospital

County Seat is a relatively isolated, medium-sized community of about 350,000 residents. The closest town is 50 miles away. County Seat has five general acute care hospitals that offer a mix of basic primary, secondary, and tertiary care services.

Five hundred physicians have medical practices based in County Seat, and all maintain active admitting privileges at one or more of County Seat's hospitals. No physician from outside County Seat has any type of admitting privileges at a County Seat hospital. The physicians represent 10 different specialties and are distributed evenly among the specialties, with 50 doctors practicing each specialty.

---

43. *See supra* Example 1.

One hundred physicians (also distributed evenly among specialties) maintain active admitting privileges at County Seat Medical Center. County Seat's other 400 physicians maintain active admitting privileges at other County Seat hospitals.

Half of County Seat Medical Center's 100 active admitting physicians propose to form an IPA to market their services to purchasers of health care services. The physicians are divided evenly among the specialties. Under the proposed arrangement, the physicians in the network joint venture would agree to meaningful cost containment and quality goals, including utilization review, quality assurance, and other measures designed to reduce the provision of unnecessary care to the plan's subscribers, and a substantial amount (in this example 20 percent) of the compensation due to the network's physician participants would be withheld and distributed only if these measures are successfully met. This physician network joint venture would be exclusive: Its physician participants would not be free to contract individually with health plans or to join other physician joint ventures.

A number of health plans that contract selectively with hospitals and physicians already operate in County Seat. These plans and local employers agree that other County Seat physicians, and the hospitals to which they admit, are good substitutes for the active admitting physicians and the inpatient services provided at County Seat Medical Center. Physicians with medical practices based outside County Seat, however, are not good substitutes for area physicians, because such physicians would find it inconvenient to practice at County Seat hospitals due to the distance between their practice locations and County Seat.

Competitive Analysis

A key issue is whether a physician network joint venture, such as this IPA, comprising 50 percent of the physicians in each specialty with active privileges at one of five comparable hospitals in County Seat would fall within the antitrust safety zone. The physicians within the joint venture represent less than 20 percent of all the physicians in each specialty in County Seat.

County Seat is the relevant geographic market for purposes of analyzing the competitive effects of this proposed physician joint venture. Within each specialty, physicians with admitting privileges at area hospitals are good substitutes for one another. However, physicians with practices based elsewhere are not considered good substitutes.

For purposes of analyzing the effects of the venture, all of the physicians in County Seat should be considered market participants. Purchasers of health care services consider all physicians within each specialty, and the hospitals at which they have admitting privileges, to be relatively interchangeable. Thus, in this example, any attempt by the joint venture's physician participants collectively to increase the price of physician services above competitive levels would likely lead third-party purchasers to recruit non-network physicians at County Seat Medical Center or other area hospitals.

Because physician network joint venture participants constitute less than 20 percent of each group of specialists in County Seat and agree to share substantial financial risk, this proposed joint venture would fall within the antitrust safety zone.

5. Physician Network Joint Venture with Financial Risk-Sharing and a Large Percentage of Physicians in a Relatively Small Community

Smalltown has a population of 25,000, a single hospital, and 50 physicians, most of whom are family practitioners. All of the physicians practice exclusively in Smalltown and have active admitting privileges at the Smalltown hospital. The closest urban area, Big City, is located some 35 miles away and has a population of 500,000. A little more than half of Smalltown's working adults commute to work in Big City. Some of the health plans used by employers in Big City are interested in extending their network of providers to Smalltown to provide coverage for subscribers who live in Smalltown, but commute to work in Big City (coverage is to include the families of commuting subscribers). However, the number of commuting Smalltown subscribers is a small fraction of the Big City employers' total workforce.

Responding to these employers' needs, a few health plans have asked physicians in Smalltown to organize a non-exclusive IPA large enough to provide a reasonable choice to subscribers who reside in Smalltown, but commute to work in Big City. Because of the relatively small number of potential enrollees in Smalltown, the plans prefer to contract with such a physician network joint venture, rather than engage in what may prove to be a time-consuming series of negotiations with individual Smalltown physicians to establish a panel of physician providers there.

A number of Smalltown physicians have agreed to form a physician network joint venture. The joint venture will contract with health plans to provide physician services to subscribers of the plans in exchange for a monthly capitation fee paid for each of the plans' subscribers. The physicians forming this joint venture would constitute about half of the total number of physicians in Smalltown. They would represent about 35 percent of the town's family practitioners, but higher percentages of the town's general surgeons (50 percent), pediatricians (50 percent), and obstetricians (67 percent). The health plans that serve Big City employers say that the IPA must have a large percentage of Smalltown physicians to provide adequate coverage for employees and their families in Smalltown and in a few scattered rural communities in the immediate area and to allow the doctors to provide coverage for each other.

In this example, other health plans already have entered Smalltown, and contracted with individual physicians. They have made substantial inroads with Smalltown employers, signing up a large number of enrollees. None of these plans has had any difficulty contracting with individual physicians, including many who would participate in the proposed joint venture.

Finally, the evidence indicates that Smalltown is the relevant geographic market for all physician services. Physicians in Big City are not good substitutes for a significant number of Smalltown residents.

Competitive Analysis

This proposed physician network joint venture would not fall within the antitrust safety zone because it would comprise over 30 percent of the physicians in a number of relevant specialties in the geographic market. However, the Agencies would not challenge the joint venture because a rule of reason analysis indicates that its formation would not likely hamper the ability of health plans to contract individually with area physicians or with other physician network joint ventures, or enable the physicians to raise prices above competitive levels. In addition, the joint venture's agreement to accept capitated fees creates incentives for its physicians to achieve cost savings.

That health plans have requested formation of this venture also is significant, for it suggests that the joint venture would offer additional efficiencies. In this instance, it appears to be a low-cost method for plans to enter an area without investing in costly negotiations to identify and contract with individual physicians.

Moreover, in small markets such as Smalltown, it may be necessary for purchasers of health care services to contract with a relatively large number of physicians to provide adequate coverage and choice for enrollees. For instance, if there were only three obstetricians in Smalltown, it would not be possible for a physician network joint venture offering obstetrical services to have less than 33 percent of the obstetricians in the relevant area. Furthermore, it may be impractical to have less than 67 percent in the plan, because two obstetricians may be needed in the venture to provide coverage for each other.

Although the joint venture has a relatively large percentage of some specialties, it appears unlikely to present competitive concerns under the rule of reason because of three factors: (1) the demonstrated ability of health plans to contract with physicians individually; (2) the possibility that other physician network joint ventures could be formed; and (3) the potential benefits from the coverage to be provided by this physician network joint venture. Therefore, the Agencies would not challenge the joint venture.

6. Physician Network Joint Venture with Financial Risk Sharing and a Large Percentage of Physicians in a Small, Rural County

Rural County has a population of 15,000, a small primary care hospital, and ten physicians, including seven general and family practitioners, an obstetrician, a pediatrician, and a general surgeon. All of the physicians are solo practitioners. The nearest urban area is about 60 miles away in Big City, which has a population of 300,000, and three major hospitals to which patients from Rural County are referred or transferred for higher levels of hospital care. However, Big City is too far away for most residents of Rural County routinely to use its physicians for services available in Rural County.

Insurance Company, which operates throughout the state, is attempting to offer managed care programs in all areas of the state, and has asked the local physicians in Rural County to form an IPA to provide services under the program to covered persons living in the County. No other managed care plan has attempted to enter the County previously.

Initially, two of the general practitioners and two of the specialists express interest in forming a network, but Insurance Company says that it intends to market its plan to the larger local employers, who need broader geographic and specialty coverage for their employees. Consequently, Insurance Company needs more of the local general practitioners and the one remaining specialist in the IPA to provide adequate geographic, specialty, and backup coverage to subscribers in Rural County. Eventually, four of the seven general practitioners and the one remaining specialist join the IPA and agree to provide services to Insurance Company's subscribers, under contracts providing for capitation. While the physicians' participation in the IPA is structured to be non-exclusive, no other managed care plan has yet entered the local market or approached any of the physicians about joining a different provider panel. In discussing the formation of the IPA with Insurance Company, a number of the physicians have made clear their intention to continue to practice outside the IPA and have indicated they would be interested in contracting individually with other managed care plans when those plans expand into Rural County.

Competitive Analysis

This proposed physician network joint venture would not fall within the antitrust safety zone because it would comprise over 30 percent of the general practitioners in the geographic market. Under the circumstances, a rule of reason analysis indicates that the Agencies would not challenge the formation of the joint venture, for the reasons discussed below.

For purposes of this analysis, Rural County is considered the relevant geographic market. Generally, the Agencies will closely examine joint ventures that comprise a large percentage of physicians in the relevant market. However, in this case, the establishment of the IPA and its inclusion of more than half of the general practitioners and all of the specialists in the network is the result of the payer's expressed need to have more of the local physicians in its network to sell its product in the market. Thus, the level of physician participation in the network does not appear to be overinclusive, but rather appears to be the minimum necessary to meet the employers' needs.

Although the IPA has more than half of the general practitioners and all of the specialists in it, under the particular circumstances this does not, by itself, raise sufficient concerns of possible foreclosure of entry by other managed care plans, or of the collective ability to raise prices above competitive levels, to warrant antitrust challenge to the joint venture by the Agencies. Because it is the first such joint venture in the county, there is no way absolutely to verify at the outset that the joint venture in fact will be non-exclusive. However, the physicians' participation in the IPA is formally non-exclusive, and they have expressed a willingness to consider joining other managed care programs if they begin operating in the area. Moreover, the three general practitioners who are not members of the IPA are available to contract with other managed care plans. The IPA also was established with participation by the local area physicians at the request of Insurance Company, indicating that this structure was not undertaken as a means for the physicians to increase prices or prevent entry of managed care plans.

Finally, the joint venture can benefit consumers in Rural County through the creation of efficiencies. The physicians have jointly put themselves at financial risk to control the use and cost of health care services through capitation. To make the capitation arrangement financially viable, the physicians will have to control the use and cost of health care services they provide under Insurance Company's program. Through the physicians' network joint venture, Rural County residents will be offered a beneficial product, while competition among the physicians outside the network will continue.

Given these facts, the Agencies would not challenge the joint venture. If, however, it later became apparent that the physicians' participation in the joint venture in fact was exclusive, and consequently other managed care plans that wanted to enter the market and contract with some or all of the physicians at competitive terms were unable to do so, the Agencies would re-examine the joint venture's legality. The joint venture also would raise antitrust concerns if it appeared that participation by most of the local physicians in the joint venture resulted in anticompetitive effects in markets outside the joint venture, such as uniformity of fees charged by the physicians in their solo medical practices.

7. Physician Network Joint Venture with No Price Agreement and Involving All of the Physicians in a Small, Rural County

Rural County has a population of 10,000, a small primary care hospital, and six physicians, consisting of a group practice of three family practitioners, a general practitioner, an obstetrician, and a general surgeon. The nearest urban area is about 75 miles away in Big City, which has a population of 200,000, and two major hospitals to which patients from Rural County are referred or transferred for higher levels of hospital care. Big City is too far away, however, for most residents of Rural County to use for services available in Rural County.

HealthCare, a managed care plan headquartered in another state, is thinking of marketing a plan to the larger employers in Rural County. However, it finds that the cost of contracting individually with providers, administering the system, and overseeing the quality of care in Rural County is too high on a per capita basis to allow it to convince employers to switch from indemnity plans to its plan. HealthCare believes its plan would be more successful if it offered higher quality and better access to care by opening a clinic in the northern part of the county where no physicians currently practice.

All of the local physicians approach HealthCare about contracting with their recently-formed, non-exclusive, IPA. The physicians are willing to agree through their IPA to provide services at the new clinic that HealthCare will establish in the northern part of the county and to implement the utilization review procedures that HealthCare has adopted in other parts of the state.

HealthCare wants to negotiate with the new IPA. It believes that the local physicians collectively can operate the new clinic more efficiently than it can from its distant headquarters, but HealthCare also believes that collectively negotiating with all of the physicians will result in it having to pay higher fees or capitation rates. Thus, it encourages the IPA to appoint an agent to negotiate the non-fee related aspects of the contracts and to facilitate fee negotiations with the group practice and the individual doctors. The group practice and the individual physicians each will sign and negotiate their own individual contracts regarding fees and will unilaterally determine whether to contract with HealthCare, but will agree through the IPA to provide physician, administrative, and utilization review services. The agent will facilitate these individual fee negotiations by discussing separately and confidentially with each physician the physician's fee demands and presenting the information to HealthCare. No fee information will be shared among the physicians.

Competitive Analysis

For purposes of this analysis, Rural County is considered the relevant geographic market. Generally, the Agencies are concerned with joint ventures that comprise all or a large percentage of the physicians in the relevant market. In this case, however, the joint venture appears on balance to be procompetitive. The potential for competitive harm from the venture is not great and is outweighed by the efficiencies likely to be generated by the arrangement.

The physicians are not jointly negotiating fees or engaging in other activities that would be viewed as per se antitrust violations. Therefore, the IPA would be evaluated under the rule of reason. Any possible competitive harm would be balanced against any likely efficiencies to be realized by the venture to see whether, on balance, the IPA is anticompetitive or procompetitive.

Because the IPA is non-exclusive, the potential for competitive harm from foreclosure of competition is reduced. Its physicians are free to contract with other managed care plans or individually with HealthCare if they desire. In addition, potential concerns over anticompetitive pricing are minimized because physicians will continue to negotiate prices individually. Although the physicians are jointly negotiating non-price terms of the contract, agreement on these terms appears to be necessary to the successful operation of the joint venture.

The small risk of anticompetitive harm from this venture is outweighed by the substantial procompetitive benefits of improved quality of care and access to physician services that the venture will engender. The new clinic in the northern part of the county will make it easier for residents of that area to receive the care they need. Given these facts, the Agencies would not challenge the joint venture.

* * *

Physicians who are considering forming physician network joint ventures and are unsure of the legality of their conduct under the antitrust laws can take advantage of the Department of Justice's expedited business review procedure announced on December 1, 1992 (58 Fed. Reg. 6132 (1993)) or the Federal Trade Commission's advisory opinion procedure contained at 16 C.F.R. §§ 1.1-1.4 (1993). The Agencies will respond to a business review or advisory opinion request on behalf of physicians who are considering forming a network joint venture within 90 days after all necessary information is submitted. The Department's

December 1, 1992 announcement contains specific guidance about the information that should be submitted.

9. Statement of Department of Justice and Federal Trade Commission Enforcement Policy on Multiprovider Networks

Introduction

The health care industry is changing rapidly as it looks for innovative ways to control costs and efficiently provide quality services. Health care providers are forming a wide range of new relationships and affiliations, including networks among otherwise competing providers, as well as networks of providers offering complementary or unrelated services.[44] These affiliations, referred to herein as multiprovider networks, can offer significant procompetitive benefits to consumers. They also can present antitrust questions, particularly if the network includes otherwise competing providers.

As used in this statement, multiprovider networks are ventures among providers that jointly market their health care services to health plans and other purchasers. Such ventures may contract to provide services to subscribers at jointly determined prices and agree to controls aimed at containing costs and assuring quality. Multiprovider networks vary greatly regarding the providers they include, the contractual relationships among those providers, and the efficiencies likely to be realized by the networks. Competitive conditions in the markets in which such networks operate also may vary greatly.

---

44. The multiprovider networks covered by this statement include all types and combinations of health care providers, such as networks involving just a single type of provider (e.g., dentists or hospitals) or a single provider specialty (e.g., orthodontists), as well as networks involving more than one type of provider (e.g., physician-hospital organizations or networks involving both physician and non-physician professionals). Networks containing only physicians, which are addressed in detail in the preceding enforcement policy statement, are a particular category of multiprovider network. Many of the issues relating to multiprovider networks in general are the same as those that arise, and are addressed, in connection with physician network joint ventures, and the analysis often will be very similar for all such arrangements.

In this statement, the Agencies describe the antitrust principles that they apply in evaluating multiprovider networks, address some issues commonly raised in connection with the formation and operation of such networks, and present examples of the application of antitrust principles to hypothetical multiprovider networks. Because multiprovider networks involve a large variety of structures and relationships among many different types of health care providers, and new arrangements are continually developing, the Agencies are unable to establish a meaningful safety zone for these entities.

A. Determining When Agreements Among Providers in a Multiprovider Network Are Analyzed Under the Rule of Reason

Antitrust law condemns as per se illegal naked agreements among competitors that fix prices or allocate markets. Where competitors economically integrate in a joint venture, however, such agreements, if reasonably necessary to accomplish the procompetitive benefits of the integration, are analyzed under the rule of reason.[45] In accord with general antitrust principles, multiprovider networks will be evaluated under the rule of reason, and will not be viewed as per se illegal, if the providers' integration through the network is likely to produce significant efficiencies that benefit consumers, and any price agreements (or other agreements that would otherwise be per se illegal) by the network providers are reasonably necessary to realize those efficiencies.[46]

---

45. In a network limited to providers who are not actual or potential competitors, the providers generally can agree on the prices to be charged for their services without the kinds of economic integration discussed below.

46. In some cases, the combination of the competing providers in the network may enable them to offer what could be considered to be a new product producing substantial efficiencies, and therefore the venture will be analyzed under the rule of reason. *See* Broadcast Music, Inc. v. Columbia Broadcasting System, Inc., 441 U.S. 1 (1979) (competitors' integration and creation of a blanket license for use of copyrighted compositions result in efficiencies so great as to make the blanket license a "different product" from the mere combination of individual competitors and, therefore, joint pricing of the blanket license is subject to rule of reason

In some multiprovider networks, significant efficiencies may be achieved through agreement by the competing providers to share substantial financial risk for the services provided through the network.[47] In such cases, the setting of price would be integral to the network's use of such an arrangement and, therefore, would warrant evaluation under the rule of reason.

The following are examples of some types of arrangements through which substantial financial risk can be shared among competitors in a multiprovider network:(1) agreement by the venture to provide services to a health plan at a "capitated" rate;[48]

(2) agreement by the venture to provide designated services or classes of services to a health plan for a predetermined percentage of premium or revenue from the plan;[49]

(3) use by the venture of significant financial incentives for its provider participants, as a group, to achieve specified cost-containment goals. Two methods by which the venture can accomplish this are:

(a) withholding from all provider participants a substantial amount of the compensation due to them, with distribution of that amount to the participants based on group performance in meeting the cost-containment goals of the network as a whole; or

(b) establishing overall cost or utilization targets for the network as a whole, with the provider participants subject to subsequent

---

analysis, rather than the per se rule against price fixing). The Agencies' analysis will focus on the efficiencies likely to be produced by the venture, and the relationship of any price agreements to the achievement of those efficiencies, rather than on whether the venture creates a product that can be labeled "new" or "different."

47. The existence of financial risk sharing does not depend on whether, under applicable state law, the network is considered an insurer.

48. A "capitated" rate is a fixed, predetermined payment per covered life (the "capitation") from a health plan to the joint venture in exchange for the joint venture's (not merely an individual provider's) furnishing and guaranteeing provision of a defined set of covered services to covered individuals for a specified period, regardless of the amount of services actually provided.

49. This is similar to a capitation arrangement, except that the amount of payment to the network can vary in response to changes in the health plan's premiums or revenues.

substantial financial rewards or penalties based on group performance in meeting the targets; and

(4) agreement by the venture to provide a complex or extended course of treatment that requires the substantial coordination of care by different types of providers offering a complementary mix of services, for a fixed, predetermined payment, where the costs of that course of treatment for any individual patient can vary greatly due to the individual patient's condition, the choice, complexity, or length of treatment, or other factors.[50]

The Agencies recognize that new types of risk-sharing arrangements may develop. The preceding examples do not foreclose consideration of other arrangements through which the participants in a multiprovider network joint venture may share substantial financial risk in the provision of health care services or products through the network.[51] Organizers of multiprovider networks who are uncertain whether their proposed arrangements constitute substantial financial risk sharing for purposes of this policy statement are encouraged to take advantage of the Agencies' expedited business review and advisory opinion procedures.

Multiprovider networks that do not involve the sharing of substantial financial risk may also involve sufficient integration to demonstrate that the venture is likely to produce significant efficiencies. For example, as discussed in the Statement Of Enforcement Policy On Physician Network Joint Ventures, substantial clinical integration among competing physicians in a network who do not share substantial financial

---

50. Such arrangements are sometimes referred to either as "global fees" or "all-inclusive case rates." Global fee or all-inclusive case rate arrangements that involve financial risk sharing as contemplated by this example will require that the joint venture (not merely an individual provider participant) assume the risk or benefit that the treatment provided through the network may either exceed, or cost less than, the predetermined payment.

51. The manner of dividing revenues among the network's provider participants generally does not raise antitrust issues so long as the competing providers in a network share substantial financial risk. For example, capitated networks frequently distribute income among their participants using fee-for-service payment with a partial withhold fund to cover the risk of having to provide more services than were originally anticipated.

risk may produce efficiency benefits that justify joint pricing.[52] However, given the wide range of providers who may participate in multiprovider networks, the types of clinical integration and efficiencies available to physician network joint ventures may not be relevant to all multiprovider networks. Accordingly, the Agencies will consider the particular nature of the services provided by the network in assessing whether the network has the potential for producing efficiencies that warrant rule of reason treatment. In all cases, the Agencies' analysis will focus on substance, not form, in assessing a network's likelihood of producing significant efficiencies. To the extent that agreements on prices to be charged for the integrated provision of services promote the venture's achievement of efficiencies, they will be evaluated under the rule of reason.

A multiprovider network also might include an agreement among competitors on service allocation or specialization. The Agencies would examine the relationship between the agreement and efficiency-enhancing joint activity. If such an agreement is reasonably necessary for the network to realize significant procompetitive benefits, it similarly would be subject to rule of reason analysis.[53] For example, competing hospitals in an integrated multiprovider network might need to agree that only certain hospitals would provide certain services to network patients in order to achieve the benefits of the integration.[54] The hospitals,

---

52. *See* Section B(1) of the Agencies' Statement Of Enforcement Policy On Physician Network Joint Ventures (pp. 71-74).

53. A unilateral decision to eliminate a service or specialization, however, does not generally present antitrust issues. For example, a hospital or other provider unilaterally may decide to concentrate on its more profitable services and not offer other less profitable services, and seek to enter a network joint venture with competitors that still provides the latter services. If such a decision is made unilaterally, rather than pursuant to an express or implied agreement, the arrangement would not be considered a per se illegal market allocation.

54. Hospitals, even if they do not belong to a multiprovider network, also could agree jointly to develop and operate new services that the participants could not profitably support individually or through a less inclusive joint venture, and to decide where the jointly operated services are to be located. Such joint ventures would be analyzed by the Agencies under the rule of reason. The Statement of Enforcement Policy On Hospital Joint Ventures Involving Specialized Clinical Or Other

however, would not necessarily be permitted to agree on what services they would provide to non-network patients.[55]

B. Applying the Rule of Reason

A rule of reason analysis determines whether the formation and operation of the joint venture may have a substantial anticompetitive effect and, if so, whether that potential effect is outweighed by any procompetitive efficiencies resulting from the venture. The rule of reason analysis takes into account characteristics of the particular multiprovider network and the competitive environment in which it operates to determine the network's likely effect on competition.

A determination about the lawfulness of a multiprovider network's activity under the rule of reason sometimes can be reached without an extensive inquiry under each step of the analysis. For example, a multiprovider network that involves substantial integration may include a relatively small percentage of the providers in each relevant product market on a non-exclusive basis. In that case, the Agencies may be able to conclude expeditiously that the network is unlikely to be anticompetitive, based on the competitive environment in which it operates. In assessing the competitive environment, the Agencies would consider such market factors as the number, type, and size of managed care plans operating in the area, the extent of provider participation in those plans, and the economic importance of the managed care plans to area providers. Alternatively, for example, if a restraint that facially appears to be of a kind that would always or almost always tend to reduce output or increase prices, but has not been considered per se unlawful, is not reasonably necessary to the creation of efficiencies, the Agencies will likely challenge the restraint without an elaborate analysis of market definition and market power.[56]

Expensive Health Care Services offers additional guidance on joint ventures among hospitals to provide such services.

55. The Agencies' analysis would take into account that agreements among multiprovider network participants relating to the offering of services might be more likely than those relating to price to affect participants' competition outside the network, and to persist even if the network is disbanded.

56. *See* FTC v. Indiana Federation of Dentists, 476 U.S. 447, 459-60 (1986).

The steps ordinarily involved in a rule of reason analysis of multiprovider networks are set forth below.

1. Market Definition

The Agencies will evaluate the competitive effects of multiprovider networks in each of the relevant markets in which they operate or have substantial impact. In defining the relevant product and geographic markets, the Agencies look to what substitutes, as a practical matter, are reasonably available to consumers for the services in question.[57]

A multiprovider network can affect markets for the provision of hospital, medical, and other health care services, and health insurance/financing markets. The possible product markets for analyzing the competitive effects of multiprovider networks likely would include both the market for such networks themselves, if there is a distinct market for such networks, and the markets for service components of the network that are, or could be, sold separately outside the network. For example, if two hospitals formed a multiprovider network with their medical and other health care professional staffs, the Agencies would consider potential competitive effects in each market affected by the network, including but not necessarily limited to the markets for inpatient hospital services, outpatient services, each physician and non-physician health care service provided by network members, and health insurance/financing markets whose participants may deal with the network and its various types of health care providers.

The relevant geographic market for each relevant product market affected by the multiprovider network will be determined through a fact-specific analysis that focuses on the location of reasonable alternatives. The relevant geographic markets may be broader for some product markets than for others.

2. Competitive Effects

In applying the rule of reason, the Agencies will examine both the potential "horizontal" and "vertical" effects of the arrangement.

57. A more extensive discussion of how the Agencies define relevant markets is contained in the Agencies' 1992 Horizontal Merger Guidelines.

Agreements between or among competitors (e.g., competing hospitals or competing physicians) are considered "horizontal" under the antitrust laws. Agreements between or among parties that are not competitors (such as a hospital and a physician in a physician-hospital organization ("PHO")), may be considered "vertical" in nature.

a. Horizontal Analysis

In evaluating the possible horizontal competitive effects of multiprovider networks, the Agencies will define the relevant markets (as discussed earlier) and evaluate the network's likely overall competitive effects considering all market conditions. Determining market share and concentration in the relevant markets is often an important first step in analyzing a network's competitive effects. For example, in analyzing a PHO, the Agencies will consider the network's market share (and the market concentration) in such service components as inpatient hospital services (as measured by such indicia as number of institutions, number of hospital beds, patient census, and revenues), physician services (in individual physician specialty or other appropriate service markets),[58] and any other services provided by competing health care providers, institutional or noninstitutional, participating in the network.

If a particular multiprovider network had a substantial share of any of the relevant service markets, it could, depending on other factors, increase the price of such services above competitive levels. For example, a network that included most or all of the surgeons in a relevant geographic market could create market power in the market for surgical services and thereby permit the surgeons to increase prices.

If there is only one hospital in the market, a multiprovider network, by definition, cannot reduce any existing competition among hospitals. Such a network could, however, reduce competition among other providers, for example, among physicians in the network and, thereby, reduce the ability of payers to control the costs of both physician and

58. Although all services provided by each physician specialty or category of non-physician provider might be a separate relevant service market, there may be instances in which significant overlap of services provided by different physician specialties or categories of providers justifies including services from more than one physician specialty or provider category in the same market.

hospital services.[59] It also could reduce competition between the hospital and non-hospital providers of certain services, such as outpatient surgery.

Although market share and concentration are useful starting points in analyzing the competitive effects of multiprovider networks, the Agencies' ultimate conclusion is based upon a more comprehensive analysis. This will include an analysis of collateral agreements and spillover effects.[60] In addition, in assessing the likely competitive effects of a multiprovider network, the Agencies are particularly interested in the ability and willingness of health plans and other purchasers of health care services to switch between different health care providers or networks in response to a price increase, and the factors that determine the ability and willingness of plans to make such changes. The Agencies will consider not only the proportion of the providers in any relevant market who are in the network, but also the incentives faced by providers in the network, and whether different groups of providers in a network may have significantly different incentives that would reduce the likelihood of anticompetitive conduct.[61] If plans can contract at competitive terms with other networks or with individual providers, and can obtain a similar quality and range of services for their enrollees, the network is less likely to raise competitive concerns.

In examining a multiprovider network's overall competitive effect, the Agencies will examine whether the competing providers in the network have agreed among themselves to offer their services exclusively through the network or are otherwise operating, or are likely to operate, exclusively. Such exclusive arrangements are not necessarily anticompetitive.[62] Exclusive networks, however, mean that the providers in the network are not available to join other networks or contract

---

59. By aligning itself with a large share of physicians in the market, a monopoly hospital may effectively be able to insulate itself from payer efforts to control utilization of its services and thus protect its monopoly profits.

60. *See* Statement of Enforcement Policy on Physician Network Joint Ventures, pp.61-105.

61. *See* discussion in Statement of Enforcement Policy on Physician Network Joint Ventures, pp. 61-105.

62. For example, an exclusive arrangement may help ensure the multiprovider network's ability to serve its subscribers and increase its providers' incentives to further the interests of the network.

individually with health plans, and thus, in some circumstances, exclusive networks can impede or preclude competition among networks and among individual providers. In determining whether an exclusive arrangement of this type raises antitrust concerns, the Agencies will examine the market share of the providers subject to the exclusivity arrangement; the terms of the exclusive arrangement, such as its duration and providers' ability and financial incentives or disincentives to withdraw from the arrangement; the number of providers that need to be included for the network and potentially competing networks to compete effectively; and the justification for the exclusivity arrangement.

Networks also may limit or condition provider participants' freedom to contract outside the network in ways that fall short of a commitment of full exclusivity. The Agencies recognize that the competitive impact of exclusive arrangements or other limitations on the ability of a network's provider participants to contract outside the network can vary greatly.

b. Vertical Analysis

In addition to the horizontal issues discussed above, multiprovider networks also can raise vertical issues. Generally, vertical concerns can arise if a network's power in one market in which it operates enables it to limit competition in another market.

Some multiprovider networks involve "vertical" exclusive arrangements that restrict the providers in one market from dealing with non-network providers that compete in a different market, or that restrict network provider participants' dealings with health plans or other purchasers. For example, a multiprovider network owned by a hospital and individually contracting with its participating physicians might limit the incentives or ability of those physicians to participate in other networks. Similarly, a hospital might use a multiprovider network to block or impede other hospitals from entering a market or from offering competing services.

In evaluating whether such exclusive arrangements raise antitrust concerns, the Agencies will examine the degree to which the arrangement may limit the ability of other networks or health plans to compete in the market. The factors the Agencies will consider include those set forth in the discussion of exclusive arrangements on pages 118-119, above.

For example, if the multiprovider network has exclusive arrangements with only a small percentage of the physicians in a relevant market, and there are enough suitable alternative physicians in the market to allow other competing networks to form, the exclusive arrangement is unlikely to raise antitrust concerns. On the other hand, a network might contract exclusively with a large percentage of physicians in a relevant market, for example general surgeons. In that case, if purchasers or payers could not form a satisfactory competing network using the remaining general surgeons in the market, and could not induce new general surgeons to enter the market, those purchasers and payers would be forced to use this network, rather than put together a panel consisting of those providers of each needed service who offer the most attractive combination of price and quality. Thus, the exclusive arrangement would be likely to restrict competition unreasonably, both among general surgeons (the horizontal effect) and among health care providers in other service markets and payers (the vertical effects).

The Agencies recognize that exclusive arrangements, whether they are horizontal or vertical, may not be explicit, so that labeling a multiprovider network as "non-exclusive" will not be determinative. In some cases, providers will refuse to contract with other networks or purchasers, even though they have not entered into an agreement specifically forbidding them from doing so. For example, if a network includes a large percentage of physicians in a certain market, those physicians may perceive that they are likely to obtain more favorable terms from plans by dealing collectively through one network, rather than as individuals.

In determining whether a network is truly non-exclusive, the Agencies will consider a number of factors, including the following:

(1) that viable competing networks or managed care plans with adequate provider participation currently exist in the market;

(2) that providers in the network actually individually participate in, or contract with, other networks or managed care plans, or there is other evidence of their willingness and incentive to do so;

(3) that providers in the network earn substantial revenue from other networks or through individual contracts with managed care plans;

(4) the absence of any indications of substantial departicipation from other networks or managed care plans in the market; and

(5) the absence of any indications of coordination among the providers in the network regarding price or other competitively

significant terms of participation in other networks or managed care plans.

c. *Exclusion of Particular Providers*

Most multiprovider networks will contract with some, but not all, providers in an area. Such selective contracting may be a method through which networks limit their provider panels in an effort to achieve quality and cost-containment goals, and thus enhance their ability to compete against other networks. One reason often advanced for selective contracting is to ensure that the network can direct a sufficient patient volume to its providers to justify price concessions or adherence to strict quality controls by the providers. It may also help the network create a favorable market reputation based on careful selection of high quality, cost-effective providers. In addition, selective contracting may be procompetitive by giving non-participant providers an incentive to form competing networks.

A rule of reason analysis usually is applied in judging the legality of a multiprovider network's exclusion of providers or classes of providers from the network, or its policies on referring enrollees to network providers. The focus of the analysis is not on whether a particular provider has been harmed by the exclusion or referral policies, but rather whether the conduct reduces competition among providers in the market and thereby harms consumers. Where other networks offering the same types of services exist or could be formed, there are not likely to be significant competitive concerns associated with the exclusion of particular providers by particular networks. Exclusion or referral policies may present competitive concerns, however, if providers or classes of providers are unable to compete effectively without access to the network, and competition is thereby harmed. In assessing such situations, the Agencies will consider whether there are procompetitive reasons for the exclusion or referral policies.

3. Efficiencies

Finally, the Agencies will balance any potential anticompetitive effects of the multiprovider network against the potential efficiencies associated with its formation and operation. The greater the network's likely anticompetitive effects, the greater must be the network's likely efficiencies. In assessing efficiency claims, the Agencies focus on net efficiencies that will be derived from the operation of the network and that result in lower prices or higher quality to consumers. The Agencies will not accept claims of efficiencies if the parties reasonably can achieve equivalent or comparable savings through significantly less anticompetitive means. In making this assessment, however, the Agencies will not search for a theoretically least restrictive alternative that is not practical given business realities.

Experience indicates that, in general, more significant efficiencies are likely to result from a multiprovider network joint venture's substantial financial risk-sharing or substantial clinical integration. However, the Agencies will consider a broad range of possible cost savings, including improved cost controls, case management and quality assurance, economies of scale, and reduced administrative or transaction costs.

In assessing the likelihood that efficiencies will be realized, the Agencies recognize that competition is one of the strongest motivations for firms to lower prices, reduce costs, and provide higher quality. Thus, the greater the competition facing the network, the more likely the network will actually realize potential efficiencies that would benefit consumers.

4. Information Used in the Analysis

In conducting a rule of reason analysis, the Agencies rely upon a wide variety of data and information, including the information supplied by the participants in the multiprovider network, purchasers, providers, consumers, and others familiar with the market in question. The Agencies may interview purchasers of health care services, including self-insured employers and other employers that offer health benefits, and health plans (such as HMOs and PPOs), competitors of the providers in the network, and any other parties who may have relevant information for analyzing the competitive effects of the network.

The Agencies do not simply count the number of parties who support or oppose the formation of the multiprovider network. Instead, the Agencies seek information concerning the competitive dynamics in the particular community where the network is forming. For example, in defining relevant markets, the Agencies are likely to give substantial weight to information provided by purchasers or payers who have attempted to switch between providers in the face of a price increase. Similarly, an employer or payer with locations in several communities may have had experience with a network comparable to the proposed network, and thus be able to provide the Agencies with useful information about the likely effect of the proposed network, including its potential competitive benefits.

In assessing the information provided by various parties, the Agencies take into account the parties' economic incentives and interests. In addition, the Agencies attach less significance to opinions that are based on incomplete, biased, or inaccurate information, or opinions of those who, for whatever reason, may be simply indifferent to the potential for anticompetitive harm.

C. *Arrangements That Do Not Involve Horizontal Agreements on Prices or Price-Related Terms*

Some networks that are not substantially integrated use a variety of "messenger model" arrangements to facilitate contracting between providers and payers and avoid price-fixing agreements among competing network providers. Arrangements that are designed simply to minimize the costs associated with the contracting process, and that do not result in a collective determination by the competing network providers on prices or price-related terms, are not per se illegal price fixing.[63]

Messenger models can be organized and operate in a variety of ways. For example, network providers may use an agent or third party to convey to purchasers information obtained individually from the providers about the prices or price-related terms that the providers are willing to accept.[64] In some cases, the agent may convey to the providers all contract offers made by purchasers, and each provider then makes an independent, unilateral decision to accept or reject the contract offers. In

---

63. *See infra* Example 4.
64. Guidance about the antitrust standards applicable to collection and exchange of fee information can be found in the Statement of Enforcement Policy On Providers' Collective Provision Of Fee-Related Information To Purchasers Of Health Care Services, and the Statement of Enforcement Policy On Provider Participation In Exchanges Of Price And Cost Information.

others, the agent may have received from individual providers some authority to accept contract offers on their behalf. The agent also may help providers understand the contracts offered, for example by providing objective or empirical information about the terms of an offer (such as a comparison of the offered terms to other contracts agreed to by network participants).

The key issue in any messenger model arrangement is whether the arrangement creates or facilitates an agreement among competitors on prices or price-related terms. Determining whether there is such an agreement is a question of fact in each case. The Agencies will examine whether the agent facilitates collective decision-making by network providers, rather than independent, unilateral, decisions.[65] In particular, the Agencies will examine whether the agent coordinates the providers' responses to a particular proposal, disseminates to network providers the views or intentions of other network providers as to the proposal, expresses an opinion on the terms offered, collectively negotiates for the providers, or decides whether or not to convey an offer based on the agent's judgment about the attractiveness of the prices or price-related terms. If the agent engages in such activities, the arrangement may amount to a per se illegal price-fixing agreement.

D. Examples of Multiprovider Network Joint Ventures

The following are four examples of how the Agencies would apply the principles set forth in this statement to specific multiprovider network joint ventures, including: 1) a PHO involving substantial clinical integration, that does not raise significant competitive concerns under the rule of reason; 2) a PHO providing services on a per case basis, that would be analyzed under the rule of reason; 3) a PHO involving substantial financial risk sharing and including all the physicians in a small rural county, that does not raise competitive concerns under the rule of reason; and 4) a PHO that does not involve horizontal agreements on price.

---

65. Use of an intermediary or "independent" third party to convey collectively determined price offers to purchasers or to negotiate agreements with purchasers, or giving to individual providers an opportunity to "opt" into, or out of, such agreements does not negate the existence of an agreement.

1. PHO Involving Substantial Clinical Integration

Roxbury is a relatively isolated, medium-sized city. For the purposes of this example, the services provided by primary care physicians and those provided by the different physician specialists each constitute a relevant product market; and the relevant geographic market for each of them is Roxbury.

Several HMOs and other significant managed care plans operate in Roxbury. A substantial proportion of insured individuals are enrolled in these plans, and enrollment in managed care is expected to increase. Many physicians in each of the specialties and Roxbury's four hospitals participate in more than one of these plans. There is no significant overlap among the participants on the physician panels of many of these plans, nor among the active medical staffs of the hospitals, except in a few specialties. Most plans include only 2 or 3 of Roxbury's hospitals, and each hospital is a substitute for any other.

One of Roxbury's hospitals and the physicians on its active medical staff establish a PHO to assume greater responsibility for managing the cost and quality of care rendered to Roxbury residents who are members of health plans. They hope to reduce costs while maintaining or improving the quality of care, and thus to attract more managed care patients to the hospital and their practices.

The PHO will implement systems to establish goals relating to quality and appropriate utilization of services by PHO participants, regularly evaluate both the hospital's and each individual doctor's and the network's aggregate performance concerning those goals, and modify the hospital's and individual participants' actual practices, where necessary, based on those evaluations. The PHO will engage in case management, preadmission authorization of some services, and concurrent and retrospective review of inpatient stays. In addition, the PHO is developing practice standards and protocols to govern treatment and utilization of services, and it will actively review the care rendered by each doctor in light of these standards and protocols.

There is a significant investment of capital to purchase the information systems necessary to gather aggregate and individual data on the cost, quantity, and nature of services provided or ordered by the hospital and PHO physicians; to measure performance of the PHO, the hospital, and the individual doctors against cost and quality benchmarks; and to monitor patient satisfaction. The PHO will provide payers with detailed reports on the cost and quantity of services provided, and on the network's success in meeting its goals.

The PHO will hire a medical director and support staff to perform the above functions and to coordinate patient care in specific cases. The doctors and the hospital's administrative staff also have invested appreciable time in developing the practice standards and protocols, and will continue actively to monitor care provided through the PHO. PHO physicians who fail to adhere to the network's standards and protocols will be subject to remedial action, including the possibility of expulsion from the network.

Under PHO contracts, physicians will be paid by health plans on a fee-for-service basis; the hospital will be paid a set amount for each day a covered patient is in the hospital, and will be paid on a fee-for-service basis for other services. The physicians will not share substantial financial risk for the cost of services rendered to covered individuals through the network. The PHO will retain an agent to develop a fee schedule, negotiate fees, and contract with payers. Information about what participating doctors charge non-network patients will not be disseminated to participants of the PHO, and the doctors will not agree on the prices they will charge patients not covered by PHO contracts.

All members of the hospital's medical staff join the PHO, including its three geographically dispersed primary care group practices that together account for about 25 percent of the primary care doctors in Roxbury. These primary care doctors generally refer their patients to specialists on the hospital's active medical staff. The PHO includes all primary care doctors and specialists on the hospital's medical staff because of those established referral relationships with the primary care doctors, the admitting privileges all have at the hospital, the quality of care provided by the medical staff, their commitment to cooperate with the goals of the PHO, and the need to provide convenient referral services to patients of the primary care doctors. Participating specialists include from 20 to 35 percent of specialists in each relevant market, depending on the specialty. Hospital and physician participation in the PHO is non-exclusive. Many PHO participants, including the hospital, already do and are expected to continue to participate in other managed care plans and earn substantial income from those plans.

Competitive Analysis

The Agencies would analyze the PHO under the rule of reason because it offers the potential for creating significant efficiencies and the price agreement among the physicians is reasonably necessary to realize those efficiencies. Prior to contracting on behalf of competing physicians, the PHO will develop mechanisms to provide cost-effective, quality care, including standards and protocols to govern treatment and utilization of services, information systems to measure and monitor both the individual performance of the hospital and physicians and aggregate network performance, and procedures to modify hospital and physician behavior and assure adherence to network standards and protocols. The network is structured to achieve its efficiencies through a high degree of interdependence and cooperation among its participants. The price agreement for physician services, under these circumstances, is subordinate to and reasonably necessary to achieve these objectives.[66]

Furthermore, the Agencies would not challenge establishment and operation of the PHO under the rule of reason. In conducting the rule of reason analysis, the Agencies would evaluate the likely competitive effects of the venture in each relevant market. In this case, the PHO does not appear likely to limit competition in any relevant market either by hampering the ability of health plans to contract individually with area hospitals or physicians or with other network joint ventures, or by enabling the hospital or physicians to raise prices above competitive levels. The PHO does not appear to be overinclusive: many primary care physicians as well as specialists are available to other plans, and the doctors in the PHO have been included to achieve the network's procompetitive potential. Many PHO doctors also participate in other managed care plans and are expected to continue to do so in the future. Moreover, several significant managed care plans are not dependent on the PHO doctors to offer their products to consumers. Finally, the venture is structured so that physician participants do not share competitively sensitive information, thus reducing the likelihood of

---

66. Although the physicians have not directly agreed among themselves on the prices to be charged, their use of an agent subject to the control of the PHO to establish fees and to negotiate and execute contracts on behalf of the venture would amount to a price agreement among competitors. The use of such an agent, however, should reduce the risk of the PHO's activities having anticompetitive spillover effects on competition among provider participants for non-network patients.

anticompetitive spillover effects outside the network where the physicians still compete, and the venture avoids any anticompetitive collateral agreements.

Since the venture is not likely to be anticompetitive, there is no need for further detailed evaluation of the venture's potential for generating procompetitive efficiencies. For these reasons, the Agencies would not challenge the joint venture. They would reexamine this conclusion, however, and do a more complete analysis of the procompetitive efficiencies if evidence of actual anticompetitive effects were to develop.

2. PHO that Provides Services on a Per Case Basis

Goodville is a large city with a number of hospitals. One of Goodville's hospitals, together with its oncologists and other relevant health care providers, establishes a joint venture to contract with health plans and other payers of health care services to provide bone marrow transplants and related cancer care for certain types of cancers based on an all inclusive per case payment. Under these contracts, the venture will receive a single payment for all hospital, physician, and ancillary services rendered to covered patients requiring bone marrow transplants. The venture will be responsible for paying for and coordinating the various forms of care provided. At first, it will pay its providers using a fee schedule with a withhold to cover unanticipated losses on the case rate. Based on its operational experience, the venture intends to explore other payment methodologies that may most effectively provide the venture's providers with financial incentives to allocate resources efficiently in their treatment of patients.

Competitive Analysis

The joint venture is a multiprovider network in which competitors share substantial financial risk, and the price agreement among members of the venture will be analyzed under the rule of reason. The per case payment arrangement involves the sharing of substantial financial risk because the venture will receive a single, predetermined payment for a course of treatment that requires the substantial coordination of care by different types of providers and can vary significantly in cost and complexity from patient to patient. The venture will pay its provider participants in a way that gives them incentives to allocate resources efficiently, and that spreads among the participants the risk of loss and the possibility of gain on any particular case. The venture adds to the market another contracting option for health plans and other payers that is likely to result in cost savings because of its use of a per case payment method. Establishment of the case rate is an integral part of the risk sharing arrangement.

3. PHO with All the Physicians in a Small, Rural County

Frederick County has a population of 15,000, and a 50-bed hospital that offers primary and some secondary services. There are 12 physicians on the active medical staff of the hospital (six general and family practitioners, one internist, two pediatricians, one otolaryngologist, and two general surgeons) as well as a part-time pathologist, anesthesiologist, and radiologist. Outside of Frederick County, the nearest hospitals are in Big City, 25 miles away. Most Frederick County residents receive basic physician and hospital care in Frederick County, and are referred or transferred to the Big City physician specialists and hospitals for higher levels of care.

No managed care plans currently operate in Frederick County. Nor are there any large employers who selectively contract with Frederick County physicians. Increasingly, Frederick County residents who work for employers in Big City are covered under managed care contracts that direct Frederick County residents to hospitals and to numerous primary care and specialty physicians in Big City. Providers in Frederick County who are losing patients to hospitals and doctors in Big City want to contract with payers and employers so that they can retain these patients. However, the Frederick County hospital and doctors have been unsuccessful in their efforts to obtain contracts individually; too few potential enrollees are involved to justify payers' undertaking the expense and effort of individually contracting with Frederick County providers and administering a utilization review and quality assurance program for a provider network in Frederick County.

The hospital and all the physicians in Frederick County want to establish a PHO to contract with managed care plans and employers operating in Big City. Managed care plans have expressed interest in contracting with all Frederick County physicians under a single risk-sharing contract. The PHO also will offer its network to employers operating in Frederick County.

The PHO will market the services of the hospital on a per diem basis, and physician services on the basis of a fee schedule that is significantly discounted from the doctors' current charges. The PHO will be eligible for a bonus of up to 20 percent of the total payments made to it, depending on the PHO's success in meeting utilization targets agreed to with the payers. An employee of the hospital will develop a fee schedule, negotiate fees, and contract with payers on behalf of the PHO. Information about what participating doctors charge non-PHO patients will not be disseminated to the doctors, and they will not agree on the prices they will charge patients not covered by PHO contracts.

Physicians' participation in the PHO is structured to be non-exclusive. Because no other managed care plans operate in the area, PHO physicians do not now participate in other plans and have not been approached by other plans. The PHO physicians have made clear their intention to continue to practice outside the PHO and to be available to contract individually with any other managed care plans that expand into Frederick County.

Competitive Analysis

The agreement of the physicians on the prices they will charge through the PHO would be analyzed under the rule of reason, because they share substantial financial risk through the use of a pricing arrangement that provides significant financial incentives for the physicians, as a group, to achieve specified cost-containment goals. The venture thus has the potential for creating significant efficiencies, and the setting of price promotes the venture's use of the risk-sharing arrangement.

The Agencies would not challenge formation and operation of the PHO under the rule of reason. Under the rule of reason analysis, the Agencies would evaluate the likely competitive effects of the venture. The venture does not appear likely to limit competition in any relevant market. Managed care plans' current practice of directing patients from Frederick County to Big City suggests that the physicians in the PHO face significant competition from providers and managed care plans that operate in Big City. Moreover, the absence of managed care contracting in Frederick County, either now or in the foreseeable future, indicates that the network is not likely to reduce any actual or likely competition for patients who do not travel to Big City for care.

While the venture involves all of the doctors in Frederick County, this was necessary to respond to competition from Big City providers. It is not possible to verify at the outset that the venture will in fact be non-exclusive, but the physicians' participation in the venture is structured to be non-exclusive, and the doctors have expressed a willingness to consider joining other managed care plans if they begin operating in the area.

For these reasons, the Agencies would not challenge the joint venture. However, if it later became apparent that the physicians' participation in the PHO was exclusive in fact, and consequently managed care plans or employers that wanted to contract with some or all of the physicians at competitive terms were unable to do so, or that the PHO doctors entered into collateral agreements that restrained competition for services furnished outside the PHO, the Agencies likely would challenge the joint venture.

4. PHO that Does Not Involve Horizontal Agreements on Price

A hospital and doctors and other health care providers on its medical staff have established a PHO to market their services to payers, including employers with self-funded health benefits plans. The PHO contracts on a fee-for-service basis. The physicians and other health care providers who are participants in the PHO do not share substantial financial risk or otherwise integrate their services so as to provide significant efficiencies. The payers prefer to continue to use their existing third-party administrators for contract administration and utilization management, or to do it in-house.

There is no agreement among the PHO's participants to deal only through the PHO, and many of them participate in other networks and HMOs on a variety of terms. Some payers have chosen to contract with the hospital and some or all of the PHO physicians and other providers without going through the PHO, and a significant proportion of the PHO's participants contract with payers in this manner.

In an effort to avoid horizontal price agreements among competing participants in the PHO while facilitating the contracting process, the PHO considers using the following mechanisms:

A. An agent of the PHO, not otherwise affiliated with any PHO participant, will obtain from each participant a fee schedule or conversion factor that represents the minimum payment that participant will accept from a payer. The agent is authorized to contract on the participants' behalf with payers offering prices at this level or better. The agent does not negotiate pricing terms with the payer and does not share pricing information among competing participants. Price offers that do not meet the authorized fee are conveyed to the individual participant.

B. The same as option A, with the added feature that the agent is authorized, for a specified time, to bind the participant to any contract offers with prices equal, to or better than, those in a contract that the participant has already approved.

C. The same as option A, except that in order to assist payers in developing contract offers, the agent takes the fee authorizations of the various participants and develops a schedule that can be presented to a payer showing the percentages of participants in the network who have authorized contracts at various price levels.

D. The venture hires an agent to negotiate prices with payers on behalf of the PHO's participants. The agent does not disclose to the payer the prices the participants are willing to accept, as in option C, but attempts to obtain the best possible prices for all the participants. The resulting contract offer then is relayed to each participant for acceptance or rejection.

Competitive Analysis

In the circumstances described in options A through D, the Agencies would determine whether there was a horizontal agreement on price or any other competitively significant terms among PHO participants. The Agencies would determine whether such agreements were subject to the per se rule or the rule of reason, and evaluate them accordingly.

The existence of an agreement is a factual question. The PHO's use of options A through C does not establish the existence of a horizontal price agreement. Nor is there sharing of price information or other evidence of explicit or implicit agreements among network participants on price. The agent does not inform PHO participants about others' acceptance or rejection of contract offers; there is no agreement or understanding that PHO participants will only contract through the PHO; and participants deal outside the network on competitive terms.

The PHO's use of option D amounts to a per se unlawful price agreement. The participants' joint negotiation through a common agent confronts the payer with the combined bargaining power of the PHO participants, even though they ultimately have to agree individually to the contract negotiated on their behalf.

APPENDIX M

1993 HORIZONTAL MERGER GUIDELINES OF THE NATIONAL ASSOCIATION OF ATTORNEYS GENERAL

1. Purpose and Scope of the Guidelines

These guidelines explain the general enforcement policy of the state and territorial attorneys general ("the Attorneys General") who comprise the National Association of Attorneys General[1] ("NAAG") concerning horizontal acquisitions and mergers[2] (collectively "mergers") subject to section 7 of the Clayton Act,[3] sections 1 and 2 of the Sherman Act[4] and

---

1. The Attorneys General of American Samoa, Guam, The Commonwealth of Northern Marianas Islands, The Commonwealth of Puerto Rico and the Virgin Islands are members of NAAG.
2. A horizontal merger involves firms that are actually or potentially in both the same product and geographic markets, as those markets are defined in Section 3 of these guidelines.
3. Section 7 of the Clayton Act, 15 U.S.C. § 18, prohibits mergers if their effect "may be substantially to lessen competition or to tend to create a monopoly."
4. Section 1 of the Sherman Act, 15 U.S.C. § 1, prohibits mergers which constitute an unreasonable "restraint of trade." Section 2 of the Sherman Act, 15 U.S.C. § 2, prohibits mergers which create a monopoly or constitute an attempt, combination or conspiracy to monopolize.

analogous provisions of the antitrust laws of those states which have enacted them.[5]

The state attorney general is the primary or exclusive public enforcer of the antitrust law in most states. The Attorneys General also represent their states and the natural person citizens of their states in federal antitrust litigation.[6]

These guidelines embody the general enforcement policy of the Attorneys General. Individual attorneys general may vary or supplement this general policy in recognition of variations in precedents among the federal circuits and differences in state antitrust laws and in the exercise of their individual prosecutorial discretion.

These guidelines serve three principal purposes. First, they provide a uniform framework for the states to evaluate the facts of a particular horizontal merger and the dynamic conditions of an industry. Second, they inform businesses of the substantive standards used by the Attorneys General to review, and when appropriate, challenge specific mergers. They help businesses to assess the legality of potential transactions and therefore are useful as a business planning tool. Third, the guidelines are designed primarily to articulate the analytical framework the states apply in determining whether a merger is likely substantially to lessen competition, not to describe how the states will conduct litigation. As such, the Guidelines do not purport to provide a complete restatement of existing merger law. Rather, the Guidelines put forward a framework for the analysis of horizontal mergers which relies upon an accurate characterization of relevant markets and which is grounded in and consistent with the purposes and meaning of section 7 of the Clayton Act, as amended by the Celler-Kefauver Act of 1950 ("section 7"), and as reflected in its legislative history and interpretation by the United States Supreme Court.

---

5. Citations to the antitrust laws of the states are set forth in 6 Trade Reg. Rep. (CCH) ¶ 30,000 et. seq.
6. The authority of the Attorneys General to invoke section 7 of the Clayton Act to enjoin a merger injurious to the general welfare and economy of the State was first articulated in Georgia v. Pennsylvania R.R., 324 U.S. 439 (1945). California v. American Stores, 110 S. Ct. 1853 (1990), confirms Attorneys General's authority to enforce Section 7 and confirms the availability of the divestiture remedy to Attorneys General.

The organizing principle of the guidelines is the application of facts concerning the marketplace and widely accepted economic theory to these authoritative sources of the law's meaning.

2. Policies Underlying These Guidelines

The federal antitrust law provisions relevant to horizontal mergers, most specifically section 7 and analogous state law provisions,[7] have one primary and several subsidiary purposes. The central purpose of the law is to prevent firms from attaining either market or monopoly power,[8] because firms possessing such power can raise prices to consumers above competitive levels, thereby effecting a transfer of wealth from consumers to such firms.[9]

Congress determined that highly concentrated industries were characterized by and conducive to the exercise of market power and prohibited mergers which may substantially lessen competition. Such mergers were prohibited even prior to the parties actual attainment or exercise of market power, that is, when the trend to harmful concentration was incipient.

These guidelines deal only with these competitive consequences of horizontal mergers, and challenges will be instituted only against

---

7. For example, *see* statutes of Hawaii, Maine, Mississippi, Nebraska, New Jersey, Ohio, Oklahoma, Texas, Washington and Puerto Rico for provisions analogous to section 7. *See* 6 Trade Reg. Rep. (CCH) ¶ 30,000 et. seq. However, all states with a provision analogous to section 1 of the Sherman Act may also challenge mergers under such authority. *See* note 6 concerning state enforcement of section 7. Appendix A contains copies of the NAAG Voluntary Pre-Merger Disclosure Compact, the Protocol for Coordinating Federal-State Merger Probes and the Program for Federal-State Cooperation in Merger Enforcement.
8. Market power is the ability of one or more firms to maintain prices above a competitive level, or to prevent prices from decreasing to a lower competitive level, or to limit output or entry.
9. A buyer or group of buyers may similarly attain and exercise the power to drive prices below a competitive level for a significant period of time. This is usually termed an exercise of "monopsony power." When the terms "buyer(s)" or "groups of buyers" are used herein they are deemed to include "seller(s)" or "groups of sellers" adversely affected by the exercise of market or monopsony power.

mergers that may lead to detrimental economic effects. Mergers may also have other consequences that are relevant to the social and political goals of section 7. For example, mergers may affect the opportunities for small and regional business to survive and compete. Although such consequences are beyond the scope of these guidelines, they may affect the Attorneys General's ultimate exercise of prosecutorial discretion and may help the states decide which of the possible challenges that are justified on economic grounds should be instituted.

Goals such as productive and allocative efficiency are generally consistent with, though subsidiary to, the central goal of preventing wealth transfers from consumers to firms possessing market power. When the productive efficiency of a firm increases (its cost of production is lowered), a firm in a highly competitive industry may pass on some of the savings to consumers in the form of lower prices. However, to the extent that a merger increases market power, there is less likelihood that any productive efficiencies would be passed along to consumers.

To the extent that Congress was concerned with productive efficiency in enacting these laws, it prescribed the prevention of high levels of market concentration as the means to this end.[10] Furthermore, the Supreme Court has clearly ruled that any conflict between the goal of preventing anticompetitive mergers and that of increasing efficiency must be resolved in favor of the former explicit and predominant concern of the Congress.[11]

---

10. There is vigorous debate whether firms in industries with high concentration are on average more or less efficient than those in industries with moderate or low levels of concentration. The theory of "x-inefficiency" predicts that firms constrained by vigorous competition have lower production costs than firms in an industry with little or no competition. Various economists have attempted to quantify production cost increases due to x-inefficiency and the theory is the subject of ongoing debate.
11. In *FTC v. Procter & Gamble Co.*, 386 U.S. 568, 580 (1967), the Court stated: "Possible economies cannot be used as a defense to illegality. Congress was aware that some mergers which lessen competition may also result in economies but it struck the balance in favor of protecting competition." In *United States v. Philadelphia National Bank,* 374 U.S. 321, 371 (1963), the Court stated: "We are clear, however, that a merger the effect of which 'may be substantially to lessen competition" is not

Although Congress was apparently unaware of allocative efficiency when it enacted section 7 and the other antitrust laws,[12] preserving allocative efficiency is generally considered an additional benefit realized by the prevention of market power, because the act of restricting output has the concomitant effect of raising prices to consumers.[13]

---

saved because, on some ultimate reckoning of social or economic debits and credits, it may be deemed beneficial. A value choice of such magnitude is beyond the ordinary limits of judicial competence, and in any event has been made for us already, by Congress when it enacted the amended § 7. Congress determined to preserve our traditionally competitive economy. It therefore proscribed anticompetitive mergers, the benign and the malignant alike, fully aware, we must assume, that some price might have to be paid."

12. Perfect "allocative efficiency" or "pareto optimality" is a state of equilibrium on the "utility-possibility frontier" in which no person can be made better off without making someone else worse off. Allocative efficiency can be achieved in an economy with massive inequalities of income and distribution, e.g., one percent of the population can receive ninety-nine percent of the economy's wealth and ninety-nine percent of the population can receive one percent. A massive transfer of wealth from consumers to a monopolist does not of itself decrease allocative efficiency. However, when a monopolist restricts its output, the total wealth of society is diminished, thereby reducing allocative efficiency. Economists term this loss of society's wealth the "deadweight loss." The term of art "consumer welfare," often used when discussing the efficiency effects of mergers and restraints of trade, refers to the concept of allocative efficiency, not the welfare of consumers who purchase the monopolist's product. Consumer welfare is diminished when a monopolist restricts output.

13. In most mergers creating market power, the dollar magnitude of the wealth transfer from consumers would be greater than the monetary measure of loss in allocative efficiency (dead weight loss). *See* note 12. It is, moreover, important to understand that a transfer of wealth from consumers to firms with market power can decrease the well-being of consumers without any decrease in so-called "consumer welfare."

2.1 The Economic Effects of Mergers

Mergers may have negative or positive competitive consequences. The following is a summary description of the most common competitive effects of mergers relevant to enforcement of section 7.

2.11 Acquisition of Market Power and Wealth Transfers

When two firms, neither possessing market power, cease competing and merge, the inevitable consequence is the elimination of the competition between them. More significantly, however, the merged entity may now possess market power, an anticompetitive outcome.

A merger may also increase the concentration level in an industry to a point at which the remaining firms can effectively engage in active collusion or implicitly coordinate their actions and thus collectively exercise market power.

When a firm or firms exercise market power by profitably maintaining prices above competitive levels for a significant period of time, a transfer of wealth from consumers to those firms occurs.[14] This transfer of wealth is the major evil sought to be addressed by section 7.[15]

The wealth transfer orientation of section 7 is the same as that of the Sherman Act. The major difference between the two provisions, and reason for the enactment of section 7, is the "incipiency" standard of section 7, which permits antitrust intervention at a point when the anticompetitive consequences of a merger are not manifest but are likely

---

14. Tacit or active collusion on terms of trade other than price also produces wealth transfer effects. This would include, for example, an agreement to eliminate rivalry on service features or to limit the choices otherwise available to consumers.

15. The predominant concern with wealth transfers was evidenced in the statements of both supporters and opponents of the Celler-Kefauver amendments. *See, e.g.,* 95 Cong. Rec. 11,506 (1949) (remarks of Rep. Bennett); Id. at 11,492 (remarks of Rep. Carroll); Id. at 11,506 (remarks of Rep. Byrne); Hearings before the Subcom. on the Judiciary, 81st Cong., lst and 2d Sess., note 260 at 180 (remarks of Sen. Kilgore); 95 Cong. Rec. 11,493 (1949) (remarks of Rep. Yates); Id. at 11,490-91 (remarks of Rep. Goodwin); 95 Cong. Rec. 16,490 (1949) (colloquy of Sen. Kefauver and Sen. Wiley).

to occur absent intervention. The Celler-Kefauver amendments retained and strengthened the "incipiency" standard by extending the coverage of the law to acquisitions of assets. In section 4 of these guidelines the Attorneys General specifically attempt to give expression to the statutory concern of "incipiency."

2.12 Productive Efficiency

A merger may increase or decrease the costs of the parties to the merger and thus increase or decrease productive efficiency. A merger which increases productive efficiency and does not produce a firm or firms capable of exercising market power should lower prices paid by consumers. An inefficient merger in an unconcentrated industry is generally of no competitive concern. The efficiency effects of mergers are easy to speculate about but hard to accurately predict. There is much disagreement among economists as to whether merged firms usually perform well and whether, on average, mergers have been shown to produce significant efficiencies. However, most efficiencies and those most quantitatively significant will be realized in mergers involving small firms. Such mergers do not raise any concern under the enforcement standards adopted in section 4 of these guidelines. Furthermore, the concentration thresholds adopted in section 4 are usually sufficient to enable firms to obtain the most significant efficiencies likely to result from growth through merger as opposed to growth through internal expansion.[16]

2.13 Allocative Efficiency

A merger which facilitates the exercise of market power results in a decrease in allocative efficiency. When firms with market power restrict their output, the total wealth of society diminishes. This effect is universally condemned by economists, and its prevention, while not a concern of the Congress which enacted section 7, is a goal consistent with the purposes of the antitrust laws.

---

16. There may be rare instances where the minimum efficient scale of production and output constitutes a significant percentage of the relevant market.

2.14 Raising Rivals' Costs

In certain circumstances, a merger may raise the costs of the competitors of the parties to the merger. For example, a merger could increase the power of a firm to affect the price that rivals must pay for inputs or the conditions under which they must operate, in a manner that creates a relative disadvantage for the rivals. If the market structure is such that these increased costs can be passed on to consumers, then the prevention of this effect is consistent with the goals of the antitrust laws. Preventing such effect will also prevent a decrease in allocative and productive efficiency.

3. Market Definition

These guidelines are concerned with horizontal mergers, that is, mergers involving firms that are actual or potential competitors in the same product and geographic markets. The primary analytical tool utilized in the guidelines is the measurement of concentration in a particular market and increase in concentration in that market resulting from a merger. The market shares used to compute these concentration factors will depend upon the market definition adopted.[17] The reasonable delineation of these market boundaries is critical to realizing the objectives of the guidelines and the antitrust laws. If the market boundaries chosen are seriously distorted in relation to the actual workings of the marketplace, an enforcement error is likely.[18] An overly

---

17. For example, consider the proposed merger of two firms producing the same product. Each has a fifty percent share of the sales of this product in a certain state but only one percent of national sales. If the proper geographic market is the state, then the competitive consequences of the merger will be far different than if the geographic market is the entire country.
18. Governmental challenge of a merger which is not likely to lessen competition substantially is frequently termed "Type I error." The failure to challenge a merger which is likely to lessen competition substantially is termed "Type II error." Type I error can be corrected by the court which determines the validity of the challenge. Type II error will most likely go uncorrected, since the vast majority of merger challenges are mounted by the government. In other areas of antitrust law, private

restricted product or geographic market definition may trigger antitrust intervention when the merger would not significantly harm competition or in other circumstances result in the failure to challenge an anticompetitive merger. An overly expansive market definition, on the other hand, may result in the failure to challenge a merger with serious anticompetitive consequences.[19] Markets should be defined from the perspective of those interests section 7 was primarily enacted to protect, i.e., the classes of consumers (or suppliers) who may be adversely affected by an anticompetitive merger. The Attorneys General will utilize historical data to identify these classes of consumers ("the protected interest group"), their sources of supply, suitable substitutes for the product and alternative sources of the product and its substitutes. The market thus defined will be presumed correct unless rebutted by empirical evidence that supply responses within a reasonable period of time will render unprofitable an attempted exercise of market power.[20]

---

actions predominate and can correct Type II error. Consumers, whose interests were paramount in the enactment of section 7 and section 1 of the Sherman Act, suffer the damage of Type II error.

19. Consider, for example, the market(s) for flexible wrapping materials. These materials include clear plastic, metallic foils, waxed paper and others. Firms A and B each produce thirty percent of the clear plastic wrap and five percent of all flexible wrapping material in a relevant geographic market. Firm C produces seventy percent of the metallic foil and sixty percent of all flexible wrap. If the proper market definition is all flexible wrapping materials, then treating clear plastic and metallic foils as separate markets may lead to an unwarranted challenge to a merger between firms A and B. The same incorrect market definition may also result in the failure to challenge a merger between Firm C and either Firm A or Firm B because of the incorrect assumption that metallic foil and clear plastic wrap do not compete. However, if the correct market definition is clear plastic wrap but the more expansive market definition of all flexible materials is chosen, this may result in the failure to challenge an anticompetitive merger of firms A and B.

20. Empirical evidence, as contrasted with expert opinion, speculation, or economic theories, is generally grounded in demonstrable, historical fact. Empirical evidence of a probable supply response would include a factual showing that this response had occurred in the past when prices increased significantly. A mere prediction based on a theoretical possibility that a manufacturer would or could shift his production from one product to

The following sections detail how these general principles will be applied to define product and geographic markets and to calculate the market shares of firms determined to be within the relevant market.

3.1 Product Market Definition

The Attorneys General will determine the customers who purchase the products or services ("products") of the merging firms. Each product produced in common by the merging parties will constitute a provisional product market. However, if a market is incorrectly defined too narrowly, the merger may appear to be not horizontal when there may be a horizontal anticompetitive effect in a broader market.[21] In short, the provisional product market will be expanded to include suitable substitutes for the product which are comparably priced.[22] A comparably

---

another to capitalize on a price increase, when unsupported by evidence of previous similar responses or other factual information of comparable probative weight, is not considered "empirical evidence."

21. For example, suppose there are two beer producers and two malt liquor producers and the merger involves the acquisition of one of the malt liquor firms by one of the beer producers. If the relevant market is defined as "beer," the merger would not be horizontal. The provisional market should be defined as beverages containing X percent alcohol.

22. The existence of a functionally suitable substitute which is significantly more expensive than the relevant product will not discipline an exercise of market power until the price of the relevant product has been raised to a level comparable to the substitute. The Attorneys General will also seek to ascertain whether current price comparability of two products resulted from an exercise of market power. For example, suppose that the provisionally defined product recently cost twenty percent less than a possible substitute, but its price has recently risen twenty percent as a result of the exercise of market power. Rather than serving as a basis for broadening the product market to include the possible substitute, this finding will provide compelling evidence that any further concentration through merger will only exacerbate the market power which already exists. To ascertain whether the price comparability of two possibly interchangeable products was the result of an exercise of market power over one product, the appropriate question to ask may be "what would happen if the price of the product in question dropped?" If a significant price decrease does not substantially increase sales, then a previous

priced substitute will be deemed suitable and thereby expand the product market definition if, and only if, considered suitable by customers accounting for seventy-five percent of the purchases.

Actual substitution by customers in the past will presumptively establish that a product is considered a suitable substitute for the provisionally defined product. However, other evidence offered by the parties probative of the assertion that customers deem a product to be a suitable substitute will also be considered.[23]

3.11 Consumers Who May Be Vulnerable to Price Discrimination

Notwithstanding the determination in Section 3.1 that a product is a suitable substitute for the provisional product pursuant to application of the seventy-five percent rule, there may be small, but significant, groups of consumers who cannot substitute or can do so only with great difficulty. These consumers may be subject to price discrimination and thus may be particularly adversely affected by a merger. In addition, some markets may contain differentiated products which are not perfect substitutes for one another but are not sufficiently differentiated to warrant separate markets. If the products of the merging firms are closer substitutes, i.e., the more the buyers of one product consider the other product to be their next choice, the consumers of these products may be more subject to an exercise of market power. Similarly, the existence of distinct prices, unique production facilities, a product's peculiar characteristics and uses, distinct customers, and specialized vendors may support the definition of narrower product markets.[24]

Evidence of the commercial reality of such a market includes price discrimination, inelasticity of demand and industry or public recognition of a distinct market.

3.2 Geographic Market Definition

---

exercise of market power has likely been detected, and the two products should probably be considered to be in separate product markets. *See* United States v. E.I. duPont de Nemours & Co., 351 U.S. 377, 399-400 (1956).

23. Recycled or reconditioned goods will be considered suitable substitutes if they meet the requirements of this section.

24. *See* Brown Shoe Co. v. United States, 370 U.S. 294, 325 (1962).

Utilizing the product market(s) defined in Section 3.1, the Attorneys General will define the relevant geographic market. First, the Attorneys General will determine the sources and locations where the customers of the merging parties readily turn for their supply of the relevant product. These will include the merging parties and other sources of supply. To this group of suppliers and their locations will be added suppliers or buyers closely proximate to the customers of the merging parties. In determining those suppliers to whom the protected interest group readily turn for supply of the relevant product, the Attorneys General will include all sources of supply within the past two years still present in the market.

Utilizing the locations from which supplies of the relevant product are obtained by members of the protected interest group, the geographic market will be defined as the area encompassing the production locations from which this group purchases seventy-five percent of their supplies of the relevant product.

The product and geographic markets as defined above will be utilized in calculating market shares and concentration levels unless additional sources of supply are recognized by application of the procedures specified in Section 3.3.

3.21 Geographic Markets Subject to Price Discrimination

The Attorneys General may define additional narrower geographic markets when there is strong evidence that sellers are able to discriminate among buyers in separate locations within the geographic market(s) defined in Section 3.2. The Attorneys General will evaluate evidence concerning discrimination on price, terms of credit and delivery, and priority of shipment.[25]

3.3 Principles for Recognizing Potential Competition

Where there is relevant empirical evidence of profitable supply and demand responses which will be likely to occur within one year of any

---

25. The Attorneys General welcome submissions by buyers concerning such discrimination or any other non-speculative evidence that a proposed merger will adversely affect them.

attempted exercise of market power, the Attorneys General will calculate market shares and concentration levels, incorporating both sources of potential supply and the firms identified as being in the market defined by the procedures outlined in Sections 3.1 and 3.11.

The Attorneys General will evaluate empirical evidence of the following sources of potential competition:

1) That current suppliers of the product will produce additional supplies for the relevant market by utilizing excess capacity;

2) That new sources of the product will be readily available from firms outside the geographic market with excess capacity.

3.31 Expansion of Output

The Attorneys General will identify current suppliers of the product that will expand their output by utilization of excess capacity within one year of any attempted exercise of market power. Proof of probable utilization of excess capacity addresses the issues of: (i) The cost of bringing the excess capacity on line; (ii) the amount of excess capacity; (iii) prior history of supplying this market or present intention to do so; and (iv) how much prices would have to rise to likely induce this supply response.

3.32 New Sources of Additional Supply

The Attorneys General will identify firms not currently supplying the product in the geographic market but which will expand their output by utilization of excess capacity within one year of any attempted exercise of market power. Proof of probable utilization of excess capacity addresses the issues of: (i) The cost of bringing the excess capacity on line; (ii) the amount of excess capacity; (iii) prior history of supplying this market or present intention to do so; and (iv) how much prices would have to rise to likely induce this supply response.

3.4 Calculating Market Shares

Using the product and geographic markets defined in Sections 3.1 and 3.2, the firms supplying the market and any additional sources of supply recognized under Section 3.3, the shares of all firms determined to be in the market will be calculated.[26]

The market shares of firms presently supplying the market shall be based upon actual data from the relevant market. If there has been a demonstration of a probable supply response as defined in Section 3.3, the market shares of firms already selling in the market will be adjusted to account for the proven probable supply response. Similarly, market shares will be assigned to firms not currently supplying the market who have been shown to be likely to expand output to provide additional sources of supply as discussed in Sections 3.32 and 3.33. The assigned market shares of such firms will be based upon the amount of the product these firms would supply. The Attorneys General will utilize dollar sales, unit sales, capacity measures or other appropriate sales measurements to quantify actual market activity.

3.41 Foreign Firms

Foreign firms presently supplying the relevant market will be assigned market shares in the same manner as domestic firms, according to their actual current sales in the relevant market. Foreign firms and their productive capacity are inherently a less reliable check on market power by domestic firms because foreign firms face a variety of barriers to continuing sales or increasing their sales. These barriers include import quotas, voluntary quantitative restrictions, tariffs and fluctuations in exchange rates. When such barriers exist, market share based upon historical sales data will be reduced appropriately.

A single market share will be assigned to the firms of any foreign country or group of countries which in fact coordinate their sales.[27]

---

26. In some situations, market share and market concentration data may either understate or overstate the likely future competitive significance of a firm or firms in the market or the impact of a merger. The Attorneys General will consider empirical evidence of recent or ongoing changes in market conditions or in a particular firm and may make appropriate adjustments to the market concentration and market share data. *See* United States v. General Dynamics Corp., 415 U.S. 486 (1974).

27. For example, an import quota may be established for a particular foreign country and the foreign government may then apportion the quota among firms engaged in the import of the relevant product.

3.411 Alternative Method for Defining Markets Utilizing the Methodology of the United States Department of Justice/Federal Trade Commission Merger Guidelines

Any party presenting a position concerning the likely competitive consequences of a merger to one or more Attorneys General may present its position and analysis using the market definition principles and methodology set forth in the Merger Guidelines of the United States Department of Justice and the Federal Trade Commission, released on April 2, 1992 (DOJ/FTC Guidelines), 62 Antitrust & Trade Reg. Rep. Special Supp. (April 2, 1992). This method will only be considered where, in the opinion of the state Attorney General, sufficient evidence is available to implement the methodology workably and without speculation. In most situations, both the NAAG and DOJ/FTC market definition methodologies will produce the same result. In the event that the two tests produce different results, the Attorneys General will rely on the test that appears most accurately to reflect the market and is based on the most reliable evidence.

There are two purposes for permitting such alternative method for defining markets. First, many of the mergers which the Attorneys General may analyze using these guidelines will also be subject to scrutiny by either the Antitrust Division of the United States Department of Justice or the Federal Trade Commission. Parties may desire to present positions concerning the likely competitive consequences of a particular transaction to both federal and state antitrust enforcement agencies. Such parties will benefit from the ability to utilize a single market definition methodology in presenting their position concerning a particular transaction. Second, the Attorneys General seek to facilitate the joint or coordinated analysis of mergers by state and federal enforcement agencies.

Consistent with these principles, the Attorneys General may utilize the market definition methodology set forth in the DOJ/FTC Guidelines as an additional or alternative method in analyzing the competitive consequences of particular transactions.

4. Measurement of Concentration

The primary tool utilized by the Attorneys General to determine whether a specific horizontal merger is likely to substantially harm competition is a measurement of the level of concentration in each market defined in Section 3 or 3A. Concentration is a measurement of the number of firms in a market and their market shares. The guidelines employ the Herfindahl Hirschman Index ("HHI") to calculate the level of concentration in an industry before and after a merger and, therefore, the increase in concentration which would result from the merger.[28]

Unlike the traditional four firm concentration ratio ("CR.") which was formerly used by enforcement agencies and courts to measure market concentration,[29] the HHI reflects both the distribution of the market shares of all the leading firms in the market and the composition of the market beyond the leading firms.[30]

The predominant concern of the Congress in enacting section 7 was the prevention of high levels of industrial concentration because it

---

28. The HHI is computed by summing the numerical squares of the market shares of all the firms in the market. For example, a market with four firms each having a market share of 25% has an HHI of 2500 calculated as follows: $25^2 + 25^2 + 25^2 + 25^2 = 2500$. A market with a pure monopolist, i.e., a firm with 100 percent of the market has an HHI of 10,000 calculated as $100^2 = 10{,}000$. If the market has four firms, each having a market share of twenty-five percent and two of these four firms merge, the increase in the HHI is computed as follows: Pre-merger $25^2 + 25^2 + 25^2 + 25^2 = 2500$. Post-merger $50^2 + 25^2 + 25^2 = 3750$. The increase in the HHI due to the merger is 1250, i.e., 3750 - 2500 = 1250. The increase is also equivalent to twice the product of the market shares of the merging firms, i.e., 25 x 25 x 2 = 1250.

29. The CR. is the sum of the market shares of the top four firms in the market. A CR. cannot be converted into any single HHI but rather includes a possible range of HHI levels. For example, consider two markets with CR. of 100 percent. The first is comprised of four firms; each with a market share of twenty-five percent. This yields an HHI of 2500, i.e., $25^2 + 25^2 + 25^2 + 25^2 = 2500$. The second market is comprised of four firms with market shares of 70%, 10%, 10% and 10%. This yields an HHI of 5200, i.e., $70^2 + 10^2 + 10^2 + 10^2 = 5200$.

30. The HHI also gives significantly greater weight to the market shares of the largest firms, which properly reflects the leading roles which such firms are likely to play in a collusive agreement or other exercise of market power. A single dominant firm's likely role as the price leader in an oligopolistic market is also reflected in the HHI. For these reasons, the HHI is now the generally preferred measure of concentration.

believed that such structure was likely to produce anticompetitive consequences. Foremost among these expected anticompetitive effects of high concentration is the exercise of market power by one or more firms. The HHI levels which trigger presumptions that mergers are likely to create or enhance market power should be set at the concentration levels likely to predict a substantial lessening of competition.[31]

Furthermore, an important component of the scholarly economic inquiry into the competitive consequences of mergers has been the correlation of concentration levels with various indicia of competition. Other theories which predict the competitive effects of mergers based upon factors other than market concentration are valuable adjuncts to market concentration analysis. The most important of the supplemental inquiries concerns "ease of entry" into the markets affected by the merger.[32]

The Attorneys General divide the spectrum of market concentration into the same three numerical regions utilized by the United States Department of Justice. They are characterized in these guidelines as "unconcentrated" (HHI below 1000) "moderately concentrated" (HHI between 1000 and 1800) and "highly concentrated" (HHI above 1800).[33]

4.1 General Standards

The Attorneys General will calculate the post-merger concentration level in the market and the increase in concentration caused by the merger.

While it may be justifiable to challenge any merger above the threshold of market concentration where successful tacit or express collusion and interdependent behavior are significantly facilitated (HHI 1000) the Attorneys General are unlikely to challenge mergers which do not significantly increase concentration. This policy recognizes section 7's prohibition of mergers whose effect "may be substantially to lessen competition." When the threshold of very high concentration is exceeded

---

31. Other characteristics of the particular industry, such as barriers to entry, may indicate that concentration measures either overstate or understate the competitive significance of the merger.

32. *See* Section 5.

33. Mergers resulting in a post-merger HHI of less than 1,000 do not create a presumption that the merger will have significant anticompetitive impact.

(HHI 1800), the likelihood of anticompetitive effects are greatly increased and the increase in concentration likely to substantially lessen competition concomitantly reduced. The concentration increases which trigger presumptions that mergers are likely to create or enhance market power have been adopted in reasonable accommodation of both the "substantiality" requirement of section 7 and the need objectively to factor in the dynamic conditions in an industry.[34]

4.2 Post-Merger HHI Between 1000 and 1800

A merger that increases the HHI by more than 100 to a level in excess of 1,000 creates a presumption that the merger will result in significant anticompetitive effects. This presumption may be overcome if the merging parties are able to demonstrate, upon consideration of all of the other factors contained in these guidelines, that the merger is not likely significantly to lessen competition. The greater the HHI increase and level, the less likely that these factors will overcome this presumption.

4.3 Post-Merger HHI Above 1800

A merger that increases the HHI by more than fifty to a level in excess of 1,800 creates a presumption that the merger will result in significant anticompetitive effects. This presumption may be overcome if the merging parties are able to demonstrate, upon consideration of all of the other factors contained in these guidelines, that the merger is not likely significantly to lessen competition. The greater the HHI increase

---

34. The decision whether or not to bring suit is ultimately within the sole discretion of each Attorney General. In addition to the economic impact of a merger on a state, Attorneys General may consider numerous other factors in deciding whether to challenge a merger that raises competitive concerns. For example, Attorneys General are more likely to be concerned about mergers in industries exhibiting a significant trend towards concentration. The existence of an in-depth examination of the merger by other antitrust enforcement agencies may be relevant to the action of an Attorney General with respect to a merger that otherwise raises competitive concerns.

and level, the less likely that these factors will overcome this presumption.[35]

4.4 Mergers Involving the Leading Firm or a New, Innovative Firm in a Market

The merger of a dominant firm with a small firm in the market may create or increase the market power of the dominant firm yet increase the HHI by an amount less than the levels set forth in Sections 4.2 and 4.3. Similarly, the merger of a new, innovative firm with an existing significant competitor in the market may substantially reduce competition yet increase the HHI by an amount less than the levels set forth in Sections 4.2 and 4.3. Therefore, mergers presumptively create or enhance market power if the proposed merger involves either a leading firm with a market share of at least thirty-five percent and a firm with a market share of one percent or more, or a firm with a market share of twenty percent or more and a new, innovative firm in a market or attempting to enter a market that is moderately or highly concentrated, unless assessment of the factors discussed in Sections 5.1 and/or 5.3 clearly compels the conclusion that the merger is not likely substantially to lessen competition.

5. Additional Factors That May Be Considered In Determining Whether to Challenge a Merger

There are additional factors aside from market share and market concentration that may make a merger more or less likely substantially to lessen competition. While the assessment of these factors would increase the flexibility of these guidelines, overemphasis on these other factors, given the current state of economic knowledge, would significantly vitiate the predictability and the consistency of enforcement under the guidelines and would greatly reduce their value as a planning and risk assessment tool for the business community.

The present state of economic theory, especially where there is an absence of supporting empirical work, is generally insufficient to

---

35. For example, this presumption will be rarely overcome if the increase exceeds 200 and the resulting HHI level exceeds 2,500.

overcome the usual presumption that increases in market concentration will increase the likelihood and degree to which industry performance is adversely affected. Increased concentration may allow the industry's constituent firms to coordinate pricing in a variety of ways, to neutralize the potential benefits of increased efficiency through output reduction and to forestall entry.

For example, many theories have been offered regarding the extent to which a particular factor may tend to increase or decrease the likelihood of collusion. In an actual merger analysis, however, a relevant market is likely to be characterized by several of these factors pointing in opposite directions, and economics offers little guidance on how the individual factors should be judged in combination. Even the significance of isolated factors remains in doubt. Many states have discovered bid-rigging among highway contractors, for example, when the characteristics of the industry might lead some to predict theoretically that collusion would be extremely difficult, if not impossible.

Because of this, the merging parties will bear a heavy burden of showing that the normal presumption of anticompetitive effect should not be applied in a particular case. This heavy burden will increase further with higher levels of concentration and increases in concentration, particularly to the extent the post-merger HHI would be greater than 1800 and the increase in HHI greater than 50.

While maintaining primary reliance on the concentration and market share analysis discussed in Section 4, the Attorneys General will, in appropriate circumstances, assess four additional factors. These are ease of entry, collusive behavior, powerful or sophisticated buyers and efficiencies.

5.1 Ease of Entry

5.11 Overview

A merger is not likely to create or enhance market power or to facilitate its exercise if entry into the market is so easy that market participants, after the merger, either collectively or unilaterally could not profitably maintain a price increase above premerger levels. Such entry likely will deter an anticompetitive merger in its incipiency, or deter or counteract the competitive effects of concern.

Entry is that easy if entry would be timely, likely and sufficient in its magnitude, character and scope to deter or counteract the competitive effects of concern. In markets where entry is that easy (i.e., where entry passes these tests of timeliness, likelihood, and sufficiency), the merger raises no antitrust concern and ordinary requires no further analysis.

The entry treated in this section is defined as new competition that requires expenditure of significant sunk costs of entry and exit ("committed entry"). The Attorneys General will employ a three-step methodology to assess whether committed entry would deter or counteract a competitive effect of concern.

This first step assesses whether entry can achieve significant market impact within a timely period. If significant market impact would require a longer period, entry will not deter or counteract the competitive effect of concern.

The second step assesses whether committed entry would be a profitable and, hence, a likely response to a merger having competitive effects of concern. Firms considering entry that requires significant sunk costs must evaluate that profitability of the entry on the basis of long-term participation in the market, because the underlying assets will be committed to the market until they are economically depreciated. Entry that is sufficient to counteract the competitive effects of concern will cause prices to fall to their premerger levels or lower. Thus, the profitability of such committed entry must be determined on the basis of pre-merger market prices over the long term.

A merger having anticompetitive effects can attract committed entry, profitable at premerger prices, that would not have occurred premerger at these same prices. But following the merger, the reduction in industry output and increase in prices associated with the competitive effect of concern may allow the same entry to occur without driving market prices below premerger levels. After a merger that results in decreased output and increased prices, the likely sales opportunities available to entrants at premerger prices will be larger than they were premerger, larger by the output reduction caused by the merger. If entry could be profitable at premerger prices without exceeding the likely sales opportunities—opportunities that include pre-existing pertinent factors as well as the merger-induced output reduction—then such entry is likely in response to the merger.

The third step assesses whether timely and likely entry would be sufficient to return market prices to their premerger levels. This end may be accomplished either through multiple entry or individual entry at a sufficient scale. Entry may not be sufficient, even though timely and likely, where the constraints on availability of essential assets, due to incumbent control, make it impossible for entry profitably to achieve the necessary level of sales. Also, the character and scope of entrants' products might not be fully responsive to the localized sales opportunities created by the removal of direct competition among sellers of differentiated products. In assessing whether entry will be timely, likely, and sufficient, the Attorneys General recognize that precise and detailed information may be difficult or impossible to obtain. In such instances, the Attorneys General will rely on all available evidence bearing on whether entry will satisfy the conditions of timeliness, likelihood, and sufficiency.

5.12 Timeliness of Entry

In order to deter or counteract the competitive effects of concern, entrants quickly must achieve a significant impact on price in the relevant market. The Attorneys General generally will consider timely only those committed entry alternatives that can be achieved within two years from initial planning to significant market impact.[36] Where the relevant product is a durable good, consumers, in response to a significant commitment to entry, may defer purchases by making additional investments to extend the useful life of previously purchased goods and in this way deter or counteract for a time the competitive effects of concern. In these circumstances, if entry only can occur outside of the two year period, the Attorneys General will consider entry to be timely so long as it would deter or counteract the competitive effects of concern within the two year period and subsequently.

5.13 Likelihood of Entry

---

36. Firms which have committed to entering the market prior to the merger generally will be included in the measurement of the market. Only committed entry or adjustments to pre-existing entry plans that are induced by the merger will be considered as possibly deterring or counteracting the competitive effects of concern.

An entry alternative is likely if it would be profitable at premerger prices, and if such prices could be secured by the entrant.[37] The committed entrant will be unable to secure prices at premerger levels if its output is too large for the market to absorb without depressing prices further. Thus, entry is unlikely if the minimum viable scale is larger than the likely sales opportunity available to entrants.

Minimum viable scale is the smallest average annual level of sales that the committed entrant must persistently achieve for profitability at premerger prices.[38] Minimum viable scale is a function of expected revenues, based upon premerger prices,[39] and all categories of costs associated with the entry alternative, including an appropriate rate of return on invested capital given that entry could fail and sunk costs, if any, will be lost.[40]

Sources of sales opportunities available to entrants include: (a) The output reduction associated with the competitive effect of concern;[41] (b) entrants' ability to capture a share of reasonably expected growth in market demand;[42] (c) entrants' ability securely to divert sales from

---

37. Where conditions indicate that entry may be profitable at prices below premerger levels, the Attorneys General will assess the likelihood of entry at the lowest price at which such entry would be profitable.
38. The concept of minimum viable scale ("MVS") differs from the concept of minimum efficient scale ("MES"). While MES is the smallest scale at which average costs are minimized, MVS is the smallest scale at which average costs equal the premerger price.
39. The expected path of future prices, absent the merger, may be used if future price changes can be predicted with reasonable reliability.
40. The minimum viable scale of an entry alternative will be relatively large when the fixed costs of entry are large, when the fixed costs of entry are largely sunk, when the marginal costs of production are high at low levels of output, and when a plant is underutilized for a long time because of delays in achieving market acceptance.
41. Five percent of total market sales typically is used because where a monopolist profitability would raise price by five percent or more across the entire relevant market, it is likely that the accompanying reduction in sales would be no less than five percent.
42. Entrant's anticipated share of growth in demand depends on incumbents' capacity constraints and irreversible investments in capacity expansion, as well as on the relative appeal, acceptability and reputation of incumbents' and entrants' products to the new demand.

incumbents, for example, through vertical integration or through forward contracting; and (d) any additional anticipated contraction in incumbents' output in response to entry.[43] Factors that reduce the sales opportunities available to entrants include: (a) The prospect that an entrant will share in a reasonably expected decline in market demand; (b) the exclusion of an entrant from a portion of the market over the long term because of vertical integration or forward contracting by incumbents; and (c) any anticipated strategic reaction, including but not limited to, sales expansion by incumbents in reaction to entry, either generalized or targeted at customers approached by the entrant, that utilized prior irreversible investments in excess production capacity. Demand growth or decline will be viewed as relevant only if total market demand is projected to experience long-lasting change during at least the two year period following the competitive effect of concern.

5.14 Sufficiency of Entry

Inasmuch as multiple entry generally is possible and individual entrants may flexibly choose their scale, committed entry generally will be sufficient to deter or counteract the competitive effects of concern whenever entry is likely under the analysis of Section 5.1. However, entry, although likely, will not be sufficient if, as a result of incumbent control, the tangible and intangible assets required for entry are not adequately available for entrants to respond fully to their sales opportunities. In addition, where the competitive effect of concern is not uniform across the relevant market, in order for entry to be sufficient, the character and scope of entrants' products must be responsive to the localized sales opportunities that include the output reduction associated with the competitive effect of concern. For example, where the concern is unilateral price elevation as a result of a merger between producers of differentiated products, entry, in order to be sufficient, must involve a product so close to the products of the merging firms that the merged firm will be unable to internalize enough of the sales loss due to the price rise, rendering the price increase unprofitable.

---

43. For example, in a bidding market where all bidders are on equal footing, the market share of incumbents will contract as a result of entry.

5.15 Entry Alternatives

The Attorneys General will examine the timeliness, likelihood, and sufficiency of the means of entry (entry alternatives) a potential entrant might practically employ, without attempting to identify who might be potential entrants. An entry alternative is defined by the actions the firm must take in order to produce and sell in the market. All phases of the entry effort will be considered, including, where relevant, planning, design, and management; permitting, licensing, and other approvals, construction, debugging, and operation of production facilities; and promotion (including necessary introductory discounts), marketing, distribution and satisfaction of customer testing and qualification requirements.[44] Recent examples of entry, whether successful or unsuccessful, may provide a useful starting point for identifying the necessary actions, time requirements, and characteristics of possible entry alternatives. Entry may be by diversion of existing supplies into the market or by new production sources of supply. The Attorneys General will evaluate empirical evidence of the following sources of entry.

5.151 Diversion of Existing Supplies into the Market

The parties to a merger may produce evidence that firms will divert supplies of the product into the market in response to a price increase or restriction of output. The Attorneys General will analyze proof concerning such probable diversions of supplies currently exported from the relevant market, supplies internally consumed by vertically integrated firms in the market and additional supplies from firms currently shipping part of their production into the market.

5.151(1) EXPORTS

A firm currently exporting the product from the relevant market may divert the supply back into the market in response to a price increase or restriction of output.

This response is unlikely from an exporter who is a party to the merger, since it is unlikely to discipline its own attempted exercise of

44. Many of these phases may be undertaken simultaneously.

market power. It is also unlikely if the exporter is an oligopolist likely to benefit from the collective exercise of market power.

Although parties wishing to prove this supply response are free to produce any empirical evidence, the most persuasive proof will be historical shipping patterns showing past diversion of exports in response to price increases or restricted supply. In addition, the parties should, at a minimum, address the following questions: Are the exports contractually committed and for what term? Are the exports otherwise obligated to current buyers?

5.151(2) INTERNAL CONSUMPTION

A vertically integrated firm producing the product for internal consumption may divert this supply to the open market. Diversion is unlikely if there are no suitable and economical substitutes for the product and/or the firm has contractual or other obligations for the goods utilizing the relevant product. The most persuasive proof of such diversion will be evidence that a vertically integrated firm already sells some of the product on the open market and has a history of transferring production intended for internal consumption to the open market.

5.151(3) INCREASED IMPORTATION

A firm shipping part of its output of the product into the relevant market may respond to an attempted exercise of market power by diverting additional production into the relevant market. In order to address the impact of such a response, the parties should, at a minimum, address the factual issues of whether and for what terms these additional supplies are contractually or otherwise obligated to buyers outside the relevant market, the percentage of the suppliers' production now sent into the market and their historical shipping patterns.

5.152 New Production Sources of Additional Supply

The parties to a merger may produce evidence that firms not currently supplying the product will do so within two years of any attempted exercise of market power. This might be shown for firms with production flexibility, firms who will erect new production facilities and firms engaging in arbitrage.

5.152(1) PRODUCTION FLEXIBILITY

The Attorneys General will evaluate proof concerning firms with flexible production facilities who are capable of switching to the production of the relevant product within two years and are likely to do so. A history of such switching in the past will be the most persuasive evidence that this response is probable.

5.152(2) CONSTRUCTION OF NEW FACILITIES

A party may attempt to demonstrate that firms not presently supplying the product will erect new plant facilities (or establish new service facilities) within two years of an attempted exercise of market power.

5.152(3) ARBITRAGE

Firms proximate to the relevant market may respond to an exercise of market power by buying the product outside the market and reselling it inside the market. This potential source of supply is unlikely if the relevant product is a service or combined product and service. A history of arbitrage in the industry will be most probative that this potential response is probable.

5.2 Collusion and Oligopolistic Behavior

If there is evidence of past collusion or anticompetitive behavior,[45] the presumptions set forth in Section 4 will rarely be overcome and a proposed merger falling below the numerical thresholds set forth in Section 4 may also be examined more closely where such evidence is present. In the face of indications that collusion or oligopolistic behavior is likely to be presently occurring, the Attorneys General will not

45. An oligopolistic market will usually be moderately to highly concentrated or very highly concentrated and will exhibit one or more of the following practices: (1) Price leadership; (2) preannounced price changes; (3) relative price rigidity in response to excess capacity or diminished demand; (4) public pronouncements regarding price; and (5) price discrimination.

consider other factors offered for the purpose of showing that the presumptions in Section 4 are overcome.

The absence of current or past collusion or oligopolistic behavior will not diminish the presumptions set forth in Section 4.

5.3 Efficiencies

To the extent that efficiency was a concern of the Congress in enacting section 7, that concern was expressed in the legislative finding that less industrial concentration would further that goal.[46] The Attorneys General find that there is no substantial empirical support for the assertion that mergers involving firms of sufficient size to raise concerns under the standards set forth in Section 4, usually or on average result in substantial efficiencies. Furthermore, the concentration thresholds adopted in Section 4 are generally high enough to enable firms to obtain the most significant efficiencies likely to result from growth through merger.

Even in those rare situations where significant efficiencies can be demonstrated, rather than merely predicted, this showing cannot constitute a defense to an otherwise unlawful merger.[47] Accordingly, efficiencies will only be considered when the merging parties can demonstrate by clear and convincing evidence that the merger will lead to significant efficiencies. Moreover, the merging parties must demonstrate that the efficiencies will ensure that consumer prices will not increase despite any increase in market power due to the merger. In highly concentrated markets, even a merger which produces efficiencies will tend to create or enhance market power and will likely increase consumer prices. In addition, the Attorneys General will reject claims of efficiencies unless the merging parties can demonstrate that equivalent or comparable savings can not be achieved through other means and that such cost savings will persist over the long

---

46. For example, see 95 Cong. Rec. 11,487 (1949) (statement of Rep. Celler, co-author of legislation). "Bigness does not mean efficiency, a better product, or lower prices." 95 Cong. Rec. 11,495-98 (1949) (statement of Rep. Boggs); Corporate Mergers and Acquisitions: Hearings on H.R. 2734 before a Subcomm. of the Senate Comm. on the Judiciary, 81st Cong. 1st & 2nd Sess. 206, 308 (1950) (statement of James L. Donnelly).
47. *See* Note 11.

5.4 Powerful or Sophisticated Buyers

Tacit or express collusion can be frustrated by the presence of powerful and sophisticated buyers if these are appropriately situated to force firms in the primary market to negotiate secretly or offer substantial concessions for large purchasers. In most circumstances, however, the Attorneys General find that the presence of powerful or sophisticated buyers is unlikely to prevent anticompetitive effects from occurring.[48] Thus, the presence of powerful or sophisticated buyers will only be considered when the buyers are uniquely positioned to enter the primary market in response to collusive pricing, or to finance or otherwise facilitate the entry of others.

6. Failing Firm Defense

The failing firm doctrine, which has been recognized by the United States Supreme Court, may be a defense to an otherwise unlawful merger.[49] Because it may allow anticompetitive mergers, the defense will be strictly construed.

The Attorneys General will only consider a failing firm defense to an anticompetitive merger where the proponents of the merger satisfy their burden of showing the following three elements: (1) That the resources of the allegedly failing firm are so depleted and the prospect of rehabilitation is so remote that the firm faces a high probability of a

---

48. For example, if some but not all of the buyers in a market are powerful and sophisticated, the former may be able to achieve price concessions while the less powerful buyers will not. In that case the merger should be evaluated by its impact on the less powerful buyers. Similarly, powerful buyers may often find it more profitable to preserve the monopoly in the primary market and share in its profits than to force competition there. This is most likely when both buyer and seller market levels are highly concentrated and each side has significant power to force the other side to behave competitively. In that case forbearance on both sides, which results in preservation of the monopoly and sharing of its profits, is a more profitable result than aggressive behavior that will eliminate monopoly profits at both levels.

49. U.S. v. General Dynamics Corp., 415 U.S. 486, 507 (1974); U.S. v. Greater Buffalo Press, Inc., 402 U.S. 549, 555 (1971).

business failure;[50] (2) that it had made reasonable good faith efforts and had failed to find another reasonable prospective purchaser; and (3) that there is no less anticompetitive alternative available.[51]

---

50. Evidence showing that the putative failing firm would not be able to reorganize successfully under Chapter 11 of the Bankruptcy Act, 11 U.S.C. §§ 1101-1174 (1988), would be highly relevant.
51. The Attorneys General may exercise their prosecutorial discretion by declining to challenge a merger which will sustain a failing division of an otherwise viable firm. Since the failing division claim is highly susceptible to manipulation and abuse, the Attorneys General will require the three elements of the "failing firm" defense to be proven by clear and convincing evidence.

APPENDIX N

Antitrust Guidelines for Collaborations among Competitors

Preamble

In order to compete in modern markets, competitors sometimes need to collaborate. Competitive forces are driving firms toward complex collaborations to achieve goals such as expanding into foreign markets, funding expensive innovation efforts, and lowering production and other costs.

Such collaborations often are not only benign but procompetitive. Indeed, in the last two decades, the federal antitrust agencies have brought relatively few civil cases against competitor collaborations. Nevertheless, a perception that antitrust laws are skeptical about agreements among actual or potential competitors may deter the development of procompetitive collaborations.[1]

To provide guidance to business people, the Federal Trade Commission ("FTC") and the U.S. Department of Justice ("DOJ") (collectively, "the Agencies") previously issued guidelines addressing several special circumstances in which antitrust issues related to competitor collaborations may arise.[2] But none of these Guidelines

---

1. Congress has protected certain collaborations from full antitrust liability by passing the National Cooperative Research Act of 1984 ("NCRA") and the National Cooperative Research and Production Act of 1993 ("NCRPA") (codified together at 15 U.S.C. §§ 4301-06). Relatively few participants in research and production collaborations have sought to take advantage of the protections afforded by the NCRA and NCRPA, however.

2. The *Statements of Antitrust Enforcement Policy in Health Care ("Health Care Statements")* outline the Agencies' approach to certain health care collaborations, among other things. The *Antitrust Guidelines for the Licensing of Intellectual Property ("Intellectual Property Guidelines")* outline the Agencies' enforcement policy with respect to intellectual property licensing agreements among competitors, among other things.

represents a general statement of the Agencies' analytical approach to competitor collaborations. The increasing varieties and use of competitor collaborations have yielded requests for improved clarity regarding their treatment under the antitrust laws.

The new Antitrust Guidelines for Collaborations among Competitors ("Competitor Collaboration Guidelines") are intended to explain how the Agencies analyze certain antitrust issues raised by collaborations among competitors. Competitor collaborations and the market circumstances in which they operate vary widely. No set of guidelines can provide specific answers to every antitrust question that might arise from a competitor collaboration. These Guidelines describe an analytical framework to assist businesses in assessing the likelihood of an antitrust challenge to a collaboration with one or more competitors. They should enable businesses to evaluate proposed transactions with greater understanding of possible antitrust implications, thus encouraging procompetitive collaborations, deterring collaborations likely to harm competition and consumers, and facilitating the Agencies' investigations of collaborations.

Section 1: Purpose, Definitions, and Overview

1.1 Purpose and Definitions

These Guidelines state the antitrust enforcement policy of the Agencies with respect to competitor collaborations. By stating their general policy, the Agencies hope to assist businesses in assessing whether the Agencies will challenge a competitor collaboration or any of the agreements of which it is comprised.[3] However, these Guidelines cannot remove judgment and discretion in antitrust law enforcement. The Agencies evaluate each case in light of its own facts and apply the

---

The *1992* DOJ/FTC *Horizontal Merger Guidelines*, as amended in 1997 (*"Horizontal Merger Guidelines"*), outline the Agencies "approach to horizontal mergers and acquisitions, and certain competitor collaborations."

3. These Guidelines neither describe how the Agencies litigate cases nor assign burdens of proof or production.

analytical framework set forth in these Guidelines reasonably and flexibly.[4]

A "competitor collaboration" comprises a set of one or more agreements, other than merger agreements, between or among competitors to engage in economic activity, and the economic activity resulting therefrom.[5] "Competitors" include firms that are actual or potential competitors[6] in a relevant market.[7] Competitor collaborations involve one or more business activities, such as research and development ("R&D"), production, marketing, distribution, sales or purchasing. Information sharing and various trade association activities also may take place through competitor collaborations.

These Guidelines use the terms "anticompetitive harm," "procompetitive benefit," and "overall competitive effect" in analyzing the competitive effects of agreements among competitors. All of these terms include actual and likely competitive effects. The Guidelines use the term "anticompetitive harm" to refer to an agreement's adverse competitive consequences, without taking account of offsetting procompetitive benefits. Conversely, the term "procompetitive benefit" refers to an agreement's favorable competitive consequences, without taking account of its anticompetitive harm. The terms "overall competitive effect" or "competitive effect" are used in discussing the combination of an agreement's anticompetitive harm and procompetitive benefit.

---

4. The analytical framework set forth in these Guidelines is consistent with the analytical frameworks in the *Health Care Statements* and the *Intellectual Property Guidelines*, which remain in effect to address issues in their special contexts.
5. These Guidelines do not address the possible exclusionary effects of agreements among competitors that may foreclose or limit competition by rivals.
6. A firm is treated as a potential competitor if there is evidence that entry by that firm is reasonably probable in the absence of the relevant agreement, or that competitively significant decisions by actual competitors are constrained by concerns that anticompetitive conduct likely would induce the firm to enter.
7. Firms also may be in a buyer-seller or other relationship, but that does not eliminate the need to examine the competitor relationship, if present.

1.2 Overview of Analytical Framework

Two types of analysis are used by the Supreme Court to determine the lawfulness of an agreement among competitors: per se and rule of reason.[8] Certain types of agreements are so likely to harm competition and to have no significant procompetitive benefit that they do not warrant the time and expense required for particularized inquiry into their effects. Once identified, such agreements are challenged as per se unlawful.[9] All other agreements are evaluated under the rule of reason, which involves a factual inquiry into an agreement's overall competitive effect. As the Supreme Court has explained, rule of reason analysis entails a flexible inquiry and varies in focus and detail depending on the nature of the agreement and market circumstances.[10]

This overview briefly sets forth questions and factors that the Agencies assess in analyzing an agreement among competitors. The rest of the Guidelines should be consulted for the detailed definitions and discussion that underlie this analysis.

Agreements Challenged as Per Se Illegal. Agreements of a type that always or almost always tends to raise price or to reduce output are per se illegal. The Agencies challenge such agreements, once identified, as per se illegal. Types of agreements that have been held per se illegal include agreements among competitors to fix prices or output, rig bids, or share or divide markets by allocating customers, suppliers, territories, or lines of commerce. The Department of Justice prosecutes participants in such hard-core cartel agreements criminally. Because the courts conclusively presume such hard-core cartel agreements to be illegal, the Department of Justice treats them as such without inquiring into their claimed business purposes, anticompetitive harms, procompetitive benefits, or overall competitive effects.

---

8. *See* National Soc'y of Prof'l. Eng'rs v. United States, 435 U.S. 679, 692 (1978).
9. *See* FTC v. Superior Court Trial Lawyers Ass'n, 493 U.S. 411, 432-36 (1990).
10. *See* California Dental Ass'n v. FTC, 119 S. Ct. 1604, 1617-18 (1999); FTC v. Indiana Fed'n of Dentists, 476 U.S. 447, 459-61 (1986); National Collegiate Athletic Ass'n v. Board of Regents of the Univ. of Okla., 468 U.S. 85, 104-13 (1984).

Agreements Analyzed under the Rule of Reason. Agreements not challenged as per se illegal are analyzed under the rule of reason to determine their overall competitive effect. These include agreements of a type that otherwise might be considered per se illegal, provided they are reasonably related to, and reasonably necessary to achieve procompetitive benefits from, an efficiency-enhancing integration of economic activity. Rule of reason analysis focuses on the state of competition with, as compared to without, the relevant agreement. The central question is whether the relevant agreement likely harms competition by increasing the ability or incentive profitably to raise price above or reduce output, quality, service, or innovation below what likely would prevail in the absence of the relevant agreement.

Rule of reason analysis entails a flexible inquiry and varies in focus and detail depending on the nature of the agreement and market circumstances. The Agencies focus on only those factors, and undertake only that factual inquiry, necessary to make a sound determination of the overall competitive effect of the relevant agreement. Ordinarily, however, no one factor is dispositive in the analysis.

The Agencies' analysis begins with an examination of the nature of the relevant agreement. As part of this examination, the Agencies ask about the business purpose of the agreement and examine whether the agreement, if already in operation, has caused anticompetitive harm. In some cases, the nature of the agreement and the absence of market power together may demonstrate the absence of anticompetitive harm. In such cases, the Agencies do not challenge the agreement. Alternatively, where the likelihood of anticompetitive harm is evident from the nature of the agreement, or anticompetitive harm has resulted from an agreement already in operation, then, absent overriding benefits that could offset the anticompetitive harm, the Agencies challenge such agreements without a detailed market analysis. If the initial examination of the nature of the agreement indicates possible competitive concerns, but the agreement is not one that would be challenged without a detailed market analysis, the Agencies analyze the agreement in greater depth. The Agencies typically define relevant markets and calculate market shares and concentration as an initial step in assessing whether the agreement may create or increase market power or facilitate its exercise. The Agencies examine the extent to which the participants and the collaboration have the ability and incentive to compete independently. The Agencies also evaluate other market circumstances, e.g. entry, that may foster or prevent anticompetitive harms.

If the examination of these factors indicates no potential for anticompetitive harm, the Agencies end the investigation without considering procompetitive benefits. If investigation indicates anticompetitive harm, the Agencies examine whether the relevant agreement is reasonably necessary to achieve procompetitive benefits that likely would offset anticompetitive harms.

1.3 Competitor Collaborations Distinguished from Mergers

The competitive effects from competitor collaborations may differ from those of mergers due to a number of factors. Mergers completely end competition between the merging parties in the relevant market(s). By contrast, most competitor collaborations preserve some form of competition among the participants. This remaining competition may reduce competitive concerns, but also may raise questions about whether participants have agreed to anticompetitive restraints on the remaining competition.

Mergers are designed to be permanent, while competitor collaborations are more typically of limited duration. Thus, participants in a collaboration typically remain potential competitors, even if they are not actual competitors for certain purposes (e.g., R&D) during the collaboration. The potential for future competition between participants in a collaboration requires antitrust scrutiny different from that required for mergers.

Nonetheless, in some cases, competitor collaborations have competitive effects identical to those that would arise if the participants merged in whole or in part. The Agencies treat a competitor collaboration as a horizontal merger in a relevant market and analyze the collaboration pursuant to the Horizontal Merger Guidelines if: (a) The participants are competitors in that relevant market; (b) the formation of the collaboration involves an efficiency-enhancing integration of economic activity in the relevant market; (c) the integration eliminates all competition among the participants in the relevant market; and (d) the collaboration does not terminate within a sufficiently limited period[11] by

---

11. In general, the Agencies use ten years as a term indicating sufficient

its own specific and express terms.[12] Effects of the collaboration on competition in other markets are analyzed as appropriate under these Guidelines or other applicable precedent. See Example 1.[13]

Section 2: General Principles for Evaluating Agreements Among Competitors

2.1 Potential Procompetitive Benefits

The Agencies recognize that consumers may benefit from competitor collaborations in a variety of ways. For example, a competitor collaboration may enable participants to offer goods or services that are cheaper, more valuable to consumers, or brought to market faster than would be possible absent the collaboration. A collaboration may allow its participants to better use existing assets, or may provide incentives for them to make output-enhancing investments that would not occur absent the collaboration. The potential efficiencies from competitor collaborations may be achieved through a variety of contractual arrangements including joint ventures, trade or professional associations, licensing arrangements, or strategic alliances. Efficiency gains from competitor collaborations often stem from combinations of different capabilities or resources. For example, one participant may have special technical expertise that usefully complements another participant's manufacturing process, allowing the latter participant to lower its production cost or improve the quality of its product. In other instances, a collaboration may facilitate the attainment of scale or scope economies beyond the reach of any single participant. For example, two firms may be able to combine their research or marketing activities to lower their cost of bringing their products to market, or reduce the time needed to

---

permanence to justify treatment of a competitor collaboration as analogous to a merger. The length of this term may vary, however, depending on industry-specific circumstances, such as technology life cycles.

12. This definition, however, does not determine obligations arising under the Hart-Scott-Rodino Antitrust Improvements Act of 1976, 15 U.S.C. § 18a.
13. Examples illustrating this and other points set forth in these Guidelines are included in the Appendix.

develop and begin commercial sales of new products. Consumers may benefit from these collaborations as the participants are able to lower prices, improve quality, or bring new products to market faster.

2.2 Potential Anticompetitive Harms

Competitor collaborations may harm competition and consumers by increasing the ability or incentive profitably to raise price above or reduce output, quality, service, or innovation below what likely would prevail in the absence of the relevant agreement. Such effects may arise through a variety of mechanisms. Among other things, agreements may limit independent decision making or combine the control of or financial interests in production, key assets, or decisions regarding price, output, or other competitively sensitive variables, or may otherwise reduce the participants' ability or incentive to compete independently.

Competitor collaborations also may facilitate explicit or tacit collusion through facilitating practices such as the exchange or disclosure of competitively sensitive information or through increased market concentration. Such collusion may involve the relevant market in which the collaboration operates or another market in which the participants in the collaboration are actual or potential competitors.

2.3 Analysis of the Overall Collaboration and the Agreements of Which It Consists

A competitor collaboration comprises a set of one or more agreements, other than merger agreements, between or among competitors to engage in economic activity, and the economic activity resulting therefrom. In general, the Agencies assess the competitive effects of the overall collaboration and any individual agreement or set of agreements within the collaboration that may harm competition. For purposes of these Guidelines, the phrase "relevant agreement" refers to whichever of these three the evaluating Agency is assessing. Two or more agreements are assessed together if their procompetitive benefits or anticompetitive harms are so intertwined that they cannot meaningfully be isolated and attributed to any individual agreement. See Example 2.

2.4 Competitive Effects Are Assessed as of the Time of Possible Harm to Competition

The competitive effects of a relevant agreement may change over time, depending on changes in circumstances such as internal reorganization, adoption of new agreements as part of the collaboration, addition or departure of participants, new market conditions, or changes in market share. The Agencies assess the competitive effects of a relevant agreement as of the time of possible harm to competition, whether at formation of the collaboration or at a later time, as appropriate. See Example 3. However, an assessment after a collaboration has been formed is sensitive to the reasonable expectations of participants whose significant sunk cost investments in reliance on the relevant agreement were made before it became anticompetitive.

Section 3: Analytical Framework for Evaluating Agreements Among Competitors

3.1 Introduction

Section 3 sets forth the analytical framework that the Agencies use to evaluate the competitive effects of a competitor collaboration and the agreements of which it consists. Certain types of agreements are so likely to be harmful to competition and to have no significant benefits that they do not warrant the time and expense required for particularized inquiry into their effects.[14] Once identified, such agreements are challenged as per se illegal.[15]

Agreements not challenged as per se illegal are analyzed under the rule of reason. Rule of reason analysis focuses on the state of competition with, as compared to without, the relevant agreement. Under the rule of reason, the central question is whether the relevant agreement likely harms competition by increasing the ability or incentive profitably to raise price above or reduce output, quality, service, or innovation below what likely would prevail in the absence of the relevant

---

14. *See* Continental TV, Inc. v. GTE Sylvania Inc., 433 U.S. 36, 50 n.16 (1977).
15. *See Superior Court Trial Lawyers Ass'n*, 493 U.S. at 432-36.

agreement. Given the great variety of competitor collaborations, rule of reason analysis entails a flexible inquiry and varies in focus and detail depending on the nature of the agreement and market circumstances. Rule of reason analysis focuses on only those factors, and undertakes only the degree of factual inquiry, necessary to assess accurately the overall competitive effect of the relevant agreement.[16]

The following sections describe in detail the Agencies' analytical framework.

3.2 Agreements Challenged as Per Se Illegal

Agreements of a type that always or almost always tends to raise price or reduce output are per se illegal.[17] The Agencies challenge such agreements, once identified, as per se illegal. Typically these are agreements not to compete on price or output. Types of agreements that have been held per se illegal include agreements among competitors to fix prices or output, rig bids, or share or divide markets by allocating customers, suppliers, territories or lines of commerce.[18] The Department of Justice prosecutes participants in such hard-core cartel agreements criminally. Because the courts conclusively presume such hard-core cartel agreements to be illegal, the Department of Justice treats them as such without inquiring into their claimed business purposes, anticompetitive harms, procompetitive benefits, or overall competitive effects.

If, however, participants in an efficiency-enhancing integration of economic activity enter into an agreement that is reasonably related to the integration and reasonably necessary to achieve its procompetitive benefits, the Agencies analyze the agreement under the rule of reason, even if it is of a type that might otherwise be considered per se illegal.[19]

---

16. *See California Dental Ass'n*, 119 S. Ct. at 1617-18; *Indiana Fed'n of Dentists*, 476 U.S. at 459-61; *NCAA*, 468 U.S. at 104-13.
17. *See* Broadcast Music, Inc. v. Columbia Broadcasting Sys., 441 U.S. 1, 19-20 (1979).
18. *See, e.g.*, Palmer v. BRG of Georgia, Inc., 498 U.S. 46 (1990) (market allocation); United States v. Trenton Potteries Co., 273 U.S. 392 (1927) (price fixing).
19. *See* Arizona v. Maricopa County Medical Soc'y, 457 U.S. 332, 339 n.7, 356-57 (1982) (finding no integration).

See Example 4. In an efficiency-enhancing integration, participants collaborate to perform or cause to be performed (by a joint venture entity created by the collaboration or by one or more participants or by a third party acting on behalf of other participants) one or more business functions, such as production, distribution, or R&D, and thereby benefit, or potentially benefit, consumers by expanding output, reducing price, or enhancing quality, service, or innovation. Participants in an efficiency-enhancing integration typically combine, by contract or otherwise, significant capital, technology, or other complementary assets to achieve procompetitive benefits that the participants could not achieve separately. The mere coordination of decisions on price, output, customers, territories, and the like is not integration, and cost savings without integration are not a basis for avoiding per se condemnation. The integration must promote procompetitive benefits that are cognizable under the efficiencies analysis set forth in Section 3.36 below. Such procompetitive benefits may enhance the participants' ability or incentives to compete and thus may offset an agreement's anticompetitive tendencies. See Examples 5 through 7.

An agreement may be "reasonably necessary" without being essential. However, if the participants could achieve an equivalent or comparable efficiency-enhancing integration through practical, significantly less restrictive means, then the Agencies conclude that the agreement is not reasonably necessary.[20] In making this assessment, except in unusual circumstances, the Agencies consider whether practical, significantly less restrictive means were reasonably available when the agreement was entered into, but do not search for a theoretically less restrictive alternative that was not practical given the business realities.

Before accepting a claim that an agreement is reasonably necessary to achieve procompetitive benefits from an integration of economic activity, the Agencies undertake a limited factual inquiry to evaluate the claim.[21] Such an inquiry may reveal that efficiencies from an agreement

---

20. *See id.* at 352-53 (observing that even if a maximum fee schedule for physicians' services were desirable, it was not necessary that the schedule be established by physicians rather than by insurers); *Broadcast Music*, 441 U.S. at 20-21 (setting of price "necessary" for the blanket license).

21. *See Maricopa*, 457 U.S. at 352-53, 356-57 (scrutinizing the defendant medical foundations for indicia of integration and evaluating the record

that are possible in theory are not plausible in the context of the particular collaboration. Some claims-such as those premised on the notion that competition itself is unreasonable-are insufficient as a matter of law,[22] and others may be implausible on their face. In any case, labeling an arrangement a "joint venture" will not protect what is merely a device to raise price or restrict output;[23] the nature of the conduct, not its designation, is determinative.

3.3 Agreements Analyzed Under the Rule of Reason

Agreements not challenged as per se illegal are analyzed under the rule of reason to determine their overall competitive effect. Rule of reason analysis focuses on the state of competition with, as compared to without, the relevant agreement. The central question is whether the relevant agreement likely harms competition by increasing the ability or incentive profitably to raise price above or reduce output, quality, service, or innovation below what likely would prevail in the absence of the relevant agreement.[24]

Rule of reason analysis entails a flexible inquiry and varies in focus and detail depending on the nature of the agreement and market circumstances.[25] The Agencies focus on only those factors, and undertake only that factual inquiry, necessary to make a sound

---

evidence regarding less restrictive alternatives).

22. *See Indiana Fed'n of Dentists*, 476 U.S. at 463-64; *NCAA*, 468 U.S. at 116-17; *Prof'l. Eng'rs*, 435 U.S. at 693-96. Other claims, such as an absence of market power, are no defense to per se illegality. *See Superior Court Trial Lawyers Ass'n*, 493 U.S. at 434-36; United States v. Socony-Vacuum Oil Co., 310 U.S. 150, 224-26 & n.59 (1940).
23. *See* Timken Roller Bearing Co. v. United States, 341 U.S. 593, 598 (1951).
24. In addition, concerns may arise where an agreement increases the ability or incentive of buyers to exercise monopsony power. *See infra* Section 3.31(a).
25. *See California Dental Ass'n*, 119 S. Ct. at 1612-13, 1617 ("What is required is an enquiry meet for the case, looking to the circumstances, details, and logic of a restraint."); *NCAA*, 468 U.S. 109 n.39 ("the rule of reason can sometimes be applied in the twinkling of an eye") (quoting Phillip E. Areeda, *The "Rule of Reason" in Antitrust Analysis: General Issues* 37-38 (Federal Judicial Center, June 1981)).

determination of the overall competitive effect of the relevant agreement. Ordinarily, however, no one factor is dispositive in the analysis.

Under the rule of reason, the Agencies' analysis begins with an examination of the nature of the relevant agreement, since the nature of the agreement determines the types of anticompetitive harms that may be of concern. As part of this examination, the Agencies ask about the business purpose of the agreement and examine whether the agreement, if already in operation, has caused anticompetitive harm.[26] If the nature of the agreement and the absence of market power[27] together demonstrate the absence of anticompetitive harm, the Agencies do not challenge the agreement. See Example 8. Alternatively, where the likelihood of anticompetitive harm is evident from the nature of the agreement,[28] or anticompetitive harm has resulted from an agreement already in operation,[29] then, absent overriding benefits that could offset the anticompetitive harm, the Agencies challenge such agreements without a detailed market analysis.[30]

If the initial examination of the nature of the agreement indicates possible competitive concerns, but the agreement is not one that would be challenged without a detailed market analysis, the Agencies analyze

---

26. *See* Board of Trade of the City of Chicago v. United States, 246 U.S. 231, 238 (1918).

27. That market power is absent may be determined without defining a relevant market. For example, if no market power is likely under any plausible market definition, it does not matter which one is correct.

28. *See California Dental Ass'n*, 119 S. Ct. at 1612-13, 1617 (an "obvious anticompetitive effect" would warrant quick condemnation); *Indiana Fed'n of Dentists*, 476 U.S. at 459; *NCAA*, 468 U.S. at 104, 106-10.

29. *See Indiana Fed'n of Dentists*, 476 U.S. at 460-61 ("Since the purpose of the inquiries into market definition and market power is to determine whether an arrangement has the potential for genuine adverse effects on competition, proof of actual detrimental effects, such as a reduction of output,'can obviate the need for an inquiry into market power, which is but a surrogate for detrimental effects.'") (quoting 7 Phillip E. Areeda, *Antitrust Law* ¶ 1511, at 424 (1986)); *NCAA*, 468 U.S. at 104-08, 110 n. 42.

30. *See Indiana Fed'n of Dentists*, 476 U.S. at 459-60 (condemning without "detailed market analysis" an agreement to limit competition by withholding x-rays from patients' insurers after finding no competitive justification).

the agreement in greater depth. The Agencies typically define relevant markets and calculate market shares and concentration as an initial step in assessing whether the agreement may create or increase market power[31] or facilitate its exercise and thus poses risks to competition.[32] The Agencies examine factors relevant to the extent to which the participants and the collaboration have the ability and incentive to compete independently, such as whether an agreement is exclusive or non-exclusive and its duration.[33] The Agencies also evaluate whether entry would be timely, likely, and sufficient to deter or counteract any anticompetitive harms. In addition, the Agencies assess any other market circumstances that may foster or impede anticompetitive harms.

If the examination of these factors indicates no potential for anticompetitive harm, the Agencies end the investigation without considering procompetitive benefits. If investigation indicates anticompetitive harm, the Agencies examine whether the relevant agreement is reasonably necessary to achieve procompetitive benefits that likely would offset anticompetitive harms.[34]

---

31. Market power to a seller is the ability profitably to maintain prices above competitive levels for a significant period of time. Sellers also may exercise market power with respect to significant competitive dimensions other than price, such as quality, service, or innovation. Market power to a buyer is the ability profitably to depress the price paid for a product below the competitive level for a significant period of time and thereby depress output.
32. *See* Eastman Kodak Co. v. Image Technical Services, Inc., 504 U.S. 451, 464 (1992).
33. *Compare NCAA*, 468 U.S. at 113-15, 119-20 (noting that colleges were not permitted to televise their own games without restraint), *with Broadcast Music*, 441 U.S. at 23-24 (finding no legal or practical impediment to individual licenses).
34. *See NCAA*, 468 U.S. at 113-15 (rejecting efficiency claims when production was limited, not enhanced); *Prof'l. Eng'rs*, 435 U.S. at 696 (dictum) (distinguishing restraints that promote competition from those that eliminate competition); *Chicago Bd. of Trade*, 246 U.S. at 238 (same).

3.31 Nature of the Relevant Agreement: Business Purpose, Operation in the Marketplace and Possible Competitive Concerns

The nature of the agreement is relevant to whether it may cause anticompetitive harm. For example, by limiting independent decision making or combining control over or financial interests in production, key assets, or decisions on price, output, or other competitively sensitive variables, an agreement may create or increase market power or facilitate its exercise by the collaboration, its participants, or both. An agreement to limit independent decision making or to combine control or financial interests may reduce the ability or incentive to compete independently. An agreement also may increase the likelihood of an exercise of market power by facilitating explicit or tacit collusion,[35] either through facilitating practices such as an exchange of competitively sensitive information or through increased market concentration.

In examining the nature of the relevant agreement, the Agencies take into account inferences about business purposes for the agreement that can be drawn from objective facts. The Agencies also consider evidence of the subjective intent of the participants to the extent that it sheds light on competitive effects.[36] The Agencies do not undertake a full analysis of procompetitive benefits pursuant to Section 3.36 below, however, unless an anticompetitive harm appears likely. The Agencies also examine whether an agreement already in operation has caused anticompetitive harm.[37] Anticompetitive harm may be observed, for example, if a competitor collaboration successfully mandates new, anticompetitive conduct or successfully eliminates procompetitive pre-collaboration conduct, such as withholding services that were desired by consumers when offered in a competitive market. If anticompetitive harm is found, examination of market power ordinarily is not required. In

---

35. As used in these Guidelines, “collusion” is not limited to conduct that involves an agreement under the antitrust laws.

36. Anticompetitive intent alone does not establish an antitrust violation, and procompetitive intent does not preclude a violation. *See, e.g., Chicago Bd. of Trade*, 246 U.S. at 238. But extrinsic evidence of intent may aid in evaluating market power, the likelihood of anticompetitive harm, and claimed procompetitive justifications where an agreement’s effects are otherwise ambiguous.

37. *See id.*

some cases, however, a determination of anticompetitive harm may be informed by consideration of market power.

The following sections illustrate competitive concerns that may arise from the nature of particular types of competitor collaborations. This list is not exhaustive. In addition, where these sections address agreements of a type that otherwise might be considered per se illegal, such as agreements on price, the discussion assumes that the agreements already have been determined to be subject to rule of reason analysis because they are reasonably related to, and reasonably necessary to achieve procompetitive benefits from, an efficiency-enhancing integration of economic activity. See supra Section 3.2.

3.31(a) Relevant Agreements That Limit Independent Decision Making or Combine Control or Financial Interests

The following is intended to illustrate but not exhaust the types of agreements that might harm competition by eliminating independent decision making or combining control or financial interests.

Production Collaborations. Competitor collaborations may involve agreements jointly to produce a product sold to others or used by the participants as an input. Such agreements are often procompetitive.[38] Participants may combine complementary technologies, know-how, or other assets to enable the collaboration to produce a good more efficiently or to produce a good that no one participant alone could produce. However, production collaborations may involve agreements on the level of output or the use of key assets, or on the price at which the product will be marketed by the collaboration, or on other competitively significant variables, such as quality, service, or promotional strategies, that can result in anticompetitive harm. Such agreements can create or increase market power or facilitate its exercise by limiting independent decision making or by combining in the collaboration, or in certain participants, the control over some or all production or key assets or

38. The *NCRPA* accords rule of reason treatment to certain production collaborations. However, the statute permits per se challenges, in appropriate circumstances, to a variety of activities, including agreements to jointly market the goods or services produced or to limit the participants' independent sale of goods or services produced outside the collaboration. *NCRPA*, 15 U.S.C. §§ 4301-02.

decisions about key competitive variables that otherwise would be controlled independently.[39] Such agreements could reduce individual participants' control over assets necessary to compete and thereby reduce their ability to compete independently, combine financial interests in ways that undermine incentives to compete independently, or both.

Marketing Collaborations. Competitor collaborations may involve agreements jointly to sell, distribute, or promote goods or services that are either jointly or individually produced. Such agreements may be procompetitive, for example, where a combination of complementary assets enables products more quickly and efficiently to reach the marketplace. However, marketing collaborations may involve agreements on price, output, or other competitively significant variables, or on the use of competitively significant assets, such as an extensive distribution network, that can result in anticompetitive harm. Such agreements can create or increase market power or facilitate its exercise by limiting independent decision making; by combining in the collaboration, or in certain participants, control over competitively significant assets or decisions about competitively significant variables that otherwise would be controlled independently; or by combining financial interests in ways that undermine incentives to compete independently. For example, joint promotion might reduce or eliminate comparative advertising, thus harming competition by restricting information to consumers on price and other competitively significant variables.

Buying Collaborations. Competitor collaborations may involve agreements jointly to purchase necessary inputs. Many such agreements do not raise antitrust concerns and indeed may be procompetitive. Purchasing collaborations, for example, may enable participants to centralize ordering, to combine warehousing or distribution functions

---

39. For example, where output resulting from a collaboration is transferred to participants for independent marketing, anticompetitive harm could result if that output is restricted or if the transfer takes place at a supracompetitive price. Such conduct could raise participants' marginal costs through inflated per-unit charges on the transfer of the collaboration's output. Anticompetitive harm could occur even if there is vigorous competition among collaboration participants in the output market, since all the participants would have paid the same inflated transfer price.

more efficiently, or to achieve other efficiencies. However, such agreements can create or increase market power (which, in the case of buyers, is called "monopsony power") or facilitate its exercise by increasing the ability or incentive to drive the price of the purchased product, and thereby depress output, below what likely would prevail in the absence of the relevant agreement. Buying collaborations also may facilitate collusion by standardizing participants' costs or by enhancing the ability to project or monitor a participant's output level through knowledge of its input purchases.

Research & Development Collaborations. Competitor collaborations may involve agreements to engage in joint research and development ("R&D"). Most such agreements are procompetitive, and they typically are analyzed under the rule of reason.[40] Through the combination of complementary assets, technology, or know-how, an R&D collaboration may enable participants more quickly or more efficiently to research and develop new or improved goods, services, or production processes. Joint R&D agreements, however, can create or increase market power or facilitate its exercise by limiting independent decision making or by combining in the collaboration, or in certain participants, control over competitively significant assets or all or a portion of participants' individual competitive R&D efforts. Although R&D collaborations also may facilitate tacit collusion on R&D efforts, achieving, monitoring, and punishing departures from collusion is sometimes difficult in the R&D context.

An exercise of market power may injure consumers by reducing innovation below the level that otherwise would prevail, leading to fewer or no products for consumers to choose from, lower quality products, or products that reach consumers more slowly than they otherwise would. An exercise of market power also may injure consumers by reducing the number of independent competitors in the market for the goods, services, or production processes derived from the R&D collaboration, leading to higher prices or reduced output, quality, or service. A central question is

40. *See NCRPA*, 15 U.S.C. §§ 4301-02. However, the statute permits per se challenges, in appropriate circumstances, to a variety of activities, including agreements to jointly market the fruits of collaborative R&D or to limit the participants' independent R&D or their sale or licensing of goods, services, or processes developed outside the collaboration. *Id.*

whether the agreement increases the ability or incentive anticompetitively to reduce R&D efforts pursued independently or through the collaboration, for example, by slowing the pace at which R&D efforts are pursued. Other considerations being equal, R&D agreements are more likely to raise competitive concerns when the collaboration or its participants already possess a secure source of market power over an existing product and the new R&D efforts might cannibalize their supracompetitive earnings. In addition, anticompetitive harm generally is more likely when R&D competition is confined to firms with specialized characteristics or assets, such as intellectual property, or when a regulatory approval process limits the ability of late-comers to catch up with competitors already engaged in the R&D.

3.31(b) Relevant Agreements That May Facilitate Collusion

Each of the types of competitor collaborations outlined above can facilitate collusion. Competitor collaborations may provide an opportunity for participants to discuss and agree on anticompetitive terms, or otherwise to collude anticompetitively, as well as a greater ability to detect and punish deviations that would undermine the collusion. Certain marketing, production, and buying collaborations, for example, may provide opportunities for their participants to collude on price, output, customers, territories, or other competitively sensitive variables. R&D collaborations, however, may be less likely to facilitate collusion regarding R&D activities since R&D often is conducted in secret, and it thus may be difficult to monitor an agreement to coordinate R&D. In addition, collaborations can increase concentration in a relevant market and thus increase the likelihood of collusion among all firms, including the collaboration and its participants. Agreements that facilitate collusion sometimes involve the exchange or disclosure of information. The Agencies recognize that the sharing of information among competitors may be procompetitive and is often reasonably necessary to achieve the procompetitive benefits of certain collaborations; for example, sharing certain technology, know-how, or other intellectual property may be essential to achieve the procompetitive benefits of an R&D collaboration. Nevertheless, in some cases, the sharing of information related to a market in which the collaboration operates or in which the participants are actual or potential competitors may increase the likelihood of collusion on matters such as price, output, or other competitively sensitive variables. The competitive concern depends on the nature of the information shared. Other things being equal, the sharing of information relating to price, output, costs, or strategic planning is more likely to raise competitive concern than the sharing of information relating to less competitively sensitive variables. Similarly, other things being equal, the sharing of information on current operating and future business plans is more likely to raise concerns than the sharing of historical information. Finally, other things being equal, the sharing of individual company data is more likely to raise concern than the sharing of aggregated data that does not permit recipients to identify individual firm data.

3.32 Relevant Markets Affected by the Collaboration

The Agencies typically identify and assess competitive effects in all of the relevant product and geographic markets in which competition may be affected by a competitor collaboration, although in some cases it may be possible to assess competitive effects directly without defining a particular relevant market(s). Markets affected by a competitor collaboration include all markets in which the economic integration of the participants' operations occurs or in which the collaboration operates or will operate,[41] and may also include additional markets in which any participant is an actual or potential competitor.[42]

3.32(a) Goods Markets

In general, for goods[43] markets affected by a competitor collaboration, the Agencies approach relevant market definition as described in Section 1 of the Horizontal Merger Guidelines. To

---

41. For example, where a production joint venture buys inputs from an upstream market to incorporate in products to be sold in a downstream market, bothupstream and downstream markets may be "markets affected by a competitor collaboration."
42. Participation in the collaboration may change the participants' behavior in this third category of markets, for example, by altering incentives and available information, or by providing an opportunity to form additional agreements among participants.
43. The term "goods" also includes services.

determine the relevant market, the Agencies generally consider the likely reaction of buyers to a price increase and typically ask, among other things, how buyers would respond to increases over prevailing price levels. However, when circumstances strongly suggest that the prevailing price exceeds what likely would have prevailed absent the relevant agreement, the Agencies use a price more reflective of the price that likely would have prevailed. Once a market has been defined, market shares are assigned both to firms currently in the relevant market and to firms that are able to make "uncommitted" supply responses. See Sections 1.31 and 1.32 of the Horizontal Merger Guidelines.

3.32(b) Technology Markets

When rights to intellectual property are marketed separately from the products in which they are used, the Agencies may define technology markets in assessing the competitive effects of a competitor collaboration that includes an agreement to license intellectual property. Technology markets consist of the intellectual property that is licensed and its close substitutes; that is, the technologies or goods that are close enough substitutes significantly to constrain the exercise of market power with respect to the intellectual property that is licensed. The Agencies approach the definition of a relevant technology market and the measurement of market share as described in Section 3.2.2 of the Intellectual Property Guidelines.

3.32(c) Research and Development: Innovation Markets

In many cases, an agreement's competitive effects on innovation are analyzed as a separate competitive effect in a relevant goods market. However, if a competitor collaboration may have competitive effects on innovation that cannot be adequately addressed through the analysis of goods or technology markets, the Agencies may define and analyze an innovation market as described in Section 3.2.3 of the Intellectual Property Guidelines. An innovation market consists of the research and development directed to particular new or improved goods or processes and the close substitutes for that research and development. The Agencies define an innovation market only when the capabilities to engage in the relevant research and development can be associated with specialized assets or characteristics of specific firms.

3.33 Market Shares and Market Concentration

Market share and market concentration affect the likelihood that the relevant agreement will create or increase market power or facilitate its exercise. The creation, increase, or facilitation of market power will likely increase the ability and incentive profitably to raise price above or reduce output, quality, service, or innovation below what likely would prevail in the absence of the relevant agreement.

Other things being equal, market share affects the extent to which participants or the collaboration must restrict their own output in order to achieve anticompetitive effects in a relevant market. The smaller the percentage of total supply that a firm controls, the more severely it must restrict its own output in order to produce a given price increase, and the less likely it is that an output restriction will be profitable. In assessing whether an agreement may cause anticompetitive harm, the Agencies typically calculate the market shares of the participants and of the collaboration.[44] The Agencies assign a range of market shares to the collaboration. The high end of that range is the sum of the market shares of the collaboration and its participants. The low end is the share of the collaboration in isolation. In general, the Agencies approach the calculation of market share as set forth in Section 1.4 of the Horizontal Merger Guidelines.

Other things being equal, market concentration affects the difficulties and costs of achieving and enforcing collusion in a relevant market. Accordingly, in assessing whether an agreement may increase the likelihood of collusion, the Agencies calculate market concentration. In general, the Agencies approach the calculation of market concentration as set forth in Section 1.5 of the Horizontal Merger Guidelines, ascribing to the competitor collaboration the same range of market shares described above.

Market share and market concentration provide only a starting point for evaluating the competitive effect of the relevant agreement. The

---

44. When the competitive concern is that a limitation on independent decision making or a combination of control or financial interests may yield an anticompetitive reduction of research and development, the Agencies typically frame their inquiries more generally, looking to the strength, scope, and number of competing R&D efforts and their close substitutes. *See supra* Sections 3.31(a) and 3.32(c).

Agencies also examine other factors outlined in the Horizontal Merger Guidelines as set forth below:

The Agencies consider whether factors such as those discussed in Section 1.52 of the Horizontal Merger Guidelines indicate that market share and concentration data overstate or understate the likely competitive significance of participants and their collaboration.

In assessing whether anticompetitive harm may arise from an agreement that combines control over or financial interests in assets or otherwise limits independent decision making, the Agencies consider whether factors such as those discussed in Section 2.2 of the Horizontal Merger Guidelines suggest that anticompetitive harm is more or less likely.

In assessing whether anticompetitive harms may arise from an agreement that may increase the likelihood of collusion, the Agencies consider whether factors such as those discussed in Section 2.1 of the Horizontal Merger Guidelines suggest that anticompetitive harm is more or less likely.

In evaluating the significance of market share and market concentration data and interpreting the range of market shares ascribed to the collaboration, the Agencies also examine factors beyond those set forth in the Horizontal Merger Guidelines. The following section describes which factors are relevant and the issues that the Agencies examine in evaluating those factors.

3.34 Factors Relevant to the Ability and Incentive of the Participants and the Collaboration to Compete

Competitor collaborations sometimes do not end competition among the participants and the collaboration. Participants may continue to compete against each other and their collaboration, either through separate, independent business operations or through membership in other collaborations. Collaborations may be managed by decision makers independent of the individual participants. Control over key competitive variables may remain outside the collaboration, such as where participants independently market and set prices for the collaboration's output.

Sometimes, however, competition among the participants and the collaboration may be restrained through explicit contractual terms or through financial or other provisions that reduce or eliminate the incentive to compete. The Agencies look to the competitive benefits and harms of the relevant agreement, not merely the formal terms of agreements among the participants.

Where the nature of the agreement and market share and market concentration data reveal a likelihood of anticompetitive harm, the Agencies more closely examine the extent to which the participants and the collaboration have the ability and incentive to compete independent of each other. The Agencies are likely to focus on six factors: (a) The extent to which the relevant agreement is non-exclusive in that participants are likely to continue to compete independently outside the collaboration in the market in which the collaboration operates; (b) the extent to which participants retain independent control of assets necessary to compete; (c) the nature and extent of participants' financial interests in the collaboration or in each other; (d) the control of the collaboration's competitively significant decision making; (e) the likelihood of anticompetitive information sharing; and (f) the duration of the collaboration.

Each of these factors is discussed in further detail below. Consideration of these factors may reduce or increase competitive concern. The analysis necessarily is flexible: the relevance and significance of each factor depends upon the facts and circumstances of each case, and any additional factors pertinent under the circumstances are considered. For example, when an agreement is examined subsequent to formation of the collaboration, the Agencies also examine factual evidence concerning participants' actual conduct.

3.34(a) Exclusivity

The Agencies consider whether, to what extent, and in what manner the relevant agreement permits participants to continue to compete against each other and their collaboration, either through separate, independent business operations or through membership in other collaborations. The Agencies inquire whether a collaboration is non-exclusive in fact as well as in name and consider any costs or other impediments to competing with the collaboration. In assessing exclusivity when an agreement already is in operation, the Agencies examine whether, to what extent, and in what manner participants actually have continued to compete against each other and the collaboration. In general, competitive concern likely is reduced to the extent that participants actually have continued to compete, either through separate, independent business operations or through membership in other collaborations, or are permitted to do so.

3.34(b) Control Over Assets

The Agencies ask whether the relevant agreement requires participants to contribute to the collaboration significant assets that previously have enabled or likely would enable participants to be effective independent competitors in markets affected by the collaboration. If such resources must be contributed to the collaboration and are specialized in that they cannot readily be replaced, the participants may have lost all or some of their ability to compete against each other and their collaboration, even if they retain the contractual right to do so.[45] In general, the greater the contribution of specialized assets to the collaboration that is required, the less the participants may be relied upon to provide independent competition.

3.34(c) Financial Interests in the Collaboration or in Other Participants

The Agencies assess each participant's financial interest in the collaboration and its potential impact on the participant's incentive to compete independently with the collaboration. The potential impact may vary depending on the size and nature of the financial interest (e.g., whether the financial interest is debt or equity). In general, the greater the financial interest in the collaboration, the less likely is the participant to compete with the collaboration.[46] The Agencies also assess direct equity investments between or among the participants. Such investments may reduce the incentives of the participants to compete with each other. In either case, the analysis is sensitive to the level of financial interest in the collaboration or in another participant relative to the level of the

---

45. For example, if participants in a production collaboration must contribute most of their productive capacity to the collaboration, the collaboration may impair the ability of its participants to remain effective independent competitors regardless of the terms of the agreement.

46. Similarly, a collaboration's financial interest in a participant may diminish the collaboration's incentive to compete with that participant.

participant's investment in its independent business operations in the markets affected by the collaboration.

3.34(d) Control of the Collaboration's Competitively Significant Decision Making

The Agencies consider the manner in which a collaboration is organized and governed in assessing the extent to which participants and their collaboration have the ability and incentive to compete independently. Thus, the Agencies consider the extent to which the collaboration's governance structure enables the collaboration to act as an independent decision maker. For example, the Agencies ask whether participants are allowed to appoint members of a board of directors for the collaboration, if incorporated, or otherwise to exercise significant control over the operations of the collaboration. In general, the collaboration is less likely to compete independently as participants gain greater control over the collaboration's price, output, and other competitively significant decisions.[47]

To the extent that the collaboration's decision making is subject to the participants' control, the Agencies consider whether that control could be exercised jointly. Joint control over the collaboration's price and output levels could create or increase market power and raise competitive concerns. Depending on the nature of the collaboration, competitive concern also may arise due to joint control over other competitively significant decisions, such as the level and scope of R&D efforts and investment. In contrast, to the extent that participants independently set the price and quantity[48] of theirshare of a

---

47. Control may diverge from financial interests. For example, a small equity investment may be coupled with a right to veto large capital expenditures and, thereby, to effectively limit output. The Agencies examine a collaboration's actual governance structure in assessing issues of control.

48. Even if prices to consumers are set independently, anticompetitive harms may still occur if participants jointly set the collaboration's level of output. For example, participants may effectively coordinate price increases by reducing the collaboration's level of output and collecting their profits through high transfer prices, *i.e.*, through the amounts that participants contribute to the collaboration in exchange for each unit of the collaboration's output. Where a transfer price is determined by

collaboration's output and independently control other competitively significant decisions, an agreement's likely anticompetitive harm is reduced.[49]

3.34(e) Likelihood of Anticompetitive Information Sharing

The Agencies evaluate the extent to which competitively sensitive information concerning markets affected by the collaboration likely would be disclosed. This likelihood depends on, among other things, the nature of the collaboration, its organization and governance, and safeguards implemented to prevent or minimize such disclosure. For example, participants might refrain from assigning marketing personnel to an R&D collaboration, or, in a marketing collaboration, participants might limit access to competitively sensitive information regarding their respective operations to only certain individuals or to an independent third party. Similarly, a buying collaboration might use an independent third party to handle negotiations in which its participants' input requirements or other competitively sensitive information could be revealed. In general, it is less likely that the collaboration will facilitate collusion on competitively sensitive variables if appropriate safeguards governing information sharing are in place.

3.34(f) Duration of the Collaboration

The Agencies consider the duration of the collaboration in assessing whether participants retain the ability and incentive to compete against each other and their collaboration. In general, the shorter the duration, the more likely participants are to compete against each other and their collaboration.

3.35 Entry

---

reference to an objective measure not under the control of the participants, (*e.g.*, average price in a different unconcentrated geographic market), competitive concern may be less likely.

49. Anticompetitive harm also is less likely if individual participants may independently increase the overall output of the collaboration.

Easy entry may deter or prevent profitably maintaining price above, or output, quality, service or innovation below, what likely would prevail in the absence of the relevant agreement. Where the nature of the agreement and market share and concentration data suggest a likelihood of anticompetitive harm that is not sufficiently mitigated by any continuing competition identified through the analysis in Section 3.34, the Agencies inquire whether entry would be timely, likely, and sufficient in its magnitude, character and scope to deter or counteract the anticompetitive harm of concern. If so, the relevant agreement ordinarily requires no further analysis.

As a general matter, the Agencies assess timeliness, likelihood, and sufficiency of committed entry under principles set forth in Section 3 of the Horizontal Merger Guidelines.[50] However, unlike mergers, competitor collaborations often restrict only certain business activities, while preserving competition among participants in other respects, and they may be designed to terminate after a limited duration. Consequently, the extent to which an agreement creates opportunities that would induce entry and the conditions under which ease of entry may deter or counteract anticompetitive harms may be more complex and less direct than for mergers and will vary somewhat according to the nature of the relevant agreement. For example, the likelihood of entry may be affected by what potential entrants believe about the probable duration of an anticompetitive agreement. Other things being equal, the shorter the anticipated duration of an anticompetitive agreement, the smaller the profit opportunities for potential entrants, and the lower the likelihood that it will induce committed entry. Examples of other differences are set forth below.

For certain collaborations, sufficiency of entry may be affected by the possibility that entrants will participate in the anticompetitive agreement. To the extent that such participation raises the amount of entry needed to deter or counteract anticompetitive harms, and assets required for entry are not adequately available for entrants to respond fully to their sales opportunities, or otherwise renders entry inadequate in

---

50. Committed entry is defined as new competition that requires expenditure of significant sunk costs of entry and exit. *See* Section 3.0 of the *Horizontal Merger Guidelines*.

magnitude, character or scope, sufficient entry may be more difficult to achieve.[51]

In the context of research and development collaborations, widespread availability of R&D capabilities and the large gains that may accrue to successful innovators often suggest a high likelihood that entry will deter or counteract anticompetitive reductions of R&D efforts. Nonetheless, such conditions do not always pertain, and the Agencies ask whether entry may deter or counteract anticompetitive R&D reductions, taking into account the following:

Where market participants typically can observe the level and type of R&D efforts within a market, the principles of Section 3 of the Horizontal Merger Guidelines may be applied flexibly to determine whether entry is likely to deter or counteract a lessening of the quality, diversity, or pace of research and development. To be timely, entry must be sufficiently prompt to deter or counteract such harms. The Agencies evaluate the likelihood of entry based on the extent to which potential entrants have (1) core competencies (and the ability to acquire any necessary specialized assets) that give them the ability to enter into competing R&D and (2) incentives to enter into competing R&D in response to a post-collaboration reduction in R&D efforts. The sufficiency of entry depends on whether the character and scope of the

---

51. Under the same principles applied to production and marketing collaborations, the exercise of monopsony power by a buying collaboration may be deterred or counteracted by the entry of new purchasers. To the extent that collaborators reduce their purchases, they may create an opportunity for new buyers to make purchases without forcing the price of the input above pre-relevant agreement levels. Committed purchasing entry, defined as new purchasing competition that requires expenditure of significant sunk costs of entry and exit-such as a new steel factory built in response to a reduction in the price of iron ore-is analyzed under principles analogous to those articulated in Section 3 of the *Horizontal Merger Guidelines*. Under that analysis, the Agencies assess whether a monopsonistic price reduction is likely to attract committed purchasing entry, profitable at pre-relevant agreement prices, that would not have occurred before the relevant agreement at those same prices. (Uncommitted new buyers are identified as participants in the relevant market if their demand responses to a price decrease are likely to occur within one year and without the expenditure of significant sunk costs of entry and exit. *See id.* at Sections 1.32 and 1.41.)

entrants' R&D efforts are close enough to the reduced R&D efforts to be likely to achieve similar innovations in the same time frame or otherwise to render a collaborative reduction of R&D unprofitable. Where market participants typically cannot observe the level and type of R&D efforts by others within a market, there may be significant questions as to whether entry would occur in response to a collaborative lessening of the quality, diversity, or pace of research and development, since such effects would not likely be observed. In such cases, the Agencies may conclude that entry would not deter or counteract anticompetitive harms.

3.36 Identifying Procompetitive Benefits of the Collaboration

Competition usually spurs firms to achieve efficiencies internally. Nevertheless, as explained above, competitor collaborations have the potential to generate significant efficiencies that benefit consumers in a variety of ways. For example, a competitor collaboration may enable firms to offer goods or services that are cheaper, more valuable to consumers, or brought to market faster than would otherwise be possible. Efficiency gains from competitor collaborations often stem from combinations of different capabilities or resources. See supra Section 2.1. Indeed, the primary benefit of competitor collaborations to the economy is their potential to generate such efficiencies.

Efficiencies generated through a competitor collaboration can enhance the ability and incentive of the collaboration and its participants to compete, which may result in lower prices, improved quality, enhanced service, or new products. For example, through collaboration, competitors may be able to produce an input more efficiently than any one participant could individually; such collaboration-generated efficiencies may enhance competition by permitting two or more ineffective (e.g., high cost) participants to become more effective, lower cost competitors. Even when efficiencies generated through a competitor collaboration enhance the collaboration's or the participants' ability to compete, however, a competitor collaboration may have other effects that may lessen competition and ultimately may make the relevant agreement anticompetitive.

If the Agencies conclude that the relevant agreement has caused, or is likely to cause, anticompetitive harm, they consider whether the agreement is reasonably necessary to achieve "cognizable efficiencies." "Cognizable efficiencies" are efficiencies that have been verified by the

Agencies, that do not arise from anticompetitive reductions in output or service, and that cannot be achieved through practical, significantly less restrictive means. See infra Sections 3.36(a) and 3.36(b). Cognizable efficiencies are assessed net of costs produced by the competitor collaboration or incurred in achieving those efficiencies.

3.36(a) Cognizable Efficiencies Must Be Verifiable and Potentially Procompetitive

Efficiencies are difficult to verify and quantify, in part because much of the information relating to efficiencies is uniquely in the possession of the collaboration's participants. Moreover, efficiencies projected reasonably and in good faith by the participants may not be realized. Therefore, the participants must substantiate efficiency claims so that the Agencies can verify by reasonable means the likelihood and magnitude of each asserted efficiency; how and when each would be achieved; any costs of doing so; how each would enhance the collaboration's or its participants' ability and incentive to compete; and why the relevant agreement is reasonably necessary to achieve the claimed efficiencies (see Section 3.36 (b)). Efficiency claims are not considered if they are vague or speculative or otherwise cannot be verified by reasonable means.

Moreover, cognizable efficiencies must be potentially procompetitive. Some asserted efficiencies, such as those premised on the notion that competition itself is unreasonable, are insufficient as a matter of law. Similarly, cost savings that arise from anticompetitive output or service reductions are not treated as cognizable efficiencies. See Example 9.

3.36(b) Reasonable Necessity and Less Restrictive Alternatives

The Agencies consider only those efficiencies for which the relevant agreement is reasonably necessary. An agreement may be "reasonably necessary" without being essential. However, if the participants could have achieved or could achieve similar efficiencies by practical, significantly less restrictive means, then the Agencies conclude that the relevant agreement is not reasonably necessary to their achievement. In making this assessment, the Agencies consider only alternatives that are practical in the business situation faced by the participants; the Agencies do not search for a theoretically less restrictive alternative that is not realistic given business realities.

The reasonable necessity of an agreement may depend upon the market context and upon the duration of the agreement. An agreement that may be justified by the needs of a new entrant, for example, may not be reasonably necessary to achieve cognizable efficiencies in different market circumstances. The reasonable necessity of an agreement also may depend on whether it deters individual participants from undertaking free riding or other opportunistic conduct that could reduce significantly the ability of the collaboration to achieve cognizable efficiencies. Collaborations sometimes include agreements to discourage any one participant from appropriating an undue share of the fruits of the collaboration or to align participants' incentives to encourage cooperation in achieving the efficiency goals of the collaboration. The Agencies assess whether such agreements are reasonably necessary to deter opportunistic conduct that otherwise would likely prevent the achievement of cognizable efficiencies. See Example 10.

3.37 Overall Competitive Effect

If the relevant agreement is reasonably necessary to achieve cognizable efficiencies, the Agencies assess the likelihood and magnitude of cognizable efficiencies and anticompetitive harms to determine the agreement's overall actual or likely effect on competition in the relevant market. To make the requisite determination, the Agencies consider whether cognizable efficiencies likely would be sufficient to offset the potential of the agreement to harm consumers in the relevant market, for example, by preventing price increases.[52]

The Agencies' comparison of cognizable efficiencies and anticompetitive harms is necessarily an approximate judgment. In

---

52. In most cases, the Agencies' enforcement decisions depend on their analysis of the overall effect of the relevant agreement over the short term. The Agencies also will consider the effects of cognizable efficiencies with no short-term, direct effect on prices in the relevant market. Delayed benefits from the efficiencies (due to delay in the achievement of, or the realization of consumer benefits from, the efficiencies) will be given less weight because they are less proximate and more difficult to predict.

assessing the overall competitive effect of an agreement, the Agencies consider the magnitude and likelihood of both the anticompetitive harms and cognizable efficiencies from the relevant agreement. The likelihood and magnitude of anticompetitive harms in a particular case may be insignificant compared to the expected cognizable efficiencies, or vice versa. As the expected anticompetitive harm of the agreement increases, the Agencies require evidence establishing a greater level of expected cognizable efficiencies in order to avoid the conclusion that the agreement will have an anticompetitive effect overall. When the anticompetitive harm of the agreement is likely to be particularly large, extraordinarily great cognizable efficiencies would be necessary to prevent the agreement from having an anticompetitive effect overall.

Section 4: Antitrust Safety Zones

4.1 Overview

Because competitor collaborations are often procompetitive, the Agencies believe that "safety zones" are useful in order to encourage such activity. The safety zones set out below are designed to provide participants in a competitor collaboration with a degree of certainty in those situations in which anticompetitive effects are so unlikely that the Agencies presume the arrangements to be lawful without inquiring into particular circumstances. They are not intended to discourage competitor collaborations that fall outside the safety zones.

The Agencies emphasize that competitor collaborations are not anticompetitive merely because they fall outside the safety zones. Indeed, many competitor collaborations falling outside the safety zones are procompetitive or competitively neutral. The Agencies analyze arrangements outside the safety zones based on the principles outlined in Section 3 above. The following sections articulate two safety zones. Section 4.2 sets out a general safety zone applicable to any competitor collaboration.[53] Section 4.3 establishes a safety zone applicable to research and development collaborations whose competitive effects are analyzed within an innovation market. These

53. *See* Sections 1.1 and 1.3 above.

safety zones are intended to supplement safety zone provisions in the Agencies' other guidelines and statements of enforcement policy.[54]

4.2 Safety Zone for Competitor Collaborations in General

Absent extraordinary circumstances, the Agencies do not challenge a competitor collaboration when the market shares of the collaboration and its participants collectively account for no more than twenty percent of each relevant market in which competition may be affected.[55] The safety zone, however, does not apply to agreements that are per se illegal, or that would be challenged without a detailed market analysis,[56] or to competitor collaborations to which a merger analysis is applied.[57]

4.3 Safety Zone for Research and Development Competition Analyzed in Terms of Innovation Markets

Absent extraordinary circumstances, the Agencies do not challenge a competitor collaboration on the basis of effects on competition in an

---

54. The Agencies have articulated antitrust safety zones in *Health Care Statements* 7 & 8 and the *Intellectual Property Guidelines*, as well as in the *Horizontal Merger Guidelines*. The antitrust safety zones in these other guidelines relate to particular facts in a specific industry or to particular types of transactions.
55. For purposes of the safety zone, the Agencies consider the combined market shares of the participants and the collaboration. For example, with a collaboration among two competitors where each participant individually holds a 6 percent market share in the relevant market and the collaboration separately holds a 3 percent market share in the relevant market, the combined market share in the relevant market for purposes of the safety zone would be 15 percent. This collaboration, therefore, would fall within the safety zone. However, if the collaboration involved three competitors, each with a 6 percent market share in the relevant market, the combined market share in the relevant market for purposes of the safety zone would be 21 percent, and the collaboration would fall outside the safety zone. Including market shares of the participants takes into account possible spillover effects on competition within the relevant market among the participants and their collaboration.
56. *See supra* notes 28-30 and accompanying text in Section 3.3.
57. *See* Section 1.3 above.

innovation market where three or more independently controlled research efforts in addition to those of the collaboration possess the required specialized assets or characteristics and the incentive to engage in R&D that is a close substitute for the R&D activity of the collaboration. In determining whether independently controlled R&D efforts are close substitutes, the Agencies consider, among other things, the nature, scope, and magnitude of the R&D efforts; their access to financial support; their access to intellectual property, skilled personnel, or other specialized assets; their timing; and their ability, either acting alone or through others, to successfully commercialize innovations. The antitrust safety zone does not apply to agreements that are per se illegal, or that would be challenged without a detailed market analysis,[58] or to competitor collaborations to which a merger analysis is applied.[59]

Appendix

Section 1.3

EXAMPLE 1 (COMPETITOR COLLABORATION/MERGER)

Facts: Two oil companies agree to integrate all of their refining and refined product marketing operations. Under terms of the agreement, the collaboration will expire after twelve years; prior to that expiration date, it may be terminated by either participant on six months' prior notice. The two oil companies maintain separate crude oil production operations.

Analysis: The formation of the collaboration involves an efficiency-enhancing integration of operations in the refining and refined product markets, and the integration eliminates all competition between the participants in those markets. The evaluating Agency likely would conclude that expiration after twelve years does not constitute termination "within a sufficiently limited period." The participants entitlement to terminate the collaboration at any time after giving prior notice is not termination by the collaboration's "own specific and express terms." Based on the facts presented, the evaluating Agency likely would analyze the collaboration under the Horizontal Merger

58. *See supra* notes 28-30 and accompanying text in Section 3.3.
59. *See* Section 1.3 above.

Guidelines, rather than as a competitor collaboration under these Guidelines. Any agreements restricting competition on crude oil production would be analyzed under these Guidelines.

Section 2.3

EXAMPLE 2 (ANALYSIS OF INDIVIDUAL AGREEMENTS/ SET OF AGREEMENTS)

Facts: Two firms enter a joint venture to develop and produce a new software product to be sold independently by the participants. The product will be useful in two areas, biotechnology research and pharmaceuticals research, but doing business with each of the two classes of purchasers would require a different distribution network and a separate marketing campaign. Successful penetration of one market is likely to stimulate sales in the other by enhancing the reputation of the software and by facilitating the ability of biotechnology and pharmaceutical researchers to use the fruits of each other's efforts. Although the software is to be marketed independently by the participants rather than by the joint venture, the participants agree that one will sell only to biotechnology researchers and the other will sell only to pharmaceutical researchers. The participants also agree to fix the maximum price that either firm may charge. The parties assert that the combination of these two requirements is necessary for the successful marketing of the new product. They argue that the market allocation provides each participant with adequate incentives to commercialize the product in its sector without fear that the other participant will free-ride on its efforts and that the maximum price prevents either participant from unduly exploiting its sector of the market to the detriment of sales efforts in the other sector.

Analysis: The evaluating Agency would assess overall competitive effects associated with the collaboration in its entirety and with individual agreements, such as the agreement to allocate markets, the agreement to fix maximum prices, and any of the sundry other agreements associated with joint development and production and independent marketing of the software. From the facts presented, it appears that the agreements to allocate markets and to fix maximum prices may be so intertwined that their benefits and harms "cannot meaningfully be isolated." The two agreements arguably operate together to ensure a particular blend of incentives to achieve the potential procompetitive benefits of successful commercialization of the new product. Moreover, the effects of the agreement to fix maximum prices may mitigate the price effects of the agreement to allocate markets. Based on the facts presented, the evaluating Agency likely would conclude that the agreements to allocate markets and to fix maximum prices should be analyzed as a whole.

Section 2.4

EXAMPLE 3 (TIME OF POSSIBLE HARM TO COMPETITION)

Facts: A group of 25 small-to-mid-size banks formed a joint venture to establish an automatic teller machine network. To ensure sufficient business to justify launching the venture, the joint venture agreement specified that participants would not participate in any other ATM networks. Numerous other ATM networks were forming in roughly the same time period.

Over time, the joint venture expanded by adding more and more banks, and the number of its competitors fell. Now, ten years after formation, the joint venture has 900 member banks and controls 60% of the ATM outlets in a relevant geographic market. Following complaints from consumers that ATM fees have rapidly escalated, the evaluating Agency assesses the rule barring participation in other ATM networks, which now binds 900 banks.

Analysis: The circumstances in which the venture operates have changed over time, and the evaluating Agency would determine whether the exclusivity rule now harms competition. In assessing the exclusivity rule's competitive effect, the evaluating Agency would take account of the collaboration's substantial current market share and any procompetitive benefits of exclusivity under present circumstances, along with other factors discussed in Section 3.

Section 3.2

EXAMPLE 4 (AGREEMENT NOT TO COMPETE ON PRICE)

Facts: Net-Business and Net-Company are two start-up companies. Each has developed and begun sales of software for the networks that link users within a particular business to each other and, in some cases, to entities outside the business. Both Net-Business and Net-Company were formed by computer specialists with no prior business expertise, and they are having trouble implementing marketing strategies, distributing their inventory, and managing their sales forces. The two companies decide to form a partnership joint venture, NET-FIRM, whose sole function will be to market and distribute the network software products of Net-Business and Net-Company. NET-FIRM will be the exclusive marketer of network software produced by Net-Business and Net-Company. Net-Business and Net-Company will each have 50% control of NET-FIRM, but each will derive profits from NET-FIRM in proportion to the revenues from sales of that partner's products. The documents setting up NET-FIRM specify that Net-Business and Net-Company will agree on the prices for the products that NET-FIRM will sell.

Analysis: Net-Business and Net-Company will agree on the prices at which NET-FIRM will sell their individually-produced software. The agreement is one "not to compete on price," and it is of a type that always or almost always tends to raise price or reduce output. The agreement to jointly set price may be challenged as per se illegal, unless it is reasonably related to, and reasonably necessary to achieve procompetitive benefits from, an efficiency-enhancing integration of economic activity.

EXAMPLE 5 (SPECIALIZATION WITHOUT INTEGRATION)

Facts: Firm A and Firm B are two of only three producers of automobile carburetors. Minor engine variations from year to year, even within given models of a particular automobile manufacturer, require re-design of each year's carburetor and re-tooling for carburetor production. Firms A and B meet and agree that henceforth Firm A will design and produce carburetors only for automobile models of even-numbered years and Firm B will design and produce carburetors only for automobile models of odd-numbered years. Some design and re-tooling costs would be saved, but automobile manufacturers would face only two suppliers each year, rather than three.

Analysis: The agreement allocates sales by automobile model year and constitutes an agreement "not to compete on output." The participants do not combine production; rather, the collaboration consists solely of an agreement not to produce certain carburetors. The mere coordination of decisions on output is not integration, and cost-savings without integration, such as the costs saved by refraining from design and production for any given model year, are not a basis for avoiding per se condemnation. The agreement is of a type so likely to harm competition and to have no significant benefits that particularized inquiry into its competitive effect is deemed by the antitrust laws not to be worth the time and expense that would be required. Consequently, the evaluating Agency likely would conclude that the agreement is per se illegal.

EXAMPLE 6 (EFFICIENCY-ENHANCING INTEGRATION PRESENT)

Facts: Compu-Max and Compu-Pro are two major producers of a variety of computer software. Each has a large, world-wide sales department. Each firm has developed and sold its own word-processing software. However, despite all efforts to develop a strong market presence in word processing, each firm has achieved only slightly more than a 10% market share, and neither is a major competitor to the two firms that dominate the word-processing software market.

Compu-Max and Compu-Pro determine that in light of their complementary areas of design expertise they could develop a markedly better word-processing program together than either can produce on its own. Compu-Max and Compu-Pro form a joint venture, WORD-FIRM, to jointly develop and market a new word-processing program, with expenses and profits to be split equally. Compu-Max and Compu-Pro both contribute to WORD-FIRM software developers experienced with word processing.

Analysis: Compu-Max and Compu-Pro have combined their word-processing design efforts, reflecting complementary areas of design expertise, in a common endeavor to develop new word-processing software that they could not have developed separately. Each participant has contributed significant assets-the time and know-how of its word-processing software developers-to the joint effort. Consequently, the evaluating Agency likely would conclude that the joint word-processing software development project is an efficiency-enhancing integration of economic activity that promotes procompetitive benefits.

EXAMPLE 7 (EFFICIENCY-ENHANCING INTEGRATION ABSENT)

Facts: Each of the three major producers of flashlight batteries has a patent on a process for manufacturing a revolutionary new flashlight battery-the Century Battery-that would last 100 years without requiring recharging or replacement. There is little chance that another firm could produce such a battery without infringing one of the patents. Based on consumer surveys, each firm believes that aggregate profits will be less if all three sold the Century Battery than if all three sold only conventional batteries, but that any one firm could maximize profits by being the first to introduce a Century Battery. All three are capable of introducing the Century Battery within two years, although it is uncertain who would be first to market.

One component in all conventional batteries is a copper widget. An essential element in each producers' Century Battery would be a zinc, rather than a copper widget. Instead of introducing the Century Battery, the three producers agree that their batteries will use only copper widgets. Adherence to the agreement precludes any of the producers from introducing a Century Battery.

Analysis: The agreement to use only copper widgets is merely an agreement not to produce any zinc-based batteries, in particular, the Century Battery. It is "an agreement not to compete on . . . output" and is "of a type that always or almost always tends to raise price or reduce output." The participants do not collaborate to perform any business functions, and there are no procompetitive benefits from an efficiency-enhancing integration of economic activity. The evaluating Agency likely would challenge the agreement to use only copper widgets as per se illegal.

Section 3.3

EXAMPLE 8 (RULE-OF-REASON: AGREEMENT QUICKLY EXCULPATED)

Facts: Under the facts of Example 4, Net-Business and Net-Company jointly market their independently-produced network software products through NET-FIRM. Those facts are changed in one respect: rather than jointly setting the prices of their products, Net-Business and

Net-Company will each independently specify the prices at which its products are to be sold by NET-FIRM. The participants explicitly agree that each company will decide on the prices for its own software independently of the other company. The collaboration also includes a requirement that NET-FIRM compile and transmit to each participant quarterly reports summarizing any comments received from customers in the course of NET-FIRM's marketing efforts regarding the desirable/undesirable features of and desirable improvements to (1) that participant's product and (2) network software in general. Sufficient provisions are included to prevent the company-specific information reported to one participant from being disclosed to the other, and those provisions are followed. The information pertaining to network software in general is to be reported simultaneously to both participants.

Analysis: Under these revised facts, there is no agreement "not to compete on price or output." Absent any agreement of a type that always or almost always tends to raise price or reduce output, and absent any subsequent conduct suggesting that the firms did not follow their explicit agreement to set prices independently, no aspect of the partnership arrangement might be subjected to per se analysis. Analysis would continue under the rule of reason.

The information disclosure arrangements provide for the sharing of a very limited category of information: customer-response data pertaining to network software in general. Collection and sharing of information of this nature is unlikely to increase the ability or incentive of Net-Business or Net-Company to raise price or reduce output, quality, service, or innovation. There is no evidence that the disclosure arrangements have caused anticompetitive harm and no evidence that the prohibitions against disclosure of firm-specific information have been violated. Under any plausible relevant market definition, Net-Business and Net-Company have small market shares, and there is no other evidence to suggest that they have market power. In light of these facts, the evaluating Agency would refrain from further investigation.

Section 3.36(a)

EXAMPLE 9 (COST SAVINGS FROM ANTICOMPETITIVE OUTPUT OR SERVICE REDUCTIONS)

Facts: Two widget manufacturers enter a marketing collaboration. Each will continue to manufacture and set the price for its own widget, but the widgets will be promoted by a joint sales force. The two manufacturers conclude that through this collaboration they can increase their profits using only half of their aggregate pre-collaboration sales forces by (1) taking advantage of economies of scale-presenting both widgets during the same customer call-and (2) refraining from time-consuming demonstrations highlighting the relative advantages of one manufacturer's widgets over the other manufacturer's widgets. Prior to their collaboration, both manufacturers had engaged in the demonstrations.

Analysis: The savings attributable to economies of scale would be cognizable efficiencies. In contrast, eliminating demonstrations that highlight the relative advantages of one manufacturer's widgets over the other manufacturer's widgets deprives customers of information useful to their decision making. Cost savings from this source arise from an anticompetitive output or service reduction and would not be cognizable efficiencies.

Section 3.36(b)

EXAMPLE 10 (EFFICIENCIES FROM RESTRICTIONS ON COMPETITIVE INDEPENDENCE)

Facts: Under the facts of Example 6, Compu-Max and Compu-Pro decide to collaborate on developing and marketing word-processing software. The firms agree that neither one will engage in R&D for designing word-processing software outside of their WORD-FIRM joint venture. Compu-Max papers drafted during the negotiations cite the concern that absent a restriction on outside word-processing R&D, Compu-Pro might withhold its best ideas, use the joint venture to learn Compu-Max's approaches to design problems, and then use that information to design an improved word-processing software product on its own. Compu-Pro's files contain similar documents regarding Compu-Max.

Compu-Max and Compu-Pro further agree that neither will sell its previously designed word-processing program once their jointly developed product is ready to be introduced. Papers in both firms' files, dating from the time of the negotiations, state that this latter restraint was designed to foster greater trust between the participants and thereby enable the collaboration to function more smoothly. As further support, the parties point to a recent failed collaboration involving other firms who sought to collaborate on developing and selling a new spread-sheet program while independently marketing their older spread-sheet software.

Analysis: The restraints on outside R&D efforts and on outside sales both restrict the competitive independence of the participants and could cause competitive harm. The evaluating Agency would inquire whether each restraint is reasonably necessary to achieve cognizable efficiencies. In the given context, that inquiry would entail an assessment of whether, by aligning the participants' incentives, the restraints in fact are reasonably necessary to deter opportunistic conduct that otherwise would likely prevent achieving cognizable efficiency goals of the collaboration.

With respect to the limitation on independent R&D efforts, possible alternatives might include agreements specifying the level and quality of each participant's R&D contributions to WORD-FIRM or requiring the sharing of all relevant R&D. The evaluating Agency would assess whether any alternatives would permit each participant to adequately monitor the scope and quality of the other's R&D contributions and whether they would effectively prevent the misappropriation of the other participant's know-how. In some circumstances, there may be no "practical, significantly less restrictive" alternative.

Although the agreement prohibiting outside sales might be challenged as per se illegal if not reasonably necessary for achieving the procompetitive benefits of the integration discussed in Example 6, the evaluating Agency likely would analyze the agreement under the rule of reason if it could not adequately assess the claim of reasonable necessity through limited factual inquiry. As a general matter, participants' contributions of marketing assets to the collaboration could more readily be monitored than their contributions of know-how, and neither participant may be capable of misappropriating the other's marketing contributions as readily as it could misappropriate know-how. Consequently, the specification and monitoring of each participant's marketing contributions could be a "practical, significantly less restrictive" alternative to prohibiting outside sales of pre-existing products. The evaluating Agency, however, would examine the experiences of the failed spread-sheet collaboration and any other facts presented by the parties to better assess whether such specification and monitoring would likely enable the achievement of cognizable efficiencies.

APPENDIX O

SELECTED HART-SCOTT-RODINO STATISTICS FY 1998 - 2002[1]

	1998	1999	2000	2001	2002
Transactions Reported	4,728	4,642	4,926	2,376	1,187
Antitrust Division					
Second Requests Issued	79	68	55	43	22
Challenges	51	47	48	32	10
Actions Filed in District Court	15	21	21	8	4[2]
Consent Agreements Issued	10[3]	20[4]	18[5]	8	2
Transactions Restructured or Abandoned	36	26	27	24	6
Federal Trade Commission					
Second Requests Issued	46	45	43	27	27
Challenges	33	30	32	23	24
Actions Filed in District Court	3		5	1	5[6]
Consent Agreements Issued	23	18	18	18	10
Transactions Restructured or Abandoned	7	12	9	4	7

1. Federal Trade Commission and Department of Justice, Annual Report to Congress Pursuant to Subsection 7A of the Clayton Act Hart-Scott-Rodino Antitrust Improvements Act of 1976, Fiscal Years 1998, 1999, 2000, 2001 and 2002.
2. Two of these cases were settled by consent decree; one transaction was abandoned after filing the complaint; and in one case (United States v. SunGuard Data Sys. Inc., 172 F. Supp. 2d. 172 (D.D.C. 2001)) DOJ did not prevail.
3. Of the five remaining transactions, one was abandoned pursuant to the consent agreement and four were abandoned after the complaints were filed.
4. The remaining case was settled in November 2000 (Press Release, Department of Justice, Department Announced Tentative Settlement in Northwest-Continental Lawsuit, (Nov. 6, 2000)).
5. Of the remaining three transactions, two were abandoned after the complaint was filed and one case (United States v. Franklin Electric Co., 130 F. Supp. 2d 1025 (W.D. Wis. 2000)) was litigated in district court; DOJ prevailed.
6. The FTC authorized staff to seek injunctive relief in five matters, only one of which was filed in district court. In addition, the FTC filed two administrative complaints.

TABLE OF CASES

A

B

C

D

E

F

G

H

I

J

K

L

M

In re Microsoft Corp. Antitrust Litigation, 127 F. Supp. 2d 702 (D.Md. 2001), 394
In re Microsoft Corp. Antitrust Litigation, 333 F.3d 517 (4th Cir. 2003), 448, 449, 463
MidCon by Occidental Petroleum, Occidental Petroleum Corp., 109 F.T.C. 167 (1986), 359
Midcon Corp. v. Freeport-McMoran, Inc., 625 F. Supp. 1475 (N.D. Ill. 1986), 452
In re Midcon Corp., 107 F.T.C. 48 (1986), 222
Mid-South Grizzlies v. NFL, 720 F.2d 772 (3d Cir. 1983), 291
Midwestern Machinery, Inc. v. Northwest Airlines, 167 F.3d 439 (8th Cir. 1999), 415
Millicom International Cellular, S.A. v. Republic of Costa Rica, 995 F. Supp. 14 (D.D.C. 1998), 422
Minnesota Association of Nurse Anesthetists v. Unity Hosp., 5 F. Supp. 2d 694 (D. Minn. 1998), *aff'd*, 208 F.3d 655 (8th Cir. 2000), 96
Minnesota Association of Nurse Anesthetists v. Unity Hospital, 208 F.3d 655 (8th Cir. 2000), 96
Minnesota Mining & Manufacturing Co. v. New Jersey Wood Finishing Co., 381 U.S. 311 (1965), 8
Mississippi River Corp. v. FTC, 454 F.2d 1083 (8th Cir. 1972), 348, 352
Missouri Portland Cement Co. v. Cargill, Inc., 498 F.2d 851 (2d Cir. 1974), 321, 322, 324, 338, 342, 343, 377, 378, 430
Monfort of Colo., Inc. v. Cargill, Inc., 591 F. Supp. 683 (D. Colo. 1983), *aff'd*, 761 F.2d 570 (10th Cir. 1985), *rev'd on other grounds*, 479 U.S. 104 (1986), 57, 79, 81, 85, 86, 100
Montreal Trading Ltd. v. Amax, Inc., 661 F.2d 864 (10th Cir. 1981), 399
Morgan, Strand, Wheeler & Biggs v. Radiology, Ltd., 924 F.2d 1484 (9th Cir. 1991), 78
Morgenstern v. Wilson, 29 F.3d 1291 (8th Cir. 1994), *cert. denied,* 513 U.S. 1150 (1995), 77, 83, 87, 89
Municipal Electric Association v. SEC, 413 F.2d 1052 (D.C. Cir. 1969), 223
Murrow Furniture Galleries, Inc. v. Thomasville Furniture Industries, Inc., 889 F.2d 524 (4th Cir. 1989), 90
Mustad International Group NV, 120 F.T.C. 865 (1995), 55

N

O

P

R

S

T

U

V

W

X

Y

Z

Other

ABA SECTION OF ANTITRUST LAW COMMITMENT TO QUALITY

The Section of Antitrust Law is committed to the highest standards of scholarship and continuing legal education. To that end, each of our books and treatises is subjected to rigorous quality control mechanisms throughout the design, drafting, editing, and peer review processes. Each Section publication is drafted and edited by leading experts on the topics covered and then rigorously peer reviewed by the Section's Books and Treatises Committee, at least two Council members, and then other officers and experts. Because the Section's quality commitment does not stop at publication, we encourage you to provide any comments or suggestions you may have for future editions of this book or other publications.